Design of Modern Highway Bridges

Design of Modern Highway Bridges

Narendra Taly, Ph.D., P.E.

Department of Civil Engineering
California State University, Los Angeles
Los Angeles, CA

THE McGRAW-HILL COMPANIES, INC.

New York   St. Louis   San Francisco   Auckland   Bogotá   Caracas   Lisbon
London   Madrid   Mexico City   Milan   Montreal   New Delhi
San Juan   Singapore   Sydney   Tokyo   Toronto

McGraw-Hill

A Division of The McGraw·Hill Companies

DESIGN OF MODERN HIGHWAY BRIDGES

2 3 4 5 6 7 8 9 0 DOC DOC 9 0 9 8

ISBN 0-07-062997-8

Permissions appear on pages 1349 to 1352, and on this page by reference.

This book was set in Times Roman by Publication Services, Inc.
The editors were B. J. Clark and John M. Morriss;
* the production supervisor was Paula Keller.*
The cover was designed by Joan Greenfield.
Project supervision was done by Publication Services, Inc.
R. R. Donnelley & Sons Company was printer and binder.

Library of Congress Cataloging-in-Publication Data

Taly, Narendra.
    Design of modern highway bridges / Narendra Taly.
        p.   cm.
    Includes bibliographical references and index.
    ISBN 0-07-062997-8 (text). — ISBN 0-07-062998-6 (SM)
    1. Bridges—Design and construction   I. Title.
    TG300.T28   1998
    624'.2—dc21   96-44557

http://www.mhcollege.com

ABOUT THE AUTHOR

Narendra Taly has been engaged in the structural engineering profession since 1959, involved in design, research, teaching, and consulting. After receiving his B.S. in engineering from Benares Hindu University in Benares (now Varanasi), India, in 1959, he worked for six years as assistant engineer for the State of Rajasthan in India, and later as assistant director of the Central Water and Power Commission, Government of India in New Delhi, for three and a half years. He received his M.S. from Bucknell University in 1971 and his Ph.D. from West Virginia University in 1976. Prior to earning his Ph.D., he worked as a bridge design engineer for the state of Pennsylvania from 1971 to 1973.

Narendra Taly has been a professor in the Department of Civil Engineering at California State University, Los Angeles, since 1977, where he has taught bridge engineering and other structural engineering courses for the past twenty years. He is a registered professional engineer in the states of California and West Virginia. He has been a member of several professional organizations for the last several years.

To my wife, Trish,

To my daughters, Neena and Beena,

and to the memory of my parents,
Bhagwandas and Sunderbai Taly

CONTENTS

PREFACE

"If I have been able to see a little farther than some others, it was because I stood on the shoulders of giants."

Sir Isaac Newton (1642–1727)
in *Philosophiae Naturalis Principia Mathematica*

This book is an attempt to convey what I have learned from others, combined with my own experience as a bridge design engineer in the state of Pennsylvania, including rating and in-depth inspection of highway bridges that followed in the aftermath of the 1967 collapse of the Point Pleasant Bridge (West Virginia); as a researcher of short-span bridges as a part of my graduate work; and as a teacher of a course in bridge design at California State University, Los Angeles, since 1977. My purpose is to present to students and practicing engineers, in an elementary manner, the basic fundamentals of the structural design of bridge superstructures.

The topic of bridge design is vast and worthy of filling many volumes. However, the purpose of this text is to cover pertinent bridge design topics in a classroom environment, during one semester or quarter. It is in this context that the scope of this text has been kept limited to the design of only the most common types of bridge superstructures encountered in practice, both simple and continuous, noncomposite and composite. Advanced topics such as prestressed segmental, cantilever, arch, cable-stayed, and suspension bridges, suitable for medium and long spans, have been purposely omitted. The topic of timber bridges has not been covered separately in this text; it can be easily handled after learning the basic principals of bridge design.

To acquaint a bridge design engineer with a variety of materials available today, the text includes design of steel, reinforced concrete, and prestressed concrete bridges. In addition to the conventional materials used to date, modern composite materials that are being investigated and developed for structural design are discussed in Chapter 2.

Several examples of different kinds of bridges with detailed longhand calculations and clear references to the pertinent AASHTO specifications have been presented in the text to familiarize first-time readers with the mechanics of bridge design calculations. An in-depth discussion on the service load design, the strength design, and the load factor design, with pertinent calculations, has been presented. Practically all contextual AASHTO equations and formulas have been derived in this book. This will help readers to develop some level of proficiency and confidence, although the experience required for designing a major bridge project cannot simply be substituted by a textbook.

Recognizing the power of modern computers in technology, reference to computer programs has been appropriately made in the book. However, the direct use of the computer is not specifically employed for computational purposes in this book. The author believes that the study of basic principles in the limited time of a quarter or a semester is of the highest priority. Once these are understood and mastered, the many computer programs available in the marketplace can be used without much difficulty.

As pointed out by A. A. Jakkula in his book *A History of Suspension Bridges in Bibliographical Form,* to make real progress in the study of any branch of engineering, it is of utmost importance for students to know where to find what has been written on their subjects and to learn something of the history of their branches of specialization. This makes the bibliography of published material on students' subjects a vital necessity. Consequently, the material presented in every chapter of this book is extensively referenced. In all, this book contains over 2300 references.

This text covers the topic of bridge design in conformance with the fifteenth edition of *AASHTO Specifications for Highway Bridges,* 1992 and the 1993 *AASHTO Interim Specifications.* Most bridges in North America are designed according to the specifications of the American Association of State Highway and Transportation Officials (AASHTO, known as AASHO, American Association of State Highway Officials, prior to November 11, 1973). Although not international in their character and format, these specifications or slightly modified versions have been extensively used throughout the world. They are well known for their simplicity and proven performance and are suitable for the span lengths, structure widths, heights, and methods of construction most commonly encountered in practice.

Emphasis has been placed on the practical aspects of design, rather than on design theory, although both are equally important. This has been done purposefully, so that during the early stages of design learning, readers can develop a certain level of confidence and interest in the subject and not get bogged down in the monotony of theory. Throughout the text, major thrust has been placed on the requirements of specifications relevant to a particular design; these have been referenced in detail—both in discussion and the example problems. Extensive information on bridge-related topics is available in many of the Transportation Research Board (TRB) Publications and in the reports of the National Cooperative Highway Research Program (NCHRP), and several of these have been referenced throughout the text. Readers are urged to read these references for in-depth information.

In its May 12, 1993, Denver, Colorado meeting, the AASHTO Subcommittee on Bridges and Structures passed this historic resolution: "To adopt the Draft NCHRP 12-23 Document as the 1994 *AASHTO LRFD Specifications for Highway Bridges* and, by 1995, consider phasing out the current *Standard Specifications,*" paving the way for the use of the *Load and Resistance Factor Design Specifications* by bridge engineers. Accordingly, references have been made throughout the text to reflect this development.

Specifications that are likely to be revised, such as those covering loads (impact) and load distribution, have been described in the text to give readers the awareness of the future trends.

Considerable space has been provided in Chapter 1 for the history of bridges. Volumes have been written on this subject by many authors in the past, and many are likely to write on it in the future; it is extremely difficult to shrink this topic into a few pages. Consequently, only the highlights of the history of bridge building have been presented in a summary form. It is believed that bridge building developed and progressed as an engineering art, rather than as an engineering science, or from practice to theory, prompted by the ever-growing transportation needs of the human race. In this context, the author hopes that readers will find reading the history of bridges interesting, stimulating, and inspiring.

While the focus of this text is limited to some specific types of superstructures, readers should always be conscious of exploring new ideas by thinking, reasoning, and observing. The power of observation is great. A provocative example is Galileo's (1564–1642) thinking[1] about the bending strength of hollow sections:

> In order to bring our daily conference to an end, I wish to discuss the strength of hollow solids which are employed in art—and still more often in nature—in a thousand operations for the purpose of greatly increasing strength without adding to weight; examples of these are seen in the bones of birds and in many kinds of reeds which are light and highly resistant both to bending and breaking. For if a stem of straw which carries a head of wheat heavier than the entire stalk were made of the same amount of material in solid form, it would offer less resistance to bending and breaking. This is an experience which has been verified and confirmed in practice where it is found that a hollow lance or a tube of wood or metal is much stronger than would be a solid one of the same length and weight, one which would necessarily be thinner; men have discovered, therefore, that in order to make lances strong as well as light they must make them hollow.

Of the eleven chapters in this book, the first five deal with the general principles of design applicable to all types of bridges. Chapters 6, 7, and 8 deal with reinforced, prestressed, and slab–steel beam bridges, respectively. Chapter 9 presents an in-depth discussion on the theory and design of plate girder bridges. Chapter 10 discusses the topics of inspection, evaluation, rehabilitation, and maintenance of bridges—issues engineers have to face once bridges are put to service. And finally, bridge engineers have to *build,* so they might as well build bridges that are *beautiful* to leave behind as their legacies. Chapter 11 discusses the aesthetics of bridges to help them in that endeavor.

Great care has been taken to eliminate errors in this text. The classroom use of this book and its thorough reading by several of my students have been extremely helpful in this regard. However, it is inevitable that some errors still occur. I will be very thankful to readers for bringing them to my attention, and I welcome any comments they wish to make.

ACKNOWLEDGMENTS

Sincere efforts have been made to acknowledge the cited material by providing proper references in the text and at the end of each chapter. Any missing reference is purely inadvertent.

Special thanks are due to the distinguished panel of authoritative reviewers for agreeing to review the manuscript and for contributing extensive suggestions that considerably improved the content of this book: Professors Ray W. James of Texas A & M University; Hany Farran of California Polytechnic State University, Pomona,

---

[1]Galilei, Galileo. (1638). *Two New Sciences,* Elzevir, Leiden; trans. H. Crew and A. de Salvio (New York, 1914). Also (1933). *Dialogues Concerning Two New Sciences,* trans. H. Crew and A. de Salvio, New York, p. 150.

California; Mr. M. G. Patel, Director, Bureau of Design, Pennsylvania Department of Transportation, Harrisburg; Mr. James Roberts, Director, Engineering Services, California Department of Transportation, Sacramento; and McGraw-Hill's anonymous reviewer.

The database on cable-stayed and suspension bridges presented in Appendix C was compiled by Dr. Walter Podolny, Jr., Senior Structural Engineer, Bridge Management Group, HNG-32, FWHA, Washington, D.C. His help is gratefully acknowledged.

Grateful acknowledgment is due to Dr. Raymond Landis, dean of the School of Engineering and Technology, California State University, Los Angeles; Dr. Raj Ramchandani, Department of Electrical Engineering; Dr. Young Kim, chairman, and my colleagues Drs. Anjan Bhaumik, Irving Kett, and Rupa Purasinghe, all of the Department of Civil Engineering, California State University, Los Angeles; and Dr. Virendra Chaudhary of Boeing Corporation, Seattle, for their encouragement and support toward writing this book.

Special thanks are extended to Dr. Amir Mirmiran, Professor, Civil and Envr. Engineering Department, University of Central Florida, who used the manuscript of this book for two years during its preparation, for his many helpful suggestions and encouragement. Thanks are due to my friend and architect, Mr. Jai Arora, for providing unlimited access to his office facilities during the preparation of this manuscript. I also gratefully acknowledge the many helpful suggestions and comments made by my graduate students.

Thanks are extended to Mr. B. J. Clark who, during his tenure at The McGraw-Hill Companies, Inc., as Executive Editor for Engineering, was very helpful and encouraging during the preparation of the manuscript for this book. The author acknowledges with thanks the comments and suggestions to eliminate errors, improve clarity, and generally improve usability by Katherine Coyle, copy editor, Kathryn D. Wright, production coordinator, and Kris Engberg, customer service representative, for this book project, all at Publication Services, Inc., Champaign, IL.

The manuscript of this text was typed by my wife, Trish, who spent many hours of her spare time on it after her regular full-time job and on weekends. Without her unrelenting encouragement and support, this work would not have been possible. And I remain forever thankful to my parents who always encouraged me to seek excellence in education—mine and that of others. To both of them, and to engineers, this book is dedicated.

Narendra Taly

ACRONYMS

The following is a list of acronyms frequently used in this text:

AASHO	American Association of State Highway Officials (now AASHTO)
AASHTO	American Association of State Highway and Transportation Officials
ACI	American Concrete Institute
AISC	American Institute of Steel Construction
AISCM	American Institute of Steel Construction Manual
AISCS	American Institute of Steel Construction Specifications
AISI	American Iron and Steel Institute
AITC	American Institute of Timber Construction
ANSI	American National Standards Institute
APA	American Plywood Association
AREA	American Railway Engineering Association
ASCE	American Society of Civil Engineers
ASD	Allowable Stress Design (in AISC specifications)
ASD	Autostress Design (in AASHTO specifications)
ASTM	American Society for Testing of Materials
AWPA	American Wood Preservers Association
AWS	American Welding Society
CRC	Column Research Council
CSCE	Canadian Society of Civil Engineering
EIC	Engineering Institute of Canada
IABSE	International Association of Bridge and Structural Engineers
ICBO	International Conference of Building Officials
LFD	Load Factor Design
LRFD	Load and Resistance Factor Design
NACA	National Advisory Committee for Aeronautics
NCHRP	National Cooperative Highway Research Program
NTSB	National Transportation Safety Board

PCA   Portland Cement Association

PD   Plastic Design

P&T   Posts and Timbers

RCSC   Research Council on Structural Connections

SAE   Society of Automotive Engineers

SAMPE   Society for the Advancement of Materials and Process Engineering

SSRC   Structural Stability Research Council

UBC   Uniform Building Code

W   Wide Flange Shape

WRC   Welding Research Council

GREEK ALPHABET

Letter		Name	Letter		Name
A	α	alpha	N	ν	nu
B	β	beta	Ξ	ξ	xi
Γ	γ	gamma	O	o	omicron
Δ	δ	delta	Π	π	pi
E	ϵ	epsilon	P	ρ	rho
Z	ζ	zeta	Σ	σ	sigma
H	η	eta	T	τ	tau
Θ	θ	theta	Υ	υ	upsilon
I	ι	iota	Φ	ϕ	phi
K	κ	kappa	X	χ	chi
Λ	λ	lambda	Ψ	ψ	psi
M	μ	mu	Ω	ω	omega

CHAPTER 1

Introduction

1.1
HISTORICAL BACKGROUND

1.1.1 General

The history of bridge building can be said to be the history of the evolution of civil engineering.

It is all but impossible to date humanity's conception and creation of the first bridge—or the "art of spanning space by artificial construction" [Steinman and Watson, 1957]. It is also debatable whether bridges were *invented* or if they just *evolved* as the basic need for transportation continually grew, owing to people's mobile and nomadic lifestyles.

Perhaps people derived the first concept in bridge building from nature. The idea of a slab bridge might have developed from a tree trunk that, uprooted by winds or weakened by erosion at its roots, had fallen across a chasm or a creek (Fig. 1.1). Or perhaps the idea of piers evolved from rocks that, jutting out of shallow streams, were used as stepping stones. As the depth of the water rose during the rainy season, larger rocks were needed to serve as the stepping stones. When people realized that walking was more convenient than hopping from stepping stone to stepping stone, for individuals, tribes, and cattle, they created the slab. Slabs of stone were laid across the stepping stones, and thus emerged a multiple-span bridge. These bridges, which came to be known as clapper bridges (Fig. 1.2), can still be found in some undeveloped areas of the world. For longer spans, vines, where available, were used to make suspension bridges. Early suspension bridges consisted of twisted vines tied to tree trunks on either side of a gorge.

Although methods of structural analysis were not known until the seventeenth century, bridges of three basic forms—beam, arch, and cantilever—were used very early in human history.

1

FIGURE 1.1
Petrified log bridge, Arizona [Edwards, 1959].

The only building materials known since the dawn of history are stone and timber—materials available in nature. Manufactured materials—plain, reinforced, and pre-stressed concrete; cast iron; wrought iron; and steel—evolved gradually, mostly within the last two centuries. Along with these stronger and varied materials evolved different forms of bridges having increasingly longer spans. The history of the development of bridges is thus intertwined with the evolution of stronger materials.

1.1.2 The Pre-Christian and Roman Periods

The earliest bridges were built from wood and had the form of a beam and cantilever, as evidenced from bridges in China and India [Steinman and Watson, 1957; Gies, 1963]. The cantilever bridges were built by extending beams out from the piers on both sides of a stream. A primitive cantilever bridge over the Jhelum River in Srinagar, India, is shown in Fig. 1.3.

Stone arch bridges are the earliest bridges built that still stand today as evidence of bridge-building skill in ancient times. Although the earliest stone arches, found in the excavations at Ur in the Middle East and in Egypt, date back to about 4000 and 3000 B.C., respectively, all these arches were parts of buildings, not bridges. The oldest extant stone arch bridge, known as the Caravan Bridge, is said to be over the Meles River at Smyrna, Turkey, and is believed to have been built about the ninth century B.C. [Gies, 1963]. Many stone arch bridges were built by engineers of the Roman empire, some of which are still in service after more than 2000 years [Gies, 1963; Heins and Firmage, 1979; Richardson, 1972]. Romans excelled in building stone arches since stone was abundantly available; timber was rather scarce and had to be used economically.

The first bridge built in Rome—the famous Pons Sublicius Bridge built by Ancus Marcius over the Tiber River, was made from wood beams, and for many years it was the only bridge across the Tiber [Planter, 1911] until it was destroyed by floods in 693 A.D. Legend has it that the bridge was made wholly in timber so as to

FIGURE 1.2
Clapper bridges of the past [Gies, 1963].

be less offensive to Father Tiber, the river god, than a permanent stone bridge would be. Even so, human sacrifices were made to appease the river gods; later on this was done by casting into the river thirty dummies made of rushes every year [Smith, 1965].

The first known stone arch built in Rome is the Pons Solarus across the Teverone in the seventh century B.C. [Gies, 1963]. However, this bridge has completely disappeared and little is known about its origin. One of the most magnificent examples of the powerful skill of the early Roman engineers is the Pont du Gard Aqueduct in France (Fig. 1.4), built about 19 B.C. [Hopkins, 1970]. This structure is part bridge and part

FIGURE 1.3
Primitive cantilever bridge over the Jhelum River at Srinagar, India [Smith, 1953].

FIGURE 1.4
The Pont du Gard Aqueduct, France [Gies, 1963].

aqueduct, built to carry water over the Gard River to the city of Nimes in southern Gaul. It is said to have been conceived by Marcus Vipranius Agrippa, administrative aide, general, and the son-in-law of Augustus Caesar. It consists of three tiers of arches, reaching to a height of 155 ft above the river (as high as the Straits of Mackinac

FIGURE 1.5
Trajan's Bridge, built over the Danube in 103 A.D., as shown in the relief on Trajan's Column [Smith, 1953].

Bridge in Michigan). The first, or the bottom, tier consists of six arches varying in width from 51 to 80 ft, the largest spanning the river. The second, or middle, tier has eleven arches of the same dimensions as those of the first, to reach across the widening valley. The third, or topmost, tier consists of thirty-five 15-ft arches, extending 885 ft across the river. Amazingly, mortar was used only in the topmost tier. In the two lower tiers, no binding material such as mortar or iron clamps was used to support the blocks of stones. Other famous contemporary arches are the Pons Augustus at Rimini, Italy, the Trajan Bridge over the Danube, and the Puente Alcantra and the Segovia Aqueduct in Spain [Gies, 1963].

Trajan's Bridge (Fig. 1.5) deserves a special mention as an outstanding example of vitality and creativity. It was built in the second century A.D. by the Roman emperor Trajan after he conquered the trans-Danubian region (modern Romania), which he added to his empire under the name of Dacia. Trajan ordered a bridge built across the 3000-ft-wide Danube River, to guarantee the supply line of his legions garrisoned in the wild, forested conquered country. It was built by Apollodorus of Damascus in 106 A.D. [Smith, 1953]. Two records, slightly at variance with each other, describe the bridge—the inscription on Trajan's Column in the Forum, and the history, written a hundred years later, by Dion Cassius. According to these records, the bridge, spanning 3000 ft, stood on twenty piers of hewn stone, each 150 ft high, 60 ft wide, and 50 ft thick, placed 170 ft apart (center-to-center). The openings between the piers were spanned by timber arches 110 ft long [Gies, 1963; Smith, 1953]. In terms of rocks cut into 2-ft cubes, probably no fewer than one million, one hundred twenty-five thousand were needed [Gies, 1963]!

Trajan's Bridge was the first to be built across the Danube. It was also the first bridge for which trusses in any form were used [Timoshenko, 1953]. Unfortunately, more than a century and a half later, it was destroyed by another Roman emperor, Aurelian, when he set fire to it to slow an enemy invasion. For well over twelve hundred years, the 170-ft spans of the Trajan Bridge remained the longest ever built in the world. Sixteen hundred years passed before another bridge was built over the Danube [Gies, 1963].

The Romans were not only great builders, but they are also credited with the discovery of natural cement. They discovered pozzolana, a loosely coherent volcanic sand found at Pozzoli (ancient Puteoli), near Naples. When pozzolana is mixed with ordinary lime, hydraulic cement is formed. The Romans discovered that, as an ingredient in mortar, pozzolana improved the quality of the resulting mortar, accelerated its setting and hardening, and gave it the property of setting under water. In the words of Vitruvius, a first century B.C. writer [Book II, Chapter VI],

> There is also a kind of powder which, by nature, produces wonderful results. It is found in the neighborhood of Baiae and in the lands of the municipalities round Mount Vesuvius. This being mixed with lime and rubble, not only furnishes strength to other buildings, but also, when piers are built in the sea, they set under water.

Knowledge of the binding properties of calcium compounds appears to have evolved more than 4000 years ago. The Egyptians used gypsum as an ingredient for mortar. The Sumerians used gypsum plaster quite early in their civilization and later refined their product by mixing calcium hydroxide with sand to produce a lime mortar that closely resembled that used later by the Greeks and Romans. The Romans' lime mortar proved more durable than that of the Greeks because the Romans were more skilled in producing it—mixing, beating, and ramming it thoroughly [Hopkins, 1970]. With time and experience, the Romans improved their technique of concrete making. Unfortunately, with the fall of the Roman Empire was lost the art of making reliable lime mortar. It was not rediscovered until the fifteenth century; the next recorded use of the pozzolanic mortar is said to be that of Fra Giovanni Giolondo in binding the foundation blocks together for the Pont Notre Dame in Paris, completed in 1499.[1]

Bridge building in China is said to have started about 2300 B.C., during the reign of the Emperor Yao. Early Chinese bridges were often of the pontoon type, made out of boats called "sampans," moored a few feet apart parallel to the stream current [Steinman and Watson, 1957]. Considerable development in stone arch bridges took place in China, although little is known about its chronology. Many arch bridges were built in the Yangtse Delta, necessitated by miles of running water in the area. Although stone was used for piers of wooden spans built in the Delta, the idea of stone arch bridges is said to have travelled from Rome to China through Chinese silk merchants of the Han Dynasty (206 B.C.–A.D. 221), who dealt with the Parthians and other people on the fringe of the Roman empire. The stone arch probably first appeared in the Far East in the center of the Han power, near Chengtu. A magnificent example was the Ten Thousand Li Bridge outside the South Gate of Chengtu; it consisted of sixty-eight arches across the wide, shallow Wei River. Interestingly, unlike the Romans, the Chinese did not use mortar; they possessed nothing comparable to Roman pozzolana. Instead, they used iron keys to clamp the arches together. A resurgence of bridge building occurred in China during the Sung Dynasty (A.D. 960–1280). Marco Polo, who is reported to have travelled to China in the later part of the thirteenth century, vividly described Chinese engineering, which some say had surpassed that of Europeans in the centuries after Rome's fall [Gies, 1963].

Although the Romans were great builders of arches, they were nevertheless empiricist builders, not scientists or engineers, who lacked understanding of structural mechanics of arches. Their arches, always semicircular in form, used extensively for roads and aqueducts, were built with only empirical rules, and without the use of any theory for determining their safe dimensions. However, even these empirical methods were forgotten in the Middle Ages when few or no bridges were constructed in Europe. No Roman bridges were built after the fourth century. Engineering practically vanished

---

[1]A brief chronological history of mortar making is given by Hopkins [1970].

from Europe for several hundred years. Consequently, during the Renaissance, when the improved economy in Europe led to renewed road and bridge construction, the lost art of building arches had to be relearned and, again, the proportions of these arches were determined empirically [Timoshenko, 1953]. Robert Hooke (1635–1703) is credited with defining arch theory in 1670 and with inventing the famous Hooke's law. Later, the arch theory was expounded upon by Thomas Young (1773–1829), who, 130 years later, defined the modulus of elasticity, E [Hopkins, 1970]. Lahire (1640–1718), a French mathematician, was the first to apply statics to analyze the arch problem [Timoshenko, 1953].

It is not known exactly when the first cantilever bridge was built, but evidence suggests that it was in China [Gies, 1963], from where it is said to have travelled to India. The Chinese cantilever bridge was characterized by stone piers and timber spans. Originally, wooden caissons were used to build piers, by filling them with stone rubble to hold the projecting timbers in place. Later, the piers were built from masonry, with slots to receive the timber. The cantilevers were built by extending heavy timbers outward from the solid stone abutment or the pier, as shown in Fig. 1.6. Gies [1963] describes these timbers as "roughly hewn tree trunks, projecting in pairs, placed with an upward slant, usually in three or four pairs, with the inner ends held by the weight of the stone abutment, the outer ends bound together." Smith [1965] provides a description of timber cantilever bridges built in North India and Tibet. In the valley of Kashmir, India, elaborate cantilever bridges were built from deodar logs piled criss-cross and were lined with shops and houses (Fig. 1.3).

Today, suspension bridges are built to span the longest distances. But the *idea* of the suspension bridge is many centuries old, although its origin is uncertain. According to the writings of famous travellers and explorers, it is evident that, in their

FIGURE 1.6
Primitive cantilever bridge, Tibet [Steinman and Watson, 1957].

primitive forms, suspension bridges existed in many distant parts of the world; these are considered to be the forerunners of the modern suspension bridge. Several of these primitive bridges have been found in North India, Burma, and Peru—some were hundreds of feet long. As Prescot described in 1847, in Peru, the cords or cables "were formed from the tough fibers of the *maguey* or of the *osier* of the country, having an extraordinary tenacity and strength. These osiers were woven into cables of the thickness of a man's body. The huge ropes, then stretched across the water, were conducted through rings or holes cut in the immense buttresses of stone raised on the opposite banks of the river, and there secured to heavy pieces of timber" [Gies, 1963]. In northeast India (Assam) and Burma, suspension bridges consisted of bamboo cables, single and multiple, stretched across the stream. According to E. C. Barber's 1881 description, the cables over Brahmaputra River were made of three strands of bamboo rope, each 1 in. thick, twisted together and spanning 600 ft. In Sikkim, cables were formed from canes $\frac{3}{4}$ in. thick and 60 to 90 ft long, from a species of *calamus*, and knotted together; from these, a floor made of loose bamboo was suspended [Smith, 1953].

Steinman and Watson [1957] classify these bridges into four types: (1) the regular roadway type, with the roadway resting directly on the cables (Fig. 1.7); (2) the hammock, or tubular, type, with four cables, in pairs of two each, all woven together into a web (Fig. 1.8); (3) the basket, or transporter, bridge on one cable (Fig. 1.9); and (4) the suspended roadway, the forerunner of the modern suspension type. The basket bridge perhaps evolved from a single-cable suspension bridge (Fig. 1.10). Such bridges, consisting of single bamboo cables, were stretched across streams in north India [Gies, 1963]. Steinman and Watson [1957] describe various kinds of these bridges: " . . . in the regions of the Himalayas, the suspension bridge builder threw over the chasm two parallel cables; from these he hung vertical suspenders made of thinner rope which carried the roadway platform. Here is the principle of the modern suspension bridge, although executed in cruder form." Pictorial illustrations of various types of these bridges have been presented by many researchers, such as Gies [1963] and Edwards [1959]. These bridges often spanned 100 ft or more. A curious primitive suspension bridge found in British Columbia was built by native Americans about 1870 over the Bulkley River Canyon at Hazelton. Wire abandoned by Western Union Telegraph was used as cable for the suspension span, and logs and poles were used as towers and truss members, resulting in a cantilever-suspension bridge. This bridge collapsed in 1915 [Steinman and Watson, 1957].

An insight into the bridge-building capability of people in the region of northern India and the Himalayas is found in the chronicles of famous Chinese travellers Fa Hsien (A.D. 399), a Buddhist monk, and Hsuan-Tsang (A.D. 630), a Buddhist scholar, each of whom made a pilgrimage to India in search of sacred writings of Buddha. Fa Hsien wrote, "Below is a river named the Indus. The men of former times had cut away the rock to make a way down. There are seven hundred rock steps, and when these and the ladders have been negotiated, the river is crossed by a suspension bridge of ropes. The two banks of rivers are somewhat less than eighty paces apart." Hsuan-Tsang chronicled reports of crossing "bridges of iron," as clear indication of bridges suspended from iron chains. Soon the iron-link suspension bridges appeared in China, an innovation exported from India to China, perhaps through the writings of Hsuan-Tsang [Gies, 1963].

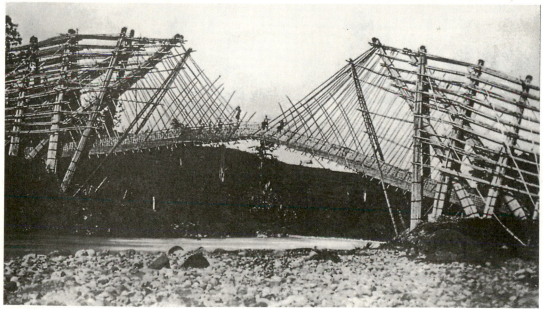

FIGURE 1.7
Primitive suspension bridges with roadway laid directly on cables [Gies, 1963].

FIGURE 1.8
Primitive hammock-type suspension bridge [Edwards, 1959].

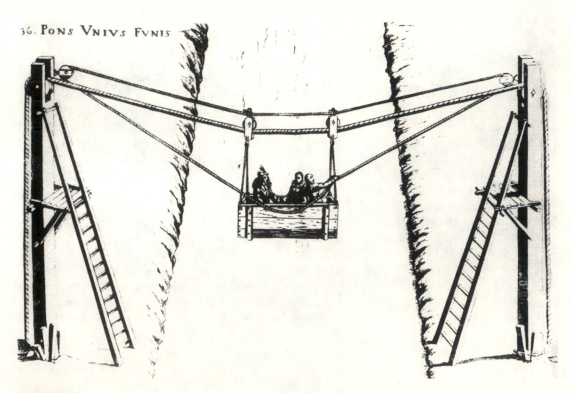

FIGURE 1.9
Ancient basket, or the transporter, bridge [Gies, 1963].

10

FIGURE 1.10
Primitive single-cable suspension bridge [Gies, 1963].

1.1.3 The Renaissance and Post-Renaissance Periods

The Renaissance period, from the 14th through the 16th centuries, is known as the age of reason and of the birth of modern science. Several renowned scientists lived during this period, including such geniuses as Leonardo da Vinci (1452–1519), Copernicus (1473–1543), and Galileo Galilei (1564–1642). Although many new scientific theories were developed during this period, relatively little advancement was made in construction. Leonardo da Vinci developed new ideas in the realms of mechanics and military bridges, and he invented many devices such as parachutes and flying machines. He was the first, through his statement of lever, to introduce the concept of the moment of a force. He also virtually wrote the principle that is now known as *Newton's third law of motion* [Kinney, 1957]. He considered the strength of beams and stated a general principle: "In every article that is supported, but is free to bend, and is of uniform cross-section, the part that is farthest from support will bend the most" [Timoshenko, 1953]. He seemed to have a correct idea of the thrust produced by an arch. However, he worked alone and did not write any books; consequently, his ideas did not influence others. Buried in his notes, his discoveries in various branches of science remained unknown for years [Timoshenko, 1953]. It was Galileo, considered to be the founder of the science of structural mechanics, who explained scientific theories that changed the methods of construction. It was his work *Two New Sciences* (1638), the first book ever written on the theory of structural mechanics, that revolutionized structural engineering and marked the beginning of the science of *strength of materials* [Timoshenko, 1953; Kinney, 1957]. In this book, Galileo discusses the fundamental principles of stress analysis for beams and framed structures, including the famous cantilever beam problem that has come to be known as *Galileo's problem*, and which was not correctly and completely solved until 1855 [Kinney, 1957]. Galileo was the first to examine how the nature, shape, and size of a member would affect its breaking strength [Hopkins, 1970].

The post-renaissance period was also an important period in the history of bridge building; for during this period lived the engineer-builder Andrea Palladio (1518–1580) and scientists such as Robert Hooke (1635–1703) and Isaac Newton (1642–1727). Other great mathematicians and scientists, such as James Bernoulli (1654-1705), his brother Johann Bernoulli (1667–1748), Johann's son Daniel Bernoulli (1700–1782), and Daniel's friend and colleague Leonard Euler (1707–1783) also lived during this period [Kinney, 1957]. Never before had so many great thinkers been born in such a short span of time. Their revolutionary scientific and mathematical discoveries created, for the first time, the theoretical basis for the construction of buildings and bridges.

Robert Hooke, now considered a co-discoverer of Newton's laws of motion, had written the following in 1666 [Timoshenko, 1953; Hopkins, 1970]:

I. That all heavenly bodies have not only a gravitation of their parts to their own proper center, but ... they also mutually attract each other within their spheres of action.

II. That all bodies, having a simple motion, will continue to move in a straight line, unless continually deflected from it by some extraneous force causing them to describe a circle, an ellipse, or some other curve.

III. That this attraction is so much greater as the bodies are nearer. As to the proportion in which those forces diminish by an increase in distance, I own I have not discovered it, although I have made some experiments to this purpose . . . .

Hooke was also the first to state the theory of arches. Having discovered these principles around 1660, he wrote in a postscript to his "Description of Helioscopes" [Hooke, 1676], which was published the following year [Hopkins, 1970],

To fill the vacancy of the ensuing page, I have here added a *decimate* of the *centesme* of the Inventions I intend to publish, though possibly not in the same order, but as I can get the opportunity and leisure; most of which I hope, will be as useful to mankind, as they are yet unknown and new.

1. A true mathematical and mechanical form of all manner of Arches for Building, with the true butment (sic) necessary to each of them. A problem which no Architecton-ick Writer hath ever yet attempted, much less performed. abcccddeeeeefggiiiiiiiillm-mmmnnnnnnooprrsssttttttuuuuuuuux [anagram]

2. The true Theory of Elasticity or Springiness and a particular Explication thereof in several subjects in which it is to be found. And the way of computing the velocity of bodies moved by them. ceiiinosssttuu [anagram]

The solution to the second anagram is "*the extension is proportional to the force.*" The solution to Hooke's first anagram was published by Richard Waller after Hooke's death: "*ut pendet continuum flesile, sic stabit contiguum rigidum inversum,*" which means "*as hangs a flexible cable, so, inverted, stand the touching pieces of an arch.*" One hundred thirty years after this discovery, Thomas Young [1773–1829] gave precise exposition of Hooke's theory of arches in his *Natural Philosophy,* lectures delivered to the Royal Institution in England in 1802 and published in 1807 [Hopkins, 1970]. In 1817, Young completed his article on bridges for the *Encyclopedia Britannica*, which, together with *Natural Philosophy*, is a significant contribution to knowledge. Young was also the first to show the importance of the dynamical effect of a load [Timoshenko, 1953].

Galileo was the first to indicate the presence of tension in beams and to correctly calculate that the bending moment caused by the weight of a uniform beam increased with the square of its length. However, his stress analysis was incorrect—he assumed uniform stresses existed throughout the beam's cross section (similar to the *plastic stress distribution* as we know it today). It was Hooke who first gave the correct linear distribution of both compression and tension across the cross section of a beam. He also implied, through sketches in his work, that sections that were plane before bending remained plane after bending, a fundamental concept in the theory of bending. This concept is now known as *Navier's hypothesis*. It was published in 1826 by the French engineer Claud Louis Marie Henry Navier (1785–1836) in his first edition of *Resume des Lecons de Mecanique*, the first great book in the mechanics of engineering. Here, Navier solved a number of problems related to flat slabs, plates, built-in beams, the two-hinged arch, and others. He was heavily influenced by the thinking of Young and by Charles Augustine Coulomb (1736–1806), who gave the first correct analysis of fiber stresses in a loaded beam. Both Coloumb and Navier are considered the founders of the science of the mechanics of materials [Kinney, 1957]. Coloumb's memoirs, published in 1773, contained the correct solutions to many problems in the mechanics of materials. But it took engineers more than forty years to understand and apply them. Navier also edited and published well-known books on bridges written by his uncle, the famous French engineer Gauthey (1732–1807), after Gauthey's death [Timoshenko, 1953].

The most significant contribution of the Renaissance to construction technology was the development of the truss as a structural principle. The truss filled the need to span longer lengths that could not be spanned with timbers, which were available in the lengths of only 50 ft or so. With trusses, shorter lengths could be used to build longer bridges [Steinman and Watson, 1957].

Andrea Palladio (1518–1580), an Italian architect, is credited with first having developed and used trusses [Smith, 1953; Timoshenko, 1953; Kinney, 1957; Steinman and Watson, 1957; Hopkins, 1970]. He built a 108-ft-span truss bridge over the Cismone between Trent and Bassano, Italy [Gies, 1963]. Palladio influenced architecture during his time so profoundly that his style came to be known as the *Palladian school of architecture*. He translated *Ten Books on Architecture* by the ancient Roman architect, Vitruvious, and, in 1570, published his own work, *Four Books on Architecture*, in which he describes the first use of trusses for bridge building. With this publication, wood truss bridges emerged.

The first covered timber bridges were built by two Swiss carpenters, brothers Hans Ulrich and Johannes Grubenmann of Tenfeu, Switzerland. Hans Ulrich built the first covered timber bridge in 1757 over the Rhine River at Schaffhausen. It was a two-span structure (171 and 193 ft) that proved strong enough to safely carry carriages weighing up to 25 tons [Timoshenko, 1953]. The second covered bridge was a 240-ft-span bridge built by Jean Grubenmann at Reichenau. In 1758, together they built a bridge over the Limmat near Wettingen (just west of Zurich), Switzerland, spanning 200 ft. All three bridges had certain general characteristics, combining trusses and arch, like all early wooden covered bridges. However, the Wettingen Bridge differed considerably from the other two in design, and is believed to be the first timber bridge using a true arch [Steinman and Watson, 1957; Hopkins, 1970]. Later, all three bridges were burned by French troops when they evacuated Schaffhausen after being defeated by the Austrians in 1799.

Many bridges of this kind, but of smaller span, were later built in Switzerland and Germany [Timoshenko, 1953; Hopkins, 1970]. However, it was in timber-rich North America that a great variety of timber bridges evolved. Credit for building the first bridges in what was to become the United States goes to Maese Francisco, the Genoese engineer of the Spanish explorer Hernando de Soto. Francisco built several bridges during the Spanish exploring expeditions of the 1530s and 1540s. One of them was destroyed by river current during a flood, marking the first bridge failure in American history [Gies, 1963, p. 291].

The first to professionally build bridges in the United States, and the pioneers of the day, were Timothy Palmer (1751–1821) of Newburyport, Massachusetts, Louis Wernwag (1770–1843), a German immigrant, and Theodore Burr (1771–1822) of Torrington, Connecticut. They built some of the most famous bridges of the times. Wernwag built the 340-foot-span arch Colossus Bridge over the Schuylkill River at Fairmount, Pennsylvania. Palmer built the Permanent Bridge at Philadelphia over the Schuylkill, a three-span (150, 185, and 150 ft) wood trussed structure (Fig. 1.11). With abutments and wingwalls 750 ft long, this bridge was 1300 ft long. After serving for about fifty years, it was destroyed by fire [Steinman and Watson, 1957]. Palmer was among the first to point out the great advantage obtained by covering wooden bridges to protect them from rot (Fig. 1.12). Burr, the most famous of the three pioneers, completed in 1815 a 360-ft arch truss bridge over the Susquehanna River at McCalls Ferry, Pennsylvania. Acclaimed to be the longest timber truss ever built in America at the time, it came to be known as Burr's masterpiece. It was destroyed after two years by an ice jam in the winter of 1817 [Steinman and Watson, 1957; Hopkins, 1970]. Each of these builders left an indelible mark on the American landscape in the form of timber bridges. Most of these structures were *indeterminate*, combining arch and truss systems. The purpose of the arch was to add rigidity to the truss, a system developed by Burr that came to be known as the Burr arch-truss (Fig. 1.13); it became for a time the most popular of all timber-bridge forms, repeated hundreds of times, especially throughout the northeastern United States [Gies, 1963]. The covered bridges of the United States are the finest examples of timber bridges built anywhere in the world [Allen, 1970a,b,c; Auvil, 1973].

In January 1820, a patent for a double-web lattice truss (Fig. 1.14) called the Town lattice mode was taken out by Ithiel Town, a New Haven, Connecticut architect. This design was significant because it could be built cheaply and quickly by a carpenter's gang in a few days. Although highly indeterminate, it was a true truss, for, unlike its predecessors, it was free from arch and horizontal thrust. It was even used for early railroad bridges [Steinman and Watson, 1957; Gies, 1963]. Town was a remarkably successful bridge builder; he not only built the lattice mode, he *peddled* it.[2] He

---

[2] See Edwards, 1959, pp. 60–61, for a description of pamphlets distributed by Ithiel Town in 1821 and 1839.

FIGURE 1.11
Palmer's Permanent Bridge at Philadelphia [Steinman and Watson, 1957].

FIGURE 1.12
Covered bridge [Steinman and Watson, 1957].

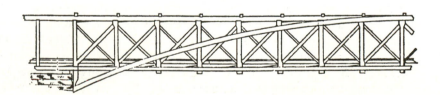

FIGURE 1.13
Theodore Burr's arch-truss [Tyrrell, 1911].

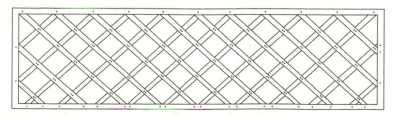

FIGURE 1.14
The Town lattice mode [Gies, 1963].

advertised claims that his bridge could be "built by the mile and cut off by the yard." He collected a dollar per foot for every bridge built under his patent; two dollars per foot for the one built without his permission.

The Town lattice was followed by the multiple king-post truss [Gies, 1963], patented in March 1830 by an army engineer, Lieutenant-Colonel Stephen Harriman Long of Hopkinton, New Hampshire. Long later received several patents for improvements to his truss (the K-truss, for example) [Edwards, 1959]. He is credited with building the first bridge that had a long truss superstructure. Called the Jackson Bridge, it was the first American structure that separated highway and railroad grades for which the K-truss was used as a lateral bracing arrangement. Long's trusses consisted of panels having either single diagonals or Xs, as the strength required. Long referred to these Xs as counterbraces by which "the truss frames are rendered stiff and unyielding" [Edwards, 1959]. However, they did not gain much popularity and were the last of the timber trusses. The truss forms of Town and Long are significant because they did not derive their rigidity from the arch, as in earlier truss forms. Thus the true form of a truss evolved.

Coincidentally, at the same time that archless trusses evolved, the railroads arrived. Although both Town's and Long's trusses could serve the railroads, they had a serious weakness, not in structure, but in material, at the connections. Wood, although strong in compression, is weak in tension, and can be pulled apart, especially if bolted at the joints. The problem was solved by William Howe of Spencer, Massachusetts, who, while retaining the wooden compression members (either single diagonals or Xs), simply replaced the wood verticals of Long's truss with wrought-iron members formed of cylindrical rods with screw ends (Fig. 1.15). Patented by Howe in 1840, this system worked well for many years, until Howe presented his designs for both highway and railroad bridges. This subjected his bridges and the theoretical problems of bridge loading to engineering scrutiny for the first time [Gies, 1963]. However, Howe's truss system was the first and the most popular truss system in America during the first half of the nineteenth century. Development of the Howe truss was followed by the Pratt truss (Fig. 1.16), patented in 1844 by brothers Caleb and Thomas Pratt. The Pratt truss system, although geometrically similar to the Howe truss, differed from it in one significant aspect: The diagonals (or the Xs) of the Pratt truss, being tensile members, were made of wrought iron, a stronger material in tension; thus the Pratt truss provided

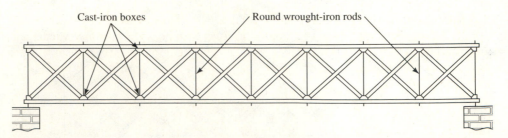

FIGURE 1.15
Howe truss with wrought-iron verticals [Hopkins, 1970].

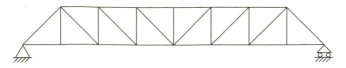

FIGURE 1.16
The Pratt truss.

a much better arrangement for the emerging all-iron trusses. Both the Howe and the Pratt trusses were not true timber trusses, however, for they both used wrought iron for tension members [Steinman and Watson, 1957; Gies, 1963]. Coincidentally, both the Howe and Pratt trusses debuted at the beginning of the railroad and automobile era. After the first metal trusses were built in England in 1845, both trusses later became all-iron trusses [Timoshenko, 1953; Steinman and Watson, 1957].

Interestingly, none of the designers or builders of the timber bridges were engineers—they were all highly skilled carpenters (Howe was a carpenter-mechanic). They had built thousands of bridges that carried loads and stood the test of time, but none were based on any rational design principles. These bridges first came under engineering scrutiny when the first American treatise on bridge building appeared in 1847— *A Work on Bridge-Building,* by Squire Whipple (1797–1886) of Utica, New York, a great ratiocinator. This book presented the stress analysis of an articulated truss, and it emphasized the fact that cast iron, being weak in tension but strong in compression, was unsuitable and uneconomical for tension members; it was more logical to use cast iron for compression members in a truss, in combination with wrought-iron tension members [Tyrrell, 1911; Timoshenko, 1953; Steinman and Watson, 1957; Hopkins, 1970]. Write Steinman and Watson [1957], "...so significant is this contribution that its date of publication marks the beginning of the era of scientific bridge design." Independently of Whipple, American engineer Colonel Herman Haupt published a theoretical treatise titled *The General Theory of Bridge Construction* in 1851. These two books are considered the foundation of modern framed structures. They were followed by Whipple's more exhaustive textbook in 1873, *An Elementary and Practical Treatise on Bridge Building* [Steinman and Watson, 1957; Kinney, 1957; Gies, 1963]. Whipple's initial form was a bowstring truss (Fig. 1.17) whose upper chords, being compression members, were made from cast iron, and whose lower chords and intermediate members, being tensile members, were made from wrought iron. Whipple did not invent this truss form, however; it had been developed some years earlier in France [Gies, 1963]. Whipple also developed a trapezoidal truss with heavy cast-iron verticals and an empirical arrangement of wrought-iron diagonals [Hopkins, 1970]. (A history of the development of various truss forms in the United States is provided by Johnson, Brywn, and Turneaure, 1926.)

Compounding the weakness of wood truss joints in tension (described earlier) was the problem of the heavier load-carrying requirement of bridges built for the developing railroads. Timber bridge builders could not produce a satisfactory answer to these problems. Notwithstanding their remarkable functionality, the timber bridges were doomed to retirement. The end of their usefulness was initiated by the collapse on March 4,

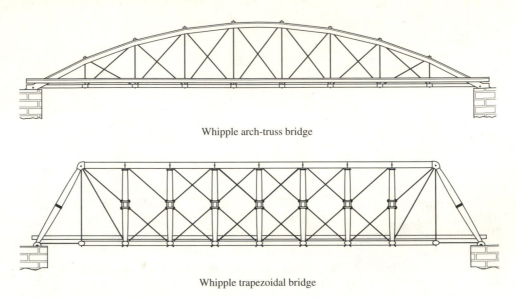

Whipple arch-truss bridge

Whipple trapezoidal bridge

FIGURE 1.17
Squire Whipple's trusses [Edwards, 1959].

1840, of the High Rock Bridge, a Town lattice bridge, over the Catskill Creek, New York, dropping a train of boxcars in the water and killing one man. This marked the first American railroad bridge fatality [Gies, 1963].

Timber bridges of the past remain, although several were destroyed by fire or floods. Some were preserved as historical landmarks, as reminders not only of the age of horse and buggy, but also of an age of great innovation. A tradition of the era of timber-bridge building in the United States was that these bridges were built on the early turnpikes by communities, not by the government; no record can be found of any state government promoting these bridges. On completion, these bridges were paid for by the collection of tolls. The old Cambridge Bridge, built in 1786 over the Charles River, Massachusetts, is said to have set the example for toll bridges in America [Steinman and Watson, 1957].

Gies [1963] gives a statewide record of covered timber bridges in the United States and Canada, listing a grand total of 1342 in the United States and 456 in Canada.

Europe was the hub of bridge-building activity during the Renaissance; Italy, France, and England were great commercial centers, and many famous bridges were built during that time in those countries. These included Ponte di Rialto (the Rialto Bridge) over the Grand Canal at Venice, designed by Antonia da Ponte in 1587 (Fig. 1.18) and hailed as the most painted bridge in the art world; Pont Notre Dame (built in 1500–1507), the first stone arch bridge to be built in Paris to replace the 1413 timber bridge; and Pont Neuf (or the New Bridge), (built in 1578–1607), only the second stone arch bridge to be built in that city [Gies, 1963]. The Rialto Bridge was hailed as the bridge of the sixteenth century, just as the Karlsbrucke was the bridge of the fifteenth and the Ponte Vecchio the bridge of the fourteenth.

FIGURE 1.18
The Ponte di Rialto (Rialto Bridge), showing, below water level, a section through the foundation, drawn in accordance with da Ponte's description and a contemporary drawing by Giacomo Guberni, "Master of Waterfront at Venice" [Smith, 1953].

One of the most outstanding bridge designers of the post-Renaissance period was Jean Randolphe Perronet (1708–1794). Born in Paris, Perronet was a friend of King Louis XV of France. His first bridge was the Pont de Neuilly over the Seine River. A five-arch bridge, each arch spanning 128 ft over piers only 13 ft thick, it had the slimmest piers ever used for an arch bridge and was hailed as the most graceful stone arch ever built. Perronet was the first to reduce the proportion of bridge piers with the principle of equilibrated thrust, and is said to be the father of modern bridge building. He was also the first director of the world's first engineering school, the *Ecole des Ponts et Chaussess* [Timoshenko, 1953]. Antoine Chezy, whose formula developed in 1769 is still applied for the open-channel flow, was a pupil and assistant of Perronet. Whereas the Roman arches almost always used a *semicircular* profile, the French developed the *elliptical* profile, and with this came flatter and more graceful arches. One of the first bridges to be built in France after the fall of the Roman empire was Pont d'Avignon over the Rhône River, whose construction began in 1177 and was completed in 1187. This bridge, some 3000 ft long, is said to have had twenty or twenty-one elliptical arches (with the long axis vertical, an effect achieved by constructing the arch of three circles, the smallest at the top) to have spanned from 65 to 115 ft, and to have had piers about 25 ft thick. Built by St. Bezenet, it was the longest masonry arch bridge ever built. Most of the bridge was destroyed over time, mainly by ice during the extremely severe winter of 1633. Only four arches remain, and its original form has been a matter of conjecture [Smith, 1953; Gies, 1963].

The first segmental arch is said to have been built by Taddeo Gaddi in 1345 in Florence, Italy, over the 300-ft-wide Arno River. This arch profile was significant from the engineering standpoint: whereas its predecessor, the semicircular arch, transmitted all loads in the downward vertical direction, the segmental arch introduced the element of horizontal thrust. The segmental arch is still an arc of a circle; it is simply a smaller arc of a larger circle. The relationship between the dimensions of arch and the resulting thrust, the required thickness of pier, and so on, were problems for which fourteenth-century mathematics had no answers. This bridge was a brilliant example of innovative engineering practice. It was followed by the legendary Ponte Vecchio, a three-span (90, 100, and 90 ft) segmental arch bridge. A single-span (236 ft) segmental arch was built in 1370–1371 over the Adda River at Trezzo, in the Duchy of Milan, Italy; it remained the longest single arch ever built in Europe for four centuries [Gies, 1963].

An important bridge was the Karlsbruck Bridge, was built in 1503 over Moldan River at Prague. It was some 2000 ft long, the longest bridge in Europe that lay entirely over the water, exceeded only by Pont d'Avignon, which rested partly on an island [Gies, 1963].

1.1.4 The Industrial Revolution

Heralded by the invention of the steam engine, the industrial revolution brought about a revolutionary change in the practice of bridge building in the nineteenth century. Iron was not a new discovery of this period—it had been known ever since the period of the pyramids, and the Persian kings are said to have obtained iron from India as early as 1500 B.C. [Hopkins, 1970]. But iron had not been developed into a structural material until now because people lacked the technology to produce it in sufficient bulk. With developed iron came many changes. Most importantly, new machines were made that aided in bridge building, and a new mode of transportation evolved—the railroad with the locomotive. The railroad demanded a revolution in bridge building; longer and stronger bridges were needed. With the advent of iron as a structural material, the history of highway and railroad bridges became intertwined.

The invention of the railroad brought new engineering challenges that forced bridge builders to think anew. Earlier bridges were short. Therefore, *dead loads,* made up of the bridges' own dead weight and, occasionally, the dead weight of houses, shops, and arcades that were built on them, were predominant. The *live load*, consisting of only two or three loaded wagons that could be hauled by a horse, pedestrians, buggies, and cattle, was relatively small, resulting in a small live load-to-dead load ratio, an important parameter in bridge design. With the arrival of the railroad, however, for the first time bridges were required to carry significantly heavier live loads. In industrial England, the need for transporting large quantities of coal and pig iron required many loaded wagons,[3] resulting in a high live load-to-dead load ratio. Also, because railroads cov-

---

[3] As a test, on July 25, 1814, George Stephenson placed his locomotive, the "Blucher," on the Killingworth Railway, England. On a slightly ascending grade, the engine drew eight loaded wagons carrying thirty tons at a speed of four miles an hour, the best record yet made by any steam engine [Stienman and Watson, 1957; Gies, 1963]. With an improved locomotive, patented by him on February 28, 1815, George Stephenson made history on September 27, 1825, when he drove the first engine from Darlington to Stocton, England, pulling a train of wagons carrying 450 passengers at a speed of 15 miles an hour [Gies, 1963].

ered increasingly longer distances and a greater number of streams, rivers, and valleys, bridges were needed in larger numbers and with longer spans.

In eighteenth century England, major development of the locomotive and the railroad took place, through the genius of George Stephenson (1781–1849), although in 1769 a French army officer had already built the first steam-powered locomotive. It was also in England that, much earlier, iron was first produced on a commercial scale and first used for bridge building.

In the first half of the seventeenth century, Dud Dudley, an Englishman, developed a method of making a better fuel for smelting his iron—he reduced coal to coke. However, its potential was not fully realized until some 100 years later, when, about 1713, Abraham Darby, an iron smelter at Coalbrookdale, in Shropshire, England, developed the use of coke for smelting iron. The eighteenth century marked the age of iron. Early in that century, experiments were begun to make iron structural shapes in the rolling mills, where metal was rolled into plates and bars. These mills were greatly improved and patented in 1783 by Henry Cort (1740–1800) who, in 1784, invented a process for producing wrought iron from pig iron [Steinman and Watson, 1957].

The world's first cast-iron bridge (Fig. 1.19) was built in 1777–1779 by Darby's grandson, Abraham Darby III (1750–1791), in Coalbrookdale, England, over the Severn River [Hopkins, 1970]. It was designed by the young Darby himself. A design by architect T. F. Prichard had been considered earlier and rejected because it combined wood with steel [Steinman and Watson, 1957]. Regarded a milestone in the history of bridge building, this 100-ft-span semicircular arch bridge is made up of five arch ribs,

FIGURE 1.19
The first iron bridge, at Coalbrookdale, England [Hopkins, 1970].

each cast in two 70-ft halves at the Coalbrookdale Iron Works [Steinman and Watson, 1957; Gies, 1963]. More than 200 years later, it is still in service, although restricted to pedestrian traffic only, and preserved by the British government as a national monument. The first iron arch in the United States was built in 1836, spanning 80 ft over Dunlap's Creep at Brownsville, Pennsylvania. Made of five tubular ribs, each of which was cast in nine segments, it was built by Captain Richard Dalefield (1798–1873) of the U.S. Engineer Corps to replace one of James Finley's suspension bridges, which had collapsed in 1820 under a combined load of heavy snow and a large road wagon [Steinman and Watson, 1957; Sealey, 1976].

Two earlier attempts to build cast-iron bridges had failed. The first attempt was made in 1755 by a French ironmaster in Lyons. The second attempt was made by Thomas Paine, author of *The Rights of Man*, who wanted to build a single-span, 400-ft iron arch over the Schuylkill, at Philadelphia. Paine's attempt was aborted because his American financial backer failed [Gies, 1963]. The second successful iron bridge, an arch spanning 130 ft, was built only three miles upstream of the first iron bridge at Coalbrookdale by Thomas Telford (1757–1834), who later came to be known as the father of suspension bridges [Steinman and Watson, 1957; Hopkins, 1970].

Iron was first used in European bridge construction in 1841. It was used in the chain cables of a suspension bridge, a 70-ft span over the Tees River in England, with the flooring supported directly on the cables in a primitive fashion [Tyrrell, 1911; Steinman and Watson, 1957].

The first all-metal trusses were built in the United States in 1840 [Mehrtens, 1908; Timoshenko, 1953]. The first all-iron bridge, designed and patented by Earl Trumbull, is the Erie Canal Bridge at Frankford, New York. Built in 1840, it is a 77-ft truss bridge combining the truss and suspension principles, and using cast-iron girders strengthened by wrought-iron bars [Tyrrell, 1911]. The second, all-iron bridge built in the United States was a 72-ft bowstring truss bridge over Erie Canal at Utica, New York, built by Squire Whipple in the same year. The first example of such a truss, it used wrought iron for tension and cast iron for compression members [Tyrrell, 1911; Edwards, 1959; Hopkins, 1970].

The first metal trusses in England were built in 1845. These were lattice trusses, similar to the American wooden trusses designed by Ithiel Town. In 1846, the multiple-system triangular truss, called the Warren truss (Fig. 1.20), was introduced. Patented in August 1848 in England by James Warren and Willoughby Theobald Monzani, this truss-type bridge was initially developed by the Belgian engineer Neuville, who had constructed bridge superstructures of this type over the Lys River, west of Ghent, Belgium, in 1846. It was improved by James Warren, who introduced it in the British Isles [Edwards, 1959, p. 60]. Relatively simple in form and devoid of any vertical members, the Warren truss consisted of top and bottom chords and diagonal members only. In contrast to the initial versions of the Howe and Pratt trusses, which consisted of verticals and Xs and were statically indeterminate, the Warren truss was statically determinate and therefore simple to analyze. The diagonals of a Warren truss are alternately in compression and tension. Because of its analytical determinacy, the Warren truss gained wide popularity among bridge engineers. In 1852, the all-iron Pratt truss was introduced. Its form was modified by replacing the Xs in panels (Fig. 1.16) with single diagonals, making it a statically determinate truss, which enhanced its popularity.

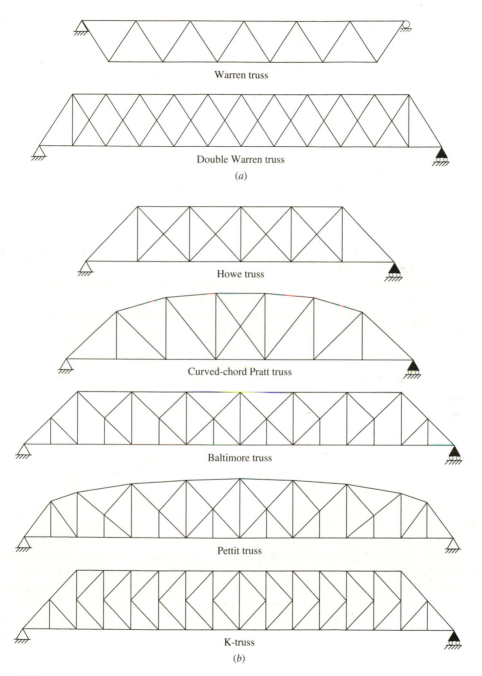

FIGURE 1.20
(a) The Warren truss. (b) Some other forms of truss bridges.

In addition to the use of iron as a new material for bridge building, advances were also made in the *mechanics* of bridge engineering. In stone arches, the dead weight is so large that the horizontal thrust is greater than that required to resist the active earth pressure of the embankments on the abutments. The cast-iron superstructure of the Coalbrookdale bridge was rather light, and hence its horizontal thrust was too small to balance the active pressure on the abutments from the embankments. Consequently, the abutments tilted inward, pushing the arch up a little at its crown. This is the reason for its upward pointing appearance (see Fig. 1.19). This behavior was noted by Telford, who corrected the problem in his designs. The arch form of the cast-iron bridge was also significant in that it embodied the skill and self-confidence of bridge builders. The arch form appeared repeatedly, as it had many times before the construction of the Coalbrookdale bridge. With every new material—stone, wood, and now iron—the *arch form* was tried first. However, iron trusses soon followed the example of iron arches.

In England, John Smeaton (1724–1792) was the first engineer to use cast iron to any great extent and is credited with introducing its systematic use in bridges. He used it in constructing windmills, water wheels, and pumps [Timoshenko, 1953]. He also was the first to use cast-iron girders in buildings, in 1755, for the floor of a factory. As an outstanding civil engineer, Smeaton came to be known as the father of civil engineering in England, and he was the first to call himself a consulting engineer. To recognize the importance of the civil engineering profession, the Smeatonian Society of Civil Engineers was created, named in Smeaton's honor [Hopkins, 1970].

Soon the limitations of cast iron—strong in *compression* and weak in *tension*—were recognized. A textbook written in the 1850s quoted the compressive, tensile, and shear strengths of cast iron[4] as 80,000–140,000, 13,000–30,000, and 3000–9000 lb/in.^{2}, respectively [Hopkins, 1970, p. 127]. On the other hand, the tensile strength of wrought iron is relatively much higher than that of cast iron—54,000 lb/in.^{2} [Singer, 1962, p. 567]. Consistent with the disparity in compressive and tensile strengths, the cast-iron beams had small top (compression) and large bottom (tension) flanges. Also, in bridge trusses, compression members were made from cast iron, whereas the tensile members were made from wrought iron, a common practice at the time. The Newark Dyke Bridge over the River Trent, near Newark, England, the earliest example of a Warren truss bridge, is an example of this practice. Having a clear span of 246 ft 6 in., and built between 1851 and 1853, the top chords (compression members) of this bridge consisted of cast-iron flanged pipes butting end-to-end. The bottom chords (tension members) were made of wrought-iron links. The diagonals, alternately compression and tension members, were made from cast iron and wrought iron, respectively [Hopkins, 1970].

The advent of railroads required sturdier bridges to control deflections and vibrations. In England, as a possible solution, tubular bridges were tried in the construction of the London–Chester–Holyhead Railroad. These bridges were to span the 400-ft-wide Conway River and the Menai Straits. The familiar arch form was ruled out for the Menai Straits by navigational considerations—the British admiralty had refused to allow the straits to be obstructed by even the temporary timber centering [Steinman and

---

[4]In today's textbooks (e.g., Singer, 1962) and handbooks, the strength of cast iron is listed separately, as for "gray cast iron" and "malleable cast iron."

Watson, 1957; Gies, 1963]. These tubular bridges through which trains could pass were suggested in 1845 by Robert Stephenson (1803–1859) and designed by William Fairbairn (1789–1874). They consisted of wrought-iron plates with side plates stiffened by vertical T-stiffeners. Figure 1.21 shows the Britannia Bridge spanning the Menai Straits, built not too far from Thomas Telford's historic suspension bridge (described later) and completed in 1850. It consists of two 1511-ft, 4680-ton continuous hollow tubes, placed side-by-side, supported on two abutments and three towers (212, 230, and 212 ft high), resulting in a four-span (230, 460, 460, and 230 ft) continuous bridge [Timoshenko, 1953; Steinman and Watson, 1957].[5] A comprehensive discussion on the

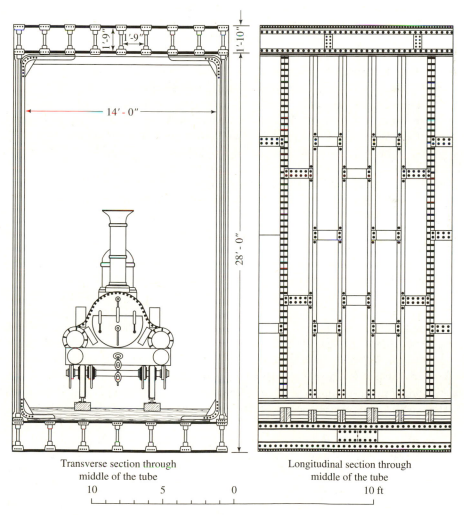

Transverse section through middle of the tube

Longitudinal section through middle of the tube

FIGURE 1.21
The Britannia Bridge [Timoshenko, 1953].

[5]More on the Britannia Bridge and the related engineering problems is discussed in Chapter 9.

design and construction of the Conway and the Britannia Bridges is provided by Fairbairn, 1849; Clark [1850] and by Rosenberg and Vincenti [1978].

The construction of the Conway and the Britannia Bridges marked a significant breakthrough in the knowledge of the strength of engineering structures. It was for these bridges that general strength was established by model tests; the strength of iron plates and riveted joints was investigated; for thin-walled structures, the buckling phenomenon was discovered; and the effects of lateral wind pressure and nonuniform solar heating were studied. Several bridges of this type were later built in England and elsewhere by Robert Stephenson [Timoshenko, 1953; Gies, 1963].[6] Eventually, however, this type of construction was abandoned in favor of more economical and efficient bridge construction. For bridges of shorter spans, thin-walled plate girders[7] were introduced by Isambard Kingdom Brunnel (1806–1859). Some of Brunnel's plate girder bridges were discussed by Fairbairn in his book *The Application of Cast and Wrought Iron to Building Purposes* [Fairbairn, 1857]. This book drew heavily on bridge-building experience and "quickly became the gospel in the British construction industry" [Rosenberg and Vincenti, 1978, p. 49].

The design of the Britannia Bridge and the phenomenon of plates buckling under compression were also studied by D. J. Jourawski (1821–1891), a Russian scientist and engineer and a contemporary of Fairbairn, who used models made from thick paper reinforced by cardboard stiffeners. Jourawski's work paved the way for stiffened-plate girder bridges. In 1842, he designed and built several bridges in Russia; one of the most important was the 180-ft, 9-span bridge built 170 ft above the waters of River Werebia for the St. Petersburg–Moscow railroad. For this bridge, he often used wooden beams of great depth as well as *built-up* wooden beams. While building timber bridges for the St. Petersburg–Moscow railroad in 1844–1850, he developed the theory of shearing stresses in rectangular beams that is still in use. During this period, the *theorem of three moments* was developed by B. P. E. Clapeyron (1799–1864), a French mathematician, as he analyzed continuous-beam bridges. This theorem was later modified by Otto Mohr (1835–1918) for bridge supports that have settlement [Timoshenko, 1953].

Certain properties of iron had been known for centuries. When it was remelted and cooled in the mold, it became hard and brittle cast iron. When most of the impurities were removed in the liquid state, it gained considerably in tensile strength and became wrought iron. Upon further remelting and reintroducing some of the removed carbon, a much stronger metal—steel—resulted. This latter part of the process was very difficult, and consequently, steel was rare and costly.

1.1.5 Modern Period

Ironmasters, both in England and America, were anxious to find a cheap steelmaking process. William Kelly (1811–1888) of Pittsburgh, Pennsylvania made wrought-iron

---

[6]Discussed in Chapter 9.

[7]Discussed in Chapter 9.

sugar kettles at his ironworks at Eddyville, Kentucky. He developed a steelmaking process in 1851, built the first of seven converters to make steel, and applied for a patent in 1856. Coincidentally, however, Henry Bessemer (1813–1898) had accidentally stumbled on the process in England and had been granted the patent before Kelly. Nonetheless, Kelly, upon producing convincing evidence of the priority of his claim, was granted a patent on June 23, 1857, resulting in the rejection of Bessemer's subsequent renewal application [Hopkins, 1970]. As it turned out, Kelly was destined to bankruptcy, and Bessemer remained the owner of the patent. The steel he produced came to be known as *Bessemer steel*. Later, Bessemer was joined by Karl Siemens and by Emile and Pierre Martin, who collaborated to develop in 1867 a better steelmaking process—the open-hearth process.

During the mid-nineteenth century, with the widespread growth of the railroads in the United States, the failures of cast-iron bridges occurred at an alarming rate. Then the tests of Hodgkinson and Fairbairn (in England) revealed the poor tensile strength of cast iron. As a result, after 1850, the use of cast iron was abandoned in favor of wrought iron. By the end of the nineteenth century, the use of wrought iron in bridges was in turn replaced by steel [Steinman and Watson, 1957].

James Eads (1820–1887), a businessman in St. Louis and one of Kelly's customers, was the first, in 1867, to use steel for bridge construction—in spite of its unproven performance, lack of research data, and uncertainty about its availability in sufficient bulk. Eads himself was not an engineer and had never before built a bridge. But as one of the great calculated risks of engineering history, in 1868–1874 he masterminded and built the triple-arch (502, 520, and 502 ft) double-decked Eads Bridge over the Mississippi at St. Louis (Fig. 1.22). Completed in 1874, the Eads Bridge is still in service, carrying two railroad tracks on the lower deck and highway traffic on the upper deck.

The Eads Bridge was a milestone in the history of bridge building, with several pioneering features. The largest and boldest of its day, the Eads Bridge marked the first extensive use of steel in bridge building.[8] Its arches were the first use of hollow tubular chord members, and its arches were the first ever to span a distance of over 500 ft. Eads used the arch form in spite of great opposition by such experienced bridge builders as John Roebling, the builder of the Brooklyn Bridge, and Robert Stephenson; being fixed-ended and indeterminate, the arches involved problems of stress analysis and erection adjustment that had not been experienced before. Construction of the Eads Bridge involved the first significant use of compressed air in America. And the compressed air was used at the greatest depth used anywhere up to that time; the caisson sunk for the east abutment foundation of the bridge remains to this day one of the deepest in which compressed-air workers have ever worked. Finally, the three great arches were built without any falsework, by cantilevering the arches out from the piers toward the span centers; this was the first extensive use of the modern-day cantilever method of bridge construction, previously proposed by Robert

---

[8]The first use of *any* steel in bridge building is reported to be for a chain suspension span of 312 ft over the Danube Canal at Vienna. It was built in 1828 by the German engineer Von Mitis, two years after the completion of Telford's Menai Strait suspension bridge in 1826, for which *wrought-iron* chains were used [Steinman and Watson, 1957, p. 166; Gies, 1963, p. 178].

FIGURE 1.22
The Eads Bridge over the Mississippi, in St. Louis, Missouri.

Stephenson and I. K. Brunel [Steinman and Watson, 1957; Gies, 1963; Hopkins, 1970].

Hailed as an engineering triumph and a monument, the Eads Bridge was pictured on a U.S. stamp, the Trans-Mississippi issue, in 1898, the first bridge to receive such philatelic recognition [Steinman and Watson, 1957]. Eads himself became a living legend. Impressed by his bridge, the journal *Scientific American* proposed Eads for President [Gies, 1963]. In 1920, when New York University inaugurated its American Hall of Fame, Eads was the first "engineer" enshrined [Smith, 1953; Gies, 1963]. And Eads *had* to convince the public of the strength and safety of the bridge. For this he gave an impressive demonstration on July 2, 1874. First, fourteen heavy locomotives, in two divisions of seven each, were moved out on two tracks and stopped over the center of each arch, side by side. Then all fourteen, seven on each track, crossed side-by-side. And finally, all fourteen crossed the bridge in single file. Their tenders were filled with coal and water during all these crossings. (Eads wanted to load the bridge with more locomotives, but none were available) [Steinman and Watson, 1957; Gies, 1963]. The bridge was formally opened on July 4, 1874, amid fireworks and fanfare [Scott, 1979]. Eads's trusted assistant and chief inspector for this bridge was the well-known Theodore Cooper (1839–1919), a New Yorker who developed Cooper's loading for railroads, which is still in use. He was also the builder of the first Quebec Bridge (described later). A detailed description of the construction of the Eads Bridge is presented by Scott and Miller [1979].

Pneumatic caissons, used for building underwater foundations, were one of the greatest developments in the construction industry in the nineteenth century. They were first used by I. K. Brunel for the Royal Albert Bridge over the Tamar River at Saltash, England, a wrought-iron structure built in 1855–1859 [Smith, 1953; Gies, 1963]. Robert Hooke is credited with developing the concept of using compressed air in caissons; he conducted experiments on the technique as early as 1664 [Hopkins, 1970].

The advent of steel and its successful use for the Eads Bridge heralded a new era in bridge building. Beginning from the mid-nineteenth century, some of the world's greatest bridges were built: cantilever bridges, arch bridges, suspension bridges, and cable-stayed bridges.

The development and increasing use of railroads as the main transportation mode led to some new service performance problems. The railway traffic imposed much heavier loads: the weight of the locomotive and the cars; the impact due to the presence of joints and irregularities; wear and tear from the hammer blows of the locomotives; the effect of lurching and nosing (the sideways push of flanges of the locomotive wheels caused by the guiding action of the tracks), and the rocking of the engine. The dynamic effects of loads were first recognized by Thomas Young, although J. V. Poncelet (1788–1867), influenced by the design of suspension bridges of his time, gave a detailed study of dynamic action in bridges. Showing how a pulsating force acting on a loaded bar could increase the amplitude of forced vibrations under conditions of resonance, he explained why a detachment of soldiers marching over a suspension bridge may be dangerous. [Timoshenko, 1953, p. 88]. Poncelet also introduced the effect of shearing forces in formulas for the deflection of beams.

An important discovery during the development of railroads was the phenomenon of *fatigue of metals* caused by a repeated cycle of stress. This phenomenon was first described in 1839 by Poncelet in his book *Industrial Mechanics* [Poncelet, 1870]. He stated that, under the action of alternating tension and compression, the most perfect spring may fail in fatigue [Poncelet, 1870]. A much more complete description of the phenomenon of fatigue was made later by A. Wohler (1819–1914). Since its discovery, fatigue analysis has played a fundamental role in the design of all structures subjected to repeated loads, especially metal bridges. Fatigue is discussed in Chapter 5.

The phenomenon of fatigue was also discussed by W. J. M. Rankine (1820–1872), who perhaps presented the first English paper in this field. Rankine's most important contribution to the theory of structures was his investigation "On the Stability of Loose Earth," in which he offers a method of designing retaining walls. His theories of earth pressure now form the fundamental principles for the design of all earth retaining structures.

Theoretical treatment of *moving* loads was another important contribution of engineers in the latter part of the nineteenth century. In 1867, E. Winkler (1835–1888) introduced the concept of *influence line* while working on problems of bridge engineering and prepared tables of the most unfavorable position of the live load for a beam with four spans [Timoshenko, 1953; Kinney, 1957].

FIGURE 1.23
The Firth of Forth Bridge, completed in 1890. (The suspension bridge under construction seen in the foreground was built in 1964) [Hopkins, 1970].

After the Tay Railway Bridge Disaster (described later) in 1877, the idea of light and flexible structures, including suspension bridges as they were then built, was completely discarded for railroad bridges. The answer to the problem of vibrations and deflections in flexible bridges due to heavy moving loads was the rigid cantilever bridge. The latter part of the nineteenth century ushered in the era of cantilever bridges.

Carl Von Ruppert, a German engineer, is reported to have been the first to design a cantilever bridge. He designed a combined arch and chain suspension bridge with piers in the stream, to span the Gulf of Bosporus in Istanbul, Turkey, but it was never built. However, some 100 years later, a suspension bridge (3524-ft main span) spanning the Bosporus was eventually completed in November 1973 [ENR, 1973; Arndt, 1975]. The first modern cast-iron truss cantilever bridge was built by Heinrich Gerber in 1867 over the Main River at Hassfurt, Germany, with a central span of 425 ft—it was known as the Gerber Bridge for some years [Steinman and Watson, 1957]. But the idea of a cantilever bridge was not new—the ancient Chinese had built cantilever bridges, and Gerber himself had derived his idea largely from Ruppert. Gerber's bridge was copied widely, especially in the United States, where the form was known not as the cantilever, but as the Gerber [Gies, 1963]. The first Gerber bridge in America was built by Charles Shaler Smith in 1876 for the Cincinnati Southern Railway—the three-span (375 ft each) Kentucky River Viaduct [Steinman and Watson, 1957; Gies, 1963]. The first great cantilever bridge, an awesome structure and the longest at the time, was built over the Firth of Forth, in England (described in the next section). (See Fig. 1.23.) Designed by Sir John Fowler and Sir Benjamin Baker, it was opened to traffic on March 4, 1890 [Hopkins, 1970]. A significant design consideration for this bridge was the allowance for wind pressure—56 lb/ft^2. One lb/ft^2 more than the 55 lb/ft^2 used by the French in their bridge designs, it was the maximum allowance used anywhere for

FIGURE 1.24
Human cantilever, adopted by Sir Benjamin Baker, to demonstrate principle of the Firth of Forth Bridge [Hopkins, 1970].

a bridge design. This was significant because the disaster of the contemporary Tay Bridge was blamed, in part, on its low-wind-pressure design (10–15 lb/ft^2). Figure 1.24 shows the brilliant method adopted by Sir Benjamin Baker to illustrate the principle of the cantilever bridge.

In addition to providing the rigidity required for long-span railway bridges, two very important factors contributed to the popularity of cantilever bridges: They were statically determinate analytically, and they did not require falsework that would obstruct a river or a waterway during construction.

Unfortunately, although success was achieved through the use of new materials—iron and steel—some historical setbacks and failures occurred in bridge building, both in Europe and in America. The first tragedy was that of the Ashtabula Bridge in Ohio. This 165-ft-span bridge, built in 1865, consisted of a 15-panel, 20-ft-high, wrought-iron Howe truss. It was built at Ashtabula, Ohio, to carry Lake Shore Railroad over a steep gorge of the Ashtabula Creek, near the shores of Lake Erie. It was also the first wrought-iron truss built by Amasa Stone Company, which had bought the Howe truss from its inventor one year after the patent was issued. After serving for 11 years, this bridge collapsed on the snowy night of December 29, 1876. A train carrying two locomotives and eleven cars with 123 passengers was crossing the bridge and the engine had almost reached the midspan. Ninety [9] people were killed. This accident reverberated throughout the United States, and, significantly, it involved a truss made from wrought iron—the newest metal at the time. Investigation into the causes of failure was inconclusive. Charles Collins, the 50-year-old chief engineer of the line, who was a surviving passenger, was made the scapegoat, along with Amasa Stone Company [Steinman and Watson, 1957; Gies, 1963].

---

[9] Accounts vary. Gies [1963] reports 80 deaths.

Two years later, another tragedy took place. The wood-and-iron Howe truss railway bridge at Tariffville, Connecticut, simply collapsed as an excursion train was crossing it. Seventeen people were killed in this mishap.

Unfortunately, during the 1870s, bridge failures had become common. About 40[10] bridges a year collapsed, representing nearly one in every four. Half of these were timber highway spans [Gies, 1963].

In the decade following the collapse of the Ashtabula Bridge, almost two hundred bridges collapsed, several involving major loss of life. In 1877, at Chattsworth, Illinois, in an accident similar to that in Ashtabula, 84 people died. Highway bridge failures were more common than those of railroad bridges [Gies, 1963]. Consequently, people soon recognized that bridge building in general lacked uniform engineering and building standards; thus *bridge specifications* were created. An interesting history of their development is provided by Edwards [1959].

Some major bridges outside the United States also failed in the nineteenth century. One of these was the famed Firth of Tay Bridge in Scotland, which failed two years after the Ashtabula collapsed. Designed and built by Thomas Bouch and opened in 1877 to carry the railroad from Edinburgh to Dundee, this bridge was considered to be one of the wonders of the modern era. The bridge consisted of 85 wrought-iron lattice trusses, with piers of cast-iron cylinders erected on a base of brick-and-stone masonry. Seventy-two of the trusses were 200-ft-span deck-type trusses (i.e., with the supporting railroad on top). The remaining 13 trusses (eleven 245-ft and two 227-ft trusses) were 27-ft deep through-type (i.e., the railroad is supported at the bottom chord level), located midstream, measuring 170 ft from their top to the water below [Steinman and Watson, 1957; Gies, 1963; Hopkins, 1970]. The successful completion of this bridge brought knighthood to Thomas Bouch. Just two years after completion, however, this bridge collapsed in the morning of Sunday, December 28, 1879. All 13 (a number long remembered in superstitious Scotland) through-trusses and 12 cast-iron piers had crashed into the Tay, carrying with them the train and 75[11] people [Hopkins, 1970]. Since none survived, the cause of the accident remains a mystery. It is said that the wind had reached a velocity of 72–80 miles per hour during the time of the accident. A court of inquiry[12] inconclusively blamed poor quality control during fabrication and construction and a disregard of wind loads in designing the bridge as factors contributing to the mishap. It was also revealed that because of lack of fit, the trusses were fabricated inaccurately. The court member Henry Cadogen Rothery declared that designer and builder Sir Thomas Bouch was mainly responsible for the mishap, saying the bridge was "badly designed, badly constructed, and badly maintained" [Steinman and Watson, 1957; Gies, 1963; Hopkins, 1970]. The failure of this bridge resulted in a series of worldwide studies on wind bracing.

Another catastrophic bridge disaster was the failure of the Quebec Bridge in Canada—a huge 3300-ft-long bridge (including the end viaducts). It was designed

---

[10]Accounts vary. Steinman and Watson [1957] report 25 bridges.

[11]Accounts vary. Steinman and Watson [1957] report about 100 deaths.

[12]The Court consisted of three members: Henry Cadogen Rothery, Wreck Commissioner; Colonel William Yolland, RE, Chief Inspector of Railways for the Board of Trade; and William Henry Barlow, President of the Institution of Civil Engineers [Hopkins, 1970].

with a main span of 1800 ft (two 600-ft cantilever spans and an 800-ft suspended span). With cantilever trusses 315 ft deep above the towers, this bridge is still the longest in the world for any type of bridge other than the suspension and cable-stayed bridges. Construction began in 1900 under the supervision of the famous Theodore Cooper, Eads's chief inspector during the building of the Eads Bridge. On August 29, 1907, as the south cantilever section was nearing completion, the bridge suddenly collapsed, taking with it more than 18,000 tons of steel and 86 men working on the bridge. Only 11 people survived [Virola, 1969]. Investigation revealed that the cause of failure was the buckling of the bottom compression chords near the piers [Tyrrell, 1911; Steinman and Watson, 1957; Gies, 1963]. Controversially, some critics attributed the failure to an initial crookedness of up to $\frac{3}{4}$ in. of the webs of some members; this crookedness reportedly increased to 2 in. after the members were installed [Smith, 1953].

Other reasons cited for the bridge failure were poor supervision and insufficient knowledge of bridge design, construction theory, and engineering mathematics. Cooper never left his New York office to inspect the bridge [Gies, 1963].

New construction began on the Quebec Bridge; this time it used a new material—nickel steel—that was 40 percent stronger than the steel originally used. The two cantilever spans had been completed in 1916, and the 4700-ton, 640-ft midspan section was assembled on shore, suspended, and carried on barges into midstream to be hoisted into position. On September 11, 1916, during the hoisting process, 30 ft in the air, the hoist machinery suddenly failed and the hoisted midspan section crashed into the river below, killing 12 people. The bridge (Fig. 1.25), was finally completed in August 1918, although one track of the bridge had been opened earlier on December 3, 1917. Initially built to carry two railroad tracks, the bridge now carries only one railroad track and three highway traffic lanes [Virola, 1969].

The Quebec Bridge, although the longest of its type, was not the first of its type to be built. Its predecessor was the famous railway bridge over the Firth of Forth, Scotland (built in 1883–1890), which carried two railway tracks (Fig. 1.26). The latter bridge has two main spans, each 1710 ft long, which, until the completion of the Quebec Bridge, were the longest spans in the world. The approaches to the main span comprise ten truss spans and four masonry arches at the southern end, and five truss spans and three masonry arches at the northern end. The bridge measures 8247 ft between the abutments [Virola, 1969].

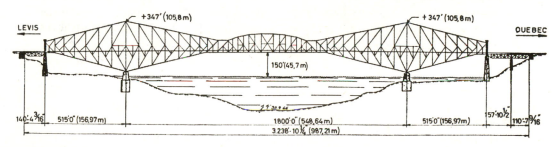

FIGURE 1.25
Quebec Bridge, Canada [Virola, 1969].

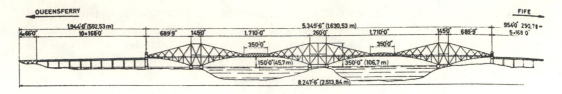

FIGURE 1.26
Firth of Forth Bridge, Scotland [Virola, 1969].

About the turn of the twentieth century, the cantilever form of construction, though not quite aesthetic, was the only possible form of construction for long-span railway bridges—it gave the required stiffness to limit deflections. Recent developments, however, have made it possible to use suspension bridges to carry railroad traffic. As the twentieth century progressed, the cantilever method of construction became simplified, making disasters such as that of the Quebec Bridge impossible. In 1917, the suspended span of the Quebec Bridge was finally lifted into position in *four days*. Only ten years later, as result of an improved and simplified procedure, the suspended span of the Carquinez Strait Bridge, in California, was lifted into position easily and safely to the same height—150 ft—in *thirty-five minutes* [Steinman and Watson, 1957].

A further catastrophe struck America again. On December 15, 1967, the U.S. 35 Highway Bridge, also popularly known as the Silver Bridge,[13] connecting Point Pleasant, West Virginia, and Kanauga, Ohio, collapsed at approximately 5 P.M. (EST). Of the 37 vehicles on the bridge, 24 fell into the Ohio River and 7 fell onto the shore. In all, 46 people were killed and 9 were injured. The bridge (380, 700, and 380 ft) was an eyebar suspension bridge built in 1927. It was unique in that the stiffening trusses of both the center span and the two side spans were framed into the eyebar chain to make up the top chord of about half of the length of the stiffening trusses. Investigation by the National Transportation Safety Board (NTSB) attributed the cause of failure to the *cleavage fracture* in the lower limb of the eye of one of the eyebars. The fracture was caused by the development of a critical-sized flaw over the 40-year life of the structure as the result of the combined action of *stress corrosion* and *fatigue* [NTSB, 1968; Fisher, 1984]. The Silver Bridge at Point Pleasant was one of two identical bridges over the Ohio River. Fearing a future catastrophe, its twin over the same Ohio River, at St. Mary's, West Virginia, was dismantled in 1969 [Fisher, 1984].

During the latter part of the nineteenth century, before engineers developed theoretical design procedures for determining shear and moment, acceptability criteria in the form of rules of thumb were developed to ensure good quality and workmanship in bridge construction. These criteria involved observing the effects of any overstress or workmanship defects under the action of combined dead and live loads by means of proof, or test, loads. The test loads for highway bridges often consisted of carts loaded with weighty materials such as stone or pig iron. Vehicles were loaded to an extent not likely to be exceeded during the life of the bridge structure. For railway bridges, the proof load consisted of two tandem locomotives for ordinary single spans, two or more locomotives followed by cars for longer spans. Theodore Cooper's specifications

---

[13]It was so named because of the shiny aluminum paint used to prevent rusting of its members.

for proof loads went a step further. They required this final test: "Before the final acceptance, the Engineer may make a thorough test by passing over each structure the specified loads, or their equivalent, at a speed not exceeding 60 miles an hour, and bringing them to stop at any point by means of the air or other brakes, or by resting the maximum load upon the structure for twelve hours" [Edwards, 1959].

Primitive suspension bridges were built in ancient times (see Secs. 1.1.1 and 1.1.2). Today's suspension bridges were preceded by rope-and-chain suspension bridges that were effectively used by military engineers during the sixteenth to nineteenth centuries, although it is believed that similar suspension bridges were built many centuries ago in India and China. The first use of a metal suspension system in Europe is reported to be that for the Oder River Bridge at Glorywitz. Built by the Saxon army in 1734, it used iron chains [Hopkins, 1970; Kavanagh, 1972]. The first metal suspension bridge in England was the Winch Bridge, a 2-ft-wide pedestrian bridge suspended on iron chains spanning 70 ft over the river Tees. Erected in 1741, it collapsed under loading in 1802 due to the corrosion of its chains. Its identical replacement lasted until 1908 [Tyrrell, 1911; Hopkins, 1970].

Some of the early suspension bridges in Europe are reported to be those built in St. Petersburg, Russia, from 1824 to 1826 [Mehrtens, 1908]. One of these bridges was a 1020-ft suspension span over the river Neva. They were built with the help of two French mathematician-scientists. One was Gabriel Lame (1795–1870), known for his *stress ellipsoid* and for his famous book *Lecons sur la Theorie Mathematique de l'Elasticitédes Corps Solides,* the first book on the theory of elasticity. The other was B. P. E. Clapeyron (1799–1864), who developed in 1848 the well-known *theorem of three moments,* which is still in use, while designing a multispan bridge in France [Timoshenko, 1953, p. 114].

Early work on the design of suspension bridges is credited to Navier. After Napoleon's defeat at Waterloo, France needed to rehabilitate its bridges, so Navier was sent to England to study the art of building suspension bridges. His three-volume report [Navier, 1823], based on his two visits (1821 and 1823), became the most widely used treatise for designing suspension bridges for the next 50 years. It contains a historical review of bridge building, a description of the most important bridges existing at the time, theoretical methods of analyzing such bridges, and a complete design for a 492-ft (150-m) suspension span to be built in Paris [Timoshenko, 1953; Billington and Nazmy, 1990].

The evolution of modern suspension bridges occurred in the United States and in Europe, most notably in England. Although in both these countries the suspension bridges were put to the rigors of regular and severe use, little theory was used in designing them [Timoshenko, 1953, p. 85].

The first suspension bridges capable of withstanding the rigors of modern times were erected in the United States [Timoshenko, 1953]. According to Charles Bender [Bender, 1872], suspension bridges were first introduced to North America by Judge James Finley. Finley was also the first to develop *stiffened* suspension bridges. Thomas Pope, a shipbuilder turned bridge builder who wrote the first American *Treatise on Bridge Architecture* [Pope, 1811], spread Finley's "ingenious invention" throughout the world. About 1810–1811, he proposed an 1800-ft wooden span, which he designated the "Flying Pendant Lever Bridge" (a cantilever bridge), to span New York's East River, between New York and Brooklyn [Hopkins, 1970]. This bridge was not built, however, and it was left for John Roebling to build the Brooklyn Bridge in the same general vicinity in 1869 (discussed later).

Finley built his first suspension bridge, the Jacob's Creek Bridge in Pennsylvania, in 1801[14] for $600.00, and he patented it in June 1808 [Finley, 1810; Tyrrell, 1911]. Made from two chains consisting of 5- to 10-ft-long 1-in.-by-1-in. wrought-iron bars, this 13-ft-wide bridge spanned 70 ft. It broke under the weight of a six-horse team load about 1825 and was repaired and put back in service [Edwards, 1959]. Finley built several other suspension bridges in Pennsylvania, Delaware, Maryland, and Washington, DC [Tyrrell, 1911].

British engineers followed the Americans, and many suspension bridges were built in England during the first quarter of the nineteenth century [Timoshenko, 1953]. In England, the first suspension bridge to carry loaded carriages, the Union Bridge at Norham Ford, was built in 1820 by Samuel Brown over the Tweed River. Consisting of 12 chains, 6 on each side, its suspension span was 449 ft. The links of the chains were made from 5-ft-long 2-in.-diameter round eyebars [Hopkins, 1970].

The first great suspension bridge, and the world's first bridge over the ocean, was built by Thomas Telford (1757–1834) over the Menai Strait, England. Its 580-ft span was a world record at the time. It used 2000 tons of wrought iron to build 16 cable chains and was opened to traffic on January 30, 1826. One week after it opened, the bridge was observed to be suffering from aerodynamic vibrations during a gale in the strait. This problem was rectified by installing transverse bracings that fastened the chain cables to each other at intervals. In another storm in January 1836, six of the suspension rods, by which the roadway was suspended, were broken and replaced. In January 1839, a hurricane hit the bridge, breaking over a third of the 444 suspension rods. The bridge was investigated and significantly retrofitted with four "strong-trussed railings," two for each carriageway. After the bridge served traffic for over 100 years, its 16 wrought-iron cables were replaced with steel ones in 1939. The bridge is still in satisfactory service, carrying highway traffic [Steinman and Watson, 1957; Gies, 1963].

The erection method used for the *eyebar chain* suspension bridge was its greatest drawback—it involved a cumbersome, sometimes huge, construction in the form of scaffoldings. The *wire* suspension bridge evolved as the answer. The first wire suspension bridges were built in 1816, one at Galashields, Scotland, and a second over the Schuylkill River, in Philadelphia [Kavanagh, 1972].

Two major suspension bridges that are considered to be hallmarks in the history of modern suspension bridges were built in the United States during the second half of the nineteenth century. A 20-ft-wide 1010-ft-long suspended span, the longest at the time, was built by Charles Ellet, Jr. (1810–1862), in 1848 over the Ohio River at Wheeling, West Virginia (then called Virginia) [Ellet, 1851]. Six years later, this great bridge was destroyed by wind [Steinman and Watson, 1957; Gies, 1963]. The other major suspension bridge was the 1595.5-ft Brooklyn Bridge designed by John Augustus Roebling (1806–1869), who is considered to be the inventor of modern suspension bridges [Smith, 1953]. Started by John Roebling in 1867 and completed in 1883 by

---

[14]Several authorities have erroneously quoted the year of construction as 1796. Edwards [1959, p. 41] has traced this error to Navier who, in 1921, personally examined and reported on developments in suspension-bridge construction in England.

his son Washington Roebling, it was the first suspension bridge to use cables of *steel wire*, and it was heralded as "the Eighth Wonder of the World" [Steinman and Watson, 1957, p. 246]. Built over the East River in New York State, it remained the longest suspension bridge for the next 20 years. It was surpassed in 1903 by the second East River bridge, the Williamsburg Bridge, designed by Leffert L. Buck. With a 1600-ft main span ($4\frac{1}{2}$ ft longer than the Brooklyn Bridge), the Williamsburg was the first large suspension bridge with *steel towers*. Preceding the construction of the Brooklyn Bridge, John Roebling had built six suspension structures of modest spans in the years 1844–1850, five of which were aqueducts. He made history by building an 821-ft suspension bridge 245 ft above the rapids of Niagara River, New York, the world's first successful *railway* suspension bridge,[15] opened to traffic on March 6, 1855. Suspended from four $10\frac{1}{4}$-in.-diameter cables, each having 3640 ungalvanized wrought-iron wires, it had an upper deck for railroad tracks and a lower deck for pedestrians and carriages [Roebling, 1846, 1855]. In the Niagara Bridge, Roebling was the first to incorporate inclined stays in conjunction with stiffening trusses to provide additional stiffness to minimize vertical undulations in a major suspension bridge [Roebling, 1855; Steinman and Watson, 1957; Buonopane and Billington, 1993]. Functional obsolescence forced the replacement of this landmark structure in 1896 by a 550-ft arch bridge designed to carry the heavier modern loads [Steinman and Watson, 1957; Gies, 1963; Hopkins, 1970].

From Telford's Menai Strait Bridge (built in 1826) to Roebling's Brooklyn Bridge (built in 1869–1883) was a period of evolution of suspension bridges. Beginning with the Brooklyn Bridge, the building of suspension bridges became an American enterprise. After World War II, the use of suspension bridge for long-span construction grew rapidly. The Brooklyn Bridge span (930, $1595\frac{1}{2}$, and 930 ft), although modest in terms of modern records, was an epoch-making span that heralded the era of suspension bridges in the United States. It was followed by many notable suspension bridges—George Washington (1931), San Francisco–Oakland Bay (1936), Golden Gate (1937), Bronx–Whitestone (1939), Tacoma Narrows I (1940), Tacoma Narrows II (1950), Delaware Memorial (1951), Mackinac Straits (1957), Walt Whitman (1957), Verazzano Narrows (1964), and others, each with a record-breaking span and a history of its own, all built in the twentieth century.[16]

Of all the great suspension bridges built in the United States, the Tacoma Narrows I Bridge (1100, 2800, and 1100 ft) over Puget Sound, Washington, is especially noteworthy. It was designed by Leon S. Moisseiff of New York, a world-renowned engineer known for his design of suspension bridges. Built at a cost of $6,400,000, it carried a two-lane roadway plus sidewalks. The third longest suspension bridge at the time, it was opened to traffic on July 1, 1940. Four months later, on November 7, 1940, it collapsed under the action of a moderate 35–42 mph wind (equivalent to 5 lb/ft^2 of static wind force) [Steinman and Watson, 1941] that caused excessive vibration and twisting of the deck [Bowers, 1940; WCN, 1940]. As it turned out, this bridge had been

---

[15]John Roebling's proposal to build a railway suspension bridge over Niagara was ridiculed as impossible by engineers all over the world. Even Robert Stephenson, the builder of the famous Britannia Bridge, said, in a letter to Roebling, "If your bridge succeeds, mine is a magnificent blunder" [Steinman and Watson, 1957, p. 218].

[16]See Appendix C, Table C2, for a complete chronology of the world's suspension bridges.

designed for a static wind force of 50 lb/ft^2, but not for its aerodynamic effects. The resulting aerodynamic instability (discussed in Chapter 3) caused the bridge to collapse due to "the cumulative dynamic effect of a wind pressure of five pounds per square foot" [Steinman and Watson, 1957, p. 362]. The board[17] of engineers appointed to investigate attributed the bridge's failure to "excessive oscillation caused by wind action, which were made possible by the extraordinary degree of flexibility of the structure and of its relatively small capacity to absorb dynamic forces." Significantly, they noted, "At the higher wind velocities, torsional oscillations, when once induced, had the tendency to increase amplitudes" [Gies, 1963, p. 247]. Several reports of this bridge failure were documented [Tacoma 1941a,b,c, 1943, 1944]. Professor F. B. Farquharson of the University of Washington filmed the actual mishap; his film has become a newsreel classic.

Locally nicknamed Galloping Gertie because of its excessive flexibility, the Tacoma Narrows Bridge was a long, narrow, shallow, and light structure. With its ribbon-like appearance, it stood as a hallmark of aesthetic excellence in bridge construction. It represented the culmination of a trend in designing and building increasingly slender suspension bridges. After the Tacoma Narrows collapsed, Roebling and his contemporaries introduced stiffening trusses and stays to minimize deflections and wind-induced vibrations in suspension bridges. With time, deeper trusses were used; this trend climaxed in 1903 in the Williamsburg Bridge, which had very deep stiffening girders and clumsy proportions. Later, introduction of the deflection theory[18] reversed this trend. Greater emphasis on artistic appearance and grace achieved through slenderness led to use of increasingly shallower stiffening trusses. As a result, beginning about 1929, stiffening girders were increasingly used instead of trusses, resulting in "maximum artistic simplicity of line." By far the most flexible of all modern suspension bridges, the Tacoma Narrows I, with its 8-ft-deep stiffening girders and center-to-center width between the suspension cables of 39 ft, had a girder depth-to-span ratio of 1:350 and a width-to-span ratio of 1:72. At the time, the recommended depth-to-span ratio for stiffening trusses of suspension bridges for spans between 2000 and 3000 ft was from 1:90 to 1:150, but no established criteria existed defining satisfactory stiffness. The new bridge, the Tacoma Narrows II, was eventually built in 1950.

---

[17]Appointed by the Federal Works Agency, the sponsor of the project, the Board consisted of Theodore von Karman of the California Institute of Technology, Glenn B. Woodruff, design engineer of the Golden Gate and Transby suspension bridges, and Othmar H. Amman, the builder in 1931 of the George Washington Bridge over the Hudson River, New York, the longest suspension bridge at the time with a main span of 3500 ft [Gies, 1963].

[18]Also referred to as the *exact* or the *second-order theory,* the *deflection theory* was first proposed by W. Ritter [1877] to allow for the deflection of stiffening trusses used in suspension bridges. Further advances were made in this respect by several investigators [Dubois, 1882]; however, it is Melan [1888] who is credited with formulating the deflection theory for practical use. In the United States, this theory was first used in 1908 by L. S. Moiseiff in the design of the Manhattan Suspension Bridge. In contrast to the *elastic* (or the *first-order*) *theory* of suspension bridge analysis, which neglects the deformations of the structural geometry under the load in the formulation of equations of equilibrium, the deflection theory accounts for the effects of deformations. Except for the preliminary design and the design of bridges with shorter spans or rigid stiffening trusses for which large distortions are not possible, the elastic theory is seldom used [Kavanagh, 1972]. A brief description of the elastic and the deflection theories is presented by Kavanagh [1972] and Buonopane and Billington [1993].

It has the same span lengths as the Tacoma Narrows I, but it is aerodynamically safe and fifty percent heavier than its predecessor. The stiffening girders of the new bridge are open-web and 33-ft-deep instead of the 8-ft-deep solid-plate girders used in the first bridge [Steinman and Watson, 1957; Gies, 1963].

As the most spectacular of all collapses, the failure of the Tacoma Narrows remains the most completely observed and minutely recorded bridge disaster. It generated unparalleled worldwide research on wind-induced forces and aerodynamic instability. However, it was not without precedents; the wind-induced vibration of suspension bridges had been a vexing problem for many years. In 1846–1849, Charles Ellet completed his record-breaking 1010-ft suspension span over the Ohio River at Wheeling, West Virginia, the first long-span wire-cable suspension bridge in the world. On May 17, 1854, the bridge was destroyed by wind for lack of aerodynamic stability. According to a reporter's eyewitness account printed in the Wheeling *Intelligencer* the next day, this disaster was an aerodynamic destruction remarkably parallel to the Tacoma Narrows catastrophe [Steinman and Watson, 1957]. The Wheeling Bridge was repaired and strengthened in 1854 and reconstructed in 1861 by John Roebling [Tyrrell, 1911]. Ironically, the Wheeling Bridge disaster had been preceded by a similar aerodynamic disaster only 18 years earlier. On November 30, 1836, one of the spans of the 1136-ft-long chain pier, with 1014 ft projecting into the sea, was destroyed at Brighton, England [Reid, 1836]. Built by Samuel Brown and opened in November 1823, the bridge consisted of four 255-ft suspension spans. The 12-ft 8-in. wide platform of its third span had been destroyed earlier in a gale on October 15, 1833, and repaired [Steinman and Watson, 1957; Hopkins, 1970]. A discussion of wind-induced failures of suspension bridges is provided by Finch [1941].

Engineers learned valuable lessons from past bridge failures. Combining these lessons with research, they developed new ways to build safe bridges. However, many older bridges in seismically active regions of the world, such as Japan, Mexico, India, New Zealand, the Philippines, and the United States, face a relatively new threat to their safety—earthquakes. Most of these bridge were designed before modern seismology was developed. Several bridges were destroyed during the February 8, 1971, San Fernando, California, earthquake, which had a magnitude of 6.6 (M 6.6) on the Richter scale. The October 17, 1989, M 7.1 earthquake in Loma Prieta, California, caused widespread and significant damage again in the San Francisco area. This earthquake caused the collapse of the 50-ft upper and lower closure spans linking, on either side, two long-span truss bridges that form part of the San Francisco–Oakland (double-deck) suspension bridge. It also caused the collapse of a large portion of the Cypress Viaduct, California's first continuous double-deck freeway, a reinforced concrete structure built in 1954–1957. Forty-eight bents of this bridge collapsed, killing 41 people [EERI, 1990; U.S. GAO, 1990]. Significant damage to bridges was observed during the January 17, 1995, M 6.8 earthquake in Hyogo-Ken Nanbu, Japan, which killed an estimated 5000 people [EERI, 1995]. Since this vulnerability to earthquakes has been recognized, several bridges are being retrofitted. Continuing studies of some of these bridges indicate that replacement, rather than retrofitting, may be a more cost-effective alternative. A discussion on seismic retrofitting of bridges is presented in Chapter 10.

While the cast-iron, wrought-iron, and steel bridges were being built during the nineteenth century, another construction material was being developed in both England

and the United States. The art of producing reliable lime mortar, known to the Romans, was lost for many centuries in the Middle Ages, as is mentioned in Sec. 1.1.2. *Natural hydraulic cement,* so called because it sets, or hardens, under water, was rediscovered in England in 1796. A builder found such a material on the Isle of Sheppy, and it came to be called Sheppy stones or Roman cement (a misnomer). Soon deposits of this material were also found in the United States. Because these deposits were widespread and reliable, the natural cement industry developed. During the nineteenth century, this new material was used extensively for bridges. For example, the masonry work for the Brooklyn Bridge was done with Rosendale Cement, from Rosendale, New York.

The real breakthrough in reliable mortar came about in the early 1820s. Joseph Adspin, a bricklayer of Leeds, England, invented the first artificial cement, called Portland cement. It was so named because its color and texture resembled a limestone found in the Isle of Portland off the southern coast of England, which is still a popular source of building stone in England [Steinman and Watson, 1957]. Adspin patented his process for making artificial cement on October 21, 1824. Isaac Charles Johnson further modified this process independently. In 1844, Johnson patented the process of heating materials of closely controlled chemical composition until they sinter at 2550 °F— virtually the same process used today. About 1850, this new product, by virtue of its controlled chemical composition and reliable physical properties, replaced the natural cement almost entirely [Hopkins, 1970]. This new material was successfully used to develop another revolutionary new building material—concrete.

In the 1860s, a Parisian gardener named Joseph Monier (1823–1906) was using the newly developed building material, concrete, to make tubs for large plants. Finding that concrete by itself had to be used in inconvenient bulk to achieve adequate strength, he hit on the idea of embedding a web of iron wire in the material during its preparation. Monier was not the first to think of combining concrete with iron or steel; the idea had been patented earlier in both France and America. However, his wire netting was the first such arrangement to work. He obtained his first patent on July 16, 1867, for the construction of basins, tubs, and reservoirs of cement in which iron netting was embedded. Within a few years, reinforced concrete was being used for dozens of structural purposes. Realizing the importance of his work, Monier secured patents in 1877 that covered floors, buildings, bridges, arches, railway sleepers, and other types of construction [Steinman and Watson, 1957; Gies, 1963]. His first bridge, built in 1875, was 13 ft wide and spanned 50 ft. Francois Hennebique, a French engineer, developed the T-shaped cross section, and he and his disciple, the Swiss engineer Robert Maillart, built several famous reinforced concrete arch bridges [Gies, 1963]. Maillart's concrete bridges are considered symbols of aesthetics (discussed in Chapter 11). Some common types of reinforced-concrete bridges are discussed in Chapter 6.

Early in the history of reinforced concrete, in 1888, an American named P. H. Jackson of San Francisco had an even better idea. He theorized that if steel wire were used in reinforcing concrete and if the wire were stretched tight to begin with, the result would be a much stronger kind of reinforced concrete that could be used in much smaller quantities. Jackson's experiments were never successful, probably because the steel wire of his day could not withstand enough tension. It was not until about 1930, when Eugene Freyssinet of France began using high-strength steel wire, that another new concept in building—*prestressed concrete*—evolved.

Prestressed concrete, although it was used widely for bridge construction in Europe during the first half of the twentieth century, had a rather slow start in the United States. The first major prestressed concrete bridge built in the United States is the Walnut Lane Bridge in Philadelphia, Pennsylvania, built in 1956. Since then, the use of prestressed concrete in bridge construction has steadily increased throughout the world. With the advent of the *cantilever,* or the *segmental, method* of construction, prestressed concrete bridges have become economically feasible for medium spans, and even spans in the 800-ft range have been built in Japan [Mathivat, 1983]. Today, prestressed concrete bridges have almost become the preferred type for short and medium spans, outbidding steel bridges [Libby and Perkins, 1976; Mathivat, 1983]. Prestressed concrete bridges are discussed in Chapter 7.

The most recent advancement in bridge building is that of cable-stayed bridges, which evolved in Europe after World War II. Germany was the pioneer in building cable-stayed bridges and is the home of some of the most impressive bridges of this type.

Credit for first using the concept of a cable-stayed bridge is generally given to C. J. Loscher, a German carpenter, who successfully built a completely timber bridge in 1784 with *inclined stays,* or *tie rods,* anchored in the tower, as shown in Fig. 1.27. However, the Loscher scheme is said to be antedated by over 150 years by the bar chain bridge of Faustus Verantius (1617) [Kavangh, 1972], a recognized leader in truss design during the Renaissance [Steinman and Watson, 1957; Brown, 1993]. The Loscher bridge was followed by the King's Meadow footbridge, having an approximate span of 110 ft, built in 1817 by the two British engineers Redpath and Brown. Another cable-stayed pedestrian bridge with a span of 259 ft (79 m) was built over Tweed River, Dryburgh-Abbey, England. This bridge collapsed in 1818 due to wind oscillations, which caused the chain stays to break at the joints. The cable-stayed bridge was again suggested by the French architect Poyet in 1821. In 1824, a 256-ft (78-m) cable-stayed bridge was built over the Saale River in Germany. This bridge also collapsed the following year, reportedly because a crowd of people overloaded the bridge, which caused the chain stays to fail, killing 25 people. Navier, perhaps influenced by the failure of these and other cable-stayed bridges, essentially ruled them out, for both structural and economic reasons, in his prestigious three-volume report on suspension bridges [Navier, 1823], even though the idea of using *stays* was known at the time.

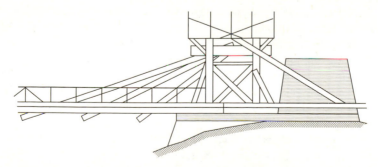

FIGURE 1.27
Loscher's bridge [Podolny and Scalzi, 1986].

These and other remarkable examples of early cable-stayed bridges are illustrated in treatises by Haseler [1900] and Mehrtens [1900].

Because of past failures, cable-stayed bridges were condemned and forgotten; almost no cable-stayed bridges were built for more than a century. They were rediscovered in 1938 by the German engineer Prof. Franz Dischinger (1887–1953) as he tried to design a two-track railway suspension bridge spanning 2460 ft (750 m) across the river Elbe near Hamburg, Germany [Dischinger, 1949a,b]. His goal was to incorporate stays into railroad suspension bridges to reduce deflections. This technique, of course, was not new. Stay ropes[19] had been used in some older suspension bridges, mainly in Roebling's Niagara Bridge (1855), the Cincinnati Bridge (1866), and in the Brooklyn Bridge (1883). But these ropes were too slack and too weak to play any significant role. However, without realizing that this was the drawback, builders omitted these stays in later suspension bridges [Leonhardt and Zellner, 1970]. It is noteworthy that, although the resurgence of cable-stayed bridges is lauded as a great innovation of the twentieth century, the concepts of using *stays* is hardly new. The basic idea of supporting and/or stabilizing a beam by ropes from a vertical support began perhaps with the booms, rigging, and masts of ancient Egyptian sailing ships.

The history and development of cable-stayed bridges in various countries is presented by Fiege [1966, 1971], Leonhardt and Zellner [1970], Taylor [1969], Thul [1966, 1972], and Podolny and Scalzi [1986]. Some important cable-stayed bridges are briefly described later in this chapter. Cable-stayed bridges can have both steel as well as prestressed concrete decks. Several cable-stayed bridges have been built throughout the world in the last twenty years, and significant advances have been made in the past decade in their spanning capabilities.

About the mid-twentieth century, many notable multiple-span bridges were built in the United States, each with a record-breaking length and a history of its own. This bridge construction activity, spurred by the demands of increased heavy traffic, was achieved as a result of cumulative knowledge in bridge engineering and the use of various structural forms and materials. Steel, reinforced concrete, and prestressed concrete were used. Some of these bridges are huge projects containing cantilever, truss, girder, and sometimes even suspension spans.

In 1935, the Huey P. Long Bridge over the Mississippi in Louisiana was completed. This 4.4-mile-long structure consists of a railroad section 22,996 ft long and a highway section 9364 ft long. Eight spans comprise the central section, the longest cantilever span being 790 ft [Steinman and Watson, 1957].

The Chesapeake Bay Bridge, nearly eight miles long and over four miles from shore to shore, was completed in 1952 and involved some of the heaviest construction attempted in the United States. Designed by the J. E. Greiner Company of Baltimore, the bridge consists of deck girders, deck trusses, deck cantilevers, a 780-ft-long through-cantilever, and a 1600-ft suspension span [Steinman and Watson, 1957].

The 15.2-mile-long Sunshine Skyway crosses Tampa Bay, Florida, from Maximo Point on the Pinellas County shore (near St. Petersburg) to Palm View on the Manatee

---

[19]The term "rope" is often used to apply exclusively to a *twisted* wire cable, in contrast to one with parallel strands.

County shore (near Brandenton). It consists of six hydraulic causeways, ranging from 3700 ft to 20,000 ft in length, and five steel-and-concrete bridges ranging from 324 ft to 22,373 ft long. It was opened to traffic in September, 1954 [Steinman and Watson, 1957]. A portion of the Sunshine Skyway Bridge was struck by a freighter in 1980, destroying a 1300-ft segment of the southbound span and killing 35 people [Garcia and Robison, 1986]. An entirely new design was provided to replace the damaged portion. Completed in 1986, the replacement bridge extends 21,877 ft (6670 m). As one of the world's most spectacular cable-stayed bridges (see book cover photo), it bridges the central navigation channel of Tampa Bay with the largest precast concrete segmental concrete bridge in the world. Its deck, designed for shipping clearance, stands 175 ft above the water [Brown, 1993].

The 24-mile-long Greater New Orleans Expressway, extending over Lake Pontchartrain, Louisiana, was completed in 1956 and remains the longest highway bridge in the world. It consists of several 56-ft-long spans of prestressed concrete (discussed in Chapter 7) and two movable bascule spans (described in Sec. 1.3.7). It is surpassed only by the 30-mile railroad trestle across Great Salt Lake, Utah.

A great bridge-building effort, the Honshu-Shikoku Bridge project, is underway (in 1996) in Japan, in an effort to connect two of Japan's four main islands by the year 2000. With its several suspension and cable-stayed bridges, when completed, this project will include 9 of the 20 longest-spanning bridges in the world [Billington, 1990; Brown, 1993].

1.1.6 Conclusion

We have come a long way from the primitive clapper bridges and suspension bridges consisting of vines hung between two trees across a river or a stream. Early bridges consisted of arches in stone or in timber with short spans. The advent of new materials—wrought iron, and later, steel—led to the development of chains and cables, which ushered in the modern suspension and cable-stayed bridges. These developments, coupled with advances in construction technology, broke new ground in the spanning capabilities of bridges.

The maximum span that can be bridged depends on the structural form adopted for a particular bridge. The limiting, or ultimate, span may be defined as the span at which a structure will be able to support its own weight. Since a bridge must support live load in addition to its own weight, the practical maximum span will always be shorter than the limiting span. The ultimate possibility in long-span bridging is discussed in Stussi [1951], Chang and Cohen [1981], Mallick [1983], and Starossek [1996].

Beginning with the Brooklyn Bridge (completed in 1883), bridges with increasing span lengths have been built all over the world. Since the 1930s, many great arch, suspension, and cable-stayed bridges of record spans have been built. These stand as symbols of civil engineering triumph. New ground in building longer spans continues to be broken. In some sense, however, the building of bridges still remains a formidable task; we have reached the moon and are striving to reach Mars, but so far we have been unable to bridge some notable gaps such as the Straits of Messina between Italy and Sicily, the Strait of Gibraltar between Spain and Morocco, and the Bering Strait between Alaska and Russia. Herzog [1982] has suggested a span of 11,483 ft

(3500 m) over the 2-mile-wide Messina Straits, a length closer to the ultimate span than is possible with our present day materials and knowledge. This bridge will most likely be the world's longest bridge. A brief summary of the proposed bridges for these gaps is provided by Brown [1993].

1.2
GLOSSARY

The following terms are frequently used in bridge design. Familiarity with these terms will help in understanding the material in this text.

Abutment   End support for bridge beams or girders, placed where the roadway ends and the bridge over the opening begins.

Access bridge   Pedestrian bridge of very short span used as a link between adjacent buildings; also used as a temporary bridge at construction sites.

Anchor span   The portion between the simple supports of a side span of a cantilever bridge (see Figs. 1.40 and 1.41).

Approach span   A span leading up to or away from the main span of a suspension or a cable-stayed bridge. Also, the first or last span of a multispan, continuous bridge.

Bailey bridge   An erector-set type of bridge developed by British engineers during World War II for temporary use.

Bearing stiffeners   Stiffeners provided at the ends of plate girders to transfer reactions to abutments or piers or, in the case of truss bridges, attach the girders to panel points of the trusses. Bearing stiffeners prevent local crippling in the web immediately adjacent to concentrated loads or reactions, and they also prevent a general vertical buckling.

Box caisson   A *box caisson* is open at the top and closed at the bottom, usually built on land and floated to the site, and sunk on a previously prepared bearing stratum.

Bracings   Members provided for lateral stability between adjacent beams or girders, or between two trusses of a bridge.

Bridge   A structure that spans an opening, or gap, 20 ft across or larger. The gap may be a waterway (river, channel, or creek), a valley, or another roadway. In general, the term *bridge* also describes structures built to span gaps in a roadway to carry loads across traffic flow or utility lines (such as pipelines for gas, water, or oil).

Bridge crossing   (Also referred to as *grade-separation structure.*) An intersection between a bridge and a roadway at a given elevation. Various bridge-crossing terms are currently used. The term used to describe a bridge-crossing depends on the particular situation.

Caisson   A special type of pier foundation used when it is necessary to carry the foundation to a considerable depth in order to reach a suitable bearing stratum. It consists of a hollow shell that is sunk into position to form a major part of a completed foundation. There are three types of caissons: *box caissons, open caissons,* and *pneumatic caissons.*

Cantilever span   The *overhang,* or cantilever, portion of the side span of a continuous bridge. The *free end* of the cantilever span supports one of the ends of the *suspended* span (see Fig. 1.39).

Continuous span   A bridge span that extends beyond two supports.

Cyclic loading   (Also called *repetitive loading.*) Alternately applying and removing loads, causing a member to endure cyclic stresses of some minimum value to some maximum value. When repeated many times, cyclic loading may cause a structural member to fail due to *fatigue.*

Deck   Flooring that supports vehicular traffic. The deck may be made of reinforced concrete, open- or filled-grid steel, steel plate, or wood.

Diaphragm   A short member, usually a channel, a W shape (for steel stringers), or a short rectangular concrete beam (for reinforced or prestressed concrete stringers) used between adjacent parallel stringers to distribute loads among them.

Double-deck bridge   A bridge carrying two levels of roadways, one above the other. Usually, but not necessarily, the two roadways carry traffic in opposite directions. This is an alternative to building two separate bridges for carrying traffic in opposite directions at the same location.

End stiffeners   Stiffeners provided at the ends of a plate girder, e.g., bearing stiffeners.

Fatigue   A fracture phenomenon resulting from a fluctuating stress cycle.

Fatigue life   The number of stress cycles that will cause failure for a specified maximum stress and specified stress ratio.

Fatigue limit   (Also sometimes referred to as *endurance limit*.) The limiting lower bound value of the fatigue strength as the fatigue life becomes very large.

Fatigue strength   The value of the maximum stress that will cause failure at a specified number of stress cycles for a given stress ratio.

Floor beams   Transverse beams (or girders) that support stringers in a truss bridge and transfer loads to panel points (i.e., points of intersection of truss members) in truss bridges.

Future wearing surface   Wearing surface that will be applied to a bridge deck in the *future* but is provided for in the *present* design to account for future dead loads.

Haunched girder   A plate girder of variable depth, with one or both ends haunched, i.e., made deeper than the remainder of the girder. When both ends of the plate girder are haunched, a considerable portion of its middle segment is straight; the bottom flanges are curved for the haunched segments.

Hybrid girders   Plate girders with flanges having higher-strength steel. They can be noncomposite, composite, or box girders.

Interchange   An intersection of two highways containing ramps and structures to provide access to traffic. An interchange may be a *two-level, three-level,* or *four-level* interchange, depending on whether the interchange involves roadways at two, three, or four different elevations.

Intermediate stiffeners   Vertical stiffeners provided at intermediate points of plate girders to prevent web buckling.

Longitudinal stiffener   Horizontal stiffener used for plate girders. When a single longitudinal stiffener is used, it is usually placed at one-fifth of the web depth from the compression flange. Its purpose is to prevent web buckling.

Main span   The span between towers of a cable-stayed or a suspension bridge.

Open caisson   A cassion that is open at both ends and built at the site where it is to be permanently positioned.

Orthotropic   A material that has different material properties at right angles to each to other. (Derived from the conjunction of two words—*orthogonal* and *anisotropic.*

Overcrossing   A structure that carries a county road or a city street over a state highway.

Overhead   A structure that carries a highway over a railroad.

Pedestrian overcrossing   An elevated pedestrian bridge over a roadway at the ground level.

Pedestrian undercrossing   A pedestrian bridge built underneath a highway bridge.

Piers   Intermediate supports consisting of one or more columns supporting a continuous bridge or a series of several simple spans.

Plate girder   A built-up steel beam of W shape consisting of two or more flange plates and a web plate.

Pneumatic caisson   A cassion that is closed at the top, open at the bottom, and filled with compressed air to force the water out. Generally used where the depth of water is between 40 and 110 ft.

Separation   A grade separation of two highways.

Side span   A span on either side of the main span of a cable-stayed or a suspension bridge. Also, the first or last span of a continuous bridge with three or more spans.

Skew bridge   A bridge whose longitudinal axis is not perpendicular to the abutments, piers caps, or both that support it.

Span   Distance between centers of bearings at supports.

Stiffeners   Steel angles or plates fastened to webs of plate girders to prevent web buckling. The edge of the plate stiffener or the leg of the angle is fastened to the face of the web (discussed in Chapter 9).

Stress cycle   As a bridge is loaded and unloaded by the live load (or fluctuating load), stresses in structural members vary from a certain minimum to a certain maximum; this is called a *stress cycle*. The minimum and the maximum stresses may be both compressive, both tensile, or alternately compressive and tensile.

Stress ratio   The ratio of algebraic minimum stress to the algebraic maximum stress in the stress cycle, usually denoted by R.

Stringers   Longitudinal beams that directly support the bridge deck. Stringers' longitudinal axes are oriented in the direction of the longitudinal axis of the roadway (i.e., parallel to traffic). Terms such as "beams" and "girders" are often used synonymously in discussion of stringers.

Substructure   Portion of the bridge that supports the superstructure. The substructure includes bridge bearings and every other bridge element below the bearings, such as abutments and piers.

Superstructure   Generally, the portion of the bridge above the bridge bearings. The superstructure may include only a few components, such as a reinforced concrete slab in a slab bridge, or it may include several components, such as the flooring, stringers, floor beams, trusses, and bracings in a truss bridge. In suspension and cable-stayed bridges, components such as suspension cables, hangers, stays, towers, bridge deck, and the supporting structure comprise the superstructure.

Suspended span   A span that is supported on the cantilever spans of a continuous span; i.e., it is supported by the free ends of the cantilever spans on each side (see Fig. 1.39).

Undercrossing   A bridge built to carry a city street or a county road under a state highway.

Viaduct   A bridge of some length that allows highways or railroads to pass over a valley. The valley may contain streets, railroads, or other features.

Wearing surface   A layer of concrete or asphaltic material provided over concrete decks to protect the structural integrity of the deck from wear and tear caused by traffic.

1.3
TYPES OF BRIDGES

To most people, describing a *bridge type* is a matter of ambiguous preference and perception, for they might be unaware of the true nature of construction of the bridge or its engineering features. Bridges can be characterized or classified in several ways, depending on the objective of classification. The necessity of classifying bridges in various ways has grown as bridges have evolved from simple beam bridges to modern suspension bridges and cable-stayed bridges. Bridges are always classified in terms of the bridge's superstructure, and superstructures can be classified according to the following characteristics:

Material of construction
Span lengths
Structural form
Span types
Load path characteristics
Usage
Position (for movable bridges)
Deck type (for combination and double-deck bridges)

1.3.1 Classification by Materials of Construction

Bridges can be identified by the materials from which their superstructures are built, namely, timber, concrete, and steel. They are described as steel bridges, concrete bridges, and timber bridges. This is not to suggest that only one kind of material is used exclusively to build these bridges in their entirety. Often, a combination of materials is used in bridge building. For example, a bridge may have a reinforced concrete deck and steel stringers, which is typical of many highway bridge superstructures. Also, recently, a new breed of materials called *advanced composite materials* (ACMs) has been developed for structural applications in bridges.

1.3.1.1 Steel bridges

Contrary to the general notion that a steel bridge is made entirely of steel, a steel bridge has a superstructure that consists, typically, of a reinforced concrete deck supported on steel stringers, one of the most common combinations of materials used for modern highway bridges. (The other common form for highway bridges is a reinforced concrete deck with prestressed concrete beams.) Truss highway and railroad bridges are built mostly from steel, although a few old timber bridges still exist. Other medium- and long-span bridges (defined later), such as cable and suspension bridges, may be truly all-steel structures. Arch bridges are built from both steel and concrete. In a few cases, in which the old concrete deck is to be rehabilitated, an open- or filled-grid deck made from steel is used to replace the deteriorated concrete deck. In some cases, the deck may consist of a steel plate deck instead of a conventional concrete deck.

Prestressed steel bridges are conceptually akin to prestressed concrete bridges. In prestressed steel bridges, steel beams are prestressed to counterbalance a certain portion of the dead-load stresses. The prestressing force is introduced in the bottom flanges of the beams by attaching to them a group of pretensioned high-strength strands (cables). The strands can be anchored to the girders, or, in the case of composite bridges, to the concrete deck. This procedure also constitutes a convenient method for strengthening existing bridges—both highway and railroad bridges [Sterian, 1969; Ferjencik, 1971; Kavanagh, 1972; Kar, 1974; Troitsky, 1988].

The concept of prestressed steel bridges actually dates back to the old days when truss bridges *underslung* by cable were used. In these bridges, the beams and trusses were underslung by a tensile system of links and rods with turnbuckles for stiffening them, a system introduced about 1851 by Albert Fink in his Fink trusses [Sterian, 1969; Kavanagh, 1972].

1.3.1.2 Concrete bridges

Concrete bridges include bridges built from both reinforced concrete and pre-stressed concrete. A reinforced concrete bridge generally has all its superstructural elements, such as deck, stringers, and parapets, built from reinforced concrete. A typical short-span prestressed concrete bridge has a reinforced concrete deck supported by prestressed concrete beams, such as I-shaped or box beams. For shorter spans, contiguously placed prestressed concrete planks (solid or hollow slabs) are used with a wearing surface of reinforced concrete. These planks simply act as prestressed concrete slabs placed longitudinally between the abutments. Several such planks are required to provide the desired bridge width. For medium-span bridges, prestressed concrete box girders are used. Their top flanges serve as a bridge deck, eliminating the need for a separate reinforced concrete deck. Often, these box girders are large enough to provide for the entire bridge width. Arch bridges are also built from reinforced concrete and, in recent years, cable-stayed bridges have also been built from prestressed concrete [Morandi, 1961; ICJ, 1963; Rothman and Chang, 1974]. Designs of both reinforced and prestressed concrete bridges are presented in ACI publications [ACI, 1969, 1977], by Heins and Lawrie [1984], and by Elliot [1990]. Design and construction of modern prestressed concrete highway bridges are discussed by Libby and Perkins [1976] and by Mathivat [1983].

Design of reinforced concrete *slab, T-beam,* and *box girder bridges* is covered in Chapter 6. Prestressed concrete *beam* and *box girder bridges* are discussed in Chapter 7.

1.3.1.3 Timber bridges

The first bridges to be built in the United States, before 1840, were timber bridges, mostly covered truss bridges. Today timber bridges are seldom built except in parks and recreational facilities, and in logging areas of forests. Typically, the deck and the supporting members (stringers and floor beams) are all-wood members. With the development of glued-laminated (or glulam) timber, both the deck and the supporting members are now built from glulam members. One of the latest developments in timber decks is the prestressing of glulam decks, a practice successfully used in Ontario, Canada, for several short-span bridges in the 40-ft range [CE, 1985].

1.3.1.4 Aluminum bridges

Very few aluminum bridges exist. At least eight aluminum bridges, including two four-span structures and two bascule bridges in England, are in service [Steinman and Watson, 1957]. High strength-to-weight ratio and high corrosion resistance are the two most significant factors in favor of aluminum as a construction material for bridges.

Structural aluminum was first used in bridge building in 1933 to replace the suspended floor (including floor beams, stringers, roadway, and sidewalks) of the two 360-ft lenticular (eye-shaped) truss spans of the Smithfield Street Bridge over the Monongahela River at Pittsburgh [Steinman and Watson, 1957]. The Smithfield Street Bridge was designed by Gustave Lindenthal and built in 1882. Use of aluminum reduced the dead load of the bridge by some 800 tons and added about 34 years to the service life of the bridge [Rogerson et al., 1967; Rothman and Chang, 1974]. As part of the bridge's rehabilitation, the deck was replaced again in 1977, this time by an aluminum *orthotropic* bridge deck [Rogerson et al., 1967]. This bridge is still in satisfactory service.

The first ever all-aluminum bridge is a 100-ft-deck plate girder bridge over the Grasse River at Messena, New York. Built in 1946 by Alcoa, it is designed for an E-60 railroad loading. Weighing only 53,000 pounds, it is much lighter than the almost identical steel span weighing 128,000 lbs.

The world's first all-aluminum highway bridge is a 290-ft-span arch, built during 1948–1950 over the Saguenay River at Arvida in Quebec, Canada [Steinman and Watson, 1957].

England is the home of the world's first two movable aluminum bridges. These are a double-leaf bascule bridge (discussed later) spanning 121 ft, built in 1948 over the Wear River at Sutherland, and a 100-ft-span double-leaf bascule bridge built in 1953 across an entrance to Victoria Dock in Aberdeen, Scotland. England is also the home of the world's first continuous aluminum bridges; among them is a three-span $310\frac{1}{2}$-ft-long pedestrian bridge with a center span of $172\frac{1}{2}$ ft [Steinman and Watson, 1957].

In the past, design of aluminum bridges was covered by *AASHTO Standard Specifications for Highway Bridges,* Sec. 11.2, *Aluminum Design—Bridges.* However, the new *Guide Specifications for Aluminum Highway Bridges* was issued by AASHTO in 1991, and a new *Aluminum Guide Specification for Division II—Construction* was proposed in 1996. The second edition of *Specifications for Aluminum Bridge and Other Highway Structures,* issued in 1976 by the Aluminum Association, Inc., forms the basis for the current AASHTO specifications for aluminum bridges.

1.3.1.5 Advanced composite materials

Long used by the aerospace, aircraft, and defense industries, *advanced composite materials* (ACMs) are now being explored for structural applications in bridges for both superstructures and substructures. Serious interest in using these materials for structural applications developed in the early 1980s, primarily as a response to the corrosion problems discovered in a large number of bridges built in the preceding 50 years that have reinforced concrete decks supported on steel beams. ACMs are high-strength, light, and corrosion-resistant, and they have desirable fatigue properties. A very complex array of properties can be achieved with ACMs, particularly when they are used compositely with concrete or steel. Bridges using ACMs may be referred to as composite bridges. ACMs are discussed in Chapter 2.

1.3.1.6 Other materials

Other materials have been tried for bridge construction, perhaps purely as experiments with new materials. A 79-ft-span pedestrian bridge with a fiberglass superstructure, reinforced with steel diagonals to carry tension, was built in Israel in 1975 [ENR, 1975]. Plastic, paper, and inflatable fabric bridges have also been reported [Product, 1970; CE, 1970b; McCormic, 1972; ENR, 1975a].

1.3.2 Classification by Span Lengths

In bridge engineering, it is customary to identify bridges as short-span, medium-span, and long-span, depending on the span lengths. Presently there are no established criteria to define the range of spans for these different classifications, and practices vary. However, the following guidelines have been suggested [Bakht et al., 1982; Bakht and Jaeger, 1990]:

1. Bridges in which the load effects are governed by a *single* actual *vehicle* on the span can be considered *short-span* bridges (up to 65 ft, or 20 m, long).
2. Bridges in which the maximum load effects are governed by a *train of moving vehicles* can be considered *medium-span* bridges (65–410 ft, or 20–125 m, long).
3. Bridges in which the maximum load effects are caused by a *train of stationary vehicles* with minimum headway distances can be considered *long-span* bridges (longer than 400 ft, or 125 m).

In the absence of any established criteria, a common practice is to classify bridges by *span lengths* as follows:

Short-span bridges	20 to 125 ft
Medium-span bridges	125 to 400 ft
Long-span bridges	Over 400 ft

Bridges with spans of 20 ft and under are classified as culverts.

This classification of bridges is made more out of necessity than for the sake of mere description. It so happens that certain types of bridges (described later by structural forms) are suitable only for a certain range of span lengths. Thus, by classifying a bridge in a particular category, certain bridge forms are automatically eliminated from consideration. For example, a suspension or a cable-stayed bridge, used for long spans, will not be considered as an alternative for a short-span bridge. Similarly, a typical slab-stringer deck bridge, suitable for short spans, cannot be used for long spans because the sizes and lengths of beams produced by the industry, as well as the construction methods and transportation, are limited. Certain prefabricated products, such as steel beams, prestressed concrete beams, and glulam beams, based on our current knowledge, are suitable only for short-span bridges. The state of the art in short-span bridges is discussed in the literature [GangaRao and Taly, 1977, 1978; Taly, 1976; Taly and GangaRao, 1974, 1977, 1978].

Short-span bridges are either single-span bridges or parts of multispan bridges (i.e., several single-span structures). Note that the *AASHTO Standard Specifications for Highway Bridges* (see the introduction of this standard) applies to ordinary highway bridges with spans up to 500 ft.

1.3.3 Classification by Structural Form

From an engineering perspective, bridges are classified by their structural form; this is necessary because the methods of analysis used depend on the structural form. Only certain types of structural forms are suitable and economically viable alternatives for certain span ranges.

Structural form refers to the load-resisting mechanism of a bridge by which it transfers gravitational and lateral loads from the deck to the foundation. In different types of bridges loads follow different paths as they are applied on the deck and finally resolved in the earth below. From this perspective, bridges can be classified as follows:

1.3.3.1 Slab-stringer bridges

In a slab-stringer bridge, the deck is supported on stringers that are themselves supported on abutments (in a single-span bridge) or piers (in a continuous-span or a multispan bridge). All bridge loads are transferred from deck to stringers to abutments or piers. The deck is usually built from reinforced concrete, except for the timber deck in the case of timber bridges. Stringers, generally simple beams, can be steel, reinforced concrete, prestressed concrete, or timber, and they are positioned with their longitudinal axes parallel to the direction of traffic. The slab is designed to bend in a direction perpendicular to the plane of bending of the stringers. The concrete slab can be cast either noncompositely or compositely, with stringers of steel, reinforced concrete, or prestressed concrete.

The slab-stringer system is most suitable for short-span bridges. Considered as a unit, it constitutes the basic unit comprising all bridges with the exception of slab bridges. In medium- and long-span bridges, the slab-stringer unit is supported on floor beams, which in turn transfer loads to other *main load-carrying elements* of the bridge, such as arches, cables in a cable-stayed bridge, or suspension cables (through *hangers*) in a suspension bridge. Design of slab-stringer bridges is covered in Chapter 8.

Other forms of bridges used for single spans, such as T-beam (*single* or *double*) and box girder bridges, are designed as simple spans, where the slab is cast monolithic with the rest of the beam (or the girder). Although these bridges are generally suitable for short spans, the prestressed box girder can be built *segmentally* to carry medium spans. In recent years, the segmental construction of prestressed box girder bridges has become popular for reasons of economy and long-term durability.

Plate girder bridges are essentially slab-stringer bridges, except that *steel plate girders* (i.e., built-up steel beams) are used instead of the rolled steel beams used for short-span slab-stringer bridges. Depending on whether they are simple-span or continuous, these bridges are economically suitable for spans in the 200-ft range, although plate girder bridges with spans exceeding 950 ft have been built. Because of their ability to span large distances, they minimize clearance problems in traffic interchanges and complex multilevel overpasses. One notable plate girder bridge is the second-largest plate girder structure, the three-span (246, 856, and 246 ft) highway bridge over the Sava River (Sava I) in Belgrade, Yugoslavia. The depth of its haunched girders varies from 14 ft 9 in. at the midspan to 31 ft 6 in. at the piers (Fig. 1.28) [AISC, 1962; Simpson, 1970; O'Connor, 1971]. Built in 1956 to replace a suspension bridge destroyed in World War II, it is still serving satisfactorily. The continuous Bonn–Beuel plate girder bridge (main span 643 ft) over the Rhine in Germany is another notable structure [AISC, 1962]. Design of plate girder bridges is covered in Chapter 9.

1.3.3.2 Orthotropic bridges

Orthotropic simply means having different elastic properties in two mutually perpendicular directions. Orthotropic bridges essentially consist of a *cross-stiffened* deck plate, a plate that has dissimilar elastic properties in two mutually perpendicular directions. This is known as an *ortho*gonal-aniso*tropic* plate, or simply an orthotropic plate. It evolved from a steel deck plate system known as the battledeck floor (Fig. 1.29), introduced in 1930 by the American Institute of Steel Construction to reduce the dead-weight of highway bridges [AISC, 1962]. This system consisted of a steel deck plate $\frac{3}{8}$

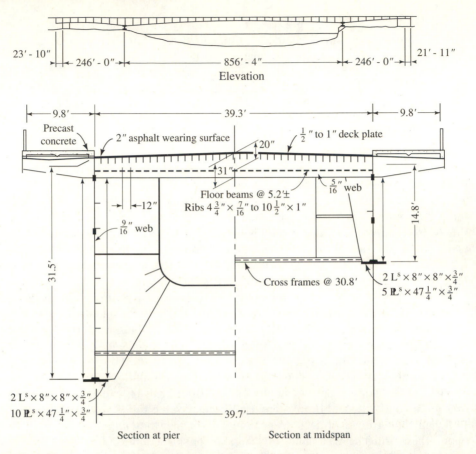

FIGURE 1.28
Sava I Bridge, Yugoslavia [AISC, 1962].

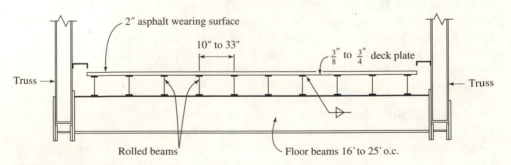

FIGURE 1.29
Cross section of typical battledeck floor bridge [AISC, 1962].

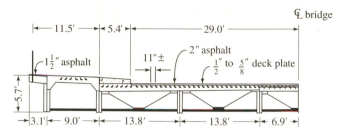

FIGURE 1.30
Cross section of the orthotropic Kurpfalz Bridge in Mannheim,
Germany [AISC, 1962].

to $\frac{3}{4}$ in. thick, welded to longitudinal I-beam stringers spaced 10 to 33 in. on centers and
supported by or framed into the transverse floor beams. The deck plate was intended to
transmit local wheel loads transversely to the stringers, and to participate in resisting the
stresses of individual stringers by acting as their top flanges. The deck plate, however,
did not participate in resisting the floor beam stresses, and therefore it did not enhance
the rigidity and the strength of the main load-carrying members of the bridge. Thus, the
system failed to realize the anticipated economy [AISC, 1962; Radojkovic, 1966].

Research on the battledeck floors, however, showed that the load-carrying capacity
of a steel plate loaded by a wheel was much greater than that predicted by the elastic theory. This system was improved by German engineers who stiffened a thin steel
plate in *both* directions by a relatively shallow gridwork of closely spaced (12- to 24-in.)
welded ribs, instead of stiffening in just the direction of the longitudinal beams. Engineers already knew that economy could be achieved only if the stiffened plate was also
a part of the main load-carrying system of the bridge. This knowledge was used after
World War II, when an economic stimulus was created by the necessity of rebuilding
long-span bridges destroyed during the war, accompanied by the shortage of steel. In
almost all long-span bridges, such as plate girder, suspension, and cable-stayed bridges,
the use of an orthotropic deck had become common. Figure 1.30 shows the cross section of the three-span (184, 246, and 184 ft) Kurpfalz Bridge over the Necker River in
Mannheim, Germany, the first bridge in which the steel plate deck was used. In 1956, a
steel plate deck was used for the Sava River Bridge in Belgrade, Yugoslavia, the longest
plate girder bridge (246, 856, and 246 ft) in the world (Fig. 1.28). By 1960, at least 40
orthotropic steel plate bridges had been built in Germany, and many more had been
built elsewhere [AISC, 1962; Troitsky, 1967; Simpson, 1970].

Orthotropic deck bridges are generally considered suitable for long-span bridges
[Rogerson et al., 1967; Simpson, 1970; Feige, 1971], and Chang [1961] has discussed
their economic feasibility for short-span bridges. Orthotropic deck bridges are not discussed in this text. A comprehensive discussion on the subject is provided by AISC
[1962], Troitsky [1967], O'Connor [1971], Hedefine [1972], and Wolchuk [1990].

1.3.3.3 Truss bridges

From a design standpoint, loads on a bridge deck are resisted essentially by the
resisting moments of the supporting beams (or girders). The sizes, and hence the resisting moments, of plate girders are limited by the problems of fabrication, erection, and

transportation. Practical maximum lengths of plate girders are in the 150-ft range, and the section depths range from 10 to 12 ft for economical design. Truss bridges provide the required answer when larger-depth girders are required. By virtue of the truss action, members are subjected primarily to direct stresses only. Thus, they can carry large amounts of force with a comparatively small amount of steel.

In the past, trusses were commonly built for spans ranging from 75 to 150 ft. With developments in materials and construction methods, other types of bridges (e.g., prestressed-concrete box girder and segmental bridges, steel box girder bridges, and cable-stayed bridges) have become more competitive with truss bridges. As a result, for spans smaller than 300 ft, trusses are hardly economical for highway bridges.

The first truss bridges were built from wood. Several of these are still in existence, although they are no longer functional for modern highway traffic. Nevertheless, some of them have been preserved as historic civil engineering landmarks. Some truss bridges were also built from wrought iron. Modern truss bridges are built mostly from steel, although a few reinforced-concrete truss bridges also exist [ACI, 1969, 1977]. *Prestressed-steel truss bridges* are a modern concept in which the bottom chords are *prestressed in compression* to counterbalance a portion of the tensile stresses caused by the loads [Troitsky, 1988]. A common method of introducing precompression in the bottom chords of trusses is to attach to them a group of pretensioned steel strands.

Truss bridges may be simple spans or continuous spans. In the latter case, the end trusses have cantilevered spans that support the central truss span (see suspended spans in Fig. 1.40).

Truss bridges can be classified in several ways. They can be classified as highway or railway bridges, depending on the loading they carry. Because railway loading is much heavier than highway loading, railway trusses are built with much heavier sections. Consequently, highway trusses are lighter than railway trusses. Since highways are generally wider than railways, truss spacing in highway bridges is relatively wider than that in railway bridges.

With their evolution, trusses were classified based on the arrangement of chords and direction of diagonals. Top chords can be parallel to the bottom chords, as in the case of the Pratt, Warren, and Howe trusses (discussed earlier), resulting in trusses with constant depth. The chords provide a couple that resists the bending moment caused by the loads. With longer spans, the required magnitude of this couple increases; this couple is economically achieved by spacing the chords farther apart at the points of the largest bending moments, with little increase in the chord forces. The result is a truss with variable depths along the span, such as a Parker truss (Fig. 1.20(*b*)). When simply supported, the Parker truss has its maximum depth at the center, the point of the maximum bending moment. For greatest economy, the top-chord profile should approximate a parabola, which is the shape of the bending-moment diagram for a uniformly loaded simple beam.

Very long spans dictate truss depths that are too great, and the slopes of their diagonals may become unacceptable. For an economic design, the desirable slope of diagonals is between 45° and 60°. A solution to this problem is the K-truss (Fig. 1.20(*b*)), which permits short panels with acceptable slopes of diagonals. Typically, each panel is provided with *two* diagonals meeting at the midheight of a vertical. Thus, each of the two diagonals in a panel has a slope only half as great as it would be if only one diagonal were provided in that panel. The short panels are also economical for the floor system. K-trusses may have constant or variable depths (similar to the Parker truss). They are economical for longer spans for which deep trusses with short panels are desirable.

Truss bridges are also described in relation to the position of the floor (or the deck) relative to the upper or lower panel points of the truss. These bridges are referred to as *deck, through-,* or *half-through*-trusses. In all truss bridges, floor loads are transferred to truss panel points through the medium of transverse floor beams that connect the two trusses composing the bridge.

In a deck truss, the floor is supported at the *upper* panel points of the trusses, which in turn are positioned wholly *underneath* the deck. Because deck trusses do not obstruct the view for motorists, they are favored for highway bridges. Deck trusses are, however, less common for railway bridges. In a through-type truss, the floor is supported at the *lower* panel points of the trusses. The *upper* panel points of the trusses are connected together laterally and diagonally, by sway bracings. This arrangement results in a three-dimensional latticed structure through which the vehicles or trains pass (hence the term through-truss). Figure 1.31 identifies various components of a typical through-truss bridge. Vertical and diagonal members of through-trusses obstruct motorists' view. As a result, through-trusses are not favored for highway bridges.

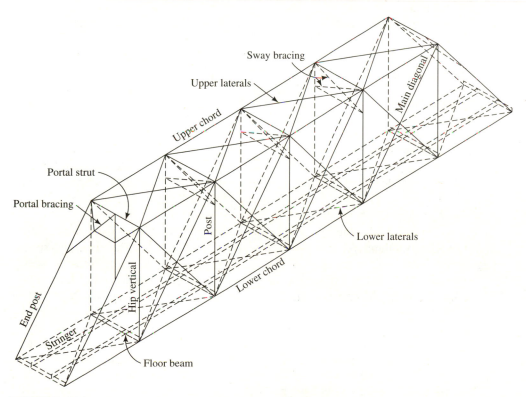

FIGURE 1.31
Typical through-truss bridge. Various members have been identified.

Clearance and the practical necessity of providing suitable sway frames usually require through-trusses to be at least 24 ft deep for highway bridges and at least 30 ft deep for railway bridges. Trusses with smaller spans require smaller depths, which makes it impractical to provide sway bracings at the top. The result is a *half-through-truss,* which is also referred to as a *pony truss.*

The absence of top bracings in half-through-trusses requires special design provisions to resist lateral forces. Upper chords are designed as columns with elastic supports at the panel points. The verticals are designed as cantilevers, subjected to a concentrated load at the top and having a rigid connection to a floor beam. Upper chords, verticals, and diagonals may buckle in compression. The development of the theory of framework stability actually started with various attempts to approach this problem. One of the first studies on the buckling of compression members was prompted by the failure in buckling of a Russian railroad truss bridge. Stability analysis of such trusses is discussed by Bleich [1952] and by Timoshenko and Gere [1961] and is summarized in the SSRC guide [1988].

The dead-load force in a bridge truss member is often a large percentage of the total member force. An extensive treatment of the weights of metal in steel trusses is provided by Waddell [1935]. Discussion of the influence lines for computing live-load forces in various members of bridge trusses can be found in many textbooks on structural analysis.

In earlier times, aesthetics was of little concern to bridge designers. As a result, many entirely functional but quite unattractive truss bridges were built. Often these bridges have heavy sections of various sizes, and the truss members appear to lie in all possible directions, giving an impression of complete disorder. This lack of aesthetics, evident from the many unattractive truss bridges in existence, is perhaps one of the reasons for their unpopularity. Always exposed to the environment, steel trusses require regular periodic maintenance and painting to prevent corrosion. Experience with steel truss bridges has shown that their life-cycle costs are prohibitively high—another reason for their lack of appeal.

Truss bridges are not discussed further in this text. Their design is discussed by Cooper [1889], Waddell [1916], and Shedd [1972].

1.3.3.4 Rigid frame bridges

Rigid frame bridges consist of superstructures supported on vertical or slanted monolithic legs (columns), and are economically suitable for moderate medium-span lengths.

From an analytical standpoint, a rigid frame bridge may be treated similar to two hinged or fixed arches [Olander, 1954; O'Connor, 1971; Heins and Firmage, 1979]. The only difference is that instead of the generally accepted form of the continuous smooth curve of an arch axis, a rigid frame bridge with inclined legs (Fig. 1.32) has an arch axis that is trapezoidal in form, and, one with vertical legs (Fig. 1.33) has a rectangular form [Kavanagh and Young, 1990]. Schematics of various forms of arch axes are shown in Fig. 1.37 [O'Connor, 1971].

Several rigid frame bridges have been built in recent years, both from steel and from concrete. The longest bridge of this type in the world is perhaps the asymmetrical 1165-ft (313, 501, and 351 ft) Grand Duchess Charlotte Bridge at Luxembourg,

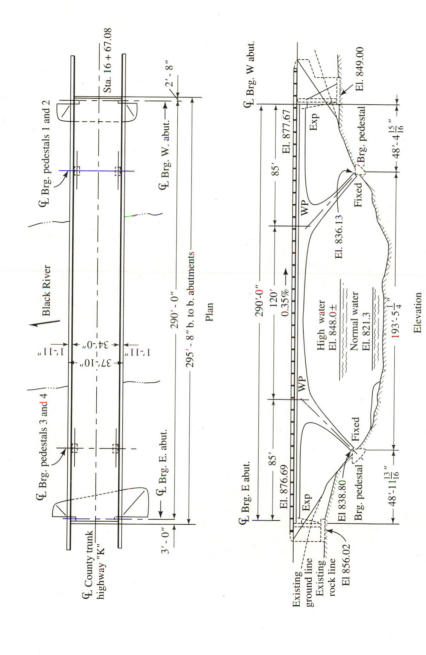

FIGURE 1.32

Rigid frame bridge with inclined legs—The Hatfield Bridge over Blake River, Wisconsin [USS, 1974].

57

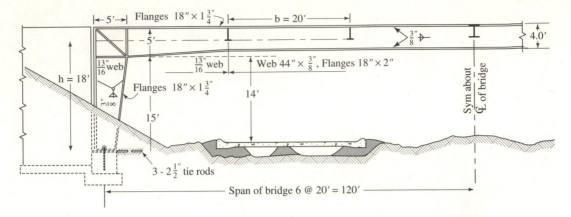

FIGURE 1.33
Rigid frame bridge with vertical legs.

a unique haunched steel box girder bridge. Its main span is also asymmetrical about the shallowest section (off midspan), which divides it into 226-ft and 275-ft segments [Hagon and Broucke, 1965]. The longest bridge of this type in the United States is the 806-ft (248, 310, and 248 ft) White Bird Canyon Bridge in Idaho, completed in 1975. The girder of this bridge consists of a steel trapezoidal box section and the legs of this section. Figure 1.33 shows the plan and elevation of the Hatfield Bridge, spanning Blake River in Jackson County, Wisconsin, a typical steel rigid frame bridge [USS, 1974].

Innovative schemes have been developed to build continuous bridges using a series of steel rigid frames instead of just one. In such schemes, the end spans become intermediate spans between the main spans (Figs. 1.34 and 1.35). With inclined legs oriented away from the main spans, these intermediate spans look like the inverted Greek letter delta (∇) and are called delta frames. Both concrete and steel have been used to build bridges of this type. Twin four-span (182 ft 7 in., 240 ft, 240 ft, and 182 ft 7 in.) steel continuous rigid frame bridges using delta frames have been built to carry Interstate 64 near Lexington, Virginia, as shown in Fig. 1.34. Fig. 1.35 shows a five-span continuous rigid frame bridge over Interstate 40 in Ozark, Arkansas.

A slant-legged prestressed concrete box girder bridge spanning South Africa's Gouritz River was completed in 1977. This 870-ft asymmetrical bridge has a main span of 361 ft, flanked by two 181-ft spans on one side and a 147-ft span on the other side [ENR, 1977]. The 230-ft long (70, 90, and 70 ft) Sollecks River Bridge in the Olympia Peninsula, Washington, has been built with precast prestressed concrete I-girders (made continuous by mild steel reinforcement) and with precast prestressed concrete hollow struts [Casad and Birkland, 1970; White et al., 1976].

Rigid frame bridges are not discussed in this text. An in-depth discussion on the topic is provided in Cheng [1960], White et al. [1976], and in Heins and Firmage [1979]. Reinforced concrete rigid frame bridges are discussed in references [PCA, 1966].

1.3.3.5 Arch bridges

Arch bridges are the oldest type of bridges ever built. Some stone arch bridges built more than 2000 years ago are still in service.

FIGURE 1.34
Interstate 64 twin four-span rigid frame bridges near Lexington, Virginia, using delta frames to create continuity.

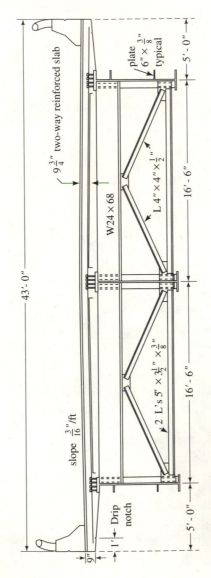

FIGURE 1.34 (continued)

FIGURE 1.35
Continuous rigid frame bridge over Interstate 40, Ozark, Arkansas (five spans: 41 ft 5$\frac{3}{8}$ in., 99 ft, 50 ft, 90 ft, 41 ft 5$\frac{3}{8}$ in.; total length is 334 ft 7$\frac{3}{4}$ in.).

A true arch transfers loads to its foundation by pure compression; however, the variable position of the live load always causes superimposed bending. When arch spans are short, the reactions can be economically transmitted to *buttresses.* In the case of large spans, the reactions are rather heavy, producing large *thrust,* the horizontal component of reaction forces. This necessitates relatively deep foundations to carry the reaction to the buttresses, as in the case of a true arch. When the foundation material is not suitable to provide the required bearing strength, the thrust can be absorbed by a *tie-rod* connecting the two ends of the arch, resulting in a *tied-arch.* To minimize the thrust for a given span, the arch should be as light as possible and its rise should be as high as possible. Figure 1.36 defines various terms related to arches. Various types of arch bridges are shown schematically in Fig. 1.37.

Like all bridges, arch bridges are classified in several different ways, depending on their purpose. From a design standpoint, they may be classified by the nature of their *ribs:* When the rib consists of a truss, the arch is called a *trussed arch;* when the rib consists of a girder, the arch is called a *solid-ribbed arch.* Analytically, arches may be classified by *degree of articulation:* An arch may be *fixed* or *two-hinged,* both types having indeterminate reactions; or it may be *three-hinged,* having determinate reactions, with the third hinge provided at the *crown* in addition to the two hinges at the supports.

Arch bridges can also be classified by the relative positions of the deck and the arch. In a *deck-arch* bridge, the arch is positioned completely below the deck, the most usual type for the true arch. The space between the deck and the arch is called the *spandrel.* The loads from the deck are transferred to the arch by *struts* (or columns) located in the spandrel. When this space is relatively open, the arch is called an *open-spandrel arch.* When the spandrel is filled with earth, the arch is called a *filled-spandrel arch.* In a *through-arch,* the arches are entirely above the deck and the tie is at the deck level. Such arch bridges are also known as *bowstring girders* or *Langer girders,* and the loads from the deck are transferred to the arch through tension hangers. In some cases, both true and tied arches are built with the deck at some intermediate level between the *springing* and the crown. Arch bridges of this type are referred to as

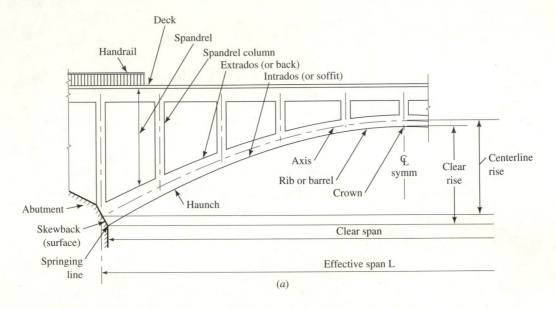

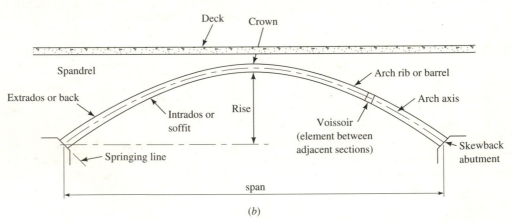

FIGURE 1.36
Arch bridge terminology; (*a*) open spandrel arch [Kavanagh and Young, 1990], (*b*) masonry arch [O'Connor, 1971].

half-through-arches. Arches can also be described by their material of construction, namely, concrete or steel arches.

An arch bridge may also be used in conjunction with other types of bridges. Many bridges have been built with three-span continuous trusses as the basic structure, with the center span being a tied arch. In some cases, the side (or the approach) spans may be slab-stringer or plate girder bridges.

To resist lateral loads, the through-type arch bridges usually need heavy overhead lateral and sway bracings provided at every panel point. These bracings are usually the truss or Vierendeel type. The truss-type bracings may consist of either the struts and diagonals between the ribs of two arches or the cross diagonals alone. The Vierendeel-

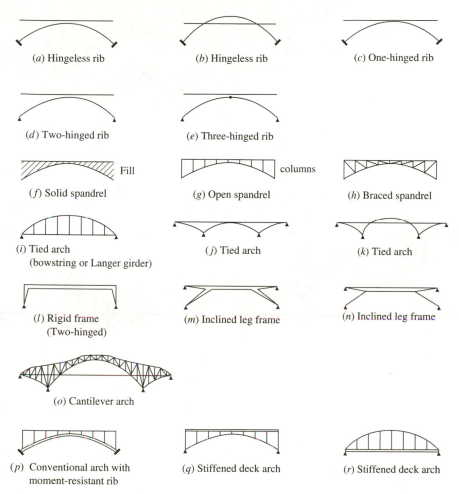

FIGURE 1.37
Various types of arch bridges [O'Connor, 1971].

type bracings consist of struts between the arches, the truss being in a curved plane. To improve their aesthetics, some arch bridges have no sway bracings, and the omission has been found to have no adverse effect on their lateral resistance. *Langer girder*-type arches, which employ a heavy tied girder and a relatively slender rib rising over the roadway, use an entirely new concept of providing lateral resistance: The arches themselves have been used to brace themselves [Nagai, Kojima, and Naruoka, 1965]. Contrary to the usual scheme of two arches lying in a vertical plane, the Langer girder arches are built in an inclined plane with their crowns almost touching, forming the shape of a basket handle. Such a system of arches has been used in the 250-ft Rio Blanco Bridge, in Rio Blanco, Mexico, and the 815-ft Fehrmarnsund Bridge on the International Highway Route between Germany and Denmark [Kavanagh and Young, 1990].

(a)

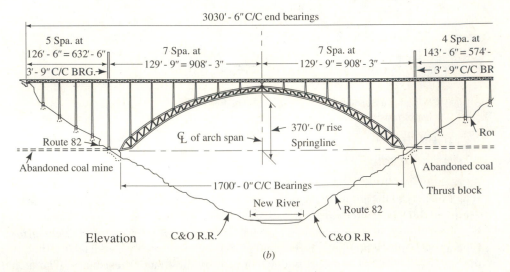

(b)

FIGURE 1.38
The New River Gorge Bridge, West Virginia; (a) during construction (photo by the author), (b) the completed arch [USS, 1978].

Arch bridges are economical for medium and long spans. The longest *steel* arch bridge ever built is the 1700-ft trussed, two-hinged, deck-type New River Gorge Bridge in West Virginia, completed in 1977 (Fig. 1.38). Its deck, 876 ft above the river [USS, 1978], is the second highest after that of the Royal Gorge Bridge over the Arkansas River in Colorado, which is 1053 ft above the water. The previous record holder is the 1652 ft 1 in., trussed, two-hinged, half-through, Kill Van Kull Bridge, at Bayonne, New Jersey (Fig. 1.39), which was completed in 1932. Also completed a few months later in 1932 is the notable Sydney Harbor Bridge in Sydney, Australia, a 1650-ft steel arch similar to the Kill Van Kull Bridge, but 2 ft shorter. A tied, solid-ribbed arch, the Port Mann Arch Bridge (1200-ft central span with two 360-ft side spans), has been built over Fraser River in Canada. Other notable arch bridges are the solid-ribbed, half-through, two-hinged Colorado River Arch Bridge (span 550 ft) in Utah, near the Garfield–San Juan county line, and the similar but tied Arkansas River Arch Bridge (span 466 ft) at Ozark, Arkansas. A noteworthy *double-deck* arch bridge is the two-hinged, tied, through-type, trussed Sherman Minton Bridge (span 800 ft) over the Ohio River, between Louisville, Kentucky, and New Albany, Indiana. Others are the 750-ft Fort Pitt Bridge over Monongahela River, a solid-ribbed, tied, through-arch, and the similar 423-ft Fort Duquesne Bridge over Allegheny River, both in Pittsburgh, Pennsylvania. Design features of these and other arch bridges are presented by O'Connor [1971], Virola [1971], Richardson [1972], and Kavanagh and Young [1990]. Construction of some of the major arch bridges built before 1950 is described by Steinman and Watson [1957].

Concrete arch bridges designed by Robert Maillart and built mostly in Switzerland are considered masterpieces of beauty and aesthetic appeal. The longest *concrete* arch bridge is the 1000-ft Gladesville Bridge in Sydney, Australia, completed in 1964 [O'Connor, 1971; Richardson, 1972]. The previous record holder is the 951-ft arch over the Parana River on the border between Brazil and Paraguay, also completed in 1964 [Richardson, 1972]. With the breed of high-strength steels presently available, arch bridges with spans in the 2000-ft-span range are economically feasible.

Arch bridges are not discussed in this text. O'Connor [1971], Richardson [1972], and Kavanagh and Young [1990] discuss the design of arch bridges.

1.3.3.6 Cantilever bridges

Cantilever bridges were the answer for long-span railway bridges in the late 1800s. They displayed the strength, rigidity, and sturdiness required to carry the heavy railroad traffic that had caused large deflections in the truss bridges of earlier times.

Essentially, a cantilever bridge consists of two simple spans (anchor spans) with a cantilever (cantilever span) on each side of either shore supporting a short *suspended span* in the middle of the stream or river (Fig. 1.40). This arrangement results in substantial reduction of moments or forces in the suspended span. Moreover, because a cantilever span can be erected without falsework, river navigation is not impeded during construction. The principle of the cantilever bridge was aptly demonstrated by Sir Benjamin Baker when he used a human cantilever (Fig. 1.24) to convince people to allow the Firth of Forth Bridge to be built in the late nineteenth century. Various arrangements for supporting suspended spans in cantilever bridges are shown in Fig. 1.41.

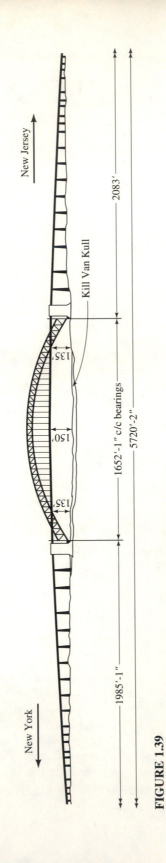

FIGURE 1.39
The Kill Van Kull Bridge, New Jersey [Salvadori and Heller, 1975].

66

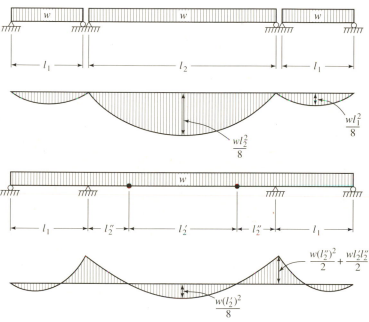

(a) Elements of a statically determinate cantilever bridge.

(b) Relative maximum moments—single span versus cantilever span.

FIGURE 1.40
Cantilever bridge principles.

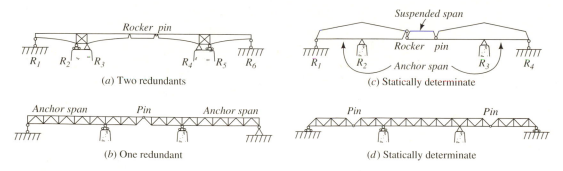

(a) Two redundants

(b) One redundant

(c) Statically determinate

(d) Statically determinate

FIGURE 1.41
Various arrangements for supporting suspended spans in cantilever bridges.

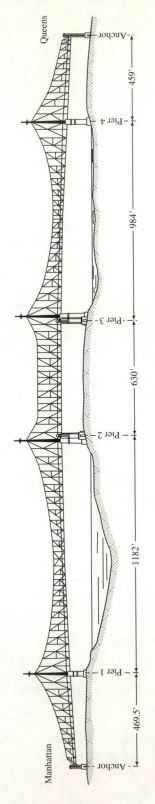

FIGURE 1.42
The Queensboro Bridge, New York [Tyrrell, 1911].

68

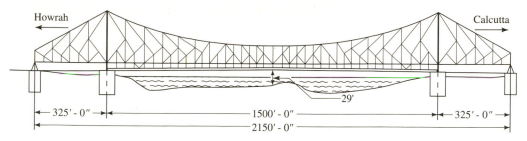

FIGURE 1.43
Howrah Bridge, Calcutta, India [Virola, 1969].

The Quebec Bridge in Canada (Fig. 1.25) and the Firth of Forth Bridge in Scotland (Fig. 1.26) are two of the longest and most famous cantilever bridges. An unusual variation on this type of bridge—a five-span continuous bridge—was built in 1901–1909 for the railroad at Queensboro over the East River, New York. This bridge consists of two unequal main spans (1182 and 984 ft), a middle 630-ft anchor span, and two shore spans (469 and 459 ft) [Tyrrell, 1911; Virola, 1969]. Designed by Gustav Lindenthal, its unusual feature is that each main span consists of two cantilever arms joined at their extremities *without* any suspended span, creating a suspension bridge-like appearance (Fig. 1.42) [Tyrrell, 1911; Steinman and Watson, 1957; Smith, 1953; Virola, 1969]. The world's longest highway cantilever bridge is the Greater New Orleans Bridge, a 1575-ft span over the Mississippi at New Orleans, Louisiana, built in 1955–1958 [Virola, 1969]. Another great cantilever bridge is the 1500-ft span Howrah Bridge in Calcutta, India (Fig. 1.43), opened to traffic in February, 1943. It has an unusual feature—the roadway is suspended *below* the bottom chords rather than supported above by them, as is usually the case [Virola, 1969].

1.3.3.7 Cable-stayed bridges

Cable-stayed bridges represent the most innovative and dramatic development of the post-World War II period. These bridges are very competitive economically for medium and long spans. They can be built with girders of either steel or prestressed concrete. Cable-stayed bridges are unique in that the superstructure is supported (or hung) at several intermediate points by *inclined cables,* or *stays,* radiating from and continuous over the towers, instead of being supported from underneath by conventional piers or bents. Cable-stayed bridges are classified by the form of the cable arrangement, as shown in Fig. 1.44.

As a structural system, cable-stayed bridges fill a gap between the deck type bridges, with the supporting girders installed *underneath* the bridge deck, and the suspension bridges. Similar in scheme to suspension bridges, cable-stayed bridges consist of three spans—two side spans and the central main span. Two towers, or *pylons,* separate the side spans from the main span. The side spans may be flanked by one or more *approach spans.* However, in contrast with this general arrangement, cable-stayed bridges with only two spans and a central tower have also been built.

Unlike suspension bridges, in which the superstructure loads are transmitted to the cables *through vertical hangers,* the loads in a cable-stayed bridge are transmitted

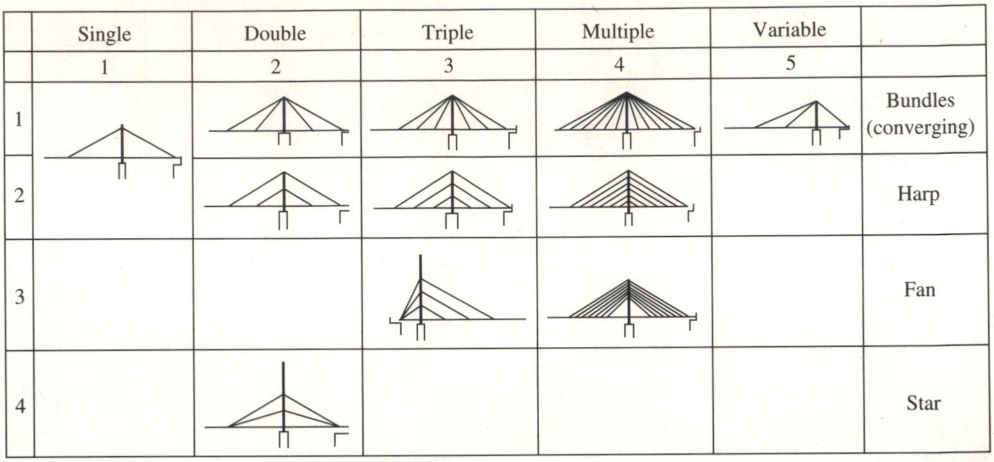

	Single	Double	Triple	Multiple	Variable	
	1	2	3	4	5	
1						Bundles (converging)
2						Harp
3						Fan
4						Star

FIGURE 1.44

Classification of cable-stayed bridges by form [Fiege, 1966].

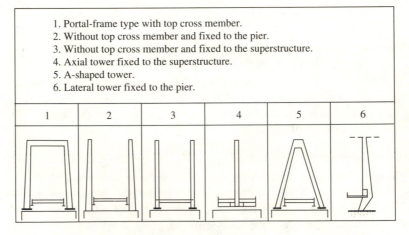

1. Portal-frame type with top cross member.
2. Without top cross member and fixed to the pier.
3. Without top cross member and fixed to the superstructure.
4. Axial tower fixed to the superstructure.
5. A-shaped tower.
6. Lateral tower fixed to the pier.

1	2	3	4	5	6

FIGURE 1.45

Shapes of towers used for cable-stayed bridges [Fiege, 1966].

directly by the inclined stays, which connect the deck to the towers. Fig. 1.45 shows various shapes of towers used for cable-stayed bridges.

Several cable-stayed bridges have been built around the world in the last forty years, mostly in Europe. Many cable-stayed bridges have been built in Germany, particularly over the Rhine and Elbe Rivers; most of these replace the many bridges destroyed in World War II and improve the highway transportation system. Development of cable-stayed bridges in various countries has been reported by several authors [Fiege, 1966; Thul, 1966; Taylor, 1969; Leonhardt and Zellner, 1970; Narouka, 1973]. Podolny and Flemming [1972] and Kavanagh [1973] examine the historical development of cable-stayed bridges. A chronological history of the construction of cable-stayed bridges and the aesthetics of some of these bridges are presented by Billington and Nazmy [1990].

FIGURE 1.46
The Maracaibo Bridge, Venezuela [Smith, 1953].

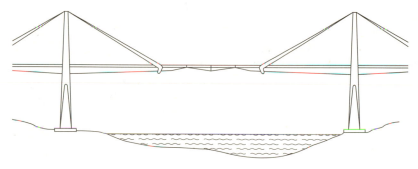

FIGURE 1.47
Combination of simply supported and cantilever arrangements for the
Maracaibo Bridge [Salvadori and Heller, 1975].

The first modern cable-stayed bridge was built in 1955 at Stroemsund, Sweden
(243, 600, and 243 ft—74, 183, and 74 m), followed in 1957 by the 853-ft (260-m)
main span North Bridge in Dusseldorf, Germany [Fiege, 1966; Leonhardt and Zellner, 1970; Podolny, 1974; Podolny and Scalzi, 1986]. Later, several other cable-stayed
bridges were built in Europe. One of the most noteworthy examples of a cable-stayed
bridge is the 135-span 5.4-mile Lake Maracaibo Bridge in Venezuela (Fig. 1.46), completed in 1962. It includes five 771-ft (235-m) *prestressed-concrete* cable-stayed girders with suspended spans, providing navigation openings. These main spans feature
cantilevered stayed sections with intermediate beams simply supported at their tips
(Fig. 1.47) [Morandi, 1961; "Bridge," 1963; ICJ, 1963; Podolny and Scalzi, 1986].

Several cable-stayed bridges were built in the United States during the past 25
years. The first is a 361-ft-long (72, 217, and 72 ft) pedestrian bridge located in
Menomonee Falls, Wisconsin. Built about 1971, this 10-ft-wide bridge is supported
on two W33 × 130 main steel girders [Woods, 1973]. The first cable-stayed highway bridge in the United States, the Sitka Harbor Bridge (150, 450, and 150 ft), was
built in 1972 in Alaska. Its total length is 1255 ft, including several 125-ft approach
spans [ENR, 1972a; Gute 1973a,b]. It was followed by the construction of the Pasco–
Kennewick Bridge (main span 981 ft) in the state of Washington, in 1978 [Grant,
1977]. The Sunshine Skyway Bridge (main span 1200 ft) was built in Tampa, Florida,

in 1986 [Garcia and Robison, 1986]. The Hale Boggs Memorial Bridge (main span 1222 ft) in Luling, Louisiana, was completed in 1983. The East Huntington Bridge (main span 900 ft) in East Huntington, West Virginia, was completed in 1985 [Grant, 1987].

Several cable-stayed bridges with record-breaking spans were built around the world, mostly in the 1980s and later. See Appendix C (Table C.1) [Podolny, 1997]. Billington and Nazmy [1990] have provided schematic elevations of 84 of the world's leading cable-stayed bridges constructed before 1987. Shanghai's Yang Pu Bridge, a 1975-ft main span cable-stayed bridge, China's longest, was completed in 1993. Presently, the longest cable-stayed bridge is France's 2808-ft (856-m) Pont de Normandie (the Normandy Bridge), with a main span of 2047 ft (624 m). It opened to traffic in January 1995. Except for the main span, which consists of orthotropic steel box girders, this entire bridge is built with 8700 psi high-performance concrete [PCA, 1995]. This innovative construction is referred to as *longitudinally composite.* Two other bridges of this type are Mexico's Tampico Bridge and Japan's Ikuchi Bridge [Robinson, 1993]. The Baytown cable-stayed bridge, in Texas (482, 1250, and 482 ft), completed in 1994, also has composite construction. With its 426-ft-high towers and two 78-ft-wide decks, this bridge has a record-setting 350,000 ft^2 of deck area [Lovett and Warren, 1992]. The longest cable-stayed bridge—under construction and due to be completed in 1999—is the Tatara Bridge in Ehime, Japan, having a 2920-ft main span. Figure 1.48 shows India's longest cable-stayed bridge (597, 1499, and 597 ft), over Hoogly River, Calcutta, completed in 1993 [ENR, 1972b, 1975b, 1978b].

The various arrangements of radiating cables (Fig. 1.44) and the imaginative forms and shapes of towers (Fig. 1.45) have made cable-stayed bridges one of the most aesthetically pleasing structures. Figure 1.49 shows the magnificent view of the stay ropes of the Friedrich Ebert Bridge, a 919-ft-main span cable-stayed bridge (394, 919, and 394 ft—120, 280, and 120 m) over the Rhine at Bonn, Germany [Leonhardt and Zellner, 1970].

Most cable-stayed bridges are stationary; however a movable 360-ft-span swing cable-stayed bridge with a swing radius of 180 ft—perhaps the only one of its kind in the world—has been built over the Sacramento River at Meridian, California.

Several variations of cable-stayed bridge principles have been adopted for construction of other bridges. A bridge type similar in appearance to the cable-stayed bridge is the *bridle chord type.* This type of bridge is actually intermediate between the cable-stayed and the *cable-suspended* (suspension) bridges. Unlike the curved cables of a

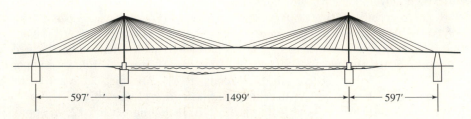

FIGURE 1.48
India's longest cable-stayed bridge, over Hoogly River, Calcutta.

FIGURE 1.49
View of stay ropes of the Friedrich Ebert Bridge over the Rhine, at Bonn, Germany [Leonhardt and Zellner, 1970].

suspension bridge, in a bridle chord bridge the main cables are *not continuous* between the towers, but are anchored to the longitudinal girder in the main span. However, like a suspension bridge, it does have hangers along the length of the cables, which provide additional support for the deck. An example of such a bridge is the Ruhrort–Homberg Bridge over the Rhine, in Germany, as shown in Fig. 1.50 [Kavanagh, 1972].

Another variation on the cable-stayed bridge is the *bi-stayed* bridge, in which the cable stays consist of both self-anchored and earth-anchored cables, and the entire midspan is supported by the stays. Figure 1.51(*a*) schematically compares the cable-stayed bridge to its bi-stayed variation. In the bi-stayed bridge system, the self-anchored

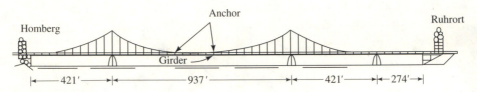

FIGURE 1.50
Bridle chord bridge over the Rhine at Ruhrort–Homberg, Germany [Kavanagh, 1972].

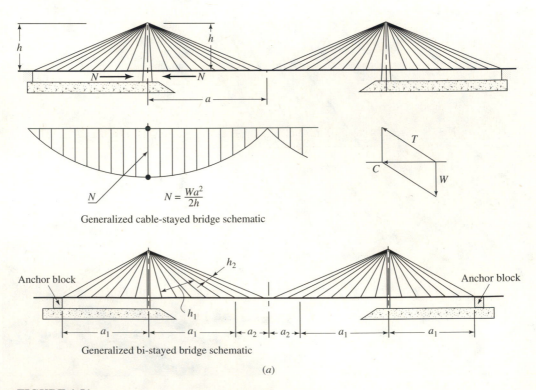

Generalized cable-stayed bridge schematic

$$N = \frac{Wa^2}{2h}$$

Generalized bi-stayed bridge schematic

(*a*)

FIGURE 1.51
(*a*) Schematic comparison of cable-stayed and bi-stayed bridges [Muller and Lockwood, 1992];

stays (h1) are located in the side spans of the bridge and also in the main span, where they are distributed over nearly the same distance from the pylon as they are in the side spans (a1). The earth-anchored stays (h2) are longer and anchor into the deck over the remainder of the main span (a2). These earth-anchored stays bend over the pylon tops and anchor into a separate anchor block away from the extremity of the bridge; hence, they cause no further compression in the bridge deck. It is suggested that a bi-stayed bridge could feasibly support clear spans extending 10,000 feet [Muller and Lockwood, 1992]. The *hybrid cable-stayed suspension bridge* (Fig. 1.51(*b*)), the *hybrid double-cantilever suspension bridge* (Fig. 1.51(*c*)), and the *spread-pylon cable-stayed bridge* (Fig. 1.51(*d*)) are other variations of cable-stayed systems proposed for longer spans (see Sec. 1.3.3.8).

Analysis and design of cable-stayed bridges is an advanced topic and is not covered in this text. Design guidelines for cable-stayed bridges are reported in *Highway Focus* [1973] and in ASCE [1977a, 1991], and a bibliography and data are

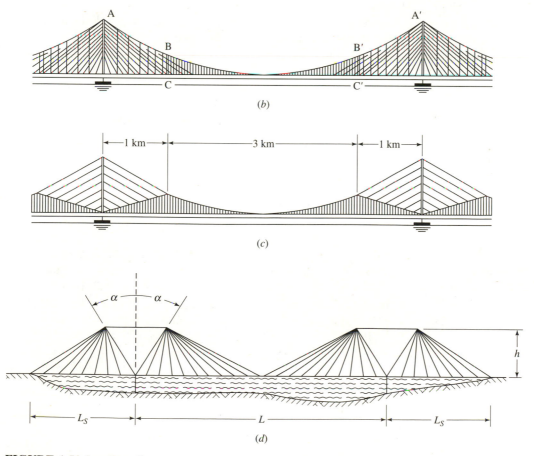

FIGURE 1.51 (continued)
(*b*) hybrid cable-stayed suspension bridge [Lin and Chow, 1991]; (*c*) hybrid double-cantilever suspension bridge [Lin and Chow, 1991]; (*d*) spread-pylon cable-stayed bridge [Starossek, 1996].

presented in ASCE [1977b]. Design and construction of cable-stayed bridges is presented by O'Connor [1971], Kavanagh [1972], Podolny and Scalzi [1986], and Heins and Firmage [1979]. Methods of analyzing cable-stayed bridges are discussed by many researchers, such as Smith [1967], Tang [1971a, 1971b], Lazer [1972], and Lazer et al., [1972]. Design, construction, and interesting features of a few cable-stayed bridges are presented by many authors, such as Simpson [1970], Thul [1966, 1972], Demers and Simonsen [1971], O'Connor [1971], Narouka [1973], Podolny [1974], and Stahl and Christopher [1992]. Prestressed concrete cable-stayed bridges are discussed by Leonhardt [1987].

1.3.3.8 Suspension bridges

Suspension bridges are recognized for spanning the longest distances and for their superior aesthetics. A cable could span the largest possible distance if it could carry just its own weight, but it would break under the smallest additional load. Assuming an optimal sag-to-span ratio of one-third to minimize the weight of the cable, it can be shown that a 200-ksi cable could span a distance of 17 miles [Salvadori and Heller, 1975]. Since the actual cable spans must carry heavy imposed loads in addition to their own weights, the span limitation of cables is reduced to only a few thousand feet.

The principle of a suspension bridge is very simple. It consists of four essential parts: the towers, the anchorages, the cables, and the deck. The deck, usually supported on stiffening trusses, is hung from the *suspension cables*. It consists of a central main span and is flanked on each side by a side span that is separated from the main span by towers. The ends of the suspension cables are secured at the *anchorages,* which are usually built of masonry or concrete.

> The roadway and the stiffening construction have local importance, but both may be wholly or partially destroyed without causing the collapse of the bridge. In all other types of bridge construction, the failure or buckling of a single truss member will precipitate the collapse of the entire structure. A suspension bridge is the safest type of construction in that local overloading or structural deficiency will not jeopardize the safety of the structure as a whole [Steinman and Watson, 1957, p. 331].

The theory and design of suspension bridges is discussed by many builders and researchers [Navier, 1823; Roebling, 1841, 1846, 1855; Barlow, 1858, 1860; Statics, 1863a,b; Bender, 1872; DuBois, 1882; Melan, 1888, 1913; Mehrtens, 1900, 1908; Suspension, 1909; Johnson et al., 1910; Steinman, 1913, 1929, 1935; Martin, 1927; Hardesty and Wessman, 1938; Gronquist, 1941; Modjeski and Masters, 1941; Steinman and Watson, 1957; Selberg, 1954; Peery, 1954; Parcel and Moorman, 1955; Pugsley, 1968; O'Connor, 1971; Kavanagh, 1972; Gimsing, 1983]. A very complete history of suspension bridges (up to 1940) in bibliographical form is provided by Jakkula [1941]. A brief description of the theory and history of suspension bridge design from 1823 to 1940 is presented by Buonopane and Billington [1993].

Suspension bridges can be classified by the type of cable anchorage as either *external* or *internal*. When the cables are anchored to massive external anchorages, the suspension bridges are *externally anchored* (Fig. 1.52). They may, however, be *self-anchored* (internally anchored), suitable for short to moderate spans (400 to 1000 ft) where foundation conditions do not permit external anchorages [Kavanagh, 1972]. In this case, the cables are attached to the stiffening trusses at the outer ends of the side

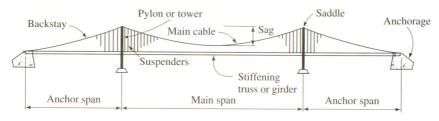

FIGURE 1.52
Externally anchored suspension bridge and terminology.

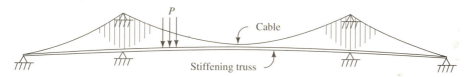

FIGURE 1.53
Self-anchored suspension bridge.

spans that rest over the supports (Fig. 1.53). The vertical component of tension in the side span cable helps reduce the dead load reaction at the end support; the horizontal component of tension creates compression in the stiffening truss. The decks are usually supported by stiffening trusses made of steel, although variations have been used. In the Hudson Hope Bridge (192, 680, and 207 ft) over Peace River in British Columbia, Canada, the stiffening girder consists of 34 *precast, prestressed concrete* box girder units; each unit is 29 ft 6 in. wide and 4 ft 1 in. deep [Osipov, 1969].

In some of the early suspension bridges built for the railroads, excessive deflection was a serious problem. To reduce these deflections, the German engineer Prof. F. Dischinger suggested adding inclined stays to the suspension cable [Dischinger, 1949a,b], but it was soon discovered that they were not very effective in reducing deflections of suspension bridges [Leonhardt and Zellner, 1970]. In some suspension bridges, inclined stays (or secondary cable systems), in addition to the conventional vertical hangers, were incorporated to increase the torsional rigidity. Some examples of this approach are Roebling's Brooklyn Bridge in New York, Deer Isle Bridge in Maine, and the Cincinnati Bridge across the Ohio River [Steinman and Watson, 1957; Hopkins, 1970; Kavanagh, 1972; Buonopane and Billington, 1993]. For the same reason, inclined stays were added to the Ellet's suspension bridge at Wheeling, West Virginia, when, after its collapse in 1854, it was rebuilt by Roebling [Hopkins, 1970]. In modern suspension bridges, additional inclined stays are generally not used, however. Figure 1.55 shows the San Marcos Bridge in El Salvador, which employs multiple inclined cables in the form of a grid or a network, known as a *cable-truss* concept [Kavanagh, 1972].

The longest suspension bridge in the United States is the Verrazano Narrows Bridge in New York (1215, 4260, and 1215 ft), completed in 1964, which outspans the Golden Gate Bridge (1125, 4200, and 1125 ft), completed in 1937. The San Francisco–Oakland Bay Bridge (Fig. 1.56), completed in 1936, is a 1.95-mile-long double-deck *twin*

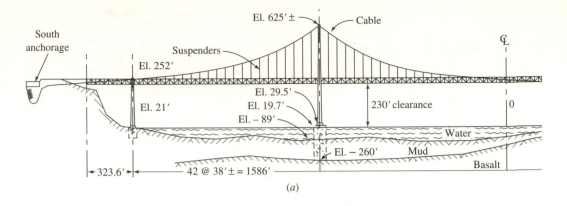

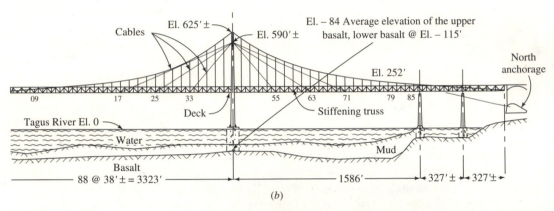

FIGURE 1.54
Salazar Bridge at Lisbon, Portugal, an example of a suspension and cable-stayed system: (*a*) Typical initial construction, for highway traffic only. (Only left half of the elevation is shown.) (*b*) Typical final construction, with cable stays, for highway and railroad traffic. (Only right half of the elevation is shown.) This bridge carries only highway traffic now. [Kavanagh, 1972].

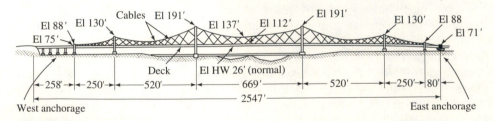

FIGURE 1.55
San Marcos cable truss bridge, El Salvador [Kavanagh, 1972].

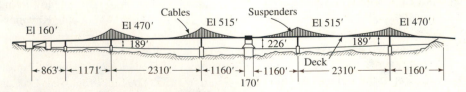

FIGURE 1.56
San Francisco–Oakland Bay Bridge, a twin suspension bridge [EERI, 1990].

suspension bridge (1171, 2310, and 1160 ft; and 1160, 2310, and 1160 ft) [O'Connor, 1971; Kavanagh, 1972; Virola, 1968]. The upper and lower decks each carry five lanes of traffic to the west and east, respectively. The lower deck was originally designed for trains. This bridge actually encompasses, in addition to the twin suspension structure, four shallow simple-span trusses on Yerba Buena Island, a long cantilever truss bridge, five deep simple-span trusses, fourteen shallow simple-span trusses, and a number of simple-span deck systems, covering a distance of 4.35 miles between San Francisco and Oakland, California.

The present recordholder for the longest suspension bridge is the Akashi–Kaikyo Bridge (main span 6529 ft, total length 12,828 ft or 3910 m) linking Akashi City in Hyogo Prefecture to Awaji Island, Japan [CE, 1975; Stahl and Christopher, 1992; CE, 1992; Brown, 1993; Podolny, 1994]. It has been designed for such engineering challenges as 80-mph wind loads and a seismic design factor of 8.5 on the Richter scale [CE, 1992]. This bridge outspans the Humber River Suspension Bridge (920, 4626, and 1739 ft) on the Humber River estuary, 160 miles north of London. [ENR, 1975b, 1976, 1978c]. Completed in 1981 after 8 years, the Humber Bridge, unlike the most modern suspension bridges, has hangers that are inclined in a zigzag pattern—a unique feature similar to that of the Severn Bridge (1000, 3240, 1000 ft) completed in 1966, also in England [Brown, 1993].

Conventional suspension bridges consist of *two* parallel cables as the main load-carrying element. A recent development is a suspension bridge with a *single* cable as the main load-carrying element. An example of this is the Hokko Bridge in Japan, a single-cable, self-anchored suspension bridge. With a main span of 984 ft (300 m) and side spans of 394 ft (120 m), it carries a four-lane highway from the Hokko Wharves to the Northern District island of Osaka's north port. Loads from the bridge superstructure are transferred to the main cable through a continuous pattern of diagonal suspenders [Billington, 1990].

In summary, both cable-stayed and suspension bridges can be characterized as cable (or cable-supported) bridges; the cable profile marks the distinction between the two types. In cable-suspended bridges, commonly referred to as suspension bridges, the main cables are curved and continuous between the towers. The deck and other vertical loading is suspended from these cables at relatively short intervals. Being relatively flexible, the main cables develop funicular shape, which is a function of the magnitude and the position of loading. On the other hand, in cable-stayed bridges, the cables are straight and extend from one tower, and they are connected directly to the deck at discrete points. Being taut, they furnish relatively inflexible supports along the span at several points, and they provide the bridge with relatively greater stiffness than that achievable in suspension bridges. Both types rely on very-high-strength steel cables or tendons. Recent research has led to the development of carbon-fiber-reinforced plastic (CFRP composite) cables that compete with steel in strength and provide excellent corrosion resistance, very high specific strength, and an equivalent elastic modulus. Such cables were proposed for use in a cable-stayed bridge under construction in 1996 in Winterthur, Switzerland [Meier and Meier, 1996].

Bridging increasingly longer spans continues to be a challenge for bridge builders, and it remains in the domain of cable bridges. This is possible because high-strength tensile elements (cables) are used. Accordingly, both cable-stayed and suspension bridges provide the solutions needed for long-span bridges. Since modern cable-stayed bridges evolved much later than suspension bridges did, suspension bridges were historically preferred over cable-stayed types because their performance had been proven and because builders had gained significantly greater knowledge and experience with their use. However, this has now begun to change, and cable-stayed bridges are considered feasible for long spans traditionally considered the domain of suspension bridges [Leonhardt and Zellner, 1972]. Also, it is believed that the greater stiffness provided by cable-stayed systems makes their limit span less susceptible to wind-induced vibrations, compared to the limit span of suspension bridges. Research continues to find new forms of towers (for suspension bridges) and pylons (for cable-stayed bridges), and more efficient cable arrangements to span yet longer spans. Some examples of these new approaches are the hybrid cable-stayed suspension bridge system (Fig. 1.51(*b*)), the hybrid double-cantilever suspension bridge system (Fig. 1.51(*c*)) [Lin and Chow, 1991], and the spread-pylon cable-stayed bridge system (Fig. 1.51(*d*)) [Starossek, 1996]. These systems promise to be economical for very large spans (in the 16,000-ft range). Discussion on the challenges posed by long-span bridge construction can be found in the literature [Mallick, 1983; Gimsing, 1988; Lin and Chow, 1991; Starossek, 1996].

Deciding on the feasibility of a particular bridge type for long spans is difficult, and there are no rules or criteria that provide a quick answer. While the cost is a major factor that may dictate the choice between a suspension bridge and a cable-stayed bridge, there are many other factors that may influence the selection process. These include aesthetics, traffic capacity and the need for future widening, structural stability, foundation conditions, erection procedures, underclearance requirements, and general civic requirements with respect to location, financing, and community values [Kavanagh, 1972].

Table C.2 (see Appendix C) gives a chronology of the world's major suspension bridges [Podolny, 1997].

1.3.4 Classification by Span Types

Bridges can be classified by the type of span used with respect to the support conditions, namely, simple or continuous. Short-span bridges are built as single spans having simple supports. In medium- or long-span bridges, depending on the site conditions, multiple simple spans can be built to span the distance. Such a bridge would consist of two end abutments and several piers as intermediate supports. As discussed earlier, distances beyond the short-span range can always be spanned by arch, cable-stayed, or suspension bridges. However, the site or the economic conditions may dictate building a multispan bridge instead.

Figure 1.40 shows schematically the behavior of a continuous beam under loads. In a *simple* beam, the moment is positive and maximum at the midspan (under gravity loads). In a *continuous* beam, the positive moments are considerably reduced in the midspan portion of the beam, but negative moments are created at the supports. These negative moments are much higher than the positive moments at the midspan, although they are still considerably smaller than the positive moment in a simple beam. Because of these larger negative moments, theoretically a larger girder cross section is required at the supports than at the midspan. Although this can be accomplished by providing a haunch at the supports (i.e., a deeper section than at the midspan), this alternative is not always economical. For spans under about 175 ft, prismatic girders may be more economical than haunched girders. This is because the cost of fabricating the haunches and the required splices to effect savings in the weight of steel may exceed the cost of additional steel required for a prismatic girder for the entire continuous span. The ends of a continuous beam are usually simply supported.

Advantages of continuous spans over simple spans include reduced weight because smaller beam cross sections are required, and greater stiffness, smaller deflections, and fewer bearings and expansion joints are needed. Continuous spans also offer redundancy and greater overload capacity than simple spans.

Continuity in bridges is obtained in a variety of ways. As Fig. 1.37 shows, the general practice is to provide a *suspended span* to be supported by *cantilever spans,* which are simply the overhangs of simple spans called *anchor spans.* This scheme can be achieved in many kinds of bridges, such as plate girder bridges, truss bridges, box girder bridges, cantilever bridges, and cable-stayed bridges. Figures 1.46 and 1.47 show the scheme of suspended spans in the cable-stayed bridge over Lake Maracaibo, Venezuela.

1.3.5 Classification by Load Path Characteristics

From the perspective of load path (or load distribution) in the bridge superstructure, bridges can be classified as one-dimensional or two-dimensional systems. A *one-dimensional system* is one in which the load is distributed in one direction only, such as a slab bridge, in which bending occurs in only one direction, about a horizontal axis perpendicular to the longitudinal axis of the bridge. However, in a slab-stringer bridge, the bending of the slab takes place in *two* mutually perpendicular directions; such a system is classified as a *two-dimensional system,* which is much more efficient and economical than a one-dimensional system.

The superstructure of a bridge can also be constructed as a *three-dimensional system,* which may be more efficient than one- or two-dimensional systems. Essentially, such a system consists of a slab (reinforced concrete or, preferably, prestressed concrete) supported on flat, skeletal, single- or double-layer, steel tetrahedrons (pyramid-shaped trusses), resulting in a three-dimensional plane grid. These tetrahedrons are arranged in a horizontal plane in two parallel grids that are interconnected by vertical or inclined web members. The external loads are distributed among the various members of the tetrahedrons omnidirectionally in space. Such a system, shown in Fig. 1.57, was suggested by Taly in 1976 and is reported in the literature [Taly and GangaRao, 1978; GangaRao and Taly, 1977, 1978]. Taly [1976] presents a comprehensive study of various patented steel tetrahedrons and of a prestressed concrete slab that can be used to build such a bridge, along with a stress analysis determined by using NASTRAN (computer program). The experimental continuous three-span (118, 131, and 118 ft) Roize Bridge over the Roize River near Grenoble, France, completed in December 1990, is based on a similar concept. The precast, pretensioned deck elements of this bridge were made from 11,500-psi concrete, although only 8700 psi was used for the design [Muller and Lockwood, 1992; Montens and O'Hagon, 1992; Muller, 1993].

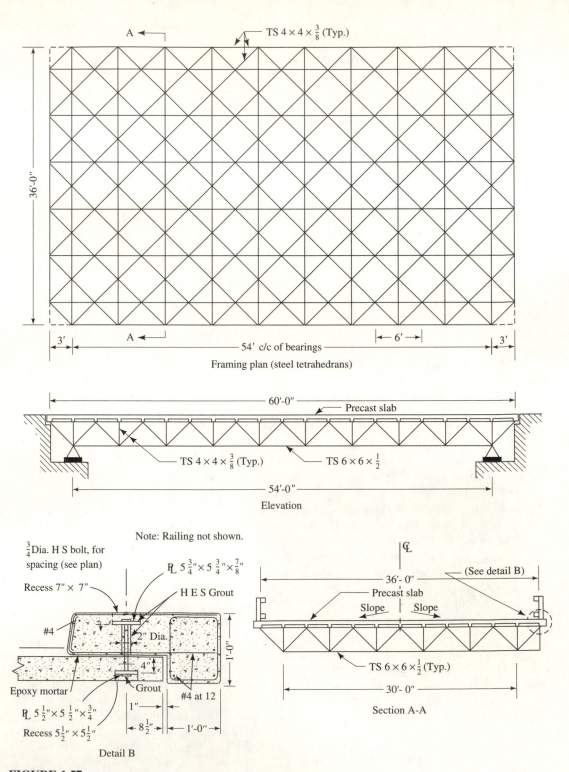

FIGURE 1.57
A three-dimensional bridge deck system. The deck slab is supported on a grid of interconnected tetrahedrons (pyramid-shaped truss modules) [Taly, 1976].

1.3.6 Utility Bridges

In addition to highway and railroad bridges, there are bridges that carry nonvehicular traffic and loads. These bridges include airport runway bridges, pipeline bridges, and conveyor bridges.

The width of airport runway bridges depends on the wingspans of the aircraft, which vary widely. The type of bridge used for runway purposes depends on the weight of the aircraft, the landing gear pattern (of the wheel base and the tread), and the wingspan (the wingtips are allowed to project past the edge of the bridge).

Pipeline bridges are built to carry fluids such as water, oil, and gas. The world's longest pipeline bridge is a 10-span, 3400-ft-long structure carrying two steel pipelines over the Fuji River in Shizuoka Prefecture, central Japan (Fig. 1.58). Each pipeline has an inner diameter of over 7 ft, and they have a combined capacity of over 234,000 gallons of water per minute. Each span is approximately 328 ft long and consists of twin tubular steel arches, each 4.5 ft in diameter [CE, 1970c]. The Santa Ana River feeder in southern California is another major water pipeline, 116 in. in diameter, supported above the Santa Ana River for a length of 1010 ft. A portion of the pipeline is supported by three 180-ft-long steel trusses designed in 1935; the remainder is supported by concrete piers spaced 50 ft apart with the pipe spanning them [Snyder et al., 1987].

A distinctive pipeline suspension bridge over the Danube, with characteristic pylons was developed by Waagner-Biro Aktiengesellschaft of Vienna (see Fig. 1.59 [CE, 1970a; Kavanagh, 1972]). Yet another unique and attractive suspension bridge is a 950-ft span (between towers) over Similkameen River Canyon in British Columbia, Canada,

FIGURE 1.58
The world's longest pipeline bridge, over the Fuji River, Japan [CE, 1970c].

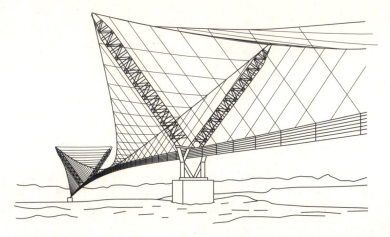

FIGURE 1.59
Pipeline bridge over the Danube, Vienna [Kavanagh, 1972].

which carries three pipelines from a copper-ore concentration plant [Chen and McMullan, 1974]. And a three-span (837 ft, or 255 m, each) suspension bridge carries a gas pipeline over the River Po, Italy [Focardi, 1971].

Utility bridges are not discussed further in this book.

1.3.7 Classification by Position—Movable Bridges

Most bridges are stationary, or fixed in place. However, to provide sufficient vertical clearance to facilitate navigation through spanned waterways, such as navigable rivers or channels, bridges are made *movable;* i.e., the superstructures of these bridges change position relative to the roads that they link. A movable bridge may be necessary when topography dictates that a roadway must be close to the surface of a navigable body of water to be spanned by the bridge. A comprehensive discussion on movable bridges is provided by Hovey [1926] and by Hool and Kinney [1943].

Movable bridges first evolved in the form of *drawbridges,* the forerunners of modern bascule bridges (to be defined shortly). Many drawbridges were built during the Middle Ages by feudal lords for defending their castles, rather than for navigational purposes for which today's movable bridges are built. A drawbridge was one of the nineteen spans of the Old London Arch Bridge completed in 1209 [Gies, 1963]. The first drawbridge built specifically for navigational purposes goes back to at least the sixteenth century. In the United States, the first bascule bridge was built in 1662 by Job Lane and Theodore Atkinson of Massachusetts. By the eighteenth century, several drawbridges were built in Europe, particularly in canal-rich regions, such as the Netherlands [Gies, 1963, p. 231].

The era of modern movable bridges began in the nineteenth century. In Chicago, the building of drawbridges started in the 1830s to provide navigation from the Chicago and Calumet Rivers to Lake Michigan. A brief history of the development of Chicago's 55 movable bridges is presented by Becker [1943] and by Ecale and Lu [1983].

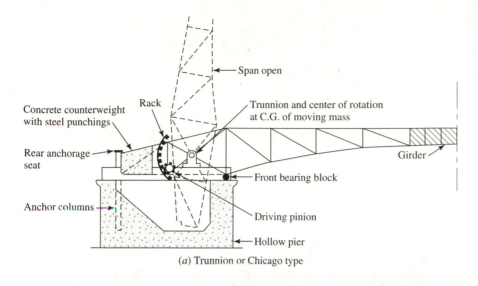

(a) Trunnion or Chicago type

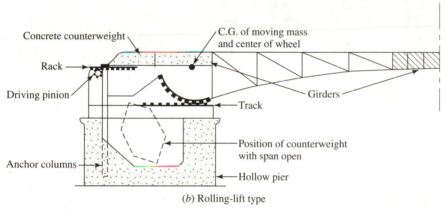

(b) Rolling-lift type

FIGURE 1.60
Bascule bridges.

In general, three kinds of movable bridges exist: the bascule bridge, the lift bridge, and the swing bridge. A movable bridge may be the only structure linking a roadway, or it may be one of the structures of a multispan bridge. The type of movable bridge used is largely dictated by the horizontal and vertical clearance requirements for navigation. Design, fabrication, and erection requirements of movable bridges are covered by the *Standard Specifications for Movable Highway Bridges* [AASHTO, 1988] and in the *Bridge Guide and Manual: Interim Specifications—1992* [AASHTO–Interim, 1992].

The *bascule bridge* (Fig. 1.60) evolved from the familiar drawbridge. It may be a *single-leaf* or a *double-leaf* type (Fig. 1.61). In the single-leaf bascule bridge, the entire span opens upward by rotating about a horizontal axis passing through one of its ends at the support. A motor-driven pinion that engages a rack opens or closes the span. The double-leaf bascule bridge consists of two halves, each of which is hinged at the

FIGURE 1.61
Double-leaf bascule bridge (Columbus Drive Bascule Bridge, Chicago).

supports, and both halves, or leaves, open upward like a double door. Bascule bridges are suitable for shorter spans having high vertical clearance requirements.

Extra care should be exercised in analyzing a bascule bridge. Because of the change in the position of the spans—horizontal when closed and vertical when open—the dead-load bar forces in certain members of a bascule bridge when the bridge is open may exceed the total bar forces exerted on the bridge when the bridge is closed and subjected to traffic.

One of the world's famous bascule bridges is the Victorian Tower Bridge of London, built in 1894 on the Thames River. This unusual bridge consists of a central double-leaf bascule span flanked by side spans of the eyebar suspension type. To eliminate pedestrian waiting while the bascule is opening, the bridge's ornate towers are provided with elevators so that pedestrians can cross on a footwalk above. Another bascule bridge is the Columbus Drive Bascule Bridge over the Chicago River. (Fig. 1.61). The 336-ft-span double-leaf bascule Canadian Pacific Railroad Bridge over the ship canal at Saulte Ste. Marie, Michigan, built in 1941, is the world's longest bascule bridge. Because of improper latching of the two leaves, this bridge collapsed on October 7, 1941, as a freight train crossed it, killing two people. Eventually, the bridge was rebuilt. A brief description of several movable bridges is provided by Steinman and Watson [1957].

A *lift bridge,* also called a vertical-lift bridge, moves vertically up and down as a whole, as shown in Fig. 1.62. The operating mechanism in a lift bridge is essentially like a window in which the sash is hung from the sash cords, and each cord passes

FIGURE 1.62
Vertical-lift bridge. (Veterans Memorial Bridge, Kaukauna, Wisconsin.)

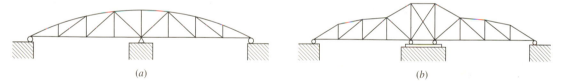

(a)   (b)

FIGURE 1.63
Horizontal-swing bridges.

over a pulley at the top and is connected to a counterweight. In a lift bridge, the cables carrying the counterweights, whose total weight equals that of the lift span, pass over large sheaves, or pulley wheels, at each end of the lift span [Steinman and Watson, 1957]. This type of movable bridge is suitable for long spans where not much vertical clearance is required.

A *swing bridge,* also called a *horizontal-swing bridge,* provides passage to ships by swinging or rotating in a horizontal plane about a vertical axis. It may rotate about a center pivot (Fig. 1.63(a)), in which case the bridge is referred to as the *center-bearing* type. Or it may open by turning on a turntable (Fig. 1.63(b)), which is the *rim-bearing* type [Norris et al., 1976]. The chief advantage of a swing bridge over other types of movable bridges is that it provides unlimited vertical clearance. An obvious disadvantage is that the center pier is a highly undesirable obstruction to the navigating vessels.

From an analytical standpoint, it is important to note the structural behavior of a swing bridge in the open and the closed positions. In the open position, the two spans of the bridge that cantilever from the center pier are statically determinate. In the closed position, the configuration is a continuous truss, and, hence, statically indeterminate.

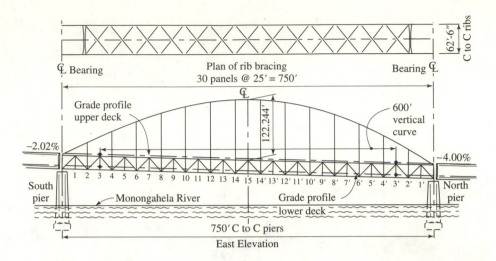

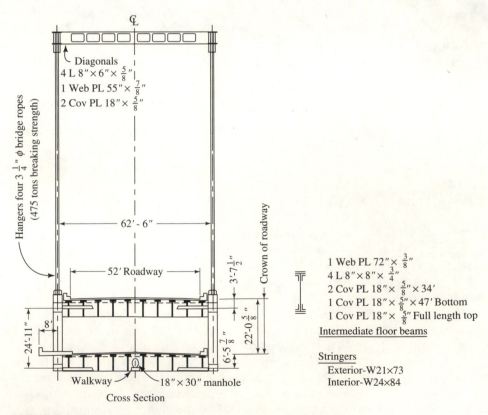

FIGURE 1.64
Double-deck arrangement of the Fort Pitt Bridge, Pittsburgh [Richardson, 1972].

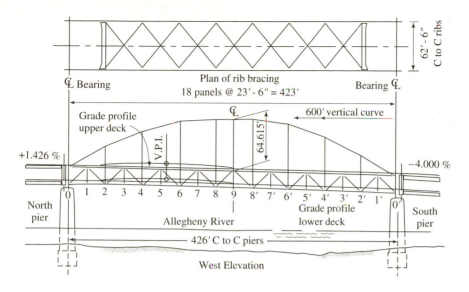

62'-6" C to C ribs

ℂ Bearing

Plan of rib bracing
18 panels @ 23'-6" = 423'

Bearing ℂ

Grade profile
upper deck

ℂ

600' vertical curve

V.P.I.

64.615'

+1.426 %

−4.000 %

North
pier

0 1 2 3 4 5 6 7 8 9 8' 7' 6' 5' 4' 3' 2' 1' 0'

Allegheny River

Grade profile
lower deck

South
pier

426' C to C piers

West Elevation

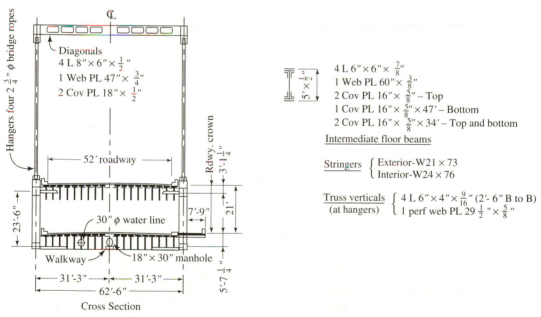

Hangers four 2 ¾" φ bridge ropes

ℂ

Diagonals
4 L 8"×6"× ½ "
1 Web PL 47"× ¾ "
2 Cov PL 18"× ½ "

52' roadway

Rdwy. crown

3'-1 ¼"

21'

23'-6"

30" φ water line

7'-9"

Walkway

18"×30" manhole

5'-7 ¼"

31'-3" 31'-3"

62'-6"

Cross Section

5'×½"

4 L 6"×6"× ⅞ "
1 Web PL 60"× ⅜ "
2 Cov PL 16"× ⅝ " – Top
1 Cov PL 16"× ⅝ "×47' – Bottom
2 Cov PL 16"× ⅝ "×34' – Top and bottom

Intermediate floor beams

Stringers { Exterior-W21×73
           { Interior-W24×76

Truss verticals   { 4 L 6"×4"× 9⁄16 " (2'-6" B to B)
(at hangers)   { 1 perf web PL 29 ½ "× ⅝ "

FIGURE 1.65
Double-deck arrangement of the Fort Duquesne Bridge, Pittsburgh [Richardson, 1972].

1.3.8 Combination and Double-Deck Bridges

Most common bridges built to carry highway or railroad traffic have only one deck. Some bridges, however, have double decks, one above the other, such as the Fort Pitt and Fort Duquesne Bridges in Pittsburgh, Pennsylvania, and the Shermon Minton Bridge in Louisville, Kentucky, all of which are steel arch bridges that carry highway traffic (Figs. 1.64, 1.65, and 1.66) [Hazelet and Wood, 1961; Kavanagh, 1972]. The twin-span

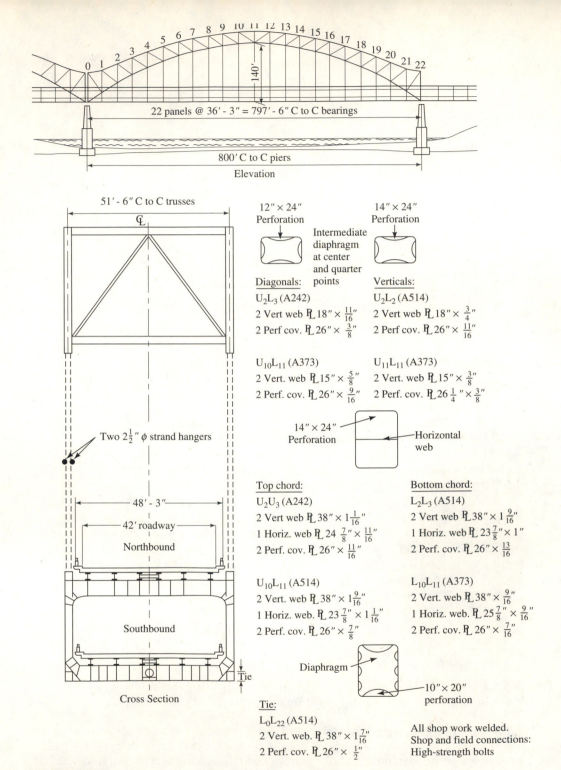

FIGURE 1.66
Double-deck arrangement of the Sherman Minton Bridge over the Ohio River between Louisville, Kentucky, and New Albany, Indiana [Richardson, 1972].

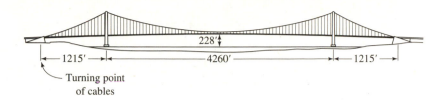

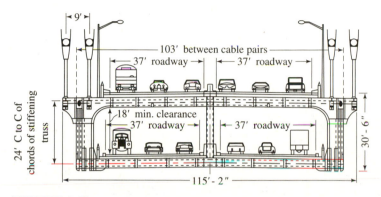

FIGURE 1.67

Cross section of the Verrazano Narrows suspension bridge, New York City, showing double-deck arrangement [Kavanagh, 1972].

San Francisco–Oakland Bay Bridge (Fig. 1.56) and the Verrazano Narrows Bridge (Fig. 1.67), both suspension bridges, are other examples of famous double-deck bridges.

Bridges have also been built to carry combinations of both highway and railroad traffic. A famous example of such a bridge is the Eads Bridge in St. Louis (see Sec. 1.1.5). Still in satisfactory service, it carries highway traffic on the upper deck and two railway tracks on the lower deck. Another example of such a bridge is the Burdekin Bridge in Queensland, Australia (Fig. 1.68). It consists of ten 250-ft simply supported Pratt truss spans, with three 60-ft and three 45-ft approach spans [Kindler, 1958]. It carries a 22-ft roadway and a single-track railway, side by side, over the Burdekin River. Japan's Akashi–Kaiko Bridge (see Sec. 1.3.3), the world's longest suspension bridge, is also a double-deck bridge, carrying both highway and railroad traffic.

1.4
AASHTO SPECIFICATIONS FOR DESIGN OF HIGHWAY BRIDGES

The American Association of State Highway and Transportation Officials (AASHTO) specifications [1992] are to highway bridge design engineers what the American Institute of Steel Construction (AISC) specifications [1989, 1994] are to designers of steel structures and the American Concrete Institute (ACI) codes [1992] are to designers of concrete structures; AASHTO specifications are the bible of highway bridge design engineers. They are intended to serve as a standard or guide for the preparation of state specifications and as a reference for bridge engineers. Because they have been adopted by all the state highway departments in the United States, they are a set of rules and

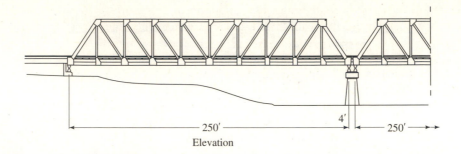

Elevation

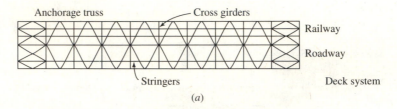

(a)

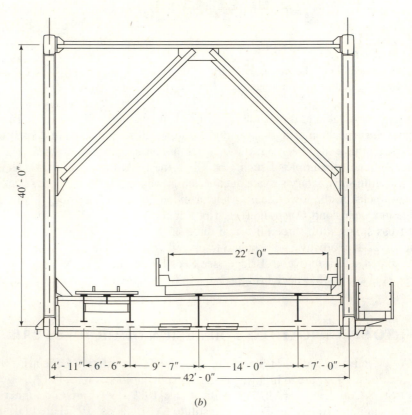

(b)

FIGURE 1.68
The Burdekin Bridge, Australia, a combined highway and railroad bridge
[O'Connor, 1971]. (a) Deck system showing the framing plan; (b) cross section
showing the railroad track (left) and the highway deck (right).

regulations to be followed in designing the nation's highway bridges. Railroad bridges are designed in accordance with the specifications adopted by the American Railway Engineering Association [AREA, 1980].

The year 1921 marked the genesis of bridge design specifications; the current form of specifications has gradually evolved for over 75 years. The first complete set of specifications was available in 1926, revised in 1928, and appeared in print in 1931 as the first edition. The specifications were periodically revised every four to six years to incorporate the new knowledge found through research and development. These revisions occurred in 1935, 1941, 1944, 1949, 1953, 1957, 1961, 1965, 1969, 1973, 1977, 1983, 1989, and 1992 (the fifteenth edition).

Interim specifications are published, usually during the middle of the calendar year. These have the same status as the AASHTO standards, although they are actually tentative revisions of the specifications, to be approved by the AASHTO Subcommittee on Bridges and Structures. If they are approved by a two-thirds majority of the subcommittee, the tentative revisions are incorporated in the new edition as the standards of the association. The AASHTO Subcommittee on Bridges and Structures is made up of the chief bridge engineers of various states. The association has fifty-two members—one from each highway or transportation department of the fifty states, one from the District of Columbia, and one from Puerto Rico.

Like all other codes and specifications, the AASHTO standards are set forth as the *minimum* requirements consistent with the current engineering practice, and they are to be used by competent professional engineers with regard to their suitability and applicability. **The AASHTO specifications apply to ordinary highway bridges up to spans of 500 ft.** For longer spans and unusual bridges, supplemental specifications are usually required.

The AASHTO specifications [1992] are contained in a voluminous document that is divided into two parts, *Division I: Design,* and *Division II: Construction.*

Division I is divided into several sections (twenty in the fifteenth edition) on the design aspects of concrete, steel, and timber bridges, both superstructures and substructures. Design methods are based on the philosophies of service load design, strength design (for concrete), and load factor design (for steel).

Division II is divided into twenty-eight sections on the construction of bridges using different materials: reinforced concrete, prestressed concrete, steel, and timber. These sections discuss testing, workmanship, construction, fabrication, and erection.

The AASHTO specifications also list various other publications prepared and published by the bridge subcommittee, as follows [AASHTO 1992]:

Construction Manual for Highway Bridges and Incidental Structures, 1973
Guide Specifications for Fracture Critical Non-Redundant Steel Bridge Members, 1978
Guide Specifications for Horizontally Curved Highway Bridges, 1980
Manual for Maintenance Inspection for Bridges, 1988
Standard Specifications for Movable Highway Bridges, 1988
Standard Specifications for Structural Supports for Highway Signs, Luminaires, and Traffic Signals, 1985
Guide Specifications for Alternate Load Factor Design Procedures for Steel Beam Bridges Using Braced Compact Sections, 1986

AASHTO/AWS D1.5-88 Bridge Welding Code, 1988

AASHTO Commentary on ANSI/AASHTO/AWS D1.5-88 Bridge Welding Code, 1991

Guide Specifications for Strength Design of Truss Bridges (Load Factor Design), 1985

Guide Specifications on Procedures for Fatigue Evaluation and Design of Steel Bridges, 1989

Guide Specifications for Strength Evaluation of Existing Steel and Concrete Bridges, 1989

Guide Specifications for Design and Construction of Segmental Concrete Bridges, 1989

Guide Specifications for Bridge Railings, 1989

Guide Specifications for Thermal Effects in Concrete Bridge Superstructure, 1989

Bridge Guide and Manual Interim Specifications, 1989

ANSI/AASHTO/AWS Bridge Welding Code D1.5-88, 1988

Foundation Investigation Manual, 1978

Guide Specifications for Fatigue Evaluation of Existing Steel Bridges, 1990 edition

Guide Specification and Commentary for Vessel Collision Design of Highway Bridges, 1991

Guide Specification for the Design of Stress-Laminated Wood Decks, 1991

The early AASHTO bridge design specifications were clearly based on the working stress design (WSD) philosophy. Beginning in 1970, these specifications were gradually modified, by adjusting design factors, to reflect the variability of certain load types, such as vehicular loads and wind forces. The result was the development of a new design philosophy referred to as the load factor design (LFD). Both the WSD, also referred to as the *service load design,* and the LFD are now permitted by AASHTO. A further refinement in design methods introduced considerations of variability in material properties, similar to load variabilities. This introduced the load and resistance factor design (LRFD), which led to the development in 1994 of the *AASHTO–LRFD Bridge Design Specifications* [AASHTO, 1994]. Bridge engineers now have a choice of two standards: the long-standing *AASHTO Standard Specifications for Highway Bridges* [1992] or the *AASHTO–LRFD Bridge Design Specifications* [1994]. Within this century, the use of the LRFD specifications will probably become mandatory for highway bridge design.

1.5
DESIGN PHILOSOPHY

1.5.1 Definitions

The following definitions, with some minor modifications, have been taken from AASHTO [1994] and will be referred to frequently in discussing various design philosophies.

Collapse   A major change in the geometry of the bridge rendering it unfit for its intended use.

Design life   Period of time on which the statistical derivation of transient load (i.e., vehicular loads that may change over time) is based. Design life is 75 years for the LRFD specifications.

Ductility   Property of a component or connection that allows inelastic response.

Extreme event limit states   Limit states related to events with return periods (i.e., the recurrence interval) in excess of the design life of the bridge, in this case, earthquakes, ice load, and truck and vessel collision.

Limit state   A condition beyond which the bridge or the component ceases to fulfill its intended function.

Load factor   A factor that accounts for the variability of loads, the uncertainty in analytical methods, and the probability of simultaneous occurrence of different loads.

Nominal resistance   Resistance of a component or connection to force effects, based on its geometrical configuration and on permissible stresses, deformations, or specified strength of materials.

Reliability   The probability of safe behavior.

Reliability index   A quantitative assessment of safety expressed as the ratio between the mean and standard deviation of the resistance minus the load effect probability distribution.

Resistance factor   A factor that accounts for material properties, structural dimensions and workmanship, and the uncertainty in predicting resistance.

Service life   The period of time that the bridge is expected to be in satisfactory operation.

Service limit states   Limit states related to stress, permanent deformation, or cracking.

Strength limit states   Limit states related to strength and stability.

1.5.2 General Concepts

In general, an acceptable structure should meet all requirements of safety and performance. A bridge design should satisfactorily accomplish the objectives of constructibility, safety, and serviceability. Simply stated, a bridge design should permit safe structural erection as planned and be able to perform its intended function, i.e., safely carry the service loads, in appropriate combination with other loads, during its design life (75 years). The useful life of a bridge, or of a structure in general, is terminated if the service conditions have changed so as to render the bridge or the structure uneconomical or if the bridge fails.

The design philosophies for various structures using members of various materials (concrete, steel, wood, aluminum, etc.) have evolved over many decades. Research in structural and material behavior, new analytical techniques, and building experience continue to result in the modification of the existing design philosophies and the development of new ones. In particular, the development of applied mechanics toward the end of the nineteenth century has greatly influenced design philosophies; more mathematical operations and more sophisticated mathematical models were introduced into design. However, the basic premise that a structure should be safe regardless of design methodology remains the cardinal principle of all design philosophies.

The foundation of every design philosophy is the known stress-strain relationship of the material. Unless otherwise mentioned, it is implied that the material is (*a*) homogeneous, i.e., has the same specific physical properties at all points; (*b*) isotropic, i.e., has the same elastic properties in all directions; and (*c*) obeys Hooke's law, i.e., the material is linearly elastic. It is known that a material such as steel behaves inelastically at higher stresses and that materials such as concrete and wood are not isotropic. For these types of materials, the design philosophies and methods are somewhat modified. Accordingly, the design philosophies are based on whether the material behaves elastically or inelastically under given loading conditions. Regardless of the type of design philosophy used, the adequate safety of a structure must be ensured.

1.5.3 Design Methods

1.5.3.1 Design methods based on elastic behavior

These design methods are sometimes called *elastic design methods* since it is assumed that the material behaves *elastically,* i.e., it obeys Hooke's law, under service loads. Certain fractions of the yield stress or the ultimate strength of the material are used as allowable stresses for design purposes. For steel, the allowable stresses are typically expressed as fractions of yield strength or the ultimate strength, denoted by F_y or F_u, respectively. For concrete, the allowable stresses are expressed as fractions of the 28-day compressive strength denoted by f_c'. This method does not consider structural performance beyond the elastic limit.

Allowable stress design (ASD). This design method refers to the elastic design method as it is used for steel structures. Allowable stress design is specified in detail in the AISC specifications [AISC, 1989] for the design of steel buildings. The allowable stresses are obtained by dividing the material strength (yield or ultimate) by a safety factor.

Service load design. This design method refers to the elastic design method as it is used for reinforced and prestressed concrete structures and for steel structures. It is recognized in the AASHTO specifications [AASHTO, 1995] for the design of highway bridges. Service load design is currently recognized as *The Alternate Method* in the ACI code [1995] for design of reinforced concrete members. This method is also used for the design of wood structures.

In the past, the allowable stress design method was called the *working stress design* method, particularly in reference to reinforced concrete design; however, this term as well as the method itself have now become obsolete.

1.5.3.2 Design methods based on inelastic behavior

The following methods are based on the inelastic behavior of material at higher loads.

Plastic design. This design method is based on the strength of steel in the inelastic range, and it is used for the design of indeterminate structures such as continuous beams and frames (not for simple beams). The maximum load that a structure can carry is based on the structural usefulness just before reaching the collapse condition. This method, known as *plastic analysis,* is used only for the design of steel structures. According to this method, the entire cross section of a structural member is at yield stress when it is subjected to collapse load conditions. The collapse loads are obtained by multiplying the dead and live loads by certain factors known as *load factors* (1.7 in this case). These increased loads are called *factored loads.* Load factors are coefficients that express the probability of variations in the normal loads for the expected service life of the bridge.

Note that in plastic design, the analysis, i.e., the determination of member forces, is based on a *collapse mechanism,* a completely different analysis method than elastic methods of analysis, such as moment distribution, slope deflection, etc.

Strength design. Initially referred to as the *ultimate strength design,* this is a design method used for reinforced and prestressed concrete structures [ACI, 1992]. According to this method, the structure is analyzed by the methods of elastic analysis using the factored loads; the member cross section is then designed assuming that concrete and reinforcing steel have reached crushing stress $(0.85 f_c')$ and yield stress (f_y), respectively. The calculated member strength is multiplied by the resistance factor ϕ (which is less than 1) to reflect the uncertainty involved in the prediction of the material strength. Unlike the plastic design method for steel, in which the *common* load factor 1.7 is used for *both* the dead and live loads, for strength design of concrete, *different* load factors are used for different kinds of loads. For example, the load factor for the dead load is 1.4, whereas the load factor for the live load is 1.7.

Strength design is completely different from plastic design, and one should not be confused with the other. However, the terms "strength design" and "load factor design" are often used synonymously.

Load and resistance factor design (LRFD) and the limit states design. A structure is built on the basic premise that it will carry certain loads *functionally* and *safely.* This raises the question, What is meant by "functionally" and by "safely"? It is this philosophical question that the load and resistance factor design (LRFD) method addresses logically.

We can infer that "functionally" means a structure performs its intended function as required. The meaning of "safely," however, is rather obscure. *Safety* can be referred to as avoidance of *structural failure.* How can we describe failure? In a popular sense, failure is associated with *collapse* [Galambos, 1981]. However, to be more meaningful, it must be precisely defined. Failure is strictly an engineer-defined phenomenon; it is based on a chosen load-induced response, i.e., a stress, or on serviceability criteria. For example, failure may be said to have occurred if the stress induced by loads exceeds yield stress; an example of this is attainment of plastic moment, or *plastic limit,* in a beam. In this context, plastic design is simply a special case of limit states design, wherein the limit state for strength is defined as the attainment of plastic moment strength, M_p. Or one can define failure as a condition in which the load-induced stress exceeds the *ultimate stress* of the material. Failure can also be defined in terms of the *serviceability* criteria; for example, we can say failure has occurred when excessive deflection of beams or floors occurs, i.e., when the *deflection limit* is exceeded, or when excessive displacement of a structure occurs, such as interstory displacement in a building. Fracture and fatigue are some of the many other examples of failure that can be cited [Galambos, 1981; Hart, 1982].

All these examples have one thing in common: They refer to the limits of a structure's usefulness. Not all of these limits cause collapse in the popular sense, and so it is appropriate to define strength as the "limit state which determines the boundary of structural usefulness" [Galambos, 1981]. A sound design philosophy, therefore, should consider various design criteria: yield, plastic, deflection, dynamic response, fatigue, and brittle failure [Kuzmanovic and Willems, 1983]. In current engineering practice, two different terms are used to denote the same general design philosophy that considers these various design criteria: "load and resistance factor design (LRFD)" is used for steel structures [AISC, 1986a,b] and "limit design" is used for reinforced concrete structures. Some engineers, e.g., those in Europe and Canada, also use the term "limit states design" in the same context [MacGregor, 1976, 1988; Haaijer, 1983].

Historically speaking, the plastic theory evolved in the early 1900s. As early as 1914, Dr. Gabor Kanzinczy of Hungary recognized that the ductility of steel permitted redistribution of stresses in an overloaded, statically indeterminate structure [Beedle, 1958]. In the United States, Prof. J. A. Van den Broek introduced a plastic theory, which he called limit design [Van den Broek, 1939]. A comprehensive discussion on various design philosophies is presented by Ellingwood et al. [1980], Galambos [1981], Galambos et al. [1982], Beedle [1986], and Pinkham [1987].

In general, the LRFD philosophy deals with the uncertainty of an event's occurrence in nature, i.e., with the probability of the occurrence of an event. In terms of design considerations, LRFD predicts how often the loads will be greater than the resistance of a structure. A comprehensive discussion on probability and statistics in science and engineering is presented by Walpole and Raymond [1982] and in the many references cited therein. Uncertainty analysis in terms of loads and safety is discussed by Hart [1982].

LRFD involves factoring both loads *and* resistance. LRFD differs from the traditional allowable stress design (ASD) method used for steel, in which only the resistance (the yield or the ultimate stress) is divided by a factor of safety (to obtain allowable stresses), and it differs from the plastic design method in which only the loads are multiplied by a common load factor. In contrast, the LRFD method uses multiple load factors and material strength modification factors in a format similar to the current ACI strength design specifications for reinforced concrete buildings [1992] and the AASHTO load factor design specifications for concrete bridges [1992].

In LRFD, to reflect concerns of structural safety, the term "limit state" is preferred over "failure," meaning that the member has reached the limit of its intended usefulness. The basic premise of the LRFD method is to provide a guide for uniform safety known as a *reliability index*. The principal new concept used in LRFD is the *first-order second moment* probabilistic mathematical model, which makes it possible to give proper weight to uncertainties in the determination of various loads and material resistance [Ellingwood et al., 1980]. This mathematical model is *not* intended to result in designs radically different from those based on the older methods, since it was tuned, or calibrated, to representative designs of the earlier methods. For example, designs of 195 existing and 41 hypothetical bridges were used to obtain the reliability indices for the proposed LRFD format of the AASHTO specifications [Vincent, 1969; ENR, 1991].

Initially developed in the seventies [Ravindra and Galambos, 1978; Galambos, 1981], the first codification of LRFD appeared in 1986 for the design of steel buildings [AISC, 1986a]. Based on years of research reported in the National Cooperative Highway Research Project (NCHRP) [1992, 1993], the first edition of *AASHTO–LRFD Bridge Design Specifications* was issued in 1994.

The LRFD method constitutes an improved design approach that uses various limits of structural usefulness, called *limit states,* as bases for design. The limit states may be dictated by many considerations:

- Functional requirements, e.g., maximum deflection or drift
- Design concepts, such as the formation of a plastic hinge or mechanism
- Collapse of the whole or part of the structure, e.g., fracture or instability

Examples of limits of structural usefulness follow:

Elastic limit (allowable stress design). The allowable stresses should not be exceeded.

Plastic limit. Enough hinges are formed in an indeterminate structure to lead to a collapse condition.

Stability limit. Stresses are limited to critical buckling stresses, F_{cr}, for stability of columns, beams, and plates.

Fatigue limit. This limit is related to the stress range, F_{sr}.

Tensile stress. F_u The stress at which a member fractures under tension.

The LRFD design criteria ensure that a limit state is violated only with an acceptably small probability, by selecting the load factors, resistance factors, nominal loads, and resistance values that will never be exceeded under the design assumptions.

Limit states can be divided into two general categories:

1. *Strength limit state.* This type of limit state is based on the load-carrying capacity of the member, on plastic strength, on probability of buckling or fracture, etc. It deals with the *limit states of strength* that define safety against extreme loads during the intended life of the structure.
2. *Serviceability limit state.* This type of limit state is based on the performance of structures under normal service loads; this includes excessive deflections, vibrations, slipping and cracking, fatigue, etc. It deals with the *functional requirements* of the structure.

LRFD is a method for proportioning that ensures that no applicable limit state is exceeded when the structure is subjected to all appropriate factored load combinations. Specifically, in designing bridges by LRFD methods, the following limit states are to be considered [AASHTO, 1994]:

1. *Service limit state.* This limit state refers to restrictions on stresses (e.g., permissible stresses), deformation (e.g., permissible deflections), and crack width under regular service conditions. Its purpose is to ensure acceptable performance of a bridge during its service life.
2. *Fatigue and fracture limit state.* Fatigue limit states are restrictions on various stress ranges under normal service conditions. These restrictions prevent premature failure of a member or a connection under the actions of repeated loads during the service life of a bridge. Fracture limit states refer to the material toughness requirements specified in the AASHTO material specifications [AASHTO–Materials, 1992].
3. *Strength limit state.* This is the strength and the stability required of various structural components to safely resist the statistically significant load combinations a bridge is likely to experience during its service life. These loading conditions may

lead to extensive distress and structural damage, but the overall structural integrity is expected to be maintained.

4. *Extreme-event limit state.* Extreme events are unique occurrences whose return period is significantly greater than the design life of the bridge. A major earthquake, a flood, or an ice flow are examples of extreme events. The design should ensure the structural survival of the bridge during these rare occurrences, although damage may be sustained.

The general notion of LRFD involves comparing the *maximum strength* of a member to the *maximum forces* that it is expected to experience during its service life. This relationship can be expressed as follows:

$$\text{Maximum strength} = \text{maximum loads} \tag{1.1}$$

Because of the uncertainties involved in the accurate determination of both the design loads and the material strengths, for safety reasons, the *calculated strength is decreased* and the *design loads are increased.* This is done by applying the resistance factor, ϕ, and the load factor, γ, respectively, and Eq. 1.1 is expressed as

$$\phi \times \text{maximum strength} = \gamma \times \text{maximum loads} \tag{1.2}$$

For design purposes, it is required that

$$\text{Factored strength} > \text{factored loads} \tag{1.3}$$

In Eq. 1.2, the ϕ factor is *less* than 1.0 and allows for uncertainties in the material strength, whereas the γ factor is *greater* than 1.0 and allows for uncertainties in load analysis. Because of the different degrees of uncertainty in predicting dead and live loads, different multipliers (i.e., load factors) are used to increase the loads, and the resulting relationship is written as

$$\phi \times \text{maximum strength} = \gamma[\beta_D D + \beta_L(L + I)] \tag{1.4}$$

where D = dead load
   L = live load
   I = live load impact
   β_D = multiplier for dead load
   β_L = multiplier for live load plus impact

The ϕ factor, the resistance factor, accounts for the uncertainties inherent in the determination of the resistance, or strength, of each member. It is intended to compensate for various uncertainties, such as the following [Vincent, 1969]:

• Analysis and calculation of the strength of a section
• Variation in material strength
• Variation in the size of a section
• Natural spread in the test results
• Applicability of test results to the actual structure
• Consequence of failure of an element

The γ factor allows for the uncertainty of the load analysis and other overall effects. Its value is taken as 1.3 to estimate the *maximum* load effects.

β_i *factors* are called the *reliability,* or *safety indices* (defined later), and subscript *i* denotes the force under consideration. The larger the value of β, the smaller the probability of exceeding the limit state, i.e., the larger the margin of safety, and vice-versa. Different values of β *factors* are used to indicate different degrees of variability of the forces (or loads) involved. The factors β_D (for dead load) and β_L (for live load plus impact) have different values for very logical reasons; it is reasonable to assume that a designer can estimate dead loads with a greater degree of certainty than he or she can estimate live loads. The values of these factors are based on statistical data [Galambos et al., 1982; Johnston et al., 1986]. For bridge design, the values of β_D and β_L are typically taken as 1.0^{20} and $\frac{5}{3}$, respectively, where the factor $\frac{5}{3}$ represents the overloads, whether authorized, unauthorized, or accidental.

The general form of Eq. 1.4 can be expressed as [Galambos, 1981; Johnston et al., 1986; Salmon and Johnson, 1990]

$$\phi R_n \geq \sum_{i=1}^{w} \gamma_i Q_i \tag{1.5}$$

where the γ_i's are the load factors by which the individual load effects, Q_i, are multiplied to account for the uncertainties of the loads. R_n is the nominal resistance (e.g., maximum axial force, $R_n = A_e F_y$, or maximum moment, $R_n = M_p = F_y Z$), and ϕ is the resistance factor. The subscript *i* indicates that different terms are used for different types of loads.

Note that Eq. 1.5 is different from the traditionally used allowable stress format,

$$\frac{R_n}{FS} \geq \sum_{1}^{i} Q_{ni} \tag{1.6}$$

where *FS* is the factor of safety. In Eqs. 1.5 and 1.6, the left side denotes the design strength, and the right side denotes the required strength.

In the AASHTO–LRFD criteria [1994], Eq. 1.5 is expressed in LRFD format as

$$\eta \sum \gamma_i Q_i \leq \phi R_n = R_r \tag{1.7}$$

where η is the load modifier related to ductility, redundancy, and operational importance, and γ and ϕ are the load and resistance factors, respectively. η is further defined as

$$\eta = \eta_D \eta_R \eta_I$$

where η_D = ductility factor. (For the strength limit state for all members, η_D equals 1.05 for nonductile components and connections, 0.95 for ductile components and connections, and 1.0 for all other limit states.)

η_R = redundancy factor. (For the strength limit state for all members, η_R equals 1.05 for nonredundant members, 0.95 for redundant members, and 1.0 for all other limit states.)

---

[20]Not always. For column design involving minimum axial load and maximum moment or maximum eccentricity, $\beta_D = 0.75$. (See AASHTO, 1992, 3.22.1A, footnotes.)

η_I = factor related to the operational importance of the bridge, to be used for the strength and the extreme-event limit states only. (η_I equals 1.05 for bridges of operational importance and 0.95 for others.) (This factor is declared by the bridge owner.)

For the service load, or the allowable stress, design, Eq. 1.7 can be rewritten as follows:

$$\frac{\phi R_n}{\gamma} \geq \sum Q_i \qquad (1.8)$$

or

$$\frac{R_n}{\gamma/\phi} \geq \sum Q_i \qquad (1.9)$$

In the service load design method, the same average variability is assumed for all loads. The term γ/ϕ (in the denominator on the left side) is the factor of safety (FS), R_n (in the numerator) is the nominal strength, and $\sum Q_i$ is (on the right side) the sum of service load effects.

Equation 1.8 is quite general and can be rewritten in more specific forms for specific designs. For example, for beam designs by the service load method, it can be written as

$$\frac{M_n}{FS} \geq M$$

where M_n = nominal beam strength
M = service load bending moment
FS = factor of safety = γ/ϕ

Equation 1.8 can also be used to express the limits of structural usefulness in the ASD, that is, the allowable stresses that must not be exceeded, as follows:

$$F_{\text{allow}} = \frac{F_{\text{lim}}}{FS} \qquad (1.10)$$

where F_{lim} is a stress that denotes a state of usefulness, such as the yield stress F_y; a critical (buckling) stress, F_{cr} (e.g., in the stability of columns, beams, and plates); the fatigue stress range, F_{sr}, in fatigue; or the tensile stress, F_u, at which the member fractures.

The reliability index referred to earlier is defined according to the first-order probabilistic method as follows [Ellingwood et al., 1980; Galambos, 1981]:

$$\beta = \frac{\ln(R/Q)}{\sqrt{V_R^2 + V_Q^2}} \qquad (1.11)$$

where Q and R are distributions of load effect and material resistance, respectively, as shown in Fig. 1.69. Both Q and R are random variables. A satisfactory structural behavior is defined when $Q \leq R$. However, the random nature of both Q and R make it theoretically impossible to state with certainty that $Q \leq R$ for any structure. This difficulty of quantifying these statistical parameters is overcome by using a simplified probabilistic approach, as shown in Fig. 1.70, in which $\ln(R/Q)$ is plotted along the

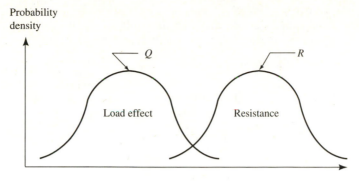

FIGURE 1.69
Probabilistic distribution of Q and R [Galambos, 1981].

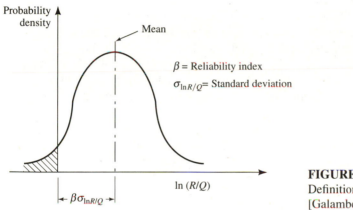

FIGURE 1.70
Definition of reliability index [Galambos, 1981].

x-axis. Because the probabilistic distributions of R and Q are known for only a few resistance and load components, they are replaced in Eq. 1.12 by their *mean values, R_m* and Q_m, whose values are based on the available data on loads and material properties. This results in the following relationship [Johnston et al., 1986]:

$$\beta = \frac{\ln(R_m/Q_m)}{\sqrt{V_R^2 + V_Q^2}} \tag{1.12}$$

where R_m = mean value of the resistance
$\quad\quad Q_m$ = mean value of the load effect
$\quad\quad V_R$ = coefficient of variation for resistance = σ_R/R_m
$\quad\quad V_Q$ = coefficient of variation for the load = σ_Q/Q_m, where σ is the standard deviation

For any given distribution of $\ln(R_m/Q_m)$, the larger the value of β, the smaller the probability of exceeding a limit state. A comprehensive discussion on the development of Eq. 1.12 is provided by Ravindra and Galambos [1978], in the LRFD commentary

TABLE 1.1
Values of objective reliability index, β

Load combinations	Objective reliability index, β
Dead load + live load (or snow load)	3.0 for members 4.5 for connections
Dead load + live load + wind load	2.5 for members
Dead load + live load + earthquake load	1.75 for members

[AISC, 1986b] and in 9 National Bureau of Standards (NBS) special publication [Ellingwood et al., 1980].

The value of β is found by a process called *calibration,* as discussed by Galambos et al. [1982] and Johnston et al. [1986]. Based on the factored loads specified by the American National Studies Institute (ANSI) [1982], the AISC Task Force and Specification Committee calibrated the AISC–LRFD specifications [AISC, 1986a, 1994] to generally agree with the experience with existing structures. In this process, the ϕ factors were set in LRFD with the objectives of obtaining the values of β shown in [Salmon and Johnson, 1990]. The smaller values of β in Table 1.1 account for the lower probability of the occurrence of wind or earthquake loads with full gravity loads. In keeping with the traditional design practice of having the connections stronger than the members, the β values for the connections are higher than those for the members.

In the LRFD criteria [AASHTO, 1994], the load factors and the load combinations are referenced to various limit states (discussed earlier) as follows:

1. *Strength limit state.*

   Strength I. Basic load combination related to normal vehicular use of the bridge without wind.

   Strength II. Load combination related to use of the bridge by permit vehicles without wind. (A permit vehicle is one whose right to travel is not administratively restricted in any way due to its weight or size.)

   Strength III. Load combination related to the maximum wind velocity that prevents the presence of significant live load on bridge.

   Strength IV. Load combination related to very high dead load-to-live load force effect ratios. This load combination is expected to govern when the force effect ratio exceeds 7.0.

   Strength V. Load combination related to normal vehicular use of the bridge with a wind velocity of 55 mph. This combination recognizes the fact that vehicles become unstable if wind velocity exceeds 55 mph. .

2. *Extreme-event limit state.* This limit state refers to a load combination related to ice load, collision by vessels and vehicles, and certain hydraulic events and earthquakes whose recurrence interval exceeds the design life of the bridge. Because the joint probability of these events is extremely low, they are specified to be applied separately. Under these loading combinations, the structure is expected to undergo considerable inelastic deformation.

3. *Service limit state.*

> *Service I.* Load combination related to normal operational use of the bridge with 55-mph wind. All loads are to be taken at their nominal values, and extreme load combinations are excluded.
>
> *Service II.* Load combination whose objective is to prevent yielding of steel structures due to vehicular live load. These load combinations are approximately halfway between those used for Service I and for Strength I limit states—cases for which the effect of wind is of no significance.
>
> *Service III.* Load combination related only to prestressed-concrete structures. Their objective is crack control.

4. *Fatigue limit state.* Fatigue and fracture load combinations are related to gravitational vehicular live load and dynamic response.

Values of the proposed load factors for various load combinations can be found in [AASHTO, 1994] and are different from those for the load factor design of current AASHTO specifications [AASHTO, 1992].

Load factor design. The tentative criteria for the load factor design of steel highway bridges were first published in Vincent [1969] and were formally introduced in 1973 in the eleventh edition of the AASHTO specifications. In AASHTO 1992, the load factor design for steel bridges is covered in Chapter 10, Part D, "Strength Design Method."

Vincent [1969] defines the load factor design as a method of proportioning structural members for multiples of design loads. To ensure serviceability and durability, consideration is given to the control of permanent deformations under *overloads* and to the fatigue characteristics and control of deflections under *service loads*. From the perspective of the LRFD criteria just discussed, the load factor design may be considered a special case of strength limit state design.

The load factor, γ, was referred to earlier in this section in conjunction with load combinations. Values of γ and β factors as stipulated in the specifications [AASHTO, 1992] are presented in Table 3.12 (Chapter 3, Sec. 3.16). Note that, in Table 3.12, the value of the γ factor for the service load design is 1.0. The loads are to be increased by the appropriate β factors, as shown in Table 3.12, *for member design only.* The load factors are *not* to be used for designing foundations (e.g., soil pressure or pile loads) or for checking foundation stability (e.g., calculating the safety factor against overturning or against sliding) for the bridge.

Note that the γ and β factors of Table 3.12 represent only general design conditions. When designing long-span structures by the load factor design method, these factors should be appropriately increased if, in the designer's judgment, the expected loads, service conditions, or materials of construction are different from those implied by the specifications.

After the members are designed for the factored loads as given in Table 3.12, they are checked for *three load levels:*

1. *Maximum design loads,* to ensure the bridge is capable of carrying a few passages of exceptionally heavy load in all lanes of the bridge. Maximum loads are loads

that are specified in AASHTO 3.22 [1992], as shown in Table 3.12 of this text. For design purposes, the maximum design loads are $1.3[D + 5(L + I)/3]$.

2. *Overload,* to ensure control of permanent deformations in a member caused by occasional overweight vehicles, which would be objectionable to the riding qualities of the bridge. Article 10.43.3 of the AASHTO specifications [1992] defines overloads as live loads that can be allowed on a structure infrequently without causing permanent damage. For design purposes, the maximum overload is $5(L + I)/3$.

3. *Service load,* to ensure that the live-load deflections and the fatigue life of a member are within acceptable limits.

As stated earlier, *the members are designed for forces obtained from elastic analysis using factored loads.*

In load factor design, *plastic stress distribution* is used to calculate the strength of a compact section, and the live load safety factor is relatively constant for all span lengths, therefore it is a more rational design method. As a result, this method has gained widespread use by bridge engineers. Load factor designs result in material savings of as much as 20 percent over materials used in service load designs; consequently, load factor designs offer competitive design alternatives for prestressed concrete designs. A comparative summary of fifteen bridges designed by both methods [Vincent, 1969] is presented in Chapter 8. Detailed designs of four continuous steel girder bridges designed by both methods and a summary of the savings in steel achieved using the load factor method are presented in an AISI publication [AISI, 1972]. A comparison of the design of a continuous, five-span, plate girder bridge designed by the two methods is reported in [ENR, 1978a].

1.5.4 Factor of Safety in Design

Regardless of the methodology used for structural design, the primary concern should be preservation of public safety. The term *"factor of safety" (FS)* was introduced in Sec. 1.6.3 in the context of LRFD methodology. Factor of safety stems from the recognition that all quantities used in the engineering calculations are associated with some degree of uncertainty. For any particular load combination, the factor of safety can be defined as [Heger, 1993]

$$FS = \frac{U}{\phi \times \text{(total nominal design load)}} \qquad (1.13)$$

where $U =$ the ultimate load, or the load that causes a limit state to be exceeded.

Since loads corresponding to the various limit states vary, the factory of safety is a variable parameter. In allowable stress design (ASD), the allowable stress is intended to be less than the calculated stress at failure by a factor of safety. However, the factor of safety varies widely because of the wide variation in calculated maximum elastic stress at failure. For example, the basic factor of safety traditionally used by AISC is 1.67 for tension members and beams, 1.92 for long columns, a slenderness ratio-dependent variable for intermediate columns, and 2.5 to 3 for connections. Consequently, for a structure to be safe, the true criterion of acceptability of a design should be strength, not stress. The factor of safety is also variable in LRFD. This stems from the basic premise of LRFD that dead load is assumed to have a lower variability than such loads as live, wind, and seismic loads. Therefore, it is logical for the factor of safety to be lower for structures in which the dead load predominates than for structures in which the live and other loads make up a large proportion of the total load. Under this concept, the relative reliability is held constant and the factor of safety varies from the lowest for all dead load to the highest, when the live load predominates. Because structural reliability criteria and the associated rational decision making are the core of LRFD standards, it is believed that these standards provide more consistent reliability in design than the traditional allowable stress design.

The general notion of variability in the determination of design loads and material strengths was introduced earlier in the context of the load and resistance factors. In general, four broad sources of uncertainty are relevant in assessing structural safety:

1. Inherent variability or randomness that may exist in the characteristics of the structure itself (e.g., material properties, member sizes, or geometry) or in the force and boundary conditions to which the structure is exposed (e.g., loads or support movements)
2. Estimation errors that arise from the incompleteness of the data and our inability to accurately estimate parameters of the probability models selected to describe the inherent variabilities
3. Model imperfection errors arising from the use of idealized mathematical models to describe complex phenomena. These errors involve both poor understanding, or ignorance, of the phenomenon itself and the use of simplified models
4. Human error arising out of human-involved processes, such as design, construction, and the operation phase of the structure

The measure of structural safety and reliability can be based only on the imperfect states of knowledge characterized by the preceding uncertainties. The methods of quantifying the uncertainties in the measure of safety that arise out of imperfect states of knowledge is described by Kiureghian [1989]. A discussion of public safety issues with regard to LRFD design standards is presented by Heger [1993].

In its annual meeting on May 12, 1993, in Denver, Colorado, the AASHTO Subcommittee on Bridges and Structures made a historic decision: The final draft of NCHRP Project 12-33 [NCHRP, 1993] was adopted as the *1994 AASHTO–LRFD Bridge Design Specifications* with a provision to consider phasing out the presently used standard specifications, AASHTO 1992, in the near future.

REFERENCES

AASHTO. (1988). *Standard Specifications for Movable Highway Bridges,* AASHTO, Washington, DC.

———. (1992). *AASHTO Standard Specifications for Highway Bridges,* 15th ed., AASHTO, Washington, DC.

———. (1994). *AASHTO–LRFD Bridge Design Specifications,* 1st ed., AASHTO, Washington, DC.

AASHTO–Interim. (1992). *Bridge Guide and Manual: Interim Specifications—1992,* AASHTO, Washington, DC.

AASHTO–Materials. (1992). *Interim Specifications for Transportation Materials and Methods of Sampling and Testing, Parts I and II, 1992,* AASHTO, Washington, DC.

ACI. (1969). *Concrete Bridge Design,* ACI pub. no. SP-23, ACI, Detroit, MI.

———. (1977). *Analysis and Design of Reinforced Concrete Bridge Structures,* ACI Com. Rep., ACI, Detroit, MI.

———. (1995). *Building Code Requirements for Structural Concrete* (ACI 318-95) and Commentary (ACI 318R-95), ACI pub. no. 318-95/ACI 318R-95, ACI, Detroit, MI.

AISC. (1962). *Design Manual for Orthotropic Steel Plate Deck Bridges,* ACI, New York.

———. (1986a). *Load and Resistance Factor Design Specification for Structural Steel Buildings* AISC, Chicago, September 1.

———. (1986b). *Commentary on the Load and Resistance Factor Design Specification for Structural Steel Buildings* AISC, Chicago, September 1.

———. (1989). *Manual of Steel Construction: Allowable Stress Design,* 9th ed., AISC, Chicago.

———. (1994). *Load and Resistance Factor Design, Vol. 1—Structural Members, Specifications, and Codes,* 2nd ed., AISC, Chicago.

AISI. (1972). *Four Design Examples—Load Factor Design of Steel Highway Bridges,* AISI pub. no. P123(PS010), New York, March.

Allen, R. S. (1970a). *Covered Bridges of the South,* Stephen Green Press, Brattleboro, VT.

Allen, R. S. (1970b). *Covered Bridges of the Northeast,* Stephen Green Press, Brattleboro, VT.

Allen, R. S. (1970c). *Covered Bridges of the Middle West,* Stephen Green Press, Brattleboro, VT.

ANSI. (1982). *American National Standard Minimum Design Loads for Buildings and Other Structures,* A58.1, ANSI, New York.

AREA. (1980). *Manual for Railway Engineering,* AREA, Chicago.

Arndt, R. (1975). "Bridge across the Bosporus," *Constructor,* January, pp. 10–16.

ASCE. (1977a). "Tentative Recommendations for Cable-Stayed Bridge Structures," ASCE Task Committee on Cable-Suspended Structures, *ASCE J. Struct. Div.,* 103(ST5), May, pp. 929–959.

ASCE. (1977b). "Bibliography and Data on Cable-Stayed Bridges," ASCE Committee on Long-Span Steel Bridges. *ASCE J. Struct. Div.,* 103(ST10), October, pp. 1971–2004.

ASCE. (1991). *Guidelines for Design of Cable-Stayed Bridges,* ASCE Committee on Cable-Suspended Bridges, ASCE, New York.

Auvil, Myrtle. (1973). *Covered Bridges of West Virginia, Past and Present,* McClain Printing Co., Parsons, WV.

Bakht, B., Cheung, M. S., and Dortan, R. A. (1982). "Discussion of 'A Comparison of Design Loads for Highways,' by P. G. Buckland and R. G. Sexsmith," *Can. J. Civ. Eng.,* 9(1), pp. 138–140.

Bakht, B., and Jaeger, L. G. (1990). "Bridge Evaluation for Multipresence of Vehicles," *ASCE J. Struct. Eng.,* 116(3), pp. 603–619.

Barlow, P. W. (1858). "On the Mechanical Effect of Combining Girder and Suspension Chains," *J. Franklin Inst.,* 35(3rd series).

Barlow, P. W. (1860). *Observations on the Niagara Railway Suspension Bridge,* John Weale, London.

Becker, Donald, N. (1943). "Development of the Chicago-Type Bascule Bridge," *ASCE Trans.,* February, pp. 263–293.

Beedle, L. S. (1958). *Plastic Design of Steel Frames,* John Wiley & Sons, New York.

Beedle, L. S. (1986). "Why LRFD?," *AISC Modern Steel Construction,* 26, 4th qtr, pp. 30–31.

Bender, C. (1872). "Historical Sketch of Successful Improvements in Suspension Bridges to the Present Time," *ASCE Trans.,* 1, pp. 27–43.

Billington, D. P. (1990). "Creative Connections: Bridges as Art," *ASCE Civ. Eng.,* March, pp. 50–53.

Billington, D. P., and Nazmy, A. (1990). "History and Aesthetics of Cable-Stayed Bridges," *ASCE J. Struct. Eng.,* 117(10), October, pp. 3103–3135.

Bleich, F. (1952). *Buckling Strength of Metal Structures,* McGraw-Hill Companies, Inc., New York.

Bowers, N. A. (1940). "Tacoma Narrows Bridge Wrecked by Wind," *Eng. News-Record,* November 14, 1940.

The Bridge Spanning Lake Maracaibo in Venezuela, (1963). Bauverlag GmbH, Berlin.

Brown, D. J. (1993). *Bridges,* Macmillan, New York.

Buonopane, S., and Billington, D. (1993). "Theory and History of Suspension Bridge Design from 1823 to 1940," *ASCE J. Struct. Eng.,* 119(3), pp. 954–977.

Casad, D. D., and Birkland, H. W. (1970). "Bridge Features Precast Girders and Struts," *ASCE Civ. Eng.,* July, pp. 42–44.

CE. (1970a). "Pipeline Bridge over the Danube Features New Design," *ASCE Civ. Eng.,* March.

CE. (1970b). "Paper Bridge Spans a Nevada Gorge," *ASCE Civ. Eng.,* October, p. 95.

CE. (1970c). "World's Longest Pipeline Bridge Spans Fuji River," *ASCE Civ. Eng.,* July, p. 89.

CE. (1975). "Japanese Structures Specialists Visit U.S.," *ASCE Civ. Eng.,* February, p. 79.

CE. (1985). "Timber Bridge Decks," *ASCE Civ. Eng.,* May, pp. 47–49.

CE. (1992). "News," *ASCE Civ. Eng.,* August, p. 12.

Chang, F.-K., and Cohen, E. (1981). "Long-Span Bridges; State of the Art," *ASCE J. Struct. Eng.,* 107(ST7), July, pp. 1145–1160.

Chang, J. C. L. (1961). "Orthotropic Plate Construction for Short-Span Bridges," *ASCE Civ. Eng.,* December, pp. 53–56.

Chen, S. C., and McMullan, J. C. (1974). "Suspension Bridge Carries Pipeline over Canyon," *ASCE Civ. Eng.,* May.

Cheng, S. (1960). "Stress Analysis of Rigid Frame Bridges with Inclined Legs," *ASCE J. Struct. Div.,* 86(ST12), December, pp. 1–22.

Clark, E. (1850). "The Britannia and Conway Tubular Bridges," 2 vols., London.

Cooper, T. (1889). "American Railway Bridges," *ASCE Trans.,* 21, p. 2.

Demers, J. G., and Simonsen, O. F. (1971). "Montreal Boasts Cable-Stayed Bridge," *ASCE Civ. Eng.,* August.

Dischinger, F. (1949a). "Hangbrucken fur schwertse Verkehrslasten" ("Suspension Bridges for Extremely Heavy Live Loads"), *Der Bauingenieur,* Berlin, 24(3), pp. 65–75 (in German).

Dischinger, F. (1949b). "Hangbrucken fur schwertse Verkehrslasten" ("Suspension Bridges for Extremely Heavy Live Loads"), *Der Bauingenieur,* Berlin, 24(4), pp. 107–113 (in German).

DuBois, A. J. (1882). "A New Theory of Suspension Bridge with Stiffening Truss," *J. Franklin Inst.,* 33(3rd series).

Ecale, H., and Lu, T.-H. (1983). "New Chicago-Type Bascule Bridges," *ASCE J. Struct. Eng.,* 109(10), October, pp. 2340–2354.

Edwards, L. N. (1959). *A Record of the History and Evolution of Early American Bridges,* C. H. Edwards (publisher), University Press, Orono, ME.

EERI. (1990). "Competing against Time," in *Report to Governor George Deukmegian,* Governor's Board of Enquiry on the 1989 Loma Prieta Earthquake, 2nd printing, May 31.

EERI. (1995). "The Hyogo-Ken Nanbu Earthquake—January 17, 1995, Preliminary Reconaissance Report," Earthquake Engineering Research Institute, Oakland, CA.

Ellet, C. (1851). "Report on the Wheeling and Belmont Suspension Bridges," in *Order of Reference of the Supreme Court of the United States,* George F. White, Saratoga Springs, New York.

Ellingwood, B., Galambos, T. V., MacGregor, J. G., and Cornell, C. A. (1980). *Development of a Probability-Based Load Criterion for American National Standard A58 Building Code*

Requirements for Minimum Design Loads in Buildings and Other Structures, special pub. 577, National Bureau of Standards, June.

Elliot, A. L. (1990). "Steel and Concrete Bridges," in *Structural Engineering Handbook,* E. H. Gaylord and C. N. Gaylord, eds., McGraw-Hill Companies, Inc., New York.

ENR. (1972a). "First U.S. Stayed-Girder Span is a Slim, Economical Crossing," *Eng. News-Record,* June 29.

ENR. (1972b). "Record Stayed-Girder Span Goes up Amid Controversy," *Eng. News-Record,* August 3, p. 13.

ENR. (1973). "Too Many Spectators Mar Gala Bridge Opening," *Eng. News-Record,* November 8, p. 19.

ENR. (1975a). "Fiberglass Pedestrian Bridge Spans Highway," *Eng. News-Record,* January 16, p. 13.

ENR. (1975b). "Caisson Problem Delays Record Span," *Eng. News-Record,* June 12.

ENR. (1976). "Tower of Record Span Rises after Caissons Sink," *Eng. News-Record,* April 1.

ENR. (1977). "Bridge Bents Lean from Steep Gorge Walls," *Eng. News-Record,* January 20, pp. 44–47.

ENR. (1978a). "One Example of a Highway Bridge Design Using Both the Load Factor Method and the Working Stress Provisions of AASHTO Specifications," *Eng. News-Record,* March 16.

ENR. (1978b). "Record Stayed-Girder Falters on Foundation Decision," *Eng. News-Record,* June 6.

ENR. (1978c). "Weather, Labor Slow Spinning of Main Cables on the Longest Span," *Eng. News-Record,* July 27, p. 20.

ENR. (1991). "Bridge Code Updated," *Eng. News-Record,* July 15.

Fairbairn, W. (1849). *An Account of the Construction of the Britannia and Conway Tubular Bridges,* John Weale, London.

Fairbairn, W. (1857). *The Application of Cast and Wrought Iron to Building Purposes,* London.

Feige, A. (1966). "The Evolution of German Cable-Stayed Bridges: An Overall Survey," *Acier-Stahl-Steel,* no. 12, December, pp. 523–532.

Feige, A. (1971). "Long-Span Highway Bridges Today and Tomorrow," *Acier-Stahl-Steel,* no. 5, May, pp. 210–221.

Ferjencik, Pavel. (1971). "Czechoslovak Contribution in the Field of Prestressed Steel Structures," *I.C.E. Monthly,* II(11).

Finch, J. K. (1941). "Wind Failures of Suspension Bridges," *Eng. News-Record,* March.

Finley, J. (1810). "A Description of the Patent Chain Bridge," *Portfolio,* 3(6), pp. 441–453.

Fisher, J. W. (1984). *Fatigue and Fracture in Steel Bridges: Case Studies,* John Wiley & Sons, New York.

Focardi. (1971). "Suspension Structure for Carrying Gas Pipeline over the River Po (Italy)," *Acier-Stahl-Steel,* September, pp. 354–357.

Galambos, T. V. (1981). "Load and Resistance Factor Design," *AISC Eng. J.,* 18, 3rd qtr., pp. 74–82.

Galambos, T. V., Ellingwood, B., MacGregor, J. G., and Cornell, C. A. (1982). "Probability-Based Load Criteria: Load Factors and Load Combinations," *ASCE J. Struct. Div.,* 108(ST5), May, pp. 959–977.

GangaRao, H. V. S., and Taly, N. (1977). "Short-Span Superstructural Systems," *ASCE Spring Conv. and Exhibit,* Dallas, TX, April 25–29, preprint no. 2839.

GangaRao, H. V. S., and Taly, N. (1978). "Conceptual Superstructural Systems for Short-Span Bridges," *ASCE Trans. Eng. J.,* TE1, paper no. 13491, January.

Garcia, A., and Robison, R. (1986). "Sunshine Skyway Nears Completion," *ASCE Civ. Eng.,* November, pp. 32–35.

Gies, J. (1963). *Bridges and Men,* Grosset and Dunlap, New York.

Gimsing, J. K. (1983). *Cable-Supported Bridges,* John Wiley & Sons, New York.

Gimsing, J. K. (1988). *Cable-Stayed Bridges with Ultra-Long Spans,* Report, Dept. of Structural Engineering, Technical Univ. of Denmark, Lyngby, Denmark.

Grant, A. (1977). "Pasco–Kennewick Bridge, the Longest Cable-Stayed Bridge in North America," *ASCE Civ. Eng.,* 47(8), 1977, pp. 62–66.

Grant, A. (1987). "Design and Construction of East Huntington Bridge," *PCI J.,* 32(1), pp. 20–29.

Gronquist, C. H. (1941). "Simplified Theory of the Self-Anchored Suspension Bridges," *ASCE Trans.,* February, pp. 177–197.

Gute, W. L. (1973a). "Design and Construction of the Sitka Harbor Bridge," *Natl. Struct. Eng. Meeting,* San Francisco, meeting preprint no. 1957, April 9–13.

Gute, W. L. (1973b). "First Vehicular Cable-Stayed Bridge in the U.S.," *ASCE Civ. Eng.,* November, pp. 50–55.

Haaijer, G. (1983). "Limit States Design—A Tool for Reducing the Complexity of Steel Structures," *AISC Natl. Eng. Conf.,* March 4.

Hagon, R., and Broucke, A. (1965). "The Grand Duchess Charlotte Bridge at Luxemburg," *Acier-Stahl-Steel,* no. 6, June, pp. 263–270.

Hardesty, S., and Wessman, H. E. (1938). "Preliminary Design of Suspension Bridges," *ASCE Trans.,* paper no. 2029, pp. 579–608.

Hart, Gary C. (1982). *Uncertainty Analysis, Loads, and Safety in Structural Engineering,* Prentice Hall, Englewood Cliffs, NJ.

Hasaler, E. (1900). *Eiserne Brucken,* Vieweg Publ.

Hazelet, C. P., and Wood, R. H. (1961). "Six-Lane Tied-Arch Bridge across the Ohio," *ASCE Civ. Eng.,* November, pp. 43–47.

Hedefine, A. (1972). "Beam and Girder Bridges," in *Structural Steel Engineers Handbook,* F. S. Merrit, ed., McGraw-Hill Companies, Inc., New York.

Heger, F. J. (1993). "Public Safety—Is It Compromised by New LRFD Design Standards?" *ASCE J. Struct. Eng.,* 119(4), pp. 1251–1264.

Heins, C. P., and Firmage, D. A. (1979). *Design of Modern Steel Highway Bridges,* John Wiley & Sons, New York.

Heins, C. P., and Lawrie, R. A. (1984). *Design of Modern Concrete Highway Bridges,* John Wiley & Sons, New York.

Highway Focus. (1973). U.S. Dept. of Transportation, Federal Highway Administration, Washington, DC, August.

Hooke, R. (1676). "Postscript," in *Descriptions of Helioscopes and Other Instruments,* pp. 26–32, London.

Hool, G. A., and Kinney, W. S. (1943). *Movable and Long-Span Steel Bridges,* McGraw-Hill Companies, Inc., New York.

Hopkins, H. J. (1970). *A Span of Bridges,* Praeger, New York.

Hovey, O. E. (1926). *Movable Bridges,* John Wiley & Sons, New York.

ICJ. (1963). "The Maracaibo Bridge in Venezuela," *Indian Concrete J.,* August, pp. 295–301.

Jakkula, A. A. (1941). *A History of Suspension Bridges in Bibliographical Form,* Agricultural and Mechanical College of Texas, 4th series.

Johnson, J. B., Brywn, C. W., and Turneaure, F. E. (1910). "Suspension Bridges," in *The Theory and Practice of Modern Framed Structures,* John Wiley & Sons, New York.

Johnston, B. G., Lin, F. J., and Galambos, T. V. (1986). *Basic Steel Design,* 3rd ed., Prentice Hall, Englewood Cliffs, NJ.

Kar, A. (1974). "Prestressing Applications in Distressed Structures," *PCI J.,* March–April, pp. 93–97.

Kavanagh, T. C. (1972). "Cable-Supported Bridges," in *Structural Designer's Handbook,* F. S. Merritt, ed., Sec. 14, McGraw-Hill Companies, Inc., New York.

Kavanagh, T. C. (1973). "Discussion of 'Historical Development of Cable-Stayed Bridges,' by W. Podolny, Jr., and J. F. Flemming," *ASCE J. Struct. Div.,* 99(ST7). July, pp. 1669–1762.

Kavanagh, T. C., and Young, R. C. Y. (1990). "Arches and Rigid Frames," in *Structural Engineering Handbook,* E. H. Gaylord and C. N. Gaylord, eds., Sec. 17, McGraw-Hill Companies, Inc., New York.

Kindler, J. E. (1958). "Burdekin Bridge Superstructure," *J. Inst. Eng.,* 30(6), pp. 169–184.

Kinney, J. S. (1957). *Indeterminate Structural Analysis,* Addison-Wesley, Massachusetts.

Kiureghian, A. D. (1989). "Measures of Structural Safety under Imperfect States of Knowledge," *ASCE J. Struct. Eng.,* 115(5), pp. 1119–1140.

Kuzmanovic, B. O., and Willems, N. (1983). *Steel Design for Structural Engineers,* 2nd ed., Prentice Hall, Englewood Cliffs, NJ.

Lazer, B. E. (1972). "Stiffness Analysis of Cable-Stayed Bridges," *ASCE J. Struct. Div.,* 98(ST7), July, proc. paper 9036, pp. 1605–1612.

Lazer, B. E., Troitsky, M. S., and Douglas, M. M. (1972). "Load Balancing Analysis of Cable-Stayed Bridges," *ASCE J. Struct. Div.,* 98(ST8), proc. paper 9122, August, pp. 1725–1740.

Leonhardt, F. (1987). "Cable-Stayed Bridges in Prestressed Concrete," *PCI J.,* 32(5), September–October, pp. 52–80.

Leonhardt, F., and Zellner, W. (1970). "Cable-Stayed Bridges—Report on Latest Developments," *Proc. Canadian Struct. Eng. Conf.,* University of Toronto.

Leonhardt, F., and Zellner, W. (1972). "Comparative Investigations between Suspension Bridges and Cable-Stayed Bridges for Spans Exceeding 600 m," *Publications IABSE,* 32-1, pp. 127–165 (in German).

Libby, J., and Perkins, N. D. (1976). *Modern Prestressed Concrete Highway Bridge Structures,* Grantville Publishing Co., San Diego.

Lin, T. Y., and Chow, P. (1991). "Gibralter Strait Crossing—A Challenge to Bridge and Structural Engineers," *Struct. Eng. Intl.,* 1(2).

Lothers, J. E. (1960). *Advanced Design in Structural Steel,* Prentice Hall, Englewood Cliffs, NJ.

Lovett, T. G., and Warren, D. W. (1992). "Double Diamonds: New Brand for a Texas Bridge," *ASCE Civ. Eng.,* April, pp. 42–45.

MacGregor, J. C. (1976). "Safety and Limit State Design for Reinforced Concrete," *Canadian J. Civ. Eng.* 3(4), December, pp. 484–513.

MacGregor, J. C. (1988). *Reinforced Concrete Design,* Prentice Hall, Englewood Cliffs, NJ.

Mallick, P. K. (1983). "Ultimate Possibility in Long-Span Bridging," *ASCE J. Struct. Eng.,* 199(11). November, pp. 2547–2560.

Martin, H. M. (1927). "The Theory of Stiffened Suspension Bridges," *Engineering,* 123, April 29.

Mathivat, J. (1983). *The Cantilever Construction of Prestressed Construction Bridges,* John Wiley & Sons, New York.

McCormick, F. C. (1972). "Why Not Plastics Bridges?" *ASCE J. Struct. Div.,* 98(ST8), August, pp. 1757–1767.

Mehrtens, G. C. (1900). *A Hundred Years of German Bridge Building,* trans. by Ludwig Mehrtens, pub. for the Paris Universal Exposition, Berlin.

Mehrtens, G. C. (1908). *Eisenbruckenbau,* Engelmann Publ., 3 vols.

Melan, J. (1888). "Theorie der eisernen Bogenbrucken und der Hangebrucken," in *Handbuch der Ingenieurwissenschaften,* Wilhelm, Leipzig, Germany, vol. 2, part 4 (in German).

Melan, J. (1913). *Theory of Arches and Suspension Bridges,* D. B. Steinman, trans., by Myron C. Clark, Chicago.

Merritt, F. S., ed. (1972). *Structural Steel Engineers Handbook,* McGraw-Hill Companies, Inc., New York.

Meier, V., and Meier, H. (1996). "CFRP Finds Use in Cable Support for Bridge," *Modern Plastics,* April, pp. 87–88.

Modjeski, R., and Masters, F. M. (1941). "Suspension Bridges and Wind Resistance," *Eng. News-Record,* October 27.

Montens, S., and O'Hagen, D. (1992). "Bringing Bridge Design into the Next Century: The Construction of the Roize Bridge," *AISC Modern Steel Constr.,* September, pp. 53–54.

Morandi, R. (1961). "Bridge Spanning Lake Maracaibo," *PCI J.,* 6(2). June, pp. 12–27.

Muller, J. M. (1993). "Bridge of the Future," *AISC Civ. Eng.,* January, pp. 40–43.

Muller, J. M., and Lockwood, J. D. (1992). "Innovations in Composite Bridge Structures," *AISC Modern Steel Constr.,* September, pp. 47–52.

Nagai, S., Kojima, H., and Naruoka, M. (1965). *Design of Langer Girder Bridge with Inclined Hangers,* National Research Council, Highway Research Board, Res. Record 103, pp. 107–113.

Narouka, M. (1973). "Cable-Stayed Bridges in Japan," *Acier-Stahl-Steel,* no. 10, October, pp. 413–418.

Navier, C. L. M. H. (1823). *Rapport a Monsieur Becqey, conseiller d'etat, directeur general des ponts et chausees et des mines; et memoire sur les ponts suspendus,* Imprimerie Royal, Paris, France, pp. 80–81 (in French).

NCHRP. (1992). *Development of Comprehensive Bridge Specifications and Commentary: Third Draft LRFD Specifications and Commentary,* NCHRP project 12-33, Transportation Research Board, Washington, DC, April.

NCHRP. (1993). *Development of Comprehensive Bridge Specifications and Commentary: Fourth Draft LRFD Specifications and Commentary,* NCHRP project 12-33, Transportation Research Board, Washington, DC, March.

Norris, C. H., Wilbur, J. B., and Utku, S. (1976). *Elementary Structural Analysis,* 3rd ed., McGraw-Hill Companies, Inc., New York.

NTSB. (1968). *Collapse of U.S. 35 Highway Bridge, Point Pleasant, West Virginia, December 15, 1967: A Report,* NTSB, Washington, DC, October 4, PB 198 139.

O'Connor, C. (1971). *Design of Bridge Superstructures,* John Wiley & Sons, New York.

Olander, H. C. (1954). "Stresses in the Corners of Rigid Frames," *ASCE Trans.,* 119, pp. 797–809.

Osipov, L. (1969). "The Hudson Hope Bridge: Its Post-Tensioned Box Girder, Stiffening Deck and Prestressed Rock Anchors," paper SP-41, in *Concrete Bridge Design,* ACI pub. SP-23.

Parcel, J. I., and Moorman, R. B. B. (1955). "Suspension Bridges" in *Analysis of Statically Indeterminate Structures,* John Wiley & Sons, New York, pp. 517–566.

PCA. (1966). *Continuous Bridges on V-Shaped Piers,* Advanced Engineering Bull. no. 19, PCA, Chicago.

PCA. (1995). "Engineered Concrete Structures," *PCA,* 8(2), August, p. 4.

Peery, D. J. (1954). "An Influence-Line Analysis for Suspension Bridges," *ASCE J. Struct. Div.,* 80(ST12), December, paper no. 558, pp. 1–19.

Pinkham, C. W. (1987) "Design Philosophies," in *Building Structural Design Handbook,* R. N. White, and C. G. Salmon, eds., John Wiley & Sons, New York, pp. 44–54.

Planter, S. B. (1911). *The Topography and Monuments of Ancient Rome,* Allyn & Bacon, New York.

PE Product. (1970). "Fabric Bridge Is Inflated and Deployed On Site," *Prod. Eng.,* 41(14), July 6.

Podolny, W., Jr. (1974). "Cable-Stayed Bridges," *AISC Eng. J.,* First qtr.

Podolny, W., Jr. (1997). Personal communication, FHWA, Washington, DC, February 3.

Podolny, W., Jr., and Flemming, J. F. (1972). "Historical Development of Cable-Stayed Bridges," *ASCE J. Struct. Div.,* 98(ST9), proc. paper 9201, September, pp. 2079–2095.

Podolny, W., Jr., and Scalzi, J. B. (1986). *Construction and Design of Cable-Stayed Bridges,* 2nd ed., John Wiley & Sons, New York.

Poncelet, J. V. (1870). *Introduction a la Mecanique Industrielle,* 3rd ed., p. 317, Paris.

Pope, T. (1811). *A Treatise on Bridge Architecture with an Historical Account and Description of Different Bridges Erected in Various Parts of the World, from an Early Period to the Present Time,* published by Thomas Pope.

Pugsley, S. A. (1968). *The Theory of Suspension Bridges,* Edward Arnold, London.

Radojkovic, M. (1966). "The Evolution of Welded Bridge Construction in Yugoslavia," *Acier-Stahl-Steel,* no. 12, December, pp. 533–541.

Rankine, W. J. M. (1857). "On the Stability of Loose Earth," *Philosophical Transactions of the Royal Society,* London, vol. 147.

Ravindra, M. K., and Galambos, T. V. (1978). "Load and Resistance Factor Design for Steel," *ASCE J. Struct. Div.,* 104(ST9), September, pp. 1337–1353.

Reid, W. (1836). "A Short Account of the Failure of a Part of the Brighton Chain Pier, in the Gale of the 30th November, 1836," *Professional Papers of the Corps of Royal Engineers,* vol. 1, pp. 99–101.

Richardson, G. S. (1972). "Arch Bridges," in *Structural Steel Designers Handbook,* Sec. 13, McGraw-Hill Companies, Inc., New York.

Ritter, W. (1877). "Versteifungsfachwerke bei Bogen-und Hangenbrucken," *Zeitschrift fur Bauwessen,* 27(4).

Robinson, R. (1993). "The French Composite: A Bridge for Normandy," *ASCE Civ. Eng.,* February, pp. 56–59.

Roebling, J. A. (1841). "Some Remarks on Suspension Bridges and on the Comparative Merits of Cable and Chain Bridges," *Amer. Railroad J. and Mechanics' Magazine,* 6 (new series), no. 6, March 15, p. 161, and no. 7, April 1, p. 193.

Roebling, J. A. (1846). "Report and Plan for a Wire Suspension Bridge," in *Order of Reference of the Supreme Court of the United States,* Geroge F. White, Saratoga Springs, New York.

Roebling, J. A. (1855). *Final Report on the Niagara Railway Suspension Bridge,* Lee, Mann & Co., Rochester, New York.

Rogerson, W. M., Sharp, M. L., Stemler, J. R., and Sommer, R. J. (1967). "Aluminum Orthotropic Bridge Deck," *ASCE Civ. Eng.,* November, pp. 65–70.

Rosenberg, N., and Vincenti, W. G. (1978). *The Britannia Bridge,* MIT Press, Cambridge, MA.

Rothman, H. B., and Chang, F. (1974). "Longest Precast Concrete Box Girder Bridge in Western Hemisphere," *ASCE Civ. Eng.,* March, pp. 56–60.

Salmon, C. G., and Johnson, J. E. (1990). *Steel Structures: Design and Behavior,* 3rd ed., Harper & Row, New York.

Salvadori, M., and Heller, R. (1975). *Structure in Architecture: The Building of Buildings,* Prentice Hall, Englewood Cliffs, NJ.

Scott, Q., and Miller, H. (1979). *The Eads Bridge,* University of Missouri Press, Columbia.

Sealey, A. (1976). *Bridges and Aqueducts,* Hugh Evelyn, London.

Selberg, A. (1954). "Design of Suspension Bridges," *Det Kongelige Norske Videnskabers Selskabs Skifrter,* No. 1 (in English).

Shedd, J. P. (1972). "Truss Bridges," in *Structural Engineering Handbook,* F. S. Merritt, ed., Sec. 12, McGraw-Hill Companies, Inc., New York.

Simpson, C. V. J. (1970). "Modern Long-Span Bridge Construction in Western Europe," *Proc. Institute Civil Eng.,* London.

Singer, F. L. (1962). *Strength of Materials,* 2nd ed., Harper & Row, New York.

Smith, B. S. (1967). "The Single Plane Cable-Stayed Girder Bridges: A Method of Analysis Suitable for Computer Use," Institution of Civil Engineers, paper no. 7011, November.

Smith, H. S. (1965). *The World's Great Bridges,* Harper & Brothers, New York.

Snyder, G. M., Lindvall, C. E., and Lyons, R. P. (1987). "Earthquakes Will Not Damage This Bridge," *ASCE Civ. Eng.,* September, pp. 54–56.

SSRC. (1988). *Guide to Stability Criteria for Metal Structures,* 4th ed., T. V. Galambos, ed., John Wiley & Sons, New York.

Stahl, F. L., and Christopher, G. (1992). "Cable Systems Investigations to Improve Corrosion Protection for the Akashi-Kaiko Bridge," *9th Annual Intl. Bridge Conf. and Exhibition,* June 15–17, Pittsburgh, PA.

Starossek, U. (1996). "Cable-Stayed Bridge Concept for Longer Spans," *ASCE J. Bridge Eng.,* 1(3), August, pp. 99–103.

"The Statics of Bridges—The Suspension Chain." (1863a). *Civ. Eng. Archit. J.,* 25, pp. 47–50, 70–71, 171–173, 236–237.

"The Statics of Bridges—The Suspension Chain." (1863b). *Civ. Eng. and Archit. J.,* 26, pp. 128–130.

Steinman, D. B. (1913). *Suspension Bridges and Cantilevers,* Science Series, no. 127, Van Nostrand, New York.

Steinman, D. B. (1929). *A Practical Treatise on Suspension Bridges: Their Design, Construction, and Erection,* 2nd ed., John Wiley & Sons, New York.

Steinman, D. B. (1935). "A Generalized Deflection Theory for Suspension Bridges," *ASCE Trans.,* 100, p. 1113.

Steinman, D. B., and Watson, S. R. (1957). *Bridges and Their Builders,* Dover Publications, New York.

Sterian, D. (1969). "Introducing Artificial Initial Forces into Steel Bridge Decks," *Acier-Stahl-Steel,* no. 1, pp. 31–37.

Stussi, F. (1951). "Long-Span Steel Bridges," in *Civil Engineering Reference Book,* pp. 761–771, Butterworth Scientific Publications, London.

"Suspension Bridges." (1909). *J. Franklin Inst.,* 19(3rd series).

Tacoma Narrows. (1941a). "Report of the Board of Investigation, Tacoma Narrows Bridge," Report to James A. Davis, Acting Director of Highways, February 17 and June 26, 1941.

Tacoma Narrows. (1941b). "The Failure of Tacoma Narrows Bridge," Report to the Hon. John M. Carmondy, Administrator, Federal Works Agency, Washington, DC, March 28.

Tacoma Narrows. (1941c). "The Failure of the Suspension Bridge over Tacoma Narrows," Report to Paul Carew, Chairman, Narrows Bridge Loss Committee, June 2.

Tacoma Narrows. (1943). "Failure of the Tacoma Narrows Bridge: Report of the Special Committee of the Board of Direction," *ASCE Proc.,* December.

Tacoma Narrows. (1944). *The Failure of the Tacoma Narrows Bridge,* Bull. no. 78, Texas Engineering Experiment Station, College Station.

Taly, N. B. (1976). *Development and Design of Short-Span Bridge Superstructural Systems,* Ph.D. dissertation, Civil Engineering Dept., West Virginia University, Morgantown.

Taly, N. B., and GangaRao, H. V. S. (1974). "Development of Standardized Short-Span Bridges," Meeting preprint 2407, *ASCE Annual and Natl. Envr. Eng. Conv.,* October 21–25, Kansas City, MO.

Taly, N. B., and GangaRao, H. V. S. (1977). "Survey of Short-Span Bridge Systems in the United States," Vol. WVDOH-2, Civil Engineering Dept., West Virginia University, Presented at the Transportation Research Board Meeting, Washington, DC, January.

Taly, N. B., and GangaRao, H. V. S. (1978). "Precast Prestressed Concrete Box Girder Bridge System with Overhangs," *8th Federation Internationale de la Precontrainte Intl. Conf.,* London, April 30–May 2.

Tang, M.-C. (1971a). "Analysis of Cable-Stayed Girder Bridges," *ASCE J. Struct. Div.,* 97(ST5). paper no. 8116, May, pp. 1481–1496.

Tang, M.-C. (1971b). "Design of Cable-Stayed Girder Bridges," *ASCE J. Struct. Div.,* 98(ST8), paper no. 9151, August, pp. 1789–1803.

Taylor, P. R. (1969). "Cable-Stayed Bridges and Their Potential in Canada," *Engineering Institute of Canada, Eng. J.,* 52(11), November.

Thul, H. (1966). "Cable-Stayed Bridges in Germany," *Proc. Conf. on Structural Steelwork,* held at the Institution of Civil Engineers, Sept. 26–28, The British Constructional Steelwork Assoc., Ltd., London.

Thul, H. (1972). "Developments of Cable-Stayed Bridges in Germany," *Der Stahlbau*, 14(6), June, pp. 161–171; 41(7), pp. 204–215 (in German).

Timoshenko, S. (1953). *History of Strength of Materials,* McGraw-Hill Companies, Inc., New York.

Timoshenko, S., and Gere, J. M. (1961). *Theory of Elastic Stability,* McGraw-Hill Companies, Inc., New York.

Troitsky, M. S. (1967). *Orthotropic Bridges: Theory and Design,* James F. Lincoln Arc Welding Foundation, Cleveland.

Troitsky, M. S. (1988). *Prestressed Steel Structures,* James F. Lincoln Arc Welding Foundation, Cleveland.

Tyrrell, H. G. (1911). *History of Bridge Engineering,* H. G. Tyrrell, Chicago.

United States GAO. (1990). *Loma Prieta Earthquake: Collapse of the Bay Bridge and the Cypress Viaduct,* United States General Accounting Office, Report GAO/RCED-90-177.

USS. (1978). "Bridge Report—New River Gorge Bridge, Fayette County, West Virginia, Structural Bridge Report, rep. no. ADUSS 88-7274-01, U.S. Steel Corp., Pittsburgh, May, 24 pp.

USS. (1974). "Hatfield Bridge, Jackson County, Wisconsin," *Bridge Structural Report,* rep. no. ADUSS 88-6323-01, U.S. Steel Corp., Pittsburgh, July.

Van den Broek, J. A. (1939). "Theory of Limit Design," *ASCE Proc.,* 65, pp. 193–216.

Vincent, G. S. (1969). *Tentative Criteria for Load Factor Design of Steel Highway Bridges,* AISI Bull. no. 15, March.

Virola, J. (1968). "The World's Greatest Suspension Bridges Before 1970," *Acier-Stahl-Steel,* no. 3, pp. 121–128.

Virola, J. (1969). "The World's Greatest Cantilever Bridges," *Acier-Stahl-Steel,* no. 4, pp. 164–170.

Virola, J. (1971). "The World's Greatest Steel Arch Bridges," *ICE Monthly,* vol. II, no. 5, 1971/72, pp. 209–221.

Waddell, J. A. L. (1916). *Bridge Engineering,* vol. 1, John Wiley & Sons, New York.

Waddell, J. A. L. (1935). "Weights of Metal in Steel Trusses," *ASCE Trans.,* 101, February, pp. 1–34.

Walpole, R. E., and Raymond, H. M. (1982). *Probability and Statistics for Engineers and Scientists,* Macmillan, New York.

WCN. (1940). "Collapse of the Tacoma Narrows Bridge," *West. Constr. News,* December, p. 1.

White, R. N., Gergely, P., and Sexsmith, R. G. (1976). *Structural Engineering,* John Wiley & Sons, New York.

Wolchuk, R. (1990). "Steel Plate-Deck Bridges," in *Structural Engineering Handbook,* E. H. Gaylord and C. N. Gaylord, eds., McGraw-Hill Companies, Inc., New York.

Woods, S. W. (1973). "Discussion of 'Historical Development of Cable-Stayed Bridges,'" *ASCE J. Struct. Div.,* 99(ST4), pp. 797–798.

CHAPTER 2

Materials of Bridge Construction

2.1
INTRODUCTION

In modern times, two materials are chiefly used for bridge construction: steel and concrete. However, to a limited extent, timber—mostly glued-laminated and stress-laminated—is used [Dickson and GangaRao, 1990; GangaRao, 1990]. In several eastern-hemisphere countries, stone masonry, with lime or cement mortar, is used for bridge substructure (abutments and piers) for economic reasons. Aluminum bridge decks are sometimes used to reduce the superstructure dead load (as much as 30 to 40 percent reductions in some cases [CE, 1996c])—usually as part of a rehabilitation or retrofit project, resulting in the bridge's enhanced live-load carrying capacity and service life. Other aluminum products are used for auxiliary applications (railings, guard rails).

In this decade, fiber-reinforced polymer composites, commonly referred to as *composite materials,* are being increasingly considered for use in infrastructure renewal in general. These lightweight materials can be used in the rehabilitation of deteriorating decks as well as for new superstructures. These materials are known to possess many desirable structural properties, such as high strength-to-weight and stiffness-to-weight ratios, corrosion resistance, environmental durability, and inherent tailorability. An overview of composites—their development and use in civil engineering infrastructures, including some bridges around the world—is presented in Sec. 2.5.

2.2
STEEL

The historical evolution of iron and steel was described in Chapter 1. In every bridge, structural steel is used in one form or another, except that decks are most commonly of

117

reinforced concrete. With the exception of concrete and timber bridges, almost every component of a bridge is made from structural steel, including stringers, floor beams, girders, truss members, cables for suspension and cable-stayed bridges, and bearings. According to the AISC–LRFD specification A2.1 [AISC, 1994], "the term *structural steel* refers to the steel elements of the structural steel frame essential to the support of the required loads." Such elements are enumerated in Sec. 2.1 of the AISC *Code of Standard Practice for Steel Buildings and Bridges* [AISC, 1994].

All structural steels are designated by ASTM designations [ASTM, 1988] as well as by such proprietary names as *Corten* steel, by U.S. Steel, and *MayariR,* by Bethlehem Steel. The AISC–LRFD *Manual* [AISC, 1994] lists 15 types of structural steel with various ASTM designations. Their specific applications are described in many references, such as [Gaylord, Gaylord, and Stallmeyer, 1992; Salmon and Johnson, 1990]. The ASTM A709 structural steel is listed as the one suitable for bridges. It is characterized by enhanced corrosion resistance and stringent impact test requirements.

Steel is mainly an alloy of iron and carbon, with varying amounts of certain other alloying elements, such as manganese, phosphorus, sulfur, silicon, aluminum, vanadium, columbium, nickel, copper, chromium, nitrogen, and boron. The element most responsible for giving steel its useful properties is carbon. It and the other elements present affect the properties of the finished steel products. Effects of various alloying elements on properties of steel are described in [Merritt, 1972; AISC Mkt, 1991]. A general discussion on classification and properties of various steels for structural applications can be found in the AISC–LRFD manual [AISC, 1994], in many texts on steel design [Gaylord, Gaylord, and Stallmeyer, 1992; Lankford et al., 1985; Kuzmanovic and Willems, 1983; Salmon and Johnson, 1990], and in handbooks [ASM, 1978; Merritt, 1972].

What makes steel a desirable material for structural use are its mechanical properties of high tensile strength, ductility (ability to flow plastically), and toughness. The most important factor affecting the mechanical properties of steels is the chemical composition. Basically, three classes of structural steels are suitable for buildings and bridges [Kuzmanovic and Willems, 1983; Salmon and Johnson, 1990]: carbon steels, high-strength low-alloy (HSLA) steels, and alloy steels. The general requirements of these steels are specified in ANSI/ASTM A6 specifications [ASTM, 1988]. Lists of common steels, their minimum yield stresses, tensile strengths, and common uses can be found in books on structural steel design [Salmon and Johnson, 1990; Gaylord, Gaylord, and Stallmeyer, 1992].

2.2.1 Carbon Steels

Carbon steel is a class of steel in which the contents of the principal strengthening agents are carefully controlled to the following maximums:

Carbon, 1.7%
Manganese, 1.65%
Silicon, 0.60%
Copper, 0.60%

Depending on the percentages of carbon content, these steels are further classified as follows [Salmon and Johnson, 1990; McCormac, 1992]:

Low-carbon steel, carbon < 0.15%
Mild-carbon steel, carbon 0.15–0.29% (category of structural carbon steels)
Medium-carbon steel, carbon 0.30–0.59%
High-carbon steel, carbon 0.60–1.70%

An increased percentage of carbon raises the yield strength but reduces ductility. The ordinary mild steel, generally referred to as ASTM A36, falls in the mild-carbon category; it has a minimum yield strength of 36 ksi. Two other kinds of carbon steels—ASTM A7 (having a minimum yield stress of 33 ksi and used extensively from 1936 to about 1965 [Gaylord, Gaylord, and Stallmeyer, 1992]) and ASTM A373—were discontinued in 1967 and 1965, respectively.

2.2.2 High-Strength Low-Alloy Steels

Structural steels included in this category have yield stresses from 40 to 70 ksi and exhibit well-defined yield points, similar to A36 steel. Essentially, steels having minimum specified yield points of 40 ksi and greater and achieving that strength in the hot-rolled condition, rather than by heat treatment, are classified as high-strength low-alloy steels [AISC Mkt, 1993]. The term "low-alloy" is used arbitrarily to describe steels for which the total of all alloying elements does not exceed 5 percent of the total composition of steel [McCormac, 1992]. The mechanical properties of steels in this category are improved compared to those of the carbon steels. These improvements are achieved by altering their chemical composition, which involves adding small amounts of alloy elements such as chromium, columbium, copper, manganese, molybdenum, nickel, phosphorus, vanadium, or zirconium. Steels in this category include ASTM A242, ASTM A440, ASTM A441, ASTM A606, and ASTM A607 and ASTM Grades 709, Grades 50, and 50W [AASHTO, 1992a, 1992b; Merritt, 1972].

2.2.3 Alloy Steels

These steels are obtained by heat-treating the low-alloy steels to obtain higher yield strengths, 80 to 110 ksi. The process of heat-treating involves quenching or rapid cooling with water or oil, from at least 1650 °F to about 300–400 °F, then tempering by reheating to at least 1150 °F, and then controlled cooling. These steels do not exhibit a well-defined yield point like the carbon and low-alloy steels; consequently, their yield strengths are determined by the 0.2-percent offset method [Gaylord, Gaylord, and Stallmeyer, 1992; Merritt, 1972; Salmon and Johnson, 1990]. Stress–strain curves for various types of steels are shown in Fig. 2.1 [AISC Mkt, 1986].

Requirements for structural steel for highway bridges are covered by AASHTO 10.2.2 [1992a]; the specifications designate structural steels by their own material specification using the letter *M*, followed by a three-digit number; these designations are also expressed in terms of the equivalent ASTM designations. A family of five types

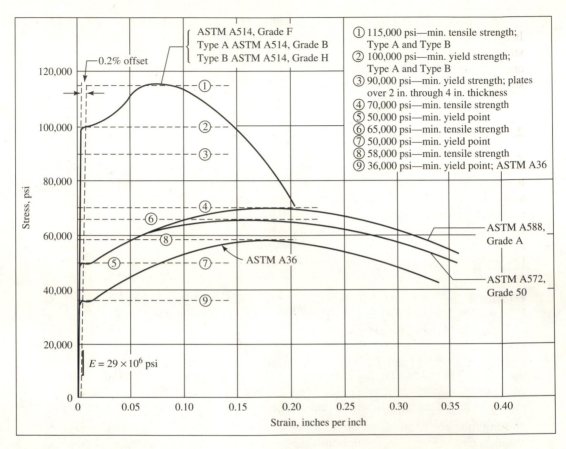

FIGURE 2.1
Stress–strain curves for various types of structural steels used in highway bridges [AMS, 1986].

of structural steels are specified:

1. Structural carbon steel
2. High-strength low-alloy columbium steels of structural quality
3. High-strength low-alloy structural steel with 50-ksi minimum yield point to 5 in. thick
4. High-strength low-alloy, quenched and tempered structural steel with 70-ksi minimum yield point to 4 in. thick
5. High-yield-strength quenched and tempered alloy steel plate, suitable for welding

In general, various factors that encourage use of higher-strength steels are

- Savings in handling, shipping, erection, and foundation costs due to savings in weight
- Superior corrosion resistance
- Use of shallower beams, permitting shallower depths of flooring and superstructure
- In buildings, possible savings in fireproofing because smaller-sized members that can be used

An important and economical use of high-strength steels is in hybrid construction. It involves the use of two or more steels of different strengths—the higher-strength steels are used where stresses are higher, and the lower-strength, lower-priced steels are used where the stresses are smaller, resulting in greatest overall economy. Hybrid structures are briefly described in Chapter 9.

2.2.4 Other Steels

Today more than 200 types of steels, with yield stresses in excess of 36 ksi, are reported to be available on the market [McCormac, 1992]. Essentially, these are special-purpose steels. For example, HY80 is an 80-ksi yield strength steel that has been widely used in ship construction; "Maraging steels" which develop yield strength in the range of 200 to 300 ksi, using a high-nickel-alloy content and a heat treatment to age the iron–nickel martensite [Errera, 1974]. However, these steels are not listed in the AISC manual [AISC, 1994] because they have not been assigned the ASTM numbers. It is believed that within a few years, steels with yield strength in the 500-ksi range will be available [McCormac, 1992, p. 21]. This possibility exists because the theoretical force between iron atoms has been estimated to be over 4000 ksi [Errera, 1974, pp. 50–51].

It is instructive to note that as the strength of steel is increased, price is usually increased and ductility is usually decreased. However, the modulus of elasticity, which governs deflections and elastic buckling, is relatively constant for all steels. Because the elastic buckling strength (discussed in Chapter 9) is directly proportional to and deflection (discussed in Chapter 5) is inversely proportional to the modulus of elasticity, any increase in strength of steel does not increase the elastic buckling resistance and stiffness of members. It is therefore felt that because of cost, buckling considerations, and greater deflections at higher stresses, the role of these very high-strength steels, although important, will be limited in structural design applications.

2.2.5 AASHTO Specifications for Structural Steel

AASHTO, Div. 2, 12.2.1 [AASHTO, 1992a] requires all steel shapes, plates, and bars to conform to AASHTO M270 (ASTM A709) Grade 36, 50, or 50W. Unless the material is galvanized or epoxy-coated, it must have a copper content of 0.2 percent. Table 2.1 (which is Table 10.2A in [AASHTO, 1992a]) gives designations and mechanical properties of various structural steels that are permitted to be used for bridges. The letter "W" following the grade of steel (as in 50W) stands for *weathering steels.* They have been used in bridges and in buildings with exposed frames. These steels are believed to have about four times the atmospheric-corrosion resistance of A36 steel [Gaylord, Gaylord, and Stallmeyer, 1992]. The corrosion problem of structural steels associated with bridges is discussed in Chapter 8.

For design purposes, the reference mechanical property specified as in AISC [1994] or AASHTO [1992a] is the yield stress in tension. It includes the *yield point,* the first stress at which an increase in strain occurs without an increase in stress, or the *yield strength,* the stress at which certain steels exhibit a specified limiting deviation from

TABLE 2.1
Mechanical properties of structural steel for bridges (AASHTO Table 10.2A) [AASHTO, 1992a]

| Type | Structural steel | Minimum material properties structural steel | | Quenched and tempered low-alloy steel | High-yield strength, quenched and tempered alloy steel | |
		High-strength low-alloy steel				
AASHTO designation[a,c]	M 270 Grade 36	M 270 Grade 50	M 270 Grade 50W	M 270 Grade 70W	M 270 Grades 100/100W	
Equivalent ASTM designation[c]	A 709 Grade 36	A 709 Grade 50	A 709 Grade 50W	A 709 Grade 70W	A 709 Grades 100/100W[b]	
Thickness of plates	Up to 4 in. incl.[e]	Up to 4 in. incl.	Up to 4 in. incl.	Up to 4 in. incl.	Up to $2\frac{1}{2}$ in. incl.	Up to $2\frac{1}{2}$ in. to 4 in. incl.
Shapes[d]	All groups[e]	All groups	All groups	Not applicable	Not applicable	Not applicable
Minimum tensile strength, F_u	58,000	65,000	70,000	90,000	110,000	100,000
Minimum yield point or minimum yield strength, F_y	36,000	50,000	50,000	70,000	100,000	90,000

[a]Except for the mandatory notch toughness and weldability requirements, the ASTM designations are similar to the AASHTO designations. Steels meeting the AASHTO requirements are prequalified for use in welded bridges.

[b]Quenched and tempered alloy steel structural shapes and seamless mechanical tubing meeting all mechanical and chemical requirements of A 709 Grades 100/100W, except that the specified maximum tensile strength may be 140,000 psi for structural shapes and 145,000 psi for seamless mechanical tubing, shall be considered as A 709 Grades 100/100W.

[c]M 270 Gr. 36 and A 709 Gr. 36 are equivalent to M 183 and A 36.
 M 270 Gr. 50 and A 709 Gr. 50 are equivalent to M 223 Gr. 50 and A 572 Gr. 50.
 M 270 Gr. 50W and A 709 Gr. 50W are equivalent to M 222 and A 588.
 M 270 Gr. 70W and A 709 Gr. 70W are equivalent to A 852.
 M 270 Gr. 100/100W and A 709 Gr. 100/100W are equivalent to M 224 and A 514.

[d]Groups 1 and 2 include all shapes except those in Groups 3, 4, and 5. Group 3 includes L-shapes over $\frac{3}{4}$ in. thick, HP shapes over 102 lb/ft, and the following W shapes: W36 × 230 to 300 incl.; W33 × 200 to 240 incl.; W14 × 142 to 211 incl.; W12 × 120 to 190 incl.; Group 4 includes the following W shapes: W14 × 219 to 550 incl. Group 5 includes the following W shapes: W14 × 605 to 730 incl. (For breakdown of Groups 1 and 2, see ASTM A 6.)

[e]For nonstructural applications or bearing assembly components over 4 in. thick, use AASHTO M 270 Gr. 36 (ASTM A 709 Gr. 36).

proportionality of stress to strain [AASHTO, 1994; AISC, 1994]. Recommended design values for material properties of steel are as follows:

1. Density of steel or cast steel: 490 lb/ft [AASHTO 3.3.6]
2. Modulus of elasticity, $E = 29 \times 10^6$ lb/in.^{2} [AASHTO 10.2.2]
3. Coefficient of expansion: 6.5×10^{-6} per degree Fahrenheit

2.3
CONCRETE

Concrete happens to be the most predominantly used material for highway bridge construction. According to U.S. National Bridge Inventory (NBI) data compiled by the Federal Highway Administration (FHWA), prestressed concrete became the most widely used U.S. material in the mid-1970s, and this trend continues [CE, 1992c; Dunker and Rabaat, 1990a,b; ENR, 1984]. With an eye on the $150 billion in Intermodal Surface Transportation Efficiency Act (ISTEA) funding, 83 percent of the respondents to a survey believe concrete bridges will be the dominant type of bridge constructed in the 1990s; steel or steel suspension bridges were named by just 23 percent [CE, 1992c].

There is hardly any bridge in which concrete is not used in some form. With the exception of orthotropic plate bridges, where an asphaltic wearing surface is used on the deck, concrete (or reinforced concrete) exclusively is used for decks, overlays, curbs, sidewalks (pedestrian walkways), parapets, and substructures (abutments, wing walls, and piers and bents).

The design of a concrete mix will depend on the strength requirements for a given design. Other factors that will affect the mix design are durability, shrinkage, freeze–thaw cycles and environmental conditions. The concrete mixture should be so proportioned as to produce a workable, finishable, durable, watertight, and wear-resistant concrete of the desired strength.

Generally speaking, concrete mixes with a 28-day compressive strength of 3000 to 4000 psi meet most design requirements satisfactorily, although concrete strength as low as 2200 psi can be used for portions of substructure such as footings, pedestals, massive pier shafts and gravity walls with none or only a small amount of reinforcement [AASHTO, 1992a]. For prestressed concrete bridges, the initial compressive strength (f_{ci}') of 3500 psi and the 28-day compressive strength of 4500 to 5000 psi are used.

The use of high-strength concrete (greater than 6000 psi) is expanding significantly throughout the United States and other industrialized nations. High-strength concretes are now commercially available on a wider geographical basis than ever before. Great strides have been made in the maximum achievable strengths to the extent that compressive strengths approaching 20,000 psi can now be obtained from commercial ready-mixed concretes, and concrete in the 26,000-psi range is being researched at the Concrete Technology Laboratory (CTL) of the Portland Cement Association in Skokie, Illinois. Although concretes of up to 19,000 psi have been used in recent years for building several highrises in various parts of the country, so far such advances have been slow in bridge construction. A 1984 report [ACI, 1984] lists only eleven bridges (five in the U.S., five in Japan, and one in Canada), built between 1967 and 1984, for which concrete strengths of up to 11,400 psi have been used.

Practices vary in the use of high-strength concrete for bridge construction in the United States. In Pennsylvania, the normal practice is to allow 6500-psi concrete (5500-psi initial strength) for prestressed concrete bridges—although strengths of up to 8000 psi (7200-psi initial strength) are also allowed. The most recent and notable use of high-strength concrete for bridge construction in the United States has been for the asymmetrical stayed-girder bridge on the Huntington (W. Va.)-to-Proctorville (Ohio) highway, for which 8000-psi concrete has been used [ENR, 1984]. For the 1250-ft main span of the Fred Hartman cable-stayed bridge (482, 1250, and 482 ft) over the Houston Ship Channel, a 7000-psi concrete for the roadway and a 6000-psi concrete for the 426-ft double-diamond towers have been specified [Lovett and Warren, 1992].

In Japan, the use of 11,400-psi concrete for two railway bridges has been reported [Nagataki, 1978]. An 11,500-psi concrete was used (8700 psi was used for calculations) for the precast, pretensioned deck panels for the Roize Bridge at Grenoble, France, for the continuous three-span (118, 131, and 118 ft) bridge completed in December, 1990 [CTL, 1992].

TABLE 2.2
Mix proportions for concrete [AASHTO, 1992a]

Class of concrete	Minimum cement content (lb/CY)	Maximum water-cement ratio (lb/lb)	Air content range (%)	Size of coarse aggregate per AASHTO M43 (square openings)	Minimum compressive strength (28 days) (lb/in.^{2})
A	611	0.49^a		1 in. to #4	3000
A(AE*)	611	0.45	$6 \pm 1\frac{1}{2}$	1 in. to #4	4000
B	517	0.58	—	2 in. to #3 and 1 in. to #4^b	2400
B(AE*)	517	0.55	$5 \pm 1\frac{1}{2}$	2 in. to #3 and 1 in. to #4^b	2400
C	658	0.49		$\frac{1}{2}$ in. to #4	4000
C(AE*)	658	0.45	$7 \pm 1\frac{1}{2}$	$\frac{1}{2}$ in. to #4	4000
P	564	0.49^a	As specified elsewhere	1 in. to #4 or $\frac{3}{4}$ in. to #4	As specified elsewhere
S	658	0.58	—	1 in. to #4	

^{a}For concrete in or over saltwater or exposed to deicing chemicals, the maximum water-cement ratio shall be 0.45.
^{b}Coarse aggregate for class B and class B(AE) shall be furnished in two separate sizes as shown.
*AE = Air-entrained.

The use of high-strength concrete is limited not because of production or availability; rather it is, in some cases, limited because of the prestressing capabilities in manufacturing plants. Reduced member stiffnesses due to the reduced cross-sectional areas of high-strength concrete members is also a concern. A joint pilot study has been conducted at the CTL involving three full-sized, 70-ft-long, prestressed concrete bulb-T girders with a compressive strength of 10,000 psi, with one of the girders having a 7000-psi cast-in-place deck [CTL, 1992].

The use of high-strength concrete in prestressed concrete bridges is discussed in Chapter 7. Current trends in the use of high-strength concrete in bridge construction can be found in several references [ACI, 1977, 1984; Adelman and Cousins, 1990; Castrodale, Kregar, and Burns, 1988; CTL, 1992; ENR, 1982; Jose and Moustafa, 1982; Rabaat and Russel, 1984; Schemmel and Zia, 1990; Shah and Ahmed, 1985].

Standard practice for concrete mix designs is described in ACI committee reports [ACI, 1991a,b]. Specifications for concrete mix design are covered under AASHTO Specifications Div. II, 8 [AASHTO, 1992a]. *Eight* classes of concrete are recognized for bridge construction. The materials are mixed by the absolute volume method as described in the AASHTO specifications [1992a]; the mix proportions are given in Table 2.2 (AASHTO 1992, Table 8.2). Table 2.3 shows the recommended practice, as suggested in *AASHTO Interim Specifications*—Bridges—1991 (commentary) for using various classes of concrete as defined in Table 2.2.

For design purposes, the following values of the modulus of elasticity of concrete, E_c (lb/in.^{2}), are recommended (AASHTO 8.7.1):

1. For w_c (weight of concrete) between 90 and 155 lb/ft^3,

$$E_c = w_c^{1.5} 33 \sqrt{f_c'}, \text{ psi} \qquad (2.1)$$

TABLE 2.3
Uses of various classes of concrete [AASHTO, 1991]

Class of concrete	Uses
Class A	For all portions of superstructure and substructure, except as noted for other types of concrete; portions include slabs, beams, girders, columns, arch ribs, box culverts, reinforced abutments, retaining walls, reinforced footings, precast piles, and cribbing.
Class B	For portions of substructure: footing, pedestals, massive pier shafts, and gravity walls, with none or only a small amount of reinforcement.
Class C	For thin reinforced sections, e.g., for reinforced railing under 4 in. thick, and for filler in steel grid floors. Class C (AE) concrete to be used in locations where concrete will be exposed to severe or moderate weather (alternate freezing and thawing).
Class P	For use when strength in excess of 4000 psi is required, e.g., for prestressed concrete members or for precast members manufactured at established plants.
Class S	For concrete to be deposited in water, e.g., to seal out water in cofferdams.

2. For the normal weight concrete ($w_c = 145$ lb/ft^3), the following approximate value of E_c (lb/in.^{2}) may be used:

$$E_c = 57,000 \sqrt{f_c'}, \text{ psi} \tag{2.2}$$

In practice, the air-entrained grades of the classes, designated AE, (classes A, B, and C) in Table 2.2, should be used in all locations (especially bridge decks) where the concrete will be exposed to severe or moderate natural weathering (alternate freezing and thawing) and where it will be exposed to saltwater or other potentially damaging environments. When reinforced concrete is exposed to salt or brackish water, deicing salts, or sulphate soils, Class S concrete should be used underwater and Class A for all other work, unless exceptions are made. The maximum water-cement ratio should be limited to 0.45. Unless otherwise indicated on plans, the clear distance from the face of the concrete to the reinforcing steel is required to be not less than 4 in. (AASHTO, 1992, II, 8.6.6).

A very important property of concrete is *creep,* which influences deflections of concrete structures under sustained loads and loss of prestress in prestressed structures. A comprehensive discussion on the subject has been provided by Hult [1966] and Neville [1970] (and many others). A brief discussion on this topic can also be found in the many texts on reinforced concrete design, such as MacGregor [1988], McCormac [1993], Nawy [1985], and others.

2.4
REINFORCING STEEL AND BARS

2.4.1 General Discussion

Deformed reinforcing bars #3 to #11 are used for general design; #14 and #18 are used only in exceptional cases. Plain bars are not permitted for load-carrying reinforcement; however, both the plain bars and smooth wire are permitted for spirals and ties. According to AASHTO 8.3.3 [AASHTO, 1992a], reinforcing steel with yield strength in excess of 60,000 lb/in.^{2} (Grade (Gr.) 60 steel) is not permitted for bridges. Exceptions exist. In some states, Gr. 60 reinforcement *only* is permitted; Gr. 40 is used only as an exception, with the permission of the chief bridge engineer. In others, reinforcing steel with a yield strength greater than 40,000 lb/in.^{2} is *not* permitted. In general, however, because of the very little difference in the prices of Gr. 40 and Gr. 60 reinforcing bars, Gr. 60 bars are the most commonly used in reinforced concrete design.

2.4.2 AASHTO Material Specifications

Material specifications for reinforcing steel are covered in AASHTO specifications, Div. II, 9 [AASHTO, 1992a] and other references [AASHTO, 1992b; ACI, 1995a]. Only deformed reinforcing bars should be used, except plain bars may be used for spirals and ties.

Both uncoated and coated bars are permitted for use in bridge construction. The following list gives the titles of the governing specifications to which the *uncoated reinforcing steel* must conform; as in the case of structural steels, both the AASHTO and the equivalent ASTM designations are given [AASHTO, 1992a].

1. Deformed and plain billet-steel bars for concrete reinforcement—AASHTO M31 (ASTM A615)
2. Deformed steel wire for concrete reinforcement—AASHTO M225 (ASTM A496)
3. Welded steel wire fabric for concrete reinforcement—AASHTO M55 (ASTM A185)
4. Cold-drawn steel wire for concrete reinforcement—AASHTO M32 (ASTM A82)
5. Welded deformed steel wire fabric for concrete reinforcement—AASHTO M221 (ASTM A497)
6. Low-alloy steel deformed bars for concrete reinforcement—ASTM A706
7. Rail-steel deformed and plain bars for concrete reinforcement—AASHTO M42 including supplementary requirement S1 (ASTM A616 including supplementary requirement S1)

In regions with a saline environment and in snowy regions where bridge decks are subjected to deicing chemicals, corrosion of reinforcing bars and consequent cracking and spalling of concrete is a matter of serious concern. To minimize corrosion, *epoxy-coated* reinforcing bars are often specified. The steel to be epoxy-coated should conform to the seven specifications just stated. Epoxy-coating of reinforcing bars is governed by requirements of AASHTO M284 (ASTM D3963), which includes the coating materials and process; the fabrication, handling, and identification of the steel; and the repair of any coating material damaged during fabrication and handling. Tests have shown that the bond strength of epoxy-coated bars is substantially reduced. As a result, AASHTO 8.25.2.3 [AASHTO, 1992a] requires that a modification factor of 1.5 be used to compute the required development length of such bars in tension when the clear concrete cover is less than $3d_b$ or the clear spacing between bars is less than $6d_b$ (d_b = diameter of the epoxy-coated bar). However, for all other cases, the modification factor is to be 1.17.

The modulus of elasticity of steel for the reinforcing bars, regardless of their grade, should be taken as 29,000 kips/in.² Poisson's ratio may be assumed as 0.2 (AASHTO 8.7.2).

2.4.3 Prestressing Steel

In bridge construction, prestressing steel is most generally used in prestressed concrete beams and decks. It is manufactured in three forms: *wires, strands,* and *bars.* AASHTO 9.3.1 [AASHTO, 1992a] requires prestressing steel to conform to the following specifications [AASHTO, 1992b]:

1. Uncoated stress-relieved wire for prestressed concrete—AASHTO M204
2. Uncoated seven-wire stress-relieved strand for prestressed concrete—AASHTO M 203
3. Uncoated high-strength steel bar for prestressing concrete—ASTM A722

Prestressing *wire,* ranging in diameters from 0.192 to 0.276 in., is made by cold-drawing high-carbon steel, followed by heat treatment for stress-relieving to develop the prescribed mechanical properties. To produce prestressing *tendons* of required strength, wires are bundled in groups of 50 individual wires. Strands (or stranded cables), ranging in diameters from 0.250 to 0.600 in., are fabricated by twisting six wires of equal diameter over a slightly larger seventh, straight, control wire; stress-relieving is achieved after the wires are twisted into the strand [Nawy, 1989]. To maximize the steel area within a given nominal diameter, the *standard strand* (Fig. 2.2(*a*)) can be "compacted" by drawing it through a die, forming a *compacted strand* (Fig. 2.2(*b*)). Wires are common in Europe; strands are common in the United States. *Alloy steel bars* for prestressing, both in the form of plain round (Type I) and deformed bars (Type II), are manufactured in diameters from 0.625 to 1.375 in. Cold-drawn in order to raise their yield strength, these bars are stress-relieved as well to increase their ductility.

Two types of strands, *low relaxation* and *stress-relieved* (normal-relaxation), are in general use for prestressing and post-tensioning purposes. These are available in two grades—250 and 270, having minimum ultimate strengths of 250 and 270 ksi, respectively, based on their nominal cross-sectional areas. For the alloy steel bars, two grades are used, 145 and 160, the former being common. Round wires are available in three grades: 235, 245, and 250, depending on diameter. All grade

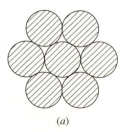

(*a*)

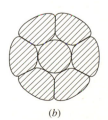

(*b*)

FIGURE 2.2
Standard and compacted seven-wire strands.

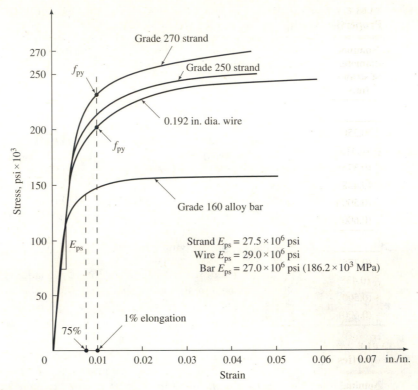

FIGURE 2.3
Typical stress–strain curves for prestressing steels [Nawy, 1989].

designations correspond to the minimum specified ultimate tensile strength in kips per square inch.

Figure 2.3 shows typical stress–strain curves for the high-strength steel used for the manufacture of prestressing wire, strands, and bars [Nawy, 1989]. Because the curves for these steels do not exhibit a well-defined yield point (as in the case of A36 steel), the yield strength is measured at 1 percent extension under load for wire and strand, and at 0.7 percent for alloy steel bars. Note that the spread between the yield strength and the tensile strength is smaller for the prestressing steels than for the reinforcing steels; consequently, the prestressing steels have significantly less ductility.

The elastic modulus of prestressing steel, E_s—in contrast to 29,000 ksi for the ordinary reinforcing steel—differs among types of prestressing products (wire, strands, and bars) and should be based on the data supplied by the manufacturer. The commonly used values of E_s are 27,000 to 28,500 ksi for strands and steel bars and 29,000 ksi for wire.

Minimum strength and geometrical properties of various strands are given in Tables 2.4 and 2.5, respectively.

Customarily, fabrication of prestressed concrete beams involves prestressing steel strands to very high stress levels—as much as 80 to 90 percent of their yield strengths.

TABLE 2.4
Properties of stress-relieved seven-wire standard strand

Nominal diameter of strand (in.)	Minimum breaking strength of strand (lb)	Nominal steel area of strand (in.²)	Nominal weight of strand (per 1000 ft)	Minimum load at 1% extension (lb)
Grade 250				
$\frac{1}{4}$ (0.250)	9000	0.036	122	7650
$\frac{5}{16}$ (0.313)	14,400	0.058	197	12,300
$\frac{3}{8}$ (0.375)	20,000	0.080	272	17,000
$\frac{7}{8}$ (0.438)	27,000	0.108	367	23,000
$\frac{1}{2}$ (0.500)	36,000	0.144	490	30,600
$\frac{3}{4}$ (0.600)	54,000	0.216	737	45,900
Grade 270				
$\frac{3}{8}$ (0.375)	23,000	0.085	290	19,500
$\frac{7}{16}$ (0.438)	31,000	0.115	390	26,350
$\frac{1}{2}$ (0.500)	41,300	0.153	520	35,100
$\frac{3}{4}$ (0.600)	58,600	0.217	740	49,800

TABLE 2.5
Properties of stress-relieved seven-wire compacted strand

Nominal diameter (in.)	Minimum breaking strength of strand (lb)	Nominal steel area (in.²)	Nominal weight (per 1000 ft)
$\frac{1}{2}$	47,000	0.174	600
0.6	67,440	0.256	873
0.7	85,430	0.346	1173

Under these conditions, unlike ordinary reinforcing steel bars, they exhibit a unique phenomenon known as *relaxation,* defined as *loss of stress* in stressed material (strands) held at constant length (between ends of the prestressed beam). In essence, it is analogous to *creep* in concrete, which refers to a *change in strain* under constant stress. The magnitude of prestress losses can be as high as 35,000 to 60,000 psi. It is this consideration that requires prestressing steels to be of *high-strength quality* so that even after the prestress losses, usable prestress will be left in the strands. Obviously, ordinary Gr. 40 or 60 reinforcing steel bars (often referred to as *nonprestressed* steel in the context of prestressed concrete design) would be left with hardly any prestress following the occurrence of prestress losses. Figure 2.4 shows typical relaxation behavior of prestressed steels [Nawy, 1989]. Relaxation losses can be reduced by a process called *stabilization;* the resulting product is called *low-relaxation steel,* having relaxation stress loss approximately 25 percent of that of the normal stress-relieved steel; consequently, it is the preferred type of prestressing steel. Note that the use of low-relaxation strands results in a reduced area of the prestress steel required and thus results in a reduced moment capacity compared to that provided by the normal relaxation strand. In such

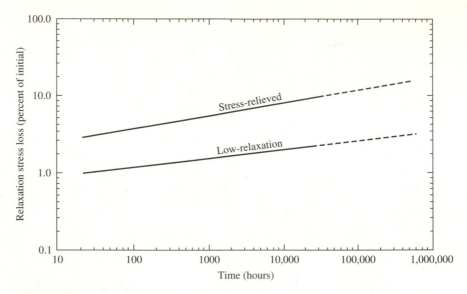

FIGURE 2.4
Loss of prestress as a result of relaxation over time in stress-relieved and low-relaxation prestressing steels [Nawy, 1989].

cases, nonprestressed steel is often used in combination with the prestressing steel to develop the required flexural strength of the beam.

Fundamentals of prestressed concrete are briefly discussed in Chapter 7. Readers are urged to refer to standard texts on prestressed concrete, such as Libby [1990], Lin and Burns [1981], Naaman [1982], Nawy [1989], and Nilson [1997], to gain thorough familiarity with prestressing steel and prestressed concrete as construction materials.

2.5
COMPOSITE MATERIALS

2.5.1 Introduction and Historical Background

"It is a truism that technological development depends on advances in the field of materials" [Chawla, 1987]. Chapter 1 discussed how the art and science of bridge building has progressed since ancient times. With the evolution of emerging materials—stone, brick, wood, iron, steel, and reinforced and prestressed concrete—bridges transformed from primitive clapper bridges to modern suspension and cable-stayed bridges. Development of new materials led to building better, longer, and stronger bridges. No doubt, the final limitation on advancement depends on materials.

For many years, demand has been growing for materials that are ever stiffer and stronger yet lighter in fields as diverse as the space, aeronautics, automotive, energy, and civil construction industries. Hardly any material, however, can satisfy demands for better overall performance in these many diverse fields. "Composite materials in this

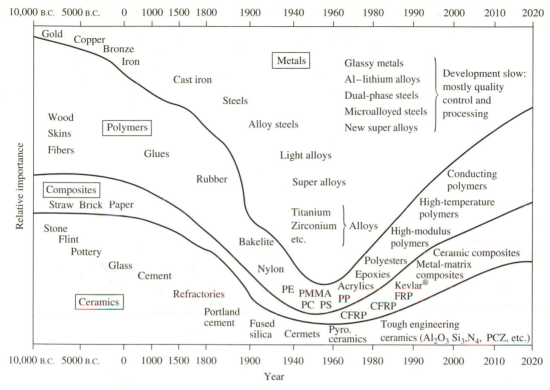

FIGURE 2.5

The relative importance of metals, polymers, composites, and ceramics with respect to historical time. The time scale is nonlinear [Ashby, 1987].

regard represent nothing but a giant step in the ever-constant endeavor of optimization in materials" [Chawla, 1987]. Over the last fifty years composites have emerged as an evolutionary link in the development of new structural materials. The relative importance of the four basic materials—metals, polymers, composites, and ceramics—are presented in a historical context by Ashby [1987] and shown schematically in Fig. 2.5. The decreasing role of metals and the steadily increasing importance of polymers, ceramics, and composites is quite apparent from this figure. Composites are the material of the future. Segal [1996] vividly describes the opportunities for advanced fibers and composites in the twenty-first century.

Interestingly, craftsmanship with fibers of molten glass is known to have existed as early as 3000 years ago among the Phoenicians and also among the early Venetians. Reinforced materials have been with us since Pithecanthropus erectus first put together a crude hut of straw-filled mud. However, most dynamic essential research of the mechanics and chemistry of composites didn't start until the twentieth century. The exponential growth of the structural composites industry really began in 1940, with the use of fiberglass.

According to Rosato [1982], the evolution of composites dates back to 1845, when A. P. Critchlow developed Florence (shellac) compound. The advent of the U.S.

plastics industry is attributed to the development of celluloid by John Wesley Hyatt in 1968. Reinforced plastics (RP) reportedly started in Leo H. Baekland's laboratory in Yonkers, New York, from 1905 to 1909. Based on his work with a mixture of phenol and formaldehyde, his public announcement of the new phenolic plastics material was made on February 5, 1909, during the American Society's New York meeting. His invention, for which he was granted a patent in 1909, was the first to make the phenol formaldehyde practical and usable. By 1910, he had started the General Bakelite Company to produce RP products. The first U.S. patent (no. 1,393,541) for a recognizable structural form was filed May 26, 1916, by inventor Robert Camp and assigned to the Westinghouse Electric and Manufacturing Company. It was for "a method of making structural elements that comprises superimposing layers of fibrous materials impregnated with a binder to form an elongated tubular body . . . and subjecting the structure thus formed to heat and pressure in a mold" [Rosato, 1982].

Much of the current composites technology is said to have evolved from aerospace applications, where the primary motivation was to improve the performance and fuel economy of aircraft. Fiberglass reinforced plastics (FRP) were first conceived, developed, and designed for light airframe structures by the Wright–Patterson Air Force Base Structures and Materials Laboratory in Dayton, Ohio, in 1943. On March 24, 1944, the BT-15 airplane, with the plastic fuselage, was first flown at Wright–Patterson Air Force Base. This was considered to be the first successful major structural component of an airplane using FRP to be developed and flown. The static tests performed on this first fabricated fuselage demonstrated the very high structural efficiency that had been predicted. Whereas severe buckling of aluminum skin would occur at 100 percent of design load, there was almost no visual or measurable skin buckling with the FRP structure at 180 percent of the design load. The properties of the FRP used in this part were impressive: tensile strength of 40,000 psi, compressive strength of 34,000 psi, flexural strength of 57,000 psi, shear strength of 19,000 psi, and elastic modulus in flexure of 2.75×10^6 psi [Rosato, 1982].

The need for high-performance composites during World War II provided the impetus for the ultimate development of composites as competitive materials. With demobilization in 1946, the commercial growth of FRP began. It became an important material for boats, automobiles, trucks, construction, appliances, containers, electrical materials, furniture, plumbing pipes, and tanks. After numerous automotive parts were produced in experimental lots in the 1940s, General Motors introduced the RP body on the Corvette in 1953. The use of RP has since exploded. The growing use of composite materials is shown schematically in Fig. 2.6.

2.5.2 Definitions

Composite materials are unique compared to such conventional materials as steel, reinforced concrete, aluminum, and wood. Many terms used in the context of composite materials are unique to the discussion of composites; hence these terms may be unfamiliar to many bridge engineers. In addition, the meanings of these terms are not self-evident. Therefore, a few selected terms are defined in this section. These terms are also listed in many handbooks on composite materials, such as Lubin [1969, 1982].

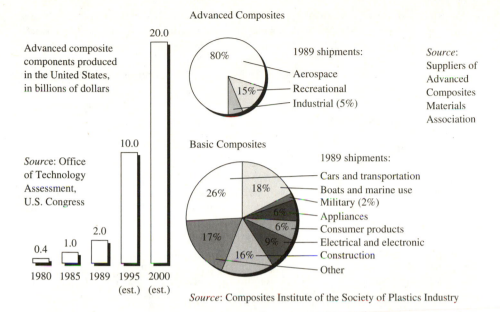

FIGURE 2.6
The growing use of composite materials. (From [NYT, 1990], *The New York Times,* March 25, 1990, Sec. F, p. 14. Copyright© by The New York Times Company. Reprinted with permission.)

The following definitions, excerpted from Schwartz [1992], are used in the discussion of composite materials presented in this section.

Adhesiveness The property defined by the adhesion stress, $A = F/S$, where F is the force perpendicular to the glue line and S is the surface.

Aging The process or the effect on materials of exposure to an environment for an interval of time.

Anisotropic Exhibiting different properties in response to stresses applied along axes in different directions.

Aramid Aromatic polyamide fibers characterized by excellent high-temperature flame resistance and by electrical properties. Aramid fibers are used to achieve high-strength, high-modulus reinforcement in plastic composites. More usually found as polyaramid, a synthetic fiber (Kevlar®).

Aspect ratio The ratio of length to diameter of a fiber.

Bidirectional laminate A reinforced plastic laminate with the fibers oriented in various directions in the plane of the laminate; a cross laminate. (*See also* Unidirectional laminate).

Boron fiber A fiber usually consisting of a tungsten-filament core with elemental boron vapor deposited on it to impart strength and stiffness.

Carbon–carbon A composite of carbon fiber in a carbon matrix.

Carbon fiber An important reinforcing fiber, known for its light weight, high strength, and high stiffness, that is produced by pyrolysis of an organic precursor fiber in an inert atmosphere at temperatures above 1800 °F (982 °C). The material may also be graphitized by heat-treating above 3000 °F (1649 °C).

Coefficient of elasticity The reciprocal of Young's modulus in a tension test.

Compatibility The ability of two or more substances combined with each other to form a homogeneous composition with useful plastic properties.

Compressive modulus, E_c   Ratio of compressive stress to compressive strain below the proportional limit. Theoretically equal to Young's modulus determined from tensile experiments.

Continuous filament   An individual flexible rod of glass of small diameter and great or indefinite length.

Creep   The change in dimension of a plastic under load over a period of time, not including the initial instantaneous elastic deformation; at room temperature it is called *cold flow.*

Critical length   The minimum length of a fiber necessary for matrix shear loading to develop fiber ultimate strength by a matrix.

D glass   A high-boron-content glass made especially for laminates requiring a precisely controlled dielectric constant.

E glass   A borosilicate glass; the type most used for glass fibers for reinforced plastics; suitable for electrical laminates because of its high resistivity. (Also called *electric glass.*)

Epoxy plastics   Plastics based on resins made by the reaction of epoxides or oxiranes with other materials such as amines, alcohols, phenols, carboxylic acids, acid anhydrides, and unsaturated compounds.

Fiber   Relatively short lengths of very small sections of various materials made by chopping filaments (converting). (Also called *filament, thread,* or *bristle.*)

Fiber-composite material   A material consisting of two or more discrete physical phases, in which a fibrous phase is dispersed in a continuous matrix phase. The fibrous phase may be macroscopic, microscopic, or submicroscopic, but it must retain its physical identity so that it could conceivably be removed from the matrix intact.

Fiberglass   An individual filament made by attenuating molten glass. (*See also* Continuous filament; Staple fibers.)

Fracture   Rupture of the surface without complete separation of laminate.

FRP   Fibrous-glass-reinforced plastic; any type of plastic-reinforced cloth, mat, strands, or any other form of fibrous glass.

Glass   An inorganic product of fusion that has cooled to a rigid condition without crystallizing. Glass is typically hard, relatively brittle, and has conchoidal fracture.

Glass fiber   A glass filament that has been cut to a measurable length. Staple fibers of relatively short length are suitable for spinning into yarn.

Glass filament   A form of glass that has been drawn to a small diameter and an extreme length. Most filaments are less than 0.005 in. (0.13 mm) in diameter.

Hybrid   The result of attaching a composite body to another material, such as aluminum or steel, on two reinforcing agents in the matrix, such as graphite and glass.

Hybrid composite   A composite with two or more reinforcing fibers.

Hygroscopic   Capable of adsorbing and retaining atmospheric moisture.

Metallic fiber   Manufactured fiber composed of metal, plastic-coated metal, metal-coated plastic, or a core completely covered by metal.

M glass   A high-beryllia-content glass designed especially for high modulus of elasticity.

Mil   The unit used in measuring the diameter of glass-fiber strands, wire, etc. (1 mil = 0.001 in.)

Molding   The shaping of a plastic composition in or on a mold, normally accomplished under heat and pressure; sometimes used to denote the finished part.

Monomer   (1) a simple molecule capable of reacting with like or unlike molecules to form a polymer. (2) The smallest repeating structure of a polymer, also called a *mer.*

Organic   Designating or composed of matter originating in plant or animal life or composed of chemicals of hydrocarbon origin, natural or synthetic.

Orthotropic   Having three mutually perpendicular planes of elastic symmetry.

Plastic   A material that contains as an essential ingredient an organic substance of high molecular weight, is solid in its finished state, and at some stage in its manufacture or processing into finished articles can be shaped by flow; made of plastic. A *rigid plastic* is one with a stiffness or apparent modulus of elasticity greater than 100 kips/in.^{2} (690 MPa) at 73.4 °F

(23 °C). A *semirigid plastic* has a stiffness or apparent modulus of elasticity between 10 and 100 kips/in.^{2} (69 and 690 MPa) at 73.4 °F (23 °C).

Plasticize   To make a material moldable by softening it with heat or a plasticizer.

Polyacrylonitrile (PAN)   A product used as a base material in the manufacture of certain carbon fibers.

Polyamide   A polymer in which the structural units are linked by amide or thioamide groupings; many polyamides are fiber-forming.

Polyesters   Thermosetting resins produced by dissolving unsaturated, generally linear alkyd resins in a vinyl active monomer, e.g., styrene, methyl styrene, or diallyl phthalate.

Polyimide   A polymer produced by heating polyamic acid; a highly heat-resistant resin (over 600 °F (316 °C)) suitable for use as a binder or an adhesive.

Polymer   A high-molecular-weight organic compound, natural or synthetic, whose structure can be represented by a repeated small unit (mer), e.g., polyethylene, rubber, cellulose. Synthetic polymers are formed by addition or condensation polymerization of monomers. Some polymers are elastomers, some plastics. When two or more monomers are involved, the product is called a *copolymer.*

Polymerization   A chemical reaction in which the molecules of a monomer are linked together to form large molecules whose molecular weight is a multiple of that of the original substance. When two or more monomers are involved, the process is called *copolymerization* or *heteropolymerization.*

Prepreg   Ready-to-mold material in sheet form, which may be cloth, mat, or paper impregnated with resin stored for use. The resin is partially cured to a B stage and supplied to the fabricator, who lays up the finished shape and completes the cure with heat and pressure.

Pultrusion   Reversed extrusion of resin-impregnated roving in the manufacture of rods, tubes, and structural shapes of a permanent cross section. After passing through the resin dip tank, the roving is drawn through a die to form the desired cross section.

S glass   A magnesia-alumina-silicate glass, especially designed to provide filaments with very high tensile strength.

SCRIMP   Seeman Composite Resin Infusion Molding Process. Used for comolding composite skins and core in one piece without the need for an oven autoclave.

Sizing   (1) Applying a material on a surface in order to fill pores and thus reduce the absorption of the subsequently applied adhesive or coating. (2) To modify the surface properties of the substrate to improve adhesion. (3) The material used for this purpose, also called *size.*

Specific modulus   Ratio of elastic modulus to the specific gravity of the material.

Specific stiffness   Stiffness-to-weight ratio.

Specific strength   Strength-to-weight ratio.

Staple fibers   Fibers of spinnable length manufactured directly or by cutting continuous filaments to relatively short lengths, generally less than 17 in. (432 mm).

Static fatigue   Failure of a part under continued static load; analogous to creep-rupture failure in metals testing, but often the result of aging accelerated by stress.

Thermoplastic   Capable of being repeatedly softened by increase in temperature and hardened by decrease in temperature; applicable to those materials whose change upon heat is substantially physical rather than chemical and can be shaped by flow into articles by molding and extrusion. Many natural resins may be described as thermoplastic.

Thermoset   A plastic that changes into a substantially infusible and insoluble material when it is cured by application of heat or by chemical means. Prior to becoming infusible, thermosetting polymers such as phenolic and melamine formaldehyde possess thermoplastic qualities that permit processing.

Tow   A large bundle of continuous filaments, generally 10,000 or more, not twisted, usually designated by a number followed by "K," indicating multiplication by 1000; for example, 12K tow has 12,000 filaments.

Transfer molding   Method of molding thermosetting materials in which the plastic is first softened by heating and pressure in a transfer chamber and then forced by high pressure through
suitable sprues, runners, and gates into the closed mold for final curing.

UDC   Unidirectional composites.

Unidirectional laminate   A reinforced plastic laminate in which substantially all the fibers are
oriented in the same direction.

Whisker   A very short fiber form of reinforcement, usually crystalline.

2.5.3 Composite Materials—Definition

What is a composite material? There appears to be no universally accepted definition of
composite materials, and definitions in the literature vary widely. The dictionary defines
a composite as something made up of disparate or separate parts. A *composite material*
is a generic term used to describe a judicious combination of two or more materials to
yield a product that is more efficient than the original constituents. According to Rosato
[1982],

> A composite is a combined material created by the synthetic assembly of two or more
> components—a selected filler or reinforcing agent and a compatible matrix binder (i.e.,
> a resin)—in order to obtain specific characteristics and properties. The components of a
> composite do not dissolve or otherwise merge completely into each other, but nevertheless
> do act in concert. The components as well as the interface between them can usually be
> physically identified, and it is the behavior and properties of the interface that generally
> control the properties of the composite. The properties of the composite cannot be achieved
> by any of the components acting alone.

Strictly speaking, everything that we use in this world is a composite material.
For example, a common metallic alloy is a composite (polycrystal) of many grains (or
single crystals). However, such a human-made material is formed at the microscopic
level, not at the macroscopic level; such materials are *not* referred to in engineering
as composites. Chawla [1987] has provided the operational definition of a composite
material as one that satisfies the following requirements:

- It is manufactured (i.e., naturally occurring materials such as wood are excluded).
- It consists of two or more physically and/or chemically distinct, suitably arranged or dis-
  tributed phases with an interface separating them.
- It has characteristics that are not depicted by any of the components in isolation.

These requirements essentially form the basic principles of designing and manufacturing composites. They are designed to give performance unattainable by the individual
constituents, and therefore they offer the tailorability for optimum design according to
specifications.

Many examples of composites can be found in nature. A common example of a
composite material is wood, which is made of cellulose fibers and a lignin matrix. The
cellulose fibers have high tensile strength but low stiffness. The lignin matrix joins the
fibers and provides the stiffness. Bone that supports the weight of the body is another
example of a natural fiber. Weight-bearing bone is composed of short and soft colla-
gen fibers embedded in a mineral matrix called apatite. A coconut palm leaf can be
viewed as a cantilever using the concept of fiber reinforcement [Chawla, 1987]. Several

examples of the structure–function relationships in the plant and the animal kingdoms are discussed by Wainwright et al. [1976].

2.5.4 Why Composite Materials?

Structural materials can be divided into four groups, namely metals, polymers, ceramics, and composites. Composites form a class of human-made material constructed from various combinations of the other three materials in macroscopic structural units [Gibson, 1994]. Composites are generally used because they have desirable properties that could not be achieved by either of the constituent materials acting alone.

An example of one of the most commonly used structural composites is concrete. Just as a concrete member involves design and preparation of concrete mix as a separate operation from the design of the member itself, composites involve designing and building not only the structure but also the structural material itself.

Some of the unique properties of composite materials are light weight, high strength-to-weight and stiffness-to-weight ratios, high energy absorption, and outstanding corrosion and fatigue damage resistance [Noton, 1974; Lubin, 1982; Chawla, 1987; Morley, 1987; Schwartz, 1992; Gibson, 1994]. A comparison of various properties of steel, aluminum, and composites is shown in Fig. 2.7. Figure 2.8 depicts dramatically the strength and stiffness of a composite.

Composites are now used to produce structural elements in a variety of components for aerospace, automotive, marine, and architectural structures (e.g., buildings and bridges). Composites offer great potential for use in bridges. Because they require low maintenance, the life-cycle costs are low. Their light weight enables a superstructure to have a larger live-load carrying capacity, a factor of great significance in rehabilitating bridge decks. The light weight of the superstructure also results in savings in the cost of the substructure. Deterioration of reinforced concrete bridge decks due to corrosion of steel reinforcing bars continues to be an expensive maintenance problem for bridge engineers (discussed in Chapter 10). Reinforcing bars made from glass-fiber-reinforced plastic (GFRP) are expected to eliminate this problem, thus reducing costs.

2.5.5 Classes of Composites

Composites include reinforced plastics (RP), fiberglass-reinforced plastics (FRP), glass-fiber-reinforced plastics (GFRP),[1] laminates, low-pressure laminates, high-pressure-laminates, and filled molding compounds. The word "composite" evolved from the industry's need for an all-inclusive term to describe the final material resulting from the many different reinforcing agents and matrices [Rosato, 1982].

In general, composites can be constructed from any combination of two or more materials, whether metallic, organic, or inorganic. Composites consist of two main elements: the body constituent, or *matrix,* that encloses the composite, giving it its bulk

---

[1]The acronym GFRC is used to denote glass-fiber-reinforced concrete.

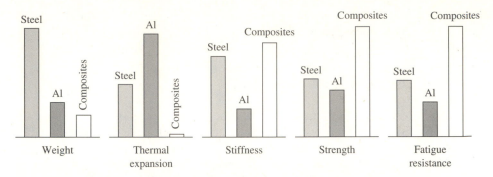

FIGURE 2.7
Comparison of various properties of steel, aluminum, and composites [Deutsch, 1978].

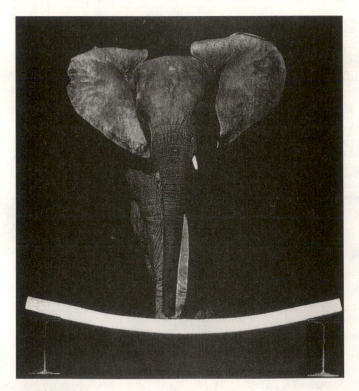

FIGURE 2.8
Graphite-fiber-reinforced cement panel displays a large
deflection before failure [Schwartz, 1992].

form, and *structural constituents,* such as fibers, particles, laminae or layers, flakes,
and fillers, which determine the internal structure of the composite. Although the possible material combinations in composites are virtually unlimited, the constituent forms
are not. However, it is obvious that the selection of a fabrication process depends on
the constituent materials in the composite. Manufacturing processes for composites
are discussed in several handbooks on composite materials [Lubin, 1969, 1982; Noton,

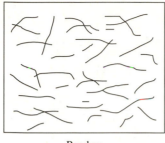

Random

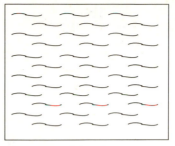

Oriented

FIGURE 2.9
Orientation of fibers [Schwartz, 1992].

1974; Katz and Milewski, 1978; Morley, 1987; Reinhart, Brinson, and Schneider, 1987; Weeton, Peters, and Thomas, 1987; Strong, 1989; Schwartz, 1992].

Composites can be classified in a number of different ways [Schwartz, 1992]: (1) by basic material combinations (e.g., metal-organic or metal-inorganic); (2) by bulk-form characteristics (e.g., matrix systems or laminates); (3) by distribution of constituents (e.g., continuous or discontinuous); or (4) by function (e.g., electrical or structural).

Depending on the distribution of the structural constituents, composites are either *homogeneous* or *graded* (or *gradient*). In homogeneous composites, the constituents are in a regular and repetitive pattern, evenly distributed throughout the matrix, with uniform cross section both in material and structure and with uniform density. In graded composites, such as laminated materials, which are composed of several different layers, the constituents have a variable pattern. In both types, the constituents can be arranged in either oriented or random fashion (Fig. 2.9).

Based on the form of the structural constituents, the composites can be grouped in five general categories (Fig. 2.10):

1. Fiber composites—composed of fibers with or without a matrix
2. Flake composites—composed of flat flakes with or without a matrix
3. Particulate composites—composed of particles with or without a matrix
4. Filled (or skeletal) composites—composed of a continuous skeletal matrix filled by a second material
5. Laminar composites—composed of layer, or laminar, constituents

In some composites, called *hybrid composites,* more than one type of fiber is used; e.g., a combination of glass and carbon fibers may be used. The goal of hybrid composites is to increase cost-effectiveness by (1) judiciously selecting different reinforcement types and by (2) placing the fibers to obtain the highest strength in highly stressed locations and directions.

Yet another class of composites is the *multifilamentary superconducting composites,* which evolved in the 1970s. *Superconductivity,* discovered in 1911 by Kammerlingh Onnes [Chawla, 1987], is a characteristic of certain metals and alloys—they lose all resistance to electricity when cooled to within a few degrees of absolute zero. Superconductors, materials that exhibit this property, are made from intermetallic

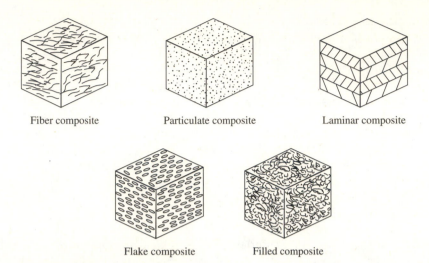

FIGURE 2.10

Classes of composites [Schwartz, 1992].

compounds (or composites) that are niobium-based (Nb-Ti and Nb$_3$Sn). A discussion on this class of composites is provided by Chawla [1987, Ch. 9].

Carbon fiber composites debuted in the 1950s. Led by the aerospace industry, the sporting goods industry is the second biggest user of carbon-fiber-reinforced polymer matrix composites. Epoxy is the most commonly used polymer matrix with carbon fibers, although polyester, polysulphone, polyimide, and thermoplastic resins are also used [Chawla, 1987].

In general, the fibers and the matrix that constitute a composite are from two different materials. There are exceptions, however, in which case the fibers and the matrix may be of the same materials, such as carbon–carbon composites. *Carbon–carbon* is a generic name for a class of composites composed of fibrous carbon reinforcements, a carbonaceous or graphitic matrix, and sometimes a filler or coating to impart specialized properties. Referred to as *CCCs*, these composites may have continuous or discontinuous reinforcement. The major attributes of the CCCs are stability and structural integrity, in a nonoxidizing environment, to temperatures approaching 2760 °C (5000 °F) [Gibson, 1994]. Because of their high costs, CCCs are used only for a few critical aerospace applications. A discussion on the evolution, development, and current uses of CCCs is presented by Schmidt, Davidson, and Theibert [1996].

Of all composite materials, the fiber type, specifically the inclusion of fibers in a matrix, has generated the most interest among engineers concerned with structural applications. The first among these were fiberglass-reinforced plastics. Because of their low cost, glass or other relatively low-modulus fibers (less than about 12,000 ksi) have found many high-volume applications, such as in automotive and sporting goods industries. Such composites are sometimes called *basic* composites. Composites made from graphite, silicon carbide, aramid polymer, boron, or other high-modulus fibers are called *advanced* or *high-performance* composites. The difference between basic and advanced composites is often blurred, and there is a growing trend toward using "advanced composites" as an inclusive term to describe all composites.

Composites can also be classified from the user's perspective. *Commercial composites* are basic composites that use unidirected high-strength composites made from helically twisted, continuous strands of glass fiber. These composites are distinguished from *aerospace composites,* which generally are advanced composites that use carbon or aramid fibers.

Because of cost considerations, basic and advanced composites are used in different industries. Advanced composites are used mainly in aircraft or aerospace structures where their higher cost can be justified based on improved weight/performance goals; the weight savings that accrues from using lighter composites results in a higher payload or reduced fuel consumption. In aerospace applications particularly, the cost per unit weight is very high because of the large amount of fuel required to lift the vehicle into orbit. Potential savings in cost due to reduced weight of aircraft and spacecraft have been discussed by Lubin and Dastin [1982] (Fig. 2.11).

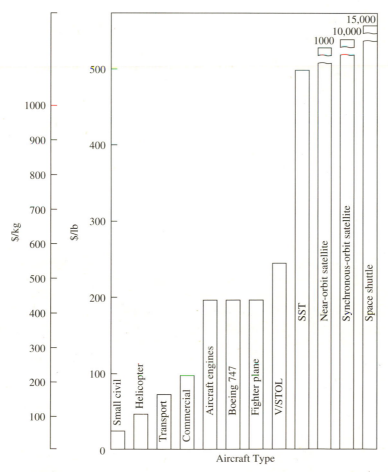

FIGURE 2.11
Value of weight saved in aircraft and spacecraft [Lubin and Dastin, 1982].

2.5.6 Constituent Materials

2.5.6.1 The matrix

The matrix forms the body constituent of a composite. Polymers, metals, and ceramics are all used as matrix materials in composites. The matrix performs important dual functions: (1) It acts as binder to hold the fibrous phase in place; i.e., it holds the fibers in a structural unit. And (2), under an applied force, it deforms and distributes the load to the high-modulus fibrous constituents that actually resist the force. In many cases, the matrix also contributes some needed property such as ductility, toughness, or electrical insulation [Chawla, 1987]. Also, since many reinforcements tend to be brittle, the matrix provides surface protection against abrasion or environmental corrosion, both of which can initiate fracture.

The matrix must be capable of developing a mechanical or chemical bond with the fiber. Chemical compatibility between the matrix and the fiber is essential so that undesirable reactions do not take place at the interface. Such reactions tend to be more of a problem in high-temperature composites. Service temperature is often the main consideration in the selection of a matrix material. The choice of a matrix for a structural fiber composite is limited by the requirement that it have a greater elongation at break than the fiber has [Schwartz, 1992].

Matrixes can be organic (polymers) or inorganic (metals and ceramics). The selection of a particular type of matrix is dictated by the application requirements. Polymers, used specifically for the fibrous composites, have been the most widely used matrix in modern composites. Composites fabricated from organic and ceramic matrixes are referred to generically as organic and ceramic matrix composites, respectively. Similarly, composites made from polymer matrixes are called polymer-matrix composites (PMCs), composites made from metal matrixes are referred to as metal-matrix composites (MMCs), and so on.

The most versatile of all engineering materials, metals are strong and tough. Metal matrixes include lightweight metals such as aluminum, titanium, and magnesium, and their alloys and intermetallics, such as titanium aluminide and nickel aluminide [Gibson, 1994]. Although the metal matrixes are higher in density than polymers, they offer greater strength, stiffness, and ductility than polymers.

Ceramic matrixes are low-density, environmentally inert materials that offer high strength and high stiffness at very high temperatures. However, these very desirable properties are overshadowed by their utter lack of toughness, which makes them prone to catastrophic failures in the presence of surface flaws (nicks or scratches) or internal flaws (inclusions, pores, or microcracks). They are also extremely susceptible to thermal shock and easily damaged during fabrication or in service. To overcome these serious drawbacks, ceramic matrixes are toughened by incorporating fibers into them, thus making them safe from catastrophic failures.

Composites using ceramic matrixes are referred to as ceramic matrix composites (CMCs). Because of limited matrix ductility and generally high fabrication temperatures, thermal mismatch between the components has a significant influence on the performance of the CMCs. Some basic differences between the CMCs and other composites should be noted. Generally, the nonceramic matrix composites are designed so that fibers bear the major portion of the load. The load sharing by the fibers and the matrix depends on the ratio of their elastic moduli, E_f/E_m. Whereas this ratio may be very high in the nonceramic composites, it may be as low as one in CMCs [Chawla, 1987].

Ceramic matrixes can withstand very high temperatures, beyond those that are tolerated by the metallic superalloys used in jet engines. For example, GeoBond, a new ceramic developed and marketed by GeoBond International of Kansas, is extremely heat-resistant and noncombustible. Made from a mixture of cement, gypsum, and a secret compound of off-the-shelf ingredients, it does not burn even when subjected to flames surpassing 2000 °F. Tests performed at Edwards Air Force Base near Los Angeles reported that GeoBond did not burn at the back of a rocket that heated to 5500 to 6000 °F. No new material has shown so much promise since asbestos, used for decades for insulation and fireproofing until it was proven to cause lung cancer in the late 1970s. GeoBond is currently being tested for roof tiles and wall boards in housing projects and for fireproofing purposes [WSJ, 1996].

Several types of organic matrixes are commercially available for use in advanced composites. The type of organic matrix determines the composite process parameters and the service operating temperatures. Most structural composites involve resin and epoxy matrix materials—i.e., polymers. Polymers are classified either as *thermosetting* (or *thermoset*) or as *thermoplastic*.

Thermosetting resins include polyesters, vinyl esters, epoxies, bismaleimides, phenolics, and polyimides. These are most commonly used for producing FRP composites. Thermosetting matrixes are relatively soft; consequently, the composites that use them are almost as strong as fibers. Therefore, to produce an efficient composite from a thermosetting matrix, it is desirable to maximize fiber content. Epoxy resins are capable of withstanding maximum service temperatures in the range of 257 °F to 347 °F [Schwartz, 1992], and thus they are more widely used than other thermosetting resins. Although epoxy resins are more expensive than polyesters, their adhesion property makes them useful in many high-performance composites.

Thermoplastic resins, sometimes also referred to as engineering plastics, include some polyesters, polyetherimide, polyamide imide, polyphenylene sulphide, polyether ether ketone (PEEK), and liquid crystal polymers. Since it is both easier and faster to heat and cool a material than it is to cure it, the thermoplastic matrixes have become very attractive to high-volume industries such as the automotive industry [Schwartz, 1992]. Unlike the processing of thermosetting resins, the processing of thermoplastics is reversible; by simply reheating it to the process temperature, the resin can be reformed into another shape, which is a great advantage.

Note that inclusion of a matrix in a composite is not an absolute necessity. For example, some textiles composites, called fiber–fiber composites, consist solely of fibers without any matrix. However, the most efficient method to produce a strong composite is to combine a fibrous material of high tensile strength and high modulus of elasticity with a lightweight bulk material (matrix) of lower strength and lower modulus of elasticity.

An important characteristic of polymer matrixes is that they are *hygrothermally sensitive.* Quite unlike metal or ceramic matrixes, polymer matrixes can degrade at moderately high temperatures and through moisture adsorption. Of the many environmental conditions that may influence the mechanical behavior of composites, changes

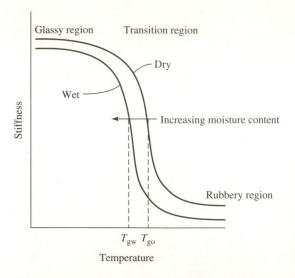

FIGURE 2.12
Variation of stiffness with temperature for a typical polymer showing the glass transition temperature, T_g, and the effect of absorbed moisture on T_g. *Note:* T_{go} = "dry" T_g, and T_{gw} = "wet" T_g [Gibson, 1994].

in temperature and moisture content are the most important because they alter the properties of polymer matrixes themselves as well as those properties of PMCs that are matrix-dominated. The combined effects of moisture (hygrospic) and temperature (thermal) are often referred to as *hygrothermal effects.* Environmental effects on composites are discussed by Staunton [1982].

A comprehensive discussion on hygrothermal degradation of the properties of PMCs is presented by Gibson [1994, Ch. 5]. Essentially, the hygrothermal environment alters the mechanical behavior of the PMCs in two ways:

1. An increase in temperature causes a gradual softening of the polymer matrix up to a point known as the glassy region (Fig. 2.12). If the temperature increase continues beyond this point, the matrix goes through a transition from glassy behavior to rubbery behavior (in the rubbery region in Fig. 2.12). In this region, the polymer becomes too soft for use as a structural material, and the matrix-dominated properties such as strength and stiffness are radically decreased. This hygrothermal degradation of mechanical properties is evident from the data shown in Fig. 2.13, which is based on tests by Browning, Husman, and Whitney [1977] on graphite–epoxy composites and epoxy matrix materials under various hygrothermal conditions. Similar results substantiating degradation of mechanical properties have been reported by Shen and Springer [1976] and by Gibson et al. [1982].

2. Hygrothermal expansion and contraction alter the stress and strain distribution in the composite. This happens because an increase in temperature or moisture causes the polymer matrix to swell, and a decrease in temperature or moisture causes it to contract. The fibers, however, do not undergo similar hygrothermal changes. As a result, the swelling or contraction of the matrix is resisted by the fibers, and residual stresses develop in the composite.

These hygrothermal effects must be duly considered in analytical modeling of the matrix-dominated properties of the PMCs.

2.5.6.2 Fibers

The most important aspect of composite materials from a structural standpoint is that the strength-contributing reinforcement need not necessarily be in the form of long continuous fibers. The fibers may be in various forms: particles, whiskers, discontinuous fibers, continuous fibers, and sheets. Most materials are stronger and stiffer in the fibrous form than in any other form, and hence the appeal of fibrous reinforcements.

Selected properties of a few advanced fibers are presented in Table 2.6. Note that accelerated development of new carbon and graphite fibers continues. For example, fibers based on pitch precursor (P-100) are now available with a modulus of 100×10^6 psi (690 GPa), more than three times that of steel [Gibson, 1994].

Included in the list is Kevlar® 29, an aramid polymer fiber produced primarily by E. I. DuPont de Nemours & Company. It was originally produced for radial tires and continues to be used for that purpose. Its higher-modulus version, Kevlar® 49, is used more extensively for structural composites. With a density of only a little more than half that of glass, the specific strength of Kevlar® is among the highest of current available fibers. These so-called advanced fibers, which possess very high strength and very high stiffness coupled with low density, are the most attractive components for advanced composites. They provide the desirable design properties of high *specific strength* and high *specific stiffness*. These properties are used in design based on particular needs: High specific strength is required when the structural design is strength-critical; high specific stiffness is required when the structural design is stiffness-critical.

The freedom of using various forms of reinforcing fibers in designing structural parts is a major advantage. For example, stiffness can be varied significantly in

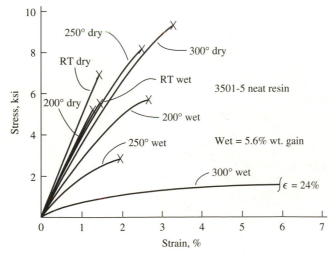

FIGURE 2.13
Stress–strain curves for 3501-5 epoxy resin at different temperatures and moisture contents. (From Browning, Husman, and Whitney [1977]. Copyright© ASTM. Reprinted with permission.)

TABLE 2.6
Selected properties of fibers and bulk metals [Gibson, 1994]

Material	Tensile strength, 10^3 psi (MPa)	Tensile modulus, 10^6 psi (GPa)	Density, lb/in.^{3} (g/cm^3)
Bulk 6061T6 aluminum	45.0 (310)	10.0 (69)	0.098 (2.71)
Bulk SAE 4340 steel	150.0 (1034)	29.0 (200)	0.283 (7.83)
E-glass fibers	500.0 (3448)	10.5 (72)	0.092 (2.54)
S-glass fibers	650.0 (4482)	12.5 (20)	0.090 (2.49)
Carbon fibers (PAN[a] precursor[b])			
AS-4 (Hercules)	580.0 (4000)	33.0 (228)	0.065 (1.80)
IM-7 (Hercules)	785.0 (5413)	40.0 (276)	0.064 (1.77)
T-300 (Amoco)	530.0 (4654)	33.5 (231)	0.064 (1.77)
T-650/42 (Amoco)	730.0 (2241)	42.0 (290)	0.064 (1.77)
Carbon fibers (pitch precursor[b])			
P-55 (Amoco)	250.0 (1724)	55.0 (379)	0.072 (1.99)
P-75 (Amoco)	300.0 (2068)	75.0 (517)	0.072 (1.99)
P-100 (Amoco)	325.0 (2241)	100.0 (690)	0.078 (2.16)
Aramid fibers			
Kevlar® 29 (DuPont)	550.0 (3792)	9.0 (62)	0.052 (1.44)
Kevlar® 49 (DuPont)	550.0 (3792)	19.0 (131)	0.053 (1.47)
Boron fibers			
0.004″ dia.[c] (Textron)	510.0 (3516)	58.0 (400)	0.093 (2.57)
0.0056″ dia.[c] (Textron)	510.0 (3516)	58.0 (400)	0.090 (2.49)
Silicon carbide fibers			
0.0056 dia.[c] (Textron)	500.0 (3448)	62.0 (427)	0.110 (3.04)

[a]PAN = polyacrylonitrile
[b]For carbon fibers, the rayon, PAN, or pitch fibers from which carbon fibers are made
[c]dia. = diameter

TABLE 2.7
Typical properties of fibers [ACI, 1974b]

Type of fiber	Tensile strength (ksi)	Young's modulus (10^3 ksi)	Ultimate elongation (%)	Specific gravity
Acrylic	30–60	0.3	25–45	1.1
Asbestos	80–140	12–20	0.6	3.2
Cotton	60–100	0.7	3–10	1.5
Glass	150–550	10	1.5–3.5	2.5
Nylon (high tenacity)	110–120	0.6	16–12	1.1
Polyester (high tenacity)	105–125	1.2	11–13	1.4
Polyethylene	~100	0.02–0.06	~10	0.96
Polypropylene	80–110	0.5	~25	0.90
Rayon (high tenacity)	60–90	1.0	10–25	1.5
Rock wool (Scandinavian)	70–110	10–17	~0.6	2.7
Steel	40–600	29	0.5–35	7.8

different areas of a composite part by selecting the type and form of fiber, by judicious orientation, and by controlling local concentrations of fibers. Thus, advanced fibers and their composites have a tremendous advantage over conventional materials in this field. For this reason, applications for composites will continue to grow in aerospace and automotive structures. Discussions on the fabrication of advanced composites can be found in the many handbooks on composite materials [Meade, 1982; Shibley, 1982; Slobodzinsky, 1982; Meyer, 1985; Strong, 1989; Schwartz, 1992].

Fibers can be broadly classified [Balguru and Shah, 1992] as

1. Metallic fibers
2. Polymeric fibers
3. Mineral fibers
4. Naturally occurring fibers

Metallic fibers are either steel or stainless steel. The polymeric fibers include acrylic, aramid, carbon, nylon, polyester, polyethylene, and polypropylene fibers. Glass fiber is the most commonly used mineral fiber. The naturally occurring fibers include various organic and inorganic fibers, such as cellulose. Asbestos, a mineral fiber, was widely used in the past for making incombustible, or fireproof, articles and in building insulation. Use of asbestos is now severely discouraged because of the high health risks involved— asbestos is carcinogenic. Its general use has already been banned in a number of industrial countries. The search for a perfect replacement for asbestos fibers continues.

Typical properties of several commonly used fibers are given in Table 2.7 for comparison. The high specific strength of several fibers (other than steel) is evident from this list.

To understand the high-performance characteristics of advanced fibers, we must understand some of the unique characteristics of fibers in general. A convenient numerical parameter describing a fiber is the *aspect ratio,* the fiber length divided by an equivalent fiber diameter.[2] Typical aspect ratios range from about 30 to 150 for length dimensions of 0.25 in. to 3 in. Diameters for various fibers in use vary widely. Typical glass fibers (chopped strands) have diameters of 0.2 to 0.6 mil. Typical plastics, such as nylon, polypropylene, polyethylene, polyester, and rayon, have been made into fibers ranging in diameter from 0.8 to 15 mil. Fibers processed from natural materials like asbestos and cotton provide a wide range of sizes. Round steel fibers have diameters varying from 10 to 30 mil. Flat steel fibers have sizes varying from 6 to 16 mil thick and 10 to 35 mil wide [ACI, 1974b]. *Whiskers* are extremely high-strength microfibers of very short length that are almost microcrystalline. Typically with a diameter of a few micrometers and a length of a few millimeters, whiskers have an aspect ratio that can vary from 50 to 10,000. However, whiskers do not have uniform dimensions or properties, and consequently the spread in their properties is very large—a great disadvantage.

The effectiveness of fibrous reinforcement stems from the fact that many materials are much stronger and stiffer in the fiber form than in the bulk form, a phenomenon first discovered by Griffith [1920]. By measuring, the tensile strengths of glass rods of

---

[2]The equivalent fiber diameter is the diameter of a circle with an area equal to the cross-sectional area of the fiber.

various diameters, he found (Fig. 2.14) that as the rods and fibers became thinner, they also became stronger. He attributed this finding to the fact that the smaller the diameter, the smaller the likelihood of failure-inducing surface cracks that are generated during the manufacturing and handling of the material. He extrapolated his results to show that, for very small diameters, the fiber strength approached the theoretical cohesive strength between adjacent layers of atoms, whereas for large diameters, the fiber strength decreased and approached the strength of bulk glass. This is called the *size effect*—the smaller the size, the lower the probability of imperfections existing in the fiber.

The geometrical configuration of fibers is another factor that contributes to the efficiency of interaction between the matrix and the fibers in a composite. Figure 2.15 [McCrum, Buckley, and Bucknall, 1988] shows the relationship between the surface area-to-volume ratio (*A/V*) and the aspect ratio of a cylindrical particle of given volume. The *A/V* ratio is greatest when a particle is in either platelet or fiber form. Thus, the fiber-matrix interfacial area available for stress transfer per unit volume of fiber increases with increasing aspect ratio of the fiber. The importance of this concept can be realized from the fact that the internal surface area occupied by the interface is quite extensive; it can be as high as 7500 in.^{2}/in.^{3} in a composite containing a reasonable fiber volume fraction [Chawla, 1987].[3]

According to Dresher [1969], the use of fibers as high-performance engineering materials is based on three important characteristics:

- Small diameter with respect to grain size, the consequence of the size effect (described in the preceding paragraph)
- High aspect ratio—this permits a large fraction of the applied load to be transferred through the matrix to the stiff and strong fibers
- Very high degree of flexibility, a characteristic of a material having a high modulus and a small diameter

It is important to recognize that composites fabricated from shorter fibers, if the fibers are properly oriented, could have significantly greater strength than those fabricated from continuous fibers. This is particularly true of whiskers, which have uniform tensile strengths as high as 1500 kips/in.^{2}, because the shorter fibers can be produced with few surface flaws. Under this condition, the fibers come close to achieving their theoretical strength. Fiber length is a critical factor in the processability of fiber composites. Although continuous fibers are easier to handle, they are more limited in design possibilities than short fibers [Schwartz, 1992].

Specific properties of a few selected fibers are discussed in the following paragraphs.

Steel fibers. Steel fibers can be classified by chemical composition into carbon steel fibers and alloy steel fibers. Carbon steel fibers are used mainly with portland cement concrete matrices and the stainless steel alloys are used in the production of refractory materials. Steel fibers are also classified according to their production techniques: cut from drawn wire, cut from sheet rock, produced directly from molten metal, and cut in a machining process from bulk steel blocks. Steel fibers are prepared according to

---

[3] A surface area of 3000 cm^2/cm^3 quoted by Chawla [1987] and converted by the author.

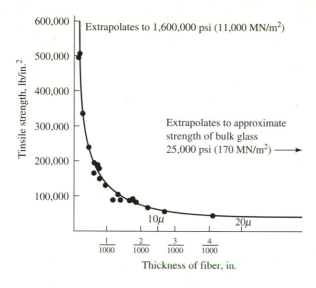

FIGURE 2.14

Griffith's measurement of tensile strength as function of the fiber thickness for glass fibers [adopted from Gibson, 1994].

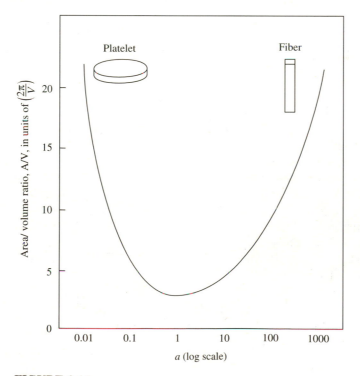

FIGURE 2.15

Surface area-to-volume ratio (A/V) of a cylindrical particle vs. the particle aspect ratio [McCrum, Buckley, and Bucknall, 1988].

ASTM A820. Depending upon the cold working (method of preparation) and the chemical composition, commercially available fibers provide yield strengths of from 50–250 ksi and sufficient ductility. Based on form and shape considerations, both longitudinal and cross-sectional steel fibers can be classified as smooth and deformed [Balguru and Shah, 1992; Shah and Skarendahl, 1986]. In typical applications, the volume percentage of steel fibers ranges from 0.5 to 2.5 percent, although higher volume percentage has also been tried successfully [Lankard and Walker, 1974; Lankard, 1985].

Glass fibers.   Developed initially for electrical applications, glass fiber is one of the most widely used reinforcing materials because of its high tensile strength; it accounts for almost 90 percent of the reinforcement in thermosetting resins. Glass fibers are available in many forms, such as rovings (continuous strands), cut or chopped strands, yarns, and milled fibers (0.032–0.125 in. long), that can be used individually or in the form of cloths, mats, or tapes, and in many commercial varieties such as *E-glass*, *S-glass*, *D-glass*, and *M-glass*. E-glass (named for its electrical insulating properties) accounts for most of the glass fiber production and is the most widely used reinforcement for composites. The second most popular glass, *S*-glass (named for its higher silica content), has 30 percent more tensile strength and 20 percent greater modulus of elasticity than that of E-glass (Table 2.6), and has the ability to withstand higher temperatures than other glasses [Chawla, 1987]. S-glass is actually stronger than most advanced fibers, but its relatively low modulus limits its application [Gibson, 1994]. C-glass (named for its corrosion resistance) has a better resistance to chemical corrosion [Chawla, 1987]. M-glass is a high-beryllia-content glass designed especially for high modulus of elasticity.

Glass-fiber-reinforced concrete (GFRC) is the general term used to define all types of cement composites reinforced with glass fibers. The matrix can be concrete, mortar, or cement paste with additives. The materials used are cement, aggregates, water, admixtures, and fibers. Glass-fiber-reinforced concrete is extensively used for architectural cladding, for which the fibers are predominantly made of alkali-resistant glass (*AR-glass*). Used for manufacturing thin sheets, glass-fiber-reinforced concrete is a growing industry, with more than $100 million in sales per year in the United States alone. A comprehensive summary on the topic of glass-fiber-reinforced concrete is reported by Balguru and Shah [1992]. Daniel [1988] reports a wide variety of applications in which GFRC has already been used or is contemplated for use.

Investigation of fiberglass as a reinforcing material had a rather slow start. Experimental work on the feasibility of using fiber glass reinforcement was initiated by I. A. Rubinsky in 1951 who experimented with glass fibers, fiberglass cords, and fiberglass rods [Rubinsky and Rubinsky, 1959; Rubinsky, 1963]. The fiberglass rods were supposed to provide better protection from the alkali attack of the cement [Nawy and Neuwerth, 1976]. Keane [1952] attempted to develop the full tensile strength of the fiberglass rods in a tensile test. In 1957, research was initiated at the Kiev Polytechnic Institute of Lenin by K. L. and U. L. Biryukovich to explore the use of glass fibers as reinforcement for concrete [1957]. N. F. Somes [1963] at the University of London in 1962 investigated the use of fiberglass as reinforcement for prestressed beams. Tests on post-tensioned beams were conducted by K. M. Gloeckner of the Virginia Department of Highways [1967]. Further experiments were conducted in 1966 by the U.S. Army Corps of Engineers at the U.S Army Engineer Waterways Experiment Station,

Vicksburg, MS. Both the reinforced concrete elements utilizing fiberglass rods as reinforcement and prestressed concrete elements using fiberglass tendons were tested [Wines and Hoff, 1966; Wines, Dietz, and Hawley, 1966]. Since the 1970s, research on glass-fiber reinforcing materials has been conducted all over the world.

Many glasses of varying compositions can be drawn into continuous filaments, where each continuous filament is an individual fiber having an indefinite length (measurable in miles). Glass fibers can also be drawn in the form of staple fibers, 8 to 15 in. long each. The longer fibers provide the greatest strength; continuous fibers are the strongest [Schwartz, 1992]. The most popular of these, E-glass, also known as the standard textile glass, has an ultimate tensile strength of about 500 kips/in.^{2} (3448 MPa) for single diameters of 0.00037 in. (0.01 mm), a Young's modulus of 10,500 kips/in.^{2} (72.4 MPa), and a density of 0.092 lb/in.^{3} (2547 kg/m^3). This is much superior to other glass varieties used for many low-performance applications. For example, window or sheet glass, which is a high-alkali glass, has a tensile strength 50 percent lower than that of E-glass. Some glass fibers have tensile strengths as high as 700 kips/in.^{2} (4827 MPa). The tensile strength of S-glass is 33 percent greater and its modulus of elasticity almost 20 percent greater than that of E-glass. Its high strength-to-weight ratio, superior strength retention at elevated temperatures, and high fatigue limit are the significant properties that qualify S-glass for aerospace applications. The mechanical properties of D-glass, an improved dielectric glass developed for high-performance electronic applications, are exceeded by those of E- and S-glass; however, its lower dielectric constant and lower density make it attractive for radome construction. Certain types of continuous glass fibers, particularly E-glass fibers, have surface protection from attack by the environment or by alkaline reaction; this has been accomplished by coatings, including resins [Schwartz, 1992]. Continuous-filament glass textile fibers normally have diameters ranging from 0.00010 to 0.00075 in. (0.003 to 0.02 mm). Although fibers of greater diameter can and have been made, they have reduced flexibility and begin to assume the properties of the bulk glass itself.

Polymeric fibers. Various types of polymeric fibers are acrylic, aramid, nylon, polyester, polyethylene, and polypropylene, developed as a result of research in the petrochemical and textile industries. They all have a very high tensile strength and high aspect ratios, the two most desirable properties for composites. But most of these fibers (with the exception of aramids) have a low modulus of elasticity. Polymeric fibers are used in very-low-volume fraction (about 0.1 percent by volume), primarily to control cracking in the early stages of casting [Balguru and Shah, 1992]. This application was developed using mainly polypropelene fibers [Zollo, 1984; Vondran, 1989].

Carbon fibers. Carbon fibers are typically produced in strands (tows) that can contain up to 12,000 individual filaments. As listed in Table 2.6, carbon fibers have elastic moduli as high as that of steel, but are two to three times stronger than steel. Yet they are very light, with a specific gravity of 1.9 (as compared to 7.83 for steel). Carbon fibers are also inert to most chemicals. They are more expensive than most other fibers, but have potential for applications that require high tensile and flexural strength. Recently, low-cost carbon fibers have been manufactured with petroleum and coal pitch [Balguru and Shah, 1992].

Naturally occurring fibers. The oldest forms of fiber-reinforced composites are said to have been made from naturally occurring fibers such as straw and horse hair. The advent of modern technology has made it possible to economically extract fibers from various plants, such as bamboo and jute, to be used for cement composites. Natural fibers used in portland cement composites include akwara, bamboo, coconut, flax, jute, sisal, sugarcane bagasse, wood, and others. In nature, bamboo is the most common example of reinforcing principle. An extensive discussion on bamboo reinforcement is provided by Subrahmanyam [1984]. A comprehensive description of these fibers and their properties is presented by Aziz, Paramasivam, and Lee [1984], and Balguru and Shah [1985]. Palm and elephant grass fibers are other naturally occurring fibers that have been tried as reinforcing materials with cement. Fibers have also been extracted from basalt rock [Balguru and Shah, 1992].

Natural fibers are abundantly available in most developing countries. They require only a small degree of industrialization for their processing. The energy required for producing natural fibers is small compared with that required for an equivalent volume of synthetic fibers, and hence the cost of composites fabricated from these fibers is also low. These economic and other related factors in developing countries where natural fibers of various kinds are abundantly available have created a need for applying modern technology to utilize these natural fibers economically and effectively for housing and other needs.

2.5.7 Mechanical Behavior of Composites

Analysis of composite materials differs from that of conventional materials. Most metallic materials are isotropic and homogeneous, whereas most composites are anisotropic, i.e., their properties depend on the orientation of fibers, and heterogeneous, i.e., their properties vary from point to point in the material. The properties in a composite vary as we move from matrix to fiber and as we change the direction along which fibers are measured. Typically, in a composite having fiber reinforcement in one direction only, the strength and stiffness along the direction of reinforcement would be greater than that in the transverse direction. Because composite materials are anisotropic, their stress-strain relationship is unconventional and much more complicated than that for conventional isotropic materials, such as steel and aluminum. For example, in an isotropic material, a normal stress will cause only normal strain, and a shear stress will cause only a shear strain. Not so in an anisotropic composite material—a normal stress may induce both normal as well as shear strain, and a shear stress may induce both shear and normal strain. In contrast to the thermal behavior of isotropic materials, which exhibit uniform expansion or contraction in all directions, a temperature change in an anisotropic material may induce nonuniform expansion or contraction plus distortion.

In dealing with composites, one must analyze both the micromechanical and macromechanical behavior of fiber-reinforced composite materials. The overall analysis process can be explained with reference to Fig. 2.16, which shows a lamina made from matrix and fibers. Several laminae are bonded together to form a laminate, which in turn is used for structural applications.

Micromechanics refers to the mechanical behavior of constituent materials such as fiber and matrix materials, the interaction of these constituents, and the resulting

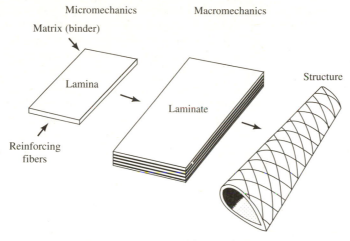

FIGURE 2.16
Micromechanics and macromechanics of composites [Gibson, 1994].

behavior of the basic composite (a single lamina, in this case). It involves the study of relationships between the effective composite properties and the effective constituent properties. The terms "structure-property relationships" and "effective modulus theories" are used in the literature to denote micromechanics [Gibson, 1994]. Many analytical approaches have been developed over the years. Chamis and Sendeckyj [1968], Christensen [1979], Hashin [1983], and Halpin [1984] have published literature surveys on this topic.

Macromechanics, on the other hand, refers to the gross behavior of composite materials and structures (in this case, lamina, laminate, and structure). Once the characteristics of a fibrous lamina are determined, its detailed microstructural nature can be ignored, and it can be treated simply as a homogeneous orthotropic sheet. A laminated composite is regarded as a body made by stacking several orthotropic sheets at specific orientations to achieve composite materials with the desired characteristics. For the final analysis of such laminated composites, the existing theories of laminated plates or shells are used [Chawla, 1987; Gibson, 1994].

The techniques required to analyze composites differ from those used to analyze conventional materials. A somewhat crude technique used to obtain composite response in the elastic range is the *rule of mixtures.* This is a rough tool based on the simple strength-of-materials approach in which the composite properties are considered to be volume-weighted averages. A key element of micromechanical analysis is the characterization of the relative volume or weight contents of various constituent materials. The rule of mixtures provides the relationships among volume fractions and weight fractions of fibers and the matrix in a composite. These relationships involve density and elastic constants. It is assumed that (1) strains in the matrix, the fibers, and the composite are equal, (2) the load carried by the composite (P_c) equals the sum of the loads carried by the fibers (P_f) and the loads carried by the matrix (P_m), and (3) there is no slip between the fibers and the matrix.

The rule of mixtures for relating the density of the composite to the densities of its constituents can be derived as follows [Chawla, 1987]. For a composite of mass m_c and volume v_c, the total mass can be expressed as the sum of total masses of the fiber and the matrix. Thus,

$$m_c = m_f + m_m \tag{2.3}$$

where the subscripts c, f, and m represent composite, fiber, and matrix, respectively. The volume of the composite can be expressed as

$$v_c = v_f + v_m + v_v \tag{2.4}$$

where v_v = volume of voids. Similarly, denoting the mass and the volume fractions by M_f, M_m, and V_f, V_m, V_v, respectively, one can write

$$M_f + M_m = 1 \tag{2.5}$$

and

$$V_f + V_m + V_v = 1 \tag{2.6}$$

Therefore, the composite density ρ_c (which equals m/v) can be expressed as

$$\rho_c = \frac{m_c}{v_c} = \frac{m_f + m_m}{v_c} = \frac{\rho_f v_f + \rho_m v_m}{v_c} \tag{2.7}$$

Equation 2.7 can be rewritten as

$$\rho_c = \rho_f V_f + \rho_m V_m \tag{2.8}$$

Equation 2.8 is known as the *rule of mixtures for density*.

The Young's modulus in the fiber direction can be derived based on the assumption that the fiber and the matrix are bonded perfectly and both have the same Poisson's ratio. Then the elongations ΔL of the fiber, the matrix, and the composite will be the same. Thus, the strain in each component can be expressed as

$$\epsilon_f = \epsilon_m = \epsilon_{cl} = \frac{\Delta L}{L} \tag{2.9}$$

where ϵ_{cl} is the strain in the composite in the longitudinal direction. Since

$$P_c = P_f + P_m \tag{2.10}$$

it can be shown that

$$E_{cl} = E_f V_f + E_m V_m \tag{2.11}$$

Equation 2.11 is the rule of mixtures for Young's modulus in the fiber direction. A similar expression can be obtained for the composite longitudinal strength:

$$\sigma_{cl} = \sigma_f V_f + \sigma_m V_m \tag{2.12}$$

The rule of mixtures for the composite strain in the transverse direction is expressed as

$$\epsilon_{cl} = \epsilon_f V_f + \epsilon_m V_m \tag{2.13}$$

Noting that $\sigma_{cl} = \sigma_f = \sigma_m$, Eq. 2.13 can be expressed as

$$\frac{1}{E_{ct}} = \frac{V_m}{E_m} + \frac{V_f}{E_f} \tag{2.14}$$

which is known as the rule of mixtures for modulus of elasticity in the transverse direction (E_{ct}).

A complete derivation of various equations under the rule of mixtures is presented by Chawla [1987].

For a rigorous analysis of composites, the micromechanical approach is followed, which is quite complex mathematically. Considering the composite as an anisotropic body, the most general case involves 21 independent elastic constants, whereas the analysis of an isotropic body involves only two independent elastic constants. The axial elongation of an isotropic body is accompanied by two equal transverse compressive strains, whereas, in a generally anisotropic body, the two transverse strains are not equal. Also, the tensile loading in an anisotropic body can result in tensile as well as shear strains. A discussion on the micromechanical analysis of composites can be found in many references: [Love, 1952; Ashton, Halpin, and Petit, 1969; Christensen, 1979; Tsai and Hahn, 1980; Lekhnitski, 1981; Vinson and Sierakowski, 1986; Chawla, 1987; Agarwal and Broutman, 1990; Gibson, 1994; Nielson, 1994].

2.5.8 Fibrous Cement-Based Composites

Although the present form of fiber-reinforced concrete is less than forty years old, the concept of reinforcing concrete with fibers evolved from ancient times when straw was used to reinforce sun-baked bricks and horse hair was used to reinforce plaster. Later, asbestos fibers were used to reinforce portland cement. Since the turn of the century, patents have been granted for various methods of incorporating metal chips or wire segments into concrete.

Portland cement concrete is one of the most commonly used materials for highway bridges and pavements. All cementitious materials—concrete, mortar, cement paste—suffer from inherent low tensile strength, low ductility, and low impact resistance because of the presence of internal flaws and voids; consequently, cementitious materials are unable to prevent small cracks. Efforts by Romualdi anda Batson to improve the flexural strength and ductility of concrete by introducing a small percentage of high-strength ductile fibers in low-strength, brittle concrete led to the development of a two-phase material—*fiber-reinforced cement-based composite,* also known as *fiber-reinforced,* or *fibrous, concrete, (FRC),* with greatly improved tensile and shear-strength properties. Romualdi and Batson suggested that fibers act as crack arresters by producing pinching forces that tend to close a crack, and that the first-crack tensile strength was inversely proportional to the geometrical spacing of fibers for a given fiber volume content [Romualdi and Batson, 1963a,b; Batson, Jenkins, and Spatney, 1972; Batson, 1985].

Essentially a composite material, fiber-reinforced concrete is a specialized concrete consisting of cement paste, mortar, or concrete with fibers of asbestos, glass, plastic, or steel. ACI Committee 544 on Fiber-Reinforced Concrete [ACI, 1974b, 1982] defines fiber-reinforced concrete as "concrete made of hydraulic cements containing fine or fine and coarse aggregate and discontinuous discrete fibers. Continuous meshes, woven fabrics, and long rods are not considered to be discrete fibre-type reinforcing elements." Unlike conventional concrete members, fiber-reinforced concrete can be thought of as a composite system in which the material as a whole carries both tensile and compressive stresses due to loads. Fiber-reinforced composite was found to provide notable improvements in the areas of shear, impact, ductility under cyclic loading, and fatigue loading. It shows good potential for earthquake-resistant structures because of the ductility it provides compared to plain concrete [Balguru and Shah, 1992].

Recommendations and guidelines regarding the various aspects of FRC are reported in several American Concrete Institute publications [ACI, 1982, 1988, 1989, 1990], developed by ACI Committee 544. A list of various applicable ASTM specifications has been provided by Balguru and Shah [1992].

Ongoing research has explored ways to use fiber-reinforced concrete in structural applications such as beams, columns, connections, plates, and prestressed concrete structures [Balguru and Ezeldin, 1987; Craig, 1987; Swamy and Bahia, 1985]. Balguru and Shah [1992] report that some of the new approaches being investigated may alter the way we design and construct concrete structures [ASTM, 1987; Krenchel and Stang, 1988; Shah, 1990; Stang and Mobasher, 1990]. The advent of high-range water-reducing admixtures has made it possible to incorporate a fiber volume of 15 percent in cement matrices. Fiber in such large quantities seems to fundamentally alter the nature of cementitious matrices.

2.5.9 Application of Composites

2.5.9.1 Industrial and commercial applications

Advanced composites constitute a new breed of materials with virtually unlimited potential for structural applications, and advocacy for their use in civil engineering structures has exploded in recent years. In general, composites encompass hundreds and thousands of materials, but only the fiber-, metal-, and ceramic-reinforced matrix composites are considered suitable for structural applications. A comprehensive treatment of various kinds of structurally suitable composites and their applications in various industries can be found in several references [Lubin, 1969, 1982; Noton, 1974; Katz and Milewski, 1978; Kelly, 1990; Morley, 1987; Reinhart, Brinson, and Schneider, 1987; Weeton, Peters, and Thomas, 1987; Strong, 1989; ACI, 1990; Schwartz, 1992].

In general, composites have been used in virtually thousands of applications, from sophisticated spacecrafts to sports and recreational equipment to consumer goods. Advanced composites have been used by the defense industries for aerospace and military aircraft since the 1940s. However, composites are prohibitively expensive. Because cost and safety are more critical concerns in civil applications, the use of composites in civil aircraft has generally lagged behind that in military aircraft. With a downward trend in costs, however, the use of composites in commercial aircraft has been steadily increasing. Advanced composites have been used in Boeing 707, 727, 737, and 747 commercial transports. The B-2 Stealth advanced technology bomber symbolizes one of the most recent applications of advanced composites. It is estimated that each B-2 aircraft uses between 40,000 and 50,000 lb of composites [PMAT, 1989; Schwartz, 1992]. Advanced composites using graphite, Kevlar,® and fiberglass have also been used in the present generation of military helicopters, such as the UH-60A, and in commercial helicopters, such as the S-76 [Immen, 1977; Rich, 1980; Schwartz and Jacaruso, 1982].

These applications are summarized by Schwartz [1992]; this summary is not repeated here.

Composites consisting of resin matrixes reinforced with mats of discontinuous glass fibers and continuous glass fibers are widely used in many forms in automobiles and trucks. Applications include such components as interior and exterior panels, under-the-hood parts, and brackets. Some structurally demanding applications of composites include bumpers and even wheels [Kulkarni, Zweben, and Pipes, 1978]. Fiber-reinforced composites have been proposed for use in special structures such as planetary and lunar facilities [Namba et al., 1988; Young and Berger, 1988] and in ultracold environments [Dutta, 1988, 1989].

2.5.9.2 Applications in bridges

In the past decade, many applications of composites in bridges have been reported in the literature. These applications have taken place in two specific areas, namely in rehabilitation and retrofitting of bridges and in new bridges. At the Second International Conference on Advanced Composite Materials in Bridges and Structures, held in August in Montreal, Canada, 119 papers contributed by 247 authors from 20 countries were presented; this indicates the growing worldwide interest in applications of composites. Applications of FRP composites in civil engineering structures is discussed by Bakht, Gilke, and Jaeger [1991], by Bakht and Jaeger [1992], and in a state-of-the-art report published by the American Concrete Institute [ACI, 1995]. More than fifty bridges that use FRP composites have been built throughout the world, mostly in Japan and Europe. Most of these are pedestrian bridges or vehicular bridges built on private roads. Many of these bridges were built as demonstration projects to validate the technology, to gain experience, and to study their long-term performance and durability. As a result, valuable insight has been gained toward using FRP reinforcing materials for highway bridges [Erki, Tadros, and Machida, 1996].

Considerable progress has been made in the 1990s toward codifying the use of FRP composites in buildings and bridges. Structural use of FRP reinforcement in Japan is discussed by Mufti, Erki, and Jaeger [1992]; by Tsuji, Kanda, and Tamura [1993]; and in reports by the Japanese Society of Civil Engineers [JSCE, 1992, 1995]. Design provisions for use of FRP composites are being written for the Canadian Highway Bridge Design Code [CHBDC, 1996a, b], which is presently under development. Drafts for the use of FRP reinforcing bars for inclusion in the ACI Code and a draft of the first edition of the CSA standard for the use of FRP reinforcing materials in building components in Canada [CSA, 1996] were presented at a recent Joint U.S.–Canadian Team Workshop in Montreal [United States–Canada Workshop, 1996]. Guidelines for the use of FRP reinforcing bars in highway bridges in the United States are also being drafted.

Composites are used in bridges in many forms. These include FRP tendons, GFRP reinforcing bars for beams and deck slabs, new pedestrian bridges using pultruded FRP structural components, and composite decks. Rehabilitation and retrofitting of existing beams and columns involves wrapping them with composite materials to enhance their service life (discussed in Chapter 10). A brief description of these applications is presented by Wilson, Vijay, and GangaRao [1996] and is summarized as follows:

Applications of FRP tendons. FRP tendons are available in the forms of glass tendons, carbon tendons, and aramid tendons and rods. A variety of surface textures are possible for FRP tendons: rough, smooth, sand-coated, braided helically wrapped, and so on. Tendons can be round or hexagonal in cross section, with a sleeve over them to contain the rods [ACI, 1995]. The advantages of FRP tendons over steel tendons are high specific strength (10–15 times higher than steel), excellent fatigue resistance of carbon and aramid tendons (which can be as much as three times more resistant than steel), noncorrosive and nonmagnetic properties, and low thermal expansion in the case of carbon and aramid tendons [ACI, 1995].

According to Aslanova and Kulesh [1996], glass fiber reinforcing rods were used for prestressing as early as 1975 in Russia. The world's first glued-laminated bridge was reportedly built in Russia, in 1981; its beams were prestressed with four 4-mm-diameter GFRP rods. In this bridge (about 40 ft long), tie rods consisting of twelve 6-mm-diameter rods were used to prestress metal beams. A third bridge (about 50 ft long), built in 1989, consisted of five prestressed concrete beams. The reinforcement in the beams was combined: four tendons of GFRP rods and one standard tendon of steel wires. The GFRP tendons consisted of twenty-four 6-mm rods. Some recently built bridges with FRP tendons follow:

- Lunen'sche-Gasse Bridge, Germany,—a 21-ft single-span slab bridge built in 1980—100 rods of glass cable were used
- Ulenberg-Strasses Bridge, Germany, the world's first large-scale bridge having 70- and 84-ft slab spans—this bridge has 59 glass tendons, each with 19 rods
- Shinmiya Bridge, Japan, built in 1988, spans 19 ft and is 23 ft wide—eight tendons composed of carbon rods were used for prestressing
- Bachigaua Minamibashi Bridge, Japan, a 60-ft, simple-span, precast, hollow-girder bridge built in 1989—post-tensioned with carbon tendons
- South Yard Country Club Suspension Bridge, Japan—post-tensioned in 1990 using flat strips of aramid
- Sumitomo Bridge, Japan, built in 1990–1991, a two-span bridge consisting of a 39-ft pretensioned composite slab and a 25-ft post-tensioned box girder—aramid tendons were used
- Hakui Cycling Road Bridge, Japan, built in 1991—its 25-ft span consists of a hollow slab pretensioned with carbon tendons
- Rapid City Bridge, South Dakota, built in 1992, this 30-ft-span bridge is 17 ft wide and consists of three pretensioned girders which support a 7-in.-thick deck slab—the girders are prestressed with three different types of materials (for performance evaluation): one-third GFRP cables, one-third CFRP cables, and one-third steel cables
- Tsukude Golf Country Club Bridge, Japan, a 325-ft-long and 12-ft-wide bridge built in 1993—carbon tendons were used to post-tension the bridge
- Lugwigshafen Bridge, Germany, a four-span (equal spans) structure having a total length of approximately 280 ft—carbon tendons were used for this prestressed concrete bridge

A discussion of various aspects of prestressed concrete beams with CFRP and GFRP tendons is presented by several researchers [Plecenik et al., 1990; Iyer, Khubchandani, and Feng, 1991; Gerritse and Werner, 1991; Rostasy and Budelmann, 1991; Meier, 1992; Grace and Abdel-Sayed, 1996; Gowripalan, Zou, and Gilbert, 1996; Jerrett, Ahmed, and Scotti, 1996; Sippel and Mayer, 1996; Yeung and Naylor, 1996]. Dolan and Burke [1996] discuss the flexural strength and design of prestressed beams with

FRP tendons. Design provisions for using FRP tendons have been drafted for the proposed Canadian Highway Bridge Design Code [CHBDC, 1996a, b].

Pedestrian bridges using FRP structural shapes. With advancement in pultrusion technology, FRP structural shapes have become available in several configurations: I-shapes, channels, angles, plates, bars, and rods. Several such products manufactured by the Morrison Molded Fiber Glass Company of Bristol, Virginia, are shown in Fig. 2.17. These are used for various building purposes [CP, 1989]. Several pedestrian bridges using these products have been built by E. T. Techtonics of Philadelphia, Pennsylvania, including single- and two-span bridges ranging in length from 30 to 80 ft. E. T. Techtonics has built about 13 such bridges at various locations in California, Hawaii, Illinois, Michigan, and Washington. For example, Fig. 2.18 shows the 80-ft-span bridge in Olympic National Park in the state of Washington and the 35-ft-span bridge in the

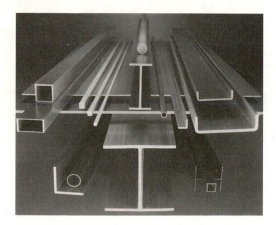

FIGURE 2.17
Fiberglass composite structural elements of various shapes formed by pultrusion. (Courtesy of Morrison.)

(a)

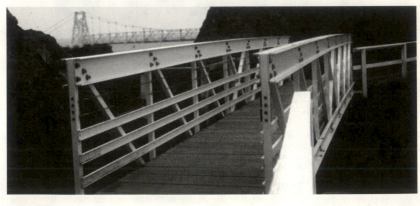

(b)

FIGURE 2.18
(a) the 80-ft-span bridge in the Olympic National Park in the state of
Washington, and (b) the 35-ft-span bridge in the Golden Gate Recreation
Area in San Francisco, California.

Golden Gate Recreation Area in San Francisco, California. A discussion on the construction of these bridges is presented by Johansen et al. [1996].

Deck slab with GFRP reinforcing bars. As an alternative to the commonly used steel reinforcing bars that cause corrosion, GFRP reinforcing bars are now beginning to be used for reinforced concrete decks. Several types of FRP bars made from fibers of glass, aramid, carbon, or a combination of these materials are commercially available. However, the majority of reinforcing bars used in civil engineering applications are produced with E-glass fibers. The matrix materials commonly used with these fibers are polyester or vinyl ester resins. The surface of the FRP bars may be smooth, sand-coated, deformed, helically wrapped, or ribbed sand-coated. The ribbed surface provides a surface texture similar to that of conventional steel reinforcing bars.

Typical of composites, the FRP reinforcing bars offer several advantages over conventional steel reinforcing bars; the most important advantages are noncorrosiveness and high specific strength. In addition, they are light, nonmagnetic, and possess excellent fatigue resistance. GFRP bars are also nonconductive.

In the United States, extensive research in the use of GFRP reinforcing bars has been conducted at the Constructed Facilities Center, West Virginia University, Morgantown. The findings are reported by several researchers: [Faza, 1991; Faza and GangaRao, 1991, 1993; GangaRao and Nivargikar, 1991; Sotiropoulos, 1991, 1995; Sotiropolous, GangaRao, and Barbero, 1991; and Sotiropolous, GangaRao, and Mongi, 1994]. High-strength concrete beams reinforced with FRP bars were reported to exhibit greater flexural strength than comparable beams with conventional steel reinforcing bars. Also, concrete beams with GFRP bars deflected three times greater than the steel-reinforced beams did, with wider and more closely spaced cracks at the ultimate loads. A discussion on deformability and ductility in concrete beams reinforced with FRP bars is reported by Mufti, Newhook, and Tadros [1996]. Maruyama and Zhao [1996] and Vijay, Kumar, and GangaRao [1996] discuss behavior of concrete beams with FRP reinforcement under shear.

Figure 2.19 shows the 177-ft-long, three-span, continuous, two-lane bridge at McKinleyville, West Virginia, the first bridge in the United States in which FRP reinforcing bars were used. Its 9-in.-thick deck consists of No. 4 FRP bars at 6-in. o.c. for transverse reinforcement and No. 3 FRP bars at 6-in. o.c. for distribution reinforcement. The clear cover for the top and the bottom bars are $1\frac{1}{2}$ and 1 in., respectively. A unique feature of this bridge is that it is an integral-abutment bridge [GangaRao, 1996].

The feasibility of using FRP reinforcing bars and FRP molded grating is discussed by Larralde [1992], Larralde, Reinbaum, and Marsi [1989], and by Tarricone [1993].

FRP composite decks. A new development in bridge superstructures is the use of FRP composites for the entire deck or as part of the actual superstructure system itself. The bridge deck has long been recognized as a critical component of the bridge superstructure. There would be several advantages to building the deck from composites. The low weight of composites would reduce the inertia forces experienced during an earthquake, and the high corrosion resistance of composites would enhance the service life of the superstructure. Several systems using composites are under investigation at the University of California at San Diego [Karbhari, 1996]. The results of this research will likely be applied for two all-composite replacement bridges being planned by the Delaware River and Bay Authority. One of these bridges will be a 70-ft span and the other a 170-ft span [CE, 1996d].

A novel FRP bridge deck has been proposed by Aref and Parsons [1996]. As shown in Fig. 2.20, it consists of a series of inner cells surrounded by an outer shell. The deck is constructed by first manufacturing the inner cells by filament winding. These cells are then held in place while the outer shell is wrapped around them. Aref and Parsons propose a simplified analysis procedure for this system based on a Ritz solution of an equivalent orthotropic plate (macromechanics aspect). Hybrid FRP bridge deck systems are discussed by Bakeri and Shyam Sunder [1990].

Composite wrappings of structural members. Several FRP products are being tried in the United States for repairs, rehabilitation, and retrofitting by the highway

(a)

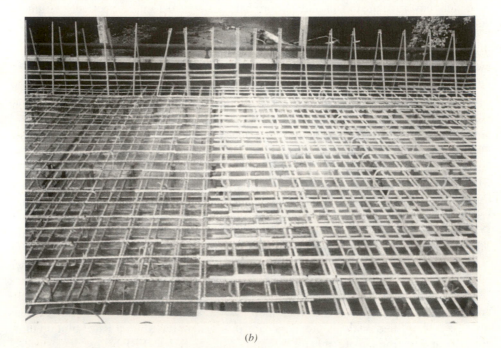

(b)

FIGURE 2.19
The McKinleyville Bridge, West Virginia—the first bridge in the United States
to use FRP reinforcing bars for the deck. (a) Courtesy of David Boyajian, Los
Angeles. (b) Courtesy of CFC, Civil Engineering Department, West Virginia University,
Morgantown.

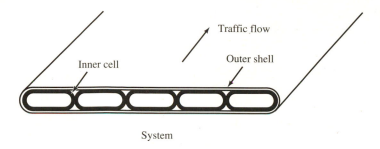

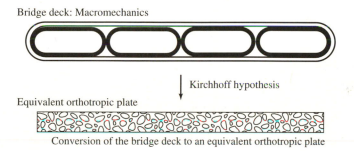

FIGURE 2.20
Structural system for proposed bridge deck consisting of a series of
inner cells and an outer shell [Aref and Parsons, 1996].

departments of such states as California, Florida, Nevada, Ohio, and Vermont. The
feasibility of using externally bonded carbon/epoxy composite plates for strengthening
concrete beams has been discussed by An, Saadatmanesh, and Ehsani [1991] and by
Saadatmanesh and Ehsani [1991a,b]. FRP composite columns are discussed by Yuan
et al. [1991].

A high-strength fiber epoxy column casing has been developed and successfully
tested at the University of California at San Diego, California. The system is made up of
carbon or glass fibers and a polyester resin composite material that can be applied like
hoops around the bridge columns [CALTRANS, 1995]. This column-wrap technique is
presently being used to retrofit bridge columns damaged during the 1989 Loma Prieta,
California, and the 1994 Northridge, California, earthquakes [Seible, 1996].

Based on the observed excellent structural response of the concrete-filled carbon-
shell columns [Burgueno, Seible, and Hegemier, 1995] investigated at the University
of California at San Diego, complete bridge systems based on the carbon-shell concept
have been proposed. One such concept is a dual-tied arch bridge in which the arches
comprise concrete-filled carbon tube segments; the tie girders consist of post-tensioned
concrete-filled carbon tubes; and the cross beams are carbon-filled tubes placed on a
link-and-log system over the beams, where only the joints are concrete filled [Seible et
al., 1995a]. Another proposed bridge is a carbon-shell space truss system that consists
of post-tensioned truss members [Seible et al., 1995b]. These bridge systems are shown
schematically in Fig. 2.21. A similar system has also been applied to a cable-stayed
bridge system [Fig. 2.22]. A summary of these innovative concepts is provided by
Seible [1996] and by Seible and Karbhari [1996].

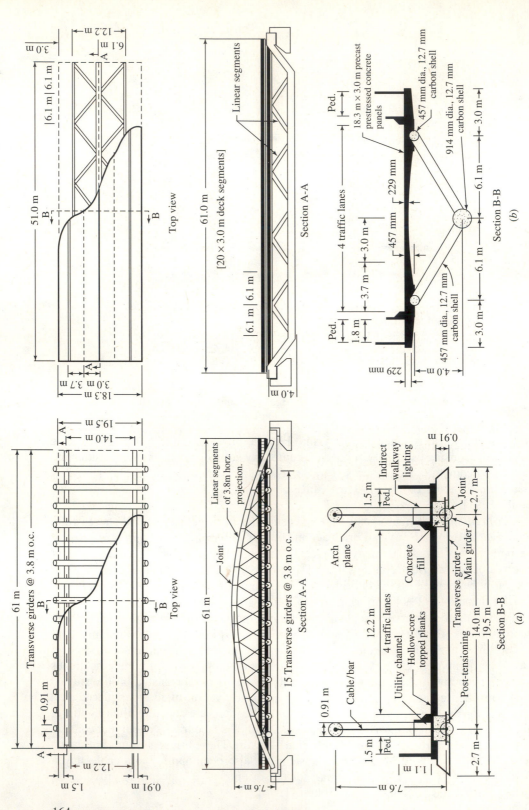

FIGURE 2.21

Carbon-shell bridge systems [Seible et al., 1995a,b]: (a) shallow dual-tied arch, (b) space truss.

164

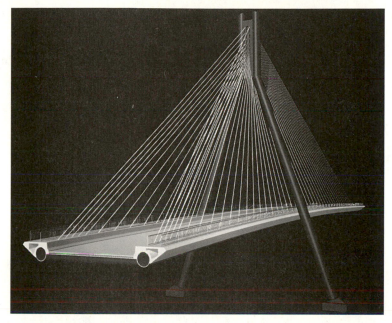

FIGURE 2.22
Carbon-shell cable-stayed bridge concept [Seible, 1996].

The Florida Dept. of Transportation has repaired many highway bridges with adhesively bonded carbon-fiber material. These fabrics allow workers to carry out repair or retrofit of concrete decks and beams at night without having to actually remove and replace the deficient beam and with significant savings in traffic-routing costs. Three kinds of carbon sheets are commercially used [Goldstein, 1996]:

1. *Tonen*—a dry fabric material with a backing paper, it is applied like a wall paper. The dry fabric is placed on wet epoxy and rolled down, so that all fibers are coated with epoxy.
2. A strip-plate-cured laminate product that may be used to strengthen flat surfaces—developed and marketed by the Swiss companies Stecelit and Sika, the product is thin but stiff, and it cannot be bent over angular surfaces.
3. *Replark*—a CFRP prepreg[4] sheet developed by Mitsubishi Chemical Corporation. It can be used to strengthen both columns and flat surfaces and can also be formed around angular surfaces.

A brief summary of current applications of CFRP and GFRP composites in bridge construction and of repair and retrofit work in the United States is provided by Goldstein [1996] and by Neuram and Kaiser [1991]. The potential for and importance of applications of FRP products for civil engineering infrastructure can be gaged from the fact that, out of a total of 119 papers presented at the Second International Conference

---

[4]Ready-to-mold material in sheet form, either cloth, mat, or paper impregnated with resin and stored for use. The resin is partially cured to B stage and supplied to the fabricator, who lays up the finished shape and completes the cure with heat and pressure.

on Advanced Composite Materials in Bridges and Structures held in August, 1996 in Montreal, 28 papers covered the subject of strengthening and repair using composites [CSCE, 1996].

The interest in FRP composites is fueled by innovative manufacturing technologies such as pultrusion, filament winding, and three-dimensional braiding [Strong, 1989]. In the United States, a shift in focus from military to civilian applications has given impetus to explore potential uses of composites in civil engineering structures. As a result, from demonstration projects in the sixties and seventies, this new material is now being applied at an unprecedented rate in actual projects involving civil engineering structures, as reported in the literature [Ballinger, 1991; Bank, 1993; CE, 1992a, 1996a,b,c,d; Chambers, 1992; Clark, 1990; Iyer and Sen, 1991; Kaempen, 1989; Kuemen, 1995; Leonard, 1990; Meier, 1992; Mobasher, Ouyang, and Shah, 1990; Muller, 1993; Plecnik, Azar, and Kabbara, 1990; PN, 1992; Saadatmanesh and Ehsani, 1989; Wilson, Vijay, and GangaRao, 1996].

REFERENCES

AASHTO. (1991). *Interim Specifications—Bridges—1991,* AASHTO, Washington, DC.

———. (1992a). *Standard Specifications for Highway Bridges—1992,* 15th ed., AASHTO, Washington, DC.

———. (1992b). *Interim Specifications for Transportation Materials and Methods of Sampling and Testing: Parts I and II, 1992,* AASHTO, Washington, DC.

———. (1994). *AASHTO–LRFD Bridge Design Specifications,* 1st ed., AASHTO, Washington, DC.

ACI. (1974a). *An International Symposium: Fiber-Reinforced Concrete,* ACI Committee 544, Pub. SP-44, American Concrete Institute, Detroit, MI.

———. (1974b). "State-of-the-Art Report on Fiber-Reinforced Concrete," in *An International Symposium: Fiber-Reinforced Concrete,* ACI Committee 544, pub. SP-44, ACI, Detroit, MI, pp. 535–550.

———. (1977). *Analysis and Design of Reinforced Concrete Bridge Structures,* ACI, Detroit, MI.

———. (1982). "State-of-the-Art Report on Fiber-Reinforced Concrete," ACI Committee 544, report ACI 544-1R-82, *Concrete International: Design and Construction,* May (reapproved 1986), ACI, Detroit, MI.

———. (1984). *State-of-the-Art Report on High-Strength Concrete,* ACI 363R-84, ACI, Detroit, MI.

———. (1988). *Design Considerations for Steel Fiber-Reinforced Concrete,* ACI Committee 544, report 544.4R-88, ACI, Detroit, MI.

———. (1989). *Measurement of Properties of Fiber-Reinforced Concrete,* ACI Committee 544, report 544.2R-89, ACI, Detroit, MI.

———. (1990). *Guide for Specifying, Mixing, Placing, and Finishing Steel Fiber-Reinforced Concrete,* ACI Committee 544, report 544.3R- 90, ACI, Detroit, MI.

———. (1991a). *Standard Practice for Selecting Proportions for Normal, Heavyweight, and Mass Concrete,* ACI Committee 211, ACI 211.1-91, ACI, Detroit, MI.

———. (1991b). *Standard Practice for Selecting Proportions for Structural Lightweight Concrete,* ACI Committee 211, ACI 211.2-91, ACI, Detroit, MI.

———. (1995). *State-of-the-Art Report on Application of FRP,* ACI Committee 440, ACI, Detroit, MI.

Adelman, D., and Cousins, T. E. (1990). "Evaluation of the Use of High-Strength Concrete Bridge Girders in Louisiana," *J. Prestressed Concrete Institute*, September–October, pp. 70–78.

Agarwal, B. D., and Broutman, L. (1990). *Analysis and Performance of Fiber Composites,* John Wiley & Sons, New York.

AISC. (1994). *Manual of Steel Construction—Load and Resistance Factor Design, Vol. I,* AISC, Chicago.

AISC Mkt. (1986). *Highway Structures Design Handbook, Vol. I,* American Marketing Services, Inc., Pittsburgh.

———. (1991). "Properties of Bridge Steels," in *Highway Structures Design Book,* vol. 1, Ch. 3, American Marketing Services, Inc., Pittsburgh.

An, W., Saadatmanesh H., and Ehsani, M. R. (1991). "RC Beams Strengthened with FRP Plates. II: Analysis and Parametric Study," *ASCE J. Struct. Eng.,* 117(11), pp. 3434–3455.

Aref, A., and Parsons, I. D. (1996). "Design and Analysis Procedures for a Novel Fiber-Reinforced Plastic Bridge Deck," *Proc. 2nd Intl. Conf. Advanced Composite Materials in Bridges and Structures,* Montreal, August 12–14, pp. 743–750.

Ashby, M. F. (1987). "Technology of the 1900s: Advanced Materials and Predictive Design," *Phil. Trans. of the Royal Soc. of London,* A322, pp. 393–407.

Ashton, J. E., Halpin, J. C., and Petit, P. H. (1969). *Primer on Composite Materials,* Technomic Publishing, Lancaster, PA.

Aslanova, L. G., and Kulesh, V. I. (1996). "Practical Applications of Glass Fiber-Reinforcing Rods in Highway Bridge Components," *Proc. 2nd Intl. Conf. Advanced Composite Materials in Bridges and Structures,* Montreal, August 12–14, pp. 271–278.

ASM. (1978). "Properties and Selection Iron and Steel" in *Metals Handbook,* 9th ed., American Society for Metals, Metals Park, Ohio.

ASTM. (1988). *Standard Specification for General Requirements for Rolled-Steel Plates, Shapes, Sheet Piling, and Bars for Structural Use,* A6-88c, ASTM, Philadelphia, PA.

Aziz, M. A., Paramasivam, P., and Lee, S. L. (1984). "Concrete Reinforced with Natural Fibers," in *New Reinforced Concretes, Vol. 2,* R. N. Swamy, ed., Surrey University Press, Glasgow, pp. 106–140.

Bakeri, P. A., and Shyam Sunder, S. (1990). "Concepts for Hybrid FRP Bridge Deck Systems," in *Serviceability and Durability of Construction Materials,* B. A. Suprenant, ed., *Proc. 1st Materials Engineering Cong.,* Denver, CO, ASCE, New York, pp. 1006–1015.

Bakht, B., Gilkie, R., and Jaeger, L. G. (1991). "Design Criteria," in *Advanced Composite Materials with Application to Bridges,* CSCE, Montreal, pp. 217–230.

Bakht, B., and Jaeger, L. G. (1992). "Design Criteria," in *Advanced Composite Materials in Bridges and Structures in Japan,* CSCE, Montreal, pp. 121–131.

Balguru, P., and Ezeldin, A. (1987). "Behavior of Partially Prestressed Beams Made with High-Strength Fiber-Reinforced Concrete," *Fiber-Reinforced Concrete Properties and Applications,* ACI pub. SP-105, ACI, Detroit, MI.

Balguru, P. N., and Shah, S. P. (1985). "Alternative Reinforcing Materials for Developing Countries," *Int. J. Developing Tech.,* 3, pp. 87–105.

———. (1992). *Fiber-Reinforced Cement-Based Composites,* McGraw-Hill Companies, Inc., New York.

Ballinger, C. A. (1991). "Development of Composites for Civil Engineering," in *Advanced Composites Materials in Civil Engineering Structures,* S. L. Iyer and R. Sen, eds., *ASCE, Proc. Specialty Conf.,* Las Vegas, January 31–February 1, pp. 288–301.

Bank, L. C. (1993). "Questioning Composites," *ASCE Civ. Eng.,* January, pp. 64–65.

Batson, G. B. (1985). "Use of Steel Fibers for Shear Reinforcement and Ductility," *Steel Fiber Concrete, United States–Sweden Joint Seminar (NSF–STU), Stockholm, June 3–5,* Elsevier Applied Science Publishers, New York.

Biryukovich, K. L., and Biryukovic, U. L. (1957). "Concrete with Reinforcement of Glass Fibers," *Stroitelnaya Promishlennet,* no. 6.

Brockenbrough, R. L. (1972). "Properties of Structural Materials: Intrinsic Properties" in *Structural Steel Designers' Handbook, Part 1, Sec. 1,* F. S. Merritt, ed., McGraw-Hill Companies, Inc., New York, pp. 1-1 to 1-27.

Browning, C. E., Husman, G. E., and Whitney, J. M. (1977). "Moisture Effects in Epoxy Matrix Composites," *Composite Materials: Testing and Design: Fourth Conference,* ASTM STP 617, ASTM, Philadelphia, pp. 481–496.

Burgueno, R., Seible, F., and Hegemier, G. (1995). "Concrete-Filled Carbon Shell Bridge Piers under Simulated Seismic Loads," *Composites Tech. Transfer Consortium Report no. ACTT-95/12,* University of California at San Diego, La Jolla.

CALTRANS. (1995). *Memo to Designers 20-4, March 1995,* California Department of Transportation, Sacramento.

Castrodale, R. W., Kregar, M. E., and Burns, N. H. (1988). *A Study of Pretensioned High-Strength Concrete Girders in Composite Highway Bridges—Design Considerations,* report no. FHWA/TX-88+381-4F, Center of Transportation Research, Austin, TX.

CE. (1992a). "Materials Key to Rehab, Conference Speakers Say," *ASCE Civ. Eng.,* October, p. 11.

———. (1992b). "Ohio Looks to Improve Bridge Deck Performance," *ASCE Civ. Eng.,* October, p. 11.

———. (1992c). "News: Survey Predicts Bridge Trends for the 1990s," *ASCE Civ. Eng.,* September, p. 12.

———. (1996a). "News: Japan Shows the Way with Aramids," *ASCE Civ. Eng.,* pp.14–15.

———. (1996b). "News: Composite Materials Edge into Mainstream Construction," *ASCE Civ. Eng.,* March, pp. 16–18.

———. (1996c). "News: New Aluminum Decks Cut Costs, Add Life," *ASCE Civ. Eng.,* August, p. 12.

———. (1996d). "Delaware Authority Puts Money on Composite Bridges," *Civ. Eng.,* October, pp. 16–17.

Chambers, R. E. (1992). "Composites Performance in the Infrastructure," in *Materials: Performance and Prevention of Deficiencies and Failures,* T. D. White, ed., ASCE, New York, pp. 532–545.

Chamis, C. C., and Sendeckyj, G. P. (1968). "Critique on Theories Predicting Thermoelastic Properties of Fibrous Composites," *J. of Comp. Materials,* 2(3), pp. 332–358.

Chawla, K. K. (1987). *Composite Materials,* Springer Verlag, New York.

CHBDC. (1996a). *Canadian Highway Bridge Design Code—Section 16, Fibre-Reinforced Structures,* final draft, July 6, 1996.

———. (1996b). "Design Provisions for Fibre-Reinforced Structures in Canadian Highway Bridge Design Code," Canadian Highway Bridge Design Code Technical Subcommittee no. 16, *Proc. 2nd Intl. Conf. Advanced Composite Materials in Bridges and Structures,* Montreal, August 12–14, pp. 391–406.

Christensen, R. M. (1979). *Mechanics of Composite Materials,* John Wiley & Sons, New York.

Clark, J. M. (1990). "Design of Fiberglass-Reinforced Plastic Underground Storage Tanks," in *Serviceability and Durability of Construction Materials,* B. A. Suprenant, ed., *Proc. 1st Materials Engineering Cong.,* Denver, CO, ASCE, Materials Eng. Div., New York, pp. 658–667.

CP. (1989). *Design Guide,* Creative Pultrusions, Inc., Pleasantville, PA.

Craig, R. J. (1987). "Flexural Behavior and Design of Reinforced Concrete Members," *Fiber-Reinforced Concrete Properties and Applications,* ACI SP-105, ACI, Detroit, MI., pp. 517–563.

CSA. (1996). "S806-97 Design and Construction of Building Components with Fibre-Reinforced Plastics," *Canadian Standards Association Technical Committee on FRP Components and Reinforcing Materials for Buildings,* 2nd revised draft, presented at the *United States–Canada Joint Workshop on FRP Reinforcement for Concrete,* Montreal, August 10–11.

CSCE. (1996). "Advanced Composite Materials in Bridges and Structures," Mamdouh El-Badry, ed., *Proc. 2nd Intl. Conf. Advanced Composite Materials in Bridges and Structures,* Montreal, August 12–14.

CTL. (1992). "Meeting the Challenge of High-Strength Concrete," *CTL Rev.,* 15(2).

Daniel, J. I. (1988). *Glass Fiber-Reinforced Concrete,* Fiber-Reinforced Concrete report no. 2493D and 2641D, Construction Technology Laboratories, Skokie, IL, pp. 5.1–5.30.

Deutsch, G. S. (1978). *23rd Ntnl. SAMPE Symp.,* May, p. 34.

Dickson B., and GangaRao, H. V. S. (1990). "Development and Testing of an Experimental Stressed-Timber T-Beam Bridge," *Trans. Res.* Rec. 1275, Transportation Research Board, National Research Council, Washington, DC, pp. 67–75.

Dolan, C. W., and Burke, C. R. (1996). "Flexural Strength and Design of FRP Prestressed Beams," *Proc. 2nd Intl. Conf. Advanced Composite Materials in Bridges and Structures,* Montreal, August 12–14, pp. 383–390.

Dresher, W. H. (1969). *J. Metals,* 21, p. 17.

Dunker, K. F., and Rabaat, B. G. (1990a). "Highway Bridge Types and Performance Patterns," *ASCE J. Performance of Constructed Facilities,* 4(3), August, pp. 161–173.

———. (1990b). "Performance of Highway Bridges," *Concrete Intl.,* 12(8), August, pp. 40–43.

Dutta, P. K. (1988). "Structural Fiber Composite Materials for Cold Regions," *ASCE J. Performance of Constructed Facilities,* September, pp. 124–134.

———. (1989). "Materials in an Arctic Environment," *Structural Materials,* J. F. Orofino, ed., ASCE, New York, pp. 216–225.

ENR. (1984). "Concrete Beats Steel by 29%," *Eng. News-Rec.,* May 14, p. 16.

Erki, M. A., Tadros, G., and Machida, A. (1996). "Avoiding Catastrophic Failure in Concrete Bridges with FRP Reinforcement," *Proc. 2nd Intl. Conf. Advanced Composite Materials in Bridges and Structures,* Montreal, August 12–14, pp. 237–243.

Errera, S. J. (1974). "Materials," in *Structural Steel Design,* Ch. 2, Lambert Tall, ed., 2nd ed., Ronald Press, New York.

Faza, S. S. (1991). *Bending and Bond Behavior and Design of Concrete Beams Reinforced with Fiber-Reinforced Plastic Bars,* PhD thesis, Dept. of Civil Engineering, West Virginia University, Morgantown.

Faza, S. S., and GangaRao, H. V. S. (1991). "Bending Response of Beams Reinforced with FRP Rebars for Varying Concrete Strengths," in *Advanced Composites Materials in Civil Engineering Structures,* S. L. Iyer and R. Sen, eds., pp. 262–270. *ASCE Proc. Specialty Conf.,* Las Vegas, January 31–February 1.

———. (1993). "Theoretical and Experimental Correlation of Behavior of Concrete Beams Reinforced with Fiber-Reinforced Plastic Rebars," *Proc. ACI Intl. Symp. on Fiber-Reinforced Plastic Reinforcement,* ACI, Detroit.

GangaRao H. V. S. (1990). "Innovative Design and Construction of Modern Bridges," *Trans. Res. News,* November–December.

———. (1996). Personal communication with H. V. S. GangaRao, Director, Constructed Facilities Center, West Virginia University, Morgantown.

GangaRao, H. V. S., and Nivargikar, R. (1991). *Workshop on Use of Composites in Construction Industry—Government, Universities, Consortium.* Constructed Facilities Center, West Virginia University, Morgantown.

Gaylord, E. H., Gaylord, C. N., and Stallmeyer, J. E. (1992). *Steel Structures,* 3rd ed., McGraw-Hill Companies, Inc., New York.

Gerritse, A., and Werner, J. (1991). "ARAPREE, A Nonmetallic Tendon: Performance and Design Requirements," in *Advanced Composites Materials in Civil Engineering Structures,* S. L. Iyer and R. Sen, eds., *ASCE Proc. Specialty Conf.,* Las Vegas, Jan. 31–Feb 1. pp. 143–154.

Gibson, R. F. (1994). *Principles of Composite Material Mechanics,* McGraw-Hill Companies, Inc., New York.

Gibson, R. F., Yau, A., Mende, E. W., and Osborn, W. E. (1982). "The Influence of Environmental Conditions on the Vibration Characteristics of Chopped-Fiber-Reinforced Composite Materials," *J. Reinforced Plastics and Composites,* 1(3), March, pp. 225–241.

Gloeckner, K. M. (1967). *Investigation of Fiberglass Prestressed Concrete,* Virginia Highway Research Council, Charlottesville, VA.

Goldstein, H. (1996). "Catching Up On Composites," *ASCE Civ. Eng.,* March, pp. 47–49.

Gowripalan, N., Zou, X. W., and Gilbert, R. I. (1996). "Flexural Behavior of Prestressed Beams Using AFRP Tendons and High-Strength Concrete," *Proc. 2nd Intl. Conf. Advanced Composite Materials in Bridges and Structures,* Montreal, August 12–14, pp. 325–334.

Grace, N. F., and Abdel-Sayed, G. (1996). Behavior of CFRP/GFRP Bridge System," *Proc. 2nd Intl. Conf. Advanced Composite Materials in Bridges and Structures,* Montreal, August 12–14, pp. 289–296.

Griffith, A. A. (1920). "The Phenomena of Rupture and Flow in Solids," *Phil. Trans. Royal Soc. of London,* 221A, pp. 163–198.

Halpin, J. C. (1984). *Primer on Composite Materials,* Technomic Publishing, Lancaster, New York.

Hashin, Z. (1983). "Analysis of Composite Materials—A Survey," *J. Applied Mech.,* 50, September, pp. 481–505.

Hult, J. (1966). *Creep in Engineering Structures,* Blaisdell Publishing, Waltham, MA.

Immen, F. H. (1977). "Army Helicopters Composites," *National Defense,* November–December.

Iyer, S. L., Khubchandani, A., and Feng, J. (1991). "Fiberglass and Graphite Cables for Bridge Decks," in *Advanced Composites Materials in Civil Engineering Structures,* S. L. Iyer and R. Sen, eds., *ASCE Proc. Specialty Conf.,* Las Vegas, January 31–February 1, pp. 371–382.

Iyer, S. L., and Sen, R., eds. (1991). *Advanced Composites Materials in Civil Engineering Structures, ASCE Proc. Specialty Conf.,* Las Vegas, January 31–February 1.

Jerrett, C. V., Ahmed, S. H., and Scotti, G. (1996). "Behavior of Prestressed Concrete Beams Strengthened by External FRP Post-Tensioned Tendons," *Proc. 2nd Intl. Conf. Advanced Composite Materials in Bridges and Structures,* Montreal, August 12–14, pp. 305–312.

Johansen, G. E., Wilson, R. J., Roll, F., Gaudini, P. G., Ribble, S. T., Fogle, A. J., Gray, K. E., Malaki, M. R., and Choy, V. M. S. (1996). "Design and Construction of Two FRP Pedestrian Bridges in Haleakala National Park, Maui, Hawaii," *Proc. 2nd Intl. Conf. Advanced Composite Materials in Bridges and Structures,* Montreal, August 12–14, pp. 975–982.

Jose, H. J., and Moustafa, S. E. (1982). "Applications of High-Strength Concrete Bridges for Highways," *J. Prestressed Concrete Inst.,* May–June, pp. 44–73.

JSCE. (1992). "Application of Continuous Fiber-Reinforcing Materials to Concrete Structures," Japanese Society of Civil Engineers Research Subcommittee on Continuous Fiber-Reinforcing Materials, *Concrete Library of JSCE,* no. 19, June, pp. 89–130.

———. (1995). *Research Committee on Continuous Fiber-Reinforcing Materials,* (English translation), Japan Society of Civil Engineers, Tokyo.

Kaempen, C. E. (1989). *Structural Applications of Composite Materials to Highway Tunnels,* Transp. Res. Rec. 1223, Transportation Research Board, Washington, DC, pp. 107–116.

Karbhari, V. M. (1996). "Fiber-Reinforced Composite Decks for Infrastructure Renewal," *Proc. 2nd Intl. Conf. Advanced Composite Materials in Bridges and Structures,* Montreal, August 12–14, pp. 759–766.

Katz, H. S., and Milewski, J. V., eds. (1978). *Handbook for Fillers and Reinforcement for Plastics,* Van Nostrand Reinhold, New York.

Keane, K. W. (1952). *Investigation of the Feasibility of Using Fiberglass for Prestressing Concrete,* MS thesis, Princeton University, May.

Kelly, A. (1990). "Composites for the 1990s," *Phil. Trans. Royal Society of London,* A322, pp. 409–423.

Kuemen, T. (1995). "World's First Advanced Composite Road Bridge Serves Heavy Trucks in England," *Roads & Bridges,* April, p. 50.

Kulkarni, S. V., Zweben, C. H., and Pipes, R. B. (1978). *Composite Materials in Automobile Industry,* ASME, New York.

Kuzmanovic, B. O., and Willems, N. (1983). *Steel Design for Structural Engineers,* 2nd ed., Prentice Hall, Englewood Cliffs, NJ.

Lankard, D. R. (1985). "Preparation, Properties, and Applications of Cement-Based Composites Containing 5 to 20 Percent Steel Fiber," *Steel-Fiber Concrete, United States–Sweden Joint Seminar (NSF–STU), Stockholm, June 3–5, 1985,* S. P. Shah and A. Skarendahl, eds., Elsevier Applied Science, New York.

Lankard, D. R., and Walker, A. J. (1974). "Bridge Deck and Pavement Overlays with Steel Fibrous Concrete," in *Fiber-Reinforced Concrete* SP-44, ACI, Detroit, MI, pp. 375–392.

Lankford, W. T., Jr., Swamis, N. L., Craven, R. F., and McGannon, H. E., eds. (1985). *The Making, Shaping, and Treating of Steel,* 10th ed., Association of Iron and Steel Engineers, Pittsburgh.

Larralde, R. J. (1992). "Feasibility of FRP-Molded Grating-Concrete Composites for One-Way Slab Systems," in *Materials: Performance and Prevention of Deficiencies and Failures,* T. D. White, ed., ASCE, New York, pp. 645–654.

Larralde, R. J., Reinbaum, L., and Morsi, A. (1989). "Fiberglass-Reinforced Plastic Rebars in Lieu of Steel," in *Structural Materials,* J. F. Orofino, ed., ASCE, New York, pp. 261–269.

Lekhnitski, S. G. (1981). *Theory of Elasticity of an Anisotropic Body,* Mir Publishing, Moscow.

Leonard, L. (1990). "Rebuilding the Infrastructure with Advanced Composites," *Advanced Composites,* May–June, pp. 43–47.

Libby, J. R. (1990). *Modern Prestressed Concrete,* 4th ed., Van Nostrand Reinhold, New York.

Lin, T. Y., and Burns, N. H. (1981). *Design of Prestressed Concrete Structures,* 3rd ed., John Wiley & Sons, New York.

Love, A. E. H. (1952). *A Treatise on the Mathematical Theory of Elasticity,* Dover, New York.

Lovett, T. G., and Warren, D. W. (1992). "Double Diamonds: New Brand for a Texas Bridge," *ASCE Civ. Eng.,* April.

Lubin, G., ed. (1969). *Handbook of Fiberglass and Advanced Composites,* Van Nostrand Reinhold, New York.

———. (1982). *Handbook of Composites,* Van Nostrand Reinhold, New York.

Lubin, G., and Dastin, S. J. (1982). "Aerospace Applications of Composites," in *Handbook of Composites,* G. Lubin, ed., Van Nostrand Reinhold, New York, pp. 722–743.

MacGregor, J. G. (1988). *Reinforced Concrete—Mechanics and Design,* Prentice Hall, Englewood Cliffs, NJ.

Maruyama, K., and Zhao, W. (1996). "Size Effects in Shear Behavior of FRP-Reinforced Concrete Beams," *Proc. 2nd Intl. Conf. Advanced Composite Materials in Bridges and Structures,* Montreal, August 12–14, pp. 227–234.

McCormac, J. C. (1992). *Structural Steel Design—ASD Method,* 4th ed., HarperCollins, New York.

———. (1993). *Design of Reinforced Concrete,* 3rd ed., HarperCollins, New York.

McCormic, F. C. (1987). "Field Studies of a Pedestrian Bridge of Reinforced Plastic," in *Bridge Needs, Design, and Performance,* Trans. Res. Rec. 1118, Transportation Research Board, Washington, DC, pp. 88–98.

———. (1988). "Advancing Structural Plastics into the Future," *ASCE J. Prof. Issues in Eng. Education and Practice,* July, pp. 335–343.

———. (1978). "Laboratory and Field Studies of a Pedestrian Bridge Composed of Glass-Reinforced Plastics," Trans. Res. Rec. 665, September, Transportation Research Board, Washington, DC, pp. 99–107.

McCrum, N. G. Buckley, C. P., and Bucknall, C. B. (1988). *Principles of Polymer Engineering,* Oxford University Press, New York.

Meade, L. E. (1982). "Fabrication of Advanced Composites," in *Handbook of Composites,* George Lubin, ed., Ch. 18, pp. 491–513.

Meier, U. (1992). "Case Histories," in *Advanced Composite Materials with Application to Bridges,* CSCE, H3A 122, Montreal.

Meyer, R. W. (1985). *Handbook of Pultrusion Technology,* Chapman & Hall, New York.

Merritt, F. S., ed. (1972). "Properties of Structural Steels, Effects of Steel Making, and Fabrication of Properties," *Structural Steel Designers' Handbook,* Section 1, Part 2, McGraw-Hill Companies, Inc., New York, pp. 1-28 to 1-39.

Morley, J. G. (1987). *High-Performance Fiber Composites,* Academic Press, New York.

Mufti, A. A., Erki, M. A., and Jaeger, L. G. (1992). "Introduction, Overview, and Case Studies," *Advanced Composite Materials in Bridges and Structures in Japan,* CSCE, Montreal, pp. 1–17.

Mufti, A. A., Newhook, J. P., and Tadros, G. (1996). "Deformability versus Ductility in Beams with FRP Reinforcement," *Proc. 2nd Intl. Conf. Advanced Composite Materials in Bridges and Structures,* Montreal, August 12–14, pp. 189-200.

Muller, J. (1993). "Bridge to the Future," *Civ. Eng.,* January, pp. 40-43.

Naaman, A. E. (1982). *Prestressed Concrete: Analysis and Design Fundamentals,* McGraw-Hill Companies, Inc., New York.

Nagataki, S. (1978). "On the Use of Superplasticisers," in *Seminar on Special Concretes, 8th FIP Congress (London, 1978),* Fédération Internationale Précontrainte, Wexham Springs.

Namba, H., Matsumoto, S., Suguhara, K., and Kai, Y. (1988). "Concrete Habitable Structure on the Moon," in *Engineering, Construction, and Operations in Space,* S. W. Johnson and J. P. Wetzel, eds., ASCE, New York, pp. 178–189.

Nawy, E. G. (1985). *Reinforced Concrete: A Fundamental Approach,* Prentice Hall, Englewood Cliffs, NJ.

———. (1989). *Prestressed Concrete: A Fundamental Approach,* Prentice Hall, Englewood Cliffs, NJ.

Nawy, E. G., and Neuwerth, G. E. (1976). "Fiberglass as Main Reinforcement for Concrete Two-Way Slabs, Plates, and Beams," *Eng. Research Bull.* No. 56, Rutgers University, New Brunswick, NJ.

Neuerm, Y., and Kaiser, H. (1991). "Strengthening of Structures with CFRP Laminates," in *Advanced Composites Materials in Civil Engineering Structures,* S. L. Iyer and R. Sen, eds., *ASCE Proc. Specialty Conf.,* Las Vegas, January 31–February 1, pp. 224–232.

Neville, A. M. (1970). *Creep of Concrete—Plain, Reinforced, and Prestressed,* American Elsevier, New York.

NYT. (1990). "Light and Tough, New Materials Head for Mass Marketing Stage," *New York Times,* March 25, sec. F, p. 14.

Nielson, L. E. (1994). *Mechanical Properties of Polymers and Composites,* 2nd ed., Marcel Dekker, New York.

Nilson, A. H. (1997). *Design of Prestressed Concrete,* John Wiley & Sons, New York.

Noton, B. R., ed. (1974). *Engineering Applications of Composites, Vol. 3,* Academic Press, New York.

Plecnik, J., Azar, W., and Kabbara, B. (1990). "Composites Applications in Highway Bridges," *Serviceability and Durability of Construction Materials,* B. A. Suprenant, ed., ASCE, New York, pp. 986–995.

Plecnik, J., Sanchez, V. F., Munely, E., Plecnik, J. M., and Ahmed, S. H. (1990). "Development of High-Strength Composite Cables," in *Serviceability and Durability of Construction Materials,* B. A. Suprenant, ed., ASCE, New York, pp. 1016–1025.

PMAT. (1989). *Performance Materials,* August 7, p. 3.

PN. (1992). "Researchers Bank on Composite Bridges," *Plastics News,* April 27, p. 3.

Rabaat, B. G., and Russel, H. G. (1984). *Proposed Replacement of AASHTO Girders with New Optimized Sections,* Transp. Res. Rec., no. 950, vol. 2, Transportation Research Board, Washington, DC, pp. 85–92.

Reinhart, T. J., Brinson, H. F., and Schneider, S. J., eds. (1987). *Engineered Materials Handbook, Volume 1—Composites,* ASM International, Materials Park, OH.

Rich, M. J. (1980). "Application of Advanced Composite Materials to Helicopter Airframe Structures," in *Fibrous Composites in Structural Design,* E. M. Leone, D. W. Oplinger, and J. J. Burke, eds., Plenum, New York.

Romualdi, J. P., and Batson, G. B. (1963a). "Mechanics of Crack Arrest in Concrete," *ASCE J. Eng. Mech. Div.,* 89(EM3), June, pp. 147–168.

———. (1963b). "Behavior of Reinforced Concrete Beams with Closely Spaced Reinforcement," *ACI J. Proc.,* 60(6), June, pp. 775–789.

Rosato, D. V. (1982). "An Overview of Composites" in *Handbook of Composites,* George Lubin, ed., Van Nostrand Reinhold, New York, pp. 1–14.

Rostasy, F. S., and Budelmann, H. (1991). "FRP Tendons for the Post-Tensioning of Concrete Structures," in *Advanced Composites Materials in Civil Engineering Structures,* S. L. Iyer and R. Sen, eds., *ASCE Proc. Specialty Conf.,* Las Vegas, January 31–February 1, New York, pp. 155–166.

Rubinsky, I. A. (1963). *Final Report—Investigation of Glass Fibers as Reinforcement for Prestressed Concrete,* Dept. of Civil Engineering, Princeton University, Princeton, NJ.

Rubinsky, I. A., and Rubinsky, A. (1959). "A Preliminary Investigation of the Use of Fiberglass for Prestressed Concrete," *Magazine of Concrete Research,* September, pp. 71–78.

Saadatmanesh, H., and Ehsani, M. R. (1989). "Application of Fiber Composites in Civil Engineering," in *Structural Materials,* J. F. Orofino, ed., ASCE, New York, pp. 526–535.

———. (1991a). "RC Beams Strengthened with GFRP Plates—I: Experimental Study," *ASCE J. Struct. Eng.,* 117(11), pp. 3417–3433.

———. (1991b). "Fiber Composites Plates for Strengthening Bridge Beams," *Composite Structures,* Elsevier Applied Science, New York.

Salmon, C. S., and Johnson, J. E. (1990). *Steel Structures: Design and Behavior,* Harper & Row, New York.

Schemmel, J. J., and Zia, P. (1990). *Use of High-Strength Concrete in Prestressed Concrete Box Beams for Highway Bridges,* Transp. Res. Rec. no. 1275, Transportation Research Board, Washington, DC, pp. 12–18.

Schmidt, D. L., Davidson, K. L., and Theibert, L. S. (1996). "Evolution of Carbon–Carbon Composites (CCC)," *SAMPE J.,* July/August, pp. 44–50.

Schwartz, M. (1992). *Composite Materials Handbook,* 2nd. ed., McGraw-Hill Companies, Inc., New York.

Schwartz, M., and Jacaruso, G. (1982). "A Giant Step Toward Composite Helicopters, " *Amer. Mach.,* March, pp. 133–140.

Segal, C. L. (1996). "Twenty-First-Century Opportunities for Advanced Fibers and Composites," *SAMPE J.,* July/August, pp. 12–19.

Seible, F. (1996). "Advanced Composites Materials for Bridges in the 21st Century," *Proc. 2nd Intl. Conf. on Advanced Composite Materials in Bridges and Structures,* Montreal, August 12–14, pp. 17–30.

Seible, F., Hegemier, G., Karbhari, V., Burgueno, R., and Davol, A. (1995a). "Shallow Dual-Tied Carbon-Shell Arch Bridge," Civil Engineering Research Foundation, *CERF 1996 Innovation Awards Program,* December.

Seible, F., Hegemier, G., Karbhari, V., Davol, A., and Burgueno, R. (1995b). "Shallow Dual-Tied Carbon-Shell Arch Bridge," Civil Engineering Research Foundation, *CERF 1996 Innovation Awards Program, Innovative Concepts Award,* December.

Seible, F., and Karbhari, V. (1996). "Advanced Composites for Civil Engineering Applications in the United States," *Proc. 1st Intl. Conf. on Composites in Infrastructure,* ICCI 96, Tuscon, AZ, January, pp. 21–37.

Shah, S. P. (1990). "Fiber-Reinforced Concrete," *Concrete Intl.,* 12(3), pp. 81–82.

Shah, S. P., and Ahmed, S. (1985). "Structural Properties of High-Strength Concrete and Its Implications for Precast Prestressed Concrete," *J. Prestressed Conc. Inst.,* 30(6) November–December, pp. 92–119.

Shah, S. P., and Balguru, P. N. (1984). "Ferrocement," in *New Reinforced Concretes, Vol. 2,* R. N. Swami, ed., Surrey University Press, Glasgow, Scotland, pp. 1–51.

Shah, S. P., and Skarendahl, A., eds. (1986). *Steel-Fiber Concrete: US–Sweden Joint Seminar (NSF–STU) Stockholm, June 3–5, 1985,* Elsevier Applied Science, New York.

Shen, C. H., and Springer, G. S. (1976). "Moisture Absorption and Desorption of Composite Materials," *J. Composite Materials,* 10, pp. 2–10.

Shibley, A. M. (1982). "Glass-Filled Thermoplastics," Sec. I, Chapter 7 in G. Lubin, ed., *Handbook of Composite Materials,* Van Nostrand Reinhold, New York, pp. 115–135.

Sippel, T. M., and Mayer, U. (1996). "Bond Behavior of FRP-Strands Under Short-Term, Reversed, and Cyclic Loading," *Proc. 2nd Intl. Conf. Advanced Composite Materials in Bridges and Structures,* Montreal, August 12–14, pp. 837–852.

Slobodzinsky, A. (1982). "Bag Molding Process," Sec. II, Chapter 14 in G. Lubin, ed., *Handbook of Composite Materials,* Van Nostrand Reinhold, New York, pp. 368–390.

Somes, N. F. (1963). "Reinforced Bonded Glass-Fiber Tendons for Prestressed Concrete," *Mag. Concrete Research,* 15(45), November.

Sotiropoulos, S. N. (1991). "Static Response of Bridge Superstructures Made of Fiber-Reinforced Plastic," M.S. thesis, Dept. of Civil Engineering, West Virginia University, Morgantown.

———. (1995). "Performance of FRP Components and Connections for Bridge Deck Systems," PhD thesis, Dept. of Civil Engineering, West Virginia University, Morgantown.

Sotiropoulos, S. N., GangaRao, H. V. S., and Barbero, E. (1991). "Static Response of Bridge Superstructures Made of Fiber-Reinforced Plastic," *Proc. Winter Annual Meeting ASME,* Atlanta, GA.

Sotiropoulos, S. N., GangaRao, H. V. S., and Mongi, A. N. K. (1994). "Theoretical and Experimental Evaluation of FRP Components and Systems," *ASCE J. Struct. Eng.,* 120(2), February, pp. 464–485.

Staunton, R. (1982). "Environmental Effects on Composites," in *Handbook of Composites,* G. Lubin, ed., Van Nostrand Reinhold, New York, pp. 513–530.

Strong, A. B. (1989). *Fundamentals of Composites Manufacturing,* ASM International, Materials Park, OH.

Subrahmanyam, B. V. (1984). "Bamboo Reinforcement for Cement Matrices," in *New Reinforced Concretes, Vol. 2,* R. N. Swami, ed., Surrey University Press, Glasgow, Scotland, pp. 141–194.

Swamy, R. N., and Bahia, H. M. (1985). "The Effectiveness of Steel Fibers as Shear Reinforcement," *Concrete Intl.: Design and Construction,* 7(3), March, pp. 35–40.

Tarricone, P. (1993). "Plastic Potential," *ASCE Civ. Eng.,* August, pp. 62–63.

Tsai, S. W., Hahn, H. T. (1980). *Introduction to Composite Materials,* Technomic Publishing, Lancaster, PA.

United States–Canada Workshop. (1996). *Joint United States–Canada Workshop on the Design of Concrete Beams and Slabs with FRP Rebars,* Montreal, August 11–12.

Vijay, P. V., Kumar, S. V., and GangaRao, H. V. S. (1996). "Shear and Ductility Behavior of Concrete Beams Reinforced with GFRP Rebars," *Proc. 2nd Intl. Conf. Advanced Composite Materials in Bridges and Structures,* Montreal, August 12–14, pp. 217–226.

Vinson, J. R., and Sierakowski, R. L. (1986). *The Behavior of Structures Composed of Composite Materials,* Martinus Nijhoff Publishers, Dordretch, Netherlands.

Vondran, G. L., (1989). "Polypropylene FRC in Steel Deck Composite Slabs," in *Structural Materials,* J. F. Orofino, ed., pp. 1–11.

Wainwright, S. A., Biggs, W. D., Currey, J. D., and Gosline, J. M. (1976). *Mechanical Design in Composites,* John Wiley & Sons, New York.

Weeton, J. W., Peters, D. M., and Thomas, K. L., eds. (1987). *Engineer's Guide to Composite Materials,* ASM International, Materials Park, OH.

Wilson, M., Vijay, P. V., and GangaRao, H. V. S. (1996). *Introduction of Advanced Fiber-Reinforced Plastic Composites for Civil Engineering Infrastructure,* final report, CFC 96-235, Dept. of Civil Engineering, West Virginia University, Morgantown.

Wines, J. C., Dietz, R. T., and Hawley, J. L. (1966). *Laboratory Investigation of Plastic-Glass Fiber Reinforcement for Reinforced and Prestressed Concrete,—Report 2,* misc. paper no. 6-779, U.S. Army Corps of Engineers, February.

Wines, J. C., and Hoff, G. C. (1966). *Laboratory Investigation of Plastic-Glass Fiber Reinforcement for Reinforced and Prestressed Concrete,—Report 1,* misc. paper no. 6-779, U.S. Army Corps of Engineers, February.

WSJ. (1996). "Burning Passion for Her Art Leads to a Hot Invention," *The Wall Street Journal,* September 26, vol. CXXXV, no. 62, p. A1.

Yeung, Y. C. T., and Naylor, A. W. (1996). "Composite Cables for Bridges and Other Structures," *Proc. 2nd Intl. Conf. Advanced Composite Materials in Bridges and Structures,* Montreal, August 12–14, pp. 245–252.

Young, F. and Berger, R. L. (1988). "Cement-Based Materials for Planetary Facilities," in *Engineering Construction and Operations in Space,* S. W. Johnson and J. P. Wetzel, eds., ASCE, New York, pp. 134–145.

Yuan, R. L., Hashem, Z., Green, A., and Bisarnsin, T. (1991). "Fiber-Reinforced Plastic Composite Columns," in *Advanced Composites Materials in Civil Engineering Structures,* S. L. Iyer and R. Sen, eds., *ASCE Proc. Specialty Conf.,* Las Vegas, January 31–February 1, ASCE, New York, pp. 205–211.

Zollo, R. F. (1984). "Collated Fibrillated Polypropylene Fibers in FRC," *Fiber Reinforced Intl. Symp.,* SP-81, ACI, Detroit, MI, pp. 397–409.

CHAPTER 3

Loads on Bridges

3.1
INTRODUCTION

Bridge structures, like buildings, must be designed to resist various kinds of loads: gravity as well as lateral. Generally, the major components of loads acting on highway bridges are dead and live loads, environmental loads (temperature-, wind-, and earthquake-induced), and other loads, such as those arising from braking of vehicles and collisions. Gravity loads are caused by the deadweight of the bridge itself, the superimposed dead load, and the live load, whereas the lateral loads are caused by environmental phenomena such as wind and earthquakes.

Bridge structures serve a unique purpose of carrying traffic over a given span; to this end they are subjected to loads that are not stationary (moving loads). Also, as a consequence, they are subjected to loads caused by the dynamics of moving loads, such as longitudinal force and impact and centrifugal forces. In the case of bridges built over waterways, the bridge substructures (but not superstructures) may be subjected to lateral loads such as earth pressure, water pressure, stream flow pressure, or ice pressure. A comprehensive discussion on loads and forces on bridges is presented in the literature [ASCE, 1981; Buckland and Sexsmith, 1981; Bakht, Cheung, and Dortan, 1982; Nowak and Hong, 1991]. ASCE [1981], with its 149 references and extensive commentary, presents a comprehensive discussion of loads on bridges and is highly recommended for a thorough reading. This important paper also discusses provisions for loads on long-span bridges, a topic not discussed in this book.

The two major components of the bridge design process are the design of the *superstructure* and the design of the *substructure*. With this perspective, the forces acting on bridges can generally be divided into two categories: (1) those acting on the *superstructure*, and (2) those acting on the *substructure*. For designing highway bridges in the United States, various kinds of loads are stipulated in AASHTO 3.2.1 [AASHTO, 1992]. These are shown in Figs. 3.1 and 3.2, respectively, and are described in the following paragraphs.

176

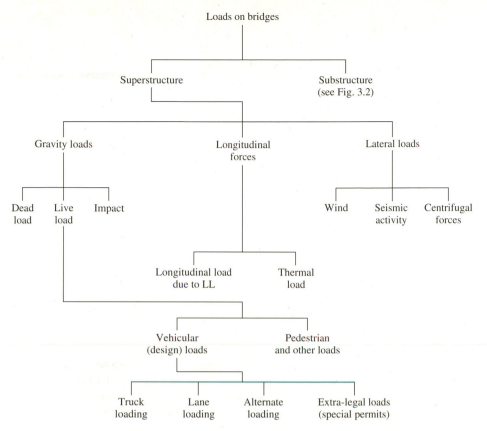

FIGURE 3.1
Loads on bridge superstructures.

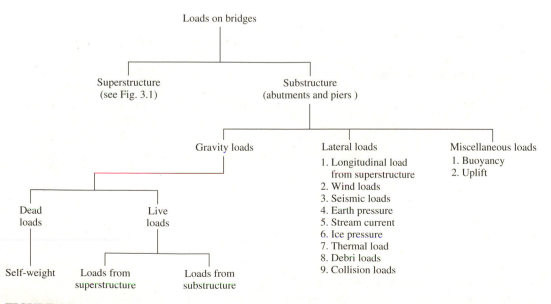

FIGURE 3.2
Loads on bridge substructures.

3.2
LOADS ON BRIDGE SUPERSTRUCTURES

3.2.1 Gravity Loads

3.2.1.1 Dead loads

The dead load on a bridge superstructure consists of the weight of the superstructure plus the weight of other items such as utility pipes (gas, water, oil, etc.), conduits, and cables, which may be carried on the side of or underneath the deck. The self-weight of the superstructure consists of the deck (including the wearing surface), sidewalks, curbs, parapets, railings, the supporting stringers, and floor beams. Depending on the type of bridge, the self-weight of the superstructure may be significant, as in the case of truss and suspension bridges, or it may be a small (but not insignificant) fraction of the total weight, as in the case of short-span slab or slab–stringer bridges. In any case, the dead load can be easily calculated from the known or the assumed sizes of the superstructural components, such as the slab, curb, and stringers. The weights of various materials as given in AASHTO 3.3.6 [AASHTO, 1992] (Appendix A, Table A1) can be used for estimating dead loads.

In the case of decks consisting of reinforced concrete slabs, it is a common practice to pour curbs, parapets, and sidewalks (where provided) *after* the slab has hardened, in order to facilitate screeding off the slab. In such cases, AASHTO 3.23.2.3.1.1, permits equal distribution of their weight (including that of railings), commonly referred to as *superimposed dead load (DL2),* to *all* stringers supporting the deck. However, this practice is reported to be questionable. Recent research on multibeam, precast, pretopped, prestressed bridges suggests that 80 percent of the sidewalk and parapet loads are taken by the exterior and only 20 percent by the interior girders, and that the asphalt wearing surface load is distributed to each beam in the ratio of its moment to the moment of inertia of all the beams [Bishara and Soegiarso, 1993]. However, a common practice is to distribute the dead load due to the self-weight of the deck (including the wearing surface) to the supporting beams on the basis of their tributary widths.

An important consideration in dead-load computations is to include anticipated future wearing surface, widening of the roadway for additional traffic lanes, and additional utilities it may have to carry. Because the top of the deck wears out in a few years, due to abrasion and deterioration from traffic contact, it is generally required to keep in the dead-load design a provision of usually 35 lb/ft^2 of the deck area (between the curbs) for the future wearing surface. This load is to be considered for all deck slabs, including decks with bituminous wearing surfaces. It is a common practice to use *permanent* deck forms (metal or prestressed concrete) for supporting the deck during its pour. These forms are left in place permanently even after the deck slab has hardened, and therefore constitute a part of the dead load that must be supported by stringers (or girders) or by the floor beams that support the deck. To account for the deadweight of these forms (and the concrete in the valleys of the metal deck forms when these are used), a load of usually 15 lb/ft^2 of the deck area is considered additional dead load for design purposes.

In cold regions that experience snowfalls, a deck may occasionally be covered by snow and ice. Snow loads on bridges are generally not critical since accumulated snow on a bridge deck would reduce both the traffic and its speed, thereby reducing the impact force. Accordingly, snow loads on bridges are considered to be offset by accompanying decreases in live loads, and no separate provision is made to consider their effect on design.

Snow shelters provided over bridges should be designed for any snow drift depth of the region. Snow loads in excess of 20 lb/ft^2 can be reduced by $(S - 20)/40$ for each degree of slope of the shelter's roof with the horizontal, a practice permitted by several building codes, such as the *Uniform Building Code* and ASCE 7-93 (formerly ANSI A58.1) [ASCE 1993]. The weight of snow can vary widely—from 5 to 12 lb/ft^3 for freshly fallen snow to 15 to 50 lb/ft^3 for moistened snow compacted by rain [ACI, 1977]. To avoid uncertainty in the weight of snow for any consideration, local officials should be consulted for the pertinent information.

3.2.2 Live Loads

For live loads on bridges as specified in the AASHTO Standard Specifications [AASHTO, 1992], note that the live loads discussed in this chapter and referred to throughout this book apply to *short-span bridges,* not to long-span bridges. This understanding is implied in the introduction to AASHTO [1992]: "Primarily, the specifications set forth the minimum requirements which are consistent with the current practice, and certain modifications may be necessary to suite local conditions. They apply to ordinary highway bridges, and supplemental specifications may be required for unusual types and for bridges longer than 500 feet." Also, note that bridge live-load models are different in different countries. A comparative study of highway bridge loadings in different countries is presented by Thomas [1975].

3.2.2.1 Definitions

A glossary of terms pertaining to descriptions of highway loading and different types of vehicles is provided by the American Association of State Highway and Transportation Officials, published in the *Guide for Maximum Dimensions and Weights of Motor Vehicles and for the Operation of Nondivisible Load Oversize and Overweight Vehicles* [AASHTO, 1991a]. It is excerpted here for reference:

Axle   The common axis of rotation of one or more wheels whether power-driven or freely rotating, and whether in one or more segments, and regardless of the number of wheels carried thereon.

Axle group   An assemblage of two or more consecutive axles considered together in determining their combined load effect on a bridge or pavement structure.

Gross weight   The weight of a vehicle and/or combination of vehicles plus the weight of any load thereon.

Height   The total vertical dimension of a vehicle above the ground surface including any load and load-holding device thereon.

Length   The total longitudinal dimension of a single vehicle, a trailer, or a semitrailer. Length of a trailer or semitrailer is measured from the front of the cargo-carrying unit to its rear, exclusive of all overhang, safety or energy efficiency devices, including air conditioning units, air compressors, flexible fender extensions, splash and spray suppressant devices, bolsters, mechanical fastening devices, and hydraulic lift gates.

Longer combination vehicle   Any combination of two or more tractors or semitrailers which operates on the Interstate System at a gross vehicle weight greater than 80,000 lb.

Quadrum axle   Any four consecutive axles whose extreme centers are not more than 192 in. apart and are individually attached to or articulated from, or both, a common attachment to the vehicle including a connecting mechanism designed to equalize the load between axles.

Semitrailer   Every single vehicle without motive power designed for carrying property and so designed in conjunction and used with a motor vehicle that some part of its own weight and that of its own load rests or is carried by another vehicle and having one or more load-carrying axles.

Single axle   An assembly of two or more wheels whose centers are in one transverse vertical plane or may be included between two parallel transverse planes 40 in. apart extending across the full width of the vehicle.

Special permit   A written authorization to move or operate on a highway a vehicle or vehicles with or without a load of size and/or weight exceeding the limits prescribed for vehicles in regular operation.

Tandem axle   Any two axles whose centers are more than 40 in. but not more than 96 in. apart and are individually attached to or articulated from, or both, a common attachment to the vehicle including a connecting mechanism designed to equalize the load between axles.

Trailer   Every single vehicle without motive power designed for carrying property wholly on its own structure, drawn by a motor vehicle which carries no part of the weight and load of the trailer on its own wheels and having two or more load-carrying axles.

Tridum axle   Any three consecutive axles whose extreme centers are not more than 144 in. apart and are individually attached to or articulated from, or both, a common attachment to the vehicle including a connecting mechanism designed to equalize the load between axles.

Truck   A single unit motor vehicle used primarily for the transportation of property.

Truck tractor   A motor vehicle used primarily for drawing other vehicles and not so constructed as to carry a load other than a part of the weight of the vehicle and load so drawn.

Variable load suspension vehicle   Axles which can be regulated by the driver of the vehicle. These axles are controlled by hydraulic and air suspension systems, mechanically, or by a combination of these methods.

Vehicle combination   An assembly of two or more vehicles coupled together for travel upon a highway.

Width   The total outside transverse dimension of a vehicle including any load or load-holding devices thereon, but excluding approved safety devices and tire bulge due to load.

3.2.2.2 AASHTO highway live loads

Highway bridges are subjected to a variety of nonstationary loads, such as those due to vehicles, motorcycles, bicycles, equestrians, and pedestrians. In the context of bridges, *"live loads"* refers to loads due to moving vehicles that are dynamic, i.e., loads that change their position with respect to time. This is unlike buildings, where live loads are the occupancy loads, which are considered static loads.

Modern highway traffic has evolved over a period of several hundred years. Today's vehicular traffic, which consists of various types of vehicles, from motorcycles and small compact cars to multi-axle vehicles carrying wide loads, has come a long way from the old days of horse-and-buggy and oxcart traffic. As a consequence, the per-wheel load of the vehicles has increased from a few hundred pounds to several thousand pounds, and the types of vehicles vary from simple two-axle vehicles to multi-axle trucks with trailers, tractor/semitrailer combinations, and longer combinations.

Highway loadings are rather complex. At any given time, a bridge deck may be loaded randomly with a multitude of vehicles. The effect of live load on a bridge is a function of several parameters, such as the gross vehicle weight, axle loads, axle configuration, span length, position (longitudinal and transverse) and number of the vehicles (multipresence) on the bridge, speed of the vehicles, stiffness characteristics of the bridge superstructure, and bridge configuration (straight, skewed, or horizontally curved). Together, these parameters introduce analytical complexity and affect force distribution in the supporting structures and its components. Live-load distribution in various portions of a bridge superstructure is discussed in Chapter 4.

From a historical perspective, the genesis of highway design live loads goes back to the mid-nineteenth century. The first live-load procedure for highway bridges was proposed and used by Squire Whipple in 1846. In his *Essay No. 2,* he regarded it "proper to consider the whole area of the roadway covered with men, which is about 100 lb to the square foot, as the greatest load to which the bridge can be exposed," and this standard continued to be in use for many years. However, after many bridge failures, the American Society of Civil Engineers created a committee to determine "the most practical means of averting bridge accidents." This committee, in its March 3, 1875, report, made recommendations for both the railroad and highway bridge loadings. It divided highway bridges into the following three categories [Edwards, 1959]:

A. City and suburban bridges and those over large rivers, where great concentration of weight is possible.
B. Highway bridges in manufacturing districts or on level, well-ballasted roads.
C. County road bridges, where roads are unballasted and the loads hauled are consequently light.

For these bridges, the following design loads were recommended:

	Loads per square foot		
Length of span	A	B	C
60 ft and under	100	100	70
60 to 100 ft	90	75	60
100 to 200 ft	75	60	50
200 to 400 ft	60	50	40

The provision for concentrated loads was made in view of the then commonly used single-axle oxcarts by these recommendations: "City bridges 6 tons; turnpikes 5 tons; country roads 4 tons" [Edwards, 1959].

At the turn of the century, the heaviest highway loading was a road roller, which continued to be used as a model for describing design live loads for highway bridges. The first American practice fixing a definite concentrated axle load for highway traffic is reported to have evolved on July 1877 through *General Specifications for Railway and Highway Bridge Combined over the Wisconsin River at Killburn City, Wisconsin* on the Chicago, Milwaukee, and St. Paul Railroad, proposed by D. J. Whittmore [Edwards, 1959]. In 1895, the Phoenix Bridge Company issued *Standard Specifications of the Phoenix Bridge Company for Steel and Iron Railway and Highway Structures,*

Edwards, [1959], in which a road roller weighing 16 tons was specified with this configuration: 6 tons concentrated on two front rolls spaced 2 ft 6 in. center-to-center, 10 tons on the rear rolls spaced 6 ft center-to-center, axles spaced 11 ft center-to-center. A more complete description of the road rollers to be used in the design of highway bridges was contained in *General Specifications for Steel and Iron Bridges and Viaducts* issued in 1896 by the Canadian Department of Railways and Canals: "Road roller of 32,000 pounds weight distributed as follows: On forward axle 16,000 pounds on wheel 4 feet 2 inches wide, on rear axle 11 feet 2 inches from forward axle 8,000 pounds on each of two wheels, spaced 5 feet 8 inches centers, and 20 inches wide" [Edwards, 1959]. With the development of the motor truck, design loadings were first based on 10-ton and 15-ton trucks. This was followed, in 1924, by a 20-ton truck loading, in anticipation of heavy traffic during the life of the bridge [ASCE, 1958].

The first serious effort to quantify highway live loads was made by the U.S. Department of Agriculture, Office of Public Roads, through its circular no. 100 of August 19, 1913: *Typical Specifications for the Fabrication and Erection of Steel Highway Bridges.* In it, a provision was made for a 15-ton road roller loading in the computation of live-load stresses. On July 1, 1919, the Office of Public Roads became the Bureau of Public Roads, which prepared and issued a revised specification [Edwards, 1959].

The American Association of State Highway Officials was created on December 12, 1914, and in July, 1922, its Committee on Bridges and Allied Structures, which studied the problem of highway live loads, was created. In the 1927 *Specifications for Highway Bridges,* the conference committee representing AASHO and AREA introduced the truck train, a heavy truck preceded and followed by trucks having three-fourths of its weight, shown in Fig. 3.3, as published in the 1935 AASHO specifications [ASCE, 1958]. The primary idea of a train of wheel loads was apparently based on the Cooper loading for railroads, derived from L. E. Moore's discussion of Hussey's paper [Hussey, 1924; Edwards, 1959]. In November 1932, AASHO (now AASHTO) adopted its first policy concerning maximum dimensions, weights, and speeds of motor vehicles [AASHTO, 1991a]. The system of truck train loadings was superseded in 1941 by equivalent lane loading, which was first used as an optional loading in the 1931 AASHO bridge specifications. This system was revised in 1941 when H20-S16 loading was introduced, a system of truck and lane loading which is still in use today [ASCE, 1958].

Since bridges are usually public property, their use is regulated by government laws in terms of maximum weight and the sizes of vehicles that can cross them. The effect of live load is dependent on many factors, such as vehicle weights, axle loads, axle configurations, span lengths, positions (transverse and longitudinal) of vehicles on the bridge, number of vehicles on the bridge (multipresence), stiffness of structural members (slab and girder), and future growth [US Congress, 1964; James et al., 1986; Moses and Ghosn, 1985; James and Heping, 1991; Nowak and Hong, 1991]. Accordingly, highway live loads can be classified as (1) legal loads and (2) design loads.

Legal loads.   A discussion on legal vehicle load and size limitations can be found in the literature [US Congress, 1964; NCHRP, 1979; Moses and Ghosn, 1985; James et al. 1986; TRB 225; James and Heping, 1991; Nowak and Hong, 1991]. The weights of all vehicles are assumed to be concentrated on the wheels and are transmitted through them

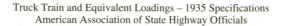

Truck Train and Equivalent Loadings – 1935 Specifications
American Association of State Highway Officials

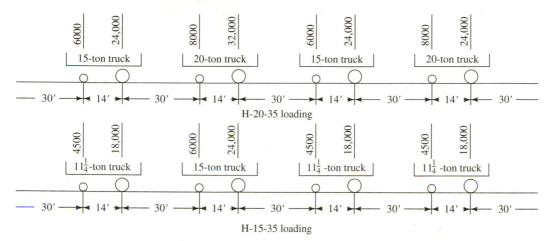

Truck Train Loading

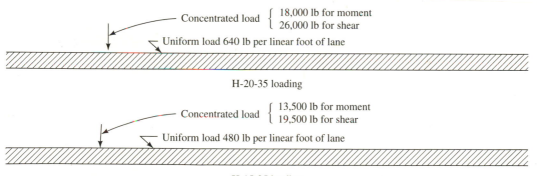

Equivalent Loading
(lane width 10 feet)

FIGURE 3.3
AASHO 1935 specification loading [ASCE, 1958].

to the axles. Figure 3.4 shows silhouettes of most basic vehicle types in use. The maximum permissible weights for wheels and axles and their sizes are as follows [AASHTO, 1991a]:

1. *Single-axle weight:* The total gross weight imposed on the highway by the wheels of any single axle of a vehicle is limited to 20 kips, including any and all weight tolerances.
2. *Tandem-axle weight:* The total gross weight imposed on the highway by a tandem axle shall not exceed 34 kips, including any and all tolerances.
3. *Maximum permissible axle group weight:* The total gross weight imposed on the highway by any group of two or more consecutive axles on a vehicle or combination

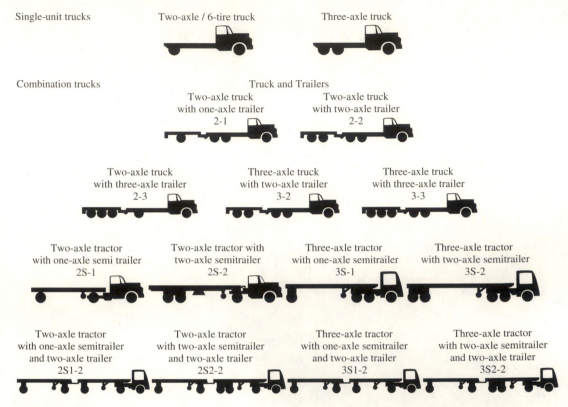

FIGURE 3.4

Typical commercial vehicle types in regular operation as designated by code based on axle arrangement [AASHTO, 1991a]. S = semitrailer. Digit following S indicates the number of axles on the semitrailer. Any digit other than the first in a combination, when not preceded by an S, indicates a trailer and the number of axles. *Example:* The designation 3S1-2 indicates a three-axle truck tractor with tandem rear axles, a semitrailer with a single axle, and a trailer with two axles.

of vehicles should not exceed the values given by Eq. 3.1:

$$W = 500\left(\frac{LN}{N-1} + 12N + 36\right) \tag{3.1}$$

where W = maximum weight, in pounds, carried on any group of two or more axles, computed to the nearest 500 pounds

L = distance, in feet, rounded off to the nearest foot, between the extremes of any group of two or more consecutive axles

N = number of axles in the group under consideration

The development of Eq. 3.1 is based on the premise that the actual stresses must not exceed the allowable design stresses for bridges designed for HS20 and HS15 trucks by more than 5 percent and 30 percent, respectively. A discussion on the proposed modification of Eq. 3.1 has been provided by several researchers [Imbsen, 1987; Moses and Verma, 1986; Moses and Ghosn, 1987; James and Heping, 1991]. It should be recognized that the weight limitations vary from state to state, although several states have adopted weight regulations generally equivalent to Eq. 3.1.

4. *Maximum permissible vehicle gross weight*: The total gross weight imposed on the highway by a vehicle or a combination of vehicles with two or more consecutive axles is to be determined by the application of the maximum permissible axle group weights listed in Table 1 of AASHTO [1991a], with one exception: two consecutive sets of tandem axles may carry a gross load of 34 kips each, provided the overall distance between the first and the last axles of such consecutive sets of tandem axles is 36 feet or more.

5. *Maximum sizes:*

- Maximum height: 13 ft 6 in.
- Maximum overall length of a single truck: 40 ft
- Maximum overall length of a single two-axle or three-axle bus: 40 ft
- Maximum overall length of a semitrailer: 53 ft

Design loads. Design live loads for highways have been and continue to be a subject of considerable research, and several models have been suggested [Harman and Davenport, 1976; ASCE, 1981; Buckland and Sexsmith, 1981; Bakht, Cheung, and Dortan, 1982; Nowak and Hong, 1991; Tabsh and Nowak, 1991]. In the United States, for designing purposes, the design vehicular live loads are divided into three categories (AASHTO 3.7):

1. Design truck loading
2. Design lane loading
3. Alternate military (or design tandem) loading

Design truck loading. Also referred to as standard truck loading, this originated in the 1920s, and although it has been revised periodically, its basic format has remained unchanged. Two systems of loadings are provided: The H loading and the heavier HS loading (the letter "S" refers to *semitrailer*). In each case, there are two standard classes of loadings (AASHTO 3.7.2), which are designated (AASHTO 3.7.3) as follows:

- H15-44 and H20-44
- HS15-44 and HS20-44

In these designations, the number 44 refers to the fact that these loadings were standardized and first published in the 1944 AASHO specifications. The H loadings consist of a two-axle truck, and the numbers 15 and 20 in the loading classification refer to the gross truck weight in tons (1 ton = 2000 lb). The HS loadings consist of a tractor truck with semitrailer (designated by the letter "S" in "HS"). The numbers following the letters "HS" indicate the total load in tons carried by the *axles* of the tractor; the load on the semitrailer is additional. The variable axle loading has been introduced for two specific reasons:

1. It approximates more closely the spacings of axles for the tractor trailer currently in use.
2. It provides a more satisfactory design loading for continuous spans. The variable spacing of axles permits positioning of heavy axles on the adjoining spans to produce maximum negative moments.

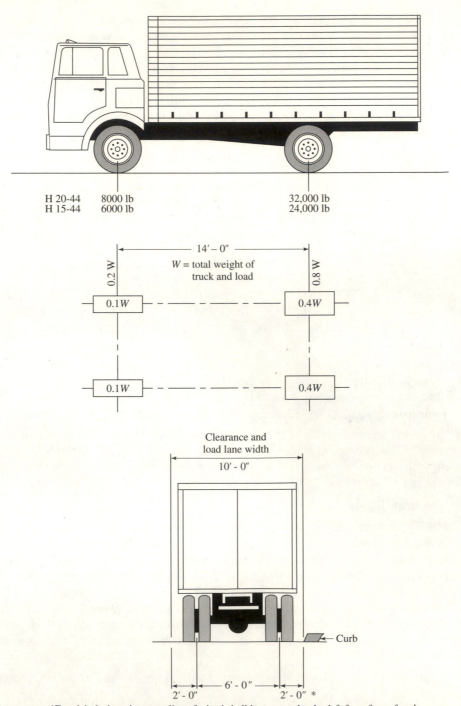

| H 20-44 | 8000 lb | 32,000 lb |
| H 15-44 | 6000 lb | 24,000 lb |

14′ – 0″

0.2 W

W = total weight of truck and load

0.8 W

0.1W — 0.4W

0.1W — 0.4W

Clearance and load lane width

10′ - 0″

Curb

2′ - 0″   6′ - 0″   2′ - 0″ *

*For slab design, the centerline of wheel shall be assumed to be 1 ft from face of curb.

FIGURE 3.5
Standard H truck loading [AASHTO, 1992].

Note that the H15 and HS15 trucks are *three-fourths* as heavy as the H20 and HS20 trucks, respectively (Figs. 3.5 and 3.6). The older versions of AASHTO specifications (then AASHO specifications) specified a smaller loading also, H10 and HS10 loading, with loads one-half as much as the corresponding H20 and HS20 loading. However, in recent years, this loading has been deleted. It is pointed out here that some agencies design their bridges for HS25 trucks, which are simply assumed to have axle loads 25 percent heavier than those of HS20 trucks. For example, the Pennsylvania Department of Transportation mandates [Penn DOT, 1993] that

> All new bridges, regardless of roadway class or funding source, shall be designed for HS25 loading (125 percent of HS20-44), 125 percent of alternate loading (two axles, 4 feet apart, with each axle carrying 30,000 pounds), or the Pennsylvania permit load (P-82) used for permit purposes, whichever produces the greatest effect for the loading combination under consideration. When using P-82, the design must be in accordance with Loading Combination Group IB in AASHTO Table A3.22.1A.

It should be recognized, however, that these vehicles are merely *model,* or *hypothetical,* vehicles and do not resemble any particular real vehicle in existence. The presumption is that any legal actual vehicle crossing the bridge should *not* cause stresses greater than those caused by the hypothetical vehicle.

Design lane loading. Lane loading was developed to better model loading on long spans, where a string of light vehicles might be critical. It approximates a 20-ton truck preceded and followed by a 15-ton truck. Essentially, the assumption of uniformly distributed lane loading obviates the necessity of having more than one design truck in a lane, regardless of the span length and the number of spans, resulting in a simple design procedure for long-span bridges.

Lane loading also has two classes of loadings, and in each class two different loadings are provided. These loadings are designated in the same manner as the truck loadings (namely, H15-44, HS15-44, H20-44, HS20-44). Basically, the lane load consists of a *uniform load* accompanied by a *concentrated load.* The value of the concentrated load is different for shear than for moment. Furthermore, as with truck loadings, the loads for H15 lane loading, including the concentrated loads, are only three-fourths as heavy as those for the HS20 lane loading. Both the concentrated and the uniform load specified for lane loading are assumed to be distributed over a 10-ft width normal to the centerline of the lane (Fig. 3.7). *Different* concentrated loads are to be used for calculating forces in the supporting members. The lighter concentrated loads are to be used for calculating bending moment; the heavier concentrated load should be used for calculating shear.

Alternate military (or design tandem) loading. This loading originated in 1956 as a Federal Highway Administration requirement for bridges on the Interstate Highway System, to provide load-carrying capacity for certain heavy military vehicles. It is applicable to certain bridges in the state highway systems. The alternate bridge loading consists of two axles spaced 4 ft apart with each axle carrying 24 kips. This load produces slightly higher live-load moments in spans under 40 ft.

AASHTO 3.7.4 [AASHTO, 1992] specifies that this alternate loading, or the HS20-44 loading, whichever produces the greater stress, be considered as the minimum design loading for highway bridges. The alternate loading is shown in Fig. 3.8.

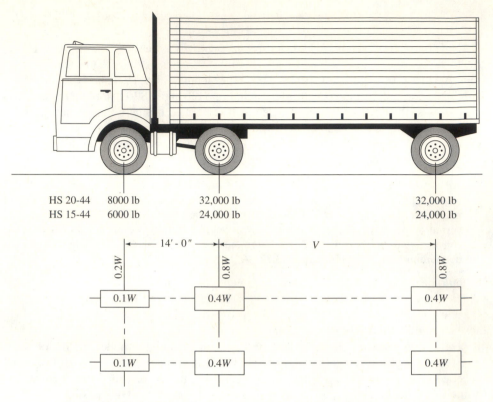

| HS 20-44 | 8000 lb | 32,000 lb | 32,000 lb |
| HS 15-44 | 6000 lb | 24,000 lb | 24,000 lb |

W = Combined weight on the first two axles, which is the same as for the corresponding H truck.
V = Variable spacing —14 ft to 30 ft, inclusive. Spacing to be used is that which produces maximum stresses.

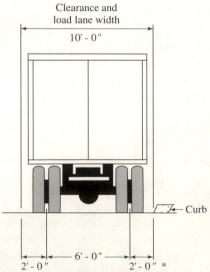

*For slab design, the centerline of wheel shall be assumed to be 1 ft from face of curb.

FIGURE 3.6
Standard HS truck loading [AASHTO, 1992].

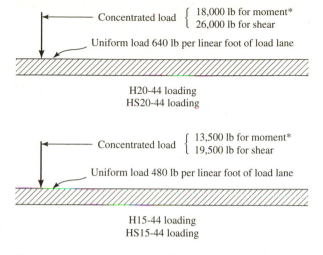

Concentrated load $\left\{\begin{array}{l}\text{18,000 lb for moment*}\\\text{26,000 lb for shear}\end{array}\right.$

Uniform load 640 lb per linear foot of load lane

H20-44 loading
HS20-44 loading

Concentrated load $\left\{\begin{array}{l}\text{13,500 lb for moment*}\\\text{19,500 lb for shear}\end{array}\right.$

Uniform load 480 lb per linear foot of load lane

H15-44 loading
HS15-44 loading

*For the loading of continuous spans involving lane loading, refer to Article 3.11.3, which provides for an additional concentrated load.

FIGURE 3.7
Standard H15 and HS15, and H20 and HS20 lane loading [AASHTO, 1992].

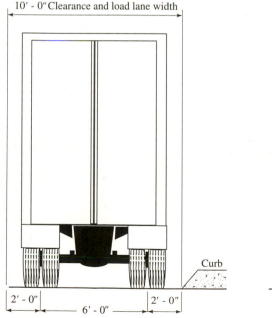

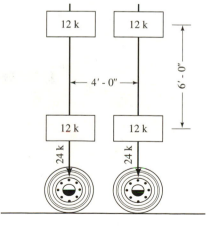

FIGURE 3.8
Alternate live loading [AASHTO, 1992].

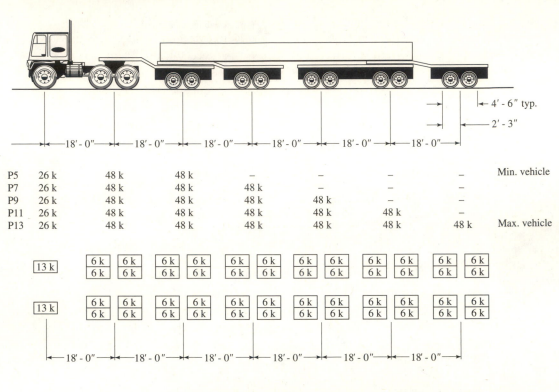

P5	26 k	48 k	48 k	–	–	–	–	Min. vehicle
P7	26 k	48 k	48 k	48 k	–	–	–	
P9	26 k	48 k	48 k	48 k	48 k	–	–	
P11	26 k	48 k	48 k	48 k	48 k	48 k	–	
P13	26 k	48 k	48 k	48 k	48 k	48 k	48 k	Max. vehicle

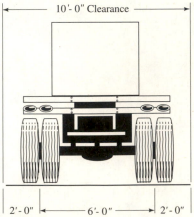

FIGURE 3.9

Permit live loads, state of California [CALTRANS 1992]. *Note:* Load occupies standard 10-ft-wide lanes. The transverse wheel location is the same as for the AASHTO HS vehicles.

Considerations should be given to local or regional modifications to design truck, design tandem, or design lane load, in view of an ever-growing demand to permit loadings on our highways that are heavier and wider than the typical AASHTO H or HS loadings. These considerations may arise from various conditions, such as

- The legal load of a given jurisdiction is significantly greater than the AASHTO design loads.
- The roadway is expected to carry unusually high percentages of truck traffic.
- Due to some unusual circumstances, many trucks can collect on certain areas of the bridge.
- Special industrial loadings are common due to the location of the bridge.

Such loadings can be described as *extralegal live loads,* and are allowed on bridges by special permits issued by the state highway agencies having jurisdictions over these bridges. The state highway agencies designate these special loadings variously, e.g., *P-loading*[1] in California (Fig. 3.9) [CALTRANS, 1992] and Pennsylvania (Fig. 3.10) [PennDOT, 1993] or *U-* or *L-loading* in Alaska (Fig. 3.11), and the loadings may differ in their gross vehicle weights and axle spacings. For example, California's P-loading consists of a family of idealized vehicles used for rating bridge capacities. The P-loading has five classes—P5, P7, P9, P11, and P13. The number following "P" indicates the total number of axles in the group. Each loading class consists of a front axle (26 kips) followed by pairs of tandems (assumed as single concentrated loads) of two each, each 48 kips and 18 feet apart. Similarly, the state of Alaska specifies special permit loads as U80 (total truck load 80 tons) and L90 (total truck load 90 tons) loadings for the design of bridges to support unusually heavy trucks in logging areas. A discussion on the modeling of extralegal live loads can be found in the literature [Kulicki and Mertz, 1991]. Nutt, Schamber, and Zokaie [1988] provide configurations of operating vehicles for several U.S. states.

It should be recognized that there are no comprehensive specifications for live loads for long-span bridges. Special considerations should be made in specifying live loads for such bridges since, by virtue of their length, they are subjected to significantly different traffic conditions compared with those for short- and medium-span bridges. For example, it is suggested that the maximum loading on long-span bridges occurs with traffic stationary; consequently, no allowance for *impact* (described later) need be made. Live loads for long-span bridges are not discussed in this text; a discussion on the subject can be found in the literature [Ivy et al., 1954; Buckland et al., 1978, 1980; Buckland, 1991; ASCE, 1981]. AASHTO 3.11.4 stipulates that, on both simple and continuous spans, the type of loading to be used, whether truck or lane load, should be the loading that would produce the maximum stress.

3.2.2.3 Selection and application of bridge live load for design

Since bridges carry multiple lanes of traffic and since several vehicles may occupy several traffic lanes on a bridge simultaneously, it is important to understand the placement of bridge loadings on a deck that will result in the greatest stress in the supporting members. With this perspective in mind, the following should be remembered:

---

[1] The letter "P" stands for *permit.*

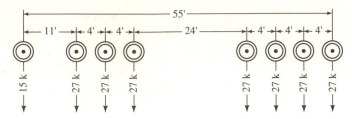

Note: Load occupies standard 10-ft-wide lane.
Transverse wheel location is the same as in HS vehicles.

FIGURE 3.10
204-k eight-axle Pennsylvania permit load (P-82) [PennDOT, 1993].

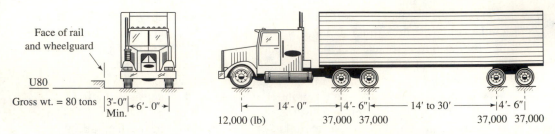

Impact on end cantilevers = 100%; Live-load deflection = $\frac{\text{SPAN}}{750}$ (Max.–U80; one truck on $\cancel{\text{L}}$)

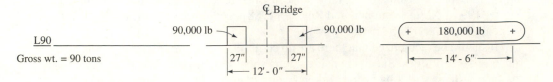

Impact on end cantilevers = 30%

Design load: HS20-44 or one U80 off-highway truck
Special permit load: one 90-ton log loader (L90)

FIGURE 3.11
Permit live loads, state of Alaska [USS, 1975].

1. The lane loading or standard truck is assumed to occupy a width of 10 ft (AASHTO 3.6.1).
2. The standard truck or lane loads are to be placed in 12-ft-wide design traffic lanes, spaced across the entire bridge roadway width measured between curbs (AASHTO 3.6.2).
3. The number of design lanes should be determined by taking the integer part of the ratio $w/12$, where w is the clear roadway width, in feet, between the curbs and/or barriers. Fractional parts of the design lanes are not permitted. Roadway widths from 20 to 24 feet can be assigned two design lanes, each equal to one-half the roadway width (AASHTO 3.6.3).

4. In computing stresses, each 10-foot lane load or single standard truck is to be used as a unit, and fractions of lane load widths or trucks should not be used (AASHTO 3.11.1).
5. The traffic lanes should be placed in such numbers and positions on the roadway, and the loads should be placed in such positions within their individual traffic lanes, that their effect will be to produce maximum stresses in the member under consideration (AASHTO 3.11.2).
6. The preceding implies that, for simple-span bridges, the *entire* length of the bridge should be loaded with the lane load (uniform load with *one* appropriate concentrated load) to calculate moment and shears in the supporting member. However, if truck

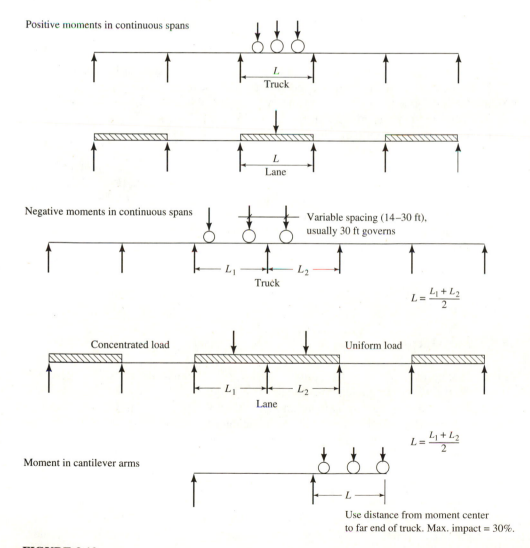

FIGURE 3.12
Loading on continuous spans for maximum positive and negative moments [CALTRANS, 1992].

loading is to be used, *only one truck per lane* (H or HS) can be placed on the entire span, regardless of its length. Because of this reason, a designer should carefully evaluate the governing design loads (truck or lane) and calculate corresponding moment and shears. It is quite likely that, for a given span, the moment may be governed by the standard lane loading, whereas the shear may be governed by the standard truck loading. Values of moments and shear for H and HS loadings on simple spans are given in the appendix (Tables A.3 through A.6). It can be seen from these tables that, beyond the spans of 56 ft for H and 140 ft for HS loadings, standard lane loading, rather than the standard truck loading, governs. *It is very important to recognize here that while design of some components in a given bridge may be governed by the truck loading, that of others in the same bridge may be governed by the lane loading.*

7. When continuous spans are involved in design, the loading as previously described needs to be modified to determine the maximum negative moments. For maximum positive moment, only one concentrated load per lane need be placed, along with the uniform load (or only one standard truck, in the case of standard truck loading), combined with as many spans loaded uniformly as are required to produce maximum moment. For maximum negative moment, a second, equal-weight concentrated load is placed in an adjacent span in the series in such a position that it will result in producing the maximum effect. Figure 3.12 shows the positions of various loads in appropriate spans for maximum positive and negative moments (AASHTO 3.11.3).

Generally, in continuous spans, the lane loading governs the maximum negative moment, except for spans less than about 45 ft in length, where the HS truck loading, with its 32-kip axles, variably spaced from 14 to 30 ft, may govern. The exact point of change of the controlling load depends on the ratio of the adjacent span lengths. For spans of more than about 110 ft, the positive moment for continuous spans is usually controlled by the lane loading.

3.3
IMPACT

3.3.1 Introduction

From an engineering standpoint, *impact load* can be defined as a *suddenly applied load.* From a vibration standpoint, impact load is defined as a load whose period of application is shorter than the fundamental period for the structure on which the load is applied. In the context of bridges, the phenomenon of impact is related to the bridge-vehicle interaction. From a designer's viewpoint, it deals with the notion of dynamic load amplification.

Major concerns about the dynamic action of moving loads evolved in the eighteenth century in the context of studying the strength of bridges. There was little, if any, agreement among engineers in the middle of the nineteenth century over the effect of a moving load on a beam. "While some assumed that a load moving with high speed acts like a suddenly applied load and may produce deflections larger than those corresponding to the static action, others argued that at very high speeds there was insufficient time for the load to drop through the distance of the expected dynamical deflection" [Timoshenko, 1952]. Historically speaking, Thomas Young, through his studies of prismatic beams, was the first to show how important the dynamical effect of a load can be. J. V. Poncelet (1788–1867), influenced by contemporary suspension bridges, made a more detailed study of this dynamic action. Dynamic tests on beams by Willis, James, and Galton[2] during the 1850s showed that deflections increased with increases in speed and that dynamic deflections two to three times larger than the static deflections were obtained at higher speeds. However, experimental investigation of actual bridges did not show the effects of speed in such a marked way. Considering only the fundamental mode of vibration, G. G. Stokes (1819–1903) was the first to show that the magnitude of dynamic deflection depended on the ratio of the period of the beam's fundamental mode of vibration to the time taken by the moving force to cross the span. Progress in this field was made by Homersham Cox, who concluded in 1849 from energy considerations that dynamic deflection was limited to twice the static deflection. Work to improve the knowledge concerning the dynamic action continued both in England and in Germany, where deflection of cast-iron bridges on the Baden Railroad were measured for various speeds of locomotives. Further improvement of the theory of impact was provided by Saint-Venant (1797–1886) [Timoshenko, 1952]. Much of the earlier work done regarding impact focused on railway bridges. It was later that attention shifted to highway bridges as their spans became larger and the loads of highway vehicles increased.

In the United States, until 1900, although it was common knowledge that loadings moving at varying speeds subjected highway bridges to dynamic action—vibration and oscillation, commonly termed *impact*—no special effort had been made to determine its intensity. Even the highway bridge specifications did not contain any empirical formulas to provide for impact. During the early years, lack of understanding of the impact phenomenon made it somewhat customary to post, even on new and sturdy bridges, signboards warning traffic to cross at a walking pace. Signs worded "Warning! Walk your horses. Penalty: $5.00 fine" or "$5.00 fine for crossing faster than a walk" were common [Edwards, 1959].

The first research dealing with highway impact forces was carried out at the Civil Engineering Department of the University of Illinois. Based on this research, the first American scientific paper on highway impact forces appears to be one entitled "Some Experiments on Highway Bridges under Moving Loads" by Prof. F. O. Daffier, presented at the Western Society of Civil Engineers in 1913 [Edwards, 1959]. Considerable research and numerous field studies have been done in this area in the past two decades; a brief summary is presented by Chan and O'Connor [1990a,b] and by Huang, Wang, and Shahawy [1992].

The interaction of moving loads and the bridge superstructure results in dynamic amplification of the moving loads, resulting in vibrations and increased stresses. This *dynamic response* is considered in design, according to AASHTO specifications [AASHTO, 1992], by ascribing *impact factor* (*I*), in terms of the static equivalent

---

[2]The Willis report describing the experiments by Prof. R. Willis, Capt. H. James, and Lt. D. Galton can be found in the appendix of Peter Barlow's (1776–1892) book *A Treatise on the Strength of Timber,* London, 1851.

of dynamic and vibratory effects. Similar provisions exist in other design codes. Recently, however, the term *impact factor* has been dropped in some codes [Chan and O'Connor, 1990a,b; OHBDC, 1993; AASHTO, 1994a] in favor of the term *dynamic load allowance,* since the phenomenon is related to the dynamic response of the bridge. Regardless of the terminology used, the dynamic effect of moving loads is described mathematically as follows:

$$\text{Dynamic response} = \text{impact factor} \times \text{maximum static response}$$

$$\text{Total response} = (1 + I) \times \text{maximum static response}$$

Consideration of the dynamic response is important for several reasons:

1. Stresses are increased above those due to static-load applications, a cause of primary concern in bridge design.
2. Excessive vibration may cause, in the minds of the vehicle occupants, a psychological fear of driving over an unsound bridge.
3. Excessive deck vibrations may cause discomfort to the pedestrian traffic.

Research [ASCE, 1958; Walker and Velestos, 1963; Biggs, 1964; Fenves, Velestos, and Siess, 1962] has shown that there are two primary causes of large vibrations of bridges:

1. Initial bounce (hammering effect) of the vehicle on its own springs as it enters the span, caused by the roughness of the approach (riding surface irregularities). This may be due to long undulations in the roadway pavement, such as those caused by the settlement of the fill, or to the resonant excitation as a result of similar frequencies of the bridge and the vehicle.
2. Dynamic response due to the surface irregularities of the bridge deck itself, such as deck joints, cracks, potholes, and delaminations.

Research has indicated that vibratory effects of moving loads on a simple-span highway bridge can be mathematically investigated based on the following assumptions:

1. The floor system, along with supporting stringers or girders, may be represented by a single beam of equivalent stiffness.
2. Of various modes of vibration, only the fundamental mode of vibration need be considered.
3. Regardless of the number of axles and the corresponding number of springs and flexible tires in a vehicle, it can be idealized as a one-degree-of-freedom system.
4. Although the weight of the vehicle is actually applied at the wheels, it is assumed, for simplicity, to be applied at the center of its mass.

It should be recognized that long-span bridges will require special analysis for wind-induced vibrations, including wind tunnel testing.

The maximum dynamic deflection of a bridge deck due to vehicle impact has been found to be a function of the initial amplitude of bounce of the vehicle and its natural frequency. However, the mathematical treatment of the dynamic deflection problem, which has been elusive for researchers, is complicated by many factors, as suggested by several researchers [Cantieni, 1984; Hwang and Nowak, 1989; Chan and O'Connor,

1990a,b; Schelling, Galdos, and Sahin, 1990; Nowak and Hong, 1991; Tabsh and Nowak, 1991; Buckland, 1991; Huang, Wang, and Shahawy, 1992; Wang and Huang, 1992]:

1. Dynamic characteristics of the bridge (i.e., type of superstructure and span length)
2. Roughness of the riding surface of the deck
3. Dynamic characteristics and configuration of various kinds of vehicles
4. Speed of vehicles
5. Multipresence of vehicles on the bridge and vehicle spacings
6. Probability of coincidence of maximum load and maximum "impact"
7. Number of spans, simple or continuous
8. Bridge configuration: straight, skewed, or horizontally curved
9. Effects of braking
10. Damping characteristics of bridge element
11. Girder position: interior or exterior

Research suggests that the most accurate indicator of the dynamic response of a bridge superstructure is its natural frequency [Shepard and Aves, 1973; Cantieni, 1984; Chan and O'Connor, 1990a,b; Schelling, Galdos, and Sahin, 1990; Huang, Wang, and Shahawy, 1992]. The first *natural* (or *flexural,* or *fundamental*) *frequency, f,* of a bridge considered as a simply supported beam is

$$f = \frac{\pi}{2L^2} \sqrt{\frac{EI_x}{m}} \tag{3.2}$$

where L = span length
I_x = moment of inertia of the structural element considered
m = mass of the structural element considered

Based on the results obtained by the Concrete Structures Section of the Swiss Federal Laboratory for Materials Testing and Research (EMPA) through static and standardized tests on 226 slab-and-beam type highway bridges conducted from 1958 to 1981, Cantieni [1984] suggested a relationship of the type

$$f = 95.4L^{-0.933} \tag{3.3}$$

A plot of Eq. 3.3 showing the relationship between the natural frequency of the bridge and its span is shown in Fig. 3.13. It is seen that a curve defined by $Lf = 100$ also fits the data points and approximates Eq. 3.3. A study shows that characteristic curves bearing the relationship Lf = constant can be drawn for various types of superstructures (constant = 60, 90, 120, and 150), as shown in Fig. 3.14.

In recognition of the significant influence of the natural frequency of the bridge superstructure (dynamic characteristics) on its dynamic response, the 1983 edition of the Ontario Highway Bridge Design Code (OHBDC) [OHBDC, 1983] specified values of impact factor based on the first flexural frequency of bridge, as shown in Fig. 3.15. However, this provision has recently been deleted, and new empirical values of the dynamic allowance have been specified, as shown in Table 3.1 [Cantieni, 1984].

The dynamic response of long-span bridges is markedly different from that of short- and medium-span bridges. Since the dynamic component of the total response results only when the traffic is *moving*, and because the distances between the *moving* vehicles

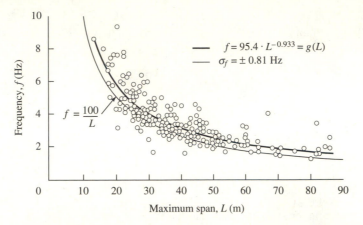

FIGURE 3.13
Natural frequency–span relationship [Cantieni, 1984; Chan and O'Connor, 1990a].

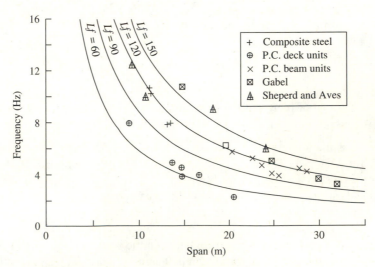

FIGURE 3.14
Natural frequency–span relationship for various superstructure types [Chan and O'Connor, 1990a].

are larger than when they are stationary, even with impact the load intensity is much reduced. For long-span bridges, the impact problem becomes even more complex, since it is recognized that for such bridges maximum loading occurs with traffic stationary, and, consequently, it is suggested that further allowance for impact is not necessary [Buckland, 1991].

Disagreement continues among researchers about the range of values of the dynamic load allowance. Observed values of impact factors higher than those given by

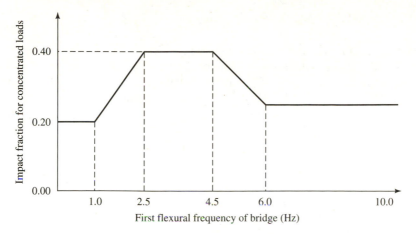

FIGURE 3.15
Impact factors according to OHBDC [Buckland, 1991].

TABLE 3.1
Dynamic load allowance [OHBDC, 1993]

Number of axles	DLA*
1	0.4
2	0.3
3 or more	0.25

*DLA = Dynamic load allowance

AASHTO [1992] have been reported by many researchers [Fleming and Romualdi, 1961; Csagoly and Dortan, 1977; Schilling, 1982; Phillips and Carr, 1984; O'Connor and Pritchard, 1985]; their findings have been summarized and discussed by Chan and O'Connor [1990b]. Based on a study of 37 different steel bridges, Schilling [1982] suggests that the value of the impact factor $(1 + I)$ could be as high as 2.0. O'Connor and Pritchard [1985] report values of $(1 + I)$ to vary randomly between 0.92 and 2.32. Phillips and Carr [1984] recorded values of $(1 + I)$ in excess of 2.0. From the observations of 226 instrumented bridges in Switzerland, impact factors as high as 1.7 in the case of undisturbed pavement and 3.5 for the case with a plank ($50 \times 300 \times 5000$ mm, or approximately $2 \times 12 \times 200$ in.) placed perpendicular to the traffic flow have been reported by Cantieni [1984]. However, based on some studies of the dynamic load allowance problem [Billing, 1982; Cantieni, 1983; O'Connor and Chan, 1988; Agarwal and Billing, 1990; Bakht and Pinjarkar, 1990], these high values are reported to be questionable [Bakht and Pinjarkar, 1989; Bakht, Billing, and Agarwal, 1992]. Amid all this controversy, the current design practice according to AASHTO [1992] is to limit the maximum value of $(1 + I)$ to 1.3; i.e., $I_{max} = 0.3$, although higher values are suggested elsewhere [OHBDC, 1993; AASHTO, 1994a].

3.3.2 Provision in AASHTO Specifications

To simplify this complex problem of evaluating the dynamic effects of moving loads, current bridge design practice is to use an empirical impact factor that varies only with span [Biggs, Suer, and Louw, 1959; Fenves, Velestos, and Seiss, 1962; Walker and Velestos, 1963; Biggs, 1964]. AASHTO 3.8.2 specifies that the dynamic effects of moving loads be expressed as a *fraction of the live loads* according to the following empirical formula:

$$I = \frac{50}{L + 125} \tag{3.4}$$

where I = Impact factor (maximum 30 percent or 0.3)
L = Length, in feet, of the portion of the span that is loaded to produce the maximum stress in the member

Equation 3.4 was first used in the Conference Committee Specifications of 1927 and is based on the results of early tests on railroad bridges made from 1907 to 1911 under the supervision and direction of the American Railway Engineering and Maintenance of Way Association (renamed in 1912 the American Railway Engineering Association, AREA) [Edwards, 1959]. The general level and the limiting value of the formula are based on A. H. Fuller's tests on highway bridges in Iowa in 1922–1925 [ASCE, 1958]. Prior to this time, various formulas, based primarily on the opinions of bridge engineers or on limited and inconclusive tests, were in use. The two most commonly used were

$$I = \frac{L^2}{L + D} \tag{3.5}$$

where L and D are computed live and dead loads, respectively; and

$$I = \frac{300}{L + 300} \tag{3.6}$$

where L is the length (ft) subjected to live load to produce the greatest stress in the member under consideration [Edwards, 1959]. Interestingly, the Japanese Specification for Highway Bridges [JRA, 1980] uses an impact formula similar in format to that of AASHTO:

$$I = \frac{20}{50 + L} \tag{3.7}$$

where L = span length (m) of a straight girder. Multiplying both the numerator and the denominator of the right side of Eq. 3.7 by 2.5 yields

$$I = \frac{50}{2.5L + 125} \tag{3.8}$$

Noting that 1 m = 3.28 ft, the similarity between Eqs. 3.4 and 3.8 is quite evident. Alternatively, dividing the numerator and the denominator of the right side of Eq. 3.7

by 3.28 yields

$$I = \frac{15.2}{L + 38} \qquad (3.9)$$

where L = span length in meters ($= L$ (ft)/3.28).

The dynamic responses in a beam, such as shear and moments, due to impact, are calculated by simply multiplying static values by the fraction I. Alternatively, total response, including the dynamic, can be obtained by multiplying the static response by the factor $(1 + I)$, as illustrated in Example 3.1.

> **EXAMPLE 3.1.** Calculate moment and shears due to HS20-44 loading for a simple span of 100 ft.
>
> **Solution.** From Table A.6 in the Appendix, for $L = 100$ ft,
>
> $$M_L = 1524.0 \text{ k-ft}$$
>
> $$V_L = 65.3 \text{ kips}$$
>
> where subscript L denotes live load. From Eq. 3.4,
>
> $$I = \frac{50}{L + 125} = \frac{50}{100 + 125} = 0.222$$
>
> Total forces, including the effect of impact, are
>
> $$M_{L+I} = M(1 + I) = 1524(1 + 0.222) = 1862 \text{ k-ft}$$
>
> $$V_{L+I} = V(1 + I) = 65.3(1 + 0.222) = 79.8 \text{ kips}$$

For uniformity of application of the impact formula, the loaded length, L, is defined in Fig. 3.14 as follows:

1. For roadway floor: the design span length
2. For transverse member, such as floor beams: the span of the member from center to center of supports
3. For computing truck load moments: the span length, or for cantilever arms, the length of the loaded portion of the span from the moment center to the farthest axle
4. For shear due to truck loads: the length of the loaded portion of span from the point under consideration to the far reaction; for cantilever arms, use a 30-percent impact factor
5. For continuous spans: the length of span under consideration for positive moment, and the average of two adjacent loaded spans for negative moment

The effect of impact is the greatest in those portions of a bridge superstructure that are in closest contact with the deck. The effect of impact should also be included in loads transferred from superstructure to substructure, as appropriate. AASHTO 3.8 identifies various portions of a bridge for which impact should or should not be considered by classifying them into two groups:

Group 1. Portions of a bridge structure for which impact must be considered:

- Superstructure, including the legs of rigid frames
- Piers, with or without bearings of all kinds
- The portions above the groundline of concrete or the steel piles supporting the super-structure

Group 2. Portions of a bridge structure for which impact can be ignored:

- Abutments, retaining walls, and piles, except as specified above
- Foundation pressures and footings
- Sidewalk loads
- Timber structures
- Culverts and structures having 3 ft or more of earth cover

One can easily calculate the length L for which the impact factor is just 0.3. This can be done by substituting 0.3 in Eq. 3.4 and solving for L. Equation 3.4 can be written as

$$\frac{50}{I} = L + 125 \tag{3.10}$$

Substitution of $I = 0.3$ in Eq. 3.10 yields

$$\frac{50}{0.3} = L + 125$$

from which one derives $L = 41.7$ ft; i.e., *for all lengths 41.7 ft and smaller, the impact factor will always be 0.3.*

The preceding AASHTO provisions for impact are applicable to straight bridges only. The behavior of curved-girder bridges is somewhat different from that of the ordinary straight-girder bridges and is not discussed in this text. Research by Shore and Rabizadeh [1974a,b] forms the basis of the current AASHTO provisions [AASHTO, 1993] relative to the dynamic impact factors for the design of horizontally curved box girder bridges. Impact factors for horizontally curved bridges are discussed by Heins [1976, 1978], Nakai and Yoo [1988], and Galdos, Schelling, and Sahin [1993]. Schelling, Galdos, and Sahin [1990] have presented a study of dynamic impact factors for some 288 representative curved bridges. These include one, two, three, and four continuous-span box girder bridges with various span lengths, numbers of spans, and span length/radius of curvature ratios (L/R) for two-, three-, and four-box combinations.

3.3.3 New Specifications for Impact Loads

The AASHTO–LRFD specifications [1994a] specify a change from the AASHTO 1992 provisions for impact loads, partly based on Page's work [1976]. These values are based on the limit states. First, the term "impact" has been replaced by a new term, "dynamic load allowance." Second, the impact formula of the current specifications has been deleted, and the magnitudes of dynamic load allowance (impact loads) are taken as shown in Table 3.2. The basic method of estimating the dynamic effects of moving loads, however, remains the same (empirical); i.e., the dynamic effects are to be taken as percentages or fractions (IM) of the live loads. The values of IM given in Table 3.2 are based on the rational assumption that in the majority of highway bridges, the dynamic component of the response does not exceed 25 percent of the static response to vehicles. However, according to the AASHTO–LRFD commentary C3.6.2.1 [1994a], the specified live-load combination of the design truck and lane load represents a group

TABLE 3.2

Dynamic load allowance, *IM*
[AASHTO, 1994a]

	IM
Deck joints—all limit states	75%
All other components	
Fatigue and fracture limit state	15%
All other limit states	33%

of exclusion vehicles at least four-thirds times that caused by the design truck alone on short- and medium-span bridges. Thus, the value of 33 percent in Table 3.2 is the product of $\frac{4}{3}$ and the basic 25 percent. The dynamic load allowance is *not* to be applied to pedestrian loads or to the design lane load.

3.3.4 Effect of Vibrations on Pedestrian Bridges

Pedestrian bridges are typically designed for pedestrian loads (discussed in the next section), which are considered static loads. However, walking across a pedestrian bridge can be characterized as a moving repetitive force that may cause the bridge to vibrate. Often, these vibrations are annoying. The problem of annoyance due to floor vibrations was recognized as early as 1828 by Tredgold [1828], who suggested that girders over long spans should be "made deep to avoid the inconvenience of not being able to move on the floor without shaking everything in the room." A comprehensive discussion on human tolerance levels for bridge vibrations has been presented by Leonard [1966].

Walking across a pedestrian bridge produces a complex dynamic response, involving different modes of vibration, as well as motion due to time variation of static deflection. A person stepping up and down at the same frequency as the fundamental frequency of the bridge will cause resonance. Jogging or more than one person walking in step constitutes more severe dynamic loading. Similarly, a large group of people walking across a bridge produces a greater dynamic loading. In the past it was common practice for soldiers to break step when marching across bridges to avoid large and potentially dangerous vibrations or resonance.

Although design criteria for vibrations due to walking on building floors have been developed [Allen and Murray, 1993], not enough data are available to codify design of pedestrian bridges for vibrations. About 30 years ago, problems due to vibrations caused by walking on the steel-joist floors that satisfied the code stiffness criteria were noted. Lenzen [1966] pointed out that damping and mass, not stiffness, were key factors in preventing unacceptable walking vibrations of these floors. Accordingly, a simple dynamic design criterion based on the heel impact response was proposed by Allen and Rainer [1976] and incorporated into an appendix to the Canadian design standard for steel structures [CSA, 1989]. Subsequently, a design criterion for pedestrian bridges based on the resonance response to a sinusoidal force was introduced in the British and the Canadian bridge standards [BSI, 1978; OHBDC, 1983]. No such design criterion exists in the AASHTO standard [AASHTO, 1992].

A simplified approach to the complex problem of a pedestrian bridge or a floor involving different modes of vibration has been proposed by Rainer, Pernica, and Allen [1988]. It is based on a single person stepping up and down at the midspan of a simply supported beam vibrating in its fundamental mode only. Maximum response will therefore occur when the natural frequency corresponds to one of the harmonic forcing frequencies. The steady-state acceleration due to harmonic resonance is given by

$$\frac{a}{g} = \left(\frac{\alpha_i P}{0.5W}\right)\left(\frac{R}{2\beta}\right)\cos(2\pi i f t)$$

$$= \left(\frac{R\alpha_i P}{\beta W}\right)\cos(2\pi i f t) \tag{3.11}$$

where a = steady-state acceleration
   g = acceleration due to gravity
   α_i = dynamic coefficient for the harmonic
   P = person's weight (taken as 0.7 kN or 160 lb for design)
   R = a reduction factor
   β = damping ratio
   W = the weight of the beam
   i = the harmonic multiple
   f = the step frequency
   t = time

In Eq. 3.11, the factor $(1/2\beta)$ represents the dynamic amplification factor for steady-state resonance, and $0.5W/g$ is the mass of an SDOF oscillator, which is dynamically equivalent to the simply supported beam of weight W vibrating in its fundamental mode. The reduction factor is introduced in Eq. 3.11 to account for two factors: (1) Full steady-state resonance is not achieved when someone *steps* along the beam instead of jumping up and down at the midspan. (2) The walker and the person annoyed are not simultaneously at the location of maximum modal displacement. A value of $R = 0.7$ is recommended for pedestrian bridges.

The OHBDC [1983] design criterion for bridges is based on a pedestrian or a jogger exerting a dynamic force of $\alpha P \cos 2\pi f t$, where $P = 0.7$ kN ($= 160$ lb) and f = step frequency (varying between 1 and 4 Hz). The bridge is modeled as an SDOF (single-degree-of-freedom system) beam that vibrates at the first frequency f_0. For a simply supported pedestrian bridge, the resonance response for flexural frequency up to 4 Hz can be determined from Eq. 3.11 with a value of R determined for the length of the bridge. The maximum acceleration is determined from Eq. 3.12:

$$\frac{\alpha_{max}}{g} = \frac{0.7(0.257)0.7}{\beta W_j}$$

$$= \frac{0.126}{\beta W_j} \tag{3.12}$$

where W_j = weight of the pedestrian bridge. The OHBDC [1983] recommends limiting values of α_{max}/g to 0.042 at $f_0 = 2$ Hz and 0.072 at $f_0 = 4$ Hz. With these recommended values, the minimum and the maximum values of βW_j in Eq. 3.12 can be evaluated as

$$\text{at } f_0 = 2 \text{ Hz:} \qquad \beta W_j = \frac{0.126}{0.042} = 3 \text{ kN} \qquad (3.13)$$

$$\text{at } f_0 = 4 \text{ Hz:} \qquad \beta W_j = \frac{0.126}{0.072} = 1.8 \text{ kN} \qquad (3.14)$$

A discussion on design criteria for vibrations due to walking is presented by Allen and Murray [1993].

3.4
PEDESTRIAN LOADING

On most bridges, sidewalks and curbs are provided, and the live load imposed on them should be given due consideration in design. AASHTO 3.14 stipulates the following loading in this regard:

1. Sidewalk floors, stringers, and their immediate supports: 85 psf
2. Girders, trusses, arches and other members:
   (a) Span 0–25 ft: 85 lb/ft^2
   (b) Span 60–100 ft: 60 lb/ft^2
   (c) Span over 100 ft: according to Eq. 3.15,

$$P = \left(30 + \frac{3000}{L}\right)\left(\frac{55 - W}{50}\right) \qquad (3.15)$$

    where P = live load per square foot (maximum 60 lb)
              L = loaded length of sidewalk (ft)
            W = sidewalk width (ft)

Note that the sidewalk live load is reducible for members or portions of a bridge superstructure spanning 60 ft or more that receive load from members that directly support the deck.
3. Pedestrian traffic: 85 lb/ft^2
4. Bicycle traffic: 85 lb/ft^2

There is no minimum or maximum sidewalk width stipulated in the specifications; widths of 3 ft to 6 ft are commonly used.

According to the AASHTO–LRFD specifications [1994a], a pedestrian design load of 75 lb/ft^2 is to be applied simultaneously with the vehicular design live load to *all sidewalks 2 ft wide or wider*; no pedestrian design live load is to be considered for sidewalks less than 2 ft wide. For bridges used for only pedestrian and bicycle traffic, the specified live load is 85 lb/ft^2, as before. Where sidewalk, pedestrian, and bicycle bridges are also to be used for maintenance or other incidental vehicles, these loads should be considered in design. However, dynamic effects due to these vehicles can be ignored (i.e., no impact factor need be considered for these vehicles) because they are very likely to be slow-moving.

3.5
REDUCTION IN LIVE-LOAD INTENSITY

3.5.1 Effect of Density of Traffic: Multipresence of Vehicles

Whereas design loads relate to the anticipated heaviest vehicle loads on the bridge, the notion of traffic density relates to the *volume* of traffic crossing a bridge and the *manner* in which it crosses it, i.e., the *multipresence* of vehicles. One may ask the question: What is the probability that a multilane bridge will simultaneously have all its lanes full of standard truck or lane loading, moving at maximum speed, and thereby subjecting the bridge to maximum loading and impact? It may be reasoned that if the bridge has only one or two lanes, the traffic conditions may frequently be as severe as stated. But on a bridge with more than two lanes, the degree of severity of traffic conditions may be assumed somewhat diminished. This logic is very similar to that adopted by building codes that permit reduction in live-load intensity for roofs and floors having tributary areas above a certain minimum. For example, the Uniform Building Code [UBC, 1994] allows reduction,[3] in accordance with certain formulas, in unit roof and floor live loads for members supporting more than 150 ft^2 (UBC Sec. 1606). However, the reduction is limited to 40 percent for members receiving load from one level only, 60 percent for others, or R as determined by the following formula (UBC 6.2):

$$R = 23.1 \left(1 + \frac{D}{L}\right)$$

where D = dead load per ft^2 of area supported by the member
L = unit live load per ft^2 of area supported by the member
R = reduction in percentage

Applying a similar logic for highway loading, it may be logical to permit reduction of the intensity of live load on a bridge if it carries more than a certain minimum number of traffic lanes.

3.5.2 Magnitude of Live-Load Reduction

The effects of multipresence of vehicles on highway bridges have been researched, and the findings are being reflected in some bridge design codes. The two important factors that need to be considered in this regard are [Jaeger and Bakht, 1987; Nutt, Schamber, and Zokaie, 1988; Bakht and Jaeger, 1990; Weschsler, 1992]:

1. Class of highway that deals with the average number of trucks and the average number of vehicles per lane per day. This will distinguish between the heavily and the lightly traveled bridges. Table 3.3 shows classification of highways according to volume of traffic, as defined in CSA [1988]—Class A is the busiest, and Class C$_2$ is

---

[3]No reduction is permitted for floors in places of public assembly and for live loads in excess of 100 lb/ft^2. The code also imposes other restrictions.

TABLE 3.3

Definitions of highway classes according to volume of traffic, Ontario [OHBDC, 1983]

Highway class	Average number of trucks per lane per day	Average number of vehicles per day	Road criteria when traffic data are unavailable
A	> 1000	> 4000	Primarily for through traffic
B	250–1000	1000–4000	Traffic and property access of equal importance
C_1	50–250	100–1000	Primarily for property access, commercial traffic moderate
C_2	< 50	< 100	Primarily for property access, commercial traffic little or none

TABLE 3.4

Reduction in live-load intensity [AASHTO, 1992; Ontario, 1983; CSA, 1988]

Code	Reduction factors for load					
	One lane	Two lanes	Three lanes	Four lanes	Five lanes	Six or more lanes
AASHTO	1.00	1.00	0.90	0.75	0.75	0.75
OHBDC	1.00	0.90	0.80	0.70	0.60	0.55
CSA	1.00	0.90	0.80	0.70	0.60	0.55

the most lightly traveled. However, no such classification is made in the AASHTO specifications.

2. Probability of multipresence of trucks in two or more lanes. This will depend on the class of highway referred to above.

Accordingly, in view of the improbability of maximum coincident loading, AASHTO 3.12 permits a reduction in the live-load intensity on a bridge deck. The *reduced* live load is obtained by multiplying the single-lane loading by the appropriate multipresence reduction factors, as shown in Table 3.4. Reduction factors specified by some other bridge design codes of North America are also given in Table 3.4 [Bakht and Jaeger, 1990]. A comprehensive discussion on this topic has been presented by Bakht and Jaeger [1985].

3.5.3 Applicability of Live-Load Reduction Provisions of the AASHTO Standard

Choosing the members or portions of a multilane bridge that should be designed for reduced live load is a decision similar to one quite commonly encountered in the design of buildings. For example, a beam supporting a roof or a floor in a building is designed for the full dead and live load (duly reduced, depending on its tributary area, if permitted by the code). At the same time, its connection with the supporting girder is designed for the corresponding dead and live-load reaction. However, the girder, which may be supporting several beams, may be designed for the full dead load plus reduced live load, the reduction being commensurate with its larger tributary area. Because the tributary area of a girder will be much larger (equal to the tributary area of one beam *times* the number of beams) than that of one of the beams supported by the girder, the girder may be permitted to have a larger reduction in the unit live load. Accordingly, the total live load supported by the girder will be smaller than the sum of the live load for which all the beams are designed. This notion of designing a girder for a live load smaller than the total live load on all beams together is based on the premise that the probability of all beams supported by the girder (i.e., the entire floor or the roof) being loaded with the full unit live load simultaneously is rather small.

The preceding logic can also be applied to bridge floors. Regardless of the number of multiple traffic lanes on a bridge, the deck and the supporting stringers should be designed to carry the *full* load, for obvious reasons. This is because standard highway live loading can be placed anywhere on a bridge deck and would cause maximum stress in the deck area in the immediate vicinity of the wheel load. Similarly, the live load can be so positioned on a bridge deck with respect to the position of a stringer that the stringer will be subjected to the maximum effect of the load. Assuming that such a maximum effect can be produced in every stringer, *all* interior and exterior stringers should be designed for their respective *maximum* loading conditions. This intent is clarified in AASHTO 3.11.2: "The number and position of the lane or the truck loads shall be as specified in Article 3.7 and, whether lane or truck loads, shall be such as to produce maximum stress, subject to the reduction specified in Article 3.12." Article 3.12.2 specifies that "the reduction in intensity of loads on transverse members such as floor beams shall be determined as in the case of main trusses or girders, using the number of traffic lanes across the width of roadway that must be loaded to produce maximum stresses in the floor beam."

The situation becomes somewhat different when the live load is transmitted to other members or portions of the bridge, such as floor beams, abutments, or piers. Abutments and piers that support stringers supporting a multilane deck can be designed for the reduced live load because of the low probability of coincident maximum loading conditions. However, one should very carefully identify portions of a bridge that can be designed for reduced loads, for in some cases reduction in live load should not be permitted:

1. Floor beams supporting a multiple-lane bridge, which receive their loads from stringers, may be designed for the reduced live load (as permitted by the specifications), but the connection between the floor beam and the stringer *must* be designed to transmit *full* stringer reaction computed on the basis of full live load on the stringer.
2. Stringer bearings should be designed to receive reactions computed for the full live load. These reactions, however, may be appropriately reduced to design floor beams, abutments, and piers of a multiple-lane bridge.

Bridge designers disagree on the correct interpretation of AASHTO 3.12 regarding the reduction of live load in longitudinal beams for bridges carrying more than two traffic lanes. Some engineers permit the reduction of live load, while others do not [Taly, 1996]. As the preceding paragraphs explain, this author believes that, when the *S*-over-*D* type distribution factors listed in AASHTO Table 3.23.1 (discussed in Chapter 4) are used, the live load in beams should *not* be reduced according to AASHTO 3.12. To avoid the ambiguity in interpreting AASHTO 3.12, some states have clarified this point in their state-modified specifications. For example, PennDOT specifications [PennDOT, 1993, p. A3-7] clearly state

> For three or more girders (in the special case of three girders, see C3.5) the "*S*-Over" lateral distribution factors may not be used as described in A3.23.2.3 and A3.23.2.2. In this case, the provisions of A3.12 (the multiple-lane reduction factors) shall *not* be used.

Alternatively, instead of using AASHTO Table 3.23.1 and Sec. 3.12, designers may use the new distribution factors specified in the AASHTO guide specifications [AASHTO, 1994b]. These new distribution factors, although relatively cumbersome to use, include the effect of the presence of multiple traffic lanes and do away with the problem of load reduction for bridges with more than two traffic lanes.

3.6
LONGITUDINAL FORCES

The term *longitudinal forces* refers to forces that act in the direction of the longitudinal axis of the bridge, specifically, in the direction of the traffic. These forces develop as a result of the braking effort (sudden stoppage, which generally governs), or the tractive effort (sudden acceleration). In both cases, the vehicle's inertia force is transferred to the deck through friction between the deck and the wheels.

The magnitude of the longitudinal force can be determined using Newton's second law of motion. The force generated by a particle of mass, *m*, in motion is given by

$$\text{Force} = (\text{mass}) \times (\text{acceleration})$$

or

$$F = m\left(\frac{dv}{dt}\right) = \left(\frac{W}{g}\right)\left(\frac{dv}{dt}\right) \tag{3.16}$$

where $m = W/g$ = mass of the particle
dv/dt = tangential acceleration or deceleration
g = acceleration due to gravity = 32.2 ft/sec^2

Provisions for calculating longitudinal forces are specified in AASHTO 3.9, which provides for them to be equal to 5 percent of all live load in all lanes carrying traffic headed in the same direction. The live load to be used in this context consists of the lane load plus the concentrated load for moment (18 kips for H20 or HS20 loading). The line of action of this force is assumed to be the center of vehicle mass, assumed to be located 6 ft above the deck slab. Furthermore, it is stipulated that this longitudinal force be transmitted to the substructure through the superstructure.

It is instructive to compare the longitudinal force as calculated according to the AASHTO specifications and the mathematical values as illustrated in the following examples:

EXAMPLE 3.2. Calculate mathematically the longitudinal force due to the braking of an HS20 standard truck that may come to a complete halt from the maximum speed of 75 mph in 8 seconds, assuming constant deceleration.

Solution.

$$75 \text{ mph} = 110 \text{ ft/sec}$$

$$F = (W/g) \times (dv/dt) = (W/32.2) \times (110/8) = 0.427W$$

$$W = \text{weight of an HS20 truck} = 72 \text{ kips}$$

$$\therefore F = 0.427 \times 72 = 30.74 \text{ kips}$$

EXAMPLE 3.3. Calculate the longitudinal force due to HS20 lane loading for a span of 100 ft per AASHTO specifications.

Solution. The lane load on a span of 100 ft for one lane is

$$0.64 \times 100 + 18 = 82 \text{ kips}$$

$$\text{Longitudinal force} = F = 0.05 \times 82 = 4.1 \text{ kips}$$

$$\text{For a two-lane bridge, } F = 2 \times 4.1 = 8.2 \text{ kips}$$

EXAMPLE 3.4. Calculate the longitudinal force due to HS20 lane loading on a two-lane bridge of 450 ft span.

Solution. Each lane load consists of a uniform load of 640 lb/ft plus a concentrated load of 18 kips. Thus, the longitudinal force due to two lanes is

$$F = 0.05(0.64 \times 450 + 18) \times 2 = 30.6 \text{ kips}$$

By comparison, the calculated value of the longitudinal force due to one HS20 standard truck, as illustrated in Example 3.2, is 30.74 kips.

It is evident from the preceding examples that AASHTO specifications for longitudinal forces give rather low values for short spans but appear to be reasonable for the medium and long spans [Heins and Firmage, 1979]. It is quite intuitive to think that on long spans, all vehicles do not brake or accelerate at *maximum* effort simultaneously; hence a low value of 5 percent appears reasonable for long spans. It may be noted that for spans under 85 ft, the standard HS20 truck results in heavier loading than the standard lane loading. Equating total lane loading to total load due to an HS20 standard truck, we have $(x)(0.64) + 18 = 72$, from which $x = 54/0.64 = 84.375$ ft.

Interestingly, the AASHTO provision for the longitudinal load (5 percent of the lane load) is far less than the longitudinal loads required by many other codes. A comparison of longitudinal loads for one 100-ft-long lane follows [ASCE 1981]:

AASHTO: 4100 lb for HS20
British: 100,000 lb for HA
Canadian: 101,000 lb for MS250
French: 66,000 lb for Type B
Ontario: 23,600 lb for OHBD truck
ASCE: 57,000 lb for HS20

Note, however, that some of these loads are applied in combinations of loadings that allow an increase in the allowable stress [ASCE, 1981].

What is the mechanism for transmission of the longitudinal force, from its origin in the live load to its final resolution in the earth below? It is assumed that longitudinal force is transmitted to the deck through the wheels of moving vehicles. The deck, in turn, transmits it to the girders, which transmit the longitudinal force to the bearings on which they are supported. This longitudinal force, along with that due to friction on bearings (arising from expansion and contraction of the superstructure), is applied at the bearings, in the direction of traffic, and is considered in the design of the substructure (abutments and/or piers, as the case may be), which finally transfers all loads to the foundation and the earth below. The effect of the longitudinal force on the members of the superstructure is very small, owing to their large axial stiffness (AE); consequently, it is not considered in their design.

3.7
CENTRIFUGAL FORCE

When a particle of mass m moves along a constrained curved path with a constant speed, there is a normal force exerted on the particle by the constraint. It is caused by the centripetal (meaning "toward the center of rotation") acceleration and acts perpendicular to the tangent to the path. For equilibrium, an equal and opposite force, called the centrifugal force, is transferred to the path. The magnitude of this force is given the following expression:

$$F = \frac{mv^2}{r} = \left(\frac{W}{g}\right)\frac{v^2}{r} \tag{3.17}$$

where $m = w/g =$ mass of the particle
   $g =$ acceleration due to gravity
   $v =$ particle velocity
   $r =$ instantaneous radius of curvature of the path

The centrifugal force thus originates from the dynamics of the vehicle motion along a curved path and is transmitted to the path itself, in this case, the bridge deck. Since this force is inversely proportional to the radius of curvature, the sharper the curve, the larger the centrifugal force.

Provision for the centrifugal force to which a curved bridge may be subjected is covered in AASHTO 3.10. Its magnitude is to be calculated by the following empirical formula:

$$C = 0.00117(S^2D) = 6.68\left(\frac{S^2}{F}\right) \tag{3.18}$$

where $C =$ the centrifugal force in percent of the live load, without impact
   $S =$ design speed in miles per hour
   $D =$ the degree of the curve[4] $= 5729.65/R$

---

[4]The *degree of curve* of a given circular curve is defined as the angle or the number of degrees subtended at the center by a chord 100 ft long.

R = the radius of the curve in feet

$F = mv^2/r$, as in Eq. 3.17

It is instructive to compare the AASHTO formula (Eq. 3.18) with the theoretical formula (Eq. 3.17):

$$F = \left(\frac{W}{g}\right)\frac{v^2}{r}$$

Substituting $g = 32.2$ ft/sec^2 and expressing velocity, v, in mph,

$$F = \left(\frac{W}{32.2}\right)\left(\frac{5280}{3600}v\right)^2\left(\frac{1}{r}\right)$$

$$= 0.0668W\left(\frac{v^2}{r}\right) \tag{3.19}$$

from which one obtains

$$\frac{F}{W} = 0.0668\left(\frac{v^2}{r}\right)$$

The right side of this expression can multiplied by 100 to express it in percentage form (AASHTO Eq. 3.2):

$$\frac{F}{W} = 6.68\left(\frac{v^2}{r}\right) \tag{3.20}$$

Note that radius R (or r) to be used in Eq. 3.17 or 3.18 refers to the curvature of the path traversed by the *centroid* of the moving load and would obviously be different for the standard trucks placed in different lanes. Accordingly, the centrifugal force exerted by two standard trucks on the same curved bridge but placed in two different lanes would be different, as illustrated in Example 3.5.

EXAMPLE 3.5.   Figure E3.5(*a*) shows the plan of the two-lane curved slab–stringer bridge showing the positions of the curved stringers. Calculate the centrifugal force on the bridge according to the AASHTO specifications.

Solution.   Positioning the wheel loads correctly on the bridge deck to produce maximum effect is the sole consideration here. In Fig. E3.5(*b*), one standard truck is placed in each of the two 12-ft lanes, with wheels of the trucks placed to produce the maximum effect on girders G_2 and G_3. Note also that the radii of girders G_2 and G_3 are shorter than the radius of girder G_1, which is positioned farthest from the center of the curved girders. Thus, the two trucks have been so positioned in their respective lanes that their centroids travel on curves with the shortest radii. Since the centrifugal force is inversely proportional to the radius (radius r appears in the denominator of Eq. 3.20), the shorter the radius, the larger the force. Note that the two trucks can also be positioned in their respective lanes so as to have a maximum effect on girders G_1 and G_2. However, in this position, the centroids of both trucks will be moving along curves with larger radii, and the corresponding centrifugal force will be smaller.

Assume that the maximum speed along the curve is limited to 35 mph. The radii of the curves on which the centroids of the right and the left truck move are calculated as

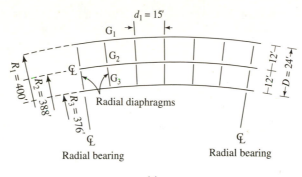

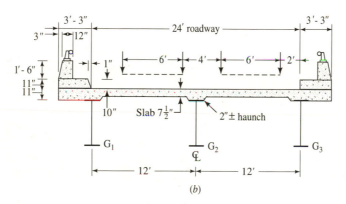

FIGURE E3.5

(a) Plan of the curved bridge showing girders; (b) cross section of the bridge.

$$R_1 = 376 + 5 = 381 \text{ ft}$$

$$R_2 = 388 + 5 = 393 \text{ ft}$$

Right truck: $C = 6.68 S^2 R$

$$= 6.68(35)^2/381 = 21.48 \text{ percent of } W$$

Left truck: $C = 6.68(35)^2/393 = 20.82$ percent of W

For the rear 32-kip axle(s), the centrifugal force will be

Right truck: $F = 32 \times 0.2148 = 6.87$ kips

Left truck: $F = 32 \times 0.2082 = 6.66$ kips

For the front 8-kip axle, the loads will be 25 percent of the preceding values:

Right truck: $F = 0.25 \times 6.87 = 1.72$ kips

Left truck: $F = 0.25 \times 6.66 = 1.67$ kips

All calculated forces are assumed to act 6 ft above the deck surface. AASHTO 3.10.3 specifies the quantity W in the preceding expressions to be that due to one standard truck in each lane. The point of application of this force is assumed to be 6 ft above the roadway surface.

Resistance to centrifugal force can be developed by a proper connection between the deck and the supporting member. When a reinforced concrete floor slab or a steel grid deck is keyed to or attached to its supporting members, the deck can be assumed to resist the centrifugal force within its own plane. It is pointed out here that lane loads are not to be used in the computation of centrifugal forces (AASHTO 3.10.4). Also, according to AASHTO–LRFD [AASHTO, 1994a], the new formula for the centrifugal force is

$$\frac{F}{W} = C = \frac{4}{3}\frac{v^2}{gr} \tag{3.21}$$

where v = highway design speed (ft/sec)
g = gravitational acceleration, 32.2 ft/sec^2
r = radius of curvature of the traffic lane

Equation 3.21 is similar to Eq. 3.20, except that it gives a value that is one-third greater. This larger value is justified to represent a group of exclusion vehicles that produce force effects at least four-thirds times those caused by the design truck alone on short- and medium-span bridges.

3.8
CURB LOADING

For curb design, AASHTO 3.14.2 stipulates a lateral force of not less than 500 pounds per linear foot of curb, applied

1. At the top of the curb, or
2. At an elevation 10 in. above the floor if the curb is higher than 10 in.

AASHTO 2.5.4 stipulates the minimum width of a curb to be 18 in.

3.9
RAILING LOADING

Railing loading depends on the purpose for which the railing is provided (e.g., vehicular, bicycle, or pedestrian railing), the geometry of the railing, and the type of parapet provided on the deck. Requirements for designing various combinations of railing and parapets are rather extensive and are covered by AASHTO 2.7.

3.10
WIND LOADS

3.10.1 General Concepts

Wind loads form a major component of lateral loads that act on all structures. In general, they are a component of the so-called environmental loads to which all structures are subjected. It is often mistakenly believed that wind load considerations are important only for long-span bridges. Statistics, however, show that bridges with spans as short as 260 ft and as long as 2800 ft have vibrated to destruction [Buckland and Wardlow, 1972; Liepman, 1952; Scanlan, 1979, 1988, 1989; Wardlow, 1970].

Bridges are frequently built on exposed sites and are subject to severe wind conditions. Wind loads on bridge superstructures depend on the type of bridge, e.g., slab–stringer, truss, arch, cable-stayed, or suspension. Other parameters that affect wind loads on bridge superstructures are the wind velocity, angle of attack, the size and shape of the bridge, the terrain, and the gust characteristics. General discussions on wind loads and their effects on structures have been presented by several researchers [ASCE, 1961, 1987; Houghton and Carruthers, 1976; Ishizaki and Chiu, 1976; Liu, 1991; Sachs, 1978; Scanlan, 1978a,b; Simui and Scanlan, 1986]. The following discussion is summarized from these references.

Wind effects on bridge structures may be threefold:

1. Static wind pressures
2. Dynamic (oscillatory) wind movements
3. Buffeting between adjacent structures

A distinction should be made between the static effects of wind, as used in designing ordinary buildings and bridges, and the dynamic effects of wind on flexible structures such as suspension and cable-stayed bridges—an aerodynamic problem [Steinman, 1941, 1945a]. The July 29, 1944, failure of the two-span, continuous truss bridge over the Mississippi River at Chester, Illinois—it was blown off its piers by wind [Steinman, 1945a]—is an example of the aerostatic effects of wind. On the other hand, the November 7, 1940, failure of the Tacoma Narrows Bridge at Puget sound [ENR, 1941] was an aerodynamic phenomenon. Aerodynamic instability means "the effect of a steady wind, acting on a flexible structure of conventional cross section, to produce a fluctuating force automatically synchronizing in timing and direction with the harmonic motions of those of the structure so as to cause a progressive amplification of these motions to dangerous destructive amplitudes" [Steinman, 1945b]. A significant force that is caused by an aerodynamic phenomenon is the wind uplift, or the vertical component of wind, known in aeronautics as lift. This force is not considered in an aerostatic problem. For example, on the morning of the Tacoma Narrows Bridge failure, the 35–42-mph gale blowing at the time amounted to a force of only about 5 lb/ft^2 on the vertical plane. The bridge had been designed for a horizontal wind pressure of 50 lb/ft^2 on the vertical plane and was structurally safe for a wind load of that magnitude. The bridge was destroyed, however, by the cumulative dynamic effects of vertical components produced by a horizontal wind pressure of only 5 lb/ft^2 [Steinman, 1941, 1954].

Static wind pressures are those that cause a bridge to deflect or deform. Dynamic wind movements affect long-span flexible bridges, such as suspension bridges and cable-stayed bridges. Such bridges are very prone to movements under wind forces, which may cause them to oscillate in a number of different modes, at low frequencies, which may be catastrophic under suitable wind conditions [Davenport, 1962a,b, 1966; Lin, 1979; Scanlan, 1978a,b, 1981, 1986; Scanlan and Wardlow, 1977]. Buffeting is caused by the close proximity of the two bridge structures. In such a case, the turbulent eddy formations from the windward bridge will excite the leeward bridge.

Buffeting is defined as the randomly forced vibration of a structure due to velocity fluctuations (i.e., unsteady loading) in the oncoming wind. It is characterized as a pure forced vibration where the forcing function is totally independent of the structure motion [ASCE, 1987, Ch. 9]. In reference to bridges, the problem of buffeting is one associated with linelike structures such as slender towers and decks of suspended-span bridges that exhibit aeroelastic effects. Analysis for buffeting forces has been discussed by Simui and Scanlan [1986].

Static wind force, the main wind force acting on a bridge structure, develops as a result of a steady wind that exerts a fairly constant pressure in the general direction of the wind. Pressure due to wind is calculated by applying the familiar principles of fluid mechanics. According to Bernoulli's theorem, when an ideal fluid strikes an object, the increase in the static pressure equals the decrease in the dynamic pressure. The intensity of this pressure is expressed by Eq. 3.22:

$$p = \tfrac{1}{2} C \rho V^2 \qquad (3.22)$$

where p = wind pressure

ρ = the mass density of air (0.00233 slugs per cubic foot at sea level and 15 °C)

V = wind velocity in feet per second

C = a coefficient of proportionality, called the *shape factor,* which depends on the shape of the obstruction

The value of coefficient C is smaller for the narrow members and streamlined surfaces, and larger for the wide members and blunt surfaces.

The resultant of the steady wind force acts not exactly in the direction of the wind, but is deflected by a force component acting at right angles to the direction to the wind. In aerodynamics, this force is called the *lift;* the component in the direction of wind is called the *drag.* The *lift* (F_L) and *drag* (F_D) on an arbitrary bluff body are shown in Fig. 3.16.

3.10.2 Variation of Wind Speed with Height and Terrain Roughness

Characteristically, the velocity of wind increases from zero at ground surface to a certain maximum at a height of approximately 0.5 to 1.0 kilometer above the ground. The surface of the earth exerts on the moving air a horizontal drag force, the effect of which is to retard wind flow. This effect decreases with the increase in height and becomes negligible above a height δ, called the boundary layer of the atmosphere. The atmosphere above the boundary layer is called the free atmosphere. The height at which this

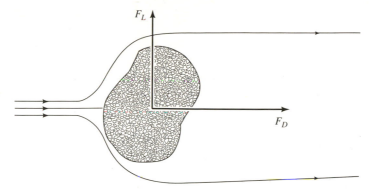

FIGURE 3.16
Lift and drag on an arbitrary bluff body.

takes place is called the gradient height, and the wind velocity at that height is called the gradient velocity, which does not vary with height [Houghton and Carruthers, 1976; Liu, 1991; Simui and Scanlan, 1986]. Generally speaking, the local mean wind velocity, used as the reference wind velocity, is the surface wind speed measured not at the ground surface, but by the anemometers mounted usually at a height of 10 m (33 ft). General variation in wind velocity with height above ground is shown in Fig. 3.17 [Liu, 1991]; Fig. 3.18 shows profiles of wind velocity over level terrains of differing roughnesses.

The wind speed profile within the atmospheric boundary level can be expressed by mathematical relationships based on fundamental equations of continuum mechanics. Historically, the first representation of the mean wind profile in horizontally homogenous terrain was proposed in 1916 [Hellman, 1916] and is called the power law, which is expressed as [Liu, 1991]

$$V(z) = V_1 \left(\frac{z}{z_1} \right)^\alpha \tag{3.23}$$

where $V(z)$ = wind velocity at height z above ground
V_1 = wind velocity at any reference height z_1 above ground, usually 10 meters
α = power law exponent that depends on the terrain characteristics

Another relationship used to approximate the wind profile is the logarithmic law, expressed as [Liu, 1991]

$$V(z) = \frac{1}{k} V_* \ln \left(\frac{z}{z_1} \right) \tag{3.24}$$

where V_* = shear velocity or friction velocity
= $\sqrt{\tau_o/\rho}$, where τ_o = stress of wind at ground level and ρ = air density = 0.07651 lb/ft^3 (or 1.2256 kg/m^3) at sea level and 15 °C
k = von Kármán constant = 0.4 approximately, based on experiments in wind tunnels and in the atmosphere

Currently, the logarithmic law is regarded by meteorologists as the more accurate representation of wind profile in the lower atmosphere; consequently, the power law

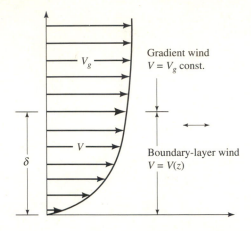

FIGURE 3.17
Variation in wind velocity with height above ground [Liu, 1991].

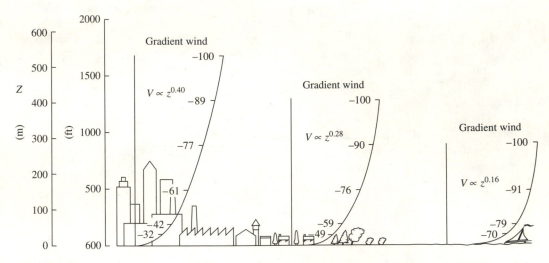

FIGURE 3.18
Profiles of mean wind velocity over level terrains of differing roughness [Davenport, 1963].

is not used in meteorological practice. However, because of its simplicity in use for wind pressure calculations, the power law formula, rather than the logarithmic law, is used in building codes, such as ASCE 7-88 (formerly ANSI 58.1) [Houghton and Carruthers, 1976; Simui and Scanlan, 1986]. A discussion on the applications of the power law formula for building structures has been presented by Mehta, Marshall, and Perry [1991].

When a structure is not very high relative to the surrounding terrain, it is satisfactory to use the surface wind speed as the reference wind speed for engineering applications [Liu, 1991]. This is true for most bridges built in rural areas whose elevations are not too high compared with the terrain in the vicinity. There are situations, however, where portions of bridges, such as towers of cable-stayed and suspension bridges, are rather tall and extend to relatively higher elevations. In such cases, the surface wind velocity alone cannot be used as the governing wind velocity for the design of the entire bridge. The increase in wind velocity with height may become an important design consideration—the elevated portions of the bridge will need to be designed for higher wind speeds than those used for the lower portions of the bridge. For example, for the Fred Hartman cable-stayed bridge, commonly referred to as the Baytown Bridge (482, 1250, and 482 ft) over the Houston ship channel, near Baytown, Texas, the 100-year design wind speed was calculated as 110 mph at 30 ft elevation, 160 mph at deck elevation (176 ft above the water level in the channel), and 195 mph at the tower tops (266 ft above the deck level). To these wind speeds, a 15 percent additional gust load factor was applied for towers and piers [Lovett and Warren, 1992]. Pertinent details of the Fred Hartman Bridge are shown in Fig. 3.19.

3.10.3 Aerodynamic Considerations

The literature is replete with discussions of aerodynamics of aircraft structures, specifically for the airfoil (cross section of the airplane's wing, Fig. 3.20). Comparatively little is known or has been written about the aerodynamic behavior of bridges, and much of the research done in this field is due to Davenport [1962a,b, 1963, 1966], Steinman [1941, 1945a,b,c,d, 1946a,b, 1947, 1950, 1954], Scanlan [1978a,b, 1979, 1981, 1983, 1987, 1988, 1989], Scanlan and Wardlow [1977], Scanlan and Tomko [1971], Scanlan and Budlong [1974], Scanlan and Gade [1977], Milne [1981], Scanlan and Jones [1990], and Ehsan, Jones, and Scanlan [1993]. With regard to bridges, the cross section of a bridge deck is treated similarly to an airfoil to understand its aerodynamic behavior [Scanlan and Tomko, 1971]. Several theories have been advanced to explain the aerodynamic behavior of bridges, i.e., the interaction between the wind and the bridge deck, and a great deal of research is in progress. Aspects of research important for bridge decks are as follows.

3.10.3.1 Vortex theory

A bridge deck is essentially a slender bluff (i.e., a nonstreamlined object), as compared with an airfoil. When a steady wind blows perpendicularly across the width of such an object, a zone of turbulent fluid flow, called a wake, whose nature depends on the Reynolds number, is created on the leeward side or past the trailing edge of the airfoil. Figure 3.21 shows the fluid flow pattern past a circular cylinder (a nonstreamlined object) and is representative of the flow on the leeward side of the bridge deck [Simui and Scanlan, 1986]. Characteristically, the pattern consists of large vortices that are shed from the top and bottom of the cylinder with a definite periodicity. The vortices trail behind the cylinder in two rows called a von Kármán vortex trail. This oscillating streamline[5] pattern caused by alternate vortex shedding, in turn, causes a fluctuating

---

[5]A streamline is defined as a path whose tangent at any point is in the direction of the velocity vector at that point.

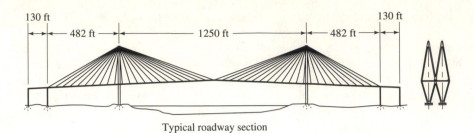

Typical roadway section

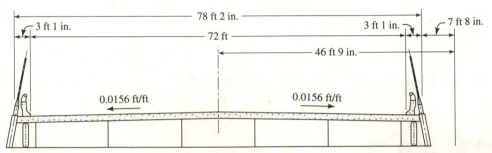

Outside girders are inclined to match the slant of cables. The steel grid and the concrete deck are fully composite.

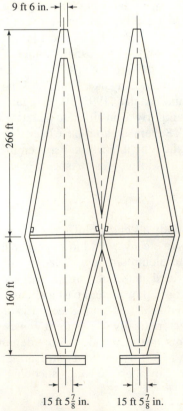

Double diamonds act like a truss to resist hurricane wind forces.

FIGURE 3.19
Fred Hartman Bridge, Texas [Lovett and Warren, 1992].

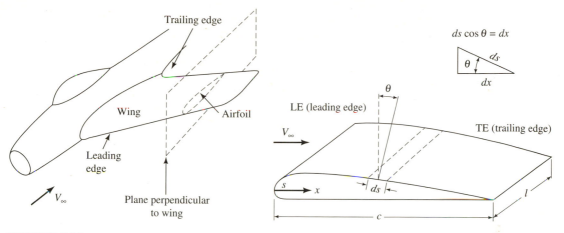

FIGURE 3.20
Airfoil—cross section of an airplane's wing [Anderson, 1985].

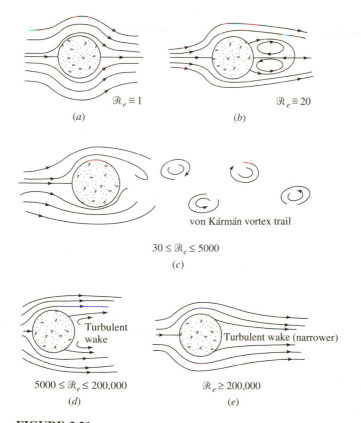

FIGURE 3.21
Flow pattern past a circular cylinder for various Reynolds numbers [Simui and Scanlan, 1986].

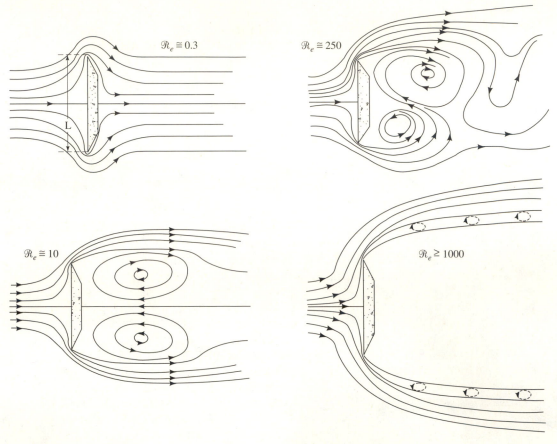

FIGURE 3.22
Flow past sharp-edged plates for various Reynolds numbers [Simui and Scanlan, 1986].

pressure on the cylinder that is dynamic (time-varying) in nature. The frequency of the fluctuating force is equal to the frequency of the vortex shedding and is proportional to the wind velocity [Buckland and Wardlow, 1972]. Figure 3.22 shows the pattern of fluid flow and the accompanying vortex formation past sharp-edged plates for various ranges of Reynolds numbers. For a very low Reynolds number ($R_e \approx 0.3$), the oncoming laminar flow turns at the sharp edges of the plate and tends to follow both the front and the rear contours of the plate. As the Reynolds number is increased by increasing the velocity of flow over the same plate ($R_e \approx 10$), the result is the separation of flow at the corners, and two large symmetric vortices are created in the wake of the flow and remain attached to the back of the plate. Further increase in the Reynolds number ($R_e \approx 250$) causes the symmetry of the vortices to be broken, only to be replaced by cyclically alternating vortices that form by turns at the top and bottom edges of the plate and are swept downstream. At still higher Reynolds numbers ($R_e \geq 1000$), a generally turbulent wake is formed behind the plate. No large vortices are formed; instead, a long series of small vortices is formed at the edges of the wake adjacent to the smooth flow region (above and below the wake) [Simui and Scanlan, 1986].

According to Strouhal, the vortex-shedding phenomenon can be described in terms of a nondimensional parameter, called the Strouhal number, defined as

$$S = \frac{N_s D}{U} \tag{3.25}$$

where S = Strouhal number
N_s = the frequency of full cycles of vortex shedding
D = the characteristic dimension of the body projected on a plane normal to the mean flow velocity
U = velocity of oncoming flow, assumed laminar

The Strouhal number, S, takes on different characteristic constant values depending on the cross-sectional shape of the prism enveloped by the flow. For assumed laminar flow, Table 3.5 lists values of S for different cross-sectional shapes for Reynolds numbers in the clear vortex-shedding range [ASCE, 1961; Simui and Scanlan, 1986].

In the case of a bridge deck, the mechanism of vortex shedding is very similar to that for an airfoil. Figure 3.23 shows wakes for square and rectangular cylinders representative of bridge decks [Simui and Scanlan, 1986]. The fluctuating pattern of wakes exerts a vertical dynamic force on the bridge deck. If the wind velocity is such that the frequency of vortex shedding approaches that of the natural frequency of the bridge deck, the latter will vibrate in a resonant manner with large amplitudes, generally referred to as galloping [Buckland and Wardlow, 1972; Houghton and Carruthers, 1976]. Thus, like torsional instability and flutter (described later), galloping is a violent instability that occurs when a critical wind is exceeded [Parkinson, 1963]. It excites a bending mode of vibration that is in a plane transverse to the wind direction. As wind velocity increases, the frequency of vortex shedding will exceed the bridge deck's natural frequency, resulting in reduced bridge vibrations. At higher wind speeds, the shedding loses its periodicity. A structural engineer must ensure that the natural frequency of the bridge deck is not too close to the vortex shedding frequency.

Vortex theory is discussed in references [Houghton and Carruthers, 1976; Lin and Ariaratnam, 1980; Scanlan, 1981; Simui and Scanlan, 1986].

3.10.3.2 Flutter theory

Flutter refers to an oscillating motion in which two or more modes of oscillation, usually bending and torsion, are combined. As wind velocity increases, a critical value is reached, which triggers the flutter motion. It is characterized by a rapid build-up of amplitude with little or no further increase in wind speed. The amplitude may reach catastrophic proportions in a few cycles of motion. Literature abounds with discussions on flutter theory [ASCE, 1961; Houghton and Carruthers, 1976; Scanlan, 1978a, 1981, 1986, 1988; Scanlan and Rosenbaum, 1951; Scanlan and Budlong, 1974; Huston, 1987]. The bridge design should be such that the critical velocity at which this motion occurs is high, and it should be ensured that wind speeds of this magnitude will not occur at the bridge site. In addition to aerodynamic factors, the flutter velocity depends on the elastic and dynamic properties of the bridge.

TABLE 3.5
Strouhal number for a variety of shapes [Simui and Scanlan, 1986]

Wind	Profile dimensions (mm)	Value of $\mathscr{S}$	Wind	Profile dimensions (mm)	Value of $\mathscr{S}$
→ ↓	$t = 2.0$, 50, 50, t (H-section)	0.120 / 0.137	↓ ↓	$t = 1.0$, 12.5, 12.5, 25, 50 (channel sections)	0.147
→	$t = 0.5$, 25, 25 (H-section)	0.120	↓	$t = 1.0$, 12.5, 12.5, 12.5, 50 (channel sections)	0.150
↓	$t = 1.0$, 25, 50 (H-section)	0.144	← ↑ ↗	$t = 1.0$, 50, 50 (L-section)	0.145 / 0.142 / 0.147
↓	$t = 1.5$, 12.5, 50 (T/H-section)	0.145	← ↑ ↗	$t = 1.0$, 25, 25 (L-section)	0.131 / 0.134 / 0.137
↓ ↑	$t = 1.0$, 25, 50 (U-section)	0.140 / 0.153	→ ↓	$t = 1.0$, 25, 25, 25, 25	0.121 / 0.143
↓ ↑	$t = 1.0$, 12.5, 50 (U-section)	0.145 / 0.168	→	$t = 1.0$, 25, 25, 12.5	0.135
→ ↓	$t = 1.5$, 50	0.156 / 0.145	→	$t = 1.0$, 50, 100 (T-section)	0.160
	Cylinder $11.800 < \mathscr{R}_e < 19.100$, 25	0.200	→ ↑	$t = 1.0$, 25, 50 (T-section)	0.114 / 0.145

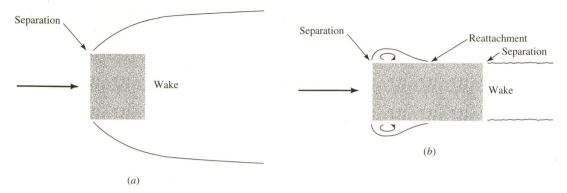

FIGURE 3.23

Flow separation and wake regions of cylinders: (a) square, (b) rectangular [Simui and Scanlan, 1986].

Note that flutter speed will be reduced if the wind velocity vector is inclined to the plane of the bridge deck, which may occur as a result of turbulence and gustiness of the wind. In such cases, the wind will be blowing at an angle to the bridge deck. It has been reported that a 5° change in the vertical wind angle, for example, will reduce the critical speed from 100 mph to 50 mph [Buckland and Wardlow, 1972]. Figure 3.24 shows schematically the phenomenon of suspension bridge flutter (Tacoma Narrows). These types of oscillations could result in catastrophic consequences. On November 7, 1940, barely four months after its completion, the two-lane, 2800-ft (main span) Tacoma Narrows suspension bridge in Tacoma, Washington, collapsed in a steady, approximately 40-mph, wind (Fig. 3.25).

Before the collapse, large deck vibrations, with amplitude as much as 15 ft, were noticed. The bridge was reported to have oscillatory problems from the beginning, attributed to its slender stiffening girder, having a span-to-depth ratio of 1/350, the *smallest ever designed.* It was so flexible that motorists frequently saw the car in front of them sink into the roadway and at times disappear completely. Some stays were added later to increase the bridge's rigidity. Meanwhile, the motorists enjoyed the roller coaster sensation and gave the bridge the jocular name "Galloping Gertie." The narrow ribbonlike bridge acted like the wing of an aircraft, and its cross section like an airfoil. The solid stiffening girder provided too much drag, and the deck, in certain positions, provided too much lift.

The collapse of the Tacoma Narrows Bridge attracted international attention, generating a tremendous amount of worldwide research on the problems of aeroelastic instability. However, this was not the first casualty of wind-induced forces. It was preceded by several similar failures in the period 1820–1870: the 449-ft-span Union Bridge at Berwick in 1820; the 225-ft-span Brighton Chain Pier, in England, in 1836 [Reed, 1844]; the 1010-ft-span Ohio River Bridge at Wheeling, West Virginia, in 1854; the 1043-ft-span Niagara River Bridge between Lewiston and Queenston in 1864 [ASCE, 1952; O'Connor, 1971]; and the Niagara–Clifton Bridge at Niagara Falls in 1889 [Steinman, 1945a]. Ironically, the principle and importance of building adequately stiffened suspension bridges [Roebling, 1852] was known since the time of John Roebling [1806–1869], whose bridges stood up while those built by his contemporaries went down.

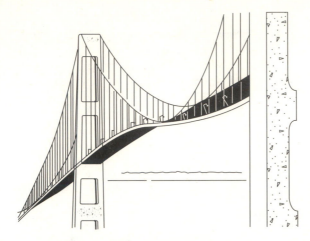

FIGURE 3.24
Aerodynamic vibrations. Note the angle between the vertical suspenders and the light posts, indicating the severity of torsional motions [Salvadori and Heller, 1975].

FIGURE 3.25
Collapse of the Tacoma Narrows Bridge due to wind loads. (Photo by UPI/Bettman Newsphotos.)

As a significant improvement in the aerodynamic stability of suspension bridges, the use of solid stiffening girders was avoided in later suspension bridges, and trusses with larger depth-to-span ratios were almost universally used instead. The goal was to avoid the von Kármán vortex effect and to foil wind forces. An example of such a design is the 3800-ft (main span) Mackinac Suspension Bridge designed by David Steinman. The stiffening trusses for this bridge are 38 ft deep, giving a depth-to-span ratio of 1/100. The trusses are spaced 68 ft apart, and the roadway is only 48 ft wide, leaving a 10-ft-wide space on either side [Merritt, 1972]. Finally, Steinman made the two outer traffic lanes solid, and the two inner lanes and the central mall open grid. This, according to Steinman, increased the critical wind velocity of the bridge to infinity. A discussion of the effects of sidewalk vents on bridge response to wind can be found in Ehsan, Jones, and Scanlan [1993].

3.10.4 Aeroelastic Stability Considerations: Summary

A discussion on aeroelastic stability can be found in several references [Houghton and Carruthers, 1976; Lin and Ariaratnam, 1980; Scanlan, 1979, 1983, 1986, 1987]. The aeroelastic stability of a bridge depends on the following factors [Simui and Scanlan, 1986]:

1. *Geometry of bridge deck.* This refers to the overall cross-sectional shape of the bridge superstructure. This shape can be aerodynamically stable or unstable. Shapes such as solid-girder or H-section types of decks form open-truss deck sections with closed, unslotted, or unvented roadways, and certain very bluff cross sections have highly unstreamlined profiles that can result in aerodynamically unstable shapes. The profile of the Tacoma Narrows Suspension Bridge, which collapsed in 1940, was an H shape. Instability can be minimized by providing streamlined *forms* (Fig. 3.26) and open cross sections that contain vents or grills through the roadway surface. The wing of an airplane is an example of a good streamlined form.

2. *Frequency of vibration of the bridge.* Bridge superstructure profiles may be torsionally soft or torsionally stiff. Examples of torsionally stiff profiles are closed box sections or deep trusses closed by roadway and wind bracing to constitute a latticed tube. H sections are considered torsionally weak sections. Aeroelastic stability

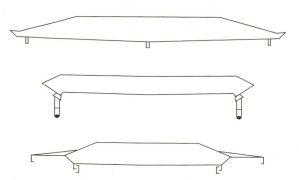

FIGURE 3.26
Streamlined deck forms (cross sections).

is enhanced by the high ratio of torsional natural frequency to the bending natural frequency [ASCE, 1952].

3. *Mechanical damping of the bridge.* Aeroelastic stability of a bridge can be enhanced by increasing the mechanical damping ratio of the bridge, defined as the ratio of the coefficients of viscous damping and critical damping. During motion, internal friction develops within the structural system and acts as a damping force [Bleich and Teller, 1952].

Several studies regarding wind loads on various kinds of bridges, and methods for their calculation, have been made and reported in the literature [ASCE, 1961; Biggs, 1953; Biggs, Naymet, and Adachi, 1955; Bucher, 1990; Pagon, 1955; Scanlan, 1987, 1988; Scanlan and Wardlow, 1977; Davenport, 1962b]. However, due to the extreme uncertainty of the wind-induced force phenomena and the corresponding complex calculations, AASHTO specifications [AASHTO, 1992] provide empirical values of wind pressures for various kinds of bridges.

The effect of wind-induced vibrations is much more pronounced on flexible bridges, such as suspension bridges, than on short-span rigid bridges, such as slab–stringer bridges. Flexibility of a bridge superstructure causes it to bend or twist (or both) under the action of aerodynamic wind loads; this action is balanced by the elastic restoring force of the bridge itself. If the force is removed, the bridge superstructure will spring back to its original shape. If the aerodynamic load fluctuates, the bridge superstructure will oscillate under the influence of the fluctuating load. The frequency and amplitude (maximum deflection) of vibration are functions of both the fluctuating wind load (forcing function) and the dynamic characteristics of the bridge. If the bridge superstructure is subjected to a fluctuating wind load with a frequency equal to that of a natural frequency of the bridge, vibrations with dangerously large amplitudes (resonant vibrations) could be generated. A comprehensive discussion on the wind excitation of suspension bridges, and related problems and possible solutions, has been provided by Steinman [1941, 1945a,b,c,d, 1946a,b, 1947, 1950, 1954] and others [Modjeski and Masters, 1941]. General discussions on vibrations of suspension bridges have been provided by Russell [1841], Timoshenko [1928, 1943], and Bleich et al. [1950].

Note that dangerous bridge vibrations can be generated due to loads other than vehicular impact and wind, for example, heavy pedestrian traffic. According to Bachman [1992], "Rhythmical human body motions lasting up to 20 seconds or more lead to almost periodic dynamic forces. The manifold different types of rhythmical human body motions constitute a large variety of possible dynamic forces. These dynamic forces increase almost linearly with the number of participants." The representative activities related to these motions are walking, running, jumping, dancing, hand clapping, and lateral body swaying [Bachman, 1992]. The normal walking rate of people varies up to 2.3 paces per second or 2.3 Hz (about 4 mph), which is also considered the upper frequency limit of a marching infantry. Undesirable bridge vibrations from marching armies on bridges have been reported in the literature [Leonard, 1966]. This phenomenon occurs because the frequency of the army's march and the pedestrians' movements approach the natural frequency of the bridge (see Fig. 3.13), leading to resonance. This was evident during the November 1973 inaugural celebration of the newly built suspension bridge over the Gulf of Bosporus (main span 3525 ft). Its bridge deck

TABLE 3.6
Bridge frequency–human discomfort relationship [Leonard, 1966]

Number of cycles per second	Type of discomfort
0.25–1	Motion sickness
2	Head resonance, motion sickness
4–6	Major resonance of the whole body
7–9	Abdominal resonance
10–12	Unspecified trunk resonances

was so jammed with the party revelers (pedestrian traffic) that their random movements (walking, running, and jumping) caused large bridge vibrations that were judged dangerous enough to warrant ordering the removal of pedestrians from the bridge [ENR, 1973]. Footbridges are particularly susceptible to human-induced vibrations, and special measures are sometimes required to avoid resonant frequencies [Leonard, 1966; Bachman, 1992]. A few case studies of structures, including footbridges, and human-induced vibrations are discussed by Leonard [1966].

Note that bridge vibrations within a certain range of frequencies also tend to affect humans (pedestrians) adversely, both physiologically and psychologically. The physiological effects, which derive from the fact that the human body is a dynamic system with its own natural frequencies, include various feelings of discomfort and body resonance that may extend beyond the normal human tolerance levels. As shown in Table 3.6, these are reported to occur in the frequency range of 1–12 Hz [Leonard, 1966]. Discomfort or annoyance may result from subjecting a human body to prolonged vibrations in which any of these frequencies predominate. As can be seen from Fig. 3.13, these frequencies are well within the frequency ranges of most bridges (1–20 Hz) [Leonard, 1966; Cantieni, 1984], although they can be as low as 0.25 Hz for suspension bridges.

The psychological effects of bridge vibrations on humans vary and are very difficult to define, the most likely effect being alarm about the ultimate safety of the bridge. A discussion on human tolerance levels for bridge vibrations can be found in [Leonard, 1966]. Because of the extreme sensitivity of the human body to vibrations, the limits of tolerance are reached at levels below those likely to cause distress in bridge structures.

Another aspect of bridge vibrations is their effect on vehicle passengers. In general, this effect is not noteworthy, except possibly on suspension bridges. This is because the passing time of a vehicle on a short- or a medium-span bridge is so short (4.5 seconds for crossing a 400-ft span at 60 mph) that any long-term effects are unlikely to be built up sufficiently to be noticed [Leonard, 1966].

3.10.5 Provisions in the AASHTO Specifications for Wind Loads

Specifications for calculating wind pressures for different kinds of bridges are covered in AASHTO 3.15, *Wind Loads*. The basic wind velocity is assumed to be 100 mph applied to the exposed area of the structure, which consists of the areas of all the members, including the floor system and railings, as seen in an elevation at 90° to the longitudinal axis of the structure. Depending on the combination of certain group loadings (described at the end of this chapter), the prescribed wind loads can be reduced or increased in the ratio of the square of the design wind velocity to the square of the basic wind velocity (100 mph), provided that the maximum probable wind velocity can be ascertained with reasonable accuracy.

Wind loads acting on a bridge consist of two components:

1. Wind load on the structure (superstructure and substructure)
2. Wind load on the moving load (vehicles on the bridge)

Separate provisions are specified for superstructures and the substructures as follows:

3.10.5.1 Wind load on superstructure

1. *Group II and group V loadings:*
   (a) *Trusses and arches:* 75 psf, but not less than 300 and 150 pounds per linear foot in the plane of the windward and leeward chords, respectively
   (b) *Girders and beams:* 50 psf, but not less than 300 pounds per linear foot
2. *Group III and VI loadings:* Loadings of case 1 above reduced by 70 percent, and a load of 100 pounds per linear foot applied at right angles to the longitudinal axis of the bridge, applied 6 ft above the deck as a wind load on the moving live load

Comments: The main difference between cases 1 and 2 is that in case 1 the wind load is applied on the moving load (vehicles).

3.10.5.2 Wind load on substructure (AASHTO 3.15.2)

Forces acting on a substructure fall in two categories:

Forces transferred from the superstructure. These forces depend on the type of superstructure, the skew angle (angle between the assumed wind direction and the normal to the longitudinal axis of the bridge), and the load group combinations. Both longitudinal and lateral loads are specified. Separate wind load values are given for group II and V loadings, and for group III and VI loadings. It should be noted that loads for group III and VI loadings are only 30 percent of the loads for the group II and V loadings, but are increased by additional wind load on moving live load per AASHTO 3.15.2.1.2, to be applied at a point 6 ft above the deck.

For the usual girder and slab bridges of spans not exceeding 125 ft, which constitute most short-span bridges, AASHTO 3.15.2.1.3 prescribes the following loadings:

(a) *On the substructure:* 50 psf transverse and 12 psf longitudinal, to be applied simultaneously
(b) *On the live load:* 100 pounds per linear foot transverse and 40 pounds per linear foot longitudinal, to be applied simultaneously

Forces applied directly to the substructure. An assumed wind pressure of 40 psf, based on a basic wind speed of 100 mph, is applied to the substructure. In the case of a skewed wind loading, the analysis can be performed by resolving the applied load into components perpendicular to the end and the front elevations of the substructure. Again, as in the case of wind loads described in the preceding paragraphs, these wind loads are different for different group loadings.

3.10.6 Overturning Wind Loads

Overturning wind loads are to be considered in addition to the preceding forces. AASHTO 3.15.3 stipulates that an upward force, to be calculated as follows, be applied at the windward quarter point of the superstructure transverse width:

1. 20 psf of the deck and sidewalk plan area for group II and V loading combinations
2. 6 psf of the deck and sidewalk plan area for group III and VI loading combinations

3.10.7 Investigation of Aerodynamic Structural Response by Wind Tunnel Tests

3.10.7.1 Application of wind tunnel tests

The responses of structures to wind-induced forces depends on the characteristics of the oncoming wind and on the geometry and mechanical properties of the structures. Based on theory and experimental data, engineers can estimate certain types of wind loads and the associated structural responses with reasonable accuracy. Some examples are the determination of mean wind loads acting on circular cylinders in a terrain with uniform roughness, or the prediction of flutter instability of certain types of suspension bridges in a horizontally homogenous wind flow. However, several situations are encountered in practice where the analytical tools are not fully capable of describing the aerodynamic properties of the structure or of taking into consideration the buffeting aspects of the oncoming wind flow.

Improvements in bridge design have added to the complexity of predicting the wind-structure response with certainty. The introduction of high-strength materials (concrete and steel) and the increased use of welding, orthotropic decks, cable-stays, and other advances in engineering have led to bridge designs that are considerably lighter, more slender, and require less damping; consequently, these bridges are also more sensitive to wind excitation [Bleich, 1948].

In view of the difficulties described in predicting the behavior under wind loads for certain types of structures, such as tall buildings and medium- and long-span bridges (arch, cable-stayed, and suspension), the required design information is obtained from wind tunnel tests on structural models. The familiar November 7, 1940, collapse of the Tacoma Narrows suspension bridge triggered serious examination of the aerodynamic behavior of bridges and led to the successful use of wind tunnel tests [Farquharson, 1949] for investigating wind-induced forces and the corresponding responses.

Wind tunnel tests are conducted extensively for aircraft structures. Their description and related information can be found in many texts on aerodynamics. Wind tunnel tests are also conducted for tall buildings; long-span bridges (such as cable-stayed and suspension bridges); tall, slender towers; large structures of unusual flexibility and light weight; major structures in special locations affected by topographical features such as hills, cliffs, valleys, and canyons; special structures such as off-shore oil platforms, tall monuments, radar stations; launch facilities for space structures; and automobiles. Wind tunnel model tests are also used to determine the effects of snow drifts on roofs having unusual geometries and to determine the alteration or amplification of winds by hills and other topographical features. They are used to test power plants, chemical plants, and factories to ensure proper dispersion of pollutants emitted from such plants and factories and to test urban environments to devise strategies to combat air pollution [Liu, 1991]. A brief discussion on wind tunnel applications is provided by Simui and Scanlan [1986, Ch. 7] and Liu [1991].

As far as model tests of a bridge are concerned, it should be recognized that the action of wind must be taken into account not only for the completed bridge, but also for the bridge during construction. In general, the same method of testing and analysis applies in the two cases. To decrease the vulnerability of a partially completed bridge to wind-induced loads, temporary ties and damping devices are used. Also, to minimize the risk of strong wind loading, construction usually takes place in seasons with low probabilities of occurrence of severe storms [Simui and Scanlan, 1986].

3.10.7.2 Types of wind tunnels

Wind tunnels can be classified in a number of ways. According to ASCE [1987], wind tunnels used for structural engineering purposes may be classified into four basic categories:

1. Long tunnels, in which the atmospheric flows are simulated by a thick boundary layer that develops naturally over a rough floor. Typically, the boundary layer has a depth of 0.5 to 1.0 m, and can be increased by placing passive devices at the test section entrance. A typical long wind tunnel has a 20–30 m test section. The design and performance of a low-cost boundary-layer wind tunnel, 2.4 m $\times$ 2.4 m $\times$ 20 m, at the University of Sydney has been discussed by Vickery [1976].
2. Short tunnels, usually 5 m long, are used for aeronautical purposes. These are designed for testing in uniform and smooth flow, conditions applicable to aircraft structures and for which the test section need not be long. Short tunnels are not suitable for testing civil engineering structures such as buildings and chimneys, which are exposed to turbulent boundary-layer winds.
3. Tunnels with passive devices, in which thick boundary layers are generated by grids, fences, or spires placed at the test section entrance. The flow is then allowed to pass over a fetch of roughness elements.
4. Tunnels with active devices, such as jets or machine-driven shutters and flaps. In tunnels equipped with jets, it is possible, within certain limits, to vary the mean velocity profile and the flow turbulence independently. Such tunnels, although expensive, may be useful for basic studies in which the effect of varying some flow characteristics independently of others can be studied in detail [Simui and Scanlan, 1986].

Wind tunnels may also be classified as open circuit or closed circuit [Liu, 1991]. Both are used for testing structural models. An open-circuit tunnel is normally a straight structure having a funnel-shaped intake at one end and a funnel-shaped outlet at the other end. The enlarged cross-sectional areas at the ends are meant to reduce head loss (energy dissipation) and prevent undesirable strong winds from being generated near the inlet and the outlet. The throat of the tunnel is the test section. The closed-circuit wind tunnel consists of loops that may be horizontal or vertical to save laboratory space. Some large closed-circuit tunnels utilize the enlarged return section as an additional test section for low-speed tests, such as those required for air pollution or wind energy studies. Closed-circuit tunnels may be built indoors or outdoors and do not suck in rain, snow, or dust. For this reason, most outdoor wind tunnels are of the closed-circuit type.

Wind tunnels may also be described in terms of wind speed. They are commonly referred to as low-speed tunnels if the Mach number is less than 0.33, which under atmospheric conditions corresponds to a wind velocity of approximately 110 m/sec (or 250 mph). They are referred to as high-speed tunnels if the Mach number is greater than 0.33, as supersonic tunnels if the Mach number exceeds 1.0, and as hypersonic tunnels if the Mach number exceeds 3.0. Wind tunnels for testing structural models are low-speed tunnels of large cross-sectional area. Wind speed is normally limited to 50 m/sec (112 mph) and often to 25 m/sec (56 mph). This is because wind speeds greater than 10 m/sec (22 mph) are considered unnecessary for testing structural models [Liu, 1991].

Most wind tunnels have rectangular or square cross sections, although a few have circular cross sections. The shape of the tunnel is unimportant for aeronautical or other tests that require uniform wind velocity. However, boundary-layer tunnels must have a square or rectangular cross section to properly simulate the variation of velocity with height in the atmospheric boundary layer.

Most wind tunnels are driven by fans, but some are driven by wall jets approximately parallel to the mean flow direction. Most tunnels generate wind of constant (uniform) temperature. Exceptions are the meteorological tunnels used to study air pollution (plume dispersion), which require vertical stratification of temperature. One such tunnel exists at Colorado State University; it measures 1.9 m × 1.9 m with a test section 28 m long. Note that stratification of temperature is not required for testing civil engineering structures.

Tunnels used for civil engineering purposes have cross sections that rarely exceed 3 m × 3 m. A notable exception is the 9 m × 9 m tunnel of the National Research Council of Ottawa, Canada, which has a test section of 39.6 m. The long-boundary-layer wind tunnel at the Public Works Research Institute in Tskuba, Japan, has a test section 39 m long. However, the largest wind tunnel, a closed-circuit type, is NASA's Ames wind tunnel in California, with a test section measuring 80 ft × 120 ft, large enough to test a full-size small aircraft.

3.10.7.3 Types of wind tunnel tests

Because aerodynamic forces, including self-excited forces, may be significantly affected by the structure of the oncoming flow (i.e., the variation of mean speed with height, and features of the flow turbulence), modern wind tunnel testing is done at facilities that attempt to simulate atmospheric flows. Experimental studies are most often performed at atmospheric boundary-layer wind tunnels, traditional wind tunnels used for studies of aircraft aerodynamics, and wind tunnels designed specifically for analyzing bridges, mostly suspended-span types.

Wind tunnel test procedures can be described by the model type (full model, taut strip model, or sectional model) and by the condition of the flow (smooth or turbulent). The tunnel model should not occupy more than 10 percent of the cross-sectional area, although models giving more blockage have been used [Houghton and Carruthers, 1976, Ch. 6].

Model tests of the full bridge. The full bridge model test involves testing the scaled model of the full bridge. It offers many advantages [Simui and Scanlan, 1986; ASCE, 1987]:

1. It represents the proper interaction of the bridge deck, piers, abutments, towers, and cables (if they exist).
2. It can represent the proper flow distortions on all parts of the bridge if the surrounding topography is modeled as well as the bridge itself.
3. In certain cases, the model scale permits the proper turbulent structure of the wind to be modeled as well.

Accuracy in scale modeling of the bridge is very important to obtain reliable results. In addition to being geometrically similar to the full bridge, such models must satisfy certain other similarity requirements. These include similarities pertaining to mass distribution, reduced frequency, mechanical damping, and shapes of vibration modes. The usual scale of such models is on the order of 1:300, although 1:100 has been used in a few cases [Farquharson, 1949; Scruton, 1948, 1952; Hirai, Okauchi, and Miyata, 1966; Davenport et al., 1969; Reinhold, 1982]. For example, for the Fred Hartman cable-stayed bridge referred to earlier, wind tunnel tests on two models, 1:250 scale (full bridge model) and 1:96 scale (section model), were conducted to study its aerodynamic behavior [Lovett and Warren, 1992]. Model tests of a few cable-stayed bridges have been described by Podolny and Scalzi [1986].

The construction of full bridge models is very elaborate and very expensive. Since the inception of wind tunnel testing of bridges, only a handful of tests on models of full bridges have been conducted [Davenport et al., 1969; Davenport, 1982; Scanlan, 1982].

Taut strip model tests. Taut strip model testing is essentially a slight simplification of full bridge model testing and is not commonly used [Davenport, 1982; Scanlan, 1982]. It was developed to study the behavior of suspension bridges at a larger scale than that which is possible with full models [Davenport, 1972; Tanaka and Davenport, 1982].

In taut strip models, short segments of the deck geometry are mounted side by side and separated by small gaps on a pair of wires. The model normally spans the wind tunnel test section. The wires are stretched across the wind tunnel and serve as the basic inner structure, which is then externally clad to resemble a given bridge geometrically. The purpose of providing tensioned wires is to permit duplication of the model frequency scale of fundamental bending and torsional frequencies of the bridge. Such models then respond to the laboratory wind flow in a manner similar to the center span of a suspension bridge [Davenport, 1972].

Section model tests. By far the most common method of testing uses section models of the bridge decks and the bridge structure. An advantage of section model tests is that they are relatively inexpensive. Section model tests are quite useful for making initial assessments, based on simple tests, of the extent to which a bridge deck shape is aeroelastically stable. Additionally, they offer the advantage of allowing the measurement of the fundamental aerodynamic characteristics of the bridge deck, on the basis of which comprehensive analytical studies can be carried out [Simui and Scanlan, 1986]. A comparison of full and section model tests has been provided by Wardlow [1978].

The section models consist of representative spanwise sections of the deck built to scale, spring-supported at the ends to permit both vertical and torsional motion, and usually enclosed between end plates to reduce aerodynamic end effects. Typically, they can be built to scales on the order of 1:50 to 1:25, so that the discrepancies between full-scale and model Reynolds numbers are smaller than in the case of full bridge tests [Simui and Scanlan, 1986].

Note that, with few exceptions, wind tunnel testing on bridge decks is performed in smooth flows [ASCE, 1987]. Details on engineering aspects of wind tunnel testing of structures can be found in many references [Davenport, 1963, 1982; Wardlow, 1969, 1970; Wardlow and Ponder, 1970; Ishizaki and Chiu, 1976, Ch. 2; Sachs, 1978, Ch. 4; Scanlan, 1981, 1982; Reinhold, 1982; Simui and Scanlan, 1986; Liu, 1991; Cermak, 1995].

3.11
TEMPERATURE-INDUCED FORCES

3.11.1 General Concepts

Like wind, temperature-induced forces constitute a kind of environmental load. As can be expected, temperature variations cause bridges to expand and contract. Traditionally, the longitudinal movements induced by maximum expected temperature variations, typically $\pm 20\,°C$, are accommodated through sliding joints, bearing displacements, or flexible pier designs. Depending on the type of superstructure, the span length, and the support conditions of the superstructure, different types of deck joints and different bearings at the supports are provided.

3.11.2 Determination of Temperature-Induced Forces

Unidirectional thermal expansion, ΔL, can be predicted by the simple expression

$$\Delta L = \alpha L \Delta T \tag{3.26}$$

where α = coefficient of thermal expansion
L = length of the bridge
ΔT = range of mean bridge temperature

If restrained, this deformation will induce an axial force, P, given by

$$P = \frac{(\Delta L)AE}{L} \tag{3.27}$$

where A = cross-sectional area of the deck
E = the modulus of elasticity of the deck material

Thus, the axial force, P, is directly proportional to the axial stiffness of the deck, AE. The current AASHTO specifications [AASHTO, 1992] specify temperature ranges for concrete and steel bridges for two climates designated as moderate and cold. However, research shows that this method of predicting bridge temperature ranges and resulting movements does not recognize the full complexity of the thermal behavior of bridges. In the past 25 years, in the wake of observed distress that was attributed to the thermal stresses in some prestressed concrete bridges [Leonhardt, Kolbe, and Peter, 1965; Leonhardt and Lippoth, 1970], there has been a growing awareness of the importance of the nonuniform temperature distribution (referred to as temperature gradient) through the superstructure. As a result, thermal loads on bridge superstructures have been a topic of extensive research [Reynolds and Emanuel, 1974; Hunt and Cooke, 1975; Ho and Liu, 1989]. Many researchers have reported on the effects of thermal loads on reinforced and prestressed concrete bridges [Priestley, 1972; Emerson, 1973; Radolli and Green, 1975; Neville, 1981; Hirst, 1982; Elbadry and Ghali, 1983, 1995; Hoffman, McClure, and West, 1983; Imbsen et al., 1985; Rao, 1986; and Mirambell and Aguado, 1990]. Emanuel and Hulsey [1978] and Dilger [1983] have discussed the effects of temperature variations on concrete deck–steel beam composite bridges. Fu and Ng [1990] have discussed thermal loads on steel box girder and orthotropic bridges. Moorty and Roeder [1991] and Li [1991] have presented analytical parametric studies of composite bridges in Canada. A general discussion on temperature-dependent movements has been presented by Priestley [1976].

The temperature-induced forces (referred to as *thermal forces* in AASHTO specifications) are generated in bridge structures as a result of repeated cycles of heating and cooling from solar radiation and the surrounding air, a phenomenon that triggers an exchange of heat energy between the surfaces of structures and their surroundings. The thermal response of bridge decks is a complex transient phenomenon influenced by many factors, chiefly the following:

1. Time-dependent solar radiation
2. Ambient temperature
3. Wind speed fluctuations
4. Material properties, such as the heat transfer coefficient for reinforced and prestressed concrete and steel
5. Variation in ambient temperature between the maximum and the minimum during a 24-hour period
6. Type of span—simple or continuous
7. Deck configurations, such as T-beam, single or multicell reinforced or prestressed concrete girders, concrete deck–steel girder composite, orthotropic bridge
8. Geometrical configuration of the deck, such as the overhang-to-web depth ratio
9. Surface characteristics of the deck

Figure 3.27 schematically shows factors affecting the thermal response of a typical two-cell concrete girder bridge [Priestley, 1976].

A major problem related to the thermal response of a bridge superstructure is the prediction of the thermal gradient resulting from solar heating and the temperature distribution through the thickness of the member. Depending on the assumptions, the heat flow in a bridge deck can be modeled as a one-, two-, or three-dimensional problem.

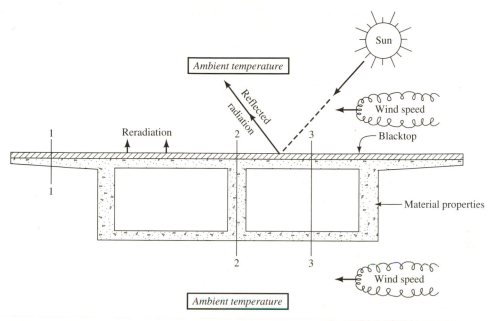

FIGURE 3.27
Factors affecting the thermal response of superstructures [Priestley, 1978].

Historically, the thermoelastic analysis of the problem of heat flow in a solid was first presented by Fourier in the form of a three-dimensional partial differential equation, which was improved upon by J. M. C. Duhamel (1797–1872) by including the effect of deformations produced by temperature changes. Duhamel defined the conditions at the boundary of the body and showed that the thermal stresses could be determined in the same manner as those due to body forces and forces applied at the surfaces; he was also the first to suggest that total stresses could be obtained by superposition [Timoshenko, 1952]. The governing equation for the flow of heat in a solid, assumed linear, is expressed as the following three-dimensional partial differential equation [Timoshenko, 1952; Ho and Liu, 1989; Fu and Ng, 1990]:

$$\frac{\partial}{\partial x}\left(k_x \frac{\partial T}{\partial x}\right) + \frac{\partial}{\partial x}\left(k_y \frac{\partial T}{\partial y}\right) + \frac{\partial}{\partial z}\left(k_z \frac{\partial T}{\partial z}\right) = c\rho \frac{\partial T}{\partial t} \tag{3.28}$$

where

x, y, z = Cartesian coordinates
t = time
c = coefficient of specific heat of the medium
ρ = density of the medium
$k_x, k_y,$ and k_z = thermal conductivity corresponding to the x, y, and z Cartesian axes

For a bridge subjected to solar radiation, it is assumed that there are no thermal variations along the longitudinal direction, z. For the material-independent properties, with $k/c\rho$ replaced by K, the diffusivity of the medium (Eq. 3.28) is reduced to a two-

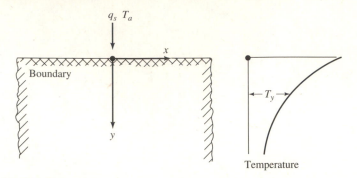

FIGURE 3.28
Coordinate definition for transient heat flow analysis [Priestley, 1978].

dimensional heat flow problem, as defined in Fig. 3.28:

$$\frac{\partial^2 T}{\partial x^2} + \frac{\partial^2 T}{\partial y^2} = \frac{1}{K}\frac{\partial T}{\partial t} \tag{3.29}$$

with the following boundary conditions [Fu and Ng, 1990]:

1. *Heat flow:* Heat flow input at specific points of the body, i.e., the boundary heat flow input, q_s:

$$q_s = k_n(\partial T/\partial_n) \tag{3.30}$$

where k_n is the median thermal conductivity in a direction normal to the surface, n.

2. *Convection:* Due to convection flow to and from the surrounding air as a result of temperature differences between the bridge surface and the air:

$$q_s = h[T_a(t) - T_0(t)] \tag{3.31}$$

The two boundary conditions given by Eqs. 3.30 and 3.31 can be jointly written as [Priestley, 1978]

$$k_n\frac{\partial T}{\partial n} + q + h(T_a - T_0) = 0 \tag{3.32}$$

where T_a = the environmental temperature
 T_0 = the solid boundary temperature, i.e., the surface temperature of the body in contact with the air
 h = boundary heat transfer coefficient or convection coefficient (a variable mainly dependent on the speed of the air across the boundary)
 n = direction normal to the boundary

Research has indicated that, for most bridges, the transverse heat flow is insignificant. Consequently, Eq. 3.29 can be transformed to a one-dimensional equation [Emerson, 1973; Hunt and Cooke, 1975; Priestley, 1978; Ho and Liu, 1989]:

$$\frac{k_n}{\rho c}\frac{\partial^2 \theta}{\partial y^2} = \frac{\partial \theta}{\partial t} \tag{3.33}$$

Priestley [1978] used Eq. 3.33 to predict the thermal response of an isotropic solid with a boundary, in contact with air, subjected to variations in ambient temperature, T_a, and radiation, q_s, as defined in Fig. 3.28.

Quantities q_s, T_a, and h are complex functions of time. Furthermore, h, the heat transfer coefficient, is a function of the following main parameters [Fu and Ng, 1990]: wind velocity, flow configuration, surface roughness, thermal properties of the air, surface area, and the temperature difference. Figure 3.29 shows the vertical distribution of longitudinal strain obtained from the finite difference solution of Eq. 3.33 in conjunction with boundary conditions given by Eq. 3.32.

Based on the preceding approach and assuming several hypotheses related to concrete (continuum, isotropy, homogeneity, and completion of concrete hardening process), a standard thermal design gradient (Fig. 3.30) was developed to predict temperature variation through the depth of concrete girders [Priestley, 1978]. Included in this development were factors based on a parametric study of the influence of wind, ambient temperature variation, blacktop (wearing surface) thickness, and surface solar absorptivity on the thermal response of a number of typical prestressed concrete bridge sections including slabs, box girders, and beam and slab bridges (multiple T's) in New Zealand. This design gradient involves two components: a fifth-power temperature decrease from a maximum T (the value of which depends on the blacktop thickness) at the concrete deck surface to zero at a depth of 1200 mm (47.4 in.) and a linear increase in temperature over the bottom 200 mm (7.9 in.) of the section. For superstructure depths less than 1400 mm (55.1 in.) these two components are superimposed. For concrete decks above enclosed air cells, a different gradient (shown by the dashed line in Fig. 3.30) is specified to represent the insulating effect of the air cell [Priestley, 1978].

The aforementioned procedure is currently being used in New Zealand, and an essentially identical design approach has been specified in AASHTO–LRFD specifications [AASHTO, 1994a] (Fig. 3.31) and is applicable to both concrete and steel superstructures in the United States. For this purpose, the values of temperatures T_1 and T_2 for decks with 2-in.- and 4-in.-thick blacktops are given in Table 3.7, for various solar radiation zones in the United States, as shown in Fig. 3.32. It should be recognized, however, that since climatic conditions are different, the conclusions and design rules drawn up for one country are, generally speaking, not applicable without modification in another.

3.11.3 Current AASHTO Provisions

Stresses resulting from governing temperature differentials should be appropriately taken into design considerations. For the sake of uniformity in considering temperature differentials, AASHTO 3.16 specifies the following ranges of temperature:

Metal structures:

Moderate climate:	0–120 °F
Cold climate:	30–120 °F

Concrete structures:

Moderate climate:	30 °F temperature rise	40 °F temperature fall
Cold climate:	35 °F temperature rise	45 °F temperature fall

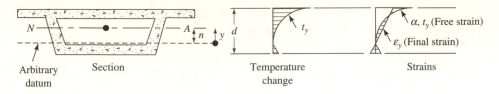

FIGURE 3.29
Vertical distribution of longitudinal thermal strain [Priestley, 1978].

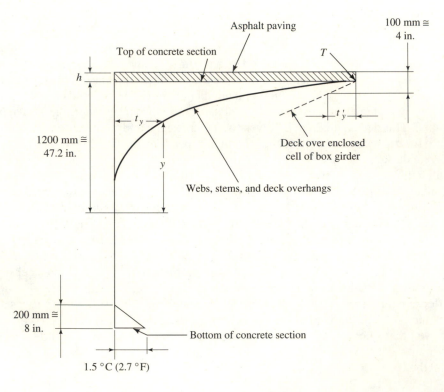

For temperature in centigrade
and y and h in millimeters:

$$T = 32 - 0.2h$$

$$t_y = T\left(\frac{y}{1200}\right)^5$$

$$t_y' = (5.00 - 0.05h)\ °C$$

For temperature in Fahrenheit
and y and h in inches:

$$T = 57.6 - 9.14h$$

$$t_y = T\left(\frac{y}{47.2}\right)^5$$

$$t_y' = (9.00 - 2.28h)\ °F$$

FIGURE 3.30
New Zealand design thermal gradient [Priestley, 1978].

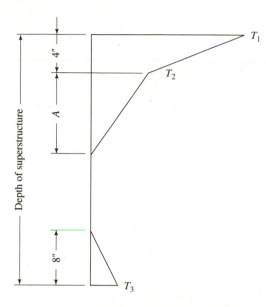

FIGURE 3.31
Thermal gradient for U.S. highway bridges (concrete and steel superstructures) [AASHTO, 1994a].

TABLE 3.7
Temperature gradients [AASHTO, 1994a]

Zone	Plain concrete surface		2-in. blacktop		4-in. blacktop	
	T_1 (°F)	T_2 (°F)	T_1 (°F)	T_2 (°F)	T_1 (°F)	T_2 (°F)
1	54	14	43	14	31	9
2	46	12	36	12	25	10
3	41	11	33	11	23	11
4	38	9	29	9	22	11

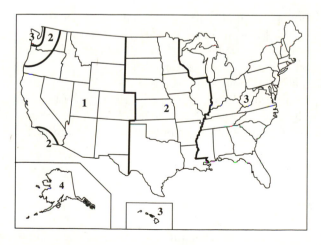

FIGURE 3.32
Solar radiation zones for the United States [AASHTO, 1994a].

3.11.4 Expansion Joints, Bearings, and Jointless Bridges

While expansion joints and support bearings are the devices commonly used in bridge superstructures to accommodate superstructural movements, extensive field observations have shown that they do not serve their intended purpose [Purvis, 1983]. Temperature-induced, or thermal, forces and their effects on a superstructure can be significant. Restraint on any movement of the superstructure due to temperature or any other cause may result in the development of forces that can be very damaging. In most cases, the major problems encountered in joints and bearings (typical for open joints, sliding plate joints, and open finger joints) are as follows [GangaRao and Thippeswamy, 1994]:

1. Corrosion of bearings and pier caps due to deicing chemicals that leak through the joints. This restricts the free movements (translation and rotation) of the superstructure and causes unusual stresses in the deck and the bridge seats.
2. Accumulation of debris and other foreign material restricts the free movement, which causes unusual stress build-up in the superstructure and substructure.
3. Differential elevation at bridge joints causes additional impact forces on the joints and the deck slab, which may lead to fracture and buckling in the deck slab.

Deck joints and support bearings are integral components of a bridge superstructure. However, it should be recognized that installation of joints and bearings during construction is time-consuming and leads to traffic interruption and delays in the completion of the project. In addition, they involve high initial and life-cycle (maintenance) costs, leading to higher toll fees for the bridge users.

To eliminate the problems caused by thermal expansion and contraction of bridge superstructures, a new design approach that involves fewer joints or the elimination of deck joints altogether is being introduced in highway bridge construction. Based on extensive research [Freyermuth, 1969; Campbell and Richardson, 1975; Zuk, 1981; Stuart, 1985; Imbsen et al., 1985; Wolde-Tinsae and Klinger, 1987; Burke, 1987, 1990a,b; Wolde-Tinsae, Klinger, and White, 1988; Dagher, Elgaaly, and Kankam, 1991], this new concept involves integrating the bridge superstructure with abutments and piers, and has been adopted by as many as 28 states, with the state of Tennessee taking the lead [Loveall, 1985; Wolde-Tinsae, 1987; Wasserman, 1987; NCHRP-SYN, 1985, 1989]. A multispan 2800-ft-long jointless bridge has been built in Tennessee (Island Bridge, at Kingsport), with joints only at the ends [Loveall, 1985]. These increasingly popular bridges are called "integral abutment" or "jointless" bridges. Analysis of jointless bridges has been given by Lee and Sarsam [1973]. An exhaustive study of jointless bridge behavior, development of design procedures, and design recommendations has been presented by GangaRao and Thippeswamy [1994].

3.12
FORCES FROM STREAM CURRENT, FLOATING ICE, AND DRIFT

Columns and piers in streams and rivers are subjected to forces due to stream flow, ice, and drift. In addition, floating logs, roots, and other debris may accumulate at piers and effectively block parts of the waterway and increase stream pressure load on the pier. Methods to evaluate debris loadings are currently being developed by the NCHRP. Meanwhile, it is suggested that the method based on the New Zealand Highway Bridge specifications be used as guidance in the absence of site-specific criteria [NCHRP, 1992].

3.12.1 Force of Stream Current on Piers

The force of stream current against the pier depends on the velocity of the flowing water and the cross-sectional shape of the pier. The more streamlined the pier, the less the force due to stream current. The flatter the nose of the pier, the larger the surface area of obstruction and the larger the force.

Fundamentally speaking, the drag F_D (force) on a blunt object due to an oncoming fluid can be expressed by the following formula [Roberson et al., 1972; Roberson and Crowe, 1990; Gerhart, Cross, and Hochstein, 1992]:

$$F_D = \tfrac{1}{2} C_D A_p \rho V_0^2 \tag{3.34}$$

where C_D = coefficient of drag
A_p = projected area of the body
ρ = fluid density
V_0 = free-stream velocity

Equation 3.34 is based on the solution of the Navier-Stokes equations for general linear viscous fluids [Frank, 1974]. The drag coefficient, C_D, is a function of the Reynolds number, the aspect ratio, and the cross-sectional shape of the blunt object. Its values for several types of cross-sectional shapes, obtained experimentally [Rouse, 1946; Morrison, 1962; Roberson et al., 1972; Frank, 1974; Roberson and Crow, 1990] are given in Table A.6 (Appendix A). For the sake of simplicity and specificity, Eq. 3.34 can be expressed as

$$F_D = K V_0^2 \tag{3.35}$$

where

$$K = \tfrac{1}{2} \rho A_p \tag{3.36}$$

According to AASHTO 3.18.1, the force of stream current is to be calculated according to

$$P = K V^2 \tag{3.37}$$

where P = pressure, psf
V = velocity of water, ft/sec
K = a constant whose value depends on the shape of the pier ends,

As shown in Fig. 3.33, the value of K is $1\tfrac{3}{8}$ for square ends, $\tfrac{1}{2}$ for pier with included nose angle of 30° or less, and $\tfrac{2}{3}$ for circular piers.

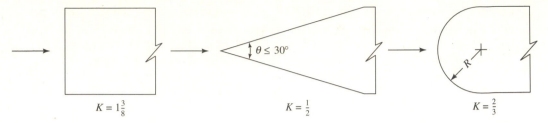

FIGURE 3.33
Values of K for various pier shapes.

3.12.2 Force of Ice on Piers

Piers may be subjected to severe forces due to ice flowing in a stream or river; these forces may be static or dynamic. Static ice pressure is created by thermal movements of continuous stationary ice sheets on large bodies of water or from ice jams. Dynamic ice pressure is created as a result of moving ice sheets and ice floes carried by stream flow, wind, or currents.

Ice jams in a river upstream of a bridge could create catastrophic conditions. Ice jams could clog the waterway, seriously impeding the flow of water, and result in floods caused by the river water jumping its banks. As an example, the March 12, 1992, issue of the *Los Angeles Times* [LA Times, 1992] reported this account of the March 11 flood in the City of Montpelier, Vermont:

> Ice jams diverted a rushing river through the heart of Vermont's capital Wednesday, and the flood forced the closing of the state offices and schools.... Governor Howard Dean... declared emergency... as the water rose rapidly during the morning to depths of up to six feet.... The downtown area filled with water as the Winooski River, obstructed by huge blocks of ice, jammed against bridges, jumped its banks and took a new course. The rushing water filled about half a mile of State Street with turbulent rapids.
>
> A railroad bridge over the Winooski collapsed Wednesday afternoon under the crush of ice pulling down most power lines in Montpelier, the nation's smallest state capital.
>
> About an hour later, however, workers using a crane repeatedly dropped a large weight on the biggest of the three ice jams and the flood waters began receding.

Considerable information on ice loads is provided by Neill [1976, 1981]; Montgomery and Lipsett [1980]; Montgomery, Girard, and Lipsett [1980]; and Montgomery et al. [1984]. The horizontal force resulting from the pressure of moving ice depends on the effective ice strength, the thickness of the contact ice sheet, the width of the pier or the diameter of a circular-shaft pier at the level of the ice, and the inclination of the pier nose to the vertical. The effective ice strength is taken to be in the range of 100 to 400 psi, based on the assumption that either crushing or splitting of the ice takes place on contact with the pier. Note that higher values of the crushing strength of ice have been determined for low temperatures—more than 800 lb/in.² has been recorded for ice at 2 °F. A study of ice pressure against dams [Rose, 1947] due to rise in temperature—the condition producing the greatest pressure—has concluded that 400 lb/in.² is an overly severe loading for dams. However, because the water behind a dam is static, an expanding ice sheet behind a dam is quite different from the floating ice forced against a bridge pier by the flow of water and possible wind drag. The actual value of the horizontal ice pressure to be used will depend on the condition of the ice at the time of movement, including the temperature, the size of the moving ice sheets and floes, and the velocity at contact. Since the last two conditions cannot be determined with a reasonable certainty, it is recommended that a conservative approach be used in estimating the ice conditions. AASHTO 3.18.2.2 recommends the following formula for calculation of horizontal forces due to ice pressure:

$$F = C_n Ptw \tag{3.38}$$

where F = horizontal force due to ice pressure, lb
C_n = coefficient for nose angle from the following table
P = effective ice strength, psi
t = thickness of ice in contact with pier, in.
w = width of pier or diameter of the circular shaft pier at the level of ice action, in.

The following values of C_n are prescribed for use in conjunction with Eq. 3.38:

Inclination of nose to vertical (degrees)	C_n
0–15	1.00
15–30	0.75
30–45	0.50

The values of the effective ice strength shown in Table 3.8 may be used as estimates for use in conjunction with Eq. 3.38 to calculate horizontal forces due to ice on piers of substantial mass and dimensions. Depending on the ratio of pier width (or diameter) to the design ice thickness, the values of effective ice strength shown in Table 3.8 may be increased or reduced as prescribed by AASHTO 3.18.2.2.4.

TABLE 3.8
Effective ice strength [AASHTO, 1992]

Movement condition of ice	Effective ice strength (psi)
Breakup occurs at melting temperatures, ice runs as small cakes and is substantially disintegrated in its structure	100±[a]
Breakup occurs at melting temperatures, but ice moves in large pieces and is internally sound	200±
At breakup, there is an initial movement of ice sheet as a whole or where large sheets of sound ice may strike the piers	300±
Breakup or major ice movement may occur with ice	400±

[a]± means plus or minus a few psi.

3.13
EARTH PRESSURE

Abutments and wing walls are portions of substructure that retain earth (or the back-fill). Consequently, both are subjected to lateral loads (earth pressure). The abutments, in addition to retaining the backfill, support gravity loads (the ends of a bridge's super-structure).

Both abutments and wing walls should be designed to withstand earth pressure as given by Rankine's formula for active earth pressure:

$$P = K_a wh \tag{3.39}$$

where P = Rankine's active earth pressure, lb
K_a = coefficient of active earth pressure
w = unit weight of soil, lb/ft^3
h = height of backfill, ft

For level backfill, the earth pressure is usually denoted by equivalent fluid pressure ($K_a w$). For a value of $K_a = 0.3$ and $w = 120$ lb/ft^3 as the weight of compacted earth, this works out to 36 lb/ft^2 per foot height of abutment or retaining walls. AASHTO 3.20.1 limits this value to 30 lb/ft^2 as a *minimum*. The distribution of this pressure is, of course, triangular or hydrostatic.

AASHTO specifications require that when highway traffic can come within a distance of one-half the wall height from the face of the wall or abutment, a live-load

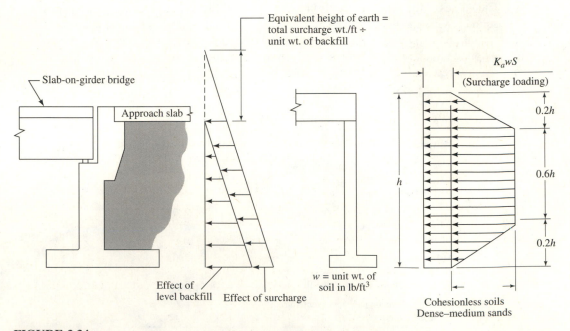

FIGURE 3.34
Earth pressure distribution for various support conditions at the top of an abutment [CALTRANS, 1992].

surcharge equal to at least 2 ft of equivalent weight of earth should be added to the earth load. However, when an adequately designed reinforced concrete approach slab supported at one end by a bridge is provided, live-load surcharge can be ignored.

The hydrostatic pressure distribution of earth pressure as discussed in the preceding paragraphs is based on the assumption that the top of the abutment or the retaining wall is unrestrained. A trapezoidal pressure distribution is used where the top of the wall is restrained, which provides a more realistic solution. Figure 3.34 shows earth pressure distributions for various conditions discussed above.

3.14
SEISMIC LOADS

Along with the wind and the thermal forces discussed earlier, seismic loads constitute yet another major component of environmental forces that all structures must be able to resist. Bridges constitute one of the most important links in the lifelines of the modern world; the others are utilities carrying electricity, gas, and water; telecommunications; roads; and hospitals. It is therefore extremely important that bridges be built earthquake safe and be in a condition to serve as such essential links at all times.

3.14.1 Historical Background

In spite of earthquake-induced damages to bridges worldwide, relatively little has been written or done in the way of research for the earthquake-resistant design of bridges. Most of the research and code development efforts toward the earthquake-resistant design of structures has been focused on buildings. Perhaps this is because of the greater social and economic consequences of earthquake damages in buildings compared with those from damaged bridges.

It is interesting to note that most knowledge for earthquake-resistant designs of structures is of rather recent origin. It was first developed for the earthquake-resistant design of buildings and, as an extension, has been applied to bridges. In Japan, a nation that suffers from the frequent occurrence of earthquakes, the first codification of seismic forces on bridges took place in 1926 as a result of substantial damage to several highway bridges during the 1923 Kanto earthquake, which was estimated at 8.3 on the Richter scale [Ohashi et al., 1979]. In spite of advanced bridge engineering knowledge, the European codes contain very little information about the earthquake-resistant design of bridges, perhaps because the moderate seismicity of the region has not warranted serious attention to the problem [Ravara, 1979]. In New Zealand, a country of moderate seismicity, the codification of earthquake-resistant designs for bridges was first made in 1971 [Chapman, 1979] as specified in the *Highway Bridge Design Brief* [NZMWD, 1978]. In the United States, the first mention of earthquake stresses in AASHTO specifications for highway bridges was made in the 1961 edition. In that edition, earthquake forces were required to be applied to a bridge structure in proportion to its weight, depending on the foundation conditions, but independent of its response characteristics. Earthquake coefficients varied from 2 percent of gravity for spread footing on sound material to 6 percent of gravity for pile foundations [Bull, 1972].

In the United States, the codification for earthquake forces in general dates back to 1906. At that time, in the aftermath of the 1906 San Francisco earthquake, that city's building code provided for a lateral load of 30 psf to compensate for the effects of wind or earthquake loads. As a result of studies following the 1925 Santa Barbara earthquake, the 1972 Uniform Building Code incorporated provisions that, for the first time, applied earthquake forces in proportion to a building's dead loads. The March 10, 1933, Long Beach earthquake (Richter magnitude 6.3) caused very significant damage to buildings, with school buildings suffering the most damage. To prevent the recurrence of similar damage to school buildings in California, the state legislature enacted the Field Act, effective April 10, 1933, which currently specifies procedures to be followed in the design and construction of public school buildings used for elementary and secondary schools and community colleges. The original seismic coefficients in this act were $0.1g$ for masonry buildings without frames, and $0.02g$ to $0.05g$ for other buildings, depending on the foundation conditions. The Riley Act required virtually all California buildings to be designed for an earthquake force equal to 2 percent of the total vertical design load; this was modified to 3 percent for buildings less than 40 ft in height. In the late 1930s, the California Toll Bridge Authority (currently the Division of Bay Toll Crossings) adopted a seismic coefficient of $0.1g$ for the San Francisco–Oakland Bay Bridge [Bull, 1972; Jephcot, 1986].

The City of Los Angeles building code was the first to recognize the importance of the flexibility of a structure when it provided, in its 1943 code, for an earthquake force as a fraction of gravity load, according to the following formula:

$$C = \frac{60}{N + 4.5} \tag{3.40}$$

where C = fraction of the gravity load (percent), 13.3 percent maximum
　　　　N = the number of stories above the story under consideration, subject to a maximum number of 13 stories

Use of Eq. 3.40 was later extended for buildings more than 13 stories tall. In 1952, the Joint Committee on Lateral Forces, composed of members of the San Francisco section of ASCE and the Structural Engineers Association for Northern California, recommended the following formula for the C coefficients, which was later incorporated in the San Francisco building code in a modified form:

$$C = K/T \tag{3.41}$$

where K = 0.015 for buildings and 0.025 for other structures
　　　　T = fundamental period of structure

with the stipulation that for buildings,

$$C_{max} = 0.06$$

$$C_{min} = 0.02$$

and for other structures,

$$C_{max} = 0.10$$

$$C_{min} = 0.03$$

In 1959, the Seismology Committee of the Structural Engineers Association of California published *Recommended Lateral Force Requirements and Commentary* [SEAOC, 1988] for buildings, which was adopted into national building codes such as ASCE [1988]. The basic base shear formula, $V = KCW$, has gone through several revisions ($V = ZKCW$ to $V = ZIKCW$ to $V = ZICW/R$) since its inception. These recommendations have since gained worldwide recognition.

It is interesting to note that in the evolutionary process of codification of earthquake forces, the focus of attention had been, generally speaking, on building structures. Although bridges had, historically, suffered damage during past earthquakes worldwide, that damage had mostly been nonvibrational, such as tilting, settlement and overturning of substructures, displacement at supports, settlement of approach fills, and wing wall damage [Gates, 1976, 1979; Penzien, 1979]. The special problems of bridges were not recognized until after the February 8, 1971, M 6.6 San Fernando earthquake, during which extremely heavy damage was sustained by freeway structures in southern California. During this earthquake, 42 bridges sustained significant damage; 5 of these collapsed [Fung et al., 1971; Jennings, 1971]. This earthquake unquestionably demonstrated the seismic vulnerability of highway bridges built according to pre-1971 AASHTO design procedures and added a new dimension to the urgent need for developing specifications for designing earthquake-resistant bridges.

Several important lessons were learned from the 1971 San Fernando earthquake. Detailed studies showed that bridges built in compliance with pre-1971 AASHO (now AASHTO) specifications, generally speaking, performed very well for moderately strong ground motion. Serious damage and collapse occurred only in the area of the strongest motion [Jennings, 1971]. Gates [1976, 1979] has made the following conclusions based on an in-depth field investigation by Fung et al. [1971] of the San Fernando earthquake bridge damage:

1. The earthquake level in San Fernando exceeded the earthquake forces specified then by the design criteria.
2. There was considerable ground movement, which caused some spans to drop off their supports.
3. Poor connections between the superstructure and the substructure were the main causes of collapse-type failures.
4. Performance of tall, slender columns was better than that of short, stiff columns, as evidenced from the shearing and bending fractures on the latter.
5. The seismic vibrations shattered concrete at the base and footings of many columns, causing longitudinal column reinforcing bars to be pulled out, which, in turn, led some structures to collapse.

The seismic loads on a bridge or on any other structure depend on many factors, chiefly

1. Dynamic response characteristics of the structure
2. Dynamic response characteristics of the soil
3. Proximity of the site to known active faults
4. Intensity of the seismic event

Generally speaking, three methods are available for analysis and design of structures for seismic loads, namely, response spectrum modal analysis, the time history method, and the equivalent static force method. Of these, the first two are called *dynamic analysis methods* [AASHTO, 1991b, 1992].

3.14.2 AASHTO Procedure for Seismic Design of Bridges

3.14.2.1 General considerations

The theoretical basis for earthquake resistance in highway bridges in the United States is a report compiled by the Applied Technology Council [ATC, 1981, 1983], titled *Seismic Design Guidelines for Highway Bridges,* and the limited analytical and experimental research done on the seismic response of bridges since 1971 [Imbsen, Nutt, and Penzien, 1978, 1979]. Although these efforts represent the best state-of-the-art knowledge of the time, there is much that remains to be studied in this field [Hall and Newmark, 1979]. Essentially, the recommended design procedure is a force design methodology based on the design philosophy that large earthquakes are to be resisted by inelastic behavior [Barenberg and Foutch, 1988].

Currently, two approaches are recognized for earthquake-resistant design of bridges [AASHTO, 1991b]: the New Zealand approach [Chapman, 1979] and the California Department of Transportation approach [Gates, 1976, 1979]. The methodology specified in the AASHTO standard [AASHTO, 1991b] is based on a combination of the two. Four additional concepts, developed as a result of observations during the 1971 San Fernando earthquake and related studies and research [Sharpe and Meyers, 1979], are included in the AASHTO standard. These concepts, which address the problem of relative displacement of various portions of superstructure and substructure, are as follows [AASHTO, 1991b]:

1. Minimum requirements are specified for the support lengths of girders at abutments, columns, and hinge seats to allow for some of the important relative displacement effects that cannot be calculated by the current state-of-the-art methods.
2. Member design forces are calculated for the directional uncertainty of seismic motions and the simultaneous occurrence of the earthquake in two perpendicular horizontal directions.
3. Design requirements and forces for foundations are intended to minimize foundation damage that is not readily detectable.
4. Methodology is applicable to all parts of the United States.

The AASHTO standard [1991b] treats the seismic design of bridges in two ways:

1. Calculation of design seismic forces
2. Detailing requirements based on required bridge performance in accordance with the seismic risk associated with its location

Figures 1 and 2 of the AASHTO standard [1991b] provide useful flowcharts outlining the steps to be followed in the specified seismic design procedures.

The 1989 AASHTO specifications provided a static equivalent method of calculating seismic forces to which a bridge structure could be subjected. This method was apparently modeled after the static equivalent method adopted by various building codes as an alternative method of seismic design. However, this method has been dropped from the 1992 AASHTO specifications [1992], and it is stipulated (AASHTO 3.21) that bridges be designed to resist earthquake motions by considering the relationship of the site to active faults, the response of the soils at the site, and the dynamic characteristics of the total structure (i.e., soil–structure interaction) in accordance with the AASHTO standard [1991b].

The need for detailing requirements based on the required bridge performance during an earthquake arose out of assessments of bridge failures during past earthquakes in Alaska, California, and Japan. The many losses of spans (i.e., failures in which the spans simply dropped off from abutments or piers) observed during these earthquakes are attributed in part to relative displacement effects [Fung et al., 1971; Jennings, 1971; Gates, 1979; Sharpe and Meyers, 1979]. Relative displacements arise from out-of-phase motions of different parts of a bridge, from lateral displacement, from rotation of the foundation, and from differential displacements of abutments. To mitigate or eliminate this type of failure, design displacement and minimum support lengths at abutments, columns, and hinge seats (measured in the direction of the span) are specified. Additionally, special ties are required between the noncontinuous segments of a bridge in the area of high seismic risk. A discussion on support conditions on abutments and piers for various kinds of bridges has been provided by Libby and Podolny [1979] and Yamadera and Yukitaka [1979]. AASHTO detailing requirements for seismic resistance of bridges are specified in the AASHTO standard [1991b]. The fundamental features of these specifications are as follows.

Importance classification (IC). According to the commentary to the AASHTO standards [1991b], "the Importance Classification (*IC*) is used in conjunction with the acceleration coefficient (*A*) to determine the *seismic performance category* (subsequently referred to as *SPC*) for bridges with an acceleration coefficient greater than 0.29. The *SPC* controls the degree of complexity and sophistication of the analysis and design requirements." Essentially, the concept of *bridge importance* arises from the fact that, depending on the location and traffic characteristics of a bridge (moderate versus heavy volume), the consequences of closure of a bridge would be vastly different. This was amply demonstrated by the collapse of the Cypress Street Viaduct and damage to the San Francisco freeway viaducts in San Francisco, both of which are heavily traveled, during the 1989 Loma Prieta earthquake. Bridge importance consideration therefore lies at the very core of the present seismic design criteria for bridges in recognition of the fact that a seriously damaged bridge may need to be closed.

Two importance classifications are specified: *IC one* for essential bridges and *IC two* for all other bridges. Essential bridges are those that must continue to function after an earthquake, as determined from the perspective of social/survival and security/defense requirements. The social/survival viewpoint requires that bridges on the following routes must continue to function after an earthquake:

1. Routes to be used by the civil defense, police, fire department, or public health agencies to respond to disaster areas
2. Transportation routes to critical facilities such as hospitals, police and fire stations, and communication centers

3. Routes to facilities such as schools and arenas, which could provide shelter or be converted to emergency aid stations
4. Routes to important utility centers such as power installations and water treatment plants

The basis for the security/defense evaluation is the *1973 Federal-Aid Highway Act* [AASHTO 1991b], which requires each state to develop a plan for a defense highway network. The network should provide connecting routes to important military installations, industries, and resources such as

1. Military bases and supply depots and National Guard installations
2. Hospitals, medical supply centers, and emergency depots
3. Major airports
4. Defense industries and those that could easily or logically be converted to such
5. Refineries, fuel storage, and distribution centers
6. Major railroad and truck terminals, railroads, and docks
7. Major power plants, including nuclear power facilities and hydroelectric centers at major dams
8. Major communication centers
9. Other facilities that the state considers important from a national defense viewpoint or during emergencies resulting from natural disasters or other unforeseen circumstances

Bridges in all of the listed categories should be classified as *essential* bridges.

The acceleration coefficients referred to previously are based on a uniform risk model of seismic hazard. The probability that the coefficient will not be exceeded at a given location during a 50-year period (chosen arbitrarily) is estimated to be about 90 percent, i.e., a 10 percent probability of exceedance. It is suggested that with this probability of nonexceedance, an event has a return period of 475 years and is called the design earthquake. Maximum probable earthquakes are sometimes referred to as those that are estimated to have a return period of 2500 years [AASHTO, 1994a].

Seismic performance categories. Each bridge is assigned a *seismic performance category (SPC)*. This classification is basically related to *seismic risk levels* in different parts of the country and the applicable design requirements, and it permits variation in the requirements for analysis techniques, minimum support lengths, column design details, and abutment and foundation design corresponding to seismic risk associated with the bridge. Four seismic performance categories—A, B, C, and D—are designated. Bridges designated as SPC A are designed for the lowest level of seismic performance; bridges designated as SPC D are designed for the highest level of seismic performance. The risk level associated with various SPCs is defined with respect to the *acceleration coefficient, A*. Based on the range of values of *A*, the SPCs are shown in Table 3.9. The values of *A* for various parts of the United States are shown in Fig. 3.35. An enlarged version of this figure can be found in AASHTO [1992].

3.14.2.2 Analysis and detailing requirements

Briefly, the analysis and detailing requirements for various kinds of highway bridges are as follows:

TABLE 3.9
Seismic performance category (SPC) [AASHTO, 1992]

Acceleration coefficient	Importance classification, *IC*	
A	I	II
$A \leq 0.09$	A	A
$0.09 < A \leq 0.19$	B	B
$0.19 < A \leq 0.29$	C	C
$0.29 < A$	D	C

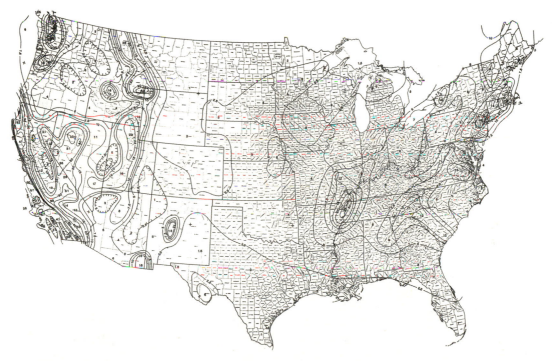

FIGURE 3.35
Acceleration coefficients—continental United States [AASHTO, 1992].

Analysis procedures. Two analysis procedures are recognized:

Procedure 1: Single-mode spectral method
Procedure 2: Multimode spectral method

For analytical purposes, bridges are classified as regular or irregular. According to AASHTO [1992], a regular bridge is defined as one that has no abrupt or unusual changes in mass, stiffness, or geometry along its span and has no large differences in these parameters between adjacent supports (abutment excluded). For example, a bridge may be considered regular if it is straight or describes a sector of an arc not exceeding 90° and has adjacent columns or piers that do not differ in stiffness by more

TABLE 3.10
Seismic analysis procedures [AASHTO, 1992]

Seismic performance category	Regular bridges (two or more spans)	Irregular bridges (two or more spans)
A	—	—
B	1	1
C	1	2
D	1	2

than 25 percent, based on the lesser of two adjacent quantities as reference. All bridges that do not satisfy this definition are defined as irregular bridges. The analysis methods to be used for analyzing bridges of various SPC designations are shown in Table 3.10.

Design requirements. To provide seismic resistance, there are two basic requirements in the case of each bridge:

1. Design for the horizontal seismic force
2. Design for adequate support lengths at bearing seats (support lengths measured in the direction of span)

Single-span bridges. Single-span bridges do not fall into any of the SPCs, and no detailed seismic analysis is required for their design. The concern for these bridges is to prevent span collapse (or span drop) failures. The end of the connection between the bridge span and the abutment should be designed both longitudinally and transversely to resist the gravity reaction at the abutment multiplied by the acceleration coefficient of the site. In addition, the minimum support lengths, as required by AASHTO [1991b], 4.9.1 (see Fig. 3.36), should be provided at the expansion ends of all girders.

Seismic performance category A bridges. No elastic analysis is required for bridges in SPC A. The only two design requirements are as follows:

1. The connection of the superstructure to the substructure should be designed to resist a horizontal seismic force equal to 20 percent of the dead-load reaction in the restrained direction.
2. The minimum support lengths as required by AASHTO Div. I-A, Seismic Design, 4.9.1 (see Fig. 3.36) should be provided.

For SPC B, C, and D, the elastic seismic forces and displacements should be determined analytically, independently along the two perpendicular axes (usually the longitudinal and transverse axes of the bridge). For a curved bridge, the chord connecting the abutments should be considered the longitudinal axis.

Seismic performance category B bridges. Design of SPC B bridges needs considerable attention from the seismic standpoint. Design forces should be calculated for several bridge components—the superstructure, its expansion joints, the connections between the superstructure and the supporting substructure (abutment and piers), and the substructure (abutment and piers) itself.

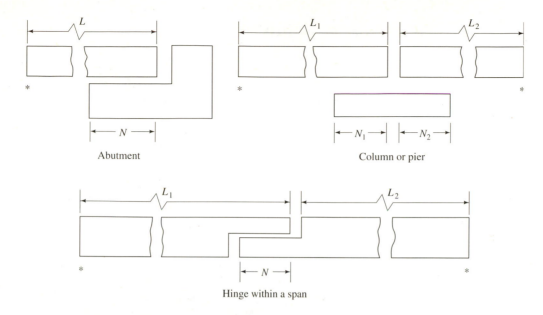

Abutment   Column or pier

Hinge within a span

*Expansion joint or end of bridge deck

$N = 8 + 0.02L + 0.08H$ (in.)

FIGURE 3.36

Dimensions for minimum support length requirements [AASHTO, 1992]. L = length in feet of the bridge deck to the adjacent expansion joint, or to the end of the bridge deck. For hinges within a span, L is the sum of L_1 and L_2, the distances to either side of the hinge. For single-span bridges, L equals the span of the bridge deck. For abutments: H = average height in feet of columns supporting the bridge deck to the next expansion joint. $H = 0$ for single-span bridges. For columns and/or piers: H = column or pier height in feet. For hinges within a span: H = average height of the adjacent two columns or piers in feet.

Design seismic forces. The AASHTO specifications for seismic design of highway bridges [AASHTO, 1991b] give a detailed procedure for determining design seismic forces for SPC B bridges. Stated briefly,

1. Elastic seismic forces are calculated from the appropriate analysis procedures referred to in previous paragraphs, for the two load cases defined as follows:

    Load case 1: Design force = absolute value of elastic seismic force in the *longitudinal* direction + 0.3(absolute value of elastic seismic force in the *transverse* direction)

    Load case 2: Design force = absolute value of the elastic seismic force in the *transverse* direction + 0.3(absolute elastic seismic force in the *longitudinal* direction)

Two significant aspects of seismic force phenomena are recognized in the preceding formulation. First, a combination of *orthogonal* seismic forces is used to account

TABLE 3.11
Response modification factor (R) [AASHTO, 1992]

Substructure[1]	R	Connections	R
Wall-type pier[2]	2	Superstructure to abutment	0.8
Reinforced concrete pile bents		Expansion joints within	
a. Vertical piles only	3	a span of a superstructure	0.8
b. One or more batter piles	2		
		Columns, piers or pile bents	
Single columns	3	to cap beam or superstructure[3]	1.0
Steel or composite steel		Columns or piers to foundations[3]	1.0
and concrete pile bents			
a. Vertical piles only	5		
b. One or more batter piles	3		
Multiple column bent	5		

[1]The R factor is to be used for both orthogonal axes of the substructure.
[2]A wall-type pier may be designed as a column in the weak direction of the pier provided all the provisions for columns in Division I-A, Seismic Design, Section 8 [AASHTO, 1992] are followed. The R factor for a single column can then be used.
[3]For bridges classified as SPC C and D, it is recommended that the connections be designed for the maximum forces capable of being developed by plastic hinging of the column or column bent as specified in AASHTO 4.8.5. These forces will often be significantly less than those obtained using an R factor of 1.

for the directional uncertainty of seismic motions and the simultaneous occurrence of seismic forces in two perpendicular horizontal directions. Second, the *absolute* rather than the *algebraic* value of seismic forces is used, since they can be positive or negative.

2. The elastic seismic forces so obtained are modified by dividing them by the appropriate response modification factor, R, shown in Table 3.11.

3. The modified seismic forces, EQM, are combined, independently, with forces due to other loads to obtain the group loading combination for the components:

$$\text{Group load} = 1.0(D + B + SF + E + EQM)$$

where
$\quad D = \text{dead load}$
$\quad B = \text{buoyancy}$
$\quad SF = \text{stream flow pressure}$
$\quad E = \text{earth pressure}$
$\quad EQM = \text{elastic seismic force for either load case 1 or load case 2 of AASHTO [1992, Division I-A, Seismic Design] 4.4 divided by the appropriate } R \text{ factor}$

Sample calculations for EQM are given in Division I-A, Seismic Design Supplement A of AASHTO [1992].

Each bridge component should be designed to withstand forces resulting from each load combination, as discussed in the next section. The group load formula previously written should be used in lieu of a group VII loading combination with γ and β factors equal to 1. For a service load design based on this load group, increases of 50 percent and $33\frac{1}{3}$ percent are permitted in the allowable stresses for structural steel and reinforced concrete, respectively. The reader is referred to Chapters 6, 7, and 8 of AASHTO [1991b][6] for full details.

Seismic design displacements. The seismic design displacements for SPC B bridges should be the larger of those shown in Fig. 3.36 (the same as for SPC A bridges), or as calculated from analysis as indicated in Table 3.10.

Seismic performance category C and D bridges. Seismic design specifications in AASHTO [1991b] 4.8.1 and 4.8.2 specify design forces for bridges in categories C and D, which essentially deal with designs of columns in the inelastic range (i.e., plastic hinging at the top and bottom of the columns, piers, or bents). These requirements are too detailed to describe here, and a thorough reading of AASHTO [1991b] is highly recommended.

The requirements for design displacements for these bridges are similar to those for SPC B bridges except that the support length, N (Fig. 3.36), is larger:

$$N = 12 + 0.03L + 0.12H \tag{3.42}$$

The design displacement should also be calculated analytically, as indicated in Table 3.11, and the larger value of the support length should be provided. The design of restraining features to limit the displacement of the superstructure (hinge ties, shear block, etc.), in general, should follow the design requirements described in the preceding paragraphs for SPC A, B, C, and D.

The contributing dead load (DL) should be determined carefully; it will depend on the direction of the EQ to be calculated. For example, in the case of a simple span fixed at one end and sliding at the other, the entire superstructure will contribute to the dead load in the longitudinal direction; for the transverse direction (perpendicular to the bridge axis), only one-half of the superstructure dead load will contribute (this is the tributary area concept).

3.14.3 Future Seismic Design Considerations

While seismic design criteria for highway bridges were still evolving in the post–1971 San Fernando earthquake period of the 1970s and 1980s, the October 17, 1989, M 6.9 Loma Prieta earthquake added a new dimension and emphasis on the seismic design procedures to be followed in the 1990s and beyond. During this earthquake, 62 people died, 3750 were injured, and more than $6 billion in property damage resulted, including $1.8 billion to the transportation systems [CA, 1990]. The most destructive impact of the earthquake was the collapse of the Cypress Street Viaduct, in which 42 people died, and the collapse of the viaducts of the San Francisco–Oakland Bay Bridge. Damage to these bridges, as well to those damaged during the 1971 San Fernando earthquake, was attributed to the engineering practice and the scant knowledge of seismic design procedures at the time of construction of these and other damaged bridges [CA, 1990; Miranda and Bertero, 1991; Mayes et al., 1992].

---

[6]This standard has now been incorporated as a part of AASHTO [1992], "Division I-A Seismic Design." The chapter numbers remain the same as in AASHTO [1991b].

Experience with the seismic behavior of bridges during these two earthquakes, and research, have led design engineers to place special emphasis on the soil–structure interaction, lateral displacement demands, and seismic isolation requirements in developing revised seismic design criteria [ATC, 1983; Buckle, Mayes, and Button, 1987; Buckle, 1993; Miranda, 1993]. For example, it is suggested that the following be introduced [Buckle, 1993]:

1. A new soil profile type, type IV, with $S = 2.0$
2. The S factor as function of earthquake magnitude
3. The response modification factors, R, as functions of importance and redundancy
4. Response modification factors for connections
5. Minimum connection force requirements for SPC A bridges
6. Requirements for minimum seat widths for skewed bridges

Because of the inherent vulnerability of existing bridges to seismic events, retrofitting of these bridges (more than 11,280 in California) has become an urgent need of the times, and separate specifications and procedures have been developed. Discussion of this topic is beyond the scope of this text; a comprehensive discussion on the subject can be found in several references [ATC, 1983; Buckle, 1993; Buckle, Mayes, and Button, 1987; Imbsen, 1992].

3.15
MISCELLANEOUS LOADS

In addition to the loads discussed in the preceding paragraphs, other loads may be present as a result of the use of a specific construction material, such as reinforced or prestressed concrete.

3.15.1 Construction, Handling, and Erection Loads

Construction, handling, and erection loads are particularly important for medium- and long-span bridges, especially when precast or prestressed concrete is used. The effects of temporary loads imposed by the sequence of construction stages, forming, falsework, construction equipment, stresses caused by lifting or placing precast members and member shortening, and redistribution of loads during prestressing should be carefully considered in analysis and design [ACI, 1977]. Construction procedures obviously differ for different kinds of bridges, and no standards can be set for any one particular type. Erection methods for precast bridge structures are determined by the bridge type, span, and height; location; topography; weight, size, and configuration of the precast units; method of jointing; and the erection equipment available. The design engineer must ensure lateral stability against twisting, buckling, and overturning, both during and after erection. Due consideration must be given to external forces on precast segments and other components during erection, such as wind, current, and waves. A contractor should rely on his or her own ingenuity for developing the fastest, most economical construction procedure, but careful consideration should be given to estimating loads resulting from construction and handling at each stage of erection.

3.15.2 Deformation Effects

Forces caused by displacement of supports and by shrinkage and creep of concrete should be carefully considered in analysis. These forces are of special significance in the construction of reinforced and prestressed concrete bridges. Forces or displacements due to shrinkage of conventionally reinforced concrete should be evaluated assuming a coefficient of shrinkage of 0.0002 (AASHTO 8.5.3). For a comprehensive discussion on deformation effects, readers should refer to ACI [1977].

3.16
COMBINATION OF LOADS FOR DESIGN

Various loads and forces acting on bridge structures have been discussed in the preceding paragraphs. An overview of loads and forces on bridges is presented in AISC publications [ASCE, 1980, 1981].

A bridge and all its components should be designed to safely resist all loads to which it may be subjected during its service life. Many of the previously described forces act on bridges simultaneously, though not to their full extent. In recognition of the improbability of the simultaneous application of all potential loads at their maximum levels, a bridge and its components should be designed for suitable combinations of these loads, determined by combining maximum levels of some loads with partial values of other loads. In general, a loading combination, designated by a *group number,* is defined by AASHTO 3.22.1 as follows:

$$\text{Group } (N) = \gamma[\beta_D D + \beta_L(L + I) + \beta_c CF + \beta_E E + \beta_B B + \beta_s SF + \beta_W W \\ + \beta_{WL} WL + \beta_L LF + \beta_R(R + S + T) + \beta_{EQ} EQ + \beta_{ICE} ICE] \tag{3.43}$$

where
$$
\begin{aligned}
N &= \text{group number} \\
\gamma &= \text{load factor (see Table 3.12)} \\
\beta &= \text{coefficient (Table 3.12)} \\
D &= \text{dead load} \\
L &= \text{live load} \\
I &= \text{live-load impact} \\
E &= \text{earth pressure} \\
B &= \text{buoyancy} \\
W &= \text{wind load on structure} \\
WL &= \text{wind load on live load (100 pounds per linear foot)} \\
LF &= \text{longitudinal force from live load} \\
CF &= \text{centrifugal force} \\
R &= \text{rib shortening} \\
S &= \text{shrinkage} \\
T &= \text{temperature} \\
EQ &= \text{earthquake} \\
SF &= \text{stream flow pressure} \\
ICE &= \text{ice pressure}
\end{aligned}
$$

TABLE 3.12
γ and β factors [AASHTO, 1992]

Col. no.		1	2	3	3A	4	5	6	7	8	9	10	11	12	13	14	
							β factors										
Group		λ	D	$(L+I)_n$	$(L+I)_p$	CF	E	B	SF	W	WL	LF	$R+S+T$	EQ	ICE	%	
Service load	I	1.0	1	1	0	1	β_E	1	1	0	0	0	0	0	0	100	
	IA	1.0	1	2	0	0	0	0	0	0	0	0	0	0	0	150	
	IB	1.0	1	0	1	1	β_E	1	1	0	0	0	0	0	0	**	
	II	1.0	1	0	0	0	1	1	1	1	0	0	0	0	0	125	
	III	1.0	1	1	0	1	β_E	1	1	0.3	1	1	0	0	0	125	
	IV	1.0	1	1	0	1	β_E	1	1	0	0	0	1	0	0	125	
	V	1.0	1	0	0	0	1	1	1	1	0	0	1	0	0	140	
	VI	1.0	1	1	0	1	β_E	1	1	0.3	1	1	1	0	0	140	
	VII	1.0	1	0	0	0	1	1	1	0	0	0	0	1	0	133	
	VIII	1.0	1	1	0	1	1	1	1	0	0	0	0	0	1	140	
	IX	1.0	1	0	0	0	1	1	1	1	0	0	0	0	1	150	
	X	1.0	1	1	0	0	β_E	0	0	0	0	0	0	0	0	100	Culvert
Load factor design	I	1.3	β_D	1.67*	0	1.0	β_E	1	1	0	0	0	0	0	0		
	IA	1.3	β_D	2.20	0	0	0	0	0	0	0	0	0	0	0		
	IB	1.3	β_D	0	1	1.0	β_E	1	1	0	0	0	0	0	0		
	II	1.3	β_D	0	0	0	β_E	1	1	1	0	0	0	0	0		
	III	1.3	β_D	1	0	1	β_E	1	1	0.3	1	1	0	0	0	Not applicable	
	IV	1.3	β_D	1	0	1	β_E	1	1	0	0	0	1	0	0		
	V	1.25	β_D	0	0	0	β_E	1	1	1	0	0	1	0	0		
	VI	1.25	β_D	1	0	1	β_E	1	1	0.3	1	1	1	0	0		
	VII	1.3	β_D	0	0	0	β_E	1	1	0	0	0	0	1	0		
	VIII	1.3	β_D	1	0	1	β_E	1	1	0	0	0	0	0	1		
	IX	1.20	β_D	0	0	0	β_E	1	1	1	0	0	0	0	1		
	X	1.30	β_D	1.67	0	0	β_E	0	0	0	0	0	0	0	0		Culvert

$(L+I)_n$ = Live load plus impact for AASHTO Highway H or HS loading

$(L+I)_p$ = Live load plus impact consistent with the overload criteria of the operation agency

* 1.25 may be used for design of outside roadway beam when combination of sidewalk live load as well as traffic live load plus impact governs the design, but the capacity of the section should not be less than required for highway traffic live load only using a β factor of 1.67. 1.00 may be used for design of deck slab with combination of loads as described in Article 3.24.2.2.

$$** \text{ Percentage } = \frac{\text{maximum unit stress (operating rating)}}{\text{allowable basic unit stress}} \times 100$$

For service load design,

$$\% \text{ (column 14)} = \text{percentage of basic unit stress}$$

No increase in allowable unit stresses shall be permitted for members or connections carrying wind loads only.

$$\beta_E = 1.00 \text{ for vertical and lateral loads on all other structures.}$$

For culvert loading specifications, see Article 6.2.

$$\beta_E = 1.0 \text{ and } 0.5 \text{ for lateral loads on rigid frames (check both loadings to see which one governs). See Article 3.20}$$

For load factor design,

$\beta_E = 1.3$ for lateral earth pressure for retaining walls and rigid frames, excluding rigid culverts.

$\beta_E = 0.5$ for lateral earth pressure when checking positive moments in rigid frames. This complies with Article 3.20.

$\beta_E = 1.0$ for vertical earth pressure

$\beta_D = 0.75$ when checking member for minimum axial load and maximum moment or maximum eccentricity

$\beta_D = 1.0$ when checking member for maximum axial load and minimum moment (for column design)

$\beta_D = 1.0$ for flexural and tension members

$\beta_E = 1.0$ for rigid culverts

$\beta_E = 1.5$ for flexible culverts

For Group X loading (culverts) the β_E factor shall be applied to vertical and horizontal loads.

260

A general discussion on various design philosophies was presented in Chapter 1 and can be found in several references [Vincent, 1969; Ravindra and Galambos, 1978; Galambos et al., 1982; Johnston, Lin, and Galambos, 1986; Salmon and Johnson, 1990]. In 1994 a new design philosophy, called the *load and resistance factor design* [AASHTO, 1994a], was proposed by AASHTO. In the AASHTO 1992 standard, two design philosophies are permitted: the service load design and the load factor design (discussed in Chapter 1). According to each of these design philosophies, various loading combinations to which a highway bridge may be subjected are identified by Roman numerals I through X, as shown in Table 3.12 (AASHTO Table 3.22.1A). Values of the γ (gamma) factor associated with various group loadings and the β (beta) factor associated with various loads within each of these groups are also shown in that table.

The whole or parts of a bridge may be subjected to several loads simultaneously. More importantly, the designer must know the various forces to which the bridge as a whole and its various components will be subjected. In the context of various group loading combinations, AASHTO 3.22.1 states "*Each* component of the structure, or the foundation on which it rests, shall be proportioned to withstand safely *all* group combinations of these forces that are applicable to the particular site or type."[7] Judging from the number of group loading combinations (10 in Table 3.12), this might appear to be a time-consuming task. Fortunately, however, such is not the case. Groups I–III pertain to superstructures and substructures. Groups IV–VI pertain primarily to the design of arches and frames. Groups VII–IX pertain to the design of substructures, and Group X pertains to culverts (as noted in the footnotes to the table). Conceptually speaking, group loadings simply include various loadings that are likely to act simultaneously.

Note that superstructure design—the primary focus of discussion in this book—is controlled by a Group I combination of $DL + LL + I$. Fortunately, these loads are relatively easy to calculate, as illustrated in various chapters that follow.

Different groups control the design of different parts of a bridge structure. It is good design practice to tabulate loads and their effects to determine the controlling loads on various members that constitute the superstructure (e.g., stringers, floor beams, and trusses) and the substructure (e.g., abutment and bent caps). Generally, it is not necessary to investigate all group loadings for a given bridge. Often, with a little practice and experience, it becomes evident by inspection that only a few group loadings will control the design of a given type of structure. The structure is then analyzed for all governing load combinations. Although the various load combinations shown in Table 3.12 were developed to cover all possible governing load combinations for highway bridge structures, it is incumbent on the design engineer to ensure that all critical load combinations are covered.

It should be noted that certain bridge owner agencies, because of the special permit loads allowed on their bridges, may use a somewhat modified form of Table 3.12. As an example, Tables 3.13 and 3.14 give values of γ and β factors for the service load design and the load factor design, respectively, used by the California Department of Transportation [CALTRANS, 1992].

As discussed in Chapter 1, the γ (gamma) multiplier in Eq. 3.43 represents the load factor, the factor by which the service loads are multiplied to obtain design loads

---

[7]Italics added.

TABLE 3.13
γ and β factors (service load design) [CALTRANS, 1992]*

Group	Gamma factor	Beta factors												
		D	L + I	CF	E	B	SF	W	WL	LF	P_s	R + S + T	ICE	%
I	1.0	1	1	1	1	1	1	0	0	0	1	0	0	100
II	1.0	1	0	0	1	1	1	1	0	0	1	0	0	125
III	1.0	1	1	1	1	1	1	0.3	1	1	1	0	0	125
IV	1.0	1	1	1	1	1	1	0	0	0	1	1	0	125
V	1.0	1	0	0	1	1	1	1	0	0	1	1	0	140
VI	1.0	1	1	1	1	1	1	0.3	1	1	1	1	0	140
VIII	1.0	1	1	1	1	1	1	0	0	0	1	0	1	140
IX	1.0	1	0	0	1	1	1	1	0	0	1	0	1	150

*Not applicable for culvert design. Use load factor design.
% indicates percentage of basic unit stress.
No increase in allowable unit stresses shall be permitted for members or connections carrying wind loads only.
P loads apply in service load design only for checking serviceablility under fatigue in structural steel.
When EQ loads are applied, load factor design shall be used to analyze their effects.

(also referred to as factored loads) for the load factor design. Its value varies—1.2, 1.25, or 1.3, depending on the type of the load combination—but *the same value applies to all the loads in a combination (or the group)*. Its basic purpose is to allow us to exercise stress control by permitting less than 100 percent of the member's ultimate capacity as a measure of safety. For example, $\gamma = 1.3$, the most commonly used value of the multiplier, permits us to use only 77 percent of the ultimate capacity of a member ($1.3 \times 0.77 \approx 1.0$). Similarly, $\gamma = 1.25$ permits us to use only 80 percent of the ultimate capacity of a member ($1.25 \times 0.80 = 1.0$). On the other hand, as discussed in Chapter 1, the β factor, called the reliability index, represents a measure of the accuracy with which various kinds of loads can be predicted, as well as the improbability of the simultaneous occurrence of various loads in a selected load combination. In contrast to the γ factor, *the β factor applies separately, with different values applied to different loads in a combination*. For example, the usual value of the β factor for dead load is 1.0 ($\beta_D = 1.0$ in Table 3.12) because it is more accurately determined and less variable. For live loads, however, its value varies from 1.0 to 2.2, as shown in Table 3.12. Of course, when it is determined that, in certain loading combinations, one type of loading may produce effects of the opposite sense to those produced by another type, the assigned β values are less than 1.0 [ACI, 1992]. For example, β is 0.75 ($\beta_D = 0.75$ in Table 3.12) for checking a compression member for minimum axial load and maximum moment (or eccentricity).

One important point should be remembered in the context of load factors in the AASHTO specifications [AASHTO, 1992]: *Although conceptually similar to those specified for the design of concrete [ACI, 1992] and steel structures [AISC, 1994], values of load factors are different for highway bridge structures. Also, they are applied differently.*

TABLE 3.14

γ and β factors (load factor design) [CALTRANS, 1992]

Group	Gamma factor	\multicolumn{14}{c}{Beta factors}
		D	$(L+I)H$	$(L+I)P$	CF	E	B	SF	W	WL	LF	PS	$R+S+T$	EQ	ICE
I_H	1.30	β_D	1.67	0	1	β_E	1	1	0	0	0	0.77	0	0	0
I_{PC}	1.30	β_D	0	1	1	β_E	1	1	0	0	0	0.77	0	0	0
I_{PW}	1.30	β_D	1	1.15	1	β_E	1	1	0	0	0	0.77	0	0	0
I_{P3D}	1.30	β_D	1	1.25	1	β_E	1	1	0	0	0	0.77	0	0	0
II	1.30	β_D	0	0	0	β_E	1	1	1	0	0	0.77	0	0	0
III	1.30	β_D	1	0	1	β_E	1	1	0.3	1	1	0.77	0	0	0
IV	1.30	β_D	1	0	1	β_E	1	1	0	0	0	0.77	1	0	0
V	1.25	β_D	0	0	0	β_E	1	1	1	0	0	0.80	1	0	0
VI	1.25	β_D	1	0	1	β_E	1	1	0.3	1	1	0.80	1	0	0
VII	1.00	1	0	0	0	β_E	1	1	0	0	0	1.00	0	1	0
VIII	1.30	β_D	1	0	1	β_E	1	1	0	0	0	0.77	0	0	1
IX	1.20	β_D	0	0	0	β_E	1	1	1	0	0	0.83	0	0	1
X*	1.30	β_D	1.67	0	0	β_E	0	0	0	0	0	0.67	0	0	0

H denotes H loads.

PC denotes P loads on closely spaced girders used only for superstructures.

PW denotes P loads on widely spaced girders and superstructures.

$P3D$ denotes P loads only on superstructures when three-dimensional analysis is used for load distribution.

$\beta_D = 0.75$ when checking columns for maximum moment or maximum eccentricities and associated axial load; and when dead load effects are of opposite sign to the net effects of other loads in a group.

$\beta_D = 1.00$ when checking columns for maximum axial load and associated moment.

$\beta_D = 1.00$ for flexural and tension members and for culverts.

$\beta_E = 0.50$ for checking positive moments in rigid frames.

$\beta_E = 1.00$ for vertical earth pressure and for rigid culverts.

$\beta_E = 1.30$ for lateral earth pressure (not for culverts).

$\beta_E = 1.50$ for flexible culverts.

* Group X applies only to culverts. Other groups do not apply to culverts.

Finally, it should be pointed out that there usually is a discontinuity in procedures for applying live loads to various members of a bridge structure. The deck slab is designed according to one loading criterion and the girders by another. The load path, the most important consideration in structural design, in a bridge structure is different from that in a building and is discussed in Chapter 4.

REFERENCES

AASHTO. (1991a). *Guide for Maximum Dimensions and Weights of Motor Vehicles and for the Operation of the Nondivisible Load Oversize and Overweight Vehicles, Revised 1991*, AASHTO, Washington, DC.

———. (1991b). *Standard Specifications for Seismic Design of Highway Bridges, 1991*, AASHTO, Washington DC.

———. (1992). *Standard Specifications for Highway Bridges,* 15th ed., AASHTO, Washington, DC.

———. (1993). *Guide Specifications for Curved Highway Bridges,* (1980 updated to 1993), AASHTO, Washington, DC.

———. (1994a). *AASHTO–LRFD Bridge Design Specifications—Customary U.S. Units,* 1st ed., AASHTO, Washington, DC.

———. (1994b). *Guide Specifications for Distribution of Loads for Highway Bridges,* AASHTO, Washington, DC.

———. (1994c). *Interim Specifications—Bridges,* AASHTO, Washington, DC.

ACI. (1977). *Analysis and Design of Reinforced Concrete Bridges,* ACI Committee Report, ACI, Detroit.

———. (1992). *Building Code Requirements for Reinforced Concrete Members (ACI 318-89) (Revised 1992) and Commentary—ACI 318R-89 (Revised 1992),* ACI, Detroit, p. 88.

Agarwal, A. C., and Billing, J. R. (1990). "Dynamic Testing of the St. Vincent Street Bridge," *Proc. CSCE Annual Conf.,* vol. IV-1, 1990, pp. 163–182.

AISC. (1994). *Manual of Steel Construction—Load and Resistance Factor Design,* 2nd ed., AISC, Chicago.

Allen, D. E., and Murray, T. M. (1993). "Design Criterion for Vibrations Due to Walking," *AISC Eng. J.,* 4th qtr., pp. 117–129.

Allen, D. E., and Rainer, J. H. (1976). "Vibration Criteria for Long-Span Floors," *Canadian J. Civ. Eng.,* 3(2), June, pp. 165–171.

Anderson, Jr., J. D. (1985). *Introduction to Flight,* McGraw-Hill Companies, Inc., New York.

ASCE. (1945). "Rigidity and Aerodynamic Stability of Suspension Bridges," *Trans. ASCE,* 110, pp. 430–580.

———. (1950). "Aerodynamic Theory of Bridge Oscillations," *Trans. ASCE,* vol. 115, pp. 1180–1260.

———. (1952). "Aerodynamic Stability of Suspension Bridges—1952 Report of the Advisory Board on the Investigation of Suspension Bridges," *Trans. ASCE,* paper no. 2761, August.

———. (1958). "Deflection Limitation of Bridges—Progress Report of the ASCE Committee on Deflection Limitations of Bridges," *Proc. ASCE,* 84(ST3), paper no. 1633, May, pp. 1633-1 to 1633-19.

———. (1961). "Wind Forces on Structures," *Trans. ASCE,* pp. 1124–1198.

———. (1980). "Loads and Forces on Bridges," preprint 80-173, *ASCE Natl. Convention, April 14–18, Portland, OR,* ASCE, New York.

———. (1981). "Recommended Design Loads and Forces on Bridges," *ASCE J. Str. Div.,* 107(ST7), pp. 1161–1213.

———. (1987). "Wind Loading and Wind-Induced Structural Response," in *Bridges: A State-of-the-Art Report,* Committee on Wind Effects of the Committee of Dynamic Effects, ASCE, New York.

———. (1988). *Minimum Design Loads for Buildings and Other Structures,* (formerly ANSI A58.1-1982), ASCE, New York.

———. (1993). *Minimum Design Loads for Buildings and Other Structures,* (formerly ANSI A58.1-1982), ASCE, New York.

ATC. (1981). *Seismic Design Guidelines for Highway Bridges,* ATC-6, Applied Technology Council, Redwood City, CA.

———. (1983). *Seismic Retrofitting Guidelines for Highway Bridges,* Applied Technology Council, publ. no. ATC-6-2 (also report no. FHWA/RD-83/007), Redwood City, CA, August.

Bachman, H. (1992). "Case Studies of Structures with Man-Induced Vibrations," *ASCE J. Str. Eng.,* 118(3), pp. 631-647.

Bakht, B., Billing, J. R., and Agarwal, A. C. (1992). "Discussion of 'Wheel Loads from Highway Bridge Strains' by Tommy Hung Tin Chan and Colin O'Connor," *ASCE J. Str. Eng.,* 118(6), June, pp. 1706–1709.

Bakht, B., Cheung, M. S., and Dortan, R. A. (1982). "Discussion of 'A Comparison of Design Loads for Highways,' by P.G. Buckland and R. G. Sexsmith," *Can. J. Civil Eng.,* 9(1).

Bakht, B., and Jaeger, L. G. (1985). *Bridge Analysis Simplified,* McGraw-Hill Companies, Inc., New York.

Bakht, B., and Jaeger, L. G. (1990). "Bridge Evaluation for Multipresence of Vehicles," *ASCE J. Str. Eng.,* 116(3), March, pp. 603–618.

Bakht, B., and Pinjarkar, S. G. (1989). *Dynamic Testing of Highway Bridges, Transp. Res. Rec.,* 1223, Transportation Research Board, Washington, DC.

Bakht, B., and Pinjarkar, S. J. (1990). "Review of Dynamic Testing of Bridges," *Transp. Res. Rec.,* 1223 Transportation Research Board, pp. 93–100.

Barenberg, M. E., and Foutch, D. A. (1988). "Evaluation of Seismic Design Procedures for Highway Bridges," *ASCE J. Str. Eng.,* 114(7), July, pp. 1588–1605.

Biggs, J. M. (1953). "Wind Loads on Truss Bridges," *Proc. ASCE.,* no. 201, July.

———. (1964). *Introduction to Structural Dynamics,* McGraw-Hill Companies, Inc., New York.

Biggs, J. M., Namyet, S., and Adachi, J. (1955). "Wind Loads on Girder Bridges," *Proc. ASCE,* no. 587, January.

Biggs, J. M., Suer, H. S., and Louw, J. M. (1959). "Vibration of Simple-Span Highway Bridges," *Trans. ASCE,* vol. 124, p. 291.

Billing, J. R. (1982). "Dynamic Loading and Testing of Bridges in Ontario, 1980," *Proc. Intl. Conf. on Short- and Medium-Span Bridges,* CSCE, Montreal, vol. 1, pp. 125–129.

Bishara, A. G., and Soegiarso, R. (1993). "Load Distribution in Multibeam Precast Pretopped Prestressed Bridges," *ASCE J. Str. Eng.,* 119(3), March, pp. 920–937.

Bleich, F. (1948). "Dynamic Instability of Truss-Stiffened Suspension Bridges under Wind Action," *Proc. ASCE,* vol. 74, October.

Bleich, F., McCullough, C. B., Rosecrans, R., and Vincent, G. (1950). *The Mathematical Theory of Vibration in Suspension Bridges,* Bureau of Public Roads, U.S. Dept. of Commerce, U.S. Govt. Printing Office, Washington, DC.

Bleich, F., and Teller, L. W. (1952). "Structural Damping in Suspension Bridges," *Trans. ASCE,* vol. 117, p. 165.

Bowers, N. A. (1940). "Tacoma Narrows Bridge Wrecked by Wind," *Eng. News-Rec.,* November 14, p. 647.

BSI. (1978). *British Standard Part 2: Steel, Concrete, and Composite Bridges: Specifications for Loads,* Appendix C, British Standards Institution, London.

Bucher, C. G. (1990). "Reliability of Bridges in Turbulent Wind," in *Structural Safety and Reliability,* A. H. Ang, M. Shinozuka, and G. I. Schueller, eds., pp. 103–106.

Buckland, P. G. (1991). "North American and British Long-Span Bridge Loads," *ASCE J. Str. Eng.,* 117(10), pp. 2972–2987.

Buckland, P. G., McBryde, J. P., Navin, F. P. D., and Zidek, J. V. (1978). "Traffic Loading of Long-Span Bridges," *Proc. Conf. Bridge Eng.,* Transportation Research Board, TRR no. 665, September, National Research Council, Washington, DC, pp. 146-154.

Buckland, P. G., Navin, F. P. D., Zidek, J. V., and McBryde, J. P. (1980). "Proposed Vehicle Loading for Long-Span Bridge," *ASCE J. Str. Div.,* 106 (STA), pp. 915–932.

Buckland, P. G., and Sexsmith, R. G. (1981). "A Comparison of Design Loads for Highway Bridges," *Can. J. Civ. Eng.,* 8(2).

Buckland, P. G., and Wardlow, R. L. (1972). "Some Aerodynamic Considerations in Bridge Design," *Eng. Inst. of Canada, Eng. J.,* vol. 5514, April, Montreal, pp. 10–16.

Buckle, I. G. (1993). "Revisions to the AASHTO Standard Specifications Division I-A: Seismic Design," *Meeting of the AASHTO Subcommittee on Bridges and Structures,* Denver, May 10–14.

Buckle, I. G., Mayes, R. L., and Button, M. R. (1987). *Seismic Design and Retrofit Manual for Highway Bridges,* report no. FHWA/IP-87/6, FHWA, Washington, DC, May.

Bull, K. D. (1972). "Seismic Design of Highway Structures," *ASCE J. Str. Div.,* ST-8, August, pp. 1741–1755.

Burke, M. P. (1987). "Bridge Approach Pavements, Integrak Bridges, and Cycle-Control Joints," *Transp. Res. Rec.,* 1113, Washington, DC, pp. 54–70.

———. (1990a). "Integral Bridges," *Transp. Res. Rec.,* 1275, Washington, DC, pp. 53–61.

———. (1990b). "Integral Bridges: Attributes and Limitations," *Transp. Res. Rec.,* 1393, Washington, DC, pp. 1–8.

CA. (1990). *Competing against Time,* Governor's Board of Enquiry on the 1989 Loma Prieta Earthquake, State of California, May.

CALTRANS. (1992). *Bridge Design Practice Manual,* California Department of Transportation, Sacramento.

Campbell, T., and Richardson, B. (1975). "A Long Curved Post-Tensioned Concrete Bridge without Expansion Joints," *Canadian J. Civ. Eng.,* vol. 2.

———. (1983). *Dynamic Load Tests on Highway Bridges; 60 Years of Experience of EMPA,* report no. 271, Swiss Federal Laboratory for Materials and Testing Research, Dubendorf, Switzerland.

Cantieni, R. (1984). "Dynamic Load Testing of Highway Bridges," *Proc. Intl. Assn. Bridge and Str. Eng.,* IABSE, Minneapolis, September, pp. 22–26.

CEQ. (1951). "The Messina Straits Bridge," *Columbia Engineering Quarterly,* January, pp. 8–30.

Cermak, J. E. (1995). "Development of Wind Tunnels for Physical Modeling of the Atmospheric Boundary Layer," in *A State of the Art in Wind Engineering, 9th Intl. Conf. on Wind Eng.,* New Delhi, organized by International Association of Wind Engineering.

Chan, T. H. T., and O'Conner, C. (1990a). "Vehicle Model for Highway Bridge Impact," *ASCE J. Str. Eng.,* 116(7), July, pp. 1772–1793.

———. (1990b). "Wheel Loads from Highway Bridge Strains," *ASCE J. Str. Eng.,* 116(7), July, pp. 1751–1793.

Chapman, H. E. (1979). "An Overview of the State of Practices in Earthquake Design of Bridges in New Zealand," *Proc. Workshop on Earthquake Resistance of Highway Bridges,* Applied Technology Council, Palo Alto, CA, January, 29–31.

CSA. (1988). *Code for Design of Highway Bridges, CAN/CSA-S6-88,* Canadian Standards Association, Rexdale, Ontario.

———. (1989). *CAN 3-S16: Steel Structures for Buildings—Limit States Design, Appendix G: Guide for Floor Vibrations,* Canadian Standard Association, Rexdale, Ontario.

Csagoly, P. F., and Dorton, R. A. (1977). "The Development of Ontario Bridge Code," Ontario Ministry of Transportation and Communications, Ontario.

Dagher, J. H., Elaaly, M., and Kankam, J. (1991). "Analytical Investigation of Slab Bridges with Integral Wall Abutments," *Transp. Res. Rec.* 1319, Washington, DC, pp. 115–125.

Davenport, A. G. (1962a). "Buffeting of a Suspension Bridge by Storm Winds," *ASCE J. Str. Div.,* 88(ST3), June, pp. 233–268.

———. (1962b). "The Response of Slender Line-Like Structures to a Gusty Wind," *Proc. Inst. Civ. Engrs.,* 23(11).

———. (1963). "The Relationship of Structures to Wind Loading," *Proc. Symp. No. 16, "Wind Effects on Buildings and Structures,"* National Physical Laboratory, London.

———. (1966). "The Action of Wind on Suspension Bridges," *Proc. Intl. Symp. on Suspension Bridges,* Laboratorio Nacional De Engenharia Civil, Lisbon.

———. (1972). "The Use of Taut Strip Models in the Prediction of the Response of Long-Span Bridges to Turbulent Wind-Flow-Induced Structural Vibrations," *Proc. IUTAM-IAHR Symp. on Flow-Induced Structural Vibrations,* Karlsruhe, West Germany, Springer Verlag, Berlin, 1974, pp. 373–382.

———. (1982). "Aeroelastic Modeling of Bridges," in *Wind-Tunnel Modeling for Civil Engineering Applications, Proc. Intl. Workshop on Wind-Tunnel Modeling Criteria and Techniques in Civil Engineering Applications,* Gaithersburg, April, Cambridge University Press, New York.

Davenport, A. G., Isyumov, N., Fader, D. J., and Bowen, C. F. P. (1969). *A Study of Wind Action on a Suspension Bridge during Erection and on Completion: The Narrows Bridge, Halifax Nova Scotia, Canada,* BLWT-3-69 with Appendix BLWT-4-70, Boundary Layer Wind Tunnel Laboratory, The University of Western Ontario, London, Canada, May 1969 and March 1970.

Dilger, W. H., Ghali, A., Chan, M., Cheung, M., and Maes, M. A. (1983). "Temperature Stresses in Composite Box Girder Bridges," *ASCE J. Str. Eng.,* 109(6), June, pp. 1460–1478.

Edwards, L. N. (1959). *A Record of History and Evolution of Early American Bridges,* University Press, Orono, ME.

Ehsan, F., Jones, N. P., and Scanlan, R. H. (1993). "Effects of Sidewalk Vents on Bridge Response to Wind," *ASCE J. Str. Eng.,* 119(2), February, pp. 484–504.

Elbadry, M. M., and Ghali, A. (1983). "Temperature Variation in Concrete Bridges," *ASCE J. Str. Eng.,* 109(10), pp. 2355–2374.

Elbadry, M. M., and Ghali, A. (1995). "Control of Thermal Cracking of Concrete Structures," *ACI Structural J.,* 92(4), July–August.

Emanual, J. H., and Hulsey, J. L. (1978). "Temperature Distributions in Composite Bridges," *ASCE J. Str. Eng.,* 104(1), January pp. 65–78.

Emerson, M. (1973). *The Calculation of the Distribution of Temperature in Bridges,* TRRL Report LR 561, Transport and Road Research Laboratory, Crowthorne, Berkshire.

ENR. (1941). "The Tacoma Bridge Report," *Eng. News-Record,* August 14, pp. 59, 61.

———. (1973). "Too Many Spectators Mar Gala Bridge Opening," *Eng. News Record,* November 8, 1973, p. 19.

Farquharson, F. B. (1949). *Aerodynamic Stability of Suspension Bridges,* Parts I-V, Bull. no. 116, University of Washington Engineering Experiment Station, Seattle, 1949–1954.

Fenves, S. J., Velestos, A. S., and Siess, C. P. (1962). *Dynamic Studies of Bridges on the AASHO Road Test,* Highway Research Board, Rep. 968, Washington, DC.

Fleming, J. F., and Romualdi, J. P. (1961). "Dynamic Response of Highway Bridges," *ASCE J. Str. Div.,* 87(7), pp. 31–61.

Frank, W. M. (1974). *Viscous Fluid Flow,* McGraw-Hill Companies, Inc., New York.

Freyermuth, C. L. (1969). "Design of Continuous Highway Bridges with Precast Concrete Girders," *ACI J.,* 14(2).

Fu, H. C., and Ng, S. F. (1990). "Thermal Behavior of Composite Bridges," *ASCE J. Str. Eng.,* 116(12), pp. 3302–3322.

Fung, G. G., LeBeau, R. J., Klein, E. D., Belvedere, J., and Goldscmidt, A. F. (1971). *The San Fernando Earthquake Field Investigation of Bridge Damage,* State of California Division of Highways, Bridge Department, Sacramento.

Galambos, T. V., Ellingwood, B., MacGregor, J. G., and Cornell, A. C. (1982). "Probability-Based Load Criteria: Load Factors and Load Combinations," *ASCE J. Str. Div.,* 108(ST-5), May.

Galdos, N. H., Schelling, D. R., and Sahin, M. A. (1993). "Methodology for the Determination of Dynamic Impact Factor of Horizontally Curved Steel Box Girder Bridges," *ASCE J. Str. Eng.,* 119(ST6), June, pp. 1917–1934.

GangaRao, H. V. S., and Thippeswamy, H. K. (1994). *Study of Jointless Bridge Behavior and Development of Design Procedures,* Constructed Facilities Center rep. no. FHWA WV 89, Civ. Eng. Dept., West Virginia University, Morgantown.

Gates, J. H. (1976). "California's Seismic Design Criteria for Bridges," *ASCE J. Str. Div.,* 102(ST-12), December, pp. 1741–1755.

———. (1979). "Factors Considered in the Development of the California Seismic Design Criteria for Bridges," in *Proc. Workshop on Earthquake Resistance of Highway Bridges,* Applied Technology Council, January 29–31.

Gerhart, P. M., Cross, R. J., and Hochstein, J. I. (1992). *Fundamentals of Fluid Mechanics,* Addison-Wesley, New York.

Hall, W. J., and Newmark, N. M. (1979). "Seismic Design of Bridges—An Overview of Research Needs," *Proc. Workshop on Earthquake Resistance of Highway Bridges*, Applied Technology Council, January 29–31.

Harman, D. J., and Davenport, A. G. (1976). *The Formulation of Vehicular Loading for the Design of Highway Bridges in Ontario,* Report presented to the Ontario Ministry of Transportation, University of Western Ontario, London.

Heins, C. P. (1976). "Curved Box Beam–Bridge Beam Analysis," *J. Computers and Structures,* 6(6), pp. 65–73.

———. (1978). "Box Girder Bridge Design—State of the Art," *AISC Eng. J.,* 2, pp. 126–142.

Heins, C. P., and Firmage, D. A. (1979). *Design of Modern Steel Highway Bridges,* John Wiley & Sons, New York.

Hellman, G. (1916). "Uber die Bewegung der Luft in den untersten Schichten der Atmosphere," *Meteorol. Z.,* 34, p. 273.

Hirai, A., Okauchi, I., and Miyata, T. (1966). "On the Behavior of Suspension Bridges under Wind Action," in *Proc. Intl. Symp. Suspension Bridges,* Laboratorio Nacional de Engenharia Civil, Lisbon, pp. 249–256.

Hirst, M. J. S. (1982). "Thermal Loadings of Concrete Bridges," in *Proc. Intl. Conf. on Short- and Medium-Span Bridges*, Toronto.

Ho, D., and Liu, C.-H. (1989). "Extreme Thermal Loadings in Highway Bridges," *ASCE J. Str. Eng.,* 115(7), July, pp. 1681–1697.

Hoffman, P. C., McClure, R. M., and West H. H. (1983). "Temperature Study of an Experimental Segmented Bridge," *PCI J.,* 28(2), pp. 78–97.

Houghton, E. L., and Carruthers, N. B. (1976). *Wind Forces on Buildings and Structures: An Introduction,* John Wiley & Sons, New York.

Huang, D., Wang, T., and Shahawy, M. (1992). "Impact Analysis of Continuous Multigirder Bridges Due to Moving Vehicles," *ASCE J. Str. Eng.,* 118(12), pp. 3427–3443.

Huang, T., and Veletsos, A. S. (1960). *Dynamic Response of Three-Span Continuous Highway Bridges,* University of Illinois Civil Engineering Studies, Structural Research Series no. 190.

Hunt, B., and Cooke, N. (1975). "Thermal Calculations in Bridge Design," in *Proc. ASCE J. Str. Div.,* 101(ST-9), September, pp. 1763–1781.

Hussey, H. D. (1924). "Proposed Loads in Highway Bridges," *Trans. Am. Soc. Civil Eng.,* paper no. 1536, vol. 87, p. 414.

Huston, D. R., (1987). "Flutter Derivatives Extracted from Fourteen Generic Deck Sections," in L. Tall, ed., *Bridges and Transmission Line Structures,* ASCE, New York.

Hwang, E. S., and Nowak, A. S. (1989). "Dynamic Analysis of Girder Bridges," *Trans. Res. Rec.* 1223, Transportation Research Board, Washington, DC.

———. (1991). "Simulation of Dynamic Load for Bridges," *ASCE J. Str. Eng.,* 117(5), May, pp. 1413–1434.

Imbsen, R. A., Liu, W. D., Shamber, R. A., and Nutt, R. V. (1987). *Strength Evaluation of Existing Reinforced Concrete Bridges,* NCHRP report no. 292, Imbsen and Associates, Sacramento.

Imbsen. R. A. (1992). *Seismic Design of Highway Bridges,* prepared for the U.S. Dept. of Trans., Federal Highway Administration, Washington DC., Imbsen & Associates, Sacramento, March.

Imbsen, R. A., Nutt, R. V., and Penzien, J. (1978). *Seismic Response of Bridges—Case Studies,* report no. 78-14, Earthquake Engineering Research Center, University of California, Berkeley.

———. (1979). "Evaluation of Analytical Procedures Used in Seismic Design Practice," in *Proc. of a Workshop on Earthquake Resistance of Highway Bridges,* Applied Technology Council, January 29–31.

Imbsen, R. A., Vandershaf, D. E., Shamber, R. A., and Nutt, R. V. (1985). *Thermal Effects in Concrete Bridge Superstructures,* NCHRP rep. no. 276, Transportation Research Board, Washington, DC.

Ishizaki, H., and Chiu, A. N. L., eds. (1976). "Wind Effects on Structures, Section V: Aerodynamics of Bridges and Other Structures," in *Proc. 2nd USA–Japan Seminar on Wind Effects on Structures,* University Press of Hawaii, Honolulu.

Ivy, R. J., Lin, T. Y., Mitchell, S., Raab, N. C., Richey, V. J., and Scheffey, C. F. (1954). "Live Loading for Long-Span Bridges," *ASCE Trans.,* paper no. 2708, June, vol. no. 119, pp. 981–994.

Jaeger, L. G., and Bakht, B. (1987). "Multipresence Reduction Factors for Bridges," in *Proc. Bridge and Transmission Line Structures,* ASCE Structures Congress, August 17–20, Orlando.

James, R. W., and Heping, Z. (1991). "Evaluation of Proposed Bridge Formula for Continuous Spans," *ASCE J. Str. Eng,* 117(4), April, pp. 1144–1158.

James, R. W., Noel, J. S., Furr, H. L., and Bonilla, F. E. (1986). "Proposed New Truck Weight Limit Formula," *ASCE J. Str. Eng.,* 112(7), July, pp. 1589–1603.

Jennings, P. C., ed. (1971). *Engineering Features of the San Fernando Earthquake, February 9, 1971,* California Institute of Technology, report no. EERL 71-02, June, Pasadena, CA.

Jephcot, D. K. (1986). "50-Year Record of Field Act Seismic Building Standards for California Schools," *Earthquake Spectra,* 2(3), May, pp. 621–629.

Johnston, B. G., Lin, F. J., and Galambos, T. V. (1986). *Basic Steel Design,* 3rd ed., Prentice Hall, Englewood Cliffs, NJ.

JRA. (1980). *The Japanese Specification for Highway Bridges,* Japanese Road Association, Maruzen, Tokyo, February.

Kulicki, J. M., and Mertz, D. R. (1991). "A New Live-Load Model for Bridge Design," in *Proc. 8th Annual Bridge Engineering Conf.,* Pittsburgh, June.

LA Times. (1992). "Vermont's Capital is Flooded as Ice Diverts River into Town," *Los Angeles Times,* March 12, 1992, p. A35.

Lee, H. W., and Sarsam, M. B. (1973). *Analysis of Integral Abutments: Final Report,* South Dakota Department of Highways, Pierre, SD, March.

Lenzen, K. H. (1966). "Vibration of Steel Joists," *AISC Eng. J.,* 3(3), pp. 133–136.

Leonard, D. R. (1966). *Human Tolerance Levels for Bridge Vibrations,* RRL report no. 34, Ministry of Transport, Road Research Laboratory, Harmondsworth, England.

Leonhardt, F., Kolbe, G., and Peter, J. (1965). "Temperature Differences Endanger Prestressed Concrete Bridges," *Beton-und Stahlbetonbau* (Berlin), no. 7, July (in German).

Leonhardt, F., and Lippoth, W. (1970). "Lessons from Damage to Prestressed Concrete Bridges," *Beton-und Stahlbetonbau* (Berlin), no. 10, October (in German).

Li, K. S. (1991). "Discussion of 'Extreme Thermal Loadings in Highway Bridges,' by D. Ho and C.-H. Liu," *ASCE J. Str. Eng.,* 117(7), July, pp. 2196–2198.

Libby, J. R., and Podolny, W., Jr. (1979). "Typical Configurations of Bridges in the United States," in *Proc. Workshop on Earthquake Resistance of Highway Bridges,* Applied Technology Council, Palo Alto, CA, Jan. 29–31.

Liepman, H. W. (1952). "On the Application of Statistical Concepts to the Buffeting Problem," *J. Aeronaut. Sci.,* 19(12).

Lin, Y. K. (1979). "Motion of Suspended Bridges in Turbulent Winds," ASCE Proc. paper no. 15044 *ASCE J. Eng. Mech.,* 105(6), Dec., p. 921.

Lin, Y. K., and Ariaratnam, S. T. (1980). "Stability of Bridge Motion in Turbulent Winds," *J. Str. Mech.,* 8(1).

Lin, Y. K., and Yang, J. N. (1983). "Multimode Bridge Response to Wind Excitation," *ASCE J. Engr. Mech.,* 109(2), April, pp. 586–603.

Liu, H. (1991). *Wind Engineering,* Prentice Hall, Englewood Cliffs, NJ.

Loveall, C. L. (1985). "Jointless Bridge Decks," *ASCE Civ. Eng.,* November, pp. 64–67.

Lovett, T. G., and Warren, D. W. (1992). "Double Diamonds: New Brand for a Texas Bridge," *ASCE Civ. Eng.,* April, pp. 42–45.

Mayes, R. L., Buckle, I. G., Kelly, T. E., and Jones, L. R. (1992). "AASHTO Seismic Isolation Design Requirements for Highway Bridges," *ASCE J. Str. Eng.,* 118(1), January, pp. 284–304.

Mehta, K. C., Marshall, R. D., and Perry, D. C. (1991). *Guide to the Use of Wind Load Provisions of ASCE 7-88 (Formerly ANSI A58.1),* ASCE, New York.

Merritt, F. S., ed. (1972). *Structural Steel Designer's Handbook,* McGraw-Hill Companies, Inc., New York.

Milne, M. (1981). "Bridge Aerodynamics," *Conf. Proc.,* Inst. Civ. Engrs., Thomas Telford Limited, London, England, March 25–26.

Mirambell, E., and Aguado, A. (1990). "Temperature and Stress Distributions in Concrete Box Girder Bridges," *ASCE J. Str. Eng.,* 116(9), September, pp. 2388–2409.

Miranda, E. (1993). "Evaluation of Seismic Design Criteria for Highway Bridges," *Earthquake Spectra,* 9(2), May, pp. 233–250.

Miranda, E., and Bertero, V. V. (1991). "Evaluation of the Failure of the Cypress Viaduct in the Loma Prieta Earthquake," *Bull. Seismological Society of America,* 81(5), October, pp. 2070–2086.

Modjeski & Masters. (1941). "Suspension Bridges and Wind Resistance," *Eng. News-Rec.,* October 23, p. 565.

Montgomery, C. J., Gerard, R., Huiskamp, W. J., and Kornglesen, R. W. (1984). "Application of Ice Engineering to Bridge Design Standards," *Proc. Cold Regions Engineering Specialty Conf.,* CSCE, Montreal, April 4-6, pp. 795–810.

Montgomery, C. J., Gerard, R., and Lipsett, A. W. (1980). "Dynamic Response of Bridge Piers to Ice Forces," *Canadian J. Civ. Eng.,* 7(2), Ottawa, pp. 345–356.

Montgomery, C. J., and Lipsett, A. W. (1980). "Dynamic Tests and Analysis of Pier Subjected to Ice Forces," *Canadian J. Civ. Eng.,* 7(3), Ottawa, pp. 432–441.

Moorty, S., and Roeder, C. W. (1991). "Temperature-Dependent Bridge Movements," *ASCE J. Str. Eng.,* 118(4), April, pp. 1091–1105.

Morrison, R. B., ed. (1962). *Design Data for Aeronautics and Astronautics,* John Wiley & Sons, New York.

Moses, F., and Ghosn, M. (1985). *A Comparative Study of Bridge Loads and Reliability,* report no. FHWA/OH-85/005, Department of Civil Engineering, Case Western Reserve University, Cleveland.

———. (1987). "Discussion of 'Proposed New Truck Weight Formula,' by R.W. James, et al.," *ASCE J. Str. Eng.* 113(11), pp. 2330–2331.

Moses, F., and Verma, D. (1986). *Load Capacity Evaluation of Existing Bridges,* Interim Report, NCHRP Project 12-28(1), Case Western Reserve University, Cleveland, May.

Nakai, H., and Yoo, C. H. (1988). *Analysis of and Design of Curved Steel Bridges,* McGraw-Hill Companies, Inc., New York.

NCHRP. (1979). *State Laws and Regulations on Truck Size and Weight,* NCHRP report 198, R. J. Hansen Associates, Transportation Research Board, Washington, DC.

———. (1992). *Development of Comprehensive Bridge Specifications and Commentary: Third Draft LRFD Specifications and Commentary,* NCHRP Project 12-33, Transportation Research Board, Washington, DC.

NCHRP–SYN (1985). *Bridge Designs to Reduce and Facilitate Maintenance and Repair,* NCHRP Synthesis report no. 123, Transportation Research Board, Washington, DC.

———(1989). *Bridge Deck Joints,* NCHRP Synthesis, report no. 141, Transportation Research Board, Washington, DC.

Neill, C. R. (1976). "Dynamic Ice Forces on Piers and Piles," An Assesment of Design Guidelines in the Light of Recent Research, *Canadian J. Civ. Eng.,* 3(2), Ottawa, pp. 305–341.

Neill, C. R., ed. (1981). *Ice Effect on Bridges,* Roads and Transportation Association of Canada, Ottawa.

Neville, A. M. (1981). *Properties of Concrete,* Pitman Press, Marshfield, MA.

Nowak, A. S., and Hong, Y. K. (1991). "Bridge Live-Load Models," *ASCE J. Str. Engr.,* 117(9), September, pp. 2757–2767.

Nutt, R. V., Schamber, R. A., and Zokaie, T. (1988). *Distribution of Wheel Loads on Highway Bridges,* final report no. 183, Imbsen & Associates, Inc., Sacramento.

NZMWD. (1978). *Highway Bridge Design Relief,* New Zealand Ministry of Works and Development pub. CDP 701D, Wellington, New Zealand, September.

O'Connor, C. (1971). *Design of Bridge Superstructures,* John Wiley & Sons, New York.

O'Connor, C., and Chan, T. H. T. (1988). "Dynamic Wheel Loads from Bridge Strains," *ASCE J. Str. Eng.,* 114(8), August, pp. 1703–1723.

O'Connor, C., and Pritchard, R. W. (1985). "Impact Studies on a Small Composite Girder Bridge," *ASCE J. Str. Eng.,* 111(3), March, pp. 641–653.

Ohashi, M., (1979). Kuribayashi, E., Iwasaki, T., and Kawashima, K. "An Overview of the State of Practices in Earthquake-Resistant Design of Highway Bridges," *Proc. Workshop on Earthquake Resistance of Highway Bridges*, Applied Technology Council, Palo Alto, CA, January 29–31.

OHBDC. (1983). *Ontario Highway Bridge Design Code,* 2nd ed., Ontario Ministry of Transportation and Communications, Toronto, Ontario.

———. (1993). *Ontario Highway Bridge Design Code,* 3rd ed., Ontario Ministry of Transportation and Communications, Toronto, Ontario.

Page, J. (1976). *Dynamic Wheel Load Measurements on Motorway Bridges,* Transportation and Road Research Laboratory, Report No. 722, Crowthorne, Berkshire, UK.

Pagon, W. W. (1955). "Wind Forces on Structures, Plate Girders, and Trusses," *Proc. ASCE,* no. 587, January.

Parkinson, G. V. (1963). "Aeroelastic Galloping in One Degree of Freedom," *Symposium No. 16, Wind Effects on Buildings and Structures,* National Physical Laboratory, UK.

Penn. DOT. (1993). *Design Manual, Part 4,* Pennsylvania Department of Transportation, Harrisburg, August.

Penzien, J. (1979). "Seismic Analysis of Multi-Span Reinforced Concrete Bridges," *Proc. Workshop on Earthquake Resistance of Highway Bridges*, Applied Technology Council, Palo Alto, CA, January 29–31.

Penzien, J., Iwasaki, T. and Clough, R. (1979). "Literature Survey: Seismic Effect on Highway Bridges," *Proc. Workshop on Earthquake Resistance of Highway Bridges,* Applied Technology Council ATC 6-1, January 29–31, Palo Alto, CA.

Phillips, M. H., and Carr, A. J. (1984). *Impact Factors and Stress Histograms for Bridges,* Road Research Unit Bull. 73, Bridge Design and Research Seminar, Road Research Unit, National Road Board, Wellington, New Zealand.

Podolny, W., Jr., and Scalzi, J. B. [1986]. *Construction and Design of Cable-Stayed Bridges,* John Wiley & Sons, New York.

Priestley, M. J. N. (1972). "Model Study of a Prestressed Concrete Box Girder Bridge under Thermal Loading," *Proc. 9th Congress Intl. Asso. Bridge and Str. Eng.,* Amsterdam.

———. (1976). "Ambient Thermal Stresses in Circular Prestressed Concrete Tanks," *J. Am. Conc. Inst.,* 73(10), pp. 553–560.

———. (1978). "Design of Concrete Bridges for Temperature Gradients," *J. Am. Conc. Inst.,* 75(5), pp. 209–217.

Purvis, R. L. (1983). "Bridge Joint Maintenance," *Transp. Res. Rec.* 399, Transportation Research Board, Washington, DC.

Radolli, M., and Green, R. (1975). "Thermal Stresses in Concrete Bridge Superstructures under Summer Conditions," *Transp. Res. Rec.* 547, Transportation Research Board, Washington, DC, pp. 23–26.

Rainer, J. H., Pernica, G., and Allen, D. E. (1988). "Dynamic Loading and Response of Footbridges," *Canadian J. Civil Eng.,* 15(1), pp. 66–71.

Rao, D. S. P. (1986). "Temperature Distributions and Stresses in Concrete Bridges," *J. Am. Conc. Inst.,* 83(4), pp. 588–596.

Ravara, A. (1979). "A European View of the Earthquake-Resistant Design of Bridges," *Proc. Workshop on Earthquake Resistance of Highway Bridges,* ATC 6-1, Applied Technology Council, Palo Alto, CA, January 29–31.

Ravindra, M. K., and Galambos. T. V. (1978). "Load and Resistance Factor Design for Steel," *ASCE J. Str. Div.,* 104(ST-9), pp. 1337–1353.

Reed, Lt. Col. W. (1844). "A Short Account of the Failure of a Part of the Brighton Chain Pier, in the Gale of the 30th November, 1836," *Papers on the Subjects Connected with the Duties of the Corps of the Royal Engineers* (professional papers of the Corps of the Royal Engineers), vol. I, p. 99.

Reinhold, T. A., ed. (1982). *Wind Tunnel Modeling for Civil Engineering Applications, Proc. Intl. Workshop, Gaithersberg, Maryland,* Cambridge University Press, New York.

Reynolds, J. C., and Emanuel, J. H. (1974). "Thermal Stresses and Movements in Bridges," *ASCE J. Str. Div.* 100(ST-1), January, pp. 63–78.

Roberson, J. A., and Crowe, C. T. (1990). *Engineering Fluid Mechanics,* Houghton-Mifflin Co., Princeton, NJ.

Roberson, J. A., Lin, C. Y., Rutherford, G. S., and Stine, M. D. (1972). "Turbulence Effect on Drag of Sharp-Edged Bodies," paper no. 9061, *ASCE J. Hydraulics Div.,* July, p. 1187.

Roebling, J. A. (1852). "Some Remarks on Suspension Bridges and on the Comparative Merits of Cable and Chain Bridges," *Amer. Railroad Journal and Mechanics' Magazine,* 6(6), March 15, p. 161, and 6(7), April 1, p. 193.

Rose, E. (1947). "Thrust Exerted by Expanding Ice Sheet," *Trans. Amer. Soc. of Civ. Engrs.* Paper no. 2314, vol. 112, pp. 871–885; Discussion, pp. 886–900.

Rouse, H. (1946). *Elementary Mechanics of Fluids,* John Wiley & Sons, New York.

Russell, J. S. (1841). "On the Vibration of Suspension Bridges and Other Structures," *Trans. Royal Scottish Soc. of Arts,* Vol. I, p. 304.

Sachs, P. (1978). *Wind Forces in Engineering,* 2nd ed., Pergamon Press, New York.

Salmon, C. G., and Johnson, J. E. (1990). *Steel Structures: Design and Behavior,* 3rd ed., Harper-Collins, New York.

Salvadori, M., and Heller, R. (1975). *Structure in Architecture—The Building of Buildings,* Prentice Hall, Englewood Cliffs, NJ.

Scanlan, R. H. (1978a). "The Action of Flexible Bridges under Wind: I: Flutter Theory," *J. Sound and Vibration.*, 60(2), September, pp. 187–200.

——. (1978b). "The Action of Flexible Bridges under Wind: II: Buffeting Theory," *J. Sound and Vibration,* 60(2), September, pp. 201–212.

——. (1979). "On the State of Stability Considerations for Suspended-Span Bridges under Wind," in *Practical Experiences with Flow-Induced Vibrations,* E. Naudascher and D. Rockwell, eds., Springer-Verlag, Berlin, pp. 595–618.

——. (1981). *State-of-the-Art Methods for Calculating Flutter, Vortex-Induced, and Buffeting Response of Bridge Structures,* report no. FHWA/RD-80-050, FHWA, Washington, DC, April.

——. (1982). "Aeroelastic Modeling of Bridges," in *Wind Tunnel Modeling for Civil Engineering Applications*, Cambridge University Press, New York.

——. (1983). "Aeroelastic Analysis of Bridges," *ASCE J. Str. Div.,* 109(5T12) December, pp. 2829–2837.

——. (1986). "Changes in Bridge Deck Flutter Derivatives Caused by Turbulence," in G. C. Hart and R. B. Nelson, eds., *Dynamic Response of Structures: Proceedings of the 3rd Conf.,* pp. 382–389.

——. (1987). "Aspects of Wind and Earthquake Dynamics of Cable-Stayed Bridges," in L. Tall, ed., *Bridges and Power Line Structures,* ASCE, New York, pp. 329–340.

——. (1988). "On Flutter and Buffeting Mechanisms in Long-Span Bridges," *Prob. Engr. Mech.,* 3(1), January.

——. (1989). "Mitigation of Severe Wind Damage Related to Ground Transportation Systems," *ASCE J. Aerospace Eng.,* 115(10), October, pp. 199–206.

Scanlan, R. H., and Budlong, K. S. (1974). "Flutter and Aerodynamic Response Considerations for Bluff Objects in a Smooth Flow," in *Flow-Induced Structural Vibrations,* E. Naudascher, ed., Springer-Verlag, New York, pp. 339–354.

Scanlan, R. H., and Gade, R. H. (1977). "Motion of Suspended Bridge Spans under Gusty Wind," *ASCE J. Str. Eng.,* 103(9), September pp. 1867–1883.

Scanlan, R. H., and Jones, N. P. (1990). "Aeroelastic Analysis of Cable-Stayed Bridges," *ASCE J. Str. Eng.,* 116(2), February, pp. 279–297.

Scanlan, R. H., and Rosenbaum, R. (1951). *Air Craft and Flutter,* MacMillan, New York.

Scanlan, R. H., and Tomko, J. J. (1971). "Airfoil and Bridge Deck Flutter Derivatives," Proc. paper no. 860, *ASCE J. Eng. Mech.,* 97(6), p. 1717.

Scanlan, R. H., and Wardlow, R. L., (1987). "Aerodynamic Stability of Bridge Decks and Structural Members," in *Cable-Stayed Bridges,* pp. 169–202. Structural Engineer, series no. 4, Bridge Division, Office of Engineering, FHWA, Washington, DC.

Schelling, D. R., Galdos, N. H., and Sahin, M. A. (1990). "Evaluation of Impact Factors for Horizontally Curved Bridges," *ASCE J. Str. Div.,* 118(11), pp. 3203–3221.

Schilling, C. G. (1982). "Impact Factors for Fatigue Design," *ASCE J. Str. Div.,* 108(9), pp. 2034–2044.

Scruton, C. (1948). "Severn Bridge Tunnel Tests," *Surveyor,* 107(2959), October, p. 555.

——. (1952). "Experimental Investigation of Aerodynamic Stability of Suspension Bridges with Special Reference to Proposed Severn Bridge," *Proc. Inst. Civ. Engrs.,* part 1, no. 2, March, pp. 189–222.

SEAOC. (1988). *Recommended Lateral Force Requirements and Commentary,* Structural Engineers Association of California, Los Angeles.

Sharpe, R. L., and Meyers, R. L. (1979). "Development of Highway Bridge Seismic Design Criteria for the United States," in *Proc. Workshop on Earthquake Resistance of Highway Bridges,* Applied Technology Council, ATC 6-1, January 29–31, Palo Alto, CA.

Shepard, R., and Aves, R. J. (1973). "Impact Factors for Simple Concrete Bridges," *Proc. Inst. Civil Engrs.,* part 2, 55, pp. 191–210.

Shore, S., and Rabizadeh, R. O. (1974a). *The Dynamic Response of Horizontally Curved Box Girders,* Curt report no. T0173, Research Project HPR-2 (111), Department of Civil Engineering, University of Pennsylvania, Philadelphia, June 3.

———. (1974b). *User's Manual for the Dynamic Response of Curved Box Girders (DYNCRB-BG),* Curt report no. T0274, Research Project HPR-2 (111), Department of Civil Engineering, University of Pennsylvania, June.

Simui, E., and Scanlan, R. H. (1986). *Wind Effects on Structures: An Introduction to Wind Engineering,* 2nd ed, John Wiley & Sons, New York.

Steinman, D. B. (1941). "Bridges and Aerodynamics," *Proc. Amer. Toll Bridge Association,* March, pp. 1–9.

———. (1945a). "Design of Bridges Against Wind. I: General Considerations—Aerostatic Stability," *ASCE Civ. Eng.,* October, pp. 446–472.

———. (1945b). "Design of Bridges Against Wind. II: Aerodynamic Instability—Historical Background," *ASCE Civ. Eng.,* November, pp. 501–504.

———. (1945c). "Design of Bridges Against Wind. III: Elementary Explanation of Aerodynamic Instability," *ASCE Civ. Eng.,* December, pp. 558–560.

———. (1945d). "Rigidity and Aerodynamic Stability of Suspension Bridges," *Trans. ASCE,* 110, pp. 439–580.

———. (1946a). "Design of Bridges Against Wind. IV: Aerodynamic Instability—Prevention and Cure," *ASCE Civ. Eng.,* January, pp. 20–23.

———. (1946b). "Design of Bridges Against Wind. V: Criteria for Assuring Aerodynamic Stability," *ASCE Civ. Eng.,* February, pp. 66–68.

———. (1947). "Problems of Aerodynamic and Hydrodynamic Stability," in *Proc. 3rd Hydraulics Conf.,* Bull. no. 31, State University of Iowa Studies in Engineering, Iowa City.

———. (1950). "Aerodynamic Theory of Bridge Oscillations," *Trans. ASCE,* 115, pp. 1180–1260.

———. (1954). *Suspension Bridges—The Aerodynamic Problem and Its Solution,* IABSE, vol. 14, pp. 209–250.

Stuart, C. F. (1985). *Long Highway Structures Without Expansion Joints,* rep. no. FHWA/CA/SD-82-08, Office of Structures Design, California Department of Transportation, Sacramento, May.

Tabsh, S. W., and Nowak, A. S. (1991). "Reliability of Highway Girder Bridges," *ASCE J. Str. Eng.,* 117(8), August, pp. 2372–2388.

Taly, N. (1996). "Clarification of AASHTO Spec. Sec. 3.12: Reduction in Load Intensity," *Annual Conf. AASHTO Highway Subcommittee on Bridges and Structures,* Philadelphia, May 13–16.

Tanaka, H., and Davenport, A. G. (1982). "Response of the Taut Strip Models to Turbulent Wind," *ASCE J. Eng. Mech. Div.,* 108(EM-1), pp. 33–49.

Thomas, P. K. (1975). "A Comparative Study of Bridge Loading in Different Countries," Transportation and Road Research Laboratory, report 135 UC, Harmondsworth, England.

Timoshenko, S. (1928). *Vibration Problems in Engineering,* D. Van Nostrand Co., New York.

———. (1943). "Theory of Suspension Bridges," *J. Franklin Inst.,* 235(3), March, p. 213, and (4), April, p. 327.

———. (1952), *History of Strength of Materials,* McGraw-Hill Companies, Inc., New York.

TRB. (1990). *Truck Weight Limits: Issues and Options,* Transportation Research Board Report no. 225, Washington, DC.

Tredgold, T. (1828). *Elementary Principles of Carpentry,* 2nd ed., publisher unknown.

UBC. (1994). *The Uniform Building Code, 1994,* International Conference of Building Officials (ICBO), Whittier, CA.

US Congress. (1964). *Maximum Desirable Dimensions and Weights of Various Vehicles Operated on Federal-Aid Systems,* House Document no. 354, U.S. Govt. Printing Office, Washington, DC.

USS. (1975). "Nine Steel Bridges for Forest Development Roads, South Tongass National Forest, Alaska," *Bridge Structural Report, ADUSS 88-5973-02,* U.S. Steel, Pittsburgh, PA.

Vickery, B. J. (1976). "The Design and Performance of a Low-Cost Boundary Layer Wind Tunnel," in *Wind Effects on Structures,* Hatsuo Ishizaki and A. N. L. Chiu, eds., University Press of Hawaii, Honolulu, pp. 99–104.

Vincent, G. S. (1969). "Tentative Criteria for Load Factor Design of Steel Highway Bridges," *Steel Research for Construction,* Bull. no. 15, AISI, March.

Walker, W. H., and Velestos, A. S. (1963). *Response of Simple-Span Highway Bridges to Moving Vehicles,* University of Illinois, Civil Engineering Studies, Structural Research Series, no. 272.

Wang, T., and Huang, D. (1992). "Cable-Stayed Bridge Vibration Due to Road Surface Roughness," *ASCE J. Str. Eng.,* 118(4), April, pp. 1354–1374.

Wardlow, R. L. (1969). *A Preliminary Wind Tunnel Study of the Aerodynamic Stability of Four Bridge Sections for the Proposed New Burrard Inlet Crossing,* NAE report LTR-LA-31, National Research Council, Canada, July.

———. (1970). *Further Wind Tunnel Studies of the Aerodynamic Stability of Four Bridge Sections for the Proposed New Burrard Inlet Crossing,* NAE report LTR-LA-54, National Research Council, Canada, June.

———. (1978). *Sectional versus Full Model Wind Tunnel Testing of Bridge Road Decks,* DME/NAE Quarterly Bull. no. 1978(4), National Research Council of Canada.

Wardlow, R. L., and Ponder C. A. (1970). *Wind Tunnel Investigations of the Aerodynamic Stability of Bridges,* LTR-LA-47, National Aeronautical Establishment, Ottawa, February.

Wasserman, E. P. (1987). "Jointless Bridge Decks," *AISC Eng. J.,* 3rd qtr., 24(3), pp. 93–100.

Weschsler, M. B. (1992). "Discussion of 'Bridge Evaluation for Multipresence of Vehicles,' by B. Bakht and L. G. Jaeger," *ASCE J. Str. Eng.,* 118(1), January, pp. 334–336.

Wolde-Tinsae, A. M. and Klinger, J. E. (1987). *Performance and Design of Jointless Bridges,* Report FHWA MD-87/OA, Department of Civil Engineering, University of Maryland, Annapolis.

Wolde-Tinsae, A. M., Klinger, J. E., and White, E. (1988). "Performance of Jointless Bridges," *ASCE J. Performance of Constructed Facilities,* 2(2), May, pp. 111–125.

Yamadera, N., and Yukitaka, U. (1979). "Special Considerations and Requirements for the Seismic Design of Bridges in Japan," in *Proc. Workshop on Earthquake Resistance of Highway Bridges,* Applied Technology Council, Palo Alto, CA, January 29–31.

Zuk, W. (1981). "Jointless Bridges," Virginia Highway and Transportation Research Council, Charlottesville, June.

CHAPTER 4

The Load Path and Load Distribution in Bridge Superstructures

4.1
INTRODUCTION

An efficient design of a bridge's superstructure is essential to achieving overall economy in the whole bridge structure, in that the superstructure deadweight may form a significant portion of the total gravity load that the bridge must transmit to the foundation. The low initial cost of a lightweight superstructure will translate into an overall economy resulting from reduced size of both the substructure and the foundation components. A clear understanding of the structural behavior of superstructures under loads is essential for efficient design.

A bridge superstructure is an integrated body of various members of reinforced concrete, prestressed concrete, or steel in the form of slabs, stringers, floor beams, diaphragms, etc.; determination of forces in these components is essential for design purposes. The term "*load distribution*" is often used in a generic sense to denote *superstructural analysis;* i.e., the determination of forces in and interaction among its components; these two terms will be used synonymously throughout this text. Discussion will be limited to the analysis of (or the load distribution in) concrete and steel superstructures only. Timber superstructures are not discussed in this text.

The advent of new construction materials led to the evolution, mostly in the last 50 years, of new structural forms, both simple and complex. Various forms of superstructures were presented in Chapter 1. Methods for their analysis, some demanding considerable mathematical theory, have been the focus of numerous studies and research efforts throughout the world in the past several decades and have been detailed in several books [Timoshenko and Woinsky-Krieger, 1959; Hendry and Jaeger, 1959; Rusch and Hergenroder, 1961; Rowe, 1962; AISC, 1963; Balas and Hanuska, 1964; Pucher, 1964; Troitsky, 1967; Bares and Massonet, 1968; ACI, 1969, 1977; O'Connor, 1971; Cusens and Pama, 1975; Bakht and Jaeger, 1985; Hambly, 1991] and in hundreds of research papers. Due to the limited scope of this text, the detailed mathematical theories of these methods are not presented here.

The advent of computers has led the analysis of bridge superstructures from hand calculations to methods that have made their complex analysis possible without recourse to complicated mathematical theory. However, a bridge engineer should be familiar with the underlying theories, not only because they provide a necessary background to understanding the physical behavior of superstructures and give a feel for the computer methods that are based on the approximate solutions of these classical methods, but also because they are useful in discerning the merits and applicability of various methods. Accordingly, an overview of these methods is presented in this chapter.

4.2
BRIDGE GEOMETRY

A brief review of the principal types of superstructures from the viewpoint of geometric and behavioral characteristics is presented in this section. Several terms will be used in the context of this discussion. As shown in Fig. 4.1, the term *longitudinal* is used to denote a direction parallel to traffic, while *transverse* denotes a direction perpendicular to it. From geometric considerations, bridges are often described as *normal* (or *right*), *skew,* and *curved*. Normal, or right, bridges are those in which the longitudinal axis of the bridge, which is parallel to the longitudinal axes of the slab, and the supporting

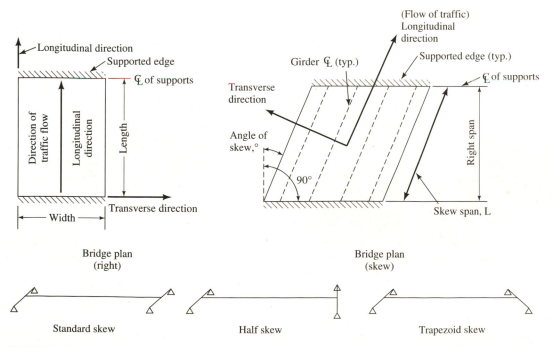

FIGURE 4.1
Definitions of right and skew bridges.

beams (when present) are normal to the centerlines of supports (abutments and/or piers). (See Fig. 4.1). Often, such a plan configuration may not be feasible because of human-created obstacles, complex intersections, space limitations, mountainous terrain, etc., and the result is a skew bridge. A skew bridge, simple or continuous, is characterized by its longitudinal axis, which forms an acute angle, instead of a right angle, with the centerlines of the supports, as shown in Fig. 4.1. *Angle of skew* (or *skew angle*) is defined as the angle between the centerline of the supports and the normal to the axis of the bridge. The skew angles at the two end supports may not necessarily be the same. As shown in Fig. 4.1, a bridge geometry with skewed but parallel lines of supports at the two opposite ends is known as the *standard skew*. Bridges with the line of support at one end normal to the bridge axis but with the other support skewed are *half-skew,* and those with different skew angles at the two supports are known as *trapezoidal skew* [Matsumoto, 1969]. Skew angle is an important parameter affecting the analysis of the bridge structure, whether simple or continuous; with torsionally stiff girders, the skew angle can have a considerable effect on the shear and bending moments in the girders. It has been suggested that, for skew angles not exceeding 20° (30° for slab-on-beam bridges, described later), bridges can be safely designed as right or normal bridges by simplified methods. However, it has been shown that, for larger skew angles, the torsional moments, which are not calculated directly in simplified analyses, are large and would invalidate the results from the simplified analyses [Kostem, 1984; Bakht and Jaeger, 1985; Hambly, 1991]. Many computer programs developed for analysis and design of bridge structures are subject to some limitations in dealing with the skewness of the bridge [Nutt, Schamber, and Zokai, 1988; NCHRP, 1992a], although there are some computer programs that can design a structure with any skew angle. The effect of skew angle on the load distribution in highway bridges continues to be the subject of numerous studies [Chen, Ciess, and Newmark, 1954; Ghali, 1969; Matsumoto, 1969; DeCastro and Kostem, 1975; Kostem, 1984; Bishara, 1986; El-Ali, 1986; Marx, Khachaturian, and Gamble, 1986; Nutt, Schamber, and Zokai, 1988; Khaleel and Itani, 1990; Bakht and Jaeger, 1992; Bishara, Maria, and Eli-Ali, 1993].

Curved bridges, also referred to as horizontally curved bridges, have become almost standard features of highway interchanges and urban expressways in recent times. They are characterized by their out-of-straightness alignment, as viewed in the plan. Curved bridges result from several factors, such as the design requirements for interchanges, the need for smooth dissemination of congested traffic, right-of-way limitations, local topography and foundation conditions, and aesthetics. Initially, curved bridges comprised a series of straight girders used as chords in forming a curved alignment. Recent developments, however, have led to the replacement of straight girders by curved girders. Curved geometry introduces considerable complexity in bridge analysis, for curved girders are subjected not only to flexural stresses, but also, due to the eccentricity of the midspan with respect to the supports, to very significant torsional stresses. Accordingly, the methods of analysis used for straight bridges cannot be used for curved bridges. Analyses and designs of curved bridges are mathematically complex topics that have warranted special specifications [AASHTO, 1980] based on a study by Culver and McManus [1971]. Generally, curved bridges can be analyzed by the grillage method, in which the curved members are idealized as curved strings of straight members, or by the space frame model and by computer methods (see Nakai and Yoo, 1988,

Appendix C). A comprehensive treatment of curved steel bridges can be found in the extensively referenced work of Nakai and Yoo [1988] and in [McManus, Nasser, and Culver, 1969; O'Connor, 1971; Heins and Firmage, 1979; AMS, 1986].

4.3
DIAPHRAGMS

Diaphragms are short structural members positioned transversely to and between adjacent stringers at various intervals and at abutments. They usually consist of channels, W shapes, cross frames, or solid vertical slabs (in the case of concrete beams). The purpose of providing diaphragms is to ensure lateral distribution of live loads to various adjacent stringers, which depends on both the stiffness of the diaphragms relative to the connected stringers and the method of connectivity. However, the extent of this structural contribution has not been quantified [DeCastro and Kostem, 1975; Degenkolb, 1977; Kostem, 1984]. The diaphragm's action comes into play when a load is placed on the deck and applied *at* the diaphragm location, a condition seldom realized in practice. Research shows that a diaphragm under the load lessens the load carried by the girder immediately under the vehicle by transferring portions of it to adjacent girders; remote diaphragms do not participate in this distributive action. For full effectiveness (i.e., more uniform distribution of live loads transversely) under highway loadings or railway loadings, several closely spaced diaphragms should be provided; this will cause the deck to act as a two-way slab. However, this distributive action does not develop unless the diaphragm spacing is as close as the girder spacing; and if so provided, the result will be an uneconomical structure [Degenkolb, 1977]. In current practice, based on experimental research, diaphragm spacings and locations relative to the span lengths are arbitrarily set by the specifications [DeCastro and Kostem, 1975; Zellin et al., 1975a,b; Degenkolb, 1977; Kostem, 1984; AASHTO, 1992]. Note that, their questionable effectiveness in straight-girder bridges notwithstanding, diaphragms and bracings constitute very important load-carrying components for curved girder bridges.

4.4
BASIC CONCEPTS

To understand the meaning of and the concern for load distribution in highway bridges, it is instructive to examine the *load path* (or the *load-transfer mechanism*) in buildings with floors supported on longitudinal beams. The dead load of the floor is assumed to be transferred to the supporting beams on the tributary area basis. The live load, such as building occupants, furniture, machines, and fixtures, although not uniform in reality, is assumed to be uniformly distributed over the floor area and is also assumed to be transferred to the supporting beams on the tributary area basis. Equally spaced interior beams, under this assumption, are assumed to share floor loads equally. The same analogy can be used for bridge decks supporting bridge live loads (vehicles), with one notable exception: the live loads (machines, fixtures, equipment, etc.) in buildings occupy relatively fixed positions (they are pseudostatic), whereas bridge live loads occupy only

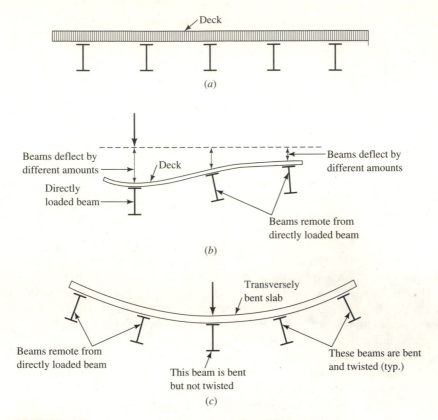

FIGURE 4.2
(*a*) A slab-on-beam deck. (*b*) Bending of the directly loaded beam in the plane
of the loads without twisting. (*c*) Transverse bending of the slab accompanied
by twisting of beams remote from the directly loaded beam.

a partial area of the decks. In fact, the live load on bridge decks, consisting of concentrated wheel loads, may occupy random positions, both longitudinally and transversely,
and thus will affect the live load shared by various beams supporting the deck. This
aspect of live-load distribution is one of the primary concerns in the analysis of bridge
decks.

Physical reasoning can be used to get a feel for the complexity involved in analysis
of bridge decks. For simplicity, a slab-on-beam type deck (discussed later), shown in
Fig. 4.2(*a*), may be used to illustrate the general nature of the problem. Again, for
simplicity, it may be assumed that the deck is loaded longitudinally by one line of
wheel loads. If these concentrated loads are placed on the deck directly over one of the
beams, that particular beam will bear a greater share of the total load than the other
parallel beams remote from it. The slab and all of the beams will bend longitudinally
in the plane containing the line of the loads (Fig. 4.2(*b*)). The slab, however, bends
transversely also, causing the remote beams (but not the directly loaded beam) to twist
along with it, to maintain the overall compatibility of displacements at the slab–beam
interfaces (Fig. 4.2(*c*)). The participatory action of these remote beams will depend on

the stiffness of the slab, and the span, spacings, and stiffnesses of beams. The determination of this participatory action of the various superstructure components is referred to as *load distribution.*

4.5
STRUCTURAL FORMS AND BEHAVIORAL CHARACTERISTICS

A bridge deck is the medium through which all bridge loads are transferred to other components. Figure 4.3 shows a typical cross section of a bridge over a waterway, in which various components are identified. The general load path (or load transfer mechanism) for most common types of bridge decks is shown in Fig. 4.4.

Depending on the purpose, bridge superstructures can be classified in several ways, as explained in Chapter 1. The applicability of an analytical method for a particular type

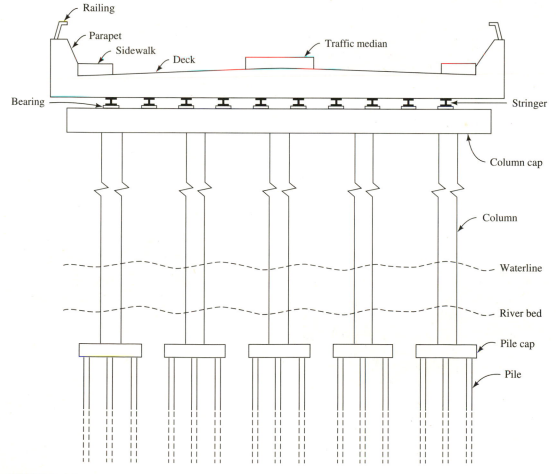

FIGURE 4.3
Typical cross section of a bridge over a waterway.

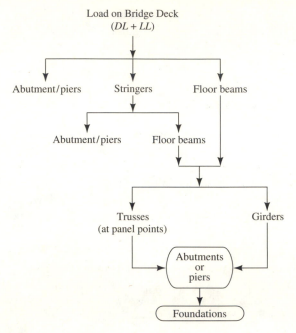

FIGURE 4.4
The load path in bridge superstructures.

of deck depends on the complexity of its structural form and behavioral characteristics; from this standpoint, the most commonly used bridge decks can be classified as follows [Hambly, 1991]:

1. Slab decks
2. Beam-and-slab decks
3. Beam decks
4. Cellular decks
5. Grid decks

4.5.1 Slab Decks

The slab deck is the most commonly used type of deck for short-span bridges. The load-carrying mechanism of a slab is analogous to that of a plate, which is characterized by its ability to transfer bending and twisting in its own plane owing to continuity in all directions. Its physical behavior is explained in Fig. 4.5, which shows the slab divided into several rectangular elements.

Application of a load on a portion of a slab causes it to deflect locally in a "dish," causing a two-dimensional system of bending and twisting moments; through this mechanism the load is transferred to the adjacent parts of the deck, which are less severely loaded. Usually, slabs are poured in place. For analytical purposes, they are said to be *isotropic* if they have similar stiffnesses in both the longitudinal and transverse directions, and *orthotropic* otherwise.

Slab decks are not economical for spans exceeding 50 ft or so, owing to the excessive deadweight resulting from large depth requirements. Hollow concrete slabs

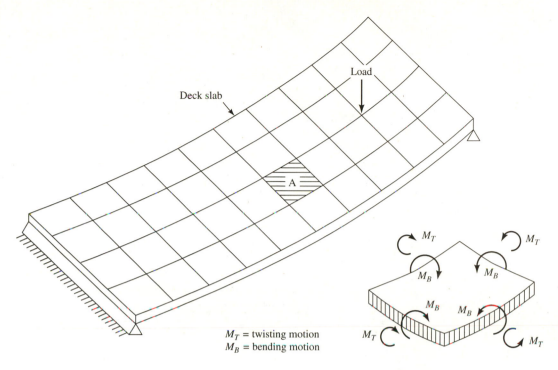

M_T = twisting motion
M_B = bending motion

Forces on element "A"

FIGURE 4.5
Plate action in a slab; distribution of forces by bending and twisting in two directions.

(voided slabs) were developed to overcome this problem, by incorporating voids of circular or rectangular cross section placed symmetrically about the neutral axis (Fig. 4.6). The scheme shown in Fig. 4.6(*b*), known as the shear-key deck, or the adjacent box beam deck,[1] entails contiguous placement of prestressed concrete box beams. The box beams are connected longitudinally by the cast-in-place shear keys. Such a scheme is ideal in situations where falsework must be avoided to prevent traffic interruptions underneath the bridge. However, this scheme is not very efficient structurally, since full continuity in the transverse direction is not developed due to a lack of transverse prestressing, and transverse distribution of the load is not as effective as in a slab.

As a two-dimensional solution, the governing equation for the lateral deflection of a loaded plate, developed by S. D. Poisson (1781–1840), with boundary conditions modified by G. R. Kirchhoff (1824–1887) [Timoshenko, 1953], is

$$D\left(\frac{\partial^4 w}{\partial x^4} + 2\frac{\partial^4 w}{\partial x^2 \partial y^2} + \frac{\partial^4 w}{\partial y^4}\right) = q \qquad (4.1)$$

---

[1]The term *adjacent box beam bridge* is used to distinguish such a design from another scheme for bridge decks in which similar box beams are spaced at intervals, without their webs touching each other. These box beams are joined transversely by a composite slab, which serves as the bridge deck.

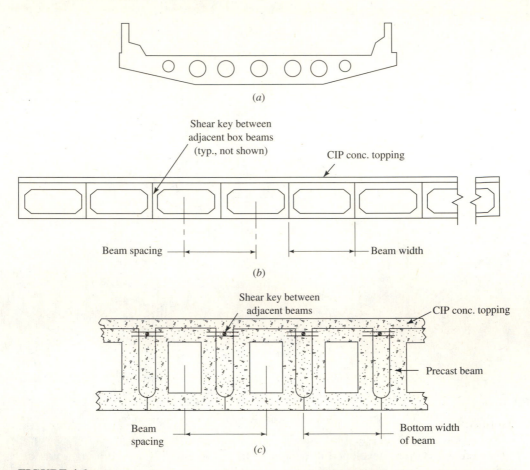

FIGURE 4.6
Voided slabs: (*a*) configurations of circular voids; (*b*) and (*c*), adjacent box beam deck with longitudinal shear keys.

where w = lateral deflection of the plate
$\quad\quad q$ = intensity of load
$\quad\quad D$ = flexural rigidity of the plate

In the absence of the closed-form solution of Eq. 4.1 for a real deck, approximate solutions have been developed [Chaudhary, 1978]. One of these is the grillage method, wherein, for analytical purposes, the real continuous plated structure (slab) is idealized by a series of discrete, orthogonally intersecting beams (Fig. 4.7). Details of these methods can be found in several references [Kerfoot and Ostapenko, 1967; Bares and Massonet, 1968; Bakht and Jaeger, 1985; Jaeger and Bakht, 1989; Hambly, 1991].

Another method is the method of influence surfaces, which uses design charts. These charts have been prepared for various shapes and support conditions by Pucher [1964], and for *skew* simply supported slabs by Rusch and Hergenroder [1961] and Balas and Hanuska [1964]. For orthotropic slabs, charts prepared by Morice and Little

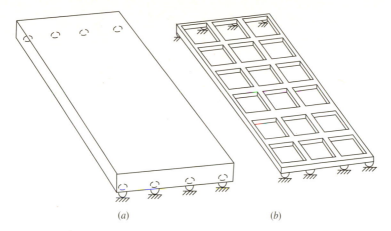

FIGURE 4.7
Grillage analysis of a slab deck: (*a*) prototype deck; (*b*) equivalent
grillage [Hambly, 1991].

[1954, 1955, 1956] and described by Rowe [1962], and charts of Cusens and Pama
[1975] are available.

Yet another method, the application of the line solution technique to the general
solution of reinforced concrete decks, has been described by Coull and Rao [1969].
Applicable to both right and skew bridge slabs, this method reduces the partial differential equation of the plate theory to a set of ordinary differential equations by replacing
the derivatives in one direction by their finite difference equivalents. Analysis of decks
formed from contiguously placed hollow box beams with longitudinal shear keys can
be found in several references [Newmark, 1938; Cusens and Pama, 1965; Nasser, 1965;
Pool et al., 1965].

4.5.2 Beam-and-Slab Decks

Figure 4.8 shows cross sections of commonly used beam-and-slab bridge decks,
schemes (*a*), (*b*), and (*c*) being the most commonly used for highway bridges in the
short-span range. Beam-and-slab decks comprise a number of usually equally spaced
(generally 6–12 ft apart) beams spanning longitudinally between supports (hence
the design is also referred to as spaced beam-and-slab decks, or parallel girder systems [O'Connor, 1971]), with a thin, structurally continuous slab spanning transversely
across the top. The slab serves the dual purpose of supporting the live load on the bridge
and acting as the top flange of the longitudinal beams. Diaphragms are provided transversely between the beams over the supports and, depending on the span, at midspan
and other intermediate locations. The slab can be noncomposite or composite, the latter
being the obvious choice for economy and structural efficiency, in which case the slab
structurally acts as the top flange of the beams. The scheme shown in Fig. 4.8(*d*), the
contiguous beam-and-slab deck (used in Europe but not popular in the United States),
consists of contiguously placed, precast prestressed concrete inverted T-beams, with a

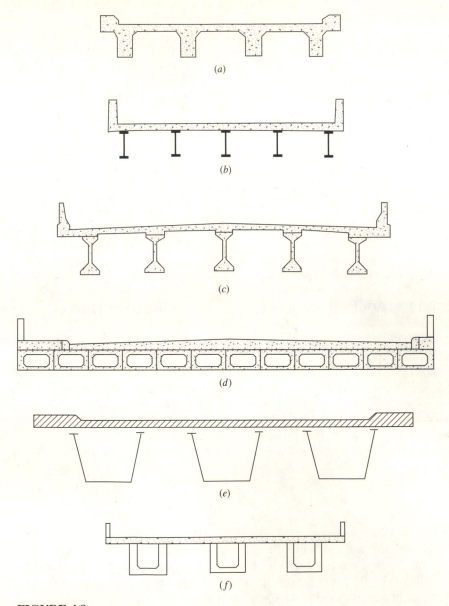

FIGURE 4.8
Cross sections of bridge-and-slab decks: (*a*) T-beam bridge, (*b*) slab-on-steel beams, (*c*) slab on prestressed concrete beams, (*d*) contiguous beam-and-slab deck, (*e*) multispine deck with steel box beams, and (*f*) multispine deck with concrete box beams.

cast-in-place reinforced concrete slab. In this scheme, under the load, the slab deflects in a single smooth wave so that the resulting structural behavior is akin to that of an orthotropic slab with longitudinal stiffening [Hambly, 1991]. In conjunction with steel beams, the concrete slab may be replaced by a stiffened steel "battledeck" fabricated from stiffened thin plate (see Chapter 1, Fig. 1.29). Such decks are known as orthotropic decks and are discussed in numerous references, such as AISC [1963], Troitsky [1967], and Cusens and Pama [1975].

A structural characteristic of the spaced beam-and-slab deck schemes of Fig. 4.8 is their use of beams of open cross section, which are inherently torsionally weak. A more efficient type of deck is the multispine deck shown in Fig. 4.8(e), which comprises girders of closed cross section (concrete or steel) and a continuous structural concrete deck at the top. In its extreme form, this type of configuration can have as few as two spine beams, concrete or steel. Of necessity, concrete spine beams are more closely spaced than steel spine beams. In a two-spine steel beam deck, the spacing of beams can be more than 40 ft, whereas the spacing of solid concrete spines is generally in the 24-ft range [Hambly, 1991].

Beam-and-slab decks of various configurations can be idealized as comprising a series of longitudinally spanning parallel T-beams connected along their edges with full continuity (Fig. 4.9). Under load, the response of a slab is characterized by longitudinal bending as flanges of T-beams, accompanied by transverse bending as a continuous beam. Mathematically, these decks can be analyzed by the grillage method, as explained in various references [Bares and Massonet, 1968; Hambly, 1991]. For analytical purposes, a transverse portion of the slab, cantilevering equally on both sides of the supporting beam, is associated with its acting in unison as its top flange. It has been shown that when a beam with an infinitely wide flange is subjected to flexure, shear strains in the wide flange cause nonlinear stress distributions of bending stresses, a phenomenon known as *shear lag*. These stress distributions are different from the linear stress distributions predicted by the simple bending theory

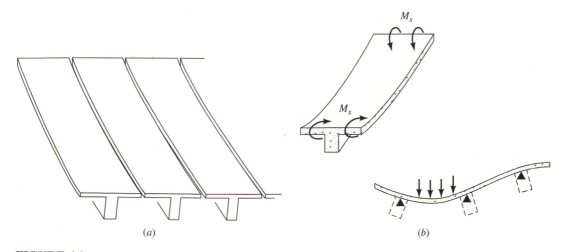

(a)   (b)

FIGURE 4.9
Response of a beam-and-slab deck. (*a*) Longitudinal bending as flanges of T-beams. (*b*) Transverse bending as a continuous beam [Hambly, 1991].

(i.e., $f = Mc/I$). For analytical simplicity, a hypothetical flange of reduced width, known as the *effective width,* is considered as the top flange of the supporting beam, resulting in a T-section [Lee, 1962; Severn, 1962, 1964; Timoshenko and Goodier, 1956; Sabins, 1979], which has been codified by the specifications [AASHTO, 1992]. The flexural stress distribution across this hypothetical flange is assumed to be uniform and can be calculated from simple bending theory ($f = Mc/I$). The spline beam decks can be analyzed by the grillage method as well as by means of harmonic analysis and folded plate theory [Hendry and Jaeger, 1956, 1959; Rowe, 1962; Muller, 1963; Hambly, 1991].

One of the early methods developed for obtaining responses (shears, moments, and deflections) of superstructures of beam-and-slab type decks is the method of distribution coefficients, which is still in use. The distribution coefficient for a certain response, defined as the ratio of the actual intensity of the response to the average intensity of the same response, is the key response quantity that forms the basis of so-called simplified methods. This method, also referred to as the D-type method in the literature [Bakht and Jaeger, 1985], is based on the analogy between a grid system and an orthotropic plate.[2] As pointed out by Bares and Massonet [1968], after World War II, a notable development occurred in the analytic approach to the grid problem: the previous solutions based on either end forces or end deformations were both abandoned, and a new method was developed based on the analogy between a grid and an orthotropic plate. The fundamentals of this new concept were established in the early 1920s by Huber [1921, 1924, 1925a,b, 1926, 1933] and followed by a variety of solutions by others [Bares and Massonet, 1968[3]]. A solution for orthotropic plates of negligible torsional rigidity was given by Guyon [1946] for loads of any variation, using coefficients of lateral distribution; he later gave a similar solution for isotropic plates [Guyon, 1949]. In this method, the loads are represented by a harmonic series, and only the first term of the series is used to obtain the coefficients. Massonet [1950] then developed solutions for orthotropic plates with torsional rigidity. For expedient use, distribution coefficients are given in either graphical form [Rowe, 1962; Morice and Little, 1956] or in tabular form [Bares and Massonet, 1968]. The accuracy of the distribution coefficients was improved by Cusens and Pama [Little, Rowe, and Morice, 1956; Cusens and Pama, 1975] by taking seven terms of the harmonic series. A brief summary of the method of harmonic analysis can be found in many references, such as Bakht and Jaeger [1985], Jaeger and Bakht [1989], and Hambly [1991]. The application of the orthotropic plate theory for bridge deck analysis can be found in the literature [Chu and Krishnamurthy, 1962; Vitols, Clifton, and Au, 1963; AISC, 1963; Troitsky, 1967; Cusens and Pama, 1975].

The method of analysis permitted in AASHTO [1992] (subsequently referred to as the *AASHTO method*) is based on the work of many researchers and is reported in the literature [Westergaard, 1930; Newmark, 1948; Jensen, 1938, 1939, 1944; Roseli, 1955; Hondros and Marsh, 1960; Severn, 1962; Pama and Cusens, 1969; Scordelis,

---

[2]An *orthotropic plate* is defined as a plate of constant thickness having different flexural and torsional rigidities in orthogonal directions.

[3]This excellent text contains 159 references on classical methods dealing with bridge deck analysis.

Davis, and Lo, 1969; Sanders and Elleby, 1970]. Although this method is by far one of the simplest, it is not without shortcomings (discussed later). Because of its widespread use by bridge engineers throughout the United States and in many other countries, the AASHTO method is the focus of discussion in this chapter, and it is also discussed in subsequent chapters. Essentially, the AASHTO method uses the concept of a wheel load distribution factor (also referred to as live-load distribution factor) of the type S/D, where S is the beam spacing in the case of slab-on-beam type decks (unit width in the case of slab bridges) and D is a deck-, type-, and geometry-related coefficient, predetermined for a variety of deck types. The quantity S/D is a dimensionless parameter, as both S and D are in units of length. To obtain design response quantities such as moments, shears, and deflections, an isolated beam is loaded with one line of wheel loads of the design vehicle, as discussed in Chapter 3, and is analyzed for the maximum response. *The required design response quantity is obtained by multiplying the maximum response by the distribution factor* (S/D). The obvious simplicity of this method is derived from the fact that the distribution factor is a function of beam spacing only and is not related to the structural characteristics of the deck. Implicit in this simple methodology are the assumptions that the transverse distribution patterns for all responses are similar, in that distribution factors can be used as multipliers for obtaining *all* design response quantities, and that the longitudinal and transverse effects of wheel loads on beams of most types of bridge decks can be treated as uncoupled phenomena.

4.5.3 Beam Decks

A bridge deck can be assumed to behave as a beam when its length-to-width ratio is such that, under loads, its cross sections displace bodily but without any distortion. Because the dominant load in such decks is concentric, distortion of the cross section under eccentric loading has relatively little influence on the principal bending stresses [Hambly, 1991]. These decks can be analyzed by classical methods of structural analysis, with stresses determined from simple bending theory and torsion of noncircular cross sections [Tung, 1969; Degenkolb, 1977; Hambly, 1991], and by folded plate theory [Defries-Skene and Scordelis, 1964; Chu and Pinjarkar, 1966; Chu and Dudnik, 1969].

4.5.4 Cellular Decks

Also referred to as box beam bridges, cellular decks have the configuration of a closed cross section comprising a number of thin slabs and thick or thin webs. Their large bending and torsional stiffness, owing to the deep closed cross-sectional configuration, make them efficient and the preferred type of deck for spans over 100 ft, for reasons of economy.

Cellular decks are usually multicellular structures whose responses depend on the provision and spacing of stiffening diaphragms. Closely spaced diaphragms prevent cross-sectional distortion, in which case the deck can be analyzed as a beam if it is narrow or as a slab if it is wide [Hambly, 1991]. However, the usefulness and stiffening action of the interior diaphragms are questionable, and for this, scant quantitative data are available. Diaphragm action was discussed in Sec. 4.3. Cellular decks can be analyzed by the grillage method or by folded plate theory [Bakht and Jaeger, 1985; Hambly, 1991; Evans, 1984].

4.5.5 Grid Decks

Resembling a waffle on the underside, a grid deck consists of a slab supported by a grid of two or more longitudinal beams and transverse beams or diaphragms. In essence, it resembles a T-beam deck with several closely spaced diaphragms (Fig. 4.10). Bending of a longitudinal beam under loads also leads to bending and twisting of the transverse beams, a phenomenon that causes load distribution in various members of the deck.

(a)

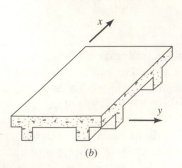

(b)

FIGURE 4.10
Grid or waffle slab decks: (*a*) Hegenburger Overpass; (*b*) a segment of a waffle slab [Lin, Kulka, and Yang, 1969].

Cumbersome falsework required for fabrication render this kind of construction rather uneconomical, and, as a result, it seems to have been abandoned in favor of slab-on-beam decks. Analysis of grid decks can be performed by the grillage analogy [Jackson, 1968; Kennedy and Bali, 1979; Bakht, 1980; Jaeger and Bakht, 1982; Bakht and Jaeger, 1985].

4.6
METHODS OF ANALYSIS

Methods of analysis of bridge decks can be classified as

- Classical methods
- Computer methods
- Simplified methods

Various methods of analyzing bridge decks, such as the grillage method, the folded plate method, and the equivalent orthotropic plate method, referred to previously, belong to the category of so-called classical methods. Burdened with cumbersome mathematics, these methods do not offer very efficient solutions, particularly for longhand calculations, and therefore they are not very appealing to design engineers. This has led to the development of so-called simplified methods, such as those used by the Ontario Highway Department [Bakht, Cheung, and Aziz, 1979; Bakht and Jaeger, 1985; OHBDC, 1983, 1992] and the method of distribution coefficients (or the AASHTO method) such as the one specified by AASHTO [1992, 1994a,b]. A comprehensive discussion on various classical methods has been provided by Bares and Massonet [1968]. An exhaustive discussion on distribution of wheel loads on highway bridges, pertinent methods, and their limitations has been presented by Nutt, Schamber, and Zokai [1988] and summarized in [NCHRP, 1992a].

By proper discretization and modeling, all types of bridge decks can be analyzed by the finite element method. Recent advances in computer methods and numerical analysis techniques have led to the development of a number of computer programs in the field of structural analysis [Lightfoot and Sawko, 1959, 1960; Scordelis, 1984]. Two types of programs are in general use: general-purpose programs, such as SAP, STRUDL, and FINITE, and special-purpose programs for analysis of specific bridge types, such as GENDEK, CELL-4, LANELL, CURVBRG, POWELL, SALOD, and MUPDI. Comprehensive discussions on the use and the results of research on bridge deck analysis based on these programs have been presented by Nutt, Schamber, and Zokai [1988]; Hambly [1991]; and Jaeger and Bakht [1989]. A summary of these results can be found in NCHRP [1992a].

In addition, a variety of computer programs are available commercially that are capable of analyzing and designing bridge superstructures. These include MERLIN DASH (for design and analysis of straight highway bridge systems) and DESCUS (for curved bridges, on PC) by Optimate, Inc. of Bethlehem, PA; MDX's AASHTO composite steel girder design program, Line Girder System, by Bridge Software Development International, Ltd. (BSDI); Bridge Design System and AASHTO BRADD-2 (a bridge automated design and drafting system) by AASHTO; and CBRIDGE, a three-dimensional analysis program for straight or curved bridges by Telos Technologies, Inc. of Syracuse, NY. Other programs, such as CRVBRG-C, STRESS, and CUGAR2, have been in use for several years. Furthermore, there are a number of computer programs developed and used in-house by various bridge owner agencies in the United States, such as highway departments or departments of transportation. The Concrete Reinforcing Steel Institute (CRSI) has developed programs such as SLABBRDG for concrete decks. In addition, there are perhaps several other computer programs used in-house by engineers in various design establishments.

4.7
AASHTO METHOD OF LIVE LOAD DISTRIBUTION—SLABS AND BEAMS

With reference to the various superstructure types (Fig. 4.8) and the load path (Fig. 4.4), we now discuss application of the AASHTO method to determine design forces in various components, such as slab, stringers, floor beams, etc.

4.7.1 Concrete Slabs

Methods prescribed in the AASHTO specifications [1992] are based on the Westergaard theory [Westergaard, 1930] and the work of Newmark [1938]; Newmark and Ciess [1943a,b]; Newmark, Ciess, and Peuman [1948]; and Jensen [1938].

4.7.1.1 Support conditions for slab

Two cases are considered, based on the direction of the span of the slab:

1. The deck consists only of a reinforced concrete slab supported on abutments and/or piers. The main reinforcement in this case runs *parallel to traffic* (Fig. 4.11(*a*)).
2. The deck slab is supported over a number of parallel steel, concrete, or timber beams. The main reinforcement in this case is oriented *perpendicular to traffic* (and beams) (Fig. 4.11(*b*), (*c*), and (*d*)).

In both cases, for analytical purposes, the loads are placed on the slab in a specified manner. The two key design forces to be determined are moment and shear in the slab. The empirical formulas used for calculating slab moments are based on the assumed position of the wheel load: one ft from the curb, or one ft from the rail if a sidewalk or curb is not provided.

4.7.1.2 Determination of moments and shear in slabs.
Case 1: Slab supported on an abutment and/or piers

This case is covered by AASHTO 3.24.3.2 under "Case B—Main Reinforcement Parallel to Traffic." For moment computations, the span (*S*) is defined as the distance between the centers of the supports, but *S* need not exceed the length of the clear span plus the thickness of the slab (AASHTO 3.24.1.1).

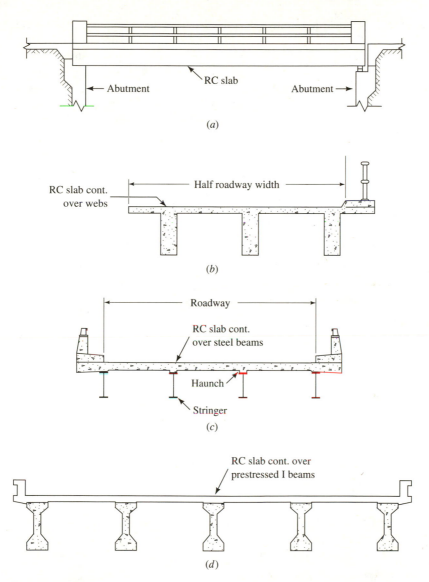

(a)

(b)

(c)

(d)

FIGURE 4.11
Support conditions for a concrete slab: (*a*) reinforced concrete slab bridge; (*b*) reinforced concrete T-beam bridge; (*c*) reinforced concrete slab supported on steel stringers; (*d*) reinforced concrete slab supported on prestressed concrete girders.

Design moment. For simple spans,

$$\text{dead-load moment} = \frac{wL^2}{8}$$

where w = dead load/ft^2 of slab and L = span (S, as previously defined).

Live-load moment (LLM). Two methods are prescribed in AASHTO 3.24.3.2 for determining slab moments.

Method 1. Moment is calculated as if it were caused by a concentrated load acting on a simple span. In reality, however, the wheel loads are not true concentrated (or point) loads, but are distributed over the tire contact area. Because of the lateral stiffness of the slab, it is assumed that the distribution area for the wheel load is larger than the actual contact area between the tire and the slab. Thus, a truck wheel load is distributed over a width of E ($= 4 + 0.06S$) ft, to a maximum of 7.0 ft. The value of the concentrated load is obtained by dividing the rear wheel load (16 kips for H20 or HS20 loading) by this distribution width. For lane loading, the concentrated load is distributed over twice the distribution width (i.e., $2E$ ft). Maximum moment is obtained by placing the concentrated load so obtained at the midspan, which gives

$$M = \frac{P'S}{4} \tag{4.2}$$

where

$$S = \text{span (ft)}$$

and

$$P' = P/E \text{ for truck loading}$$
$$= P/2E \text{ for lane loading}$$

where

$$E = 4 + 0.06S \text{ (ft)}$$

and

$$P = P_{15} = 12,000 \text{ lb for H15 truck loading}$$
$$= P_{20} = 16,000 \text{ lb for H20 truck loading}$$
$$= 13,500 \text{ lb for H15 lane loading}$$
$$= 18,000 \text{ lb for H20 lane loading}$$

Note that in the case of lane loading, the uniform lane loading should also be distributed over the width of $2E$ and moment ($wS^2/8$), calculated accordingly.

Method 2. Alternatively, for HS20 loading, the maximum live-load moment (*LLM*) per foot width of slab can be closely approximated by the following empirical formulas:

1. For spans up to 50 ft, $LLM = 900S$ ft-lb
2. For spans > 50 to 100 ft, $LLM = 1000(1.3S - 20.0)$ ft-lb

The obvious approximate nature of these values of moments should be recognized. For HS15 loading, *LLM* can be taken as three-fourths of the preceding values.

Both methods are illustrated in Example 6.1 (Chapter 6).

The edges of the deck slab should be stiffened. This can be accomplished by either providing an additionally reinforced slab section, a beam integral with and deeper than the slab, or an integrally reinforced section composed of slab and curb. This portion of the slab, known as the *longitudinal edge beam*, is designed for a live-load moment equal to $0.1PS$, where $P = P_{15}$ or P_{20}, respectively, for slabs designed for H15 or HS15, or H20 and HS20 loadings. According to AASHTO, the *value of moment for the edge beam is not to be increased for impact considerations.*

The requirement that a wheel load should not be placed closer than 1 ft from the curb or the parapet was noted earlier. These distances are sometimes called the edge distances and have an important bearing on the analytical aspects of the slab. The stiffened section at the edges of the slab essentially acts as an L-beam whose neutral axis is higher than that of the slab. Discussions on this subject have been provided by Bakht and Jaeger [1985] and by Hambly [1991]. *For continuous spans, the simple-span moment can be reduced by 20 percent, both for positive and negative moments.*

Note that values of moment obtained by the two methods are different, and no preference of one over the other is suggested in the AASHTO specifications.

Shear and bond. Deck slabs designed according to the preceding methods are considered safe in shear and bond; accordingly, no check is required for this design consideration (AASHTO 3.24.4).

4.7.1.3 Determination of moments and shear in slabs.
Case 2: Slab supported on beams and stringers

This case is covered by AASHTO 3.24.3.1, "Case A—Main Reinforcement Perpendicular to Traffic."

Span. In this case, the slab is usually continuous over several parallel stringers or beams, which can be reinforced concrete (T-beams), prestressed concrete, steel, or timber. The effective span, S, is different in each case, as follows (AASHTO 3.24.1.2):

1. When the supporting beams are made from reinforced concrete, the slab is usually cast monolithic with them, resulting in a T-beam section. In such cases, S equals the clear span (Fig. 4.12(a)). This specification also applies in the case of slabs supported on rigid top flange prestressed concrete beams, where the ratio of top flange width to minimum thickness is less than 4.0.
2. When the slab is supported on steel stringers, S equals the clear span plus half the width of the stringer flange (Fig. 4.12(b)). In a case where the widths of the top and the bottom flanges are different (e.g., in a composite plate girder), the top flange width should be considered in computing S. This specification also applies in the case of slabs supported on thin top flange prestressed concrete beams, where the ratio of top flange width to minimum thickness is 4.0 or larger.

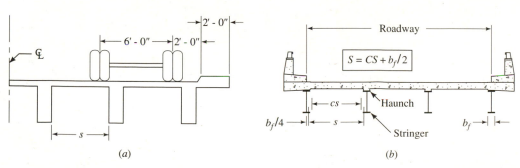

(a)   (b)

FIGURE 4.12
Effective span for stringer-supported slabs.

Design moment

$$\text{Dead load moment} = M_D = \frac{wL^2}{8} \quad \text{or} \quad \frac{wS^2}{8}$$

where w = dead load/ft^2 of slab and L = effective span (S, as defined in Fig. 4.12).

Live-load moment (LLM). LLM is determined from Eq. 4.3:

$$LLM = \frac{P(S + 2)}{32} \text{ ft-lb} \tag{4.3}$$

where $P_i = P_{20} = 16{,}000$ lb (load on one rear wheel of an HS20 truck)
$= P_{15} = 12{,}000$ lb (load on one rear wheel of an HS15 truck)

Note that Eq. 4.3 gives design moment per foot width of a simple slab, and the span, S, is in foot units. These moments are to be reduced by 20 percent when the slab is continuous over *three or more* stringers, which is generally the case for concrete decks. This reduction of moments is specified in AASHTO 3.24.3.1, which permits a continuity factor of 0.8 to be applied to Eq. 4.3. In a general sense, this is analogous to using, for uniform load, $M = wL^2/10$ for a continuous span instead of $M = wL^2/8$ for a simple span ($0.8wL^2/8 = wL^2/10$).

Applications of these formulae are illustrated by numerical examples in Chapters 6 through 9.

4.7.2 Forces in Stringers

Stringers are the longitudinal beams supported on abutments and piers. They receive their loads directly from the slab which they support. The two outside stringers on each side of the bridge deck are called the *exterior* stringers; the remaining stringers are the *interior* stringers. In this section, the load path and the distribution of dead and live loadings to stringers are discussed.

4.7.2.1 Dead-load forces

Dead load is distributed to various stringers in proportion to their tributary widths. In most cases, the stringers are spaced equally, resulting in equal tributary widths for all interior stringers. Consequently, all interior stringers are assumed to carry equal amounts of dead load. Essentially, the dead load consists of the deck slab, the wearing surface, sidewalks, curbs, parapets, and railings. Usually, the slab is poured first, and after the slab has hardened, the pouring of the curb, sidewalk, and parapet follows. The dead load due to these components, also referred to as superimposed dead load (usually denoted as *DL2* in computations), is assumed to be shared equally by all stringers, although, in reality, they are positioned in closer proximity to the exterior stringers (AASHTO 3.23.2.3.1.1). For multibeam precast, pretopped, prestressed concrete bridges, Bishara and Soegiarso [1993] have found that

1. For the right bridges, 80 percent of the sidewalk and parapet loads are taken by the exterior beams, and 20 percent by the interior beams;
2. The asphalt wearing surface load is distributed to each beam in the ratio of its moment of inertia to the total moment of inertia of all the beams.

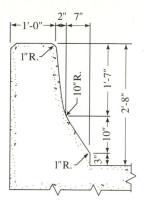

FIGURE 4.13
A typical parapet section.

The tributary area of the exterior stringers is usually smaller than that of the interior stringers. Also, as shown in Fig. 4.11, the deck slab, with edges stiffened by an integrally cast curb, parapet, or sidewalk, generally overhangs from the exterior stringers in the transverse direction. In such cases, the load on the exterior stringer can be calculated as a reaction by considering the slab (with an overhang) as simply supported on both the exterior and the first interior stringer (i.e, by the lever rule method). Figure 4.13 shows one of the commonly used concrete parapet curbs (the mounted aluminum railing not shown), weighing about 505 lb/ft. Other variations are also used.

4.7.2.2 Live-load forces

The problem of determining shears and moments in stringers due to live loads received from the slab is highly indeterminate owing to the fact that moving loads, generally speaking, can literally occupy any position on the deck; the only exception to this is the portion of the slab covered by the sidewalk, curb, and parapet. Although live loading is assumed to occupy and move in the designated lanes, such specification is hardly enforceable. This complexity and uncertainty in application of the live load on the slab has led to simplifying assumptions regarding the transverse position of the moving load on the deck. The conclusion is that the live load shared by the exterior stringer would be different from that shared by the interior stringer. This is evident because the exterior stringers support the portion of the slab covered by the sidewalk, curb, and railing, thereby precluding the possibility of the live load occupying this portion of the slab.

Owing to the presence of the slab, the loads are not applied directly to the stringers; rather, the stiffness of the slab causes lateral distribution of the moving loads to the adjacent stringers. The lateral distribution, however, is a highly indeterminate coupled phenomenon that depends on the stiffness and the type of the deck, the type and spacing of supporting stringers, and the stiffness of diaphragms. A discussion on the analysis of these beam-on-slab decks was presented in Sec. 4.5. In view of the theoretical complexity involved in load distribution to stringers, AASHTO 3.23 provides a simplified, but empirical, method to determine the lateral distribution of moving loads to both exterior and interior stringers. This method is referred to as *distribution of loads,* and, although simple, it does have some limitations (discussed in a later section). According to this method of analysis, shear and moments in stringers are obtained first as if they are directly loaded by the axle (or wheel) loads. These values are then multiplied by the appropriate *live-load distribution factors,* DF, (listed in AASHTO Table 3.23.1) and by the impact factors $(1 + I)$, to obtain design shear and moments in stringers.

In the case of lane loading, the uniform load is assumed to be distributed over a lane width of 10 ft. This stipulation also applies to the concentrated loads associated with the lane loading. For example, in the case of HS20 lane loading, the 0.64-k/ft lane load is assumed to be distributed over a width of 10 ft on a line normal to the center-line of the lane, resulting in a uniform load intensity of 0.064 k/ft^2 on the loaded lane. The concentrated loads associated with HS20 lane loading are 18 kips for moment and 26 kips for shear (AASHTO 3.7.1.3). These concentrated loads are also assumed to be distributed over a width of 10 ft, giving a line load of 1.8 k/ft for moment and 2.6 k/ft for shear (AASHTO 3.7.1.2). Note that, as far as the live-load distribution factors are concerned, no distinction is made in the AASHTO specifications between noncomposite and composite construction.

Shear and moment in a stringer due to moving loads can be easily determined from influence lines. As an example, Fig. 4.14 shows a multi-axle truck with a trailer with only six axles occupying a bridge. The maximum moment in a simple beam subjected to a series of moving concentrated loads occurs under the load closest to the resultant of the load system on the beam when the resultant and the closest load are placed equidis-tant from the centerline of the beam. Methods of drawing influence lines (*IL*) are rather simple and are discussed in the many texts on structural analysis. For design expedi-ency, values of maximum moments and shears in stringers due to H15, HS15, H20, and HS20 highway loadings, for various spans to 300 ft, are tabulated in *Appendix A* of the AASHTO specifications, with the governing live loading (truck or lane) identi-fied in parenthesis (see Appendix A, Tables A.3–A.6 of this text). Examples 4.1 and 4.2, although elementary, illustrate this methodology. For continuous beams, maximum moments, positive or negative, can be determined from influence lines, tables [AISC, 1966], or by other methods [Memari, West, and Belegundu, 1991; Zuraski, 1991].

It is incumbent on a designer to apply bridge live loads on the deck in specific manners outlined in the AASHTO specifications. The following points must be noted in this context:

1. In the case of single-span bridges, regardless of the span length of the bridge, only one H or HS truck is assumed to occupy the bridge. The distance between the two rear axles is kept as a variable between 14 and 30 ft, as shown in Fig. 4.15; this dis-tance should be chosen so as to cause maximum stresses in the supporting members.
2. In the case of lane load, the entire span is assumed to be occupied by uniform lane loading in the designated lane. The line load due to concentrated loads is to be posi-tioned, along with the uniform live load, to cause the most critical stress conditions in the member under consideration.
3. In the case of continuous spans, they should be loaded so as to cause maximum effects (stresses and deflections) in the member under consideration.

Note that shears and moments tabulated in the AASHTO specifications have been com-puted for the governing truck or the lane loading. In the case of truck loading, only one truck is assumed to be present on the span, and the tabulated values of moments and shears are computed for the corresponding axle loads (8 kips and 32 kips for H20; and

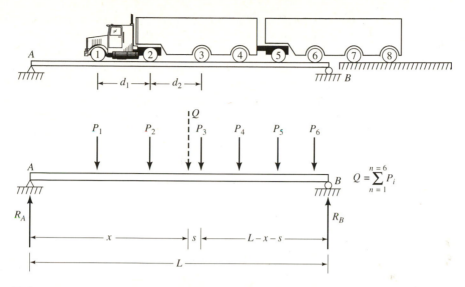

FIGURE 4.14

Maximum moment in a simple beam due to moving concentrated loads. Maximum moment occurs under load P_3, placed such that $x = (L - S)/2$. Q is the resultant of the load system on the beam.

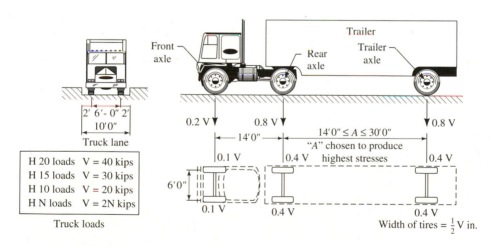

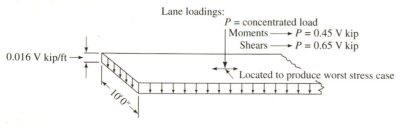

FIGURE 4.15

Positioning of truck loads for maximum effects [Lay, 1974].

8 kips, 32 kips, and 32 kips for HS20 loading; all spaced 14 ft apart). The effect of multipresence of vehicles (i.e., two or more lanes loaded simultaneously) is not included in these values. The effect of multilane loading is considered by multiplying the single-lane loading by the multipresence reduction factor, as given in AASHTO 3.12 (explained in Chapter 3). However, it is reiterated that the multipresence reduction factors are not to be used in conjunction with the distribution factors, except where the lever rule is used or where special requirements for the exterior beams in beam–slab bridges as specified in AASHTO–LRFD 4.6.2.2.2d are used [AASHTO, 1994a, Ch. 3, p. 15].

4.7.2.3 Distribution of live load in parallel stringers (parallel to traffic)

Separate distribution factors are provided in the AASHTO specifications for the interior and the exterior stringers with their longitudinal axes oriented parallel to traffic. In this context, two cases are identified:

1. For the most common types of parallel stringer systems supporting a slab, such as steel, reinforced concrete (T-beam), prestressed, or timber beams, the live-load distribution factors for the interior stringers are given in AASHTO Table 3.23.1 and are discussed under "general case" in the following paragraphs.
2. For prestressed concrete and steel box girders supporting a slab (referenced in AASHTO Table 3.23.1), referred to as the multi-beam decks, the live-load distribution factors are specified in AASHTO 3.23.4. These are discussed under "special cases" in this chapter.

Interior stringers, general case: bending moment. Distribution factors for live-load moment in the interior stringers are given in AASHTO Table 3.23.1 (see Appendix, Table A.7 of this text). This table provides distribution factors for stringers of different materials—concrete (such as T- or prestressed beams), steel, and timber (solid sawn or glued-laminated)—supporting various kinds of floorings—concrete slab, steel grid, and timber. In each case, separate distribution factors are given for the single-lane and two-lane bridges. AASHTO 3.23.2.1 specifies: "In calculating bending moments in longitudinal beams or stringers, no longitudinal distribution of wheel loads shall be assumed . . . ." This simply means that the wheel loads should be assumed as concentrated (or knife-edge) loads acting directly on stringers; the loads should not be distributed over certain lengths of the deck slab, although, in reality, the slab does act as a load-distributing medium for the stringers.

The tabulated live-load distribution factors (S over a constant) are given as fractions of average spacing, S, of stringers. Stringers are generally equally spaced; however, if for some specific reason the spacings are unequal, the *average* spacing should be used. AASHTO Table 3.23.1 is rather extensive and heavily footnoted; it is suggested that distribution factors for the given combination of flooring and stringers be carefully selected. In this context, reference is made to various kinds of deck systems shown in Fig. 4.16.

Note that the symbol S is used in many formulae in the AASHTO specifications to denote span in the same general context. In some cases, the same span *appears* to be used in the formulas, but its definitions are different. For example, in the context of distribution factors, S denotes the average spacing of stringers. However, for calculating moments in a reinforced concrete slab supported by a series of parallel stringers

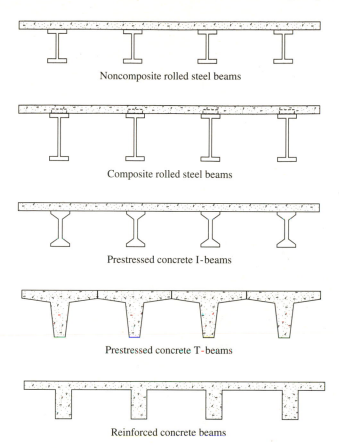

Noncomposite rolled steel beams

Composite rolled steel beams

Prestressed concrete I-beams

Prestressed concrete T-beams

Reinforced concrete beams

FIGURE 4.16
Various slab–stringer systems.

(slab reinforcement perpendicular to traffic, discussed earlier), in which case the slab is treated as a continuous element spanning several stringers, span (S) is variously defined as specified in AASHTO 2.24.1.2. In this case, it is related to, but not the same as, the average stringer spacing.

Interior stringers, general case: shear. Distribution factors for live-load shear in stringers are specified in AASHTO 3.23.1. According to this specification, different distribution factors are to be used for

- Shear due to the wheel load at the end of a stringer
- Shear due to wheels at other positions on the span

Determination of shear in a beam due to the wheel load at the end of a beam can be explained with reference to Fig. 4.17. One can intuitively see that, longitudinally, both the truck and the lane loading should be positioned on the span as shown in Fig. 4.17(*a*). The transverse position of the truck wheels on the span is shown in Figs. 4.17(*b*) and

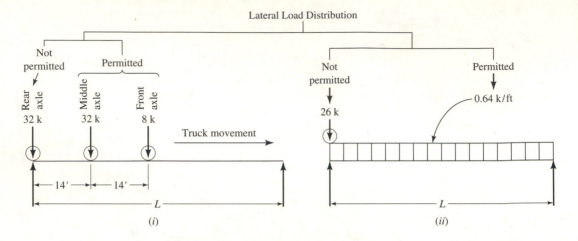

(a) Longitudinal positions of loads for maximum end shear in a beam or a stringer: (i) HS20 truck loading, (ii) HS20 lane loading.

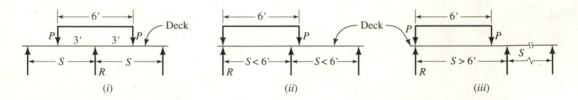

(b) Transverse axle positions of one AASHTO truck for maximum possible value of beam reaction, R: (i) axle centered over a beam, (ii) one wheel directly over a beam, S < 6 ft, (iii) same as (ii), but S > 6 ft.

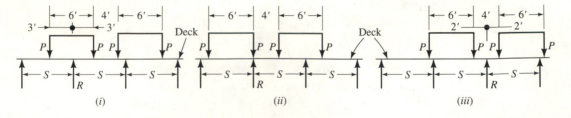

(c) Transverse axle positions of two AASHTO trucks for maximum value of beam reaction, R: (i) truck axle centered over a beam, (ii) one wheel load positioned directly over a beam, (iii) axles of two trucks positioned symmetrically about a beam, with 4-ft distance between the two axles. Note that in all three cases, 7 ft < S ≤ 8 ft for illustrative purposes only.

FIGURE 4.17
Positions of wheel loads for maximum end shear in a beam or a stringer: (a) longitudinal positions of axles; (b) transverse positions of axles for one AASHTO truck only; (c) transverse axle positions of two adjacent AASHTO trucks. $S_{max} = 14$ ft in all cases.

4.17(c). For computation of shear, a simplifying assumption is made that each portion of the slab between the two adjacent supports is considered to be simply supported so that the reaction, R, in the beam under consideration is a determinate quantity that can be easily computed by the *lever rule method*. AASHTO 3.23.1.1 specifies: "End shears and reactions in transverse floor beams and stringers shall be calculated assuming that the wheel or axle load adjacent to the end being analyzed is not distributed longitudinally." This simply means that, for the purposes of calculating maximum shear in a stringer or floor beam, the rear wheel load (which must be placed closest to the end of the beam, i.e., directly over the support, to cause maximum shear, as shown in Fig. 4.17(a)), should be treated as a concentrated (or a knife-edge) load acting directly on the member. It is not to be distributed over any length of the slab, even though the load is actually transmitted to the beam through the medium of the slab.

AASHTO 3.23.1.2 specifies methods for lateral distribution of live load for shear due to wheel loads positioned at the end of the member and to wheel loads at other positions on the span:

Wheel loads at ends of member

Figures 4.17(b) and 4.17(c) show, for one and two AASHTO trucks, respectively, the critical transverse positions of the wheel loads (i.e., the whole axle with its 16-kip loads 6 ft apart) at the ends of a stringer or a floor beam. In Fig. 4.17(b)(i), the two wheel loads are positioned symmetrically about the stringer under consideration. In Fig. 4.17(b)(ii), one of the wheels is positioned directly over the stringer, and the other is 6 ft away from it. The value of the reaction, R, caused by these wheel loads is the desired beam shear due to wheel loads positioned at the end of the beam. The value of R is computed by considering the slab as a series of simple spans between the adjacent supports (the lever rule method, AASHTO 2.23.1.2). In Fig. 4.17(b)(i), for $S \geq 6$ ft,

$$R = 2P\left(\frac{S-3}{S}\right) = 2P\left(1 - \frac{3}{S}\right) \qquad (4.4a)$$

Similarly, in Fig. 4.17(c)(iii), for $S \geq 6$ ft,

$$R = P + P\left(\frac{S-6}{S}\right)$$

$$= 2P\left(\frac{S-3}{S}\right)$$

which is the same as Eq. 4.4a. The spacing, S, between the adjacent beams or stringers is generally greater than or equal to 6 ft. In cases where S is less than or equal to 6 ft, as in Fig. 4.17(c)(ii), obviously $R = P$. Note that Eq. 4.4a can also be used to determine shear due to special permit vehicles, in which case only one vehicle may be placed on the deck.

When two AASHTO trucks are placed on the deck, the wheel loads of the adjacent truck should be placed as permitted by AASHTO. This requires maintaining a minimum distance of 4 ft between the centers of gravity of the inside wheels of the two axles. Figure 4.17(*c*) shows three intuitively selected transverse positions of two AASHTO trucks on the deck. For illustrative purposes, the beam spacing, *S*, has been chosen so that 7 ft ≤ *S* ≤ 8 ft. In each of the three cases, the wheel loads have been intuitively positioned on the deck to cause the maximum value of the beam reaction, *R*, given by Eqs. 4.4b, 4.4c, and 4.4d, as follows:

In Fig. 4.17(*c*)(*i*),

$$R = 2P\left(\frac{S-3}{S}\right) + P\left(\frac{S-7}{S}\right)$$

$$= P\left(3 - \frac{13}{S}\right) \tag{4.4b}$$

In Fig. 4.17(*c*)(*ii*),

$$R = P + P\left(\frac{S-6}{S}\right) + P\left(\frac{S-4}{S}\right)$$

$$= P\left(3 - \frac{10}{S}\right) \tag{4.4c}$$

In Fig. 4.17(*c*)(*iii*),

$$R = 2P\left(\frac{S-2}{S}\right)$$

$$= P\left(2 - \frac{4}{S}\right) \tag{4.4d}$$

A comparison of these three equations shows that Eq. 4.4c gives the largest value of *R* for the load positions considered. The parenthetical quantities in each of Eqs. 4.4b, 4.4c, and 4.4d may be thought of as the DF for the wheel load at the end of a beam. Clearly, these equations are not general, but they can be easily derived for a given beam spacing *S*. It is important to recognize that, depending on the beam spacing *S*, the number of wheel loads contributing to *R* vary. For example, in the case of Fig. 4.17(*c*)(*iii*), all four wheel loads will contribute to *R* if 8 ft < *S* ≤ 14 ft.

Wheel loads away from ends of member

For wheel loads at other positions, distribution factors given in AASHTO Table 3.23.1 (the same as for moment) should be used.

The preceding discussion should help one recognize that the procedure for determination of maximum design shear in a beam involves an important difference from that used for the live-load moment. Determination of the design live-load moment in a beam or a stringer is a one-step procedure. The maximum live-load moment due to one truck, obtained from the influence lines (or from tables), is simply multiplied by one-half, by the distribution factor (DF), and by (1 + *I*) to obtain the design live-load moment. But determination of maximum design live-load shear is a two-step procedure because the distribution factors are applied to wheel loads differently in the case of shear. For the case of live-load moment, the *same* load distribution factor is applied to all wheel loads, whereas for the case of shear, the load distribution factors for the loads at the *end* of the span are different from those for the loads that are *on* the span. For the latter, the same lateral load distribution factor is used as for the live-load moment.

Caution should be exercised in using the values of maximum moments and shears tabulated in AASHTO tables (Tables A.3–A.6 in Appendix A of this text) for design purposes. These tabulated values are simply the maximum moments and shears in simple spans for the governing type of loading (truck or lane type). These values can also be determined easily from the influence lines. These are not the design values, since the effects of load distribution and impact are not included. The following points should be remembered when using these tables:

- The tabulated values for moments are those caused by the entire truck, i.e., the axle loads. To account for the wheel load distribution, these values should be multiplied by a factor of $\frac{1}{2}$ and by the appropriate distribution factor (DF) from the AASHTO table (Table A.7, Appendix A). To obtain the design live-load moment, these values should be further multiplied by $(1+I)$ to account for impact. Thus,

$$M_{L+I} = \text{(tabulated moment value)}(\tfrac{1}{2})(DF)(1 + I)$$

- Alternatively, if the live-load moment is computed from influence lines for wheel loads (which are half of the axle loads), the design live-load moment can be obtained by multiplying it by the DF and by $(1 + I)$. Thus,

$$M_{L+I} = \text{(moment from influence lines for wheel loads)}(DF)(1 + I)$$

Application of this methodology is illustrated in Examples 4.1 and 4.2.

> **EXAMPLE 4.1.** Determine the maximum moment and shear due to HS20 loading in a T-beam of a two-lane T-beam bridge having a simple span of 100 ft. The T-beams are spaced at 7.5 ft o.c.

> *Solution*

> **Truck loading—maximum moment.** First, determine the centroid of loads on the span. By inspection, it can be seen that the centroid will lie between the two 32-kip loads, as shown in Fig. E4.1a. The sum of all loads is

> $$G = \sum P = 8 + 2 \times 32 = 72 \text{ kips}$$

> Taking moments about the central 32-kip load, we have

> $$72x = 32 \times 14 - 8 \times 14$$
> $$x = 4.667 \text{ ft}$$

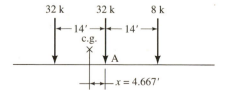

> The wheel loads are so placed that the centerline of the span bisects the centroidal distance from the nearest 32-kip load, as shown in Fig. E4.1a.

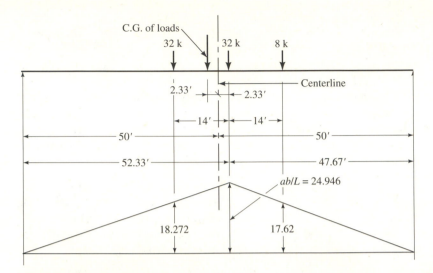

FIGURE E4.1a
Influence-line diagram for maximum moment due to truck loading.

The maximum moment occurs under the central 32-kip load, and the IL diagram for this system is simply a triangle with the ordinate equal to ab/L under the central 32-kip load closest to the centroid, located at distances a and b from the left and the right supports, respectively. Thus,

$$\frac{ab}{L} = \frac{47.67 \times 52.33}{100} = 24.946$$

The ordinates under the other two loads are calculated by proportion and shown in the IL diagram (Fig. E4.1a).

$$M_{\max} = \sum P_i(\text{IL ordinate})_i$$
$$= 8 \times 17.62 + 32 \times (24.946 + 18.272) = 1524 \text{ k-ft}$$

This value of live-load moment could also have been obtained from Table A.6 (Appendix A). However, it is important to recognize that this value of maximum moment (1524 k-ft) is due to one HS20 truck (which consists of two lines of wheels). It does *not* include the effect of lateral distribution of other wheel loads on the span or the effect of impact. Therefore, the design live-load moment is obtained as explained in the preceding paragraph.

With a T-beam spacing of 7.5 ft ($S = 7.5$ ft), the distribution factor (DF) is

$$DF = \frac{S}{6} = \frac{7.5}{6} = 1.25$$

The impact factor for $L = 100$ ft is

$$I = \frac{50}{L + 125} = \frac{50}{L + 125} = 0.222$$

Then the design live-load moment for the T-beam would be

$$M_{L+I} = \text{(live-load moment due to one truck)} \times \tfrac{1}{2} \times (DF) \times (1 + I)$$
$$= 1524 \times \tfrac{1}{2} \times 1.25 \times (1 + 0.222)$$
$$= 1164 \text{ k-ft}$$

Truck loading—maximum shear. The maximum shear in a simple beam equals the maximum support reaction for which the IL is a triangle with ordinate equal to 1.0 at the support (Fig. E4.1b). With the truck entering the span, the wheel loads are positioned so that the centroid of the rear 32-kip axle is located directly over the left support. Since 6 ft $\leq S \leq$ 8 ft, the shear due to the rear axle is computed from Eq. 4.4c. Thus,

$$R = P\left(3 - \frac{10}{S}\right)$$
$$= 16\left(3 - \frac{10}{7.5}\right)$$
$$= 26.72 \text{ kips}$$

Shear due to the middle and the front wheel loads is computed in two steps. First, these loads are multiplied by $DF = 1.25$, which was computed earlier for the live-load moment. Therefore, the modified values of the middle and the front wheel loads are

$$P_{\text{middle}} = 16 \times DF = 16 \times 1.25 = 20 \text{ kips}$$
$$P_{\text{front}} = 4 \times DF = 4 \times 1.25 = 5 \text{ kips}$$

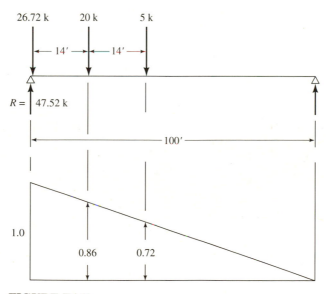

FIGURE E4.1b
Influence-line diagram for maximum shear due to truck loading.

Next, these two loads are multiplied by their respective IL ordinates to obtain the maximum shear at the support:

$$V_{support} = 20 \times 0.86 + 5 \times 0.72 = 20.8 \text{ kips}$$

Thus, the total live-load shear, without impact, is

$$V_L = 26.72 + 20.8 = 47.52 \text{ kips}$$

To obtain the design live-load shear at the support due to the HS20 truck, the above value is now multiplied by $(1 + I)$ to include the effect of impact. Thus,

$$V_{L+I} = V_L \times (1 + I) = 47.52 \times (1 + 0.222) = 58.07 \text{ kips}$$

Lane loading—maximum moment. In this case, the entire span should be loaded with uniform load equal to 0.64 kip/ft and with a concentrated load of 18 kips at the midspan (Fig. E4.1c). The IL ordinate under the load is

$$\frac{ab}{L} = \frac{50 \times 50}{100} = 25$$

$$M_{max} = P \times \text{(IL ordinate)} + \text{unit load} \times \text{area under the IL diagram}$$
$$= 18 \times 25 + 0.64\left(\tfrac{1}{2} \times 100 \times 25\right)$$
$$= 1250 \text{ k-ft} < M_{max,truck}(= 1524 \text{ k-ft})$$

To this value, we apply the DF and the impact factor. Thus, due to the lane load, the design moment is

$$M_{L+I} = 1250 \times \tfrac{1}{2} \times 1.25 \times 1.222$$
$$= 954.7 \text{ k-ft} < 1164 \text{ k-ft (truck loading)}$$

Hence, the truck loading governs, and $M_{L+I} = 1164$ k-ft.

Lane loading—maximum shear. The IL diagram for this case is the same as that for the truck loading. The 26-kip load is placed at the left support, and the entire span is covered

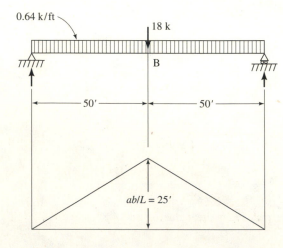

FIGURE E4.1c
Influence-line diagram for maximum moment due to lane loading.

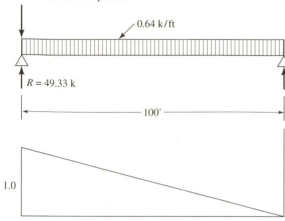

17.33 k due to 26-kip concentrated load

0.64 k/ft

$R = 49.33$ k

100'

1.0

FIGURE E4.1d
Influence-line diagram for maximum shear due to lane loading.

with the uniform load (Fig. E4.1d). It should be intuitively obvious that maximum shear will occur when the lane loading is positioned symmetrically about one of the stringers. This gives a line load of 2.6 k/ft, spread over a length of 5 ft on each side (total 10 ft) of the stringer under consideration. Assuming both sides of the slab are simply supported, the corresponding reaction is

$$R = 2wa\left(1 - \frac{a}{2S}\right) \qquad (4.5)$$

where w = uniform line load = 2.6 k/ft
   a = loaded length of the slab = 5 ft
   S = stringer spacing = 7.5 ft

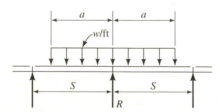

Substitution of these values into the preceding expression yields

$$R = 2 \times 2.6 \times 5.0\left(1 - \frac{5.0}{2 \times 7.5}\right) = 17.33 \text{ kips}$$

Due to the uniform lane load of 0.64 k/ft², the shear at the end is

$$V = \text{unit load} \times (\text{area under IL diagram})$$
$$= 0.64 \times (\tfrac{1}{2} \times 100 \times 1.0)$$
$$= 32 \text{ kips}$$

Therefore, the total shear is

$$V = 17.33 + 32 \text{ kips}$$
$$= 49.33 \text{ kips}$$

To this value, we apply the DF and the impact factor $(1 + I)$ to obtain the design shear due to the lane loading. Thus,

$$V_{L+I} = 49.33 \times \tfrac{1}{2} \times 1.25 \times 1.222$$
$$= 37.68 \text{ kips} < 58.07 \text{ kips due to truck loading}$$

Again, the truck loading governs, and $V_{L+I} = 58.07$ kips.

EXAMPLE 4.2. Determine the maximum live-load moment and shear in a typical interior steel stringer due to the truck loading shown in Fig. E4.2a. The steel beams are placed at 8.25 ft at centers. The transverse configuration of the vehicle is the same as that for the AASHTO vehicle. The bridge superstructure is a slab–steel stringer type with a simple span of 80 ft. Assume only one vehicle is on the bridge.

Solution

Maximum moment. Find the centroid of all loads on the span. By inspection, it is obvious that it lies in the 14-ft segment between the two 37-kip loads. Take moments about O (Fig. E4.2b, part (a)):

The sum of all loads is

$$\sum P = 160 \text{ kips}$$
$$160x = 37(14 + 18.5) - 37 \times 4.5 - 12 \times 18.5$$
$$x = 5.088 \text{ ft}$$

The loads are placed on the beam so that the centerline of the beam bisects the centroidal distance from the nearest 37-kip load and the centroid of the load group. Thus, maximum moment occurs under the 37-kip load closest to the centroid, located at distances a and b from the left and right supports, respectively. The IL ordinate under this load, ab/L (Fig. E4.2b, part (b)), is given by

$$\frac{ab}{L} = \frac{37,456 \times 42.545}{80} = 19.92$$

$$M_{\max} = \sum P_i(\text{IL ordinate})_i$$
$$= 37(19.92 + 17.526 + 13.356 + 11.258) + 12 \times 10.08$$
$$= 2417.5 \text{ kip-ft}$$

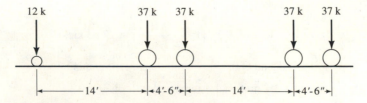

FIGURE E4.2a
Truck loading for Example 4.2.

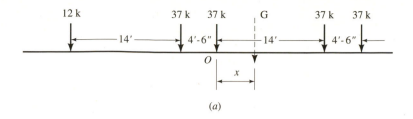

(a)

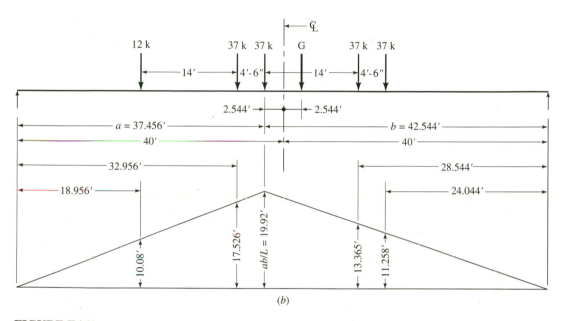

(b)

FIGURE E4.2b

Parts *(a)* and *(b)*: Influence-line diagram for maximum moment.

Note that the transverse configuration of the given vehicle is the same as that of the AASHTO vehicle (i.e., the distance between the centroids of the wheels of an axle is 6.0 ft). This is noteworthy because only under this condition can the AASHTO load distribution factors be applied.

For a slab–steel stringer superstructure and a beam spacing of $S = 8.25$ ft,

$$DF = \frac{S}{5.5} = \frac{8.25}{5.5} = 1.5$$

The impact factor is

$$I = \frac{50}{L + 125} = \frac{50}{80 + 125} = 0.244 < 0.3$$

Therefore, the maximum moment in the beam due to live load plus impact is

$$M_{L+I} = M_L \times \tfrac{1}{2} \times DF \times (1 + I)$$
$$= 2417.5 \times \tfrac{1}{2} \times 1.5 \times 1.244$$
$$= 2255.5 \text{ kip-ft}$$

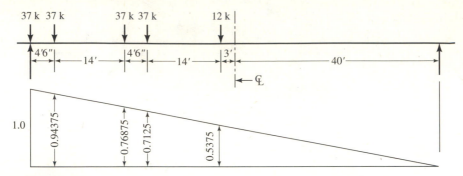

FIGURE E4.2c
Influence-line diagram for maximum shear.

Note that a factor of $\frac{1}{2}$ has been applied in the above calculation in conjunction with the DF because $M = 2417.5$ k-ft used in the calculation is due to the axle loads, not the wheel loads.

Maximum shear. As explained in the previous example, the maximum beam shear in a simple beam equals the maximum support reaction for which the IL diagram is a triangle with the ordinate equal to unity at the support (Fig. E4.2c). With the entire truck on the span, the wheel loads are so positioned that the rear 37-kip load is located directly over the left support. The maximum shear due to this axle load is computed from Eq. 4.4a:

$$V_{\text{Rear}} = 2P\left(1 - \frac{3}{S}\right) = 37 \times \left(1 - \frac{3}{8.25}\right) = 23.55 \text{ kips}$$

For all loads *on the span, DF* $= 1.5$ (the same value as for the moment). Therefore, maximum shear due to these loads is

$$
\begin{aligned}
V_{\text{max}} &= \left[\sum P_i \times (\text{IL ordinate})_i\right] \times \tfrac{1}{2} \times DF \\
&= [37(0.94375 + 0.76875 + 0.7125) + 12 \times 0.5375] \times \tfrac{1}{2} \times 1.5 \\
&= 72.13 \text{ kips}
\end{aligned}
$$

Thus, total live-load shear is

$$V_L = 23.55 + 72.13 = 95.68 \text{ kips}$$

Special cases: box girder bridges: prestressed concrete spread box girders. The live-load distribution factor (*DF*) for prestressed concrete spread box beams (Fig. 4.18(*a*)) referred to in AASHTO Table 3.23.1 is given by AASHTO 3.28.1 (AASHTO Eq. 3.33):

$$DF = \frac{2N_L}{N_B} + \frac{kS}{L} \tag{4.6}$$

where N_L = number of design traffic lanes
N_B = number of beams ($4 \leq N_B \leq 10$)
S = beam spacing ($6.57 \leq S \leq 11.0$ ft)

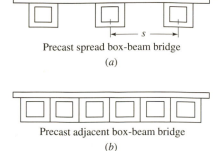

Precast spread box-beam bridge

(a)

Precast adjacent box-beam bridge

(b)

FIGURE 4.18

Prestressed concrete box beams.

L = span in feet

$k = 0.07W - N_L(0.10L - 0.26) - 0.20N_B - 0.12$ (AASHTO Eq. 3.34)

W = numerical value of roadway width between curbs expressed in feet ($32 \le W \le 66$)

Special cases: box girder bridges: prestressed concrete adjacent box beams. AASHTO 3.23.4 refers to this type of construction as a multibeam deck, a deck formed by placing several box beams contiguously (see Fig. 4.18(*b*)). The interaction between the beams is developed by continuous longitudinal shear keys and lateral bolts that may or may not be prestressed (discussed in Chapter 7). In this type of construction, no longitudinal distribution of wheel load is permitted. The live-load bending moment is determined by applying to the beam the fraction of a wheel load (both front and rear) determined from the following expression (AASHTO Eq. 3.11):

$$\text{Load distribution factor} = \frac{S}{D} \qquad (4.7)$$

where S = width of the precast member

$D = (5.75 - 0.5N_L) + 0.7N_L(1 - 0.2C)^2$,

   when $C \le 5$ (AASHTO Eq. 3.12)

$D = (5.75 - 0.5N_L)$,   when $C > 5$ (AASHTO Eq. 3.13)

N_L = number of traffic lanes

$C = K(W/L)$ (AASHTO Eq. 3.14)

W = overall width of bridge measured perpendicular to the longitudinal girders, in feet

L = span length measured parallel to the longitudinal girders, in feet; for girders with cast-in-place diaphragms, use the length between diaphragms.

$K = \sqrt{[(1 + \mu)I]/J}$, where

I = moment of inertia

J = Saint-Venant torsion constant

μ = Poisson's ratio for girders

Note that a special investigation may be necessary for precast members having widths S of less than 4 ft or greater than 10 ft. The constant, K, as defined above, may be considered a stiffness parameter. The value of St. Venant's torsional constant, J, for various cross sections may be computed from the following expressions [AASHTO 1994a, p. 4-23]:

1. For thin-walled open beams,

$$J = \frac{1}{3}\sum bt^3 \left[1 - 0.63\left(\frac{t}{b}\right) - 0.052\left(\frac{t}{b}\right)^2\right] \qquad (4.8)$$

For small values of t/b, Eq. 4.8 is reduced to

$$J \approx \frac{1}{3}\sum bt^3 \qquad (4.9)$$

2. For stocky open sections, e.g., prestressed I-beams, T-beams, etc., and for solid sections,

$$J \approx \frac{A^4}{40.0I_p} \qquad (4.10)$$

3. For closed thin-walled shapes, such as box beams and voided slabs,

$$J \approx \frac{2A_o^2}{\sum s/t} \qquad (4.11)$$

where b = width of the plate element
$\quad\quad t$ = thickness of the plate-like element
$\quad\quad A$ = area of cross section
$\quad\quad I_p$ = polar moment of inertia
$\quad\quad A_o$ = area enclosed by centerlines of elements
$\quad\quad s$ = length of a side element

For a box beam, the value of J may be computed with reference to the following figure:

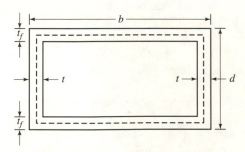

$$A_o = \text{(Average width)(Average depth)}$$
$$= (b - t)(d - t_f) \qquad (4.12)$$

$$\sum_t^s = 2\left[\left(\frac{b-t}{t_f}\right) + \left(\frac{d-t_f}{t}\right)\right]$$

$$= 2\left[\frac{bt + dt_f - t^2 - t_f^2}{tt_f}\right] \qquad (4.13)$$

TABLE 4.1
Values of K for multibeam decks [AASHTO, 1992]

Beam type	K
Nonvoided rectangular beams	0.7
Rectangular beams with circular voids	0.8
Box section beams	1.0
Channel beams	2.2

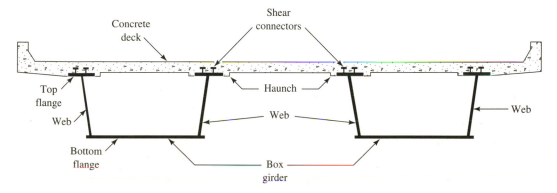

FIGURE 4.19
A steel box girder bridge [AMS, 1986].

Substitution of Eqs. 4.12 and 4.13 into Eq. 4.11 yields

$$J \approx \frac{2tt_f(b-t)^2(d-t_f)^2}{bt + dt_f - t^2 - t_f^2}$$

(4.14)

AASHTO 3.23.4.3 suggests the K values as shown in Table 4.1 for the preliminary design of various kinds of multibeam decks.

Steel box girders

For steel box girders built compositely with reinforced concrete slab (Fig. 4.19), DF is given by the following expression (AASHTO 10.39.2.1, Eq. 10.96, referred to as W_L)

$$DF \text{ (or } W_L) = 0.1 + 1.7R + \frac{0.85}{N_W}$$

(4.15)

where $R = N_W$/number of box girders, $0.5 \le R \le 1.5$
$N_W = W_c/12$ reduced to the nearest whole number
$W_c =$ roadway width between curbs (or barriers, if curbs are not provided) in feet.

Exterior stringers: steel, concrete, timber beams and T-beams. Generally speaking, the live-load bending moment in the outside (or the exterior) roadway stringers is determined by applying to them the reactions of the wheel loads obtained by assuming the deck is a simple span between the exterior and the adjacent interior stringers. This method is referred to as the *lever rule*. It involves summing moments about one support to find the reaction at another by assuming that the supported component is hinged at the interior supports [AASHTO, 1994a]. For the case of a concrete deck supported by four or more steel stringers, AASHTO 3.23.2.3.1.5 makes three separate provisions for the distribution of live loads in exterior stringers.

For $S \leq 6$ ft, $DF = S/5.5$

For $6 < S < 14$ ft, $DF = S/(4 + 0.25S)$

For $S \geq 14$ ft, the load on each stringer should be calculated as the reaction of the wheel loads, assuming the flooring between the stringers to act as a simple beam; i.e., the lever rule should be used (see footnote f to AASHTO Table 3.23.1; see Appendix A, Table A.7 in this text).

Three separate requirements are stipulated for determining the size of the exterior stringer; the largest size determined is the final choice:

1. If the exterior stringer has to carry both sidewalk and traffic live load (and all dead loads), its size can be determined by allowing 25 percent overstress based on service load (or allowable stress) design
2. The size can be determined ignoring the sidewalk (and hence no sidewalk dead and live loads)
3. The size of the exterior stringer must be at least as large as the interior stringer (AASHTO 3.23.2.3.1.4).

Exterior stringers: concrete box girders. The DF is assumed as $W_e/7$, where W_e is the width of exterior girder, taken as the top slab width, measured from the midpoint between the girders to the outside edge of the slab. The cantilever dimension of any slab extending beyond the outside face of the exterior girder should, preferably, not exceed half the girder spacing.

4.7.3 Limitations on the Applicability of AASHTO Load Distributions Factors

The empirical load distribution method for forces in stringers and longitudinal beams has appeared in the AASHTO specifications since 1931 with only minor changes [NCHRP, 1992]. Although fraught with many simplistic assumptions, the method, with some exceptions, continues to be in widespread use in view of the proven safety record of bridges that have stood the test of time. Initially, this method was developed for bridges with simple geometry: straight, simply supported, nonskewed bridges, and for a specific loading type (the AASHTO H and HS family of trucks). The method does not consider several parameters such as bridge skew angle, span length, bridge total width, number of loaded traffic lanes, spacing and stiffness of intermediate diaphragms or cross frames, or influence of noncomposite or composite construction. Furthermore, each girder, acting compositely or noncompositely, with an effective width of the concrete deck and carrying a fraction of the wheel load laterally distributed to the girder, is designed as a two-dimensional element, although, in reality, the superstructure resists loads as a complex three-dimensional structure [Tiedman, Albretch, and Cayes, 1993].

The method of distribution factors is not applicable to bridges that [Bakht and Jaeger, 1985; Hambly, 1991]

- have deck slabs of nonuniform width
- have slabs with a few isolated supports
- have slabs with a skew angle exceeding 20°
- have curved decks
- have nonuniform cross sections or nonuniform sections in the middle half of the span
- are slab-on-beam bridges with three or fewer beams
- have cellular girders with fewer than three cells

In the absence of other procedures, the same basic method, with only minor modifications, is applied to bridges continuous over interior supports, bridges with skewed supports, and those on curved alignments. The subject of load distribution factors continues to be one of active ongoing research [Zellin, et al. 1975a,b; Imbsen and Nutt, 1978; Hays, Sessions, and Berry, 1986; Kuzmanovic and Sanchez, 1986; Bakht and Moses, 1988; Hays, 1990; Kukreti and Rajpaksa, 1990; Fang, et al., 1990; Jackson, 1992; Tarhini and Fredrick, 1992]. Recent investigations [Nutt, Schamber, and Zokai, 1988] suggest that the current AASHTO procedures, although simpler, do not give the degree of accuracy expected in view of the sophistry of today's available methods. It is reported that in some cases, the AASHTO formulae can result in highly unconservative results (more than 40 percent), while in other cases they may be highly conservative (more than 50 percent) [NCHRP 1992a]. Accordingly, a new set of distribution factors (Table A.8, Appendix A) have been specified in the *AASHTO Guide Specifications* [AASHTO, 1994b], which are permitted to be used in conjunction with the AASHTO 1992 specifications. However, even these new distribution factors have limited applicability, which designers should clearly understand. These new distributions factors are applicable for

1. Specific truck types—the AASHTO H and HS trucks
2. Single and multilane loading
3. The same type of AASHTO trucks in all lanes; not applicable if one permit truck in one traffic lane is combined with an AASHTO truck in another lane
4. Bridges of common types and dimensions—where the width of the deck and the superstructure cross section are constant, and where beams are parallel and have approximately the same stiffness
5. Unless otherwise specified, bridges where the number of beams is not less than four
6. Unless otherwise specified, cases where the roadway part of the overhang does not exceed 3.0 ft
7. Bridges where the curvature in the plan is less than the specified limits:
   a. Segments of horizontally curved superstructure with torsionally stiff closed sections whose central angle subtended by a curved span is less than 12°
   b. For open sections, the radius is such that the central angle subtended by each span is less than the value given in Table 4.2

If the bridge parameters fall outside the ranges considered, the accuracy is reduced and the application of these load distribution factors becomes questionable. Recommenda-

TABLE 4.2
Limiting central angles for neglecting the influence of curvature for determining primary bending moments in beams [AASHTO, 1994a]

Number of beams	Angle for one span	Angle for two or more spans
2	2°	3°
3 or 4	3°	4°
5 or more	4°	5°

tions for more accurate analysis can be found in Appendix A.2, "Partial Commentary" [AASHTO, 1994b].

Note that, while the load path for bridge superstructures (Fig. 4.4) appears to be simple enough, the analysis is not. The complexities of load distribution in bridge superstructures has long been recognized. The AASHTO method, in reality, is not a tool for an exact analysis of forces in various superstructure components. Rather, it is a uniform method of analysis that, based on many years of experience, has been found to be quite satisfactory.

4.8
DISTRIBUTION OF LIVE LOAD IN FLOOR BEAMS

Unless specified otherwise, the floor beams considered here are those bending members that are positioned perpendicular to the direction of traffic. This is unlike stringers and girders, discussed in the preceding paragraphs, which are oriented parallel to the direction of traffic.

The load path shown in Fig. 4.4 demonstrates that live load can be transmitted to floor beams in one of the two ways, depending on the support conditions of the deck slab:

1. It can be supported over stringers which may, in turn, be supported by the floor beams
2. It may be supported directly by the floor beams

Loads on the floor beams in the two cases are calculated by different methods. Generally speaking, two schemes are used for supporting stringers:

1. Supported directly on abutment and/or piers
2. Supported on transversely positioned floor beams

The latter practice is used for steel stringers (usually W shapes) used for truss bridges, girder bridges, and other types of medium-span bridges. When floor beams (W shapes or plate girders) are used to support stringers (usually W shapes), the latter are either supported on the top flanges of floor beams or are framed into their webs, similar to a building floor system. In the first case, the stringers can be simply supported or continuous over the floor beams. In the latter case, the stringers are assumed to be simply supported (with shear connections) on floor beams. Both schemes are shown in Fig. 4.20.

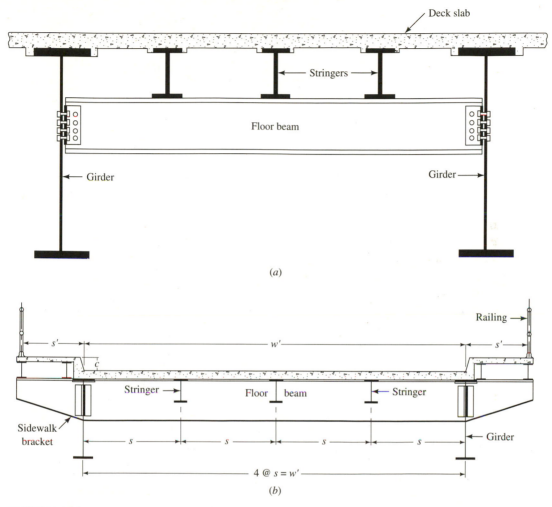

FIGURE 4.20
A floor beam supporting stringers and deck: (*a*) stringers supported on top flange of floor beams; (*b*) stringers framed into the floor beams [AMS, 1986].

4.8.1 Load on Floor Beams Transmitted by Stringers

4.8.1.1 Dead load

Dead load is transmitted to floor beams in the form of concentrated loads (reactions from stringers). In the case of equally spaced stringers (which is usually the case), the dead-load reactions from all interior stringers are equal; their determination was explained earlier for stringer design. Alternatively, the dead-load moment can be determined by treating the dead load due to the slab, stringer, and floor beam as uniformly distributed load over the floor beam. Certainly, the moments obtained by the two methods will be different, but will not have significant influence on the design of the floor beams.

4.8.1.2 Live load

The load transmitted to the floor beams by stringers is determined by a two-step method. First, maximum stringer reactions are calculated by the appropriate positioning of the moving load in the longitudinal direction (the direction of traffic or along the longitudinal axis of the stringers). This position should be consistent with the load position for maximum shear in the stringer (or maximum stringer reaction). Regardless of the number of floor beams in a bridge and bridge span, the maximum stringer reaction is determined by assuming that either (1) only one truck is placed on the whole bridge, or (2) the whole bridge is loaded by the uniform live load, including the concentrated load (i.e., the lane loading). As explained earlier, the maximum stringer reaction can be determined from influence lines or from Tables A.3 through A.6 (Appendix A).

Second, to obtain the maximum moment in the floor beam, careful consideration should be given to the longitudinal position of the wheel loads of the truck, as well as to the lateral positions of the axles of different trucks. The truck wheel loads should be placed laterally and longitudinally so as to cause the maximum effect. The positions of wheel and axle loads for critical loading conditions are spelled out in AASHTO specifications. In this regard, it is pointed out that

1. The centers of gravity of wheel loads of an axle can only be 6 ft apart.
2. The truck or lane loadings must be in their individual traffic lanes so as to produce the maximum stress in the member under consideration (AASHTO 3.6.4).
3. Within the designated traffic lanes (each being 10 ft wide according to AASHTO 3.6.1), the H or HS truck (axle) is placed symmetrically about the centerline of the traffic lane. This position gives a clearance of 2 ft between the boundary lines of traffic lanes and the centers of gravity of the wheel loads. In a multilane bridge, the minimum distance between the centers of gravity of the adjacent wheel loads of two different trucks will be 4 ft. This positioning of wheel loads is consistent with AASHTO 3.7.5 and 3.7.6.

Figure 4.21 shows the load positions consistent with the above requirements, for the maximum moment in the floor beam (span = 32 ft) supporting several parallel stringers (span = 25 ft) for a two-lane bridge. Figure 4.22 shows in plan view the positioning of these loads. Based on the longitudinal positions of the wheel loads of the truck, the concentrated loads (stringer reactions) applied to the floor beams are

$$P = 16 + \left(\frac{11}{25}\right)(16) + \left(\frac{11}{25}\right)(4)$$

$$= 24.8 \text{ kips}$$

To obtain the maximum moment in the floor beam, the truck loads are now placed transversely on the floor beam in the design traffic lanes, symmetrically about the centerline of the bridge, and separated by 4 ft, as shown in Fig. 4.21(b). At each stringer–floor beam junction, two stringer reactions (from the stringers on either side of the floor beam) are transferred to the floor beam. Thus, the reaction, R, developed on the floor beam is

$$R = 2 \times 24.8 = 49.6 \text{ k}$$
$$M_{max} = 49.6 \times 16 - 24.8(2 + 8) = 545.6 \text{ k-ft}$$

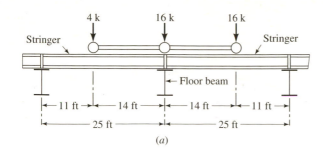

(a)

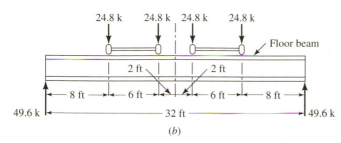

(b)

FIGURE 4.21
Positions of truck loads in a two-lane bridge for the maximum live-load moment: (a) position of HS20 truck for maximum stringer reactions on the floor beam; (b) position of loads for maximum live-load moment in the floor beam.

In computing the effect of wheel loads in the floor beams, AASHTO 3.23.3.1 does not permit a transverse distribution of wheel loads; i.e., the stiffness of the slab is ignored. The slab is considered to be a continuous beam supporting wheel loads aligned along the longitudinal axis of the floor beam. The loads are assumed to act as concentrated loads in the plane of the web of the floor beam.

A different position of wheel loads should be assumed for determining the maximum shear in the floor beams. For this purpose, the wheel loads should be placed as close to the ends as possible, consistent with AASHTO 3.6.4. Accordingly, the outside wheels of the truck should be placed 2 ft from the curb. In the case of multilane bridges, the trucks (or the lane loads, whichever governs) should be placed in their 10-ft wide design lanes, but as close as possible to the floor beam support under consideration.

4.8.2 Load on Floor Beams Transmitted Directly by Slab

In some designs (Fig. 4.23), the slab is supported directly over the floor beams; the stringers are not provided. A typical example of this type of construction entails a series of parallel longitudinal girders supported over abutments or piers and connected by transverse floor beams, which, in turn, support the slab. Another example of a similar scheme is a steel rigid frame bridge with slant legs, connected transversely by floor beams. In such cases, shear and moments in the floor beam are obtained by multiplying the simple-span moments by the distribution factors listed in AASHTO Table 3.23.3.1 (Table A.9, Appendix A, this text), as specified by AASHTO 3.23.3.2.

Usually, the floor beams are steel W shapes or plate girders; however, exceptions can always be found in practice. Figure 4.24 shows the plan and cross section of the Fechingertal Bridge, near Saarbrucken, Germany, in which the floor beams are open

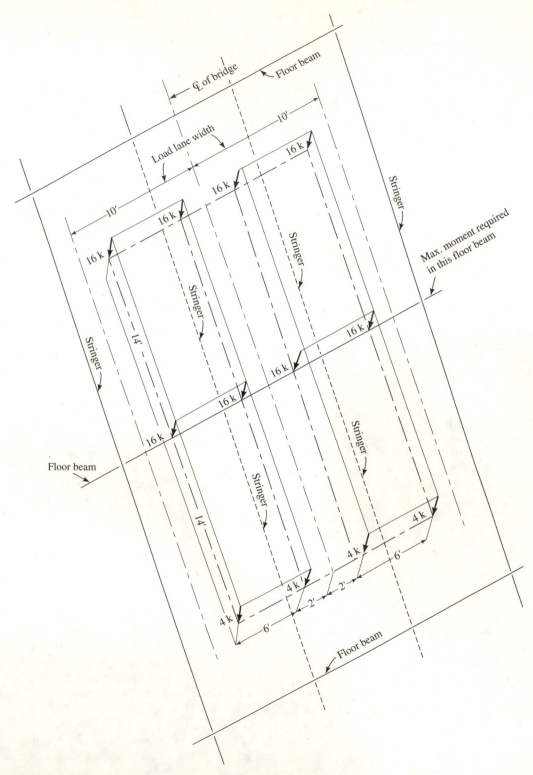

FIGURE 4.22
Positions of truck loads on a two-lane highway for maximum floor beam moments.

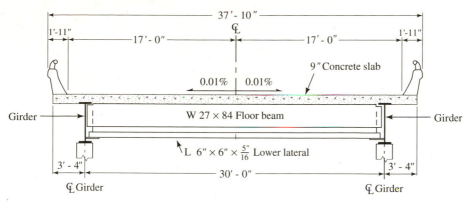

FIGURE 4.23
Deck supported directly on floor beams for the Hatfield Bridge, Jackson County, Wisconsin [USS, 1974].

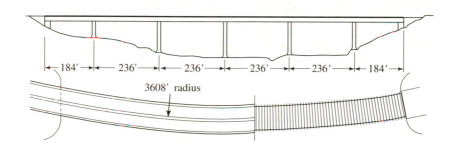

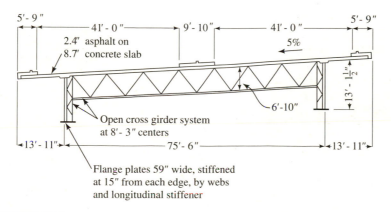

FIGURE 4.24
Fechingertal Bridge, near Saarbrucken, Germany [O'Connor, 1971].

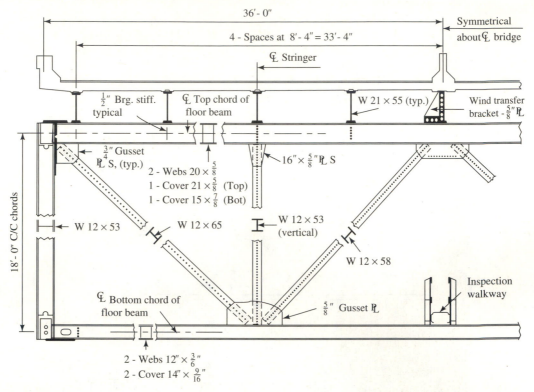

FIGURE 4.25
Floor beam for the New River Gorge arch bridge [USS, 1978].

steel web girders [O'Connor, 1971]. An unusual floor beam design (Fig. 4.25) was adopted in the construction of the New River Gorge Bridge, West Virginia, the world's longest (1700 ft) steel arch bridge. The floor beam consists of a truss, the top chord of which supports longitudinal stringers, which, in turn, supports the deck slab. An unusual construction feature is that, contrary to common practice, not all stringers are supported at the truss panel points; i.e., some are supported on the chord directly in between the top panel points. Because of this unusual arrangement, the top chord had to be designed as a beam column, rather than as an axially loaded member [USS, 1978]. In both the preceding cases, truss-type floor beams rather than W shapes are provided to stiffen the deck system, but at the same time to expose the smallest possible area to the wind so as to minimize lateral forces.

4.9
OPEN AND FILLED STEEL GRID DECKS

Open and filled steel grid decks are often used for medium- and long-span bridges. (See Figs. 4.26 and 4.27). They offer two main advantages: (1) They are lighter than the conventional reinforced concrete decks, and (2) the open steel grid minimizes wind loads on the deck. Consequently, they are often used in bridge rehabilitation projects

FIGURE 4.26
Open steel grid deck being installed on a suspension bridge [Reliance Steel].

that warrant replacement of old and deteriorated reinforced concrete decks. Being much lighter than the solid reinforced concrete deck they replace, steel grid decks reduce the dead load on the bridge, resulting in the increased live-load capacity of the superstructure. They are also used for decks of long-span bridges to reduce the effects of wind loads, as in the George Washington, Walt Whitman, and Mackinac Straits suspension bridges, for example. The open steel grid decks consist of perpendicularly placed and interlocking steel ribs and are available in the form of panels of standard sizes which can be bolted or welded to stringers. If necessary, these grids (available in pan type) can be filled with concrete (normal weight or lightweight, as necessary) and screeded

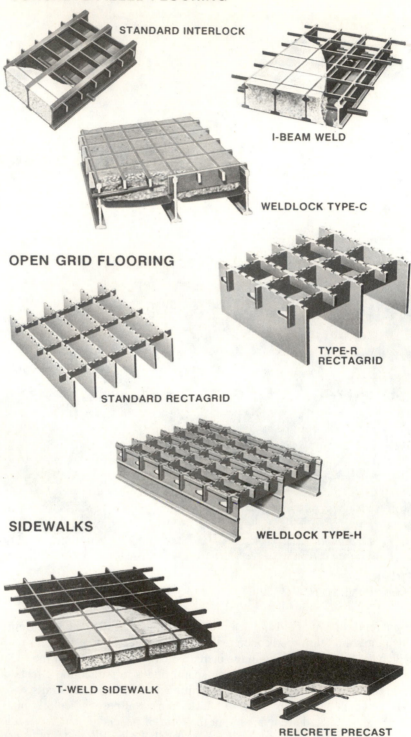

FIGURE 4.27
Open and filled grid deck systems [Reliance Steel].

flush to the top of the steel grid (Fig. 4.26). Live-load distribution factors for stringers and floor beams with steel grid decks are given in Tables A.7–A.9 (Appendix A).

4.10
MISCELLANEOUS TOPICS

4.10.1 Deck Slab Overhangs

It is common for the single-cell or multicell box girder bridges and spine-beam bridges (steel or concrete) to have cantilevered decks, with their longitudinal free edges usually stiffened with monolithically cast curbs or parapets. Their design has been the subject of study by many researchers [Sawko and Mills, 1971; Bakht and Holland, 1976; Bakht, 1981; Cheung, 1986; Li, Cheung, and Tham, 1986]. For simplicity, the cantilever decks are usually designed by treating them as simple cantilever slabs, without considering the response of the complete box itself, such as local distortion or transverse membrane forces. Discussions on this topic have been presented by Bakht and Jaeger [1985] and by Hambly [1991]. Chang and Gang [1990] have compared the test results of a plexiglass model that has a span length of 1200 mm ($\approx$ 4 ft) and a cantilever deck of 92 mm ($\approx$ 3⅝ in.) to the theoretical values obtained from the spline finite strip method.

4.10.2 The Load Path and Design Procedures

It is instructive to compare the load path and the load distribution in a bridge structure with that in a building and to note some important differences. In a typical building, the gravity loads are applied to the floor and, in turn, are transmitted to the supporting beams. The same load is then transmitted to either the supporting walls or to the floor beams. The floor beams, in turn, transfer their loads to the supporting columns or to the walls. Finally, both the walls and the columns transfer their loads to the foundation and to the earth below. All structural elements of the building are therefore designed for the *same* loading criteria. Thus, from their origin to their final destination (the foundation), loads follow a continuous path, and a continuity in the design procedure is maintained. In a bridge structure, a continuous load path is also maintained. However, the loading criteria for which various structural components are designed are different, causing a discontinuity in the design procedures. For example, the deck slab is designed for one loading criterion and the stringers (or girders) for another. The live-load reactions from these loads are then discarded, and new design criteria are used to design the substructure. Different load combinations may govern design at different locations. As loads are transmitted to the substructure, they are further distributed, and the effect of impact dissipates as the loads move down through the substructure. Also, the intensity of the live load is reduced to take into account the improbability of several heavy vehicles crossing a bridge simultaneously. As a result, the total load considered for designing a foundation may be less than that applied to the superstructure. In the case of bridges designed for three or more lanes, the total load to be considered for the foundation design is always less than that applied to the superstructure [CALTRANS, 1992].

Applications of the principles of distribution of dead and live loads in designing bridge superstructures are presented through several examples in Chapters 6 through 9.

4.10.3 Vehicles with Other Geometrical and Wheel Load Configurations

The preceding discussion has focused on the AASHTO method of load distribution and its limitations. Here, we consider the extent of error involved if this method were also used to determine forces in the superstructure components when non-AASHTO vehicles (i.e., vehicles with other geometrical and wheel load configurations) are allowed to use a bridge. The reader is again referred to AASHTO Appendix A.2, "Partial Commentary" [1994b], which states,

> The formulas [of the AASHTO method] are developed for a specific truck, namely AASHTO HS family of trucks, and the effects of other truck configurations should be kept in mind. Limited investigation on this matter has revealed that if the gauge width is the same and the longitudinal axis positions do not change, the distribution factors are not affected greatly. However, if two different truck types are considered simultaneously, e.g., one permit truck along with an HS 20 truck, the formulas are not applicable.

REFERENCES

AASHTO. (1980). *Guide Specifications for Horizontally Curved Bridges,* AASHTO, Washington, DC.

———. (1992). *Standard Specifications for Highway Bridges,* 15th ed., AASHTO, Washington, DC.

———. (1994a). *AASHTO–LRFD Bridge Design Specifications, Customary U.S. Units,* 1st ed., AASHTO, Washington, DC.

———. (1994b). *Guide Specifications for Distribution of Loads for Highway Bridges,* AASHTO, Washington, DC.

ACI. (1969). *Concrete Bridge Design,* ACI Pub. SP-23, ACI, Chicago.

———. (1977). "Analysis and Design of Reinforced Concrete Bridge Structures," *ACI Committee Report,* ACI, Detroit.

AISC. (1963). *Design Manual for Orthotropic Steel Plate Deck Bridges,* AISC, Chicago.

———. (1966). *Moments, Shears, and Reactions for Continuous Highway Bridges,* AISC, Chicago.

AMS. (1986). *Highway Structures Design Handbook,* Vols. I and II, American Marketing Services, Inc., Pittsburgh.

Bakht, B. (1980). "Discussion on Rigidities of Concrete Waffel-Type Slab Bridges," *Canadian J. Civil Eng.,* 7(1), January, pp. 198–200.

———. (1981). "Simplified Analysis of Edge-Stiffened Cantilever Slabs," *ASCE J. Str. Div.,* 107(3), March, pp. 535–550.

Bakht, B., Cheung, M. S., and Aziz, T. S. (1979). "The Application of a Simplified Method of Calculating Longitudinal Moments to the Proposed Ontario Highway Bridge Design Code," *Canadian J. Civil Eng.,* 6(1), January, pp. 36–50.

Bakht, B., and Holland, D. A. (1976). "A Manual Method for the Elastic Analysis of Wide Cantilever Slabs of Linearly Varying Thickness," *Canadian J. Civil Eng.,* 3(4), April, pp. 523–530.

Bakht, B., and Jaeger, L. G. (1985). *Bridge Analysis Simplified,* McGraw-Hill Book Companies, Inc., New York.

———. (1992). "Discussion of 'Live-Load Moments for Continuous Skew Bridges,' by M. A. Khaleel and R. A. Itani," *ASCE J. Str. Eng.,* 118(3), March, pp. 870–871.

Bakht, B., and Moses, F. (1988). "Lateral Distribution Factors for Highway Bridges," *ASCE J. Str. Eng.,* 114(8), August, pp. 1785–1803.

Balas, J., and Hanuska, A. (1964). *Influence Surfaces for Skew Plates,* Vydaratelstvo Slovenskej Akademic Vied, Bratislava.

Bares, R., and Massonet, C. (1968). *Analysis of Beam Grids and Orthotropic Plates by the Guyon-Massonet-Bares Method,* Frederick Unger Publishing Co., New York.

Bishara, A. G. (1986). "Analysis for Design of Bearings at Skew Bridge Supports," final report, Federal Highway Administration, Washington, DC.

Bishara, A. G., Maria, C. L., and Eli-Ali, N. D. (1993). "Wheel Load Distribution on Simply Supported Skew I-Beam Composite Bridges," *ASCE J. Str. Eng.,* 119(2), February, pp. 399–419.

Bishara, A. G., and Soegiarso, R. (1993). "Load Distribution in Multibeam Precast Pretopped Prestressed Bridges," *ASCE J. Str. Eng.,* 119(3), March, pp. 920–937.

CALTRANS. (1992). *Bridge Design Practice Manual,* California Department of Transportation, State of California, Sacramento.

Chang, S. T., and Gang, J. Z. (1990). "Analysis of Cantilever Decks of Thin-Walled Box Girder Bridges," *ASCE J. Str. Eng.* 116(9), September, pp. 2410–2418.

Chaudhary, V. K. (1978). "Analysis of Plates with Various Shapes and Boundaries," Ph.D. dissertation, West Virginia University, Morgantown.

Chen, T. Y., Ciess, C. P., and Newmark, N. M. (1954). "Studies of Slab and Beam Highway Bridges, Part IV: Moments in Simply Supported Skew I-Beam Bridges," *Engineering Experiment Station Bull.* no. 439, University of Illinois, Urbana.

Cheung, Y. K. (1986). "Application of Spline-Finite-Strip Method in the Analysis of Curved Slabs Bridge," *Proc. Inst. Civ. Engr., Part 2,* 1986, pp. 111–124.

Chu, K. H., and Dudnik, E. (1969). "Concrete Box Girder Bridges Analyzed as Folded Plates," *Concrete Bridge Design,* ACI publication SP-23, ACI, Detroit, pp. 221–244.

Chu, K. H., and Krishnamurthy, G. (1962). "Use of Orthotropic Plate Theory in Bridge Design," *Proc. ASCE, J. Str. Div.,* 88(ST3), June, pp. 35–77.

Chu, K. H., and Pinjarkar, S. G. (1966). "Multiple Folded Plate Structures," *ASCE Proc., J. Str. Div.,* 92(ST2), April, pp. 297–321.

Coull A., and Rao, K. S. (1969). "The Analysis of Reinforced Concrete Bridge Decks by the Line-Solution Technique," *Concrete Bridge Design,* ACI publication SP-23, ACI, Detroit, pp. 19–38.

Culver, C. G., and McManus, P. F. (1971). *Instability of Horizontally Curved Members, Lateral Buckling of Curved Plate Girders,* project report submitted to the Pennsylvania Department of Transportation, Department of Civil Engineering, Carnegie-Mellon University, Pittsburgh, September.

Cusens, A. R., and Pama, R. P. (1965). "Design of Concrete Multibeam Bridge Decks," *Proc. ASCE J. Str. Div.,* 91(ST5), October, pt. 1, paper 4518, pp. 255–278.

———. (1975). *Bridge Deck Analysis,* John Wiley & Sons, New York.

DeCastro, E. S., and Kostem, C. N. (1975). *Load Distribution in Skewed Beam–Slab Highway Bridges,* Fritz Engineering Laboratory, report no. 378A.7, Lehigh University, Bethlehem, PA.

DeFries-Skene, A., and Scordelis, A. C. (1964). "Direct Stiffness Solution of Folded Plates," *ASCE Proc., J. Str. Div.,* 90(ST4), August, pp. 15–47.

Degenkolb, O. H. (1977). *Concrete Box Girder Bridges,* ACI, Detroit.

El-Ali, N. D. (1986). *Evaluation of Internal Forces in Skew Multi-Stringer Simply Supported Bridges,* Ph.D. thesis, Ohio State University, Columbus.

Evans, R. (1984). "Simplified Methods for the Analysis and Design of Bridges of Cellular Construction," in *Analysis and Design of Bridges,* C. Yilmitaz and S. Tanvir Wasti, eds., NATO ASI Series, Martinus Nijhoff Publishers, Boston, pp. 95–118.

Fang, I. K., Worley, J., Burns, N. H., and Klingner, R. E. (1990). "Behavior of Isotropic R/C Bridge Decks on Steel Girders," *ASCE J. Str. Eng.,* 116(3), March, pp. 659–678.

Ghali, A. (1969). "Analysis of Continuous Skew Concrete Girder Bridges," *Concrete Bridge Design,* ACI publication SP-23, ACI, Detroit, pp. 137–170.

Guyon, Y. (1946). "Calcul Des Ponts Larges a Poutres Multiples Solididarisees par des Entretoises," *Annals des Ponts et Chaussees,* no. 24, pp. 553–612.

———. (1949). "Calcul des ponts-dalles," *Annals des Ponts et Chaussees de France*, no. 119, pp. 555–589, 683–718.

Hambly, E. C. (1991). *Bridge Deck Behavior,* 2nd ed., E & FN Spon, London, (Van Nostrand Reinhold, New York).

Hays, C. O., Jr. (1990). "Discussion of 'Lateral Distribution Factors for Highway Bridges' by B. Bakht and F. Moses," *ASCE J. Str. Eng.,* 116(3), March, pp. 868–871.

Hays, C. O., Jr., Sessions, L. M., and Berry, A. J. (1986). "Further Studies on Lateral Load Distribution Using Finite Element Methods," Trans. Res. Rec. 1072, Transportation Research Board, Washington, DC.

Heins, C. P., and Firmage, A. (1979). *Design of Modern Steel Highway Bridges,* John Wiley & Sons, New York.

Hendry, A. W., and Jaeger, L. G. (1956). "The Analysis of Interconnected Bridge Girders by the Distribution of Harmonics," *Str. Eng.* (England), 34(7), July, pp. 241–256.

———. (1959). *The Analysis of Grid Frameworks and Related Structures*, Prentice Hall, Englewood Cliffs, NJ.

Hondros, G., and Marsh, J. G. (1960). "Load Distribution in Composite Girder–Slab Systems," *Proc. ASCE J. Str. Div.*, 86(ST11), November, paper 2645, pp. 79–109.

Huber, M. T. (1921). "Teorie plyt prostokatnie roznokierunkovych," Lwów, Poland.

———. (1924). "Uber die Biegung einer Rechteckplatte von ungleicher Biegungsfestigket in der Langs und Querrichtung," *Bauingenieur 6,* pp. 259, 305.

———. (1925a). "Uber die genaue Berchnungeiner orthotropen Platte," *Bauingenieur 7,* p. 878.

———. (1925b), "Uber die Biegung einer sehr langen Eisenbetonplatte," *Bauingenieur 7,* p. 7.

———. (1926). "Einige Anwendungen der Biegungstheorie orthotroper Platten," *Zangew. Math. Mech.,* p. 229.

———. (1933). "Die Theorie der kreuzweise bewehrten Eisenbetonplatte nebst Anwendungen auf mehrese bautechnisch wichtige Aufgaben uber rechteckige Platten," *Bauingenieur 4,* pp. 354, 392.

Imbsen, R. A., and Nutt, R. V. (1978). "Load Distribution Study on Highway Bridges Using STRUDL F.E.A. Capabilities," *Conf. on Computing in Civil Engr.,* ASCE, New York.

Jackson, N. (1968). "The Torsional Rigidity of Concrete Bridge Decks," *Concrete,* 2(11), November, pp. 468–474.

Jackson, P. A. (1992). "Discussion of 'Behavior of Isotropic R/C Bridge Decks on Steel Girders' by I. K. Fang, J. Worley, N. H. Burns, and R. E. Klingner," *ASCE J. Str. Eng.,* 118(3), March.

Jaeger, L. G., and Bakht, B. (1982). "The Grillage Analogy in Bridge Analysis," *Canadian J. Civil Eng.,* 9(2), February, pp. 224–235.

———. (1989). *Bridge Analysis by Microcomputer,* McGraw-Hill Companies, Inc., New York.

Jensen, V. P. (1938). "Solutions for Certain Rectangular Slabs Continuous over Flexible Supports," *University of Illinois Eng. Exper. Station Bull.* no. 303, University of Illinois, Urbana.

———. (1939). "Moments in Simple Span Bridge Slabs with Stiffened Edges," *University of Illinois Eng. Exper. Station. Bull.* no. 315, University of Illinois, Urbana.

———. (1944). "Highway Slab Bridges with Curbs: Laboratory Tests and Proposed Design Method," *University of Illinois Eng. Exper. Station Bull.* no. 346, University of Illinois, Urbana.

Kennedy, J. B., and Bali, S. K. (1979). "Rigidities of Waffel-Type Slab Structures," *Canadian J. Civil Eng.,* 9(1), January, pp. 65–74.

Kerfoot, R. P., and Ostapenko, A. (1967). "Grillages under Normal and Axial Loads—Present Status," *Fritz Eng. Lab. Report 323.1,* June, Lehigh University, Bethlehem, PA.

Khaleel, M. A., and Itani, R. A. (1990). "Live-Load Moments for Continuous Skew Bridges," *ASCE J. Str. Eng.,* 116(9), September, pp. 2361–2373.

Kostem, C. (1984). "Lateral Live-Load Distribution in Prestressed Concrete Highway Bridges," in *Analysis and Design of Bridges*, C. Yilmitaz and S. Tanvir Wasti, eds., NATO ASI Series, Martinus Nijhoff Publishers, Boston, pp. 213–224.

Kukreti, A. R., and Rajpaksa, Y. (1990). "Analysis Procedure for Ribbed and Grid Plate Systems Used for Bridge Decks," *ASCE J. Str. Eng.,* 116(2), February, pp. 372–391.

Kuzmanovic, B. O., and Sanchez, M. R. (1986). "Lateral Distribution of Live Loads on Highway Bridges," *ASCE J. Str. Eng.,* 112(8), August, pp. 1847–1862.

Lay, M. G. (1974). "Bridges," in *Structural Steel Design,* 2nd ed., Lamber Tall, ed., Ronald Press, New York, pp. 94–143.

Lee, J. A. N. (1962). "Effective Width of T-Beams," *Str. Eng.,* 40(1), January, pp. 21–27.

Li, W. Y., Cheung, Y. K., and Tham, L. G. (1986). "Spline Finite Strip Analysis of General Plates," *ASCE J. Engr. Mech.,* 112(1), January, pp. 43–54.

Lightfoot, E., and Sawko, F. (1959). "Structural Frame Analysis by Electronic Computer: Grid Frameworks Resolved by Generalized Slope Deflection," *Engineering,* 187, London, pp. 18–20.

———. (1960). "Analysis of Grid Frameworks and Floor Systems by Electronic Computer," *Structural Engineering,* 38(3), March, London, pp. 79–87.

Lin, T. Y., Kulka, F., and Yang, Y. C. (1969). "Post-Tensioned Waffle and Multispan Cantilever System with Y-Piers Composing the Henenberger Overpass," *Concrete Bridge Design,* ACI Pub. SP-23, ACI, Detroit, MI.

Little, G., Rowe, R. E., and Morice, P. B. (1956). "Load Distribution in Right Highway Bridges," *Intl. Assoc. Bridge Str. Eng.,* 5th Congress, Lisbon.

Marx, H. J., Khachaturian, N., and Gamble, W. L. (1986). "Development of Design Criteria for Simply Supported Skew Slab-and-Girder Bridges," *Struct. Res. Series* no. 522, University of Illinois, Urbana.

Massonet, C. (1950). "Methode de Calcul des ponts a Poutres Multiples Tenant Compte de leur Resistance a la Torsion" ("Methods of Calculation of Bridges with Several Longitudinal Beams, Taking into Account Their Torsional Resistance"), *Pub. Intl. Assoc. Bridge and Str. Eng.,* vol. 10, pp. 147–182.

Matsumoto, Y. (1969). "Skew Girders," in *Concrete Bridge Design,* pub. SP-23, ACI, Detroit, pp. 171–191.

McManus, P. F., Nasser, G. A., and Culver, C. G. (1969). "Horizontally Curved Girders—State-of-the-Art," *ASCE J. Str. Div.,* 95(ST5), May, pp. 853–870.

Memari, A. M., and West, H. H., and Belegundu, A. D. (1991). "Methodology for Automation of Continuous Highway Bridge Design," *ASCE J. Str. Eng.,* 117(9), September, pp. 2584–2599.

Morice, P. B., and Little, G. (1954). "Load Distribution in Prestressed Concrete Bridge Systems," *Struct. Eng.,* 32(3), March, Nr. 1, pp. 83–111.

———. (1955). "Discussion of 'Load Distribution in Prestressed Concrete Bridge Systems,' by P. B. Morice and G. Little," *Struct. Eng.,* 33, Nr. 1.

———. (1956). *The Analysis of Right Bridge Decks Subjected to Abnormal Loading,* Cement and Concrete Association, London.

Muller, J. (1963). "Concrete Bridges Built in Cantilever," *J. Inst. Hwy. Engrs.,* 10(4), October, pp. 159–171; 11(1), January 1964, pp. 19–30.

Nakai, H., and Yoo, C. H. (1988). *Analysis and Design of Curved Steel Bridges,* McGraw-Hill Companies, Inc., New York.

Nasser, K. W. (1965). "Design Procedure for Lateral Load Distribution in Multibeam Bridges," *J. Prestressed Concrete Inst.,* 10(4), August, pp. 54–68.

NCHRP. (1992a). "Distribution of Wheel Loads on Highway Bridges," *Res. Results Digest,* no. 187, NCHRP Project 12-26, May.

NCHRP. (1992b). *Development of Comprehensive Bridge Specifications and Commentary: Third Draft LRFD Specifications and Commentary,* NCHRP proj. 12-33, Transportation Research Board, National Research Council, Washington, DC, April 1992.

Newmark, N. M. (1938). "A Distribution Procedure for Analysis of Slabs Continuous over Flexible Beams," *University of Illinois Eng. Exper. Station Bull.* no. 304, University of Illinois, June 17.

———. (1948). "Design of I-Beam Bridges, Highway Bridge Floor Symposium," *ASCE J. Str. Div.,* 74(ST1), March, pp. 305–331.

Newmark, N. M., and Ciess, C. P. (1943a). "Moments in I-Beam Bridges," *University of Illinois Eng. Exper. Station Bull.* no. 336, University of Illinois, Urbana.

———. (1943b). "Design of Slab and Stringer Highway Bridges," *Public Roads,* pp. 157–164.

Newmark, N. M., Ciess, C. P., and Peuman, R. H. (1948). "Studies of Slab–Beam Highway Bridges," *University of Illinois Eng. Exper. Station Bull.* no. 375, University of Illinois, Urbana.

Nutt, R. V., Schamber, R. A., and Zokai, T. (1988). *Distribution of Wheel Loads on Highway Bridges,* final report, NCHRP project 12-26, April, Transportation Research Board, National Research Council, Washington, DC.

O'Connor, C. (1971). *Design of Bridge Superstructures*, Wiley-Interscience, John Wiley & Sons, New York.

OHBDC. (1983). *Ontario Highway Bridge Design Code (OHBDC),* 2nd ed., Ministry of Transportation and Communications, Downsview, Ontario.

———. (1992). *Ontario Highway Bridge Design Code (OHBDC),* 2nd ed., Ministry of Transportation and Communications, Downsview, Ontario.

Pama, R., and Cusens, A. R. (1969). "Load Distribution in Multibeam Concrete Bridges," *Concrete Bridge Design,* pub. SP-23, ACI, Detroit.

Pool, R. B., Arya, A. S., Robinson, A. R., and Khachaturian, N. (1965). "Analysis of Multibeam Bridges with Beam Elements of Slab and Box Section," *Univ. of Illinois Eng. Exper. Station Bull.* no. 483, University of Illinois, Urbana.

Pucher, A. (1964). *Influence Surfaces of Elastic Plates,* Springer Verlag, Vienna.

Reliance Steel. (undated). *Catalog No. RSL-18B,* Reliance Steel Products Co., McKeesport, PA.

Roseli, A. (1955). *Lateral Load Distribution in Multibeam Bridges,* Prestressed Concrete Bridge Members progress report no. 10, Fritz Eng. Lab., Lehigh University, Bethlehem, PA.

Rowe, R. E. (1962). *Concrete Bridge Design,* C. R. Books, London.

Rusch, H., and Hergenroder, A. (1961). *Influence Surfaces for Moments in Skew Slabs,* Technological University, Munich, (translated from German by C. R. Amerongen, Linden, Cement and Concrete Association).

Sabins, G. M., ed. (1979). *Handbook of Composite Construction Engineering,* Van Nostrand Reinhold Co., New York.

Sanders, W. W., and Elleby, H. A. (1970). *Distribution of Wheel Loads on Highway Bridges,* Highway Research Program Synthesis of Highway Practice III, report no. 83, Transportation Research Board, National Research Council, Washington, DC.

Sawko, F., and Mills, J. H. (1971). "Design of Cantilever Slabs for Spline Beam Bridges," *Developments in Bridge Design and Construction, Proc. Cardiff Conf.,* Crosby Lockwood & Son, Ltd., London, pp. 1–26.

Scordelis, A. (1984). "Berkeley Computer Programs for Analysis of Concrete Box Girder Bridges," in *Analysis and Design of Bridges,* C. Yilmitaz and S. Tanvir Wasti, eds., NATO ASI Series, Martinus Nijhoff Publishers, Boston, pp. 119–190.

Scordelis, A. C., Davis, R. E., and Lo, K. S. (1969). "Load Distribution in Concrete Box Girder Bridges," *Concrete Bridge Design,* pub. SP-23, ACI, Detroit, pp. 117–136.

Severn, R. T. (1962). "The Deformation of a Rectangular Slab Stiffened by Beams under Transverse Load," *Mag. Concrete Research,* 14(41), July, pp. 73–78.

———. (1964). "Effective Width of T-Beams," *Mag. Concrete Research,* 16(47), June, pp. 99–102.

Tarhini, K. M., and Fredrick, G. R. (1992). "Wheel Load Distribution in I-Girder Highway Bridges," *ASCE J. Str. Eng.,* 116(3), March, pp. 1285–1294.

Tiedeman, J. L., Albretch, P., and Cayes, L. R. (1993). "Behavior of Two-Span Continuous Bridge under Truck Axle Loading," *ASCE J. Str. Eng.,* 119(4), April, pp. 1234–1250.

Timoshenko, S. P. (1953). *History of Strength of Materials,* McGraw-Hill Companies, Inc., New York.

Timoshenko, S. P., and Goodier, J. N. (1951). *Theory of Elasticity,* McGraw-Hill Companies, Inc., New York, pp. 262–268.

Timoshenko, S. P., and Woinsky-Krieger, S. (1959). *Theory of Plates and Shells,* 2nd ed., McGraw-Hill Companies, Inc., New York.

Troitsky, M. S. (1967). *Orthotropic Bridges: Theory and Design,* The James F. Lincoln Arc Welding Foundation, Cleveland.

Tung, D. H. (1969). "Torsional Analysis of Single Thin-Walled Trapezoidal Concrete Box Girder Bridges," *Concrete Bridge Design,* pub. SP-23, ACI, Detroit, pp. 205–220.

USS. (1974). *Hatfield Bridge, Jackson County, Wisconsin,* USS Bridge Report no. ADUSS 88-6323-01, U.S. Steel, Pittsburgh, July.

———. (1978). *New River Gorge Bridge, Fayette County, West Virginia,* USS Bridge Report no. ADUSS 88-7274-01, U.S. Steel, Pittsburgh, May.

Vitols, R. J., Clifton, R. J., and Au, T. (1963). "Analysis of Composite Beam Bridges by Orthotropic Plate Theory," *Proc. ASCE J. Str. Div.,* 89(ST4), August, pt. 1, paper 3584, pp. 71–94.

Westergaard, H. M. (1930). "Computation of Stresses in Bridge Slabs Due to Wheel Loads," *Public Roads,* March.

Zellin, M. A., Kostem, C. N., Vanhorn, D. A., and Kulicki, J. M. (1975a). *Lateral Distribution of Live Load in Prestressed Concrete I-Beam Bridges,* Fritz Engineering Laboratory, report no. 387.2A, Lehigh University, Bethlehem, PA.

———. (1975b). *Live-Load Distribution Factors for Prestressed Concrete I-Beam Bridges,* Fritz Engineering Laboratory, report no. 387.2B, Lehigh University, Bethlehem, PA.

Zuraski, P. D. (1991). "Continuous-Beam Analysis for Highway Bridges," *ASCE J. Str. Eng.,* 117(1), January, pp. 80–99.

CHAPTER 5

Serviceability Criteria: Deflection and Fatigue

5.1
INTRODUCTION

Functional considerations are the very reason for creating a structure. Structural design can be considered optimal if it can simultaneously satisfy the requirements of function, safety, economy, and aesthetics [Kuzmanovic and Willems, 1983]. Although all of these requirements are important, that of functionality carries the most weight, because it is the very reason for creating a structure. Toward that end, designers provide highway bridges not merely with adequate strength but also with service lives uninterrupted by fatigue damage; durable riding surfaces; and comfortable crossings for pedestrians and occupants of moving vehicles. The importance of functionality implies, in addition to other considerations, that the design of a structure should primarily be performance-based. *Deflection, slenderness and flexibility of structure,* and *fatigue* are three elements of the design matrix that are related to the performance of a bridge structure during its service life. Together, they form a part of the design criteria, generally known as the *serviceability criteria.*

There are other considerations that affect serviceability and, in time, lead to functional obsolescence of a bridge. These include changed traffic patterns, increased size and weight limitations of live load, and material deterioration (corrosion of steel or reinforcing bars, spalling and cracking of concrete, etc.) due to either poor maintenance or old age.

5.2
DEFLECTION AND DEPTH-SPAN RATIOS

5.2.1 Historical Development

Limiting the *deflection-to-span* and the *depth-to span* (slenderness) ratios had been recognized early on by both railroad and highway bridge engineers as the key to providing bridges with durable riding surfaces as well as comfort to the occupants of moving vehicles. However, how these criteria contribute to those qualities has not been very clear [Wright and Walker, 1971].

Both the deflection-to-span and the depth-to-span ratio limitations have evolved over more than 100 years. During the early years, because of the widespread use of railroads and the much heavier loadings involved, railroad engineers took the lead in establishing the two limitations. In the United States the evolution of deflection limitations can be traced back to the 1870s. According to a landmark study [ASCE, 1958][1] on deflection limitations of bridges, the first serious effort in this regard appears to be that of the Phoenix Bridge Company, which, in 1871, limited the deflection due to the passage of a train and locomotive at 30 miles per hour to $\frac{1}{1200}$ of the span. In 1905, the AREA specifications provided that

> pony trusses and plate girders shall preferably have a depth not less than $\frac{1}{10}$ of the span and the rolled beams and channels used as girders shall preferably have depth not less than $\frac{1}{12}$ of the span. When these ratios are decreased, proper increases shall be made to the flange section.

The limiting depth-to-span ratios were modified from time to time as follows [ASCE, 1958]:

Year	Trusses	Plate Girders	Rolled Beams
1913, 1924	1:10	1:10	1:12
1907, 1911, 1915	1:10	1:12	1:12
1919, 1921, 1953	1:10	1:12	1:15

Early highway bridge specifications followed the railroad's lead regarding the depth-to-span ratio limitations, with minor modifications; not until the 1930s were specific limitations developed for the distinctive problem of highway bridge design. The U.S. Department of Agriculture Circular no. 100, issued in 1913 by the Bureau of Public Roads, set limiting depth-to-span ratios at 1:10, 1:12, and 1:20 for trusses, plate girders, and rolled beams, respectively. The same limitations were contained in the U.S. Department of Agriculture Bulletin no. 1259, issued in October 1924 (AASHTO specifications). Over the years, these requirements were modified as follows [ASCE, 1958]:

Year	Trusses	Plate Girders	Rolled Beams
1913, 1924	1:10	1:10	1:20
1931	1:10	1:15	1:20
1935, 1941, 1949, 1953	1:10	1:25	1:25

These limitations were quite possibly set and modified arbitrarily, because no record exists as to any bases for a particular value for them. In fact, in 1905 the AREA

---

[1]This report contains a bibliography of 108 references, chronologically listed, pertaining to the deflections due to live load in highway and railroad bridges.

Committee explained the somewhat ambiguous wording of their provisions for design, which reduced depths, as follows [ASCE, 1958]:

> We established the rule because we could not agree on any. Some of us in designing a girder that is very shallow in proportion to its length, decrease the unit stress or increase the section according to some rule which we guess at. We put it there so that a man would have a warrant for using whatever he pleased.

The ASCE Committee [ASCE 1958] concluded that "Neither the reasons for these changes nor the original basis for the limitation on depth-span ratios have been determined by the Committee."

5.2.2 Purpose of Deflection Limitations

Deflection limitations for highway bridges appear to have evolved in the early 1930s, when reports of objectionable vibrations of steel girder highway bridges began to appear. The Bureau of Public Roads made a statistical study to correlate the reported vibrations with the properties of the bridges involved. According to this study, the bridges for which objectionable vibrations were reported usually had computed live load deflections of more than $\frac{1}{800}$ of the span for simple and continuous spans and more than $\frac{1}{400}$ of the span for cantilever spans. Accordingly, in the design specifications issued by the Bureau of Public Roads in November 1936, the allowable deflections due to live load plus impact were limited to $\frac{1}{800}$ of the span for bridges carrying light traffic and to $\frac{1}{1100}$ for bridges in or adjacent to populous centers and for bridges carrying heavy traffic. In 1939 the specification was extended to limit the deflection for cantilever arms to $\frac{1}{300}$ of the arm except at locations of dense traffic, where the limit was kept to $\frac{1}{400}$ of the arm. These specifications were adopted in the meetings of the AASHO (now AASHTO) Committee in 1938. With minor modifications, nearly the same limitations continue to be used today.

While suggesting that its goal might have been to reduce human discomfort by limiting large deflections, the ASCE Committee [ASCE, 1958] pointed out two reasons for limiting deflections for railroad bridges:

- To avoid excessive vibration of the structure in resonance with the recurring hammer blows of the locomotive driving wheels
- To avoid objectionable oscillation of the rolling stock induced when the deflections of the successive spans tended to set up a harmonic excitation of the sprung weight

The ASCE Committee [ASCE, 1958] also gave the following reasons for limiting deflections for highway bridges:

1. To avoid undesirable structural effects, including
   - Excessive deformation stresses in secondary members or connections resulting either from the deflection itself or from induced rotations at joints or supports
   - Excessive dynamic stresses of the type considered in design by the use of conventional "impact" factors
   - Fatigue effects resulting from excessive vibration

2. To avoid undesirable psychological reactions by

- Pedestrians, whose reactions are clearly a consequence of the motion of the bridge alone
- Passengers in vehicles, whose reactions are affected as a result of the motion of the vehicle in combination with the bridge, or by the motion of the bridge when the vehicle is at rest on the span

However, the 1958 Committee [ASCE, 1958] noted several shortcomings in the stated approaches by pointing out the following:

The limited survey conducted by the Committee revealed no evidence of serious structural damage that could be attributed to excessive deflection. The few examples of damaged stringer connections or cracked concrete floors could probably be corrected more effectively by changes in design than by more restrictive limitations on deflections. On the other hand, both the historical study and the results from the survey indicate clearly that unfavorable psychological reaction to bridge deflection or vibration is probably the most important source of concern regarding the flexibility of bridges. However, those characteristics of bridge vibration which are considered objectionable by pedestrians or passengers in vehicles are yet to be defined.

Extensive research has been conducted on human response to motion [Pain and Upstone, 1942; Reiher and Meister, 1946; Janeway, 1948; Goldman, 1948; Oehler, 1957; Dieckmann, 1958; Walley, 1959; Wright and Green, 1959a,b, 1963; Guignard and Irving, 1960; Lenzen, 1966; Leonard, 1966; Peterson, 1972; Allen and Rainer, 1976; Matthews, Montgomery, and Murray, 1982; Murray, 1981, 1991; Pernica and Allen, 1982; Bachmann, 1984, 1992; Allen, Rainer, and Pernica, 1987; Bachmann and Ammann, 1987; Baumann and Bachmann, 1987; Vogt and Bachmann, 1987; Ohlson, 1988; Rainer, Pernica, and Allen, 1988; ISO, 1989, 1992; Wyatt, 1989; Allen and Murray, 1993]. These studies show that human reaction to vibrations is a complicated phenomenon that is not completely understood. The psychological effects derive from the fact that the human body is a dynamic system which has natural frequencies of its own, as shown by Dieckmann [1958] and by Guignard and Irving [1960]. It acts as an extremely sensitive pickup device that is able to detect very small levels of vibration. This extreme sensitivity tends to exaggerate personal reactions, making individual assessments of intensity unreliable [Leonard, 1966]. Nevertheless, it is now generally agreed that the primary factor affecting human sensitivity is acceleration, rather than deflection, velocity, or the rate of change of acceleration of bridge structures. Thus, there are as yet no simple, definitive guidelines for the limits of tolerable static deflection or dynamic motion. Among current specifications the Ontario Highway Bridge Design Code [OHBDC, 1983] contains the most comprehensive provisions regarding vibrations tolerable to humans [AASHTO, 1994].

In summarizing the purposes of limiting deflections for highway bridges, the ASCE Committee noted that "...it should first be noted that the safety of structure is not involved, even to the extent that more flexible bridges may be adequate to carry the live load with safety" [ASCE, 1958]. This line of thought is echoed in *Commentary C2.5.2.6.1* in the AASHTO–LRFD specifications [AASHTO, 1994]: "service load deformations may cause deterioration of wearing surfaces and local cracking in concrete slabs and in metal bridges which could impair serviceability and durability, even if self limiting and not a potential source of collapse." Accordingly, the deflection limitations constitute a serviceability criterion, not a strength criterion.

It is pertinent to note the trend in bridge design during the period in which deflection-to-span and depth-to-span requirements evolved as just described. When the first limitations were proposed, the standard floor was plank; the supporting members were either simple beams, pony trusses, or pin-connected through trusses; and questions concerning the effects of vibration centered on individual members. These questions were largely eliminated with the advent of more substantial members, riveted and bolted joints, and welded and composite construction. However, vibrations of the bridge as a whole were noted with some concern at about the time unit stresses were increased, and cantilever and continuous construction began to appear.

Along with changes in the bridge design practices, there were also changes in the design highway live loads from time to time. At the turn of the century the heaviest loading was a road roller. With the development of motor trucks, design loadings were first based on 10-ton and 15-ton trucks. This was followed by introduction of 20-ton trucks in 1924 for bridges on which heavy traffic was anticipated during their service life. Three years later, the Conference Committee representing AASHTO and AREA introduced the truck train—a heavy truck preceded and followed by trucks having three-fourths of its weight—which appeared in the 1927 *Specifications for Steel Highway Bridges*. This was superseded in 1941 by the equivalent lane loading, which was first used as an optional loading in the 1931 AASHO bridge specifications. Finally, the H20-S16 (now designated as HS20-44) was introduced in in the 1941 AASHO specifications [ASCE, 1958]. The evolution of highway live loadings in the United States is discussed in Chapter 3.

It should be noted that deflection-to-span and the depth-to-span (slenderness) ratios are not independent but are related by the following expression [Wright and Walker, 1971]:

$$\frac{\delta}{L} = K\sigma\frac{L}{d} \tag{5.1}$$

where δ = deflection
  σ = flexural stress producing deflection δ
  L = span
  d = member depth
  K = a factor depending on the distribution of loading.

A discussion on the values of K has been presented by Bressler, Lin, and Scalzi [1968]; Wright and Walker [1971] have discussed the interrelationships between the two parameters δ/L and d/L.

5.2.3 Deflection Requirements

Although deflections are caused by both dead and live loads, the deflection limitations have historically always been linked to live loads. Note that the deflection criteria in the AASHTO specifications for bridges other than orthotropic bridges are optional [AASHTO, 1994, 2.5.2.6.2]. Calculated deflections of structures have often

TABLE 5.1

AASHTO-specified limitations on deflection due to live load plus impact [AASHTO, 1992]

Member having simple or continuous spans	$L/800$
For urban-area bridges, used in part by pedestrians	$L/1000$
Deflection of cantilever arms due to service load plus impact (no pedestrians)	$L/300$
Same as above but with pedestrians	$L/375$

been found to be difficult to verify in the field, because many sources of stiffness are not accounted for in calculations.

For both steel and reinforced concrete bridges, AASHTO 8.9.3 (for reinforced concrete beams) and 10.6 (for steel stringers/girders) limit the deflections resulting from live load plus impact, as shown in Table 5.1.

The effect of impact is to contribute the dynamic part of the deflection, caused by the suddenness and bouncing effect of the moving load. This was alluded to in Chapter 3 in the context of impact. Historically, it is interesting to note that until the middle of the 19th century there was no agreement among engineers on the effect of a moving load (i.e., dynamical action) on a beam. The first experiments to determine deflections caused by impact were reportedly conducted for railroad bridges in England and Germany in the 1840s and 1850s. A summary discussion of these tests has been provided by Timoshenko [1953, pp. 173–178].

5.2.4 Depth-to-Span Ratio Requirements

Another criterion employed in the design of highway bridges is the limitation on the slenderness and the flexibility of the superstructure. This requirement is expressed in terms of the *depth-to-span ratio* for members supporting the bridge flooring.

5.2.4.1 Steel members

The depth-span requirements for steel members are shown in Table 5.2.

TABLE 5.2

AASHTO-specified depth-span limitations for steel members [AASHTO, 1992, 10.5]

Member	Limiting D/L ratio[*]
Beams or girders	1/25
Composite girders	
Overall (concrete slab + steel girder)	1/25
Steel girder alone	1/30
Trusses	1/10

[*]D = Total or overall girder depth

L = Span length

For continuous span-depth ratios, the span length should be considered as the distance between the dead load points of contraflexure.

TABLE 5.3
Recommended minimum depths for constant-depth members
[AASHTO, 1992, Table 8.9.2]

Superstructure type	Minimum depth (ft),[a] simple spans	Continuous spans
Bridge slabs with main reinforcement parallel to traffic	$1.2(S + 10)/30$	$(S + 10)/30 \geq 0.542$
T-girders	$0.070S$	$0.065S$
Box girders	$0.060S$	$0.055S$
Pedestrian-structure girders	$0.033S$	$0.033S$

[a]When variable-depth members are used, values may be adjusted to account for change in relative stiffness of positive- and negative-moment sections.
S = span length, ft

5.2.4.2 Reinforced concrete members

For reinforced concrete members, the approach to deflection limitation is similar to that specified by the ACI Code [ACI 1995], i.e., to limit the minimum depth of members. AASHTO 8.9.2 specifies the member depth limitations as shown in Table 5.3. A slightly different version of these requirements was recommended in the earlier specifications [ACI, 1977].

It may be noted that the above-stated minimum depth limitations first appeared in the 1977 AASHTO specifications (1.5.40(B)), which specified the same minimum depth requirements for slabs with reinforcement either *perpendicular* or *parallel* to traffic. However, this stipulation was revised in the 1989 AASHTO specifications by dropping the words "and perpendicular," as shown in Table 5.3.

Deflections are significantly influenced by the support conditions. For example, for a simple span, $\Delta_{\text{midspan}} = 5wL^4/384EI$, whereas for a fixed span it is $wL^4/384EI$, only one-fifth that for the simple span. Thus, the depth requirements vary depending upon the support conditions; this aspect is reflected in Table 5.3.

5.2.5 Deflections Due to Dead Load and Camber

In the preceding paragraphs the discussion focused on live load– and impact-induced deflection. Of course, there will be deflection caused by the dead load, but no limitation is set for it in the AASHTO specifications.

It is generally agreed that perceptibly deflected beams are unsightly and give the appearance of inherent weakness to passing motorists. If the thickness of the concrete slab over the supporting stringers is kept constant, the resulting flooring will also have an undesirable deflected profile. Consequently, the beam dead load deflections must be accommodated during the concrete placement for the slab.

An acceptably level floor can be achieved in many ways [Larson and Huzzord, 1990]:

1. Providing a slab of varying thickness over the sagged beams
2. Providing stiffer (overdesigned) beams to minimize deflections

3. Shoring the beams before concrete placement
4. Cambering the beams (forming them with an initial upward deflection)

The relative economy of these methods should dictate the choice. In general, it has been found that cambering the beams is the most cost-effective method of accommodating dead-load deflections. In addition, the resulting relatively straight profile of stringers also adds to the overall aesthetic appeal.

In practice, the stringers are cambered an amount equal to dead-load deflections plus or minus enough additional camber that the stringers will be a constant distance below the roadway surface under the full dead load. AASHTO 10.14 specifies that "girders should be cambered to compensate for dead load deflections and vertical curvature required by profile grade." For spans under 50 ft or so using rolled beams, the dead-load deflections are relatively small, and cambering will be of little value [AASHTO,1991; AISC Mkt., 1986b].

Rolled beams may have a slight mill camber when received from the rolling mill. This mill camber should be turned upward when no cambering is required [AASHTO, 1991]. The maximum lengths that can be cambered depend on the length to which a given section can be rolled, with a maximum of 100 ft. Table 5.4 gives the maximum and minimum *cold cambering* of beams (that is, cambering subsequent to rolling) to produce a predetermined dimension [AISC, 1989].

For specific cambers or lengths outside those listed in Table 5.4, the producer or the supplier should be consulted. Mill camber in beams of smaller depth than tabulated should not be specified. While specifying camber, the following rules should be observed [AISC, 1989]:

- A single minimum value for camber, within the ranges shown for the length ordered, should be specified.
- Camber should be specified by the ordinate at the midlength of the portion of the beam to be curved. Ordinates at other points should not be specified.
- Camber will approximate a simple regular curve nearly the full length of the beam or between any two specified points.
- Camber is measured at the mill and will not necessarily be present in the same amount in the member as received, because of release of stress induced during the cambering operation. In general, 75% of the specified camber is likely to remain.
- Permissible variations (mill tolerances) for camber ordinates are given in Table 5.5.

TABLE 5.4
Maximum and minimum acceptable induced camber (in.) [AISC, 1989]

Sections, nominal depth (in.)	Specified length of beam (ft)				
	30–42	42–52	52–65	65–85	85–100
W shapes, 24 and over	1–2	1–3	2–4	3–5	3–6
W shapes, 14 to 21, inclusive, and S shapes, 12 in. and over	¾–2 ½	1–3	2–4	2 ½–5	Inquire

TABLE 5.5
Permissible variation for camber ordinates [AISC, 1989]

Lengths	Plus variation	Minus variation
50 ft or less	$\frac{1}{2}$ in.	0
Over 50 ft	$\frac{1}{2}$ in. plus $\frac{1}{8}$ in. for each 10 ft or fraction thereof in excess of 50 ft	0

Precambering of steel beams, nevertheless, adds to the total cost, and it is not required for steel beam bridges in the short span range. A preferable method in such a case is to provide variable coping depth over the beams, i.e., providing the correct depth thickness of concrete slab and final deck elevations for the uncambered beam. The cost of additional coping concrete thus required will be more than offset by the cost of precambering. Full details regarding cambering are presented in reference [AISC, 1989].

5.2.6 Deflection Calculations

Because the deflections are essentially serviceability criteria, they are calculated for *service load conditions* by using the elastic design formulas that can be found in texts on strength of materials and handbooks.

5.2.6.1 Dead-load deflections

Steel members. The following general formula may be used for calculating deflection of steel stringers due to dead loads [AISC Mkt, 1986]:

$$\Delta = \left(\frac{72wL^4}{E_sI}\right)ab[1 + ab - 4(C_R - C_L)(1 + a) - 12C_L] \tag{5.2}$$

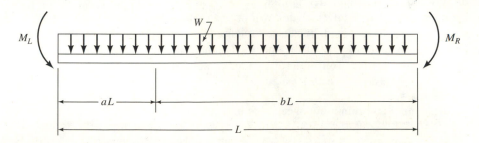

where Δ = deflection, in., at distance aL from left support
$b = 1 - a$
w = dead load, kips/ft
L = span, ft
E_s = modulus of elasticity of steel
I = moment of inertia, in.^{4}, of steel section or of composite section with modular ratio $3n$, computed at the point of maximum positive moment

$$C_R = M_R/wL^2$$
$$C_L = M_L/wL^2$$
$$M_R = \text{bending moment at right support, kip-ft}$$
$$M_L = \text{bending moment at left support, kip-ft}$$

Substitution of $E_s = 29,000$ ksi and $a = L/2$ (for midspan) in Eq. 5.2 yields

$$\Delta_{\text{midspan}} = \frac{45wL^4}{2E_sI} = \frac{wL^4}{1300I} \tag{5.3}$$

Composite members. Steel-concrete composite beams (or girders) may involve *shored* or *unshored* construction. In the case of shored construction, the *composite* section resists both dead and live load. Long-term or permanent loads, such as dead loads, cause concrete to creep and thereby reduce the effectiveness of the concrete portion of the cross section in resisting stresses. This can be accounted for approximately by using a reduced value of the modulus of elasticity of concrete, E_c, which essentially increases the value of the modular ratio, $n = E_s/E_c$. For sustained loads the AASHTO specifications stipulate that the value of the modulus of elasticity of concrete, E_c, be reduced to $\frac{1}{3}E_c$, so that the effective modular ratio is increased to $3n$. Thus, the dead-load deflection can be calculated using Eq. 5.2 and the properties of the composite section ($I_{\text{composite}}$) are calculated with modular ratio equal to $3n$.

Reinforced concrete members. An exhaustive discussion on deflection of concrete structures can be found in many papers published in ACI special publication SP-43 [ACI, 1974a]. Two types of deflections should be considered for serviceability of reinforced concrete members: *immediate deflections* and *long-term deflections*.

Immediate deflections are defined to be those that occur during the normal service life of the member as a result of *sustained* load. Under this condition, the stresses in concrete remain within the elastic range. Accordingly, deflections can be calculated from the elastic properties of the member cross section. AASHTO 8.13.3 stipulates that immediate deflections can be calculated based on the *gross moment of inertia*, I_g, or the *effective moment of inertia*, I_e, based on the properties of both the *uncracked* and the *cracked* sections as follows:

$$I_e = \left(\frac{M_{\text{cr}}}{M_a}\right)^3 I_g + \left[1 - \left(\frac{M_{\text{cr}}}{M_a}\right)^3\right] I_{\text{cr}} \le I_g \tag{5.4}$$

where $M_{\text{cr}} = f_r I_g / y_t$
M_a = maximum moment at stage for which the deflection is being computed
I_g = moment of inertia of gross section, neglecting reinforcement
$\quad = bd^3/12$
f_r = modulus of rupture of concrete [AASHTO 8.15.2.1.1]
$\quad = 5.5\sqrt{f_c}$ for normal-weight concrete
$\quad = 6.3\sqrt{f_c}$ for sand-lightweight concrete
$\quad = 5.5\sqrt{f_c}$ for all-lightweight concrete
y_t = distance from the centroidal axis of the gross section, neglecting reinforcement, to extreme fiber in tension

Equation 5.4 is subject to the following stipulations:

- For continuous members the effective moment of inertia may be taken as the average of values of I_e, obtained for the critical positive- and negative-moment section.
- For prismatic members the effective moment of inertia may be the value of I_e, obtained at midspans of simple or continuous spans.
- For cantilever spans the effective moment of inertia may be taken at the support.

AASHTO 8.13.4 stipulates that the *long-term* deflections be calculated by multiplying the immediate deflections by the following factors:

1. Where the immediate deflection has been based on I_g, the multiplier is 4.
2. Where the immediate deflection has been based on I_e, the multiplier is $[3 - 1.2(A_s'/A_s)] \geq 1.6$,

   where $A_s' =$ area of compression reinforcement, in.^{2}
   $A_s =$ area of tension reinforcement, in.^{2}

A comprehensive discussion on long-term deflections can be found in the many texts on reinforced concrete such as Ferguson [1979], MacGregor [1988], Nawy [1985], Nilson [1978], and Wang and Salmon [1973].

Prestressed concrete members. Deflection calculations for prestressed members involve several steps owing to the presence of prestressing force. The beams would generally have a net initial upward deflection, generally referred to as "camber," resulting from a combined effect of dead load and the prestressing force, before the application of live load.

Deflections due to dead load can be calculated using the moment of inertia of *gross section,* since under the service load conditions the member cross section remains *uncracked* because of the presence of prestressing force.

The prestressing force creates additional deflection in beams, usually upward, with positive eccentricity.[2] The path followed by the prestressing force along the span may be straight (*constant* eccentricity) or parabolic (*variable* eccentricity); or it may be constant in the midspan area and zero or positive at ends. The magnitude of upward deflection (camber) will depend on the magnitude and the profile of the path of prestressing force, as shown in Fig. 5.1. Deflections due to prestressing force can be calculated based on the elastic methods (such as the conjugate beam method) using the moment of inertia of gross section. The effect of presence of reinforcement (prestressed or nonprestressed) is rather small and, in view of the uncertain nature of concrete behavior, may be ignored.

The time-dependent changes in deflection include those due to creep and shrinkage of concrete and to relaxation of steel—factors that cause loss of some prestressing force, and are covered in AASHTO 9.16.2.1. A provision for the lump-sum values of loss of

---

[2]Eccentricity is defined as *positive* when it is located *below* the neutral axis in a simply supported prestressed concrete beam. The term *upward deflection* rather than *camber* is used to describe deflection due to prestressing force. The term *camber* is used to denote intentionally induced upward deflection, as in the case of steel beams.

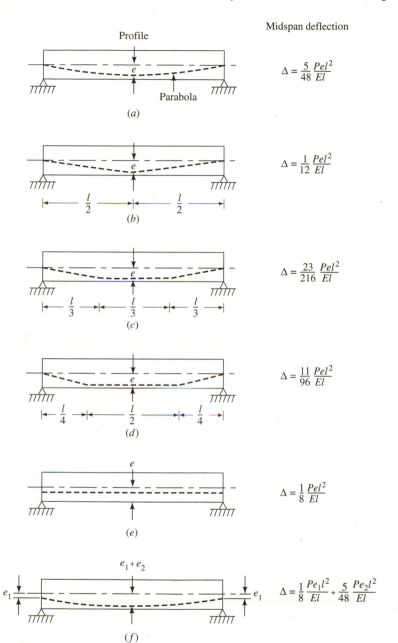

FIGURE 5.1
Deflection of prestressed beams for various tendon profiles [Nilson, 1978].

prestressing force is made in AASHTO 9.16.2.2; it can be used in lieu of the rigorous approach of 9.16.1.1.

The net deflection of a prestressed concrete member can be determined by superposing the individual effects. A discussion on deflection of prestressed concrete members can be found in several references, such as Libby [1976], Lin and Burns [1981], Naaman [1982a], Nawy [1989], and Nilson [1978].

Trusses. AASHTO 10.6.6 specifies that the *gross* area of each truss member be used to calculate truss deflections. In the case of perforated plates the effective area should be computed by dividing the net volume by the length measured from center to center of perforations.

5.2.6.2 Live-load deflections

Live-load deflections should be computed for the governing loading conditions—truck or lane—by the usual methods of computing deflections. For composite beams the moment of inertia of the composite section, I_c, with a modular ratio n, should be used. Because of the usually large moment of inertia of a composite beam, deflections seldom control the design of composite beams.

For H20 loading, deflection should be calculated by placing the 16-kip wheel at midspan, with the 4-kip wheel at 14 ft away from it. When multiple loads are placed on a span, the conjugate beam method can be conveniently used for calculating deflections. The resulting deflection should be multiplied by the appropriate distribution and impact factors.

In the case of HS20 loading it is difficult, although theoretically possible, to determine the exact positions of the three wheel loads that will result in maximum deflection. As a practical matter, however, one may calculate deflection by placing the two 16-kip loads (the heaviest loads) symmetrically about the center line of the stringer; the 4-kip load can be placed at 14 ft away from one of the 16-kip loads, if it can be placed on the span at all (depending on the span length). For such a load positioning, the following formulas can be used [AISC Mkt, 1986]:

1. For the two symmetrically placed loads, case 9 of reference [AISC, 1989] applies:

$$\Delta = \frac{Pa}{24EI}(3L^2 - 4a^2), \qquad \text{where } a = \left(\frac{L}{2} - 7\right) \tag{5.5}$$

This deflection is obviously maximum at the midspan. Substituting of $P = 16$ kips, $E = 29,000$ ksi, and converting all lengths into inch units, Eq. 5.5 can be approximately, but conservatively, expressed as

$$\Delta_{\text{max}} = \frac{a(3L^2 - 4a^2)}{25I} \tag{5.6}$$

2. For the 4-kip load, placed away from the center, case 8 of reference [AISC, 1989] applies:

$$\Delta = \frac{Pab(a + 2b)\sqrt{3a(a + 2b)}}{27EIL} \tag{5.7}$$

This deflection is maximum *not at the midspan* but at a point given by

$$x = \sqrt{\frac{a(a + 2b)}{3}}, \qquad \text{when } a > b \tag{5.8}$$

Substituting $P = 4$ kips, $E = 29{,}000$ ksi, and converting all lengths to inch units, Eq. 5.8 can be approximately, but conservatively, expressed as

$$\Delta_{\text{max}} = \frac{ab(a + 2b)\sqrt{3a(a + 2b)}}{110IL} \tag{5.9}$$

The difference between the maximum and the midspan deflection is, fortunately, not a significant one. Consequently, the total maximum deflection can be found by summing up the deflection values given by these formulas.

Reference [AISC Mkt, 1986] gives the following formula for computing midspan deflections of a continuous stringer due to the HS loading:

1. HS truck loading:

$$\Delta = \frac{324}{E_s I_c}\left[P_T(L^3 - 555L + 4780) - \tfrac{1}{3}(M_R + M_L)L^2\right] \tag{5.10}$$

where Δ = deflection at midspan, in.
$\quad\;\; P_T$ = weight of one front wheel, kips, multiplied by the live-load distribution factor, plus impact
$\quad\quad\;$ = 4 kips × 2 wheels per truck × number of lanes × distribution factor ×(1 + impact factor)
$\quad\;\; I_c$ = moment of inertia, in.^{4}, of the composite section with modular ratio n, computed at point of maximum positive moment × number of beams
$\quad\; w_L$ = one-half weight of uniform lane load for moment, kips, multiplied by the distribution factor, plus impact
$\quad\;\; L$ = span in ft

For a simple span, $M_R = M_L = 0$, and Eq. 5.10 simplifies to

$$\Delta = \frac{324P_T}{E_s I_c}(L^3 - 555L + 4780) \tag{5.11}$$

Substitution of $E_s = 29{,}000$ ksi in Eq. 5.11 yields

$$\Delta = \frac{P_T}{90I_c}(L^3 - 555L + 4780) \tag{5.12}$$

2. For lane loading, the expression for the midspan deflection for a continuous stringer is

$$\Delta = \frac{45L^2}{2E_s I_c}[L(w_L + 1.6P_L) - 4.8(M_R + M_L)] \tag{5.13}$$

where P_L = one-half weight of concentrated lane load for moment, kips, multiplied by the distribution factor, plus impact. For a simple span $M_L = M_R = 0$, and with $E_s = 29,000$ ksi, Eq. 5.13 yields

$$\Delta = \frac{L^3}{1300 I_c}(w_L L + 1.6 P_L) \tag{5.14}$$

For noncomposite construction I_c, the moment of inertia of the composite section, may be replaced by I_s, the moment of inertia of the steel section, in these formulas.

In the end span of a continuous stringer the maximum deflection occurs approximately at $0.4L$. The live-load deflection at this point may be computed by the following expressions. For HS truck loading,

$$\Delta_{0.4L} = \frac{300}{E_s I_c}[P_T(L^3 + 3.89L^2 - 680L + 5910) - 0.32ML^2] \tag{5.15}$$

For lane loading,

$$\Delta_{0.4L} = \frac{43L^2}{2E_s I_c}[L(w_L L + 1.5P_L - 4.5M)] \tag{5.16}$$

where $\Delta_{0.4L}$ = deflection at $0.4L$ from the simple support, in.
$\quad\quad M$ = bending moment at continuous support, kip-ft

Yet another method of calculating live load deflections is the use of charts. Figure 5.2 presents a nomograph from which live-load deflection for HS20 loading can be calculated graphically [PennDOT, 1970]. The procedure involves first connecting appropriate points on the moment-of-inertia and span axes (the two axes on the left side of the nomograph) and extending the connecting line toward the right to intersect the middle (unmarked) axis. Next, this intersection point is connected to the load-distribution-factor axis (far right); the intersection of this connecting line on the deflection axis gives the total stringer deflection, including the effect of impact. The following example is illustrated on the nomograph.

EXAMPLE 5.1. Span, $L = 64 ft$, $I = 20,000$ in.^{4}, live load dist. factor = 1.00.

Solution. To solve, connect $I = 20,000$ in.^{4} and $L = 64$ ft on the two far left axes and extend the line to intersect the middle unmarked axis. Connect this intersection point to DF = 1.0 on the far right axis; intersection of this line with the deflection axis gives $\Delta = 0.65$ in. This value is less than the allowable value of $L/800$ or $L/1000$ (as the case may be), as seen in the nomograph.

This result can be verified from the formulas presented earlier as follows: Substituting $L = 64$ ft, $I = 20,000$ in.^{4}, distribution factor = 1.0, and impact factor = 0.265, we have (from Eq. 5.12)

$$\Delta = \frac{P_T(L^3 - 555L + 4780)}{90I}$$

$$= \frac{4.0 \times 1.0 \times 1.265(64^3 - 555 \times 64 + 4780)}{90 \times 20,000}$$

$$= 0.65 \text{ in.}$$

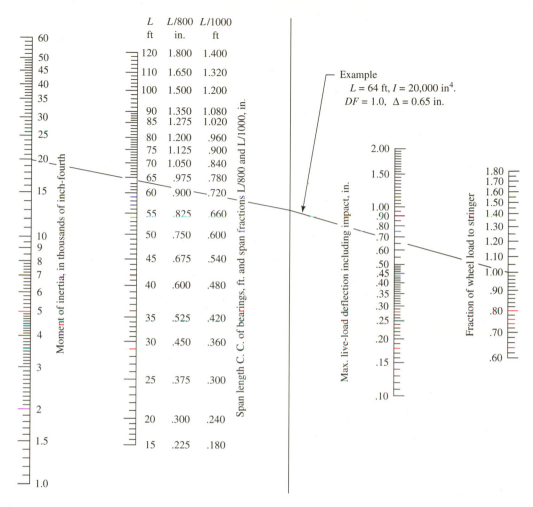

Note:
Deflections are computed for HS20-44 live load, assuming constant
cross section (EI) of stringers and modulus of elasticity, $E = 29{,}000$ ksi.

FIGURE 5.2
Nomograph for bridge beam deflections (HS20 loading) [PennDOT, 1970].

The same results can be found from the formulas of [AISC, 1989] as discussed earlier.
For the two symmetrically placed 16-kip loads, $a = 25$ ft, and from Eq. 5.6

$$\Delta = \frac{a(3L^2 - 4a^2)}{25I}$$

$$= \frac{25(3 \times 64^2 - 4 \times 25^2)}{25 \times 20{,}000}$$

$$= 0.489 \text{ in.}$$

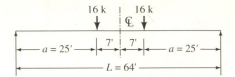

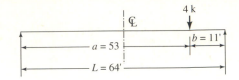

For the 4-kip load, $a = 53$ ft, $b = 11$ ft, and from Eq. 5.9

$$\Delta = \frac{ab(a + 2b)\sqrt{3a(a + 2b)}}{110\,IL}$$

$$= \frac{53 \times 11(53 + 2 \times 11)\sqrt{3 \times 53(53 + 2 \times 11)}}{110 \times 20{,}000 \times 64}$$

$$= 0.034 \text{ in.}$$

Total deflection is obtained by adding the two quantities and multiplying the result by the distribution factor plus impact:

$$\Delta = (0.489 + 0.034) \times 1.0 \times 1.265$$

$$= 0.66 \text{ in., as before.}$$

The use of these expressions will be illustrated in several following chapters.

5.3
FATIGUE IN STEEL BRIDGES

5.3.1 Introduction

The most disastrous failure of a highway bridge in recent times was that of the Point Pleasant Bridge, West Virginia, on December 15, 1967. The cause of this failure was determined to be stress corrosion and fatigue (discussed in Chapters 1 and 10). This failure focused the attention of engineers worldwide on fatigue research.

Fatigue can be broadly defined as a phenomenon of reduced material resistance under fluctuating stresses. Some engineers define *fatigue* as the fracture of structural components caused by a number of load fluctuations or reversals. ASTM E206-62T defines fatigue as

> the process of progressive localized permanent structural change occurring in a material subjected to conditions which produce fluctuating stresses and strains at some point or points, and which may culminate in cracks or complete fracture after a sufficient number of fluctuations.

Stated differently, the *fatigue limit* is the maximum stress that can be repeated indefinitely without causing fatigue failure when applying fluctuating loads.

The credit for introducing the term *fatigue* is generally given to J. V. Poncelet (1788–1867), who used it in his lectures to the workers of Metz (France) to explain certain failure phenomena under the repeated action of tension and compression. The first reports of fatigue failure date back to the early days of railroads; after locomotives and railroad cars had been running satisfactorily for several years, thin cracks appeared in their axles at points of sudden change in the cross-sectional dimensions, particularly at sharp, re-entrant corners. It was mistakenly believed that repetitive loading (and hence stressing) of axles caused the fibrous texture of malleable iron gradually to assume a crystallized structure, until Rankine [1843] observed in 1843 that a gradual deterioration took place without loss of fibrous texture. The close relationship between the failure of metal parts (axles) and the repetitiveness of loading was amply recognized by Mc-Connell [1849], whose exhaustive study of the failure of railway axles concluded:

> Our experience would seem to prove that, even with the greatest care in manufacturing, these axles are subject to a rapid deterioration, owing to the vibration and jar which operates with increased severity, on account of their peculiar form. So certain and regular is the fracture at the corner of the crank from this cause that we can almost predict in some classes of engines the number of miles that can be run before signs of fracture are visible.

His advice:

> All my experience has proved the desirableness of maintaining ... (journals of axles) as free as possible from sharp, abrupt corners and sudden alteration in diameter or sectional strength.

The French engineers recommended a careful inspection of coach axles after 70,000 km of service to avoid problems of sudden fracturing. The first scientific investigation of fatigue of metals began with the work of A. Wohler (1819–1914), who performed many experiments and designed and built many of the necessary machines and measuring instruments. He was the first to introduce the concept of limiting stress, popularly known today as the fatigue limit of a material [Timoshenko, 1953].

5.3.2 Glossary

The following terms will be used to discuss the phenomenon of fatigue and the related design aspects:

Corrosion fatigue   A phenomenon involving combined action of corrosion and cyclic loading that results in larger reduction in material resistance than either acting alone.

Endurance limit   Maximum stress below which materials under fluctuating stresses will not fail up to a quasi-infinite number of cycles.

Fatigue   A phenomenon of reduced material strength due to repetitive loading involving fluctuating tensile stresses.

Fatigue life   The number of stress cycles that will cause failure for a maximum stress and specified stress ratio.

Fatigue limit   The limiting value of the fatigue strength as the fatigue life becomes very large, also called the *endurance limit*.

Fatigue strength   The value of the maximum stress (tensile or compressive) that will cause failure at a specified number of stress cycles for a given stress ratio.

Fretting fatigue   A complex phenomenon involving a combination of wear and fatigue that occurs when two metal surfaces in contact are subjected to small repetitive *sliding movement* (e.g., in the strands of a wire rope), initiating surface cracks that may eventually grow into ordinary fatigue cracks. It also involves chemical action [Heywood, 1962; Hanson and Parr, 1965; Fuchs and Stephens, 1980].

Nonredundant-load-path structure   A structure that could collapse from the failure of a single element.

Redundant-load-path structure   A structure having load path such that a single fracture in a member *cannot* lead to collapse.

S–N **diagram**   A plot, on a semilogarithmic (or logarithmic) scale, of fatigue test results of similar specimens at the same stress ratio but at different magnitudes of maximum stress, with the maximum stress as the ordinate and the fatigue life as abscissa.

S_R–*N* **curves**   A plot on log-log scale of the number of stress cycles N (as abscissa) and the fatigue stress range S_R (as ordinate).

Stress category   Denotes the type of connection details, such as mechanically fastened or welded connections or built-up members, including plain material, as given in AASHTO Table 10.3.13, denoted alphabetically A through F.

Stress cycle   Fluctuation of stress in a member from a certain minimum to a certain maximum. The minimum and maximum stresses can be either of the same type (tensile *or* compressive) or of different types—one tensile and the other compressive. They may or may not be equal. Various kinds of stress cycles are shown in Fig. 5.3. The number of stress cycles that a member undergoes is denoted by N.

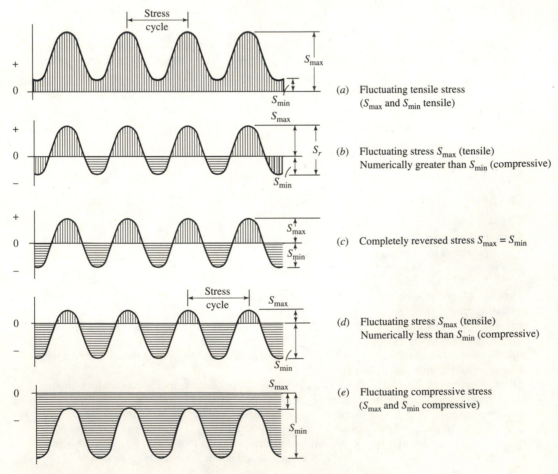

FIGURE 5.3
Various kinds of stress cycles [AISC Mkt, 1986].

Stress range   The algebraic difference between the maximum and minimum calculated stresses due to dead load, live load, impact, and centrifugal force, denoted by S_R. Tension and compression stresses are assigned opposite signs.

Stress ratio   The ratio of the algebraic minimum stress to the algebraic maximum stress in a stress cycle, usually denoted as R.

5.3.3 Mechanism of Fatigue Failure: Steel

The phenomenon of fatigue is related to the fact that a cyclic repetitive stressing of a metal bar can produce fracture by much smaller forces than are required for failure under a static load. Fatigue is commonly classified as *high-cycle* or *low-cycle*. High-cycle fatigue is defined as the fatigue caused by more than 10,000 cycles, whereas the low-cycle fatigue occurs within 10,000 cycles [Liu, 1991]. Cyclic stresses are known to initiate and then to propagate cracks in structural members, eventually weakening them. This phenomenon occurs when the cyclic stresses are above the fatigue limit. The cracks initiate after a certain number of cycles and then grow at an increasing rate, culminating in complete fracture. For cyclic stresses below the fatigue life, this phenomenon is not known to occur, nor do existing cracks propagate further. Although no definite relationship is known to exist between the ultimate strength and the endurance limit, tests show that the latter is between 40 and 50 percent of the former.

Even under cyclic load, the potential of crack initiation and growth increases in the presence of stress raisers. Stress raisers can be characterized as imperfections that create local stress concentrations. Stress raisers are generally present in most structural members as a result of the manufacturing and fabrication processes. They are very difficult to eliminate, and efforts to remove them may cause worse conditions than those originally present [Fisher, 1977; Barsome, 1981]. Some examples of stress raisers are sudden changes in the geometry of a member's cross section, welds or mechanical fasteners, and features that interrupt the smooth flow of stresses in a member. Structural details behave differently because of different stress concentration conditions present in them. Welded components or members, such as a coverplated beam or a stiffener, are examples of discontinuous members. Figure 5.4 shows a few examples of stress concentration regions caused by the geometrical discontinuities in the fabricated joints [Rolfe and Barsom, 1987]. Internal discontinuities are characterized by presence of porosity, slag inclusions, cold lops, and other comparable conditions. Surface roughness and residual stresses are also known to act as stress raisers. A discussion on the influence of various properties and composition characteristics of steel on fatigue behavior has been provided by Hanson and Parr [1965].

In bridge structures, load fluctuations, and hence stress reversals, are generally caused by the random movements of vehicles on the decks. However, a much less known phenomenon is *wind-induced fatigue*. It is felt that both low-cycle and high-cycle fatigue can be produced by high winds. Low-cycle fatigue may dominate in case of tornado and thunderstorm straight-line winds, which have short duration and generate high stresses. In areas frequented by tropical cyclones (hurricanes or typhoons) or by mountain downslope winds, both low- and high-cycle fatigues may have significant vibrational effects, causing stress reversals. The 1940 collapse of the Tacoma Narrows

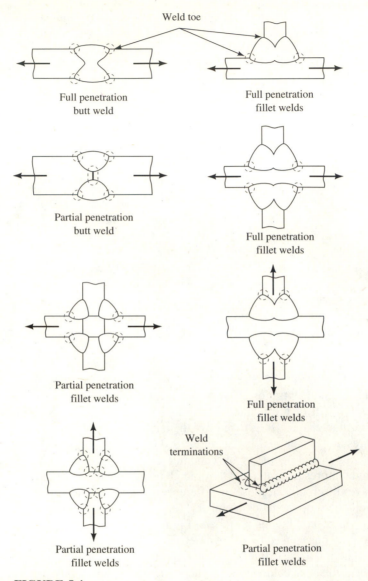

FIGURE 5.4
Stress concentration regions (indicated by dashed circles) in welded
joints [Rolfe and Barsom, 1987].

Bridge, only four months after its opening, is a classic example of wind-induced fatigue
failure. Prior to its collapse the bridge was seen having large-amplitude vibrations, both
in linear and torsional modes caused by wind [Liu, 1991]. Only limited knowledge
exists in the field of wind-induced fatigue.

A fatigue crack is characterized by the absence of apparent large deformation prior
to failure, which also makes its timely discovery difficult. This is in contrast to the popular notion of failure as a phenomenon that occurs when the material undergoes plastic

deformation. About 90 percent of all cracks usually develop in regions of high stress concentrations at the surface and subsequently propagate into the section. Sometimes the cracks are initiated at weld defects, which do not necessarily occur at the surface [Kuzmanovic and Willems, 1983].

5.3.4 Classification of Fatigue

Research has indicated that fatigue failure is not simply a behavior under fluctuating load alone; it is also highly influenced by such factors as initial discontinuities, residual stresses, variable stress cycles, and connection details. One major fatigue problem, discovered more than two decades ago, involved cracking from secondary stresses and displacement-induced stresses [Fisher, 1977; Fisher et al., 1990]. Accordingly, two types of fatigue phenomena are recognized: *load-induced fatigue,* as described earlier and recognized in present and past specifications, and *distortion-induced fatigue* [NCHRP, 1992]. The latter fatigue phenomenon, recognized in the last two decades, occurs as the result of the secondary and the displacement stresses. According to Fisher [1977], the problem developed because many bridges are essentially linear structures and are designed for in-plane loading and deflection of the main girders and the cross framing. Generally, the effects of secondary and displacement-induced stresses are seen at connections to main members. A comprehensive discussion on distortion-induced fatigue, with recommendations for its mitigation, can be found in the literature [AISC Mkt, 1986; Fisher, 1977; Fisher et al., 1990]; a summary from these references follows.

Secondary stresses are caused by the interaction of various structural components in response to the live load. These secondary stresses generally have little effect on the structural behavior of a bridge and are therefore not considered in design. However, they contribute to fatigue failure of main members, secondary bracing members, and joints. A case in point is the stringer-to-floor-beam connection, which is typically designed as a flexible connection—that is, the connection would resist only shear, not moment. However, a perfectly flexible connection is only an idealization; some end restraint or resisting moment, whose magnitude depends on the relative flexibility of the connection and the connected parts, is always developed as the connected parts resist the rotation of the end of the beam. Lateral bending of the web results from the twisting or lateral movement of the flange. Lateral bending of gusset plates is caused by the out-of-plane movements of the connected members. Bridge superstructures commonly feature a system of several parallel stringers or girders, transversely connected by cross bracings or diaphragms; when these adjacent stringers or girders deflect by different amounts, their webs are subjected to out-of-plane movement caused by the connected cross bracings or diaphragms.

When lower lateral bracings are provided to resist lateral loads caused by wind, live loading, and lateral movement, they are required to be attached to the web or the lower flanges with lateral gussets. Such connection details have low fatigue resistance and qualify for detail category E (described later). These attachments are subjected to both longitudinal stresses in the girders, due to live loads, and transverse stresses applied to the gussets by wind forces in the bracing. In a two-girder design, only one line of wind bracing is provided. With this arrangement, the wind bracings and attachments

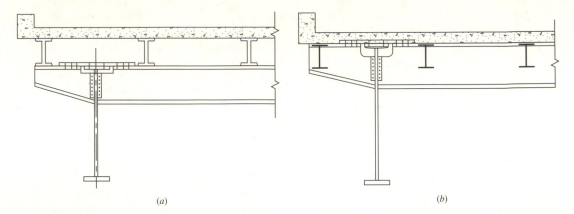

FIGURE 5.5
Typical floor beam-girder bridge sections.

are subjected to stress reversals as the wind blows from either side of the girders. In multigirder bridges, however, two lines of lateral bracings (one on each side of the bridge) are provided. With this arrangement the bracings carry wind loads from only one side and thus are not subjected to stress reversals.

Vibration of lateral bracings caused by traffic loadings can also cause out-of-plane movements, resulting in the fatigue cracking.

Another factor to recognize in the context of lateral bracings is the fact that these members are commonly built with unsymmetrical sections such as angles and tees. When axial forces develop in the bracings due to wind loads, a rotation occurs at the gusset because the neutral axes of the bracing and the gusset, being in different planes, do not coincide.

Some configurations of girder bridges involve placement of floor beams that cantilever beyond the outside of the longitudinal girders, as shown schematically in Fig. 5.5. Two stringer-placing schemes commonly used in these configurations are (1) placing stringers on top of the floor beams (Fig. 5.5(*a*)) and (2) framing stringers into the floor beams (Fig. 5.5(*b*)). In both cases, because the girders and the floor beams are perpendicular to each other, the deformation of one affects the other, resulting in out-of-plane deformations and higher secondary stresses.

Skewed and orthotropic bridges have some unusual features that give rise to secondary stresses [Wolchuck, 1990]. Skewed steel bridges are significantly more prone to out-of-plane distortions than right-angle bridges are. In orthotropic steel bridges the frequency of loading and the proportion of stress due to live load are very high. Many details are subjected to more than one cycle per truck; each axle (or wheel) may cause a stress cycle [Fisher, 1977].

The load-induced fatigue problem can be mitigated by adopting the *stress range concept*—that is, by limiting the allowable stresses to a level for which a given number of loading cycles will not cause fatigue failure. It has been recognized that the severity of the distortion-induced stresses often depends on the connection details, which the designer can control. It is therefore very important that recommended details be used in designing connections as to preclude the probability of fatigue failure.

5.3.5 Fatigue Strength of Steel: Test Results

Tests [AISC Mkt, 1986] performed on a large number of different steels indicate that

1. Up to tensile strength of 200 ksi, the fatigue limit of steel is about 50 percent of its tensile strength.
2. Fatigue strength of steel increases with tensile strength of steel; the higher the tensile strength, the higher the fatigue strength.
3. The fatigue strength decreases with increasing number of loading cycles; e.g., it is greater for 100,000 cycles than it is for 2,000,000 cycles.

Test results referring to items 2 and 3 above are shown in Figs. 5.6 and 5.7 [AISC Mkt, 1986].

4. The presence of a weld in a specimen reduces its fatigue strength considerably, as can be seen from comparison of Figs. 5.6 and 5.7. The decrease in fatigue strength is greater for steels with greater tensile strength, as indicated by the much flatter slopes of the curves in Fig. 5.7 as compared to those in Fig. 5.6.
5. For the same maximum stress, the number of stress cycles required to produce failure increases with increasing stress ratio, as shown in Fig. 5.8 [AISC Mkt, 1986].

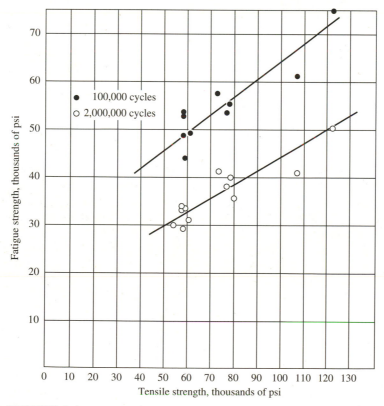

FIGURE 5.6

Comparison of fatigue strength for various cycles of loading on steel plates (as received) [AISC Mkt, 1986].

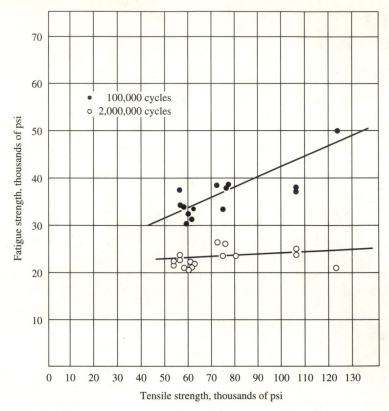

FIGURE 5.7
Comparison of fatigue strengths for various cycles loading on steel plates with transverse butt-welded joints [AISC Mkt, 1986].

Figure 5.9 shows a very useful design chart that presents a relationship between the maximum and minimum stresses (and hence the stress ratio R) and the number of stress cycles N. A point P on such a chart, corresponding to S_{max} and S_{min} and lying below the curve for N cycles, indicates that for such values of S_R and R, the fatigue failure will not occur at N cycles.

5.3.6 Design Approaches

Osgood [1982] describes two design approaches for preventing fatigue failures: "safe-life" and "fail-safe" designs. The first approach requires that no fatigue cracks develop during the whole design life of the structure. Hence, this approach assumes that the fatigue life of a structure can be predicted and that before the end of that time the structure can be repaired, replaced, or retired. If the analysis/synthesis can be accomplished sufficiently early in the design schedule, deficiencies can be eliminated to achieve the desired life of the structure. For the "safe-life" design to be successful, several elements of the design matrix must be properly considered, such as the following [Kuzmanovic

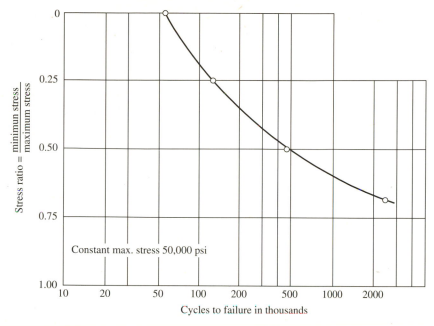

FIGURE 5.8

Results of fluctuating tension fatigue tests on transverse butt-welded joints [AISC Mkt, 1986].

and Willems, 1983]:

- The modes and frequencies of working loads during the whole operational life of the structure
- The size and shape of all components and their connections, which must be planned so as to provide sufficient reserve strength as compared to real loading
- Systematic fatigue tests of various structural groups, which must be performed to prove "safe life" experimentally
- Additional measures of environmental effects on fatigue strength

It is recognized that some structural damage and failures will inevitably occur but that catastrophic failures are unacceptable and must be prevented. This line of thought led to the concept of "fail-safe" or "damage-tolerant" design [Osgood, 1982]. This procedure is based on the concept that damage from failed components could be made tolerable by providing alternate load-carrying members and sizing them so that those remaining after the partial failure would sustain reasonable load levels. For this design approach, the elements of the design matrix that need to be considered are the following [Kuzmanovic and Willems, 1983]:

- Timely inspection of the structure and its parts to detect a crack of a predetermined minimum size so that its propagation will be slow
- Arresting a crack before it can propagate completely through a life-important structural part

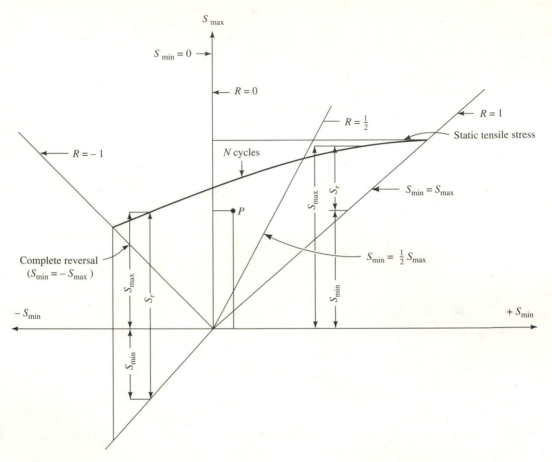

FIGURE 5.9
AWS–WRC Diagram [AISC Mkt, 1986].

- Making additional stress paths available and thus guarding against damage from failure of one structural member by providing structural redundancy, i.e., design a *redundant-* rather than a *nonredundant-*path structure

Two main parameters that form the nucleus of design for fatigue are the load (or stresses) and the fatigue life. The objective of all fatigue analysis, calculations, testing, and second-guessing is an acceptable combination of load and life. Prediction of the fatigue life of a structural member involves (1) finding a proper expression for load and its relationship with time or frequency in order to establish the allowable stress level, and (2) controlling the hardware design such that geometry and material properties do not force the actual stress at some location above that allowable value. A comprehensive discussion on methods of predicting fatigue life has been provided by Osgood [1982].

Generally speaking, four design approaches are currently in use to prevent fatigue failure [AISC Mkt, 1986]:

1. Fracture mechanics approach
2. Strain-life approach (widely used in automotive applications)

3. Stress-life reduction-factor approach (widely used in machine design)
4. Stress-life detail-category approach (generally used for structural applications, such as bridges and buildings)

The last category involves two options: limiting the stress range to acceptable levels (that is, using the stress-range concept to minimize load-induced fatigue), and choice of an appropriate connection detail that would introduce minimum stress concentration effect and secondary stresses (to minimize distortion-induced fatigue). Substantial test data have been developed that show that the two most important factors governing the fatigue strength are the stress range and the type of detail [Fisher et al., 1974]. Many different types of connection details have been worked out to improve their fatigue performance; a comprehensive assessment has been provided by Smith and Hirt [undated]. A discussion on various fatigue design approaches, as well as design and fabrication principles and practices, can be found in several references including McConnell [1849], Hall and Viest [1967], Gurney [1968], Fuchs and Stephens [1980], Rolfe and Barsom [1987], Osgood [1982], ASCI Mkt [1986], and FHWA [1990].

5.3.7 AASHTO Fatigue Design Approach

In the United States, fatigue specifications evolved from the designs of railroad bridges, which required reductions in allowable stresses for members subjected to stress reversals. During the 1940s both AREA and AASHTO (then AASHO) used the AWS bridge specifications for welded structures, which specified maximum allowable stresses in relation to the stress ratio R for three load cycle conditions: 100,000 cycles, 600,000 cycles, and 2,000,000 cycles, which was considered to be the infinite-life condition. New specifications for fatigue design of steel bridges, based on newly accumulated data and a reexamination of the old data, were adopted in 1965. These specifications provided for maximum allowable stresses for various connection and fabrication details for three load cycle conditions: 100,000 cycles, 500,000 cycles, and 2,000,000 cycles. As further data became available, minor changes were introduced, but the general format of the specifications remained the same [Fisher, 1977].

The AASHTO fatigue specifications are based on the basic premise that the

minimum life expectancy under the worst possible combination of loading cycles and the resulting stress range is between 60 and 70 years if all stress cycles are assumed to cause damage. Obviously, the minimum life is even greater since many stress cycles are below the fatigue crack growth threshold and cause no damage at all. Since highway bridges are subjected to both deterioration and obsolescence, 60 to 70 years seems a reasonable life to anticipate should fatigue be the controlling factor. For the vast majority of bridges and their components, no crack growth is expected at all.

[Fisher, 1977]. AASHTO Table 10.3.2A prescribes design life for fatigue in terms of stress (or loading) cycles for various types of roads (freeways, major highways, streets, etc.) for two average daily truck traffic (ADTT) conditions (2500 or more and less than 2500); however, the types of the trucks have not been defined. The load cycles that represent the design fatigue life therefore represent neither the total number of trucks likely to cross a bridge during its life, nor the number of 72-kip trucks (HS20 trucks) expected to cross it. Rather, they are artificial numbers corresponding to the allowable stress ranges that are expected to provide designs with a life expectancy of 60 to 70 years [AISC Mkt, 1986]. Bruhwiler, Smith, and Hirt [1990] have provided results of fatigue tests on riveted bridge members with up to 20,000,000 cycles of loading.

The allowable fatigue stress ranges for various stress categories are based on the load path characteristics of the bridge structure, which are redundant or nonredundant. A *redundant-load-path structure* is a bridge whose configuration has multiple load paths, such as a multigirder bridge or a truss bridge with multi-element eye bars. Such bridges are not likely to collapse simply from the failure of one of their components. For example, a slab-stringer bridge is not likely to collapse if one of the several stringers supporting the deck fails, because the load carried by the failed stringer will be redistributed to other stringers. On the other hand, there are structures configured such that failure of one structural element would cause the entire structure to collapse. Such structures belong to the *nonredundant-load-path structure* category, which includes flange and web plates in one- or two-girder bridges, main one-element truss members, hanger plates, and caps at single- or two-column bents. If a bridge deck is supported by only two girders, failure of one of them will cause the bridge to collapse. Similarly, the failure of a joint or a main member of the trusses of a truss bridge will also cause the bridge to collapse. Because redundant-load-path structures are relatively safer than nonredundant-load-path structures, the allowable fatigue stress ranges for various stress categories are higher for the former than for the latter. A discussion on redundancy in highway bridges has been provided by Frangopol and Nakib [1991].

Cyclic loadings, which cause cyclic stress in loaded members as shown in Fig. 5.3, can be described by various kinds of stress parameters, such as the following:

1. Maximum stress, S_{max}
2. Minimum stress, S_{min}
3. Average stress, $S_{avg} = \frac{1}{2}(S_{max} + S_{min})$
4. Stress range, $S_r = S_{max} - S_{min}$
5. Stress ratio, $R = S_{min}/S_{max}$

The current bridge design specifications [AASHTO, 1992] use the cyclic-variation parameter "stress range" (S_r) as the basic design parameter, because the other stress parameters have much smaller influence on the fatigue life [AISC Mkt, 1986].

The fatigue design approach for highway bridges is specified in AASHTO, 10.3.2. (see Tables A.10 through A.14 in Appendix A of this book for the allowable fatigue stress range and the corresponding stress cycles). Basically, four *design-life categories* are considered: 100,000, 500,000, 2,000,000, and over 2,000,000 cycles. For each of these categories, eight stress categories for redundant- and nonredundant-path structures are given.

The AASHTO fatigue design stress range values are based on studies that show that the fatigue life N_i (in numbers of cycles) and the applied stress range S_{ri} (in ksi) bear the following relationship [Fisher, 1977; AISC Mkt, 1986]:

$$N_i = AS_{ri}^{-3} \qquad (5.17)$$

or

$$S_{ri} = \left(\frac{A}{N_i}\right)^{1/3} \qquad (5.17a)$$

TABLE 5.6
A values for detail categories
[NCHRP, 1992]

Detail category	Constant A
A	2.5×10^{10}
B	1.2×10^{10}
B'	6.1×10^{9}
C	4.4×10^{9}
C'	4.4×10^{9}
D	2.2×10^{9}
E	1.1×10^{9}
E'	3.9×10^{8}

where the constant A is a function of the fatigue behavior of a connection detail whose values are shown in Table 5.6 [NCHRP, 1992].

In Fig. 5.10 the design stress ranges are shown by parallel stress-life curves (the allowable S–N curves); results obtained from these curves are given in Appendix A (Tables A.10 and A.11). The allowable stresses for redundant-load-path structures correspond to those given by the curves, whereas those for nonredundant-load-path structures are somewhat smaller (about 80%). The allowable stress ranges for the nonredundant-load-path structures for the "over 2,000,000 cycles" design-life category are about the same as, or somewhat smaller than, the corresponding values for the redundant-load-path structures [AISC Mkt, 1986].

Experimental data overwhelmingly show that the most important factors governing the fatigue strength are the stress range and the type of connection detail [Fisher, 1977]. Accordingly, the current bridge specifications [AASHTO, 1992] specify maximum stress ranges for various kinds of connection detail. The eight stress categories, A through F (including B' and E', which were created later and added to the six initial categories) are characterized by details of welding (i.e., the manner in which the two components are welded together) as encountered in practice. AASHTO Table 3.10.1B (Table A.12, Appendix A) describes various kinds of welded connections, each of which corresponds to a specific stress category. These stress categories can be summarized as follows [Fisher, 1977; AISC Mkt, 1986]:

1. Stress category A consists of plain material: base metal with rolled or cleaned surfaces or good quality flame-cut edges with *ANSI smoothness* of 1,000 or less. This category provides the highest fatigue strength.

2. Stress category B covers built-up members and such connections as (1) continuous longitudinal filled or groove welds, (2) full-penetration transverse groove welds ground flush, (3) tapered splices with the weld reinforcement removed, (4) 24-inch-radius curved transitions for flange plates or groove-welded attachments, and (5) bolted joints. The allowable $S_{R,\text{fat}}$–N curve (Fig. 5.10) for category B represents 95 percent confidence limits for the lower 95 percent survival, applied to data obtained from tests conducted at Lehigh University. Confidence limits and structural reliability, as related to the probabilistic design approach, have been discussed by Osgood [1982].

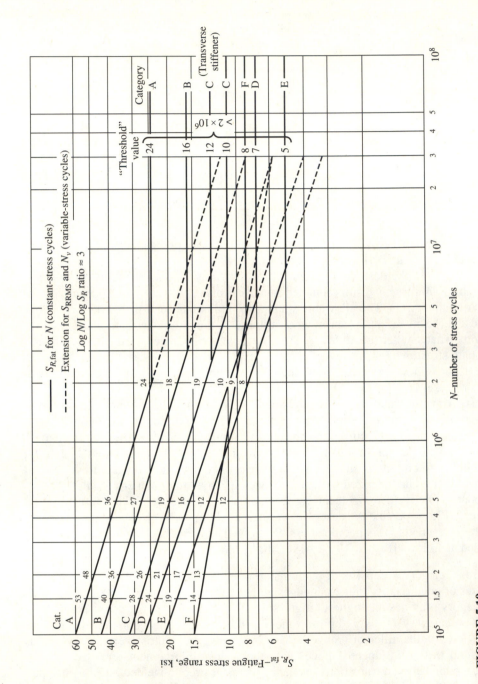

FIGURE 5.10

S_R–N curves [Fisher, 1977].

364

3. Stress category B' covers bare metal and weld metal in coverplated rolled or built-up members connected by full-penetration groove welds with reinforcement left in place, or by continuous partial-penetration groove welds parallel to the direction of applied stress.

4. Stress category C covers (1) transverse stiffeners or attachments, (2) full-penetration transverse groove welds with the reinforcement not removed, (3) 6-in. radius curve transitions for groove-welded attachments, and (4) stud-type shear connectors. The allowable $S_{R,\text{fat}}$–N curve (Fig. 5.10) for this category represents the lower 95 percent confidence limit from tests of welded beams and girders with transverse stiffeners welded to either the web alone or to the web and tension flange, conducted at Lehigh University [Fisher et al., 1974].

5. Stress category D covers (1) 4-in. attachments, (2) 2-in. radius curved transitions for groove or filled welded attachments, and (3) riveted joints. The $S_{R,\text{fat}}$–N curve for this category is based on the lower 95 percent confidence limit on test data obtained from tests at Lehigh University.

6. Stress category E covers (1) ends of cover plates fillet-welded to flanges not greater than 0.8 in. thick, (2) attachments longer than 4 in., (3) intermediate longitudinal fillet welds, and (4) fillet-welded lap joints. The test specimens included partial-length cover plates welded to rolled beams, rolled beams with full-length cover plates, and welded beams. The $S_{N,\text{fat}}$–R curve for this category is based on the lower 95 percent confidence limits on the Lehigh University tests. Category E details are not permitted with nonredundant structures, because the allowable stresses derived as discussed previously would be too low for practical use [AISC Mkt, 1986].

7. Stress category E' covers (1) ends of cover plates fillet-welded to flanges greater than 0.8 in. thick and (2) girder flanges greater than 1 in. thick that pierce through the web of another girder and are fillet-welded to each side of that web. The $S_{N,\text{fat}}$–R curve for this category is based on the lower 95 percent confidence limits on the Lehigh University tests.

8. Stress category F covers only shear stress on the throat of fillet welds and applies to continuous or intermittent longitudinal or transverse fillet welds. The allowable $S_{N,\text{fat}}$–R curve for this category is based on data obtained from tests at the University of Illinois [Wilson, 1944].

A comprehensive discussion on various kinds of stress categories can be found in reference AISC Mkt [1986]. Munse, Stallmeyer, and Drew [1968] and Fisher [1984] have provided valuable discussion on the fatigue behavior of riveted and bolted joints. Example 5.2 illustrates the application of Eqs. 5.17 and 5.17a for calculating allowable fatigue stresses according to AASHTO 1992 specifications.

EXAMPLE 5.2. Calculate the allowable fatigue stresses for (1) joints in stress categories C and E, with $N = 2 \times 10^6$ cycles in each case and (2) joints in stress category E', with $N = 2 \times 10^6$ and 500,000 cycles.

Solution. The allowable fatigue stress can be determined from Eq. 5.17a:

$$S_{\text{ri}} = \left(\frac{A}{N}\right)^{1/3} \tag{5.17a}$$

Values of constant A for various stress categories (i.e., for the type of weld details as described in Appendix A, Table A.13) are obtained from Table 5.6. All cases pertain to the redundant load path structures.

For stress category C, $A = 4.4 \times 10^9$. With $N = 2 \times 10^6$ cycles,

$$S_{\text{ri}} = \left(\frac{4.4 \times 10^9}{2 \times 10^6}\right)^{1/3} = 13 \text{ ksi}$$

For stress category E, $A = 1.1 \times 10^6$. With $N = 2 \times 10^6$ cycles,

$$S_{\text{ri}} = \left(\frac{1.1 \times 10^9}{2 \times 10^6}\right)^{1/3} = 8.2 \text{ ksi}$$

For stress category E', $A = 3.9 \times 10^6$. With $N = 2 \times 10^6$ cycles,

$$S_{\text{ri}} = \left(\frac{3.9 \times 10^8}{2 \times 10^6}\right)^{1/3} = 5.8 \text{ ksi}$$

However, with $N = 500,000$ cycles,

$$S_{\text{ri}} = \left(\frac{3.9 \times 10^8}{0.5 \times 10^6}\right)^{1/3} = 9.2 \text{ ksi}$$

These allowable fatigue stresses can be verified from Appendix A, Table A.10. Note that in this table, the stress value of 8.2 ksi has been rounded off to 8 ksi.

5.3.8 Application of Fatigue Specifications to Design

A comprehensive discussion on design of highway bridges for fatigue and related AASHTO design philosophy can be found in Fisher [1977, with examples], AISC Mkt [1986], and Dexter and Fisher [1997]; a brief summary has been provided by Fisher et al. [1978]. Design for fatigue involves limiting the actual stress range to those specified in AASHTO Table 10.3.1A (allowable stresses for various stress categories). The loadings, lateral load distribution factors, and impact factors used for computing the stress range for fatigue check are the same as those used for the normal strength considerations. AASHTO 10.3.2 mandates the following:

1. The number of cycles of maximum stress range to be considered from AASHTO Table 10.3.2A (see Tables A.10 and A.11 in Appendix A of this book) unless traffic and loadometer survey or other considerations indicate otherwise.

AASHTO Table 10.3.2A (Appendix Tables A.13 and A.14) separately specifies the design life categories for the main (longitudinal) load-carrying members, transverse members, and details subjected to wheel loads. The main load-carrying members should be checked for two separate AASHTO highway loadings: the truck loading and the lane loading. However, the transverse members and details subjected to wheel loads are to be checked for truck loading only.

The footnote to AASHTO Table 10.3.2A calls for a special procedure to be used for computing the stress ranges for the main (longitudinal) load-carrying members in the design-life category of "over 2,000,000 cycles." For such cases the stress range is to be calculated by placing a *single truck* on the bridge and distributing its weight to the girders as specified in AASHTO 3.23, which would result in a lateral load distribution factor of $S/7$ instead of $S/5.5$. For this loading case, the shear in steel girders is limited to $0.58F_yDt_wC$, where C is the *web buckling coefficient* (ratio of the buckling shear stress to the yield shear stress) as specified in AASHTO, 10.34.4.

2. Allowable fatigue stresses shall apply to those Group Loadings that include live load or wind load.

   Dead loads are of permanent nature, so they do not cause stress variations and therefore do not affect the stress range. Accordingly, the dead loads are not included in the group loadings considered for fatigue design.

3. The number of cycles of stress range to be considered for wind loads in combination with dead loads is to be 100,000 cycles, except for structures where other considerations indicate a substantially different number of cycles.

   The specific members and details that require a fatigue check should be carefully identified to satisfy the design requirements and avoid potential future failure problems. *Fatigue problems arise only when tensile stresses are involved*, so only those members need to be fatigue-checked that are expected to undergo a large number of stress reversals or a large number of variations of tensile stress. For example, the top chords of a simply supported truss bridge are always in compression under the dead load and the dead-plus-live-load conditions; accordingly, these members need not be fatigue-checked. On the other hand, stresses in the bottom chords of the same truss are always tensile and vary under the live load condition. Thus, these members would need to be fatigue-checked. In the case of continuous-span trusses, the chord members that will be subjected to stress reversal or fluctuations in tensile stresses should be carefully identified for fatigue checking. The diagonal and vertical members are usually subjected to stress reversals as the live load passes from one side of the truss to the other side; therefore, they would need to be fatigue-checked.

   Similar principles can be applied to simple or continuous-span beams and girders to determine the need for fatigue checking. The top flange of a simple span beam is always in compression regardless of the loading conditions; hence, it need not be fatigue-checked. The bottom flange, however, is always in tension, which increases as the live load is applied; therefore, it would need to be fatigue-checked.

   In continuous beams, the stress conditions are markedly different. Near the interior supports, the negative dead-load moments are usually larger than the positive live-load moments in the same region, resulting in net compressive stress in the bottom flange in this region. Thus, the bottom flange in this portion of the beam need not be fatigue-checked, but the top flange should be. Stress conditions in the midspan segments of these beams are just the opposite. The positive dead-load moments in these regions are usually larger than the negative live-load moments, which keep the top flange in this portion of the beam always in compression, obviating the need to check it for fatigue. Between these two regions, tensile stresses occur in both the top and the bottom flanges, which, obviously, would need to be fatigue-checked.

5.4
FATIGUE IN REINFORCED AND PRESTRESSED CONCRETE BRIDGES

Since concrete, unlike steel, is essentially a composite material, its fatigue strength is related to the fatigue strength of its constituent materials. The subject of fatigue strength of concrete structures therefore has three components: concrete, steel, and combination of the two. A comprehensive discussion on various topics related to fatigue of reinforced and prestressed concrete structures can be found in ACI [1974c, 1982]; brief summaries can be found in texts on reinforced and prestressed concrete structures.

5.4.1 Concrete

It is recognized that, for all practical purposes, concrete does not have a fatigue limit. Studies [McCall, 1958; Murdock and Kesler, 1958; Nordby, 1958; Stelson and Cernica, 1959; Hilsdorf and Kesler, 1966; Siriaksorn and Naaman, 1979] indicate that, in general, concrete in direct tension or compression can sustain a fluctuating stress of between 0 and 50 to 55 percent of its static strength for about ten million cycles. To design for a fatigue life of ten million cycles, the ACI Committee on Fatigue recommends [ACI, 1974b,c; PCI, 1977] the following expression:

$$f_{cr} = 0.4 f_c' - \frac{f_{min}}{2} \tag{5.18}$$

For the *S–N* relationship, the following has been suggested by Aas-Jakobson and Lenschow [1973] and modified by Tepfers and Kutti [1979], who suggested the value 0.0685 for β:

$$\frac{f_{max}}{f_c'} = 1 - \beta \left(1 - \frac{f_{min}}{f_{max}} \right) \log N \tag{5.19}$$

Unlike steel, the fatigue life of concrete depends on many loading parameters, such as f_{min}/f_{max}, f_{mean}/f_{max}, f_{mean}/f_c', f_{max}/f_c', and $(f_{max} - f_{min})/f_c'$. In view of the poor correlation between the test data and the predicted fatigue life, Park [1990] suggested a probability-based method.

A comprehensive summary of fatigue strength of plain concrete has been presented by Neville [1981]. According to this summary, fatigue strength of concrete is improved by cyclic loading below its fatigue limit. It is theorized that this increase in strength is due to densification of concrete caused by the initial low-stress level cycling. The fatigue behavior of concrete in compression and flexure is similar. Both in compression and in flexure-tension, the frequency of the alternating load (at least within the limits of 70 to 2,000 cycles per minute) does not affect the resulting fatigue strength (higher frequency is of little practical significance). Tests have indicated that at a given number of cycles, fatigue failure occurs at the same fraction of the ultimate strength and is thus independent of the magnitude of this strength and the age of concrete. According to Helgason et al. [1975], the deterioration of the bond between the cement paste and the aggregate is responsible for this failure, as evidenced by high-speed fatigue tests on small specimens of plain concrete, which showed fewer broken aggregate particles than did specimens that failed in a static test [Assimacopoulos, Warner, and Ekberg, 1959]. Air-entrained concrete and lightweight concrete exhibit the same fatigue behavior as the normal-weight concrete. Interestingly, with the exception of loading involving stress reversals, the fatigue strength of concrete is *increased* by rest periods; the increase is proportional to the rest periods' duration between 1 and 5 minutes, beyond which there is no increase in the fatigue strength. It should be recognized, however, that any fatigue cracks caused in concrete will act as stress raisers for reinforcement in a concrete member.

5.4.2 Reinforced Concrete Members

A comprehensive discussion on the fatigue strength of reinforced concrete can be found in ACI [1974b,c; 1982], and Helgason et al. [1975]; brief summaries have been presented in [ACI, 1977] and in [Nilson and Winter, 1991]. Test results show that (1) the fatigue strength at which two million or more cycles can be applied without causing failure is independent of the grade of steel, (2) the sustainable stress range ($f_{max} - f_{min}$) without causing fatigue failure depends on the magnitude of f_{min}, and (3) in deformed bars the degree of stress concentration at the junction of the rib and the cylindrical body of the bar plays a significant role in reducing the safe stress range.

Fatigue failure of concrete requires both (1) cyclic loading generally in excess of 1 million load cycles and (2) a change of reinforcement stress in each cycle of about 20 ksi. Since in most concrete structures dead load stresses (i.e., f_{min}) account for a significant portion of the service load stresses, case (2) is infrequent (i.e., the stress range $f_{max} - f_{min}$ is small). Consequently, reinforced concrete structures rarely fail in fatigue.

Essentially, the ribs and the lugs cause sudden discontinuity in the surface of the bar, act as stress raisers, and cause stress concentrations in the reinforcing bar. This stress concentration depends on the geometry of the lug, which is defined by the lug's r/h ratio (Fig. 5.11). The value of this ratio is typically in the order of 0.25 for the North American deformed bars [Jhamb and MacGregor, 1974]. Based on the results of extensive tests [Corley, Hanson, and Helgason, 1978], ACI Committee 343 [ACI, 1977] has recommended the following formula for safe fatigue strength of reinforcing bars for more than two million cycles:

$$f_{sr} = 21 - 0.33 f_{min} + 8\left(\frac{r}{h}\right) \qquad (5.20)$$

where f_{sr} = safe stress range, in ksi
f_{min} = minimum stress, positive in tension, negative in compression, in ksi
r = lug-base radius—radius of the circular transition curve (Fig. 5.11)
h = height of lug, measured from the base of the lug away from the transition curve (Fig. 5.11)

The value of the ratio r/h, when unknown, is recommended to be 0.3. It is pointed out, however, that the current AASHTO specifications [AASHTO, 1992] do not contain this provision, but it is included in the AASHTO–LRFD specifications [AASHTO, 1994].

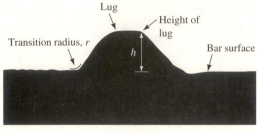

(*a*) Lug profile

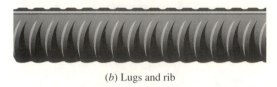

(*b*) Lugs and rib

FIGURE 5.11
Base radius r, and lug height, h, of a deformed reinforcing bar: (*a*) lug profile, (*b*) lugs and rib [Corley, Hanson, and Helgason, 1978].

5.4.3 Prestressed Concrete Members

Considerable research has been done on fatigue life of prestressing strands [Lane and Ekberg, 1959; Tide and Van Horn, 1966; Edwards and Picard, 1972; Gylltoft, 1978, 1979] and prestressed concrete beams (both pretensioned and post-tensioned) [Ozall and Ardaman, 1956; Ekberg, Walther, and Slutter, 1957; Ruble and Drew, 1962; Warner and Hulsbos, 1962; Sawko and Saha, 1968; Bennet and Dave, 1969; Hanson, Hulsbos, and Van Horn, 1970; Price and Edwards, 1970; Fauchart and Trinh, 1973; Fauchart, Kavyrchine, and Trinh, 1975; Dave and Garwood, 1975; Irwin, 1977; Rabaat et al., 1978, 1979; Overmann, Breen, and Frank, 1984; Harajli and Naaman, 1985; Naaman, 1987, 1989; Al-Zaid, Naaman, and Nowak, 1988] in the last forty years. Tests on prestressed concrete beams (model and full-scale) included both fully prestressed and partially prestressed beams, under both constant and random-amplitude fatigue loading [Naaman and Founas, 1991]. For reasons of economy, partially prestressed beams are typically designed with a combination of ordinary reinforcing bars and prestressing strands. These beams are designed for zero or little tension (uncracked sections) under dead loads and as cracked beams under working (live) loads. The risk of fatigue failure in the partially prestressed beams is considered greater than for the fully stressed beams for several reasons. Under repetitive loads, stresses and stress ranges in the partially prestressed concrete beams are generally higher than those in the equivalent fully prestressed beams. Opening and closing of structural cracks causes the possibility of fretting between the concrete and steel and between the wires of the same strands (due to twisting and untwisting of strands during the cyclic loading) [Naaman, 1982b, 1989; Harajli and Naaman, 1985]. Tests under cyclic loading on full-scale pretensioned prestressed concrete composite beams by Rabaat et al. [1978] indicated failure of some specimens at about three million cycles; the calculated first-cycle stress range in the strands of these specimens was only

13 ksi, a low value. This concern led to several recent investigations of partially pre-stressed concrete beams, discussed by Naaman [1982b,], Reese [1983], and Harajli and Naaman [1984]. Design considerations for fatigue life of partially prestressed concrete beams and researchers' recommendations are presented by Siriaksorn and Naaman [1979], Naaman and Siriaksorn [1979], Naaman [1985], and Naaman and Founas [1991].

The fatigue strength of prestressing steel depends on its type (that is, the wire, strand, bars, etc.), steel treatment, anchorage type, and the degree of bond. The fatigue strengths of wires, for a given number of loading cycles, is higher than for the rolled steels. Stress relieving of prestressing steels is reported to significantly increase their fatigue life [Naaman, 1989]. The test data for cyclic loading of prestressing steels can be shown by typical S–N curves as shown in Fig. 5.12 [Naaman, 1980], or by a

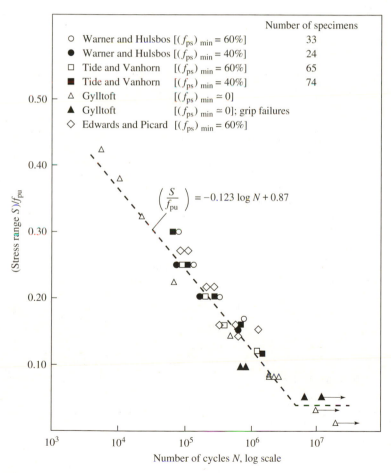

FIGURE 5.12

Typical S–N curve for prestressing strands [Naaman, 1980].

Goodman diagram [Ekberg, Walther, and Slutter, 1957] as shown in Fig. 5.13 [Eckberg, Walther and Slutter, 1957]. These diagrams are essentially similar to those used for fatigue data of steels discussed earlier. FIP Commission [1976] recommends using a *Smith diagram,* as shown in Fig. 5.14, which is a modification of the Goodman diagram; it uses mean stress instead of the minimum stress as abscissa [Naaman, 1982a]. Presently, two million cycles are considered as normal for most applications. Tests on prestressed concrete beams by various researchers [Bennet and Dave, 1969; Fauchart and Trinh, 1973; Fauchart, Kavyrchine, and Trinh, 1975; Dave and Garwood, 1975; Irwin, 1977] have shown that specimens under cyclic loading sustained more than three million cycles without failure. Tests by Harajli and Naaman [1985] on 4.5×9 in. $\times 9$ ft long, fully and partially prestressed concrete beams indicate a fatigue life of over five million cycles. When tested to failure after five million cycles of loading, these beams showed practically no reduction in their ultimate load capacity, although a reduction in ductility was generally observed. Tests by Roller et al. [1995] on two 70-ft-long 54-in.-deep bulb-T (10-ft-wide top flange) high-strength (10,000 psi) prestressed concrete beams showed that the beams withstood more than 5 million cycles of fatigue loading and also satisfied all serviceability requirements. Tests [Naaman, 1982a; Harajli and Naaman, 1985; Naaman and Founas, 1991] indicate that fatigue failure in fully and partially prestressed concrete beams results from the fatigue fracturing of either the prestressing strands or the reinforcing steel. The fatigue life of prestressed concrete beams can therefore be predicted on the basis of the fatigue lives of prestressing and reinforcing steels.

The higher risk associated with the partially prestressed concrete beams, pointed out in an earlier paragraph, should not be construed to mean that such beams should not be used in practice. In fact, partially prestressed beams have several advantages over fully prestressed beams, such as better control of camber; economy, resulting from savings in prestressing steel and the work of tensioning and end anchorages; economical utilization of mild steel; and possible greater resilience in the structure [Leonhardt, 1977; Lin, 1977; Lin and Burns, 1981]. Such beams can be designed for *small* values of stress changes due to repeated loads (stress range), leading to improved and acceptable fatigue life. This can be accomplished by appropriate selection of the partial prestressing ratio and the detailing of the reinforcement. Design of partially prestressed concrete beams is now a well-understood concept. A comprehensive treatment of the subject has been presented by Lin and Burns [1981]; a summary of the design procedures has been provided by Siriaksorn and Naaman [1979].

From a practical standpoint, it should be recognized that there is no fundamental difference between fully and partially prestressed beams, except that concrete in partially prestressed beams would have some tension in the precompressed tensile zone. For that matter, even the fully prestressed beams, typically designed for no tensile stresses under any loading conditions, may have some tension when subjected to overload conditions. For example, such an overload condition may occur in bridges during the passage of exceptionally heavy vehicles. Although the term "partially prestressed" is not explicitly mentioned in the AASHTO specifications [1992], they do permit (9.15.2.2) a tensile stress of $6\sqrt{f_c'}$ in the precompressed tensile zone of members with bonded reinforcement. This aspect of the specifications is clarified in AASHTO–LRFD specifications, 5.9 [1994]. Of course, if concrete is not permitted to carry any

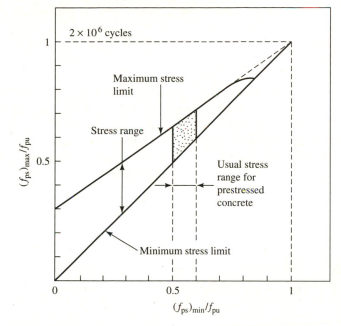

FIGURE 5.13
Typical Goodman diagram for prestressing wires and strands
[Ekberg, Walther, and Slutter, 1957].

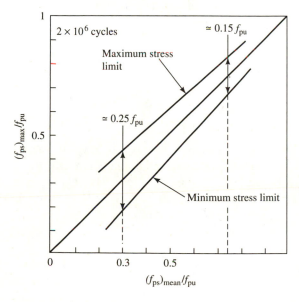

FIGURE 5.14
Typical Smith diagram for
prestressing strands [FIP, 1976].

tension at the cracked sections, the entire tension force must be carried by the non-prestressed reinforcement.

Studies suggest that prestressing steel has practically no endurance limit [Tide and Van Horn, 1966; Edwards and Picard, 1972; Sawko and Saha, 1968; Price and Edwards, 1970]. It should be recognized that stress range is the most significant parameter affecting the fatigue life of both reinforcing and prestressing steels. However, a significant difference between reinforced and prestressed concrete should be recognized. In a reinforced-concrete beam there may be significant stress variation in stresses in the reinforcing bar under dead and live load conditions, particularly if the live loads are large. However, in prestressed concrete beams the variation in stresses in prestressing steel due to live load seldom exceeds about 10,000 psi. Thus, as long as concrete does not crack (as in fully prestressed beams), there exists very little possibility of fatigue failure in prestressed concrete beams. Test data from fatigue studies indicate a fatigue life of about two million cycles at a stress range of 10 percent of the ultimate strength of the prestressing steel and a minimum strength not above 60 percent of the ultimate. For fatigue life at other stress ranges, Naaman [1982b] and Harajli and Naaman [1985] suggest (Fig. 5.12) the following expression for the S-N curve for prestressing strands derived from the data of several researchers:

$$\frac{\Delta f_{\text{ps}}}{f_{\text{pu}}} = -0.123 \log N + 0.87 \tag{5.21}$$

where Δf_{ps} = range of stress in prestressing steel
$\quad\quad\; f_{\text{pu}}$ = ultimate strength of prestressing steel
$\quad\quad\;\; N$ = number of loading cycles

ACI Committee 215 [ACI, 1974b] suggests a maximum stress range of $0.10 f_{\text{pu}}$ for prestressing wire and $0.12 f_{\text{pu}}$ for prestressing steels [Naaman, 1982a]. The current AASHTO specifications do not contain any provisions for the permissible stress range in prestressed beams; however, the following limits are proposed for prestressing strands of curved profile [AASHTO, 1994, 5.5.3.3]:

1. For radius of curvature 12 ft and under: 10 ksi
2. For radius of curvature exceeding 30 ft: 18 ksi
3. For radius of curvature between 12 and 30 ft, use linear interpolation.

Ekberg, Walther, and Slutter [1957] suggest a rational method of predicting the fatigue life of prestressed concrete beams. This method uses the fatigue failure envelopes of concrete and prestressing steel and relates them to the stress-moment diagram for a prestressed concrete beam. It is to be noted that the fatigue envelopes for different steels vary [Lane and Ekberg, 1959; Ruble and Drew, 1962; Warner and Hulsbos, 1962]. A summary of this methodology is presented in [Lin and Burns, 1981].

REFERENCES

AASHTO. (1991). *Guide Specifications for Alternate Load Factor Design Procedures for Steel Beam Bridges Using Braced Compact Sections—1991*, AASHTO, Washington, DC.

———. (1992). *Standard Specifications for Highway Bridges,—1992,* 15th ed., AASHTO, Washington, DC.

———. (1994). *AASHTO–LRFD Bridge Design Specifications,* 1st ed., AASHTO, Washington, DC.

Aas-Jakobson, K., and Lenschow, R. (1973). "Behavior of Reinforced Columns Subjected to Fatigue Loadings," *ACI. Proc.,* March, pp. 635–652.

Abeles, P. W., Barton, F. W., and Brown, E. I. (1969). "Fatigue Behavior of Prestressed Concrete Bridge Beams," First Intl. Symp. Concrete Bridge Design, *ACI Special Pub. SP–23,* ACI, Chicago, pp. 579–600.

ACI. (1974). "Consideration for Design of Concrete Structures Subjected to Fatigue Loading," report by ACI Committtee 215, *ACI J. Proc.,* 71 (3), March, pp. 97–121.

———. (1974a). "Deflection of Concrete Structures," ACI Special Pub. SP-43, ACI, Detroit, MI.

———. (1974b). "Consideration for Design of Concrete Structures Subjected to Fatigue Loading," report by ACI Committee 215, *ACI J. Proc.,* 71(3), March, pp. 97–121.

———. (1974c). "Abeles Symposium: Fatigue of Concrete," ACI Special Pub. SP–41, ACI, Detroit, MI.

———. (1977). "Analysis and Design of Concrete Bridges," ACI Report 343R–77, ACI Committee 343, Detroit, MI.

———. (1982). "Fatigue of Concrete Structures," ACI Special Pub. SP–75, ACI, Detroit, MI.

———. (1995). *Building Code Requirements for Structural Concrete (ACI 318-95) and Commentary (318R-95),* ACI, Farmington Hills, MI.

AISC. (1989). *Manual of Steel Construction—Allowable Stress Design,* 9th ed. AISC, New York.

AISC Mkt. (1986). *Highway Structures Design Handbook,* vols. I and II, AISC Marketing, Inc., Pittsburgh.

Allen, D. E., and Rainer, J. H. (1976). "Vibration Criteria for Long-Span Floors," *Canadian J. Civ. Eng.,* 3(2), pp. 165–171.

Allen, D. E., Rainer, J. H., and Pernica, G. (1987). "Building Vibrations Due to Human Activities," *Proc. Structures Congress of Amer. Soc. Civ. Eng.* (ASCE), New York.

Allen, D. E., and Murray, T. M. (1993). "Design Criterion for Vibrations Due to Walking," *AISC Eng. J.,* 30(4), 4th qtr., pp. 117–129.

Al-Zaid, R. Z., Naaman, A. E., and Nowak, A. S. (1988). "Partially Prestressed Composite Beams under Sustained and Cyclic Loads," *ASCE J. Str. Eng.,* 114(2), February, pp. 269–291.

ASCE. (1958). "Deflection Limitations of Bridges—Progress Report of the Committee on Deflection Limitations of Bridges of the Structural Division," *Proc. ASCE J. Str. Div.,* 84(ST3) paper no. 1633, May, pp. 1633-1–1633-20.

Assimacopoulos, B. M., Warner, R. E., and Ekberg, C. E. (1959). "High-Speed Fatigue Tests on Small Specimens of Plain Concrete," *J. Prestressed-Concrete Inst.,* 4(2), February, pp. 52–70.

Bachmann, H. (1984). "Vibrations of Building Structures Caused by Human Activities; Case Study of a Gymnasium," *Techincal Translation 2077,* National Research Council of Canada, Ottawa, Ontario.

Bachmann, H. (1992). "Case Studies of Structures with Man-Induced Vibrations," *ASCE J. Str. Eng.,* 118(3), March, pp. 631–647.

Bachmann, H., and Ammann, W. (1987). "Vibrations in Structures Induced by Man and Machines," *Structural Engineering Document No. 3e,* IABSE, Zurich, Switzerland.

Barsom, J. M. (1981). "Fatigue Considerations for Steel Bridges," *ASTM STP738,* ASTM, Philadelphia.

Baumann, K., and Bachmann, H. (1987). "Durch Menschen verursachte dynamische Lasten und deren Auswirkungen auf Balkentragwerke (Man-Induced Dynamic Loads and Their Influence on Beam Structures)," in Basel Birkhauser, ed., *Report No. 7501-3,* Institute of Structural Engineering (IBK), Swiss Federal Institute of Technology (ETH), Zurich (in German).

Bennet, E. W., and Dave, N. J. (1969). "Test Performance and Design of Concrete Beams with Limited Prestress," *Struct. Eng.* (London), 47(12), December, pp. 487–496.

Bresler, B., Lin, T. Y., and Scalzi, J. B. (1968). *Design of Steel Structures,* 2nd ed., John Wiley & Sons, New York.

Bruhwiler, E., Smith, I. F. C., and Hirt, M. A. (1990). "Fatigue and Fracture of Riveted Bridge Members," *ASCE. J. Str. Eng.,* 116(1), January, pp. 198–214.

Burns, N. H. (1993). "Static and Fatigue Behavior of Pretensioned Composite Bridge Girders Made with High-Strength Concrete," *PCI J.,* 38(3), pp. 116–129.

Corley, W. G., Hanson, J. M., and Helgason, T. (1978). "Design of Reinforced Concrete for Fatigue," *ASCE J. Str. Div.,* 104(ST6), pp. 921–932.

Dave, N. H., and Garwood, J. J. (1975). "The Limit State Behavior of 'Class-3' Post-tensioned Beams under Short-Term, Sustained, and Fatigue Loadings," *Behavior in Service of Concrete Structures,* Colloq. Intl. Assoc. Bridge and Struct. Eng. (IABSE), FIP, CEB, RILEM, IASS, Liege, Belgium, June, pp. 319–330.

Dexter, R., and Fisher, J. M. (1997). "Fatigue and Fracture," in *Steel Design Handbook—LRFD Method,* McGraw-Hill Companies, New York, pp. 8-1–8-53.

Dieckmann, D. A. (1958). "Study of the Influence of Vibration on Man," in *Ergonomics,* I, 4, Taylor and Francis, London, pp. 347–355.

Edwards, A. D., and Picard, A. (1972). "Fatigue Characteristics of Prestressing Strands," Proc. *Inst. Civ. Eng.,* 53, September, pp. 323–336.

Ekberg, C. E., Jr., Walther, R. E., and Slutter, R. G. (1957). "Fatigue Resistance of Prestressed Concrete Beams in Bending," *ASCE J. Str. Div.,* 83(ST4), July, pp. 1–17.

Fauchart, J., Kavyrchine, M., and Trinh, J. (1975). *Annales de L'Institut Technique du Batiment et des Travaux Publics,* March, pp. 23–32.

Fauchart, J., and Trinh, J. (1973). "Comportement Sous Charges Repetees de Poutrelles en Beton Arme Preconstraint," *Annales de L'Institut Technique du Batiment et des Travaux Publics,* Paris, September–October, pp. 87–132.

Ferguson, P. M. (1979). *Reinforced Concrete Fundamentals,* John Wiley & Sons, New York.

FHWA. (1990). "Economical and Fatigue-Resistance Steel Details," *Pub. No. FHWA-HI-90-043,* Federal Highway Administration, Washington, DC.

FIP. (1976). *Report on Prestressing Steels: Types and Properties,* Federation Internationale de la Precontrainte Commission on Prestressing Steel Systems, Waxham Spring, England, August.

Fisher, J. W. (1977). *Bridge Fatigue Guide: Design and Details,* American Institute of Steel Construction, New York.

———. (1984). *Fatigue and Fracture in Steel Bridges: Case Studies,* John Wiley & Sons, New York.

Fisher, J. W., Albrecht, P. A., Yen, B. T., Klingerman, D. J., and McNamee, B. M. (1974). "Fatigue Strength of Steel Beams with Welded Stiffeners and Attachments," *NCHRP Report 147,* Transportation Research Board, Washington, DC.

Fisher, J. W., Hanson, J. M., Lally, A., Scheffey, C., and Salgo, M. N. (1978). "Fractures—Problem for Welded Bridges," ASCE Civ. Eng., September, pp. 70-73.

Fisher J. W., Jian, J., Wagner, D. C., and Yen, B. T. (1990). "Distortion-Induced Fatigue Cracking in Steel Bridges," NCHRP Report no. 336, Transportation Research Board, Washington, DC.

Frangopol, D. M., and Nakib, R. (1991). "Redundancy in Highway Bridges," *AISC Eng. J.,* 28(1), 1st qtr., pp. 45–50.

Fuchs, H. S., and Stephens, R. I. (1980). "Metal Fatigue in Engineering," John Wiley & Sons, New York.

Goldman, D. E. (1948). "A Review of Subjective Responses to Vibratory Motion of the Human Body in Frequency Range 1 to 70 c.p.s., Report NM-004-001, Naval Medical Research Institute, Annapolis, Maryland.

Grant, A., and Clark, J. H. (1969). "Performance Evaluation of a Partially Prestressed Rigid-Frame Concrete Bridge," *First Intl. Symp. Concrete Bridge Design,* ACI Special Pub. SP-23, ACI, Chicago, pp. 625–630.

Guignard, J. C., Irving, A. (1960). "Effects of a Low-Frequency Vibration on Man," *Engineering,* 190, pp. 364–67.

Gurney, R. T. (1968). *Fatigue of Welded Structures,* Cambridge University Press, Cambridge.

Gylltoft, K. (1978). "Fatigue Tests of Concrete Sleepers," Report No. 1978: 13, Div. of Structural Engineering, University of Lulea, Sweden.

———. (1979). "Bond Properties of Strands in Fatigue Loading," Report No. 1979: 22, Div. of Structural Engineering, University of Lulea, Sweden.

Hall, D. H., and Viest, I. M. (1967). "Design of Steel Structures for Fatigue," *Proc. ASCE Natnl. Meet. on Water Resources Eng.,* New York, October 16–20, p. 2.

Hanson, A., and Parr, J. G. (1965). *The Engineer's Guide to Steel,* Addison-Wesley Publishing Co., Palo Alto, CA.

Hanson, J. M., Hulsbos, C. L., and Van Horn, D. A. (1970). "Fatigue Tests of Prestressed-Concrete I-Beams," *ASCE J. Str. Div.,* 96 (ST11), November, pp. 206–226.

Harajli, M. H., and Naaman, A. E. (1984). "Deformation and Cracking of Partially Prestressed Concrete Beams under Static and Cyclic Fatigue Loading," Report No. UMEE 84RI, Department of Civil Engineering, University of Michigan, Ann Arbor, August.

———. (1985). "Static and Fatigue Tests on Partially Prestressed Beams," *ASCE J. Str. Eng.,* 111(7), July, pp. 1602–1618.

Helgason, T., Hanson, J. M., Somes, N. J., Orely, W. G., and Hognested, E. (1975). "Fatigue Strength of High-Yield Reinforcing Bars," *Report for NCHRP Projects 4-7 and 4-7/1,* PCA, Research and Development Laboratories, Skokie, IL, March.

Heywood, R. B. (1962). *Designing against Fatigue in Metals,* Van Nostrand Reinhold, New York.

Hilsdorf, H. K., and Kesler, C. E. (1966). "Fatigue Strength of Concrete under Varying Flexural Stresses," *ACI J. Proc.,* 63(10), October, pp. 1059–1075.

Irwin, C. A. K. (1977). "Static and Repetitive Loading Tests on Full-Scale Prestressed-Concrete Bridge Beams," *Report no. 802,* Transport and Road Research Laboratory, Bridge Design Div., Crowthorne, Berkshire, England.

ISO. (1989). *International Standard ISO 2631-2, Evaluation of Human Exposure to Whole-Body Vibration—Part 2: Human Exposure to Continuous and Shock-Induced Vibrations in Buildings (1 to 80 Hz),* International Standards Organization, Geneva, Switzerland.

———. (1992). *International Standard ISO 10137, Basis for Design of Structures—Serviceability of Buildings against Vibration,* International Standards Organization, Geneva, Switzerland.

Janeway, R. N. (1948). "Vehicle Vibration Limits to Fit the Passenger," *J. Soc. Automotive Engrs.,* 56(8).

Jhamb, I. C., and MacGregor, J. G. (1974). "Stress Concentrations Caused by Reinforcing Bar Deformations," *Abeles Symp.—Fatigue of Concrete,* ACI Special Pub. SP-41, ACI, Detroit, MI.

Kuzmanovic, B.O., and Willems, N. (1983). *Steel Design for Structural Engineers,* 2nd ed., Prentice Hall, Englewood Cliffs, NJ.

Lane, R. E., and Ekberg, Jr., C. E. (1959). "Repeated Load Tests on 7-Wire Prestressed Strands," *Fritz Eng. Lab. Rep.,* Lehigh University, Bethlehem, PA.

Larson, J. W., and Huzzord, R. K. (1990). "Economical Use of Cambered Steel Beams," *AISC Natnl. Steel Const. Conf.,* March.

Lenzen, K. H. (1966). "Vibration of Steel Joists," *AISC Eng. J.,* 3(3), pp. 133–136.

Leonard, D. R. (1966). "Subjective Tests on Human Reaction to Bridge Vibrations," RRL Report no. 34, Harmondsworth Road Research Laboratory, Ministry of Transport, Harmondsworth, England.

Leonhardt, F. (1977). "Recommendations for the Degree of Prestressing in Prestressed Concrete Structures," *FIP Notes,* 69, July–August, pp. 9–14.

Libby, J. R. (1976). *Modern Prestressed Concrete: Design Principles and Construction,* Van Nostrand Reinhold, New York.

Lin, T. Y. (1977). "Partial Prestressing Design Philosophies," *FIP Notes,* 69, July–August, pp. 5–9.

Lin, T. Y., and Burns, N. H. (1981). *Design of Prestressed-Concrete Structures,* 3rd ed., John Wiley & Sons, New York.

Liu, H. (1991). *Wind Engineering: A Handbook for Structural Engineers,* Prentice Hall, Englewood Cliffs, NJ.

MacGregor, J. G. (1988). *Reinforced Concrete: Mechanics and Design,* Prentice Hall, Englewood Cliffs, NJ.

Marks, J. D., and Keifer, Jr., O. (1969). "Long-Term Field Study of Stresses in a Post-Tensioned Concrete Bridge Girder," *First Intl. Symp. Concrete Bridge Design,* ACI Special Pub. SP-23, ACI, Chicago, pp. 631–654.

Matthews, C. M., Montgomery, C. J., and Murray, D. W. (1982). "Designing Floor Systems for Dynamic Response," *Struct. Eng.* Rep. No. 106, Department of Civil Engineering, University of Alberta, Edmonton, Alberta, Canada.

McCall, J. T. (1958). "Probability of Fatigue Failure of Plain Concrete," *ACI J. Proc.* 55(2), August, pp. 233–244.

McConnell, J. E. (1849). "On Railway Axles," *Proc. Inst. Mech. Engrs.,* October, 1847–1849, London.

Munse, W. H., Stallmeyer, J. E. and Drew, F. P. (1969). "Structural Fatigue and Steel Railroad Bridges," AREA, Chicago.

Murdock, J. W., (1961). "The Mechanism of Fatigue Failure in Concrete," Ph.D. thesis, Civil Engineering Department, University of Illinois, Urbana, IL.

Murdock, J. W., and Kesler, C. E. (1958). "Effect of Stress on Fatigue Strength of Plain Concrete Beams," *ACI J. Proc.* 55(2), August, pp. 221–231.

Murray, T. M. (1981). "Acceptability Criterion for Occupant-Induced Floor Vibrations," *AISC Eng. J.,* 18(2), 2nd qtr., pp. 62–70.

———. (1991). "Building Floor Vibrations," *AISC Eng. J.,* 28(3), 3rd qtr., pp. 102–109. (See also correction to this paper in *AISC Eng. J.,* 28(4), 4th qtr., 1991, p. 176.)

Naaman, A. E. (1980). "Fatigue of Partially Prestressed Beams," Preprint, *Symp. on Fatigue in Concrete Structures, ACI Annual Conv.,* Puerto Rico, September.

———. (1981). "A Proposal to Extend Some Code Provisions on Reinforcement to Partial Prestressing," *PCI J.* 26(2), March–April, pp. 74–91.

———. (1982a). *Prestressed Concrete Analysis and Design,* McGraw-Hill Companies, Inc., New York.

———. (1982b). "Fatigue in Partially Prestressed Concrete" *Fatigue of Concrete Structures,* ACI SP-75, ACI, Detroit, MI, pp. 25–46.

———. (1985). "Partially Prestressed Concrete: Review and Recommendations," *PCI J.,* 30(5), pp. 54–81.

———. (1987). "Discussion of 'Fatigue of Partially Prestressed Concrete,' by M. E. Shahawi and B. deV Batchelor," *ASCE J. Str. Eng.,* 113(11), November, pp. 2328–2329.

———. (1989). "Fatigue of Reinforcement in Partially Prestressed Beams," *Proc. ASCE Structures Congress, 1989— vol. Structural Materials,* ASCE, New York, pp. 337–381.

Naaman, A. E., and Founas, M. (1991). "Partially Prestressed Beams under Random Amplitude Fatigue Loading," *ASCE J. Str. Eng.,* 117(12), December, pp. 3742–3761.

Naaman, A. E., and Siriaksorn, A. (1979). "Serviceability Based Design of Prestressed Beams— Part 1: Analytic Formulation," *PCI J.* 24(2), April, pp. 64–89.

Nawy, E. G. (1985). *Reinforced Concrete: A Fundamental Approach,* Prentice Hall, Englewood Cliffs, NJ.

———. (1989). "Prestressed Concrete: A Fundamental Approach," Prentice Hall, Englewood Cliffs, NJ.

NCHRP. (1992). "Development of Comprehensive Bridge Specifications and Commentary: Third Draft LRFD Specifications and Commentary," 1992, NCHRP Project 12-33, Transportation Research Board, Washington, DC.

Neville, A. M. (1981). *Properties of Concrete,* 3rd ed., Pittman, Marshfield, MA.

Nilson, A. H. (1978). *Design of Prestressed Concrete,* John Wiley & Sons, New York.

Nilson, A. H., and Winter, G. (1991). *Design of Concrete Structures,* John Wiley & Sons, New York.

Norby, G. M. (1958). "Fatigue of Concrete—A Review of Research," *ACI J. Proc.,* 55(2), August, pp. 191–219.

Oehler, L. T. (1957). "Vibration Susceptibilities of Various Highway Bridge Types," *Proc. ASCE J. Struct. Div.,* 83(ST4), paper no. 1318.

OHBDC. (1983). *Ontario Highway Bridge Design Code, 1983,* Highway Engineering Div., Ministry of Transportation and Communications, Toronto, Ontario.

Ohlson, S. V. (1988). "Ten Years of Floor Vibration Research—A Review of Aspects and Some Results," Proc. Symp./Workshop on Serviceability of Buildings, vol. 1, Ottawa, Ontario, pp. 435–450.

Osgood, C. C. (1982). *Fatigue Design,* 2nd ed., Pergamon Press, New York.

Overmann, T. R., Breen, J. E., and Frank, K. H., "Fatigue Behavior of Pretensioned Concrete Girders," Research Rep. no. 300-2f, Center for Highway Research, University of Texas, Austin.

Ozall, A. M., and Ardaman, E. (1956). "Fatigue Tests of Pretensioned Prestressed Beams," *ACI J. Proc.,* 53(4), October, pp. 413-424.

Pain, J. F., and Upstone, T. J. (1942). "Some Considerations Affecting the Minimum Depth of Small Highway Bridge Girders," *Proc. Inst. Civ. Engrs.,* London.

Park, Y. J. (1990). "Fatigue of Concrete under Random Loadings," *ASCE J. Str. Eng.,* 116(11), pp. 3228–3235.

PCI Com. (1977). "Volume Changes in Precast Prestressed-Concrete Structures," PCI Committee on Design Handbook, *PCI J.,* 22(5), September–October, pp. 38–53.

PennDOT. (1970). "Standards for Design of Steel Bridges–BD 100," Pennsylvania Department of Transportation, Harrisburg, PA.

Pernica, G., and Allen, D. E. (1982). "Floor Vibration Measurements in a Shopping Center," *Canadian J. Civ. Eng.,* 92, pp. 149–155.

Peterson, C. (1972). "Theorie der Zufallsschwingungen und Anwendungen (Theory of Random Vibrations and Applications)," Work Rep. no. 2/72, Structural Engineering Laboratory, Technical University of Munich, Munich, Germany.

Price, K. M., and Edwards, A. C. (1970). "Fatigue Strength of Prestressed-Concrete Flexural Members," *Proc. ICE* (London), 47, October, pp. 205-226.

Rabaat, B. G., Karr, P. H., Russell, H. G., and Bruce, R. N., Jr. (1978). "Fatigue Tests on Full-Size Prestressed Girders," *Tech. Rep. No. 113,* Portland Cement Assocation Research and Development Laboratories, June.

———. (1979). "Fatigue Tests of Pretensioned Girders with Blanketed and Draped Strands," *PCI J.,* 24(4), July–August, pp. 88–114.

Rainer, J. H., Pernica, G., and Allen, D. E. (1988). "Dynamic Loading and Response of Footbridges," *Canadian J. Civ. Eng.,* 15(1), pp. 66–71.

Rankine, W. J. M. (1843). *Proc. Inst. Civ. Engrs.,* vol. 2, London, p. 105.

Reese, G. A. (1983). "Fatigue Strength of Prestressed Girders," Ph.D. thesis, Department of Civil Engineering, University of Texas at Austin, August.

Reiher, H. J., and Meister, F. J. (1946). "Human Sensitivity to Vibration," *1931 Forsch auf dem Geb. des Ing.,* 2(11), pp. 381–386. (Translation report F-TS-616-RE, Wright Field).

Rolfe, S. T., and Barsom, J. M. (1987). *Fracture and Fatigue Control in Structures—Application of Fractural Mechanics,* 2nd ed., Prentice Hall, Englewood Cliffs, NJ.

Roller, J. J., Russell, H. G., Bruce, R. N., and Martin, B. T. (1995). "Long-Term Performance of Prestressed, Pretensioned, High-Strength Concrete Bridge Girders," *PCI J.,* 40(6), November–December, pp. 48–59.

Rosli, A. (1969). "Experiences from Fatigue and Rupture Tests on a Prestressed Concrete Bridge," *First Intl. Symp. Concrete Bridge Design,* ACI Special Pub. SP-23, ACI, Chicago, pp. 601–624.

Ruble, E. J., and Drew, F. P. (1962). "Railroad Research on Prestressed Concrete," *PCI J.,* 7(6), December, pp. 46–59.

Sawko, F., and Saha, G. P. (1968). "Fatigue of Concrete and Its Effect upon Prestressed Concrete Beams," *Mag. of Conc. Res.* 20(62).

Shahawi, M. E., and Batchelor, B. deV. (1986). "Fatigue of Partially Prestressed Concrete," *ASCE, J. Str. Eng.,* 112(3), March, pp. 524–537.

Siriaksorn, A., and Naaman, A. E. (1979). "Serviceability-Based Design of Prestressed Beams, Part 2: Computerized Design and Evaluation of Major Parameters," *PCI J.* 24(3), May–June, pp. 40–60.

Smith, I. F. C., and Hirt, M. A. (undated). "Methods of Improving the Fatigue Strength of Welded Joints," *Publication ICOM 114,* ICOM-Construction Metallique, Institut de Statique et Structures, Ecole Polytechnique, Federale de Lausanne, Lausanne, Switzerland.

Stefens, R. J. (1965). *Symp. Vibration in Civ. Eng.,* Imperial College, London, April.

Stelson, T. E., and Cernica, J. N. (1958). "Fatigue Properties of Concrete Beams," *ACI J. Proc.* 55(2), August, pp. 255-259.

Tepfers, R., and Kutti, T. (1979). "Fatigue Strength of Plain, Ordinary, and Lightweight Concrete," *ACI J. Proc.,* 76(5), pp. 635–652.

Tide, H. R., and Van Horn, D. A. (1966). "A Statistical Study of the Static and Fatigue Properties of High-Strength Prestressing Strands," Rep. no. 309-2, Fritz Engineering Laboratory, Lehigh University, June, Bethlehem, PA.

Timoshenko, S. (1953). *History of Strength of Materials,* McGraw-Hill Companies, Inc., New York.

Vogt, R., and Bachman, H. (1987). "Dynamische Lasten durch rhythmisches Klatschen, Fussstampfen, und Wippen (Dynamic Loads from Rhythmic Hand Clapping, Foot Stamping, and Moving Up and Down)," Rep. no. 7501-4, Institute of Structural Engineering (IBK), Swiss Federal Institute of Technology (ETH), Zurich.

Walley, F. (1959). "St. James' Park Bridge." *J. Inst. Civ. Engrs.,* 12(2), London, pp. 217–22.

Wang, C. K., and Salmon, C. G. (1973). "Reinforced Concrete Design," Intext Publishing Co., New York.

Warner, R. F., and Hulsbos, C. L. (1962). "Probable Fatigue Life of Prestressed-Concrete Flexural Members," Fritz Engineering Laboratory Report, Lehigh University, Bethlehem, PA.

Wilson, W. M. (1944). "Fatigue Strength of Fillet-Weld and Plug-Weld Connections in Steel Structural Members," Bull. no. 350, 41(30), Engineering Experimentation Station, University of Illinois, March 14, Urbana, IL.

Wolchuck, R. (1990). "Lessons from Weld Cracks in Orthotropic Decks in Three European Bridges," *ASCE J. Str. Eng.,* 116(1), January, pp. 75–84.

Wright, D. T., and Green, R. (1959a). "Highway Bridge Vibrations—Part 1: A Review of Previous Studies," Rept. no. 4, Queen's University, Kingston, Ontario.

———. (1959). "Human Sensitivity to Vibration," Rept. no. 7, Queen's University, Kingston, Ontario.

———. (1963). "Highway Bridge Vibrations, Part II: Ontario Test Programme," Rept. no. 5, Queen's University, Kingston, Ontario.

Wright, R. N., and Walker, W. H. (1971). "Criteria for Deflection of Steel Bridges," *AISI Bull.,* no. 19, November.

Wyatt, T. A. (1989). "Design Guide on the Vibration of Floors," *Steel Const. Inst.,* Pub. 076, Silwood Park, Ascot, Berkshire, England.

CHAPTER 6

Design of Reinforced Concrete Bridges

6.1 INTRODUCTION

It was pointed out in Chapter 1 that in a vast majority of cases, a bridge deck consists of a reinforced concrete flooring supported by a system of longitudinal beams—concrete (reinforced or prestressed), steel, or timber. These decks are usually cast in place with concrete of about 3000 to 4000 psi compressive strength. The curbs and parapets are normally cast after the deck has sufficiently hardened, to facilitate screeding off the slab. To enhance the service life of the deck, a wearing surface, usually $\frac{1}{2}$-in.-thick integral concrete, or $1\frac{1}{2}$-to 2-in.-thick ($1\frac{1}{4}$ in. minimum) asphalt concrete or latex-modified concrete [NCHRP–SYN, 1992],[1] is applied directly over the entire deck [AASHTO, 1992a; CRSI, 1983; PCI, 1975]. Detailed specifications covering the wearing surface are provided in AASHTO Div. II, 28 [AASHTO, 1992a]. Treatment of various types of reinforced concrete bridges can be found in several references such as [ACI, 1991; ACI, 1969, 1977, 1995; PCI, 1975; CRSI, 1983; Heins and Lawrie, 1984].

Reinforced concrete bridges possess several advantages over other types, the major one being the adaptability of concrete to a wide variety of structural shapes and forms. Cast-in-place structures are continuous and monolithic, attributes which translate into easy construction, low costs, and good seismic resistance. They are ideally suited for curved alignments, skewed piers, abutments, superelevations, and transitions at the freeway connector ramps, and can be given the desired aesthetic appearance. According to the National Bridge Inventory (NBI) data for the years 1950–1989

---

[1]Latex-modified concrete, also called polymer-modified concrete, is a mixture of cement, aggregate, and a latex emulsion admixture of which there are several varieties. This type of concrete is less porous and more durable than asphalt concrete; consequently, it requires less thickness than asphalt concrete and is preferred over asphalt concrete for overlays.

[FHWA, 1979, 1988], reinforced concrete bridges were the preferred types for spans in the 20 to 60-ft range before the advent of prestressed concrete technology, and they are still built in that span range in many cases. In the span range of 60 to 120 ft, steel bridges were the preferred type, followed by reinforced concrete bridges. This trend has, of course, been changing in favor of prestressed concrete bridges due to the economics of the life cycle costs. Table 6.1 gives various kinds of bridges built in the United States in the 1950–1989 period [Dunker and Rabbat, 1990, 1992], of which 29 percent are reinforced concrete bridges [Dunker and Rabbat, 1992].

For very short spans, say, under 35 ft for simple spans and 45 ft for continuous spans, an economical highway bridge superstructure may consist of a simple, longitudinal, one-way slab, spanning between the abutments [ACI, 1977]. In such a case, the slab acts as the principal load-supporting element of the superstructure, and can be characterized as a one-dimensional structure. For slightly longer spans, thicker slabs are required, which are uneconomical. However, they are made economical by providing voids in them. Voided slabs, considered economical for spans in the 40 to 65-ft range [ACI, 1977], are usually of the precast prestressed type, fabricated in plants in standard widths, transported to the site for erection, and possibly transversely post-tensioned. These are described in Chapter 7.

Alternatively, slab bridges can be designed as continuous structures to achieve longer spans. When designed as a continuous structure, the end spans are made shorter than the center span (ratio of approximately 1 to 1.25), an arrangement known as *balanced spans*. Such an arrangement results in the design positive moment in the end span about equal to the design negative moment at the intermediate supports [PCI, 1975]. For a single-span cast-in-place concrete bridge, an alternative for a longer span is a reinforced concrete deck supported over reinforced or prestressed concrete girders, resulting in a T-beam structure. T-beam bridges with simple spans are used for lengths up to about 60 ft and for continuous spans up to about 80 ft [ACI, 1977]. In this case, the slab is treated as a continuous element supported over the longitudinally spanning webs of T-beams. The slab also provides a broad compression flange (top flange) for the girders. In such an arrangement, because the bendings of the slab and that of the T-beam occur in the same plane but perpendicular to each other, a T-beam structure may be characterized as a two-dimensional structure.

A third type of structure is a reinforced concrete *box beam* in which the webs of a T-beam structure are all connected by a common bottom flange, resulting in a cellular superstructure. Depending on the number of interior webs, box girders can be single-cell or multicell structures. They are usually economical for spans in excess of 50 ft. In the 50 to 100-ft-span range, they cost about one-third more than T-beam structures, although, based on experience, some contractors claim that they could build box girder bridges just as economically as they could build T-beams [Elliot, 1990]. Often prestressed (post-tensioned), this arrangement enhances the moment-carrying capacity of the superstructure, which makes it suitable for relatively longer spans.

The designs of reinforced concrete slab, T-beam, and box girder bridges are discussed in this chapter; the designs of prestressed concrete bridges are presented in Chapter 7. Various reinforced concrete bridge superstructure configurations are shown in Fig. 6.1. Note that regardless of the type of longitudinally supported beams (webs of T-beams, steel stringers, or prestressed concrete girders) that support the deck

TABLE 6.1
Number of highway bridges by year built and span range (1950–1989) [Dunker and Rabbat, 1992]

Year built	Material	Span range (ft*)											Total built all spans
		< 20	20–39	40–59	60–79	80–99	100–119	120–139	140–159	160–179	180–199	≥ 200	
1950–1954	Timber	3826	2948	81	9	7	2	0	0	0	0	1	6874
	Steel	1069	6734	4030	2588	1194	446	266	127	76	49	210	16,789
	Reinf. conc.	1592	5655	1717	587	203	83	32	14	7	1	16	9907
	Prestr. conc.	30	350	146	56	18	6	1	1	0	0	0	608
	Total	6517	15,687	5974	3240	1422	537	299	142	83	50	227	34,178
1955–1959	Timber	2904	1773	51	4	2	2	2	0	0	1	1	4740
	Steel	473	4699	4778	3883	2032	832	374	201	112	65	224	17,673
	Reinf. conc.	2335	7487	3529	1341	464	186	51	12	9	6	21	15,441
	Prestr. conc.	75	1172	1400	1100	241	45	7	3	3	3	5	4054
	Total	5787	15,131	9758	6328	2739	1065	434	216	124	75	251	41,908
1960–1964	Timber	3201	2022	65	6	8	1	2	1	0	0	1	5307
	Steel	671	5415	4898	4998	2850	1205	489	285	132	96	238	21,277
	Reinf. conc.	2443	7741	3653	1888	892	364	116	37	16	14	28	17,192
	Prestr. conc.	85	2381	3043	2565	555	128	24	6	7	3	5	8802
	Total	6400	17,559	11,659	9457	4305	1698	631	329	155	113	272	52,578
1965–1969	Timber	2799	1589	57	13	5	3	3	1	0	1	0	4471
	Steel	442	3935	3789	4371	3244	1663	815	354	158	105	292	19,168
	Reinf. conc.	2316	6123	3307	1530	918	508	183	71	11	6	20	14,993
	Prestr. conc.	83	2749	3538	3195	1199	384	107	57	28	11	7	11,358
	Total	5640	14,396	10,691	9109	5366	2558	1108	483	197	123	319	49,990
1970–1974	Timber	2162	1267	51	16	2	0	0	0	1	0	2	3501
	Steel	400	3446	2463	2172	2463	1961	1196	522	257	137	282	15,299
	Reinf. conc.	2019	4583	1971	606	420	326	157	65	25	7	19	10,198
	Prestr. conc.	124	2882	3134	2493	1816	874	408	304	125	61	54	12,275
	Total	4705	12,178	7619	5287	4701	3161	1761	891	408	205	357	41,273
1975–1979	Timber	1738	1192	55	25	4	2	0	1	0	0	0	3017
	Steel	280	2811	1785	1283	1130	1115	841	462	202	91	211	10,211
	Reinf. conc.	1495	3909	1617	339	223	143	99	47	16	6	27	7921
	Prestr. conc.	79	3067	3260	2270	1571	793	326	154	86	69	58	11,733
	Total	3592	10,979	6717	3917	2928	2053	1266	664	304	166	296	32,882
1980–1984	Timber	791	820	37	18	1	2	1	0	0	0	0	1670
	Steel	229	2123	1441	878	854	779	641	374	200	98	227	7844
	Reinf. conc.	1156	3363	1530	296	143	94	68	30	16	4	16	6716
	Prestr. conc.	105	2631	3696	2347	1611	783	372	99	62	36	56	11,798
	Total	2281	8937	6704	3539	2609	1658	1082	503	278	138	299	28,028
1985–1989	Timber	684	833	40	9	6	1	0	1	0	1	1	1576
	Steel	192	1970	1358	900	640	584	487	307	172	105	212	6927
	Reinf. conc.	740	3145	1676	268	140	86	53	28	7	4	9	6156
	Prestr. conc.	60	2249	3932	2677	1609	1077	426	149	70	51	64	12,364
	Total	1676	8197	7006	3854	2395	1748	966	485	249	161	286	27,023

*Metric (SI) conversion factor: 1 ft = 0.305 m.

(see Fig. 4.11), the methods of designing reinforced concrete decks are the same (AASHTO 3.24.3.1, Case A, main reinforcement perpendicular to traffic) [AASHTO, 1992a].

6.2
MATERIALS OF CONSTRUCTION

The two materials used for the construction of reinforced concrete bridges are concrete and reinforcing steel, which were both discussed in Chapter 2. Design-related details of reinforcing bars are presented in a later section in this chapter.

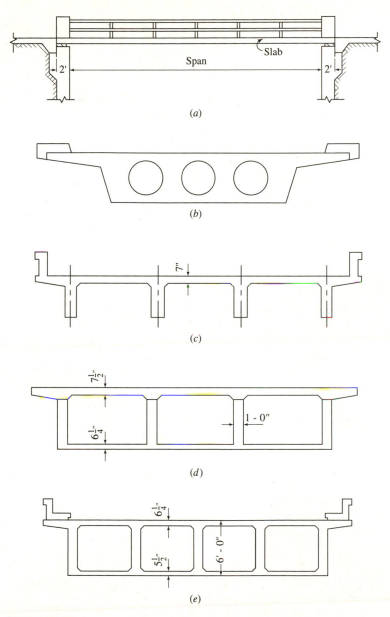

FIGURE 6.1
Various reinforced concrete bridge deck sections: (*a*) slab, (*b*) voided slab, (*c*) T-beam, (*d*) a three-cell box girder, (*e*) a four-cell box girder.

6.3
DESIGN METHODS

6.3.1 General

Structural design of reinforced concrete bridges can be performed by the service load design method (AASHTO 8.15) or by the strength (or load factor) design method (AASHTO 8.16). This design approach is stipulated in AASHTO 8.14. AASHTO 8.14.1.3 further stipulates that the strength and serviceability requirements of the strength design are satisfied by the service load design if the service load stresses are limited to values prescribed by AASHTO 8.15 (discussed in the following sections). The service load requirements include requirements for deflection control, stresses at service loads, fatigue stress limits, and distribution of flexural reinforcement to control flexural cracking of concrete, which negatively affects driver and pedestrian comfort. These design aspects are covered by AASHTO 8.16.8.

6.3.2 The Service Load Design Method

6.3.2.1 General

Various aspects of reinforced concrete design, including principles of designing structural elements such as slabs and T-beams, are covered in texts on reinforced concrete design [Ferguson, 1979; Nawy, 1985; Nilson and Winter, 1986; McCormac, 1993] and will not be repeated here. However, various formulae to be used in design calculations are presented here for a brief review. Figure 6.2 presents definitions of various parameters used in the service load design of reinforced concrete based on the cracked-section theory using the transformed area. For analysis of a cracked rectangular reinforced concrete section, the neutral axis factor, k, is given by

$$k = \sqrt{(pn)^2 + 2pn} - pn \qquad (6.1)$$

where $p = A_s/bd$ (reinforcement ratio)
$n = E_s/E_c$ = modular ratio
$j = 1 - k/3$ (lever-arm factor)

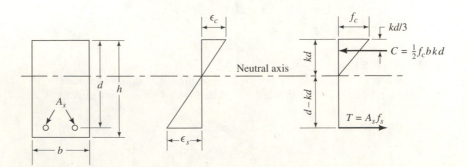

FIGURE 6.2
Definitions of parameters used in service load design.

Values of the modular ratio, n, are defined by AASHTO 8.7 and 10.38.1.3 and given in Table A.14 (Appendix A). Variations in these values are sometimes made by certain agencies. For example, the California DOT specifications [CALTRANS, 1993a] stipulate the following values of n:

$$
\begin{aligned}
f_c' &= 2000\text{–}2400 \text{ psi} & n &= 15 \\
&= 2500\text{–}2900 & &= 12 \\
&= 3000\text{–}3900 & &= 10 \\
&= 4000\text{–}4900 & &= 8 \\
&= 5000 \quad \text{or more} & &= 6
\end{aligned}
$$

Knowing the beam cross section, the area of reinforcing steel, and the design strength of concrete (f_c'), the value of k in Eq. 6.1 can be computed easily. Alternatively, it can be read from tables given in Appendix A (Table A.15). Finally, the allowable moment for a cross section may be obtained by considering independently the allowable concrete or steel stresses:

$$ M_c = \tfrac{1}{2} f_c k j b d^2 \tag{6.2} $$

$$ M_s = A_s f_s j d \tag{6.3} $$

The smaller of the two values given by Eqs. 6.2 and 6.3 should be taken as the allowable moment for the section. For design of a rectangular section, the following relationships should be used:

1. The depth of the slab or of a rectangular beam:

$$ d = \sqrt{\frac{2M}{f_c b k j}} \tag{6.4} $$

2. Area of reinforcing steel required:

$$ A_s = \frac{M}{f_s j d} \tag{6.5} $$

where $b = 12$ in. for a slab.

The values of the *design coefficients* k and j to be used in conjunction with Eqs. 6.4 and 6.5 can be computed from the following expressions:

$$ k = \frac{n}{n + f_s/f_c} \tag{6.6} $$

$$ j = 1 - \frac{k}{3} \tag{6.7} $$

where f_c = allowable stress in concrete
$\quad\;\; f_s$ = allowable stress in steel reinforcement

Note that, for given values of the concrete strength (f_c') and the grade of steel reinforcement (f_y), both f_c and f_s, which appear in Eq. 6.6, are known quantities. As a solution to Eq. 6.6, Table A.16 (Appendix A) gives values of the design coefficients k and j for the commonly used values of f_c and f_s.

The slab thickness, h, should be varied in increments of $\frac{1}{2}$ in. As a first step, the slab thickness should be assumed based on the *minimum* thickness requirements for deflection control (AASHTO 8.9.2; see Ch. 5, Table 5.3). However, note that some agency specifications may mandate a larger *minimum* slab thickness for reasons other than structural requirements. After finalizing the slab thickness, its moment of resistance should be checked (from Eqs. 6.2 and 6.3) as a final step, to ensure that it is not smaller than the design moment.

6.3.2.2 Allowable stresses (AASHTO 8.15): Flexure

Allowable stresses in concrete

Extreme fiber stress in compression $0.40 f_c'$

Extreme fiber stress in tension for plain concrete $0.21 f_r$

The fact that tensile stress in plain concrete is permitted by AASHTO should not be construed to imply that the use of plain concrete is permitted for structural members. In fact, plain concrete is not generally permitted for any structural use (and is even prohibited in many states, Pennsylvania, for example) unless the concrete members are fully supported for their entire length and they are not subjected to temperature variation. Cracking of concrete, plain or reinforced, is a very serious problem which affects the life of a structure, and every effort should be made to avoid it at the design stage.

The modulus of rupture, f_r, should be obtained from tests. In the absence of test results, the following values of modulus of rupture should be used:

Normal-weight concrete $7.5 \sqrt{f_c'}$

Sand-lightweight concrete $6.3 \sqrt{f_c'}$

All-lightweight concrete $5.5 \sqrt{f_c'}$

Bearing stress, f_b $0.30 f_c'$

A higher value of the bearing stress is permitted when the supporting surface is wider on all sides than the loaded area; in such a case the allowable bearing stress on the loaded area may be multiplied by a factor of $\sqrt{(A_2/A_1)}$ but not one greater than 2.

Allowable stress, f_s, in steel reinforcement

Grade 40 reinforcement   20,000 psi

Grade 60 reinforcement   24,000 psi

Certain states or agencies may specify their own allowable stress values, which may be lower than those specified previously. For example, the California Department of Transportation specifies the following stresses [CALTRANS, 1993a]:

Extreme fiber stress in compression for
transversely reinforced deck slabs, f_c: 1200 psi

Grade 60 reinforcement for transversely
reinforced deck slabs: 20,000 psi

Because of the relatively insignificant difference between the costs of Grade 40 and Grade 60 reinforcing steel, the latter is generally used in practice. In some states, use of Grade 60 reinforcement is mandated for highway bridges; Grade 40 reinforcement is used as an exception with the special approval of the chief bridge engineer.

6.3.2.3 Allowable stresses (AASHTO 8.15): Shear

Shear stress in a reinforced concrete beam can be calculated from Eq. 6.8:

$$v = \frac{V}{b\,jd} \tag{6.8}$$

Allowable stresses and design for shear are covered in AASHTO 8.15.2. In members subjected to flexure and shear, the allowable shear is given by Eq. 6.9:

$$v_c = 0.95 \sqrt{f_c'} \tag{6.9}$$

A more detailed calculation of the allowable shear stress can be made from Eq. 6.10:

$$v_c = 0.9 \sqrt{f_c'} + 1100\rho \left(\frac{Vd}{M}\right) \leq 1.6 \sqrt{f_c'} \tag{6.10}$$

where M = design moment occurring simultaneously with V at the section being considered, and $Vd/M \leq 1.0$

AASHTO specifications stipulate *two* conditions for providing shear reinforcement:

1. Shear reinforcement is to be provided when the design shear stress, v, exceeds the allowable shear stress for concrete, v_c (AASHTO 8.15.5.3).
2. Minimum shear reinforcement is to be provided when the design shear exceeds one-half the allowable shear stress (AASHTO 8.19).

Both cases are discussed in the next section.

Design for shear. When the design shear exceeds the allowable shear stress, the excess shear must be carried by shear reinforcement. However, this excess shear is limited in such a way that the excess shear stress, $(v - v_c)$, does not exceed $4 \sqrt{f_c'}$ (AASHTO 8.15.5.3.9); if it does, a larger beam cross section is indicated. The required shear reinforcement, perpendicular to the beam's longitudinal axis (vertical stirrups), can be calculated from Eq. 6.11:

$$A_v = \frac{(v - v_c)b_w s}{f_s} \tag{6.11}$$

where A_v = cross-sectional area of all legs of stirrups
s = spacing of stirrups.

AASHTO 8.19.3 stipulates that the stirrup spacing should not exceed the smaller of $d/2$ or 24 in. These spacings are to be reduced by half, i.e., to the smaller of $d/4$ or 12 in., if the excess shear stress, $(v - v_c)$, exceeds $2 \sqrt{f_c'}$.

The minimum shear reinforcement is calculated by the following expression, with stirrup spacing limited to $d/2$ or 24 in.:

$$A_v = \frac{50 b_w s}{f_y} \tag{6.12}$$

For requirements for other kinds of shear reinforcements, such as inclined stirrups or bars, readers are urged to refer to the appropriate AASHTO specifications.

6.3.3 Strength Design Method (Load Factor Design Method)

The *load factor design* method calls for designing reinforced concrete members by the *strength design* method, for which the relevant design requirements are covered in AASHTO 8.16, and the design assumptions are stipulated in AASHTO 8.16.2. The philosophy of load factor design was presented in Chapter 3. Details of strength design of reinforced concrete members are covered in several references [Nawy, 1985; Nilson and Winter, 1986; MacGregor, 1988; McCormac, 1993] and will not be repeated here, except that the principles will be presented. Essentially, the method is similar to that used for reinforced concrete buildings. Design loads (force, moment, shear, or stress) are obtained by multiplying service loads by the load factors, as stipulated in AASHTO 3.22.3 (see Chapter 3, Table 3.12). It is required that the nominal strength of a member, multiplied by the strength reduction factor, ϕ, should not be less than the design forces. Note that in both cases—service load design and load factor design—the methods of structural analysis are the same. Various ϕ factors as stipulated by AASHTO 8.16.1.2.2 are given in Table 6.2. Note that these ϕ factors have the same values as those used for the strength design of reinforced concrete buildings [ACI, 1995].

In spite of similarities in the application of strength design principles to buildings and bridges, different load factors are used in the two cases because of differences in the variability of loads involved. For example, for reinforced concrete buildings, the load factors for the dead and the live load are 1.4 and 1.7, respectively [ACI, 1995], whereas those for a bridge are to be taken as 1.3 for the dead load and 6.5/3 ($1.3 \times 5/3$) for live load plus impact [AASHTO, 1992a]:

$$\text{For buildings:} \qquad \sum \gamma_i Q_i = 1.4D + 1.7L \tag{6.13}$$

$$\text{For bridges:} \qquad \sum \gamma_i Q_i = 1.3\left[D + \tfrac{5}{3}(L + I)\right] \tag{6.14}$$

TABLE 6.2
ϕ factors [AASHTO, 1992a]

	Design parameter	ϕ
a	Flexure	0.90
b	Shear	0.85
c	Axial compression with	
	spirals	0.75
	ties	0.70
d	Bearing on concrete	0.70

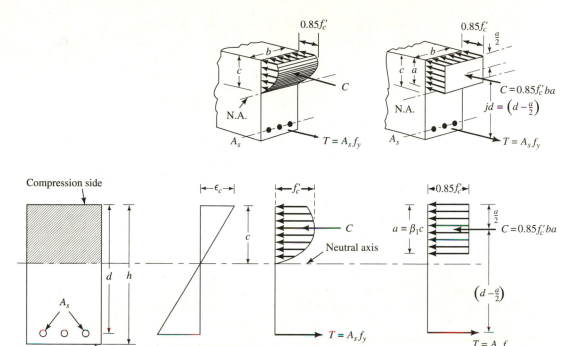

FIGURE 6.3
Strength design of a rectangular reinforced concrete section [Nawy, 1985].

Figure 6.3 shows a rectangular reinforced concrete section for which Whitney's rectangular stress distribution is applied. Equilibrium of horizontal forces under the balanced conditions yields

$$C = T$$

$$\text{or} \quad 0.85 f_c' ab = A_s f_y$$

Substituting $A_s = \rho bd$ and solving for a, the depth of the rectangular stress block (AASHTO Eq. 8.17) gives

$$a = \frac{A_s f_y}{0.85 f_c' b} \tag{6.15a}$$

$$= \frac{\rho f_y d}{0.85 f_c'} \tag{6.15b}$$

The moment equilibrium yields

$$M_n = T\left(d - \frac{a}{2}\right) = A_s f_y\left(d - \frac{a}{2}\right) \tag{6.16}$$

Equation 6.16 gives the nominal strength of the section, which, multiplied with ϕ, the strength reduction factor, is equated to the factored design loads, M_u (AASHTO Eq. 8.16):

$$M_u = \phi M_n = \phi A_s f_y \left(d - \frac{a}{2} \right) \qquad (6.17)$$

In Eq. 6.17, one substitutes the value of a from Eq. 6.15a to yield

$$M_u = \phi M_n = \phi A_s f_y d \left(1 - 0.588 \frac{\rho f_y}{f'_c} \right) \qquad (6.18)$$

The constant 0.588 in the right-hand-side parenthetical term in Eq. 6.18 is rounded off to 0.59 in the ACI building code [ACI, 1995] and to 0.6 in AASHTO Eq. 8.15. Thus

$$M_u = \phi M_n = \phi A_s f_y d \left(1 - 0.6 \rho \frac{f_y}{f'_c} \right) \qquad (6.19)$$

Equation 6.19 is the fundamental expression used for designing rectangular reinforced concrete sections in bending by the strength design method. For computational efficiency, this expression is written slightly differently by substituting $A_s = \rho b d$:

$$M_u = \phi \rho b d f_y d \left(1 - 0.6 \frac{\rho f_y}{f'_c} \right) \qquad (6.20)$$

Rearranging the terms, we obtain

$$\frac{M_u}{\phi b d^2} = \rho f_y \left(1 - 0.6 \frac{\rho f_y}{f'_c} \right) \qquad (6.21)$$

Equation 6.21 is very convenient for use in design. For a given set of material strengths (f'_c and f_y), and for trial values of b and d, the left-hand term ($M_u/\phi b d^2$) of Eq. 6.21 is completely known from values of the corresponding steel ratio, ρ, and hence the required amount of reinforcement can be calculated. As a practical matter, such values are tabulated for various combinations of f'_c and f_y, as given in Appendix A (Table A.17), which is extremely helpful in design. The term $M_u/\phi b d^2$ is sometimes called the *flexural*, or the *moment of resistance, factor* and is denoted by R.

The value of the *balanced steel ratio*, ρ_b, obtained from compatibility of balanced strains in concrete ($\epsilon_c = 0.003$, AASHTO 8.16.3.1.2) and reinforcement ($\epsilon_y = f_y/E_s$, $E_s = 29,000$ ksi) at ultimate conditions, is given by AASHTO Eq. 8.18:

$$\rho_b = \frac{0.85 \beta_1 f'_c}{f_y} \left(\frac{87,000}{87,000 + f_y} \right) \qquad (6.22)$$

A reinforced concrete section must be designed as an underreinforced section to ensure yielding failure of reinforcement before crushing failure of concrete occurs. Consequently, the maximum reinforcement ratio, ρ, should not exceed $0.75 \rho_b$ (AASHTO 8.16.3.1.1).

Since ρ_b is clearly a function of the given design parameters, namely, f_y, f_c', and β_1 (which again is a function of f_c'), its value is known in advance. For computational convenience and efficiency in the design process, values of ρ_b are tabulated for various combinations of f_c' and f_y, as given in Appendix A (Table A.18). This table also gives values of $0.5\rho_b$, a value which may be used for the initial design trial. Note that the depth of Whitney's rectangular stress block, a, is related to the depth of the neutral axis, c, by the relationship $a = \beta_1 c$, where β_1 is a coefficient whose value, subject to a minimum of 0.65, is given by Eq. 6.23 (AASHTO 8.16.2.7):

$$\beta_1 = 0.85 - 0.05\left(\frac{f_c' - 4000}{1000}\right) \tag{6.23}$$

The design of a reinforced concrete slab is initiated by selecting $b = 12$ in. and a depth (d) to meet the minimum recommended depth requirements, as shown in Table 5.3 (Chapter 5). With the design moment, M_u, known, the value of $M_u/\phi bd^2$ is calculated, and the corresponding value of ρ is determined from Table A.17 (Appendix A). Knowing the required values of b, d, and ρ, the value of A_s is calculated and the required bar spacing selected from Table A.19 (Appendix A).

When a reinforced concrete member is designed according to the load factor design, AASHTO 8.16.8 stipulates that the following serviceability requirements be satisfied.

6.3.3.1 Service load stresses

Stresses under service load conditions should not exceed the allowable stresses, as presented in the earlier sections.

6.3.3.2 Fatigue stress limits

Tests indicate that reinforcing bars in bridge superstructures are more likely to be subjected to critical fatigue stresses than is the surrounding concrete; consequently, longitudinal forces in all types of bridges are checked for fatigue at locations of maximum service stress range and bar cutoffs. In regions where stress reversal takes place, the slabs are doubly reinforced.

AASHTO 8.16.8.3 stipulates that the range between a maximum tensile stress and the minimum stress in straight reinforcement should not exceed f_f, given by AASHTO Eq. 8.60, as discussed in Chapter 5:

$$f_f = 21 - 0.33 f_{\min} + 8\left(\frac{r}{h}\right) \tag{6.24}$$

where f_f = stress range, ksi
   $f_{\min}$ = algebraic minimum stress level, ksi (tension positive and compression negative)
   r/h = ratio of base radius (r) to height (h) of rolled-on transverse deformations, equal to 0.3 when the actual value of r/h is not known.

This fatigue stress limit is waived when the deck slab, with primary reinforcement perpendicular to traffic, is designed in accordance with AASHTO 3.24.3, Case A.

6.3.3.3 Distribution of flexural reinforcement

To control flexural cracking of concrete, tension reinforcement should be well distributed within the maximum flexural zones. This requirement is critical only when the yield strength of flexural reinforcement exceeds 40,000 psi. In such a case, the bar sizes and their spacing at the maximum positive and negative moment sections should be so chosen that the stress in reinforcing steel under service load conditions does not exceed the following value (AASHTO 8.16.8.4, Eq. 8.61):

$$f_s = \frac{z}{\sqrt[3]{d_c A}} \leq 0.6 f_y \qquad (6.25)$$

where A = effective area, in.^{2}, of concrete surrounding the flexural tension reinforcement and having the same centroid as the reinforcement, divided by the number of bars or wires. When the flexural reinforcement consists of several bar or wire sizes, the number of bars or wires are to be calculated by dividing the total reinforcement area by the area of the largest bar used

d_c = thickness of concrete cover measured from extreme tension fiber to the center of the closest bar or wire, in., limited to 2 in. maximum for calculations

It is instructive to note that this requirement is similar to that required for the reinforced concrete buildings [ACI, 1995].

Careful attention should be paid to quantities A and d_c, defined in Fig. 6.4. Note that for a single layer of tensile reinforcement, the depth (t) of the concrete area surrounding the reinforcing bars equals $2d_c$, whereas, for a multiple-layered reinforcement, d_c is measured from the tension face of the beam to the centroid of the *nearest* layer of tension reinforcement.

Considerable research has been done on control of crack widths in reinforced concrete structures because of their extreme importance in relation to associated corrosion problems. An exhaustive discussion on the causes, mechanisms, and controls of cracking in concrete can be found in texts on reinforced concrete design [Ferguson, 1979; Nawy, 1985; Nilson and Winter, 1986; MacGregor, 1988; McCormac, 1993] and in several other references [Broms, 1965; Gergely and Lutz, 1968; Nawy, 1968, 1972; ACI, 1972; Nawy and Blair, 1973; Lutz, 1974].

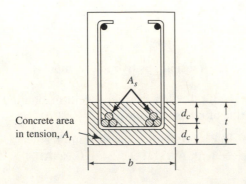

FIGURE 6.4
Definitions of A and d_c in Eq. 6.25 [Nawy, 1985].

A major parameter affecting the crack width in a reinforced concrete member is the bond stress between the reinforcing bars and the surrounding concrete. When the bars are bundled together, the contact area between the bundled bars and the concrete is smaller than that between the concrete and the single bars. To provide for this eventuality, the Gergely–Lutz formula is expressed in a modified form [Nawy, 1972, 1985; Lutz, 1974]:

$$w_{max} = 0.076\beta f_s \sqrt[3]{d_c A'} \qquad (6.26)$$

where $A' = bt/\gamma'_{bc}$

γ_{bc} = number of bars if all are of the same diameter, or the total area of reinforcing steel divided by the area of the largest bar if more than one size is used. The term γ'_{bc} is essentially a perimetric reduction of γ_{bc} and is defined in Fig. 6.5.

AASHTO Eq. 6.61 is the Gergely–Lutz formula [Gergely and Lutz, 1968] derived from the general formula based on a statistical study of test data of several investigations [Nawy, 1985]:

$$w_{max} = 0.076\beta f_s \sqrt[3]{d_c A} \qquad (6.27)$$

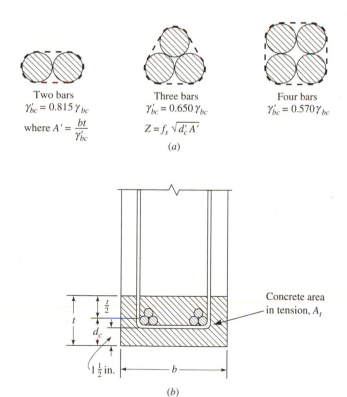

FIGURE 6.5
Perimetric reduction factors with bundled bars: (*a*) perimetric factors; (*b*) section geometry of concrete area in tension [Nawy, 1985].

where w_{max} = crack width in units of 0.001 in.

$\beta = (h - c)/(d - c)$ = depth factor, average value = 1.20

f_s = maximum stress (ksi) in steel at service load level, $0.6 f_y$ to be used if no computations are available

It is important to note that $f_s = 0.6 f_y$, in lieu of actual stress in reinforcing steel, is applicable to normal structures only.

For computational simplicity, a parameter, z, is introduced in Eq. 6.27 [Nilson and Winter, 1986]:

$$z = \frac{w}{0.076 \times 12} = \frac{w}{0.091} \tag{6.28}$$

The z-w relationship of Eq. 6.28 can be expressed as

$$w = (0.091)z \tag{6.29}$$

Note that the units of z are kips per inch. The AASHTO specifications [AASHTO, 1992a] prescribe the following upper and lower limits on the value of z:

z = 170 kips/in. for members in moderate exposure conditions

z = 130 kips/in. for members in severe exposure conditions

The terms "moderate" and "severe" are not defined, however. For reinforced concrete culverts, the value of z is to be taken as 98 kips/in. (AASHTO 17.6.4.7). The California specifications [CALTRANS, 1993b] are somewhat more prescriptive with regard to the environmental conditions prevalent in various geographical state areas (not shown here) as follows:

Area I: Mild climate, where frost is rare, or where, because of light traffic volumes, salt is applied infrequently. This area includes all portions of the state not specifically itemized as Areas II and III.

Area II: Moderate climate, where frost or light freezing occurs, but where chains are seldom used. Salting of the deck is only done in rare or emergency instances.

Area III: Severe climate, where freeze-thaw cycles and heavy salting occur frequently and where chains are used.

The upper limits on values of z, based on environmental conditions, are prescribed as follows:

1. 100 kips/in. for structures in direct contact with sea water or subjected to sea water spray
2. 130 kips/in. for structures not in direct contact with sea water or subjected to sea water spray but located within 1000 ft of ocean or tidal water, and for bridge decks located in environmental Area III (severe climate)
3. 170 kips/in. for all cases other than those previously listed

Specifications [CALTRANS, 1993b] suggest additional protective measures where members are exposed to very aggressive or corrosive environments, such as deicer chemicals. In such cases, protection should be provided by increasing the denseness or imperviousness to water, or by furnishing other protection such as waterproofing protection systems.

TABLE 6.3
Tolerable crack widths for reinforced concrete [ACI, 1972, 1980]

Exposure condition	Tolerable crack width		
	(in.)	(mm)	$z = w/0.091*$
Dry air or protective membrane	0.016	0.41	176
Humidity, moist air, soil	0.012	0.30	132
Deicing chemicals	0.007	0.18	77
Seawater and seawater spray; wetting and drying	0.006	0.15	66
Water-retaining structures, excluding nonpressure pipes	0.004	0.10	44

*Values in this column added in the table by the author.

With the z value limits of 100, 170, and 130, the permissible crack width can be calculated from Eq. 6.29 as follows:

$$z = 100, \qquad w = 0.091 \times 100 \times 0.001 = 0.009 \text{ in.}$$

$$z = 170, \qquad w = 0.091 \times 170 \times 0.001 = 0.015 \text{ in.}$$

$$z = 130, \qquad w = 0.091 \times 130 \times 0.001 = 0.012 \text{ in.}$$

It can be seen that the smaller value of z corresponds to the smaller permissible crack width and has been used in examples where applicable. Tolerable crack widths for various environmental conditions are shown in Table 6.3 [ACI, 1972, 1980]. Also shown are the corresponding values of z for comparison purposes.

6.4
REINFORCEMENT

6.4.1 General

Requirements for providing reinforcement are covered in the respective design specifications for concrete members (AASHTO Sec. 8, Part D). In all cases, attention should be paid to minimum sizes and types of bars permitted for use. For example, compression reinforcement used to increase the strength of flexural members is to be enclosed by ties or stirrups of at least #3 bar for longitudinal bars that are #10 or smaller, and at least #4 bar for #11, #14, #18, and bundled longitudinal bars. Similarly, for compression members, at least six longitudinal bars in a square arrangement are required. The minimum size of bars should be #5 (AASHTO 8.18.1.2). Because of practical and economic considerations, the use of #3 bar is generally not practical for longitudinal reinforcement in slab construction. Table A.20 (Appendix A) gives the area of a group of bars in a concrete member. Table A.21 (Appendix A) gives the minimum required beam widths for a given number of bars in a single layer. Table A.22 gives the maximum number of bars that can be placed in a single layer in a given beam width, with concrete having $\frac{3}{4}$ in. and 1 in. size aggregates.

6.4.2 Flexural Reinforcement

6.4.2.1 Minimum reinforcement

AASHTO 8.17.1 requires that at any section of a flexural member where tension reinforcement is required by analysis, the actual reinforcement provided should be sufficient to develop a moment at least 1.2 times the cracking moment, calculated on the basis of modulus of rupture for normal weight concrete (AASHTO 8.15.2.1.1):

$$f_r = 7.5 \sqrt{f_c'} \qquad\qquad (6.30)$$

$$M_{cr} = f_r S \qquad\qquad (6.31)$$

where S = section modulus, based on uncracked section.

6.4.2.2 Spacing limits

Spacing limits for reinforcing bars for bridges, different and generally more conservative than those for reinforced concrete buildings as recommended by the ACI [1995], are covered in AASHTO 8.20:

1. For cast-in-place concrete, the clear distance between parallel bars in a layer should not be less than $1\frac{1}{2}$ times the bar diameters, $1\frac{1}{2}$ times the coarse aggregate, or $1\frac{1}{2}$ in.
2. Where bars are placed in two or more layers, the bars in the upper layers should be placed directly above the ones in the lower layers. The clear distance between the bars in the two layers should not be less than 1 in.
3. Bundling of bars in a group is permitted. For bars #10 and smaller, a maximum of four bars can be bundled; for bars #11, #14, and #18, the number of bars in a bundle is limited to two. When the spacing limitations are based on bar diameter, a unit of bundled bars should be treated as a single bar of a diameter derived from the equivalent total area (AASHTO 8.21.5).

6.4.2.3 Protection against corrosion

The ability of a structure to satisfactorily carry design loads over its design life with a minimum of maintenance problems is the intended goal of a good structural design; i.e., structures should possess both strength and durability. Unfortunately, durability cannot be ensured by producing concrete of appropriate strength alone. It must be supplemented by providing adequate protection of concrete from aggressive media. Corrosion of both the reinforcing and the prestressing steel is a disruptive phenomenon that is the cause of the most frequent and the most serious forms of degradation of reinforced and prestressed concrete structures.

Corrosion of reinforcing steel can be attributed to four main causes: carbonation or sulphation, chloride attack, inadequate cover, and cracks. It is an electrochemical phenomenon that initiates in the presence of chlorides, carbonates or sulfides, oxygen, and water that is generally furnished by the water in the pores of the concrete. When reinforcing bars are embedded in fresh concrete, with cement mortar surrounding steel, a thin coating of ferro-ferrous hydroxide forms on the surface of steel. This acts as a protective layer, thus passivating the steel surface [Mehta, 1986; Gerwick, 1993]; chloride ions are the most common materials which can break down this passive protective layer. In addition to their presence in the water of the concrete mix, chlorides come from marine environments and from salt spread on bridge decks to prevent icing. Sodium chloride from washed deicing salts can be splashed (by tires, for example) sideways over the parapets, bridge piers, and columns, with subsequent absorption up to 8 in. deep into the concrete [Bennison, 1987].

Corrosion adversely affects durability of concrete and is generally manifested by cracking or spalling of concrete, rust staining, corrosion of reinforcing steel, excessive deflection, and in extreme cases, failure of the member. Often, these phenomena are interactive, in that cracking of concrete leads to accelerated corrosion of reinforcing steel, followed by further spalling of concrete cover, exposing more steel [Gerwick, 1993]. In reinforced concrete, two broad categories of environmental factors affect durability: those causing or accelerating disintegration of or change in the concrete, and those causing or accelerating corrosion of steel. With proper design and good construction practice, corrosion damage can be mitigated. A detailed discussion of this topic is beyond the scope of this book, but discussions can be found in several references [FIP, 1975; ACI, 1975, 1988; Gerwick, 1990; Mehta, 1991].

The single most effective measure to prevent corrosion of reinforcement in concrete is to produce concrete of very low permeability. Low permeability limits the penetration of chlorides and restricts the flow of oxygen and, in effect, lengthens the time for chlorides to reach reinforcing bars. Lower permeability and consequent increase in resistivity of concrete can be achieved by lower water-cement ratios. Most generally, corrosion involves concrete with water-cement ratios above 0.45 or 0.50. With the advent of superplasticizers, it is now possible to achieve water-cement ratios of 0.37 to 0.38. A summary of precautions and several countermeasures that can be taken to prevent corrosion of steel reinforcing bars in concrete is discussed by Gerwick [1993].

An adequate protection to steel against fire and corrosion can be provided by a sufficient depth of concrete cover over the reinforcing bars. The minimum cover requirements can be based on several criteria, namely, the compressive strength of concrete, the condition of exposure, the water-cement ratio, and the minimum cement content [Bennison, 1987]. AASHTO 8.22 requires the following minimum clear cover (in inches), outside of the outermost steel, for protection of reinforcing bars from the environment:

Concrete cast against and permanently exposed to earth	3
Concrete exposed to earth or weather	
Primary reinforcement	2
Stirrups, ties, and spirals	$1\frac{1}{2}$
Concrete deck slabs in mild climates	
Top reinforcement	2
Bottom reinforcement	1
Concrete deck slabs that have no positive corrosion protection and are frequently exposed to deicing salts	
Top reinforcement	$2\frac{1}{2}$
Bottom reinforcement	1
Concrete not exposed to weather or in contact with ground	
Primary reinforcement	$1\frac{1}{2}$
Stirrups, ties, and spirals	1
Concrete piles cast against or permanently exposed to earth	2

Note that these cover requirements are the minimum requirements recommended by AASHTO. In many states, depending on the environmental conditions, greater cover is mandated. For bundled bars, the minimum concrete cover is required to be equal to the equivalent diameter of the bundle, subject to a maximum of 2 in. If the bundled bars are used for concrete cast permanently exposed to earth, the clear cover is to be 3 in.

Some states specify cover requirements based on the type of environment with respect to chloride concentration and call for increased concrete protection in corrosive or marine environments, or in other severe exposure conditions, by increasing the denseness and imperviousness to water of the protecting concrete, or by other means. For example, the California Department of Transportation requires that elements in direct contact with ocean water or ocean water spray conform to chloride concentrations between 10,000 and 20,000 ppm (parts per million) [CALTRANS, 1993a]. Its cover requirements for corrosion protection are shown in Table 6.4; the marine environment applies to other structural elements within 1000 ft of ocean or tidal water. Similarly, the British specifications [BSI, 1985] require different depths of concrete cover depending on the conditions of exposure (classified as mild, moderate, severe, very severe, and extreme) and the grade of concrete (C30, C35, C40, C45, and C50).

TABLE 6.4
Minimum cover for reinforcement, (in.) [CALTRANS, 1993a]

Structural member or surface		Environment		Chloride concentration (ppm)		
		Normal	Marine	1000 to 5000	5000 to 10,000	10,000 to 20,000
Concrete cast against and/or permanently exposed to earth:	Piles	2	3	3	3	3
	Footings	3	4	3	4	5
	Walls	2	4	2	3	5
	Columns:					
	Flat and curved surfaces	2	4	3	4	5
	Corners	2	5	3	5	6
Concrete exposed to weather:	Top surfaces of deck slabs[1]	2	2.5	—	—	2.5
	Bottom surfaces of deck slabs	1.5	1.5	—	—	2.5
	Bottom slabs of box girder bridges	1.5	1.5	—	—	2.5
	I- and T-beam webs and outside faces of box girder webs	1.5	3	—	—	3
	Bottom flange bulb of precast I- and T-beams	1.5	3	—	—	3
	Curbs and railings	1	1[2]	—	—	—
	Columns and caps:					
	Flat surfaces	2	4	—	—	—
	Corners	2	5	—	—	—
	Walls	2	3	—	—	—
Concrete not exposed to weather or not in contact with earth:	Principal reinforcement	1.5	1.5	—	—	—
	Stirrups, ties, and spirals	1	1	—	—	—

[1] Special considerations are required in freeze/thaw areas.
[2] Use epoxy-coated rebar.

6.4.3 Shrinkage and Temperature Reinforcement

AASHTO 8.20 stipulates that a minimum of 0.125 in.^{2} of reinforcement per foot in each direction be provided for shrinkage and temperature near exposed surfaces of walls and slabs not otherwise reinforced. The spacing of such reinforcement is limited to a maximum of the smaller of three times either the wall or the slab thickness, or 18 in. To satisfy this requirement, it is a common practice to provide #4 bar @ 18 inches o.c. in each direction; this gives a reinforcing area of 0.133 in.^{2} in each direction.

6.4.4 Transverse Reinforcement

AASHTO 3.24.10 stipulates that all reinforced concrete slabs be provided with distribution reinforcement, near the bottom fibers, placed perpendicularly to the main reinforcement, to distribute concentrated loads laterally. The amount of such reinforcing steel is governed by the orientation of the main reinforcement with respect to direction of traffic:

- For main reinforcement parallel to traffic (AASHTO Eq. 3.21):

$$\text{Percentage of reinforcement} = \frac{100}{\sqrt{S}} \qquad \text{but} \not> 50\% \qquad (6.32)$$

where S = effective span length. This requirement applies to slab bridges; the reinforcement is to be provided in the bottom mat, placed above the main reinforcement.

- For main reinforcement perpendicular to traffic (AASHTO Eq. 3.22):

$$\text{Percentage of reinforcement} = \frac{220}{\sqrt{S}} \qquad \text{but} \not> 67\% \qquad (6.33)$$

This reinforcement is required to be placed in the middle half of the span. Additionally, 50 percent of this reinforcement is to be provided in the outer quarters of the span (AASHTO 3.24.10.3). This requirement is applicable to slabs of T-beams and slabs supported over steel stringers.

6.5 CONSTRUCTION DETAILS

In addition to the structural design of the slab and the T-beams, there are several constructional details that are common to all types of bridges and that should be carefully considered in designing a bridge superstructure. These details are described briefly in the following paragraphs and will not be repeated in other chapters.

6.5.1 Diaphragms

The subject of diaphragms was discussed in Chapter 4. In T-beam construction, they are provided between the beams at the ends and at some intermediate points along the span, and they are cast integrally with the slab and the webs. At the intermediate points, they provide lateral support to beams, and when the abutment does not extend above the bridge-seat level, the end diaphragms support the backfill.

AASHTO 8.12 recommends providing diaphragms at the ends and at points of maximum positive moments for spans exceeding 40 ft. Generally, diaphragms are provided at midspan or at the third-points. In the absence of any specific design requirements, they are arbitrarily made 6 to 8 in. thick and provided with a nominal amount of reinforcement. When provided, the weights of diaphragms should be considered concentrated dead loads to be carried by T-beams (and by any other beam or girder, for that matter).

6.5.2 Deck Joints

To provide for expansion and contraction of the deck due to temperature and other causes, it is common practice to provide expansion joints in a bridge deck at the expansion ends and at other desirable locations. Details for the expansion and contraction deck joints are spelled out in AASHTO Div. II, 8.9. In humid climates and areas subject to freezing, joints should be sealed to prevent erosion, filling with debris, and freezing-induced spalling. Experience has shown that expansion joints are a major source of superstructural maintenance problems as they malfunction over time. Consequently, there is a growing tendency to provide expansion joints at much greater intervals than before and, possibly, to provide jointless decks [Loveall, 1985; Wasserman, 1987; NCHRP-SYN, 1985, 1989].[2] The provision of expansion joints is a matter of construction details and practices that vary regionally; these provisions can be found in standard plans of bridge-owner agencies and are not discussed here. Because of the importance of the deck joints in bridges, special deck-joint systems are available from the industry [Koch, 1992].

6.5.3 Bearings

Bearings are devices provided at the abutments or piers and positioned between the bottom flanges of the beams and the top of the bridge seats. Basically, they serve the following important functions:

1. Uniformly distribute the concentrated horizontal and vertical loads due to beam reactions over bearing areas to eliminate highly localized stresses and resulting structural damage
2. Allow movements between the superstructure and the substructure (abutments and piers), and minimize the effects of loads due to volume changes resulting from shrinkage, creep, and temperature
3. For longer spans, allow rotations at the supports that will be caused by the deflection of the loaded beam

A comprehensive discussion on the subject of bridge bearings can be found in the literature [Stanton and Roeder, 1982, 1983; Roeder and Stanton, 1983, 1991; Iversion

---

[2]For additional discussion on the subject, please see Chapter 3, Sec. 3.11—Temperature-Induced Forces.

and Pfeifer, 1985; Pfeifer and Iversion, 1985; NCHRP, 1987; PBQD, 1992]. Design methods and requirements for bearings for highway bridges in the United States are given in AASHTO 14, 15, 19, 20, and Div. II, 18 [AASHTO, 1992a]. As opposed to the bearing devices of the past, which involved pins, rollers, rockers, and plates that required costly periodic maintenance [PBQD, 1992], the current trend is to use self-lubricating elastomeric bearing pads such as PTFE (polytetrafluoroethylene, Teflon being a brand name version) bearing pads, which are fabricated from elastomers (elastic substances occurring naturally or produced synthetically, such as chloroprene or poly-chloroprene, manufactured and patented by du Pont under the trade name Neoprene). These pads are of two types: plain, or unreinforced (consisting of elastomers only, generally in single layer), and reinforced (consisting of alternate layers of steel, fiberglass, or fabric reinforcement—and elastomer, bonded together). These types of modern bearing pads have been found to be virtually maintenance free and highly effective in accommodating the necessary superstructural movements. The isolation of shock loads on structural members and minimization of vibrations between the contacting surfaces are some of the other important advantages of the elastomeric bearing pads. Of late, design of bearing pads has become somewhat specialized and left to vendors [Voss, 1989, 1991; PBQD, 1992].

6.5.4 Sidewalks, Curbs, Parapets, and Railings

Sidewalks are usually provided for pedestrian traffic on bridges, generally carrying urban expressways, and wherever necessary. They should be of such widths as required by the controlling and concerned public agencies, but preferably not less than 4 ft [ACI, 1969]. When sidewalks are provided, they should be separated from the bridge roadway by the use of a suitable railing (AASHTO 2.7.3).

Curbs and parapets are safety barriers provided parallel to the longitudinal axis of the bridge on both sides of the roadway, designed to prevent a moving vehicle from leaving the roadway. Both may be designed to form a combination curb and gutter section. Curbs are of two general types: parapets (nonmountable) and mountable curbs (also called brush curbs). Curbs are generally made 9 in. wide (maximum) and 8 to 10 in. high (AASHTO 2.2.5) with their inside faces sloping toward the roadway. Parapets are made of varying heights, but generally not less than 2 ft 6 in. high, and may be used in combination with the curbs. A typical parapet section (New Jersey type) is shown in Fig. 4.13.

Curbs and sidewalks are poured after the hardening of the deck. Both should have vertical slits or other provisions of discontinuity to prevent them from resisting deck bending moments; this avoids any structural cracking.

AASHTO 2.7 mandates that railings be provided along the edges of the roadway for protection of traffic and pedestrians. Essentially, railings are safety devices provided to contain the vehicles. However, they also serve to protect the vehicle occupants in collision with the railing, to protect other vehicles near a collision, and to protect the vehicles or pedestrians on roadways underneath the bridge. Various kinds of railings are referred to as pedestrian railings, bicycle railings, traffic railings, combination traffic and pedestrian railings, and combination traffic and bicycle railings. AASHTO specifications [1989, 1992b] provide current guide specifications for highway bridge railings.

6.5.5 Medians

Lanes carrying the opposing traffic should preferably be carried on two separate structures. However, when the width limitations dictate the use of the same bridge for lanes of opposing traffic, they should be separated by traffic separators known as medians, usually of parapet sections 12 to 27 in. high.

6.5.6 Drainage

Effective means of drainage, both transverse and longitudinal, should be provided on a bridge roadway. In those regions of the country where salts or deicing chemicals are not used, drainage of the deck is required only to prevent ponding of water in the travelled lanes. However, in the parts of the country subject to snow where salt is used as a deicing agent, positive drainage is a must to reduce high maintenance costs.

General guidelines for drainage can be found in pertinent AASHTO specifications [AASHTO, 1991a,b]. However, most agencies with jurisdiction over bridges have their own specific policies and procedures for drainage. Vertical openings or drains through the deck are not efficient solutions for drainage because they invariably get clogged and become nonfunctional. The simplest solution to the drainage problem is to allow water to discharge over the side of the bridge. Transverse drainage is provided by a suitable crown in the deck (about $\frac{1}{8}$ in./ft), and the longitudinal drainage by camber or gradient (AASHTO 1.5), all of which can be easily accomplished mechanically. For longitudinally horizontal bridges, a camber of 0.50 to 1.0 percent is generally provided to carry the water in the gutters to the ends of the span. Bridges built on a grade usually do not require any specific provisions for drainage. However, water flowing downgrade in a gutter section should not be permitted to run onto the bridge. Instead, it should be intercepted and discharged into a catch basin located off the bridge. Longitudinal drainage on long bridges should be provided by a sufficient number of scuppers or inlets of proper sizes. The details of deck drains should be such as to prevent the discharge of drainage water against any portion of the structure or on moving traffic below, and to prevent erosion at the outlet of the downspout. Overhanging portions of the deck should be provided with a drip bead or notch to prevent water from returning onto the bottom of the superstructure.

6.5.7 Roadway Width

The width of the roadway on a bridge is defined as the clear width measured at right angles to the longitudinal centerline of the bridge between the bottom of the curbs, or in their absence, the distance between the nearest faces of the bridge railing (AASHTO 2.1.2). The actual roadway width to be provided would depend on the number of traffic lanes and on the shoulder width, which in turn depend on the volume of traffic. General guidelines for roadway widths suitable for various volumes of traffic are spelled out in pertinent AASHTO documents [AASHTO, 1992c,d]; however, practices may vary among states having jurisdictions over bridges. Usually, the roadway widths are at least the distances between the approach guardrails, if guardrails are provided, or they equal the width of the approach roadway section, including shoulders. Where a curbed roadway section approaches a bridge, the same section is carried across the bridge [AASHTO, 1992a, Article 2.3.1].

6.6
DESIGN OF SLAB BRIDGES

Slab bridges are characterized by simple or continuous concrete slabs spanning in the direction of traffic. They constitute the simplest type of highway bridges. Design of a reinforced concrete one-way slab to carry highway bridge loading is initiated by assuming a suitable thickness based on the minimum thickness requirements for deflection control, as stipulated in AASHTO 8.9.2 (see Chapter 5, Table 5.3). This gives the first estimate of the dead load due to the self-weight of the slab, to which the weight due to the wearing surface, say 25 to 35 lb/ft^2, is added to obtain the total dead load. The live load moments and shears are calculated according to the methods described in Chapter 4 and are multiplied by the factor $(1 + I)$ to account for the effect of impact. Note that, since the spans of the one-way slab bridges are usually under 35 ft, the value of the impact factor is 0.3. The slab is then designed for the sum of the dead and the live load moments (including impact). Note that the cost difference between a short span designed for HS15 and HS20 loading is generally less than 2 percent. The differences in reinforcing for continuous slab bridges designed for HS15 or HS20 loading, having 20-ft, 30-ft, and 40-ft end spans are only 0.3, 0.6, and 1.5 lb/ft^2 of the deck area, respectively. It is therefore recommended that all short-span concrete bridges be designed for HS20 loading [PCI, 1975]. Since the difference in the cost of Grade 40 and Grade 60 bars is not significant, it is also recommended that Grade 60 reinforcements be used for designing concrete bridges. Example 6.1 illustrates the design of a typical single-span reinforced concrete slab bridge. Both methods of design—the service load method and the load factor design—are illustrated.

EXAMPLE 6.1. Design a two-lane reinforced concrete slab bridge for a clear span of 20 ft to carry HS20 loading. A provision of 30 lb/ft ^{2} of dead load should be made in the design for the future wearing surface. The following data are given: $f_c' = 3000$ psi, Grade 40 reinforcement, clear width = 40 ft.

Calculations. The design of a slab bridge essentially consists of two parts: design of the slab and design of the longitudinal edge beams.

Design by the service load method: Design of slab. Assume 6 in. to the center of the bearings from the face of the abutments:

$$L = S = 20 + 2 \times (\tfrac{6}{12}) = 21 \text{ ft}$$

The minimum slab thickness is given by AASHTO 8.9.3 (Table 5.3 in this text) for deflection control:

$$t_{min} = 1.2\left(\frac{S + 10}{30}\right)$$

$$= 1.2\left(\frac{21 + 10}{30}\right)$$

$$= 1.24 \text{ ft}$$

Therefore, try a 15-in.-thick slab.

$$\begin{aligned}
\text{Self-weight of slab} &= 1 \times 1.25 \times 150 = 187.5 \text{ lb/ft}^2 \\
\text{Wearing surface} & \qquad\qquad\qquad\quad = 30.0 \text{ lb/ft}^2 \\
\hline
\text{Total load} & \qquad\qquad\qquad\quad = 217.5 \text{ lb/ft}^2
\end{aligned}$$

Dead-load moment $M_D = wL^2/8 = 0.2175 \times (21)^2/8 = 11{,}990$ lb-ft

To calculate live-load moment, the weight of one rear wheel of the HS20 truck (16 kips) is distributed over a width, E, per AASHTO 3.24.3.2:

$$E = 4 + 0.06S = 4 + 0.06 \times 21 = 5.26 < 7.0 \text{ ft}$$

$$\text{The weight on a unit width of slab} = \frac{\text{weight of one rear wheel}}{E}$$

$$= \frac{16{,}000}{5.26}$$

$$= 3042 \text{ lb}$$

This 3042-lb load is treated as a concentrated load on a span of 21 ft, and the corresponding live-load moment is

$$M_{L,\text{truck}} = \frac{PS}{4} = 3042 \times \frac{21}{4} = 15{,}970 \text{ lb-ft}$$

Compare this with moment due to HS20 lane loading. The lane load (both the uniform and the concentrated) is distributed over a width of $2E$; thus,

$$w = \frac{640}{2 \times 5.26} = 60.8 \text{ psf}$$

The live-load moment due to this load is

$$M_w = \frac{wL^2}{8} = \frac{60.8 \times (21)^2}{8} = 3352 \text{ lb-ft}$$

The concentrated load is

$$P = \frac{18}{2 \times 5.26} = 1.711 \text{ kips}$$

The moment due to this load is given by

$$M_{\text{conc load}} = \frac{PL}{4} = \frac{1.711 \times 21}{4} = 8.98 \text{ kip-ft}$$

The total live-load moment due to lane loading is

$$M_L = 3.352 + 8.98 = 12.332 \text{ kip-ft} < 15.97 \text{ kip-ft (truck loading)}$$

Therefore, the truck loading governs. Use $M_L = 15.97$ kip-ft (the larger value):

$$\text{Impact:} \; I = \frac{50}{L + 125} = \frac{50}{21 + 125} = 0.342 > 0.3$$

Hence, use $I = 0.3$ (maximum value). Thus,

$$\begin{aligned}
M_I &= 0.3 \times 15.97 &&= 4.79 \text{ kip-ft} \\
M_{\text{total}} &= 11.99 + 15.97 + 4.79 &&= 32.75 \text{ kip-ft}
\end{aligned}$$

For $f'_c = 3000$ psi, $n = 9$ (Table A.14, Appendix A). For the design of rectangular sections, $k = 0.351$ and $j = 0.883$ (Table A.16, Appendix A). Thus, from Eq. 6.4,

$$d = \sqrt{\frac{2M}{f_c k j b}} = \sqrt{\frac{2 \times 32.75 \times 12}{1.2 \times 0.351 \times 0.883 \times 12}} = 13.2 \text{ in.}$$

Assuming #8 for main reinforcing bar, and 1 in. as clear cover, the total required slab thickness is $h = 13.2 + 0.5 + 1 = 14.7$ in. Use $h = 15$ in., required for deflection control. Then, the effective depth is $d = 15 - 0.5 - 1.0 = 13.5$ in. From Eq. 6.5,

$$A_s = \frac{M}{f_s j d} = \frac{32.75 \times 12}{20 \times 0.883 \times 13.5} = 1.65 \text{ in.}^2$$

Therefore, provide #9 @ 7 in. o.c., $A_s = 1.71$ in.^{2} (Appendix A, Table A.19).

Distribution reinforcement (AASHTO 3.24.10.2)

Percentage of reinforcement $= 100/\sqrt{S} = 100/\sqrt{21} = 21.82\% < 50\%$ max.

Therefore, $A_s = 0.2182 \times 1.65 = 0.36$ in.^{2} Provide #6 @ 15 in. o.c., $A_s = 0.36$ in.^{2}, directly above and perpendicular to the main reinforcement.

Temperature reinforcement (AASHTO 8.20.1)

$$A_s = \tfrac{1}{8} \text{ in.}^2 \text{ per ft}$$

in each direction. Provide #4 @ 18 in. o.c. in each direction below the top face of the slab. All reinforcement details are shown in Fig. E6.1b.

Shear and bond (AASHTO 3.24.4). Slab designed for bending by the previous method is considered satisfactory in shear and bond; hence, no further checking is necessary.

Check for minimum reinforcement (AASHTO 8.17.1.1)

$$f_r = 7.5 \sqrt{f'_c} = 7.5 \sqrt{3000} = 410.8 \text{ psi}$$

$$I_{cr} = \frac{bh^3}{12} = \frac{12 \times 15^3}{12} = 3375 \text{ in.}^4$$

$$M_{cr} = \frac{f_r I_{cr}}{h/2} = \frac{410.8 \times 3375}{7.5 \times 12,000} = 15.41 \text{ kip-ft}$$

$$1.2 M_{cr} = 1.2 \times 15.41 = 18.5 \text{ kip-ft}$$

$$M_{design} = 32.75 \text{ kip-ft} > 1.2 M_{cr} = 18.5 \text{ kip-ft; OK.}$$

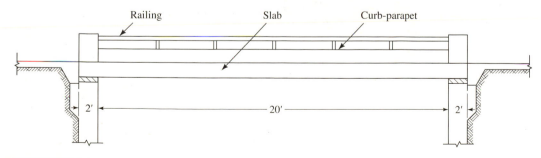

FIGURE E6.1a
A reinforced concrete slab bridge.

Fatigue stress limits (AASHTO 8.16.8.3). Fatigue stress limits are to be checked for the service load conditions, as provided by AASHTO Eq. 8.60.

$$f_f = 21 - 0.33 f_{min} + 8\left(\frac{r}{h}\right)$$

The minimum stress level, f_{min}, is caused by dead loads only. From service load design calculations, $M_D = 11.99$ kip-ft.

$$A_s = 1.71 \text{ in.}^2, \rho = \frac{A_s}{bd} = \frac{1.71}{12 \times 13.5} = 0.0106$$

From Table A.15 (Appendix A), for $n = 9$ and $\rho = 0.0106$ (by interpolation), $k = 0.351$ and $j = 0.883$. Therefore, the minimum stress, f_{min}, is

$$f_{min} = f_s = \frac{M}{A_s jd} = \frac{11.99 \times 12}{1.71 \times 0.883 \times 13.5} = 7.05 \text{ ksi}$$

The maximum stress is caused by the live load plus impact; the corresponding moment, including the dead-load moment, is $M_{total} = 32.75$ kip-ft. The corresponding stress in the main reinforcement is

$$f_s = \frac{M}{A_s jd} = \frac{32.75 \times 12}{1.71 \times 0.883 \times 13.5} = 19.28 \text{ ksi}$$

Thus, the actual stress range is $f_f = 19.28 - 7.05 = 12.23$ ksi. According to AASHTO Eq. 8.60,

$$f_f = 21 - 0.33 \times 7.05 + 8 \times 0.3 = 21.08 \text{ ksi} > 12.23 \text{ ksi}$$

Hence, the fatigue stress limit requirements are satisfied.

Design of longitudinal edge beams. AASHTO 3.24.8 stipulates that edge beams be provided for all slabs having primary reinforcement parallel to traffic. Three alternatives are suggested for providing edge beams:

1. A slab section additionally reinforced
2. A beam integral with and deeper than the slab
3. An integrally reinforced section of slab and curb

Although a safety curb would be provided for the bridge, it will be poured only after the slab has hardened (to facilitate screeding off the slab). As such, the curb is not considered an integral part of the longitudinal edge beam, which eliminates the second and the third alternatives. One would, therefore, choose the first alternative—an additionally reinforced section of the slab—as the longitudinal edge beam. Choose $b = 24$ in., so that the cross section of the longitudinal edge beam is 24 in. $\times$ 15 in. Provide a curb 10 in. high (standard depth), which gives the total height of the beam as 25 in. (for computing the self-weight).

$$\text{Self-weight (including the curb)} = 24 \times 25 \times \tfrac{150}{144} = 625 \text{ lb/ft}$$
$$\text{Weight of railing (assumed)} \qquad\qquad = \quad 15 \text{ lb/ft}$$

$$\text{Total dead load} \qquad\qquad\qquad\qquad = 640 \text{ lb/ft}$$

$$M_D = 0.64 \times (21)^2/8 = 35.28 \text{ kip-ft}$$

The live-load moment in a longitudinal edge beam is given by AASHTO 3.24.8.2:

$$M_L = 0.10 P_{20} S = 0.10 \times 16{,}000 \times 21 = 33.6 \text{ kip-ft}$$

$$M_{total} = 35.28 + 33.6 = 68.88 \text{ kip-ft}$$

The required beam depth, with $b = 24$ in., can now be calculated from Eq. 6.4. With $k = 0.351$ and $j = 0.883$ for $n = 9$ (Table A.16, Appendix A),

$$d = \sqrt{\frac{2M}{f_c k j b}} = \sqrt{\frac{2 \times 68.88 \times 12}{1.2 \times 0.351 \times 0.883 \times 24}} = 13.53 \text{ in.}$$

With 1 in. cover and #8 as the main reinforcing bar, $h_{required} = 13.53 + 1 + 0.5 = 15.03$ in., say 15 in., as provided. The required reinforcement can now be calculated from Eq. 6.5:

$$A_s = \frac{M}{f_s j d} = \frac{68.88 \times 12}{20.0 \times 0.883 \times 13.5} = 3.47 \text{ in.}^2$$

Therefore, provide four #9 bars, $A_s = 4.0$ in.$^2 > 3.47$ in.^{2} (Table A.20, Appendix A).

Check for minimum reinforcement (AASHTO 8.17.1.1). From Eq. 6.30:

$$f_r = 7.5 \sqrt{f_c'} = 7.5 \sqrt{3000} = 410.8 \text{ psi}$$

$$I_{cr} = \frac{24 \times 15^3}{12} = 6750 \text{ in.}^4$$

Then, from Eq. 6.31:

$$M_{cr} = \frac{f_r I_{cr}}{h/2} = \frac{410.8 \times 6750}{7.5 \times 12,000} = 30.81 \text{ kip-ft}$$

$$1.2 M_{cr} = 1.2 \times 30.81 = 36.97 \text{ kip-ft}$$

$$M_{design} = 68.88 \text{ kip-ft} > 1.2 M_{cr} = 36.97 \text{ kip-ft; OK.}$$

Fatigue stress limits (AASHTO 8.16.8.3). Fatigue stress limits will be checked for the service load conditions. The permissible stress range is given by AASHTO Eq. 8.60:

$$f_f = 21 - 0.33 f_{min} + 8 \left(\frac{r}{h} \right)$$

The minimum stress level, f_{min}, is caused by dead loads only. From service load design calculations, $M_D = 35.28$ kip-ft.

$$A_s = 4.00 \text{ in.}^2, \rho = A_s/bd = 4.00/(24 \times 13.5) = 0.0123$$

From Table A.15 (Appendix A), for $n = 9$ and $\rho = 0.0123$ (by interpolation), $k = 0.373$, $j = 0.875$. The minimum stress, therefore, is (from Eq. 6.5)

$$f_{min} = f_s = \frac{M}{A_s j d} = \frac{35.28 \times 12}{4.0 \times 0.875 \times 13.5} = 8.96 \text{ ksi}$$

The maximum stress is caused by the live load plus impact; the corresponding moment, including the dead-load moment, is $M_{total} = 68.88$ kip-ft. The corresponding stress in the main reinforcement is

$$f_s = \frac{M}{A_s j d} = \frac{68.88 \times 12}{4.0 \times 0.875 \times 13.5} = 17.49 \text{ ksi}$$

Thus, the actual stress range, $f_f = 17.49 - 8.96 = 8.53$ ksi. According to AASHTO Eq. 8.60, the permissible stress range is $f_f = 21 - 0.33 \times 7.84 + 8 \times 0.3 = 20.81$ ksi > 8.53 ksi. Hence, the fatigue stress limit requirements are satisfied.

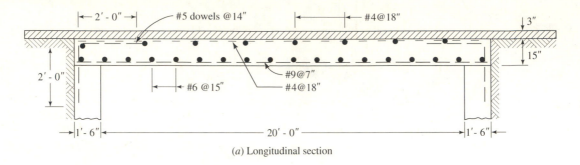

(a) Longitudinal section

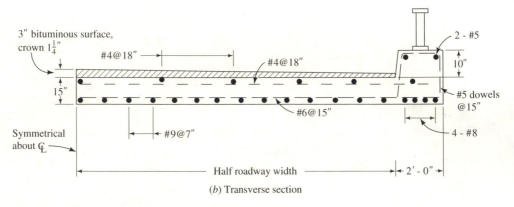

(b) Transverse section

FIGURE E6.1b
Reinforcement details (slab and the edge beams).

Reinforcement details are shown in Fig. E6.1b. #5 dowels @ 18 in. o.c., along with two #5 hanger bars, are provided for the entire lengths of longitudinal edge beams.

Miscellaneous details. For effective drainage, the roadway surface is crowned by providing varying thicknesses of the wearing surface across the deck cross section. According to AASHTO 8.5.1, devices for expansion and contraction due to temperature changes are to be provided at supports only for spans exceeding 40 ft. Thus, bearing pads are not required to be provided for slab bridges. Instead, the slab rests directly on the abutments—on the bridge seat precoated with a bituminous mixture—and fixed bearings are provided by placing vertical dowels usually @ 12 in. o.c. along the length of the abutments. As shown in Fig. E6.1b, these dowels extend vertically 24 in. into the abutment and bend to extend 24 in. horizontally inside the slab. This detail also acts as a preventive measure against cracking that may occur near the abutment edges.

Design by the load factor method: Design of slab. The following service load moments were calculated earlier:

$$M_D = 11.99 \text{ kip-ft}$$

$$M_L = 15.97 \text{ kip-ft}$$

$$M_I = 4.79 \text{ kip-ft}$$

These moments will be appropriately factored for a Group I loading combination per AASHTO 3.22.1 (see Table 3.12, Chapter 3).

$$M_u = \gamma[\beta_D \times D + \beta_L(L + I)]$$

where $\gamma = 1.3$

$\beta_D = 1.0$ for flexural members (see footnotes to Table 3.12)

$\beta_L = 1.67$ (or $\frac{5}{3}$)

Thus, $M_u = 1.3[11.99 + 1.67(15.97 + 4.79)] = 60.66$ kip-ft. For flexure, $\phi = 0.9$ (AASHTO 8.16.1.2). For a slab, $b = 12$ in., $d = 13.5$ in. (based on the minimum depth requirements, determined earlier). Thus,

$$\frac{M_u}{\phi b d^2} = \frac{60.66 \times 12{,}000}{0.9 \times 12 \times (13.5)^2} = 369.82 \text{ lb/in.}^2$$

From Table A.17 (Appendix A), for $M_u/\phi b d^2 = 369.0$ lb/in.^{2} (close enough to 369.82 lb/in.^{2}), $\rho = 0.0100$, from which $A_s = 0.010 \times 12 \times 13.5 = 1.62$ in.^{2} Therefore, provide #9 @ 7 in. o.c., $A_s = 1.71$ in.^{2} (as in the case of the service load design method).

Distribution reinforcement. This requirement is the same as in the case of service load design. Provide #6 @ 15 in. o.c. directly above and perpendicular to the main reinforcement.

Temperature and shrinkage reinforcement. This requirement is the same as in the case of service load design. Provide #4 @ 18 in. o.c. in each direction under the top face of the slab.

Check for minimum reinforcement (AASHTO 8.17.1.1). Calculations are the same as provided earlier for the service load design.

Fatigue stress limits (AASHTO 8.16.8.3). Fatigue stress limits are to be checked for the service load conditions. Calculations are the same as provided earlier for the service load design.

Design of longitudinal edge beams. From calculations for the service load design, one has the following values of design moments:

$$M_D = 35.28 \text{ kip-ft}$$

$$M_L = 33.6 \text{ kip-ft}$$

Thus,

$$M_u = \gamma[\beta_D \times D + \beta_L(L + I)]$$

$$= 1.3[1.0 \times 35.28 + 1.67 \times (33.6)]$$

$$= 118.81 \text{ kip-ft}$$

$$\frac{M_u}{\phi b d^2} = \frac{118.81 \times 12{,}000}{0.9 \times 24 \times (13.5)^2} = 362.2 \text{ lb/in.}^2$$

From Table A.17 (Appendix A), for $M_u/\phi b d^2 = 362.2$ lb/in.^{2}, $\rho = 0.0098$, from which $A_s = \rho b d = 0.0098 \times 24 \times 13.5 = 3.17$ in.^{2} Therefore, provide four #9 bars, $A_s = 4.0$ in.$^2 > 3.17$ in.^{2} (Table A.15, Appendix A).

Check for minimum reinforcement (AASHTO 8.17.1.1). These calculations are the same as provided earlier for the service load design.

Fatigue stress limits (AASHTO 8.16.8.3). Fatigue stress limit is to be checked for the service load conditions. Calculations for this are the same as provided earlier for the service load design. Since there has been no change in any type of reinforcement as a result of design by the load factor design method, the reinforcement details remain the same as those for design by the service load method (Fig. E6.1b).

6.7
DESIGN OF T-BEAM BRIDGES

6.7.1 General

T-beams are proportioned to conform to requirements as stipulated in AASHT0 8.10.1. Design of a T-beam consists of two parts: design of the transverse slab and design of the longitudinal beam of a T-section. The basic design procedure, similar to that used for T-beams in buildings, involves determination of three dimensions: the slab thickness, the spacing of webs, and the size of webs. Accordingly, the design of a T-beam is a two-step process. The first step is to design the slab, spanning continuously over the webs, per AASHTO 3.24.3.1, case A (main reinforcement perpendicular to traffic). The T-beam, spanning longitudinally between abutments or piers, with a portion of the slab acting as its top flange, is designed next.

Design of a T-beam for highway bridges is initiated by selecting a suitable flange thickness as stipulated in AASHTO 8.11.1. For one-way slabs (main reinforcement parallel to traffic), the minimum thickness is governed by deflection control requirements (AASHTO 8.9.2); the earlier editions of the AASHTO specifications stipulated the same minimum thickness requirements for the flanges of T-beams (main reinforcement perpendicular to traffic) also. However, these requirements for T-beam flanges were deleted in the later editions, and there are none in the current AASHTO specifications [AASHTO, 1992a]. The reasoning behind this deletion appears to be the fact that, for a continuous slab spanning (transversely) over closely spaced supports (webs of T-beams), the deflection, being very small, does not constitute the governing factor. In the absence of any specifics, some engineers still use the same old requirements as a guide for the initial selection of the flange thickness, however. This minimum thickness may be superseded on the higher side by the regional or the agency requirements, for various reasons.

The slab is designed to resist transverse bending due to loads that include its own weight, the wearing surface, and the live load plus impact. In a T-beam construction, the slab is cast monolithically with the webs; accordingly, the span is taken as the clear distance between the webs (S). Because this distance is rather small, the value of the impact factor for slab design is always 0.3. In the absence of a definite expression to be used for calculating the dead-load moments (none are given in the AASHTO specifications), a coefficient of $\frac{1}{10}$ is generally used for both the positive and the negative design moments (i.e., $M = \pm wS^2/10$).

For the T-beam design, the usual trial and error procedure is followed. Initially, a suitable (but minimum) depth of the T-section is selected based on the requirements of deflection control (AASHTO Table 8.9.2). A web width in the 12 to 15-in. range is selected arbitrarily for the initial trial section, to be modified later as necessary. A portion of the transverse slab is assigned to the T-section as its compression flange. The width of this portion of the slab that can be associated with the T-section as its compression flange is known as the effective flange width and was discussed in Chapter 4. A comprehensive discussion of the concept of effective flange width can be found in the literature [Wang, 1953; Lee, 1962; Severn, 1962, 1964; Timoshenko and Goodier, 1970; Cheung and Chan, 1978; Sabins, 1979; Bakht and Jaeger, 1985]. For design purposes, the effective flange width should be the *least* of the following (AASHTO 8.10.1.1):

1. $\frac{1}{4}L$, where $L =$ span
2. Twelve times the slab thickness + web thickness ($12t_s + b_w$)
3. The distance between the centerlines of adjacent webs

Having selected the initial cross section of the T-beam, the self-weight of the beam is calculated. The sidewalks (where provided), safety curbs, and parapets are cast after the T-beams have hardened; accordingly, their weight, including that of the railings and the wearing surface, often referred to as the superimposed dead load, can be distributed equally to all T-beams. The dead-load moments are caused by the self-weight of the beam and the superimposed dead load. Moments and shear due to the live load and impact are calculated as discussed in Chapter 4, and the T-beam is designed for the total loads. The span length is taken as the clear span plus the depth of the T-beam, which need not exceed the distance between the centers of supports (AASHTO 8.8.1).

The spacing of T-beam webs is a crucial factor affecting the economics of the T-beam flooring, which must be decided by the designer; however, there are no relevant criteria in the specifications. Although a larger web spacing would result in a smaller number of T-beams (and less formwork), it will also result in a relatively thicker slab and a deeper web. This is so because the live-load moment in the slab and the live-load distribution factor for the T-beam are both directly proportional to the clear web spacing. The determination of a specific combination of these parameters that would result in the least weight of a T-beam flooring is a problem of structural optimization. One should remember, however, that the least weight does not necessarily translate into the least cost, because the solution of the least-weight problem does not involve the cost function. Variations in local prices and in the availability of skilled labor and materials render the cost function highly indeterminate, which makes coupling the least-weight and the least-cost parameters almost impossible. From a practical standpoint, however, one may select initially a desirable slab thickness ($7\frac{1}{2}$ to $8\frac{1}{2}$-in. range) based on the deflection and vibration control, or any other requirements (e.g., the minimum depth set by the owner agencies for practical reasons), and determine the slab span (web spacing) for which this thickness would be adequate. The spacing of webs should also be such that, preferably, the exterior T-beams would have the same flange widths as the interior ones. The clear roadway width to be carried across the bridge also influences the spacing of the webs to some extent. The total width of the slab, which equals the clear roadway width plus the widths of two parapet curbs, should be divided by a suitable whole number to arrive at the required number of webs. A few trials should give reasonably satisfactory spacings of the webs, usually in the $5\frac{1}{2}$ to 8.0-ft range.

6.7.2 Examples

Example 6.2 illustrates the basic design procedure for a two-lane highway bridge carrying HS20 loading. Although the calculation of maximum design moment in the slab and the T-beam is simple and straightforward according to the AASHTO method, the maximum design moment and shear in the T-beam at various locations along the span involves lengthy computations involving influence lines owing to the moving nature of the highway loads.

> **EXAMPLE 6.2.** Design a reinforced concrete T-beam bridge for a span of 40 ft between centers of bearings for HS20–44 loading carrying two traffic lanes 10-ft wide each and 6-ft shoulder widths on each side. Sidewalks are not required but standard parapets should be provided with railing (15 lb/ft) on each side. A provision of 15 lb/ft^2 of dead load should be made in the design for the wearing surface. Use $f_c' = 4000$ psi and Grade 40 reinforcement. The deck and the webs of the T-beams are to be cast monolithically. Assume the distance between the centerline of bearings and the face of the support is 12 in. Live-load deflection is to be limited to $L/800$.
>
> *Calculations.* The slab is to be supported as shown in Fig. E6.2a. A curb-to-curb roadway width of 32 ft has been arbitrarily selected (two 10-ft-wide lanes plus two 6-ft-wide shoulders) for this example. With the bottom width of the parapet curbs at 1 ft 9 in. on each side, the total width of the slab comes to 35 ft 9 in. The slab is assumed to be supported by six T-beams, so that each would have a flange width of 5 ft 11 in. A width of 3 in. has been added on each side of the parapet curb, resulting in a total slab width of 36 ft and a flange width of 6 ft, a convenient number (instead of 5 ft 11 in.).

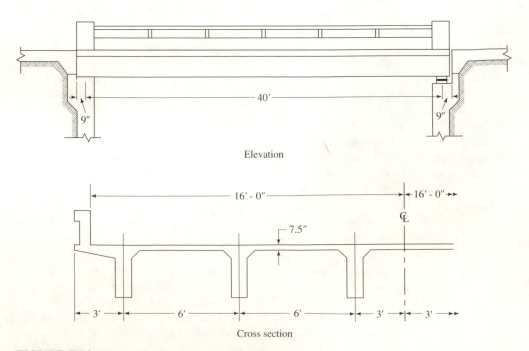

FIGURE E6.2a
Bridge cross section.

Service load design (AASHTO 8.15): Design of slab

$$\text{Spacing of T-beams} = 6 \text{ ft } 0 \text{ in.}$$

$$\text{Estimated stem size} = 15 \times 33$$

$$\text{Estimated concrete slab thickness} = 7\tfrac{1}{2} \text{ in.}$$

$$\text{Asphalt wearing surface} = 15 \text{ lb/ft}^2$$

$$\text{Slab span: } S = \text{clear span} = 6.00 - \tfrac{15}{12} = 4.75 \text{ ft}$$

Minimum slab thickness (AASHTO Table 8.9.2 and Chapter 5 of this text):

$$t_s = \frac{S + 10}{30} = \frac{4.75 + 10}{30} = 0.492 \text{ ft} = 5.9 \text{ in.}$$

This is less than the assumed slab thickness of 7.5 in. Hence, use a 7.5-in.-thick slab.

$$\text{Self-weight of slab} = \left(\frac{7.5}{12}\right) \times 1 \times 150 \qquad = \quad 94 \text{ lb/ft}$$

$$\text{Wearing surface} \qquad\qquad\qquad\qquad\qquad = \quad 15 \text{ lb/ft}$$

$$\text{Total load} \qquad\qquad\qquad\qquad\qquad w = \quad 109 \text{ lb/ft}$$

$$M_D = \pm\frac{wL^2}{10} = \pm\frac{0.109(4.75)^2}{10} = \pm 0.25 \text{ k-ft}$$

$$M_L = \pm 0.8\left(\frac{S + 2}{32}\right)P_{20}$$

$$= \pm 0.8 \times \left(\frac{4.75 + 2}{32}\right) \times 16.0$$

$$= \pm 2.70 \text{ kip-ft}$$

$$\text{Impact factor, } I = \frac{50}{L + 125}$$

$$= \frac{50}{4.75 + 125}$$

$$= 0.39 > 0.3 \text{ (maximum value permitted)}$$

Therefore, use $I = 0.3$ (maximum value). Hence, $M_{L+I} = 2.70 \times 1.3 = 3.51$ kip-ft. Total design moment, $M_T = 0.25 + 3.51 = 3.76$ kip-ft. With $f_c = 0.4 \times 4000 = 1600$ psi and $f_s = 20{,}000$ psi, the design coefficients are (Table A.14, Appendix A)

$$j = 0.87$$

$$k = 0.39$$

$$d = \sqrt{\frac{2M}{f_c k j b}}$$

$$= \sqrt{\frac{2 \times 3.76 \times 12{,}000}{1600 \times 0.39 \times 0.87 \times 12}}$$

$$= 3.72 \text{ in.}$$

Assuming #5 bars for the main reinforcement and 2 in. clear cover, $t_{reqd} = 3.72 + \frac{1}{2} \times 0.625 + 2 = 6.03$ in. < 7.5 in. (min.). With $t = 7.5$ in., $d = 7.5 - 0.31 - 2 = 5.19$ in.

$$A_s = \frac{M}{f_s jd}$$

$$= \frac{3.76 \times 12}{20 \times 0.87 \times 5.19}$$

$$= 0.5 \text{ in.}^2$$

Provide #5 @ 7 in. o.c. both at top and bottom.

$$A_s = 0.53 \text{ in.}^2 > 0.5 \text{ in.}^2, \text{reqd.}$$

Distribution steel: AASHTO 3.24.10. According to AASHTO Eq. 3.22

$$A_s = \frac{220}{\sqrt{S}} = \frac{220}{\sqrt{4.75}} = 92\% > 67\% \text{ (maximum required)}$$

Hence, provide 67 percent of the main reinforcement as the distribution reinforcement.

$$A_{s,\,dist} = 0.67 \times 0.53 = 0.36 \text{ in.}^2$$

Therefore, provide #5 @ 10 in. o.c., $A_s = 0.37$ in.^{2} This reinforcement is to be provided directly over and perpendicular to the main reinforcement in the middle half of the deck span. At least half of this reinforcement should be placed in the outer quarters of the spans, to act as temperature and shrinkage reinforcement.

Temperature steel: AASHTO 8.20

$$A_s = \tfrac{1}{8} \text{ in.}^2/\text{ft of slab}$$

Provide #4 @ 18 in. o.c. ($A_s = 0.13$ in.^{2}) directly under and perpendicular to the top reinforcement. All slab reinforcing details are shown later in Fig. E6.2b.

Interior girders

Distance between the center line of the bearing to the face of the support $= 12$ in.

Span (between centers of bearings) $= 40$ ft

Spacing of T-beams $= 6$ ft 0 in.

Depth of T-beam $= 0.07S$ (AASHTO Table 8.9.2)

$= 0.07 \times 40 = 2.8$ ft $= 33.6$ in.

Assume a total beam depth of 33 in. and a stem width of 15 in. as the initial trial section. In the absence of any controlling design criteria for the web size, its dimensions will be selected on the basis of shear, as shown later.

Dead load

Weight of slab @ 109 lb/ft$^2 = 0.109 \times 6.0$ $= 654$ lb/ft

Weight of T-beam stem $= 15 \times 25.5 \times \frac{150}{144}$ $= 398$ lb/ft

Total dead load $w = 1052$ lb/ft

$= 1.052$ k/ft

$$M_D = \tfrac{1}{8}wL^2 = \tfrac{1}{8} \times 1.052 \times (40)^2 = 210.4 \text{ k-ft}$$

$$V_D = \tfrac{1}{2} \times 1.052 \times 40 \qquad = 21.04 \text{ kips}$$

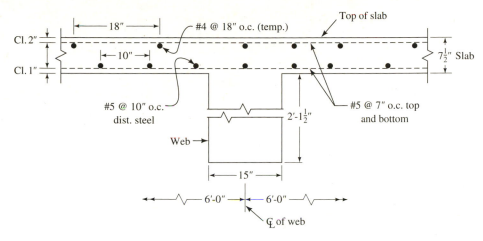

FIGURE E6.2b
Slab reinforcing details (web reinforcing not shown).

Live load. The maximum live-load moment (LLM) can be computed from the influence line (IL, Fig. E6.2c). The maximum LLM occurs at 17.67 ft from support. The maximum dead-load moment is calculated at this point to be combined with the maximum live-load moment. The LLM due to one HS20 truck is $M_L = 32(9.864 + 3.68 + \frac{1}{4} \times 2.409) = 449.8$ k-ft. Alternatively, the maximum LLM due to one HS20 truck can be read directly from Table A5 (Appendix A) for HS20–44 loading: $M_{40} = 449.8$ ft-kips.

$$\text{Distribution factor, } DF = \frac{S}{6} = \frac{6.0}{6} = 1.0$$

$$\text{Impact factor, } I = \frac{50}{L + 125} = \frac{50}{40 + 125} = 0.3$$

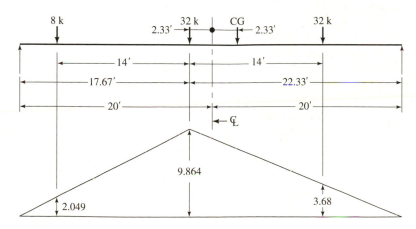

FIGURE E6.2c
Influence line for maximum live-load moment.

Therefore, the design live-load moment including the impact is

$$M_{L+I} = (\text{LLM due to one truck}) \left(\tfrac{1}{2}\right) (\text{Dist. factor}) (1 + I)$$

$$= 449.8 \times \tfrac{1}{2} \times 1.0 \times (1 + 0.3) = 292.5 \text{ k-ft}$$

In this calculation, the factor $\tfrac{1}{2}$ has been used to convert the LLM due to *one truck* (two wheel lines) to LLM due to *one line* of wheels, and the factor 1.0 (distribution factor $= S/6$) has been used to take into effect the number of wheel lines associated with one T-beam based on spacing of T-beams.

The maximum dead-load moment at $x = 17.67$ ft from the support can be computed from the same IL diagram as for the live load.

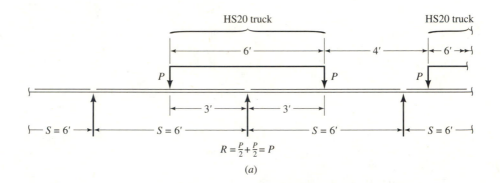

(a)

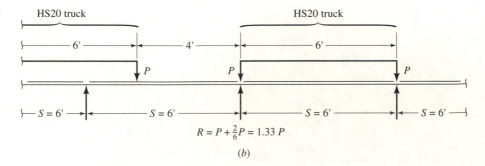

(b)

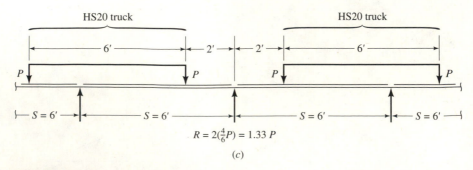

(c)

FIGURE E6.2d
Critical transverse positions of truck due to wheel loads at the end of the beam.

$$M_D = w \times \text{area under the IL diagram}$$
$$= 1.052 \times (\tfrac{1}{2} \times 40 \times 9.864)$$
$$= 207.5 \text{ k-ft}$$
$$M_{\text{Total}} = 207.5 + 292.5 = 500.0 \text{ k-ft}$$

The maximum shear in the T-beam is to be computed according to the provisions of AASHTO 3.23.1 (see discussion in Chapter 4, Sec. 4.7.2.2. and Fig. 4.17). Transversely, the HS20 truck (i.e., the axles) can be placed laterally in any one of the three positions shown in Fig. E6.2d. Axle positions in Figs. E6.2d(b) and E6.2d(c) give the same maximum reaction R, which is larger than that given by axle positions in Fig. E6.2d(a). Note that Fig. E6.2d is similar to Fig. 4.17(c), drawn for the specific case of $S = 6$ ft. Thus, $R = 1.33P = 1.33 \times 16 = 21.33$ kips. Note also that according to AASHTO, the rear wheel is positioned at the end of and directly over the T-beam (or the girder) (Fig. 4.17(a)), and it is assumed that it is not laterally distributed to other T-beams.

The load due to the middle and the front wheels is assumed to be laterally distributed to other T-beams (see Example 4.1 in Chapter 4). Therefore, values of the middle and the front wheel loads associated with one T-beam (or girder) are obtained by multiplying the actual values of wheel loads by the same distribution factor as used for moment (i.e., $S/6.0 = 6.0/6 = 1.0$). The maximum live-load shear in the T-beam is obtained from the IL for maximum reaction at support (Fig. E6.2e). Thus,

load at the end   inf. line ordinates

$$V_{L,\text{support}} = 21.33 + (16 \times 1.0 \times 0.65) + (4 \times 1.0 \times 0.3) = 32.93 \text{ kips}$$

distribution factors

$$V_{L+I} = 32.93 \times (1 + 0.3) = 42.81 \text{ kips}$$

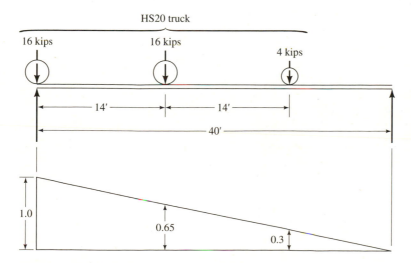

FIGURE E6.2e
Influence line for maximum shear at the support.

The maximum shear at the support due to the dead load is also computed from the IL for maximum reaction:

$$V_{D,\text{support}} = w \times \text{ area under the IL diagram}$$
$$= 1.052 \times (\tfrac{1}{2} \times 40 \times 1.0)$$
$$= 21.04 \text{ kips}$$
$$V_{\text{Total}} = 21.04 + 42.81 = 63.85 \text{ kips}$$

As pointed out earlier, before designing the section for flexure, the web will be checked for shear. The reason for this first step is that the web must have a certain minimum cross-sectional area to resist shear. If the selected cross section of the T-beam works out to be adequate for this purpose, proceed with the flexural design. If not, the cross section of the T-beam will need to be revised, and rechecked for shear before proceeding to flexural design. The allowable shear stress in concrete is (AASHTO 8.15.5.2.1)

$$v_c = 0.95 \sqrt{f_c'}$$

The allowable shear to be carried by shear reinforcement is (AASHTO 8.15.5.3.9)

$$v - v_c = 4.0 \sqrt{f_c'}$$

Therefore, the total allowable shear is given by

$$v = 4.95 \sqrt{f_c'}$$
$$= 4.95 \sqrt{4000}$$
$$= 313 \text{ psi}$$

Since $v = V/b_w d$ (AASHTO Eq. 8.3), the minimum web area required to resist shear is

$$b_w d = \frac{V}{v_c}$$
$$= \frac{63.85}{0.313}$$
$$= 204 \text{ in.}^2$$

Assuming that two or more layers of flexural reinforcement will be required, a distance of 6 in. is assumed from its centroid to the bottom of the web; thus $d = 33 - 6 = 27$ in., and $b_w d = 15 \times 27 = 405$ in.$^2 > 204$ in.^{2}, as required.

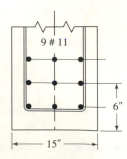

Calculate A_s for flexure assuming $d = 27$ in. and the compression resultant at $\frac{1}{2}t$ ($t =$ slab thickness) from the top fibers:

$$A_s = \frac{M}{f_s(d - t/2)} = \frac{500 \times 12}{20X(27 - 7.5/2)} = 12.38 \text{ in.}^2$$

Provide eight #11 bars ($A_s = 12.50$ in.², Table A.20, Appendix A) as shown; their centroid is located at 2.98 in. above the centroid of the bottom layer:

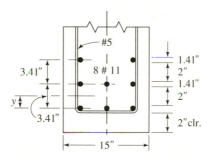

$$y = \tfrac{1}{8}(2 \times 6.82 + 3 \times 3.41) = 2.98 \text{ in.}$$

$$d = 33 - 2 - 0.625 - 1.41/2 - 2.98$$

$$= 33 - 6.31 = 26.69 \text{ in.}$$

Now, calculate the moment of resistance of the cross section of the T-beam. Check whether the neutral axis lies in the flange or the web by taking about the flange-web interface the moments of the flange and that of the transformed area of the reinforcement ($n = 8$). The effective flange width b_e is to be the least of the following (AASHTO 8.10.1.1):

1. $L/4 = 40 \times 12/4 = 120$ in.
2. c/c of webs $= 6 \times 12 = 72$ in.
3. $2(6 \times t) + b_w = 2 \times 6 \times 7.5 + 15 = 105$ in.

Hence, $b_e = 72$ in. Check if the neutral axis (N.A.) is located in the flange or the web. This is easily done by comparing the moments of areas of the flange and the transformed area of tensile reinforcement (nA_s) taken about the flange-web interface:

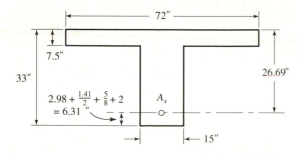

Beam cross section

$$72 \times 7.5 \times 7.5/2 \stackrel{?}{=} 8 \times 12.5 \times (26.69 - 7.5)$$

$$2025 > 1919, \text{ hence, the N.A. lies in the flange.}$$

Taking moments about the top fibers, one has $72 \times y^2/2 = 8 \times 12.5 \times (26.69 - y)$, which yields $y = 7.33$ in.; i.e., $kd = 7.33$ in.

$$jd = d - \frac{kd}{3}$$
$$= 26.69 - \frac{7.33}{3}$$
$$= 24.25 \text{ in.}$$

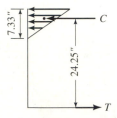

$$M = A_s f_s jd = \frac{12.5 \times 20 \times 24.25}{12}$$
$$= 505.2 \text{ k-ft} > 500.0 \text{ k-ft; OK}$$

Now, check shear stress. Shear reinforcement is to be designed for shear at a distance $d = 26.69$ in. from the face of support (or $26.69 + \frac{12}{2} = 32.69$ in., say, 33 in. from the center of support, which is 55.07 kips (AASHTO 8.15.5.1.4)). Note that the support width has been assumed to be 12 in.

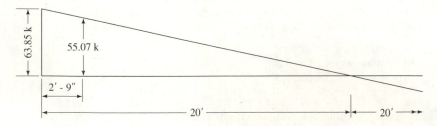

Shear at a distance $d = 2$ ft 9 in. from the support

The maximum shear stress in the beam is

$$v_{max} = \frac{V}{b_w d} = \frac{55.07 \times 1000}{15 \times 26.69} = 137.6 \text{ psi}$$

The shear stress that can be carried by concrete alone is

$$v_c = 0.95 \sqrt{f_c'} = 0.95 \sqrt{4000} = 60 \text{ psi}$$

Therefore, the shear stress to be carried by web reinforcement is

$$v_{steel} = v_{max} - v_c = 137.6 - 60 = 77.6 \text{ psi}$$

Maximum shear permitted to be carried by web reinforcement is (AASHTO 8.15.5.3.9)

$$4\sqrt{f_c'} = 4\sqrt{4000} = 253 \text{ psi} > 77.6 \text{ psi; OK}$$

Hence, the web section is adequate for shear.

Select #5 U-stirrups, $A_v = 0.61$ in.^{2} The required spacing is calculated from AASHTO Eq. 8.7:

$$s = \frac{A_v f_s}{(v - v_c)b_w} = \frac{0.61 \times 20{,}000}{77.6 \times 15} = 10.48 \text{ in.}$$

Maximum permissible spacing $= d/2 \,(\text{AASHTO } 8.19.3) = 26.69/2 = 13.35$ in. > 10.48 in. Therefore, provide #5 U-stirrups at 9 in. o.c.

Minimum shear reinforcement is to be provided according to AASHTO 8.19.1.1(b) in the region where $\frac{1}{2}v_c \leq v_c$. With #5 U-stirrups, this spacing is calculated from AASHTO Eq. 8.64:

$$s = \frac{A_v f_y}{50 b_w} = \frac{0.61 \times 40{,}000}{50 \times 15} = 32.53 \text{ in.}$$

The next step will be to calculate the moment at selected points along the span, by determining the required flexural reinforcement at those points and the points of cutoff of flexural reinforcement. This step is demonstrated for the load factor design method, which follows the calculations for the exterior girder.

Exterior girders. For simplicity in design and construction, the exterior girders are provided the same cross section as the interior girders. In addition to the dead-load moment due to the wearing surface and its own weight, it is assumed, conservatively (see Chapter 4), that the weight of the parapet curb is carried entirely by the exterior girder.

Dead load

From calculations for the interior girder, $w_d = 1052$ lb/ft

Weight of the parapet curb (see Chapter 4) $= 505$ lb/ft

Total $w_d = 1557$ lb/ft

$$M_D = \tfrac{1}{8}wL^2 = \tfrac{1}{8} \times 1.557 \times (40)^2 = 311.4 \text{ k-ft}$$

It was determined earlier that the maximum live-load moment occurs at 17.67 ft from the support. The dead-load moment at this point is found from the influence line as before. By proportion to dead-load for the interior girder (1.052 k/ft),

$$M_D = 207.5 \times \left(\frac{1.557}{1.052}\right) = 307.1 \text{ k-ft}$$

Live load. For the live-load moment, the wheel loads are to be placed as shown in Fig. 3.7.7A of AASHTO [1992a], and the live-load distribution factor will be calculated in accordance with AASHTO 3.23.2.3.1.2 (discussed in Chapter 4). For our case, the position of live load will be as shown in Fig. E6.2f.

The distribution factor, by the lever rule, $DF = 5.25/6 = 0.875$.

$$I = 0.3$$

$$M_{L+I} = 449.8 \times \tfrac{1}{2} \times 0.875 \times 1.3 = 255.8 \text{ k-ft}$$

$$M_{\text{Total}} = 307.1 + 255.8 = 562.9 \text{ k-ft}$$

This value is higher than the moment of resistance of the interior girder (505.2 k-ft). The required increase is provided by an extra #11 bar (for 9 total #11 bars, $A_s = 14.06$ in.^{2},

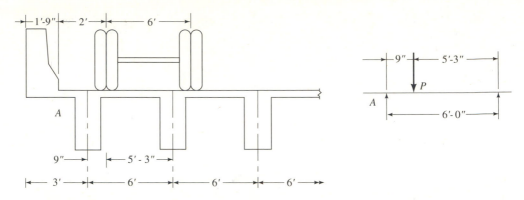

FIGURE E6.2f
Position of live load for the exterior girder.

Table A.20, Appendix A) for the flexural reinforcement, as shown. The centroid of reinforcing steel now passes through the middle row of the reinforcement.

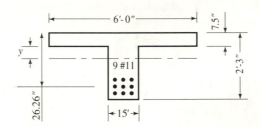

$$d = 33 - 2 - 0.625 - 1.41 - 2 - 1.41/2$$
$$= 26.26 \text{ in.}$$

Determine the location of the N.A. Check if it is located in the flange or the web, by comparing the moments of areas of the flange and the transformed area of tensile reinforcement (nA_s) taken about the flange-web interface:

$$72 \times 7.5^2/2 \gtreqless 8 \times 14.06 \times (26.26 - 7.5)$$

$$2025 < 2110; \text{ hence, the N.A. lies in the web.}$$

$$72 \times 7.5 \times (3.75 + y) + 15y^2/2 = 8 \times 14.06 \times (18.76 - y)$$

$$7.5y^2 + 652.48y - 85 = 0$$

which yields

$$y = 0.13 \text{ in. (inside the web), which is very small.}$$

For simplicity, this small distance of 0.13 in. will be ignored and the N.A. will be assumed to lie at the flange-web interface.

Calculate the moment of inertia of the cracked section and check stresses.

$$I_{cr} = 72 \times (7.5)^3 + 8 \times 14.06 \times (26.26 - 7.5)^2 = 49,711 \text{ in.}^4$$

$$f_c = \frac{M\,y_t}{I_{cr}} = \frac{562.9 \times 12{,}000 \times 7.5}{49{,}711} = 1019 \text{ psi}$$

$$f_s = n\left(\frac{M\,y_b}{I_{cr}}\right) = 8 \times \left(\frac{562.9 \times 12{,}000 \times 18.76}{49{,}711}\right) = 20{,}393 \text{ psi}$$

The overstress in tensile reinforcement is

$$\text{Overstress} = \left(\frac{20{,}393 - 20{,}000}{20{,}000}\right) \approx 2\%$$

In view of the conservative approach used here, this slight overstress is considered insignificant and acceptable.

Shear. The dead load is $w = 1.557$ k/ft, and $V_D = \frac{1}{2}wL = \frac{1}{2} \times 1.557 \times 40 = 31.14$ kips. The live-load shear is computed in the same manner as for the interior T-beam (see Fig. E6.2g for the influence line). The rear wheel (16.0 kips) is positioned just at the support, and is not subject to lateral distribution.[3] The middle (16.0 kips) and the front wheel (4.0 kips) are positioned 14 ft and 28 ft, respectively, away from the rear wheel. Both these loads are subject to lateral distribution. Thus

load at end ↙   inf. line ordinates ↙   ↘

$$V_{L,\text{support}} = 16.0 + (16.0 \times 0.875 \times 0.65) + (4.0 \times 0.875 \times 0.3)$$

↖ distribution factor ↗

$$= 26.15 \text{ kips}$$

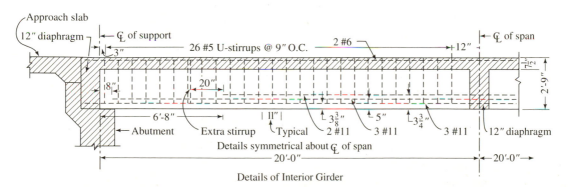

Details of Interior Girder

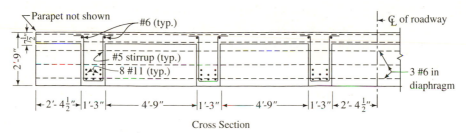

Cross Section

FIGURE E6.2g
Reinforcing details for the T-beam bridge.

[3] To be conservative, the lever rule has not been applied here.

$$V_{L+I} = 26.15 \times (1 + 0.3) = 34.0 \text{ kips}$$

$$V_{\text{Total}} = V_D + V_{L+I}$$
$$= 31.14 + 34.0 = 65.14 \text{ kips}$$

The maximum shear permitted in the T-beam is

$$V_{\max} = v_{\max} b_w d$$

$$= \frac{313 \times 15 \times 26.26}{1000}$$

$$= 123.3 \text{ kips} > 65.14 \text{ kips}$$

Hence, the section is adequate for shear.

Calculations for bar cutoffs for the flexural reinforcement and the web reinforcement are not shown here; these are similar to those for the interior girders. Details of reinforcement are shown later in Fig. E6.2g.

Load factor design (AASHTO 8.16). All loads (moments and shears) were calculated earlier. These values will be used for calculating the factored loads.

Design of slab

$$\text{Group } (N) = \gamma[\beta_D D + \beta_L(L + I)] \qquad \text{(AASHTO Eq. 3.10)}$$

For group I, $\gamma = 1.3$, $\beta_D = 1.0$, $\beta_L = 1.67$

From previous calculations, $M_D = 0.25$ k-ft, $M_{L+I} = 3.51$ k-ft

$$M_u = 1.3(1.0 \times 0.25 + 1.67 \times 3.51) = 7.95 \text{ k-ft}$$

With the minimum slab thickness of 7.5 in., #5 bar for flexural reinforcement, and 2 in. cover, $d = 5.19$ in., as before. Thus,

$$\frac{M_u}{\phi b d^2} = \frac{7.95 \times 12,000}{0.9 \times 12 \times (5.19)^2} = 327.94 \text{ psi}$$

With $f_c' = 4.0$ ksi and $f_y = 40$ ksi, $\rho = 0.0086$ by interpolation (Appendix A, Table A.17).

$$A_s = \rho b d = 0.0086 \times 12 \times 5.19 = 0.54 \text{ in.}^2$$

Therefore, provide #5 @ 6.5 in. o.c., $A_s = 0.57$ in.^{2} The distribution of steel is 67 percent of main reinforcement, as before:

$$A_s = 0.67 \times 0.54 = 0.36 \text{ in.}^2$$

Therefore, provide #5 @ 10 in. o.c., $A_s = 0.37$ in.^{2}
The temperature steel $= \frac{1}{8}$ in.^{2}/ft of slab, so provide #4 @ 18 in. o.c.

Fatigue stresses. Fatigue stresses need not be checked for deck slabs with primary reinforcement perpendicular to traffic and designed in accordance with AASHTO 3.24.3.

Design of interior girders. From calculations for the service load design, $M_D = 207.5$ k-ft, and $M_{L+I} = 292.5$ k-ft. Therefore,

$$M_u = 1.3[\beta_D D + \beta_L(M_{L+I})]$$
$$= 1.3[1 \times 207.5 + 1.67 \times 292.5] = 904.8 \text{ k-ft}$$

$$M_n = M_u/\phi = 904.8/0.9 = 1005.33 \text{ k-ft}$$

For the initial trial, use the same section as that for the service load design, and revise it as necessary. Assume nine #11 bars in three rows, and assume $d = 33 - 7 = 26$ in. Assume the lever arm, z, as the larger of $0.9d$ or $(d - h_f/2)$, where h_f is the thickness of the compression flange:

$$z = 0.9d = 0.9 \times 26 = 23.4 \text{ in.} \leftarrow \text{ use (larger value)}$$

$$z = d - h_f/2 = 26 - 7.5/2 = 22.5 \text{ in.}$$

$$\text{Trial steel area, } A_s = \frac{M}{f_y z} = \frac{1005.33 \times 12}{40 \times 23.4} = 12.89 \text{ in.}^2$$

The corresponding value of the compression area is

$$A_c = \frac{f_y A_s}{0.85 f_c'} = \frac{40 \times 12.89}{0.85 \times 4} = 151.65 \text{ in.}^2$$

The flange area of the T-section is $A_f = 72 \times 7.5 = 540 \text{ in.}^2 > 151.65 \text{ in.}^2$ Hence the compression block lies entirely in the flange, and

$$a = \frac{A_c}{b} = \frac{151.65}{72} = 2.11 \text{ in.}$$

This gives a new trial value of $z = d - a/2 = 26 - 2.11/2 = 24.95$ in.

$$A_s = \frac{1005.33 \times 12}{40 \times 24.95} = 12.09 \text{ in.}^2$$

$$A_c = \frac{f_y A_s}{0.85 f_c'} = \frac{12.09 \times 40}{0.85 \times 4} = 142.23 \text{ in.}^2$$

$$a = \frac{142.23}{72} = 1.98 \text{ in.}$$

This gives a new trial value of $z = d - a/2 = 26 - 1.98/2 = 25.01$ in.

$$A_s = \frac{1005.33 \times 12}{40 \times 25.01} = 12.06 \text{ in.}^2$$

$$A_c = \frac{f_y A_s}{0.85 f_c'} = \frac{40 \times 12.06}{0.85 \times 4} = 141.88 \text{ in.}^2$$

$$a = \frac{141.88}{72} = 1.97 \text{ in.}$$

This gives a new trial value of $z = d - a/2 = 26 - 1.97/2 = 25.02$ in.

$$A_s = \frac{1005.33 \times 12}{40 \times 25.02} = 12.05 \text{ in.}^2 \approx 12.06 \text{ in.}^2, \text{ as before.}$$

Provide eight #11 bars ($A_s = 12.5 \text{ in.}^2$, Table A.20, Appendix A) as in the case of service load design, and check the nominal moment capacity of the beam. For this reinforcement layout, d had been calculated as 26.69 in.

$$a = \frac{A_s f_y}{0.85 \times f_c' b} = \frac{12.50 \times 40}{0.85 \times 4 \times 72} = 2.04 \text{ in.}$$

$$M_n = A_s f_y (d - a/2) = 12.5 \times 40(26.69 - 2.04/2)/12 = 1069.6 \text{ k-ft}$$

which is greater than the required value of $M_n = 1005.33$ k-ft, and is therefore acceptable.

Check for ρ_{max}. Calculate the depth of the neutral axis from the strain diagram (AASHTO 8.16.3.1.2).

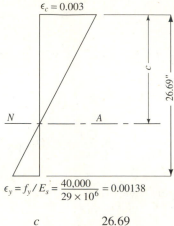

$$\epsilon_y = f_y / E_s = \frac{40,000}{29 \times 10^6} = 0.00138$$

$$\frac{c}{0.003} = \frac{26.69}{0.003 + 0.00138}$$

$$c = 18.28 \text{ in.}$$

$$a = \beta_1 c = 0.85 \times 18.28 = 15.54 \text{ in.}$$

Hence, the compression area extends inside the web by $(15.54 - 7.5) = 8.04$ in. The total compression area, A_c, is

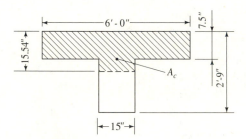

$$A_c = 72 \times 7.5 + 15 \times 8.04 = 660.6 \text{ in.}^2$$
$$C = 0.85 \times f_c' A_c = 0.85 \times 4 \times 660.6$$
$$= 2246 \text{ kips}$$
$$T_{max} = 0.75 \times 2246 \qquad \text{(AASHTO 8.16.3.1.1)}$$
$$= 1684.5 \text{ kips}$$
$$T_{actual} = A_s f_y = 12.50 \times 40$$
$$= 500 \text{ kips} < 1684.5 \text{ kips; OK}$$

Check for ρ_{min}. Unlike the requirements for buildings (per ACI code, $\rho_{min} = 200/f_y$), the requirements for the minimum reinforcements are given by AASHTO 8.17.1.1:

$$\phi M_n \geq 1.2 M_{cr} \qquad \text{(AASHTO Eq. 8.62)}$$
$$f_r = 7.5 \sqrt{f_c'} \qquad \text{(AASHTO 8.15.2.1.1)}$$
$$= 7.5 \times \sqrt{4000}$$
$$= 474.34 \text{ psi}$$

Locate the centroid of the concrete section (to calculate the moment of inertia of the gross section) by taking moments about the top fibers:

$$A = 72 \times 7.5 + 15 \times 25.5 = 922.5 \text{ in.}^2$$

$$922.5\bar{y} = \frac{72 \times (7.5)^2}{2} + 15 \times 25.5 \times \left(7.5 + \frac{25.5}{2}\right)$$

$$= 2025 + 7745.6$$

$$= 9770.6$$

from which $\bar{y} = 10.59$ in.

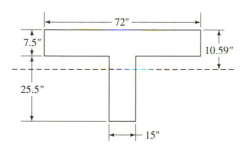

$$I_g = \frac{1}{12} \times 72 \times (7.5)^3 + 72 \times 7.5 \times \left(10.59 - \frac{7.5}{2}\right)^2$$

$$+ \tfrac{1}{3} \times 15 \times (10.59 - 7.50)^3 + \tfrac{1}{3} \times 15 \times (33.0 - 10.59)^3$$

$$= 2531.25 + 25{,}264.22 + 147.52 + 56{,}274.42$$

$$= 84{,}217 \text{ in.}^4$$

Alternatively, the gross moment of inertia of the T-beam can be calculated from Table A.23 (Appendix A). For the present case, $t/h = 7.5/33 = 0.2273$, and $b'/b = \frac{15}{72} = 0.2083$. For these values, $C = 0.39059$ (by interpolation). Therefore,

$$I_g = \tfrac{1}{12} bh^3 (C)$$

$$= \tfrac{1}{12} \times 72 \times (33)^3 \times 0.39059$$

$$= 84{,}220 \text{ in.}^4$$

which is almost the same as the preceding value of I_g.

$$M_{cr} = \frac{f_r I_g}{y_t} \qquad \text{(AASHTO Eq. 8.2)}$$

$$= \frac{474.34 \times 84{,}217}{22.41 \times 12{,}000}$$

$$= 148.55 \text{ k-ft}$$

$$1.2 M_{cr} = 1.2 \times 148.55 = 208.13 \text{ k-ft}$$

$$\phi M_n = 0.9 \times 1069.6 = 962.6 \text{ k-ft} > 1.2 M_{cr} = 208.13 \text{ k-ft; OK}$$

Fatigue stress limits (AASHTO 8.16.8.3). Due to service loads, $M_{L+I} = 292.5$ k-ft. The centroid of the cracked section is located at 7.33 in. from the top of the flange (see calculations for the service load design).

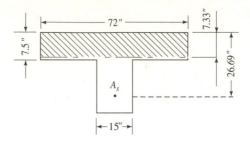

$$I_{cr} = \tfrac{1}{3} \times 72 \times (7.33)^3 + 8 \times 12.5 \times (26.69 - 7.33)^2$$
$$= 46{,}933 \text{ in.}^4$$

Stress in reinforcement due to M_{L+I} is

$$f_{L+I} = (8)\frac{292.5 \times 12{,}000 \times 19.36}{46{,}933}$$
$$= 11{,}583 \text{ psi}$$

The minimum stress, f_{min}, occurs due to dead load, $M_D = 207.5$ k-ft. By proportion, $f_{min} = 11{,}583 \times (207.5/292.5) = 8217$ psi.

$$f_f = 21 - 0.33 f_{min} + 8(r/h) \tag{6.24}$$
$$= 21 - 0.33 \times 8.271 + 8(0.3) = 20.688 \text{ ksi} > f_{L+I} = 11.583 \text{ ksi, OK}$$

Check for shear. Refer to the calculations for service load design.

$$V_u = 1.3[\beta_D D + \beta_L (L + I)]$$
$$= 1.3(1.0 \times 21.04 + 1.67 \times 42.81) = 120.3 \text{ kips}$$
$$V_n = V_u/\phi = 120.3/0.85 = 141.53 \text{ kips}$$

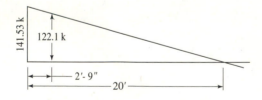

Shear at a distance d from face of left support.

At a distance $d = 26.69$ in. from the face of support (i.e., 33 in. or 2.75 ft from the centerline of support), V_n is calculated to be

$$V_n = 141.53 \times \left(\frac{20.0 - 2.75}{20.0}\right) = 122.1 \text{ kips}$$

The shear resistance of concrete is calculated from AASHTO Eq. 8.49 because of its simplicity, instead of from AASHTO Eq. 8.48:

$$V_c = 2\sqrt{f_c'}b_w d \qquad \text{(AASHTO Eq. 8.49)}$$
$$= 2\sqrt{4000} \times 15 \times 26.69 = 50.6 \text{ kips}$$
$$V_s = V_n - V_c = 122.1 - 50.6 = 71.5 \text{ kips}$$

$$V_{s,\text{max}} = 8\sqrt{f'_c}b_wd \qquad \text{(AASHTO 8.16.6.3.9)}$$

$$= 8 \times \sqrt{4000} \times 15 \times 26.69 = 202.6 \text{ kips} > V_s = 71.5 \text{ kips; OK}$$

$$4\sqrt{f'_c}b_wd = 4 \times \sqrt{4000} \times 15 \times 26.69 = 101.3 \text{ kips} > V_s = 71.5 \text{ kips}$$

Hence, $s_{\text{max}} \leq d/2$ (AASHTO 8.16.6.3.8 and 8.19.3).

With #5 U-stirrups, $A_v = 0.61 \text{ in.}^2$

$$s = \frac{A_v f_y d}{V_s} = \frac{0.61 \times 40 \times 26.69}{71.5} = 9.2 \text{ in.}$$

From Eq. 6.12 for minimum web reinforcement,

$$s = \frac{A_v f_y}{50 b_w}$$

$$= \frac{0.61 \times 40,000}{50 \times 15}$$

$$= 32.5 \text{ in.}$$

$$s_{\text{max}} = d/2 = 26.69/2 = 13.35 \text{ in.} > 9.2 \text{ in. (governs)}$$

Therefore, provide #5 U-stirrups @ 9 in. o.c., and place the first stirrup at 3 in. from the end. Since $s_{\text{max}} = 13.35$ in., use $s = 9$ in. (< 9.2 in.) throughout the beam. There is no need for calculating spacing of stirrups at other locations in the beam in this problem. This is certainly a conservative approach. Alternatively, spacing of stirrups may be increased per AASHTO 8.19.1.1(a).

Check for deflection (AASHTO 8.13). Although AASHTO 8.13.3 permits *either* the gross *or* the effective moment of inertia (i.e., I_g or I_e) for deflection computations, the smaller (conservative) value will be used in this example. The effective moment of inertia, I_e, of the T-section is

$$I_e = \left(\frac{M_{cr}}{M_a}\right)^3 I_g + \left[1 - \left(\frac{M_{cr}}{M_a}\right)^3\right] I_{cr} \leq I_g \qquad \text{(AASHTO Eq. 8.1)}$$

$M_{cr} = 148.55$ k-ft (computed earlier)

$M_a = 500$ k-ft (see calculations for the service load design)

Hence

$$I_e = \left(\frac{148.55}{500}\right)^3 \times 84,217 + \left[1 - \left(\frac{148.55}{500}\right)^3\right] \times 46,933$$

$$= 2208 + 45,702$$

$$= 47,910 \text{ in.}^4 < I_g = 84,217 \text{ in.}^4; \text{ OK}$$

According to AASHTO 8.13.2, deflection is to be calculated on the basis of equal sharing by all beams (six in this case) supporting the deck loaded by all lanes (two in this case). The formula for deflections presented in Chapter 5 will be used. Calculate E_c.

$$E_c = 57,000\sqrt{f'_c} \qquad \text{(AASHTO 8.7.1)}$$

$$= 57,000\sqrt{4000}$$

$$= 3.6 \times 10^6 \text{ lb/in.}^2$$

Therefore, deflection due to the live load is

$$\Delta = \frac{324}{EI_e}\left[P_T(L^3 - 555L + 4780)\right]$$

$$= \frac{324 \times (4 \times 2 \times 2) \times 1.0 \times 1.3[(40)^3 - 555 \times 40 + 4780]}{3.6 \times 10^3 \times 6 \times 47,910}$$

$$= 0.30 \text{ in.}$$

The allowable live-load deflection is

$$\Delta_{LL} = \frac{L}{800} = \frac{40 \times 12}{800} = 0.6 \text{ in.} > 0.30 \text{ in.}$$

Thus, the section so designed satisfies all requirements of the AASHTO specifications.

Moments and shears at intermediate points. It is customary to determine maximum moments and shears at several points along the span, usually at every tenth point (i.e., at $L/10$), to determine points of cutoff for the flexural reinforcement and for spacing of stirrups. Points of cutoff for flexural reinforcement are best determined by plotting the moment capacity of the continuing reinforcement on the moment envelope for the beam. In this 40-ft span bridge, the maximum moment occurs at 17.67 ft from one of the supports. For illustration, maximum moments at 5 and 10 ft from the support are calculated from influence lines.

Maximum moment at 5 ft from support

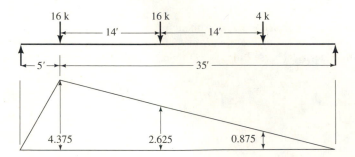

Influence line for M_{max} at 5 ft from the left support.

$$\begin{aligned}
M_D &= 1.052 \times \tfrac{1}{2} \times 4.375 \times 40 & &= 92.05 \text{ k-ft} \\
M_L &= 16(4.375 + 2.625) + 4 \times 0.875 &&= 115.5 \text{ k-ft} \\
M_{L+I} &= 115.5 \times 1.3 &&= 150.15 \text{ k-ft} \\
M_u &= 1.3(92.05 + 1.67 \times 150.15) &&= 445.64 \text{ k-ft}
\end{aligned}$$

Maximum moment at 10 ft from support

$$\begin{aligned}
M_D &= 1.052 \times \tfrac{1}{2} \times 7.5 \times 40 & &= 157.8 \text{ k-ft} \\
M_L &= 16(7.5 + 4.0) + 4 \times 0.5 &&= 186.0 \text{ k-ft} \\
M_{L+I} &= 186.0 \times 1.3 &&= 241.8 \text{ k-ft} \\
M_u &= 1.3(157.8 + 1.67 \times 241.8) &&= 730.1 \text{ k-ft}
\end{aligned}$$

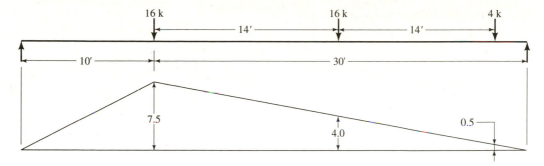

Influence line for M_{max} at 10 ft from the left support.

Some bars of the flexural reinforcement will be cut off where they are no longer required along the span. Calculate the nominal moment capacities of the T-sections with only three bars in the bottom layer, and with only six bars in the bottom two layers. All bars, however, will be extended to full development length beyond the points at which they are not theoretically required. The extension requirements are intended to compensate for unforeseen shifts or changes in the moment envelope.

M_n with 3 #11 bars

$$d = 29.54 \text{ in.}, \quad A_s = 4.68 \text{ in.}^2$$

$$0.85 f_c' a b = A_s f_y$$

$$a = \frac{4.68 \times 40}{0.85 \times 4 \times 72} = 0.765 \text{ in.}$$

$$M_n = A_s f_y \left(d - \frac{a}{2} \right) = \frac{1}{12} \times 4.68 \times 40 \left(29.66 - \frac{0.765}{2} \right) = 456.7 \text{ k-ft}$$

$$M_u = \phi M_n = 0.9 \times 456.7 = 411.03 \text{ k-ft}$$

M_n with 6 #11 bars

$$d = 27.96 \text{ in.}, \quad A_s = 9.37 \text{ in.}^2$$

$$0.85 f_c' a b = A_s f_y$$

$$a = \frac{9.37 \times 40}{0.85 \times 4 \times 72} = 1.53 \text{ in.}$$

$$M_n = A_s f_y \left(d - \frac{a}{2} \right) = \frac{1}{12} \times 9.37 \times 40 \left(27.96 - \frac{1.53}{2} \right) = 849.39 \text{ k-ft}$$

$$M_u = \phi M_n = 0.9 \times 849.39 = 764.45 \text{ k-ft}$$

The bars can be cut off as follows:

1. At 10 ft from the support, $M_u = 730.1$ k-ft, whereas the M_u of the section with six #11 bars is 764.45 k-ft. Hence, out of the eight total #11 bars, the top two #11 bars can be theoretically stopped at this point.
2. At 5 ft from the support, $M_u = 445.64$ k-ft, whereas the M_u of the section with three #11 bars in the bottom layer is only 411.03 k-ft (smaller); hence, the additional three #11 bars cannot be cut off at this point. Calculate the maximum moment at 4 ft from the support and check if the bars can be cut off at this point.

Maximum moment at 4 ft from support

$$M_D = 1.052 \times \tfrac{1}{2} \times 3.6 \times 40 \qquad = 75.7 \text{ k-ft}$$

$$M_L = 16(3.6 + 2.2) + 4 \times 0.8 \quad = 96.0 \text{ k-ft}$$

$$M_{L+I} = 96.0 \times 1.3 \qquad\qquad = 124.8 \text{ k-ft}$$

$$M_u = 1.3(75.7 + 1.67 \times 124.8) = 369.3 \text{ k-ft}$$

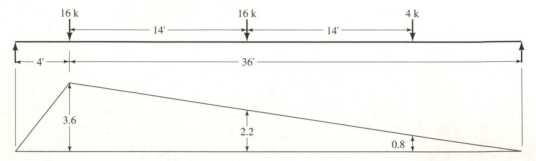

Influence line for $M_{\max}$ at 4 ft from the left support.

This is *smaller* than the M_u (411.03 k-ft) of the section with three #11 bars. Hence, of the six #11 bars, the three #11 bars in the upper layer can be cut off at this point. The three #11 bars in the bottom layer will be extended the full length of the beams to satisfy the requirements of AASHTO 8.24.2.1 that at least one-third the positive moment reinforcement in simple members shall extend along the same face of the member into the support.

Development lengths. The required development lengths of flexural reinforcement are governed by AASHTO 8.24 and 8.25.

- The *basic* development length (AASHTO 8.25.1), l_{db}, is

$$l_{db} = \frac{0.04 A_b f_y}{\sqrt{f_c'}}$$

$$= \frac{0.04 \times 1.56 \times 40,000}{\sqrt{4000}} = 39.46 \text{ in.}$$

but not smaller than $0.0004 d_b f_y = 0.0004 \times 1.41 \times 40,000 = 22.56$ in., or 12 in. (AASHTO 8.25.4). Hence, $l_{db} = 39.46$ in., say, 40 in.—governs. The two #11 bars must be extended 40 in. in the direction of decreasing moment, beyond the point of maximum stress.

- According to AASHTO 8.24.1.2.1, the cutoff bars should also extend, in the direction of decreasing moment, a distance equal to the *greater* of the following beyond the point where they are no longer required:

  15 bar diameters, $15 d_b = 15 \times 1.41 = 21$ in.

  $\tfrac{1}{20}$ of clear span, $L/20 = 40 \times \tfrac{12}{20} = 24$ in.

  Effective depth, $d = 26.69$, say, 27 in. ← governs

Hence, two #11 bars that are theoretically not required at 10 ft from the support must be extended 27 in. toward the support from this point.

- According to AASHTO 8.24.2.2, the continuing reinforcement (six #11 bars) must have development lengths at least equal to l_d (40 in. in this case) beyond the point where they are no longer required to resist tension.
- AASHTO 8.24.2.3 requires that the bar sizes should be such that l_d computed for f_y per AASHTO 8.25 satisfies the following equation:

$$l_d \leq 1.3(M/V) + l_a \qquad \text{(AASHTO Eq. 8.65, modified)}$$

where M = computed moment capacity, assuming all positive tension reinforcement at the section as fully stressed

V = maximum shear force at the section

l_a = embedment length beyond the center of support

1.3 = coefficient giving 30 percent increase in the value of M/V in the development length limitation, to account for the confinement of the end reinforcement by compressive reaction, which tends to prevent splitting and bond failure along the bars

Flexural capacity of three #11 bars (M_u = 411.03 k-ft) and maximum shear force at the support (V_u = 120.3 kips) had been calculated earlier.

The value of l_a is kept 6 in. (AASHTO 8.24.2.1). Then

$$l_d \leq 1.3\frac{M_u}{V_u} + l_a = \frac{1.3 \times 411.03 \times 12}{120.3} + 6 = 59.3 \text{ in.}$$

The actual l_d of 40 in. meets this restriction.

- When flexural reinforcement is cut off at some points in the tension zone of a beam, provisions of AASHTO 8.24.1.4 must be satisfied to prevent the tendency of formation of premature flexural cracks in the vicinity of the cut ends. To this end, the criteria stipulated in AASHTO 8.24.1.4.2 will be satisfied as follows:

  a. Extra stirrup will be provided along each terminated bar over a distance from the termination point equal to three-fourths of the effective depth of the member, i.e., $0.75 \times 26.69 = 20$ in.

  b. The excess stirrup area, A_v, required is not to be less than

$$A_v = \frac{60b_w s}{f_y}$$

  c. The spacing, s, should not exceed $d/8\beta_b$, where β_b is the ratio of the area of reinforcement cut off to the total area of the reinforcement at the section. In the present case, with $d = 26.69$ in., the values of $d/8\beta_b$ are as follows:

  Eight #11 bars, $A_s = 12.5$ in.^{2}
  Six #11 bars, $A_s = 9.37$ in.^{2}, $\beta_b = (12.5 - 9.37)/12.5 = 0.21$,
  $d/8\beta_b = 15.9$ in.
  Three #11 bars, $A_s = 4.68$ in.^{2}, $\beta_b = 4.69/9.37 = 0.5$, $d/8\beta_b = 7.4$ in.

The shear reinforcement provided consists of #5 @ 11 in. o.c. Provide one extra #5 stirrup each at locations of points of cutoff of the flexural reinforcement. This will satisfy both the area and the spacing requirement at those locations.

Distribution of flexural reinforcement. To control flexural cracking of concrete, tension reinforcement should be well distributed within the maximum flexural zones. When the design yield strength, f_y, of tension reinforcement exceeds 40,000 psi, provisions of AASHTO 8.16.8.4 must be satisfied. However, this condition need not be considered in the present case because $f_y = 40,000$ psi for the reinforcing steel. Various reinforcing details are shown in Fig. E6.2g.

Design of exterior girders. For simplicity in design and construction, the exterior girders are to have the same cross section as the interior ones. In addition to the dead-load moment due to the wearing surface and its own weight, it is conservatively assumed that the weight of parapet curbs is also carried entirely by the exterior girder. The following values of the dead-load and the live-load moment were computed earlier for the service load design:

$$M_D = 307.1 \text{ k-ft}$$
$$M_{L+I} = 255.8 \text{ k-ft}$$
$$M_u = 1.3[\beta_D D + \beta_L (L + I)]$$
$$= 1.3(1.0 \times 307.1 + 1.67 \times 255.8) = 954.6 \text{ k-ft}$$

The required nominal capacity of the beam, $M_n = M_u/\phi = 954.6/0.9 = 1060.7$ k-ft. For the interior beam, $M_n = 1069.6$ k-ft (calculated earlier).

$$V_D = \tfrac{1}{2}wL = \tfrac{1}{2} \times 1.557 \times 40 = 31.14 \text{ kips}$$

Maximum live load shear in the exterior girder due to service load plus impact was calculated earlier as 34.0 kips. Therefore,

$$V_u = 1.3[\beta_D D + \beta_L (L + I)]$$
$$= 1.3(31.14 + 1.67 \times 34.0) = 114.3 \text{ kips}$$

For the interior girder, V_u was calculated to be 120.3 kips, which is greater than the value of V_u for the exterior girder. Hence, the section provided is adequate. Detailed design of the exterior girders can be made following the same procedure as for the interior girders. It must be remembered, however, that per AASHTO 3.23.2.3.1.4, the exterior girder *must* have at least as much load-carrying capacity as the interior girder. Accordingly, the design details for the exterior girder will be made similar to those of the interior girders.

Miscellaneous construction details. Practices vary among various bridge owner agencies, but the following practice is representative:

1. **Diaphragms:** 12-in.-wide full-depth diaphragms, transversely placed between all girders, should be provided at both ends and at the midspan. The bottom of the beams and the diaphragm will be at the same level. The diaphragms will have three #6 bars through them, continuing transversely through the beams, and will be cast integrally with them.
2. **Bearings:** The beams will have a fixed bearing at one end and an elastomeric expansion bearing at the other end. At the fixed bearing end, the end diaphragm is supported directly on the bridge seat. Vertical dowels, projecting from the abutment, are bent so as to project inside the webs or the flange of the T-beams. At the expansion end, the end diaphragm is supported on an elastomeric bearing pad placed on the bridge seat.
3. **Drainage, Parapet Curbs and Railings:** These are provided according to the prevailing practices of the bridge owner agencies.

There are many other details that have not been covered in this discussion. Readers should refer to FHWA [1968][4] or other similar references for typical details for concrete superstructures. All state highway departments and other design organizations have standard plans for use on bridges in their jurisdiction, and they should be consulted as necessary to prepare detailed drawings.

---

[4]The agency should be contacted for the latest revisions.

6.8
DESIGN OF BOX GIRDER BRIDGES

6.8.1 General

Since the construction of the first reinforced concrete bridge in the United States in 1937, the popularity of concrete box girder bridges (reinforced and prestressed) has steadily increased, generally in the western states, and particularly in California, where nearly 90 percent of all bridges built on the state highway system are concrete box girders, about 80 percent of them prestressed. Various box girder configurations are shown in Fig. 6.8.

Although cast-in-place box girder bridges have been built for spans as long as 460 ft, for simple spans, they are generally economical for spans in the 95 to 140-ft range, limited by excessive dead-load deflections [Degenkolb, 1977]. This makes them ideally suited for highway interchange structures for which the general span range is 50 to 150 ft. For longer spans, prestressed concrete box girders are more economical. Note, however, that a considerable overlap exists in the economics of reinforced and prestressed concrete box girder bridges, and both can be competitive under certain circumstances; variations can be found regionally.

Lightweight concrete is used to reduce the deadweight of the superstructure in cases where the normal-weight concrete is too heavy from a practical standpoint. For example, it is ideally suited for very high-level bridges where the dead load of the superstructure would result in unduly large columns and footings to resist seismic forces. It has also been found useful for multilevel interchange structures, where minimum structure depths are required and locations for columns are limited. The reduced deadweight of concrete translates into reduced reinforcement in the superstructure, and reduced reinforcing and concrete in the substructure. The corresponding reduction in material costs can more than offset the higher cost of lightweight concrete [AASHTO, Degenkolb, 1977]. Note that the differences in the physical properties of normal-weight and lightweight aggregates cause their design factors to vary (e.g., modulus of rupture, f_r, modular ratio, n, for deflection, and the multiplier for shear strength); however, the design procedures are identical. A thorough discussion on the use of lightweight concrete is presented in an ACI committee reports [ACI, 1967, 1992].

Concrete box girder bridges have several advantages over other types:

1. The relative shallow depth requirement of a box girder bridge is a definite advantage where headroom is limited, a condition frequently encountered in urban areas.
2. Monolithic construction of the superstructure and the substructure offers structural advantages as well as enhanced aesthetics. The pier caps, in the case of continuous box girders, can be placed within the box, facilitating rigid connection to the pier shaft to develop continuity.
3. They provide ideal space for utilities such as gas and water pipelines; power, telephone and cable ducts; storm drains; and sewers; all of which can be easily and safely placed inside the large cells and completely hidden from view. In some cases, the cells of box girders have been used as culverts to carry large amounts of drainage. If necessary, the spacing of webs can be easily adjusted to facilitate the placement of these utilities at desired locations [Degenkolb, 1977; Elliot, 1990]. However,

precautionary measures must be taken to prevent leakage, which might cause environmental and costly maintenance problems. In some cases, it may be prudent to avoid their use for carrying utilities and drainage.

4. A significantly important characteristic of box girders is their high torsional stiffness, which makes them ideally suited for bridges on curved alignments. This is especially important for interchanges on freeways where the ramp structures typically require sharp curved alignment, the main reason for their preference throughout the United States. In states such as California, about 70 to 80 percent of all bridges are multicell concrete box girder bridges. Their high torsional stiffness also makes it possible to design them as a unit rather than as individual girders.

5. Box girder structures lend themselves to easy aesthetic treatment through smooth finishing of the soffit and the sides (Fig. 6.6) [Degenkolb, 1977]. Their requirement for economical depth-to-span ratio is much less than other types of bridges, resulting

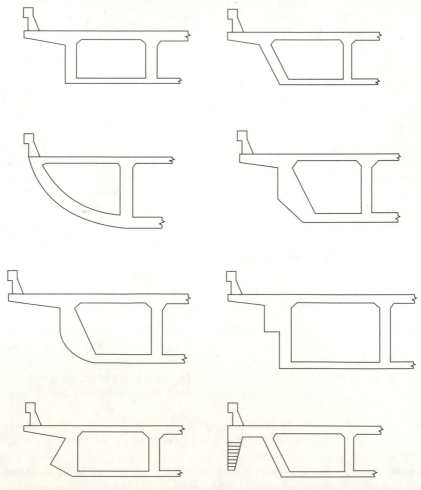

FIGURE 6.6
Aesthetic treatment on the sides of box girders [Degenkolb, 1977].

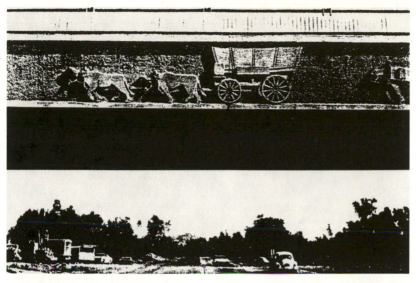

FIGURE 6.7
Mural formed in the exterior face of box girder bridge using different thickness of plywood [Degenkolb, 1977].

in a slender and aesthetically pleasing appearance. Any desired profile and architectural treatment can be given to the exterior faces of the box girders by giving them the desired surface finishes, as shown in Fig. 6.7 and as discussed in Chapter 11. Specially treated forms for the outer surfaces of the box girder have been used to obtain a smooth high-grade surface that does not require additional finishing.

6. In box girders, only the soffit and the faces of the exterior girders (webs) need to be given a high-quality finish; thus, savings result from the reduced costs of finishing.

6.8.2 General Design Considerations

6.8.2.1 Structural behavior

A reinforced concrete box girder is essentially a T-beam with a transverse bottom flange similar to the top flange, resulting in a closed, torsionally stiff multicell configuration. Figure 6.8 shows configurations of several commonly used multicell box girder bridges [Libby and Perkins, 1976].

The top deck, supported on webs (also referred to as girders), performs two basic functions similar to a T-beam bridge: It supports the live load on the bridge, and it acts as the top flange of the longitudinal girders. Thus, the deck is subjected to simultaneous bending both transversely as well as longitudinally. No special consideration is made, however, for the simultaneous effects of maximum stresses occurring in concrete in both directions.

The interior webs resist shear and often only a small portion of girder moments. Consequently, they are usually thinner than the webs of T-beams. This is so because, in the case of continuous T-beam spans, the webs must resist the negative girder moments,

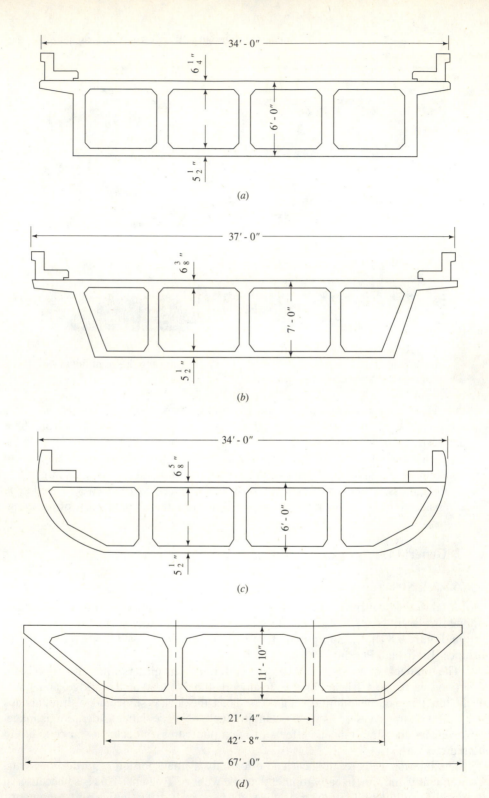

FIGURE 6.8
Configurations of various multicell box girders [Libby and Perkins, 1976].

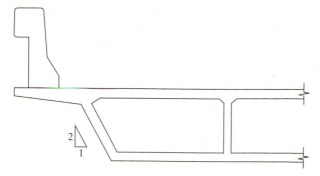

FIGURE 6.9
Sloped exterior webs of a box girder.

as well as all the shear, and contain all the reinforcement for positive moments. While the interior webs are all vertical, the exterior webs may be vertical, inclined, curved, or otherwise profiled as shown in Fig. 6.6, often to improve aesthetics. When the exterior webs are inclined, their slope should preferably be 1:2 (Fig. 6.9) [CALTRANS, 1993c].

The bottom slab (soffit) of the box girder contains reinforcement for the positive moment and also acts as a compression flange in the negative-moment regions of continuous spans. The bottom slab also affords a superstructure considerably thinner than a T-beam bridge of the same span and permits even longer spans to be built.

6.8.2.2 Proportions

A comprehensive discussion on the proportioning of highway box girder bridges can be found in several references [Heins and Lawrie, 1984; Degenkolb, 1977; Elliot, 1990]. In general, a multicell box girder can be viewed as a T-beam structure with the webs connected by a transverse continuous bottom flange. The first box girder bridges were therefore designed on the basis of modified specifications for T-beam bridges.

Depth. The recommended depths of box girders are dictated by deflection requirements. For constant-depth box girders, AASHTO 8.9.2 recommends a minimum depth-span ratio of $0.060S$ for simple spans and $0.055S$ for continuous spans, as shown in Table 5.3 (Chapter 5). Parabolic soffits may be provided for continuous spans with even smaller depth-span ratios, as recommended by the Portland Cement Association [PCA, 1941, 1951].

Top slab thickness. As was pointed out earlier, the current specifications make no recommendations for the minimum thickness of the top slab except that they satisfy the design requirements, i.e., carry the loads as a continuous slab for the selected web spacings. However, many designers use greater deck thickness, varying from 6 to 9 in. and as required by the standards and manuals in use, for the same web spacings. Cover requirements per AASHTO 8.22 should be satisfied. Since the underside of the deck is well-protected by the cell of the box, a 1-in. cover for the lower layer of reinforcement is adequate; however, the cover for the top reinforcing steel should be 2 in. or more, as warranted by the environmental conditions. Designers should consult variations in these requirements as prescribed by specific states. For example, the California specifications [CALTRANS, 1993a] require a minimum thickness of 6 in. for cast-in-place box girders, but permit a minimum of $5\frac{1}{2}$ in. for plant-produced girders.

Bottom slab thickness. The bottom slab or the soffit essentially performs three important functions: (1) It contains reinforcement for positive moment, (2) it functions as a compression flange for the negative moments for continuous box girders, and (3) it provides the desired architectural features of the girder.

Historically, the thickness requirements for the bottom slab evolved without any criteria except an arbitrary thickness of $5\frac{1}{2}$ in. required for placing concrete around #4 bars above and below a #11 main girder reinforcement with $1\frac{1}{2}$ in. cover [Degenkolb, 1977]. The cover for the bars near the top can be 1 in. (or even less) because it has better protection than the one at the bottom. With the adequacy of this design proven by experience, the arbitrary $5\frac{1}{2}$-in. thickness for the bottom slab became a standard AASHTO requirement for minimum thickness, with only the minor modification that it should be the larger of $\frac{1}{16}$ of the clear span between the webs or $5\frac{1}{2}$ in., but need not be thicker than the top slab, unless dictated by design (AASHTO 8.11.2). Local variations exist. For example, the California specifications [CALTRANS, 1993a] require a minimum thickness of $5\frac{1}{2}$ in. for cast-in-place box girders but permit a minimum of 5 in. for plant-produced girders.

Vent holes, 4 to 5 in. in diameter, should be provided in the bottom slab in each cell, adjacent to piers and abutments, to facilitate drainage of curing or of rain water, leakage through the top deck, and condensation. Each diaphragm, when provided, should also have a 6-in. opening. Occasionally, there is leakage from utilities. Inadequate drainage can result in accumulation of water and consequent serious overloads leading to possible failures.

To increase the stiffness of the box girder, the soffit is thickened from the inside while maintaining a constant depth of the girder. In continuous spans, the stiffness requirements at the supports are higher to resist the negative moments; this is accomplished by thickening the soffit at the supports as required.

Webs. There are no provisions in the AASHTO specifications governing the spacing and thickness of webs (or girders). Their primary purpose is to resist shear and only a small portion of moments. Web spacings may vary between 7 and 8 ft. Optimum web spacings are suggested to be between 7 and 9 ft for spans to 150 ft, and as much as 12 ft for longer spans [Elliot, 1990]. Although webs as thin as 6 in. have been built [Elliot, 1990], a thickness of 8 in. is considered a desirable minimum for practical considerations, to facilitate placement of two-legged shear stirrups and concrete. Some designers use a rule of thumb of 1 in. for each foot of height, with an 8-in. minimum. For prestressed concrete, a minimum width of 12 in. is usually provided in order to accommodate large-diameter prestressing ducts [Degenkolb, 1977].

For relatively deep flexural members, it is good engineering practice to provide some auxiliary longitudinal reinforcement near the vertical faces in the tension zone to control cracking in the web. Without such reinforcement, the width of the cracks in the web may greatly exceed the crack width at the level of the flexural reinforcement. Both ACI 318-95 (10.6.7) [ACI, 1995] and AASHTO 8.17.2.1.3 [AASHTO, 1992a] *require* such reinforcement, called the skin reinforcement, A_{sk}, to be provided in the deep webs of the girders. The requirements in both codes are identical. According to these requirements, the skin reinforcement, $A_{sk} \geq 0.012(d - 30)$ per foot of height, is required to be provided on each face along the height of a concrete member, provided the depth of the side face exceeds 3 ft. Such reinforcement is to be uniformly distributed along side faces of a member for a distance of $d/2$ nearest the flexural tension reinforcement. The maximum spacing of this reinforcement is limited to the lesser of $d/6$ or 12 in. Practices vary, however. In California, this requirement applies to members exceeding 2 ft in depth, and no exception is made for the height; i.e., the reinforcement is to be provided along the full web height, with spacing limited to the lesser of web width or 12 in. [CALTRANS, 1993a, 8.17.2.1.4]. In all cases, the skin reinforcement can be included in computing the flexural capacity of the member based on the stresses in individual bars, which are based on the stress and strain compatibility analysis.

A reduction in the number of girder webs can be accomplished by cantilevering the deck beyond the exterior webs. An overhang half as long as the girder spacing usually gives an aesthetically pleasant as well as a more economical structure [Degenkolb, 1977].

The interior webs are always vertical, whereas the exterior webs can be vertical or sloped. When sloped, the thickness of the webs is kept at 10 in. for practical considerations [CALTRANS, 1993d]. In addition, the exterior webs can have extra thickness as required by the architectural features. Webs may be flared to meet the shear requirements, for example, in areas in the vicinity of supports. When this option is used, AASHTO 8.11.3 requires that the web thickness be tapered over a minimum distance of 12 times the difference in the web thickness.

Fillets. Historically, it has been thought that a state of stress concentration exists, at least theoretically, at the junction of various inside surfaces of the box girder (webs, the top, the soffit slab, diaphragms, caps, etc.). Longitudinal fillets evolved, in the opinion of some engineers, as a desirable means to provide for the smooth flow of stresses around these corners, which may develop when an arrangement of live loads on the structure causes differential deflections between adjacent girders [Degenkolb, 1977]. Experience from many box girders built without any fillets between the soffit slab and the webs shows that they are not necessary. Consequently, they remain a feature of questionable structural effectiveness, and providing them has become purely a matter of judgment based on personal experience and preference. Requirements for fillets are covered by AASHTO 9.8.2.3, which requires that adequate fillets be provided at the intersection of all surfaces within the cell of a box girder, except at the junction of the web and the bottom flange, where none are required. The usual practice is to provide 4 in. by 4 in. fillets where necessary. California, which builds box girder bridges more than any other state, has similar requirements [CALTRANS, 1993a].

Reinforcement. General requirements for reinforcement are covered by AASHTO 8.17.2.3 as follows:

1. A minimum of distributed reinforcement of 0.4 percent of the flange area should be placed in the bottom slab parallel to the girder span. A single layer of reinforcement may be provided. Spacing of bars should not exceed 18 in.

2. A minimum distributed reinforcement of 0.5 percent of the cross-sectional area of the slab, based on the least slab thickness, should be placed in the bottom slab transverse to the girder span, and distributed on both faces of the slab. Spacing of bars should not exceed 18 in. All transverse reinforcement in the slab should extend to the exterior face of the outside girder webs in each group and should be anchored by a 90° hook.

Because the preceding reinforcement requirements are standard for box girders used for highway bridges, most design organizations maintain this information in a tabulated form for quick selection of bars. Figures 6.10a and 6.10b show such tables taken from [CALTRANS, 1993c].

The top slab ordinarily requires four layers of reinforcing steel. The transverse reinforcement at the top and the bottom of the slab is required to resist transverse bending of the slab and to transfer loads to the main girders. In addition, two layers of longitudinal bars are provided: one is placed on the top of the bottom transverse reinforcement, which acts as the distribution reinforcement, and the other is placed under the top transverse reinforcement, to resist negative girder moments in the case of continuous spans.

3. Girder reinforcement: The most commonly used size of the reinforcing steel in the girder is #11 bars when it is designed by the service load method. Use of #14 and #18 bars may be warranted if the number of smaller bars causes undesirable congestion. When designed by the load factor design method, the result generally is a smaller total amount of reinforcement, and usually #10 and #11 bars can be used [Degenkolb, 1977].

The layout of bars in the soffit is important. Experience shows a tendency for the cracks to form in concrete at the ends of tensile reinforcing steel. When a number of bars are terminated at the same location, the cracks tend to join and form a larger crack. It is therefore considered a good practice to place the main reinforcing bars so that their ends are staggered, as shown in Fig. 6.11, rather than have them progressively shorter.

In continuous reinforced concrete box girders, reinforcement for the negative moment is required in the top slab, whereas that for the positive moment is required in the bottom slab. To simplify shop detailing, cutting, handling, and placement, as few bar lengths as possible should be used. Because 60-ft bar lengths are available in most areas, the maximum bar lengths should be kept shorter than 60 ft to facilitate handling. Also, when the bar cutoffs are calculated, it is possible to use many bars of the same length by adding a foot or two to the required lengths. The additional cost of extra bar lengths (steel) is usually offset by savings in fabricating, handling, and placing a number of different lengths.

For cast-in-place reinforced or post-tensioned concrete box girders, it is customary to cast the top slab some time after the soffit slab and the webs are cast, thus forming a horizontal construction joint at the top of webs. During the interval of time after the web concrete has set to some degree and the girder reinforcement is capable of resisting longitudinal stresses, any settlement of the falsework, compression of the falsework members, or additional take-up in the falsework joints produces negative moments in the uncompleted structure consisting of the soffit slab and the webs. These moments can cause tensile stresses and cracking in the girder webs unless longitudinal reinforcement (called *interim* reinforcement) is provided just below the horizontal construction joints

S Effective span	T Top slab	Dim. F	Trans. bars Size	Trans. bars Spacing	D #5 bars	G #4 bars
4'-0"	6 1/2"	6"	#5	13"	4	2
4'-3"	6 5/8"	7"		13"	4	2
4'-6"	6 3/4"	7"		12"	4	2
4'-9"	6 7/8"	7"		12"	4	3
5'-0"	6 7/8"	8"		12"	4	
5'-3"	7"	8"		12"	4	
5'-6"	7 1/8"	9"		11"	4	
5'-9"	7 1/8"	9"		11"	4	
6'-0"	7 1/4"	9"		11"	4	
6'-3"	7 3/8"	10"		11"	5	
6'-6"	7 1/2"	10"		11"	5	
6'-9"	7 1/2"	11"		10"	5	
7'-0"	7 5/8"	11"		10"	6	
7'-3"	7 3/4"	11"		10"	6	
7'-6"	7 3/4"	1'-0"	#5	10"	6	3
7'-9"	7 7/8"	1'-0"	#6	13"	7	4
8'-0"	8"	1'-1"		13"	7	
8'-3"	8 1/8"	1'-1"		13"	7	
8'-6"	8 1/8"	1'-1"		13"	8	
8'-9"	8 1/4"	1'-2"		13"	8	
9'-0"	8 3/8"	1'-2"		13"	8	
9'-3"	8 3/8"	1'-2"		12"	10	
9'-6"	8 1/2"	1'-3"		12"	10	
9'-9"	8 5/8"	1'-3"		12"	10	
10'-0"	8 5/8"	1'-4"		12"	10	
10'-3"	8 3/4"	1'-4"		12"	11	
10'-6"	8 7/8"	1'-4"		12"	11	4
10'-9"	8 7/8"	1'-5"		11"	12	5
11'-0"	9"	1'-5"		11"	12	
11'-3"	9 1/8"	1'-6"		11"	12	
11'-6"	9 1/8"	1'-6"		11"	13	
11'-9"	9 1/4"	1'-6"		11"	13	
12'-0"	9 3/8"	1'-7"	#6	11"	13	5
12'-3"	9 1/2"	1'-7"		11"	13	
12'-6"	9 1/2"	1'-7"		10"	15	
12'-9"	9 5/8"	1'-8"		10"	15	
13'-0"	9 3/4"	1'-8"		10"	15	
13'-3"	9 3/4"	1'-9"		10"	15	
13'-6"	9 7/8"	1'-9"		10"	16	
13'-9"	10"	1'-9"		10"	16	
14'-0"	10 1/8"	1'-10"		10"	16	
14'-3"	10 1/4"	1'-10"	#6	10"	16	
14'-6"	10 3/8"	1'-11"	#7	13"	17	
14'-9"	10 1/2"	1'-11"		13"	17	
15'-0"	10 1/2"	1'-11"		13"	18	5
15'-3"	10 5/8"	2'-0"		13"	18	6
15'-6"	10 3/4"	2'-0"		13"	18	
15'-9"	10 7/8"	2'-1"		12"	19	
16'-0"	10 7/8"	2'-1"		12"	19	
16'-3"	11"	2'-1"		12"	20	
16'-6"	11 1/8"	2'-2"		12"	20	
16'-9"	11 1/8"	2'-2"		12"	20	
17'-0"	11 1/4"	2'-3"		12"	20	
17'-3"	11 3/8"	2'-3"		12"	20	6
17'-6"	11 1/2"	2'-3"		11"	22	7
17'-9"	11 1/2"	2'-4"		11"	22	
18'-0"	11 5/8"	2'-4"		11"	22	
18'-3"	11 3/4"	2'-4"		11"	23	
18'-6"	11 7/8"	2'-5"		11"	23	
18'-9"	11 7/8"	2'-5"		11"	23	
19'-0"	12"	2'-6"		11"	23	
19'-3"	12 1/8"	2'-6"		11"	23	
19'-6"	12 1/4"	2'-6"		11"	23	
19'-9"	12 1/4"	2'-7"		11"	24	
20'-0"	12 3/8"	2'-7"	#7	10"	26	7

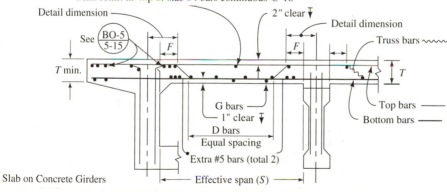

Min. reinf. in top of slab #4 bars continuous @ 18"

Detail dimension

2" clear

Detail dimension

See BO-5 / 5-15

F

F

Truss bars

T min.

T

G bars

1" clear

Top bars

D bars

Equal spacing

Bottom bars

Extra #5 bars (total 2)

Slab on Concrete Girders

Effective span (S)

Detail data:

Designers to specify span to be used and girder width.
⊗ Extra D bars to be added when S > 11 ft.

Effective overhang shall not be greater than $\frac{1}{2}$ the effective span(s).
↧ Increase cover over bars and adjust slab thickness if required for environmental conditions. See BDS 8.22 and Memo to Designers 8-2.

Notes:

For culverts or bridge slabs supporting fill, note provisions of BDS 6.4. Design based on decks having three or more girders. For two girder decks a special design is required.

Design data:

Design stresses: See BDS 8.15
$f_s = 20,000$ lbs. per sq. in.
$f_c = 1200$ lbs. per sq. in.
$n = 10$

Design loads: See BDS 3.24

$M_{DL}(\text{ft-k}) = \frac{wS^2}{10}$

$M_{LL}l(\text{ft-k}) = \frac{P(S+2)}{32} \times 1.30 \times 0.80 = .52(S+2)$

$w =$ Weight per lin. ft width of slab (includes 35 #/ft.^{2} deck overlay allowance)
$S =$ Effective span
Impact factor 1.30
Continuity factor 0.8
$P =$ Wheel load = 16k
Distribution Reinforcement:
$220/\sqrt{s}$, max = 67%. See BDS 3.24.10.

FIGURE 6.10a
Deck slab reinforcement [CALTRANS, 1993c].

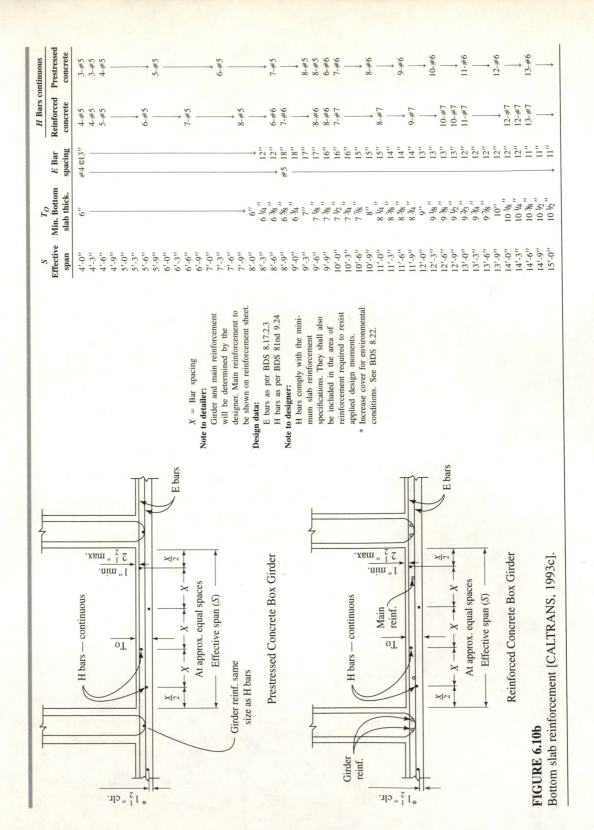

S Effective span	T_O Min. Bottom slab thick.	E Bar spacing	H Bars continuous — Reinforced concrete	H Bars continuous — Prestressed concrete
4'-0"	6"	#4 @13"	4-#5	3-#5
4'-3"			4-#5	3-#5
4'-6"			5-#5	4-#5
4'-9"				
5'-0"				
5'-3"				5-#5
5'-6"			6-#5	
5'-9"				
6'-0"			7-#5	
6'-3"				
6'-6"			8-#5	6-#5
6'-9"				
7'-0"				7-#5
7'-3"				
7'-6"				
7'-9"				
8'-0"	6"	12"		
8'-3"	6 ¼"	12"		8-#5
8'-6"	6 ⅜"	18"	6-#6	8-#5
8'-9"	6 ⅝"	18"	7-#6	6-#6
9'-0"	6 ¾"	17"		7-#6
9'-3"	7"	17"		
9'-6"	7 ⅛"	16"	8-#6	
9'-9"	7 ⅜"	16"	8-#6	
10'-0"	7 ½"	16"	7-#7	
10'-3"	7 ¾"	15"		8-#6
10'-6"	7 ⅞"	15"		
10'-9"	8"	15"	8-#7	8-#6
11'-0"	8 ¼"	14"		
11'-3"	8 ⅜"	14"		9-#6
11'-6"	8 ⅝"	14"	9-#7	
11'-9"	8 ¾"	13"		
12'-0"	9"	13"		10-#6
12'-3"	9 ⅛"	13"	10-#7	
12'-6"	9 ⅜"	13"	10-#7	
12'-9"	9 ½"	12"		11-#6
13'-0"	9 ¾"	12"	11-#7	
13'-3"	9 ⅞"	12"		
13'-6"	10"	12"		
13'-9"				12-#6
14'-0"	10 ⅛"	12"	12-#7	
14'-3"	10 ¼"	12"	12-#7	
14'-6"	10 ⅜"	11"	13-#7	
14'-9"	10 ½"	11"		
15'-0"	10 ½"	11"		13-#6

X = Bar spacing

Note to detailer:
Girder and main reinforcement will be determined by the designer. Main reinforcement to be shown on reinforcement sheet.

Design data:
E bars as per BDS 8.17.2.3
H bars as per BDS 8.1nd 9.24

Note to designer:
H bars comply with the minimum slab reinforcement specifications. They shall also be included in the area of reinforcement required to resist applied design moments.
* Increase cover for environmental conditions. See BDS 8.22.

Prestressed Concrete Box Girder

Reinforced Concrete Box Girder

FIGURE 6.10b
Bottom slab reinforcement [CALTRANS, 1993c].

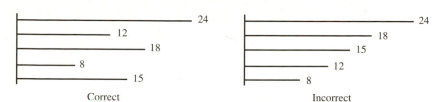

FIGURE 6.11

Layout of bottom slab reinforcement [CALTRANS, 1993c].

at the top of webs. AASHTO specifications require that this interim reinforcement consist of 10 percent of the negative reinforcing steel, or two #8 bars placed at the top of the web for the full length of the girders. When the webs are narrow (e.g., 8 in. wide), one of the bars is placed about 4 in. below the other, leaving enough clearance for the vibrator to function properly [Degenkolb, 1977].

Diaphragms. The subject of diaphragms was discussed in Chapter 4 in some detail and will not be repeated here. Diaphragms are not required for box girders unless the box girders are sharply curved. AASHTO 8.12.3 stipulates that diaphragms are not required for straight box girder bridges and curved box girder bridges with an inside radius of 800 ft or greater. However, diaphragms do improve torsional resistance of curved box girders. Consequently, for box girder bridges with radii smaller than 800 ft, diaphragms spaced no greater than 40 ft apart are required, unless shown otherwise by tests or structural analysis. Some states have somewhat different spacing requirements based on their experience. For example, the California Department of Transportation [CALTRANS, 1993a] requires maximum diaphragm spacing to be 40 ft for radii 400 ft or less, and 80 ft for radii between 400 and 800 ft.

Only nominal reinforcement is needed in diaphragms, at the top and bottom, to support stirrups, as the transverse steel in the top and bottom slab of the box girder provides for their continuity at the girders. Except when the diaphragms have utility openings, nominal shear reinforcement (say, #4 @ 12 in.) is sufficient. Both intermediate and end diaphragms with openings should be designed for loads, usually a truck wheel midway between girders [Elliot, 1990].

Construction. Most generally, box girder bridges are cast in place on falsework. In the case of multispan structures, two or more spans are made continuous over the intermediate supports. However, for practical reasons, the entire box girder cannot be poured in one operation, and construction joints have to be provided, out of necessity. Requirements and practices vary from state to state. Two alternatives are in use: (1) Pour the soffit and webs together without a construction joint between them, and (2) have the soffit poured first, followed by the pouring of the webs and the top slab. In the first case, it is important to let the concrete in the soffit harden sufficiently before pouring concrete in the web forms, so that the soffit can resist the fluid forces of the fresh web concrete. After the web concrete has hardened, the forms are removed, the forms for the top slab are installed, and concrete for it is poured. In this case, a construction joint is created near the junction between the webs and the top slab. The forms used for the top slab are thus left in place. In the second case, a construction joint is created near the junction of the soffit and the webs [Degenkolb, 1977].

6.8.3 Design Procedure and Example

At the option of the designer, a box girder can be designed as a structure consisting of several T-beams, or the entire superstructure can be designed as a unit. With the advent of computers, the latter practice has gained wide acceptance and is presented in the following example. The early box girder bridges were designed as modified T-beams. Since a box girder has a bottom slab in addition to a top slab, a better load distribution is obtained as compared to that in a simple T-beam bridge. Consequently, the load distribution factors for box girders are smaller than those for T-beam structures (*S*/7 vs. *S*/6 for two or more traffic lanes).

EXAMPLE 6.3. Design a reinforced concrete box girder for a simple span of 100 ft for a two-lane highway bridge for HS20 loading. The typical cross section is shown in Fig. E6.3a. Use $f_c' = 4000$ psi and Grade 60 reinforcement.

Calculations. The minimum depth is selected to satisfy AASHTO 8.9.2.

$$h_{min} = 0.055S = 0.055 \times 100 = 5.5 \text{ ft}$$

A total depth of 6 ft 6 in. is selected as required to satisfy stress criteria, as shown later. A thickness of $8\frac{1}{8}$ in. is selected for the top slab, required to support loads in transverse bending, supported over webs spaced at 9 ft 6 in. Its design is similar to that of a T-beam slab, as illustrated in Example 6.2, and is not repeated here. Provision has been made for a 3-in. asphalt concrete overlay for future wearing surface. The web thickness is selected as 12 in. Longitudinal fillets (4 in. by 4 in.) have been provided in all cells at the junctions of webs and the top and the soffit slabs, although none is required at the bottom according to specifications.

The bottom flange thickness, *t*, is computed according to AASHTO 8.11.2:

$$\text{Clear span between girder webs } = 9.5 - 1.0 = 8.5 \text{ ft}$$

$$t = \frac{8.5 \times 12}{16} = 6.375 \text{ in. or } 6\frac{3}{8} \text{ in.}$$

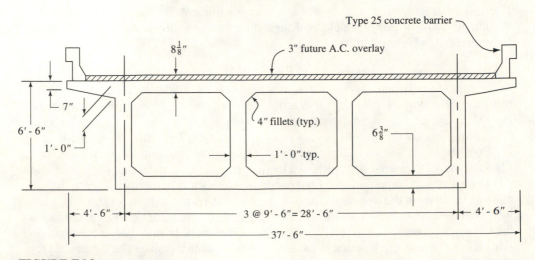

FIGURE E6.3a
Typical cross-section of a box girder.

Reinforcement parallel to girder. The minimum distribution reinforcement in the bottom slab, which can be provided in a single layer, is computed to satisfy the requirement of AASHTO 8.17.2.3.1. The width between the outside faces of the exterior webs is 29.5 ft.

$$A_s = 0.004 \times 6.375(29.5 \times 12) = 9.03 \text{ in.}^2$$

With bar spacings limited to 18 in. (i.e., 1.5 ft), the minimum number of spacings is 29.5/1.5 $\approx$ 20. Therefore, provide twenty-one # 6 bars, $A_s = 21 \times 0.44 = 9.24$ in.$^2 > 9.03$ in.^{2}; OK.

Reinforcement transverse to girder span. This reinforcement is provided to satisfy the requirement of AASHTO 8.17.2.3.2:

$$A_s = 0.005 \times 6.375 \times 12 = 0.38 \text{ in.}^2/\text{ft}$$

For each face of the bottom slab, $A_s = \frac{1}{2} \times 0.38 = 0.19$ in.^{2} Use #5 @ 9 in. alternating at top and bottom, resulting in a maximum permissible spacing of 18 in. and $A_s = 0.41$ in.^{2} This reinforcement will be anchored in the exterior faces of the outside girders as required by AASHTO 8.17.2.3.2.

Design for main flexural reinforcement

Dead load. The cross-sectional area, A, of the girder is

$$
\begin{aligned}
A &= \text{Top slab} + \text{bottom slab} + \text{overhangs} + \text{webs} + \text{fillets} \\
&= 29.5 \times 8.125/12 + 29.5 \times 6.375/12 + 2 \times \tfrac{1}{2} \times 4(7 + 12)/12 \\
&\quad + 4 \times 12(78 - 8.125 - 6.375)/144 + 12 \times \tfrac{1}{2}(4 \times 4)/144 \\
&= 19.974 + 15.672 + 6.333 + 21.167 + 0.667 \\
&= 63.813 \text{ ft}^2
\end{aligned}
$$

Therefore, self-weight $= 63.813 \times 0.15 = 9.57$ k/ft. Weight of the asphaltic concrete overlay @ 35 lb/ft^2 = $(37.5 - 2 \times 1.75) \times 0.035 = 1.19$ k/ft. Weight of the Type 25 concrete barrier rail (California standard)[5] $= 0.392$ k/ft.

$$\text{Total dead load} = 9.57 + 1.19 + 2 \times 0.392 = 11.544 \text{ k/ft}$$

$$
\begin{aligned}
\text{Maximum moment due to dead load, } M_D &= \tfrac{1}{8}wL^2 \\
&= \tfrac{1}{8} \times 11.544 \times 100^2 \\
&= 14{,}430 \text{ k-ft}
\end{aligned}
$$

$$\text{Maximum shear due to dead load, } V_D = \tfrac{1}{2} \times 11.544 \times 100 = 577.2 \text{ kips}$$

Live load. For $L = 100$ ft and HS20–44 loading (Table A.5, Appendix A),

$$M_{LL} = 1524 \text{ k-ft}$$

$$V_{LL} = 65.3 \text{ kips}$$

---

[5]Used here for illustrative purposes only.

The entire box girder will be designed as a unit, for which the distribution factors for the exterior and the interior girders are combined. The distribution factor is obtained by dividing the out-to-out slab width by seven (i.e., $S/7$) per AASHTO 3.23.2.2, Table 3.23.1 (see Appendix A, Table A.7): The number of LL lanes $= 37.5/7 = 5.38$ lines of wheels (or 2.69 lanes).

$$I = \frac{50}{L + 125} = \frac{50}{100 + 125} = 0.22$$

$$M_{LL+I} = 1524 \times 2.69 \times 1.22$$
$$= 5001 \text{ k-ft}$$

$$V_{LL+I} = 65.3 \times 2.69 \times 1.22$$
$$= 214.3 \text{ kips}$$

Total design loads are

$$M_{Total} = 14{,}430 + 5001 = 19{,}431 \text{ k-ft}$$

$$V_{Total} = 577.2 + 214.3 = 791.5 \text{ kips}$$

Calculate the area of steel assuming $j = 0.9$ and $d = \pm 74$ in.

$$A_s = \frac{M}{f_s jd}$$
$$= \frac{19{,}431 \times 12}{24 \times 0.9 \times 74} = 145.9 \text{ in.}^2$$

Try #14 bars, $A_s = 2.25$ in.^{2} per bar (Appendix A, Table A.20). The number of bars required $= 145.9/2.25 = 64.84$, say 65 bars.

$$A_s = 65 \times 2.25 = 146.25 \text{ in.}^2 > 145.9 \text{ in.}^2; \text{ OK.}$$

Serviceability check

Check for moment. Check stresses in the concrete and the reinforcement. Analyze the girder as a cracked section. Check if the neutral axis lies in the flange or the web by taking the moment of areas about the bottom face of the top slab. The overhangs are assumed to have rectangular cross section for this computation. For $f_c' = 4000$ psi and $f_y = 60$ ksi, $n = 8$ (Appendix A, Table A.14).

$$37.5 \times 12 \times 8.125 \times (\tfrac{1}{2} \times 8.125) \gtreqless 8 \times 146.25 \times (74 - 8.125)$$

$$14{,}853.5 < 77{,}073.8$$

Hence, the neutral axis lies in the web, and the section has to be analyzed as a T-beam. For simplicity, the overhangs and the fillets are neglected in this computation as shown in Fig. E6.3b.

Assuming #5 stirrups and 2 in. clear cover,

$$d = 78 - 2.0 - 0.75 - 0.63 = 74.62 \text{ in.}$$

Taking the moment about the neutral axis,

$$348 \times 8.125 \times (y - \tfrac{1}{2} \times 8.125) + 4 \times 12 \times \tfrac{1}{2} \times (y - 8.125)^2$$

$$= 8 \times 146.25 \times (74.62 - y)$$

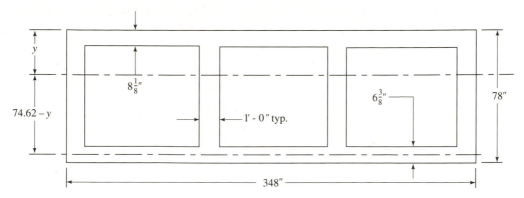

FIGURE E6.3b
Cross section of the box girder.

$$2827.5y - 11{,}486.7 + 24y^2 - 390y + 1584.4 = 87{,}305.4 - 1170y$$

$$24y^2 + 3607.5y - 97{,}207.7 = 0$$

$$y^2 + 150.3y - 4050.3 = 0$$

$$\text{Solving, } y = 23.33 \text{ in.}$$

The transformed moment of inertia of the cracked section is

$$\begin{aligned}
I_{cr} &= 348 \times 8.125^3/12 + 348 \times 8.125(23.33 - 8.125/2)^2 \\
&\quad + 4 \times 12 \times (23.33 - 8.125)^3/3 + 8 \times 146.25 \times (74.62 - 23.33)^2 \\
&= 15{,}555 + 1{,}049{,}671 + 56{,}244 + 3{,}077{,}877 \\
&= 4{,}199{,}347 \text{ in.}^4
\end{aligned}$$

Stresses in concrete and reinforcement can now be calculated from the flexure formula:

$$\begin{aligned}
f_c &= \frac{M y_t}{I_{cr}} \\
&= \frac{(19{,}431 \times 12) \times 23.33}{4{,}199{,}347} \\
&= 1.295 \text{ ksi} < 0.4 \times 4000 \text{ psi} = 1600 \text{ psi; OK}
\end{aligned}$$

$$\begin{aligned}
f_s &= n\left(\frac{M y_b}{I_{cr}}\right) \\
&= 8 \times \left(\frac{(19{,}431 \times 12) \times (74.62 - 23.33)}{4{,}199{,}347}\right) \\
&= 22.783 \text{ ksi} < 24 \text{ ksi; OK}
\end{aligned}$$

Note that, in view of the above stresses, which are close to those permissible, a shallower section would not have been adequate.

Check for shear. $V_{max} = 791.5$ kips. Assuming that entire shear is resisted by all four webs,

$$b = 4 \times 12 = 48 \text{ in., } d = 74.62 \text{ in.}$$

$$\text{Shear stress, } v = \frac{V}{b_w d} \qquad \text{(AASHTO Eq. 8.12)}$$

$$= \frac{791.5}{48 \times 74.62}$$

$$= 0.221 \text{ ksi or } 221 \text{ psi}$$

$$v_c = 0.95 \sqrt{f_c'} = 0.95 \times \sqrt{4000} = 60 \text{ psi}$$

$$v - v_c = 221 - 60 = 161 < 4\sqrt{4000} = 256 \text{ psi; OK}$$

Use #5 two-legged stirrups, $A_s = 4(2 \times 0.31) = 2.48$ in.^{2} (in 4 webs). The required spacing is

$$s = \frac{A_v f_s}{(v - v_c) b_w}$$

$$= \frac{2.48 \times 24,000}{161 \times 48} = 7.7 \text{ in.}$$

Provide #5 two-legged stirrups @ 7 in. o.c. Check for minimum shear reinforcement (AASHTO 8.19.1):

Check for minimum reinforcement for flexure

$$s = \frac{A_v f_y}{50 b_w}$$

$$= \frac{2.48 \times 60,000}{50 \times 48} = 62 \text{ in.} \gg 7.0 \text{ in. provided; OK}$$

$$\phi M_n \geq 1.2 M_{cr} \qquad \text{(AASHTO Eq. 8.62)}$$

$$M_{cr} = f_r I_g / y_t \qquad \text{(AASHTO Eq. 8.2)}$$

Locate the centroidal axis of the concrete section (Fig. E6.3c). Moments are taken about the top fibers.

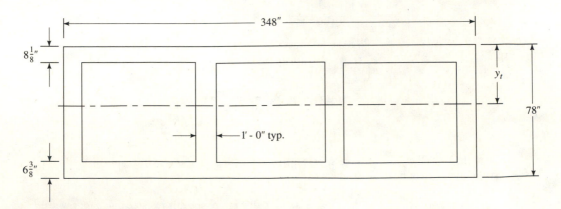

FIGURE E6.3c
Cross section of centroidal axis.

$$348 \times 8.125(y_t - 8.125/2) + 4 \times 12 \times \tfrac{1}{2}(y_t - 8.125)^2 = 348 \times 6.375$$
$$\times (78 - y_t - 6.375/2) + 4 \times 12 \times \tfrac{1}{2}(78 - y_t - 6.375)^2$$

$$2827.5y_t - 11{,}486.7 + 24y_t^2 - 390y + 1584.4 = 165{,}971.5 - 2218.5y_t$$
$$+123{,}123.4 - 3438y_t + 24y_t^2$$

$$y_t \times (2827.5 - 90 + 2218.5 + 3438) = 11{,}486.7 - 1584.4 + 165{,}971.5 + 123{,}123.4$$

$$8094y_t = 298{,}997.2, \text{ which gives } y_t = 36.94 \text{ in.}$$

$$
\begin{aligned}
I_g &= [348 \times 8.125^3/12 + 348 \times 8.125 \times (36.94 - 8.125/2)^2] \\
&\quad + 4 \times 12(36.94 - 8.125)^3/3 + 4 \times 12 \times (78 - 36.94 - 6.375)^3/3 \\
&\quad + [348 \times 6.375^3/12 + 348 \times 6.375 \times (78 - 36.94 + 0.5 \times 6.375)^2] \\
&= 15{,}555 + 3{,}056{,}330 + 382{,}803 + 667{,}644 + 7513 + 4{,}343{,}471 \\
&= 8{,}473{,}316 \text{ in.}^4
\end{aligned}
$$

$$f_r = 7.5\sqrt{f_c'}$$
$$= 7.5\sqrt{4000} \text{ psi} = 474.34 \text{ psi}$$

$$M_{cr} = \frac{f_r I_g}{y_t}$$
$$= \frac{474.34 \times 8{,}473{,}316}{36.94 \times 12{,}000}$$
$$= 9048 \text{ k-ft}$$

$$1.2M_{cr} = 1.2 \times 9048 = 10{,}858 \text{ k-ft}$$

$$\phi M_n = 46{,}669 \text{ k-ft} > 1.2M_{cr} = 10{,}858 \text{ k-ft; OK.}$$

Check for fatigue stress limits. Fatigue stress limits are to be checked according to AASHTO 8.16.8.3, as was illustrated in the design of the T-beam bridge. The range between the maximum tensile stress and the minimum stress is that caused by live load plus impact, whereas the minimum tensile stress is caused by dead-load moment alone.

$$M_D = 14{,}430 \text{ k-ft}$$

$$M_{LL+I} = 5001 \text{ k-ft}$$

$$f_{min} = n\left(\frac{M_D y_b}{I_{cr}}\right)$$

$$= 8 \times \left(\frac{14{,}430 \times 12 \times 51.29}{4{,}199{,}347}\right)$$

$$= 16.92 \text{ ksi}$$

Stress due to live load plus impact:

$$f_{\text{LL}+I} = 8 \times \left(\frac{5001 \times 12 \times 51.29}{4,199,347}\right) = 5.86 \text{ ksi}$$

$$f_f = 21 - 0.33 f_{\min} + 8(r/h) \quad \text{(AASHTO Eq. 8.60)}$$

$$= 21 - 0.33 \times 16.92 + 8 \times 0.3$$

$$= 17.82 \text{ ksi} > 5.86 \text{ ksi; OK}$$

Check for control of crack widths. Since $f_y = 60$ ksi in this example, distribution of flexural reinforcement should be checked according to AASHTO 8.16.8.4:

$$f_s = \frac{z}{\sqrt[3]{d_c A}} \quad \text{(AASHTO Eq. 8.61)}$$

Various terms in the previous formula were described earlier and are defined in Fig. E6.3d.

Total number of reinforcing bars in flexure is 65.

$$A = [4 \times 2 \times 12 \times 3.38 + (348 - 48) \times 6.38]/65 = 34.44 \text{ in.}^2$$

$$f_s = f_s \le 0.6 f_y = 0.6 \times 60 = 36 ksi$$

$$d_c = 78 - 74.62 = 3.38 \text{ in., use 2.0 in. (maximum permitted)}$$

$$z = 130 \text{ kips/in. for severe exposure conditions (AASHTO 8.16.8.4)}$$

$$f_s = \frac{130}{\sqrt[3]{2.0 \times 34.44}} = 31.7 \text{ ksi} < 36 \text{ ksi; OK}$$

Note that the smaller value of $z = 130$ kips/in. has been used, instead of the higher value of 170 kips/in., to limit the cracks to the smaller permissible widths.

Check for strength. The section so designed will now be checked for strength by the load factor method.

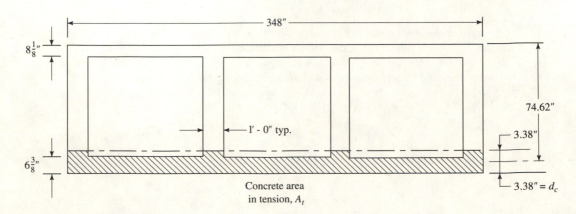

FIGURE E6.3d
Showing d_c and concrete area, A, in tension.

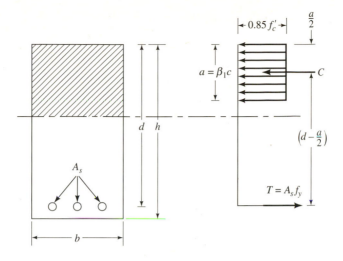

Moment

Group I loading:

$$M_u = \gamma[\beta_D D + \beta_L(L + I)]$$
$$= 1.3[1 \times D + 1.67(L + I)]$$
$$= 1.3[14{,}430 + 1.67 \times 5001]$$
$$= 29{,}616 \text{ k-ft}$$

$$A_s = 146.25 \text{ in.}^2, \quad f_y = 60 \text{ ksi}$$

$$C = T$$

$$0.85 f_c' ab = A_s f_y$$

$$a = \frac{A_s f_y}{0.85 \times f_c' \times b} = \frac{146.25 \times 60}{0.85 \times 4 \times 348} = 7.416 \text{ in.} < t = 8.125 \text{ in.}$$

Hence, the compression block lies entirely in the flange, and M_u can be calculated as for a rectangular section.

$$M_n = A_s f_y(d - a/2) \qquad \text{(AASHTO Eq. 8.16)}$$
$$= 146.25 \times 60(74.62 - 7.416/2)/12$$
$$= 51{,}854.4 \text{ k-ft}$$
$$\phi M_n = 0.9 \times 51{,}854.4 = 46{,}669 \text{ k-ft} > M_u = 29{,}616 \text{ k-ft; OK}$$

Shear

$$V_u = 1.3(577.2 + 1.67 \times 214.3)$$
$$= 1215.6 \text{ kips}$$

$$V_c = 2\sqrt{f_c'}b_w d \qquad \text{(AASHTO Eq. 8.49)}$$
$$= 2\sqrt{4000} \times 48 \times 74.62$$
$$= 453 \text{ kips}$$

$$V_s = A_s f_y d/S \qquad \text{(AASHTO Eq. 8.53)}$$

$$= 2.48 \times 60 \times 74.62/7$$

$$= 1586.2 \text{ kips}$$

$$V_n = V_c + V_s$$

$$= 453 + 1586.2 = 2039.2 \text{ kips}$$

$$\phi V_n = 0.85 \times 2039.2 = 1733.3 > V_u = 1215.6 \text{ kips; OK}$$

Longitudinal skin reinforcement over the web heights. According to AASHTO 8.17.2.1.3, skin reinforcement should be provided for a distance of $d/2$ along the height of the girder. However, according to California practice, this reinforcement should be provided for the full height.

$$A_{sk} \geq 0.012(d - 30) = 0.012(6.5 \times 12 - 30) = 0.58 \text{ in.}^2/\text{ft height}$$

Provide #5 bar @ 12 in. (lesser of $d/6$ or 12 in.) o.c. each face,

$$A_{sk} = 2 \times 0.31 = 0.62 \text{ in.}^2 > 0.58 \text{ in.}^2; \text{ OK}$$

The preceding calculations illustrate that all design criteria have been satisfied. Reinforcement details for the midspan section are shown in Fig. E6.3e. Details of development lengths and bar cutoff points can be worked out as illustrated earlier for the T-beam bridge design example.

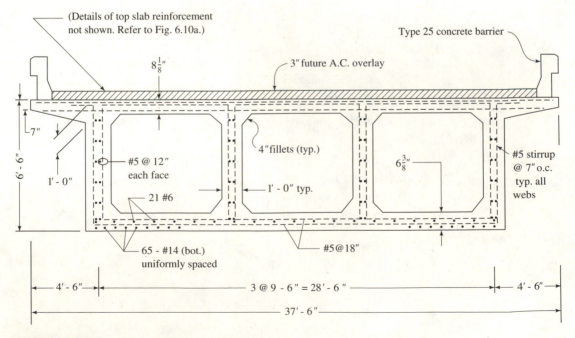

FIGURE E6.3e
Reinforcement details for cross section at midspan.

REFERENCES

AASHTO. (1989). *Guide Specifications for Bridge Railings,* AASHTO, Washington, DC.

——. (1991a). *Model Drainage Manual,* AASHTO, Washington, DC.

——. (1991b). *Highway Drainage Guidelines,* Volumes 1–8, AASHTO, Washington, DC.

——. (1992a). *Standard Specification for Highway Bridges,* 15th ed., AASHTO, Washington, DC.

——. (1992b). *Bridge Guide and Manual Interim Specifications—1992,* AASHTO, Washington, DC.

——. (1992c). *A Policy on Geometric Design of Highways and Streets,* AASHTO, Washington, DC.

——. (1992d). *A Policy on Design Standards—Interstate System,* AASHTO, Washington, DC.

ACI. (1967). "Guide for Structural Lightweight Aggregate Concrete," ACI Committee 213, *ACI J.,* 64(8), August, pp. 443–447.

——. (1969). "Concrete Bridge Design," *ACI Publication SP-23,* ACI, Detroit.

——. (1972). "Control of Cracking in Concrete Structures," ACI Committee 224, Proc. vol. 69, December, pp. 717–753.

——. (1975). "Durability of Concrete," *ACI Publication SP-47,* ACI, Detroit.

——. (1977). "Analysis and Design of Reinforced Concrete Bridge Structures," *ACI Committee Report,* ACI Committee 443, ACI, Detroit, p. 116.

——. (1980). "Control of Cracking in Concrete Structures," *Concrete International,* 2(10), October 1980, pp. 35–76.

——. (1988). "Concrete in Marine Environment," *ACI Publication SP-109,* ACI, Detroit.

——. (1991). "Recommended Practice for Concrete Highway Bridge Deck Construction," *ACI Report 345,* ACI, Detroit.

——. (1992). *Structural Lightweight Aggregate Concrete Performance,* ACI, Farmington Hills, MI.

——. (1995). *Analysis and Design of Reinforced Concrete Bridge Structures,* ACI Committee Report, ACI, Farmington Hills, MI.

——. (1995). *Building Code Requirements for Structural Concrete,* (ACI 318-95) and Commentary (ACI 318-R95), ACI, Farmington Hills, MI.

Bakht, B., and Jaeger, L. G. (1985). *Bridge Analysis Simplified,* McGraw-Hill Companies, Inc., New York.

Bennison, P. (1987). "Repair and Protection of Reinforced Concrete Bridges," in *Concrete Bridge Engineering: Performance and Advances,* R. J. Cope, ed., Elsevier Applied Science, New York, pp. 107–141.

Broms, B. B. (1965). "Crack Width and Crack Spacing in Reinforced Concrete Members," *ACI J.,* 62(10), October, pp. 1237–1256.

BSI. (1985). *BS 8110: Part I 1985, Structural Use of Concrete, Code of Practice for Design and Construction,* British Standard Institution, London.

CALTRANS. (1993a). *Bridge Design Specifications Manual* (rev. 1993), State of California, Department of Transportation, Sacramento.

——. (1993b). *Memo to Bridge Designers,* State of California, Department of Transportation, Sacramento.

——. (1993c). *Bridge Design Details* (rev. 1993), State of California, Department of Transportation, Sacramento.

——. (1993d). *Bridge Design Practice—A Design Manual,* State of California, Department of Transportation, Sacramento.

Cheung, M. S., and Chan, M. Y. T. (1978). "Finite Strip Evaluation of Effective Flange Width of Bridge Girders," *Canadian J. Civil Eng.,* 5(2), February, pp. 174–185.

CRSI. (1983). *A New Look at Short-Span Reinforced Concrete Bridges,* Concrete Reinforcing Steel Institute, Schaumburg, IL.

Degenkolb, O. H. (1977). *Concrete Box Girder Bridges,* ACI, Detroit.

Dunker, K. F., and Rabbat, B. G. (1990). "Highway Bridge Type and Performance Patterns," *ASCE Journal of Performance of Constructed Facilities*, 4(3), August, pp. 161–173.

——. (1992). "Performance of Prestressed Concrete Highway Bridges in the United States—The First 40 Years," *PCI J.,* 37(3), May/June, pp. 48–64.

Elliot, A. L. (1990). "Steel and Concrete Bridges," section 18 in *Structural Engineering Handbook,* E. H. Gaylord and C. N. Gaylord, eds., McGraw-Hill Companies, Inc., New York.

Ferguson, P. M. (1979). *Reinforced Concrete Fundamentals,* 4th ed., John Wiley & Sons, New York.

FHWA. (1968). *Standard Plans for Highway Bridges: Volume 1. Concrete Superstructures,* U.S. Department of Transportation, Federal Highway Administration, Bureau of Public Roads, Washington, DC.

——. (1979). *Recording and Coding Guide for the Structure Inventory and Appraisal of the Nation's Bridges,* Bridge Management Branch, Bridge Division, Federal Highway Administration, Washington, DC.

——. (1988). *Recording and Coding Guide for the Structure Inventory and Appraisal of the Nation's Bridges,* Bridge Management Branch, Bridge Division, Federal Highway Administration, Washington, DC.

FIP. (1975). "Practical Construction," *FIP Guides to Good Practice,* Federation Internationale de la Precontrainte, London.

Gergely, P., and Lutz, L. A. (1968). "Maximum Crack Width in Reinforced Concrete Flexural Members," in *Causes, Mechanisms, and Control of Cracking in Concrete, ACI Special Publication SP-20,* ACI, pp. 1–17.

Gerwick, B. C., Jr. (1990). "International Experience in the Performance of Marine Concrete," *Concrete International*, ACI, May 1990; *F.I.P. Notes* 1991/1, Federation Internationale de la Precontrainte, London.

——. (1993). *Construction of Prestressed Concrete Structures,* 2nd ed., John Wiley & Sons, New York.

Heins, C. P., and Lawrie, R. A. (1984). *Design of Modern Concrete Highway Bridges,* John Wiley & Sons, New York.

Iversion, J. K., and Pfeifer, D. W. (1985). "Criteria for Design of Bearing Pads," *Tech. Rep. No. 4,* Prestressed Concrete Institute, Chicago, June.

Koch. (1992). *Koch Bridge Joint System,* a brochure, Koch Materials Co., Stroud, OK.

Lee, J. A. N. (1962). "Effective Width of T-Beams," *Structural Engineering*, 40(1), January, pp. 21–27.

Libby, J. R., and Perkins, N. D. (1976). *Modern Prestressed Concrete Highway Bridge Superstructures: Design Principles and Construction Methods,* Grantville Publishing Co., San Diego.

Loveall, C. L. (1985). "Jointless Bridge Decks," *ASCE Civ. Eng.,* November, pp. 64–67.

Lutz, L. A. (1974). "Crack Control Factor for Bundled Bars and for Bars of Different Sizes," *ACI J.,* 71(1), January, pp. 9–10.

MacGregor, J. G. (1988). *Reinforced Concrete—Mechanics and Design,* Prentice Hall, Englewood Cliffs, NJ.

McMormac, J. (1993). *Design of Reinforced Concrete,* HarperCollins College Publishers, New York.

Mehta, P. K. (1986). *Concrete: Structure, Properties, and Materials,* Prentice Hall, Englewood Cliffs, NJ.

——. (1991). "Concrete—50 Years of Progress," *ACI Publication SP 126, Proc. 2nd Int. Conf. on Durability of Concrete,* ACI, Detroit.

Nawy, E. G. (1968). "Crack Control in Reinforced Concrete Structures," *ACI J. Proc.,* vol. 65, October, pp. 825–838.

———. (1972). "Crack Control in Beams Reinforced with Bundled Bars," *ACI J. Proc.,* vol. 69, October, pp. 637–640.

———. (1985). *Reinforced Concrete—A Fundamental Approach,* Prentice Hall, Englewood Cliffs, NJ.

Nawy, E. G., and Blair, K. W. (1973). "Further Studies on Flexural Crack Control in Structural Slab Systems," a discussion by ACI Code Committee 318, and "Authors' Closure," *ACI J. Proc.,* vol. 70, January, pp. 61–63.

NCHRP 298. (1987). "Performance of Elastomeric Bearings," *NCHRP Report No. 298,* Transportation Research Board, Washington, DC.

NCHRP-SYN. (1985). "Bridge Designs to Reduce and Facilitate Maintenance and Repair," *National Cooperative Highway Research Program Synthesis Report No. 123,* Transportation Research Board, Washington, DC.

———. (1989). "Bridge Deck Joints," by Burke, M. P., Jr., *National Cooperative Highway Research Program Synthesis of Highway Practice Report 141,* Transportation Research Board, National Research Council, Washington, DC.

———. (1992). "Latex-Modified Concretes and Mortars," *National Cooperative Highway Research Program Synthesis of Highway Practice Report 179,* Transportation Research Board, National Research Council., Washington, DC.

Nilson, A. H., and Winter, G. (1986). *Design of Concrete Structures,* 10th ed., McGraw-Hill Companies, Inc., New York.

PBQD. (1992). Parsons, Brinkerhoff, Quade, and Douglas, and staff. *Bridge Inspection and Rehabilitation: A Practical Guide,* Louis G. Silano, ed., John Wiley & Sons, New York.

PCA. (1941). *Continuous Hollow Girder Concrete Bridges,* Portland Cement Association, Chicago.

———. (1951). *Continuous Concrete Bridges,* 2nd ed., Portland Cement Association, Chicago.

PCI. (1975). *Short-Span Bridges: Spans to 100 Ft,* Prestressed Concrete Institute, Chicago.

Pfeifer, D. W., and Iversion, J. K. (1985). "Bearing Pads for Precast Concrete Buildings," *PCI J.,* September–October.

Roeder, C. W., and Stanton, J. F. (1983). "Elastomeric Bearings: State of the Art," *ASCE J. Str. Div.,* 109(12), September, p. 2853.

———. (1991). "State-of-the-Art: Elastomeric Bridge Bearing Design," *ACI J.,* 88(1), January–February.

Sabins, G. M., ed. (1979). *Handbook of Composite Construction Engineering,* Van Nostrand Reinhold Co., New York.

Severn, R. T. (1962). "The Deformation of a Rectangular Slab Stiffened by Beams under Transverse Load," *Magazine of Concrete Research,* 14(41), July, pp. 73–78.

———. (1964). "Effective Width of T-Beams," *Magazine of Concrete Research,* 16(47), June, pp. 99–102.

Stanton, J. F., and Roeder, C. W. (1982). "Elastomeric Bearings, Design, Construction, Materials," NCHRP Report No. 248, Transportation Research Board, Washington, DC, August, p. 82.

———. (1983). "Elastomeric Bridge Bearing Specifications: Review of the Present and Proposals for the Future," Title No. 80-47, *ACI J.,* November–December, p. 514.

Timoshenko, S. P., and Goodier, J. N. (1970). *Theory of Elasticity,* McGraw-Hill Companies, Inc., New York, pp. 262–268.

Voss. (1989). *Fiberlast—The Omni Direction Bearing Pad of Tommorow,* Voss Engr. Inc., Chicago, p. 14.

———. (1991). *Sorbtex—Fiberlast, a Design Manual,* Voss Engr. Co., Chicago.

Wang, C. T. (1953). *Applied Elasticity,* McGraw-Hill Companies, Inc., New York.

Wasserman, E. P. (1987). "Jointless Bridge Decks," *AISC Engr. J.,* 3rd qtr., pp. 93–100.

CHAPTER 7

Prestressed Concrete Bridges

7.1
INTRODUCTION

The credit for discovering the concept of prestressing goes to San Francisco, California, engineer P. H. Jackson, who patented the concept in 1886 and used it for tightening concrete blocks and concrete arches to serve as floor slabs. About 1888, German engineer C. E. W. Doehring independently obtained a patent for prestressing concrete slabs with metal wires. However, these early attempts were unsuccessful, because the prestressing was lost through shrinkage and creep of concrete. The credit for successfully developing the modern concept of prestressed concrete goes to the French engineer E. Fressynet (1879–1962), who, about 1927, demonstrated the usefulness of prestressing using high-strength steel to control prestress losses [Steinman and Watson, 1957; Raafat, 1958; Lin, 1963; O'Connor, 1971; Naaman, 1982]. Starting in 1941 with a 180-ft, segmentally constructed, two-hinged, portal-framed bridge of arch form over river Marne at Luzancy, France, and followed by five other nearly identical bridges, Fressynet convincingly proved and popularized the virtues of prestressed concrete as a new building material. His methods also provided the model for modern segmental bridge construction methods [Nilson, 1978; Podolny and Muller, 1982].

In the United States, the practice of prestressing was introduced by R. E. Dill for producing concrete planks and fence posts in 1925 [Naaman, 1982]. Prestressed concrete bridge construction evolved with a small two-span (20–30 ft) bridge built in 1950 in Madison County, Tennessee [Steinman and Watson, 1957; PTI, 1985], in two weeks' time, at a savings of nearly 40 percent over conventional reinforced concrete. The first major prestressed concrete bridge, the three-span (74, 160, and 74 ft), cast-in-place, post-tensioned Walnut Lane Memorial Bridge in Philadelphia, Pennsylvania, was completed in 1951 [Schofield, 1948, 1949; Magnel, 1950; Zollman, 1981; Zollman et al., 1992]. Following its construction, the Bureau of Public Roads, now the Federal Highway Administration (FHWA) published "Criteria for Prestressed Concrete Bridges," which was revised in 1954 [PCI, 1981a]. Since then, prestressed concrete bridges have been progressively replacing reinforced-concrete and steel-girder bridges as bridges of choice in the small- and medium-span range. According to the National Bridge Inventory (NBI), prestressed concrete bridges are the most commonly built bridges of any type during the past 40 years. A new type in 1950, prestressed concrete bridges today account for almost 50 percent of all bridges built in the United States [Dunker and Rabbat, 1990, 1992].

As discussed in Chapter 1, definitions of short, medium, and long spans vary. For prestressed concrete bridges, these terms are generally used in the context of *lengths of plant-precast elements.* For example, spans up to 50 ft can be defined as short, those of 50–100 ft (15–30 m) as moderate (medium), and above 100 ft as long [Naaman, 1982]. Some define spans up to 20 m as short, 20–35 m as medium, and over 35 m as long [Taylor, 1987].

7.2
TERMINOLOGY

The following terms, whose definitions have been adapted from those in AASHTO 9.1.3 [AASHTO, 1992], will be used throughout this chapter:

Anchorage seating   Deformation of the anchorage, or seating of tendons in the anchorage device, that takes place when prestressing force is transferred from the jack to the anchorage device.

Bonded tendon   A prestressing tendon that is bonded to concrete, either directly or through grouting.

Coating   Material used to protect prestressing tendons against corrosion, to reduce friction between tendon and duct, or to debond prestressing tendons.

Couples (couplings)   The means by which prestressing force is transmitted from one partial-length prestressing tendon to another.

Creep of concrete   Time-dependent deformation of concrete under sustained load.

Curvature friction   Friction resulting from bends or curves in the specified prestressing tendon profile.

Debonding (blanketing)   Wrapping, sheathing, or coating a prestressing strand to prevent bond between the strand and surrounding concrete.

Duct   A hole or void formed in the prestress member to accommodate a tendon for post-tensioning.

Effective prestress   Stress remaining in concrete due to prestressing after all calculated losses have been deducted, excluding effects of superimposed loads and weight of the member; the stress remaining in prestressing tendons after all losses have occurred, excluding effects of dead load and superimposed load.

Elastic shortening of concrete   Shortening of a member caused by application of forces induced by prestressing.

End anchorage   A length of reinforcement, mechanical anchor, hook, or combination thereof, beyond the point of zero stress in reinforcement; a mechanical device to transmit prestressing force to concrete in a post-tensioned member.

End block   An enlarged end section of a member, designed to reduce anchorage stresses.

Friction (post-tensioning)   Surface resistance between the tendon and its duct in contact during stressing.

Grout opening, or vent   Temporary force exerted by the device that introduces tension into prestressing tendons.

Post-tensioning   A method of prestressing in which tendons are tensioned after concrete has hardened.

Precompressed zone   The portion of flexural member cross section that is compressed by prestressing force.

Prestress, loss of   Reduction in prestressing force resulting from combined effects of strains in concrete and steel, including effects of elastic shortening; creep and shrinkage of concrete; relaxation of steel stress; and, for post-tensioned members, friction and anchorage seating.

Prestressed concrete   Reinforced concrete in which internal stresses have been introduced to reduce potential tensile stresses in the concrete resulting from loads.

Pretensioning   A method of prestressing in which tendons are tensioned before concrete is placed.

Shear lag   Nonuniform distribution of bending stress over the cross section.

Shrinkage of concrete   Time-dependent deformation of concrete caused by drying and chemical changes (hydration process).

Tendon   Wire, strand, bar, or bundle of such elements, used to impart prestress to concrete.

Tendon stress, relaxation of   Time-dependent reduction of stress in a prestressing tendon at constant strain.

Transfer   Act of transferring stress in prestressing tendons from jacks or pretensioning bed to concrete member.

Transfer length   The length over which prestressing force is transferred to concrete by bond in pretensioned members.

Wobble friction   Friction caused by unintended deviation of a prestressing sheath or duct from its specified profile or alignment.

Wrapping, or sheathing   The enclosure around a prestressing tendon to prevent temporary or permanent bond between a prestressing tendon and surrounding concrete.

7.3
MATERIALS OF CONSTRUCTION

The three main materials used in construction of prestressed concrete girders—concrete, reinforcing bars, and prestressing steel—were discussed in Chapter 2. In addition, grout is used around prestressing steel in post-tensioned concrete beams.

7.3.1 High-Strength Concrete

There is no clear-cut definition of high-strength concrete; its definition varies internationally and even regionally within a country [Lane and Podolny, 1993]. Some define it as concrete having a 28-day compressive strength of 8000 psi or more, and concretes having compressive strengths higher than 10,000 psi are sometimes referred to as *ultra high-strength* concretes. Others classify concrete between 50 and 80 MPa as high-strength, between 80 and 120 MPa as very-high-strength, and above 120 MPa as ultra- or super-high-strength concrete.[1] Bridge engineers often consider over-6000-psi

---

[1]1 ksi = 6.895 MPa.

concretes as high-strength [Dolan, Ballinger, and LaFraugh, 1993] to distinguish them from most conventional concrete, having strengths in the range of 3000 to 6000 psi. Consistent production of specially formulated over-6000-psi concretes requires more stringent quality control and more care in the selection and proportioning of materials (such as plasticizers, mineral admixtures, type and size of aggregates). Also, test studies show that in many respects the microstructure and properties of over-6000-psi concretes differ from those of conventional concrete [Mehta, 1986]. A comprehensive discussion on high-strength concrete is presented in the 1984 report of ACI Committee 343 [ACI, 1984] and ACI special publication SP-87 [Russell, 1985] and by Burg and Ost [1992].

The specified compressive strength requirement of concrete, f_c', for prestressed concrete girders evolved from 4000 to 5000 psi in the 1950s to 5000 to 6000 psi in the 1970s and beyond. In the last decade, significant advances have been made in the technology of producing high-strength concrete. Use of microsilica (also known as silica fume or condensed silica fume), very-high-quality aggregate, and extremely low water-cement ratios (less than 0.3) using high-range water reducers (known as superplasticizers) have made it easy to produce over-10,000-psi concretes (referred to as superplasticized concretes) with a very high consistency (8 to 10 in. of slump). Compressive strengths of 8500 to 9500 psi with slumps of 2 to 5 in. are attainable without the use of superplasticizers [Mehta, 1986; Adelman and Cousins, 1990]. Concretes in the 7000–15,000-psi range are being produced in many countries; concrete with compressive strengths in the 15,000–20,000 psi range are now commercially available in North America; and application of concrete in 9000–11,000 psi range is considered both practical and economically feasible [Lane and Podolny, 1993; Russell, 1994].

In the United States there appears to be a growing trend toward using high-strength concrete, generally in the range of 6000–10,000 psi, for prestressed concrete bridge construction [Abdel-Karim and Tadros, 1992a; CTL, 1992; Durning and Rear, 1993; Dolan and LaFraugh, 1993; Lane and Podolny, 1993; Russell, 1994]. Bold advances have been made in the use of high-strength concretes in high-rise building construction; over-10,000-psi concretes have been successfully used. Chicago's 311 South Wacker building, a 70-story, 969-ft high-rise and the world's tallest concrete frame, was completed in 1990 with concrete having compressive strength ranging up to 12,000 psi. The 759-ft-tall Two Union Square Building in Seattle, Washington, completed in 1988, used concrete with compressive strengths averaging over 19,000 psi.

In North America, bridge design specifications for concrete strengths often vary from state to state. Some states, such as Illinois, Idaho, Montana, and Florida permit 6000-psi concrete in their state specifications; others, such as Texas, Washington, and Pennsylvania, permit 7000- to 8000-psi concrete for their bridges [Dolan, Ballinger, and LaFraugh, 1993]. In Texas a test program set up by the Texas Department of Highways and Public Safety (now the Texas Department of Transportation) is under way to assess the viability and performance of high-strength concrete, with the primary goal of reducing overall costs [Castrodale, Kreger, and Burns, 1988]. As a part of this program the Braker Lane Bridge over Interstate 35 at Austin, Texas, was designed and built using Texas Type C girders fabricated with high-strength concrete; the compressive strengths required were 7400 psi within 17 hours and 9600 psi at 28 days

[Durning and Rear, 1993]. AASHTO 9.15 [AASHTO, 1993] limits the concrete compressive strength to 5000 psi, with a 6000-psi threshold when special inspection requirements are imposed, to ensure consistency in quality of concrete. Consequently, few states or suppliers exceed the 6000-psi limitation. However, concrete strengths up to 8000 psi are permitted in Ontario, Canada [OHBDC, 1992].

Although ACI code 318-89 and ACI report 363R-84 [ACI, 1984] effectively limit U.S. concrete strength to 10,000 psi, some countries are revising their codes to permit higher strengths. For example, the Norwegian standard for the design of concrete standard, NS 3473, was revised in 1989 to permit maximum concrete strengths up to 15,200 psi and 12,300 psi, for normal-weight and lightweight concrete, respectively. Similarly, in Finland the building code is being revised to permit increased concrete strength, from 8700 psi to 14,500 psi [Lane and Podolny, 1993]. In Japan, 7100-psi concrete is used regularly for plant-precast pretensioned girders, 5700-psi concrete for site-cast post-tensioned girders, and 8500 psi for plant-precast post-tensioned box girders [Yamane, Tadros, and Arumugasaamy, 1994]. An international overview of high-strength concrete, including a summary of 290 papers on the subject, is reported in [FIP, 1990a]. In Europe, a new FIP/CEB group consisting of 16 members from 14 countries is working in the area of high-strength concrete [Helland, 1994].

The advantages and performance of high-strength concrete in bridge girders, as well as continuing research to implement its use, are reported in the literature [Rabbat, Takayanage, and Russell, 1982; Shah and Ahmed, 1985; Carrasquillo and Carrasquillo, 1986; Jobse, 1987; Luther and Bauer, 1987; Russell, Gebler, and Whiting, 1989; Smith and Rad, 1989; Zia, Schemmel, and Tallman, 1989; Leming et al., 1990; Fiorato, 1991; ENR, 1991; MacGregor, 1992; Towles, 1992; Roller et al. 1993] and summarized in several references [Gerwick, 1993; Lane and Podolny, 1993; Russell, 1985, 1994]. Since the modulus of elasticity of concrete is proportional to the square root of the strength, high-strength concrete results in high flexural stiffness, leading to improved deflection characteristics. The tensile strength of concrete, which is also proportional to the square root of the compressive strength, is higher for high-strength concrete, resulting in improved behavior under overload or partial-prestress conditions. The reduced porosity and permeability of high-strength concrete enhance durability.

Thus, increased compression and flexural capacities are major advantages of using high-strength concrete. Several recent corroborating studies have indicated increased span capabilities of high-strength concrete girders.

A study conducted by the Construction Technology Laboratories, Inc. (CTL) showed that increasing concrete strength from 5000 psi to 7000 psi could result in an increase of about 15 percent in span capability [Rabbat, Takayanage, and Russell, 1982]. A similar study of various I- and bulb-T beams using 10,000-psi concrete also showed increased span capabilities, as shown in Figs. 7.1 and 7.2 [Jobse, 1987; Roller et al., 1995].

A study by Castrodale, Kreger, and Burns [1988] of 12 different girder cross sections, fabricated from concretes having strengths varying from 6000 psi to 15,000 psi, reports an increase of 10 to 40 percent in span for a given section. Figure 7.3 shows a comparison of girder spacings for 150-ft simple span bridges using 6000-psi and 10,000-psi concrete girders [Jobse, 1987].

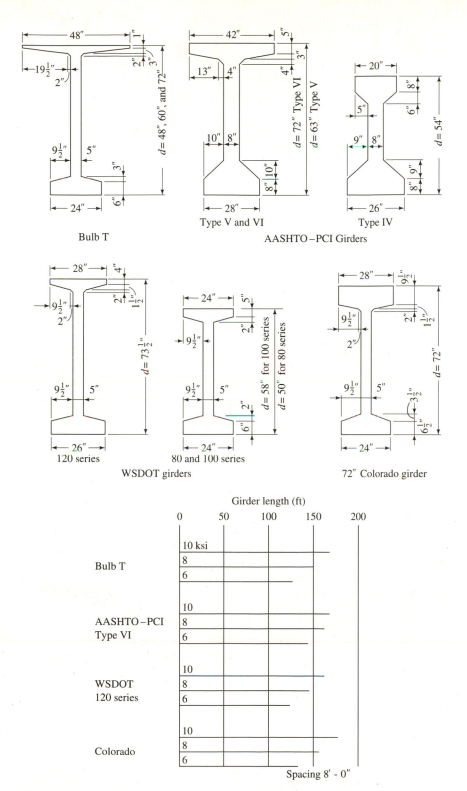

FIGURE 7.1
Span capabilities for basic 72-in.-deep girders with cast-in-place decks [Jobse, 1987].

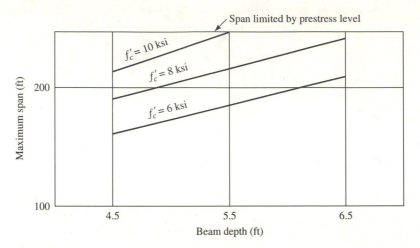

FIGURE 7.2
Span capabilities for two-span continuous box girder bridge [Jobse, 1987].

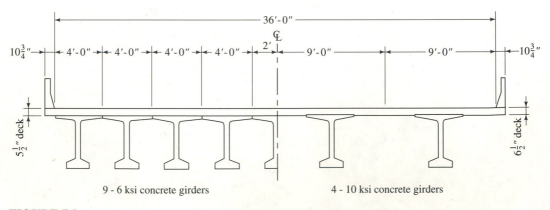

FIGURE 7.3
Two 150-ft simple span bridge designs with different concrete strengths [Jobse, 1987].

Figure 7.4(*a*) shows the influence of concrete strength on the span capabilities of a Texas Type C girder. It is seen that, with a girder spacing of 10 ft, a 6000-psi concrete girder of this type can span approximately 63 ft, whereas a similar 10,000-psi concrete girder can span approximately 80 ft—an increase of about 27 percent. Figure 7.4(*b*) shows a similar trend for the AASHTO–PCI Type IV girder with 4-ft and 7-ft spacings. For example, such a girder made from 6000-psi concrete can span about 108 ft with a spacing of 7 ft, as compared to a span of about 130 ft for a 10,000-psi concrete girder with the same spacing—an increase of nearly 20 percent. Figure 7.4(*c*) shows interrelationships between the concrete strength and girder spacings for selected spans of 100, 120, and 140 ft. For example, for a span of 120 ft, the 10,000-psi concrete AASHTO–PCI Type IV girders would need spacings of 9 ft, more than double the 4-ft spacings required for 6000-psi concrete girders of the same type. The corresponding layout of girders is shown in Fig. 7.5 [Durning and Rear, 1993].

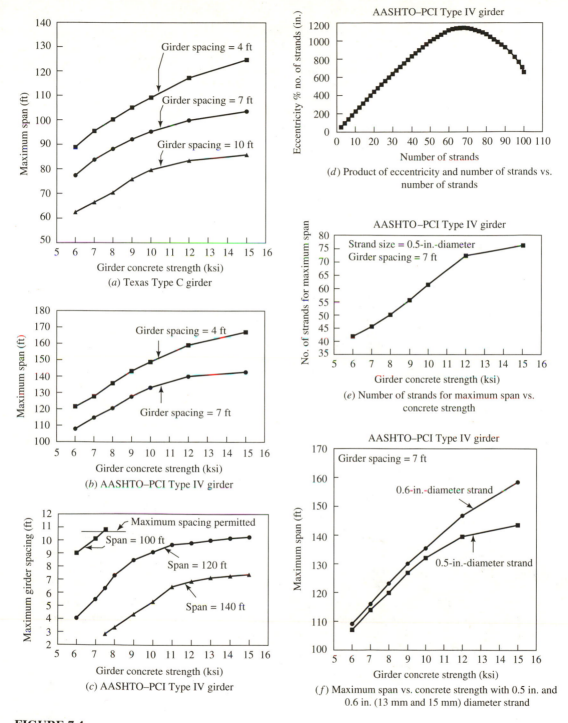

FIGURE 7.4

Influence of concrete strength on simple-span prestressed concrete girder bridges [Durning and Rear, 1993].

467

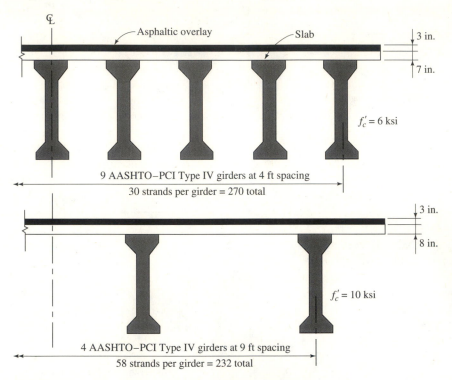

FIGURE 7.5
Bridge design comparison, 10 ksi vs. 6 ksi concrete [Durning and Rear, 1993].

It is noteworthy in Figs. 7.4(*a*) through 7.4(*c*) that the influence of high-strength concrete becomes less pronounced for concrete strengths above 10,000 psi. The reason is that a larger number of prestressing strands is required for longer-span girders. Because of the space limitations in the bottom flanges of these girders, any added strands must be placed higher up in the web, in effect reducing the eccentricity of the prestressing force, as shown in Fig. 7.4(*d*). As a result, although this larger number of strands increases the moment of resistance, it does so much less effectively, as evidenced by the decreasing (flatter) positive slopes of the curves in Figs. 7.4(*a*) through 7.4(*c*). Figure 7.4(*e*) shows the influence of concrete strength on the number of $\frac{1}{2}$-in.-diameter prestressing strands required for AASHTO–PCI Type IV high-strength prestressed concrete girders spaced at 7 ft. Maximum span lengths for this girder and spacing, for various concrete strengths, are shown in Fig. 7.4(*b*). Figure 7.4(*e*) shows that, for a 10,000-psi AASHTO–PCI Type IV girder, some 62 strands are required. This is roughly the point in Fig. 7.4(*d*) at which the product of the number of strands and the eccentricity starts to level off (and then starts decreasing). To increase the span capabilities of girders made from concretes over 10,000 psi efficiently, the eccentricity of the prestressing force must be increased; that is, the centroid of prestressing strands should be located as close to the bottom flange of the girder as possible. This is accomplished by using a smaller number of 0.6-in.-diameter strands instead of a larger number of $\frac{1}{2}$-in.-diameter strands. Placing relatively fewer strands of 0.6-in. diameter in the web (and the majority of the strands in the flange) locates the centroid of pre-stressing strands closer to the bottom flange, leading to increased eccentricity and correspondingly greater span capabilities, as shown in Fig. 7.4(f).

Table 7.1 shows the results of a Louisiana study [Adelman and Cousins, 1990] of the economics of superstructures built from various 6000- and 10,000-psi concrete AASHTO girder types, shown in Fig. 7.6. According to this study, the larger girders have the potential of greater span increase capabilities. Average span increases of 5 to 10 ft can be seen for girder Types II and III and of 10 to 15 ft are shown for girder Types III, IV, IV-S, IV-Modified, and the bulb-T. Despite the increased cost of high-strength concrete (see Table 7.2) due primarily to the increased constituent costs and the cost of the superplasticizer, the study showed savings of about $17,000 in the cost of the superstructure, or approximately 5 percent of the total bridge construction cost.

Results from similar studies by Russell [1994] for concrete strength in the 6000–14,000-psi range are presented in Fig. 7.7 for AASHTO Type IV girders using $\frac{1}{2}$-in.-diameter strands, commonly used for bridges in the 100-ft range. It shows that, for a span of 110 ft, a 6000-psi concrete would require a girder spacing of 6 ft. However, for the same span, an 8000-psi concrete would require a girder spacing of 10 ft. Effectively, this means that, for a typical 40-ft-wide bridge (two 12-ft traffic lanes plus two 8-ft-wide shoulders) designed for HS20-44 loading (with an impact factor of 1.25 and a distribution factor of $S/5.5$), the number of girders is reduced from seven to four by using 8000-psi concrete instead of 6000-psi concrete.

Use of higher-strength concrete for the same girder spacings also increases span capabilities, as can be seen from Fig. 7.7. For example, an AASHTO Type IV girder, which has a span capability of 112 ft at 6-ft spacing when made from 6000-psi concrete, can span 129 ft if made from the 8000-psi concrete—an increase of over 15 percent. Increased span capabilities are also seen if 0.6-in.-diameter strands are used instead of conventional $\frac{1}{2}$-in.-diameter strands. As previously explained, this increase is attributed to the fact that most of a smaller number of 0.6-in.-diameter strands can be placed in the bottom flange, resulting in greater eccentricity than is possible with a larger number of $\frac{1}{2}$-in.-diameter strands, some of which must be placed in the web, reducing eccentricity (and thus requiring a greater amount of prestressing force and hence an even greater number of $\frac{1}{2}$-in.-diameter strands). Similar results can be seen in Fig. 7.8 for the AASHTO Modified Type IV girder. For both sizes of strands, it is assumed that they are placed on 2-in. grid lines, as is the common practice.

The cost savings that accrue from using high-strength concrete can be attributed to several factors. The increased flexural capacity of high-strength concrete girders lends them to larger girder spacings (and hence a smaller number of girders) for a bridge superstructure of a given span, leading to economical construction [Degenkolb, 1997]. Substantial savings accrue in the nonmaterial costs associated with girders, such as the fabrication costs and handling, transportation, and erection costs. Although the basic unit cost of concrete is higher for high-strength concrete, it may be partially or even fully offset by reduced quantities of concrete as a result of the smaller number of girders used. Although high-strength concrete girders have more prestressing strands per girder, the total number of strands for all of the girders is less than that required for the larger number of normal-strength concrete girders, as shown in Fig. 7.5 (232 versus 270 strands for the 115-ft simple-span bridge).

TABLE 7.1
Increase in span capabilities with 10,000-psi concrete [Adelman and Cousins, 1990]

Girder type	Number of girders (transverse spacing)	Maximum span (ft)		Increase (ft)	Percent increase
		6 ksi	10 ksi		
II	4(11.25)	40	40	0	0.0
	5 (8.75)	50	55	5	10.0
	6 (7.33)	55	60	5	9.1
	7 (6.33)	60	65	5	8.3
	8 (5.58)	65	70	5	7.7
					Avg = 7.0
III	4(11.25)	60	65	5	8.3
	5 (8.75)	70	75	5	7.1
	6 (7.33)	80	85	5	6.3
	7 (6.33)	85	90	5	5.9
	8 (5.58)	90	100	10	11.0
					Avg = 7.7
IV	4(11.25)	80	90	10	13.0
	5 (8.75)	90	100	10	11.0
	6 (7.33)	100	110	10	10.0
	7 (6.33)	105	115	10	9.5
	8 (5.58)	110	125	15	14.0
					Avg = 12.0
IV-S	4(11.25)	75	85	10	13.0
	5 (8.75)	85	95	10	12.0
	6 (7.33)	100	110	10	10.0
	7 (6.33)	100	115	15	15.0
	8 (5.58)	105	120	15	14.0
					Avg = 13.0
IV-MOD	4(11.25)	90	95	5	5.5
	5 (8.75)	100	110	10	10.0
	6 (7.33)	115	125	10	8.7
	7 (6.33)	120	130	10	8.3
	8 (5.58)	120	135	15	13.0
					Avg = 9.1
Bulb-T	4(11.25)	85	95	10	12.0
	5 (8.75)	100	110	10	10.0
	6 (7.33)	110	120	10	9.1
	7 (6.33)	120	130	10	8.3
	8 (5.58)	125	140	15	12.0
					Avg = 10.0
					Overall average = 9.6

Metric (SI) conversion factors: 1 ksi = 6.90 MPa; 1 ft = 0.305 m.

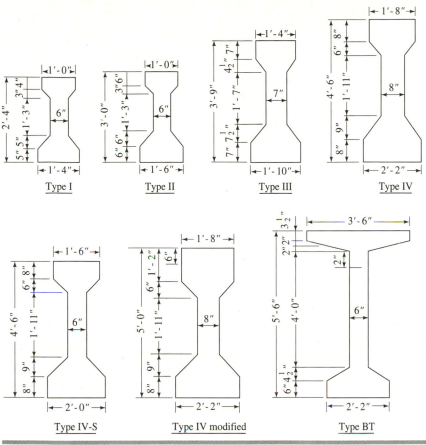

Beam type	Type IV-S		Type IV modified			Type BT		
	Area (in.²)	Area (ft²)	X (in.)	Y (in.)	Moment of inertia (in.⁴)	Weight (lb)	Bottom sect. mod. (in.³)	Top sect. mod. (in.³)
I	276	1.9167	12.5	12.59	22.750	288	1.805	1.307
II	369	2.5625	16.5	15.83	50.980	384	3.220	2.527
III	560	3.8889	21.0	20.27	125.390	583	6.186	5.070
IV	789	5.4792	25.5	24.73	260.730	822	10.543	8.908
IV-S	681	4.7292	25.5	24.39	233.528	709	9.575	7.887
IV mod.	909	6.3125	31.5	28.99	369.320	947	12.740	11.910
BT	731	5.0764	31.5	33.64	439.683	761	13.070	13.587

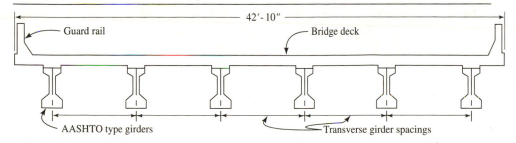

FIGURE 7.6

Typical bridge cross section and the standard AASHTO bridge girders used in the Louisiana study [Adelman and Cousins, 1990].

TABLE 7.2
Constituent cost* of mix design [Adelman and Cousins, 1990]

Mix constituents	Mix design cost ($/yd³)	
	Normal strength	High strength
Cement	18.33	16.88
Fly ash	—	3.12
Sand	2.44	2.52
Aggregate	7.17	12.73
Water reducer	0.52	0.00
Superplasticizer	0.00	4.00
Subtotal	28.45	39.25
6% waste	1.71	2.36
Total	30.16	41.61

*Average figures for the State of Louisiana. Cost figures in other states may be different.

7.3.2 Structural Lightweight Concrete

Structural lightweight concrete, technically referred to as *structural lightweight-aggregate concrete,* is defined as concrete having a 28-day compressive strength in excess of 2500 psi and a 28-day air-dried unit weight not exceeding 115 lb/ft³ [ACI, 1967, 1979]. It may consist entirely of lightweight aggregates or of a combination of both lightweight and normal-weight aggregate. The compressive and tensile strength and unit weight requirements are specified in ASTM C 330 [ASTM, 1983].

The use of structural lightweight concrete in bridge construction has increased steadily since the 1960s. Its high durability and lightness make it ideally suited for bridge superstructures. Generally, lightweight concrete is used to reduce the dead-weight of the superstructure in cases where normal-weight concrete is too heavy from a practical standpoint. For example, it is ideally suited for very-high-level bridges, where the dead load of the superstructure would result in unduly large columns and footings to resist seismic forces. It has also been found useful for multilevel interchange structures, where minimum structure depths are required and locations for columns are limited. The reduced deadweight of concrete translates into reduced reinforcing and prestressing steel in the superstructure and reduced reinforcing and concrete in the substructure. The corresponding reduction in material costs more than offsets the higher cost of lightweight concrete [Degenkolb, 1977]. A discussion on prestressed lightweight concrete can be found in several references [ACI, 1979; Lin, 1985; Gerwick, 1993].

The reduced mass of the superstructure made from lightweight concrete (which typically can be 25 to 30 percent lighter than its normal-weight concrete counterpart) permits longer spans and deeper sections while maintaining the same dead load and an increased live load capacity. A significant design advantage of lightweight structural concrete is that the reduced mass of the superstructure can help minimize earthquake-

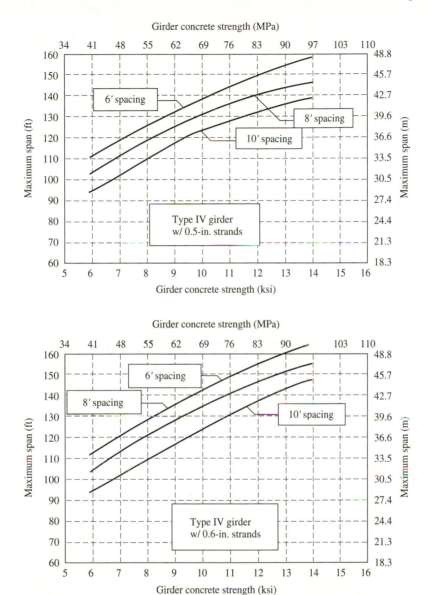

FIGURE 7.7
Relationship between maximum span and concrete strength for AASHTO
Type IV girders [Russell, 1994].

induced forces—an important consideration in the design of bridges in areas of high
seismicity. Unfortunately, designers have not fully exploited this potential because of
the long-held view that structural lightweight concrete is too expensive compared to
other viable alternatives such as steel or normal-weight concrete [Quade, 1952; Anderson, 1957, 1972; Lamarre, 1967; Lazlo, 1967; Casad and Birkland, 1970].

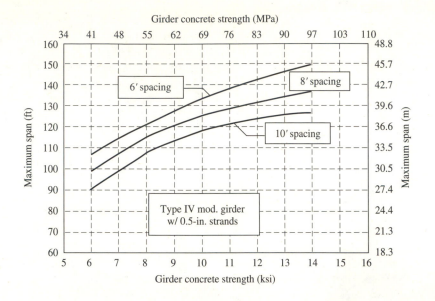

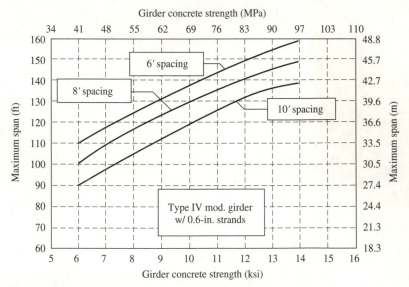

FIGURE 7.8

Relationship between maximum span and concrete strength for AASHTO Modified Type IV girders [Russell, 1994].

The smaller self-weight of structural lightweight concrete components provides very important advantages for precast prestressed girders: It makes it economical to transport sizeable precast sections; reduces the need for extensive falsework; speeds erection; and allows for use of smaller, lighter, and more economical equipment. A lighter superstructure also results in a lighter substructure and foundation, which translate into additional cost savings.

For example, to reduce weight and facilitate handling, semi-lightweight concrete weighing 125 to 130 lb/ft^3 was used for the 63 prestressed, post-tensioned I-beam segments (108 ft long, 102 in. deep, weighing 135,000 to 145,000 lb) used in the five-span, 986-ft-high level Shelby Creek spliced segmental bridge in eastern Kentucky [Caroland et al., 1992]; they were hauled 140 miles from the fabrication plant to the job site.

Lightweight concrete prestressed box girders were one of four options considered in the preliminary study for the proposed 1.2-mile, $93.1-million Benicia-Martinez segmental bridge, which will carry the northbound half of Interstate 680 and probably heavy rail traffic across San Pablo Bay between the cities of Benicia and Martinez, California. This lightweight concrete option cost between $8 to $42 million less than the other three options (a steel truss bridge with a concrete deck, a steel box girder bridge, and a cable-stayed bridge) [Murrillo, Thoman, and Smith, 1994].

Structural lightweight concrete, however, is not without disadvantages. The higher modulus of elasticity of normal-weight concrete, which permits a shallower depth at the midspan while meeting the deflection criteria, is certainly an advantage over lightweight concrete. Because of its lower modulus of elasticity, a lightweight concrete member can produce more than twice the amount of deflection of a normal-weight concrete member for a given load, consequently requiring a higher amount of prestressing.

While some engineers embrace lightweight concrete as a cost cutter, its performance and durability in certain geographical locations, such as the industrial belts of New Orleans and Baton Rouge, Louisiana, are reported to have been poor. Lightweight concrete decks built in these areas barely ten years ago are deteriorating, necessitating their replacement with normal-weight concrete and precluding lightweight concrete from future use for bridge work altogether [Huval, 1994a].

The differences between the physical properties of normal-weight and lightweight aggregates cause their design factors (e.g., modulus of rupture, f_r) to vary, although the design procedures are identical. The lower shear strength of lightweight concrete permitted by AASHTO 8.15.5.2.4 and 8.16.6.2.4 [AASHTO, 1992] for reinforced concrete, and by AASHTO 9.22.5 [AASHTO, 1993] for prestressed concrete, should be noted.

7.3.3 Prestressing Steel

7.3.3.1 General

Properties of prestressing strands were described in Chapter 2 and will not be repeated here. The $\frac{1}{2}$-in.-diameter 270-k strand is the most commonly used prestressing reinforcement for bridge girders, whereas deformed bars are used for stirrups and non-prestressed steel.

Cover and spacing requirements for prestressed concrete girders are stipulated in AASHTO 9.25 [AASHTO, 1992]. It calls for a minimum clear concrete cover of $1\frac{1}{2}$ in. for prestressing steel and main reinforcement, and 1 in. for stirrups and ties. Clear cover is to be appropriately increased if dictated by the environmental conditions. With #5 deformed bar for stirrups having 1 in. clear cover, the centroid of the lowest row of $\frac{1}{2}$-in.-diameter prestressing strands will be located approximately $1\frac{7}{8}$ in. from the extreme bottom fibers of the beam.

The AASHTO specifications [AASHTO, 1992] stipulate no minimum horizontal or vertical spacing of parallel pretensioning strands, except that at the ends of the beam (within the development length), the minimum clear spacing for them is to be the greater of three times the diameter of the strand or $1\frac{1}{3}$ times the maximum size of the concrete aggregate (AASHTO 9.25.2). However, in general engineering practice a center-to-center spacing of 2 in. is maintained both horizontally and vertically, creating a grid at 2-in. centers (Fig. 7.9).

Bundling of prestressing strands is permitted only in the middle third of the beam (AASHTO 9.25.3.2), with the stipulation that the deflection points be investigated for secondary stresses. The AASHTO–LRFD specifications [AASHTO, 1994] (AASHTO 5.10.3.3.1) requires that the minimum clear distance between the groups of bundled strands be not less than either 1.33 times the maximum size of the aggregate or 1.0 in. The number of $\frac{1}{2}$-in. or smaller diameter strands that can be bundled linearly touching one another in a vertical plane is limited to eight. The number of strands bundled in any other manner is limited to four. The minimum clear spacing for the post-tensioning ducts is to be $1\frac{1}{2}$ in. or $1\frac{1}{2}$ times the maximum size of the concrete aggregate.

Premature deterioration of reinforced concrete bridge decks, owing primarily to corrosion of the reinforcing steel and to freeze-thaw action, has become a problem of major proportion confronting bridge engineers. The problem is further compounded in the presence of aggressive environments, which expose decks to deicing salts or marine environments.

Reinforcing corrosion and concrete deterioration are believed to be initiated by the penetration of chlorides, moisture, and oxygen through the cracks commonly associated with reinforced concrete. It is therefore believed that a "crack-free" design will mitigate, if not altogether eliminate, these problems by providing the uncracked concrete as a necessary barrier to inhibit the corrosion mechanism. Such a crack-free design can be produced by providing adequate concrete cover, good concrete quality, and adequate compaction (to reduce porosity). Studies [Poston, Carrasquillo, and Breen, 1985, 1987; Poston et al., 1988] have shown that proper concrete cover and quality by themselves, although absolutely essential, are not enough to ensure the long-term durability of the deck. Use of prestressing—transversely, longitudinally, or both—in concrete decks, along with good concrete quality and adequate cover, is considered a desirable and viable approach to this goal [Poston, Breen, and Carrasquillo, 1989]. In addition to providing precompression (and hence a tightly compacted concrete) necessary to maintain a crack-free deck under live loads, prestressing of decks has other advantages, which are discussed in a later section.

7.3.3.2 Corrosion of prestressing steels and its mitigation

A serious factor affecting durability of prestressed concrete members is corrosion associated with prestressing steels. The term *corrosion* is used to describe deterioration of a metal by chemical or electrochemical reaction with its environment [Uhlig, 1948]; corrosion of reinforcing steel was discussed in Chapter 6. Corrosion of prestressing steel is similar to that of ordinary reinforcing steel, albeit more serious; it has become a matter of great concern in the context of safety of prestressed concrete bridges. In view of its serious ramifications, the corrosion problem is discussed in detail in the following paragraphs.

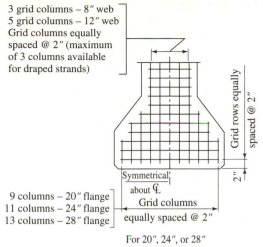

3 grid columns – 8″ web
5 grid columns – 12″ web
Grid columns equally
spaced @ 2″ (maximum
of 3 columns available
for draped strands)

Grid rows equally
spaced @ 2″

2″

Symmetrical
about ℄

9 columns – 20″ flange
11 columns – 24″ flange
13 columns – 28″ flange

Grid columns
equally spaced @ 2″

For 20″, 24″, or 28″
bottom flange width
(straight or draped strand designs)

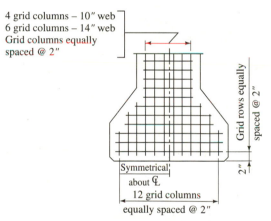

4 grid columns – 10″ web
6 grid columns – 14″ web
Grid columns equally
spaced @ 2″

Grid rows equally
spaced @ 2″

2″

Symmetrical
about ℄
12 grid columns
equally spaced @ 2″

For 26″ bottom flange width
(straight strand designs)

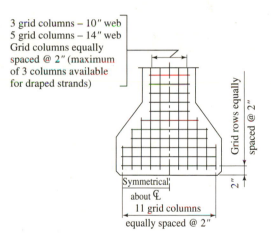

3 grid columns – 10″ web
5 grid columns – 14″ web
Grid columns equally
spaced @ 2″ (maximum
of 3 columns available
for draped strands)

Grid rows equally
spaced @ 2″

2″

Symmetrical
about ℄
11 grid columns
equally spaced @ 2″

For 26″ bottom flange width
(draped strand designs)

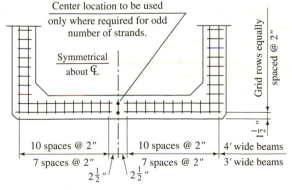

Center location to be used
only where required for odd
number of strands.

Symmetrical
about ℄

Grid rows equally
spaced @ 2″

1½″

10 spaces @ 2″   10 spaces @ 2″   4′ wide beams
7 spaces @ 2″   7 spaces @ 2″   3′ wide beams
2½″   2½″

Typical strand grid for a box girder

FIGURE 7.9
Spacing of prestressing strands in precast prestressed concrete girders [PennDOT, 1993b].   477

Prestressing tendons, being bare, bright steel, go through an oxidation process when exposed to atmosphere, resulting in formation of a superficial brownish-red coating (hydrated iron oxide), commonly known as rust. This atmospheric corrosion does not adversely affect the properties of the strand or its durability. On the contrary, it is said to improve the bond by corroding the mill scale and evaporating lubricating compounds used in the cold-drawing process during manufacture [Uhlig, 1948; Sason, 1992]. The degree of rust allowable is often defined as "that which can be removed by wiping with a soft dry cloth" [Uhlig, 1948].

The most common types of corrosion that affect prestressing steel are uniform corrosion, localized or pitting corrosion, and stress corrosion. Other types of corrosion are hydrogen embrittlement, fretting corrosion, crevice corrosion, and stray-current corrosion [Uhlig, 1948; Wranglen, 1985; Podolny, 1992].

The term *hydrogen embrittlement* refers to the effect of monomolecular hydrogen ions that penetrate into the metal structure, where they combine with electrons drawn from the steel to form hydrogen gas molecules, which exert internal pressure that acts like a tensile stress. Such embrittlement may also occur when dissimilar metals, such as aluminum or zinc, are used in the vicinity of steel (as when aluminum powder is used in grout to cause expansion). Metal cracking ensues from the internal pressure developed by the hydrogen, either alone or in combination with a critical external tensile stress. The causative chemical reaction occurs over a period of time and has been responsible for tendon rupture after several years of installation [Podolny, 1992].

Stress corrosion refers to a highly localized phenomenon that produces cracking owing to the simultaneous presence of corrosion and tensile stress [Monfore and Verbeck, 1960]. Essentially, it is enhanced propagation of a microcrack that was originally produced in steel by high local stresses (e.g., around a bend). It is associated with minute traces of chlorides and sulfides, and possibly other negative ions, occurring in the atmosphere [Gerwick, 1993] and can occur at stress levels within the design range [Podolny, 1992].

Both hydrogen embrittlement and stress corrosion are very serious phenomena, but fortunately they rarely occur [Gerwick, 1993]. Higher-strength steel is inherently more susceptible to the possibility of brittle fracture caused by stress corrosion or hydrogen embrittlement [Tanaka, Yamaoka, and Kurauchi, 1981], and either phenomenon can lead to sudden fracture of steels that are under high stress. However from a practical standpoint, these two forms of corrosion have been almost eliminated by adoption of strict codes, quality assurance in manufacturing, and good construction practices [Yamaoka, Tsubono, and Kurauchi, 1988; Gerwick, 1993].

The forms of corrosion that are due to chlorides and carbonation are much more likely to have detrimental effects on the durability of prestressing steel. A concentration of 0.2 percent by weight of cement is considered enough to cause chloride corrosion in extreme cases; values of 0.4 to 0.5 percent at the surface of the steel are considered the threshold level (defined as the lowest level of chloride that will initiate electrochemical corrosion). Penetration of chlorides is proportional to the permeability and diffusivity of concrete and is accelerated by high temperatures [Gerwick, 1993]. The presence of chlorides, as a cause of corrosion, has been discussed in several references [Stark, 1984; Hope, Page, and Poland, 1985; Hope and Ip, 1987; Pfeifer, Perenchio, and Hime, 1992].

In general, corrosion of prestressing steels in prestressed concrete structures can be much more serious than corrosion of reinforcing steel in conventional reinforced concrete structures because the prestressing strands have relatively smaller cross-sectional area under very high stress. Pitting may concentrate stresses, leading to early fracture.

Whereas deterioration of concrete bridges associated with corrosion of conventional reinforcement is well known, the extent of corrosion of prestressing reinforcement, particularly in highway bridges, is only beginning to be uncovered [Podolny, 1992; Kaminkar, 1993]. Because of its crack-free character, prestressed concrete has traditionally been regarded as a corrosion-free material in comparison to conventional reinforced concrete. Experience, however, has proved otherwise. Cases of distress in prestressed concrete associated with corrosion of prestressing steel have steadily increased since it came into use in the 1950s [Szilard, 1969a; FIP, 1986a, b; Podolny, 1992]. According to a statistical evaluation of 242 incidents of corrosion damage of prestressing steel during the 1951–1979 period [Nurnberger, 1980; FIP, 1986], buildings, pipes, storage structures, and bridges comprised 27, 24, 19, and 13 percent of the cases, respectively. Research findings on corrosion of prestressing steels are reported in the literature [Szilard, 1969a, b; Moore, Klodt, and Hensen, 1970; Schupack, 1978, 1982; Nurnberger, 1980; Peterson, 1980; Wrangler, 1985; FIP, undated, 1986a, b], but little is known about the extent of corrosion of prestressing steels in bridges.

In post-tensioned bridges, the tendons are placed inside flexible, galvanized, corrugated ferrous-metal ducts and grouted with neat cement grout (a suspension of water and cement with a water-cement ratio of 0.45 or less) with or without admixtures. This grout remains in suspension until initial set and is subject to sedimentation, commonly referred to as the "bleed" phenomenon, for 1 to 10 hours. Bleeding occurs because the specific gravity of water is only one-half that of cement. Thus, sedimentation tends to take place, and lenses of bleed water may be left in the ducts, where they tend to migrate and collect at high points in the profile, as shown in Figs. 7.10 [Schupack, 1982] and 7.11 [Lab. Reg., 1986]. This entrapped water may freeze and rupture the member, or it may be reabsorbed and leave air voids, which permit an oxygen gradient to develop, leading to corrosion [Gerwick, 1993]. This bleed phenomenon is of particular concern in long-span girders, in which the tendons have a substantial vertical rise. Study of distressed bridges shows that air tends to be trapped at high and low points on profiled tendons, especially at anchors [New CE, 1992b]. Fortunately, though, the tendons at the top of the negative-moment curve are tightly stressed against the bottom of the duct, so the bleed water is generally above them [Gerwick, 1993].

Improper grouting practices and high chloride content in the grout are believed to be serious sources of corrosion that can trigger a collapse without warning. Such a mishap occurred on December 4, 1985, when all nine of the interior I-girders (each consisting of eight precast segmental sections) of the 60-ft-long, simply supported, segmental Ynys-y-Gwas Bridge, built in 1953 in Great Britain, collapsed [Woodward and Williams, 1988]. The exterior box girders, however, did not collapse. The mishap was attributed to tendons that had experienced a considerable progression of corrosion, believed to have been caused by chlorides that penetrated through mortar and reached tendons (thus, by improper protection treatment). Post-failure examinations showed chlorides on the fractured surfaces of tendons. Ten repeated inspections, the last of which was made in June 1985, only six months before the collapse, had been ineffective in detecting the corrosion problem.

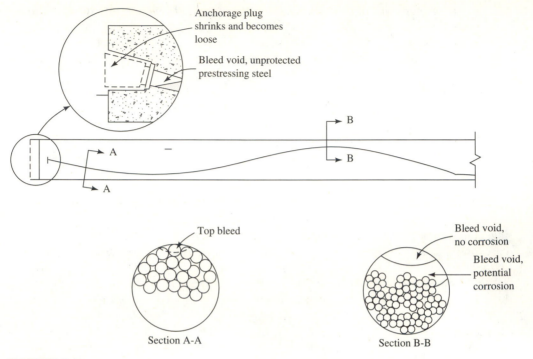

FIGURE 7.10
Poor details leading to corrosion in bonded tendons [Schupack, 1978].

The entire superstructure of the Azergues River Bridge in France, a post-tensioned concrete structure built in 1962, had to be replaced as a result of the serious corrosion of prestressing steel resulting from chloride penetration [Rimboeuf and Salzmann, 1980]. A prereplacement inspection of this bridge in 1972, prompted by serious cracking of the girders showed, that of the 144 tendons investigated, 16 were fully grouted, 38 were partially grouted, 80 were ungrouted, and *10 were neither stressed nor grouted,* indicating poor workmanship [Podolny, 1992]. One account [CT, 1988] reports failure of nine out of 240 galvanized 50-mm Macalloy (high-strength) bars as a result of hydrogen embrittlement, even though the resistance of galvanized wire is believed to be about 22 times that of the bare wire. However, a cracked galvanization layer or improper handling of bars or tendons can completely ruin this enhanced resistance [Yamaoka, Tsubono, and Kurauchi, 1988].

Poor grouting practices also dictated the strengthening of the 935-ft-long Grand-Mere Bridge over the St. Maurice River near Grand-Mere, Quebec, Canada, built in 1977. This segmentally built, single-cell box girder bridge was prestressed longitudinally with 284 straight bars, $1\frac{1}{4}$-in. (32 mm) in diameter, located in the top slab in addition to the 80 slightly curved bars in the bottom flange and 48 draped bars in the webs for continuity. It is reported that post-tensioning duct injection of grout was completely achieved with certainty only on 80 percent of the bars; the remainder were partially filled or not filled at all, leaving up to 20 percent of the top bars virtually unprotected against corrosion. Out of concern caused by the excessive deflection and

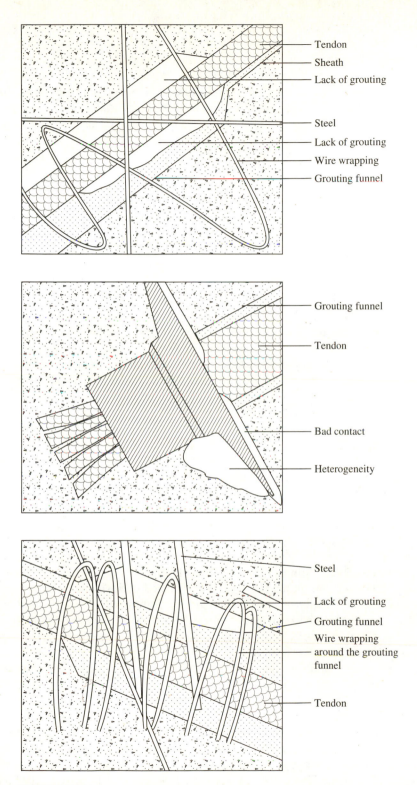

FIGURE 7.11
Locations of various potential grout voids [Lab. Reg., 1986].

481

transverse cracking in the top slab with evidence of chloride efflorescence, this bridge was strengthened in 1991 [Massicotte et al., 1994; Massicotte and Picard, 1994].

A combination of poor grouting practices and high chloride content in the grout is also believed to be the source of corrosion noted in a recent study [Schupack, 1993; PTI, 1993] of the post-tensioned T-beams of the Bissel Bridge over the Connecticut River at Windsor, Connecticut, completed in 1958 [CE, 1992]; the beams had been salvaged when the bridge was widened. An early example of longer-span post-tensioned bridges, this 1680-ft bridge consisted of fourteen 120-ft simple spans having a cast-in-place post-tensioned superstructure with a T-beam framing. The prestressing system consisted of 12 Fressynet grouted 0.276-in.-diameter 240-ksi stress-relieved wires (strands were not used then) in a flexible bright metal sheath in each web, using the now obsolete Fressynet anchorage. The 1992 study of the bridge's superstructure showed that longitudinal web cracks, first noticed in 1971, had occurred in 41 of the 112 T-beam webs. These cracks generally followed the trajectory of a tendon and sometimes extended through to the other side of the web and the soffit. The outward appearance of the structure had no tell-tale manifestations of tendon corrosion. However, the exhumed tendons had startling revelations: They exhibited generalized corrosion of wires and sheaths; corrosion occurred intermittently; and wire breakages were random, with up to three wires having failed at any one cross section. Some wires lost about half their cross section, although they did not fail. Several instances of poorly grouted tendons were observed: Often grout did not fill the spaces between wires and between the wires and the sheath; a number of tendons were never grouted or had blockages that were never grouted.

The grout itself was found to be highly contaminated with chlorides, up to 8000 parts per million [Schupack, 1993]. For comparison, typical specifications limit the amounts of chlorides in the mixing water to 650 ppm (parts per million) or 0.065 percent, and soluble chlorides in the aggregates are limited to 0.02 percent by weight of cement [Gerwick, 1993]. For bridges, AASHTO 10.3.4.3 [AASHTO, 1992] limits chlorides in admixtures to 0.005 percent, or 50 ppm, and requires that water in grout be potable, clean, and free of injurious quantities of substances known to be harmful to portland cement and prestressing steel. As a practical matter, total chloride content in grout should be limited to 100 ppm [Schupack, 1993].

Concerns growing from the Ynys-y-Gwas Bridge failure [New CE, 1992a] and from inspections of several other bridges that revealed corrosion problems with post-tensioned tendons [New CE, 1992b] resulted in a 1992 ban in Great Britain on new construction of prestressed bridges using post-tensioned tendons. Additionally, it has been required that tendons be inspectable and replaceable, and the once-rejected design with unbonded tendons has been pronounced the preferred design option [Schupack, 1993]. It is strongly believed that such restrictions are unnecessary and that a well-prepared grout mix and proper grouting practices can alleviate much of the problem. Recommendations for grouting of tendons are reported in the literature [PCIJ, 1972; PTI, 1985; FIP, 1990b].

Discussion on corrosion protection systems for prestressing steel can be found in several references [Szilard, 1969b; Moore, Klodt, and Hensen, 1970; Brown and Fitzgerald, 1971; Pfeifer and Scali, 1981; Schupack, 1982, 1991; FIP, 1986a, b; Pfeifer, Landgren, and Zoob, 1987; Perenchio, Fraczek, and Pfeifer, 1989; Podolny, 1990; Gerwick, 1993]. A summary of various types of corrosion and corrosion protection systems for prestressing steels can be found in references [Podolny, 1992; Gerwick, 1993]. Generally, the corrosion mitigation systems fall into two broad categories: those that improve or enhance concrete durability and improve its properties, and those that provide direct corrosion protection to steel. Epoxy-coated strands are suggested as one of the means to mitigate corrosion of prestressing steels [Dorstein, Hunt, and Preston, 1984; PCI, 1993]. Zinc coating or galvanizing is another means that provides protection to steel; however, it is believed that the galvanizing process adversely affects the mechanical properties of prestressing steel—it reduces the strand's ultimate strength by about 15 percent, lowers its modulus of elasticity depending on the amount of zinc coating used, and increases the ultimate elongation and long-term relaxation [Bruggeling, 1982; Lin and Burns, 1981]. Also, the fatigue strength may be reduced as much as 20 percent [Phoenix, Johnson, and McGuire, 1986]. Galvanized tendons are also felt to be at an increased risk of hydrogen embrittlement; however, scientific evidence to support such a fear is so far lacking [Yamaoka, Tsubono, and Kurauchi, 1988; Bassi, 1989; Podolny, 1992; Gerwick, 1993].

Because corrosion is an electrochemical phenomenon, the resistivity of concrete is a measure of the rate at which corrosion can occur. This principle has led to a recent development that uses fully encapsulated and completely *electrically isolated tendons* (*EIT*), including the anchorages, with or without grout [Perenchio, Fraczek, and Pfeifer, 1989; Schupack, 1982, 1991, 1993; PTI, 1993]. This system usually uses a plastic sheath, plastic-coated anchorage hardware, and plastic anchorage cover and is claimed to provide a relatively higher level of corrosion protection. It can be electrically monitored by measuring the initial resistance of the EIT, and the resistance at some later time; a change in resistance indicates a compromised corrosion protection system [Schupack, 1993]. In view of the growing concern over corrosion in prestressed concrete girders, use of various types of fiber-reinforced plastic (FRP) tendons and the required anchorage systems is increasingly advocated [Dolan, 1990; Minosaku, 1992; Taerwe, Lambotte, and Miesseler, 1992; Tsuji, Kanda, and Tamura, 1993].

7.4
ADVANTAGES AND DISADVANTAGES
OF PRESTRESSED CONCRETE

7.4.1 Advantages

Prestressed concrete bridges have become the preferred type in all states in the United States, primarily for reasons of economy and savings in life-cycle costs [Dunker and Rabbat, 1992; Freyermuth, 1992]. Various *advantages* of utilizing prestressed concrete bridges are the following:

1. Prestressed concrete products are usually produced in plants using high-strength concrete under controlled conditions, resulting in higher-quality products with longer life expectancy. Even for longer spans, the girders can be cast in segments in the plant and later post-tensioned at site to erect the entire structure. This technique is now being used extensively for segmentally built prestressed concrete bridges. Alternatively, under favorable circumstances it is possible to cast the *entire* structure in the plant and transport it to the site for erection as a whole. This was exemplified

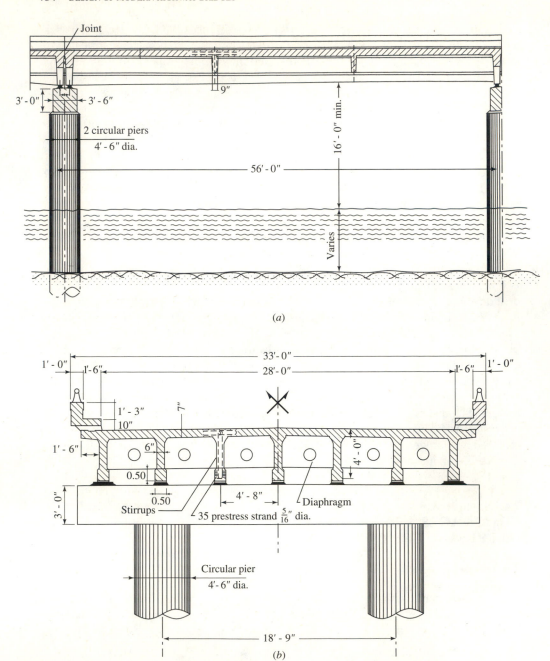

FIGURE 7.12
Bridge over Lake Pontchartrain, Louisiana, the longest multi-span bridge in the world. (*a*) Longitudinal section, (*b*) transverse section [Podolny and Muller, 1982].

in the construction of the 24-mile Lake Pontchartrain Bridge near New Orleans, Louisiana. For this longest bridge in the world, shown in Fig. 7.12, each 56-ft-long, 33-ft-wide span was precast in a yard and floated by barges to site for final erection [Smith, 1955; Van Buren, 1961].

Although the notion of precasting bridge girders in a plant is generally associated with prestressed concrete members, the possibilities of precasting bridge beams and slabs in a plant and assembling them on-site were recognized in the "General Specifications for Concrete Bridges," written by Wilbur J. Watson and published in 1908. The San Mateo Bridge over San Francisco Bay, built in the 1920s, is a notable example of the use of precasting; it comprises 1054 30-ft and 116 35-ft precast girder spans. Another spectacular use of precasting from the earlier years is the Tampa Bay Bridge at St. Petersburg, Florida [Steinmann and Watson, 1957].

2. Tension cracking can be eliminated in a prestressed structure, thereby minimizing the penetration of water and air, leading to improved durability and enhanced service life of concrete and reinforcement. The uncracked section results in a much more efficient design than that from conventional reinforced concrete members.

3. Prestressing permits a more efficient use of concrete as a structural material, because the entire section, not just the uncracked portion, is made to resist compression.

4. Prestressing reduces the diagonal tension. Use of inclined tendons reduces the shear carried by the webs. As a result, a thinner web, requiring fewer stirrups and, consequently, a lighter section, can be achieved. The saving in dead load lowers the handling and transportation costs and increases bridge rating.

5. During prestressing, both concrete and steel are proof-loaded, ensuring safety under service loads. It was the successful full-scale on-site testing, first ever in the United States, of the 160-ft post-tensioned concrete girder for the Walnut Lane Bridge in October 1949 that convinced bridge engineers of the potential of prestressed concrete technology. That test girder supported about 10 times the design load and deflected about 25 in. before total failure [Fornerod, 1950; Zollman, 1978]. Various recent tests on prestressed and post-tensioned concrete girders removed from dismantled bridges have confirmed the safety of prestressed concrete bridges with regard to the ultimate loads [Fornerod, 1950; Riessauw and Taerwe, 1980; Rabbat, 1984; Olson and French, 1990; Shenoy and Frantz, 1991; Tabatabai and Dickson, 1993; Labia, Saiidi, and Douglas, 1993].

6. The smaller girder depths that are possible with prestressed concrete are advantageous under the constraints of limited overhead clearance (for grade separation structures) and free board (for bridges over waterways).

7. Prestressing greatly reduces (practically eliminates) cracking due to fatigue. This aspect was discussed in detail in Chapter 5.

8. When box girders are used, their shallow depths, slenderness, and uncluttered exterior and underside appearance reflect good aesthetics.

9. Prestressed concrete girders with large top flange widths, such as bulb T-beams, adjacent and spread box beam systems, and other box girders, provide ready-made working space during erection, thus either eliminating or minimizing the need for falsework. Falsework not only slows down traffic, but also tends to be a traffic hazard and becomes overly expensive if detours have to be provided. Often, falsework has to be provided over roads where traffic is maintained; in such cases, extra clearance

TABLE 7.3

Span ranges for various types of prestressed concrete bridges [Podolny and Muller, 1982]

Span (ft)	Bridge types
0– 150	Pretensioned I-girder
100– 300	Cast-in-place post-tensioned box girder
100– 300	Precast balanced cantilever, segmental, constant depth
250– 600	Precast balanced cantilever, segmental, variable depth
200–1000	Cast-in-place cantilever, segmental
800–1500	Cable-stay with balanced cantilever, segmental

must be provided for the final bridge in order to maintain the required clearance for the false beams, and this can mean a significant increase in cost. In such cases the preferred option is to use precast concrete or steel box girders, which can be erected quickly without falsework and with a minimum of traffic interference.

10. Prestressed concrete bridges have relatively longer service life. Inspection results indicate that most of the early prestressed concrete bridges, built in the 1950s following the construction of the Walnut Lane Memorial Bridge, although approaching their planned 50-year service life, are not only in active use today but are expected to serve for many more years [Gustaferro, Hillier, and Janney, 1983; Dunker and Rabbat, 1992]. Even in the adverse marine environment, which would be ruinous to reinforced concrete and steel bridges, prestressed concrete bridges have been found to have performed satisfactorily [Novokshchenov, 1990, 1991; Schupack and Suarez, 1991; Murray and Frantz, 1992; Dickson, Tabatabai, and Whiting, 1993]. With new technologies available for protection from corrosion, both reinforced and prestressed concrete bridges would achieve longer service life [Pfeifer, Landgren, and Zoob, 1987].

11. Cast-in-place post-tensioned construction is adaptable to large interchanges with complex geometries involving curved, superelevated (banked), skewed, multilevel sections, and sections of varying width. Longer spans and shallower depths are more economically feasible than with conventional reinforced concrete. Table 7.3 gives approximate ranges of application of bridge type by span lengths achievable from prestressed construction.

7.4.2 Disadvantages

1. A major disadvantage of prestressed concrete, compared to steel, is its own deadweight. Dead load, more than live load, dominates in long-span bridges, resulting in supporting substructures that are heavier and, consequently, uneconomical. However, the advent of high-strength concretes is providing a solution to this problem. High-strength concretes are now being evaluated to reduce deadweights, to permit longer spans or fewer girders for equivalent loading, and to provide improved durability. Current practice in the use of high-strength concrete in highway bridge construction was discussed in Sec. 7.3.1.

2. Prestressed concrete is more sensitive to quality of materials and workmanship.
3. Prestress losses, due to various sources such as creep and shrinkage of concrete or relaxation of prestressing steel, are an important consideration, which a designer must consider very carefully.

The intent here is not to present a complete discussion on the theory and design of prestressed concrete structures; for that purpose, readers are urged to refer to several excellent texts on the subject [Magnel, 1954; Guyon, 1960; Lin, 1963; Libby, 1976a; Nilson, 1978; Lin and Burns, 1981; Naaman, 1982; Nawy, 1989]. Nevertheless, the basic principles of prestressed concrete design are presented in the subsequent paragraphs for a quick review. For the material presented in this chapter, it is assumed that readers are sufficiently familiar with the principles of design of reinforced and prestressed concrete using both the service load and the load factor design (strength design) methods.

7.5
TYPES OF PRESTRESSED CONCRETE BRIDGES

7.5.1 General

The scope of this book has intentionally been limited to design of prestressed concrete bridges of the most common types, such as slab, slab–girder, spread and adjacent box girder, and conventional box girder bridges. A brief discussion on design of prestressed concrete bridges can be found in several references [O'Connor, 1971; ACI, 1973, 1974, 1977, 1995; Tokerud, 1979; PCI, 1981b; Naaman, 1982; Elliot, 1990]. Libby and Perkins [1976] and Heins and Lawrie [1984] have presented a comprehensive discussion on the design of reinforced and prestressed concrete highway bridges. A thorough reading of ACI [1995], PCI [1981b], and Sections 8 and 9 of AASHTO [1992, 1996] is highly recommended for obtaining insight into design practices for reinforced and prestressed concrete highway bridges. Description of the salient features of a few pre-1970 prestressed concrete bridges can be found in O'Connor [1971].

Generally, the lengths of precast prestressed concrete girders are limited by the constraints of transportation and handling systems, which dictate the maximum segment size produced at the fabrication plant. Hauling girders from the casting yard to the confines of cities is always a tricky problem that involves navigating freeway on and off ramps, getting around streets, and turning around street corners while clearing utility poles. A trend toward longer spans with single-length members has resulted in a need for deeper I- and bulb-T beam sections. However, the center of gravity of these members is high above the roadway, making their transportation difficult. The presence of tensile stresses in the top flanges requires that these beams be laterally supported near their ends during hauling to minimize or prevent lateral instability during transit.

The lateral stability problem is also encountered during handling of I-, T- or bulb-T beams with large depths in that they may be tipped sideways, forcing the web out of the vertical plane, thus initiating their buckling. The lateral buckling problem of prestressed concrete beams is of a different type than that of steel members with thin-walled open cross sections (such as I-beams, which generally have low torsional stiffness and are rigidly restrained from rotation at their supports). Prestressed girders, with their thick flanges and webs, generally have large torsional stiffnesses—100 to 1000 times those of steel I-beams. However, during lifting, a prestressed beam hangs from flexible supports (such as lifting loops embedded in the top flange near the ends). The presence of the sweep tolerances in the precast beam, together with imprecise placement of the lifting loops (i.e., not exactly in the plane of the minor axis of the web), causes the center of gravity of the beam to be displaced slightly on one or the other side of the roll axis, as shown in Fig. 7.13. As a result, the beam is tipped about the roll axis by a small angle $\theta_i = e_i/y_r$,

where θ_i = initial roll angle, radians, of a rigid beam

e_i = initial eccentricity of the center of gravity from the roll axis

y_r = distance from the center of gravity to the roll axis, measured along the (original) vertical axis of the beam.

This tipping causes a component $W \sin \theta_i$ of the weight of the beam, W, along the beam's x-axis. This force causes lateral deflection of the beam, which in turn further shifts the center of gravity of the beam's mass. This further shift causes *additional* increase in the initial roll angle θ_i, which causes further increase in the lateral load component $W \sin \theta_i$, causing, in turn, further lateral deflection, and the cycle continues. Consequently, the final angle θ may reach a value at which the lateral bending of the beam is sufficient to destroy it. Mast [1989] has shown that the critical length for roll equilibrium without initial imperfection is given by

$$y_t = \frac{wL_{cr}^4}{120EI_y} \tag{7.1}$$

where y_t = distance from the centroid of girder to the top fibers

w = weight of the beam per linear foot

L_{cr} = critical length

E = elastic modulus of concrete

I_y = moment of inertia about the weak axis

This expression is valid for cases when the lifting loops are located near the ends of the beam—a conservative assumption. Nevertheless, this expression can be conveniently used to estimate the critical lengths for beams from the standpoint of lateral stability; hence, these critical lengths constitute the upper limits of practical lengths for the precast prestressed beams for bridge construction. Moving the location of lifting loops slightly away from the ends (and toward the center of the beam) increases the beam's stability. A comprehensive discussion on stability of I-girders during lifting, transportation, and erection can be found in the literature [Muller, 1962; Swann and Godden, 1966; Anderson, 1971; Swann, 1971; Libby, 1976; Mast, 1966, 1989, 1993, 1994; Imper and Lazlo, 1987; Gerwick, 1993; Castrodale et al., 1994]. A mathematical treatment of the behavior of long precast prestressed concrete beams during transportation and handling, and ways of increasing their stability during these operations, has been presented by Mast [1989, 1994].

In the United States, some states limit the transportable lengths to about 130 ft. Because of the heavy weight of long-span precast girders, the process of obtaining the permit to transport them across the interstate is critical; some long girders may have weight exceeding the capacities of the bridges on the shipping routes. Precast prestressed girders (bulb-T and I-beams), generally 100–115 ft long in the early 1950s,

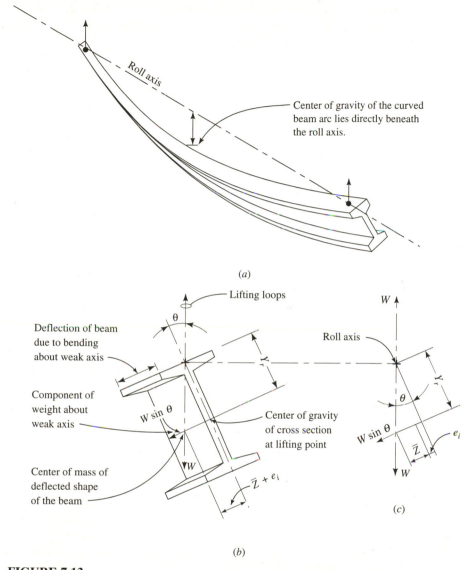

FIGURE 7.13

Equilibrium of a prestressed concrete I-beam in tilted position: (*a*) perspective of a beam free to roll and deflect laterally, (*b*) end view, (*c*) equilibrium diagram [Mast, 1989].

are now being produced up to 160 ft [Abdel-Karim and Tadros, 1992b; Dunker and Rabbat, 1992; Freyermuth, 1992]. According to CE [1993], 138-ft-long bulb-T girders were used for the continuous four-span bridge carrying I-294 (the Tri-State Tollway) over I-290 (the Eisenhower Expressway) in Chicago. Spans in the range of 140–150 ft have been completed in Florida [ENR, 1985; Csagoly and Nickas, 1987; Garcia, 1993]. And 151-ft-long AASHTO Type V girders have been used for one of the five spans of Florida's Turnpike over I-595 and the North New River Canal [PCIJ, 1989b]. Type 81 I-girders (i.e., 81 in. deep) as long as 154 ft 6 in. (with only 6-in.-thick web) have been used for Bridge No. 86005 over the Mississippi River in Elk River, Minnesota [Endicott, 1995]. Plant-precast girders ranging to 167 ft have been shipped in the states of Minnesota, Pennsylvania, and Washington. By comparison, in Japan the maximum transportable length of a precast concrete girder is limited to just 71 ft by transportation authorities—in effect limiting the length of precast, pretensioned girder bridges to under 69 ft [Yamane, Tadros, and Arumugasaamy, 1994]. With the proliferation of the drop-in segment (or suspended-span) design, spans in the 250-ft range may become common. High-strength concrete, leading to higher flexural capacities, should also result in increased economical span lengths.

The maximum lengths of precast girders produced in a plant are generally smaller than those of cast-on-site girders, which can be floated to the erection site. For longer spans, it is necessary to precast on site or in short segments in a plant, and subsequently post-tension at site. Most short-span bridges are built from prestressed beams that are generally precast in a plant and transported to site for erection.

7.5.2 Description of Various Types of Prestressed Concrete Bridges

Since the 1950s, various configurations of precast prestressed concrete beams been developed in different parts of the world. Practices vary because of differences in live loads, in available technology, and in the prevailing practices that have evolved over time. Prestressed concrete bridges are classified by the physical characteristics of their superstructures (usually the shape of the girders supporting the deck) and are variously referred to as I-beam, T-beam, double T-beam, multibeam, box girder bridges, and so forth. To conform to the terminology used in the AASHTO specifications [AASHTO, 1992, 1996], the term *stringer,* often used to describe steel-beam bridges, is not used in conjunction with prestressed concrete bridges.

Generally, most short- and medium-span highway bridges built with precast prestressed concrete girders have two basic forms:

1. Precast prestressed concrete I-, bulb-T, or U-girders are used to support a cast-in-place concrete deck about 7″ or thicker. These girders have stirrups projecting from their top flanges, to be embedded in the cast-in-place deck to develop composite action. Diaphragms between girders are usually cast in place, but girders with integrally cast diaphragms with post-tensioning operations have also been reported [Quade, 1952; Lamarre, 1967]. A layer of asphalt surfacing about $1\frac{1}{2}$ in. to 2 in. thick or a $\frac{1}{2}$-in. thick additional integrally cast concrete layer is provided as a wearing surface. Among the various prestressed concrete bridge superstructures, the I-beam construction has become the most preferred form because the supported deck can be replaced relatively easily after it has reached its service life—an often-cited advantage.

2. Precast prestressed concrete box, T-, or channel beams can be laid contiguously where little or no field concreting is required for the deck slab. The top flanges of these members are sufficiently thick to serve as ready-made decks. Longitudinal shear keys are provided between adjacent beams for transverse continuity. An asphalt concrete or modified-latex concrete wearing surface is normally applied directly to the top surface of these concrete units. Of all the shapes, box beam construction has been used most widely.

Generally, in either case the preferred type of superstructure is dictated by several factors such as feasibility of construction, economics, product availability (which may vary locally or regionally), time constraint, technical development, and the environment. Experiences and preferences of the bridge owners/designers are other factors that affect the bridge type selection process. Accordingly, practices and preferences for using one or the other type, and the applicable economical span range, vary widely from state to state.

The dual advantages of inherent economies and quality control achievable with precast prestressed members have made prestressed concrete a material of choice since the 1950s for short-span bridges in the span range of 70 to 120 ft [Dunker and Rabbat, 1992]. During the early stages of development, different shapes and sizes of girders were designed for each new bridge, but the popularity and frequent use of precast prestressed girders led various states to standardize their own girder shapes [Taly and GangaRao, 1974, 1977; Taly, 1976]. Recognizing the need for standardization, in 1956 the Bureau of Public Roads (now known as the Federal Highway Administration) adopted two shapes for standardization: the I-beam and the box sections, which came to be known as the AASHO–PCI girders (now AASHTO–PCI, or simply AASHTO girders). All of these initial efforts and developments, however, were targeted for simple short spans approximately 100 ft, but more commonly 40 to 80 ft, for which precast pretensioned girders were ideal [Podolny and Muller, 1982]. As demand for longer-span and continuous bridges grew with time, it soon became apparent that these girders were not suitable for them. In continuous beams the design is often governed by the negative moments. The inadequacy of these existing sections (insufficient concrete area for compression in the bottom flange, and webs too narrow to accommodate ducts for continuity post-tensioning tendons) limited their span capabilities, transverse girder spacing, or both. These drawbacks led to the development of new sections and modification of the existing sections. These include several versions of so-called bulb-T beams (I-beams with large top flanges) [Lin and Burns, 1981; Garcia, 1993; Geren and Tadros, 1994] and U-beams [Ralls, Ybanez, and Panek, 1993], with capabilities for longer spans and claims of better sectional efficiency over the existing sections.

The standardization of configurations and section properties of precast concrete girder sections is comparable to that found in the steel industry with its industrywide I-beam, channel, angle, and tube sections. Typically, depending on span length, prestressed concrete superstructures can be built from a wide variety of longitudinally prestressed concrete members as follows (in order of increasing, albeit overlapping, span length):

1. Solid slab and voided slab
2. Channel, inverted channel, and U-beam
3. T-beam (single, double, multiple, and bulb-T)
4. I-beam
5. Box beam (spread and adjacent)
6. Multicell box girder
7. Segmental box beam

Several of these superstructure types are described in the following paragraphs. Table 7.4 summarizes span ranges for various precast pretensioned beam sections used in the

TABLE 7.4
Precast pretensioned beam sections used for short-span bridges in the United States [Yamane, Tadros, and Arumugasaamy, 1994]

Typical section		Width mm (in.)	Depth mm (in.)	Span range m (ft)	Cast-in-place to precast concrete weight ratio
	Solid slab	910 to 2440 (36 to 96)	250 to 460 (10 to 18)	up to 9.1 (up to 30)	0.0*
	Voided slab	910 to 1220 (36 to 48)	380 to 530 (15 to 21)	7.6 to 15.2 (25 to 50)	0.0*
	Multistem	1220 (48)	410 to 530 (16 to 21)	7.6 to 16.8 (25 to 55)	0.0*
	Double stem	1520 to 2440 (60 to 96)	410 to 580 (16 to 23)	6.1 to 18.3 (20 to 60)	0.0†
	Single stem	1220 to 1830 (48 to 72)	610 to 1220 (24 to 48)	12.2 to 24.4 (40 to 80)	0.0†
	Box girder	910 to 1220 (36 to 48)	690 to 1070 (27 to 42)	18.3 to 30.5 (60 to 100)	0.0*
	Deck bulb-T‡	1220 to 2130 (48 to 84)	740 to 1040 (29 to 41)	18.3 or more (60 or more)	0.0†
	I-girder‡	460 to 660 (18 to 26)	910 to 1370 (36 to 54)	12.2 to 30.5 (40 to 100)	0.6 to 1.2
	AASHTO–PCI bulb-T‡	1070 (42)	1370 to 1830 (54 to 72)	24.4 to 42.7 (80 to 140)	0.6 to 1.2
	Local standard I-girder‡	610 to 1520 (24 to 60)	710 to 2740 (28 to 108)	up to 50.9 (up to 167)	0.6 to 1.2

*Bridges built without topping concrete or diaphragms.
†In some cases, with topping concrete and cast-in-place concrete diaphragms.
‡When post-tensioning is used in combination with pretensioning, these girders may be spliced to reach longer spans up to 76 m (250 ft).

492

TABLE 7.5
Precast pretensioned beam sections used for short-span bridges in Japan [Yamane, Tadros, and Arumugasaamy, 1994]

Typical section		Width mm (in.)	Depth mm (in.)	Span range m (ft)	Cast-in-place to precast concrete weight ratio
	Pretensioned solid box girder*	700 (28)	325 to 400 (13 to 16)	5 to 9 (16 to 30)	0.10
	Pretensioned voided box girder*	700 (28)	425 to 800 (17 to 32)	10 to 21 (33 to 69)	0.10
	Pretensioned T-girder*	750 (30)	800 to 1050 (32 to 41)	14 to 21 (46 to 69)	0.25
	Post-tensioned T-girder*	1500 (59)	1050 to 2150 (41 to 85)	20 to 40 (66 to 131)	0.23
	Post-tensioned box girder*	1000 to 1600 (39 to 63)	800 to 1600 (32 to 63)	24 to 40 (79 to 131)	0.14
	Post-tensioned I-girder†	650 to 1050 (26 to 41)	1550 to 2450 (61 to 97)	20 to 40 (66 to 131)	0.60 to 1.20

*Used with noncomposite bridge deck.
†Used with composite bridge deck.

United States. For comparison, Table 7.5 summarizes the precast prestressed concrete beam sections used in Japan.

Figure 7.14 shows standard sections for a span range of 50 to 105 ft (16 to 32 m) used in England, where the M, U, and box beams (in that order) are more popular and the I-section is rarely used [Somerville, 1970; Manton and Wilson, 1975; PCA UK, 1984; Cope, 1987]. The design of these sections is covered in BS 5400 [BSI, 1984]. Figure 7.15 shows deck configurations with these beams and a cast-in-place concrete slab. Note the use of a UM-beam as a special edge beam; its additional vertical web produces a desirable aesthetic appearance [Taylor, 1987].

Several characteristics of highway bridge superstructures built from these precast prestressed concrete beams in the United States are notable [Taly, 1976; ACI, 1977; PCI, 1981b].

Section no.	Depth (mm)	Area (mm²)	Ht. N.A. (mm)	I_{NA} (mm⁴ ×10⁻⁶)	Self-weight (kN/m)
B1	510	337,550	251	9765	7.95
B2	585	356,300	287	14,095	8.39
B3	660	375,050	323	19,430	8.84
B4	735	396,925	361	26,175	9.36
B5	810	418,800	400	33,995	9.87
B6	885	437,550	435	42,450	10.31
B7	960	456,300	471	52,200	10.75
B8	1035	478,175	510	63,970	11.26
B9	1110	500,050	548	76,930	11.79
B10	1220	527,550	600	97,240	12.43
B11	1220	604,625	580	105,800	14.25
B12	1260	616,625	598	114,810	14.53
B13	1310	633,501	623	127,660	14.93
B14	1360	651,001	649	141,660	15.34
B15	1410	667,877	674	149,830	15.74
B16	1460	682,876	697	170,330	16.09
B17	1510	697,876	720	185,415	16.44

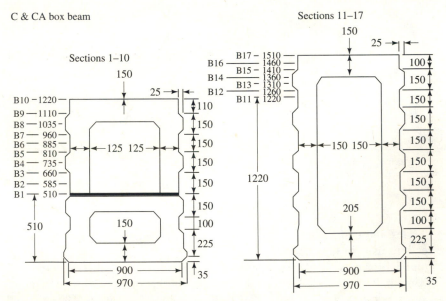

(*Note*: All dimensions are in millimeters.)

FIGURE 7.14
Cross sections and section properties of precast prestressed concrete beams used in England [Manton and Wilson, 1975].

Section no.	Depth (mm)	Area (mm²)	Ht. N.A. (mm)	I_{NA} (mm⁴ ×10⁻⁶)	Self-weight (kN/m)
WB1	510	419,032	251	12,556	9.88
WB2	585	447,245	290	18,300	10.54
WB3	660	465,995	326	25,172	10.98
WB4	735	487,870	364	33,716	11.50
WB5	810	500,282	398	42,923	11.79
WB6	885	528,495	439	54,419	12.46
WB7	960	547,245	475	66,718	12.90
WB8	1035	569,120	513	81,310	13.42
WB9	1100	581,532	545	95,794	13.71
WB10	1220	622,495	607	123,490	14.67
WB11	1220	707,270	579	133,235	16.67
WB12	1260	719,270	598	144,475	16.95
WB13	1310	736,770	623	160,455	17.37
WB14	1360	753,645	648	177,062	17.76
WB15	1410	770,520	673	194,566	18.16
WB16	1460	785,520	696	212,027	18.52
WB17	1510	800,520	719	230,464	18.87

DOW MAC wide box beam

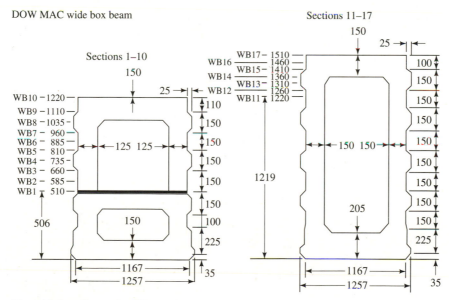

(*Note*: All dimensions are in millimeters.)

FIGURE 7.14 (continued)

Section no.	Depth (mm)	Area (mm²)	Ht. N.A. (mm)	I_{NA} (mm⁴ ×10⁻⁶)	Self-weight (kN/m)
U1	800	469,390	354	30,010	11.08
U2	850	485,895	377	35,640	11.44
U3	900	502,400	400	41,880	11.85
U4	950	518,905	424	48,760	12.24
U5	1000	535,325	447	56,270	12.61
U6	1050	551,830	471	64,450	13.00
U7	1100	568,335	495	73,320	13.40
U8	1200	601,345	543	93,220	14.19
U9	1300	634,270	590	116,100	14.96
U10	1400	667,280	638	142,200	15.72
U11	1500	700,205	687	171,500	16.52
U12	1600	733,215	735	204,400	17.29

DOW MAC U beam
  U-beam standard sections

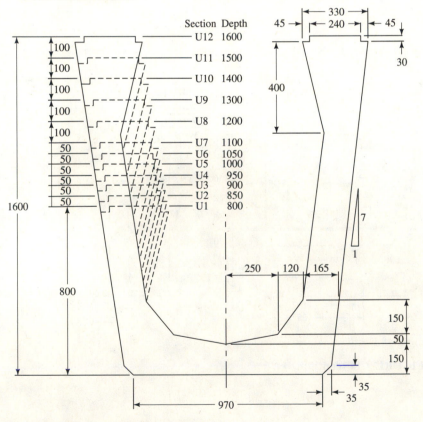

(*Note*: All dimensions are in millimeters)

FIGURE 7.14 (continued)

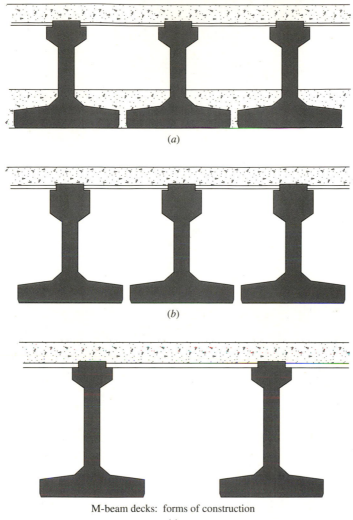

(a)

(b)

M-beam decks: forms of construction

(c)

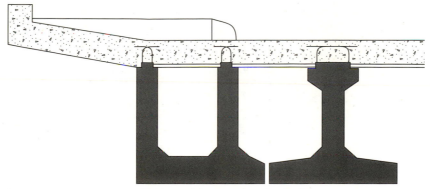

UM-beam giving attractive edge detail

(d)

FIGURE 7.15
Forms of M-beam bridge superstructures used in England [Taylor, 1987].

497

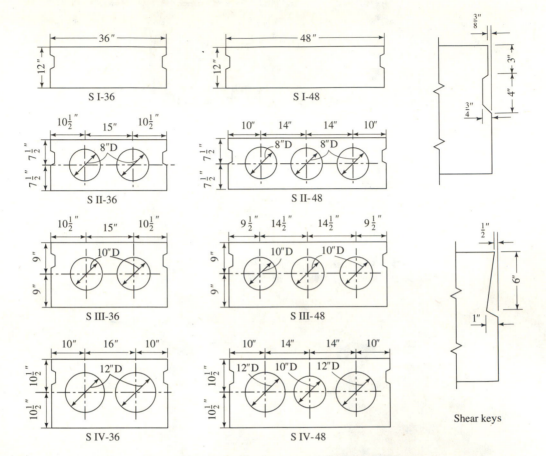

Section	Area (in.²)	Moment of inertia (in.⁴)	Section modulus (in.³)	Range of span (ft)	
				HS20-44	H20-44
SI-36	432	5180	864	20–28	20–29
SII-36	439	9720	1296	27–35	28–38
SIII-36	491	16,510	1835	34–42	37–46
SIV-36	530	25,750	2452	41–49	45–54
SI-48	576	6910	1152	20–28	20–29
SII-48	569	12,900	1720	27–35	28–38
SII-48	628	21,850	2428	34–42	37–46
SIV-48	703	34,520	3287	41–50	45–55

FIGURE 7.16
AASHTO–PCI solid and voided slabs: (*a*) solid slab units, (*b*) voided slab units.

7.5.2.1 Solid slab and voided slab bridges

These slabs (or *planks*), usually 3 to 8 ft wide and 10 to 18 in. deep, are economical for short spans in the 30-ft range because of their flexibility and depth limitations. Deeper slabs are made economical for slightly longer spans (20 to 55 ft) by providing longitudinal voids to reduce their deadweight (such voided slabs are also referred to as cored slabs). Both types of slab units are produced in standard widths of 3 and 4 ft and various standardized depths. Details and cross-sectional properties of AASHTO–PCI solid and voided slabs are shown in Fig. 7.16.

Figures 7.17(*a*) and (*b*) show transverse sections of bridges built from solid and voided slab units. The slab elements are placed contiguously for the full width of the deck, essentially resulting in what are often referred to as *multibeam decks*. A combination of slab units of different standard widths can be used to attain the desired deck width. When necessary, these slab elements can be precast with shear stirrups projecting from the top fibers, to be bonded to the cast-in-place concrete for composite action and lateral continuity.

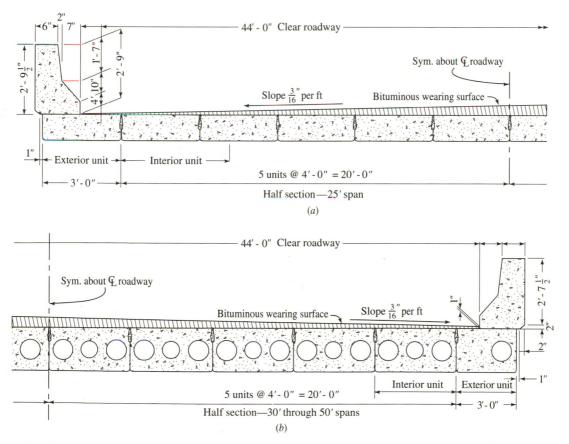

FIGURE 7.17
Half transverse sections of bridges built from (*a*) solid and (*b*) voided slab units.

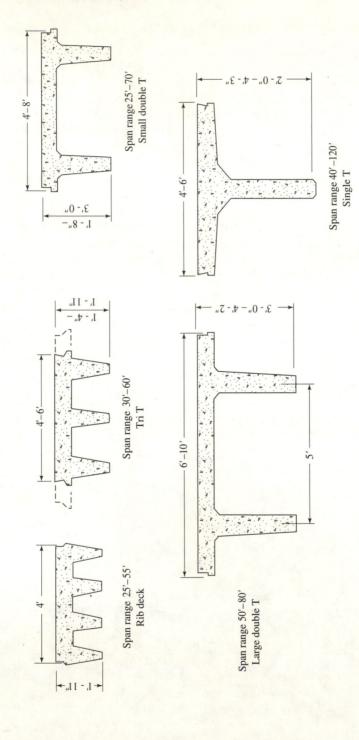

FIGURE 7.18
Various forms of T-girders used for short-span highway bridges [Tokerud, 1979].

Span range 25'–70'
Small double T

Span range 40'–120'
Single T

Span range 30'–60'
Tri T

Span range 50'–80'
Large double T

Span range 25'–55'
Rib deck

7.5.2.2 T-beam bridges

Various forms of precast prestressed T-beams have evolved over the past 40 years to build short-span highway bridges [Curtis, 1967; Kwei, 1967]. These include contiguously placed *single-T, double-T,* and *multiple-T* sections (Fig. 7.18) and are suitable for bridges in the span range of 20 to 80 ft; some single-T beam sections can span 120 ft. These precast sections are produced in standardized widths, usually 4, 6, and 8 ft.

Advancement in post-tensioning technology has led to the emergence of *double-T beams*, previously used only for rural and secondary roads, as potential systems for bridges on state and interstate-class highways in Florida for simple spans up to 80 ft. The fully precast beams are transported to the site, erected adjacent to each other, V-joints between the edges of their flanges are filled with nonshrink mortar grout, and they are transversely post-tensioned to provide for lateral resistance and continuity (load transfer) [Shahawy, 1990; Arokiasamy et al., 1991; Shahawy and Issa, 1992]. Figure 7.19 shows details of the Florida double-T beam used for full-scale testing [Shahawy and Issa, 1992], which in most respects is similar to that used in practice in that state.

Figure 7.20 shows a system of precast prestressed double-T beams used in California. With 2-in.-thick, 8-ft-wide flanges, they are precast in standardized depths of 18, 24, and 32 in., with projecting web reinforcement that is embedded in the cast-in-place slab ($5\frac{1}{2}$ in. minimum) to develop composite action for live load. Obviously, the beams act noncompositely for all dead load that is applied before the deck concrete hardens.

For increased span capabilities, the Concrete Technology Corporation developed the *bulb-T* series, having a 4-ft-wide top flange and several standardized depths, in 1959 (Fig. 7.21). Arthur R. Anderson improved this design in 1969, developing the innovative *decked bulb-T* series with large standardized flange widths of 5 to 10 ft, each with several standardized depths from 29 to 77 in. (Fig. 7.22), with span capabilities up to 190 ft [Anderson, 1957, 1972]. Placed contiguously, these girders provide a ready-made deck, eliminating the need for a costly cast-in-place deck. The unique feature of this series is that the top flange is cast with 120-lb/ft^3, lightweight 6000-psi concrete, whereas the rest of the section is cast from 160-lb/ft^3, high-strength 8500-psi concrete. The section properties of this series are calculated based on a transformed section in which the transformed width of the deck is half of its actual width (i.e., in the ratio of the modulus of elasticity of the top flange concrete to that of the web and bottom flange concrete). Anderson also developed the *Washington series 14 bulb-T*, which was standardized with some modifications in 1988 as the *AASHTO–PCI bulb-T* series (Fig. 7.23) [Geren and Tadros, 1994]. Noteworthy are the details of the prefabricated, galvanized steel, K-shaped diaphragms, which are field-bolted to the steel plates anchored in these girders. Roller et al. [1995] have presented the results of an experimental investigation of 70-ft-long, 54-in-deep pretensioned high-strength (10,000-psi) concrete bulb-T girders having a 10-ft-wide top flange. These girders are reported to have withstood more than 5 million cycles of fatigue loading and satisfied all serviceability requirements.

Although girder sections with large depths are generally preferable because of their large moments of inertia and enhanced spanning capabilities, certain practical considerations may warrant girders of shallow depths. The five-span, 500-ft-long (100 ft each span), 40-ft-wide Fargo-Moorhead Toll Bridge over the Red River linking Fargo, North Dakota, and Moorhead, Minnesota, completed in June 1988, is an example of

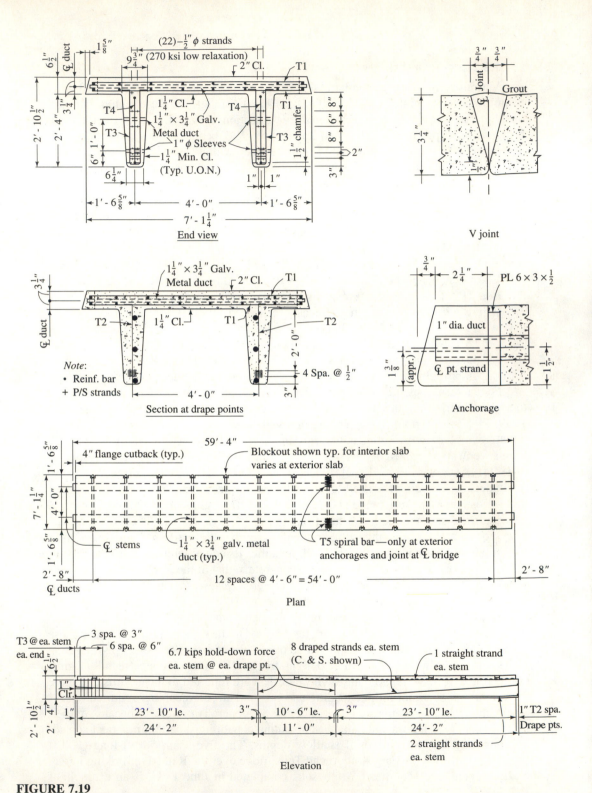

FIGURE 7.19
Typical details of the precast double-T beam used by the Florida Department of Transportation [Shahawy and Issa, 1992].

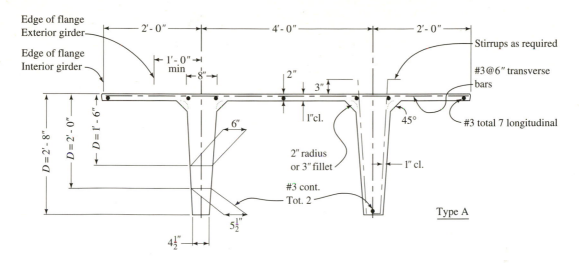

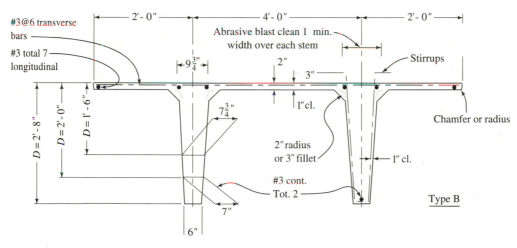

FIGURE 7.20
Precast prestressed double T-beams used in California.

Depth d (in.)	Area (in.^{2})	y_b (in.)	Moment of inertia (in.^{4})
24	380	12.14	28,900
30	410	14.95	51,100
36	440	17.78	80,700
48	500	23.51	164,000
60	560	29.29	283,200
72	620	35.12	442,800

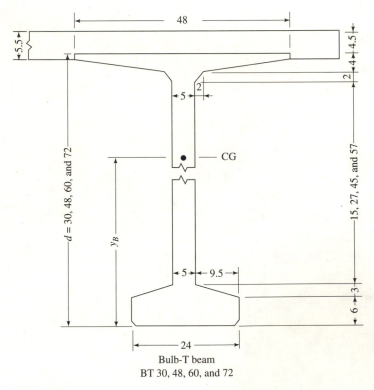

Bulb-T beam
BT 30, 48, 60, and 72

FIGURE 7.21
Section properties of bulb-T beams [Anderson, 1972].

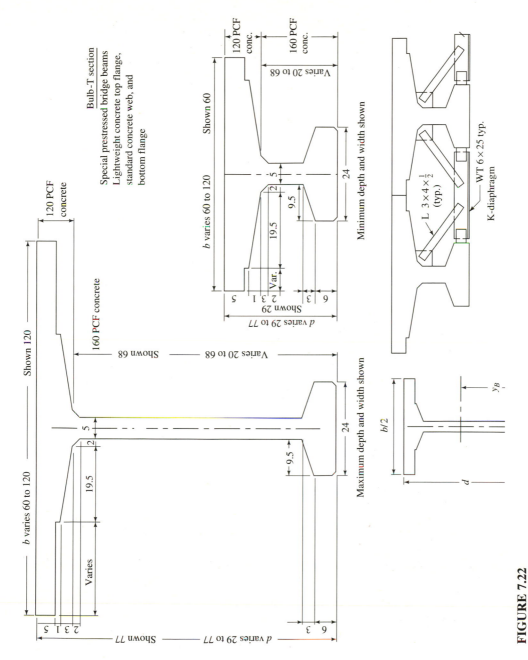

FIGURE 7.22

Prestressed decked bulb-T beams [Anderson, 1972].

$\frac{b}{2}$ (in.)	Transformed section beam properties			
	d (in.)	Area (in.^{2})	y_b (in.)	Moment of inertia (in.^{4})
30	29	456	15.24	48,200
	35	486	18.35	78,900
	41	516	21.46	118,400
	53	576	27.63	225,700
	65	636	33.77	374,400
	77	696	39.89	568,900
36	29	486	15.93	51,800
	35	516	19.17	84,600
	41	546	22.39	126,700
	53	606	28.76	240,600
	65	666	35.07	398,100
	77	726	41.32	603,400
42	29	516	16.54	55,100
	35	546	19.91	89,700
	41	576	23.23	134,100
	53	636	29.79	254,200
	65	696	36.25	419,800
	77	756	42.63	635,200
48	29	546	17.09	58,000
	35	576	20.56	94,300
	41	606	23.99	140,800
	53	666	30.72	266,600
	65	726	37.33	439,700
	77	786	43.85	664,600

FIGURE 7.22 (continued)

shallow-depth bulb-T girders. Ordinarily, for 100-ft simple spans, AASHTO Type IV or Type V I-girders (Fig. 7.24), with total superstructure depth in excess of 62 in., would be required. Those girders were judged as an impracticable alternative for this bridge, where considerations of flooding problems necessitated shallow bridge girders. As a result, 10 contiguously placed, 39-in.-deep (decked) bulb-T girders, post-tensioned *transversely* using the manufacturer's Dywidag post-tensioning system, were used to enhance the durability and strength of the deck (Fig. 7.24). Air holes were cast in the deck to minimize buoyancy likely to be caused by flooding [PCIJ, 1989c].

It is interesting to note that, while single T-beam bridges are rarely built in the United States, they are very common in Japan for short and medium spans (Table 7.5). Precast pretensioned single T-beams are used for short spans (41 to 69 ft), whereas precast post-tensioned single T-beams are used for medium spans (66 to 131 ft). In both cases the superstructure is built as noncomposite. Also, in both cases, not only are the girders transversely post-tensioned at diaphragm locations, but the T-beam flanges are transversely post-tensioned at frequent intervals (500 mm) at relatively high levels of prestressing force. Some important details of these bridge systems are shown in Figs. 7.25a and b.

Type*	A (in.^{2})	I (in.^{4})	y_b (in.)
BT-54	659	268,077	27.6
BT-63	713	392,638	32.1
BT-72	767	545,894	36.6

*Numbers refer to the total depth of cross section.

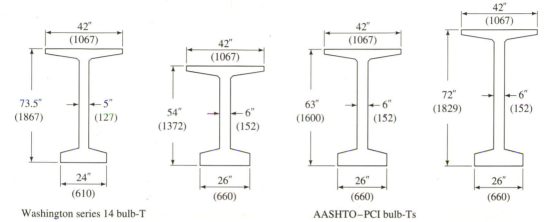

Washington series 14 bulb-T   AASHTO–PCI bulb-Ts

(*Note*: Dimensions are in millimeters.)

FIGURE 7.23
Washington series 14 bulb-T and AASHTO–PCI bulb-T girders [Geren and Tadros, 1994].

7.5.2.3 Prestressed channel girder bridges

The prestressed channel shape is similar to the double-T beam section except for the overhanging flange (i.e., smaller flange). The reduction in web width is not practical; certain minimum width is required for pouring concrete, placing reinforcements, vibrating, and stability [Mast, 1966]. Furthermore, the reduced flange width reduces concrete area in the compression zone of the section, with consequent shortening of the lever arm of the resisting couple. The channel section is therefore less efficient than a double-T section of the same size and hence is comparatively uneconomical.

The type of construction with beams of channel sections is similar to that for the double-T beams. A typical superstructure built from channel sections is shown in Fig. 7.26a [USDOT, 1990]. Figure 7.26b shows cross-sectional details of a channel section used for the fascia girder for an overpass in Canada [Ragan, 1969].

7.5.2.4 Box beam bridges

Box beams are prefabricated in standardized widths of 3 and 4 ft to accommodate various bridge widths and several standardized depths suitable for span ranges of 60 to 100 ft. Figure 7.27 shows configurations and section properties of the AASHTO–PCI box girders, commonly used in the United States [Elliot, 1990].

Two types of girder layouts may be used for superstructures built from box girders: (1) the spread box beam bridge and (2) the adjacent box beam bridge.

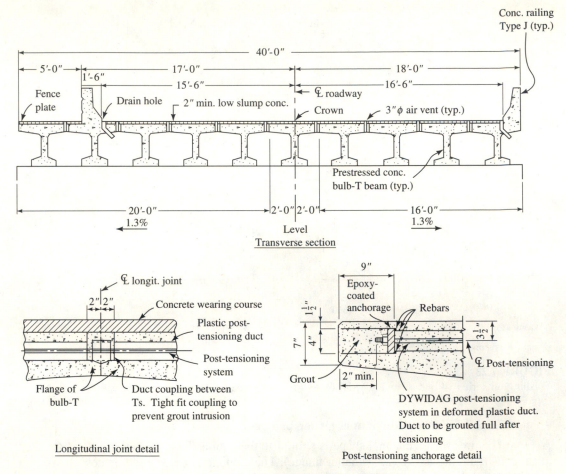

FIGURE 7.24
Cross section and transverse post-tensioning details of the Fargo-Moorhead Bridge [PCIJ, 1989c].

Spread box beam bridge. Beams are placed at selected transverse spacings (but not contiguously) to support a cast-in-place deck. Reinforcement from the webs of the precast box girders may be extended above the top flange, to be embedded into the deck to develop composite action. Intermediate diaphragms are provided as required by the specifications. A typical section through a spread box bridge is shown in Fig. 7.28 [USDOT, 1990].

Adjacent box beam bridge. In this design, box beams are placed contiguously to provide the desired bridge width, as shown in Fig. 7.29, resulting in a superstructure commonly referred to as a multibeam deck. The two exclusive advantages of adjacent box beam systems are that (1) their shallow depths provide easy solutions where only limited superstructure depths are possible, and (2) 3- and 4-ft-wide sections can be combined to produce arbitrary deck widths. In addition, like the solid and voided slabs, they provide a ready-made deck that can be advantageously used as working space for other construction work, thus eliminating the need for costly falsework.

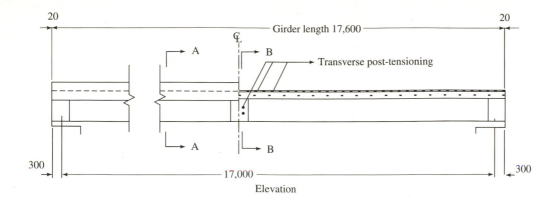

Elevation

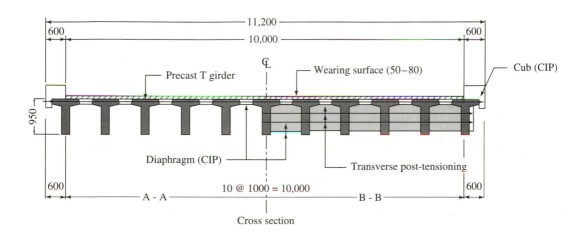

Cross section

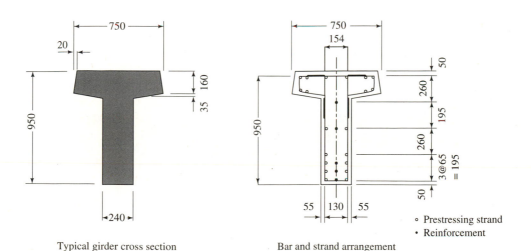

Typical girder cross section   Bar and strand arrangement

(*Note*: All dimensions are in millimeters.)

FIGURE 7.25a
Precast, pretensioned T-girder bridge system used for simple short spans in Japan [Yamane, Tadros, and Arumugasaamy, 1994].

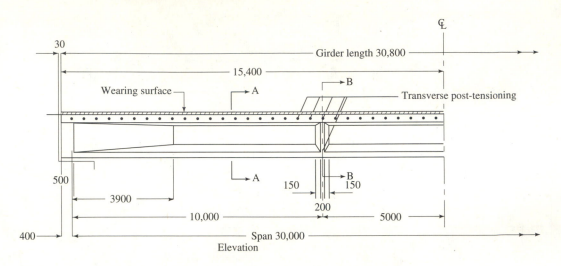

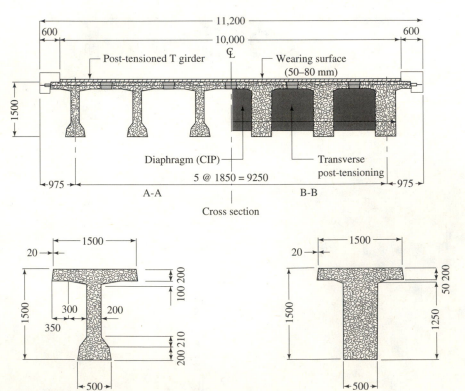

Typical girder cross section

FIGURE 7.25b
Precast, post-tensioned T-girder bridge system used for simple medium spans in Japan [Yamane, Tadros, and Arumugasaamy, 1994].

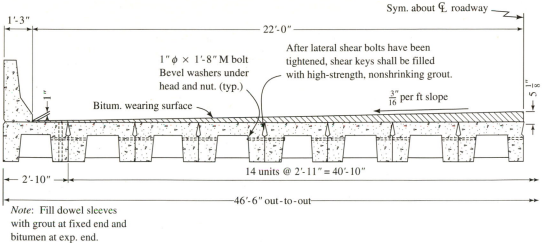

(a) Half section

Note: Fill dowel sleeves
with grout at fixed end and
bitumen at exp. end.

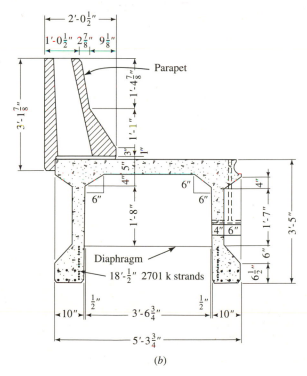

(b)

FIGURE 7.26
Precast prestressed channel beam bridge [USDOT, 1990; Ragan, 1969].

Section	Area (in.²)	Moment of inertia (in.⁴)	c_b, (in.)*	Span limit (ft)	
				Draped strand	Straight strand
BI-36	560	50,330	13.35	74	62
BI-48	692	65,940	13.37	73	63
BII-36	620	85,150	16.29	86	73
BII-48	752	110,500	16.33	86	74
BIII-36	680	131,140	19.25	97	83
BIII-48	812	168,370	19.29	96	83
BIV-36	710	158,640	20.73	103	87
BIV-48	842	203,090	20.78	103	88

* From center of gravity to bottom surface.

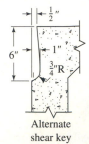

Alternate shear key

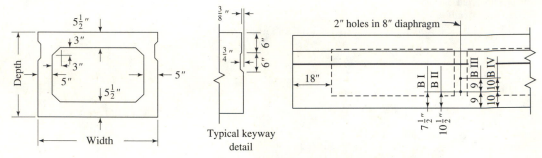

Typical keyway detail

FIGURE 7.27
Section properties of standard AASHTO–PCI box sections [Elliot, 1990].

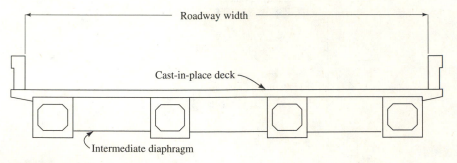

FIGURE 7.28
Typical cross section through a spread box beam bridge [USDOT, 1990].

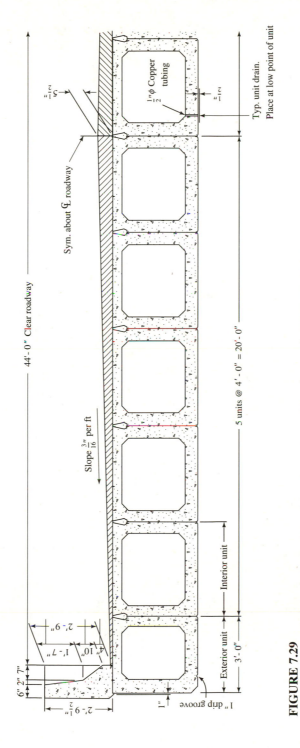

FIGURE 7.29

Typical cross section through an adjacent box beam (or multibeam) bridge [USDOT, 1990].

513

combined to produce arbitrary deck widths. In addition, like the solid and voided slabs, they provide a ready-made deck that can be advantageously used as working space for other construction work, thus eliminating the need for costly falsework.

Two construction schemes are used for adjacent box beam bridge superstructures:

1. Composite construction, in which case the deck, formed from cast-in-place concrete, acts compositely with the girders. Often, the box beams are cast with stirrups projecting from the top flanges, to be embedded in the poured-in-place deck to develop a composite action. In such cases the girders act noncompositely in resisting dead load. The composite action, which comes into play only after the concrete has hardened, is beneficial for resisting live load and any other superimposed loads. A 2 to $2\frac{1}{2}$-in.-thick topping of bituminous concrete or equivalent, which also acts as a wearing surface, is provided over the entire deck surface for leveling and creating a smooth riding surface.
2. Noncomposite construction, which does not require cast-in-place concrete; the top flanges of the girders themselves serve as the deck.

Box beams are usually fabricated with *interior* diaphragms at the middle or third points. Transverse rods about $1\frac{1}{4}$-in. in diameter are inserted through these diaphragms and post-tensioned to hold the girders together. Diaphragms for the adjacent box beam bridges are required only if necessary for slab end support, or to contain or resist transverse tension ties (AASHTO 9.10.3.2).

A common feature of these superstructures is the built-in longitudinal shear keys provided at the edges of T-beam flanges, the sides of solid and voided slabs, on the webs of box beams along their entire lengths, as shown in Figs. 7.17, 7.27, and 7.29. To preserve aesthetics, the exterior beams are cast with shear keys only on the inside edge of the T-beam flange or on the inside face of the box girder. Following the contiguous placement of these girders, the shear keys are filled with a high-strength nonshrink grout to provide lateral resistance and load transfer. For T-beams the shear keys are formed by filling the V-joints between the adjacent edges of the flanges, followed by transverse post-tensioning of the entire deck [Shahawy, 1990].

Many studies on various kinds of shear transfer connections are reported in the literature [Hanson, 1960; Gaston and Kriz, 1964; Birkland and Birkland, 1966; Mast, 1968; Walker, 1969; Ventury, 1970; Mattock and Hawkins, 1972; Moustafa, 1981; PCI, 1992; Foerster, Rizkalla, and Hoeval, 1989; Serrette et al., 1989; Gangatharan and Brown, 1990]. However, it must be pointed out that no rational basis exists for computing shear resistance and lateral load transfer provided by the wide variety of shear keys used in practice; the connection details have been arrived at through practice and experience, essentially by a trial-and-error process, over the years.

In addition to these longitudinal shear keys, the interaction between adjacent beams is developed by transverse ties or bolts, which may or may not be prestressed and may consist of post-tensioned tendons. Different schemes are used for adjacent box and T-beams. For box girders, some specifications (PennDOT [1993a] for example) call for providing a 270-ksi, $\frac{1}{2}$-in.-diameter tendon with a force of 30,000 lb for these ties at each diaphragm. Alternatively, ties equivalent to a $1\frac{1}{4}$-in.-diameter mild-steel bar tensioned to 30,000 lb may be used [Elliot, 1990]. Such ties may typically be provided at each end as well as at one or more intermediate points along the span; they are required to be placed 48 hours after the placement of shear keys, but not before the grout has attained a strength of at least 2500 psi. Tendons are tightened at the midspan first and progressively toward the ends.

Vents, usually $1\frac{1}{4}$-in. in diameter, are provided in the bottom flanges of each void in box beams to drain the trapped moisture [Bender and Kriesel, 1969].

7.5.2.5 I-beam bridges

Figure 7.30 shows the standard AASHTO–PCI I-beams (also referred to simply as AASHTO I-beams), used by many states in the United States, and their section properties and span ranges. The AASHTO Type I beam is seldom used because of its lack of cost-effectiveness; the noncomposite voided slabs are more economical for its span range. Several states (such as Illinois, Iowa, Minnesota, Missouri, Nebraska, Ohio, Pennsylvania, Texas, Washington, and Wisconsin) use their own standard I- and box sections, whose section properties (compiled by the author), are reported in the literature [Taly and GangaRao, 1974, 1977; Taly, 1976]. There appears to be a growing trend toward using lighter and more slender sections, prompting development of new and more efficient I-section configurations (Fig. 7.31) in certain states to serve specific needs [Garcia, 1993; Geren and Tadros, 1994]. Also, for bridges continuous over the piers, newer shapes are often designed to resist both negative and positive moments.

A striking difference among the standard sections adopted by various states lies in their web thicknesses, which vary from 5 in. for the Washington State I-girders (Fig. 7.32), to $6\frac{1}{2}$ or 7 in. for the Florida State standard beams (Fig. 7.33), to 8 to 14 in. for the Pennsylvania State I-girders (Fig. 7.34). The thin webs are preferred because they reduce the deadweight of the girders (and hence, their dead-load moment), obviously resulting in increased flexural capacity for the live load. The reduced shear capacity of the thinner webs can be compensated by providing the necessary shear (or web) reinforcement. Thin webs, however, may require extra care during transportation and handling to maintain stability, and they may be too narrow to accommodate ducts for post-tensioning steel.

In all these beam configurations, a particular section is selected as applicable for a span range, and then varying amounts of prestressing force can be applied as required for a specific span. For example, the AASHTO–PCI Type V beam is suitable for a span range of 90 to 120 ft, but the amount of prestressing force required, and hence the number of prestressing strands, would be different for different spans.

It is a common practice to have a cast-in-place deck to act compositely with the supporting I-girders. This is accomplished by embedding in the deck the stirrups that extend from the girder's top flange. Precast prestressed form panels (discussed in a later section) are commonly used to support the deck during the pour-in phase. Figure 7.35 shows typical transverse sections through a prestressed I-beam bridge with AASHTO Type V girders.

7.5.2.6 Trapezoidal box and U-beam bridges

Beams having the shape of an inverted channel section (with vertical or slant webs), and thus referred to as *U-beams* or *trapezoidal box beams,* are also feasible for short-span bridges [Taly and GangaRao, 1974, 1978; Taly, 1976]; they may or may not

AASHTO beam type	Area (in.²)	I (in.⁴)	y_b* (in.)	Recommended span limits (ft)
I	276	22,750	12.59	30–45
II	369	50,980	15.83	40–60
III	560	125,390	20.27	55–80
IV	789	260,730	24.73	70–100
V	1013	521,180	31.96	90–120
VI	1085	733,320	36.38	110–140

*From center of gravity to bottom fibers.

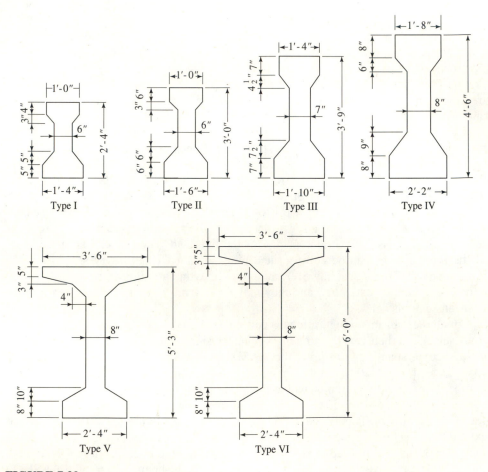

FIGURE 7.30

Cross sections and section properties of standard AASHTO–PCI I-sections [Lin and Burns, 1981].

I-sections

Agency	Type	D1	D2	D3	D4	D5	D6	B1	B2	B3	B4	A	I	y_b
AASHTO	Type VI	72	5	3	4	10	8	42.9	26.9	6.9	4	1006	699,093	36.4
AASHTO–PCI	BT-72	72	3.5	2	2	4.5	6	42.9	26.9	6.9	2	832	573,909	36.6
Canada	1728 mm	68.0	5.0	2.5	—	3.5	7	25.5	29.9	6.9	—	802	478,762	31.7
	2000 mm	78.7	3.9	3.9	—	5.5	7.1	34.9	29.4	6.9	—	930	758,791	37.6

I-sections with curved surfaces

Agency	Type	D1	D2	D3	D4	D5	B1	B2	B3	R1	R2	R3	R4	A	I	y_b
Florida	BT-72	72	2	4	5.5	7.5	48.4	30.4	6.9	8	8	0	0	930	651,190	34.4
Kentucky*	BT-1800	70.9	3	3.9	6.9	8.9	58.9	27.6	6.9	7.5	7.5	0	7.5	996	696,975	36.5
	NU750	29.5	2.6	1.8	5.5	5.3	49.2	39.4	6.9	7.9	7.9	2.0	2.0	643	71,554	13.6
	NU900	35.4	2.6	1.8	5.5	5.3	49.2	39.4	6.9	7.9	7.9	2.0	2.0	684	114,178	16.2
	NU1100	43.3	2.6	1.8	5.5	5.3	49.2	39.4	6.9	7.9	7.9	2.0	2.0	738	189,390	19.7
Nebraska	NU1350	53.1	2.6	1.8	5.5	5.3	49.2	39.4	6.9	7.9	7.9	2.0	2.0	806	315,398	24.1
University	NU1600	63.0	2.6	1.8	5.5	5.3	49.2	39.4	6.9	7.9	7.9	2.0	2.0	874	480,111	28.6
	NU1800	70.9	2.6	1.8	5.5	5.3	49.2	39.4	6.9	7.9	7.9	2.0	2.0	928	642,003	32.3
	NU2000	78.7	2.6	1.8	5.5	5.3	49.2	39.4	6.9	7.9	7.9	2.0	2.0	982	832,521	36.0
	NU2400	94.5	2.6	1.8	5.5	5.3	49.2	39.4	6.9	7.9	7.9	2.0	2.0	1091	1,306,244	43.4

*Kentucky girder section properties were computed from a straight-line approximation of curved surface.
Note: Units are in inches and 1 in. = 25.4 mm.

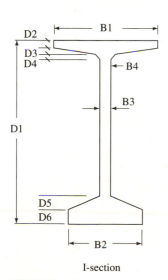

I-section

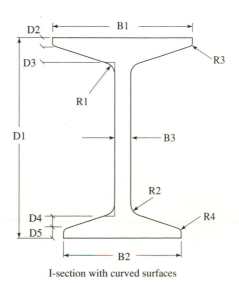

I-section with curved surfaces

FIGURE 7.31

New I-girder series developed by Nebraska University for the Nebraska Department of Roads, to be used for future state bridges [Geren and Tadros, 1994].

Beam properties			
Type	Area (in.²)	y_b (in.)	Moment of inertia (in.⁴)
40	253	15.16	31,000
60	332	18.63	70,100
80	476	22.53	154,900
100	546	27.90	249,000
120	626	35.60	456,000

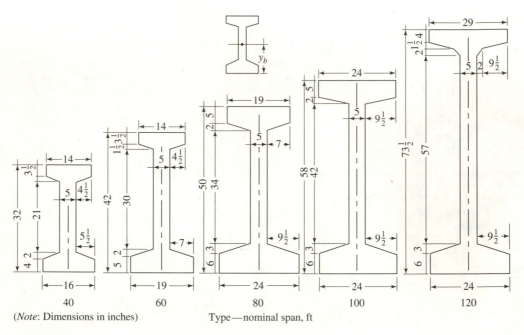

(*Note*: Dimensions in inches)   Type—nominal span, ft

FIGURE 7.32
Washington State standard I-girders.

have cantilevered top flanges extending beyond the webs on each side. They are used in Canada [MRA, 1973; Batchelor et al., 1976; Campbell and Batchelor, 1977; PCI, 1977; PCIJ, 1980; Campbell and Bassi, 1994] and England [Somerville, 1970; Manton and Wilson, 1975; Cope, 1987] (Fig. 7.14) but have not been popular in the United States. However, they are beginning to gain some attention lately as viable alternatives for bridges in the 120- to 180-ft span range. Generally referred to as multispine bridges [Bakht and Jaeger, 1985], such bridges consist of precast prestressed open cross sections (i.e., without precast top flange) and a cast-in-place concrete deck on top, essentially resembling spread box beam superstructures.

In the United States, feasibility studies for the use of prestressed U-beam super-structures (*contiguously* placed as in Fig. 7.36) were conducted at the University of

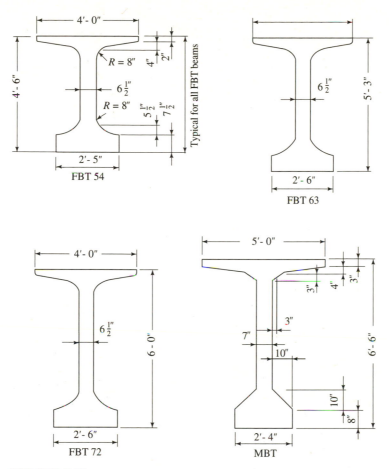

FIGURE 7.33
Florida Department of Transportation (DOT) standard beams [Garcia, 1993].

Missouri at Columbia in the early 1970s. It was concluded that this bridge system was uneconomical, and further work on its development was abandoned [MCHRP, 1969; Salmons and Kagay, 1971; Salmons and Mokhtari, 1971]. However, spaced U-beam systems with cast-in-place decks (similar to the spread box beam superstructure) and contiguously placed U-beams (for longer spans) are popular in Great Britain, where they were introduced in 1973 [Chaplin et al., 1973; Curen and Round, 1973; CE, 1974b; Taylor, 1987]. Figure 7.37 shows a typical trapezoidal box beam bridge used in Canada [Campbell and Bassi, 1994], where this type was introduced in 1973 for spans to 147 ft (45 m) with a depth-to-span ratio of 1:25. Its overall configuration resembles the section used in England, except that the inside faces of the webs are straight for the sake of simplicity in precasting. The U-section girder (Fig. 7.38) used by the Louisiana Department of Transportation and Development has a configuration identical

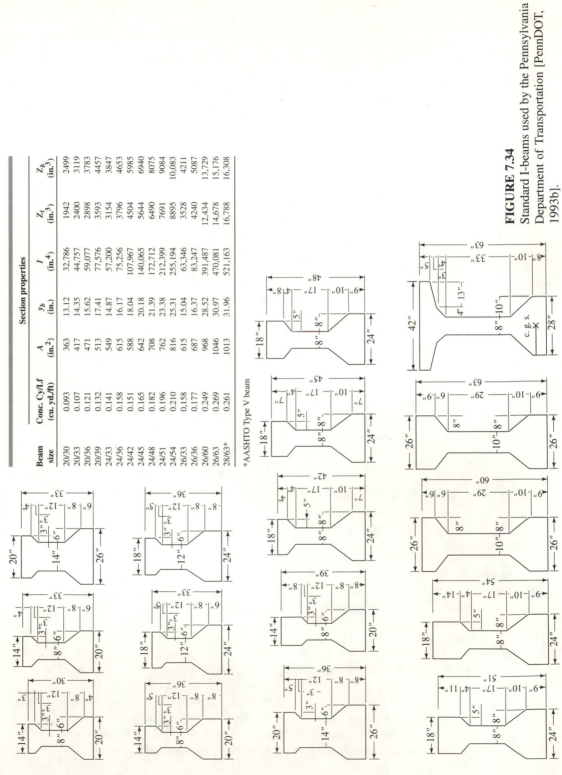

Section properties

Beam size	Conc. Cy/Lf (cu. yd/ft)	A (in.^{2})	y_b (in.)	I (in.^{4})	Z_t (in.^{3})	Z_b (in.^{3})
20/30	0.093	363	13.12	32,786	1942	2499
20/33	0.107	417	14.35	44,757	2400	3119
20/36	0.121	471	15.62	59,077	2898	3783
20/39	0.132	513	17.41	77,576	3593	4457
24/33	0.141	549	14.87	57,200	3154	3847
24/36	0.158	615	16.17	75,256	3796	4653
24/42	0.151	588	18.04	107,967	4504	5985
24/45	0.165	642	20.18	140,065	5644	6940
24/48	0.182	708	21.39	172,712	6490	8075
24/51	0.196	762	23.38	212,399	7691	9084
24/54	0.210	816	25.31	255,194	8895	10,083
26/33	0.158	615	15.04	63,346	3528	4211
26/36	0.177	687	16.37	83,247	4240	5087
26/60	0.249	968	28.52	391,487	12,434	13,729
26/63	0.269	1046	30.97	470,081	14,678	15,176
28/63*	0.261	1013	31.96	521,163	16,788	16,308

*AASHTO Type V beam

FIGURE 7.34

Standard I-beams used by the Pennsylvania Department of Transportation [PennDOT, 1993b].

520

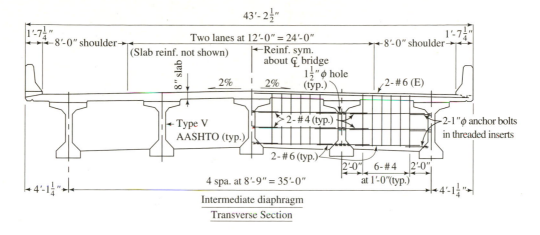

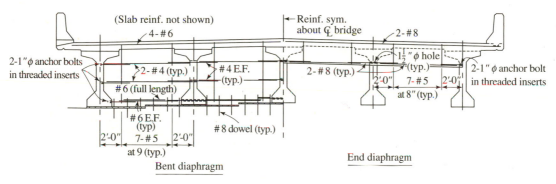

FIGURE 7.35
Typical transverse section through a bridge with prestressed AASHTO Type V girders [USDOT, 1990].

to one used in Canada [Huval, 1994]. A beam with a similar cross section is under consideration for use by the California Department of Transportation. Use of the open cross section (of the U-beam) is attractive because it permits replacement of a cast-in-place deck that has served its useful life.

Figure 7.39 shows a prestressed U-beam superstructure proposed by the Texas Department of Transportation, capable of spans in the 100- to 120-ft range, as an aesthetic alternative to the AASHTO Type IV I-beam. Its cross-sectional shape is essentially similar to the Canadian U-beam section (with minor modification in the upper part of the webs). With inclined webs 5 in. thick and a 4.6-ft-wide bottom flange, the section is proposed in two depths: 40 in. with 6.22-in.-thick bottom flange and 54 in. with 8.19-in.-thick bottom flange. This system envisages using precast panel forms (instead of falsework) to support the cast-in-place concrete deck [Ralls, Ybanez, and Panek, 1993].

One of the advantages of the U-beam is its adaptability to horizontally curved bridges: Its webs can be precast with different depths to accommodate the transverse

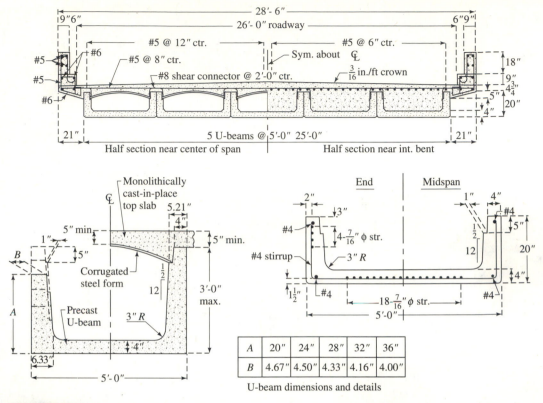

FIGURE 7.36
U-beam bridge developed at the University of Columbia, Missouri, but abandoned as being uneconomical [Salmons and Kagay, 1971].

deck slope required for superelevation. The absence of the top flange leads to lighter girder weights. Handling, transportation, and erection are consequently easier and thus more economical in terms of equipment and construction costs. Collapsible void forms can be reused to minimize fabrication costs, because the top is not covered—another economical advantage.

This type of beam is not without drawbacks, however. One apparent drawback is that it would act compositely to share only the live load; the dead load would be carried by the girder alone, because the beam is installed before the deck is cast. As a result, the material in compression (top portions of the webs) is not efficiently utilized. Because the stiffness of an open box section is smaller than that of a closed box section, its span capability is less than that of a trapezoidal section with integrally precast top flange (described next), even though the final configuration is similar. Also, the cast-in-place deck may pose durability problems associated with corrosion of reinforcing steel. Long-term behavior and service performance of these types of bridges in the United States are not well known because of the lack of a wider sample of urban bridges of these types under service.

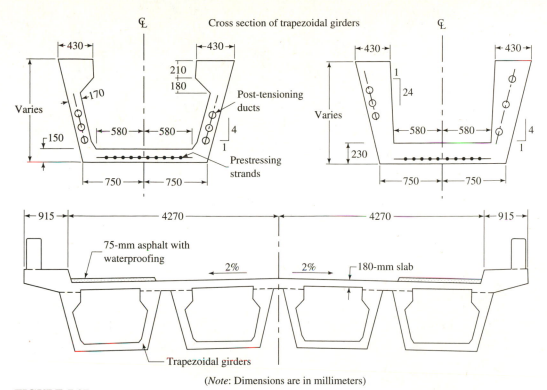

(*Note*: Dimensions are in millimeters)

FIGURE 7.37

Typical transverse section through a prestressed trapezoidal girder bridge [Campbell and Bassi, 1994].

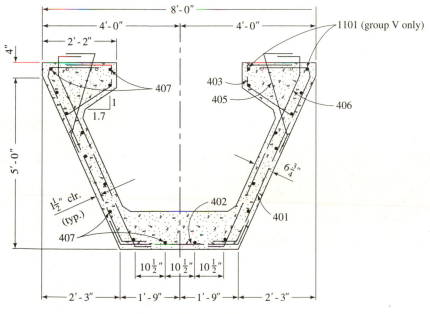

(*Note*: Numbers 401, 402, . . . , and 1101 refer to specific bar types.)

FIGURE 7.38

Prestressed U-beam used by the Louisiana Department of Transportation and Development [Knapp, 1995].

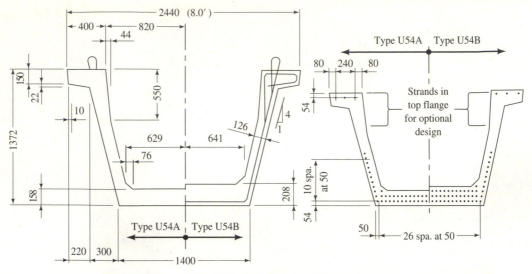

(*Note*: All dimensions are in millimeters.)

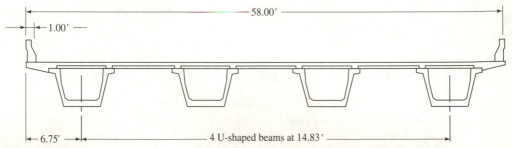

FIGURE 7.39
Precast prestressed concrete U-beam proposed by the Texas Department of Transportation [Ralls, Ybanez, and Panek, 1993].

Figure 7.40 shows a deck configuration, proposed by Taly about 1976, that uses T-box girders (trapezoidal box girders with overhanging top flanges) suitable for short- and medium-span bridges [Taly and GangaRao, 1974; Taly, 1976]. This system consists of precast prestressed units of standard widths (of top flange, 6 and 8 ft) and standard depths (30, 36, and 42 in.) to achieve a deck of specified width in 2-ft increments. The structural efficiency of these T-box girders varies from 0.515 to 0.56, which is quite high. Wider units, e.g., 12 ft wide, can also be designed to achieve the desired deck widths, although they would be relatively heavier. The beam's box configuration with inclined webs leads to an aesthetic appearance. Edge beams can be precast with special details having the required parapet profiles.

Because of the high torsional rigidity, the stability of T-box girders during handling, transportation, and erection is not a problem. This system can be ideal for building short- and medium-span bridges in congested urban areas in high seismic zones. When properly designed, T-box girders can also be used for horizontally curved girder bridges [ABAM, 1988].

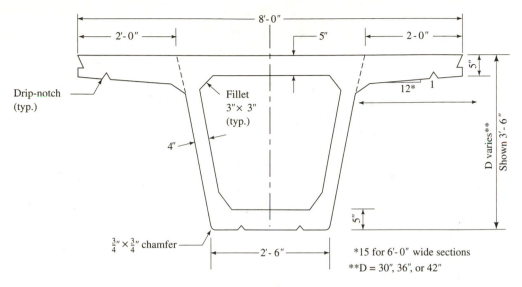

Drip-notch
(typ.)

Fillet
3″ × 3″
(typ.)

12*   1

D varies**
Shown 3′ - 6″

4″

$\frac{3}{4}″ \times \frac{3}{4}″$ chamfer

2′ - 6″

*15 for 6′- 0″ wide sections
**D = 30″, 36″, or 42″

Typical section

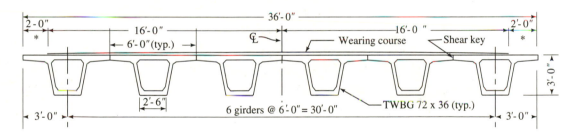

Typical arrangement with 6-ft-wide girders

*Clearance for railing system

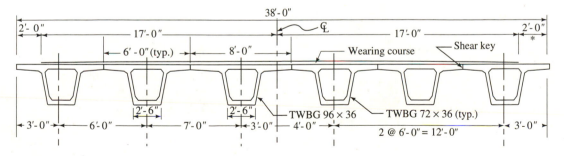

Typical arrangement with a combination of 6-ft and 8-ft-wide girders

FIGURE 7.40
Precast trapezoidal T-box girder [Taly, 1976].

The advantage of T-box girders over U-beam girders is that T-box girders enhance the durability of the precast deck, leading to savings in the life-cycle costs of the superstructure. An apparent drawback of this system is the increased self-weight of the member due to the integrally precast overhanging top flanges; this can increase hauling and erection costs. This factor makes the T-box girders unappealing for use in single-member lengths for medium-span bridges. However, this difficulty can be overcome by using lightweight structural concrete. Alternatively, smaller-length segments that can be spliced by post-tensioning in the field (described in a later section), can be used to build a medium-span bridge [Abdel-Karim and Tadros, 1992a, 1992b]. Yet another method is to use a drop-in segment simply supported over the cantilevered end of the side or the end spans; this method was used in building the Tlalpan Freeway bridges in Mexico City [PCIJ, 1991; Rioboo Martin, 1992].

In spite of its superior structural efficiency, this T-box girder system has rarely been used. About three thousand T-box girders of similar but larger cross section have been used for the twin-girder bridges of the 27-mile Bay Area Rapid Transit (BART) System, in San Francisco, California [Riggs, 1966]. Similar girders were used again in 1994 for its Pittsburgh–Antioch Extension segment. A typical cross section of these girders is shown in Fig. 7.41 [Grafton, 1994b].

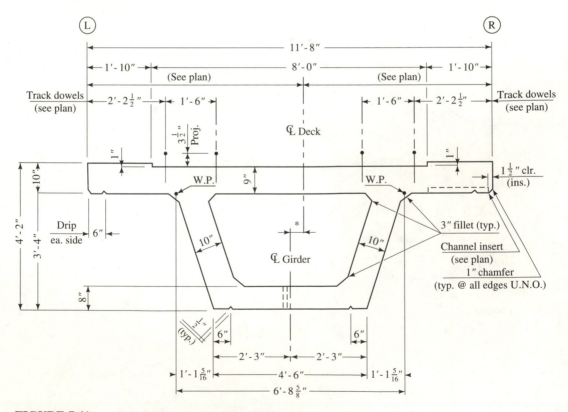

FIGURE 7.41
Prestressed T-box girder for the Bay Area Rapid Transit (BART) System, San Francisco, California [Grafton, 1994].

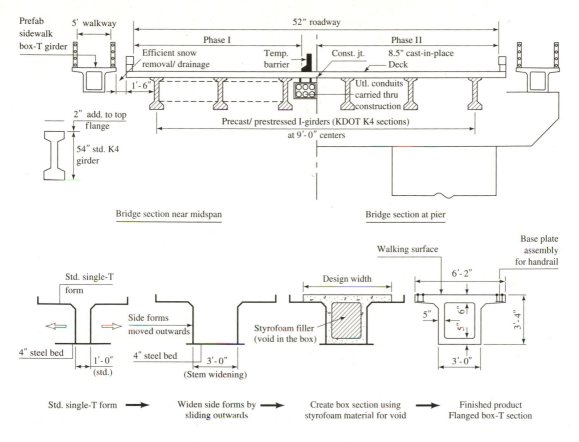

Fabrication process for the flanged boxed-T section

FIGURE 7.42

T-box girder used for the sidewalks of the 47th Street Bridge over the Arkansas River, Wichita, Kansas [Govindaswamy, 1989].

Figure 7.42 shows a modified version (having vertical, instead of inclined, webs) of the T-box girder used for the sidewalks of the 47th Street Bridge over the Arkansas River, Wichita, Kansas, completed in 1987. These box girders were cast using the existing single-T forms by spreading the stem walls and placing a Styrofoam section to create the void. The entire sidewalk was erected in less than two weeks' time at a cost of about $135 per ft, much cheaper than about $220 per ft (in 1987 dollars) for the alternate cast-in-place deck over the I-girders [Govindaswamy, 1989].

An excellent example of the use of T-box girders is the construction of two 1539-ft bridges (two 39, two 63, two 115, two 131, and one 170 ft) on the Tlalpan Freeway in Mexico City, a highly congested city in a highly seismic area [PCIJ, 1991; Rioboo Martin, 1992]. The superstructure system used for these bridges, which is similar to Taly's (described earlier), consists of three longitudinal girders, each 12 ft wide, resulting in a 36-ft-wide deck, as shown in Fig. 7.43. The thickness of the top flange varies from 3 to 5 in., and that of the bottom flange varies from 9.8 to 19.7 in. The webs are 5.9 in.

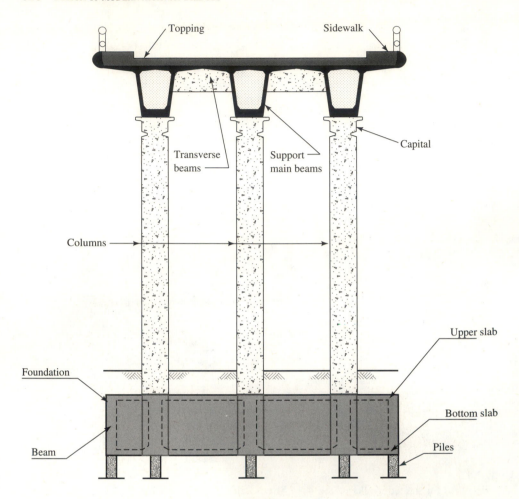

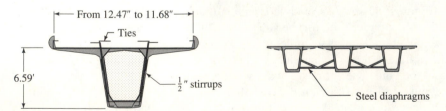

FIGURE 7.43
Transverse section of the Tlalpan Freeway Bridge, Mexico City, built from precast prestressed concrete trapezoidal T-box girders [Rioboo Martin, 1992].

thick, with $\frac{1}{2}$-in. ties projecting from them above the top flange for embedment in the 3.15-in.-thick cast-in-place topping reinforced with $\frac{1}{2}$-in. reinforcing bars. The exterior overhang of the two edge girders is integrally precast with a special curb parapet.

To meet the AASHTO diaphragm requirements, prefabricated diaphragms consisting of 4-in.-diameter structural tubing were provided at each end and at midspan. These diaphragms were welded to precisely positioned embedments in the precast concrete girders. The largest members used were 125 ft long, 12.5 ft wide, and 6.6 ft deep, and they weighed 154 tons each. The central and longest span of 170 ft—a new record then for precast girders—was attained by the Gerber-type structural system: simply supporting the 125-ft suspended (or drop-in) segment of the center span on the cantilevered ends of the girders of the side spans (Fig. 7.44). An identical structural system is being used for many other bridges in Mexico City and elsewhere in Mexico [Riobboo Martin, 1992]. This innovative use of precast and prestressed concrete in bridge construction won a special award by the Prestressed Concrete Institute in 1991 [PCIJ, 1991].

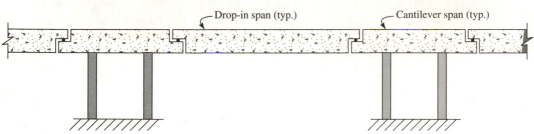

FIGURE 7.44
Schematic showing the arrangement of the support and the suspended spans using the Gerber-type structural system for the Tlalpan Freeway Bridge, Mexico City [Rioboo Martin, 1992].

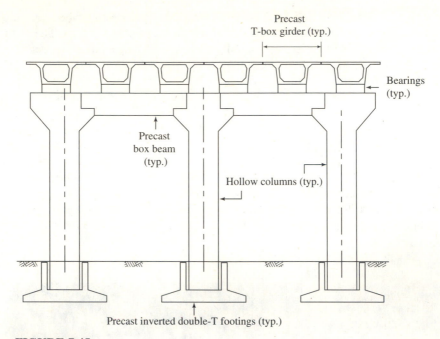

FIGURE 7.45
Cross section of the T-box girder bridge, Queretaro City, Mexico [ASCENT, 1994].

Figure 7.45 shows the cross section of the 71-ft 3-in. wide three-span (40.5, 71.5, and 40.5 ft) bridge built in 1993 in Queretaro City, Queretaro State, Mexico, for which a total of 36 precast prestressed T-box girders (twenty-four 40.5-ft and twelve 71.5-ft) were used. These girders are supported on neoprene bearing pads on the corbels of the hollow columns, which in turn are supported by inverted double-T precast footings. The bridge's substructure employs retaining and load-bearing walls at each end comprising 396 precast hollow-core sections standing on end. This precast "erector set" approach, also used for other bridges in Queretaro City, enabled completion of the bridge in about 90 days—considerably faster than the cast-in-place alternative [ASCENT, 1994].

Figure 7.46 shows a standardized trapezoidal box girder used in California for a span range of 80 to 210 ft. The top flange width is the same as its height, and the bottom flange is half as wide as the top flange. The top flange has standardized widths that vary from 4 to 8 ft, in 1-ft increments, and the depth and the bottom flange width vary accordingly. Girder spacings vary from 8 to 16 ft, in 2-ft increments [CALTRANS, 1993a].

7.5.2.7 Box girder bridges

It has been determined that simple-span AASHTO I-beam bridges cannot compete in span ranges over 150 ft. Instead, box girders with single- or multiple-cell cross sections (with and without cantilevered extensions of top flange) are used for medium- and long-span bridges [Libby and Perkins, 1976]. Box bridges described in this section should be distinguished from the box beam bridges (the spread box and the adjacent box beam type) described in Sec. 7.5.2.4.

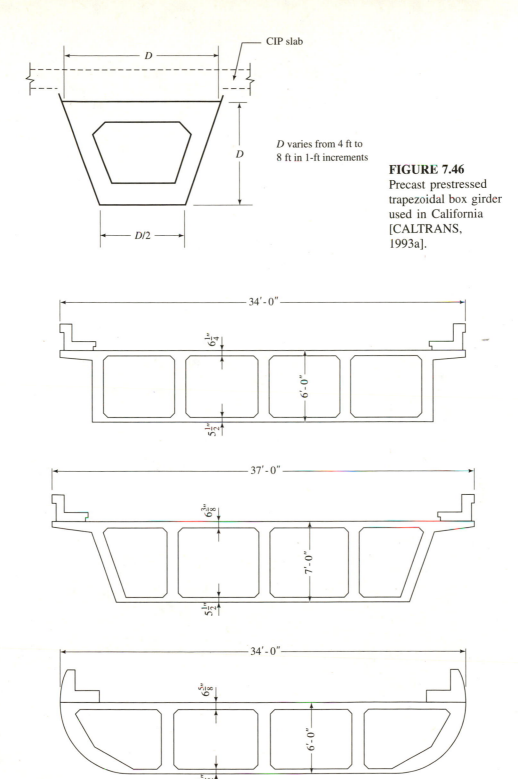

CIP slab

D

D

D/2

D varies from 4 ft to
8 ft in 1-ft increments

FIGURE 7.46
Precast prestressed
trapezoidal box girder
used in California
[CALTRANS,
1993a].

34'- 0"

$6\frac{1}{4}''$

6'- 0"

$5\frac{1}{2}''$

37'- 0"

$6\frac{3}{8}''$

7'- 0"

$5\frac{1}{2}''$

34'- 0"

$6\frac{5}{8}''$

6'- 0"

$5\frac{1}{2}''$

FIGURE 7.47
Various types of box girder cross sections [Libby and Perkins, 1976].

Two basic forms of construction are used for box girder bridges. For simple and continuous spans, box girders are cast-in-place, often integrally with the supporting pier shafts, and subsequently post-tensioned. Typical cross sections are shown in Fig. 7.47 [Libby and Perkins, 1976].

For long spans, the segmental construction technique (described later) is used; the single-cell section is the more common type. Often a single-cell box section can be used for deck widths of about 35 ft. For wider decks, multiple-cell box girders (Fig. 7.48) are recommended; cross sections with as many as four cells without overhangs have been used. Cross sections of several box girders used for some well-known segmentally constructed bridges are shown in Figs 7.49a and 7.49b [PCI, 1981b; Podolny and Muller, 1982]. Alternatively, two single-cell box sections can be placed side-by-side. In the latter case, the single-cell sections may be connected by a common middle slab which, depending on the bridge cross section, can be quite wide [Libby and Perkins, 1976; Podolny and Muller, 1982]. Figure 7.50 shows details of the Chaco-Corrientes Bridge (537, 804, and 537 ft), also known as the General Manuel Belgrano Bridge, over the Parana River, Argentina. Built in 1973, this cable-stayed bridge was then the longest precast concrete box girder bridge in South America. It has a middle slab spanning 22 ft $7\frac{1}{2}$ in. between the two box girders [Rothman and Chang, 1974; Muller, 1975]. Figure 7.51 shows the elevation and the cross section of the main span and the approaches of the Chesapeake and Delaware Canal Bridge, built in 1995. Situated on U.S. 13 near

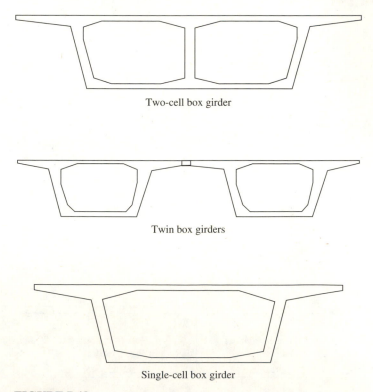

Two-cell box girder

Twin box girders

Single-cell box girder

FIGURE 7.48
Typical cross sections for segmental bridges [Libby and Perkins, 1976].

Bridge	Cross section	Type of construction	Span (ft)
Rio Niteroi, Brazil	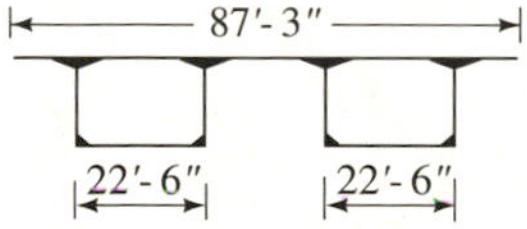	Precast	262
Pine Valley, U.S.A.	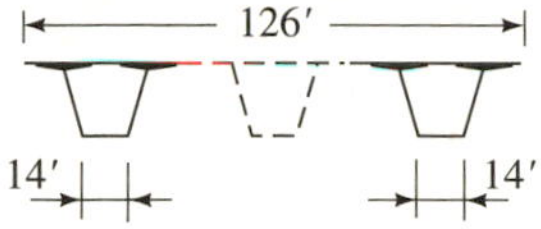	Cast-in-place	450
Kipapa, U.S.A.	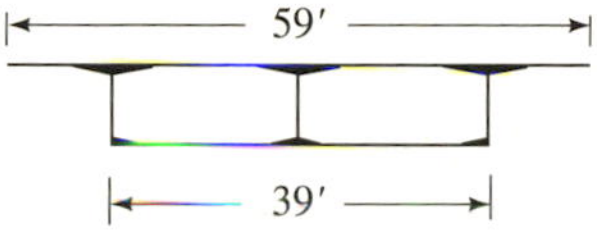	Cast-in-place	250
Kishwaukee, U.S.A.	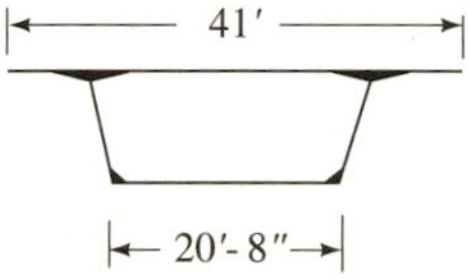	Precast	250
Long Key, U.S.A.	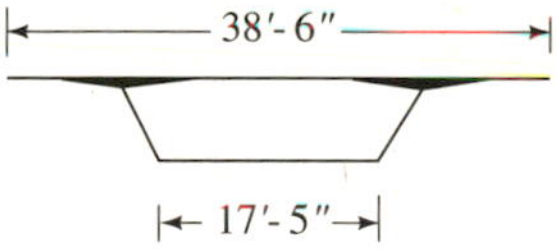	Precast	118
Seven Mile, U.S.A.	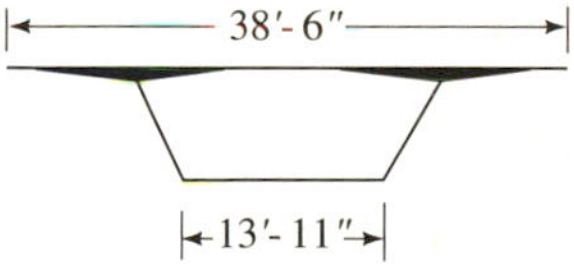	Precast	135
Columbia River, U.S.A.	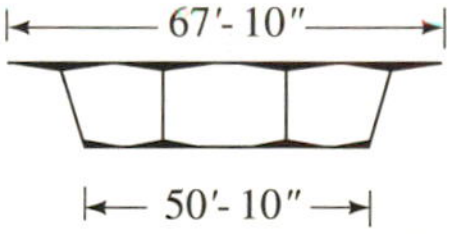	Cast-in-place and precast	600
Zilwaukee, U.S.A.	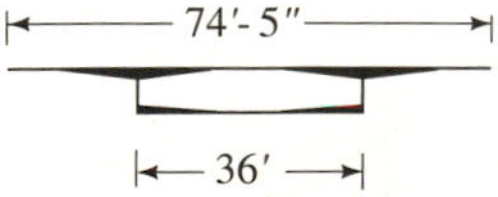	Precast	375
Houston Ship Channel, U.S.A.	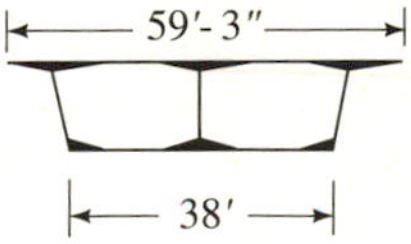	Cast-in-place	750

FIGURE 7.49a

Typical cross sections of some segmental cantilever bridges in the Americas [Podolny and Muller, 1982].

Bridge (and maximum span)	Cross section (dimensions in meters)	Segment length	Maximum segment wt. (tons)
Choisy-le-Roi 55 m (180 ft)		2.50 m 8.20 ft	25
Seudre 79 m (259 ft)		3.30 m 10.80 ft	75
Blois 91 m (299 ft)		3.50 m 11.50 ft	75
Chillon 104 m (341 ft)		3.20 m 10.50 ft	80
Saint Andre de Cubzac 95 m (312 ft)		3.40 m 11.20 ft	80
B 3 South 50 m (164 ft)		2.50–3.40 m 8.20–11.20 ft	50
Saint-Cloud 106 m (348 ft)		2.25 m 7.40 ft	130

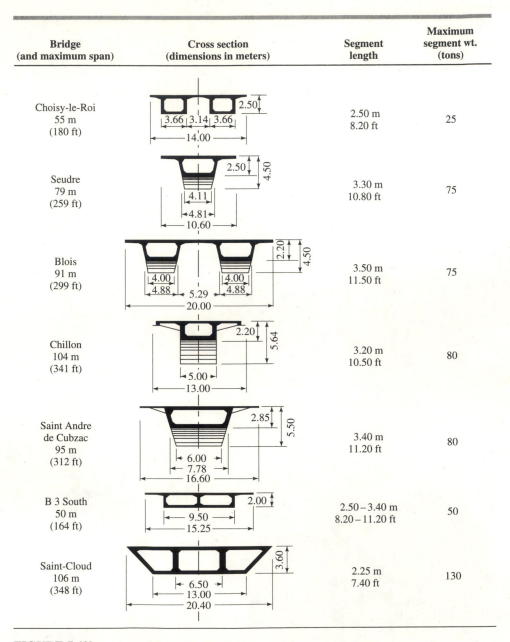

FIGURE 7.49b

Typical cross sections of some early European segmental bridges [Muller, 1975].

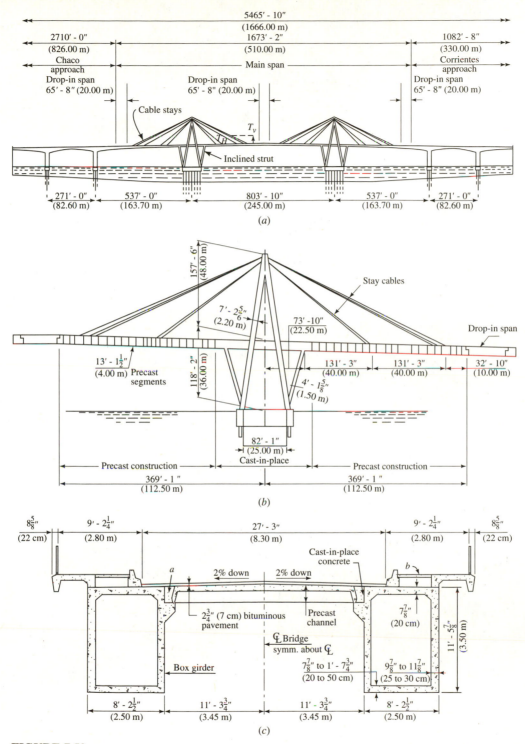

FIGURE 7.50
The Chaco-Corrientes Bridge (537, 804, and 537 ft) over the Parana River, Argentina:
(*a*) Elevation, (*b*) details of the bridge near the tower, (*c*) transverse section through the deck
showing precast deck sections laid on ledges of precast box girders [Rothman and Chang, 1974].

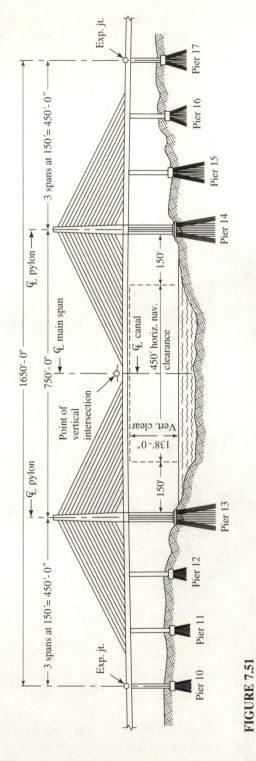

FIGURE 7.51
The Chesapeake and Delaware Canal Bridge near St. Georges, Delaware [Pate, 1995].

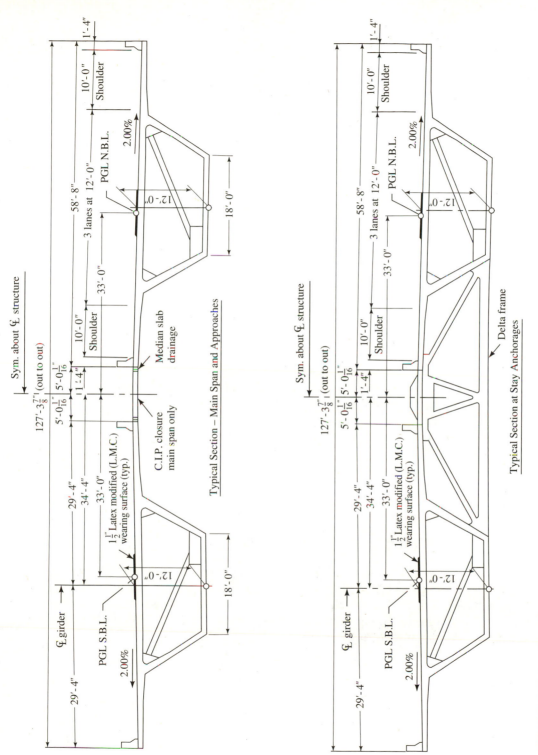

FIGURE 7.51 (continued)

537

St. Georges, Delaware, this $58 million, 4650-ft-long structure is considered to be the first major all-present, prestressed concrete segmental cable-stayed bridge built in the northeast United States. A total of 984 trapezoidal single-cell box sections—each 10 ft long × 58 ft 8 in. wide × 12 ft deep—were match-cast to ensure tight tolerances during erection. For cost comparison, note that the cost of the steel alternate for this bridge, which also involved a cable-stayed system for the main span, was bid at $64 million—$6 million higher than the precast prestressed concrete segmental alternative that was built [Pate, 1995].

Thanks to advancements in prestressing and construction technology, segmental construction techniques are now also used for other types of bridges such as arch, rigid frames, truss, cable-stayed, and suspension. Several examples of these types of bridges are described by Podolny and Muller [1982].

Initially used for straight bridges, the versatility of the segmental construction method has led to its use for arch bridges, using precast segments. The first application of truly segmental construction was the Fressynet's arch-shaped Luzancy Bridge over the Marne River, France. A recent record in segmentally built prestressed concrete arch bridges is the twin arch, 1572-ft-span Natchez Trace Bridge over Route 96 near Franklin, Tennessee. Both the superstructure and the two arches were built using precast trapezoidal hollow box sections [Corven and Jordon, 1993]. Examples of several segmentally built arch bridges are discussed by Podolny and Muller [1982].

The major advantage of the segmental construction technique is that it does not require costly and cumbersome falsework, and it avoids associated problems such as interfering with existing traffic and creating detours. The method becomes extremely efficient when precast units are used, resulting in reduced construction time. Growing experience with segmental construction technique has led to its adaptation for most new bridge sites. This technique has also made medium-span bridges more economically feasible where single-length girders are not practical or where site conditions do not permit shoring and formwork.

7.6
POST-TENSIONED PRESTRESSED CONCRETE BRIDGES

In previous sections, we have discussed bridge superstructures built from precast prestressed concrete girders. Other forms of bridge superstructure construction that have become very popular are cast-in-place (situ-cast), post-tensioned, prestressed box girders and precast or situ-cast segments that are post-tensioned before or after erection by a technique known as segmental construction.

7.6.1 Cast-in-Place Post-Tensioned Prestressed Concrete Box Girder Bridges

7.6.1.1 General considerations

The cast-in-place, post-tensioned, prestressed concrete box girders are typically built on falsework and are extensively used for medium- and long-span bridges. Outwardly, their appearance is similar to that of reinforced concrete box girders except that, in most cases, the prestressed box girders would be relatively slender for the same span. For longer spans, prestressed girders would be the choice.

The cross-sectional details of both the reinforced and prestressed box girders are similar. However, the deck and the soffit slab of the reinforced concrete box girder have a considerable amount of conventional longitudinal reinforcement within them, whereas the prestressed box girders have a large number of prestressing tendons placed in girder stems. These strands are placed in *ducts*, which may or may not be grouted (Fig. 7.52). To accommodate these ducts, the webs (often referred to as girders, or as stems) of prestressed box girders are made wider than those of the reinforced concrete box girders, although oval ducts can be used for the thinner webs. The design of the deck is the same for both prestressed box girders and reinforced concrete box girders, and the cost due to girder (web) spacing and deck overhangs (the portion of the deck that extends beyond the exterior girders) is also the same for both types [Degenkolb, 1977].

FIGURE 7.52
Reinforcing-cage and tendon (inside the ducts) layout of typical post-tensioned concrete girders.

Most short- and medium-span situ-cast prestressed box girder bridges are built on falsework, just as the nonprestressed bridges are, and they are post-tensioned by means of tendons encased in ducts placed inside the stems. In single-span box girders, the tendons may also be placed in the soffit slab. After tensioning the tendons, the ducts are grouted under pressure. The hardened grout serves two purposes: It protects the tendons from corrosion and bonds them to the ducts to develop integral action with concrete.

Continuity is a common feature for multispan box girder bridges, usually of four or more spans; the trend is to stretch the length of continuity as far as possible, even around the horizontal curves. This results in fewer expansion joints and, in turn, minimum maintenance problems with consequent savings in life-cycle costs. One major maintenance problem is the pier bearing assemblies on longer-span structures; their removal and replacement are very time-intensive and expensive. Designing a cast-in-place post-tensioned box girder to act integrally as a frame through monolithic construction with piers is an economical way to eliminate the pier bearing assembles. Another significant advantage of cast-in-place post-tensioned box girders is the enhanced durability of the post-tensioned structure achieved through control or elimination of cracking; a post-tensioned structure will essentially remain crack-free under service loads.

Tendons in prestressed concrete box girders may be internal, that is, embedded in the girders and the soffit, or external. External tendons are placed in girder cells as shown in Fig. 7.53, or even outside the primary girders, and are not bonded to them. Placement of tendons outside the girders results in two significant advantages: It permits girders to be thinner, which reduces the deadweight of the box girder, and it allows tendons to be replaced if they are damaged or deteriorated. However, the accompanying reduced ultimate load capacity is a disadvantage. And providing proper protection from corrosion of external tendons is always a matter of concern.

External tendons can also be used for increasing the load-carrying capacity of existing bridges, as discussed in Chapter 10. The St. Adele Bridge, the first North American

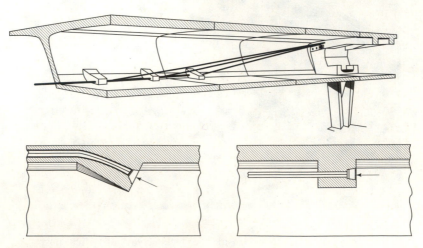

FIGURE 7.53
Placement of external tendons inside the cell of a box girder [PTI, 1985].

cast-in-place segmental bridge, was built in 1964 and strengthened in 1988 [Ouellet and Gaumond, 1990]; the Lierve River Bridge, the first North American precast segmental bridge, was built in 1967 and strengthened in 1987; and the Grand-Mere Bridge, a cast-in-place post-tensioned segmental bridge, was built in 1977 and strengthened in 1991. These are a few recent examples of existing segmental bridges strengthened through external post-tensioning [Massicotte et al., 1994; Massicotte and Picard, 1994].

Internal tendons—both bonded and unbonded—have some advantages and disadvantages. When subjected to overloads, post-tensioned box girders with bonded tendons develop clearly spaced fine cracks that disappear or close completely upon removal of the overload. But when girders with unbonded tendons are overloaded, widely spaced large cracks appear that do not close upon removal of the overload. This problem can be alleviated by placing reinforcement in girders with unbonded tendons to reduce the size and spacing of cracks caused by overloading. Another consequence of choosing whether to use bonded or unbonded tendons is the effectiveness of the tendon when it breaks. Whereas a broken unbonded tendon becomes ineffective for its entire length, a broken bonded tendon is rendered ineffective only for a short distance, which may or may not be serious [Degenkolb, 1977].

In addition to its unsurpassed aesthetic potential, a major advantage of the cast-in-place construction method is the elimination of heavy transport and erection equipment needed for transporting and erecting the heavy precast members. Easy adaptability to accomodate changes in alignment, cross section, and span length, and the ease of making transitions, adjustments, and construction joints, are other advantages of this method that contribute to the overall economy of the structure [Gerwick, 1993]. In California, where a majority of bridges are cast-in-place post-tensioned box girders built on falsework, experience has demonstrated that this is an economical alternative for bridge spans in the range of 100–300 ft and for falsework heights of at least 150 ft. The main disadvantages of this method include deformations as concrete weight is applied to supports, and effects of thermal strains, shrinkage, and plastic deformation of young concrete.

Salient features of several cast-in-place post-tensioned prestressed concrete box girder bridges built in the United States are presented in publications of the Post-Tensioning Institute [PTI, 1978, 1985]. Figure 7.54 shows a typical simple-span undercrossing using a box girder structure. The dramatic three-span (227, 300, and 183 ft) East Fork Chowchilla River Bridge in Mariposa, California, shown in Fig. 7.55, is 150 ft above the valley of the Chowchilla River, one of the highest concrete bridges in the United States. A PTI–PCI joint publication [PTI/PCI, 1971/1990] gives important design and cost data for some 200 bridges of this type built in California in the late 1960s.

For cast-in-place box girders with normal slab–span and girder spacing, the slabs can be considered an integral part of the girder, and the entire slab width can be assumed to be effective in compression as permitted in AASHTO 9.8.2.1 [AASHTO, 1992]. Accordingly, bending stresses can be calculated by simple bending theory. However, as specified in AASHTO 9.8.2.2, for box girders of unusual proportions, including segmental box girders, effects of shear lag must be considered in determining bending stresses. A discussion on the shear lag effects on bending stresses in continuous box girder bridges has been presented by Chang [1992].

FIGURE 7.54
A typical simple-span post-tensioned prestressed concrete box girder undercrossing.

7.6.1.2 Design considerations

The fundamental design considerations for cast-in-place box girder bridges, which are constructed on falsework, are very similar to those for the conventional reinforced concrete bridges discussed in Chapter 6. Design parameters and the proportions of various components of post-tensioned concrete box bridges, which have evolved from experience in California, are discussed by Degenkolb [1977] and in design manuals [PTI, 1978], and are specified in AASHTO 9.8.2 and 9.9 [AASHTO, 1992].

(a) Depth-to-span ratio. The suggested depth-to-span ratios for a preliminary design are shown in Table 7.6.

(b) Thickness of top and bottom slab and of web (girder). Typically, the top slab thickness is kept as the greater of 6 in. or $\frac{1}{30}$th of the clear distance between fillets or girders (AASHTO 9.9.1). The overhang is usually nonprismatic, where the minimum thickness (at the free end) is the same as the top-slab thickness, and where the

FIGURE 7.55
East Fork Chowchilla River Bridge in Mariposa, California.

TABLE 7.6
Depth-span ratios for cast-in-place post-tensioned concrete box girders constructed on falsework [PTI, 1978]

Type of structure	Depth-span ratio
One- and two-span structures	0.04–0.045
Multispan structures	0.035–0.04
Haunched structures at pier	±0.048
Haunched structures at centerline of span	±0.024

thickness uniformly increases toward its junction with the outside girder (web). The bottom slab is kept as the greater of $5\frac{1}{2}$ in. or $\frac{1}{30}$th of the clear distance between webs or fillets (AASHTO 9.9.2). However, the California requirements, which are more stringent than AASHTO's, require the minimum thickness of both the top and bottom slabs to be $\frac{1}{16}$th of the clear distance between fillets or girders [CALTRANS, 1993b].

The girder, or web thickness, although not specified in the AASHTO specifications [AASHTO, 1992], is typically kept as 12 in. and optionally flared near the anchorages to provide end blocks for the tendon anchorages. Girder (web) spacings are usually kept as 8 ft, but no more than two times the structure depth [CALTRANS, 1993c, p. 3–38], with the slab overhang equal to half this spacing. Much larger girder spacings and overhangs are made possible by transverse post-tensioning of the slab. AASHTO 9.8.2.3 [AASHTO, 1992] requires that adequate fillets be provided at the intersections of all surfaces within the cell of a box girder, except at the junction of the web and the bottom flange, where none are required. Preliminary sizing of the box girder is illustrated in Example 7.1.

(c) Load distribution. Evolved over a long period of time, the load distribution procedures for box girders are based on analytical and test studies, on engineering judgment, and, most importantly, on experience with the large number of box girder bridges designed and built in California. Load distribution in a box girder bridge is influenced by the number and dimensions of the cells, the depth-span ratio, the width-span ratio, the number of diaphragms, and by other factors. Certainly, a box girder bridge is inherently stiffer in the transverse direction than a slab-on-beam bridge, which lacks transverse continuity in the bottom flange [Scordelis, Davis, and Lo, 1969].

AASHTO Table 3.23.1 (Appendix A, Table A.7) gives the distribution factor (DF) for a box girder bridge as $S/7$. Therefore, the live load per girder is given by

$$LL/\text{girder} = \frac{S}{2 \times 7} = \frac{S}{14}$$

For cast-in-place box girders with normal span and girder spacing, the slabs can be considered integral parts of the girders (i.e., webs), and the entire slab width can be considered to be effective in compression (AASHTO 9.8.2.1). This assumption permits designing the entire box girder as a unit instead of designing the girder as several modified T-beams, as in past practice. Therefore, the equivalent DF for the entire box girder can be expressed as [PTI, 1978]

$$DF = \frac{(\text{Web spacing}) \times (\text{Number of webs})}{14} = \frac{\text{Width}}{14} \tag{7.2}$$

The distribution factor given by Eq. 7.2 is applied either to the live-load moment due to the truck or to that due to the lane load, whichever governs.

(d) Tendon requirements. A graphical design aid for quickly estimating the amount of post-tensioning steel required is suggested in design manuals such as CALTRANS [1993a] and PTI [1978]. For a given span length and appropriate depth-to-span ratio, the approximate amount (in lb/ft^2 of the deck) of post-tensioning steel is determined from graphs (see Appendix B, Figs. B.1–B.6); the required concrete strength is given by the dashed lines in the graph. Generated by computer for HS20 loading, these graphs are valid for the zero allowable tensile stress. However, they can also be used when the allowable tensile stress is $6\sqrt{f_c'}$—by using 85 percent of the indicated value for simple spans and 75 percent of the indicated value for multiple spans [PTI, 1978]. The use of this methodology is illustrated in Example 7.5.

Typically, in post-tensioned construction, several post-tensioning strands are encased in a conduit, the diameter of which depends on the number of strands encased. The minimum duct size is governed by AASHTO 9.25.4 [AASHTO, 1992], which requires that the duct area be at least twice the net area of prestressing steel if the tendons consist of several wires, bars, or strands. For tendons made from a single wire, bar, or

TABLE 7.7

Typical strand tendons in galvanized semirigid post-tensioning ducts [PTI, 1978]

Number of strands	Size of duct (in.)	Working force at approximate stress level of $0.6f_s'$ (kips)
9–12	$2\frac{5}{8}$	223–296
13–18	3	322–446
19–24	$3\frac{1}{2}$	471–595
25–31	4	620–768

strand, the duct diameter is required to be at least $\frac{1}{4}$ in. larger than the nominal diameter of the wire, bar, or strand. Bundling of post-tensioning ducts is permitted—in groups of three maximum—if post-tensioning steel is draped or deflected (AASHTO 9.25.3). A minimum clear spacing of the greater of $1\frac{1}{2}$ in. or $1\frac{1}{2}$ times the size of concrete aggregate must be maintained at the ends of the beam (AASHTO 9.25.2.1).

According to PTI [1978], a large majority of post-tensioned bridges have been built in the United States with tendons made of seven-wire ASTM A416-74, Grade 270, $\frac{1}{2}$-in.-diameter stress-relieved strand (cross-sectional area = 0.153 in.^{2}), ducted in a galvanized semirigid conduit. The number of strands per tendon is usually left to the post-tensioning supplier.

With the maximum stress in post-tensioning strands of $0.7f_s'$ (or $0.7 \times 270 = 189$ ksi for 270-ksi strands), and with a prestress loss of 33 ksi for 5000 psi concrete (AASHTO Table 9.16.2.2), the approximate tendon stress after losses works out to be 156 ksi. Assuming this stress value to be approximately $0.6f_s'$ (or $0.6 \times 270 = 162$ ksi), a $\frac{1}{2}$-in. strand will carry $0.153 \times 162 = 24.786$ kips. Based on this assumption, Table 7.7 gives typical ranges of the number of $\frac{1}{2}$-in. tendons, the corresponding working force, and the duct size requirements. (Larger tendons are available for special applications.)

(e) Tendon location. Graphical design aids are used to estimate the eccentricities of the post-tensioning force in the box girder. Two problems are involved here. First, the centroid of the group of strands in the duct must be determined. The random position of the post-tensioning strands in the duct make determination of the centroid of the group of strands a difficult problem. In practice, depending on the required number of strands and the size of the post-tensioning duct, the location of the centroid of the group of strands (distance Z between the centroid and the center of the duct) are assumed as shown in Table 7.8.

TABLE 7.8

Location of centroid of strands in a post-tensioning duct [PTI, 1978; CALTRANS, 1993d; AASHTO, 1994]

Duct size (outer diameter) (in.)	Distance Z (in.)
3 or less	$\frac{1}{2}$
3–4	$\frac{3}{4}$
Over 4	1

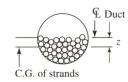

C.G. of strands

The second step involves locating the tendon profile and the centroid of post-tensioning steel in the box girder's cross section; these are determined from a design aid given in PTI [1978]. For preliminary design location of the tendon profile, the tendon's center of gravity for all practical tendon and duct configurations is taken from the guide in Fig. 7.56. The D dimension defined in this figure is obtained from Fig. B.7 (Appendix B) for *simple-span* bridges. Figure B.7 provides a range of D values to permit flexibility in the final details selected for the post-tensioning tendons. Figure B.8 (Appendix B) provides the D values for *continuous* bridges. Similar charts/design aids are commonly used in practice by bridge design professionals [CALTRANS, 1993a]. The K distance varies depending on the location of the deck or the bent reinforcing steel.

(f) Friction: straight girders. When strands are pulled through ducts during post-tensioning, loss of prestressing force occurs due to friction between strands and the surrounding ducts. Total loss of prestress due to friction may be considered as

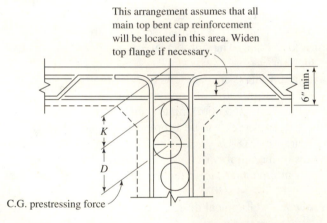

This arrangement assumes that all main top bent cap reinforcement will be located in this area. Widen top flange if necessary.

6" min.

K

D

C.G. prestressing force

K –varies depending on location of deck or bent reinf. steel
D –see D charts

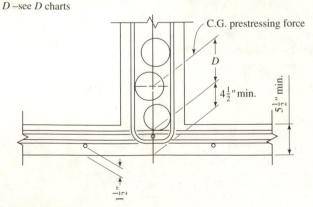

C.G. prestressing force

D

$4\frac{1}{2}''$ min.

$5\frac{1}{2}''$ min.

$1\frac{1}{2}''$

FIGURE 7.56
Guide for assuming the center of gravity of ducted prestressing strands [PTI, 1978].

consisting of two parts: friction due to local deviations in the tendon alignment, referred to as the *wobble effect,* and friction due to the tendon form or alignment, referred to as the *curvature effect.* Theoretically, the wobble effect occurs because neither the tendon nor the duct are ever exactly linear as a result of accidental or unavoidable misalignment, and the corresponding friction loss occurs regardless of whether the alignment of the tendon or duct is straight or draped. The curvature effect results from the necessarily curved alignment of tendons along the span. This effect is similar in character to *belt friction,* which follows the laws of dry friction and for which the familiar classical expression $T_1 = T_2 e^{\mu\alpha}$ is used to determine the load T_1 necessary at the other end to initiate slippage (in the direction of T_1) when a load T_2 is applied at one end (where $T_1 > T_2$). Both effects are shown schematically in Fig. 7.57.

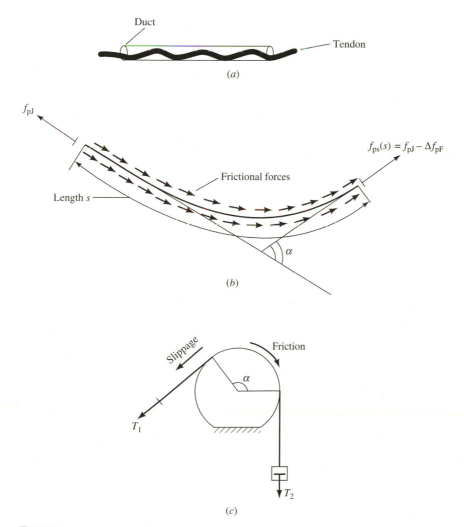

FIGURE 7.57
Wobble and curvature effect causing prestress loss due to friction: (*a*) wobble effects, (*b*) curvature effect, (*c*) belt friction [Naaman, 1982].

It is convenient to treat the wobble effect as an additional curvature effect [Naaman, 1982] and to use a single expression to determine total friction loss due to both effects, as given by AASHTO Eq. 9.1:

$$T_o = T_x e^{(KL+\mu\alpha)} \tag{7.3}$$

where T_o = steel stress at the jacking end

T_x = steel stress at point x on the curved path of the tendon

K = friction wobble coefficient per foot of post-tensioning steel

L = Length of the post-tensioning steel element from the jacking end to point x on the curved path of the tendon

μ = friction curvature coefficient

α = total angular change of prestressing of post-tensioning steel profile, in radians, from jacking end to point x on the curved path of the tendon

Equation 7.3 can be expressed as

$$T_x = T_o e^{-(KL+\mu\alpha)} \tag{7.3a}$$

which gives steel stress at any point x on the curved path of a tendon. The quantity $e^{-(KL+\mu\alpha)}$ may be called the *friction loss coefficient.*

Equation 7.3. can be simplified somewhat as follows:

$$e^x = 1 + x + \frac{x^2}{2} + \frac{x^3}{3} + \frac{x^4}{4} + \cdots \tag{7.4}$$

which, for small values of x, becomes

$$e^x = 1 + x \tag{7.5}$$

Thus, for small values of KL and $\mu\alpha$,

$$T_o = T_x(1 + KL + \mu\alpha) \tag{7.6}$$

or

$$T_x = \frac{T_o}{(1 + KL + \mu\alpha)} \tag{7.6a}$$

which is AASHTO Eq. 9.2. Because approximation is involved in Eq. 7.5, AASHTO 9.16 restricts the use of Eq. 7.6 to values of $(KL + \mu\alpha)$ that are less than or equal to 0.3. For computational purposes, either Eq. 7.3 or Eq. 7.6 may be used. A detailed discussion on loss of prestress due to friction can be found in texts on prestressed concrete design.

An alternative to this classical method is the *equivalent-load method,* based on the equivalent-load approach [PTI, 1978] suggested by Keyder [1990]. According to this method, the tendon profile is converted into an equivalent load that causes the tendon to bear against the surrounding material. The equivalent load thus causes equal and opposite normal, or contact, forces. The friction force is simply the normal force multiplied by the coefficient of friction. Thus, it is necessary only to compute the equivalent load, as in the *load-balancing method,* which is discussed in the literature [Lin, 1961, 1963a, 1963b; Lin and Burns, 1981; Nawy, 1989].

For a harped tendon, with an angle θ with the horizontal, the vertical component of the prestressing force P is $P\sin\theta$, which, since θ is usually small, can be assumed to be equal to $P\theta$. For draped or curved tendons having the usual parabolic profile, the equivalent load is given by $w = 8Pe/L^2$. Examples of calculating prestress losses by this method have been presented by Keyder [1990].

The values of K and μ vary greatly, depending on the type of steel (wires, strands, or bars), the type of duct (flexible, semirigid, or rigid), and the surface conditions of both (rusted, greased or mastic-coated tendons, bright or galvanized metal sheathing, or greased or asphalt-coated and wrapped duct). In addition, the value of K depends on the length of the tendon and the workmanship in the alignment of the duct.

A variety of ducts, tendons, and wrapping materials are available, so the values of the coefficients K and μ should be carefully chosen. Where a rigid duct is used, the wobble coefficient K can be taken as zero. Its value can also be taken as zero for large tendons in a semirigid duct [ACI, 1995a]. Values of these coefficients to be used for particular types of tendons should be obtained from the tendon manufacturers. The ACI code [ACI, 1995a] recommends a range of values of K and μ, as shown in Table 7.9, to serve as a guide.

AASHTO 9.16.1 requires that friction losses in post-tensioned steel be based on experimentally determined wobble and curvature coefficients and that friction losses should be verified during the stressing operations. Results of extensive investigation of friction characteristics of semirigid ducts based on actual tests on a representative portion of the post-tensioned box girder bridges by the California Department of Transportation are summarized in Table 7.10. From these tests, it was concluded that $\mu = 0.25$ and $K = 0.0002$ ft^{-1}. The values of μ and K recommended by AASHTO 9.16.1 [AASHTO, 1992] are presented in Section 7.13 (Table 7.16). The California Department of Transportation uses $K = 0$ for the galvanized rigid ducts most widely used for cast-in-place post-tensioned bridges in California [CALTRANS, 1993c]. Example 7.1 (also discussed in CALTRANS [1993c]) illustrates the use of the design aids (tables and charts) referred to in the preceding discussion.

TABLE 7.9
Friction coefficients for post-tensioned tendons [ACI, 1995a]

Type of steel	Wobble coefficient, K (ft)$^{-1}$	Curvature coefficient (μ)
Wire tendons	0.0010–0.0015	0.15–0.25
High-strength bars	0.0001–0.0006	0.08–0.30
Seven-wire strand	0.0005–0.0020	0.15–0.25
Unbonded tendons		
Mastic-coated wire tendons	0.001–0.002	0.05–0.15
Seven-wire strand	0.001–0.002	0.05–0.15
Pregreased wire tendons	0.0003–0.002	0.05–0.15
Seven-wire strand	0.0003–0.002	0.05–0.15

TABLE 7.10
Summary of tests to determine friction characteristics of semirigid ducts [PCI/CRSI, 1969]

Structure	Duct size (in.) and type	Number of tendons tested	Average total tendon angle change for tendons tested (rad)	Average tendon length (ft)	Average measured force (kips) Live end	Average measured force (kips) Dead end	Average calculated force, dead end (kips)
Northwest Connector Bridge #53-1907	$2\frac{3}{4}$ A	15	1.34	394	372	250	246
12/80 Separation Bridge #23-16L	$2\frac{3}{4}$ A	8	0.99	392	372	280	269
Telegraph U.C. Bridge #33-413R	$2\frac{3}{4}$ A	7	0.37	273	372	324	320
Sand Hill Rd. O.C. Bridge #35-07	$2\frac{5}{8}$ B	8	1.21	553	300	202	199
Del Paso Park Sep. Bridge #24-193R	$2\frac{5}{8}$ C	12	0.93	548	300	251	213
California Aqueduct Bridge #50-323	$3\frac{1}{2}$ D	7	0.84	394	590	441	432
R Street U.P. Bridge #24-211	$3\frac{1}{2}$ D	14	3.67	418	682	289	251
Eel River Br. R&L Bridge #4-155	$4\frac{1}{2}$ E	6	0.76	698	960	801	690

Calculated force at the dead end is based on $\mu = 0.25$ and $K = 0.0002$.
Duct description:

A = $2\frac{3}{4}$-in.-diameter duct made from 24-gauge galvanized material and seamed with a continuous longitudinal resistance weld.

B = $2\frac{5}{8}$-in.-diameter duct made from 26-gauge galvanized material and seamed with a helical interlocking joint.

C = $2\frac{5}{8}$-in.-diameter duct made from 26-gauge galvanized material and seamed with a longitudinal interlocking joint.

D = $3\frac{1}{2}$-in.-diameter duct made from 24-gauge galvanized material, corrugated and seamed with a helical interlocking joint.

E = $4\frac{1}{2}$-in.-diameter duct made from 24-gauge galvanized material, corrugated and seamed with a helical interlocking joint.

EXAMPLE 7.1. Figure E7.1a shows the elevation of a two-span continuous (162 and 150 ft) cast-in-place post-tensioned concrete box girder bridge. The total deck width is to be kept as 37 ft 6 in. Determine the preliminary size of the box girder, and estimate the required amount of post-tensioning steel and prestress loss due to friction.

Solution

Preliminary size of the box girder

Proportion of cross section of box girder. For this continuous bridge, a depth-span ratio of 0.04 is selected from Table 7.6. The overall depth of the box girder will be selected based on the length of the longer span: $D = 0.04 \times 162 = 6.48$ ft ≈ 6.5 ft. Use $D = 6$ ft 6 in.

Girder spacing. $S < 2 \times D = 2 \times 6.5 = 13$ ft maximum. Assume 4-ft overhangs. Assuming 12-in.-wide girders, the center-to-center distance between the outside girders is $37.5 - 2 \times 4.0 - 2 \times 0.5 = 28.5$ ft.

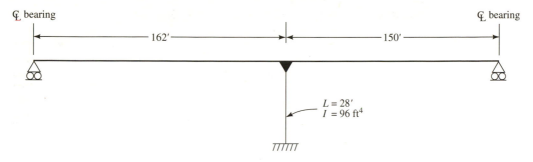

FIGURE E7.1a
Elevation of bridge for Example 7.1.

With a maximum spacing of 13 ft, the number of bays required is 28.5/13, or 2.2. Provide three bays (and, hence, four webs) with a spacing of 28.5/3 = 9.5 ft < 13 ft, OK. Provide girder spacing = 9 ft 6 in., girder thickness = 12 in.

Top and bottom slab thickness. The top slab thickness is based on the clear distance between the girders. In this example, this clear distance = $9.5 - 2 \times 0.5 = 8.5$ ft. The corresponding slab thickness for this clear spacing, $8\frac{1}{8}$ in., is selected from Fig. 6.10a. Similarly, the soffit thickness of $6\frac{3}{8}$ in. is selected from Fig. 6.10b. These thicknesses satisfy the minimum thickness requirements of both AASHTO and the State of California Department of Transportation for both top and bottom slabs. Provide top slab $8\frac{1}{8}$ in., bottom slab $6\frac{3}{8}$ in.

Four-in. fillets are provided at the junction of the top slab with girders, as required by AASHTO 9.8.2.3. The typical cross section of the box girder arrived at from the above procedure is shown in Fig. E7.1b.

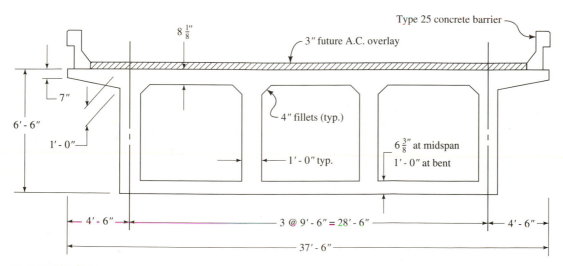

FIGURE E7.1b
Cross section of box girder for Example 7.1.

Estimate of the amount of post-tensioning steel. For a depth-to-span ratio of 0.04 and an average span of 156 ft (average of 162 and 150 ft), the estimated amount of post-tensioning steel per square foot of deck area is found from Fig. B.2 (Appendix B) to be 4.1 lb/ft^2. Weight of P/S steel $= 4.1 \times 37.5 \times (162 + 150) = 47{,}970$ lb.

The following expression, suggested in CALTRANS [1993c], will be used for estimating P_j. Assuming low relaxation strands, a maximum prestressing stress of 0.75 f_s' is used (AASHTO 9.15.1). Thus, with $f_s' = 270$ ksi as the ultimate strength of prestressing steel,

$$\text{Total lb of P/S steel} = \frac{P_j}{(0.75 \times 270)} \times \text{Total bridge length} \times 3.4$$

$$P_j = \frac{0.75 \times 270 \times 47{,}970}{312 \times 3.4} = 9157 \text{ kips}$$

This total post-tensioning force is to be distributed equally to all girders, four in this example. Thus,

$$P_j = 9157/4 = 2290 \text{ kips/girder}$$

Estimate of prestress loss due to friction. To estimate friction losses, Eq. 7.3a will be used (although Eq. 7.6a could also have been used) and the friction loss coefficient $e^{-(KL+\mu\alpha)}$ will be computed. For this purpose, the tendon (or cable) profile (or layout) will be determined first. Determine the K and D distances (as defined in Fig. 7.56). The K distance is assumed to be $4\frac{7}{8}$ in. at the midspan and $6\frac{5}{8}$ in. at the bent. The D distance is found from Fig. B.8 (Appendix B) for $P_j = 2290$ kips.

Thus, at midspan, the minimum distance $= K + D = 4\frac{7}{8} + 7\frac{1}{2} = 12\frac{3}{8}$ in. Use 12 in. At bent, the minimum distance $= K + D = 6\frac{5}{8} + 7\frac{1}{2} = 14\frac{1}{8}$ in. Use 15 in. $= 1.25$ ft.

These distances are shown in Fig. E7.1c for the tendon path at 0.4L from each support and the centerline of the bent. The final step in defining the tendon path is to find the vertical position of two inflection points located at 0.1L in each span measured from the centerline

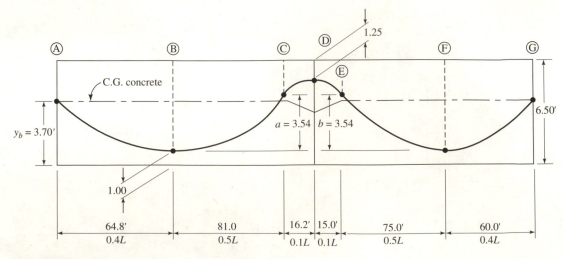

FIGURE E7.1c
Tendon profile in the two-span continuous beam.

of bent. This location results in a reasonable radius of curvature for placing the semirigid duct, and it maintains the forces on the duct within the acceptable limits during stressing.

Dimension a and b in Fig. E7.1c can be found because the inflection points of two parabolas lie on a straight line. By similar triangles,

$$\frac{a}{81} = \frac{4.25}{97.2} \rightarrow a = 3.54 \text{ ft}$$

$$\frac{b}{75} = \frac{4.25}{90} \rightarrow b = 3.54 \text{ ft}$$

With the tendon path thus completely defined, the friction loss coefficients, $e^{-(KL+\mu\alpha)}$, are calculated as follows. Assuming that angles are small (i.e., $\tan\alpha \approx \alpha$), the angle change α is defined as

$$\alpha = 2e/L$$

where e is the vertical distance of the parabola between control points, and L is the horizontal distance between the control points.

The angle α between the horizontal and the tangent to the parabola at the control points is shown, for various control points, in the following table:

Point	e (ft)	L (ft)	$\alpha = 2e/L$ (rad)
B	2.70	64.8	0.0833
C	3.54	81.0	0.0874
D	0.71	16.2	0.0874
E	0.71	15.0	0.0944
F	3.54	75.0	0.0944
G	2.70	60.0	0.0900

The values of the friction loss coefficients to be used in conjunction with Eq. 7.3a are tabulated as follows for various segments of the tendon. The value of the wobble coefficient, K, is assumed to be 0, and the value of the friction coefficient, μ, is assumed to be 0.2 in this example so that $e^{-(KL+\mu\alpha)} = e^{-\mu\alpha}$.

Segment	α (rad)	Cumulative α (rad)	$-\mu\alpha$	$e^{-\mu\alpha}$
AB	0.0833	0.0833	−0.0167	0.983
BC	0.0874	0.1707	−0.0341	0.966
CD	0.0874	0.2581	−0.0516	0.950
DE	0.0944	0.3525	−0.0705	0.932
EF	0.0944	0.4469	−0.0894	0.914
FG	0.0900	0.5369	−0.1074	0.898

(g) Friction: horizontally curved girders. Note that the friction losses discussed above occur in straight post-tensioned girders with tendons that have a parabolic profile in a *vertical* plane. Additional friction losses should be considered for such bridges if the tendons are on a *horizontal* curve. Experience in California has shown serious problems associated with horizontally curved prestressed post-tensioned box girders. In one case, the *deviation forces* exerted laterally by the tendons (on the inside of the curvature) caused extensive concrete spalling of the girder web. In another case, the tendons broke free of the web in the curved section [CALTRANS, 1993d]. The magnitude of the in-plane deviation force, $F_{u\text{-in}}$, can be estimated by Eq. 7.7 [AASHTO, 1994]:

$$F_{u\text{-in}} = \frac{P_u}{R} \tag{7.7}$$

where $F_{u\text{-in}}$ = the in-plane deviation force effect per unit length of tendon, in kips/ft
P_u = the factored tendon force, in kips, with a load factor for the jacking force—1.3 (See Article 3.4.3 of AASHTO–LRFD specifications, 1994)
R = the radius of curvature of the tendon at the considered location

These deviation forces would normally be resisted by the concrete cover. According to AASHTO [1994], the shear resistance of concrete cover against pull-out by these deviation forces, V_r, is given by

$$V_r = \phi V_n \tag{7.8}$$

where
$$V_n = 0.125 d_c \sqrt{f'_c} \tag{7.9}$$

and where V_n = nominal shear resistance per unit length, kips/in.
ϕ = resistance factor for shear—0.9 for normal-weight concrete
d_c = the minimum concrete cover over the tendon duct, plus one-half of the duct diameter, in.
f'_c = specified compressive strength of concrete at the time of loading or prestressing

If the shear resistance of the concrete cover, V_r, is exceeded by the factored in-plane deviation forces, it is required that fully anchored tie-backs, in the form of either non-prestressed or prestressed reinforcement, be provided to resist these forces [AASHTO, 1994].

The effect of horizontal curvature may be considered as a portion of the friction loss due to the angular change of the prestressing steel. As such, its magnitude can be determined in the same manner as determining the effect due to the vertical curvature, and the general expression $T_x = T_o e^{-(KL + \mu\alpha)}$ can be used, where

α = total angular change of prestressing profile in radians from jacking end to point X; α is the *vectorial* summation of the tendon drape and the horizontal curvature.

The California practice [CALTRANS, 1993c] is to use Eq. 7.10 for determining α:

$$\alpha = \sqrt{(\alpha_V)^2 + (\alpha_H)^2} \tag{7.10}$$

where
$$\alpha_V = \frac{2\delta}{L} \tag{7.11}$$

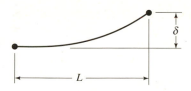

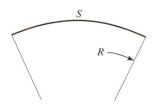

FIGURE 7.58
Definitions of terms for tendon with drape and horizontal curvature [CALTRANS, 1993c].

and
$$\alpha_H = \frac{S}{R} \qquad (7.12)$$

where (see Fig. 7.58) δ = tendon drape in length L
$\qquad\qquad\qquad\quad L$ = distance from jacking point to point X
$\qquad\qquad\qquad\quad S$ = length of curve from jacking point to point X
$\qquad\qquad\qquad\quad R$ = radius

Example 7.2 illustrates the calculation of friction losses due to the combined tendon drape and horizontal curvature.

EXAMPLE 7.2. A 4-ft-deep cast-in-place post-tensioned concrete box girder spanning 100 ft, shown in Fig. E7.2, is horizontally curved. The radius of curvature from end A to midpoint B is 150 ft, and from midpoint B to end C is 300 ft. Compute the loss in prestress due to friction.

Solution. Solve for T_x at B. From end A to midpoint B,

$$\alpha_V = \frac{2\delta}{L} = \frac{2(2.5 - 0.75)}{50} = 0.07 \text{ radians}$$

$$\alpha_H = \frac{S}{R} = \frac{50}{150} = 0.33 \text{ radians}$$

$$\alpha = \sqrt{\alpha_V^2 + \alpha_H^2} = \sqrt{(0.07)^2 + (0.33)^2} = 0.34 \text{ radians}$$

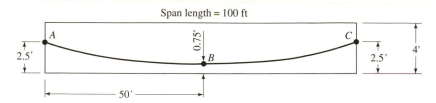

FIGURE E7.2
Horizontally curved post-tensioned concrete box girder.

$$T_o = 0.75 f_s' \text{ for low-relaxation strands (AASHTO 9.15.1)}$$
$$= 0.75 \times 270 = 202.5 \text{ ksi}$$
$$\mu = 0.2$$
$$K = 0$$

$$T_x = T_o e^{-(KL+\mu\alpha)}$$

$$T_x = T_o e^{-(0.20)(0.34)}$$

$$= 202.5 e^{-(0.20)(0.34)}$$

$$= 202.5 \times 0.93$$

$$= 189.2 \text{ ksi} \qquad \text{or} \qquad 0.93 P_j$$

Similarly, solve for T_x at C. From midpoint B to end C,

$$\alpha_V = \frac{2(2.5 - 0.75)}{50} = 0.07 \text{ radians}$$

$$\alpha_H = \frac{50}{300} = 0.17 \text{ radians}$$

Total $\alpha_V = 0.07 + 0.07 = 0.14$ radians
Total $\alpha_H = 0.33 + 0.17 = 0.50$ radians

$$\alpha = \sqrt{(0.14)^2 + (0.50)^2} = 0.52 \text{ radians}$$

$T_x = 202.5 e^{-(0.20)(0.52)} = 202.5 \times 0.90 = 182.5$ ksi or $0.90 P_j$, where P_j = prestressing force at the jacking end.

(h) Anchorage zones. In both pretensioned and post-tensioned beams, the pre-stressing force is transferred to beams in their end portions known as the *end zones,* or the *anchorage zones.* In the pretensioned beams, the prestressing force is transferred to the surrounding concrete gradually over a certain length from the end of the beam. In post-tensioned beams, the prestressing force is transferred directly on the ends of the beam through bearing plates and anchors. As a result, in both cases, the ends of the beam are subjected to concentrated forces. The area immediately behind the bear-ing plate is subjected to high bursting stresses that generate high tensile stresses in the transverse direction away from the plate. Along the longitudinal axis of the beam, the zone of this high stress concentration extends for a distance approximately equal to the depth of the beam. Beyond this distance, the bursting stresses become negligible [Naaman, 1982].

Stress analysis for an anchorage is very complex; compressive stresses in its im-mediate vicinity are believed to be of the same order as the strength of concrete and, hence, are subjected to inelastic strains and deformations. Methods for determining these stresses based on elastic analysis can be found in the literature [Guyon, 1960; Zielinski and Rowe, 1960; Leonhardt, 1964; Abeles, Bardhan-Roy, and Turner, 1976]. A general discussion on the nature, magnitude, and control of these stresses can be found in texts on prestressed concrete; this topic is not discussed here.

In some cases, it becomes necessary to increase the area of the beam's cross sec-tion in the end portion of the beam in order to accommodate the raised tendons, their

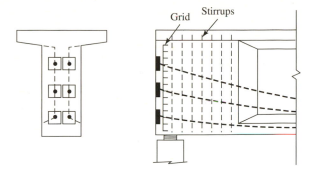

FIGURE 7.59
Typical end block of a prestressed concrete beam
[Naaman, 1982].

anchorages, and the support bearing. This is accomplished by gradually increasing the web width to that of the flange, as shown in Fig. 7.59; the resulting enlarged section is called the *end block*. Contrary to expectation, research by Gergeley and Sozen [1967] has shown that in spite of the enlarged area of this end section, the transverse tensile stresses in the end block *increase* instead of decrease. However, AASHTO 9.21 mandates that end blocks be used to distribute the concentrated prestressing forces at the anchorage in post-tensioned beams. Preferably, they should be as wide as the narrower flange of the beam and as long as three-fourths of the depth of the beam or 24 in., whichever is greater. This anchorage zone is required to be adequately reinforced by a closely spaced grid of both vertical and horizontal bars placed near the face of the end block to resist bursting stresses. Details of such reinforcement should follow the recommendations of the supplier of the anchorages. In the absence of such recommendations, this reinforcement should consist of, as a minimum, #3 bars on 3-in. centers in each direction, placed not more than $1\frac{1}{2}$ in. from the inside face of the anchor bearing plate.

AASHTO specifications [1992] permit rather high bearing stresses at the anchorages of post-tensioned beams—limited to the smaller of 3000 psi or $0.9f_c'$ at service loads (AASHTO 9.16.1). Such high bearing stresses are believed to be justifiable on two grounds [Lin and Burns, 1981]:

1. Since the highest value of the post-tensioning force occurs at the time of transfer, the highest bearing stresses that will ever exist at the anchorage will also occur at that time. Thereafter, the bearing stress will gradually decrease with the loss of prestress.
2. While the post-tensioning force has its maximum value at the time of transfer, the concrete strength is at its minimum. After transfer, the concrete strength gradually increases to its highest value at 28 days, while the prestressing force decreases due to losses. Hence, if failure does not occur at the time of transfer, it is quite unlikely to occur in the future.

In practice, anchorages are generally supplied by vendors according to their own standards for different tendons. Based on successful practice and experience, the vendors'

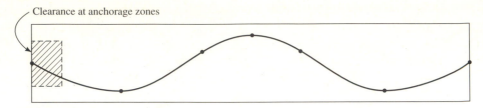

Clearance at anchorage zones

FIGURE 7.60
Anchorage zone clearances [CALTRANS, 1993d].

designs are considered reliable, so the engineer need not design the anchorages. According to CALTRANS [1993d], the anchorage zone clearances shown in Fig. 7.60 and in Table 7.11 are recommended for cast-in-place post-tensioned box girders.

7.6.2 Precast Post-Tensioned Prestressed Concrete Segmental Bridges

A significant and innovative development of modern bridge construction technology is segmental construction, which has led to full exploitation of the potential of prestressed concrete. Segmental construction is a method of construction in which the primary superstructure members (the girders) are composed of individual members called *segments* that are post-tensioned together in place [PCIJ, 1975a]. The method uses both precast and cast-in-place segments that are post-tensioned at various stages of construction.

Segmental construction technique evolved in Europe in the aftermath of World War II for the replacement of thousands of war-damaged bridges. The acute shortage of steel in post-war Europe gave the impetus to use prestressed concrete in replacing bridges throughout much of Europe.

Precast segmental construction was used in 1941 by the French pioneer in engineering, Eugene Fressynet, in constructing the 180-ft two-hinged portal-framed bridge over the Marne River, near Luzancy, France. Precast I-shaped segments were used [Nilson, 1978]. In the United States, a similar system progressed in the 1950s. The first prestressed concrete bridge built in California was a 110-ft-span pedestrian bridge built in

TABLE 7.11
Recommendations for anchorage zone clearances [CALTRANS, 1993d]

P/T force, P_j (kips/girder)	Stem thickness (in.)	Anchorage space requirements	
		Width (in.)	Height (in.)
0–1000	12	27	27
1000–1500	12	27	41
1500–2000	12	27	54
2000–2500	12	27	68
2500–3000	12	27	81
3000–3500	12	27	89
3500–4000	12	27	105

1951 over Arrayo Seco (a flood channel) near Los Angeles. Designed by the CAL-TRANS engineer Jim Jurkovich and by T. Y. Lin of the University of California at Berkeley, the bridge comprised two 55-ft precast segments joined at midspan. A temporary falsework bent provided support until the post-tensioning was completed [Thorkildsen and Holombo, 1995]. However, the first application of precast segmental construction technology for a highway bridge in the United States began with the construction in 1952 of the 50-ft-span, 24-ft-wide East Koy Creek Bridge near Sheldon, New York, designed by the Fressynet Company. In this project, the bridge girders were match-cast into three equal longitudinal segments (in contrast to the European transverse segments), to limit maximum lifting weight to 5.5 tons. The center segment was cast first, followed by the end segments, which were cast directly against it. Keys were cast at the joints between the segments so that the three precast segments could be joined at the site in the same position they had been in in the precasting yard. After curing, the segments were transported to the construction site where they were reassembled and post-tensioned with cold joints. This bridge also represents the first practical application of match-casting technique [Mathivat, 1966, 1979; Muller, 1969, 1975; PTI/PCI, 1978].

Several schemes of segmental construction are in use. The scheme used determines both the design and the calculations and forms the basis of classifying bridges as follows [Mathivat, 1979]:

1. Cantilever bridges (or bridges made of a succession of cantilevers)
2. Bridges with concrete precast beams
3. Incrementally launched bridges
4. Bridges built on self-supporting and self-launching centering

The most widely used method in segmental construction is the cantilever method, in which a bridge superstructure is built by a succession of segments. Figure 7.61(a) illustrates the principles of cantilever construction. Conceptually, this technique is similar to that used in the past to build timber cantilever bridges—by setting tree trunks orthogonally in horizontal rows, as in Fig. 7.61(b). Bridges of this type can still be found in India, China, and Tibet (discussed in Chapter 1).

The first segment of the bridge is supported on a rigid abutment or pier. This supports the next segment, including the weight of the formwork or the construction equipment, as a cantilever. After it gains sufficient strength (if cast-in-place), this second segment is integrated with the first one by post-tensioning, which makes the whole assembly self-supporting. And in turn, this assembly is used as the starting point for the next segment. At each construction sequence, the resulting cantilever is stabilized by prestressed tendons, which are set in the upper fibers of the girder. These tendons increase in length as the number of installed segments increases and the work progresses. The system can be used with the precast segments alone or in combination with cast-in-place segments. In the latter case, each segment is cast directly against the preceding one, a scheme that lends itself to the most efficient construction method that can be used for complex and variable-shaped structures [Gerwick, 1993].

Initially developed for steel structures, the cantilever construction method was used for building reinforced concrete bridges as early as the 1930s. In 1928, Fressynet used this concept for the Plougastel Bridge, France. The credit for the first application of the balanced cantilever method is given to E. Baumgart, a Brazilian engineer, who designed

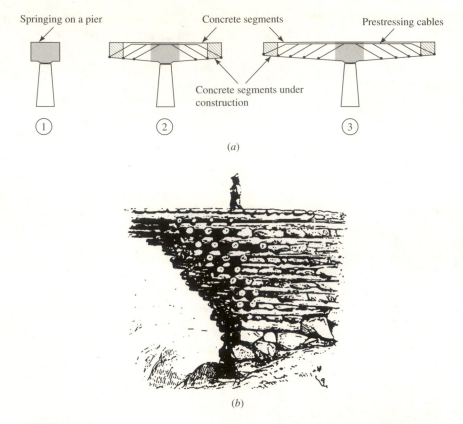

FIGURE 7.61
Principle of cantilever construction [Mathivat, 1979]: (*a*) segmental construction by cantilever method, (*b*) cantilevered timber bridge (an impression from the art historian Viollet Le Duc).

and built the Hervel Bridge, a reinforced concrete structure, over the Rio Piexe in Brazil in 1930 [Podolny and Muller, 1982; Mathivat, 1979; PTI/PCI, 1978]. Also known as the *progressive cantilever method* in Europe, the balanced cantilever method evolved in Germany in the early 1950s. It was first used by Ulrich Finsterwalder for building in 1950 the 203-ft-span prestressed concrete bridge over the Lahn River at Balduinstein. Later, several other bridges in Balduinstein and Neckarrens, Germany, were built in collaboration with the German firm of Dycherhoff & Widmann, leading the way to construction of prestressed concrete bridge spans in excess of 700 ft [Gerwick, 1964; Finsterwalder, 1965; Finsterwalder and Schambeck, 1965]. An exhaustive discussion of the cantilever method, along with several notable bridges built by this technique, is presented by Mathivat [1979] and by Podolny and Muller [1982].

The development of the cantilever method of segmental construction using *precast segments* began in France in 1962 with the three-span (123, 180, and 123 ft) continuous Choisy-le-Roi Bridge over the Seine River near Paris. The design was prepared by Enterprises Campenon Bernard to replace a war-damaged bridge originally built in 1870, which in turn had been built to replace an old bridge built by the famous French mathematician Navier [Mathivat, 1966; Muller, 1969]. Its remarkable speed of construction, which ensued from simultaneously casting the superstructure segments and constructing the substructure, led to the construction of several other similar structures in France by the same contractor. Since then, this has become the preferred construction method for bridges with spans of 200–400 ft.

In North America, the first application for segmental construction technology was the *cast-in-place segmental construction* in 1964 of the single-cell box girder continuous three-span (132.5, 265, and 132.5 ft) Ste. Adele Bridge, crossing the River of the Mules near Ste. Adelein, Quebec, Canada. This was followed by the three-span (130, 260, and 130 ft) Lievre Bridge, also in Quebec, completed in 1967. However, the first major use of the precast segmental box girder construction was for the eight-span (one 203.75, six 265, and one 203.75 ft) Bear River Bridge, near Digby, Nova Scotia, opened to traffic in December 1972. The geometry of this bridge included a variety of circular, spiral, and parabolic curves and tangent sections.

In the United States, this method evolved with the construction of the three-span (100, 200, and 100 ft) Corpus Christi Bridge (also known as the JFK Memorial Causeway) in Texas, which was opened to traffic in February 1973. A year later, this was followed by the construction of the 1716-ft five-span (270, 340, 450, 380, and 276 ft) Pine Valley Creek Bridge on Interstate 8 near San Diego, California. Designed by the California Department of Transportation, this dramatic bridge had pier heights ranging from 140 to 340 ft and a roadway height of about 450 ft above water level in Pine Valley Creek [Podolny and Muller, 1982; PTI/PCI, 1978; PTI, 1985].

With continuing refinement in segmental construction technology came a major innovation—the launching gantry, which was used for the first time for the 46-span (one 94, seven 130, one 194, twenty-six 259, one 194, nine 130, and one 94 ft), 9600-ft-long Oleron Viaduct, France, built between 1964 and 1966 [ENR, 1965; PTI/PCI, 1978]. Typically used for a steel-framed bridge of cantilever-truss or cable-stayed truss type, it permits movements of segments over the completed part of the structure and places them in cantilever over successive piers [Gerwick, 1993]. A comprehensive description of this method, used for two parallel 11-span bridges over the Connecticut River, has been presented by Sofia and Homsi [1994]. Known as the Raymond E. Baldwin Bridge, each bridge is an 11-span continuous unit 2522.5 ft long. The span lengths vary between 177.5 and 275 ft. The single-cell segments used for these bridges have top widths of 77 and 86 ft for the two bridges.

The other variable aspect of the segmental construction method is the segments (or sections) themselves. Most commonly consisting of box cross sections, these concrete segments may be precast, cast-in-place, or, in some cases, a combination of both.

Apart from the cantilever method, other schemes are also used when they are more practical. Precast segments may be erected in their final position on falsework. In this scheme, joints are made after adjusting for deadweight deflection to the final deck profile, and the span is post-tensioned, followed by the removal of the falsework. Alternatively, the precast segments may be assembled on a barge or other support located immediately below the final position. After all segments are jointed and post-tensioned together, the entire span is lifted into the final position.

Variations of the above schemes have been used. All or a large portion of the entire span can be precast and post-tensioned in a plant. These large segments are then transported to the site and erected by crane barges that have a capacity of several thousand tons. Based on the double cantilever scheme and used earlier in the former Soviet Union for 100-m spans, this concept permits augmentation of span lengths by a span suspended between the ends. Typically, construction is initiated by fixing, either permanently or temporarily, a prefabricated *hammerhead* (double cantilever) section on top of a pier, and then construction progresses from both ends. This concept has been used to erect 62 full-width highway bridge girders and 62 double-track railroad girders, each 110 m long, and 124 hammerhead girders over 100 m long, weighing about 6000 tons each, on the Great Belt Western Bridge in Denmark [Gerwick, 1993]. This method will also be used for the 250-m-long girders in Canada. In the United States, over 2200 identical 56-ft-long, 33-ft-wide, 185-ton spans were floated into position by barges and erected for the 24-mile-long bridge across Lake Pontchartrain, near New Orleans. As shown in Fig. 7.12, each segment consisted of seven prestressed AASHTO Type III girders cast integrally with a reinforced concrete deck in a casting yard near the bridge site [Smith, 1955; Van Buren, 1961].

Depending on the site conditions, the geometry of the bridge, and the span lengths, several construction methods may have to be used for the same project. For example, three different methods were used for the Biloxi Interstate 110 Viaduct, Biloxi, Mississippi, completed in February 1988. Conventional cast-in-place concrete box girders were used for the sharply curved portion over the Gulf of Mexico, and the remainder of the bridge was built by precast concrete segmental box girder construction, partly by the span-by-span method and partly by the balanced cantilever method [Phipps and Spruill, 1990].

In North America, the explosive growth of segmental and cable-stayed bridges represents probably one of the most significant current developments in prestressed concrete structural systems. In recognition of this revolutionary and versatile construction technology, a new organization, The American Segmental Bridge Institute (ASBI) was formed December 3, 1988, at Wichita, Kansas, to advance design and construction technology and to provide a database of information for designers and builders [PCIJ, 1989; Breen, 1990]. Also, under the leadership of the Post-Tensioning Institute, a comprehensive new design and construction guide [AASHTO, 1989] was developed under an NCHRP contract [PTI, 1988] and adopted as an interim standard by AASHTO. (It was revised in 1993 through the *AASHTO Interim Specifications for Bridges—1993*.)

The design of post-tensioned prestressed concrete segmental bridges is beyond the scope of this book, but the topic is discussed in several references [Leonhardt, 1965; Muller, 1969, 1975; Lacey and Breen, 1969, 1975; PTI/PCI, 1971/1990; Lacey, Breen, and Burns, 1971; Libby, 1976a,b; Libby and Perkins, 1976; Podolny and Muller, 1982; Ballinger, Podolny, and Abrams, 1977; PTI, 1978; Podolny, 1979]. An exhaustive list of references can be found in Podolny and Muller [1982].

7.6.3 Prestressed Concrete Segmental Cable-Stayed Bridges

The advent of segmental construction technology has made it possible to use prestressed concrete for cable-stayed bridges in the long-span range that had hitherto been reserved for structural steel. Table 7.12 compiled by Podolny and Muller [1982] presents a summary of important concrete cable-stayed bridges.

TABLE 7.12

Concrete cable-stayed bridges—general data [Podolny and Muller, 1982]

Bridge	Location	Type	Spans (ft)[d]	Year completed
1. Tempul	Guadalete River, Spain	Aqueduct	66–198–66	1925
2. Benton City	Yakima River, Washington, U.S.	Highway	two@57.5–170–two@57.5	1957
3. Lake Maracaibo	Venezuela	Highway	525–five@771–525	1962
4. Dnieper River	Kiev, Ukraine	Highway	216.5–472–216.5	1963
5. Canal du Centre	Obourg, Belgium	Pedestrian	two@220	1966
6. Polcevera Viaduct	Genoa, Italy	Highway	282–664–689–460	1967
7. Magliana	Rome, Italy	Highway	476–176	1967
8. Danish Great Belt[a]	Denmark	Highway and rail	multispans 1132	Delayed by funding
9. Danish Great Belt[b]	Denmark	Highway and rail	multispans 1148	Delayed by funding
10. Pretoria	Pretoria, South Africa	Pipe	two@93	1968
11. Barwon River	Geelong, Australia	Pedestrian	180–270–180	1969
12. Mount Street	Perth, Australia	Pedestrian	two@116.8	1969
13. Wadi Kuf	Libya	Highway	320–925–320	1971
14. Richard Foyle	Londonderry, Northern Ireland	Highway	230–689	Project abandoned
15. Mainbrücke	Hoechst, West Germany	Highway and rail	485.6–308	1972
16. Chaco/Corrientes	Panara River, Argentina	Highway	537–803.8–537	1973
17. River Waal	Tiel, Holland	Highway	312–876–312	1974
18. Barranquilla	Barranquilla, Columbia	Highway	228–459–228	1974
19. Danube Canal	Vienna, Austria	Highway	182.7–390–182.7	1974
20. Kwang Fu	Taiwan	Highway	220–440–440–220	1977
21. Pont de Brotonne	Normandy, France	Highway	471–1050–471	1977
22. Carpineto	Province Poetenza, Italy	Highway	100–594–100	1977
23. Pasco-Kennewick	State of Washington, U.S.	Highway	406.5–981–406.5	1978
24. M-25 Overpass	Chertsey, England	Rail	two@180.5	1978
25. Ruck-A-Chucky[c]	Auburn, California, U.S.	Highway	1300	Design completed
26. Dame Point[c]	Jacksonville, Florida, U.S.	Highway	650–1300–650	1988
27. East Huntington[c]	East Huntington, West Virginia, U.S.	Highway	158–300–900–608	1985
28. Weirton-Steubenville[c]	Weirton, West Virginia, U.S.	Highway	820–688	1990

[a]Design by White Young and Partners.
[b]Design by Ulrich Finsterwalder.
[c]Alternative design with structural steel.
[d]1 ft = 0.305 m.

563

The credit of first using cable stays for a concrete structure goes to Professor E. Torroja for the Tempul Aqueduct, which crosses the Guadalete River in Spain [Torroja 1958]. Built in 1925, it has a classical three-span symmetrical cable-stayed bridge configuration. Several years later, Homer M. Hadley designed a 400-ft cable-stayed bridge (two 57.5, one 170, and two 57.5 ft] that was built in 1957 over the Yakima River at Benton City, Washington [Hadley, 1958; Podolny and Scalzi, 1976]. An all-concrete stayed girder bridge, probably the world's first, was built in 1978 over the Omoto River in northern Japan for a single-track railroad crossing that is 1333 ft long. The stayed center portion has a main span of 281 ft, flanked by 153-ft side spans. Other concrete box girder spans complete the crossing [ENR, 1978]. However, the modern cable-stayed bridge evolved with the construction in 1962 of the Lake Maracaibo Bridge over Lake Maracaibo, in Venezuela. Its designer, Riccardo Morandi, led the way for the acceptance of the cable-stayed bridge as a viable alternative for long spans [ENR, 1962; Morandi, 1969; Leonhardt, 1974, 1984]. Morandi designed five other bridges of similar style. Others emulated his bridge style in their designs. A discussion on design and construction of various cable-stayed bridges can be found in the literature [Podolny and Scalzy, 1976; Podolny and Muller, 1982; Leonhardt, 1984; Strasky, 1993; PCIJ, 1994; Pate, 1995].

A striking example of a cable-stayed bridge in which prestressed concrete is used is the unusual and graceful hanging-arc Ruck-A-Chucky Bridge (Fig. 7.62) built over the American River, California, and designed by T. Y. Lin International/Hanson Engi-

FIGURE 7.62
Ruck-A-Chucky Bridge over the American River, California (Courtesy of T. Y. International, San Francisco) [Prog. Arch., 1979].

neers. A cable-stayed bridge with a curved main span of 1312 ft, the Ruck-A-Chucky is hung by cables from the rocky mountain slopes of the canyon it crosses [Prog. Arch., 1979]. The potential of prestressed concrete for use in medium- and long-span bridges is reported in several references such as Leonhardt [1974], Lin and Kulka [1975], and Kozak and Bezouska [1976].

7.6.4 Prestressed Concrete Suspension Bridges

Prestressed concrete suspension bridges are generally of the *self-anchored* type (see discussion in Chapter 1 and Fig. 1.53) that use prestressed concrete girders instead of steel girders; i.e., the force in the external cables is used by anchoring the cables into the concrete girders. An example of this type of bridge is the Merelbeck Bridge near Ghent, Belgium, with a center span of 328 ft [Vandpitte, 1957; ENR, 1960]. A recent example is a precast, prestressed concrete suspension footbridge (98.4, 826.7, 98.4 ft) over the Vranov Reservoir in the Czech Republic [PCIJ, 1994].

The segmental construction technique has also been successfully used for building suspension bridges. An example is the unique single-span 680-ft Hudson Hope Bridge over the Peace River in northern British Columbia, Canada, which opened to traffic in September 1964. The deck of this bridge consists of 34 precast concrete box girder segments, each 20 ft long and 4 ft 1 in. deep, post-tensioned at site. This deck served as both the bridge roadway and the stiffening girder for the suspension system. The first of its kind, this bridge was conceived by H. H. Minshall, a well-known British Columbian erector [Osipov, 1969].

7.6.5 Miscellaneous Prestressed Concrete Bridge Types

Many different types of prestressed concrete bridges, such as stress-ribbon, truss, through-girder, and inverted suspension bridges have been built. But these are rather uncommon types that may adapt to special situations. These applications arise from the fact that the concept of prestressing can be used as a most desirable alternative to carry loads in tension instead of in flexure [Naaman, 1982]. Morandi successfully used this concept in his bridges that feature prestressed concrete elements in the form of cable stays [Morandi, 1969].

7.6.5.1 Stress-ribbon bridges

The origin of the stress-ribbon bridge, although of uncertain antiquity, can be traced to the primitive suspension bridges built in India, China (Fig. 7.63), and Peru (Fig. 7.64), as described in Chapter 1. Construction of these bridges involved simply tying two or more fiber ropes at each end across a span forming a catenary, which supported an overlaid walkway made from transversely laid bamboo sticks [Steinman and Watson, 1957; Edwards, 1959]. Alexander De Humbolt and Aime Bonpland describe bridges of this type that they found in their 1799–1804 explorations of the equatorial areas of South America. They describe the Penipe River Bridge (Fig. 7.64) as being 100 ft long and 7 or 8 ft wide, and they note other similar bridges of much larger dimensions [Edwards, 1959].

FIGURE 7.63
Early stress-ribbon bridge in China [Podolny and Muller, 1982].

In principle, a stress-ribbon bridge is similar to these primitive suspension bridges, except that modern construction uses high-strength materials and engineering technology involving precasting and prestressing. The fundamental idea is to produce a suspended, but tightly stretched, ribbon of prestressed concrete that is anchored in the abutments and laid across intermediate supports provided with cantilever arms. The modern version of this concept was reinvented in the late 1950s by the German engi-

FIGURE 7.64
Humbolt's view of the "Rope Bridge over the Penipe River," in Peru [Edwards, 1959].

FIGURE 7.65
Stress-ribbon bridge concept for the Bosporous Bridge [Finsterwalder, 1969].

neer Ulrich Finsterwalder as the innovative stress-ribbon bridge suitable for light loads and long span [Finsterwalder, 1965, 1969; Walther, 1971/1972; Nehse, 1973]. In 1958, Finsterwalder proposed the first modern attempt to implement this concept—a shallow funicular-shaped prestressed concrete stress-ribbon tensile member spanning 190 m for the central span of the three-span (396, 408, and 396 m) Bosporus Bridge (Fig. 7.65). He proposed this design again in 1961 for the Zoo Bridge at Cologne [Podolny and Muller, 1982; Finsterwalder, 1965]. Both bridges were unsuccessful. The first successful realization of this type of bridge was the construction of the 710-ft conveyor belt bridge at the Holderbank-Wildeck Cement Works from 1963–1964 in Switzerland. This was followed in 1969–1970 by the construction of the 448-ft (130-ft main span) footbridge in Freiburg, Germany (Fig. 7.66), which is 14.4 ft wide and has a deck thickness of 10 in. [Tang, 1976; Podolny and Muller, 1982]. A single-span, 446-ft-long and 10.2-ft-wide stress-ribbon bridge (Fig. 7.67) was built in 1971 in Germany over the Rhône River near Lingon-Leox to carry a pipeline and pedestrian traffic [Nilson, 1978; Podolny and Muller, 1982; CE, 1974a; Wilson and Wheen, 1974; Strasky, 1987]. Strasky and Pirner [1986] and Strasky [1987] discuss nine precast stress-ribbon pedestrian bridges built in Czechoslovakia in the mid 1980s. These bridges vary from one

FIGURE 7.66
Freiburg stress-ribbon footbridge [Podolny and Muller, 1982].

FIGURE 7.67
Stress-ribbon bridge carrying pedestrian traffic and a pipeline over the Rhône River near Lingon-Leox [CE, 1974a; Nilson, 1978].

to four spans; the longest span is 472 ft and the maximum bridge length is 1329 ft. A stress-ribbon bridge has been built in North America recently. The slender appearance of the stress-ribbon bridges notwithstanding, wind-tunnel tests have shown that they are safe against torsional oscillations [Finsterwalder, 1969; Tilly, Cullington, and Eyre, 1984].

The superstructure of a stress-ribbon bridge generally consists of a prestressed band attached to rigid end abutments. The deck is formed from precast concrete segments that are suspended on high-strength steel bearing cables and then shifted along the cables to the specified position. Joints between the segments are concreted in place, followed by prestressing of the whole deck, thus developing compression and rigidity sufficient to carry the dead and the live loads. Generally, high-strength cables are passed through a series of precast concrete components, the deck assembly of which can be tensioned from stiff abutments. The stress-ribbon superstructure differs from that of the conventional suspension bridge in that both the cable and the deck can be independently tensioned; in a suspension bridge, the main load-carrying element is the cable, with the deck acting as a stiffening element.

7.6.5.2 Prestressed concrete truss bridges

A few examples of prestressed concrete used to build truss bridges are reported in the literature [Carroll, Beaufait, and Byran, 1978; Gerwick, 1978; Naaman, 1982].

FIGURE 7.68
Iwahana Bridge, Japan, a prestressed concrete railway truss bridge [Gerwick, 1978].

These bridges can be successfully built from precast prestressed concrete elements, which can be assembled on site and connected by post-tensioning. Several truss railway bridges have been built in Japan. An notable example of a prestressed concrete truss bridge is the 260-ft Warren type truss Iwahana Bridge, the first prestressed concrete truss railway bridge built in Japan (see Fig. 7.68). A 12-ksi high-strength concrete was used for its chords and diagonals, which were match-cast in plant and then joined on site by post-tensioning [Gerwick, 1978]. Another example is the three-span (241, 600, and 241 ft) Rip Bridge in Australia, which consists of a three-arch-shaped cantilever truss system spanning the entrance to Brisbane Waters, north of Sydney [Wheen, 1979]. In both cases, the precast elements were joined on site by post-tensioning.

7.6.5.3 Prestressed concrete through-girder bridges

A prestressed concrete through-girder bridge is characterized by a single open-section girder of trapezoidal form resembling a U-section with inclined legs. The purpose of inclined legs, which act as the load-carrying girders, is to reduce the span of the transverse slab (i.e., the bottom width of the U-girder), thus reducing both slab thickness and pier widths. Starting with the first through-girder bridge in 1959, several railroad bridges of this type have been built in Japan. The railroad track is laid on the bottom slab, and the trains run in between the two inclined side girders. Design and construction details of prestressed concrete through-girder bridges are presented by Tanaka [1965], Ozaka and Koike [1965], and Kono and Ozaka [1969].

FIGURE 7.69
The Rio Colorado inverted suspension bridge, Costa Rica [Lin and Kulka, 1973].

7.6.5.4 Prestressed concrete inverted suspension bridges

Two well-known examples of the inverted suspension bridge using prestressed concrete are the Rio Colorado Bridge, Costa Rica (Fig. 7.69) [Lin and Kulka, 1973], and the Hayahi-No-Mine Bridge, Japan [Matsushita and Sato, 1979]. The Rio Colorado Bridge uses a catenary-shaped prestressed concrete ribbon to support the horizontal deck. The bridge is 669 ft (204m) long with a main span of 380 ft (116 m) [Naaman, 1982]. Conceptually, these bridges are similar to the suspension bridges except that the cables are used below the deck. This proves that prestressed concrete is one of the most desirable alternatives for carrying the load mostly in tension instead of in flexure [Naaman, 1982]. Experience from these bridges has led to the development of a self-anchoring inverted suspension bridge believed to be a low-cost solution for spans ranging from 200–400 ft over deep valleys [ENR, 1972; Loh, 1974; Matsushita and Sato, 1979].

In the United States, the most commonly built prestressed concrete superstructure for short and medium spans consists of I-beams, and the second most commonly built type is box girders, as dictated by economics. The use of other types, such as various types of T-beam configurations, is limited to only a few states. In the Northwest and West-Coast states, cast-in-place, post-tensioned box girders are more common than any other type. Design of these three types of bridges is presented in detail in the remainder of this chapter.

7.7
PRECAST PRESTRESSED CONCRETE COMPOSITE DECK PANELS

As previously stated, the cast-in-place reinforced concrete deck supported by precast prestressed concrete I-beams is the most common type of prestressed concrete bridge built in the United States. The beams used in this type of bridge have stirrups projecting from their top flanges that are embedded in the cast-in-place concrete for the deck to develop composite action.

Various methods may be used to support fresh deck concrete until it hardens. Contractors generally have the option of using conventional forms, *stay-in-place* (*SIP*) *metal deck forms,* or *prestressed concrete deck panels.* Forming costs for the conventional forms are high, and installation and removal of these forms is time-consuming; therefore, conventional forms are not preferred. Instead, the current practice is to use either the stay-in-place cold-formed light-gauge steel forms [Burdick, 1966; Wolford, 1971] or the thin, precast prestressed concrete form panels, which can act compositely with the poured-in-place concrete [ENR, 1973; PCIJ, 1975b; Barker, 1975; Kluge and Sawyer, 1975]. Although both types of forms eliminate the need for costly removal of falsework, the precast prestressed form panels are preferred over the steel forms because the steel forms suffer from two disadvantages: They do not replace or reduce the bottom transverse slab reinforcement since they do not act compositely with the concrete slab, and they are subject to long-term corrosion problems.

Figure 7.70 shows typical details of the precast prestressed concrete composite deck panels used as forms to support a cast-in-place concrete deck. Often referred to simply as *deck panels,* they offer a convenient and cost-effective method of construction for concrete bridge decks. Usually they are precast in a plant, trucked to the site, and lifted by cranes onto concrete or steel girders. There they span the adjacent girders to serve as a form surface for the cast-in-place upper layer (topping) that completes the bridge deck and contains the reinforcement for the negative moment. Upon hardening, the cast-in-place topping integrates structurally with the deck panels. The deck panels contain all the positive reinforcement required to resist transverse bending of the deck between the girders due to dead and live loads.

Because deck panels are a significant part of bridge superstructures, extensive research has been done on their behavior, design, and service performance [Jones and Furr, 1970; Buth, Furr, and Jones, 1972; PCIJ, 1975b; Barnoff et al., 1977; Barnoff and Sutherland, 1978; Csagoly, Holokawa, and Dorton, 1978; Reed, 1978; Beal, 1981; Bieschke and Klingner, 1982, 1988; Hays and Lybas, 1982; Buckner and Turner, 1983; Hays and Tabatabai, 1985; PCIJ, 1978, 1987; Fagundo et al. 1985; Ross, 1988; Fang et al., 1990; Klingner et al., 1990]. The use of deck panels began with about 80 bridges on the East-West Illinois Tollway Extension, some bridges on the Northwest Tollway near Chicago built in the early 1950s, and some bridges in Texas. Experience with deck panels has shown that they are reliable and safe [Barker, 1975; PCIJ, 1975b]. These panels can be installed rapidly, and in addition to serving as formwork, they also provide a convenient and safe working surface for the remaining cast-in-place deck construction. Consequently, their use is preferred by contractors in many states for constructing decks on most prestressed concrete girder superstructures.

Design of deck panels is covered by AASHTO 9.12. In addition to their own dead-weight, deck panels are designed compositely with the cast-in-place portion of the slab to support additional dead load and live loads. Design live-load moments for deck panels are calculated in accordance with AASHTO 3.24.3.

The design concrete strengths for deck panels are governed by AASHTO 9.22, which requires a minimum concrete strength at the time of transfer of 4000 psi; AASHTO 9.15 requires a minimum design concrete strength of 5000 psi. In keeping with the practice that evolved over several years, these panels are *concentrically* prestressed, although eccentric prestressing would be more cost effective.

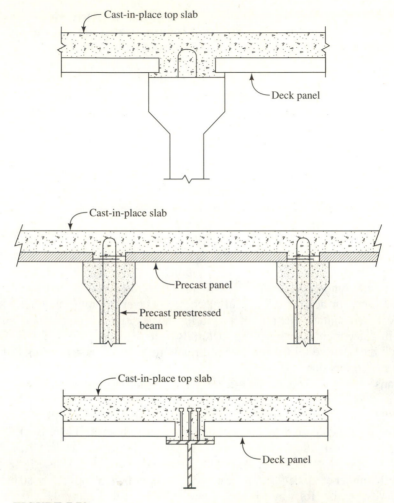

FIGURE 7.70
Typical details of precast prestressed deck panels on prestressed girder (top), with prestressing strand projections (center), and on steel girder (bottom).

AASHTO 9.23 covers general requirements for reinforcement for deck panels. It mandates (1) prestressing of deck panels in a direction transverse to the beams on which they are supported (i.e., in the direction of the span of the deck panels), (2) roughening of the top surface of the deck panels to ensure composite action with the cast-in-place concrete, and (3) providing reinforcing bars or equivalent mesh, at least 0.11 in.^{2} per ft of deck panel, transverse to the strands. AASHTO 9.25.2.2 requires that the prestressing strands be placed symmetrically and uniformly across the width of the panel, with their spacing limited to the smaller of $1\frac{1}{2}$ times the composite slab thickness or 18 in.

Specifications [AASHTO, 1992] require that precast panels be checked for flexural and shear strengths. AASHTO 9.17.4.2 requires that (1) at ultimate load, the stress in the prestressing strands of these panels be limited to that given by AASHTO Eq. 9.19,

$$f_{su}^* = \frac{l_x}{D} + \frac{2}{3} f_{se} \tag{7.13}$$

and that (2) it not exceed the stress given by AASHTO Eq. 9.17:

$$f_{su}^* = f_s' \left[1 - \left(\frac{\gamma^*}{\beta_1} \right) \left(\frac{p^* f_s'}{f_c'} \right) \right] \tag{7.14}$$

where D = nominal diameter of strand, in inches

f_{se} = effective prestress, in ksi, in prestressing strand after losses

l_x = distance from end of prestressing strand to center of panels

A comprehensive discussion on design practices for deck panels is presented by Ross Bryan Associates [1988]. Panels are designed to be as light as possible for ease in handling and erection. Their thickness varies from $2\frac{1}{2}$ to $4\frac{1}{2}$ in.: 3 in. is the minimum recommended thickness, and $2\frac{1}{2}$ in. is the absolute minimum thickness. Panel thickness is an important factor in selecting the prestressing strand to be used. Based on past satisfactory service performance, the recommended ratio of panel thickness to strand diameter is 8:1, as shown in Table 7.13.

Deck panels have been cast in widths (measured parallel to the girders) ranging from 2 to 10 ft, with 4 and 8 ft being the most common and preferred. Two-ft-wide panels may be used at the edges or as required by the bridge geometry. Trapezoidal or triangular pieces may be used at ends on skewed bridges. Continuity at the transverse joints between the two panels is provided by the cast-in-place portion of the deck.

A recent example of the use of prestressed precast deck panels is the five-span 986-ft-long Shelby Creek Bridge, a spliced, segmental, prestressed concrete I-beam structure built 179 ft above the bed of Shelby Creek in eastern Kentucky, and completed in December 1991. This bridge has 744 precast prestressed deck panels, each 10 ft $5\frac{1}{2}$ in. long (span), $3\frac{1}{2}$ in. thick, and 2 ft 9 in. to 8 ft wide, with a design concrete strength of 6000 psi. Forty-two $\frac{3}{8}$-in.-diameter strands were also used [Caroland et al., 1992].

No mechanical shear stirrups are required to develop bond at the interface of the deck panels and the cast-in-place topping. A roughened top surface of the panels without any contaminant is sufficient to develop the required bond for composite action, which is mandated by AASHTO 9.23: "The top surface of the panels shall be roughened in such a manner as to ensure composite action between the precast and the cast-in-place concrete" [AASHTO, 1992].

It is recommended that the panels be raked in the direction parallel to the strands in order to minimize the reduction in section modulus. Hooks projecting from the top face of the panels are provided for lifting purposes. A typical reinforcing detail of deck

TABLE 7.13
Recommended strand sizes for various panel thicknesses [Ross, 1988]

Panel thickness (in.)	Maximum strand size (in.)
3	$\frac{3}{8}$
$3\frac{1}{2}$	$\frac{7}{16}$
4	$\frac{1}{2}$

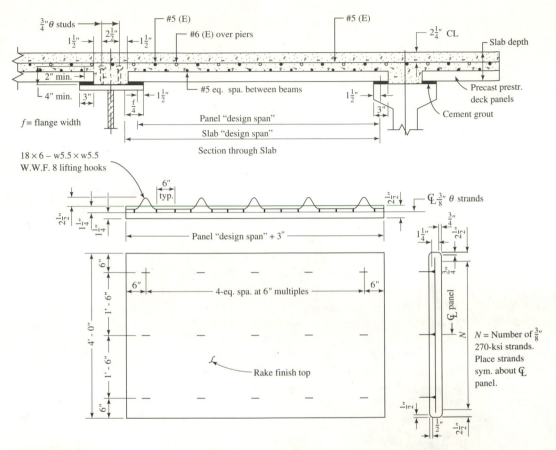

FIGURE 7.71
Precast prestressed panel-reinforcing details.

panels is shown in Fig. 7.71. Research has shown that the behavior of bridges with deck-panel strand projections is very nearly the same as that of bridges without the projections [Bieschke and Klingner, 1988].

Deck panels designed according to the methodology described above have performed well under fatigue test conditions. Consequently, no special provisions are needed for fatigue [Buckner and Turner, 1983; Hays and Tabatabai, 1985; Fang et al., 1990].

Proper design of bearing between the deck panels and the supporting girders is one of the most important components of the overall design process. The panels are placed continuously along the girder length and are supported on the adjacent girders over their entire lengths. A permanent, continuous, firm support is required between the deck panels and the supporting girders, as shown in Fig. 7.70. This permanent bearing material may be grout, mortar, or concrete. Grout may be a high-strength low-slump mix, or it may be nonshrink with a maximum strength of 5000 psi. Until these permanent materials reach their design strength, deck panels are supported by some compressible materials, such as high-density foam strips of expanded polystyrene, fiberboard, or bituminous fiberboard [Ross, 1988].

The profile of the top of the finished concrete deck is usually different from the profile of the top of the cambered prestressed girder. Vertical curvature and superelevation are other parameters that influence the profile of the top of the deck. As a result, special techniques are required to provide good bearing to the flat underside of the panels. One of two methods can be used: (1) A variable-thickness topping can be provided over the panels, which are supported over constant-thickness bearings, or (2) variable-thickness bearings can be used under the constant-thickness panels, with a constant topping. If the first option is used, the weight of the additional concrete thickness should be considered in the design of panels as well as in the design of girders.

7.8
TRANSVERSELY AND LONGITUDINALLY PRESTRESSED DECKS

In prestressed concrete bridges, the term "prestressing force" generally refers to the *longitudinal* prestressing force that is applied through tendons present in the bottom flanges and in the webs of girders. In addition to this longitudinal force, the deck, which forms the top flange of these girders, may also be prestressed in transverse or longitudinal directions or both. The reason for this prestressing is simply to introduce precompression to counteract tension cracks caused by loads or any other sources.

Transverse prestressing is usually applied to the top flanges of box girder bridges through post-tensioning, which offers the following advantages [Tedesko, 1976; PTI, 1978; PTI/PCI, 1978]:

1. A transversely post-tensioned deck will remain uncracked under the action of normal loads, and any cracks that might form will remain tightly closed because of the post-tensioning force. Transverse post-tensioning enhances durability of the deck against temperature and shrinkage cracks by providing precompression in the top face of the deck, a desirable approach for the design of bridge decks exposed to an aggressive environment.

    An example of a transversely prestressed deck is the 500-ft-long, five-span (100 ft each) Fargo–Moorhead Toll Bridge over the Red River, Minnesota. Its ten contiguously placed bulb-T girders that form the superstructure are transversely post-tensioned to improve durability and structural strength with a minimum effective prestress of 15.34 kips per linear ft of deck (Fig. 7.24) [PCIJ, 1989c].

2. A transversely post-tensioned deck provides greater load capacity of the top slab in the transverse direction. The deck slab thickness is reduced, leading to reduced concrete quantities and reduced dead-load moments and shears.

3. Transverse prestressing of decks permits longer spans of slab between girders (webs), which reduces the number of webs required in wide structures. This reduces forming costs and concrete quantities. The cost savings for multiweb box girder bridges cast on falsework results mainly from a thinner top slab and fewer webs.

4. Transverse prestressing of decks is particularly advantageous for box girders with large overhanging flanges because it permits longer lengths of the overhangs.

5. For wide segments, transverse post-tensioning usually results in reduced overall structure cost.

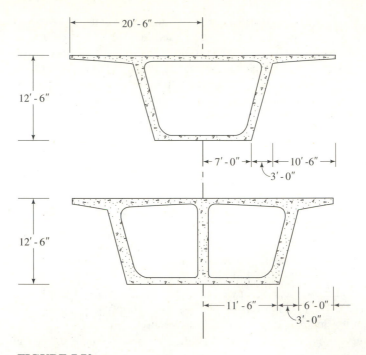

FIGURE 7.72

Cross section of the Eel River Bridge, California. Redesigned transversely post-tensioned superstructure (top), and original design without transverse post-tensioning (bottom) [Tedesko, 1976].

Some early examples of notable structures in which decks were transversely pre-stressed include the Eel River Bridge; the Napa River and the Pine Valley Creek Bridges in California; the Denny Creek Bridge in Washington; the Bendorf Bridge over the Rhine River, about 5 miles north of Koblenz, Germany; and the Saint Jean Bridge over the Garonne River at Bordeaux, France.

Several examples of transverse post-tensioning of the top slab of box girder super-structures are reported in the literature (see Figs. 7.72–7.74). Figure 7.72 shows a cross section of one of the twin box girders of the five-span (ranging from 201.5 ft to 310 ft), curved, Eel River Bridge, a cast-in-place segmental bridge in northern California. The redesigned single-cell box girder configuration permitted the cantilever of the top slabs to be increased from 6.0 ft to 10.5 ft on either side of the exterior girders, and it allowed the interior girder to be eliminated. Although the redesigned superstructure increased the post-tensioning costs by 40 percent, from $600,000 to $1 million, it saved about 3000 cu. yd of concrete and 560,000 lb of post-tensioning steel [PTI, 1978].

The twenty-span (sixteen spans 188 ft long and four spans varying from 143 ft 7 in. to 166 ft) Denny Creek Bridge, located in the Snoqualmie National Forest about 70 miles east of Seattle, Washington, in the Cascade Mountains, is a cast-in-place box girder bridge with a transversely post-tensioned deck. The single-cell box section of this bridge has 15-ft 4$\frac{3}{8}$-in. overhangs on each side, permitting a clear roadway width of 52 ft (Fig. 7.73) [PTI, 1978].

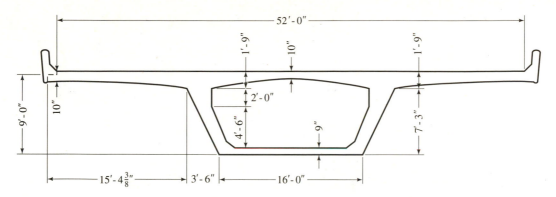

FIGURE 7.73
Transversely post-tensioned cross section of the Denny Creek Bridge, Snoqualmie National Forest, Washington [PTI, 1978].

Figure 7.74 shows a cross section of the typical transversely post-tensioned Biloxi Interstate 110 Viaduct in Biloxi, Mississippi, completed in February 1988 at a cost of $40.2 million. Transversely prestressed with $\frac{1}{2}$-in.-diameter strands spaced at 7 in. on centers, it has a 9-in.-thick slab for a clear span of 21 ft 4 in. between the girders, with overhangs about 10 ft long on each side of the girder [Phipps and Spruill, 1990].

Figure 7.75 shows the alternate cross sections of the Preferential Bridge in Chicago, with and without transverse post-tensioning of the deck [Tedesko, 1976].

The 13-span (lengths varying from 120 to 250 ft), 2230-ft-long Napa River Bridge, located just south of Napa, California, is a cast-in-place, segmentally built, lightweight concrete structure that carries a 68-ft-wide roadway. Transverse post-tensioning of the box girder permitted the number of webs (girders) to be reduced from seven, which would have been required for the cast-in-place prestressed concrete alternative, to three; and it allowed 10-ft overhangs to be built on each side of the three-girder box section. Transverse tendons consist of four $\frac{1}{2}$-in.-diameter strands encased in flat ducts measuring 2.25 by 0.75 in. (Fig. 7.76) with proper splay at both ends to accommodate a flat bearing at the end of the deck slab [PTI, 1978].

Opened to traffic in 1974, the Pine Valley Creek Bridge on Interstate 8 between El Centro and San Diego, California, was the first prestressed concrete cast-in-place segmental bridge built in the United States. The five-span (255, 340, 450, 380, and 266 ft), 1716-ft-long superstructure of this bridge consists of twin two-lane single-cell trapezoidal box girders, each 42 ft wide (out-to-out). The center span is 450 ft above the creek bed. Its deck is transversely prestressed, permitting the 24-ft span of the deck between the webs and permitting 10-ft overhangs [Podolny and Muller, 1982].

The Saint Jean River Bridge, built in 1965, is a six-span, 1560-ft-long structure with a deck consisting of three single-cell box girders, the top slabs of which are transversely prestressed with tendons that have twelve 8-mm strands at 2.5-ft intervals. Built in 1964, the 3378-ft Bendorf Bridge, in Germany, with a navigation span of 682 ft, consists of a single-cell box girder with a top flange of 43.3 ft, including 10-ft-wide overhangs. This design was made possible by the transverse prestressing of the top flange [Podolny and Muller, 1982].

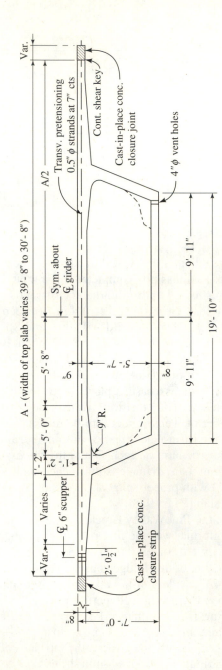

FIGURE 7.74
Transversely post-tensioned cross section of the box girder for the Biloxi Viaduct, Biloxi, Mississippi [Phipps and Spruill, 1990].

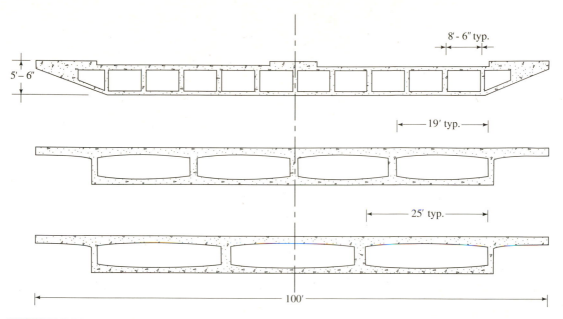

FIGURE 7.75
Alternate cross sections for the Preferential Bridge, Chicago: conventional prestressed box girder (top), transversely post-tensioned section (center and bottom) [Tedesko, 1976].

Most of the transverse post-tensioning of a deck slab is accomplished in one of two ways: either by 270-ksi $\frac{1}{2}$-in.-diameter strands or by bar tendons. Note that transversely post-tensioned deck slabs also normally have longitudinal and transverse non-prestressed reinforcement near the top and bottom of the slab. This reinforcement serves two functions: (1) It provides the necessary flexural capacity to permit removal of the section from the forms and to allow handling prior to transverse post-tensioning, and (2) it contributes to the flexural capacity of the slab at the ultimate conditions.

FIGURE 7.76
$2\frac{3}{4} \times \frac{3}{4}$ flat ducts for four-strand tendons [PTI, 1978].

An important design consideration for transverse post-tensioning of the deck slab is the transverse elastic shortening of the deck slab, which generates additional transverse moments and stresses. The lateral bending of the web caused by transverse post-tensioning sets up fixed-end moments that are required to be distributed throughout the transverse frame [PTI/PCI, 1978]. An analysis of this problem is discussed by Leonhardt and Lipproth [1970]. The strength of concrete slabs prestressed in two directions is discussed in several references [Fressynet, 1951; Rogers, 1952; Scordelis, Samarzich, and Pirtz, 1960; Scordelis, Pister, and Lin, 1956; Lin, Scordelis, and Itaya, 1959; Hemakon, 1975].

There is growing recognition of the advantages of transverse post-tensioning to establish continuity between adjoining edges of flanged girders such as precast, pretensioned single-T, and double-T girders. Strands or bars are used in post-tensioning to provide a more positive lateral tie than that in other types of connectors. The prestressing tendons are usually located at about $4\frac{1}{2}$-ft centers at mid-depth of the connection, and they are stressed to produce a compressive stress of 75 psi across the joints.

Shahawy and Issa [1992] conducted limited laboratory tests on a simply supported half-scale bridge model with three double-Ts joined together by simple V-joints and transversely post-tensioned. Their study concluded that (1) an average effective post-tensioning of 150 psi across the longitudinal joints between the double-Ts results in monolithic behavior and provides punching shear resistance similar to that of a cast-in-place concrete slab in a multigirder bridge, (2) an average transverse post-tensioning value of 300 psi in the end zone helps to strengthen the free end of the slab and eliminates the need for diaphragms, and (3) a transverse effective prestress of 150 psi appears to have potential for providing adequate fatigue life of the longitudinal joints.

Results of tests on two identical 60-ft-long, 30-ft-wide simple-span bridges, the Texas Street Bridge and the Gains Street Bridge in Tallahassee, Florida, are reported by Shahawy and Issa [1992]. These bridges, built from precast prestressed $85\frac{1}{2}$-in.-wide double-Ts that were post-tensioned with 270-ksi $\frac{1}{2}$-in.-diameter strands spaced at 54 in. o.c. (Fig. 7.19), *had no intermediate or end diaphragms,* a key feature that indicates additional savings in cost and construction time. The V-joints between the adjacent flanges of double-Ts were filled with nonshrink grout designed to attain a strength of 6500 psi in five days. The strands were then stressed with an initial prestressing force of 29 kips per strand, to result in an effective transverse post-tensioning stress of 200 psi. The tests concluded that "transverse post-tensioning transformed the separate slab of each beam into a large continuous slab which behaves very similar to cast-in-place construction" [Shahawy and Issa, 1992]. Satisfactory fatigue strength of the longitudinal V-joints between the flanges of adjacent double-T girders is reported by Arokiasamy et al. [1991]. Based on satisfactory results from these tests, several bridges using this system have been built in the state of Florida.

Transverse prestressing of decks is more common in segmentally constructed bridges than in other bridge types. Its potential, only sparingly realized in the past, is being increasingly exploited in the construction of segmental bridges, and the practice is also recommended by AASHTO 9.7.3.2 [AASHTO, 1992].

An extensive experimental and analytical study, jointly sponsored by the Texas State Department of Highways and Public Transportation and the Federal Highway Administration, was conducted at the University of Texas at Austin in the mid-1980s to develop criteria for the design of durable bridge decks [Poston, Carrasquillo, and

Breen, 1985, 1987, 1989; Poston et al., 1988]. The study's suggested specifications, provisions, and examples are reported by Poston, Breen, and Carrasquillo [1989]. It had been claimed that a transversely prestressed bridge deck designed in accordance with these specifications would be free of cracks in the *longitudinal* direction, thus eliminating one likely mechanism by which freeze-thaw deterioration of concrete and the corrosion of reinforcement take place. Ironically, the Texas bridge decks were developing cracks primarily in the *transverse* direction; thus transverse prestressing would hardly be beneficial.

To solve this problem, the study also evaluated the minimum levels of longitudinal deck prestressing required to minimize transverse cracking. In 1986, a trial transversely post-tensioned slab-and-girder bridge was built at LaGrange, Texas, for a field study, using single-strand unbonded tendons. This experiment revealed that (1) the construction process for this type of deck was both time- and labor-intensive, (2) the placement tolerances required for post-tensioned strands to produce the desired level of precompression in the deck were too great to be achieved in the field with typical construction practices, and (3) increased construction cost and complexity outweighed the potential benefit of increased deck durability. Consequently, further work on transverse post-tensioning of decks was abandoned.

In Japan, unlike in the United States, most precast pretensioned girder bridges are built as noncomposite structures. Transversely post-tensioned cast-in-place slab and diaphragms are required for all these bridges in order to produce a more durable bridge deck system and a more efficient load distribution. In both the pretensioned and post-tensioned T-girders, the basic spacing of transverse post-tensioning is 20 in. The prestressing steel is positioned in the slab such that the eccentricity at the midspan of the slab is zero or downward, and the eccentricity at the negative moment section is upward because of the change in the slab thickness. Figure 7.77 shows details of the Japanese practice of transverse post-tensioning for a pretensioned T-girder bridge [Yamane, Tadros, and Arumugasaamy, 1994].

No specifics are given in the AASHTO specifications [1992] for the transverse prestressing of decks. However, the potential advantage of transverse prestressing in minimizing the longitudinal cracking of the deck is recognized by ACI Code 318-95, Sec. 7.12.3, which recommends that prestressing tendons used for shrinkage and temperature reinforcement be proportioned to provide a minimum average compressive stress of 100 psi on the gross area using effective prestress after losses. The tendon spacing is not to exceed 6 ft. However, when the tendon spacing exceeds 54 in., additional bonded shrinkage and temperature reinforcement is to be provided between the tendons at slab edges extending from the slab edge for a distance equal to the tendon spacing.

7.9
CONTINUITY IN PRESTRESSED CONCRETE BRIDGES

7.9.1 General Considerations

In the United States, building bridges with precast pretensioned concrete girders evolved following the construction of Philadelphia's famed cast-in-place, post-tensioned Walnut Lane Memorial Bridge in 1950. The main factors in the evolution

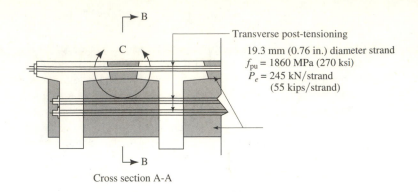

Transverse post-tensioning
19.3 mm (0.76 in.) diameter strand
f_{pu} = 1860 MPa (270 ksi)
P_e = 245 kN/strand
(55 kips/strand)

Cross section A-A

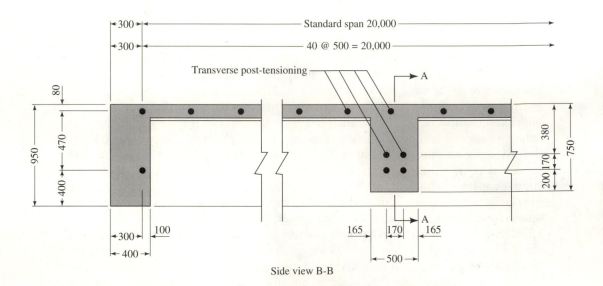

Side view B-B

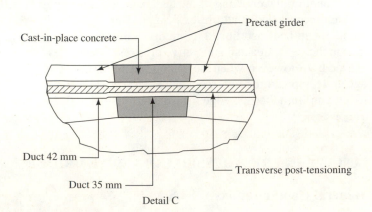

Detail C

FIGURE 7.77
Typical transverse post-tensioning scheme for a pretensioned T-girder bridge, Japan [Yamane, Tadros, and Arumugasaamy, 1994].

and the subsequent rapid growth of this method were the inherent economies and the high level of quality control achievable with plant-produced members. As a result, during the 1950s and early 1960s, the trend in the United States was to build multispan bridges with precast pretensioned concrete girders for spans up to 100 ft, and the advantages of continuous cast-in-place bridges were abandoned in favor of the simpler constructability offered by prefabricated standardized units [Anderson, 1973; Podolny and Muller, 1982]. Common highway overpass structures consisted of three or four short-span superstructures.

In these multispan bridges, however, the presence of piers, which served as intermediate supports near the shoulders or in the middle of a highway or a waterway, was soon recognized as a safety hazard. This concern was echoed in the AASHTO Traffic Safety Committee report in 1967, which called for the "adoption and use of two-span bridges for overpass crossings in divided highways ... to eliminate the bridge piers normally placed adjacent to the shoulders" [AASHTO, 1967]. This led to a trend in constructing two-span grade separation structures with longer spans. This type of structure is desirable and aesthetically superior because it creates a more open effect for better visibility, and it reduces the hazard to traffic safety by reducing the number of supporting substructure units [AASHTO 1967; Leonhardt, 1984]. The increased roadwidths of today's interstate highways demand grade-separation structures with two, three, or four spans with a total length of 180 ft or longer. Longer-span bridges measuring 300 ft or longer are required over rivers and waterways. Other factors that contributed to the desirability of building continuous bridges are the problems and the associated costs of maintaining the expansion joints between the two adjacent simple spans. As a result, continuity is almost always employed for bridges longer than one span and is usually provided for bridges with four spans or more. The current practice is to stretch out the length for continuity as far as possible, even around horizontal curves [Gerwick, 1993].

The AASHTO–PCI I-girder bridges became the system of choice for engineers, but it soon became apparent that transportability was seriously limited by the girder length and weight required for longer spans. These concerns prompted the Prestressed Concrete Institute to suggest building simple spans up to 140 ft, and continuous spans up to 180 ft, from precast girders up to 80 ft long by *splicing* [PCI, 1968]. Use of extended abutments (Fig. 7.78, top) or inclined or haunched piers (Fig. 7.78, bottom) was suggested for achieving longer spans [Anon, 1967b]. Figure 7.78 (bottom) illustrates a scheme used for the 231-ft long Hobbema Bridge in Alberta, British Columbia, Canada. The center portion of this bridge consists of a cast-in-place reinforced concrete frame with outward-sloping legs that create a stable center support. The drop-in segments are supported on the abutments and the cantilevered ends of this frame; this reduces the end-span lengths by 29 ft. Although the superstructure of this bridge consists of precast channel girder sections, the I-girders or box girders could also have been used. A similar scheme was also used for the 242-ft-long Adrossan Overpass (also built with channel girder sections) in Alberta, except the central frame was also built by post-tensioning precast units [Ragan, 1969].

The central frame can have many graceful and elegant configurations, limited only by the engineers' creativity and imagination. The piers can be V-shaped (also referred to as *Morandi column* [Leonhardt, 1984], X-shaped, or Y-shaped (Fig. 7.79), which are all aesthetically pleasing [Lin, Kulka, and Yang, 1969; Leonhardt, 1984; Gerwick,

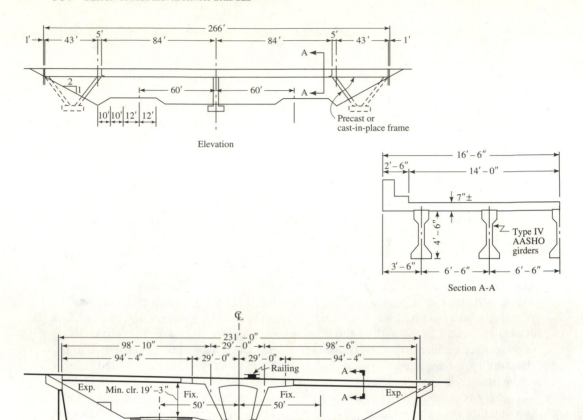

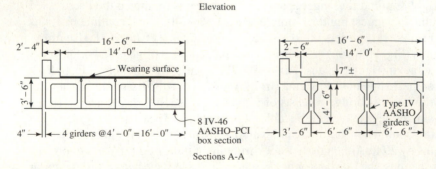

FIGURE 7.78
Schemes for achieving longer spans for prestressed concrete bridges: extended abutments (top), median frame with inclined legs supporting the drop-in girders (bottom) [PCI, 1967].

FIGURE 7.79
Configurations of aesthetically pleasing interior supports for continuous prestressed concrete bridges:
(*a*) V-shaped piers, (*b*) X-shaped piers.

FIGURE 7.79 (continued)
Configurations of aesthetically pleasing interior supports for continuous
prestressed concrete bridges: (*c*) Y-shaped piers [Leonhardt, 1984], and
(*d*) Y-shaped piers for the Alsea River Bridge, Oregon [Gerwick, 1993].

1993]. The V portion (the top of the Y) of these piers carries the pier-segment cantilevering on both sides to support the drop-in beam segments.

Building increasingly longer-span-bridges at low initial cost is a goal that engineers have continued to pursue. In addition to being a challenging task, there are many
advantages to building multispan continuous bridges instead of one or several single-
span simply supported bridges for the same total span length. Construction techniques
for building continuous spans depend on various factors, mainly the site conditions,
the span lengths, and the available equipment [Lin and Gerwick, 1969; Lundgren and
Hansen, 1969; Muller, 1969; Gerwick, 1993]. A discussion on the advantages and disadvantages of continuous bridges is presented in several texts on design of prestressed

concrete structures referenced in earlier paragraphs. A summary of these advantages and disadvantages follows:

Advantages

1. Long-span continuous bridges result in the elimination of deck joints that have the potential for long-term maintenance problems.

   Joints and bearings are costly to buy and install. With time, they allow water and salt to leak down on to the superstructure and the pier caps below, causing costly maintenance problems. This has led to a general trend, and in some cases, to regular state highway department practices, to design bridges as continuous structures from end to end. No intermediate joints are introduced in the bridge deck other than the cold joints required for construction. This applies to both longitudinal and transverse joints. Concrete superstructures up to 800 ft and sometimes longer are built with no joints, not even at the abutments. When expansion joints are necessary, they are generally provided only at abutments. For example, the multispan 2800-ft-long Island Bridge in Kingsport, Tennessee, is continuous and jointless, with joints only at the abutments [Loveall, 1985]. (This topic is discussed in detail in Chapter 3, Section 3.11.)
2. Post-tensioning, when used to develop continuity, leads to the virtual elimination of cracking in decks, thus enhancing the durability of decks.
3. Continuous spans satisfy the safety requirements imposed by federal highway regulations that dictate the elimination of piers adjacent to roadway shoulders at overpasses, as shown in Fig. 7.80.

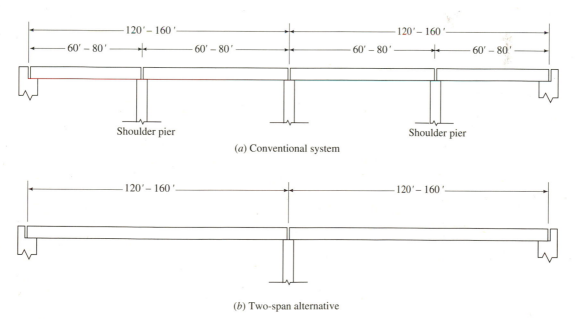

(a) Conventional system

(b) Two-span alternative

FIGURE 7.80
Conventional and alternative highway overpass bridges [Abdel-Karim and Tadros, 1992b].

4. Longer spans, made possible by continuity, require fewer piers and are thus more economical to construct than conventional bridge systems that comprise two or more simple spans and require a greater number of piers. Continuous superstructures are also lighter, leading to a lighter substructure and consequent cost savings [Lin and Gerwick, 1969].

5. For bridges over waterways, AASHTO [1991] dictates that all river piers be designed for ship or barge impact loads, a requirement that leads to costly designs. Longer-span and continuous bridges reduce the number of piers subject to these impact loads, resulting in cost savings.

6. Moments are smaller in continuous beams than in simple beams of the same span length. As a result, continuous beams are shallower, and hence lighter, than those required for simple spans of the same length. The shallower beams require less material, less prestressing force, and hence are comparatively cheaper.

7. In earthquake-prone areas, the lower weight of the superstructure is particularly important in reducing the resulting lateral loads that the structure must resist [Lount, 1969]. Cast-in-place continuous prestressed concrete structures, such as the hollow box girder bridges commonly built in California and other Western States, continue to be the most economical and the most aesthetic methods of construction for longer-span intermediate-sized bridges.

8. Continuity allows redistribution of stresses under overload conditions, which ensures a higher margin of safety against collapse.

9. Deflections are smaller in continuous beams than in comparable simple spans. Hence, for continuous beams, smaller depth is sufficient not only for strength but also for rigidity.

10. Continuity provides better dynamic response. Joint rigidity in continuous frames (when girders are made continuous with columns) provides an important mechanism to resist horizontal loads such as those induced by wind, blast, or earthquakes [Nilson, 1978].

11. In continuous beams, several spans can be prestressed with the same continuous tendon (i.e., the same tendons can be used to resist both positive and negative moments) by providing an undulating profile; only two anchorages per tendon are required for this, resulting in savings in material and labor costs.

12. Cast-in-place continuous prestressed concrete hollow box girder bridges, rigid frames, and slabs all have longer economical span ranges.

13. Continuous spans, because of improved span-depth ratio, are relatively slender and, hence, graceful and aesthetically superior to the simple-span structures [Leonhardt, 1984].

14. Cast-in-place continuous structures are the most economical and the most aesthetic solutions for bridges on sharp skew crossings and at interchanges with complicated geometrics, including bridges on curves.

Disadvantages

1. In continuous girders, the prestressing tendons are relatively longer and follow a curved path through a large number of bends, usually parabolic, with positive eccentricity in the midspan region and negative eccentricity at the support. As a result, frictional losses are excessive.

2. Undulating tendons create practical difficulties in grouting.
3. If the girders are rigidly connected to columns (and thus creating a frame action), excessive lateral forces and moments are created in supporting columns on account of elastic shortening due to prestress.
4. Effects of secondary stresses owing to shrinkage, creep, temperature variation, and settlement of supports could be serious if not properly controlled or allowed for in design.
5. Concurrence of maximum moments and shear at the same section of the girder, which occurs over the supports of most continuous beams, may decrease the ultimate capacity of the girder.
6. The difficulty in handling moment reversals makes designing a continuous girder unappealing. Continuous girders can be subjected to serious reversal of moments if the live loads are much heavier than dead loads and if partial span loadings are considered. However, this can often be controlled by designing girders as partially prestressed.
7. In continuous beams, the maximum negative moments at supports, which are generally larger than the maximum positive moments near the midspan, may sometimes control the number of strands required for the entire beam length. However, this can be avoided either by providing a deeper section at the support or by providing additional, nonprestressed reinforcement at the support. In a simply supported beam, this situation does not arise; the beam design is controlled by the maximum positive moment that occurs at the midspan.
8. A relatively more complex design procedure, in which the secondary moments should be accounted for, is required for designing a continuous structure. However, with the advent of simpler methods, such as the load-balancing method, and by using computers, the design of continuous beams can be handled with less difficulty.
9. Suspended spans are particularly vulnerable to seismic shaking, as evidenced by the collapse of several bridges in California during the 1989 Loma Prieta and the 1994 Northridge earthquakes. Curved and skewed alignments greatly increase the span's vulnerability.

7.9.2 Methods of Achieving Continuity

In prestressed concrete superstructures, continuity is generally accomplished by post-tensioning at the site. Methods of achieving continuity, i.e., the type of tendon layout and the method of framing that should be used, in prestressed concrete superstructure construction are discussed in such references as Freyermuth [1969], O'Connor [1971], Nawy [1989], and Abdel-Karim and Tadros [1992a,b]. A brief description of these methods, illustrated by several diagrams showing typical tendon profiles for various schemes for achieving continuity, follows. Note that, in general, the tendon profile follows the deflected shape of the girder, or the moment diagram due to uniform load plotted positive downward.

Generally, two methods are used for achieving continuity, depending on the construction method used, the site conditions, the length of the adjacent spans, and the engineers' judgment and skill.

7.9.2.1 Monolithic continuity

Monolithic continuity involves *cast-in-place* construction. Usually all or most tendons are continuous throughout all or most of the spans. The principles of providing *monolithic* continuity by several methods are illustrated in Fig. 7.81. In the simple continuity scheme shown in Fig. 7.81(*a*), all spans are prismatic and cast-in-place, and continuity is provided for the full length of the girder by post-tensioning after the concrete hardens. Figure 7.81(*b*) shows a similar system, but with nonprismatic girders. Increased girder depths over the piers may be needed for providing the required shear resistance, or for architectural or aesthetic considerations. Such a scheme, however, is more costly because of the increased cost of formwork. Figure 7.81(*c*) shows a prismatic

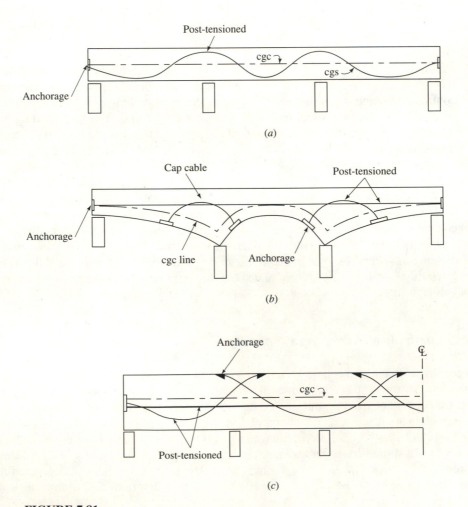

FIGURE 7.81
Tendon layout in continuous beams with monolithic continuity: (*a*) prismatic girder, (*b*) nonprismatic girder, and (*c*) prismatic girder with overlapping tendons [Nawy, 1989].

continuous girder with overlapping tendons. In all these cases, the monolithic construction provides continuity for both the dead and the live loads, a significant advantage over nonmonolithic continuity.

7.9.2.2 Nonmonolithic continuity

Nonmonolithic continuity involves *precast* pretensioned elements. By this methodology, continuity is achieved at the support sections through cast-in-place concrete (in conjunction with post-tensioning or nonprestressed reinforcement), which provides the desired level of continuity to resist superimposed dead load and the live loads. However, continuity can also be achieved for total loads, at a cost, by shoring the precast beams before placing the composite concrete topping and the continuity reinforcement [Nawy, 1989].

Various methods of achieving nonmonolithic continuity are illustrated in Fig. 7.82. A common feature of all these methods is that continuity is achieved through the cast-in-place joint between the precast pretensioned beam segments located over the piers.

In Fig. 7.82(*a*), the precast girders themselves are designed as pretensioned members to resist their own loads as well as to transport and handle stresses. The necessary duct work and anchorage system to receive the post-tensioning tendons are also cast into the girders. After erection, the duct work is coupled between the beams, and the concrete diaphragms and the deck are cast. After the cast-in-place concrete attains its required strength, the tendons are immediately stressed and anchored. The amount of post-tensioning is based on that required to develop continuity for all stages of loading, which includes the dead load of the girder as well as the superimposed loads.

Figure 7.82(*b*) shows a variation of the same basic scheme as in Fig. 7.82(*a*), but with the post-tensioning applied for the full length of the structure. The precast girders are pretensioned with only sufficient capacity to resist the positive moments due to the self-weight of the girders and the slab, as well as any other loads that may be applied or anticipated during construction but prior to the post-tensioning operation. The additional moment capacity required for the positive moments and the total negative moments is introduced by post-tensioning [Jacobson, 1969].

Figure 7.82(*c*) shows the use of couplers for providing post-tensioning continuity between *prismatic* beam segments. Figure 7.82(*d*) shows the use of nonprestressed continuity reinforcement provided in the negative moment region of the girders (over the piers). In such construction, the dead load is resisted by the simply supported precast prestressed concrete member only, while the live load and other superimposed dead loads are resisted by the composite action in the continuous girder [Freyermuth, 1969]. Figure 7.82(*e*) shows a method of providing post-tensioning continuity in *nonprismatic* beams.

Because of its relative simplicity, the method shown in Fig. 7.82(*d*) has been one of the most popular methods of developing nonmonolithic continuity. However, it is not the most efficient method because it provides for continuity for only those loads (such as live loads and superimposed loads) that are applied only after the deck hardens and acts compositely with the girders. It also suffers from the drawback that cracks develop near the top surface of the deck in the vicinity of piers due to negative continuity moments. When exposed to traffic and deicing chemicals, these cracks can promote rapid deck deterioration.

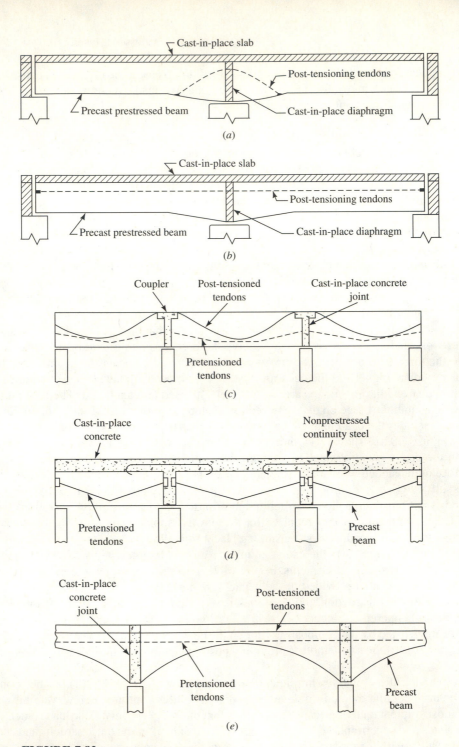

FIGURE 7.82
Methods of achieving continuity using precast pretensioned girders:
(*a*) post-tensioning in the negative-moment region of a two-span girder, (*b*) full-length post-tensioning in a two-span girder, (*c*) post-tensioning using couplers, (*d*) nonprestressed steel, and (*e*) post-tensioning in nonprismatic beams [Jacobson, 1969; Nawy, 1989].

7.9.3 New Techniques for Creating Continuity

A new technique developed by Tadros et al. at the University of Nebraska in Lincoln to create nonmonolithic continuity in precast prestressed concrete girders appears to offer significant advantages over the other methods previously described. This technique, shown in Fig. 7.83 [Tadros et al., 1993], essentially uses the scheme shown in Fig. 7.82(c). During casting, the pretensioning strands of the precast beams, depressed at the midspan and elevated at the ends, are kept extended beyond their interior ends, long enough to permit their appropriate cutting for staggered splicing.

Two methods are used to achieve the interior joint continuity (Fig. 7.83). In the first method, after the girders are erected into position, strand extensions are spliced using mechanical splices with contiguous hardware, followed by uniform tightening of all coupled strands via the slack recovery hardware. Next, the ends of the joined members are pushed outward using appropriate jacking apparatus; thus appropriate tensile forces are *simultaneously* introduced into *all* coupled strands in the joint. This step is followed by pouring of the high early-strength and low-shrinkage concrete in the joint, while the jacking apparatus still maintains the appropriate tensile forces in the spliced strands. The precompression is introduced into the joint by releasing the jacking force after the joint concrete has sufficiently hardened.

In the second method, after the girders are erected into position, appropriate brackets and spacer struts are installed at the top and bottom of girders to maintain end positions during strand tensioning. *Individual* strands are spliced and prestressed using appropriate mechanical splices, followed by casting of the joint. After sufficient hardening of joint concrete, precompression is introduced into the joint by removing spacer struts, brackets, and other temporary hardware. This method, like other methods of creating nonmonolithic continuity, provides continuity for superimposed dead loads and live loads only.

The cost-effectiveness of this methodology arises from the fact that the same pretensioning strands of the precast beam, which are depressed at the midspan, can be elevated near the supports to provide for the negative moments, resulting in lower levels of prestressing and camber, and, in turn, smaller long-term upward creep. Consequently, a very small camber (or none, in some cases) results, which leads to smoother riding characteristics of the deck, with less of a roller-coaster profile. In addition, the precompression of interior cast-in-place joint concrete (over the piers) minimizes, if not altogether eliminates, flexural cracking in the joint area, thus minimizing future costly maintenance problems. Two bridges have been built recently in Lincoln, Nebraska using this methodology—a 555-ft-long, five-span (90, 125, 125, 125, and 90 ft) continuous pedestrian and bicycle overpass and a 744-ft-long, six-span (114, 172, 172, 114, 86, and 86 ft) highway bridge. These bridges are described by Fiecenec et al. [1993].

7.9.4 Spliced I-Girder Continuous Bridges

Yet another method of developing nonmonolithic continuity is the segmental construction method, which involves jointing, or *splicing,* several precast, pretensioned beam segments by post-tensioning [Abdel-Karim and Tadros, 1992a, 1992b]. Simply

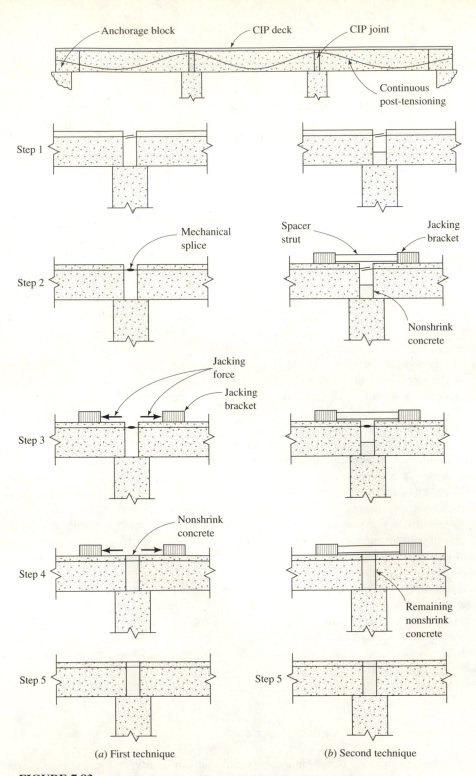

(a) First technique   (b) Second technique

FIGURE 7.83
A new method of providing nonmonolithic continuity in precast prestressed concrete girders developed at the University of Nebraska in Lincoln [Tadros et al., 1993].

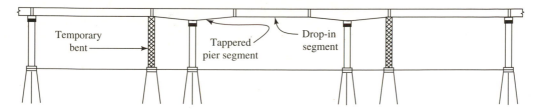

FIGURE 7.84
Principle of developing continuity by spliced-girder technique.

speaking, girder splicing is a technique in which more than one segment is spliced to produce span lengths greater than the girder segments.

In the United States, this technique evolved with the construction of the single-span East Koy Bridge in Sheldon, New York, in 1952. The technique was needed to simplify transportation and handling problems [Muller, 1969, 1975]. Each girder was cast in three segments and assembled on site. The center segment was cast first, and then the two side segments were cast directly against the center segment. Keys were provided in the joints to facilitate their site placement in the same relative position in which they were initially cast. This particular technique is generally referred to as *match-casting*. In Europe, match-casting evolved with the construction in 1962–1964 of the three-span (123, 180, and 123 ft), continuous Choisy-le-Roy Bridge over the Seine River, just east of the Orly Airport. This bridge was designed by Jean Muller and built by Enterprises Campenon Bernard. [Muller, 1969; Podolny and Muller, 1982]. The refined form of this concept has spread from this French project to all parts of the world.

Figure 7.84 illustrates the principles of this splicing technique. Essentially, it entails splicing in the field a series of girders that are simply supported between the piers and the abutment to achieve continuity. The continuity thus achieved may be likened to that of *segmental construction* of medium-span bridges, in which (usually) box girder segments are jointed together in the field to develop continuity through the joint. Continuity is achieved for the superimposed dead load and live load by full-length post-tensioning of the entire continuous girder (but not necessarily throughout the whole bridge). Continuity under the deck dead load can be achieved through casting diaphragms prior to pouring the deck [Harvey, 1986]. One significant advantage of this technique over the conventional method of providing continuity (by providing nonprestressed reinforcement in the negative-moment region) is that the deck has roughly 15 percent greater spanning capability (Fig. 7.85) [Abdel-Karim and Tadros, 1992b].

The girder segments are of two basic types: the *pier segment* and the *drop-in segment*. While the drop-in segments are usually prismatic, the pier segments may be either prismatic or nonprismatic. First, the pier segments are installed on the piers, with equal overhangs on each side supported on temporary bents. These segments are stabilized in position through transverse post-tensioning with the piers. The drop-in segments are placed next, with their ends supported on the ends of the adjacent pier segments, which are already supported on *temporary* bents. After splicing the joints between the pier segments and the drop-in segments, the temporary bents are removed.

Ideally, girder splices should be located at points of dead-load contraflexure, or at locations of small moments. This, however, may not always be possible, and splices may have to be located as dictated by site considerations. Maximum segment lengths

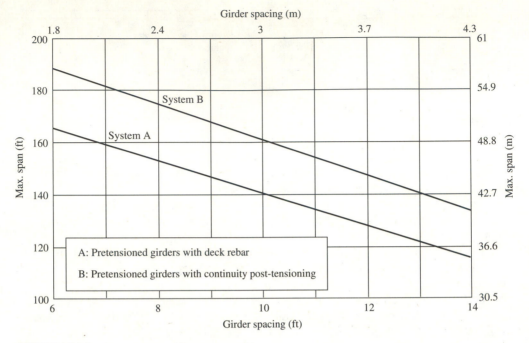

FIGURE 7.85
Span capability vs. girder spacing for the two methods used for achieving continuity [Geren and Tadros, 1994].

are usually governed by the transportation and handling constraints, accessibility at the construction site, and other site conditions. Although it is undesirable to do so, if site conditions so dictate, field splices may be located on piers where the negative moments are maximum. Design criteria and details for splices over the piers are discussed by Oesterle, Gilkin, and Larson [1989].

Occasionally, splicing between the adjacent ends of two girders may not be feasible for such reasons as high costs of the temporary supports, site limitations (i.e., construction over rivers or existing traffic lanes), etc. In such cases, although the desired lengths of side spans may be achieved by splicing, the drop-in ends may be left unspliced by forming a hinge. In such a case, the drop-in segment would simply act as a suspended span (simple span) between the cantilevered ends of the pier segments. An example of such a bridge is the Sebastian Inlet Bridge in Brevard County, Florida, built in 1964 (Fig. 7.86) [PCI, 1967b; PCA, 1978a].

Finally, note that it is possible to have *different* types of girders for the drop-in segments and the pier segments for the same bridge, as dictated by their individual span requirements during and after construction. Figure 7.87 shows the elevation and cross sections of the girders for the two types of segments for the three-span, 389-ft-long Cascade Orchards Bridge in Levanworth, Washington, completed in October 1965. The central drop-in 110-ft-long precast segments consist of prismatic I-girders, whereas the end-span girders, with anchor spans (cantilevered arms) of 32.5 ft each, consist of cast-in-place, nonprismatic box sections [Grant and Clark, 1969]. Different types of girders have also been used for the five-span (65, 160, 120, 160, and 75 ft), 580-ft-long

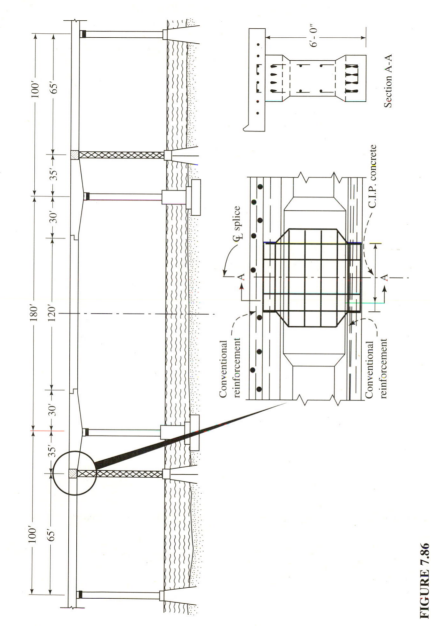

FIGURE 7.86
The Sebastian Inlet Bridge, Florida, with spliced girders in the side spans and a suspended center span [PCI, 1967].

597

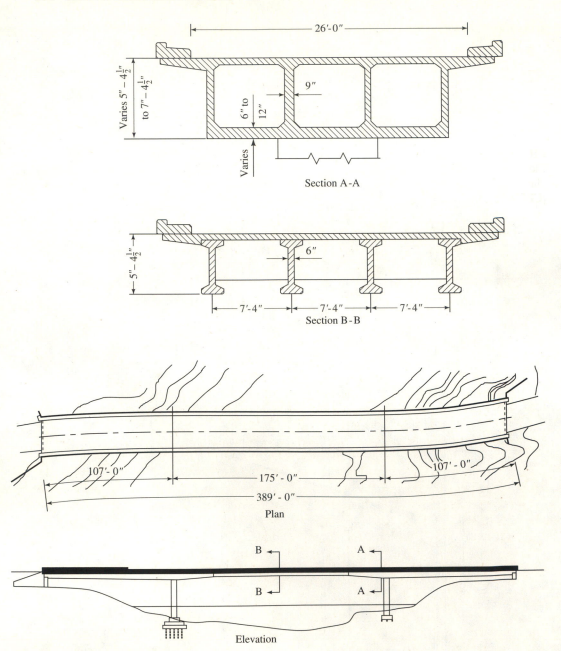

FIGURE 7.87
Plan, elevation, and sections of the Cascade Orchards Bridge in Levanworth, Washington, with different types of girders in the drop-in span and the side spans [Grant and Clark, 1969].

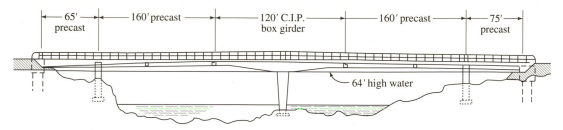

FIGURE 7.88

Elevation of the Umpqua River Bridge, near Sutherlin, Oregon. The pier segment consists of the cast-in-place, nonprismatic box girder, whereas the drop-in segments of the side spans consist of precast I-girders [CE, 1972].

Umpqua Bridge near Sutherlin, Oregon. The 120-ft-long central pier segment consists of a cast-in-place nonprismatic box girder, whereas the 160-ft-long side span girders consist of 80-ft-long spliced precast I-girders (Fig. 7.88) [PCI Br. Bull., 1970; CE, 1972]. Obviously, the webs of the I- and the box girders in such cases must be aligned for placement of ducts for post-tensioning. After the drop-segments are erected, they are integrated into a single structural unit by field post-tensioning with the pier or with the supporting segments.

The splicing technique can be illustrated by several examples reported in the literature. Although ideally suited for continuous bridges, this splicing technique can also be used for building longer-span simple-span bridges, such as the 164-ft-span Esker Overhead in northwestern British Columbia, Canada, completed in September 1990 by splicing three equal beam segments. Figure 7.89 shows various stages of erection in the construction process of this bridge [Mills, Chow, and Marshall, 1991].

A detailed discussion of this methodology, including a survey (see Appendix C, Table C.3) and brief descriptions and salient features of several bridges built by this technique, is presented by Abdel-Karim and Tadros [1992b]. This discussion is summarized in Abdel-Karim and Tadros [1992a]. This technique has been found feasible for building continuous bridges by splicing *I-girder* segments in the range of 150 to 280 ft; spliced girders spanning 263 ft have been already built. The technique has been developed only for I-girders since they are preferred by most engineers; when I-girders are used, the deck slab can be replaced more easily after it reaches its service life and without negatively affecting the girders. Figure 7.90 shows the general layout of the sharply curved, 1345-ft nine-span Annacis Channel East Bridge in British Columbia, Canada, over the Frase River, just south of Vancouver, with a main span of 233 ft and a drop-in segment of 167 ft [Marshall and Pelkey, 1986; Pierce, 1988]. This bridge was completed in 1984.

Economic superiority of the spliced-girder bridge system is well-documented in the literature [Caroland and Depp, 1990; Caroland et al., 1992; Abdel-Karim and Tadros, 1992b]. Figure 7.91 shows salient features of the 970-ft-long, five-span (one 162.25, three 218.5, and one 162.25 ft), high-level Shelby Creek Bridge over a narrow valley in eastern Kentucky, completed in December 1991. The spliced-girder method adopted for this bridge was the most economical method compared to such other alternates as a steel delta-frame girder, a steel deck truss, twin post-tensioned segmental concrete box

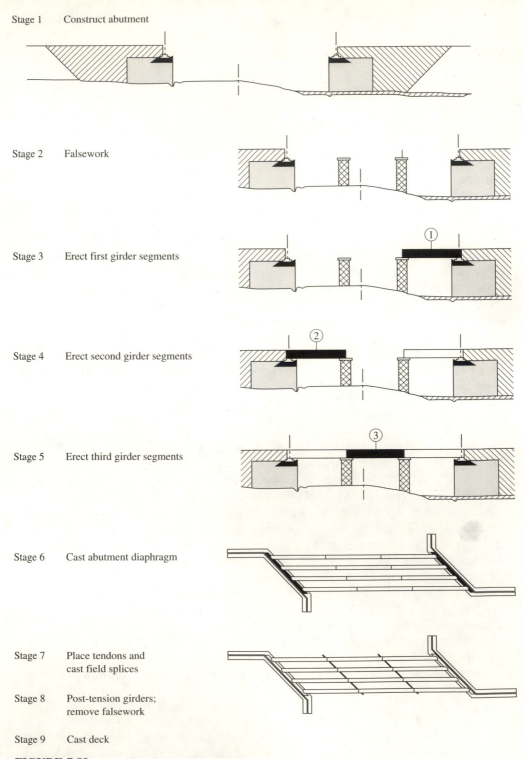

Stage 1   Construct abutment

Stage 2   Falsework

Stage 3   Erect first girder segments

Stage 4   Erect second girder segments

Stage 5   Erect third girder segments

Stage 6   Cast abutment diaphragm

Stage 7   Place tendons and
                   cast field splices

Stage 8   Post-tension girders;
                   remove falsework

Stage 9   Cast deck

FIGURE 7.89
Various stages of erection in the spliced-girder construction of the Esker Overhead in British Columbia, Canada [Mills, Chow, and Marshall, 1991].

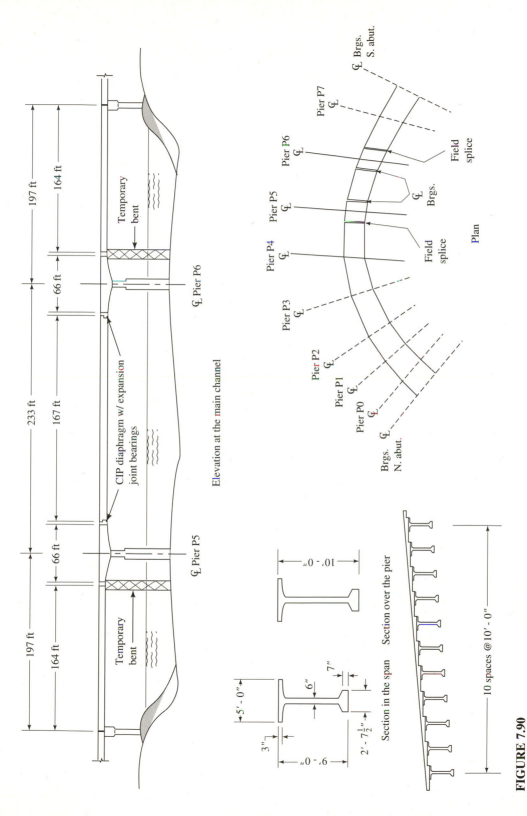

FIGURE 7.90
Annacis Channel East Bridge, British Columbia, Canada [Abdel-Karim and Tadros, 1992b].

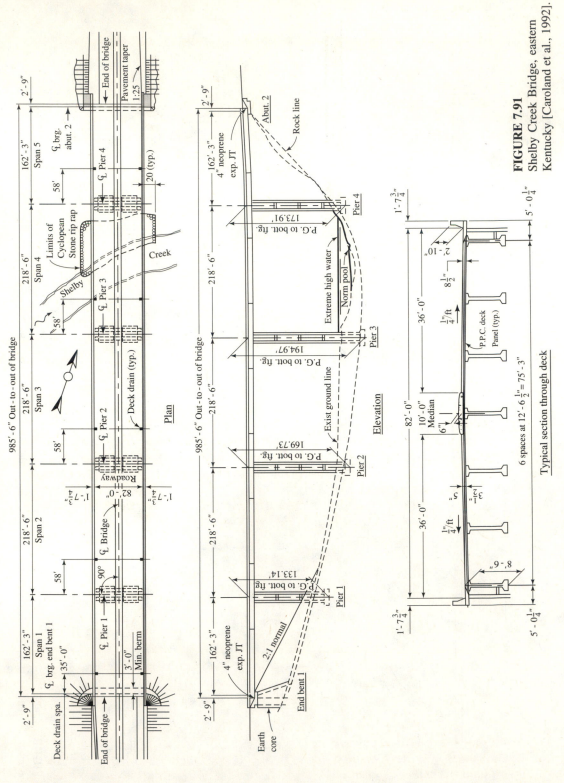

FIGURE 7.91
Shelby Creek Bridge, eastern Kentucky [Caroland et al., 1992].

602

girders, and a continuous composite welded-steel plate girder using load factor design. The spliced-girder technique cost about $417,000 less than the second low bid for the continuous composite welded steel plate girder [Caroland et al., 1992].

Similarly, the spliced-girder option was the most economical and feasible solution for the 540-ft-long, five-span (85, 105, 160, 105, and 85 ft) Salt River Bridge in Fort Knox, Kentucky, designed in 1987 for military loading (a convoy of 100-ton tanks, 2.4 to 2.7 times as heavy as the AASHTO HS20 truck loading). The four alternates for this bridge were a five-span, V-strut, post-tensioned concrete, segmental I-beam; a three-span, continuous, composite-steel plate girder; a three-span, post-tensioned concrete, segmental box beam; and a six-span prestressed concrete, continuous I-beam bridge [Caroland and Depp, 1990].

Details of several other bridges built by this technique are reported in the literature [PCA, 1978b; PCIJ, 1988; Pierce, 1988; Janssen, 1989; Bakht et al., 1990; Caroland and Depp, 1990; Janssen and Spans, 1994].

7.10
OPTIMIZATION OF PRECAST PRESTRESSED CONCRETE BRIDGE SYSTEMS

An engineer's cherished goal is to develop an optimal solution for the structural design under consideration, and bridges are no exception to this general philosophy. The selection of a particular superstructure type depends on several factors, such as its feasibility, its span capability, the limitation of depth-to-span ratio, the system availability from precasters or suppliers, its performance history, the engineer's own experience and preferences (e.g., prestressed concrete vs. steel), regional trends, construction time constraints, aesthetics, and cost. Within these constraints, the type of superstructure selected may not necessarily reflect an optimum design. Satisfied with the proven success of some well-established specific types of superstructure systems, many engineers prefer to continue to use those systems and are reluctant to use new and innovative solutions, their superiority notwithstanding. Compounding this problem is the fact that the fabricators, who have invested in their specific systems, are just as reluctant to innovate, produce, and supply new systems. In most cases, therefore, the designs prepared by the engineers may not be the optimum solutions.

According to Cohn and Dinovitzer [1994], some 150 books and 2500 papers have been published since 1960 on various topics related to structural optimization. However, documentation in a comprehensive catalog of examples [Cohn and Dinovitzer, 1994], shows that, in practice, very little work has been done in the area of optimizing prestressed concrete superstructures. The answer to the question of selecting the best system for a given project has always been elusive. Key considerations that may play a major role in the selection of the "best system" are to rely on existing practices and accumulated experience, or to minimize costs under the specific conditions of the project.

In general, the structural problems of optimal design may be identified by (a) uncertainty consideration (deterministic or probabilistic), (b) design variables, such as materials, geometry, and loading, and (c) problem formulation, which involves objectives, limit states, and constraints [Cohn and Dinovitzer, 1994]. In most cases involving bridge superstructures, the general approach appears to be optimizing girders for an arbitrarily selected superstructure system rather than optimization of the entire system.

Lounis and Cohn [1993] have addressed the optimization-specific question as follows:

> What is the optimal prestressed concrete stringer system for given bridge length, width, traffic loading, and standard provisions? Specifically, what are the longitudinal and transverse configurations that result in minimum superstructure cost, and what are the corresponding prestressed and nonprestressed reinforcements?

They define the optimal bridge superstructure as "one of minimum total cost, using standardized girder sections and traffic loading." In this context, they identify three levels of optimization:

Level 1, member optimization. Member optimization is the optimization of girder cross sections of specific structure types. Examples in this category follow:

- Optimization of concrete slabs [Kirsch, 1973]
- Single-span steel girders [Wills, 1973; Mafi and West, 1986]
- Single-span prestressed concrete girders [Torres, Brotchie, and Cornell, 1966; Naaman, 1972; Rabbat and Russell, 1982a; Cohn and Mac Rae, 1984]
- Single-span box girders [Tempelman and Winterbottom, 1975]
- Single-span multibeam bridges [Fereig, 1994]
- Multispan simple girders [Aguilar, Movassaghi, and Brewer, 1973; Bond, 1975]
- Continuous prestressed concrete box girders [Aziz and Edwards, 1966; Bond, 1975, 1983]
- Frame bridges [Adin, Cohn, and Pinto, 1979]

Level 2, configuration or layout optimization. This involves determining the best combination of longitudinal and transverse member arrangement within a given bridge system. Specific items considered include the number of spans, the position of intermediate supports, the type of members—simply supported or continuous, etc. Relatively much less work has been done on this type of optimization [Aziz and Edwards, 1966; Bond, 1975].

Level 3, system optimization. This involves overall features of the structural system. Various parameters include materials, structural type and configuration, member cross-section and span lengths, combined longitudinal and transverse member arrangement, etc. Only a few attempts have been made to address this problem, including studies on medium two-span continuous prestressed concrete bridge systems [Kulka and Lin, 1982, 1984], short simple-span bridge systems [Mafi and West, 1986], the surface effect of vehicles [Gellatly and Dupree, 1976], tall building systems [McDermott, Abrams, and Cohn, 1972a,b], and general cost considerations [Lounis and Cohn, 1992; Scott, 1983; Geren, Abdel-Karim, and Tadros, 1992].

A discussion on all three levels of optimization for a structural system that uses precast, prestressed girders is presented in Lounis and Cohn [1993]. In practice, a $7\frac{1}{2}$-in. by $8\frac{1}{2}$-in.-thick concrete slab is arbitrarily selected, and the spacing of longitudinal girders is adjusted so that the selected slab is sufficiently thick as a continuous element to span the girders. This approach is used in several examples that follow.

7.11
PRINCIPLES OF PRESTRESSED CONCRETE DESIGN

7.11.1 General Considerations

The term "prestressing" refers to a process of imposing a state of stress on a structural body prior to its placement in service, to enhance its load-carrying capacity and service performance. In concrete, this process is used to develop a state of precompression through stretched tendons. The tendons may be high-strength steel wire, strands made of high-strength steel wire, or high-strength alloy bars. As described in Chapter 2, carbon-, aramid-, and alkali-resistant glass tendons have also been used experimentally.

The two forms of prestressing commonly used are pretensioning and post-tensioning. The prefixes "pre" and "post" refer to the fabrication phase of the concrete member when the tendons are stressed (or stretched). In *pretensioned* concrete members, the tendons are stretched and anchored to abutments *before concrete is poured*. After the concrete has hardened and gained a substantial portion of its ultimate strength, known as the release strength, the tendons are released, transferring stresses to the concrete. Post-tensioning is the process of imposing prestress by stressing and anchoring tendons against *already hardened concrete*. In the most common construction practice, ducts are formed in the body of an otherwise-reinforced concrete member by means of thin-walled, flexible, semirigid or rigid sheaths. After the concrete hardens to sufficient strength, the tendons are inserted and stretched by jacking. Then wedges are seated to transfer the load from the jacks to the anchors at the ends of the concrete member. Pretensioning is most commonly applied to plant-produced concrete elements, whereas post-tensioning is most commonly applied to cast-in-place concrete members. Post-tensioning is also applied to precast segments of a concrete member. These segments may be plant-produced or cast at site and then post-tensioned in position. For example, segmental bridges are built by post-tensioning precast segments or by using a combination of precast and cast-in-place segments.

The tendons may be classified as *bonded* or *unbonded*. *Bonded* tendons refer to tendons that are substantially bonded to the concrete, by direct contact, throughout their entire length. Pretensioned tendons are almost always bonded. Post-tensioned tendons passing though ducts that are grouted are also classified as bonded. However, in some cases of post-tensioned tendons, the force is applied only at the anchorages—such tendons are *unbonded*. Bond along the length of tendons is intentionally prevented in several ways. Tendons may be coated with a corrosion-resistant grease and then encased in plastic sheaths. Alternatively, when the post-tensioned tendons are placed in ducts, the ducts may be filled with grease.

7.11.2 Flexural Analysis

7.11.2.1 Flexural strength

Flexural analysis of prestressed members differs significantly from that of reinforced concrete members because it is assumed that the presence of prestressing force keeps the member uncracked. Consequently, it is further assumed that the member can be analyzed as homogeneous and elastic under service loads, that all assumptions of simple bending theory apply, and that the following Navier's formula can be applied:

$$\frac{M}{I} = \frac{f}{y} = \frac{E}{R} \tag{7.15}$$

where R is the radius of curvature of the bent beam.

A prestressing force, P, applied at the centroid of the beam's cross section will introduce a uniform compressive stress across its entire depth. However, to take full advantage of the prestressing force, it is generally applied eccentrically, say, with an eccentricity, e, with the result that the beam is also subjected to a moment, Pe, in addition to the compressive stress. The presence of this moment causes tension and compression on the opposite faces of the beam, resulting in a linearly varying (generally compressive) stress distribution across the beams's cross section. The net stresses in a transversely loaded prestressed concrete beam can be calculated, treating the beam as a beam-column, by the principle of superposition:

Net flexural stress = stress due to transversely applied loads
    + stress due to prestressing force

The stress due to the transverse loads can be calculated by the simple flexure formula:

$$f = \frac{My}{I} = \frac{M}{S} \tag{7.16}$$

where S is the section modulus of the beam.

As a matter of general convention, when the prestressing force is located below the centroid of the beam, the eccentricity is considered to be *positive;* if this force is located above the centroid, it is *negative*. A prestressing force, P, with a positive eccentricity, e, introduces in the beam a combination of axial compressive force (equal to P) and a negative moment ($M = Pe$) that causes tensile stresses in the top fibers and compressive stresses in the bottom fibers. In the following discussion, compressive and tensile stresses are assigned positive and negative signs, respectively. Subscripts t and b denote the top and the bottom fibers of the cross section. Substituting into Eq. 7.16, we obtain

$$f_t = \frac{P}{A} - \left(\frac{Pe}{S_t}\right)$$
$$= \frac{P}{A}\left[1 - \frac{eA}{S_t}\right] \tag{7.17}$$

$$f_b = \frac{P}{A} + \left(\frac{Pe}{S_b}\right)$$
$$= \frac{P}{A}\left[1 + \frac{eA}{S_b}\right] \tag{7.18}$$

where f_t = stress in the top fibers
   f_b = stress in the bottom fibers
   A = cross-sectional area of beam
   S_t = section modulus for the top fibers
   S_b = section modulus for the bottom fibers

Equation 7.17 shows that, depending on the value of the eccentricity, e, of the pre-stressing force, the top fiber stress, f_t, can be compressive or tensile. Generally, all codes such as AASHTO, ACI, CEB–FIP, etc. specify the maximum allowable *tensile* stress under the service load. It is therefore important to define the limiting eccentricity that, when prestressing force is acting alone, will not cause any tensile stress in the cross section. The limiting condition of no tensile stress in the top fibers can be established by equating the right side of Eq. 7.17 to zero. Thus,

$$\frac{P}{A}\left(1 - \frac{eA}{S_t}\right) = 0 \tag{7.19}$$

Since P/A cannot be zero, the parenthetical quantity in Eq. 7.19 must be zero:

$$e = \frac{S_t}{A} = k_t \tag{7.20}$$

Similarly, the limiting condition of no tensile stress in the bottom fibers, when prestressing force is acting alone, can be established by equating the right side of Eq. 7.18 to zero. Thus

$$e = -\frac{S_b}{A} = -k_b \tag{7.21}$$

The minus sign in Eq. 7.21 simply means that the eccentricity e is measured upward from the centroid of the concrete cross section.

Quantities k_t and k_b are defined as

$k_t = S_b/A$ = kern distances for the top fibers of the beam
$k_b = S_t/A$ = kern distances for the bottom fibers of the beam

The *kern distances* are the limiting values of eccentricities that define an envelope, also known as the *kern section,* within which the prestressing force, acting alone, can be applied without causing tension in the extreme fibers of a rectangular beam. This does not imply that the prestressing force must remain in the kern section. However, it is convenient to use these quantities as reference points in design calculations. Introducing k_b and k_t in Eqs. 7.17 and 7.18, respectively, we obtain

$$f_t = \frac{P}{A}\left(1 - \frac{e}{k_b}\right) \tag{7.22}$$

$$f_b = \frac{P}{A}\left(1 + \frac{e}{k_t}\right) \tag{7.23}$$

To obtain total stresses, the stresses due to the prestressing force should be algebraically added to those due to loads. For example, at the midspan, where the eccentricity of the prestressing force is positive, the top and bottom fiber stresses are

$$f_{t,\text{final}} = \frac{M_D}{S_t} + \frac{M_L}{S_t} + \frac{P}{A}\left(1 - \frac{e}{k_t}\right) \tag{7.24}$$

$$f_{b,\text{final}} = -\frac{M_D}{S_b} - \frac{M_L}{S_b} + \frac{P}{A}\left(1 + \frac{e}{k_t}\right) \tag{7.25}$$

The minus sign in Eq. 7.25 indicates tensile stresses in the bottom fibers due to applied dead and live loads.

The stresses given by Eqs. 7.24 and 7.25 should not exceed the allowable stresses for an acceptable design. Stresses at any other section in the beam can be similarly checked by these equations. Note that at the ends of a *simple* beam, the moment due to applied loads is zero, and the final stresses would exist only as a result of the prestressing force, which may be concentric or eccentric. However, at an interior support of a *continuous* beam, the moment due to the applied loads would be negative and, hence, the eccentricity would also be negative to introduce compressive stresses in the top fibers in order to counter the tensile stresses generated by the negative moment.

Although the computation of stresses in a prestressed concrete beam due to any loading conditions is simple and straightforward, the stresses do need to be computed at various stages of loading because of losses in prestress that occur over time. Typically, when a prestressing force, P_i, is applied to a beam initially (hence, it is known as the *initial prestressing force*), the net stresses are those due to the dead load of the beam and the initial prestressing force. At this initial stage, the strength of concrete is f'_{ci}, known as the *initial compressive strength,* or the strength at release, which is smaller than the 28-day compressive strength, f'_c. At this stage, the loading should be checked to ensure stresses are within the allowable limits. When live loads are applied, the losses in prestress are assumed to have already taken place, leading to a reduction in the value of the initial prestressing force. This reduced prestressing force is known as the *effective prestress*, P_e. Under the action of the live load, then, the final stresses present are those due to dead and live loads and those due to the effective stress, P_e.

The principles of determining the flexural strength of a prestressed concrete beam are similar to those used in determining that of a reinforced concrete beam, as discussed in Chapter 6. The applicable formulas are covered in AASHTO 9.17 [AASHTO, 1992]. For a rectangular section with prestressing steel only, the depth of the compression block, a, is obtained from Fig. 7.92: Since $C = 0.85 f'_c ba$ and $T = A_{ps} f_{ps}$, we have, assuming $f_{ps} = f^*_{su}$,

$$a = \frac{A^*_s f^*_{su}}{0.85 f'_c b} \tag{7.26}$$

The permitted moment capacity, or the design strength, ϕM_n, should be greater than the factored design moment (i.e., the moment due to all loads):

$$\phi M_n = \phi \left[A^*_s f^*_{su} d \left\{ 1 - 0.6 \left(p^* \frac{f^*_{su}}{f'_c} \right) \right\} \right] \tag{7.27}$$

where M_n = nominal moment capacity of beam
     A^*_s = area of prestressing steel
     f^*_{su} = average stress in prestressing steel at the ultimate load
     f'_c = compressive strength of concrete
     p^* = A^*_s/bd = ratio of prestressing steel to concrete section
     ϕ = strength reduction factor

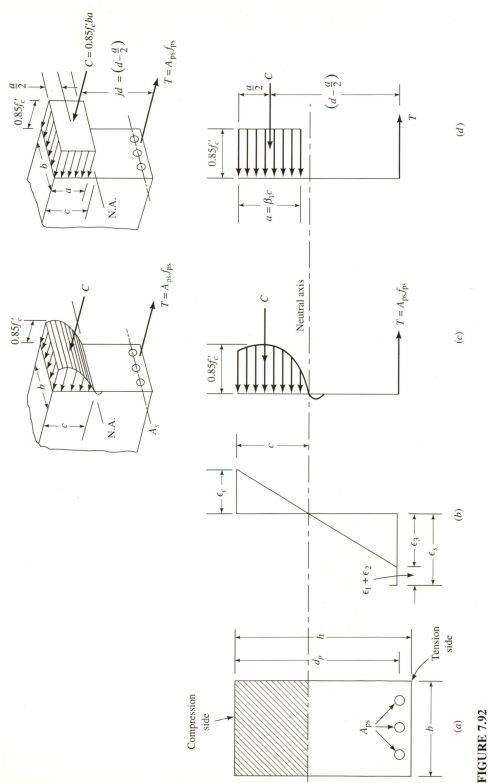

FIGURE 7.92

Stress and strain distribution across the beam depth: (a) beam cross section, (b) strains, (c) actual stress distribution, and (d) idealized equivalent stress block [Nawy, 1989].

Eq. 7.27 is AASHTO Eq. 9.13. By substituting $A_s^* = p^* bd$, Eq. 7.27 can be conveniently written as

$$\phi M_n = \phi \left[p^* bd f_{su}^* d \frac{f_c'}{f_c'} \left\{ 1 - 0.6 \left(\frac{p^* f_{su}^*}{f_c'} \right) \right\} \right]$$
$$= \phi f_c' bd^2 q(1 - 0.6q) \tag{7.28}$$

where

$$q = \frac{p^* f_{su}^*}{f_c'} \tag{7.29}$$

The quantity q defined by Eq. 7.29 is called the *reinforcing index*. Eq. 7.28 can be rewritten as

$$\frac{M_n}{f_c' bd^2} = q(1 - 0.6q) \tag{7.30}$$

Knowing the value of the reinforcement index, q, the nominal flexural capacity of a rectangular beam, M_n, can be readily calculated from Table 7.14.

The strength-capacity reduction factor, ϕ, in Eq. 7.28 should be taken per AASHTO 9.14:

For factory-produced, precast prestressed concrete members, $\phi = 1.0$

For post-tensioned cast-in-place concrete members, $\phi = 0.95$

For shear, $\phi = 0.90$

The actual moment capacity, ϕM_n, may be smaller than the factored design moment (i.e., the required value), and therefore unacceptable. To augment this moment capacity, nonprestressed reinforcement, A_s, is added in the beam, and the total increased nominal moment capacity of the beam becomes

$$M_n = A_s^* f_{su}^* d \left\{ 1 - 0.6 \left(\frac{p^* f_{su}}{f_c'} + \frac{d_t}{d} \frac{p f_{sy}}{f_c'} \right) \right\}$$
$$+ A_s f_{sy} d_t \left\{ 1 - 0.6 \left(\frac{d}{d_t} \frac{p^* f_{su}^*}{f_c'} + \frac{p f_{sy}}{f_c'} \right) \right\} \tag{7.31}$$

Provided that the value of the effective prestress after losses is not less than $0.5 f_s'$, the value of f_{su}^* in Eqs. 7.28 and 7.31 can be taken as follows: For bonded members with prestressing steel only,

$$f_{su}^* = f_s' \left[1 - \left(\frac{\gamma^*}{\beta_1} \right) \left(\frac{p^* f_s'}{f_c'} \right) \right] \tag{7.32}$$

which is AASHTO Eq. 9.17. For bonded members with prestressing steel and nonprestressed reinforcement,

$$f_{su}^* = f_s' \left[1 - \frac{\gamma^*}{\beta_1} \left\{ \frac{p^* f_s'}{f_c'} + \frac{d}{d_t} \left(\frac{p f_{sy}}{f_c'} \right) \right\} \right] \tag{7.33}$$

Equation 7.33 is the same as AASHTO Eq. 9.17a.

TABLE 7.14

Numerical values of the reinforcing index, q, vs. $M_u/\phi f_c' bd^2$ [Naaman, 1982]

q	0.000	0.001	0.002	0.003	0.004	0.005	0.006	0.007	0.008	0.009
0.0	0	0.0010	0.0020	0.0030	0.0040	0.0050	0.0060	0.0070	0.0080	0.0090
0.01	0.0099	0.0109	0.0119	0.0129	0.0139	0.0149	0.0159	0.0168	0.0178	0.0188
0.02	0.0197	0.0207	0.0217	0.0226	0.0236	0.0246	0.0256	0.0266	0.0275	0.0285
0.03	0.0295	0.0304	0.0314	0.0324	0.0333	0.0343	0.0352	0.0362	0.0372	0.0381
0.04	0.0391	0.0400	0.0410	0.0420	0.0429	0.0438	0.0448	0.0457	0.0467	0.0476
0.05	0.0485	0.0495	0.0504	0.0513	0.0523	0.0532	0.0541	0.0551	0.0560	0.0569
0.06	0.0579	0.0588	0.0597	0.0607	0.0616	0.0625	0.0634	0.0643	0.0653	0.0662
0.07	0.0671	0.0680	0.0689	0.0699	0.0708	0.0717	0.0726	0.0735	0.0744	0.0753
0.08	0.0762	0.0771	0.0780	0.0789	0.0798	0.0807	0.0816	0.0825	0.0834	0.0843
0.09	0.0852	0.0861	0.0870	0.0879	0.0888	0.0897	0.0906	0.0915	0.0923	0.0932
0.10	0.0941	0.0950	0.0959	0.0967	0.0976	0.0985	0.0994	0.1002	0.1011	0.1020
0.11	0.1029	0.1037	0.1046	0.1055	0.1063	0.1072	0.1081	0.1089	0.1098	0.1106
0.12	0.1115	0.1124	0.1133	0.1141	0.1149	0.1158	0.1166	0.1175	0.1183	0.1192
0.13	0.1200	0.1209	0.1217	0.1226	0.1234	0.1243	0.1251	0.1259	0.1268	0.1276
0.14	0.1284	0.1293	0.1301	0.1309	0.1318	0.1326	0.1334	0.1342	0.1351	0.1359
0.15	0.1367	0.1375	0.1384	0.1392	0.1400	0.1408	0.1416	0.1425	0.1433	0.1441
0.16	0.1449	0.1457	0.1465	0.1473	0.1481	0.1489	0.1497	0.1506	0.1514	0.1522
0.17	0.1529	0.1537	0.1545	0.1553	0.1561	0.1569	0.1577	0.1585	0.1593	0.1601
0.18	0.1609	0.1617	0.1624	0.1632	0.1640	0.1648	0.1656	0.1664	0.1671	0.1679
0.19	0.1687	0.1695	0.1703	0.1710	0.1718	0.1726	0.1733	0.1741	0.1749	0.1756
0.20	0.1764	0.1772	0.1779	0.1787	0.1794	0.1802	0.1810	0.1817	0.1825	0.1832
0.21	0.1840	0.1847	0.1855	0.1862	0.1870	0.1877	0.1885	0.1892	0.1900	0.1907
0.22	0.1914	0.1922	0.1929	0.1937	0.1944	0.1951	0.1959	0.1966	0.1973	0.1981
0.23	0.1988	0.1995	0.2002	0.2010	0.2017	0.2024	0.2031	0.2039	0.2046	0.2053
0.24	0.2060	0.2067	0.2075	0.2082	0.2089	0.2096	0.2103	0.2110	0.2117	0.2124
0.25	0.2131	0.2138	0.2145	0.2152	0.2159	0.2166	0.2173	0.2180	0.2187	0.2194
0.26	0.2201	0.2208	0.2215	0.2222	0.2229	0.2236	0.2243	0.2249	0.2256	0.2263
0.27	0.2270	0.2277	0.2284	0.2290	0.2297	0.2304	0.2311	0.2317	0.2324	0.2331
0.28	0.2337	0.2344	0.2351	0.2357	0.2364	0.2371	0.2377	0.2384	0.2391	0.2397
0.29	0.2404	0.2410	0.2417	0.2423	0.2430	0.2437	0.2443	0.2450	0.2456	0.2463
0.30	0.2469	0.2475	0.2482	0.2488	0.2495	0.2501	0.2508	0.2514	0.2520	0.2527
0.31	0.2533	0.2539	0.2546	0.2552	0.2558	0.2565	0.2571	0.2577	0.2583	0.2590
0.32	0.2596	0.2602	0.2608	0.2614	0.2621	0.2627	0.2633	0.2639	0.2645	0.2651
0.33	0.2657	0.2664	0.2670	0.2676	0.2682	0.2688	0.2694	0.2700	0.2706	0.2712
0.34	0.2718	0.2724	0.2730	0.2736	0.2742	0.2748	0.2754	0.2760	0.2766	0.2771
0.35	0.2777	0.2783	0.2789	0.2795	0.2801	0.2807	0.2812	0.2818	0.2824	0.2830
0.36	0.2835	0.2841	0.2847	0.2853	0.2858	0.2864	0.2870	0.2875	0.2881	0.2887
0.37	0.2892	0.2898	0.2904	0.2909	0.2915	0.2920	0.2926	0.2931	0.2937	0.2943
0.38	0.2948	0.2954	0.2959	0.2965	0.2970	0.2975	0.2981	0.2986	0.2992	0.2997
0.39	0.3003	0.3008	0.3013	0.3019	0.3024	0.3029	0.3035	0.3040	0.3045	0.3051

Notes: 1. Enter $M_u/\phi f_c' bd^2$ and get q or vice versa.
  2. $M_u/\phi f_c' bd^2 = q(1 - 0.59q)$.
  3. $q = (A_{ps} f_{ps} + A_s f_y - A_s' f_y')/bd f_c'$.

To preserve adequate ductility in the beam, the maximum amount of prestressing steel in the beam is limited by the specifications. This is done by limiting the value of the reinforcement index, q, to a maximum of $0.36\beta_1$, where β_1 is a factor for the concrete strength as defined in Chapter 6 (Eq. 6.23). The factor β_1 is the ratio of the compression-block depth, a, to the neutral-axis depth, c (i.e., $\beta_1 = a/c$). For rectangular beams with reinforcement index greater than $0.36\beta_1$, the design flexural strength is limited to

$$\phi M_n = \phi(0.36\beta_1 - 0.08\beta_1^2)f_c'bd^2 \tag{7.34}$$

which is the same as AASHTO Eq. 9.22. For a value of $\beta_1 = 0.85$, Eq. 7.34 is reduced to

$$\phi M_n = \phi(0.25f_c'bd^2) \tag{7.35}$$

In AASHTO–LRFD 5.7.3.3 [AASHTO, 1994], Eq. 7.35 is expressed as $c/d_e \leq 0.42$, where c is the depth of the neutral axis and d_e is the depth of the combined prestressed and nonprestressed steel areas. Skogman, Tadros, and Grasmick [1988] have shown that the maximum reinforcement index can be approximated by $c/h \leq 0.36$, where h is the total girder depth. For $d_e = 0.86h$, this limit gives results identical to those of the AASHTO–LRFD specifications [AASHTO, 1994].

Similarly, to preclude the possibility of brittle failure, the girders must contain a certain amount of minimum flexural reinforcement. To ensure this, AASHTO 9.18.2 requires that the total amount of prestressed and nonprestressed reinforcement be adequate to develop an ultimate moment at the critical section at least equal to 1.2 times the cracking moment, M_{cr}^*; i.e.,

$$\phi M_n \geq 1.2M_{cr}^* \tag{7.36}$$

where

$$M_{cr}^* = (f_r + f_{pc})S_c - M_{d/nc}\left(\frac{S_c}{S_b} - 1\right) \tag{7.37}$$

The various quantities in Eq. 7.37 are defined as follows:

f_r = the modulus of rupture of concrete

f_{pc} = compressive stress in concrete (see the definition in AASHTO 9.1.2)

S_b = noncomposite section modulus for the extreme fiber of the section, where the tensile stress is caused by externally applied loads

S_c = composite section modulus for the extreme fiber of the section, where the tensile stress is caused by externally applied loads

$M_{d/nc}$ = noncomposite dead-load moment at the section

An important step in the preliminary design of prestressed concrete beams is estimating the required prestressing force and the corresponding eccentricity, which depend on allowable stresses as well as stresses due to loads. The methods of determining these parameters are discussed in texts referred to earlier on the design of prestressed concrete structures, and these methods are not repeated here.

Lin [1963a], and Lin and Burns [1981] suggest a simple and quick procedure for the preliminary design of a prestressed concrete beam based on the knowledge of the internal $C - T$ couple acting in the section (where C is the total compressive force

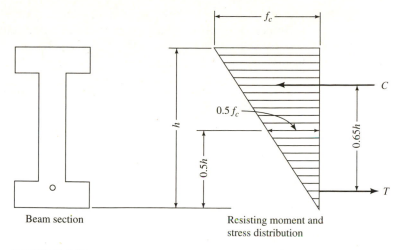

FIGURE 7.93
Preliminary design of a beam section [Lin, 1963a].

and T is the total tensile force). Under the service-load condition, the lever arm of this couple could vary between $0.65h$ and $0.8h$ (depending on the shape of the section), with an average value of $0.65h$, as shown in Fig. 7.93. Given a total design moment, M_T, and the depth, h, of the beam section (either known or assumed), and assuming the lever arm of $0.65h$, the effective P_e can be computed from Eq. 7.38:

$$P_e = T = \frac{M_T}{0.65h} \tag{7.38}$$

For an effective unit prestress of f_{se} in prestressing steel, the beam's area can be computed as

$$A_{ps} = \frac{P_e}{f_{se}} = \frac{M_T}{0.65h f_{se}} \tag{7.39}$$

For horizontal equilibrium, the total prestress (or the total tensile force) $T = A_{ps} f_{se}$ must be equal to the total compressive force, C. The average unit stress on concrete area A_c due to these forces can be expressed as

$$\frac{C}{A_c} = \frac{T}{A_c} = \frac{A_{ps} f_{se}}{A_c} \tag{7.40}$$

Under service-load conditions, the top fiber stress, f_c, according to AASHTO 9.15.2.2, is limited to $0.4 f_c'$. If the average fiber stress in A_c is assumed to be $0.5 f_c$, i.e., half the maximum allowable compressive stress f_c, then Eq. 7.40 can be expressed as

$$\frac{A_{ps} f_{se}}{A_c} = 0.50 f_c$$

$$A_c = \frac{A_{ps} f_{se}}{0.50 f_{se}} \tag{7.41}$$

In bridge superstructure design, for a given span, the total design moment is known, and the beam shape and size are generally chosen based on experience. Hence, this procedure can be followed very easily for estimating the effective prestress and the corresponding eccentricity, and their final values can be found after a few iterations.

7.11.2.2 Shear strength

Discussions on the shear cracking behavior of prestressed concrete girders can be found in several texts on prestressed concrete, and this topic is not repeated here. In spite of extensive research [Sozen, 1957; Bresler and Pister, 1958; Evans and Hosny, 1958; Walther, 1958; MacGregor, 1958; Walther and Warner, 1958; Sozen, Swoyer, and Siess, 1959; MacGregor, Sozen, and Siess, 1960, 1965; Lorensten, 1965; Kani, 1966; Bresler and MacGregor, 1967; MacGregor and Hanson, 1969; Mattock and Hawkins, 1972; Taylor, 1972; ASCE–ACI, 1973], the problem of shear cracking of both reinforced and prestressed concrete girders remains as complex as ever. For simplicity, it is assumed that the structural cracking of concrete ensues when the concrete's tensile strength, which is much smaller than its compression strength, is exceeded.

As a consequence of external loading, both shear and moment are present in a beam, and the type of cracking that can precipitate will depend on many variables, mainly the magnitudes of shear and moment at the section under consideration, the span-depth ratio of the girder, and the compressive strength of concrete. Research suggests that two types of shear-related cracks can develop in prestressed concrete girders. Generally, *flexural cracks*, which are almost perpendicular to the longitudinal axis of the beam, develop in the regions of large moments. However, in the presence of high shear due to diagonal tension, the flexural cracks extend as inclined cracks and are called *flexure-shear cracks*. That is, these cracks occur as a result of the combined effect of flexure and shear. The second type of shear-associated cracking occurs in the regions of high shear and small moments (e.g., close to supports). In these regions, the magnitude of principal tension is relatively high compared to that of the flexural stresses, leading to *web-shear cracking*. Both types of cracks are shown in Fig. 7.94.

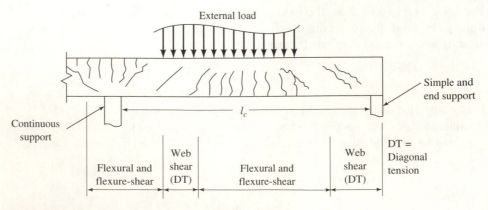

FIGURE 7.94
Cracking in a prestressed concrete beam [Nawy, 1989].

Because of the uncertainties involved in analyzing the shear cracking mechanism, the current philosophy is to evaluate both the *flexure-shear strength*, V_{ci}, and the *web-shear strength*, V_{cw}, and take the smaller of the two as the shear strength, V_c, of the member's cross section. If this value (multiplied by the strength reduction factor, ϕ) falls short of the factored design shear, V_u, then web reinforcement must be provided to resist the difference, V_s. Typically, the design procedure for shear consists of designing the beam for flexure first, then evaluating for shear strength, and then providing the necessary web reinforcement. For most commonly used simple-span bridges, the girders are prismatic. By comparison, in Japan, the web thicknesses of post-tensioned I- and T-girders are increased gradually toward the ends, for a distance of $0.15L$ to $0.2L$ from the girder ends, to enhance shear capacity and to provide post-tensioning anchorages in these regions [Yamane, Tadros, and Arumugasamy, 1994].

The design philosophy described above is similar to that followed for ordinary reinforced concrete beams. However, in a prestressed concrete beam, the compression due to prestressing forces markedly reduces the effect of the flexural shear, resulting in lower principal tensile stresses, a phenomenon that is not present in an ordinary reinforced concrete beam. Additionally, when prestressing tendons are inclined, the prestressing force introduces a shear that acts in the direction opposite to that of the load-induced shear (i.e., a negative shear is introduced). Thus, the net shear in a prestressed concrete beam is

$$V_{net} = V_{loads} - V_P \tag{7.42}$$

where V_P is the vertical component of the prestressing force (Fig. 7.95). Consequently, the net shearing force to be carried by concrete is reduced by V_P:

$$V_c = V - V_P \tag{7.43}$$

Design provisions for shear of prestressed concrete bridge girders are contained in AASHTO 9.20. The shear strength of a prestressed concrete member is taken as the sum of the shear strength provided by the concrete and by the web reinforcement. For design purposes, this relationship is written as

$$V_u \le \phi(V_c + V_s) \tag{7.44}$$

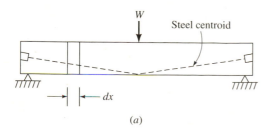

(a)

(b)   (c)

FIGURE 7.95
Effect of inclined tendons on net shear in a prestressed concrete beam [Nilson, 1978].

which is the same as AASHTO Eq. 9.26,

where V_u = factored shear force at the section considered
V_c = nominal shear strength provided by concrete
V_s = nominal shear strength provided by web reinforcement
ϕ = strength reduction factor for shear = 0.90 (AASHTO 9.14)

The value of shear strength, V_c, as explained above, is taken as the smaller of V_{ci} or V_{cw}. The expressions for V_{ci} and V_{cw} are as follows. This method is semiempirical in that some terms in the formulas for both quantities are based on test data.

The shear strength V_{ci} is computed from AASHTO Eq. 9.28:

$$V_{ci} = 0.6 \sqrt{f_c'} + V_d + \frac{V_i M_{cr}}{M_{max}} \qquad (7.45)$$

but V_{ci} need not be less than $1.7 \sqrt{f_c'} b' d$, and d need not be less than $0.8h$,

where b' = width of web of a flanged member
V_d = shear at section due to unfactored dead load
V_i = factored shear at section due to externally applied loads occurring simultaneously with M_{max}
M_{max} = maximum factored moment at section due to externally applied loads
M_{cr} = cracking moment due to externally applied loads, which is computed from the following formula:

$$M_{cr} = \frac{I}{Y_t}(6 \sqrt{f_c'} + f_{pe} - f_d) \qquad \text{(AASHTO Eq. 9.28)}$$

where f_{pe} = compressive stress in concrete due to effective prestress only (after allowance for all prestress losses), at the extreme fibers of the section where tensile stress is caused by externally applied loads
f_d = stress due to unfactored dead load, at the extreme fibers of the section where tensile stress is caused by externally applied loads
Y_t = distance from the centroidal axis of the gross section, neglecting reinforcement, to the extreme fibers in tension

The shear strength V_{cw} is computed from AASHTO Eq. 9.29:

$$V_{cw} = (3.5 \sqrt{f_c'} + 0.3 f_{pc})b' d + V_P \qquad (7.46)$$

but d need not be less than $0.8h$,

where f_{pc} = compressive stress in concrete (after allowance for all prestress losses), at the centroid of the cross section resisting externally applied loads, or at the junction of the web and the flange, when the centroid lies within the flange
V_P = vertical component of effective prestress at the cross section

Note that the quantity V_P, the vertical component of prestressing force at the cross section, is included in AASHTO Eq. 9.29 but not in AASHTO Eq. 9.27. This is due to the fact that the slope of the tendon in the region of flexure-shear cracking is generally very small, and the value of V_P therefore is negligible.

The required web reinforcement is designed in accordance with AASHTO 9.20.3. The shear strength of the web reinforcement, V_s, is computed from AASHTO Eq. 9.39,

$$V_s = \frac{A_v f_{sy} d}{s} \tag{7.47}$$

but is not greater than $8\sqrt{f_c'}b'd$,

where A_v = area of web reinforcement

  s = spacing of web reinforcement, not to exceed $0.75h$ or 24 in. However, when V_s exceeds $4\sqrt{f_c'}b'd$, this maximum spacing is to be reduced by one-half

  f_{sy} = design yield strength of web reinforcement, not to exceed 60,000 psi

And finally, regardless of whether or not the calculations indicate the necessity of web reinforcement, a minimum area of web reinforcement must be provided per AASHTO Eq. 9.31:

$$A_v = \frac{50b's}{f_{sy}} \tag{7.48}$$

Note the obvious similarity of the above formula to AASHTO Eq. 8.64 for reinforced concrete beams.

As a matter of general design practice, prestressed concrete structures are typically designed to satisfy initial and final stresses (due to moment and shear) at service-load conditions. This is followed by a check for flexural and shear capacity of the section, and then required web reinforcement is provided for shear at the ultimate conditions. Because of the presence of camber, deflections are usually not a problem, but they should be calculated to determine the final camber.

7.11.2.3 Composite construction

In the context of prestressed concrete, composite construction usually refers to a two-stage placement of concrete, often leading to two different unit weights and properties. In its most general form, *composite construction* involves construction in which a precast member (usually a girder) acts in combination with cast-in-place concrete (usually a slab acting as a top flange), that is poured at a later time and bonded to the member, with stirrups if necessary, to develop composite action. AASHTO 8.14.2.1 [AASHTO, 1992] defines a composite flexural member as one that "consists of precast and/or cast-in-place concrete elements constructed in separate placements but so interconnected that all elements respond to superimposed loads as a unit."

Since the early fifties, composite construction has been researched and extensively used for prestressed concrete highway bridges [Siess, 1949; Samuely, 1952; Evans and Parker, 1955; ACE–ASCI, 1960; Hanson, 1960; Kaar, Kriz, and Hognested, 1960; Mattock and Kaar, 1961; Grossfield and Birnstiel, 1962; Kriz and Raths, 1965; Hofbeck, Ibrahim, and Mattock, 1969; Branson, 1974, 1977; Pauley, Park, and Phillips, 1974; Saeman and Washa, 1985; Mattock, 1987; Patnaik, 1992; Loov and Patnaik, 1994]. Various forms of composite construction using prestressed concrete members, such as single- or double-T beams and box beams, were mentioned in Sec. 7.2. A frequently used form of composite construction involves precast prestressed I-beams and a cast-in-place reinforced concrete slab, resulting in a superstructure that can be idealized, for design purposes, as several contiguously placed T-beams. A pretensioned composite member may be further post-tensioned after the cast-in-place slab has hardened.

Advantages and disadvantages of composite construction. From a structural standpoint, composite structures are inherently more efficient than noncomposite ones because a composite section is stiffer than a noncomposite section. A major advantage of composite construction is the economy achieved through combining precast and cast-in-place concrete while retaining the continuity and efficiency of the monolithic construction. A composite beam is relatively smaller, shallower, and lighter, and hence more economical, than a noncomposite beam. Use of shallower sections for greater spans results in reduced heights of fill for approach roadways at grade separation structures and interchanges. Another advantage of composite construction is that products of superior quality are obtained through precasting; plant fabrication is under good quality control, forms are reused for standardized sections, and strands are tensioned long-line. At site, the precast units are erected first—without any scaffolding—which permits rapid erection of the structure with little or no interruption to the traffic below. These precast units are conveniently used to support the formwork required to support the cast-in-place slab. Further economy can be achieved by using *stay-in-place forms,* instead of reusable forms, to support the cast-in-place slab, thus eliminating the time required to remove the reusable forms. The use of precast prestressed concrete stay-in-place forms (also referred to as *deck panels*) for this purpose was described in Sec. 7.7 and illustrated in Fig. 7.70. As shown in Fig. 7.96, in multiple-span structures, the cast-in-place slab can be poured continuously over the supports of precast beams placed in series to develop continuity. The cast-in-place slab also offers an effective means of distributing loads laterally.

A disadvantage of composite construction is that the restraint provided by the cast-in-place slab causes an increase in the prestress losses of the precast element and thus influences the time-dependent deflections [Branson, 1974; Tadros, Ghali, and Dilger, 1975, 1977]. A summary of various advantages and disadvantages of composite construction using precast prestressed concrete members can be found in many texts referenced earlier on the design of reinforced and prestressed concrete structures.

Initial cost is often a factor in selecting a composite or a noncomposite superstructure. While it is common practice in the United States to build composite bridge superstructures for short and medium spans, such a practice is not universal. For example, because of high labor costs, the majority of bridges in Japan are noncomposite and transversely post-tensioned [Yamane, Tadros, and Arumugasaamy, 1994].

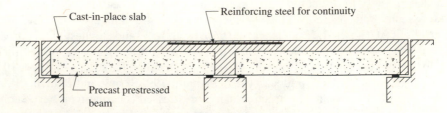

FIGURE 7.96
Precast prestressed beams made continuous for live loads by a cast-in-place slab.

Flexural stresses in composite sections. In most common types of prestressed concrete bridge superstructures, construction proceeds with the installation of precast girders, followed by the pouring of concrete for the deck. This sequence has an important bearing on the stress history of the girder. In such a construction sequence, the girder must support the dead load of the deck in addition to its own weight. Stresses on the *noncomposite* section include stresses due to prestress and those due to the moment caused by the girder's self-weight, the deadweight of the deck, and any other superimposed loads applied *prior* to the curing of the deck. After the deck hardens, the stresses due to the live load and to the superimposed dead loads (such as the intermediate diaphragms, wearing surface, and parapets) are resisted by the *composite* section. Final stresses are then calculated by superposition.

Variations in this loading history are possible. To create a more efficient structural system, the girder may be shored so that stresses due to the deadweight of the deck are also borne by the composite section. In such a case, "the entire composite member or portions thereof may be used in resisting the shear and moment" (AASHTO 8.14.2.2 [AASHTO, 1992]). For example, the girder may be shored at midspan before the deck is poured. This would create a *negative moment* in the girder at the (temporary) support, causing compression in the bottom fibers and tension in the top fibers of the beam. The deck is poured, and the temporary support is removed after the deck hardens. Loads resulting from the removal of the temporary support (i.e., the deadweight of the slab) would then be resisted by the composite section of the deck and the girder, and because of its enhanced section properties, the stresses would be smaller. The net result is that the stress level in the girder is greatly reduced compared to that of the traditional, unshored design and construction methods. Note that shoring should not be removed until the supported elements (the deck, in this case) have developed the design properties required to support all loads, limit deflections, and prevent cracking.

This technique can be used to increase the span capability of a given girder, as in the case of the 151-ft span of the five-span (130, 151, 99, 99, and 99 ft) bridge in Broward County, Florida, built in 1988–1989, that carries the Florida Turnpike over I-595 and the North New River Canal. By temporarily supporting at midspan the AASHTO Type V girders, which can span in the range of 130 ft, the girders were able to span 150 ft, resulting in a savings of $104,000 (in 1988 dollars) [PCIJ, 1989b]. The stresses in such cases can be easily calculated by using the superposition principle, as illustrated in Example 7.3.

EXAMPLE 7.3. The following values are given:

AASHTO Type V girder: $S_t = 16{,}790$ in.^{3} $S_b = 16{,}306$ in.^{3}
Composite section: $S_t = 41{,}038$ in.^{3} $S_b = 20{,}704$ in.^{3}

$$w_{\text{girder}} = 999 \text{ lb/ft}, \, w_{\text{deck}} = 553 \text{ lb/ft}, \, L = 149.6 \text{ ft}$$

Stresses due to prestress: $f_t = -758$ psi $f_b = 3692$ psi
Superimposed dead load stresses: $f_t = 111$ psi $f_b = -220$ psi
Stresses due to live load: $f_t = 457$ psi $f_b = -904$ psi

Calculate and compare stresses for the unshored and midspan-shored construction.

Solution. Stresses due to the self-weight of the girder (noncomposite) are

$$M = \tfrac{1}{8}wL^2 = \tfrac{1}{8} \times 999 \times (149.6)^2 = 2794.72 \text{ k-ft}$$

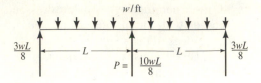

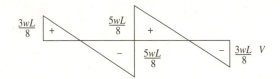

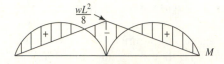

FIGURE E7.3

Stresses in the top and the bottom fibers of the noncomposite section are

$$f_t = M/S_t = 2794.72 \times 12{,}000/16{,}790 = 1997 \text{ psi}$$

$$f_b = M/S_b = 2794.72 \times 12{,}000/16{,}306 = -2057 \text{ psi}$$

Due to the deadweight of the slab on the unshored girder, the stresses in the top and the bottom fibers are

$$M = \tfrac{1}{8} \times wL^2 = \tfrac{1}{8} \times 553 \times (149.6)^2 = 1547.03 \text{ k-ft}$$

$$f_t = 1547.03 \times 12{,}000/16{,}790 = 1106 \text{ psi}$$

$$f_b = 1547.03 \times 12{,}000/16{,}306 = -1138 \text{ psi}$$

A temporary midspan support reduces the span length to $149.6/2 = 74.8$ ft, with the negative moment at the central support $= -\tfrac{1}{8}wL^2$. (See Fig. E7.3). The top and the bottom fiber stresses (noncomposite action) are

$$M = -\tfrac{1}{8} \times 553 \times (74.8)^2 = 386.96 \text{ k-ft}$$

$$f_t = -386.96 \times 12{,}000/16{,}790 = -277 \text{ psi}$$

$$f_b = 3867.57 \times 12{,}000/16{,}306 = 285 \text{ psi}$$

The midspan reaction at the temporary support is

$$P = 1.25wL = 1.25 \times 553 \times 74.8 = 51.705 \text{ kips}$$
$$\text{Point load due to diaphragm} \qquad \underline{1.705 \text{ kips}}$$
$$\text{Total load} \qquad 53.41 \text{ kips}$$

Final stresses are computed from the superposition principle. Due to the concentrated load P at the midspan, the maximum moments and stresses are

$$M = \tfrac{1}{4}PL = \tfrac{1}{4} \times 53.41 \times 149.6 = 1997.53 \text{ k-ft}$$

$$f_t = -1997.53 \times 12{,}000/41{,}038 = 584 \text{ psi}$$

$$f_b = -1997.53 \times 12{,}000/20{,}754 = -1155 \text{ psi}$$

Net stresses on the unshored girder are

$$f_t = -758 + 1997 + 1106 + 111 + 457 = 2913 \text{ psi}$$
$$f_b = 3692 - 2057 - 1138 - 220 - 904 = -627 \text{ psi}$$

Net stresses on the shored girder are

$$f_t = -758 + 1997 - 277 + 584 + 111 + 457 = 2114 \text{ psi}$$
$$f_b = 3692 - 2057 + 285 - 1155 - 220 - 904 = -359 \text{ psi}$$

Compare these stresses with the allowable stresses: With $f_c' = 6000$ psi, the allowable stresses are

$$f_c = 0.4 \times 6000 = 2400 \text{ psi} > 2114 \text{ psi}$$
$$f_t = -6\sqrt{f_c'} = 6 \times \sqrt{6000} = -465 \text{ psi} > -359 \text{ psi}$$

Horizontal shear in composite sections. Flexural shear due to external loads causes a tendency for horizontal slip (or shear) to occur at the interface between the cast-in-place slab and the precast girder. To develop resistance to this slip, i.e., to develop composite action between the cast-in-place slab and the precast girder, it is essential to have a good bond at their interface. Natural adhesion and friction between the surfaces at the interface provide considerable resistance to horizontal shear. Extensive laboratory testing shows that surface roughness plays a major role in providing the necessary horizontal shear strength. Thus, it is customary when using members with wide contact surfaces at the interface, such as single- or double-T beams, hollow-core slabs, or panels, to leave the top surface of the precast members rough (and to intentionally roughen them, if necessary) to enhance the shear transfer ability through friction and mechanical interlock. This rough surface can be attained during the precasting phase of the girders through careful vibration and by ensuring that coarse aggregate is firmly embedded but protrudes from the top face of the girders.

In cases of members with narrow contact surfaces at the interface, such as between a prestressed I-girder and a cast-in-place slab, the required resistance to horizontal shear at the interface is developed by anchoring into the cast-in-place slab the web reinforcement ties extending from the top of the precast girders; this provides dowel action to resist slip. The main function of the ties, or the dowels, is to prevent separation of the components at the interface in a direction normal to the contact surface. Accordingly, it is considered good practice to provide ties if a danger of separation exists [Lin and Burns, 1981].

Considerable research has been done to estimate the shear strength of composite concrete beams with rough surfaces. The major parameters affecting the shear strength of composite beams are the roughness of the top of the precast beam, the concrete strength, and the amount of reinforcing steel crossing the joint at the interface. Tests indicate that an as-cast surface with the coarse aggregate left protruding from the top of the precast beam, but without an intentionally roughened surface, can develop shear resistance on the order of 220–290 psi [Loov and Patnaik, 1994], and that stirrups are typically unstressed and ineffective until the horizontal shear stresses exceed these values.

The design of ties that cross the interface between the precast beams and the cast-in-place slab evolved with the research of Hanson [1960] and Kaar, Kriz, and Hognested [1960], which was summarized in the ACI–ASCE Committee 333 Report [1960], and formed the basis of the design provisions that first appeared in the 1963 ACI code. Later, based on push-off tests [Birkland and Birkland, 1966; Mast, 1968; Kriz and Raths, 1965; and Hofbeck, Ibrahim, and Mattock, 1969], the concept of *shear friction* was introduced in the 1970 ACI code. Since then, more than 30 shear-friction equations have been proposed by various researchers. A detailed literature review and a summary, with proposed revision to the ACI code, are reported by Loov and Patnaik [1994].

From a design standpoint, note that, because the design for shear is based on the limit state at failure due to factored loads, the design stipulations that apply for the composite sections are the same as those that apply for the precast sections. Provisions for horizontal shear transfer in prestressed composite members are contained in AASHTO 9.20.4. These are similar to the provisions for reinforced concrete flexural members (AASHTO 8.16.6.5), and they require that horizontal shear be fully transferred at the contact surfaces:

$$V_u = \phi V_{\text{nh}} \tag{7.49}$$

where V_{nh} = nominal horizontal shear strength
ϕ = strength reduction factor for shear = 0.90 (AASHTO 9.14)

Equation 7.49 is the same as AASHTO Eq. 9.31a.

For purposes of design, empirical values have been set based on test results. For example, the ACI code [ACI 1995] allows at factored loads the following horizontal strengths based on tests discussed by Hanson [1960]; Kaar, Kriz, and Hognested [1960]; and Saeman and Washa [1964]. The same values are also adopted in the 1992 AASHTO specifications (AASHTO 9.20.4.3):

- 80 psi for contact surfaces that are clean, free of laitance, and intentionally roughened; i.e., $V_{\text{nh}} = 80 b_v d$
- 80 psi for contact surfaces that are clean and free of laitance, not intentionally roughened but with minimum ties provided; i.e., $V_{\text{nh}} = 80 b_v d$
- 350 psi when contact surfaces are clean and free of laitance, intentionally roughened to a full amplitude of approximately $\frac{1}{4}$ in., and with minimum ties provided; i.e., $V_{\text{nh}} = 350 b_v d$

where b_v = width at the contact surface
d = depth of the entire composite section

The terms "clean" and "free of laitance" are used in the above specification to recognize the fact that surface preparation of the interface has a significant influence on the horizontal shear capacity of composite structural members. Extension of the web reinforcement across the interface (into the slab) by itself may not be adequate to prevent bond failure at the interface if contact surfaces are not properly roughened [Evans and Parker, 1955].

The minimum area of ties, according to AASHTO 9.20.4.5, is required to be not less than $50 b_v s / f_y$, with tie spacing s limited to the smaller of four times the least web width, or 24 in.

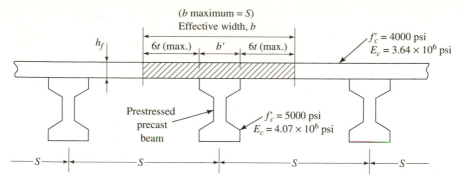

(a) Composite structural system

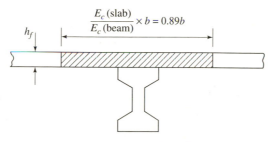

(b) Section for elastic analysis
modified for different f_c' values

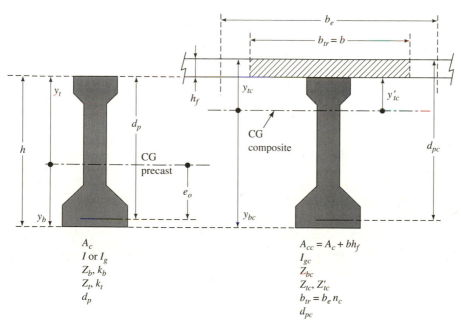

A_c
I or I_g
Z_b, k_b
Z_t, k_t
d_p

$A_{cc} = A_c + bh_f$
I_{gc}
Z_{bc}
Z_{tc}, Z_{tc}'
$b_{tr} = b_e n_c$
d_{pc}

(c) Section properties required for composite design

FIGURE 7.97

Composite structural system showing transformation of the effective width of the flange: (a) given superstructure system, (b) transformed section, and (c) section properties required for composite design [Lin and Burns, 1981; Naaman, 1982].

It is a common practice to specify a smaller value of f_c' (usually 3500–4000 psi) for the cast-in-place deck concrete than that for the superior-quality concrete (usually 6000 psi or higher) of the precast girder. These differences in concrete compressive strengths result in different moduli of elasticity for the two members, which must be properly accounted for in flexural design calculations. This is typically done by *transforming* one of the two elements (the cast-in-place slab, in this case) into a fictitious element having the same modulus of elasticity as the other (the precast girder, in this case). The cast-in-place slab section that has thickness h_f and effective width b_e is transformed into an equivalent section that has the same thickness, h_f, and a transformed width, b_{tr}, according to the following relationship [Naaman, 1982]:

$$b_{tr} = b_e \frac{(E_c)_{CIPC}}{(E_c)_{PPC}} = b_e n_c \qquad (7.50)$$

where $(E_c)_{CIPC}$ = modulus of elasticity of concrete for the cast-in-place slab
$(E_c)_{PPC}$ = modulus of elasticity of concrete for the precast prestressed girders
n_c = ratio of the modulus of elasticity of precast concrete to that of concrete of precast girders

Note that the modulus of elasticity of concrete, E_c, is proportional to the square root of its compressive strength. Because the value of $(E_c)_{CIPC}$ is usually smaller that that of $(E_c)_{PPC}$, the value of n_c is usually less than 1.0. However, some designers (for example, Texas Department of Transportation), use the value of $n = 1.0$ for $f_c \leq 7500$ psi for the precast girders. Principles of determining the effective width, b_e, were presented in Chapter 6. Both b_e and b_{tr} are shown in Fig. 7.97.

7.12
ALLOWABLE STRESSES

The allowable stresses for designing precast prestressed concrete members are covered by AASHTO 9.15. The design strength of concrete is usually taken as 5000 psi. Higher-strength concrete, discussed in Section 7.3.1, may be used if it can be obtained consistently.

7.12.1 Prestressing Steel

Allowable stresses for prestressing steel and for concrete are outlined in this section. The following stresses for prestressing steel are permitted in the specifications (AASHTO 9.15.1):

7.12.1.1 Stress at anchorages after seating
Pretensioned members

Stress-relieved strands $0.70 f_s'$
Low-relaxation strands $0.75 f_s'$

where f_s' = ultimate strength of prestressing steel

Post-tensioned members

$$0.70 f_s'.$$

Slight overstressing up to $0.85 f_s'$ for short periods of time may be permitted to offset seating losses and to accommodate the stress increase due to a drop in temperature, provided that the stress after seating does not exceed the above values.

Overstressing up to $0.90 f_y^*$ for short periods of time may be permitted to offset seating and friction losses provided that the stress at the anchorage does not exceed the above value. The stress at the end of the seating-loss zone must not exceed $0.83 f_y^*$ immediately after seating.

7.12.1.2 Stress at service load after losses

$$0.80 f_y^*$$

Includes bonded prestressed strands.

The new LRFD specifications [AASHTO, 1994] are more specific about stress limits for various kinds of prestressing steel, as shown in Table 7.15.

TABLE 7.15
Stress limits for prestressing steel [AASHTO, 1994]

	Tendon type		
	Stress-relieved strand and plain high-strength bars	Low-relaxation strand	Deformed high-strength bars
At jacking (f_{pj}):			
Pretensioning	$0.72 f_{pu}$	$0.78 f_{pu}$	
Post-tensioning	$0.76 f_{pu}$	$0.80 f_{pu}$	$0.75 f_{pu}$
At transfer (f_{pt}):			
Pretensioning	$0.70 f_{pu}$	$0.74 f_{pu}$	
Post-tensioning at anchorages and couplers immediately after anchor set	$0.70 f_{pu}$	$0.70 f_{pu}$	$0.66 f_{pu}$
Post-tensioning, general	$0.70 f_{pu}$	$0.74 f_{pu}$	$0.66 f_{pu}$
At service limit state (f_{pe}):			
After losses	$0.80 f_{py}$	$0.80 f_{py}$	$0.80 f_{py}$

7.12.2 Concrete

The following stresses for concrete are permitted in the specifications (AASHTO 9.15.2).

7.12.2.1 Temporary stresses before losses due to creep and shrinkage

Compression

Pretensioned members	$0.60 f_{ci}'$
Post-tensioned members	$0.55 f_{ci}'$

Tension

Precompressed tensile zone   None

Other areas

Tension areas with no bonded reinforcement   200 psi or $3\sqrt{f'_{ci}}$

Where the calculated tensile stress exceeds the above value, bonded reinforcement must be provided to resist the total tension force in the concrete computed on the assumption of an uncracked section. However, the maximum tensile stress is not to exceed $7.5\sqrt{f'_{ci}}$.

Concrete strength at the transfer of prestressing force to the concrete member is an important parameter to consider for design of prestressed concrete girders. AASHTO 9.22 requires that, unless otherwise specified, the prestressing force should not be transferred to concrete until the compressive strength of the concrete, as indicated by the test cylinders, cured by a method identical with that used to cure the members, is at least 4000 psi for pretensioned members (other than piles) and 3500 psi for post-tensioned members and pretensioned piles.

7.12.2.2 Stress at service load after losses have occurred

Compression $0.40\,f'_c$

Tension in the precompressed tensile zone

(*a*) For members *with* bonded reinforcement, including bonded prestressing strands $6\sqrt{f'_c}$

For severe corrosive exposure conditions, such as coastal areas $3\sqrt{f'_c}$

(*b*) For members *without* bonded reinforcement   None

Tension in other areas is limited by allowable temporary stresses specified in AASHTO 9.15.2.1.

Cracking stress

Use the modulus of rupture from tests, or, if that is not available, use the following values:

Highway bridges

For normal-weight concrete $7.5\sqrt{f'_c}$
For sand-lightweight concrete $6.3\sqrt{f'_c}$
For all other lightweight concrete $7.5\sqrt{f'_c}$

Anchorage bearing stress

Post-tensioned anchorage at service load is 3000 psi (but not to exceed $0.9\,f'_{ci}$).

Table A.24 (Appendix A) lists values of various allowable stresses in concrete as functions of f'_c and $\sqrt{f'_c}$.

7.13
PRESTRESSING LOSSES

Calculation of losses in prestress, defined as the difference between the initial stress in the prestressing steel and the stress at any time, *t*, due to various causes, is an extremely important design consideration for calculating effective prestress in tendons. In design

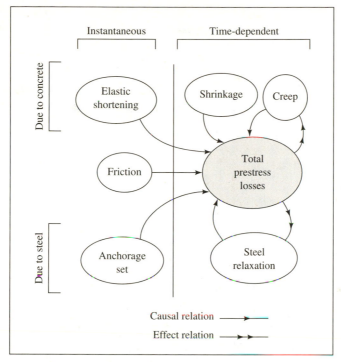

FIGURE 7.98
Interrelationships of causes and effects among prestress losses
[Naaman and Hamza, 1993].

computations, total prestress losses expected at the end of the service life of a structure are calculated and applied as a safe value in design. Their magnitude, however, does not affect the ultimate flexural strength of a member. For a detailed discussion on prestress losses, readers should refer to texts on prestressed concrete (referenced earlier) and to other references [ACI–ASCE, 1958; ACI, 1971; Branson and Kripanarayana, 1971; Glodowski and Lorenzetti, 1972; Grouni, 1973; Hernandez and Gamble, 1975; PCIJ, 1975c; Tadros, Ghali, and Dilger, 1975, 1977; Naaman and Siriaksorn, 1979a,b; Zia et al., 1979; Huang, 1982; FIP, 1984; PennDOT, 1985; Tadros, Ghali, and Meyer, 1985; Ghali and Favre, 1986; ACI, 1989; Naaman and Hamza, 1991, 1993].

Prestress losses are both instantaneous and time-dependent. They occur *cumulatively* as a result of elastic shortening, shrinkage and creep of concrete, and the relaxation of steel. The interrelationship of causes and effects among various types of losses is shown in Fig. 7.98 [Naaman, 1982; Naaman and Hamza, 1993].

Several methods have been developed to predict prestress losses for fully prestressed beams made from normal-strength concretes and normal stress-relieved strands [Naaman and Hamza, 1993]. These include methods to calculate the following:

- Estimate of total losses on a lump-sum basis
- Lump-sum estimate of separate prestress losses due to individual effects, such as shrinkage, creep, or relaxation
- Accurate determination of cumulative losses by the time-step method

However, for most practical purposes, a common engineering practice is to use a lump-sum estimate of total prestress losses in design; detailed separate calculations for each type of prestress loss is not necessary. This is an acceptable practice, according to both the ACI code [ACI 1995] and the AASHTO specifications [AASHTO, 1992]. The ACI–ASCE Joint Committee 423 [ACI–ASCE, 1958] has suggested expressions to approximate prestress losses. It also suggested using the lump-sum values—35 ksi for pretensioned members and 25 ksi for post-tensioned members—as the total prestress losses due to elastic shortening, creep and shrinkage of concrete, and relaxation of steel. The losses due to friction and anchorage set are additional.

For design of prestressed concrete bridge members, AASHTO 9.16.2 specifies the following method to determine prestress losses, excluding those due to friction (AASHTO Eq. 9.3):

$$\Delta f_s = SH + ES + CR_C + CR_S \tag{7.51}$$

where Δf_s = total loss excluding friction, psi
SH = loss due to concrete shrinkage, psi
ES = loss due to elastic shortening, psi
CR_C = loss due to creep of concrete, psi
CR_S = loss due to relaxation of prestressing steel, psi

For estimating each of the above losses, formulas are given in the AASHTO specifications. The formula for losses due to creep of concrete is the same for both pretensioned and post-tensioned concrete members. However, separate formulas are given for losses of prestress in pretensioned and post-tensioned concrete members due to shrinkage, elastic shortening, and relaxation of steel. The loss due to relaxation of prestressing of steel also depends on whether the strands are the stress-relieved or low-relaxation type.

In addition to the losses discussed above, post-tensioned members have losses due to friction, which are to be determined based on the experimentally determined wobble and curvature coefficients. In the absence of experimental data, the AASHTO-prescribed values of the wobble coefficient, K, and the curvature coefficient, μ, shown in Table 7.16, are to be used in conjunction with Eq. 7.3 (AASHTO Eq. 9.1) and Eq. 7.6 (AASHTO Eq. 9.2). Loss of prestress due to friction is covered by AASHTO 9.16.1. This topic was discussed in Sec. 7.6.1.2, and the pertinent AASHTO method was illustrated by Example 7.1.

TABLE 7.16
Values of K and μ for use in Eq. 7.3 (AASHTO Eq. 9.1) and Eq. 7.6 (AASHTO Eq. 9.2)

Type of steel	Type of duct	K/ft	μ
Wire or ungalvanized strand	Bright metal sheathing	0.0020	0.30
	Galvanized metal sheathing	0.0015	0.25
	Greased or asphalt-coated and wrapped	0.0020	0.30
	Galvanized rigid	0.0002	0.25
High-strength bars	Bright metal sheathing	0.0003	0.20
	Galvanized sheathing	0.0002	0.15

TABLE 7.17
Estimate of prestress losses (AASHTO Table 9.16.2.2) [AASHTO, 1992]

Type of prestressing steel	Total loss (psi)	
	f'_c = 4000 psi	f'_c = 5000 psi
Pretensioning strand	—	45,000
Post-tensioning		
wire or strand	32,000	33,000
bars	22,000	23,000

Alternatively, if the preceding method for computing prestress losses cannot be used for lack of data, the AASHTO specifications [AASHTO, 1992] permit prestress losses to be estimated on a lump-sum basis. For prestressed concrete members made from normal-weight concrete, having normal prestress levels, and subjected to average exposure conditions, the prestress losses may be taken as given in Table 7.17 (AASHTO Table 9.16.2.2). These losses are based on use of normal-strength concrete (as shown in Table 7.17), normal stress-relieved strands, normal prestress levels (i.e., within the AASHTO-permitted limits), and average environmental conditions.

A parametric study [Naaman and Hamza, 1993] suggests that for high-strength concrete (6–10 ksi) partially prestressed flexural members,[2] the time-dependent prestress losses are also influenced by the type of cross section of the flexural member (such as I-girder, box beam, rectangular beam, double-T beams), the *partial prestressing ratio* (PPR), and the compressive strength of concrete. PPR is defined as the ratio of the contribution of resistance of the prestressing steel to the total resistance of the section, and it is numerically expressed as

$$\text{PPR} = \frac{A_{\text{ps}} f_{\text{py}}}{A_{\text{ps}} f_{\text{py}} + A_s F_y} \tag{7.52}$$

where A_{ps} = cross-sectional area of prestressing steel
     A_s = cross-sectional area of ordinary tensile reinforcing steel
     f_{py} = yield strength of prestressing steel
     f_y = yield strength of ordinary reinforcing steel

Thus, for a fully prestressed beam, $A_s = 0$ and PPR $= 1$.

This study makes the following points:

1. Prestress losses are sensitive to the partial prestressing ratio, PPR. However, the variation in PPR has opposite effects on prestress losses due to creep and on prestress losses due to relaxation of prestressing steel. A decrease in the value of PPR is accompanied by a decrease in prestress loss due to creep, but it is also accompanied by an increase in prestress loss due to relaxation of prestressing steel.

---

[2]Members having both prestressing and ordinary reinforcing steel, as opposed to fully prestressed beams, which would have negligible or no ordinary reinforcing steel.

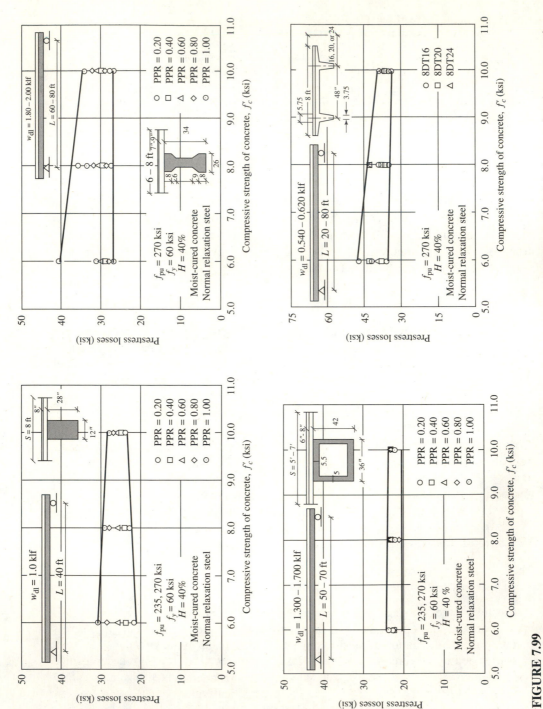

FIGURE 7.99

Influence of concrete compressive strength on time-dependent prestress loss (upper and lower limits) in beams of various geometric configurations [Naaman and Hamza, 1993].

2. Time-dependent stress losses generally decrease with an increase in the compressive strength of concrete. Up to 20 percent decrease was observed when f'_c varied from 6 to 10 ksi. However, for box girders, I-girders, and solid rectangular beams, the effect of concrete compressive strength up to 10 ksi was found to be negligible. Figure 7.99 shows the influence of concrete compressive strength on prestress losses.

3. The geometry of the member's cross section influences prestress losses—highest losses for fully prestressed double-T beams and hollow-core slabs primarily used for buildings, average losses for the rectangular and the AASHTO Type I beams, and the lowest losses for box girders. Figure 7.99 shows, for various concrete compressive strength, the influence of cross-sectional geometry on the time-dependent prestress losses. Figure 7.100 shows, for a rectangular beam with various values of PPR, the influence of age on prestress losses. Also, typical variation of time-dependent prestresses losses with level of prestress is shown in Fig. 7.101.

4. Loss due to elastic shortening, which is instantaneous, decreases with the decrease in the level of prestress (i.e., the value of PPR). For the specific parameters used in this study, the value of PPR varied from 0 to 19 ksi. With an initial prestress of 189 ksi ($= 0.7 \times 270$ ksi), this represents about a 10-percent decrease. Accordingly, the study recommends that, in any lump-sum estimate of losses, the effect of elastic shortening, since it is not time-dependent, should be calculated separately.

In the absence of specific information about the geometry of a member cross section, the study recommends, for design, the following expression in terms of f'_c and PPR for estimating the *average lump-sum time-dependent losses* (TDL):

$$ \text{TDL} = 33\left(1 - 0.15\frac{f'_c - 6}{6}\right) + 6(\text{PPR}) \text{ ksi} \qquad (7.53) $$

This expression is valid for members made from normal-weight concrete and normal-relaxation prestressing steel. For members made from structural-lightweight concrete, the values of TDL estimated from this expression are recommended to be *increased* by 5 ksi, but *reduced* by 6 ksi for low-relaxation strands and wires.

Table 7.18 [AASHTO, 1994] gives recommended expressions based on the Naaman–Hamza study [1993] for estimating lump-sum average time-dependent losses (TDL) for beams of various geometric configurations, subject to the following adjustments:

- Reduce by 4 ksi for box girders
- Reduce by 6 ksi for beams, solid slabs, and I-girders
- Reduce by 8 ksi for single T's, double T's, hollow-core slabs, and voided slabs

In conjunction with these recommendations, the instantaneous prestress loss due to elastic shortening can be calculated from the expressions provided in the AASHTO specifications [1992] or from the expression recommended in the Naaman–Hamza study [1993]. Both are reported to give close numerical values. These recommendations have been adopted in the new LRFD specifications [AASHTO, 1994] for future use, in place of the current lump-sum provisions, for the following reasons [Naaman

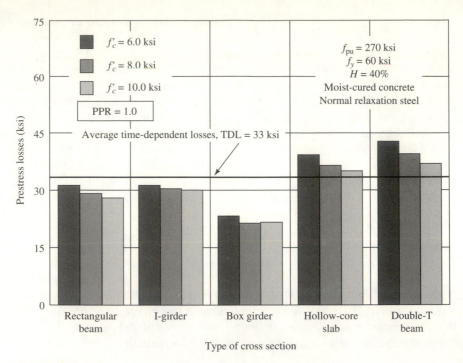

FIGURE 7.100
Effect of beam cross section geometry on time-dependent losses in fully prestressed beams [Naaman and Hamza, 1993].

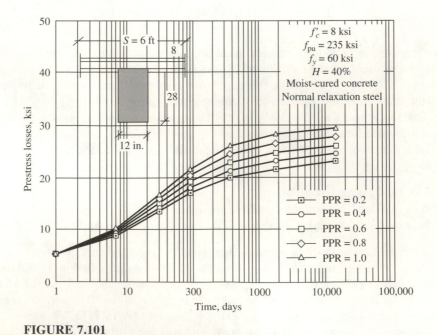

FIGURE 7.101
Typical variation of time-dependent prestress losses with time and level of prestress [Naaman and Hamza, 1993].

TABLE 7.18
Recommended lump-sum estimates of time-dependent losses (ksi) due to creep, shrinkage, and relaxation [Naaman and Hamza, 1993; AASHTO, 1994]

Type of beam section	Level	For wires and strands with f_{pu} = 235, 250, or 270 ksi	For bars with f_{pu} = 145 or 160 ksi
Rectangular beams, solid slab	Upper bound	29.0 + 4.0 PPR	19.0 + 6.0 PPR
	average	26.0 + 4.0 PPR	
Box girder	Upper bound	21.0 + 4.0 PPR	15.0
	average	19.0 + 4.0 PPR	
I-girder	Average	$33.0\left[1.0 - 0.15\dfrac{f'_c - 6.0}{6.0}\right] + 6.0\,\text{PPR}$	19.0 + 6.0 PPR
Single-T, double-T, hollow-core and voided slab	Upper bound	$39.0\left[1.0 - 0.15\dfrac{f'_c - 6.0}{6.0}\right] + 6.0\,\text{PPR}$	$31.0\left[1.0 - 0.15\dfrac{f'_c - 6.0}{6.0}\right] + 6.0\,\text{PPR}$
	Average	$33.0\left[1.0 - 0.15\dfrac{f'_c - 6.0}{6.0}\right] + 6.0\,\text{PPR}$	

and Hamza, 1993]: The current provisions

- Do not distinguish instantaneous from time-dependent losses
- Do not consider the influence of the geometry of the beam cross section
- Do not recognize the effect of the partial prestressing ratio (PPR)
- Do not consider concrete compressive strength beyond 6000 psi

7.14
DEVELOPMENT LENGTH OF PRESTRESSING STRANDS

Bond is the primary mechanism by which the force in a prestressing strand is transferred to the surrounding concrete in the end portion of a pretensioned concrete beam. The distance from the end of the member over which the effective prestressing force develops is referred to as the *transfer length*. The *flexural bond length* is the additional bond length required to develop the strand stress from effective prestress to the ultimate stress at the ultimate flexural strength of the beam. The sum of these two lengths is referred to as the *development length*. Based partly on past research [Janney, 1963; Over and Au, 1965] but mainly on the test results of Hanson and Kaar [1959] and Kaar, LaFraugh, and Mass [1963], the equation combining these two lengths is

$$L_d = \frac{f_{se}}{3}D + (f_{ps} - f_{se})D \qquad (7.54)$$

The first term, $(f_{se}/3)D$, represents the transfer length, and the second term, $(f_{ps} - f_{se})D$, represents the flexural bond length. AASHTO 9.27.1 requires that prestressing strands be bonded to the surrounding concrete beyond the critical section for a *minimum* development length. This minimum length, given by the above expression, is written in simplified form as (AASHTO Eq. 9.32)

$$L_d = (f_{su}^* - \tfrac{2}{3} f_{se})D \qquad (7.55)$$

where D = nominal diameter of strand, in.

f_{su}^* = average stress in prestressing at ultimate load

f_{se} = effective steel prestress after losses

According to this expression, for 270-ksi, $\frac{1}{2}$-in.-diameter strands, assuming an initial prestress of $0.7 f_{pu}$ and a 20-percent loss, the transfer length would be 50 strand diameters, and the flexural bond length would be 110 strand diameters—thus a total development length of at least 160 strand diameters.

The current expression is based on the test of prestressed concrete beams with strands of $\frac{1}{2}$-in. diameter, so its applicability is questionable for 0.6-in.-diameter strands. Research shows that the transfer length and development increase almost linearly with the strand diameter. To prevent average bond strength from reaching a limiting bond stress that causes bond failure, the development for 0.6-in.-diameter strands should logically be greater than 160 strand diameters. A comparison of values recommended by several researchers [Hanson and Kaar, 1959; Martin and Scott, 1976; Zia and Mostafa, 1977; Russell and Burns, 1993] for the development length of 0.6-in.-diameter strands is shown in Fig. 7.102. A comprehensive discussion on the transfer and development length of prestressing strands *has been* presented by Cousins, Johnston, and Zia [1990].

Requirements for the development length for prestressing steel are currently under research. Based on the results of tests to failure of twenty full-scale AASHTO Type I beams, the following expression for the development length has been suggested [Bazant, 1972; Bakos et al., 1982; Deatherage and Burdette, 1991; Deatherage, Burdette, and Chew, 1994]:

$$L_d = \left[\frac{f_{si}}{3} + 1.5(f_{ps} - f_{se}) \right] D \qquad (7.56)$$

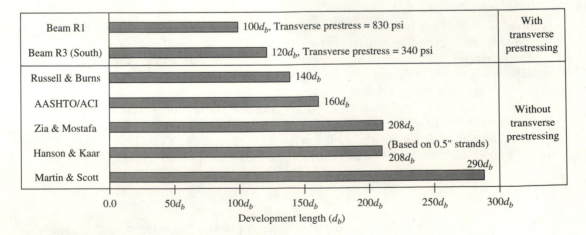

FIGURE 7.102
Comparison of recommended values for development length of 0.6-in. diameter seven-wire strand [Aboutaha and Burns, 1994].

where f_{se} and f_{ps} (same as f_{su}^*) are defined as above, and f_{si} is the prestressing stress at transfer. The net effect of this proposed equation, in comparison to AASHTO's current equation, is to increase the required development length; this is done by increasing the transfer length portion of the equation by using f_{si} instead of f_{se} (since $f_{si} > f_{se}$) and multiplying the flexural bond length portion by 1.5. These studies also indicate that there is no significant difference in the flexural strength of beams with $\frac{1}{2}$-in.-diameter prestressing strands spaced at 2-in. spacings and that of similar beams with $\frac{1}{2}$-in.-diameter prestressing strands spaced at $1\frac{3}{4}$-in. spacings. While this and other related research is undergoing engineering scrutiny and evaluation, the current AASHTO Eq. 9.32 [AASHTO, 1992] continues to be used. The current equation is also specified in the AASHTO–LRFD specifications [AASHTO, 1994]. A state-of-the-art summary of the strand development lengths has been presented by Buckner [1995].

7.15
DEFLECTIONS

Deflections in beams were discussed in Chapter 5. Here, the time-dependent effects for prestressed concrete in service-load range are presented. Being more slender than their reinforced concrete counterparts, deflections of prestressed concrete beams are an important consideration for the serviceability of bridges.

It is convenient to consider the total deflection of a prestressed concrete beam as consisting of two parts: instantaneous deflection and long-term deflection. The *instantaneous deflection* is elastic and is caused by transient loads such as live loads, and it does not vary with time. The *long-term deflection,* a complex phenomenon governed by several parameters, is caused by sustained loads and increases with time due to the creep phenomenon. The long-term creep deformations of prestressed concrete beams are seriously affected by the ever-present (sustained) eccentric compression due to prestressing force. Failure to predict and control such deformations could result in poor ride characteristics of the deck, which is supported on prestressed concrete girders. Because of its importance, the subject of long-term deflection continues to be researched. A comprehensive discussion on long-term deflections can be found in several references [Corley and Sozen, 1966; Bazant, 1972; Bakos et al., 1982; Alwis, Olorunnivw, and Ang, 1994].

Dead-load deflections of both reinforced and prestressed concrete girders are affected by several factors, such as the type, quality, and proportions of materials in concrete, the amount and placement of reinforcing steel, the method of curing, the age and strength of concrete, the time history of loading, and other factors [Tadros, Ghali, and Dilger, 1975; Bazant and Panula, 1980]. It is believed that by properly controlling these factors, deflections can be predicted with reasonable accuracy.

Deflections of prestressed concrete beams are calculated by the conventional methods available in texts on strength of materials. This is based on the premise that the sections are prismatic; made of materials that are homogeneous, isotropic, and elastic; and follow Hooke's law. These assumptions are obviously approximations, and estimated deflections of prestressed concrete beams are replete with uncertainties. For a prestressed concrete beam, the load-deflection relationship, prior to rupture, can be

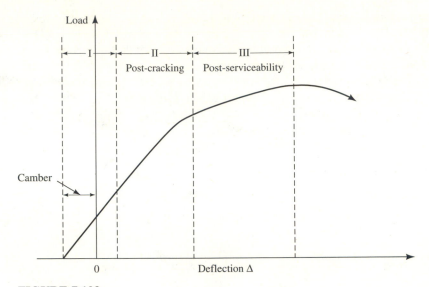

FIGURE 7.103
Beam load-deflection relationship. Region I, precracking stage, region II, postcracking stage, region III, post-serviceability stage [Nawy, 1989].

ideally characterized as *trilinear* as it goes through the three stages of cracking: precracking stage, postcracking stage, and the post-serviceability stage, as shown in Fig. 7.103 [Nawy, 1989].

Practical determination of E_c, the elastic modulus of concrete, is difficult within an accuracy of 10 percent or even 20 percent [Lin and Burns, 1981]. The value of E_c for beams, which is obtained from tests on sample cylinders, may differ from the E_c value for the cylinders themselves. It is known that E_c varies with the age of and stress levels in concrete. According to Naaman [1982], the *effective,* or *equivalent,* modulus of elasticity of concrete as influenced by creep, $E_{ce}(t)$, is given by

$$E_{ce}(t) = \frac{E_c(t)}{1 + C_C(\tau)} \qquad (7.57)$$

where $E_c(t)$ = instantaneous elastic modulus of concrete at time t
   t = age of concrete in days
   $C_C(\tau)$ = creep coefficient at time t
   τ = time after loading = $t - t_A \geq 0$
   t_A = age of concrete at loading

However, the effective elastic modulus is affected by *aging,* a phenomenon that refers to the change in properties of concrete with progress of its hydration. The *age-adjusted effective modulus,* proposed by Trost [1967] and modified by Bazant [1972], is given by

$$E_{ce}(t, t_A) = \frac{E_c(t_A)}{1 + \chi(t, t_A)C_C(t, t_A)} \qquad (7.58)$$

where $E_{ce}(t, t_A)$ = age-adjusted effective modulus at time t when loading occurs at time t_A

$\qquad E_c(t_A)$ = instantaneous elastic modulus at time t_A

$\qquad \chi(t, t_A)$ = aging coefficient at time t

$\qquad C_C(t, t_A)$ = creep coefficient at time t for a concrete member loaded at time t_A

Further refinement in computing long-term deflections has been suggested by Bazant and Oh [1984] using the BP-2 model [Bazant, 1988] after simplifying with the effective modulus method and accommodating a nonlinear moment-curvature relationship. A comprehensive discussion on mathematical modeling of creep and shrinkage of concrete can be found in Bazant [1988].

The moment of inertia also varies with the stage of loading, i.e., whether the section is uncracked or cracked. The AASHTO specifications [1992] suggest using the following value of effective moment of inertia, I_e, as originally suggested by Branson [Branson, 1968, 1977; Naaman and Siriaksorn, 1979a,b]:

$$I_e = \left(\frac{M_{cr}}{M_a}\right)^3 I_g + \left[1 - \left(\frac{M_{cr}}{M_a}\right)^3\right] I_{cr} \leq I_g \qquad (7.59)$$

or

$$I_e = I_{cr} + \left(\frac{M_{cr}}{M_a}\right)^3 (I_g - I_{cr}) \leq I_g \qquad (7.60)$$

where I_{cr} = moment of inertia of cracked section

$\qquad I_g$ = gross moment of inertia

$\qquad M_{cr}$ = cracking moment of inertia for the beam at the section of maximum moment M_a

$\qquad M_a$ = maximum moment acting on the span at the stage for which deflection is computed (essentially same as M_{max} at section of maximum moment)

Several methods have been proposed by researchers for computing I_{cr}. For example, PCI [1992] suggests the following expression for I_{cr} for a fully prestressed beam in a cracked state:

$$I_{cr} = n_p A_{ps} d_p^2 (1 - \sqrt{\rho_p}) \qquad (7.61)$$

where $n_p = E_{ps}/E_c$

The above expression can be modified as follows to apply for the partially prestressed beams:

$$I_{cr} = (n_p A_{ps} d_p^2 + n_s A_s d_s^2)(1 - \sqrt{\rho_p + p_p}) \qquad (7.62)$$

where $n_s = E_s/E_c$

Naaman and Siriaksorn [1979a,b] have suggested the following expression for moment of inertia of a cracked section:

$$I_{cr} = \frac{c^3 b}{3} + n_p A_{ps}(d_p - c)^2 + n_s A_s(d_s - c)^2 - \frac{(b - b_w)(c - h_f)^3}{3} \qquad (7.63)$$

where c = distance from the extreme compressive fiber to the neutral axis at the loading considered

Estimating the effect of creep on deflections with any degree of precision is very difficult [Lin and Burns, 1981]. Thus, deflections of both reinforced and prestressed concrete beams can be estimated only imprecisely. However, in view of the imprecisely defined allowable deflections, the approximations used in deflection calculations have become an accepted norm.

Methods of computing deflections of prestressed concrete beams are discussed in several texts referred to in earlier sections on prestressed concrete structures. Exhaustive treatments of deflections are presented by Naaman [1982] and Nawy [1989], who discuss the calculation of short-term deflections of beams with cracked sections by the *effective-moment-of-inertia computation method* or the *bilinear computation method,* and the long-term effects on camber and deflection by the *PCI-multipliers method* [PCI, 1985] or the *incremental time-steps method.* The PCI-multiplier method allows one to include both the creep effect and other factors, such as the presence of sustained precompression and composite topping. These multipliers are listed in Table 7.19 [Martin, 1977]; their application is illustrated in Example 7.4. It has been suggested [Shaikh and Branson, 1970; Branson, 1974] that long-term camber in prestressed concrete beams can be reduced by addition of nonprestressed reinforcement, in which case a reduced multiplier, C_2, can be used:

$$C_2 = \frac{C_1 + A_s/A_{ps}}{1 + A_s/A_{ps}} \tag{7.64}$$

where C_1 = multiplier from Table 7.19
A_s = area of nonprestressed reinforcing
A_{ps} = area of prestressing steel

Flexural cracking and deflection behavior of pretensioned and post-tensioned beams has been reported by Nawy and Potyondy [1971], Nawy and Huang [1977], Nawg and Chiang [1980], Cohn [1986], and Nawy [1985, 1986].

TABLE 7.19
C_1 multipliers for long-term deflection and camber [PCI, 1992]

Loading stage	Without composite topping	With composite topping
At erection		
1. Deflection (downward) component— apply to the elastic deflection due to the member weight at the time of release of prestress.	1.85	1.85
2. Camber (upward) component— apply to deflection calculated in (1) above.	1.80	1.80
Final		
3. Deflection (downward) component— apply to deflection calculated in (1) above.	2.7	2.4
4. Camber (upward) component— apply to camber calculated in (2) above.	2.45	2.2
5. Deflection (downward)— apply to elastic deflection due to superimposed dead load only.	3.0	3.0
6. Deflection (downward)— apply to elastic deflection caused by the composite topping.	—	2.30

There appears to be no consensus or uniformity in adopting specific values of the coefficient of creep, and practices vary nationally. For example, Degenkolb [1977] has suggested the following approximate percentages of the ultimate deflection at various ages for cast-in-place concrete box girder bridges:

- 25 percent when falsework released—continuous spans
- 33 percent when falsework released—simple spans
- 70 percent at 6 months
- 82 percent at 1 year
- 90 percent at 2 years
- 93 percent at 3 years
- 95 percent at 4 years
- 100 percent at ultimate

The AASHTO–LRFD specifications [1994, p. 5-42] give the following multipliers, C_c, depending on whether the gross moment of inertia (I_g) or the effective moment of inertia (I_e) is used for computing the *instantaneous* deflections. For deflections calculations based on the gross moment of inertia, I_g, $C_c = 4.0$. For deflections calculations based on the effective moment of inertia, I_e, $C_c = 3.0 - 1.2(A'_s/A_s) \geq 1.6$,

where A'_s = area of compression reinforcement
A_s = area of nonprestressed tension reinforcement

The California Department of Transportation, the largest builder of cast-in-place prestressed concrete box girder bridges in the United States, recommends the following values of coefficient of creep for precast prestressed concrete I-beam bridges [CAL-TRANS, 1993c, pp. 3–37]:

Time (weeks)	Coefficient of creep
2	1.25
9	1.50
20	1.75

According to California practice, it is commonly assumed that the value of coefficient creep is 1.5 and that the prestress force has relaxed to a value to about $0.89P_i$. However, for determining camber for cast-in-place box girder structures, a value of coefficient of creep of 3.0 is applied [CALTRANS, 1993d, p. 11-3].

Shear lag is an important consideration for computing deflections in cross sections of concrete box girders. Both reinforced and prestressed concrete girders represent thin-walled structures whose deflections can be predicted with reasonable accuracy by the simple beam theory from a designer's point of view. However, the presence of prestress complicates the effect of shear lag on maximum stress and deflection induced in the beam cross section. A rigorous analysis of such a structure would normally consider both membrane and thin-plate actions [Hambly, 1991]. A simplified method of arriving at shear lag coefficients of two-span continuous and prestressed concrete box girder bridges subjected to uniform loading on the deck slab is discussed in the literature [Chang, 1992; Narasimham, 1993].

7.16
DESIGN EXAMPLES

Three examples with detailed long-hand calculations are presented in the remainder of this chapter. These include a single-span, precast, prestressed composite I-beam bridge, a single-span cast-in-place box girder bridge, and a two-span cast-in-place post-tensioned box girder bridge. All calculations conform to the 1992 AASHTO specifications and the 1993 Interim AASHTO specifications.

7.16.1 Design of Simple-Span, Precast, Prestressed, Composite I-Beam Bridges

Example 7.4 presents a detailed design of a simple-span, precast, prestressed, composite I-beam bridge, perhaps the most widely used bridge type for short-span bridges. I-beam bridges were discussed in Sec. 7.5.2.5. Typically, the bridge consists of parallel precast, prestressed I-beams and a cast-in-place deck. Composite action is developed through the stirrups that project from the tops of precast I-beams and are anchored into the cast-in-place deck.

EXAMPLE 7.4. Design an interior girder for a precast, prestressed composite I-beam bridge superstructure to carry HS20 loading over a span of 75 ft between the centers of bearings, assuming unshored construction. Use $f_{ci}' = 4000$ psi and $f_c' = 5000$ psi for the girder, and use $f_c' = 4000$ psi for the deck.

Calculations. For the purpose of this bridge, a precast prestressed AASHTO Type IV girder, capable of spanning distances in the 70 to 100-ft range (see Fig. 7.30) is selected. For a clear roadway width of 28 ft, an arbitrary spacing of 7 ft 8 in. is selected as shown in Fig. E7.4a, requiring four equally spaced girders to support the superstructure.

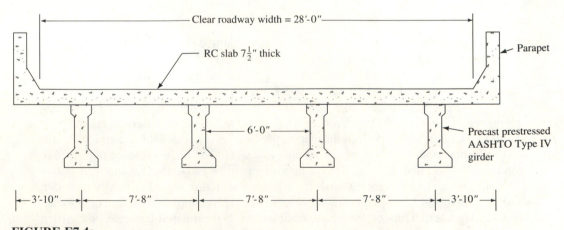

FIGURE E7.4a
Typical cross section for bridge in Example 7.4.

Deck slab. Calculations for design of the deck slab are not illustrated in this example, since they are very similar to the design of the slab for the reinforced concrete T-beam bridge presented in Chapter 6. Instead, in this example, Fig. 6.10 (Chapter 6) is used to pick out the required slab thickness. A girder spacing of 7 ft 8 in. gives the clear span (measured as the distance between the inside edges of the 20-in.-wide top girder flanges) for the slab as 6 ft ($92 - 20 = 72$ in.). From Fig. 6.10, the slab thickness required for an effective span of 6 ft is $7\frac{1}{4}$ in. However, for this bridge, a slab thickness of $7\frac{1}{2}$ in. has been adopted, which is often the minimum required thickness. This actual slab will consist of 3-in.-thick precast prestressed concrete deck panels (see Sec. 7.7) with a $4\frac{1}{2}$-in.-thick cast-in-place concrete topping. Intermediate diaphragms, 8 in. thick and 4 ft deep, will be provided between all girders at midspan, as required by the specifications.

Effective width, b_e (AASHTO 8.10.1.1). The effective width, b_e, is to be the *least* of the following values (AASHTO 8.10.1.1). Note that the top flange width ($b_v = 20$ in.), instead of the web thickness ($b_w = 8$ in.), has been considered to determine the effective width, b_e.

$$\tfrac{1}{4}L = \tfrac{1}{4} \times 75 \times 12 = 225 \text{ in.}$$

$$c/c \text{ of beams} = 7 \text{ ft-8 in.} = 92 \text{ in.}$$

$$12t_s + b_v = 12 \times 7.5 + 20 = 110 \text{ in.}$$

$\tfrac{1}{2} \times$ clear distance between the top flanges of I-beams $= \tfrac{1}{2} \times (92 - 20) = 36$ in.

Therefore,

$$b_e = 36 \times 2 + 20 = 92 \text{ in.}$$

where $b_v = 20$ in. $=$ the width of the top flange of the AASHTO Type IV girder. Hence $b_e = 92$ in.

Section properties. The geometry of the AASHTO Type IV girder is shown in the following figure, and section properties are recalculated from statics.

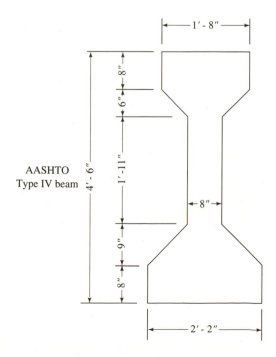

Section properties

Section	A (in.^{2})	y_b (in.)	Ay_b (in.^{3})	d (in.)	Ad^2 (in.^{4})	I_o (in.^{4})
20×8	160	50	8000	25.3	102,500	853
$2 \times \frac{1}{2} \times 6 \times 6$	36	44	1584	199.3	13,400	72
38×8	304	27	8200	2.3	1600	36,581
$2 \times \frac{1}{2} \times 9 \times 9$	81	11	890	13.7	15,200	364
26×8	208	4	932	20.7	89,000	1109
$\sum$ girder	789		19,506		221,700	38,979
Composite girder	789	24.73	19,506	14.45	164,745	260,680
Slab^a	614	57.75	35,459	18.57	211,735	2879
$\sum$ Composite girder	1403		54,965		376,480	263,559

^{a}Transformed area of slab $= 0.89 \times 92 \times 7.5 = 6.14$ in.^{2}, where 0.89 is the ratio of the moduli of elasticity of the 4000-psi concrete for the slab and the 5000-psi concrete for the girder.

$$E_{c,\text{slab}} = 33w_c^{1.5}\sqrt{f_c'} = 33 \times (145)^{1.5} \times \sqrt{4000} = 3.64 \times 10^6 \text{ psi}$$

$$E_{c,\text{girder}} = 33w_c^{1.5}\sqrt{f_c'} = 33 \times (145)^{1.5} \times \sqrt{5000} = 4.07 \times 10^6 \text{ psi}$$

Hence the modular ratio is

$$n = \frac{E_{c',\text{slab}}}{E_{c',\text{girder}}} = \frac{3.64}{4.67} = 0.89$$

Girder (noncomposite)
$y_b = 19,506/789 = 24.73$ in.
$y_t = 54 - 24.73 = 29.27$ in.

Composite section
$y_b = 54,965/1403 = 39.18$ in.
$y_t = 61.5 - 39.18 = 22.32$ in.

Girder

$$I_G = 221,700 + 38,979 \qquad = 260,680^3 \text{ in.}^4$$
$$S_t = 260,680/29.27 \qquad = 8906 \text{ in.}^3$$
$$S_b = 260,680/24.73 \qquad = 10,541 \text{ in.}^3$$
$$k_t = S_b/A = 10,541/789 \qquad = 13.36 \text{ in.}$$
$$k_b = S_t/A = 8906/789 \qquad = 11.29 \text{ in.}$$

Composite section

$$I = 376,480 + 263,559 \qquad = 640,039 \text{ in.}^4$$
$$S_{t,\text{slab}} = 640,039/22.32 \qquad = 28,678 \text{ in.}^3$$
$$S_b = 640,039/39.18 \qquad = 16,336 \text{ in.}^3$$
$$S_{t,\text{girder}} = 640,039/14.82 \qquad = 43,188 \text{ in.}^3$$

Allowable stresses: AASHTO 9.15.2 [AASHTO, 1992]

1. Prestressing steel. Stress at anchorages after seating $= 0.7f_s' = 0.7 \times 270 = 189$ ksi.
2. Concrete

---

[3]Standard tabulated value of the moment of inertia of the AASHTO Type IV girder is listed as 260,730 in.^{4}, with $y_b = 24.73$ in. (see Fig. 7.30), and may be used instead.

(a) Temporary stresses before losses due to creep and shrinkage (using $f'_{ci} = 4000$ psi at release):

Compressive stress in concrete $0.6 f'_{ci} = 0.6 \times 4000 = 2400$ psi

Tension in precompressed tensile zone   None

Tension in tension areas with no bonded reinforcement   200 psi or $3 \sqrt{f'_{ci}} = 3 \times \sqrt{4000}$ psi $= 190$ psi (Use 190 psi.)

Maximum tensile stress $7.5 \sqrt{f'_{ci}} = 7.5 \times \sqrt{4000}$ psi $= 474$ psi

(b) Stresses at service load after losses have occurred:

Compression $= 0.4 f'_c \times 5000 = 2000$ psi
Tension in precompressed tensile zone (for members with bonded reinforcement) $= 6 f'_c = 6 \times \sqrt{5000} = 424$ psi

Design moments

Dead-load moments. For normal-weight concrete, $\gamma_{conc} = 150$ lb/ft^3.

Self-weight of the girder $= (789/144) \times (0.15) = 0.822$ k/ft

$$M_G = \tfrac{1}{8} \times 0.822 \times (75)^2 \times 12 = 6936 \text{ kip-in.}$$

Deadweight of the slab $= (92 \times 7.5)/144 \times 0.15 = 0.719$ k/ft

$$M_S = \tfrac{1}{8} \times 0.719 \times (75)^2 \times 12 = 6067 \text{ kip-in.}$$

Total dead-load moment, $M_{D1} = 6936 + 6067 = 13{,}003$ kip-in.
Distance between the inside faces of the girder webs $= 7$ ft
Deadweight of the diaphragm is

$$P_D = \tfrac{8}{12} \times \tfrac{48}{12} \times 7.0 \times 0.15 = 2.8 \text{ kips}$$

The deadweight of each parapet, including railing, is assumed to be 500 lb/ft for this example and will be distributed equally to the four girders. Depending on the type of parapet selected, this weight would vary (see Chapter 4, Sec. 4.7.2.1). With the weight of the future wearing surface as 25 lb/ft^2 (some designers use 35 lb/ft^3), the superimposed dead load on the girder is

$$w_{si} = (500 \times 2)/4 + 25 \times 7.67 = 441.75 \text{ lb/ft} = 0.442 \text{ k/ft}$$

It is assumed that the dead load due to the diaphragms, future wearing surface, and the parapets will be borne equally by all girders. Hence, the moment due to superimposed load is

$$M_{D2} = \frac{PL}{4} + \frac{w_{si}L^2}{8}$$

$$= \frac{2.8 \times 75}{4} + \frac{0.442 \times (75)^2}{8}$$

$$= 363.28 \text{ k-ft}$$

$$= 363.28 \times 12 = 4360 \text{ k-in.}$$

$$M_{D,\text{Total}} = M_{D1} + M_{D2} = 13{,}003 + 4360 = 17{,}363 \text{ kip-in.}$$

Live-load moments

Spacing, $S = 7$ ft 8 in. $= 7.67$ ft

Distribution factor $= S/5.5$
$$= 7.67/5.5 = 1.395 \text{ (Appendix A, Table A.7)}$$

For $L = 75$ ft, $M_{LL} = 1075.1$ kip-ft (Appendix A, Table A.6)

$$I = \frac{50}{L + 125} = \frac{50}{75 + 125} = 0.25$$

$$M_{LL+I} = 1075.1 \times 1.25 \times 1.395 \times \tfrac{1}{2} \times 12 = 11{,}244 \text{ kip-in.}$$

Total design moment, $M_T = 17{,}363 + 11{,}244 = 28{,}607$ kip-in.

Stresses under various loading conditions are tabulated as follows and shown schematically in Fig. E7.4b:

| | Stresses | | |
Loading	f_b (psi)	f_t (psi)	Section
D.L. (girder)	−658	+779	Noncomposite
D.L. (girder + slab)	−1234	+1460	Noncomposite
Superimposed D.L.	−267	+101	Composite
Live load	−688	+260	Composite
Full-service load, $\sum$	−2189	+1821	

Sign convention: + indicates compression, − indicates tension.

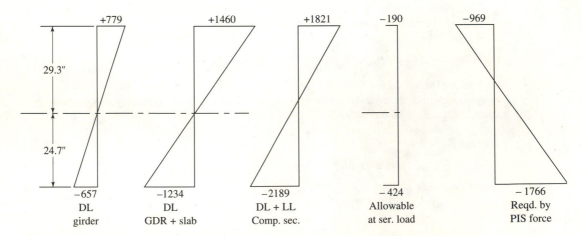

FIGURE E7.4b

Stress distribution in girder and the desired state of stresses at various stages of loading.

Estimate the required amount of effective prestressing force P_e: $M_T = P_e d'$, where $d' =$ lever arm (see Fig. 7.93) The lever arm will be assumed to vary between $0.7h$ and $0.8h$, where h is the total depth of the composite section: $h = 54 + 7.5 = 61.5$ in. Assume prestress loss = 45 ksi (AASHTO Table 9.16.2.2). Effective prestress = $189 - 45 = 144$ ksi or $144/189 = 76.2$ percent. Therefore,

$$P_e = 0.762 P_i$$

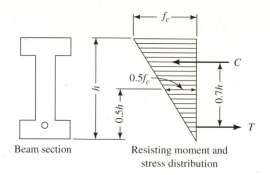

Beam section

Resisting moment and stress distribution

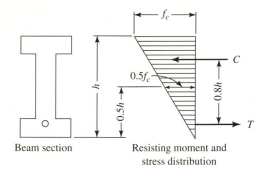

Beam section

Resisting moment and stress distribution

With $d' = 0.7h$,

$$P_e = \frac{M_T}{0.7h} = \frac{28,607}{0.7 \times 61.5} = 664.5 \text{ kips}$$

$$P_i = \frac{664.5}{0.762} = 872.0 \text{ kips}$$

If $d' = 0.8h$,

$$P_e = \frac{M_T}{0.8h} = \frac{28,607}{0.8 \times 61.5} = 581.4 \text{ kips}$$

$$P_i = \frac{581.4}{0.762} = 763 \text{ kips}$$

Use $\frac{1}{2}$-in. ϕ 270-k strands: $A = 0.153$ in.^{2} (Appendix A, Table A.25). Initial prestressing force per strand $= 0.153 \times 189 = 28.9$ kips

For $P_i = 872.8$ kips, number of strands $= 872.8/28.9 = 30.2$
For $P_i = 763$ kips, number of strands $= 763/28.9 = 26.4$

Trial design
Try 26 strands. With a 26-in.-wide bottom flange, 12 strands can be placed at 2-in. grid lines. Arrange 26 strands as shown.

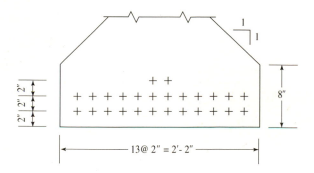

Compute the centroid of strands (CGS) from the bottom fibers in order to compute the eccentricity, e.

$$\text{CGS from the bottom fibers} = \frac{2 \times 6 + 12 \times 4 + 12 \times 2}{26} = 3.23 \text{ in.}$$

$$e = 24.73 - 3.23 = 21.5 \text{ in.}$$
$$P_i = 26 \times 28.9 = 751.4 \text{ kips}$$
$$P_e = 751.5 \times 0.762 = 572.6 \text{ kips}$$

Check stresses at transfer

At midspan

$$f_t = \frac{P_i}{A}\left(1 - \frac{e}{k_b}\right) = \frac{751.4}{789}\left(1 - \frac{21.5}{11.29}\right) = -0.861 \text{ ksi}$$

Net $f_t = -861 + 779 = -82 \text{ psi} < -190 \text{ psi}$, OK

$$f_b = \frac{P_i}{A}\left(1 + \frac{e}{k_t}\right) = \frac{751.4}{789}\left(1 + \frac{21.5}{13.36}\right) = 2.485 \text{ ksi}$$

Net $f_b = 2485 - 657 = 1828 \text{ psi} < 2400 \text{ psi}$, OK

At ends (*DL* moment $= 0$)

$$\text{Excess tension at ends} = -861 - (-190) = -671 \text{ psi}$$

This excess tension can be avoided by (1) debonding certain strands near the ends, or (2) reducing eccentricity at the ends. We will use the second option because the beneficial effect of the vertical component of the prestressing force will help reduce shear in the beam. To have the maximum slope of the strands, we will provide negative eccentricity at the ends. Note that because of the limited thickness of the web (only 8 in.), only the six centrally located strands (in three rows) can be harped, and the remaining twenty strands will have to remain straight. At the ends, the centroid of the six harped strands will be at 4 in. from the top of the girder. In such a case, the eccentricity of all strands can be determined by taking moments about the bottom of the girder:

$$e = \frac{(6 \times 50) + (10 \times 2) + (10 \times 4)}{26}$$
$$= 10.90 \text{ in. below the CGC}$$

With $e = 10.90$ in., the stresses at the top and the bottom are

$$f_b = \frac{P_i}{A}\left(1 + \frac{e}{k_t}\right) = \frac{751.4}{789}\left(1 + \frac{10.90}{13.26}\right) = 1729 \text{ psi} < 2400 \text{ psi}, \text{ OK}$$

$$f_t = \frac{P_i}{A}\left(1 - \frac{e}{k_b}\right) = \frac{751.4}{789}\left(1 - \frac{10.90}{11.29}\right) = 32 \text{ psi (no tension)}, \text{ OK}$$

Final stresses at midspan due to the service load, where $P_e = 572.6$ kips, are

$$f_b = \frac{P_e}{A}\left(1 + \frac{e}{k_t}\right) = \frac{572.6}{789}\left(1 + \frac{21.5}{13.36}\right) = 1.894 \text{ ksi}$$

Net $f_b = 1.894 - 2.189 = -0.295 < -0.424 \text{ ksi}$, OK.

$$f_t = \frac{P_e}{A}\left(1 - \frac{e}{k_b}\right) = \frac{572.6}{789}\left(1 - \frac{21.5}{11.29}\right) = -0.656 \text{ ksi}$$

Net $f_t = -0.656 + 1.821 = 1.165 \text{ ksi} < 2.00 \text{ ksi } (= 0.4f_c')$, OK. Hence, all stress requirements are satisfied.

Check for the ultimate capacity. According to AASHTO 9.17.2 (for rectangular sections or for flanged sections with neutral axis within the flange, $c \leq 7.5$ in.),

$$M_u = A_s^* f_{su}^* d(1 - 0.6p^* f_{su}^*/f_c')$$
$$A_s^* = 26 \times 0.153 = 3.98 \text{ in.}^2$$

$$p^* = \frac{A_s}{bd} = \frac{3.98}{92 \times (61.5 - 3.23)} = 0.000742$$

f_{su}^* is computed from AASHTO Eq. 9.17.

From AASHTO 9.1.2, $\gamma^* = 0.28$ for a low-relaxation strand, and $\beta_1 = 0.85$ (for $f_c' = 4000$ psi in slab)

$$f_{su}^* = f_s'\left[1 - \left(\frac{\gamma^*}{\beta_1}\right)\left(\frac{p^* f_s'}{f_c'}\right)\right]$$

$$= 270\left[1 - \left(\frac{0.28}{0.85}\right)\left(\frac{0.000742 \times 270.0}{4.0}\right)\right]$$

$$= 265 \text{ ksi}$$

$A_s^* f_{su}^* = 3.98 \times 265 = 1056$ kips. With $b_e = 92$ in. and $f_c' = 4.0$ ksi,

$$a = \frac{A_s^* f_{su}^*}{0.85 f_c' b} = \frac{1056}{0.85 \times 4.0 \times 92} = 3.38 \text{ in.}$$

$$c = \frac{a}{\beta_1(\text{slab})} = \frac{3.38}{0.85} = 3.97 \text{ in.} < 7.5 \text{ in.} \ (= \text{slab thickness})$$

Hence, the neutral axis lies in the flange, and the section can be analyzed as a rectangular section. With the centroid of prestressing steel at 3.23 in. from the bottom fibers, $d = (54 + 7.5 - 3.23) = 58.27$ in.,

$$M_n = A_s^* f_{su}^* d\left(1 - 0.6\frac{p^* f_{su}^*}{f_c'}\right)$$

$$= 1056.5 \times 58.27\left(1 - 0.6 \times \frac{0.000742 \times 265}{4.0}\right)$$

$$= 59{,}718 \text{ kip-in.}$$

$\phi = 1.0$ for factory-produced precast prestressed concrete members (AASHTO 9.14)

$\phi M_n = 1.0 \times 59{,}718 = 59{,}718$ kip-in.

Group $(N) = \gamma[\beta_D, +\beta_L(L + I)]$, (AASHTO 3.22), where $\gamma = 1.3$, $\beta_D = 1.0$, and $\beta_L = 1.67$.
Therefore,

$$M_u = 1.3[D + 1.67(L + I)]$$
$$= 1.3(17{,}363 + 1.67 \times 11{,}244)$$
$$= 44{,}934 < 59{,}718 \text{ kip-in., OK}$$

Check for ductility

1. Maximum steel (AASHTO 9.18.1):
   Check that the steel is yielding as the ultimate capacity (i.e., the point where the deck concrete crushes) is approached.

   For the amount of prestressing steel provided, $p^* = 0.000742$. Therefore, the reinforcement index, q, is

   $$q = \frac{p^* f_{su}^*}{f_c'} = \frac{(0.000742)(265)}{4.0} = 0.0492 < 0.36\beta_1 = 0.36 \times 0.85 = 0.306$$

2. Minimum steel (AASHTO 9.18.2.1):

   $$\phi M_n \geq 1.2 M_{cr}^*$$

   $$M_{cr}^* = (f_r + f_{pe})S_c - M_{d/nc}\left(\frac{S_c}{S_b} - 1\right)$$

   where
   $f_r = 7.5\sqrt{f_c'} = 7.5 \times \sqrt{5000} = 530$ psi (AASHTO 9.15.2.3)
   $f_{pe} = P_e/A_c = 572.6/1403 = 0.408$ ksi
   $M_{d/nc}$ = noncomposite dead-load moment at the section
   $= 13,003$ kip-in.
   S_b = noncomposite section modulus for the extreme fibers of section where tensile stress is caused by externally applied loads
   $= 10,541$ in.^{3}
   S_c = composite section modulus for the extreme fibers of section where tensile stress is caused by externally applied loads
   $= 16,336$ in.^{3}
   $M_{cr}^* = [(0.530 + 0.408)16,336 - 13,003(\frac{16,336}{10,541} - 1)]$
   $= [15,323 - 7148]$
   $= 8175$ kip-in.
   $1.2 M_{cr}^* = 1.2 \times 8175 = 9810$ kip-in.
   $\phi M_n = 59,718$ kip-in. $> 1.2 M_{cr}^* = 9810$ kip-in., OK

Check for shear

Check shear at $h/2$ from the face of support (AASHTO 9.20.2.4):

Dead loads: Girder: $w_G = 0.822$ k/ft
              Slab: $w_s = 0.719$ k/ft
Superimposed dead load $= 0.442$ k/ft
Total dead load $= \overline{1.983}$ k/ft

Dead load due to intermediate diaphragm: $P = 2.8$ kips

Assume a 10-in.-long (measured parallel to girder) bearing pad with $d = 61.5$ in.; the critical section for shear is located at $10/2 + 61.5/2 = 35.75$, or 36 in. (rounded-off) from the centerline of the bearings (see Fig. E7.4c).

$$V_d = 1.983(L/2 - x) + P/2$$

$$= 1.983\left(\frac{75}{2} - 3\right) + \frac{2.8}{2}$$

$$= 69.81 \text{ kips}$$

Live-load shear at the critical section is determined from the influence line (see Fig. E7.4d).

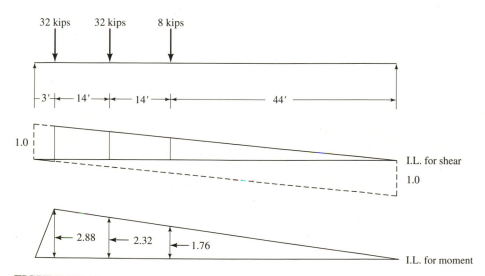

5 in.

$61.5/2 = 30.75'' = d/2$

Bearing
pad

$35.75'' \approx 3''$

Section at $d/2$ from
face of support   **FIGURE E7.4c**

Loaded length $= 75 - 3 = 72$ ft.

$$V_L = 32(\tfrac{72}{75} + \tfrac{58}{74}) + 8 \times \tfrac{44}{75}$$

$$= 60.16 \text{ kips}$$

$$I = \frac{50}{72 + 125} = 0.254$$

$$V_{L+I} = 60.16 \times 1.254 \times \frac{1}{2} \times \frac{7.67}{5.5} = 52.60 \text{ kips}$$

$$V_u = 1.3[V_D + \tfrac{5}{3}V_{L+I}]$$

$$= 1.3[69.81 + \tfrac{5}{3} \times 52.60]$$

$$= 204.72 \text{ kips}$$

Calculate shear strength provided by concrete alone, V_c, as the *smaller* of V_{ci} and V_{cw} (AASHTO 9.20.2). Compute V_{ci}:

$$V_{ci} = 0.6\sqrt{f_c'}b'd + V_d + \frac{V_i M_{cr}}{M_{max}} \qquad \text{(AASHTO Eq. 9.27)}$$

32 kips   32 kips   8 kips

3′   14′   14′   44′

1.0

I.L. for shear

1.0

2.88   2.32   1.76

I.L. for moment

FIGURE E7.4d
Influence-line diagram for shear and moment at critical section of beam.

where d = depth of composite section = $61.5 - 3.23 = 58.27$ in., b' = width of web = 8 in.

V_d = shear due to the dead load of the composite section

= $1.541(\frac{1}{2} \times 75 - 3) = 53.16$ kips

V_i = factored shear force due to the superimposed dead load and live load

The superimposed dead load is

w_{SDL} = 0.442/ft + weight of intermediate diaphragm

V_{SDL} = $0.442(\frac{1}{2} \times 75 - 3) + \frac{1}{2} \times 2.8 = 16.65$ kips

The same value for V_{SDL} could have been obtained from the influence-line diagram for shear at that section: $V_{SDL} = 0.442 \times [\frac{1}{2}(72 \times 0.96 - 3 \times 0.04)] + 0.5 \times 2.8 = 16.65$ kips.

$$V_i = 1.3[16.65 + \tfrac{5}{3}(52.47)] = 135.33 \text{ kips}$$

The maximum moments due to these externally applied loads are

1. *Due to superimposed loads* (from the influence-line diagram)

$$M_{SDL} = 0.442 \times \frac{1}{2} \times 2.88 \times 75 + 2.88 \times 2.2 \times \frac{37.5}{72} = 51.94 \text{ kip-ft}$$

2. *Due to live load* (from the influence-line diagram)

$$M_L = 32 \times (2.88 + 2.32) + 8 \times 1.76 = 180.48 \text{ kip-ft}$$

$$M_{L+I} = 180.48 \times 1.254 \times \frac{1}{2} \times \frac{7.67}{5.5} = 157.81 \text{ kip-ft}$$

The factored moment due to the externally applied loads is $M_{max} = 1.3 \times [51.94 + \frac{5}{3} \times 157.81] = 409.44$ kip-ft.

The moment causing flexural cracking at a section due to externally applied load is given by (AASHTO Eq. 9.28)

$$M_{cr} = \frac{I}{Y_t}(6\sqrt{f_c'} + f_{pe} - f_d)$$

$$= \frac{260,680}{21.5}(6\sqrt{5000} + 1894 - 1234) \times \frac{1}{12,000}$$

$$= 1095.53 \text{ kip-ft}$$

$$V_{ci} = \frac{0.6\sqrt{5000} \times 8 \times 50.77}{1000} + 53.16 + \frac{135.33 \times 1095.53}{409.44}$$

$$= 432.49 \text{ kips}$$

Compute V_{cw}:

$$V_{cw} = (3.5\sqrt{f_c'} + 0.3f_{pc})b'd + V_P \qquad \text{(AASHTO Eq. 9.29)}$$

$$f_{pc} = \frac{P_e}{A_{comp}}$$

$$= \frac{572.6}{1403}$$

$$= 408 \text{ psi}$$

with the third-point harping of the strands (see Fig. E7.4e).

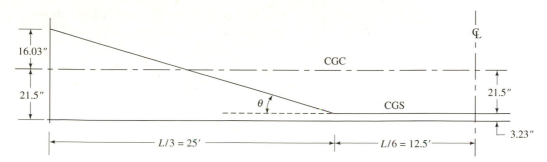

FIGURE E7.4e
Tendon profile with third-point harping.

$$\tan \theta = \frac{16.03 + 21.5}{25 \times 12} = 0.1251$$

$$\theta = 7.13066°, \ \sin \theta = 0.1241$$

$$V_P = P_e \sin \theta = 572.6 \times 0.1241 = 71.06 \text{ kips}$$

$$V_{cw} = (3.5 \sqrt{5000} + 0.3 \times 408) \times ([8 \times (0.8 \times 54)]/1000) + 71.06$$

$$= 198.9 \text{ kips} < V_{ci} = 432.49 \text{ kips}$$

Therefore, the shear strength of the concrete section alone is $V_C = V_{cw} = 198.9$ kips.

$$V_u = \phi V_n = \phi(V_c + V_s) = 0.9V_c + 0.9V_s$$

$$204.72 = 0.9 \times 198.9 + 0.9V_s \rightarrow V_s = 28.57 \text{ kips}$$

The maximum shear that can be permitted with web reinforcement is

$$8\sqrt{f_c'}b'd = 8 \times \sqrt{5000} \times 8 \times (54 - 3.23) \times \tfrac{1}{1000}$$

$$= 229.76 \text{ kips} > V_s = 5.82 \text{ kips, OK}$$

Since

$$4\sqrt{f_c'}b'd = \tfrac{1}{2} \times 229.76 = 114.88 \text{ kips} > V_s = 5.82 \text{ kips}$$

the maximum permissible spacing for stirrups is

$$s_{max} = 0.75h = 0.75 \times 54 = 40.5 \text{ in.} > 24 \text{ in.} \quad \text{(AASHTO 9.20.3.2)}$$

Hence, provide stirrups at $s = 24$ in.
Provide Gr. 60 #4 two-legged stirrups, $A_v = 0.39$ in.^{2} (see Appendix A, Table A.20). Therefore, the maximum spacing of web reinforcement is

$$s = \frac{A_v F_{sy} d}{V_s} \qquad \text{(AASHTO Eq. 9.30)}$$

$$= \frac{0.39 \times 60 \times 50.77}{28.57} = 41.58 \text{ in.} > 24 \text{ in. max.}$$

With Gr. 60 #A two-legged stirrups, the minimum spacing is

$$s_{min} = \frac{A_v f_{sy}}{50b'} = \frac{0.39 \times 60,000}{50 \times 8} = 58.5 \text{ in.} > 24 \text{ in.}$$

Hence, provide #4 two-legged stirrups at 24-in. o.c. throughout the beam. These stirrups should be extended above the top of the girder for anchoring into the cast-in-place slab to resist the horizontal shear.

Horizontal shear (AASHTO 9.20.4). $V_u = 204.72$ kips. For a clean, laitance-free, but *not* intentionally roughened contact surface (with d = depth of the entire composite section = $71.5 - 3.23 = 58.27$ in.),

$$V_{nh} = 80 b_v d \qquad \text{(AASHTO 9.20.4.3(b))}$$

$$= 80 \times 20 \times \frac{58.27}{1000}$$

$$= 109.2 \text{ kips} < V_u = 204.72 \text{ kips}$$

As specified above, Gr. 60 #4 two-legged stirrups at 24 in. o.c., extending from the top of the girders, will be anchored into the cast-in-place slab. This reinforcement will serve as the minimum tie reinforcement ($A_v = 50 b_v s / f_y$, calculated above) and satisfy the requirements of AASHTO 9.20.4.5(a). However, the top of the girders, in addition to being clean and laitance-free, must be intentionally roughened to a full amplitude of approximately $\frac{1}{4}$ in. for the horizontal shear resistance to be increased to

$$V_{nh} = 350 b_v d \qquad\qquad \text{(AASHTO 9.20.4.3(c))}$$

$$= 350 \times 20 \times 58.27 = 407.89 \text{ kips} > 204.72 \text{ kips, OK}$$

Hence, no additional ties are required to resist horizontal shear.

Development length required (AASHTO 9.27.1)

$$l_d = (f_{su}^* - \tfrac{2}{3} f_{se}) D \qquad\qquad \text{(AASHTO Eq. 9.32)}$$

$f_{su}^* = 266.21$ ksi (calculated earlier), $f_{se} = 144$ ksi

$$l_d = (266.21 - \tfrac{2}{3} \times 144) \times 0.5 = 85 \text{ in.}$$

Additional reinforcement in girder

1. Provide two #6 bars as hanger bars.
2. Provide three equally spaced #4 bars on each face of the web, as shown in Figure E7.4f.

Deflection and camber

1. Due to the dead load of girder, $w_G = 822$ lb/ft

$$\Delta_G = \frac{5wL^4}{384EI_G} = \frac{5 \times 0.822 \times (75)^4 \times (12)^3}{384 \times 4.07 \times (10)^3 \times 260{,}680} = 0.55 \text{ in. } (\downarrow)$$

2. Camber due to the initial prestressing force, $P_i = 751.4$ kips

$$\Delta_P = -\left(\frac{5}{48}\right) \frac{P(e_1 + e_2)L^2}{EI_G} + \frac{1}{8} \frac{Pe_2 L^2}{EI_G}$$

$$= -\left(\frac{5}{48}\right) \frac{751.4 \times (21.5 + 16.03) \times (75)^2}{4.07 \times 10^3 \times 260{,}680} + \left(\frac{1}{8}\right) \frac{751.4 \times 16.03 \times (75)^2}{4.07 \times 10^3 \times 260{,}860}$$

$$= -1.06 + 0.1$$

$$= -1.05 \text{ in. } (\uparrow)$$

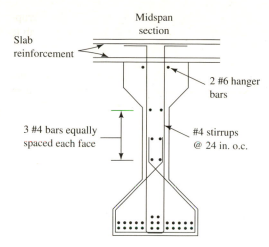

Slab
reinforcement

Midspan
section

2 #6 hanger
bars

3 #4 bars equally
spaced each face

#4 stirrups
@ 24 in. o.c.

FIGURE E7.4f

3. Net initial camber $= -1.05 + 0.55 = -0.5$ in. ($\uparrow$)
4. Deflection due to slab: $w_{\text{slab}} = 0.719$ k/ft

$$\Delta_{\text{slab}} = \frac{5wL^4}{384EI_G} = \frac{5 \times 0.719 \times (75)^4 \times (12)^3}{384 \times 4.07 \times 10^3 \times 260,680} = 0.48 \text{ in. } (\downarrow)$$

5. Deflection due to the superimposed dead load: $w_{\text{SDL}} = 0.422$ k/ft

$$\Delta_{\text{SDL}} = \frac{5wL^4}{384EI_G} = \frac{5 \times 0.442 \times (75)^4 \times (12)^3}{384 \times 4.07 \times 10^3 \times 640,039} = 0.12 \text{ in. } (\downarrow)$$

6. Net deflection $-0.5 + 0.48 + 0.12 = 0.1$ in. ($\downarrow$)
7. For deflection based on I_g, creep coefficient $C_c = 4.0$ (AASHTO 1994, p. 5-42)
   Net deflection due to total load $= 0.1 \times 4.0 = 0.4$ in. ($\downarrow$)
8. Live-load deflection (see formula in Chapter 5) is

$$\Delta_L = \frac{324}{EI_g} P_T (L^3 - 555L + 4780)$$

where $P_T =$ weight of one front truck wheel $\times$ LL distance factor $\times (1 + I)$

$$= 4 \times \frac{7.67}{5.5} \times 1.25 = 6.973 \text{ kips}$$

$$\Delta_L = \frac{324 \times 6.973 \times [(75)^3 - 555 \times 75 + 4780]}{4.07 \times 10^3 \times 640,039} = 0.33 \text{ in. } (\downarrow)$$

Compare with allowable live-load deflection (AASHTO 10.6.1):

$$\Delta_{\text{allowable}} = \frac{L}{800} = \frac{75 \times 12}{800} = 1.125 \text{ in. } > 0.33 \text{ in., OK}$$

It is instructive to compute the time history of deflection as follows, using the deflection multipliers suggested by Martin [1977]:

1. *At transfer*

   Due to prestress, $\Delta_P = -1.05$ in. ($\uparrow$)
   Due to girder weight, $\Delta_G = 0.55$ in. ($\downarrow$)
   Estimate of camber at transfer $= -1.05 + 0.55 = -0.50$ in. ($\uparrow$)

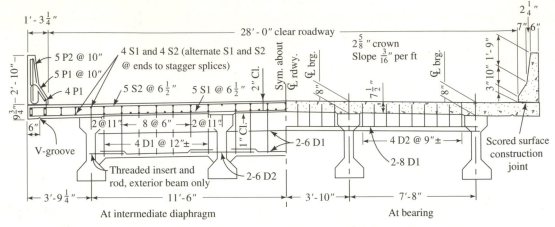

FIGURE E7.4g
Transverse section through the bridge.

2. *At erection* (sustained load due to girder weight for 30 days), using multipliers from Table 7.19:

$$\Delta_P = -1.05 \times 1.8 = -1.89 \text{ in. } (\uparrow)$$
$$\Delta_G = 0.55 \times 1.85 = 1.02 \text{ in. } (\downarrow)$$
Estimate of camber at erection $= -1.89 + 1.49 = -0.87$ in. $(\downarrow)$

3. *At end of three years* (sustained load due to slab and the superimposed dead load)

$$\Delta_P = -1.05 \times 2.45 = -2.57 \text{ in. } (\uparrow)$$
$$\Delta_G = 0.55 \times 2.70 = 1.49 \text{ in. } (\downarrow)$$
$$\Delta_{SDL} = (0.48 + 0.12) \times 3 = 1.80 \text{ in. } (\downarrow)$$
Estimated final deflection $= -2.57 + 1.49 + 1.80 = 0.72$ in. $(\downarrow)$

A typical transverse section of the bridge is shown in Fig. E7.4g.

7.16.2 Design of Post-Tensioned Concrete Box Girder Bridges

General description and design philosophy of box girder bridges was presented in Sec. 7.6.1.1. Two examples of box girder bridge design are presented henceforth: a single-span box girder bridge in this section, and a two-span continuous box girder bridge in the next. Both types of bridges are some of the most commonly built in the State of California.

Example 7.5 illustrates design of a cast-in-place, single-span post-tensioned, concrete box girder bridge. The design calculations for this example have been adopted from PTI [1978]. Extensive explanatory comments are provided wherever necessary for clarification.

EXAMPLE 7.5. Design a cast-in-place, post-tensioned, concrete box girder bridge for a simple span of 162 ft to carry HS20 loading. The out-to-out width of the bridge is 42 ft. Use $f_c' = 4500$ psi and $\frac{1}{2}$-in.-diameter 270-ksi strands for post-tensioning.

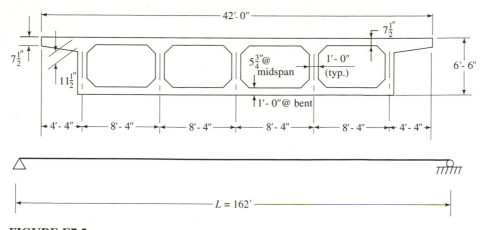

FIGURE E7.5
Cross section of box girder.

Solution. The cross section of a cast-in-place concrete box girder is shown in Fig. E7.5. The minimum thicknesses of top and bottom flanges and webs are selected to satisfy the requirements of AASHTO 9.9. Based on practical considerations, the top slab is made $7\frac{1}{2}$ in. thick, the webs are arbitrarily kept 12 in. thick, and the bottom slab is made $5\frac{3}{4}$ in. thick. Fillets are provided at the junctions of all webs with top and bottom flanges; however, their presence is neglected in calculations to simplify the calculations. The width of the cantilever slab extending beyond the exterior girder has been limited to half the girder spacing (AASHTO 3.23.2.3.2.1).

Calculate section properties. Take the moments of areas about the bottom fibers to determine the centroid of the section.

Section	A (ft²)	y_b (ft)	Ay_b (ft³)	d (ft)	Ad^2 (ft⁴)	I_o (ft⁴)
42×0.625	26.25	6.19	162.48	2.53	168.88	0.854
$\frac{1}{2} \times 3.83 \times 0.33 \times 2$	1.26	5.76	7.28	2.1	5.57	0.01
$5 \times 1.0 \times 5.4$	27.00	31.8	85.86	0.48	6.22	65.61
34.33×0.479	16.44	0.24	3.95	3.42	191.60	0.310
Σ	70.95		259.57		372.27	66.784

The center of gravity of concrete (CGC) is located at y_b from the bottom fibers:

$y_b = 259.57/70.95 = 3.66$ ft from the botton fibers
$y_t = 6.5 - 3.66 = 2.84$ ft from the top fibers

Moment of Inertia

$I = I_o + Ad^2 = 66.784 + 372.27 = 439.05$ ft⁴
Section modulus (top fibers), $S_t = 439.05/2.84 = 154.6$ ft³
Section modulus (bottom fibers), $S_b = 439.05/3.66 = 119.96$ ft³
Radius of gyration, $r^2 = I/A = 439.05/70.95 = 6.19$ ft²

Stresses in top and bottom fibers, f_t and f_b, respectively, are expressed in terms of design moment, M (kip-ft):

$$f_t = \frac{M}{S_t} = \frac{1000 \times M}{144 \times 154.6}$$

$$= 0.045M \text{ (ksi)}$$

$$f_b = \frac{M}{S_b} = \frac{1000 \times M}{144 \times 119.96}$$

$$= 0.058M \text{ (ksi)}$$

These two expressions will be used throughout this example to calculate stresses due to loads.

Design moments. Assuming normal-weight concrete, $\gamma_c = 150$ lb/ft^3. Therefore,

Dead load $= 70.95 \times 0.15 = 10.64$ kips/ft
Diaphragms and fillets (assumed) $= 0.03$
Total dead load, $w = 10.64 + 0.03 = 10.67$ kips/ft
$M_D = \frac{1}{8} \times 10.67 \times (162)^2 = 35{,}003$ kip-ft

Live-load distribution. The entire box girder will be designed as one unit for which the distribution factors of the exterior and the interior girders are combined. This methodology conforms to the practice followed by the California Department of Transportation [CALTRANS, 1993c].

Equivalent distribution factor, DF_{eq}, for the entire structure is given by Eq. 7.2:

$$DF_{eq} = \frac{\text{web spacing} \times \text{no. of webs}}{14}$$

$$= \frac{\text{Deck width}}{14} = \frac{42}{14} = 3.0$$

$$\text{Impact factor, } I = \frac{50}{L + 125} = \frac{50}{162 + 125} = 0.174$$

Live-load moment is determined by interpolation from Table A.6 (Appendix A):

$$M_{L=162} = 2768 + (3077 - 2768) \times \tfrac{2}{10} = 2830 \text{ kip-ft}$$

$$M_{LL+I} = 2830 \times 3.0 \times 1.174 = 9967 \text{ kip-ft}$$

$$M_{\text{Total}} = M_D + M_{LL+I} = 35{,}003 + 9967 = 44{,}970 \text{ kip-ft}$$

Post-tensioning requirements: stresses at midspan due to $DL + LL$. Top and bottom fiber stresses due to loads are calculated from expressions calculated earlier:

$f_t = 0.045M = 0.045 \times 44{,}970 = 2024$ psi (compression)
$f_b = 0.058M = 0.058 \times 44{,}970 = -2608$ psi (tension)

Allowable stresses for $f_c' = 4500$ psi are

Compression $= 0.40 f_c' = 0.4 \times 4500 = 1800$ psi
Tension $= 6\sqrt{f_c'} = 6 \times \sqrt{4500} = 402$ psi

Approximate amount of post-tensioning steel required is calculated from Fig. B.1 (Appendix B). This chart is valid for the zero allowable tension condition. When the allowable tension is $6\sqrt{f_c'}$ (as in this example), the chart values are to be multiplied by 0.85 [PTI, 1978].

$L = 162$ ft and $D = 6.5$ ft; $D/L = 6.5/162 = 0.04$. From the chart, the approximate amount of post-tensioning steel required for a span of 162 ft is 4.7 lb/ft^2.

Amount of steel required $= 0.85 \times 4.7 = 4.0$ lb/ft^2 of deck area. Weight of pre-stressing steel required per linear foot of the bridge $= 4.0 \times 42 = 168$ lb/ft

Cross-sectional area of a $\frac{1}{2}$-in.-diameter strand $= 0.153$ in.^{2} (Appendix A, Table A.25). With density of steel as 490 lb/ft^3, the weight of one strand is $w = 0.153 \times 490/144 = 0.52$ kip/ft

Number of strands required $= 168/0.52 = 323$ strands

Calculate the prestressing force (after losses) in each girder (or web, five in the present case). With a total of 323 strands, and assuming average stress of $0.6f_s'$, the force in each girder is

$$P_f = 323 \times (0.6 \times 270) \times 0.153/5 = 1601 \text{ kips/girder}$$

From Fig. B.7 (Appendix B), for $P_f = 1601$ kips, minimum $D = 3\frac{1}{2}$ in.

As shown in Fig. 7.56, the maximum distance from the CGS to the bottom fiber $(x) = 3\frac{1}{2} + 4\frac{1}{2} = 8$ in. Therefore $e = 3.66 \times 12 - 8 = 35.92$ in., or $= 2.99$ ft.

Post-tensioning force and concrete strength required. With the eccentricity of prestressing force, $e = 2.99$ ft, calculate the maximum prestressing force (after losses) that can be permitted to control stresses.

Net tensile stress at bottom $= 2608 - 402 = 2206$ psi

$$f_b = \frac{P_f}{A} + \frac{P_f e}{S_b} = 2206 \text{ psi}$$

Therefore,

$$\frac{P_f}{70.95 \times 144} + \frac{P_f \times 2.99 \times 12}{119.96 \times (12)^3} = 2.206$$

or

$$P_f = 8141 \text{ kips}$$

Hence, P_f/girder $= 8141/5 = 1628.2$ kips.

Assume $P_f = 1601$ kips (close enough, OK). Minimum D required (Fig. B.7, Appendix B) for 1628 kips $\approx 3\frac{5}{8}$ in. $\approx 3\frac{1}{2}$ in. required for the assumed $P_f = 1601$ kips. Therefore tendons will fit inside the duct.

Calculate the design concrete strength required. The stress in top fibers due to post-tensioning is

$$f_t = \frac{8141}{70.95 \times 144} - \frac{8141 \times 2.99 \times 12}{154.6 \times (12)^3}$$

$$= -296 \text{ psi}$$

Therefore, final stress at the top is $f_t = 2024 - 296 = 1728$ psi.

Since the allowable concrete stress is $f_c = 0.4f_c'$, the concrete strength required is $f_c' = f_c/0.4 = 1728/0.4 = 4320$ psi, whereas the concrete strength used to calculate the allowable tension of $6\sqrt{f_c'}$ is 4500 psi (close enough, OK). Thus, there is no need for recycling the design. However, if necessary, the design procedure could be recycled, which could reduce the required P_f by about 1 percent.

Number of $\frac{1}{2}$-in.-ϕ 270-ksi strands required. Assume prestress loss = 33,000 psi* (see Table 7.17). (*Assume the same value as for 5000-psi concrete, since the value for 4500-psi concrete is not given.)

Allowable strand stress before losses = $0.7 \times 270 = 189$ ksi
Effective prestress = $f_e = 189 - 33 = 156$ ksi

Area of a $\frac{1}{2}$-in.-diameter 270-ksi strand = 0.153 in.^{2} (Appendix A, Table A.25)

$$\text{Number of strands per girder} = \frac{8141}{5 \times 156 \times 0.153}$$

$$= 68.2 \text{ strands}$$

Actually, 68 strands will be provided per girder. $P_{f.\text{total}}$ (before losses) = $68 \times 5 \times 189 \times 0.153 = 9832$ kips.

Required concrete strength at stressing. The required ultimate strength of the concrete at the time of stressing will be governed by either the initial flexural stresses or the bearing stresses induced by the tendon anchorages. A discussion of the anchorage bearing stresses was presented earlier in Sec. 7.6.1.2g. The compressive stresses in the post-tensioned girder, other than in the immediate area of the anchorage, are limited to $0.55 f_c'$ and the tensile stresses are limited to $7.5\sqrt{f_{ci}'}$ (AASHTO 9.15.2.1). Top and bottom stresses will be computed from the expressions derived earlier.

Dead-load fiber stress at midspan

At top, $f_t = 0.045M = 0.045 \times 35,003 = 1575$ psi (compressive)
At bottom, $f_b = 0.058M = 0.058 \times 35,003 = 2030$ psi (tensile)

Stresses at midspan due to the post-tensioning force of 9832 kips (before losses) are

$$f_t = \frac{9832 \times 1000}{70.95 \times 144} - 0.045 \times 9832 \times 2.99$$

$$= -321 \text{ psi (tensile)}$$

$$f_b = \frac{9832 \times 1000}{70.95 \times 144} + 0.058 \times 9832 \times 2.99$$

$$= 2667 \text{ psi (compressive)}$$

Therefore, the net stresses are

At top, $f_t = 1575 - 321 = 1254$ psi (compressive)
At bottom, $f_b = 2667 - 2030 = 637$ psi (compressive)

Required strength at stressing = $f_c/0.55 = 1254/0.55 = 2280$ psi. Hence, the anchorage bearing stresses will govern.

Check for strength. Ultimate-moment requirements normally do not control simple-span design. The procedures to check ultimate-moment capacity and typical web reinforcement calculations are omitted here but are shown for the two-span bridge in the next example.

Deformations and friction. The amount of shortening as a result of post-tensioning approximates a total (elastic + plastic + shrinkage) of 1 in. per 100 ft of structure. On this structure, provision should be made at one abutment to allow for movement due to shortening.

Deflections due to dead load and prestressing should be calculated separately in the normal manner, as illustrated in Example 7.4. To find the net deflection at a particular point in time, consideration must be given to the magnitude of the active prestressing force. For instance, to compute initial deflections, the initial prestressing force should be used, and while calculating ultimate deflections, the final prestressing force should be used.

The friction effects can generally be neglected in the design of a simple-span structure. However, the post-tensioning contractor should make friction calculations and submit them on the fabrication drawings. See Example 7.1 for the calculation procedure.

7.16.3 Design of Cast-in-Place Continuous Post-Tensioned Box Girder Bridges

The design and details of continuous prestressed members differ from the simple beam design in that *secondary moments* are introduced as the member is stressed. Also called the *parasitic* or *hyperstatic moments,* these moments are byproducts of prestressing; they do not exist in determinate beams (hence the term "secondary"). The term "secondary" is rather misleading, however, because these moments are not secondary in magnitude and must be accounted for in the design.

The tendon path is usually longer and has more angle change in continuous prestressed members than in simple beam design; thus friction and anchor seating losses must be considered in the design calculations. The design procedure illustrated by the next example accounts for secondary moments, friction losses, and anchor seating losses.

Example 7.6 illustrates the preliminary design of a two-span continuous box girder bridge taken from CALTRANS [1993c] (also discussed in PTI [1978]). Explanatory notes, wherever necessary, are provided.

EXAMPLE 7.6. A TWO-SPAN CONTINUOUS BOX GIRDER BRIDGE. Prepare a preliminary design for a two-span (150–162 ft) cast-in-place, continuous post-tensioned box girder bridge, as shown in Fig. E7.6a for HS20-44 loading. Use normal-weight concrete and $\frac{1}{2}$-in.-diameter 270-ksi strands, $f_c' = 5000$ psi.

Design calculations. This structure will be designed as a unit with live load applied, which is equivalent to individual girder design.

Section properties at midspan. Take the moments of the areas about the bottom fibers to determine the centroid of the section.

Section	A (ft²)	y_b (ft)	Ay_b (ft³)	d (ft)	Ad^2 (ft⁴)	I_o (ft⁴)
42×0.625	26.25	6.19	162.48	2.53	168.02	0.854
$\frac{1}{2} \times 3.83 \times 0.33 \times 2$	1.26	5.76	7.28	2.1	5.56	0.01
$5 \times 1.0 \times 5.39$	26.99	31.8	85.83	0.48	6.22	65.64
34.33×0.477	16.38	0.24	3.93	3.42	191.59	0.310
Σ	70.88		259.52		371.39	66.714

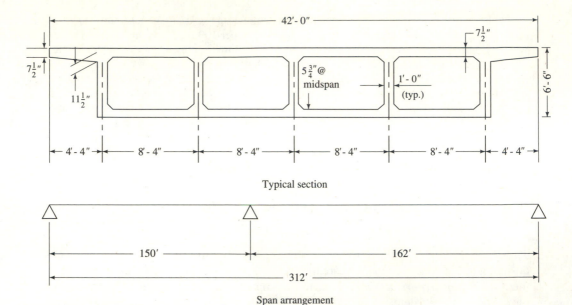

Typical section

Span arrangement

FIGURE E7.6a
A two-span continuous post-tensioned box girder bridge.

The location of the center of gravity of concrete (CGC) is determined as follows:

$y_b = 259.52/70.88 = 3.66$ ft from bottom fibers
$y_t = 6.5 - 3.66 = 2.84$ ft from top fibers
$I = 371.39 + 66.714 = 438.11$ ft^4
$S_t = 438.11/2.84 = 154.26$ ft^3
$S_b = 438.11/3.66 = 119.70$ ft^3

Stresses in top and bottom fibers are expressed in terms of design moment, M (kip-ft).

$$f_t = \frac{M}{S_t} = \frac{1000 \times M}{144 \times 154.26}$$

$$= 0.045M$$

$$f_b = \frac{M}{S_b} = \frac{1000 \times M}{144 \times 119.70}$$

$$= 0.058M$$

The coefficients 0.045 and 0.058 in the above expressions are referred to as *stress coefficients*.

Section properties at bent (see Fig. E7.6a). The cross section at the bent is similar to the one at midspan, except that the bottom slab thickness has been increased from $5\frac{3}{4}$ in. at the midspan to 12 in. at the bent.

Take the moment of areas about the bottom fibers to determine the centroid of the section.

Section	A (ft^2)	y_b (ft)	Ay_b (ft^3)	d (ft)	Ad^2 (ft^4)	I_o (ft^4)
42×0.625	26.25	6.19	162.48	2.53	168.02	0.854
$\frac{1}{2} \times 3.83 \times 0.33 \times 2$	1.26	5.76	7.28	2.1	5.56	0.01
$5 \times 1.0 \times 4.785$	24.38	3.43	83.61	0.29	2.05	48.27
34.33×1.0	34.33	0.50	17.16	2.64	239.27	2.86
Σ	86.22		270.53		414.90	51.994

$y_b = 270.53/86.22 = 3.14$ ft from the bottom fibers
$y_t = 6.5 - 3.14 = 3.36$ ft from the top fibers

Moment of inertia of the entire box section

$I = 51.994 + 414.90 = 466.90$ ft^4
Section modulus (top), $S_t = 466.90/3.36 = 138.96$ ft^3
Section modulus (bottom), $S_b = 466.90/3.14 = 148.69$ ft^3

The stresses in the top and bottom fibers are expressed in terms of the design moment, M (kip-ft):

$$f_t = \frac{M}{S_t} = \frac{1000M}{138.96 \times 144} = 0.0500M$$

$$f_b = \frac{M}{S_b} = \frac{1000M}{148.69 \times 144} = 0.0467M$$

The coefficients 0.50 and 0.0467 in the above expressions may be referred to as stress coefficients.

Design moments. With normal-weight concrete, $\gamma_c = 150$ lb/ft^3.

$$\begin{aligned} \text{Dead load} &= 70.88 \times 0.15 = 10.63 \text{ k-ft} \\ \text{Diaphragms and fillets} &= \underline{0.33 \text{ k-ft}} \\ \text{Total} &= 10.66 \text{ k-ft} \end{aligned}$$

Live-load distribution. The distribution factor,

$$\text{LL per girder} = \frac{S}{2 \times 7} = \frac{S}{14}$$

For the entire structure, use width/14. LL distribution factor $= \frac{42}{14} = 3.0$ lanes.
No multiple-lane live-load reduction is applicable because the computed distribution is an equivalent girder loading.

Design moments (from moment envelopes)

At 0.4L span 1	*At 0.6L span 2*	*At centerline of bent*
$M_D = 15{,}151$ k-ft	$M_D = 19{,}940$ k-ft	$M_D = -34{,}078$ k-ft
$M_L = 6980$ k-ft	$M_L = 7597$ k-ft	$M_L = -9230$ k-ft
$M_T = \overline{22{,}131}$ k-ft	$M_T = \overline{27{,}537}$ k-ft	$M_T = \overline{-43{,}308}$ k-ft

Preliminary post-tensioning requirements. These calculations are similar to those for Example 7.5. From Fig. B.2 (Appendix B), for 162 ft (or longer[3]) span and $D/L = 6.5/162 = 0.04$, the amount of post-tensioning steel required per ft^2 of deck $= 0.75 \times 4.2 = 3.15$ lb/ft^2. Note that the multiplier 0.75 has been used since the allowable tension is $6\sqrt{f_c'}$ (instead of zero), as explained in Sec. 7.6.1.2d. Also, note that Fig. B.2 is valid for the case of two *equal* spans. However, it has been used in this example of a two-span box girder with unequal spans for estimating purposes. For the entire deck (width $= 42$ ft), the amount of post-tensioning steel required $= 42 \times 3.15 = 132.3$ lb/ft of bridge.

Here, $\frac{1}{2}$-in.-diameter prestressing strands will be used, with the density of steel as 490 lb/ft^2, and the weight of the $\frac{1}{2}$-in.-diameter strand ($A = 0.153$ in.^{2}) is $w = 0.153 \times 490/144 = 0.52$ lb/ft. Therefore,

$$\text{Number of } \tfrac{1}{2}\text{-in.-diameter prestressing strands required} = 132.3/0.52 = 255 \text{ strands}$$

The box sections contain five girders. Therefore,

$$\text{Number of strands per girder} = \tfrac{255}{5} = 51$$
$$f_c' \text{ required} = 3700 \text{ psi}$$

(from Fig. B.2, Appendix B, by interpolation between curves for $f_c' = 3500$ psi and 5000 psi).

With fifty-one $\frac{1}{2}$-in. strands (0.153 in.^{2} each) and a prestressing stress of $0.75 f_s'$, the jacking force per girder, P_j, is

$$P_j = 51 \times (0.75 \times 270) \times 0.153 = 1580 \text{ kips/girder}$$
$$\text{Total } P_j = 1580 \times 5 = 7900 \text{ kips}$$

From Fig. B.8 (Appendix B), $D = 5\frac{1}{2}$ in. Refer to Fig. 7.56 to locate the CGs of prestressing steel—distances ($D + 4\frac{1}{2}$ in.) at the bottom and ($D + K$) at the top of the box section.

The minimum distance from the CG of the prestressing force to the bottom fibers of the box girder, $D + 4\frac{1}{2}$ in. $= 5\frac{1}{2} + 4\frac{1}{2} = 10$ in. The minimum distance from the CG of the prestressing force to the top fibers of the box girder, $D + K = 5\frac{1}{2} + (7\frac{1}{2} - 1) = 12$ in.

Inflection points along the tendon path are located at $0.1L$ from the bent. This results in a reasonable radius of curvature for placing a semirigid duct and maintains the forces on duct material within the acceptable limits during stressing.

Due to the presence of secondary moments, the most efficient location of the low point along the tendon path is near $0.5L$ in a two-span structure. For this example, the point at $0.5L$ will be used. The tendon profile is shown in Fig. E7.6b. From this figure, dimensions a and b can be found because the inflection points of two parabolas lie on a straight line. The distance between the CGs at $0.5L$ and at the support is $6.5 - 1 - 0.83 = 4.67$ ft. Thus,

$$a = 4.67 \times \frac{60}{75} = 3.74 \text{ ft}$$

$$b = 4.67 \times \frac{64.8}{81} = 3.74 \text{ ft}$$

Friction losses. Friction losses will be calculated similar to Example 7.1. Values of the wobble coefficient, K, and the friction coefficient, μ, will be taken as 0.0002 and 0.25,

---

[3]One could have also selected the required amount of prestressing steel for the average span length of 156 ft (average of 150 and 162 ft) for this preliminary design.

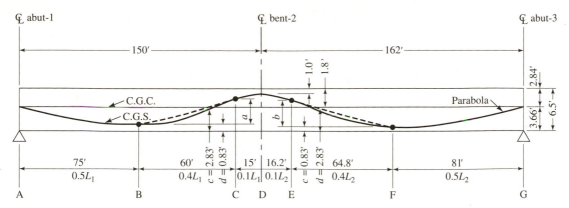

Tendon (C.G.S.) profile

Note: Dimensions *a* and *b* can be found because the inflection point of two parabolas lies on a straight line.

$$a = \tfrac{60}{75} \times 4.67 = 3.74'$$

$$b = \tfrac{64.8}{81} \times 4.67 = 3.74'$$

FIGURE E7.6b
Tendon (CGS) profile.

respectively. Angle changes will be computed as illustrated in Example 7.1. The angle change, α, was defined as $\alpha = 2e/L$, where e is the vertical distance of the parabola between control points, and L is the horizontal distance between the control points.

Angle change in span 1 (in radians)

$$\text{Segment } AB, \frac{2B}{L} = \frac{2 \times 2.83}{75} = 0.075$$

$$\text{Segment } BC, \frac{2B}{L} = \frac{2 \times 3.74}{60} = 0.125$$

$$\text{Segment } CD, \frac{2B}{L} = \frac{2 \times 0.93}{15} = 0.125$$

Therefore,

$$\alpha = 0.075 + 0.125 + 0.125 = 0.325 \text{ radian}$$

(*Note:* The angle change, α, in segments *BC* and *CD* will always be equal.)

Angle change in span 2 (in radians)

$$\text{Segment } DE, \frac{2B}{L} = \frac{2 \times 0.93}{16.2} = 0.115$$

$$\text{Segment } EF, \frac{2B}{L} = \frac{2 \times 3.74}{64.8} = 0.115$$

$$\text{Segment } FG, \frac{2B}{L} = \frac{2 \times 2.83}{81} = 0.07$$

Therefore,

$$\alpha = 0.1150 + 0.115 + 0.07 = 0.300 \text{ radian}$$

Span 1. $L = 150$ ft, $K = 0.0002$, $\mu = 0.25$, and $\alpha = 0.325$ radian (computed above). Therefore,

$$KL + \mu\alpha = 0.0002 \times 150 + 0.25 \times 0.325 = 0.11$$
$$P_j = P_x e^{(KL+\mu\alpha)} \quad \text{(see Eq. 7.3)}$$
$$= P_x e^{0.11}$$
$$= 1.116 P_x$$

Hence, $P_x = (1/1.116)P_j = 0.896P_j$; i.e., tension at bent $= 89.6$ percent of P_j. Note that the use of Eq. 7.6 (instead of Eq. 7.3) would give $P_j = 1.11P_x$ instead of $1.116P_x$ (close enough).

Span 2. $L = 162$ ft, $K = 0.0002$, $\mu = 0.25$, and $\alpha = 0.30$ radian (computed above). Therefore,

$$KL + \mu\alpha = 0.0002 \times 162 + 0.25 \times 0.300 = 0.107$$
$$P_j = P_x e^{0.107}$$
$$= 1.113 P_x$$

Hence, $P_x = (1/1.113)P_j = 0.898P_j$; i.e., tension at bent $= 89.8$ percent of P_j. Use T_j at bent $= 89.8P_j$.

Anchor set. The effect of anchor set on the cable stress is as follows:

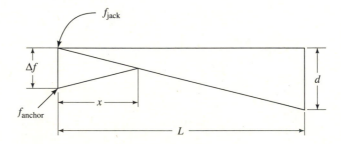

Δf = Change in stresses due to anchor set (ksi)
S = Length influenced by anchor set (ft)
d = Friction loss in length L (ksi)
L = Length to a point where loss is known (ft)
ΔL = Anchor set (in.)
E = Modulus of elasticity (ksi)

From Hooke's law, average unit stress $= E \times$ unit strain.

$$\frac{\Delta f}{2} = E\frac{\Delta L}{12x}$$

$$\Delta f = \frac{E\Delta L}{6x}$$

By similar triangles,

$$\frac{x}{\Delta f/2} = \frac{L}{d}$$

or

$$\Delta f = \frac{2\,dx}{L}$$

Equating the above two values of Δf yields

$$\frac{E\Delta L}{6x} = \frac{2\,dx}{L}$$

so that

$$x = \sqrt{\frac{E(\Delta L)L}{12d}}$$

Stress variation along tendon. Given $f_s' = 270$ ksi. For this example, assume[4] $\Delta L = \frac{5}{8}$ in. The recommended method of detailing requires jacking the tendons to $0.75\,f_s'$ (the stress after anchor set is not to exceed $0.70\,f_s'$ per AASHTO 9.15.1).

$$f_{jack} = 0.75\,f_s' = 0.75 \times 270 = 202 \text{ ksi}$$
$$f_j \text{ at bent} = 0.898\,f_{jack} = 0.898 \times 202 = 181 \text{ ksi}$$
$$d = 202 - 181 = 21 \text{ ksi}$$

The distance x influenced by the anchor set is computed from the previously derived expression.

Span 1

$$x = \sqrt{\frac{29 \times 10^3 \times 0.625 \times 150}{12 \times 21}} = 104 \text{ ft}$$

$$\frac{104}{150} = 0.7L_1$$

$$\Delta f = \frac{2\,dx}{L} = \frac{2 \times 21 \times 104}{150} = 29 \text{ ksi}$$

or

$$\Delta f = \left(\frac{29}{0.75 \times 270}\right)P_j = 0.14P_j$$

Span 2

$$x = \sqrt{\frac{29 \times 10^3 \times 0.625 \times 162}{12 \times 21}} = 108 \text{ ft}$$

$$\frac{108}{162} = 0.7L_2$$

$$\Delta f = \frac{2\,dx}{L} = \frac{2 \times 21 \times 108}{150} = 28 \text{ ksi}$$

---

[4]The anchor set may vary with different post-tensioning systems. Anchor set values may be obtained from post-tensioning materials supplier.

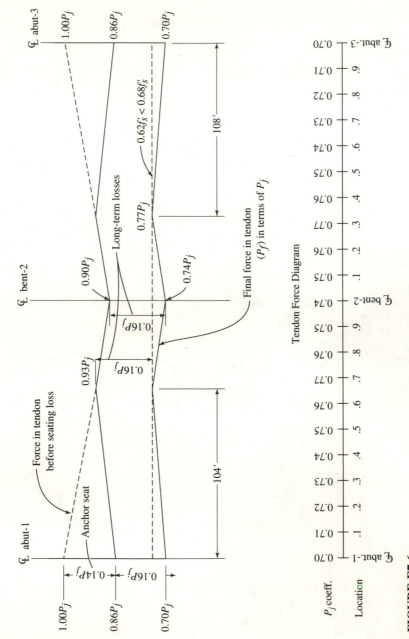

FIGURE E7.6c
Tendon force diagram.

666

or

$$\Delta f = \left(\frac{28}{0.75 \times 270}\right)P_j = 0.14P_j$$

Assume long-term losses = 33 ksi (AASHTO Table 9.16.2.2).

$$\Delta f_{LT} = \frac{33}{0.75 \times 270} = 0.16P_j$$

By assuming the jacking force, P_j, to be unity at a stress of 202 ksi (0.75×270 ksi), the force along the tendon and the prestress losses can be expressed in terms of P_j. Also, the internal moment due to the prestress force being applied at an eccentricity can be expressed in terms of the same P_j. The long-term losses are assumed to be 33 ksi per AASHTO 9.16.2.2. The tendon force diagram is shown in Fig. E7.6c.

Secondary moments are combined with $P_f e$ moments to provide the total moment effect of the post-tensioning. The secondary moments can be computed by several methods, such as slope deflection or by influence coefficients. The method contained in this example uses the influence coefficients appearing in Appendix B [PTI, 1978].

The $P_f e$ moments and the secondary moments were computed neglecting the flare in the bottom slab. No appreciable error is introduced with this procedure since the increased e and increased I tend to compensate for each other. The flare properties are used for computing the dead-load and live-load moments and the stresses.

Secondary moments. Equivalent loads are calculated per Appendix B, Sec. B.1 and are shown in Fig. E7.6d. The profile of the tendon is shown in Fig. E7.6b.

Span 1. From Fig. E7.6b, $a_1 = 0.5$, $L_1 = 150$ ft, $b_1 = 0.1$, $d = 2.83$ ft, and $c = 6.5 - 0.83 - 1.0 = 4.67$ ft. The equivalent load W_{e1} is given by

$$W_{e1} = \frac{2Pd}{a_1^2 L_1^2} = \frac{2 \times 0.72P_j \times 2.83}{(0.5)^2 \times (150)^2} = 0.00072P_j$$

$$W_1 = \frac{2Pc}{(1 - a_1)(1 - b_1 - a_1)L_1^2}$$

$$= \frac{2 \times 0.76P_j \times 4.67}{(1 - 0.5)(1 - 0.1 - 0.5)(150)^2} = 0.001577P_j$$

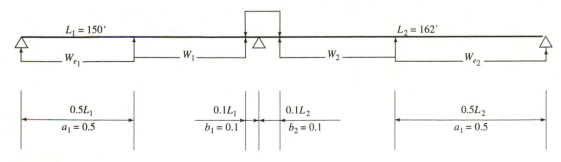

FIGURE E7.6d
Equivalent loads for calculating secondary moments.

Span 2. As before, $a_2 = 0.5$, $L_2 = 162$ ft, $b_2 = 0.1$, $d = 2.83$ ft, and $c = 4.67$ ft.

The equivalent load W_{e2} is given by

$$W_{e2} = \frac{2Pc}{a_2^2 L_2^2} = \frac{2 \times 0.72 P_j \times 2.83}{(0.5)^2 \times (162)^2} = 0.000621 P_j$$

$$W_2 = \frac{2Pc}{(1 - a_2)(1 - b_2 - a_2)L_2^2}$$

$$= \frac{2 \times 0.76 P_j \times 4.67}{(1 - 0.5)(1 - 0.1 - 0.5)(162)^2} = 0.001352 P_j$$

$$\begin{aligned}
\text{Total } M &= (0.022513 \times 0.00072 P_j + 0.019657 \times 0.001577 P_j \\
&\quad + 0.024809 \times 0.000621 P_j + 0.028413 \times 0.001352 P_j) \times (162)^2 \\
&= 2.651 P_j \text{ kip-ft}
\end{aligned}$$

The coefficient 2.651 is shown as -2.651 at bent in Fig. E7.6f. Now,

$$\begin{aligned}
\text{Total } M &= M_{\text{primary}} + M_{\text{secondary}} \\
&= P_f e + M_s
\end{aligned}$$

where $M_s = M_{\text{secondary}}$, from which

$$\begin{aligned}
M_s &= M - P_f e = 2.651 P_j - 0.74 P_j \times 1.84 \\
&= 1.289 P_j \approx 1.29 P_j
\end{aligned}$$

The coefficient 1.29 is shown as -1.29 at bent in Fig. E7.6f.

Figures E7.6e and E7.6f show, respectively, $P_j e$ and $P_f e$ diagrams. Figures E7.6g and E7.6h show, respectively, the top and bottom fiber stresses due to dead load and live load plus impact.

Solution for prestressing force. As in simple-span prestressing, the prestressing force must be large enough to bring the concrete stresses within the allowable limits. For $f_c' = 5000$ psi,

$$\text{Allowable tension} = 6\sqrt{f_c'} = 6 \times \sqrt{5000} = 424 \text{ psi}$$
$$\text{Allowable compression} = 0.4 f_c' = 0.4 \times 5000 = 2000 \text{ psi}$$

The stresses in the concrete due to prestressing are computed from the following equation:

$$f = \frac{P}{A} + \frac{Pec}{I}$$

These terms can be written as

$$\frac{P_j \times \text{force coefficient}}{\text{area}} + P_j \times \text{moment coefficient} \times \text{stress coefficient} = f_t$$

In the preceding equation, the force and the moment coefficients are obtained from Figs. E7.6e and E7.6f, respectively. The stress coefficients for the box section at the midspan and at bent was computed earlier.

The point of maximum tension in the top fiber is at the centerline of bent 2 = 1849 psi. The required change in stress due to post-tensioning = $1849 - 424 = 1425$ psi. Substituting in the above equation,

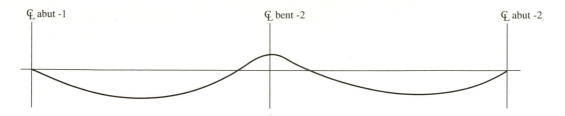

P_je	P_j coeff.	e	Location	P_je	P_j coeff.	e	Location	P_je	P_j coeff.	e	Location
0	0.70	0	0	1.45	0.77	1.89	0.7	1.98	0.76	2.60	1.4
0.72	0.71	1.02	0.1	0.55	0.76	0.73	0.8	2.12	0.75	2.83	1.5
1.30	0.72	1.81	0.2	−0.68	0.75	−0.91	0.9	2.00	0.74	2.71	1.6
1.74	0.73	2.38	0.3	−1.36	0.74	−1.84	1.0	1.74	0.73	2.38	1.7
2.00	0.74	2.71	0.4	−0.68	0.75	−0.91	1.1	1.30	0.72	1.81	1.8
2.12	0.75	2.83	0.5	0.55	0.76	0.73	1.2	0.72	0.71	1.02	1.9
1.98	0.76	2.60	0.6	1.45	0.77	1.89	1.3	0	0.70	0	1.0

FIGURE E7.6e
P_je diagram.

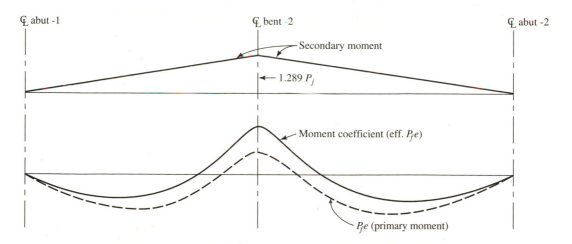

Moment coeff.	M_s	P_je	Moment coeff.	M_s	P_je	Moment coeff.	M_s	P_je
0	0	0	1.45	−0.90	0.55	1.98	−0.77	1.21
0.72	−0.13	0.59	0.55	−1.03	−0.48	2.12	−0.64	1.48
1.30	−0.26	1.04	−0.68	−1.16	−1.84	2.00	−0.51	1.49
1.74	−0.39	1.35	−1.36	−1.29	−2.65	1.74	−0.39	1.35
2.00	−0.51	1.49	−0.68	−1.16	−1.84	1.30	−0.26	1.04
2.12	−0.64	1.48	0.55	−1.03	−0.48	0.72	−0.13	0.59
1.98	−0.77	1.21	1.45	−0.90	0.55	0	0	0

FIGURE E7.6f
Effective P_fe diagram.

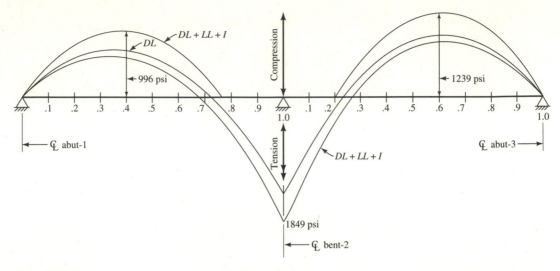

FIGURE E7.6g
Top fiber dead load + live load + impact stresses.

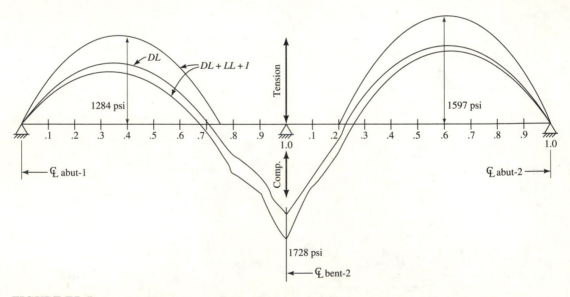

FIGURE E7.6h
Bottom fiber dead load + live load + impact stresses.

$$\frac{1000 \times 0.74P_j}{86.22 \times 144} + P_j \times 2.65 \times 0.0500 = 1425$$

$P_j = 7418$ kips. Post-tensioning force per girder $= \frac{7418}{5} = 1484$ kips/girder, which is less than 1580 kips/girder computed earlier. Hence, $P_j = 7418$ kips, governs.

In the above calculation, the force coefficient, 0.74, and the moment coefficient, 2.65, have been taken from Figs. E7.6e and E7.6f, respectively. The stress coefficient (0.0500) was computed earlier for maximum stress in the top fibers at bent. $A = 86.22$ ft^2 is the cross-sectional area of the box girder at the bent section.

Check D from Fig. B.8 (Appendix B): $D = 5\frac{1}{2}$ in. Hence, the tendon will work at the estimated eccentricity.

Check bottom fiber stress at $0.6L$ in span 2: Post-tensioned stress required $= 1597 - 424 = 1173$ psi.

$$\frac{1000 \times 0.74P_j}{70.88 \times 144} + 1.49P_j \times 0.580 = 1173$$

Solving for P_j, we have $P_j = 2233$ kips.

Check bottom fiber stress at $0.4L$ in span 1: Post-tensioned stress required $= 779 - 424 = 355$ psi.

$$\frac{1000 \times 0.74P_j}{70.88 \times 144} + 1.49P_j \times 0.0580 = 355$$

Solving for P_j, we have $P_j = 2233$ kips.

The stresses due to post-tensioning are plotted directly on the stress diagram already constructed for $DL + LL + I$. Note that the sign convention used for plotting stresses due to prestressing should be opposite those used for stresses due to $DL + LL + I$. The final stresses are found by scaling between stress lines, as shown in Figs. E7.6i and E7.6j.

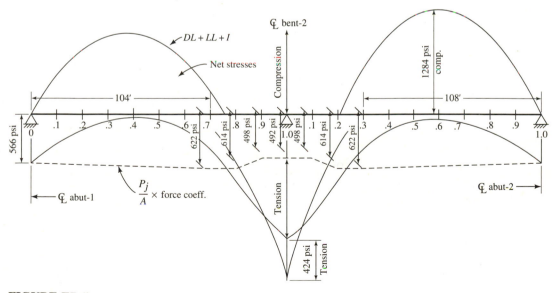

FIGURE E7.6i
Top fiber combined stresses.

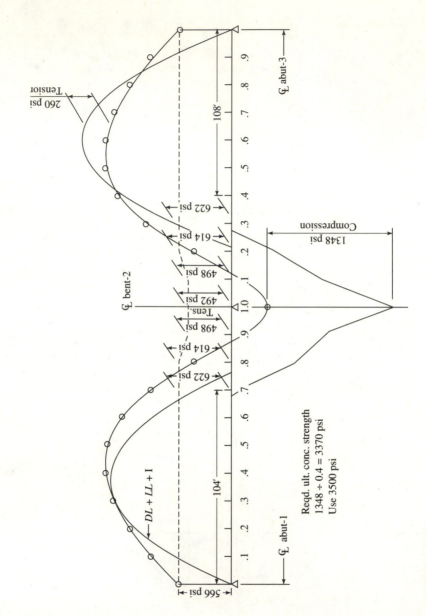

FIGURE E7.6j
Bottom fiber combined stresses.

672

The stress plots show that the required ultimate strength of the concrete due to compression in the bottom slab at the bent is 3370 psi. The designer therefore has a choice of designing the structure for a lower-strength concrete and somewhat more post-tensioning steel, or a higher-strength concrete with inherently better durability characteristics and a little less post-tensioning steel.

Ultimate load considerations. AASHTO specifications require that post-tensioned members be designed by the elastic method and their capacity for ultimate loads be verified for a factored ultimate design moment (M_u). Structures are proportioned for shear on the basis of ultimate load considerations only.

$$M_u = \text{Moment due to factored loads} + \text{secondary moment}$$

$$= 1.3\left[DL + \tfrac{5}{3}(LL + I)\right] + 0.51 P_j$$

$$= 1.3\left[15{,}151 + \tfrac{5}{3} \times 6980\right] + 0.51 \times 7418$$

$$= 38{,}603 \text{ kip-ft}$$

where the coefficient -0.51 for the secondary moment at $0.4L$ is taken from Fig. E7.6f. Compare this value with the nominal moment capacity, M_n, which is computed as follows:

Nominal moment capacity, M_n

$$f_{su}^* = f_s'\left[1 - \left(\frac{\gamma^*}{\beta_1}\right)\left(\frac{p^* f_s'}{f_c'}\right)\right] \qquad \text{(AASHTO Eq. 9.17)}$$

$$p^* = \frac{A_s^*}{bd}, \qquad A_s^* = \frac{P_j}{0.75 P_s'} = \frac{7418}{0.75 \times 270} = 36.6 \text{ in.}^2$$

$$p^* = \frac{36.6}{42 \times 5.55 \times 144} = 0.00109$$

$$\gamma^* = 0.28 \text{ for low-relaxation steel} \qquad \text{(AASHTO 9.1.2)}$$

For $f_c' = 5000$ psi,

$$\beta_1 = 0.85 - \frac{f_c' - 4000}{1000} \times (0.05)$$

$$= 0.85 - \frac{5000 - 4000}{1000} \times (0.05)$$

$$= 0.80$$

Thus,

$$f_{su}^* = 270\left[1 - \left(\frac{0.28}{0.80}\right)\left(\frac{0.00109 \times 270}{5}\right)\right] = 264.4 \text{ ksi}$$

Locate NA (neutral axis): According to AASHTO 9.17.2, the NA will fall in the flange if the flange thickness (5.75 in.) is greater than a, the depth of the compression block, which is given by

$$a = \frac{A_s^* f_{su}^*}{0.85 f_c' b} = \frac{36.6 \times 264.4}{0.85 \times 5 \times (42 \times 12)} = 4.52 \text{ in.}$$

Hence, the neutral axis falls in the flange, and the section can be analyzed as a rectangular one. The nominal moment capacity, M_n, is

$$M_n = A_s^* f_{su}^* d \left(1 - \frac{0.6 p^* f_{su}^*}{f_c'} \right)$$

$$= 36.6 \times 264.4 \times 5.55 \times \left(1 - \frac{0.6 \times 0.00109 \times 264.4}{5} \right)$$

$$= 51{,}850 \text{ kip-ft}$$

For a post-tensioned, cast-in-place concrete member, $\phi = 0.95$ (AASHTO 9.14). $\phi M_n = 0.95 \times 51{,}850 = 49{,}258$ kip-ft, $> M_u = 38.603$ kip-ft, OK.

Check maximum steel percentage (AASHTO 9.18.1):

$$p^* \frac{f_{su}^*}{f_c'} = 0.00109 \times \frac{262}{5} = 0.06$$

For 5000-psi concrete, $\beta_1 = 0.80$, $0.36\beta_1 = 0.36 \times 0.8 = 0.29$. Since $0.29 > 0.06$, steel will yield before concrete fails, and ductility is assured, OK.

Compute cracking load and check minimum steel (AASHTO 9.18.2): Modulus of rupture $= 7.5 \sqrt{f_c'} = 7.5 \sqrt{5000} = 530$ psi.

$$f_{cr} = \frac{P_j \times \text{force coefficient}}{A} + P_j \times \text{moment coefficient}$$
$$\times \text{stress coefficient} - M_{cr} \times \text{stress coefficient}$$

In the above expression, the force coefficient $= 0.74$ (Fig. E7.6e), the moment coefficient $= 1.49$ (Fig. E7.6f), and the stress coefficient $= 0.058$ was computed earlier.

$$-530 = \frac{1000 \times 8248 \times 0.74}{144 \times 70.88} + 8248 \times 1.49 \times 0.058 - M_{cr} \times 0.058$$

$$M_{cr} = 31{,}738 \text{ kip-ft}$$

$$1.2 M_{cr} = 38{,}085 \text{ kip-ft} < 52{,}345 \text{ kip-ft}$$

Hence, A_s^* provided is greater than the minimum required, OK.

Check ultimate moment at bent:

$$M_u = \text{Moment due to factored loads} + \text{secondary moment}$$

$$= 1.3 \left[DL + \tfrac{5}{3}(\ll + I) \right] - 1.29 P_j$$

$$= 1.3 \left[34{,}078 + \tfrac{5}{3} \times 9230 \right] - 1.29 \times 7418$$

$$= 54{,}731 \text{ kip-ft}$$

where the coefficient -1.29 for the secondary moment at support is taken from Fig. E7.6f.

Moment capacity, M_n. Locate neutral axis, NA.

$$f_{su}^* = f_s^* \left[1 - \left(\frac{\gamma^*}{\beta_1} \right) \left(\frac{p^* f_s'}{f_c'} \right) \right]$$

$$p^* = \frac{A_s^*}{bd} = \frac{36.6}{34.33 \times 5.5 \times 144} = 0.00135$$

$$f^*_{su} = 270 \left[1 - \left(\frac{0.28}{0.8} \right) \left(\frac{0.00135 \times 270}{5} \right) \right]$$

$$= 263.1 \text{ ksi}$$

The depth of the compression block, a, is

$$a = \frac{A^*_s f^*_{su}}{0.85 f'_c b} = \frac{36.6 \times 263.1}{0.85 \times 5 \times (42 \times 12)} = 4.5 \text{ in.} < 12 \text{ in. (flange thickness)}$$

Hence, NA lies in the flange, and the section can be analyzed as a rectangular section.

$$M_n = A^*_s f^*_{su} d \left(1 - \frac{0.6 p^* f^*_{su}}{f'_c} \right)$$

$$= 36.6 \times 263.1 \times 5.5 \times \left(1 - \frac{0.6 \times 0.00135 \times 263.1}{5} \right)$$

$$= 50,705 \text{ kip-ft}$$

$$\phi M_n = 0.95 \times 50,705 = 48,170 \text{ kip-ft} < M_u = 54,731 \text{ kip-ft, NG}$$

Hence, nonprestressed steel is required. Excess moment to be resisted by nonprestressed steel is $(1/\phi)M = (54,731 - 48,170)/0.95 = 6906$ kip-ft.

Use Grade 60 steel, $f_y = 60,000$ psi. With the depth of compression block $a = 4.5$ in., the center of compression is 2.25 in. up from the bottom of the box, and the center of gravity of the mild steel is about 3.5 in. from the top surface, so that the distance from extreme compression fiber to the centroid of nonprestressed tension reinforcement, d_t, is

$$d_t = 6.5 - 0.19 - 0.29 = 6.02 \text{ ft} = 72.24 \text{ in.}$$

With Grade 60 reinforcing bars,

Resisting $M = A_s f_y d_t = A_s \times 60 \times 6.02 = 361.2 A_s$
$361.2 A_s = 6906 \rightarrow A_s = 19.12 \text{ in.}^2$

Provide twenty #9 bars ($A_s = 20$ in.^{2}) (four #9 bars in each girder).
Check total reinforcement index (AASHTO 9.18.1):

$$\text{Prestressed steel: } \frac{p^* f^*_{su}}{f'_c} = \frac{0.00135 \times 263.1}{5} = 0.071$$

$$\text{Nonprestressed steel: } \frac{p f_{sy}}{f'_c} = \frac{20 \times 60}{(34.33 \times 12) \times 72.24 \times 5} = 0.008$$

where $b = 34.33$ ft is the bottom width of the box girder, and $d = 72.24$ in. for the nonprestressed steel.

$$\text{Total reinforcement index} = 0.071 + 0.008$$

$$= 0.079 < 0.36 \beta_1 = 0.36 \times 0.8 = 0.29, \text{ OK}$$

Therefore, the steel will yield before the concrete ruptures, and ductility is assured.

Note that when nonprestressed reinforcement is provided, AASHTO 9.17.4.1 requires the value of f^*_{su} to be recalculated from AASHTO Eq. 9.17a. However, in the present case, the influence of nonprestressed reinforcement on the value of f_{su}^* is very small and can be safely ignored. Its revised value is

$$f_{su}^* = f_s' \left\{ 1 - \frac{\gamma^*}{\beta_1} \left[\frac{p^* f_s'}{f_c'} + \frac{d_t}{d} \left(\frac{p f_{sy}}{f_c'} \right) \right] \right\}$$

$$= 270 \left[1 - \frac{0.28}{0.8} \left(0.071 + \frac{72.24}{66} \times 0.008 \right) \right]$$

$$= 269.2 \text{ ksi}$$

compared to 263.1 ksi.

To determine the cut off point for mild steel and length of flare required, plot the negative portion of the ultimate moment envelope.

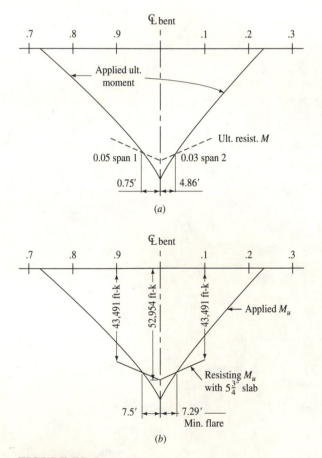

FIGURE E7.6k
(*a*) Ultimate moment diagram near bent, (*b*) bottom slab flare length diagram.

Span 1. At point

$$0.7L, \ M_u = 1.44[1330 + \tfrac{5}{3} \times (-3575.24)] + 0.90 \times 7418 = +10.8 \text{ k-ft}$$
$$0.8L, \ M_u = 1.44[-8074 + \tfrac{5}{3} \times 4086] + 1.03 \times 7418 = -13,792.4 \text{ k-ft}$$
$$0.9L, \ M_u = 1.44[-19877 - \tfrac{5}{3} \times 5847] + 1.16 \times 7418 = -34,050.8 \text{ k-ft}$$

At bent $M_u = 60,812$ k-ft,

$$0.1L, \ M_u = 1.44[-18081 - \tfrac{5}{3} \times 5419] + 1.16 \times 7418 = -30,437.4 \text{ k-ft}$$
$$0.2L, \ M_u = 1.44[-4882 - \tfrac{5}{3} \times 3339] + 1.03 \times 7418 = -7403.1 \text{ k-ft}$$
$$0.3L, \ M_u = 1.44[552 - \tfrac{5}{3} \times 2886] + 0.9 \times 7418 = +7698.6 \text{ k-ft}$$

Ultimate capacity: at bent, resisting $M_u = 48,170$ kip-ft.

When the ultimate moment is controlled by the steel, it is nearly proportional to d. Therefore, at point

M_u at 0.9L, span 1 = 4.57/5.5 × 48,170 = 40,025 kip-ft
M_u at 0.8L, span 1 = 2.93/5.5 × 48,170 = 25,661 kip-ft
M_u at 0.1L, span 2 = 4.57/5.5 × 48,170 = 40,025 kip-ft
M_u at 0.2L, span 2 = 2.93/5.5 × 48,170 = 25,661 kip-ft

Figure E7.6k shows theoretical lengths of 7 ft 6 in. in span 1 and 4 ft 10 in. in span 2. Therefore, the mild steel must be placed to these lengths plus the development lengths, as required by AASHTO.

Flare lengths. This design is based on the bottom slab flare extending out $0.1L$ from the centerline of the bent. The length required to provide adequate ultimate moment capacity can now be found.

Moving away from the bent, the slab thickness is reduced while A_s remains constant. At the point where the normal bottom slab thickness is adequate, the neutral axis usually falls in the web. By neglecting the small compression area in the web, the ultimate strength based on failure in the concrete can be conservatively estimated.

The ultimate moment capacity varies along the span because d changes. M_u can be computed at any specific point using the minimum slab thickness and can be assumed to vary on a straight line between them. The required flare length can then be found graphically using the ultimate moment diagram, as shown in Fig. E7.6k.

Span 1

At point 0.8L, $t = 5\tfrac{3}{4}$ in., $\tfrac{1}{2}t = 0.24$ ft, $d = 2.93$ ft
$M_u = 0.85 \times 5 \times 34.33 \times 12 \times 5.75(2.93 - 0.24) = 27,081$ kip-ft

At point 0.9L, $t = 5\tfrac{3}{4}$ in., $d = 4.57$ in.
$M_u = 0.85 \times 5 \times 34.33 \times 12 \times 5.75(4.57 - 0.24) = 43,591$ kip-ft

Span 2

At point 0.2L, $t = 5\tfrac{3}{4}$ in., $\tfrac{1}{2}t = 0.24$ ft, $d = 2.93$ ft
$M_u = 0.85 \times 5 \times 34.33 \times 12 \times 5.75(2.93 - 0.24) = 27,081$ kip-ft

At point 0.1L, $t = 5\tfrac{3}{4}$ in., $\tfrac{1}{2}t = 0.24$ ft, $d = 4.57$ ft
$M_u = 0.85 \times 5 \times 34.33 \times 12 \times 5.75(4.57 - 0.24) = 43,451$ kip-ft

At bent: $t = 5\tfrac{3}{4}$ in., $\tfrac{1}{2}t = 0.24$ ft, $d = 5.50$ ft
$M_u = 0.85 \times 5 \times 34.33 \times 12 \times 5.75(5.50 - 0.24) = 52,954$ kip-ft

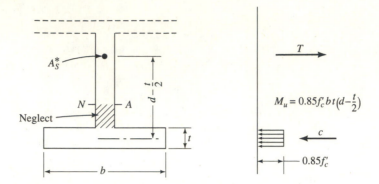

$$M_u = 0.85 f'_c \, b \, t \left(d - \frac{t}{2}\right)$$

Shear capacity. AASHTO specifications will be used for determining shear capacity, except that rather than using d = distance from compression face to the centroid of the prestressing force, we will consider $d = 0.8$ times the total girder depth for the full length of the structure. The cable shear will be the vertical component of P_f. These assumptions generally result in a slightly more conservative design than the more complex procedure specified in the ACI code [ACI, 1995].

Applied shear. Below are $DL + LL + I$ shears from normal analysis.

Span no.	Dead-load shear (K)	
	Left	**Right**
1	572.3	−1026.7
2	1073.8	−653.0

Span no.	Live-load shear plus impact (K)		
	Left end	**Midspan**	**Right end**
1	241.0	+92.5 −141.9	−310.7
2	318.7	+139.0 −72.4	−249.4

The secondary moments resulting from prestressing cause a change in reaction, which affects shear values:

where ΔR = change in reaction = M_s/L

Span 1: $\Delta R = 1.289 \times \frac{7428}{150} = 63.7^k$

Span 2: $\Delta R = 1.289 \times \frac{7418}{162} = 59.0^k$

Span 1

$$V_u = \frac{1.3}{\phi}\left[DL + \frac{5}{3}(LL + I)\right]$$

For shear in cast-in-place post-tensioned members, $\phi = 0.9$ which gives $1.3/\phi = 1.44$. Maximum shears at critical locations are as follows:

Abutment 1

$$V_u = 1.44(572.3 + \tfrac{5}{3} \times 241) + 63.7 = 1466.2 \text{ kips}$$

Centerline span

$$V_u = 1.44 \times \tfrac{5}{3} \times 92.5 + 63.7 = 285.7 \text{ kips}$$

Bent

$$V_u = 1.44(1073.8 + \tfrac{5}{3} \times 310.7) - 63.7 = 2228.3 \text{ kips}$$

Span 2

Bent

$$V_u = 1.44(1073.8 + \tfrac{5}{3} \times 318.7) - 59.0 = 2252.2 \text{ kips}$$

Centerline span

$$V_u = 1.44 \times \tfrac{5}{3} \times 139.0 - 59.0 = 274.6 \text{ kips}$$

Abutment 3

$$V_u = 1.44(653.0 + \tfrac{5}{3} \times 249.4) + 59.0 = 1597.9 \text{ kips}$$

Cable shears

$$V = (\text{force coefficient})(P_j)(\sin\alpha) = (\text{force coefficient})(P_j)(\alpha, \text{ radian})$$

Location	Cable slope α (rad)	Force coefficient	P_j (kips)	Cable shear, V (kips)
Abut. 1	0.075	0.70	7418	389
0.5L Span 1	0	0.75	7418	0
0.9L Span 1	0.125	0.75	7418	695
Bent 2	0	0.74	7418	0
0.1L Span 2	0.115	0.75	7418	640
0.5L Span 2	0	0.75	7418	0
Abut. 3	0.070	0.70	7418	363

Concrete shear resistance (AASHTO 9.20.2.1). $V_{ci} = 1.7\sqrt{f'_c}b'd$ (conservatively taken for this preliminary design).

For five 12-in.-wide webs, $b' = 12 \times 5 = 60$ in., $d = 0.8h = 0.8 \times 78 = 62.4$ in. Thus, with $f'_c = 5000$ psi, the shear strength provided by concrete is

$$V_{ci} = (1.7\sqrt{5000})(60)(62.4) \text{ lb}$$

$$= 450 \text{ kips}$$

Shear resistance to be provided by the web reinforcement (AASHTO 9.20.3) is

$$V_s = V_u - V_c = \frac{A_v f_{sy} d}{S} \qquad \text{(AASHTO Eq. 9.30)}$$

With Grade 60 #5 two-legged stirrups in five webs,

$$A_v = 2 \times 5 \times 0.31 = 3.1 \text{ in.}^2$$

$$V_s = \frac{3.1 \times 60 \times 62.4}{S} = \frac{11606}{S}$$

Check for maximum permissible spacing of stirrups (AASHTO 9.20.3.2).

$$4\sqrt{f_c'} b'd = 4\sqrt{5000} \times 60 \times 62.4 \text{ lb} = 1059 \text{ kips}$$

$$8\sqrt{f_c'} b'd = 8\sqrt{5000} \times 60 \times 62.4 \text{ lb} = 2118 \text{ kips}$$

Maximum shear occurs at bent 2: $V_u = 2228.3$ kips

$$V_s = V_u - V_c = 2228.3 - 450 = 1778.3 \text{ kips}$$

which is smaller than 2118 kips but greater than 1059 kips. Hence, the maximum stirrup spacing should be the smaller of

$$\tfrac{1}{2} \times (0.75h) = \tfrac{1}{2} \times 0.75 \times 78 = 29.25 \text{ in.}$$

or

$$\tfrac{1}{2} \times 24 = 12 \text{ in. (governs)}$$

At bent, the required stirrup spacing is

$$S = \frac{11606}{V_s} = \frac{11606}{1778.3} = 9.85 \text{ in.}$$

Hence, provide $S = 9$ in. for this preliminary design.

Minimum stirrup area (AASHTO 9.20.3.3):

$$\text{Minimum } A_v = \frac{50b'S}{f_y}$$

$$S_{\max} = \frac{A_v f_y}{50b'}$$

$$= \frac{3.1 \times 60,000}{50 \times (5 \times 12)}$$

$$= 62 \text{ in.}$$

The preceding design for spacing of web reinforcement is obviously conservative in that the lower bound value of $v_c = 1.7\sqrt{f_c'}$ has been used as a first approximation. A detailed analysis for spacing of web reinforcement may be made using AASHTO Eqs. 9.27, 9.28, and 9.29, as illustrated in Example 7.4. Note that the maximum spacing of stirrups would very likely be governed by AASHTO 9.20.3.2, as computed above.

Deflections. Deflections due to prestressing can be calculated from the effective $P_f e/EI$ diagram using the slope deflection method. As with simple spans, one must note the level of the prestressing force at the time at which the deflection is to be calculated. Abutment details normally allow for movement to accommodate structure shortening.

7.17
SOME TRIAL DESIGN PARAMETERS

Structural design is a paradoxical problem in that load-carrying components must be designed before their sizes are known. The dead load of a structure cannot be known until it has been designed. However, a structure cannot be designed until all loads, including dead loads, are completely known in advance. In practice, this problem is solved by assuming (or actually guessing) the sizes of various structural components such as floor or slab, beams, and girders in the initial design trial. These assumed sizes are verified by calculating their structural adequacy. If these sizes are found to be deficient or oversized, new trial sizes are assumed, and the design is recycled.

In common types of short- and medium-span bridges, the designer is required to assume trial dimensions of design parameters, such as thickness of slab, and sizes and spacing of beams and girders. Most design organizations, such as professional offices and state, county, and city highway departments, follow their own in-house practices for certain minimum sizes for slab thickness, beam web widths, standard beam spacings, etc. These practices are based on experience from designs that have withstood the test of time.

Naaman [1982] has suggested several rules of thumb (summarized in Table 7.20) for quick selection of numerical values of several design parameters to facilitate a quick preliminary design. These are related to the deck slab thickness, h_f, the beam depth, h, web thickness, b_w, and spacing, S.

TABLE 7.20

Common range of main design parameters in bridge superstructures [Naaman, 1982]

Variable		Design range
Depth, h	Slab	Simple-span: $0.03 \leq h/L \leq 0.04$ Continuous: $0.025 \leq h/L \leq 0.035$
	Beams (T, box)	Simple-span: $0.035 \leq h/L \leq 0.055$ Continuous: $0.03 \leq h/L \leq 0.045$
	I-beams (Composite)	Simple-span: $0.045 \leq h/L \leq 0.06$ Continuous: $0.040 \leq h/L \leq 0.055$
Web thickness, b_w	Pretensioned beams	Minimum value: $b_w \approx 4$ in. Common range: $5 \leq b_w \leq 8$ in.
	Post-tensioned beams	Precast: $b_w \approx \phi + 5$ in. Cast-in-place: $b_w \approx \phi + 8$ in.
Top slab thickness, h_f		Range: $S/15 \leq h_f \leq S/12$ in. Most common range: $6 \leq h_f \leq 9$ in.
Beam spacing, S		Range: $2 \leq S \leq 16$ ft Most common range: $5 \leq S \leq 10$ ft

REFERENCES

AASHTO. (1967). "Highway Design and Operational Practices Related to Highway Safety," *Report to the Special AASHTO Traffic Safety Committee,* February.

——. (1989). *Guide Specifications for Design and Construction of Segmental Concrete Bridges,* AASHTO, Washington, DC.

——. (1991). *Guide Specifications and Commentary for Vessel Collision Design of Highway Bridges,* AASHTO, Washington, DC.

——. (1992). *AASHTO Standard Specifications for Highway Bridges,* 15th ed., AASHTO, Washington, DC.

——. (1993). *AASHTO Interim Specifications for Bridges—1993,* AASHTO, Washington, DC.

——. (1994). *AASHTO–LRFD Bridge Design Specifications,* Customary U.S. Units, 1st ed., AASHTO, Washington, DC.

——. (1996). *AASHTO Standard Specifications for Highway Bridges,* 16th ed., AASHTO, Washington, DC.

ABAM Engineers, Inc. (1988). "Precast Prestressed Concrete Horizontally Curved Bridge Beams—Special Report." *PCI J.,* 33(5), September–October, pp. 50–123.

Abdel-Karim, A. M., and Tadros, M. K. (1992a)."Design and Construction of Spliced I-Girder Bridges," *PCI J.,* 37(4), July–August, pp. 114–122.

——. (1992b). "State of the Art of Precast/Prestressed Concrete Spliced-Girder Bridges," ACI Special Pub. SP-92, Prestressed Concrete Institute, Chicago, October.

Abeles, P. W., Bardhan-Roy, B. K., and Turner, F. H. (1976). *Prestressed Concrete Designer's Handbook,* 2nd ed., Viewpoint Publishers, Cement and Concrete Association, Wexham Springs, Slough, England.

Aboutaha, R. S., and Burns, N. H. (1994). "Strengthening of Prestressed Concrete Composite Beams Using External Prestressed Stirrups," *PCI J.,* 39(4), July–August 1994, pp. 64–73.

ACI. (1963). *Building Code Requirements for Reinforced Concrete,* ACI Committee 318, ACI, Detroit.

——. (1967). "Guide for Structural Lightweight Aggregate Concrete," ACI Committee 213, *ACI J. Proc.,* 64(8), August, pp. 443–467.

——. (1970). *Building Code Requirements for Reinforced Concrete,* ACI Committee 318, ACI, Detroit.

——. (1971). "Prediction of Creep, Shrinkage, and Temperature Effects in Structures," ACI Committee 209, Special Pub. SP-27, *Designing for Creep, Shrinkage, and Temperature,* ACI, Detroit, pp. 51–93.

——. (1973). "Preliminary Design and Proportioning of Reinforced Concrete Bridge Structures," ACI Committee 443, *ACI J. Proc.,* 70(5), May, pp. 328–336.

——. (1974). "Analysis and Design of Reinforced Concrete Bridge Structures," ACI Committee 443, *ACI J. Proc.,* 71(4), May, pp. 171–200.

——. (1977). *Analysis and Design of Reinforced Concrete Bridge Structures,* ACI Committee 443, ACI, Detroit.

——. (1979). "Guide for Structural Lightweight Aggregate Concrete," ACI Committee 213, *ACI 213R-79, Concrete International,* 1(2), February, pp. 33–62.

——. (1984). State-of-the-Art Report on High-Strength Concrete," ACI Committee 363, ACI 363R-84, *ACI J. Proc.,* 81(4), July–August, pp. 364–411.

——. (1989). "Prediction of Creep, Shrinkage, and Temperature Effects in Concrete Structures," ACI Committee 209, *ACI Manual of Concrete Practice—Part 1,* ACI, Detroit.

——. (1989). *Building Code Requirements for Reinforced Concrete,* ACI 318-89, ACI Committee 318, ACI, Detroit.

——. (1995a). *Building Code Requirements for Structural Concrete* (ACI 318-95) *and Commentary* (ACI 318R-95), ACI Committee 318, ACI, Farmington Hills, MI.

———. (1995b) *Analysis and Design of Reinforced Concrete Bridge Structures,* ACI Committee 443, ACI, Detroit.

ACI–ASCE (1958). "Tentative Recommendations for Prestressed Concrete," ACI–ASCE Committee 423, *ACI J.,* 54(7), January, pp. 545–578.

———. (1960). "Tentative Recommendations for Design of Composite Beams and Girders for Buildings," ACI–ASCE Committee 333, *ACI J.,* 57(12), December, pp. 609–628.

Adelman, D., and Cousins, T. E. (1990). "Evaluation of the Use of High-Strength Concrete Bridge Girders in Louisiana," *PCI J.,* 35(5), September–October, pp. 70–78.

Adin, M., Cohn, M. Z., and Pinto, M. (1979). "Comprehensive Optimal Design of Reinforced Concrete Bridges," *Intl. Symp. on Nonlinear Design of Concrete Structures,* University of Waterloo, Ontario, pp. 349–377.

Aguilar, R. J., Movassaghi, K., and Brewer, J. A. (1973). "Computerized Optimization of Bridge Structures," *Computer and Structures, Vol. 3,* Pergamon Press, New York, pp. 429–442.

Alwis, W. A. M., Olorunnivw, A., and Ang, K. K. (1994). "Long-Term Deflections of RC Beams," *ASCE J. Struct. Eng.,* 120(7), July, pp. 2220–2226.

Anderson, A. R. (1957). "How Beam Design Affects Prestressed Concrete Bridge Costs," *Eng. News-Record,* October, pp. 326–328.

———. (1971). "Lateral Stability of Long Prestressed Concrete Beams," *PCI J.,* 16(3), May–June, pp. 7–9.

———. (1972). "Systems Concepts for Precast Prestressed Concrete Bridge Construction," *Special Report 132,* Highway Research Board, Washington, DC, pp. 9–21.

———. (1973). "Stretched-Out AASHTO–PCI Beams, Type III and IV, for Longer-Span Highway Bridges," *PCI J.,* 18(5), September–October, pp. 32–49.

Arockiasamy, M., Reddy, M., Badve, D. V., and Rao, B.V. (1991). "Fatigue Strength of Joints in Precast Prestressed Double-T Bridges," *PCI J.,* 36(1), January–February, pp. 84–97.

ASCE–ACI. (1973). "The Shear Strength of Reinforced Concrete Members," ASCE–ACI Joint Committee 426 report, *ASCE J. Struct. Div.,* 99(ST6), June, Chs. 1–4, pp. 1091–1197.

ASCENT. (1994). "Best Bridge Spanning 65–135 ft: Bridge 'Peñelas,' Queretaro City, Queretaro State, Mexico," *Ascent,* Fall 1994, p. 32.

ASTM. (1983). *Annual Book of ASTM Standards,* ASTM, Sec. 4, Vol. 04.02, "Concrete and Mineral Aggregates," Philadelphia.

Aziz, E. M., and Edwards, A. D. (1966). "Some Aspects of the Economics of Continuous, Prestressed Concrete Bridge Girders," *Struct. Eng.,* 44(2), February, pp. 49–54.

Bakht, B., and Jaeger, L. J. (1985). *Bridge Analysis Simplified,* McGraw-Hill Companies, Inc., New York.

Bakht, B. et al., eds. (1990). "Provencher Bridge over the Red River, Winnepeg, Manitoba," *Developments in Short- and Medium-Span Bridge Engineering, Vol. 1, 3rd Intl. Conf. Short- and Medium-Span Bridges,* Toronto, Ontario, August 7–10.

Bakos, S. L. et al. (1982). "Long-Term Deflections of Reinforced Concrete Beams," *Mag. Conc. Res.,* 34(121), pp. 203–212.

Ballinger, C. A., Podolny, W., and Abrams, M. J. (1977). *A Report on the Design and Construction of Segmental Bridges in Western Europe—1977,* International Road Federation, Washington, DC. (Also available from Federal Highway Administration, Washington, DC, Report No. FHWA-RD-78-44, June 1978).

Barker, J. M. (1975). "Research, Application, and Experience with Precast Prestressed Bridge Deck Panels," *PCI J.,* 20(6), November–December, pp. 66–85.

Barnoff, R. M., Orndorff, J. A., Jr., Harbaugh, R. B., and Rainly, D. E. (1977). "Full-Scale Tests of a Prestressed Bridge with Precast Deck Planks," *PCI J.,* 22(5), September–October, pp. 66–83.

Barnoff, R. M., and Sutherland, F. G. (1978). "Readers' Comments on 'Tentative Design and Construction Specification for Bridge Deck Panels,' by PCI Bridge Committee," *PCI J.*, 23(6), November–December, pp. 80–82.

Bassi, K. G. (1989). "Comments on 'Effect of Galvanizing on Hydrogen Embrittlement of Prestressing Wire,' by Yamakoa, Y., Tsubono, H., and Kurauch, M.," *PCI J.*, 34(3), May–June 1989, pp. 162–164.

Batchelor, B. de V., Campbell, T. I., McEwen, D. W., and Csagoly, P. (1976). "Model Study of New Standard Prestressed Concrete Bridge," *ASCE J., Struct. Div.*, 102 (ST9), September, pp. 1789–1806.

Bazant, Z. P. (1972). "Prediction of Creep Effects Using Age-Adjusted Effective Modulus Method," *ACI J.*, 69(4), April, pp. 212–217.

———. ed. (1988). *Mathematical Modeling of Creep and Shrinkage of Concrete,* John Wiley & Sons, New York.

Bazant, Z. P., and Oh, B. H. (1984). "Deformation of Progressively Cracking Reinforced Concrete Beams," *ACI J.*, 81(3), May–June, pp. 268–278.

Bazant, Z. P., and Panula, L. (1980). "Creep and Shrinkage Characterization for Analyzing Prestressed Concrete Structures," *PCI J.*, 25(3), May–June, pp. 86–122.

Beal, D. B. (1981). "Strength of Concrete Bridge Deck," *Research Report 89,* New York State Department of Transportation, July.

Bender, B. F., and Kriesel, W. J. (1969). "Precast, Prestressed Box Beams—A State-of-the-Art Report," *PCI J.*, 14(1), January–February, pp. 72–95.

Bieschke, L. A., and Klingner, R. E. (1982). *The Effects of Transverse Strand Extensions on the Behavior of Precast Prestressed Panel Bridges,* Research Report 303-1F, Center for Transportation Research, University of Texas at Austin, June.

———. (1988). "Effects of Transverse Panel Strand Extensions on the Behavior of Precast Prestressed Panel Bridges," *PCI J.*, 33(1), January–February, pp. 68–88.

Birkland, P. W., and Birkland, H. W. (1966). "Connections in Precast Concrete Construction," *ACI J.*, 63(3), March, pp. 345–367.

Bond, D. (1975). "An Examination of the Automated Design of Prestressed Concrete Decks, by Computer," *Proceed. Inst. Civ. Engrs.*, part 2, vol. 59, pp. 669–697.

———. (1983). "Optimal Design of Continuous Prestressed Concrete Bridges," *Intl. Symp. Nonlinearity and Continuity in Prestressed Concrete,* vol. 3, (M. Z. Cohn, ed.), University of Waterloo, Ontario, pp. 201–234.

Branson, D. E. (1968). "Design Procedures for Computing Deflections," *ACI J.*, 75(9), September, pp. 730–742.

———. (1974). "The Deformation of Noncomposite and Composite Prestressed Members," *Deflection of Concrete Structures,* ACI Special Pub. SP-43, ACI, Detroit, pp. 83–127.

———. (1977). *Deformation of Concrete Structures,* McGraw-Hill Companies, Inc., New York.

Branson, D. E., and Kripanarayana, A. (1971). "Loss of Prestress, Camber, and Deflection of Noncomposite and Composite Prestressed Concrete Structures," *PCI J.*, 16(5), September–October, pp. 22–52.

Breen, J. E. (1990). "Prestressed Concrete: The State of the Art in North America," *PCI J.*, 35(6), November–December, pp. 62–67.

Bresler, B., and Pister, K. S. (1958). "Strength of Concrete under Combined Stresses," *ACI J.*, 55(9), September, pp. 321–345.

Bresler, B., and MacGregor, J. G. (1967). "Review of Concrete Beams Failing in Shear," *ASCE J. Struct. Div.*, 93(ST1), February, pp. 343–372.

Brown, R. P., and Fitzgerald, J. H. (1971). "A Practical Approach to Counteracting Corrosion of Bridge Structures," *Public Works,* 102(11), November, pp. 63–66.

Bruce, R. N., Martin, B. T., Russell, H. G., and Roller, J. J. (1992). *Feasibility of Utilizing High-Strength Concrete in Design and Construction of Highway Bridge Structures,* Louisiana

Department of Transportation and Development, Interim Reports, Tulane University, New Orleans, December.

Bruggeling, A. S. G. (1982). "FIP Commission on Prestressing Steels and Systems—Chairman's Report," *Proc. Ninth Congress of the FIP,* vol. 3, Stockholm, pp. 63–73.

BSI. (1984). "BS 5400: Steel, Concrete, and Composite Bridges: Part 4—Code of Practice for Concrete Highway Bridges," British Standards Institute, London.

Buckner, C. D. (1995). "A Review of Strand Development Length for Pretensioned Concrete Members," *PCI J.,* 40(2), March–April, pp. 84–105.

Buckner, C. D., and Turner, H. T. (1983). *Performance of Full-Span Panel-Form Bridges under Repetitive Loading,* Final Report 80-1C, Department of Civil Engineering, Louisiana State University, Baton Rouge.

Burdick, E. B. (1966). *A Survey of the Use and Performance of Permanent Steel Bridge Forms,* AISI, October.

Burg, R. G., and Ost, B. W. (1992). "Engineering Properties of Commercially Available High-Strength Concretes," *R&D Bull.* RD104T, PCA, Chicago.

Buth, E., Furr, H. L., and Jones, H. L. (1972). *Evaluation of a Prestressed Panel, Cast-in-Place Concrete Bridge,* Research Report 145-3, Texas Transportation Institute, Texas A&M University, College Station, September.

CALTRANS. (1993a). *Bridge Design Aids Manual,* California Department of Transportation, Office of Structure Design, Sacramento.

———. (1993b). *Standard Specifications for Highway Bridges with Revisions by State of California,* California Department of Transportation, Office of Structure Design, Sacramento.

———. (1993c). *Bridge Design Practice Manual,* California Department of Transportation, Office of Structure Design, Sacramento.

———. (1993d). *Memo to Designers,* California Department of Transportation, Office of Structure Design, Sacramento.

Campbell, T. I., and Bassi, K. (1994). "Comments on 'The New Texas U-Beam Bridges: An Aesthetic and Economical Design Solution,' by M. L. Ralls and J. J. Panek," *PCI J.,* 38(5), September–October 1993, pp. 20–29, and 39(2), March–April, pp. 122–123.

Campbell, T. I., and Batchelor, B. de V. (1977). "Load Testing of a Model Two-Span Continuous Prestressed Concrete Trapezoidal Girder," *PCI J.,* 22(6), November–December, pp. 62–79.

Caroland, W. B., and Depp, D. C. (1990). "Salt River Bridge," *PCI J.,* 35(1), January–February, pp. 108–119.

Caroland, W. B., Depp, D. C., Janssen, H. H., and Spaans, L. (1992). "Spliced Segmental Prestressed I-Beams for Shelby Creek Bridge," *PCI J.,* 37(5), September–October, pp. 22–33.

Carrasquillo, P. M., and Carrasquillo, R. L. (1986). *Guidelines for Use of High-Strength Concrete in Texas Highways,* Research Report 367-1F, Project 3-5-85-367, Center of Transportation Research, University of Texas at Austin, August.

Carroll, W. T., Beaufait, F. W., and Byran, R. H. (1978). "Prestressed Concrete Trusses," *ACI J.,* 75(8), August.

Casad, D. D., and Birkland, H. W. (1970). "Bridge Features Precast Girders and Struts," *ASCE Civ. Eng.,* July, pp. 42–44.

Castrodale, R. W., Kreger, M. E., and Burns, N. H. (1988). *A Study of Pretensioned High-Strength Concrete Girders in Composite Highway Bridges—Design Considerations,* Research Report 381-4F, Project 3-5-84-381, Center of Transportation Research, University of Texas at Austin, January.

Castrodale, R. W., May, H. R., Nagle, J. W., and Zandegui, S. (1994). "Readers' Comments on 'Lateral Stability of Long Prestressed Concrete Beams, Part 2,' by R. F. Mast," *PCI J.,* 39(1), January–February, pp. 96–100.

CE. (1972). "Oregon Gets a Segmental Post-Tensioned Bridge," *ASCE Civ. Eng.,* March, pp. 67–69.

CE. (1974a). "World's Top Prestressed Concrete Structures—1970–1974," *ASCE Civ. Eng.,* August, pp. 68–71.

———. (1974b). "Precast U-Beams Used for Bridge over Canal," *Civ. Eng.,* November, p. 21.

———. (1992). "Bridge Construction Goes Gently down the River," *ASCE Civ. Eng.,* November, p. 23.

———. (1993). "Long Time Coming for Long-Span Bridges," *ASCE Civ. Eng.,* June, p. 26.

Chang, S. T. (1992). "Prestress Influence on Shear-Lag Effect in Continuous Box Girder," *ASCE J. Struct. Eng.,* 118(11), November, pp. 3113–3121.

Chaplin, E. C., Garret, R. J., Gordon, J. A., and Sharpe, D. J. (1973). "The Development of a Design for a Precast Bridge Beam of U-Section," *Structural Engineer*, 10(51), October, pp. 383–388.

Cohn, M. Z. (1986). *Partial Prestressing from Theory to Practice, Vols. I and II,* NATO–ASI Applied Science Series, Martinus Nijhoff Publishers, in Cooperation with NATO Scientific Affairs Division, Dordrecht, vol. I, p. 405; vol. II, p. 425.

Cohn, M. Z., and Dinovitzer, A. S. (1994). "Application of Structural Optimization," *ASCE J. Struct. Eng.,* 120(2), February, pp. 617–648.

Cohn, M. Z., and Mac Rae, J. (1984). "Prestressing Optimization and Design Practice," *PCI J.,* 29(4), July–August, pp. 68–83.

Cope, R. J., ed. (1987). *Concrete Bridge Engineering: Performances and Advances,* Elsevier Applied Science, London.

Corley, W. G., and Sozen, M. A. (1966). "Time-Dependent Deflections of Reinforced Concrete Beams," *ACI J.,* 63(3), March, pp. 373–386.

Corven, J. A., and Jordon, J. W. (1993). "Arches for a Parkway," *ASCE Civ. Eng.,* November, pp. 44–47.

Cousins, T. E., Johnston, D. W., and Zia, P. (1990). "Transfer and Development of Epoxy Coated and Uncoated Prestressing Strand," *PCI J.,* 35(4), July–August, pp. 92–103.

Csagoly, P. F., Holokwa, M., and Dorton, R. A. (1978). *The True Behavior of Thin Concrete Bridge Decks,* Trans. Res. Rec. no. 664, Transportation Research Board, Washington, DC, pp. 153–161.

Csagoly, P. F., and Nickas, W. N. (1987). "Florida Bulb-T and Double-T Beams," *Concrete Intl.,* 9(11), November, pp. 18–23.

CT. (1988). "Bypass Brings Back Brick," *Construction Today,* July–August, p. 53.

CTLR. (1992). "Meeting the Challenges of High-Strength Concrete," *CTL Rev.,* (Construction Technology Ltd.), 15(2), April, p. 1.

Curen, A. R., and Round, J. L. (1973). "Tests of a U-Beam Bridge Deck," *Struct. Engineer* (London), 51(10), October, pp. 377–382.

Curtis, R. B. (1967). "Single-T Bridges," *PCI J.,* 12(2), March–April, pp. 76–81.

Deatherage, J. H., and Burdette, E. G. (1991). *Development Length and Lateral Spacing Requirements for Prestressing Strand for Prestressed Concrete Bridge Products,* Final Report, Precast/Prestressed Concrete Institute, University of Tennessee, Knoxville, September.

Deatherage, J. H., Burdette, E. G., and Chew, C. K. (1994). "Development Length and Lateral Spacing Requirements for Prestressing Strand for Prestressed Concrete Bridge Girders," *PCI J.,* 39(1), January–February, pp. 70–83.

Degenkolb, O. H. (1977). *Concrete Box Girder Bridges,* Iowa State University Press, Ames, and ACI, Detroit.

Dickson, T. J., Tabatabai, H., and Whiting, D. A. (1993). "Corrosion Assessment of a 34-Year-Old Precast Post-Tensioned Concrete Girder," *PCI J.,* 38(6), November–December, pp. 44–51.

Dolan, C. W. (1990). "Developments in Nonmetallic Prestressing Tendons," *PCI J.,* 35(5), September–October, pp. 80–88.

Dolan, C. W., Ballinger, C. A., and LaFraugh, R. W. (1993). "High-Strength Prestressed Concrete Bridge Girder Performance," *PCI J.,* 38(3), May–June, pp. 88–97.

Dolan, C. W., and LaFraugh, R. W., (1993). "High-Strength Concrete in Precast Industry," *PCI J.,* 38(3), May–June, pp. 16–19.

Dorstein, V., Hunt, F. F., and Preston, H. K. (1984). "Epoxy Coated Seven-Wire Strand for Prestressed Concrete," *PCI J.,* 29(4), July–August, pp. 120–129.

Dunker, K. F., and Rabbat, B. G. (1990). "Highway Bridge Type and Performance Patterns," *ASCE J. Performance of Constructed Facilities,* 4(3), August, pp. 161–173.

———. (1992). "Performance of Prestressed Concrete Highway Bridges in the United States—The First 40 Years," *PCI J.,* 37(3), May–June, pp. 48–64.

Durning, T. A., and Rear, K. B. (1993). "Braker Lane Bridge—High-Strength Concrete in Prestressed Concrete Girders," *PCI J.,* 38(3), May–June, pp. 46–51.

Edwards, L. N. (1959). *A Record of History and Evolution of Early American Bridges,* University Press, Orono, ME.

Elliot, A. L. (1990). "Steel and Concrete Bridges," Sec. 18, in E. H. Gaylord, Jr., and C. N. Gaylord, eds. *Structural Engineering Handbook,* McGraw-Hill Companies, Inc., New York.

Endicott, W. A. (1995). "Precast Alternate Leaves Steel Design Behind—Case Study," *Ascent,* Summer 1995, pp. 28–30.

ENR. (1960). "Suspended Span is Prestressed Concrete," *Eng. News-Record,* April 21, pp. 40–42.

———. (1962). "Maracaibo Bridge Opens to Traffic," *Eng. News-Record,* August 30, p. 30.

———. (1965). "European Prestress Specialists Perfect Their Bridge Technique," *Eng. News-Record,* October, pp. 110–112.

———. (1972). "Inverted Suspension Span is Simple and Cheap," *Eng. News-Record,* May 11, pp. 27–31.

———. (1973). "Nonreinforced Concrete Road Offers Economy," *Eng. News-Record,* December 13, pp. 16–18.

———. (1978). "Rail Bridge Has Concrete Stays," *Eng. News-Record,* Oct. 26, p. 16.

———. (1985). "Test Girder Shows Strength," *Eng. News-Record,* December 19, p. 29.

———. (1991). "High-Strength Concrete in High-Seismic Zone?" *Eng. News-Record,* May 6, pp. C-76–C-78.

Evans, R. H., and Hosny, A. H. H. (1958). "The Shear Strength of Post-Tensioned Prestressed Concrete Beams," *Proc. Third Congress Intl. Fed. Prestressing,* Berlin.

Evans, R. H., and Parker, A. S. (1955). "Behavior of Prestressed Concrete Composite Beams," *ACI J.,* 52(6), June, pp. 861–881.

Fagundo, F. E., Tabatabai, H., Soongswang, K., Richardson, J. M., and Callis, E. G. (1985). "Precast Panel Composite Bridge Decks," *Concrete Intl.,* 7(5), May, pp. 59–65.

Fang, I. K., Tsui, C. K. T., Burns, N. H., and Klingner, R. E. (1990). "Fatigue Behavior of Cast-in-Place and Precast Panel Bridge Decks with Isotropic Reinforcement," *PCI J.,* 35(3), May–June, pp. 28–39.

Fereig, S. M. (1994). "Preliminary Design of Precast Prestressed Concrete Box Girder Bridges," *PCI J.,* 39(3), May–June, pp. 82–90.

Ficenec, J. A., Kneip, S. D., Tadros, M. K., and Fischer, L. G. (1993). "Prestressed Spliced I-Girders: Tenth Street Viaduct Project, Lincoln, Nebraska," *PCI J.,* 38(5), September–October, pp. 38–48.

Finsterwalder, U. (1965). "Prestressed Concrete Bridge Construction," *ACI J.,* 62(9), September, pp. 1037–1046.

———. (1969). "Free-Cantilever Construction of Prestressed Concrete Bridges and Mushroom-Shaped Bridges," *First Intl. Symp. Concrete Bridge Design,* SP-23, ACI, Detroit, pp. 467–494.

Finsterwalder, U., and Schambeck, H. (1965). "Die Spannbetonbruecke ueber den Rhein bei Bendorf," *Beton und Stahlbetonbau,* 60(3), March , pp. 55–62.

Fiorato, A. E. (1991). "Current Research on High-Performance Concrete at the Portland Cement Association," presentation at *Federal Executive Seminar,* Arlington, VA, October.

FIP. (1984). *Practical Design of Reinforced and Prestressed Concrete Structures, FIP recommendations based on CIB-FIP Model Code MC 78,* Federation Internationale de la Precontrainte, Thomas Telford, Ltd., London, SW1X 8BH.

——. (1986a). *FIP State-of-the-Art Report: Corrosion and Corrosion Protection of Prestressed Ground Anchorages,* Federation Internationale de la Precontrainte, Thomas Telford, Ltd., London, SW1X 8BH.

——. (1986b). *Corrosion Protection of Unbonded Tendons—FIP Recommendations,* Federation Internationale de la Precontrainte, Thomas Telford, Ltd., London, SW1X 8BH.

——. (1990a). "High-Strength Concrete: State-of-the-Art Report," *Bulletin d'Information,* No. 197, Federation Internationale de la Precontrainte, Thomas Telford, Ltd., London, SW1X 8BH.

——. (1990b). "Grouting of Tendons in Prestressed Concrete," in *FIP Guide to Good Practice,* Federation International de la Precontrainte, Thomas Telford, Ltd., London, SW1X 8BH.

——. (undated). "Corrosion Protection of Prestressing Steel," *FIP State-of-the-Art Report: Draft Report,* Federation Internationale de la Precontrainte, Thomas Telford, Ltd., London, SW1X 8BH.

Foerster, H. R., Rizkalla, S., and Hoeval, J. S. (1989). "Behavior and Design of Shear Connections, for Load-Bearing Wall Panels," *PCI J.,* 34(1), January–February, pp. 102–119.

Fornerod, M. (1950). "Load and Destruction Test of 160-ft Girder Designed for First Prestressed Concrete Bridge in U.S.A.," *Publications, International Association for Bridge and Structural Engineering,* Vol. 10.

Fressynet, E. (1951). "The Deformation of Concrete," *Mag. Concrete Res.,* December.

Freyermuth, C.L. "Design of Continuous Highway Bridges with Precast Prestressed Concrete Girders," *PCI J.,* 14(2), March–April, pp. 14-36.

——. (1992). "Building Better Bridges: Concrete vs. Steel," *ASCE Civ. Eng.,* July, pp. 68–71.

Gangatharan, A., and Brown, R. C. (1990). "Shear Strength of Post-Tensioned Grouted Keyed Connections," *PCI J.,* 35(3), May–June, pp. 64–73.

Garcia, A. M. (1993). "Florida's Long-Span Bridges: New Forms, New Horizons," *PCI J.,* July–August, 38(4), pp. 34–49.

Gaston, J. R., and Kriz, L. B. (1964). "Connections in Precast Structures—Scarf Joints," *PCI J.,* 9(3), June, pp. 37–59.

Gellatly, R. A., and Dupree, D. M. (1976). "Examples of Computer-Aided Optimal Design of Structures," *IABSE Tenth Congress—Introductory Report,* Tokyo, pp. 77–105.

Geren, K. L., Abdel-Karim, A. M., and Tadros, M. K. (1992). "Precast Prestressed Concrete Bridge I-Girders: The Next Generation," *Concrete Intl.,* 14(6), June, pp. 25–28.

Geren, K. Y., and Tadros, M. K. (1994). "The NU Precast Prestressed Concrete Bridge I-Girder Series," *PCI J.,* 39(3), May–June, pp. 26–39.

Gergeley, P., and Sozen, M. A. (1967). "Design of Anchorage Zone Reinforcement in Prestressed Concrete Beams," *PCI J.,* 12(2), March–April, pp. 63–75.

Gerwick, B. C. (1964). "Precast Segmental Construction for Long-Span Bridges," *ASCE Civ. Eng.,* January, pp. 43–47.

——. (1978). "Prestressed Concrete Developments in Japan," *PCI J.,* 23(6), November–December, pp. 66–76.

——. (1993). *Construction of Prestressed Concrete Structures,* John Wiley & Sons, New York.

Ghali, A., and Favre, R. (1986). *Concrete Structures: Stresses and Deformations,* Chapman and Hall, London.

Glodowski, R. J., and Lorenzetti, J. J. (1972). "A Method for Predicting Prestress Losses in a Prestressed Concrete Structure," *PCI J.,* 17(2), March–April, pp. 17–31.

Govindaswamy, R. (1989). "47th Street Bridge over Arkansas River," *PCI J.,* 34(6), November–December, pp. 126–133.

Grafton, J. (1994). Pomeroy Corp., Petaluma, CA, April. Personal correspondence.

Grant, A., and Clark, J. H. (1969). "Performance Evaluation of a Partially Prestressed Rigid-Frame Concrete Bridge," *First Intl. Symp. Concrete Bridge Design,* ACI Publication SP-23, ACI, Chicago, pp. 625–630.

Grossfield, B., and Birnstiel, C. (1962). "Tests of T-Beams with Precast Webs and Cast-in-Place Flanges," *ACI J. Proc.,* 59(6), June, pp. 843–851.

Grouni, H. N. "Prestressed Concrete: A Simplified Method for Loss Computation," *ACI J. Proc.,* 70(2), February, pp. 15–29.

Gustaferro, A., Hillier, M. A., and Janney, J. R. (1983). "Performance of Prestressed Concrete on the Illinois Tollway after 25 Years of Service," *PCI J.,* 28(1), January–February, pp. 50–67.

Guyon, Y. (1960). *Prestressed Concrete,* Vols. 1 and 2, John Wiley & Sons, New York.

Hadley, H. M. (1958). "Tied-Cantilever Bridge—Pioneer Structure in U.S.," *ASCE Civ. Eng.,* January, pp. 48–50.

Hambly, E. C. (1991). *Bridge Deck Behavior,* Van Nostrand Reinhold, New York.

Hanson, N. W. (1960). "Precast-Prestressed Concrete Bridges: Part 2—Horizontal Shear Connections," *J. Res. and Dev. Lab., Portland Cement Assoc.,* 2(2), May, pp. 38–58; *PCA Devel. Dept. Bull. D35,* 1960.

Hanson, N. W., and Kaar, P. H. (1959). "Flexural Bond Tests of Pretensioned Prestressed Beams," *ACI J.,* 56(1), January, pp. 783–802.

Harvey, D. I. (1986). *Spliced Segmental Precast Concrete Bridges Using Staged Post-Tensioning,* ACI Special Pub. SP-93-32, ACI, Detroit.

Hays, C. O., and Lybas, J. M. (1982). "Full-Span Form Panels for Highway Bridges," *Transportation Research Record 871, Segmental and Systems Bridge Construction—Concrete Box Girder and Steel Design,* Transportation Research Board, Washington, DC, pp. 23–29.

Hays, C. O., and Tabatabai, H. (1985). "Summary of Research on Florida Precast Panel Bridges," *Report No. 85-1,* University of Florida, Quincy, August.

Heins, C. P., and Lawrie, R. A. (1984). *Design of Modern Concrete Highway Bridges,* John Wiley & Sons, New York.

Helland, S. (1994). "Readers' Comments on High-Strength Concrete," *PCI J.,* 39(4), July–August, p. 103.

Hemakon, R. (1975). *Strength and Behavior of Post-Tensioned Flat Plates with Unbonded Tendons,* Ph.D. dissertation, University of Texas at Austin, December.

Hernandez, H. D., and Gamble, W. L. (1975). "Time-Dependent Losses in Pretensioned Concrete Construction," *Structural Research Series No. 417,* Civil Engineering Studies, University of Illinois, Urbana, May.

Hofbeck, J. A., Ibrahim, I. O., and Mattock, A. H. (1969). "Shear Transfer in Reinforced Concrete," *ACI J.,* 66(2), February, pp. 119–128.

Hope, B. B., and Ip, A. K. C. (1987). "Chloride Corrosion Threshold in Concrete," *Materials J.,* ACI, 84(4), July–August, pp. 306–314.

Hope, B. B., Page, J. A., and Poland, J. S. (1985). "The Determination of the Chloride Content of Concrete," *Cement and Concrete Res.* 15(5), September, pp. 863–870.

Huang, T. (1982). "Study of Prestressed Losses Conducted by Lehigh University," *PCI J.,* 27(5), September–October, pp. 48–61.

Huval, D. S. (1994). Retired Chief Bridge Engineer, Department of Transportation and Development, State of Louisiana, June. Personal communication.

Imper, R. R., and Laszlo, G. (1987). "Handling and Shipping of Long-Span Bridge Beams," *PCI J.,* 32(6), November–December, pp. 86–101.

Jacobson, F. K. (1969). "Continuous Precast Prestressed Concrete Bridge Stringers (a New Orleans Paper)," *First Intl. Symp. Concrete Bridge Design,* ACI Special Pub. SP-23, ACI, Chicago, pp. 655–664.

Janney, J. R. (1963). "Report of Stress-Transfer-Length Studies on 270-ksi Strand," *PCI J.,* 8(1), January–February, pp. 41–45.

Janssen, H. H. (1989). "Design and Construction of Segmental I-Girders," *Sixth Annual Intl. Bridge Conf.,* Pittsburgh, June 12–14.

Janssen, H. H., and Spans, L. (1994). "Record Span Spliced Bulb-T Girders Used in Highland View Bridge," *PCI J.,* 39(1), January–February, pp. 12–19.

Jobse, H. J. (1987). *Application of High-Strength Concrete for Highway Bridges—Executive Summary,* Publication No. FHWA/RD-87/079, Federal Highway Administration, Washington, DC, October.

Jones, H. L., and Furr, H. L. (1970). *Study of In-Service Bridges Constructed with Prestressed Subdecks,* Research Report 145-1, Texas Transportation Institute, Texas A&M University, College Station, July.

Kaar, P. H., Kriz, L. B., and Hognested, E. (1960). "Precast Prestressed Bridges: (1) Pilot Tests of Continuous Girders," *J. Res. and Dev. Lab.,* 2(2), May, pp. 21–37; *Devel. Dept. Bull. D34,* PCA, 1960.

Kaar, P. H., LaFraugh, R., and Mass, M. (1963). "Influence of Concrete Strength on Strand Transfer Length," *PCI J.,* 8(5), September–October, pp. 47–67.

Kaminker, A. J. (1993). "Comments on 'Corrosion of Prestressing Steels and Its Mitigation,' by W. Podolny, Jr.," *PCI J.,* 38(4), July–August, pp. 102–103.

Kani, G. N. J. (1966). "Basic Facts Concerning Shear Failure," *ACI J.,* 63(6), June, pp. 675–692.

——. (1969). "A Rational Theory for the Function of Web Reinforcement," *ACI J.,* 66(3), March, pp. 185–197.

Keyder, E. (1990). "Friction Losses in Prestressed Steel by Equivalent Load Method," *PCI J.,* 35(2), March–April, pp. 74–77.

Kirsch, U. (1973). "Optimum Design of Prestressed Plates," *ASCE J. Struct. Div.,* 99(ST6), June, pp. 1075–1090.

Klingner, R. E., Fang, I. K., Tsui, C. K. T., and Burns, N. H. (1990). "Load Capacity of Isotropically Reinforced, Cast-in-Place and Precast Panel Bridge Decks," *PCI J.,* 35(4), July–August, pp. 104–113.

Kluge, R. W., and Sawyer, H. A. (1975). "Interacting Pretensioned Concrete Form Panels for Bridge Decks," *PCI J.,* 20(3), May–June, pp. 34–61.

Knapp, N. (1995). Chief Bridge Engineer, Louisiana Department of Transportation and Development, Baton Rouge. Personal communication.

Kono, M. and Ozaka, Y. (1969). "Design and Construction of Prestressed Concrete Through-Girder Bridges in Japan," ACI Special Pub. SP-23-20, *First Intl. Symp. Concrete Bridge Design,* pp. 549–561.

Kozak, J. J., and Bezouska, T. J. (1976). "Twenty-Five Years of Progress in Prestressed Concrete Bridges," *PCI J.,* September–October, pp. 90–110.

Kriz, L. B., and Raths, C. H. (1965). "Connections in Precast Concrete Structures—Strength of Corbels," *PCI J.,* 10(1), January–February, pp. 16–61.

Kulka, F., and Lin, T. Y. (1982). "Comparative Study of Medium-Span Box Girder Bridges with Other Precast Systems," *First Intl. Conf. on Short- and Medium-Span Bridges, Vol. 1,* Toronto, Ontario, pp. 81–94.

——. (1984). "Comparative Study of Medium-Span Box Girder Bridges with Other Precast Systems," *Canadian J. Civ. Eng.,* 11, pp. 396–403.

Kwei, G. C. S. (1967). "Discussion of 'Single T-Beam Bridges,' by R. B.Curtis," *PCI J.,* 12(5), September–October, pp. 82–83.

Labia, Y., Saiidi, M., and Douglas, B. (1993). "Retrofitting and Structural Evaluation of Prestressed Concrete Bridges," *Progress Report,* Department of Civil Engineering, University of Nevada, Reno, March.

Lab. Reg. (1986). *Scorpion II is a Modern and Powerful System of X-Ray Radiography and Radioscopy for the Inspection of Reinforced or Prestressed Concrete Engineering Structures,* Laboratoire Regional des Ponts-et-Chaussees de Blois, February.

Lacey, G. C., and Breen, J. E. (1969). "Long-Span Prestressed Concrete Bridges of Segmental Construction: State of the Art," Research Report 121-1, Center for Highway Research, University of Texas at Austin, May.

———. (1975). "The Design and Optimization of Segmentally Precast Prestressed Box Girder Bridges," Research Report 121-3, Center for Highway Research, University of Texas at Austin, August.

Lacey, G. C., Breen J. E., and Burns, N. H. (1971). "State of the Art for Long-Span Bridges of Segmental Construction," *PCI J.,* 16(5), September–October, pp. 53–77.

Lamarre, B. (1967). "Highway Built with Prestressed Concrete in Montreal," *PCI J.,* 12(5), October, pp. 67–80.

Lane, S. N., and Podolny, W. (1993). "The Federal Outlook for High-Strength Concrete Bridges," *PCI J.,* 38(3), May–June, pp. 20–33.

Lazlo, G. (1967). "A Prestressed Lightweight Concrete Bridge 131 ft Long," *ASCE Civ. Eng.,* April, pp. 64–65.

Leming, M. L., Ahmed, S. H., Zia, P., Schemmel, J. J., Elliot, R. P., and Naaman, A. E. (1990). *High-Performance Concretes—An Annotated Bibliography, 1974–1989,* Report No. SHRP-C/WP-90-001, Strategic Highway Research Program, National Research Council, Washington, DC, March.

Leonhardt, F. (1964). *Prestressed Concrete: Design and Construction,* 2nd ed., Wilhelm, Ernest, & Sohn, Berlin.

———. (1965)."Long-Span Prestressed Concrete Bridges in Europe," *PCI J.,* 10(1), February, pp. 62–75.

———. (1974). "Latest Development of Cable-Stayed Bridges for Long Spans," *Saetryk af Bygingsstatiske Meddelelser,* 45(4), Denmark, Danmarko Teckniske Hojskole.

———. (1984). *Bridges—Aesthetics and Design (Brucken—Asthetik und Gestaltung),* MIT Press, Cambridge, MA (in English and German).

Leonhardt, F., and Lipproth, W. (1970). "Conclusions Drawn from Distress of Prestressed Concrete Bridges," *Beton-und Stahlbetonbau,* 65(10), October, pp. 231–244 (in German).

Libby, J. R. (1976a). *Modern Prestressed Concrete Design Principles and Construction Methods,* Van Nostrand Reinhold, New York.

———. (1976b). "Segmental Box Girder Bridge Superstructure Design," *ACI J.,* 73(5), May, pp. 279–290

Libby, J. R., and Perkins, N. D. (1976). *Modern Prestressed Concrete Highway Bridge Superstructures—Design Principles and Construction Methods,* Grantville Pub., San Diego, CA.

Lin, T. Y. (1961). "A New Concept for Prestressed Concrete," *Constr. Rev.,* Sydney, Australia, pp. 21–31 (reprinted in *PCI J.,* December, pp. 36–52); also in T. Y. Lin, "Revolution in Concrete," *Architectural Forum Part I,* May 1961 pp. 121–127, and *Architectural Forum Part II,* June 1961, pp.116–121.

———. (1963a). *Design of Prestressed Concrete Structures,* 2nd ed., John Wiley & Sons, New York.

———. (1963b). "Load Balancing Method for Design and Analysis of Prestressed Concrete Structures," *ACI J.,* 60(6), June, pp. 719–742.

———. (1985). *Criteria for Designing Lightweight Concrete Bridges,* Final Report, No. FHWA/RD-85/045, by T. Y. Lin Intl., National Technical Information Service, Springfield, VA, August.

Lin, T. Y., and Burns, N. H. (1981). *Design of Prestressed Concrete Structures,* 3rd ed., John Wiley & Sons, New York.

Lin, T. Y., and Gerwick, B. C. (1969). "Design of Long-Span Concrete Bridges with Special Reference to Prestressing, Precasting, Erection, Structural Behavior, and Economics (a New Orleans Paper)," *First Intl. Symp. Concrete Bridge Design,* ACI Special Pub. SP-23, ACI, Chicago, pp. 693–704.

Lin, T. Y., and Kulka, F. (1973). "Construction of Rio Colorado Bridge," *PCI J.,* 18(6), November–December, pp. 92–101.

———. (1975). "Fifty-Year Advancement in Concrete Bridge Construction," *ASCE J. Construction Div.,* 101(C03), September, pp. 491–510.

Lin, T. Y., Kulka, F., and Yang, Y. C. (1969). "Post-Tensioned Waffle and Multispan Cantilever System with Y Piers Composing the Hennerberger Overpass," *First Intl. Symp. Concrete Bridge Design,* ACI Special Pub. SP-23, ACI, Chicago, pp. 495–506.

Lin, T. Y., Scordelis, A. C., and Itaya, R. (1959). "Behavior of Continuous Slab Prestressed in Two Directions," *ACI J. Proc.,* 56, pp. 441–459.

Loh, E. (1974). "Comments on 'Construction of Rio Colorado Bridge,' by T. Y. Lin and F. Kulka," *PCI J.,* 19(2), March–April, pp. 131–133.

Loov, R. E., and Patnaik, A. K. (1994). "Horizontal Shear Strength of Composite Concrete Beams with a Rough Interface," *PCI J.,* 39(1), January–February, pp. 48–69.

Lorensten, M. (1965). "Theory of Combined Action of Bending Moment and Shear in Reinforced and Prestressed Concrete Beams," *ACI J.,* 62(4), April, pp. 403–419.

Lounis, Z., and Cohn, M. Z. (1992). "Optimal Design of Prestressed Concrete Highway Bridge Girders," *Proc. Third Intl. Symp. Concrete Bridge Design,* Washington, DC, March.

Lounis, Z., and Cohn, M. Z. (1993). "Optimization of Precast Prestressed Concrete Bridge Girder Systems," *PCI J.,* 38(4), July–August, pp. 60–78.

Lount, A. M. (1969). "The Practical Design of Redundant Prestressed Concrete Bridges," *First Intl. Symp. Concrete Bridge Design,* ACI Special Pub. SP-23, ACI, Chicago, pp. 537–547.

Loveall, C. L. (1985). "Jointless Bridge Decks," *ASCE Civ. Eng.,* November, pp. 64–67.

Lundgren, A., and Hansen, F. (1969). "Three-Span Continuous Prestressed Concrete Bridge Constructed of Precast Units in Free-Cantilever Construction (a New Orleans Paper)," *First Intl. Symp. Concrete Bridge Design,* ACI Special Pub. SP-23, ACI, Chicago, pp. 665–680.

Luther, M. D., and Bauer, K. C. (1987). "Using High-Strength Concrete Simplifies Column Design," *Concrete Construction,* 32(6), June, pp. 546–547.

MacGregor, J. G. (1958). "Effect of Draped Reinforcement on Behavior of Prestressed Concrete Beams," *Structural Research Series No. 154,* University of Illinois, Urbana, May.

———. (1992). "Canadian Network of Centres of Excellence on High-Performance Concrete," *Concrete Intl.* 15(2), February, pp. 60–61.

MacGregor, J. G., and Hanson, J. M. (1969). "Proposed Changes in Shear Provisions for Reinforced and Prestressed Concrete Beams," *ACI J.,* 66(4), April, pp. 276–288.

MacGregor, J. G., Sozen, M. A., and Seiss, C. P. (1960). "Strength and Behavior of Prestressed Concrete Beams with Web Reinforcement," *Structural Research Series 210,* University of Illinois Civil Engineering Studies, Urbana, August.

———. (1965). "Strength of Concrete Beams with Web Reinforcement," *ACI J.,* 62(12), December, pp. 1503–1519.

Mafi, M., and West, H. H. (1986). "Cost-Effective Short-Span Bridge Systems: A Selection Concept and an Optimization Procedure," *Second Intl. Conf. Short- and Medium-Span Bridges, Vol. 2,* Ottawa, Ontario, pp. 117–131.

Magnel, G. (1950). "Prototype Prestressed Beam Justifies Walnut Lane Bridge Design," *ACI J.,* 46(12), December, pp. 301–316.

———. (1954). *Prestressed Concrete,* McGraw-Hill Companies, Inc., New York.

Manton, B. H., and Wilson, C. B. (1975). *MOT/C&CA Standard Bridge Beams,* Cement and Concrete Association, London.

Marshall, S. L. and Pelkey, R. E. (1986). *Production, Transportation, and Installation of Spliced Prestressed Concrete I-Girders for the Annacis Channel East Bridge,* ACI Special Pub. SP-93-33, ACI, Detroit.

Martin, L. D. (1977). "A Rational Method of Estimating Camber and Deflection of Precast Prestressed Concrete Members," *PCI J.,* 22(1), January–February, pp. 100–108.

Martin, L. D., and Scott, N. L. (1976). "Development of Prestressing Strand in Pretensioned Members," *ACI J.,* 73(8), August, pp. 453–456.

Massicotte, B., and Picard, A. (1994) "Monitoring of a Prestressed Segmental Box Girder Bridge during Strengthening," *PCI J.,* 39(3), May–June, pp. 66–80.

Massicotte, B., Picard, A., Gaumond, Y., and Ouellet, C. (1994). "Strengthening of a Long-Span Prestressed Segmental Box Girder Bridge," *PCI J.,* 39(3), May–June, pp. 52–65.

Mast, P. E. (1966). "Elastic Stability of Flanges of Typical Prestressed Single Ts," *PCI J.,* 11(4), August, pp. 64–76.

Mast, R. F. (1968). "Auxiliary Reinforcement in Concrete Connections," *ASCE J. Struct. Div.,* 94(ST6), June, pp. 1485–1503.

———. (1989). "Lateral Stability of Long Prestressed Concrete Beams: Part 1," *PCI J.,* 34(1), January–February, pp. 34–53.

———. (1993). "Lateral Stability of Long Prestressed Concrete Beams, Part 2," *PCI J.,* 38(1), January–February, pp. 70–83.

———. (1994). "Lateral Bending Test to Destruction of a 149-ft Prestressed Concrete I-Beam," *PCI J.,* 39(4), July–August pp. 54–62.

Mathivat, J. (1966). "Reconstruction du Pont de Choisy-le-Roi," *Travaux,* no. 372, January.

———. (1979). *The Cantilever Construction of Prestressed Concrete Bridges,* John Wiley & Sons, New York.

Matsushita, H., and Sato, M. (1979). "The Hayashi-No-Mine Prestressed Bridge," *PCI J.,* 24(2), March–April, pp. 90–109.

Mattock, A. H. (1987). "Anchorage of Stirrups in Thin Cast-in-Place Topping," *PCI J.,* 32(6), November–December, pp. 70–85.

Mattock, A. H., and Hawkins, N. M. (1972). "Shear Transfer in Reinforced Concrete—Recent Research," *PCI J.,* 17(2), March–April, pp. 55–75.

Mattock, A. H., and Kaar, P. H. (1961). "Precast Prestressed Concrete Bridges— 4. Shear Tests on Continuous Girders," *J. PCA Res. and Dev. Lab.,* 3(1), January, pp. 19–46; *PCA Devel. Dept. Bull. D45,* 1961.

McDermott, J. F., Abrams, J. I., and Cohn, M. Z. (1972a). "Some Results in the Optimization of Tall Building Systems," *IABSE Ninth Congress—Preliminary Report,* Amsterdam, pp. 855–861.

———. (1972b). "Computer Program for Selecting Structural Systems," *Preprint 1863, ASCE Annual Meeting*, Houston, TX.

MCHRP. (1969). *Study of a Proposed Precast Prestressed Composite Bridge System,* Final Report, Report 69-2, Missouri Cooperative Highway Research Program, University of Missouri, Columbia.

Mehta, P. K. (1986). *Concrete: Structure, Properties, and Materials,* Prentice Hall, Englewood Cliffs, NJ.

Mills, D., Chow, K. T., and Marshall, S. L. (1991). "Design Construction of Esker Overhead," *PCI J.,* 36(5), September–October, pp. 44–51.

Minosaku, K. (1992). "Using FRP Materials in Prestressed Concrete Structures," *Concrete Intl.,* 14(8), August, pp. 41–44.

Moktharzadeh, A., and French, C. W. (1993). "Bibliography on High-Strength Concrete," *PCI J.,* 38(3), May–June, pp. 130–137. (Lists 205 references.)

Monfore, G. E., and Verbeck, G. J. (1960). "Corrosion of Prestressed Wire in Concrete," *ACI J.,* 57(5), November, pp. 491–515.

Moore, D. G., Klodt, D. T., and Hensen, R. J. (1970). "Protection of Steel in Prestressed Concrete Bridges," *NCHRP Report 90,* Transportation Research Board, National Research Council, Washington, DC.

Morandi, R. (1969). "Some Types of Tied Bridges in Prestressed Concrete," *First Intl. Symp. Concrete Bridge Design,* paper SP-23, ACI, Detroit, pp. 447–465.

Moustafa, S. E. (1981). "Effectiveness of Shear-Friction Reinforcement in Shear-Diaphragm Capacity of Hollow-Core Slabs," *PCI J.,* 26(1), January–February, pp. 118–132.

MRA. (1973). *Precast Beams for Bridges,* Report to Ontario Precast Concrete Manufacturers' Association, McCormic, Rankin, and Associates, Ltd., Rexdale, Ontario.

Muller, J. (1962). "Lateral Stability of Precast Members during Handling and Placing," *PCI J.,* 7(1), January–February, pp. 21–23.

———. (1969). "Long-Span Precast Prestressed Concrete Bridges Built in Cantilever," *First Intl. Symp. Concrete Bridge Design,* paper SP-23-40, ACI Pub. SP-23, ACI, Detroit, pp. 705–740.

———. (1975). "Ten Years of Experience in Precast Segmental Construction—A Special Report," *PCI J.,* 20(1), January–February, pp. 28–61.

Murillo, J. A., Thoman, S., and Smith, D. (1994). "Lightweight Concrete for a Segmental Bridge," *ASCE Civ. Eng.,* May, pp. 68–70.

Murray, V. E., and Frantz, G. C. (1992). "Chloride Testing of 27-Year-Old Prestressed Concrete Bridge Beams," *PCI J.,* 37(5), September–October, pp. 68–79.

Naaman, A. E. (1972). "Computer Program for Selection and Design of Simple-Span Prestressed Concrete Girders," *PCI J.,* 17(1), January–February, pp.73–81.

Naaman, A. E. (1982). *Prestressed Concrete Analysis and Design: Fundamentals,* McGraw-Hill Companies, Inc., New York.

Naaman, A. E., and Hamza, A. M. (1991). *Evaluation of Prestress Losses for Partially Prestressed High-Strength Concrete Beams,* Report no. UMCE 91-18, Department of Civil and Environmental Engineering, University of Michigan, Ann Arbor.

———. (1993). "Prestress Losses in Partially Prestressed High-Strength Concrete Beams," *PCI J.,* 38(3), May–June, pp. 98–114.

Naaman, A. E., and Siriaksorn, A. (1979a). "Serviceability-Based Design of Partially Prestressed Beams, Part I: Analytic Formulation," *PCI J.,* 24(2) March–April, pp. 64–89.

———. (1979b). "Serviceability-Based Design of Partially Prestressed Beams, Part II" *PCI J.,* 24(3), May–June, pp. 64–89.

Narasimham, S. V. (1993). "Discussion on 'Prestress Influence on Shear-Lag Effect in Continuous Box Girder Bridge,' by S. T. Chang," *ASCE J. Struct. Eng.,* 119(7), July, pp. 1681–1682.

Nawy, E. G. (1985). "Flexural Cracking Behavior of Pretensioned and Post-Tensioned Beams: The State of the Art," *ACI J.,* 82(12), December, pp. 890–900.

———. (1986). "Flexural Cracking Behavior and Crack Control of Pretensioned and Post-Tensioned Prestressed Beams," *Proc. NATO–NSF Advanced Research Workshop, Vol. 2,* Dordrecht–Boston, Martinus Nijhoff, pp. 137–156.

———. (1989). *Prestressed Concrete: A Fundamental Approach,* Prentice Hall, Englewood Cliffs, NJ.

Nawy, E. G., and Chiang, J. Y. (1980). "Serviceability Behavior of Post-Tensioned Beams," *PCI J.,* 25(1), January–February, pp. 74–95.

Nawy, E. G., and Huang, P. T. (1977). "Crack and Deflection Control of Pretensioned Prestressed Beams," *PCI J.,* 22, pp. 30–47.

Nawy, E. G., and Potyondy, J. G. (1971). "Flexural Cracking Behavior of Pretensioned Prestressed Concrete I- and T-Beams," *ACI J.,* 65, pp. 335–360.

Nehse, H. (1973). "Spannbandbrucken," in *Festschrift Ulrich Finsterwalder 50 Jahre fur Dywidag,* Dyckerhoff & Widman, Munich (in German).

New CE. (1992a). *New Civ. Eng.,* October 8.

———. (1992b). *New Civ. Eng.,* October 15.

Nilson, A. H. (1978). *Design of Prestressed Concrete,* John Wiley & Sons, New York.

Novokshchenov, V. (1990). "Prestressed Concrete and Marine Environment," *ASCE J. Struct. Eng.,* 116(11), November, pp. 3193–3205.

———. (1991). "Prestressed Concrete Bridges in Adverse Environments," *Concrete Intl.,* 13(5), May, pp. 44–48.

Nurnberger, U. (1980). "Analyse und Auswertung von Schadensfallen an Spannstahlen, (Analysis and Evaluation of Damage to Prestressing Steels)," Forschungs bericht aus dem Forschungsprogramm des Bundesministers fur Verkehr und der Forschungs-gesellschaft fur das Strassenwesen e.V., Heft 308, Bundesminister fur Verkehr, Bonn-Bad Godesberg (in German).

O'Connor, C. (1971). *Design of Bridge Superstructures,* John Wiley & Sons, New York.

Oesterle, R. G., Gilkin, J. D., and Larson, S. C. (1989). *Design of Precast Prestressed Bridge Girders Made Continuous,* NCHRP Report No. 322, Transportation Research Board, Washington, DC, November.

OHBDC. (1992). *Ontario Highway Bridge Design Code,* Ontario Ministry of Transportation and Communication, Toronto, Ontario.

Olson, S. A., and French, C. W. (1990). "Prestressed Concrete Girders after 20 Years in Service," in *Bridge Evaluation, Repair, and Rehabilitation,* A. S. Nowak, ed., University of Michigan, Ann Arbor, pp. 391–403.

Osipov, L. (1969). "The Hudson Hope Bridge—Its Post-Tensioned Box Girder Stiffening Deck and Prestressed Rock Anchors," *First Intl. Symp. Concrete Bridge Design,* ACI Pub. SP-23, ACI, Detroit, pp. 741–753.

Ouellet, C., and Gaumond, Y. (1990). "Strengthening of Two Prestressed Segmental Box Girder Bridges," in *Development in Short- and Medium-Span Bridge Engineering—1990,* B. Bakht, R. A. Dorton, and L. G. Jaeger, eds., *Third Intl. Conf. Short- and Medium-Span Bridges, Vol. 2,* Toronto, Ontario, August.

Over, R. S., and Au, T. (1965). "Prestress Transfer Bond of Pretensioned Strands in Concrete," *ACI J.,* 62(11), November, pp. 1451–1460.

Ozaka, Y., and Koike, S, (1965). "Design of Arakawa Bridge of Tohoku Line," *Prestressed Concrete,* 7(6), September (in Japanese).

Pate, D. (1995). "The Chesapeake and Delaware Canal Bridge—Design-Construction Highlights," *PCI J.,* 40(5), September–October, pp. 20–30.

Patnaik, A. K. (1992). *Horizontal Shear Strength of Composite Concrete Beams with a Rough Interface,* Ph.D. thesis, Department of Civil Engineering, The University of Calgary, Alberta, December.

Pauley, T., Park, R., and Phillips, M. H. (1974). "Horizontal Construction Joints in Cast-in-Place Reinforced Concrete," *Shear in Reinforced Concrete,* ACI Spec. Pub. SP-42, Vol. 2, ACI, Detroit, pp. 599–616.

PCA. (1978a). "Florida Spliced I-Girder Bridge Construction," *PCA Bridge Report,* PCA, Skokie, IL.

———. (1978b). "Kingston Road Bridge, Scarborough, Ontario," *PCA Bridge Report,* PCA, Skokie, IL.

——. (1984). *Prestressed Concrete Bridge Beams,* 2nd ed., PCA, British Precast Concrete Federation, Leicester, England.

PCI. (1967). "Long Spans with Standard Bridge Girders," *PCI Bridge Bulletin,* Prestressed Concrete Institute, March–April.

PCI. (1968). *Prestressed Concrete for Long-Span Bridges,* Prestressed Concrete Institute, Chicago.

——. (1977). *Precast Trapezoidal Box Girders and Spliced I Girders,* PCI Committee on Bridges, Preliminary Report, Prestressed Concrete Institute, Chicago, October.

——. (1981a). *Reflections on the Beginnings of Prestressed Concrete in America,* Prestressed Concrete Institute, Chicago.

——. (1981b). *Precast Prestressed Concrete Short-Span Bridges—Spans to 100 Feet,* 2nd ed., Prestressed Concrete Institute, Chicago.

——. (1992). *PCI Design Handbook,* 4th ed., Precast/Prestressed Concrete Institute, Chicago.

——. (1993). "Guidelines for the Use of Epoxy-Coated Strand," *PCI Committee Report,* PCI Ad Hoc Committee on Epoxy-Coated Strand, *PCI J.,* 38(4), July–August, pp. 27–33.

PCI Br. Bull. (1970). "Umpqua River Bridge Segmentally Constructed," *PCI Bridge Bull.,* Prestressed Concrete Institute, January–February.

PCI/CRSI. (1969). *Post-Tensioned Box Girder Bridges, Design and Construction,* a joint publication by the Prestressed Concrete Institute, Chicago, and Concrete Reinforcing Steel Institute, Schaumburg, IL.

PCIJ. (1972). "Recommended Practice for Grouting of Post-Tensioned Prestressed Concrete," PCI Committee on Post-Tensioning, *PCI J.,* 17(6), November–December, pp. 18–25.

——. (1975a). "Recommended Practice for Segmental Construction in Prestressed Concrete," PCI Committee Report on Segmental Construction, *PCI J.,* 20(2), March–April.

——. (1975b). "Investigation to Determine Feasibility of Using In-Place Precast Prestressed Form Panels for Highway Bridge Decks," Sponsored by Texas Transportation Institute, Texas Highway Department and the Federal Highway Administration, Washington, DC, *PCI J.,* 20(3) May–June, pp. 62–67.

——. (1975c). "Recommendations for Estimating Prestress Losses," PCI Committee on Prestress Losses, *PCI J.,* 20(4), July–August, pp. 43–75.

——. (1978). "Tentative Design and Construction Specifications for Bridge Deck Panels," PCI Bridge Committee, *PCI J.,* 23(1), January–February, pp. 32–39.

——. (1980). "Precast Trapezoidal Girder Spliced with Post-Tensioning for Highway Underpass," *PCI J.,* 25(2), March–April, pp. 132–133.

——. (1987). "Precast Prestressed Concrete Bridge Deck Panels," PCI Committee on Bridges, Special Report, *PCI J.,* 32(2), March–April, pp. 26–45.

——. (1988). "Joseph Palmer Knap Bridge," *PCI J.,* 33(4), July–August, pp. 160–169.

——. (1989a). "American Segmental Bridge Institute Formed," *PCI J.,* 34(1), January–February, p. 180.

——. (1989b). "Florida's Turnpike over I-595 and North New River Canal, Broward County, Florida," *PCI J.,* 34(2), March–April, pp. 38–47.

——. (1989c). "Fargo-Moorhead Toll Bridge," *PCI J.,* 34(3), May–June, pp. 144–154.

——. (1991). "PCI Delegation Tours Tlalpan Freeway," *PCI J.,* 36(4), July–August, p. 108.

——. (1994). "FIP Outstanding Structures Award," *PCI J.,* 39(4), July–August, p. 31.

PennDOT. (1985). *Prestressed Concrete,* Vols. 1 and 3, Pennsylvania Department of Transportation, Part B, Sec. 9.

——. (1993a). *Standard Adjacent Box Beam Details (BD-654),* Bureau of Design, Commonwealth of Pennsylvania, Department of Transportation, Harrisburg, July.

——. (1993b). *Standard for Bridge Design BD-201,* Bureau of Design, Commonwealth of Pennsylvania, Department of Transportation Harrisburg, July.

Perenchio, W. F., Fraczek, J., and Pfeifer, D. W. (1989). *NCHRP Report 313: Corrosion Protection of Prestressing Systems in Concrete Bridges,* Transportation Research Board, National Research Council, Washington, DC, February.

Peterson, C. A. (1980). "Survey of Parking Structure Deterioration and Distress," *Concrete Intl.* 1(3), March, pp. 53–61.

Pfeifer, D. W., Landgren, J. R., and Zoob, A. B. (1987). *Protective Systems for New Prestressed and Substructure Concrete,* Final Report No. FHWA/RD-86/193, U.S. Department of Transportation, Federal Highway Administration, Washington, DC, April.

Pfeifer, D. W., Perenchio, W. F., and Hime, W. G. (1992). "A Critique of the ACI 318 Chloride Limits," *PCI J.,* 37(2), March–April, pp. 68-71.

Pfeifer, D. W., and Scali, M. J. (1981). *Concrete Sealers for Protection of Bridge Structure,* NCHRP Report No. 244, Transportation Research Board, Washington, DC, December.

Phipps, A. R., and Spruill, Q. D., Jr. (1990). "Biloxi Interstate-110 Viaduct," *PCI J.,* 35(1), January–February, pp. 120–132.

Phoenix, S. L., Johnson, H. H., and McGuire, W. (1986). "Conditions of Steel Cable after Period of Service," *ASCE J. Struct. Eng.,* 112(6), June, pp. 1263–1279.

Pierce, L. F. (1988). "Annacis Channel East Bridge," *PCI J.,* 33(1), January–February, pp. 148–155.

Podolny, W., Jr., (1979). "An Overview of Precast Prestressed Segmental Bridges," *PCI J.,* 24(1) January–February, pp. 56–87.

———. (1990). "Corrosion Protection of Prestressing Steels, Vol. 2," *FIP—Eleventh Intl. Congress on Prestressed Concrete,* Hamburg, June 4–9, pp. T57–T61.

———. (1992). "Corrosion of Prestressing Steels and Its Mitigation," *PCI J.,* 37(5), September–October, pp. 34–55.

Podolny, W., Jr., and Muller, J. (1982). *Construction and Design of Prestressed Concrete Segmental Bridges,* John Wiley & Sons, New York.

Podolny, W., Jr., and Scalzi, J. B. (1976). *Construction and Design of Cable-Stayed Bridges,* John Wiley & Sons, New York.

Poston, R. W., Breen, J. E., and Carrasquillo, R. L. (1989). "Design of Transversely Prestressed Concrete Bridge Decks," Special Report, *PCI J.,* 34(5), September–October, pp. 68–109.

Poston, R. W., Carrasquillo, R. L., and Breen, J. E. (1985). *Durability of Prestressed Bridge Decks,* Report 316-1, Center for Transportation Research, University of Texas at Austin, July.

———. (1987). "Durability of Post-Tensioned Bridge Decks," *ACI Materials J.,* 87(4), July–August, pp. 315–326.

Poston, R. W., Phipps, A. R., Breen, J. E., and Carrasquillo, R. L. (1988). "Effects of Transverse Prestressing in Bridge Decks," *ASCE J. Struct. Eng.,* 114(4), April, pp. 743–764.

Prog. Arch. (1979). "Ruck-A-Chucky Bridge," (First prize of the 26th Progressive Architecture Award), *Progressive Architecture,* January, pp. 68–69.

PTI. (1978). *Post-Tensioned Box Girder Bridge Manual,* Post-Tensioning Institute, Phoenix.

———. (1985). *Post-Tensioning Manual,* 4th ed., Post-Tensioning Institute, Phoenix.

———. (1988). *Design and Construction Specifications for Segmental Concrete Bridges,* National Cooperative Highway Research Program Report No. 20-7/32, Post-Tensioning Institute, Phoenix.

———. (1993). "Autopsy of 35-Year-Old Post-Tensioned Bridge," *Post-Tension Institute Newsletter,* Fall/Winter, pp. 4–6.

PTI/PCI. (1978). *Precast Segmental Box Girder Bridge Manual,* a joint publication by the Post-Tensioning Institute and the Prestressed Concrete Institute, Chicago.

Quade, M. N. (1952). "Fifteen-Mile Toll Bridge Under Construction across Lower Tampa Bay," *ASCE Civ. Eng.,* April, pp. 25–30.

Raafat, A. A. (1958). *Reinforced Concrete in Architecture,* Reinhold, New York.

Rabbat, B. G. (1984). "25-Year-Old Prestressed Concrete Girder Tested," *PCI J.,* 29(1), January–February, pp. 177–179.

Rabbat, B. G., and Russel, H. G. (1982a). "Optimized Sections for Pretensioned Concrete Bridge Girders," *PCI J.,* 27(4), July–August, pp. 88–104.

Rabbat, B. G., and Russel, H. G. (1982b). "Optimized Sections for Pretensioned Concrete Bridge Girders in the United States," *First Intl. Conf. on Short- and Medium-Span Bridges, Vol. 2,* Toronto, Ontario, pp. 97–111.

Rabbat, B. G., Takayanage, T., and Russell, H. G. (1982). *Optimized Sections for Major Prestressed Concrete Bridge Girders,* Publication No. FHWA/RD-82/005, Federal Highway Administration, Washington, DC, February.

Ragan, H. S. (1969). "A Package Concrete Overpass in Alberta," *First Intl. Symp. Concrete Bridge Design,* ACI Special Pub. SP-23, ACI, Chicago, pp. 681–692.

Ralls, M. L., Ybanez, L., and Panek, J. J. (1993). "The New Texas U-Beam Bridges: An Aesthetic and Economical Design Solution," *PCI J.,* 38(5), September–October, pp. 20–29.

Reed, R. L. (1978). *Application and Design of Prestressed Deck Panels,* Trans. Res. Rec. No. 665, Transportation Research Board, Washington, DC, pp. 164–171.

Riessauw, F. G., and Taerwe, L. (1980). "Tests on Two 30-Year-Old Prestressed Concrete Beams," *PCI J.,* 25(6), November–December, pp. 70–73.

Riggs, L. W. (1966). "Twenty-Seven Miles of Aerial Structures for the San Francisco Bay Area Rapid Transit System," *PCI J.,* 11(4), July–August, pp. 28–39.

Rimboeuf, M., and Salzmann, C. (1980). "Bridge over the River Azergues," *IABSE Congress,* Vienna, pp. 27–31.

Rioboo Martin, J. M. (1992). "A New Dimension in Precast Prestressed Concrete Bridges for Congested Urban Areas in High Seismic Zones," *PCI J.,* 37(2), March–April, pp. 44–65.

Rogers, G. J. (1952). "Validity of Certain Assumptions in the Mechanics of Prestressed Concrete," *ACI J. Proc.,* 49, pp. 317–330.

Roller, J. J., Martin, B. T., Russell, H. G., and Bruce, R. N. (1993). "Performance of Prestressed High-Strength Concrete Bridge Girders," *PCI J.,* 38(3), May–June, pp. 34–45.

Roller, J. J., Russell, H. G., Bruce, R. N., and Martin, B. T. (1995). "Long-Term Performance of Prestressed High-Strength Concrete Bridge Girders," *PCI J.,* 40(6), November–December, pp. 48–58.

Ross. (1988). "Recommended Practice for Precast Prestressed Concrete Composite Bridge Deck Panels," Prepared for the PCI Bridge Committee by Ross Bryan Associates, Inc., Nashville, Tennessee, *PCI J.,* 33(2), March–April, pp. 67–109.

Rothman, H. B., and Chang, F. K. (1974). "Longest Precast Concrete Bridge in Western Hemisphere," *ASCE Civ. Eng.,* March, pp. 56–60.

Russell, B. W. (1994). "Impact of High-Strength Concrete on the Design and Construction of Pretensioned Girder Bridges," *PCI J.,* 39(4), July–August, pp. 76–89.

Russell, B. W., and Burns, N. H. (1993). *Design Guidelines for Transfer, Development, and Debonding of Large-Diameter Seven-Wire Strands in Pretensioned Concrete Girders,* Research Report 1210-5F, Center of Transportation Research, University of Texas at Austin, January, pp. 21–81.

Russell, H. G., ed. (1985). *High-Strength Concrete,* ACI Special Pub. SP-87, ACI, Detroit.

Russell, H. G., Gebler, S. H., and Whiting, D. (1989). "High-Strength Concrete: Weighing the Benefits," *ASCE Civ. Eng.,* November, pp. 59–61.

Saemann, J. C., and Washa, G. W. (1964). "Horizontal Shear Connections between Precast Beams and Cast-in-Place Slabs," *ACI J.,* 61(11), November, pp. 1383–1409; "Discussion," *ACI J.,* 62(6), June, pp. 1807–1810.

Salmons, J. R., and Kagay, W. J. (1971). "The Composite U-Beam Bridge Superstructure," *PCI J.,* 16(3), May–June, pp. 20–32.

Salmons, J. R., and Mokhtari, S. (1971). "Structural Performance of Composite U-Beam Bridge Superstructure," *PCI J.,* 16(4), July–August, pp. 21–33.

Samuely, F. J. (1952). "Some Recent Experience in Composite Precast and In Situ Concrete Construction with Particular Reference to Prestressing," *Proc. Inst. Civ. Engrs.,* vol. 1, part 1, no. 30, pp. 222–259.

Sason, A. S. (1992). "Evaluation of Degree of Rusting on Prestressed Concrete Strand," *PCI J.,* 37(3), May–June, pp. 25–30.

Schofield, E. R. (1948). "First Prestressed Bridge in the U.S.," *Eng. News-Record,* December, pp. 16–18.

———. (1949). "Construction Starts on Prestressed Concrete Bridge in Philadelphia," *ASCE Civ. Eng.,* July, p. 32.

Schupack, M. (1978). "A Survey of the Durability Performance of Post-Tensioning Tendons," *ACI J.,* 75(10), October, pp. 501–510.

———. (1982). "Protecting Post-Tensioning Tendons in Concrete Structures," *ASCE Civ. Eng.,* December, pp. 43–45.

———. (1991). "Corrosion Protection of Unbonded Tendons," ACI, *Concrete Intl.,* February, pp. 51–57.

———. (1993). "Bonded Tendon Debate," *ASCE Civ. Eng.,* August, pp. 64–66.

Schupack, M., and Suarez, M. G. (1982). "Some Recent Corrosion Embrittlement Failures of Prestressing Systems in the United States," *PCI J.,* 27(2), March–April, pp. 38–55.

———. (1991). "Discussion of 'Prestressed Concrete Bridges in Adverse Environments'," *Concrete Intl.,* 13(12), pp. 11–14.

Scordelis, A. C., Pister, K. S., and Lin, T. Y. (1956). "Strength of Concrete Slab Prestressed in Two Directions," *ACI J. Proc.,* 53(9), September, pp. 241–256.

Scordelis, A. C., Samarzich, W., and Pirtz, D. (1960). "Load Distribution on Prestressed Concrete Slab Bridge," *PCI J.,* 5(3), June.

Scordelis, A. C., Davis, R. E., and Lo, K. S. (1969). "Load Distribution in Concrete Box Girder Bridges," ACI, ACI Pub. SP-23, pp. 117–133.

Scott, N. L. (1983). *Suggestions for Reducing Costs in Prestressed Concrete Bridges,* Highway Res. Rec. No. 34, pp. 117–129.

Serrette, R. L., Rizkalla, S., Atiogbe, E. K., and Huevel, J. S. (1989). "Multiple Shear Key Connections for Shear Wall Panels," *PCI J.,* 34(2), March–April, pp. 104–120.

Shah, S. P., and Ahmed, S. H. (1985). "Structural Properties of High-Strength Concrete and Its Implications for Precast Prestressed Concrete," *PCI J.,* 30(6), November–December, pp. 92–119.

Shahawy, M. E. (1990). "Feasibility Study of Transversely Prestressed Double-T Bridges," *PCI J.,* 35(5), September–October, pp. 56–69.

Shahawy, M. E., and Issa, M. (1992). "Load Testing of Transversely Prestressed Double-T Bridges," *PCI J.,* 37(2), March–April, pp. 86–99.

Shaikh, A. F., and Branson, D. E. (1970). "Nontensioned Steel in Prestressed Concrete Beams," *PCI J.,* 15(1), January–February, pp. 14–36.

Shenoy, C. V., and Frantz, G. C. (1991). "Structural Tests of 27-Year-Old Prestressed Concrete Bridge Beams," *PCI J.,* 36(5), September–October, pp. 80–90.

Siess, C. P. (1949). "Composite Construction for I-Beam Bridges," *ASCE Transactions,* 114, pp. 1023–1045.

Skogman, B. C., Tadros, M. K., and Grasmick, R. (1988). "Ductility of Reinforced and Prestressed Concrete Flexural Members," *PCI J.,* 33(6), November–December, pp. 94–107.

Smith, G. J., and Rad, F. N. (1989). "Economic Advantages of High-Strength Concretes in Columns," *Concrete Intl.,* April, pp. 37–43.

Smith, W. H. (1955). "Longest Vehicular Bridge Starts across Lake Pontchartrain," *ASCE Civ. Eng.,* 25(5), May, pp. 282–285.

Sofia, M. J., and Homsi, E. H. (1994). "Fabrication and Erection of Precast Concrete Segmental Bridges for Baldwin Bridge," *PCI J.,* 39(6), November–December, pp. 36–52.

Somerville, G. (1970). *Standard Bridge Beams for Spans from 7 m to 36 m,* Cement and Concrete Association, London.

Sozen, M. A. (1957). *Shear Strength of Prestressed Concrete Beams without Web Reinforcement,* Structural Research Series No. 139, University of Illinois, Urbana, August.

Sozen, M. A., Swoyer, E. M., and Siess, C. P. (1959). "Strength in Shear of Beams without Web Reinforcement," *Engr. Experiment Station Bull.,* No. 452, April.

Stark, David (1984). "Determination of Permissible Chloride Levels in Prestressed Concrete," *PCI J.,* 29(4), July–August, pp. 106–119.

Steinman, D. B., and Watson, S. R. (1957). *Bridges and Their Builders,* Putnam, New York.

Strasky, J. (1987). "Precast Stress-Ribbon Bridges in Czechoslovakia," *PCI J.,* 32(3), May–June, pp. 53–73.

———. (1993). "Design and Construction of Cable-Stayed Bridges in the Czech Republic," *PCI J.,* 38(6), November–December, pp. 24–43.

Strasky, J., and Pirner, M. (1986). *DS-L Stress-Ribbon Footbridges,* Dopravni stvby, Brno, Czechoslovakia.

Swann, R. A. (1971). "Readers' Comments on 'Lateral Stability of Long Prestressed Concrete Beams'," *PCI J.,* 16(6), November–December, pp. 85–87.

Swann, R. A., and Godden, W. G. (1966). "The Lateral Buckling of Concrete Beams Lifted by Cables," *Structural Engineer,* 44(1), January, pp. 21–33.

Szilard, R. (1969a). "Corrosion and Corrosion Protection of Tendons in Prestressed Concrete Bridges," *ACI J.,* 66(1), January, pp. 42–59.

———. (1969b). "Survey on Durability of Prestressed Concrete Structures in the United States, Canada, and Pacific and Far Eastern Countries," *PCI J.,* 14(5), October, pp. 62–73.

Tabatabai, H., and Dickson, T. J. (1993). "Structural Evaluation of a 34-Year-Old Precast Post-Tensioned Concrete Girder," *PCI J.,* 38(5), September–October, pp. 50–63.

Tadros, M. K., Ghali, A., and Dilger, W. H. (1975). "Time-Dependent Prestress Loss and Deflection of Prestressed Concrete Members," *PCI J.,* 20(3), May–June, pp. 86–98.

———. (1977). "Effect of Nonprestressed Steel on Prestress Loss and Deflection," *PCI J.,* 22(2), March–April, pp. 50–63.

Tadros, M. K., Ficenec, J. A., Einea, A., and Holdsworth, S. (1993). "A New Technique to Create Continuity in Prestressed Concrete Members," *PCI J.,* 38(5), September–October, pp. 30–37.

Tadros, M. K., Ghali, A., and Meyer, A. W. (1985). "Prestress Loss and Deflection of Precast Members," *PCI J.,* 30(1), January–February, pp. 114–141.

Taerwe, L. R., Lambotte, H., and Miesseler, H.-J. (1992). "Loading Tests on Concrete Beams Prestressed with Glass Fiber Tendons," *PCI J.,* 37(4), July–August, pp. 84–97.

Taly, N. (1976). *Development and Design of Standardized Short-Span Bridge Superstructural Systems,* Ph.D. dissertation, Civil Engineering Department, West Virginia University, Morgantown.

Taly, N., and GangaRao, H. V. S. (1974). *Development of Standardized Short-Span Bridges,* Meeting Preprint 2407, *ASCE Annual and Natl. Environ. Eng. Conv.,* October 21–25, Kansas City, MO.

———. (1977). *Survey of Short-Span Bridge Systems in the United States,* WVDOH 50-Interim Report, Civil Engineering Department, West Virginia University, Morgantown, presented at the Transportation Research Board meeting, Washington, DC, January.

————. (1978). "Precast Prestressed Concrete Box Girder Bridge System with Overhangs," *8th FIP Intl. Conf.,* London, April 30–May 2.

Tanaka, Y. (1965). "A Study on the Design and Construction of Railway Structures for Grade Separation between a Highway and a Railway, Especially on a New Type of Prestressed Concrete Viaduct—Railway Technical Research Report," *Japanese Natl. Railways,* 502, November (in Japanese).

Tanaka, Y., Yamaoka, Y., and Kurauchi, M. (1981). "Effects of Tensile Strength on the Stress Corrosion Behavior of Steel Wires," *Proc. FIP Third Symp.,* Madrid, September.

Tang, M. C., (1976). "Stress-Ribbon Bridge in Freiburg, Germany, Features Prestressed Concrete Deck Slab," *ASCE Civ. Eng.,* May, pp. 75–76.

Taylor, H. P. J. (1972). "The Fundamental Behavior of Reinforced Concrete Beams in Bending and Shear," *Shear in Reinforced Concrete,* Special Pub. SP-42, Vol. 1, ACI, Detroit, pp. 43–77.

Taylor, H. P. J. (1987). "Prestressed Precast Concrete Bridges," in *Concrete Bridge Engineering: Performances and Advances,* R. J. Cope, ed., Elsevier Applied Science, London, pp. 247–287.

Tedesko, A. (1976). "Bridge Decks: Transverse Post-Tensioning and Other Successful Experiences," *ACI J.,* 73(12), December, pp. 665–670.

Templeman, A. B., and Winterbottom, S. K. (1975). "Optimum Design of Concrete Cellular Spine Beam Bridge Decks," *Proc. Inst. Civil Engrs.,* England, Part 2, Vol. 59, pp. 669–697.

Thorkildsen E., and Holombo, J. (1995). "Innovative Prestressed Concrete Bridges Mark CALTRANS Centennial," *PCI J.,* 40(6), pp. 34–38.

Tilly, G. P., Cullington, D. W., and Eyre, R. (1984). *Dynamic Behavior of Footbridges,* IABSE Surveys S-26/84.

Tokerud, R. (1979). "Precast Prestressed Concrete Bridges for Low-Volume Roads," *PCI J.,* 24(4), July–August, pp. 42–56.

Torres, G. B., Brotchie, J. F., and Cornell, C. A. (1966). "A Program for the Optimum Design of Prestressed Concrete Highway Bridges," *PCI J.,* 11(3) May–June, pp. 63–71.

Torroja, E. (1958). *Philosophy of Structures,* trans. by J. J. Polivka and Milos Polivka, University of California Press, Berkeley.

Towles, T. T. (1992). "Advantages in the Use of High-Strength Concretes," *ACI J. Proc.,* 28(9), May, pp. 607–612.

Trost, E. (1967). "Implications of the Superposition Principle in Creep and Relaxation Problems for Concrete and Prestressed Concrete (Auswirkungen des Superpositionsprinzips auf Kriech und Relaxation-sprobleme bei Beton und Spannbeton)," *Beton und Stahlbetonbau,* 10, pp. 230–238, 2261–2269.

Tsuji, Y., Kanda, M., and Tamura, T. (1993). "Applications of FRP Materials to Prestressed Concrete Bridges and Other Structures in Japan," *PCI J.,* 38(4), July–August, pp. 50–58.

Uhlig, H. H., ed. (1948). *Corrosion Handbook,* John Wiley & Sons, New York.

USDOT. (1990). "Standard Plans for Highway Bridges, Concrete Superstructures," U.S. Department of Transportation, Federal Highway Administration, Washington, DC, January.

Van Buren, M. (1961). "Concrete Bridge across Lake Pontchartrain," *Municipal. Eng. J.,* 47, 2nd qtr., paper 307, pp. 70–81.

Vandepitte, D. C. (1957). "Prestressed Concrete Suspension Bridges," *Proc. World Conf. Prestressed Concrete,* San Francisco.

Ventury, W. (1970). "Diaphragm Shear Connectors between Flanges of Prestressed Concrete T-Beams," *PCI J.,* 15(1) January–February, pp. 67–78.

Walker, H. C. (1969). "Summary of Basic Information on Precast Concrete Connections," PCI Committee on Connection Details, *PCI J.,* 14(12), December, pp. 14–58.

Walther, R. E. (1958). "The Shear Strength of Prestressed Concrete Beams," *Proc. Third Congress Intl. Fed. Prestressing,* Berlin.

———. (1971/1972) "Stress-Ribbon Bridges," *Intl. Civ. Eng. Monthly,* 2(1), pp. 1–7.

Walther, R. E., and Warner, R. F. (1958). " Ultimate Strength Tests of Prestressed and Conventionally Reinforced Concrete in Combined Bending and Shear," Fritz Engr. Lab., Institute of Research, Lehigh University, September.

Wheen, R. J. (1979). "The Rip Bridge—A Unique Australian Structure," *Concrete Intl.,* 1(11), November, pp. 12–15.

Wills, J. (1973). *A Mathematical Optimization Procedure and Its Applications to the Design of Bridge Structures,* Report LR 555, Transport and Road Research Laboratory, Crowtone, Berkshire, England, pp. 1–28.

Wilson, A. J., and Wheen, R. J. (1974). "Direct Design of Taut Cables under Uniform Loading," *ASCE J. Struct. Div.,* 100(ST3), March, pp. 565–578.

Wolford, D. S. (1971). "Steel Highway Accessary Structures," *ASCE J. Struct. Div.,* 97(ST7), July, pp. 1991–2008.

Woodward, R. J., and Williams, F. W. (1988). "Collapse of Ynys-y-Gwas Bridge, West Glamorgan," *Proc. Inst. Civ. Engrs.,* part I, vol. 84, August, pp. 635–669.

Wranglen, G. (1985) *Korrosion und Korrosionsschutz (An Introduction to Corrosion and Protection of Metals),* Institute fur Metallskydd, Stockholm 26, Springer Verlag, Berlin (in German).

Yamane, T., Tadros, M. K., and Arumugasaamy, P. (1994). "Short- to Medium-Span Prestressed Concrete Bridges in Japan," *PCI J.,* 39(2), March–April, pp. 74–100.

Yamaoka, Y., Tsubono, H., and Kurauchi, M. (1988). "Effect of Galvanizing on Hydrogen Embrittlement of Prestressing Wire," *PCI J.,* 33(4), July–August, pp. 146–158.

Zia, P., and Mostafa, T. (1977). "Development Length of Prestressing Strands," *PCI J.,* 22(5), September–October, pp. 54–65.

Zia, P., Preston, H. K., Scott, N. L., and Workman, E. B. (1979). "Estimating Prestress Losses," *Concrete Intl.,* 1(6), June, pp. 32–38.

Zia, P., Schemmel, J. J., and Tallman, T. E. (1989). *Structural Applications of High-Strength Concrete,* Pub. No. FHWA/NC/89/006, Federal Highway Administration, Washington, DC, June.

Zielinski, J., and Rowe, R. E. (1960). *An Investigation of the Stress Distribution in Anchorage Zones of Post-Tensioned Concrete Members,* Research Report No. 9, Pub. 41.009, Cement and Concrete Association, Wexham Springs, Slough, England, September.

Zollman, C. C. (1978). "Magnel's Impact on the Advent of Prestressed Concrete," in *Reflections on the Beginnings of Prestressed Concrete in America*, Precast/Prestressed Concrete Institute, Chicago, 1981, pp. 5–32; also *PCI J.,* 23(3), May–June, pp. 21–48.

Zollman, C. C., Depman, F., Nagle, J., and Hollander, E. F. (1992). "Building and Rebuilding of Philadelphia's Walnut Memorial Bridge—Part 1: A History of Design, Construction, and Service Life," *PCI J.,* 37(3), May–June, pp. 66–82.

CHAPTER 8

Slab–Steel Beam Bridges

8.1 INTRODUCTION

History was made when Abraham Darby the third (1750–1791) built the world's first iron bridge during 1776–1779 at Coalbrookdale, England. This nearly semicircular arch bridge, with its approximately 100-ft main span, is still in service, albeit limited to pedestrian traffic only. In the United States, the first cast-iron bridge was an 80-ft-span structure made of five tubular arch ribs; it was built in 1836 by Richard Delafield (1798–1873) of the U.S. Engineers Corps [Steinman and Watson, 1957]. However, the modern era in bridge building began in the United States with the construction of the famed double-deck Eads' Bridge over the Mississippi (built in 1868–1874) in St. Louis, Missouri; this marked the first extensive use of structural steel in bridges. Steel bridges then became the most common type of highway structures built in the United States, and steel continued to dominate bridge construction until the advent of reinforced concrete, and, later, prestressed concrete, some fifty years ago.

The most common type of short- and medium-span highway structures, variously referred to as *slab–steel beam, slab-stringer,* or simply *steel bridges,* consist of rolled steel beams, usually equally spaced, placed longitudinally (parallel to traffic) to span the bridge (Fig. 8.1). For longer spans, built-up beams known as *plate girders*, which have webs deeper than those available with the deepest rolled beams, are used. In all span lengths, slab–steel beam bridges are usually transversely spanned by a cast-in-place reinforced concrete slab that serves as a bridge deck and provides lateral stability to stringers. Diaphragms are provided at intermediate points and at the ends to provide lateral stability. Orthotropic bridges, which are characterized by their steel plate deck, and steel box girder bridges, referred to in the following paragraphs, are outside the scope of this book, and their design is not discussed.

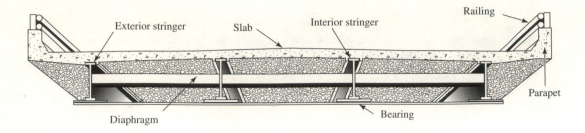

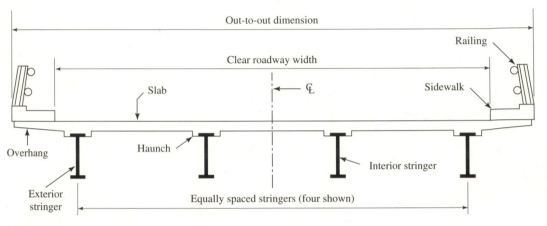

FIGURE 8.1
Typical slab–steel beam bridge.

Interestingly, since the beginning of this conventional slab–steel beam type of bridge construction some 100 years ago, not much has changed in either the design or the construction methodology of these bridges. However, a few innovations, such as the *space truss* bridge [Taly and GangaRao, 1974; Taly, 1976; Montens and O'Hagan, 1992; Muller and Lockwood, 1992; Muller, 1993], the *prefabricated press-formed steel T-box girder bridge* system [Taly and GangaRao, 1979], and the post-tensioned segmental steel bridge, referred to as the *tension arch system* [Weaver and Bonasso, 1994], are reported in the literature.

A new approach to deck design for slab–steel beam bridges is being tried in the world's first demonstration project, built in 1995 in Canada [Newhook and Mufti, 1996]. Its structural system uses *polypropylene-fiber-reinforced concrete,* which enables the bridge deck to be built totally free of all internal reinforcement; i.e., the deck slab is completely steel-free [Bakht and Mufti, 1996]. Although the cast-in-place slab remains the usual method of building a bridge deck, occasionally precast, prestressed concrete deck panels and prefabricated steel grid panels, open or concrete-filled, are being used as a low-weight, time-saving alternative for deck replacement in bridge rehabilitation projects. These new systems are described in the last section of this chapter.

8.2
USING STEEL BEAMS IN BRIDGES—ADVANTAGES, DISADVANTAGES, AND THE EFFECTS OF CORROSION

8.2.1 Advantages of Steel Beam Bridges

Several advantages of steel beam bridges can be noted [Schilling, 1985]:

- Steel has the most desirable properties of any construction material that can be commercially used. It is a high-quality, homogeneous, isotropic material that is perfectly elastic to its yield point. It has high compressive and tensile strength. Past the yield point, it offers considerable ductility to provide a large reserve strength unmatched by any other construction material. It can accommodate local stress raisers and imposed deformations, such as secondary bending, and it can absorb seismic loading.
- Steel bridges can be built faster than reinforced or prestressed concrete bridges. They can be erected with relative ease over land or water and under various weather conditions, thus minimizing construction costs.
- Because the use of steel in bridges has a long history, high-quality erection and fabrication procedures have been developed over time.
- Steel superstructures are usually lighter than comparable concrete superstructures. This translates into reduced substructure costs, which can be significant when soil conditions are poor.
- Steel superstructures can usually be designed with shallower depths than comparable concrete superstructures. This is an important consideration when overhead clearances are involved.
- Steel bridges are easy to repair, and repairs can be made more quickly than in concrete bridges. For example, in a slab–steel beam bridge, a concrete deck supported by steel stringers can be repaired or replaced without shoring.

8.2.2 Disadvantages of Steel Beam Bridges

Steel beam bridges have some major disadvantages that have made them much less favorable than prestressed concrete bridges:

- Corrosion of steel beams has been an endless and costly bridge maintenance problem, and it is one of the major causes of deterioration of steel bridges. Numerous failures of steel bridges due to corrosion and related phenomena have been reported in the literature. Some of these failures are discussed in Chapter 10. Contrary to expectations, even the corrosion-resistant, or so-called weathering, steel has not been found to be satisfactory and cost-effective, as the steel industry generally claims. Corrosion and its effects on steel beam bridges are discussed in Sec. 8.2.3.
- The end result of corrosion is a weak superstructure.
- Painting costs of steel bridges over the design life are high. Environmental and health concerns about the removal and disposal of lead-based paints have increased costs related to the painting of steel bridges. When oil-based paints are used, the emissions of volatile organic compounds (VOCs) pose a dangerous health hazard. Removal of

the coatings of old paint and disposal of the contaminated blast-cleaning debris over the life span of the structure are prohibitively costly. In some cases, the estimated cost of the collection and disposal of materials from a structure repainting project was high enough to justify either abandoning the bridge or replacing it with a new one. Because painting poses such a serious problem, AASHTO is currently considering issuing guidelines for painting steel bridges.

- In the past two decades, the use of weathering steel (A588) has increased in bridge construction as a means of economizing by eliminating painting. With time, rust turns brown, which is one of the least aesthetic colors (discussed in Chapter 11). Rust from steel bridge beams and other steel components usually ends up staining abutments and piers, making them unsightly.

8.2.3 Corrosion of Steel Beams and Its Effects on Bridges

Corrosion control of steel highway bridges and other steel appurtenances, and mitigating the corrosion-related damage, have become a serious national problem. General discussion about corrosion and its effects can be found in several references [Uhlig, 1948; Karpenco and Vasilenko, 1985]. Issues pertaining to the corrosion of steel in highway bridges, such as maintenance and rehabilitation, are discussed in Chapter 10. Corrosion of prestressing steel was discussed in Chapter 7. Corrosion of steel beams in highway bridges is reported in the literature [ENR, 1978a,b; Zoccola, 1978; Brockenbrough, 1983; Komp, 1983; Bellenoit, Yen, and Fisher, 1984; Fisher, 1984; McCrum, Reincke, and Lay, 1984; MIDOT, 1985; Kayser and Nowak, 1987, 1989; Kayser, 1988; Kulkarni, 1994] and is summarized in the following paragraphs.

The accumulation of salt and water is considered the primary cause of corrosion of steel beams in highway bridges. The sources of water and salt are either leakage from the deck or the accumulation of road spray and condensation. Kayser and Nowak [1987, 1989] have identified five main forms of corrosion that can affect steel:

- General corrosion
- Pitting corrosion
- Galvanic corrosion
- Crevice corrosion
- Stress corrosion

The components of a steel bridge can be affected by more than one form of corrosion.

General corrosion, the most prevalent form of corrosion, refers to the general loss of surface material over time, leading to gradual thinning of members. This form of corrosion accounts for the largest percentage of corrosion damage.

Pitting corrosion also causes loss of material, although it is localized and restricted to small areas. *Pits* can be characterized as rolled-in imperfections, and they can be dangerous, for they inconspicuously extend into the metal. Their presence in high-stress regions is a potential source of stress concentration.

Galvanic corrosion occurs when two dissimilar metals, i.e., steels with different chemical compositions, are electrochemically coupled, e.g., in bolted or welded connections, in which the base metal is different from the weld metal [Uhlig, 1948]. Mill scale (surface scale or iron oxide that forms on structural steel after hot rolling) can galvanically encourage corrosion of the underlying base metal.

Crevice corrosion occurs in small confined areas, such as under peeling paint, between faying surfaces, or at pit locations.

Stress corrosion refers to tensile loading of metal in a corrosive environment. An existing crack on a metal's surface spreads gradually under repetitive loading. However, formation of rust at the crack tip accelerates this spreading of the crack. For mild carbon steel in ordinary bridge environments, stress corrosion is usually not a problem. However, corrosion fatigue has been identified as a corrosion problem [Kayser and Nowak, 1989]. It is a phenomenon that is actually a combination of pitting corrosion, crevice corrosion, and stress corrosion. This phenomenon was believed to be the cause of the sudden collapse of the Point Pleasant Bridge in West Virginia on December 15, 1967 [Kayser, 1988]. The bridge had been built in 1929. The effect of corrosion fatigue is a reduction in the fatigue life of the metal.

Rusting at a crack tip of a stressed steel member may be dangerous even under static loads, or even if the steel is heat-treated and has high strength and low ductility. Together, corrosion and stress may cause an initially harmless crack to extend to the point where it can initiate a brittle fracture. The various forms of possible corrosion and corresponding structural damage, and the type of bridge components affected, are discussed by Kayser and Nowak [1987, 1989]. In general, the net result of corrosion of steel members is the loss of material, resulting in thinner members. Consequently, section properties, such as cross-sectional area, section modulus, moment of inertia, and radius of gyration, are reduced. Except for the sectional area, these reductions occur nonlinearly because these properties may be proportional to the square or the cube of the dimensions involved. Reduction in metal thickness can adversely affect the buckling capacity of members. Corroded flanges can result in reduced flexural capacity of a steel beam. A beam's shear and bearing capacities may be affected if the web is corroded. In continuous composite girders, a corroded (and hence weakened) lower flange in the negative moment region creates the additional possibility of compression flange buckling.

Corrosion can cause other forms of damage. For example, buildup of corrosion products may exert pressure at the interface of the connected parts, which, in some cases, can be as high as 1200 psi [Brockenbrough, 1983]. This pressure can cause connected plates to pry apart, subjecting them to eccentricities and additional stresses. Accumulation of rust around bearings or hinges can freeze them, render them nonfunctional, and thus cause unintended stress in the structure [Bellenoit, Yen, and Fisher, 1984].

The rate of corrosion in different environments has been evaluated in several studies [Zoccola, 1978; Komp, 1983; McCrum, Reincke, and Lay, 1984]. The rate of corrosion can accelerate significantly in the presence of a marine environment. For example, in Michigan, because highways are laden with salt and debris, average corrosion losses have been observed to range from a mere 0.2 to 0.6 mils/year/surface (one mil = 1/1000 of an inch) to a significant 1.20 mils/year/surface, with portions of certain beams approaching a structurally serious 2.5 to 5.0 mils/year/surface [MIDOT, 1985].

Several cases of extensive repairs prompted by the corrosion of steel bridge components are reported in the literature. For example, rapid deterioration of main cables forced emergency reconstruction in 1978 on the General U.S. Grant suspension bridge (main span 700 ft) that carries U.S. Route 23 over the Ohio River at Portsmouth, Ohio. This bridge had initially suffered from quick corrosion of its main cables, which were repaired in 1940, barely 12 years after the bridge was completed in 1927 [ENR, 1978a, 1978b].

All 88 cable-stays of the 1705-ft Kohlbrand cable-stayed bridge over the Hamburg River in Germany, completed in 1974, showed signs of possible corrosion as early as 1976. These cables were protected from possible corrosion by a plastic-based protective coating, but the coating soon developed hairline cracks. Rain soaking in from the top permeated the cables, and salt that was kicked up from the roadway surface by traffic during the winter also worked its way into the cables. A report by the Swiss Office for Materials Testing, which inspected only five stays, indicated that in spite of the plastic-based protective coating on the cables, humidity and salt had worked their way into the strands of the steel stays. All 88 stays were replaced in 1979 by galvanized cables at a cost of over $6 million [ENR, 1978a]. Atmospheric corrosion is discussed in references [ASM, 1978].

In some cases, corrosion might so adversely affect a steel bridge that replacing it may be more cost-effective than rehabilitation. An example of such a bridge, inspected by Taly in 1972, is discussed in Chapter 10 (see Figs. 10.1 and 10.2).

Several steel bridges in the state of Michigan are reported to be seriously affected by corrosion, including some unpainted bridges built from the corrosion-resistant A588 steel (weathering steel). In one case, pitting in the web of one of the state's oldest steel beam bridges was measured to exceed 0.300 in. (half the web thickness, in this instance). This apparently resulted from corrosion preferentially following the pathway of impurities that had supposedly been rolled into the beam during manufacturing. Initially hidden, this pitting was revealed when sandblasting was carried out as surface preparation for repainting the beam [MIDOT, 1985].

The corrosion problems found on steel bridges in the state of Michigan [Kulkarni, 1994] have prompted researchers to make the following observations and recommendations [MIDOT, 1985]:

1. Rates of corrosion have been measured that are sufficient to cause perforation of bridge members during their service lives.
2. Unpainted A588 steel (weathering steel) should not be used in Michigan's highway environments.
3. An effort should be made to paint or otherwise protect those structures exposed to significant amounts of salt (from either leakage or spray) by the time they reach 15 or 20 years of age.

Corrosion problems are not restricted to northern climates. Built from weathering steel and completed in 1983, the Hale Boggs Memorial cable-stayed Bridge (also called the Luling Bridge), with a main span of 1222 ft, in Luling, Louisiana, is already showing rust formation in an unusually short time; this has caused concern among the state's bridge engineers [Knapp, 1994].

Failure to repair or replace the corroded components of a bridge in time may result in disastrous consequences. On October 21, 1994, a 157-ft segment of a steel box girder bridge over the Han River, South Korea, collapsed under the morning rush-hour traffic, killing at least 32 people. The cause of this tragedy was attributed to corroded extension hinges that broke under heavy loads.

According to several studies [NJDOT, 1968; Yura, Frank, and Polyzois, 1978; Cosaboom, Mehalchick, and Zoccola, 1979; Culp and Tinklenbuerg, 1980; DOT, UK, 1981; AISI, 1982; Albrecht and Naeemi, 1984; Zoccola, 1976; Zoccola et al., 1976; Bethlehem, 1988; Aulthouse, 1989; FHWA, 1989; Bethlehem, 1993; Penn DOT, 1993], poor performance of weathering steel in highway structures is attributed to application of this material in improper locations or under improper conditions, lack of understanding of the limitations of weathering grade steel, or poor detailing. Concern about the poor performance of weathering steel bridges prompted the Federal Highway Administration (FHWA) to sponsor the *Weathering Steel Forum* in July 1988, to better define the performance record of this material and to provide engineers guidelines for proper and cost-effective applications of uncoated (unpainted) weathering steel in highway bridges. As a result of research data and of case histories presented in this forum, the FHWA suggested guidelines for improving weathering steel bridges. These guidelines, entitled "Uncoated Weathering Steel Structures" [Bethlehem, 1990a], were incorporated into the FHWA *Technical Advisory* [1989]. The guidelines recommend against using weathering steel in certain environments that are not conducive to the weathering process—the formation of a durable adherent protective oxide coating on the surface that changes with time from a rusty red-orange to a dark, rich, purple-brown patina under appropriate atmospheric conditions. These environments are as follows [Bethlehem, 1990a]:

Marine coastal areas. Salt-laden air that is generated along the Atlantic, Pacific, and Gulf Coasts may be transported inland by prevailing winds. Factors that affect the corrosion of steel are the level of chloride concentration in the salt-laden air, the direction of the prevailing winds, the distance of the structure from the shore line, and the topographical and environmental characteristics of the area. Thus, the weathering behavior of uncoated weathering steel structures can vary significantly from one location to another along the three coastlines. Methods are available to determine the daily ambient chloride concentration in the surrounding atmosphere. According to DOT UK [1981], uncoated steel should not be used when chloride levels exceed 0.1 mg/100 cm^2/day, average.

Areas of frequent high rainfall, high humidity, or persistent fog. These climatic conditions can result in excessive condensation and prolonged periods of wetness of steel, resulting in the potential for increased corrosion. Examples of such areas are portions of the Pacific Northwest, west of the Cascade Mountains, where high annual rainfall can contribute to excessive corrosion of uncoated steel.

Industrial areas. In heavy industrial areas with chemical and other manufacturing plants, the air may contain impurities that can be deposited on and decompose steel surfaces. According to DOT UK [1981], when the threshold for sulfur trioxide exceeds 2.1 mg/100 cm^2/day average, uncoated weathering steel should not be used.

Prolonged continuous contact with water is not good for the expected performance of weathering steel. For example, weathering steel is not recommended in cases where it may be continuously submerged in water, buried in soil, or on bridges where water runoff contaminated with deicing salts (used during winter months) drains through leaky seals, open joints, or expansion dams. Timber decking is another application for which weathering steel is not recommended; timber retains moisture and may be treated with salt-bearing preservatives that will promote corrosion [Bethlehem, 1993].

Certain locations and geometries greatly influence the performance of weathering steel in highway structures. These include tunnel-like grade separation structures characterized by narrow, depressed roadway sections between vertical retaining walls, narrow shoulders, minimum vertical clearances, and deep abutments adjacent to the shoulders. Such a geometric configuration prevents roadway spray from being dissipated by air currents and can result in excessive salt in the spray being deposited on the bridge steel. To preclude such a possibility, minimum vertical clearances are mandated by various states for their bridges. For example, the Pennsylvania Department of Transportation mandates a minimum vertical clearance of 20 ft above the depressed roadway sections if weathering steel is to be used [PennDOT, 1993]. For water crossings, it is important to maintain sufficient clearance over water to avoid prolonged periods of wetness of steel through spray or condensed water vapor. Recommended clearances are at least 10 ft over sheltered, stagnant water, and at least 8 ft over running water [Bethlehem, 1990a].

To avoid or minimize corrosion problems related to unpainted A588 (weathering) steel, state highway or transportation departments maintain strict guidelines for its use. For example, it cannot be used without written approval of the chief bridge engineer. In general, the use of A588 steel is not permitted for bridges located in corrosive environments or for bridge types in which salt spray and dirt accumulation may be a concern, e.g., trusses, inclined-leg bridges, or bridges with open steel decking. Where A588 steel is permitted, special design criteria are used, and the structure must be specially detailed to avoid retention of water and debris and to protect the substructure from possible staining. For example, the number of expansion joints is minimized, and steel is painted to a length of at least 5 ft on each side of the expansion joint. Special attention is paid in the selection of fasteners [PennDOT, 1993]. Mechanical fasteners made of A325 and A490 Type III weathering steel and stainless steels are considered suitable for weathering steel bridges; zinc and cadmium galvanized carbon steel bolts are not suitable for weathering steel bridges [Yura, Frank, and Polyzois, 1978].

8.3
GENERAL DESIGN CONSIDERATIONS

8.3.1 Analysis for Loads

Loads on bridge steel superstructures and related analysis techniques were discussed, respectively, in Chapters 3 and 4; readers should be familiar with the material presented in those chapters to derive the maximum benefit from this chapter. Techniques for analyzing bridge loads are discussed in several references [Bares and Massonet,

1968; Bakht and Jaeger, 1985; Hambly, 1991]. Bridge superstructures in this and other chapters in this book have been designed by the AASHTO method, according to the *Standard Specifications for Highway Bridges* published by the American Association of State Highway and Transportation Officials (AASHTO) in Washington, DC [1992]. The AASHTO method is practiced in the United States and in many other countries.

8.3.2 Bridge Types

Various types of bridges were described briefly in Chapter 1. What are generally referred to as *steel bridges* are not all-steel bridges, but composite bridges, in that most of them have a concrete or some other kind of deck supported by a steel framing. Bridges of this general configuration can be classified as follows:

8.3.2.1 Noncomposite or composite steel beam bridges

Slab–steel beam bridge superstructures may be built either as noncomposite or composite structures. In a *noncomposite* structure, the steel beams act independently of the deck slab in resisting both the dead as well as the live loads. In *composite* construction, the dead loads are resisted by steel beams alone (assuming unshored construction), whereas the superimposed dead loads and the live loads are resisted by the composite action of the slab and the steel beam acting as a unit. Designs of both types of superstructures, simple as well as continuous, are presented in this chapter. *Plate girder* superstructures, which may also be characterized as slab–steel beam bridges, are suitable for medium and long spans; these are covered in Chapter 9.

8.3.2.2 Orthotropic bridges

Orthotropic bridges (also called orthotropic steel deck bridges), mentioned in Chapter 1, are superstructures built with a steel plate deck instead of the commonly used concrete deck. Except for the $1\frac{1}{2}$-in. to $2\frac{1}{2}$-in. asphalt wearing surface, these bridges may be regarded as true all-steel superstructures.

In an orthotropic bridge, the steel deck plate is usually stiffened in two mutually perpendicular directions (Fig. 8.2). In the most common form of construction, the steel plate either is attached to reinforcing steel ribs or is continuous over relatively closely spaced supports that are placed parallel to the traffic. This support system transforms the structural behavior of the deck plate from isotropic to anisotropic. If these longitudinal ribs are supported on perpendicular floor beams, the behavior of the plate changes further from anisotropic to *orthogonal-isotropic,* referred to as orthotropic, for short. Conventional bridge design methods, discussed in detail in this and other chapters of this book, consider the bridge deck to act as a series of separate units. In a significant departure from this, the orthotropic design method considers the entire bridge superstructure to act as a *single unit.* As a result, orthotropic bridges result in substantial reductions in dead-load moments, and thus they are particularly suitable for long-span bridges where the ratio of dead-load to live-load moments is high.

Design of orthotropic-deck superstructures is covered in AASHTO 10.41 and discussed exhaustively in references [Loveys, 1963; Wolchuck, 1963; Troitsky, 1967; Hall, 1971; Hedefine, 1972].

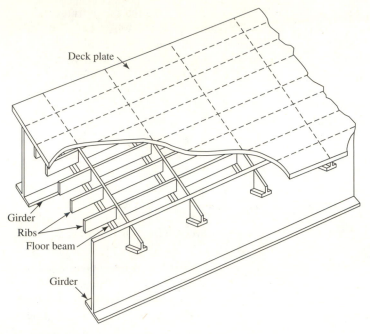

FIGURE 8.2
A typical orthotropic deck [Wolchuck, 1990].

8.3.2.3 Prestressed steel bridges

Prestressed steel bridges are a type of bridge in which prestressing force is used to augment the capacity of load-carrying members, as in prestressed concrete members. A prestressed steel member usually consists of high-tensile steel tensioned against an ordinary carbon-steel beam, girder, or truss, in order to develop a stronger and more efficient structure. In the context of steel,

> prestressing is defined as a means of efficiently utilizing various strength steels in girders, trusses, and other structures so that significant savings in the depth of their components can be achieved. The term "prestressed steel" means the application of a predetermined concentric or eccentric force to a steel member so that the state of stress in the member resulting from this force, and from any other anticipated external loading, will be restricted to certain specified limits [ASCE–AASHO, 1968].

In its present form, the concept of prestressed steel structures evolved in Europe to optimize the use of steel that was in short supply during the post–World War II years; prestressed steel was used both for building new bridges and strengthening existing ones [Troitsky, 1988].

Application of prestressing in steel bridges is not really a new idea; the principle had been applied to steel structures long before high-strength steel made prestressed concrete possible. One of the earliest applications of prestressing was made at the turn of the century to bridges with a wrought-iron truss rod underneath each main girder (comprising a trussed-beam), which could be tightened with a turnbuckle. Tightening the rod created a negative bending moment in the main girder that counteracted positive moments due to the applied loads. In addition, these rods also resisted live-load stresses by acting as the bottom chords of a truss [Troitsky, 1988].

In 1840, William Howe of Spencer, Massachusetts, introduced a composite truss that consisted of wooden top and bottom chords and the X-diagonals, but with wrought-iron verticals (see Fig. 1.15) that were tightened (or prestressed) with nuts and bolts, a form of prestressed truss. The concept of prestressing steel structures was applied on a grand scale by Robert Stephenson for the great Britannia Bridge to carry the Chester and Holyhead railway across the Menai Straits in England. These twin four-span (230, 460, 460, and 230 ft), tubular wrought-iron structures, large enough to permit trains to pass through them (see Fig. 1.21), were completed in 1850. *Continuity* was introduced in all four riveted tubes through prestressing (although not so described then) by means of special erection procedures. The purpose of prestressing was to introduce a system of internal forces that would act opposite to the applied loads, particularly the self-weight of the tubes themselves, thus saving material and cost [Timoshenko, 1953; Francis, 1980; Troitsky, 1988].

Prestressing may be applied for building new bridges as well as for strengthening such main load-carrying members as girders, trusses, and the deck structure of existing bridges. The first application of prestressing for strengthening a steel bridge is said to have been made in 1939 on the Paris–Lyon Mediterrance Railroad in France [Carpentier, 1962]. Prestressing techniques are adaptable to both noncomposite and composite bridges [Hoadley, 1963; Finn, 1964; Reagan and Krahl, 1967; Troitsky, Zielinski, and Rabbani, 1989] and to simple as well as continuous bridges [Troitsky, Zielinski, and Rabbani, 1989; Troitsky, 1990]. It is also possible to obtain a *prestressed hybrid beam* by prebending the rolled beam and welding prebent, high-strength steel plates to its flanges [ASCE–AASHO, 1968]. Comprehensive coverage of prestressed steel bridges and related bibliographies can be found in the literature [ASCE–AASHO, 1968 (an excellent summary containing 55 references); Troitsky, 1988, 1990; Magnel, 1950].

Several prestressed steel bridges, for both highways and railways, have been built in many European countries, most notably Germany, as well as in England, the former Soviet Union, and a few in the United States and Mexico [Troitsky, 1988]. Some of the notable prestressed steel highway bridges built in the United States include the Des Moines Bridge, a three-span continuous bridge (73.25, 93.5, and 73.25 ft) in Des Moines, Iowa [ENR, 1961; Steel Constr., 1961]; the Bentalon Bridge, a 106-ft single-span bridge over Bentalon Avenue in Baltimore, Maryland [Levine and McLoughlin, 1967]; and Bonners Ferry Bridge, the 1378-ft, eleven-span (110 to 155 ft) fully continuous, cable-stressed plate girder bridge over Kootenay River in Idaho, built in 1984, the first of its kind in the United States [ENR, 1983; Loveall, 1987; Schilling, 1985; Troitsky, 1988].

In summary, prestressed steel enables a designer to achieve a greater elastic range than is possible for an identical nonprestressed steel member. A prestressed steel member can resist relatively large overloads without suffering permanent distortion. Prestressing is a means of efficiently using various strength steels in built-up beams and girders, so that significant savings in weight and depth of members can be achieved. Although this is achieved without reducing the margin of safety against yielding of steels, it does reduce the margin of safety against plastic mechanism [ASCE–AASHO, 1968].

8.3.2.4 Preflex bridges

Preflex bridges [Troitsky, 1988, 1990; ARBED, year unknown] are bridge super-structures that use prestressed steel beams commonly referred to as *preflex beams.* These beams are prestressed by the *predeflection technique* developed in 1949 by Lipski [Baes and Lipski, 1958], which enables the use of concrete-encased high-strength steel beams where deflection or cracking of concrete, or both, would otherwise be excessive. The technique (Fig. 8.3) involves initially deflecting a beam in the direction of the design loads and then encasing the tension flange in high-strength concrete while the beam is in the deflected and stressed state. Predeflection loads are removed after the concrete encasement achieves the required strength, thus precompressing the encased concrete on the tension flange. Prior to deflection, the beam is precambered to the desired level, and shear connectors are welded for composite action, if required. After erection, the web and the top flange are also encased in concrete, usually monolithically with the deck slab [Troitsky, 1988, 1990].

Although prestressed concrete has found all kinds of structural applications in North America, the application of prestressed steel structures technology is presently

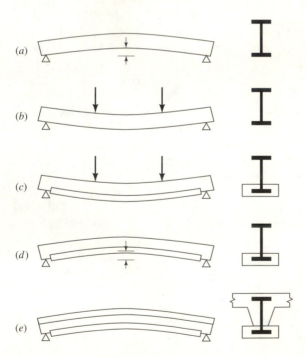

(*a*) Prebent steel girder

(*b*) Application of preflection load

(*c*) Concreting of lower concrete chord and setting

(*d*) Prestressing of lower concrete chord by removal of preflection load. The girder is brought to site in this state.

(*e*) Extension to preflex girder as double composite girder (example)

FIGURE 8.3
Preflex bridges.

limited mostly to large-span roofs [Troitsky, 1988]. In the United States, post-tensioning of steel beams and girders is widely accepted for rehabilitation projects and for strengthening of existing bridges, but not for new bridges. The lack of commercialization and progress in the use of this technology can partly be attributed to reasons such as unfamiliarity of designers and contractors with the techniques of prestressing steel structures [Troitsky, 1988] and the potential of steel bridges for corrosion [Spaans, 1994].

8.3.2.5 Composite steel box girder bridges

Composite steel box girder bridges, suitable for single spans of 75 ft or longer, or for continuous spans of 120 ft or longer, are tubular bridge superstructures in which the bottom flange and webs are made from steel plate, and the deck is made from reinforced concrete (hence the term "composite") [Hedefine, 1972; Heins and Firmage, 1979; AISC Mkt., 1987; Wolchuck, 1990]. As shown in Fig. 8.4a, a steel box girder

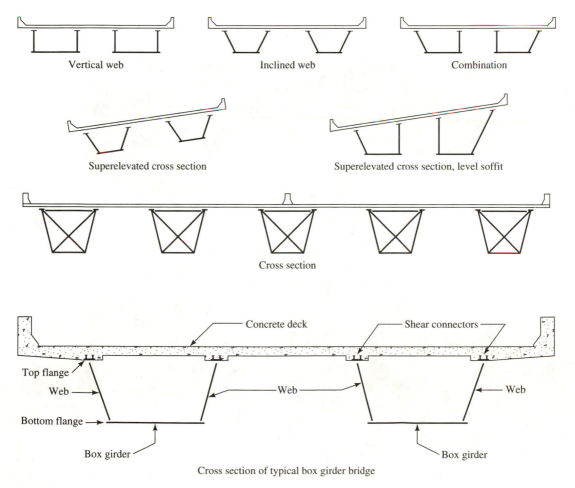

FIGURE 8.4a
Various types of composite box girder bridges.

may be a single-cell, twin-cell, or multiple-cell structure (also referred to as a structure with *multicellular decks*) [Hambly, 1991]. Alternatively, a steel box girder bridge may have two or more separate closed cross sections with a reinforced concrete deck, also known as a *multispine bridge* [Bakht and Jaeger, 1985]. The webs may be vertical or inclined; the latter gives the advantage of a narrower bottom flange. The top flange widths are usually large—wide enough to provide the necessary bearing surface for the concrete deck supported on them—and the required number of shear studs are welded for composite action. In composite box girder bridges with a vertical axis of symmetry, each half-section of the box girder can be considered equivalent to a plate girder section. In continuous steel box girder bridges, either the interior support can be a simple support, or the box girder can be supported on and rigidly connected to a central steel pier, resulting in a rigid frame structure [AISC Mkt., 1987].

Box girder superstructures offer several advantages. Because the cross sections are closed, they possess high torsional stiffness and strength, compared with an equal

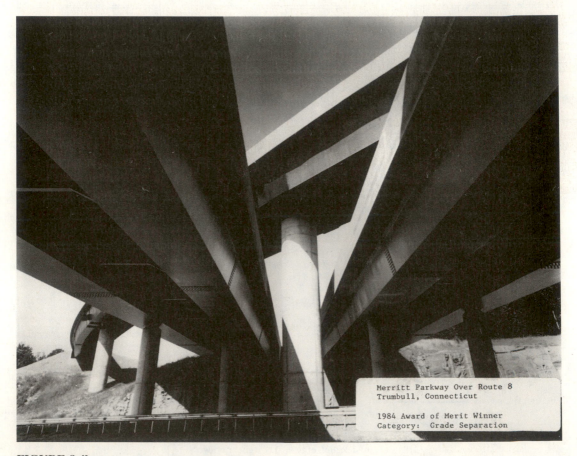

FIGURE 8.4b
Twin box girder bridges for grade separation—Merritt Parkway over Route 8, Trumbull, Connecticut (Courtesy of AISC).

FIGURE 8.4c
The three-span, slant-leg Whitebird Canyon Bridge in Idaho [Courtesy of Idaho Transportation Department].

number of open cross sections, such as rolled beams or plate girders. Their high torsional stiffness makes them especially suitable for curved bridges that are subjected to torsional moments. Consequently, they are preferred for multi-level grade separation structures in urban areas (Fig. 8.4b). The interior of a box girder, which makes up about half the total steel surface, is automatically protected from a corrosive environment, and therefore maintenance is relatively easier than for plate girder bridges. The box shape, especially with inclined webs, offers an aesthetically pleasing structure, often a reason for selecting a composite box girder bridge. Figure 8.4c shows the 806-ft, three-span (248, 310, and 248 ft) Whitebird Canyon Bridge. Completed in 1975 in the state of Idaho, it is a slant-leg steel trapezoidal box girder bridge, the longest of its kind in the United States.

Design of composite steel box girder superstructures is outside the scope of this book and not discussed further. Their design is covered by AASHTO 10.39 and discussed in several references [Hedefine, 1972b; Heins and Firmage, 1979; AISC Mkt., 1978, 1987; FHWA, 1980a; Wolchuck, 1990]. Curved box girder bridges, very complex structures from an analytical standpoint, are exhaustively discussed by Heins and

Firmage [1979] and by Nakai and Yoo [1988]. Specifications for their design are contained in AASHTO [1993].

8.3.3 Steels for Bridge Superstructures

Various kinds of steels used in construction were discussed in Chapter 2. The selection of the steel grade to be used for the bridge superstructures is one of the most important factors affecting bridge costs. The two types of steel generally used for bridge construction are carbon steel (ASTM 36), generally referred to as the *primary* or the *basic structural steel,* and the high-strength, low-alloy steel (ASTM A572). The latter is available in four different grades, that is, yield-strength levels: 42, 50, 60, and 65 ksi. Product availability of certain shape groups is covered in ASTM A6/A6M [ASTM, 1988] and listed in other references [AISC, 1989, 1994]. Both steels are weldable.

When considering the economics of a bridge superstructure, the least-weight design should not be confused with the least-cost design. A proper cost comparison should include not only cost per unit of weight, but also fabrication and erection costs. Although the cost per pound of high-strength steel (A572 Gr. 50) is greater than that of carbon steel (A36)—about 7 percent more for lighter sections to about 11 percent more for heavier sections [Bethlehem, 1990c]—the fabrication and erection costs per piece are about the same for both steels. Because of the significant increase in the design stress resulting from increased yield point (50 ksi vs. 36 ksi—approximately 39 percent increase in stress), smaller and lighter sections of high-strength steel can be used in place of A36 steel, resulting in a lighter superstructure. Thus, although initially a lighter superstructure made from high-strength steel is more expensive per pound, it is likely to be less costly overall than a comparable superstructure made from heavier A36 steel. Therefore, a preliminary cost comparison can be based solely on the cost of mill material of similar members. A judicious use of high-strength steel is likely to result in net savings in the cost of the superstructure [Bethlehem, 1990c]. A comparison of costs for a 50-ft simple-span noncomposite bridge is presented in Example 8.2.

High-strength steel is also advantageous in many other ways. Because of the higher strength, rolled sections may be used instead of the built-up members made from carbon steel, thus saving fabrication costs. For example, a high-strength steel rolled section can be used instead of a coverplated steel beam. This is especially true when strength, rather than the stiffness, is the design criterion. Because of their higher design stress, shallower depths are usually possible with high-strength beams and girders, producing a relatively slender, more attractive structure. Lower weight reduces transportation and handling costs. High-strength steel offers an important choice when the ratio of dead load to the total load is high. A lighter superstructure resulting from using high-strength steel members would also result in lower substructure costs.

It may be economical to use different grades of steel in the same steel bridge superstructure, which may consist of many components, all of which may not be subjected to the same kinds of loads and stresses. For example, a truss bridge consists of trusses having many different members, such as chords, verticals, and diagonals, which are subjected to tension or compression. It also has a deck that is supported by a system of stringers and floor beams, which are flexural members. For cost effectiveness, different grades of steel may be used for these different members.

8.4
DESIGN OF NONCOMPOSITE STEEL BEAM BRIDGES

From a construction perspective, a noncomposite steel beam bridge superstructure, commonly used for spans in the 40-ft range, is one of the simplest to design and build. The most common form of steel beam superstructure consists of a few equally spaced parallel rolled beams, commonly referred to as *stringers,* supporting a reinforced concrete slab that functions as a deck. In this context, the steel industry defines short-span bridges as those that can be built from rolled beams, generally in the range of 80 ft [AISC Mkt., 1987].

The design of a steel beam superstructure involves four components: deck slab, stringers, diaphragms, and bearings. These are discussed in the following paragraphs.

8.4.1 Deck Slab

The load distribution for the deck slab was discussed in Chapter 4 (Sec. 4.5.2). The *effective span* of the slab supported on the steel stringers was defined as the center-to-center distance between the adjacent stringers minus one-half the top flange width of the stringer (Fig. 4.12). Design procedure for the deck slab is covered by AASHTO 3.24.3.1, *Case A—Main Reinforcement Perpendicular to Traffic,* subsequently referred to as the AASHTO method. The procedure is similar to that used for the design of the deck slab for a reinforced concrete T-beam bridge discussed in Chapter 6, and it is not repeated here. Readers are urged to gain familiarity with these portions of this book before proceeding with the rest of this chapter.

The deck slab behaves as a continuous transverse bending element supported over several stringers. Consequently, it is subjected to positive moment in its middle portion between the stringers and to negative moment in the portion adjacent to and over the stringers. Thus, the middle portion of the slab requires reinforcement at the bottom, and the portion of the slab adjacent to and over the stringers requires reinforcement at the top. This would be an ideal arrangement of reinforcement if the position of the inflection point were fixed. Such is not the case, however, because a wheel load can occupy a random position on the slab and cause a change in the location of the inflection points in the moment diagram. Because of this behavior, some reinforcement, both at the top and the bottom, should be straight for the full width of the slab. In practice, two types of reinforcement layout are in vogue: the straight-bar method [Fig. 8.5(*a*)] and the bent-bar method [Fig. 8.5(*b*)]. In the *straight-bar method,* reinforcement for maximum moment in the slab is provided at the top as well as at the bottom (i.e., the same size bars at the same spacings). In the *bent-bar method,* every alternate bar is bent to provide, in the middle portion of the slab, bottom reinforcement twice that in the top, and vice-versa over the beams. The purpose of bending the alternate bars is to achieve some degree of economy by not providing reinforcement for the maximum slab moment, both at the top and the bottom of the slab for its entire width. However, whether savings in steel so obtained would offset the cost of bending the bars remains questionable.

The maximum moment in the slab, and hence its thickness, obviously depends on the spacings of stringers. It was pointed out in Chapter 6 (Sec. 6.7) that, in practice, a

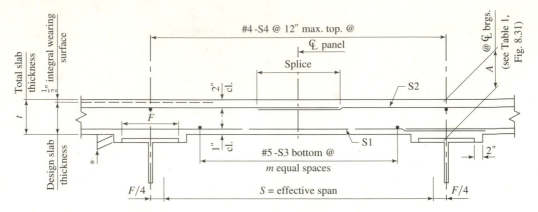

* Bars S3 and S4 to be spaced symmetrically about ℄ panel.
∗ Haunches vary to compensate for irregularities in camber.

(a)

Main reinforcement
for negative moment
Temperature steel
Distribution steel
Main reinforcement
for positive moment
Bend up every
other bar

(b)

FIGURE 8.5
Slab reinforcement: (*a*) straight bar method [PennDOT, 1970], (*b*) bent-bar method [Heins and Firmage, 1979].

slab thicker than that required to resist the moment, based on the designer's mandatory thickness requirements, may be provided. Most state highway departments have provisions for *minimum slab thickness* (based on practical considerations and experience) in their specifications, a practice that varies from state to state.

Shear and bond in the slab designed according to the AASHTO method are considered satisfactory, and no further calculations are required (AASHTO 3.24.4). At the ends and at each expansion joint, the concrete slab should be thickened to form a beam, running perpendicular to traffic, to protect the end of the slab.

8.4.2 Steel Stringers

8.4.2.1 Gravity loads

Steel stringers, which receive their loads from the deck slab, were discussed in Chapter 4, and that discussion is not repeated here. The design of steel stringers is simple and straightforward. Once the moments and shears are calculated, the stringer size, usually a wide flange beam (W-shape), is obtained from AISC's *Manual of Steel*

Construction [AISC, 1989, 1994]. Because the stringers are usually equally spaced, the interior stringers are all the same size. And in general, because the exterior stringers are required to be at least as large as the interior stringers, the practice is to provide all stringers of the same size, assuming that the required size of the exterior stringer turns out to be smaller than that of the interior stringer.

Forces in stringers due to both dead load and live load depend on their spacings. In general, an *interior stringer* is proportioned to carry the following loads:

1. Dead load due to the tributary portion of the slab and the *haunch* (the haunch is shown in Fig. 8.5 and is explained next). The tributary portion lies between the center lines of the stringers. This portion of the dead load is usually denoted as DL1
2. The stringer's share of the superimposed dead load: e.g., wearing surface, sidewalk, parapet and railing, etc. This portion of the dead load is usually denoted as DL2
3. The live load, including impact

The top flanges of all steel beams are embedded in a layer of concrete between the top flange and the bottom of the deck slab. This layer of concrete is called a haunch (Fig. 8.5). Typically, the haunch is 2 to 4 in. thick and about 6 in. wider than the width of the top flange of the steel beam (i.e., it extends 3 in. beyond the edges of the flange). Essentially, the haunch provides lateral support to the top flange of the steel beam that is in compression in simple spans, and it prevents lateral buckling. This arrangement permits steel stringers to be treated as fully laterally supported beams. While dead load due to the haunch must be included in the design, it is a common practice to disregard its presence in computing the section properties of the composite section.

The superimposed dead load, usually applied after the slab has been cured, is distributed equally to all stringers. Therefore, the larger the stringer spacing, the larger its share of the total load and, consequently, the larger its size. The spacing of stringers is, thus, a critical design parameter that affects sizes of both the deck slab and the stringer. The designer has the option of choosing several smaller stringers at close spacings, or a few relatively larger stringers at large spacings. The latter option usually results in an economical design through less steel, fewer diaphragm connections and bearings, and fewer girders to erect. From a practical standpoint, however, the spacing should be chosen so that the required minimum slab thickness, usually $7\frac{1}{2}$ in. or thicker, would be able to carry loads safely. Even with a chosen slab thickness, a range of stringer spacings is possible, as shown in Fig. 8.3(*a*). For example, with an 8-in.-thick slab, stringer spacing can vary from 5 ft 10 in. to 6 ft 10 in. For a bridge of a given width, any spacing may be chosen from this range to result in equally spaced stringers. It is best to provide an even number of beams or girders in the superstructure—a minimum of four for greater redundancy [PennDOT, 1993]—to facilitate redecking or replacing half the superstructure while using the other half to maintain traffic temporarily, during possible future rehabilitation. As a check, the selected stringer size should conform to the following requirements:

1. AASHTO 10.5.1, which requires that the ratio of girder depth to span be not less than 1:25
2. AASHTO 10.8.1, which requires that all structural steel be at least $\frac{5}{16}$ in. thick, except the web thickness of rolled beams or channels, which may not be less than 0.23 in. (0.25 in. in the new LRFD specifications [AASHTO, 1994a]); a perusal of

the AISC manual [AISC 1989] shows that, except for a few very small sizes that are too small to be used for bridge loads, most W shapes satisfy this requirement

Design of the *exterior stringers* can be similarly performed. Loads on the exterior stringer were discussed in Chapter 4. AASHTO 2.23.2.3.1.4 requires that the exterior stringer must be at least as large as the interior stringer. Consequently, the size of the exterior stringer is kept the same as that of the interior stringer, unless the design calculations indicate otherwise.

Shear in either interior or exterior stringers that consist of W shapes is usually not a problem.

Deflection due to dead and live loads should be checked as discussed in Chapter 5. Methods of computing deflections in various kinds of beams due to various kinds of loads can be found in [Ku, 1986]. These methods cover simple and continuous beams, with various end conditions and cross sections (prismatic and nonprismatic). According to AASHTO 10.14, girders should be cambered to compensate for dead-load deflections and vertical curvature required by the profile grade. Maximum lengths that can be cambered depend on the length to which a given section can be rolled, with a maximum of 100 ft [AISC, 1989]. Camber of steel rolled beams was discussed in Chapter 5.

Permissible deflections due to live load plus impact are specified in AASHTO 10.6. Because deflection limitations are based on the serviceability criteria, they are the same regardless of whether a bridge is simple or continuous, noncomposite or composite. A comprehensive discussion on the deflection of steel beam bridges can be found in the literature [Wright and Walker, 1971, 1972]. In general, for simple and continuous spans, the deflection due to service live load plus impact should not exceed 1/800 of the span. Exceptions to this requirement are bridges in urban areas that are used in part by pedestrians; in this case, this ratio should preferably be limited to 1/1000. In some cases, even stricter limitations may be imposed by some bridge owner agencies. For example, the state of Illinois limits live-load deflections of heavily traveled composite structures carrying pedestrian traffic to $L/1440$.

8.4.2.2 Wind loads

In addition to the gravity loading due to dead and live loads, beams and girders are also subjected to lateral loads due to wind. Wind loads are assumed to act horizontally from any direction. According to AASHTO 10.21.2, a horizontal wind force of 50 lb/ft^2 is applied to the area of the superstructure exposed in elevation whose height is measured from the bottom of the beam or the girder to the top of the parapet.[1,2] When the units are converted to linear feet of the bridge, AASHTO 3.15.1.1.2 requires that this force be not less than 300 lb/ft. Arbitrarily, half of this force is applied in the plane of each flange of the exterior beam or girder and is eventually transferred to the reactions at the supports of beams or girders (Fig. 8.6).

---

[1] The value of 50 lb/ft^2 is applicable for beams and girders only. For trusses and arches, the intensity of wind force is to be 75 lb/ft^2.

[2] The wind load on the live loading is assumed to be transferred entirely to the deck slab and is therefore zero for the bottom flange of the beam or girder.

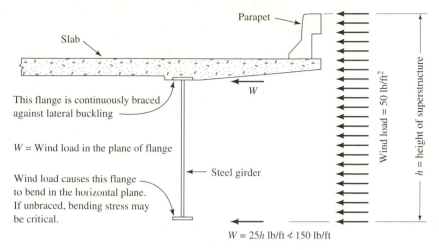

FIGURE 8.6
Wind loads on the superstructure.

When the top flange is rigidly attached to the deck, sufficient stiffness in the plane of the wind loads is present at the flange level, and it is assumed that wind loads are transferred to the diaphragms or to the cross frames at the ends of the span, which, in turn, transmit the wind loads to the bearings. Because of the stiffness of the deck, lateral bracings are not required in the plane of the top flange (AASHTO 10.21.1), although such bracings may be required during construction. However, wind loads transferred to the bottom flange cause it to bend in the horizontal plane, so it should be laterally braced, as required. For the lateral bracings to be effective, AASHTO 10.21.3 requires that the lateral bracings be placed in the exterior bays (i.e., between the exterior beam and the first interior beam, and in the plane of their bottom flanges). Bracings may consist of angles (not smaller than $3 \times 2\frac{1}{2}$ in.), other shapes, or welded sections.

A rational method of computing stresses due to horizontal wind loads in the bottom flanges of beams and girders first appeared in the 1982 AASHTO specifications. When lateral bracings are not present, the moment M in the beam due to wind load, which causes bending of the bottom flange in the horizontal plane, may be computed as that for a simple beam:

$$M = \frac{WL^2}{8} \tag{8.1}$$

where L = length of span (ft)
      W = wind load in the plane of the bottom flange (lb/ft)
         = 50 lb/ft^2 × ($\frac{1}{2}$ × height of superstructure) ≥ 150 lb/ft

The corresponding bending stress in the flange is computed by the simple bending formula $f = M/S$, where S is the section modulus of the bottom flange, taken about an axis parallel to and in the plane of the longitudinal axis of the beam:

$$S = \frac{t_f b_f^2}{6} \tag{8.2}$$

where t_f = flange thickness (in.)
   b_f = flange width (in.)

Assuming elastic (i.e., linear) distribution of stresses, the tips of the bottom flange will be subjected to maximum stresses, with zero stress at the center of the flange. Because both t_f and b_f are usually small for steel beams, the bending stress so computed turns out to be significantly larger than the permitted stress. However, when diaphragms or cross frames are provided, the bottom flange, under the action of wind load, bends in a horizontal plane and behaves as a continuous plate element supported by the diaphragms or the cross frames. As a result, both the moment and the stress are reduced considerably. The moment caused by this wind load is computed by Eq. 8.3 (AASHTO Eq. 10.9):

$$M_{cb} = 0.08 W S_d^2 \text{ (ft-lb)} \tag{8.3}$$

where W = wind loading along the exterior flange (lb/ft)
   S_d = diaphragm spacing (ft)

The bending stress due to the moment M_{cb} can be computed from Eq. 8.4 (AASHTO Eq. 10.8):

$$
\begin{aligned}
F_{cb} &= \frac{M_{cb}}{S} \\
&= \frac{12 M_{cb}}{t_f b_f^2 / 6} \text{(psi)} \\
&= \frac{72 M_{cb}}{t_f b_f^2} \text{(psi)}
\end{aligned}
\tag{8.4}
$$

where the value of S has been substituted from Eq. 8.2.

This stress should be added to those due to the gravity loads (dead and live loads plus impact) on the beam. Regardless of which design method is followed—the service-load or the load-factor method—if the resulting stress exceeds the permitted stress, measures must be taken to limit the total stress below that permitted. This can be done as follows:

• Reduce the moment due to the wind loading in the bottom flange, M_{cb}, thus reducing the stress it causes.
• Increase the section modulus of the bottom flange by increasing its width, b_f. Note that because the section modulus of the bottom flange varies as the square of its width, b_f, but only in direct proportion to its thickness, t_f, a change in thickness would not help much.
• Provide wind bracing.

The maximum wind-induced stress, F, in the bottom flange of *each* beam or girder is computed from Eq. 8.5 (AASHTO Eq. 10.5):

$$F = R F_{cb} \tag{8.5}$$

where R is a coefficient whose value is determined as follows: When bottom lateral bracings *are not* provided,

$$R = \frac{0.2272L - 11}{(S_d^2)^{1/3}} \qquad \text{(AASHTO Eq. 10.6)} \qquad (8.6)$$

When bottom lateral bracings *are* provided,

$$R = \frac{0.059L - 0.64}{\sqrt{S_d}} \qquad \text{(AASHTO Eq. 10.7)} \qquad (8.7)$$

where L = span length (ft).

When wind bracings are provided, they are usually connected to the bottom flange at the locations of the diaphragms or the cross frames, resulting in complex connection details. Not only are such connections costly, but they are also prone to fatigue problems. Consequently, wind bracings should be avoided as much as possible, and the other two options—using the largest permissible flange width, or reducing the diaphragm or cross-frame spacing—should be seriously considered to control flange stresses due to wind loads. It is important to note that the moment in the bottom flange, M_{cb}, due to wind load, depends on the spacings of the diaphragms or the cross frames, S_d, and not on the bridge span, L. Therefore, the flange stresses can be easily controlled by adjusting the diaphragm or cross-frame spacings.

In short-span bridges with a series of parallel beams, stress in the exterior stringer due to wind loads is usually very small (usually 1 ksi or less) and is unlikely to affect beam design, if at all. Thus, it may even be ignored in the calculations. However, in medium- and long-span bridges such as plate girders, stress induced by wind loads is large and may affect beam design, and, consequently, wind loads should be properly accounted for. A comprehensive discussion on wind load computations for plate girder bridges can be found in [AISC Mkt., 1987].

8.4.3 Diaphragms

The general philosophy of providing diaphragms was discussed in Chapter 4 (Sec. 4.1). Requirements for providing diaphragms, covered in AASHTO 10.20.1, are as follows:

- Rolled beams and plate girders must be provided with cross frames or diaphragms at each support and at intermediate points in all bays (i.e., between all adjacent stringers). These diaphragms or cross frames should be spaced not more than 25 ft apart.
- For rolled beams, the depth of diaphragms should preferably be half the beam depth, but not less than one-third the beam depth. For shallow beams, diaphragms usually consist of wide flange I- or channel-sections. For deeper beams, cross frames are provided, which should be as deep as practicable.
- Intermediate cross frames should preferably be of the cross type or V-type.
- End diaphragms or cross frames should be proportioned to adequately transmit all of the lateral forces to the bearings. Also, the diaphragm should be capable of supporting the concrete edge beam provided to protect the end of the concrete slab.

Diaphragms are subjected to horizontal wind loads that are transferred to them by the lateral wind bracings. According to AASHTO 10.20.2.2, the maximum horizontal force, F_D, in the transverse diaphragms and the cross frames is obtained from Eq. 8.8 (AASHTO Eq. 10.10):

$$F_D = 1.14WS_D \qquad\qquad (8.8)$$

where W = wind loading along the exterior flange (lb/ft)
$\quad S_d$ = diaphragm spacing (ft)

8.4.4 Bearings

Provision should be made at one of the two supports of a simply supported span for expansion of the deck due to temperature and other causes. It is common practice to build one end as fixed and the other end with a bearing system to accommodate expansion or contraction. As discussed in Chapter 6, bearings may be made of steel, or they may be elastomeric pads.

8.5
DESIGN OF COMPOSITE STEEL BEAM BRIDGES

8.5.1 Advantages of Composite Construction

Composite construction, now in general use for spans over 40 ft, came into practice in the 1950s. For shorter spans in the 40- to 60-ft range, composite construction is not economical.

Composite steel beams are characterized by mechanical anchorages that are attached to their top flanges and embedded in the concrete deck. The most important consideration for composite design is economics. With composite construction, shallower steel stringers can be used than those used in noncomposite construction. For a certain range of spans, the cost of welding shear connectors is more than offset by the savings in the weight of steel stringers. In addition, a composite girder results in a flexural member with a large moment of inertia; consequently, the live-load deflections are minimal. Embedment of shear connectors in the bottom of the concrete slab provides positive continuous lateral bracing for the compression flanges of the steel stringers; this permits full stresses to be used for compression flange design. The shallower superstructure also results in a lighter, slender, and graceful design. The lighter superstructure also translates into savings in the design of the substructure. Figure 8.7 shows the weight–span-length relationship for simple-span I-beam noncomposite and composite bridges [USDOC, 1990].

Composite construction may not be desirable under certain conditions. As an alternative, a continuous structure may be considered. Continuity in stringers may result in reduced moments, which may be carried by noncomposite construction; continuity will also result in smaller deflection. In some cases, lighter members are not desirable from the viewpoint of reduced resistance to vibratory forces, such as wind.

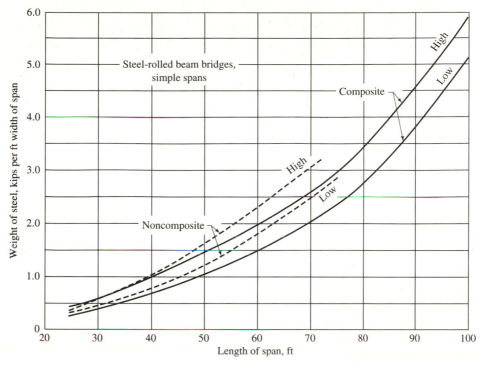

FIGURE 8.7
Relationship between weight of steel and span length, for noncomposite and composite beams [USDOC, 1990].

8.5.2 Design of Composite Sections

Composite construction is known to have evolved in the early 1900s in the form of concrete-encased beams (steel beams totally encased in concrete) used as a fire protection measure. These beams, designed both as noncomposite and composite, were used widely until the advent of lightweight fireproofing materials that were more economical; these made concrete encasement unnecessary. These totally encased members depend upon natural bond and friction between concrete and steel for interaction with concrete, and they are considered to act as composite beams—without additional anchorages—if designed according to AISC specifications [AISC, 1989]. However, fireproofing usually is not required for bridges. And, because the natural bond between concrete and steel is easily broken by the heavy impactive loads of bridges (and hence is unreliable), it precludes the use of encased beams as composite beams for bridges. It is also for this reason that, in a composite beam, the entire horizontal shear must be resisted by mechanical anchorages. Furthermore, since encased beams lack the ductility of shear connectors, they cannot be designed by the strength theory methods [Slutter, 1974].

Encased beams are permitted for buildings [AISC, 1989] but not for highway bridges, and no reference to this type of construction is made in the AASHTO specifications [AASHTO, 1992]. In the 1930s, research in composite construction led to the development of mechanical anchorages (also referred to as shear connectors) to provide interaction between concrete and steel. For practical and economical reasons, this form of construction became widely accepted. Mechanical anchorages are not used in conjunction with encased beams, since relatively large deformations are necessary before mechanical anchorages transmit any sizeable horizontal shear.

The first approval of composite construction for building floors was in the 1952 AISC specifications, and the first for highway bridges was in the 1944 AASHO specifications [Kuzmanovic and Willems, 1983; McMormac, 1992]. A discussion on the many forms of composite construction can be found in the ASCE report [Viest, 1974], in many texts on steel design [McGuire, 1968; Kuzmanovic and Willems, 1983; Johnston, Lin, and Galambos, 1986; Salmon and Johnson, 1990; McMormac, 1992; and many others], and in many other references [Hacker, 1957; Viest, Fountain, and Seiss, 1957; Viest, Fountain, and Singleton, 1958; ASCE, 1960; ASCE–ACI, 1960; Viest, 1960; Vitols, Clifton, and Au, 1963; Ketchek, 1963; Chapman, 1964; Slutter and Driscoll, 1965; Toprac, 1965a,b; Daniels and Fisher, 1967; McGarraugh and Baldwin, 1971; Hedefine, 1972; Slutter, 1974; Hamada and Longworth, 1976; Lorenz, 1983, 1988; ASCE, 1984a,b; Johnson and Buckby, 1986; Hooper, Grubb, and Viest, 1990]. Typical composite construction used for highway bridges is presented in the following paragraphs.

Composite construction involves three major elements:

1. Reinforced concrete deck
2. Longitudinal steel girders supporting the deck
3. Shear connectors to resist the horizontal shear

The deck is provided by a continuous reinforced concrete slab, spanning transversely and supported by several parallel steel stringers. The main reinforcement in the slab is, therefore, placed perpendicular to traffic. Thus, the design of the slab is identical in noncomposite and composite construction. However, there is a major difference in the bending of the beam: In composite construction, *longitudinally,* the slab and the steel stringer are assumed to act in unison or compositely; i.e., no slippage occurs at the concrete slab–steel beam interface. The slab is assumed to act simply as a cover plate attached to the compression flange of the beam. In other words, a portion of the slab functions much like a steel cover plate over the compression flange of the stringer, adding significantly to the compression flange's strength and stiffness. Thus, a composite beam section comprises a concrete slab at the top and an I-beam at the bottom. In simple spans, the slab, acting as the top flange of the composite section, is always in longitudinal compression at working loads. Therefore, no tensile reinforcement is required in the slab in the longitudinal direction. In contrast, in noncomposite construction, the slab bends *transversely,* i.e., in a plane perpendicular to the bending of the beam, as a continuous structural member supported by several beam supports. Consequently, the slab must be adequately reinforced, as explained earlier.

It is important to recognize the economy provided by composite construction. The concrete slab essentially acts as a heavy top steel plate; thus substantial savings may be made through the use of unsymmetrical steel sections. In unsymmetrical beams, the bottom flange can be larger than the top flange; because this involves no additional fabrication costs, the use of unsymmetrical, rather than symmetrical, built-up beams is always more economical. When rolled beams are used, the unsymmetrical section may be obtained by welding a cover plate on the bottom flange [Hooper, Grubb, and Viest, 1990].

According to the allowable stress design method, a composite beam section, consisting of a concrete slab at the top and a steel I-beam at the bottom, is designed using the conventional flexure formula: $f = Mc/I$. The elementary theory of bending that yields this formula assumes that the bending stresses are proportional to the distance from the neutral axis and that the stresses are uniform across the width of the flange. But it is known that, if this width is very large, parts of the flange at some distance away from the web do not participate fully in resisting the moment. It is a usual practice in such cases to replace the actual width by a certain reduced width, such that the elementary theory of bending applied to such a transformed beam cross section gives the correct value of the maximum bending stress. This reduced width of the flange is referred to as the *effective width*, a concept first developed by von Karman [1924] that has been the subject of considerable theoretical and experimental research ever since [Metzer, 1929; Miller, 1929; Chwalla, 1936; Rusch, 1953; Girkmann, 1954; Dischinger and Mehmel, 1955; Adekola, 1968; Abdel-Sayed, 1969a, b; Cheung and Chan, 1978; and others]. A comprehensive discussion on the theory and analysis for determining the effective width of the flange, is presented by Timoshenko and Goodier [1951], Girkmann [1954], Lee [1962], Wolchuck [1963], and Troitsky [1967].

In the case of a composite beam section, the slab acts as the top flange of the beam, and the effective width is defined as that width of the slab that can be considered in its entirety in computing its moment of inertia. Implicit here are two assumptions:

- The strain distribution across the effective width is uniform.
- There is no slip at the slab–beam interface.

If slip occurs, the flexure formula, $f = Mc/I$, cannot be used to compute bending stresses in the composite section. A rigorous analysis that accounts for the strain incompatibility at the slab–beam interface owing to the lack of full composite action is presented by Knowels [1973]. Effective width is also required to calculate the compression resultant, C, in concrete that would balance the tensile force resultant, T, in steel when the load factor design is used.

Application of the flexure formula requires knowledge of the section properties of the composite section, which, in turn, requires knowledge of two things: (1) The extent (i.e., the width) of the top slab, which can be associated as a part of the composite section, must be defined, and (2) the slab concrete must be converted into an equivalent area of steel. Thus, defining the cross section of a composite section is a two-step procedure. First, a certain width of the slab, commonly referred to as the *effective width*, b_e, is defined based on certain assumptions. Second, this effective width is converted into the equivalent width of the steel flange, called the *transformed effective width*. Because the basic material is steel, this is achieved by dividing the effective width by the modular ratio. Thus,

$$b_{\text{tr}} = \frac{b_e}{n} \tag{8.9}$$

and

$$A_{\text{tr}} = b_{\text{tr}} t_{\text{slab}} \tag{8.10}$$

where b_e = effective width

$\quad\quad\quad b_{tr}$ = transformed flange width

$\quad\quad\quad n$ = modular ratio, E_s/E_c

$\quad\quad\quad E_s$ = modulus of elasticity of steel

$\quad\quad\quad E_c$ = modulus of elasticity of concrete

$\quad\quad\; t_{slab}$ = thickness of the slab

$\quad\quad\; A_{tr}$ = transformed area of the slab associated with the composite beam section

With the enlarged compression flange provided by the transformed area of the concrete slab, the whole deck is assumed, for purposes of design, to act as a series of T-beams. A_{tr} may be considered the equivalent area of steel for calculating the section properties of the composite section.

In the absence of slip at the slab–beam interface, what actually happens to a slab supported by a steel beam can be visualized by physical reasoning. As the load is applied, the slab and the beam deflect together, and shearing stresses are generated at the slab–beam interface (this is the so-called horizontal shear). The slab acquires its longitudinal compressive stresses from these shear stresses. The distribution of compressive stresses across the width, however, is not uniform. They are, as Fig. 8.8 shows, higher in the vicinity of the flange of the steel beam and lower away from the flange. This departure from the conventional bending theory is known as *shear lag*, since it involves shear deformation in the flange [Timoshenko and Goodier, 1951].

While these mathematical theories give the effective width, b_e, for an infinite flange width as a function of the span length, in practical situations other variables are important as well. These include spacing of the beams, relative thickness of the slab with

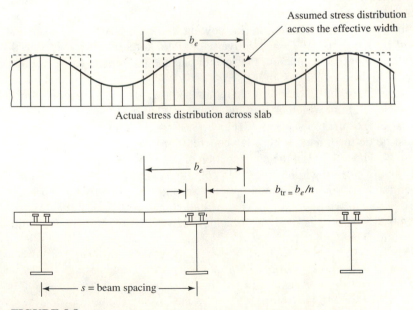

FIGURE 8.8
Effective width of composite steel beam and stress distribution.

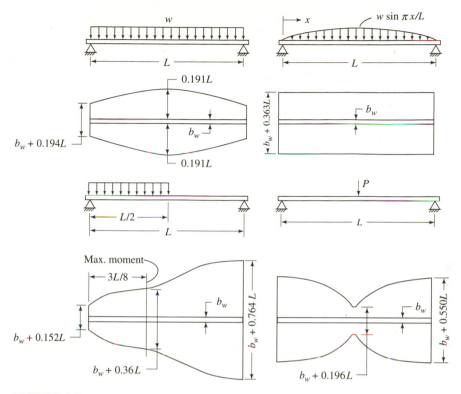

FIGURE 8.9

Equivalent flange widths for infinite actual width beams with a rib cross-sectional area of $0.1tL$ [adapted from Girkmann, 1954].

respect to the total beam depth, width of the web (in the case of T-beams), and loading conditions. Figure 8.9 [Girkmann, 1954] shows the variation of the effective flange projection for a flange of zero stiffness between beams (i.e., for $t/h = 0$).

A summary of various factors that influence the determination of effective width is presented by Brendel [1964]. A discussion on how the concept of effective width applies to beams with flange and web of dissimilar materials (e.g., where a concrete flange and a steel web are used for the composite steel beam) can be found in Johnson and Lewis [1966]. Heins and Fan [1976], Vallenilla and Bjorhovde [1985], Fisher [1970], and Grant, Fisher, and Slutter [1977] present discussion on the strength of composite steel beams using a formed steel deck, or steel stay-in-place forms (shown in Fig. 8.10), to support the slab. Heins and Fan [1976] and Cheung and Chan [1978] investigate effective flange width for various bridge configurations and loading conditions.

To ensure that the slab and the supporting stringers act in unison, slippage between them must be prevented. The required bonding, or the *shear resistance* at the interface, is developed by providing shear connectors on the compression flange of the stringers, which are embedded in concrete. As a result of such a construction, both the slab and the steel beam act *compositely,* hence the term "composite design." Details of composite design can be found in several texts on steel design and in other references cited earlier,

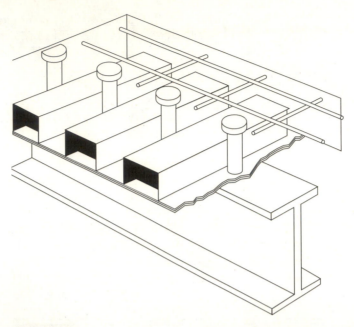

FIGURE 8.10
Formed steel deck with shear studs in a composite steel beam.

and these details will not be repeated here; however, some important aspects of the subject are discussed here.

8.5.2.1 Concrete slab

- The slab thickness is determined by the transverse flexural requirement. The principal reinforcement, therefore, is in the direction perpendicular to the bridge axis, and it provides for both positive and negative moments.
- In the longitudinal direction, the distribution steel is provided at the bottom and the temperature and shrinkage steel is at the top.
- The slab design is carried out in the same manner as in the case of noncomposite construction. The design of reinforced concrete slabs was discussed in detail in Chapter 6.

8.5.2.2 Steel beams

- Steel beams span between abutments and/or piers.
- Rolled sections, rolled sections with cover plates, or built-up girders with cover plates on tension flanges, are used.
- Depth ratios per AASHTO 10.5 should be observed.

8.5.2.3 Composite section

Essentially, the design of a composite steel beam, like any other design, is a trial-and-error procedure that involves selecting the steel beam section and investigating the stresses in concrete and steel. Initially, a steel section is selected based on engineering judgment, and the stresses are computed. These stresses are compared with those permitted to indicate to what extent, if any, the steel section should be adjusted until an optimum stress condition is reached. The following considerations apply to composite beam design construction.

Type of construction—unshored and shored. Construction of a composite steel beam bridge may be carried out with or without shoring. In unshored construction, steel stringers must be designed to resist their own load in addition to the dead load of fresh concrete and the formwork. The composite section supports all loads placed *after* the concrete has hardened. Such loads include superimposed dead load due to wearing surface, curb, parapet and railing, and live load plus impact. The bending stress computations should reflect this sequence of load applications. If effective temporary supports, used to support stringers before the concrete deck slab is poured, are kept in place until the concrete has attained 75 percent of its required 28-day strength, stresses due to all loads can be calculated on the basis of the composite section (AASHTO 10.38.4.1).

In shored construction, beams are temporarily shored to support the uncured concrete of the deck while it undergoes the curing, or setting, process. During this stage, the weight of uncured concrete and the supporting beams is transferred directly to ground through shores, thus relieving beams of any stresses due to the deck slab and their own weight; it is assumed that the beams are not stressed until after the shores are removed. Therefore, shores should be sufficiently strong to support these loads, and their design and spacing must ensure that the beam deflections are insignificant while the beams are shored. Shores are removed after the slab concrete has set, and now the beam is assumed to act compositely. Stresses due to *all* loads are then computed on the basis of section properties of the composite section. Therefore, the design procedures for beams using shored construction differ from those used for unshored construction; the procedures are considerably simpler for shored construction.

Design considerations

Section properties of composite section

A portion of the dead load and the live load is to be resisted by the composite section. The section properties of the composite section are determined based on the *transformed section*. The concrete area is transformed into an equivalent steel area by dividing the effective width by the modular ratio, n (or by $3n$, if necessary, as discussed later). Values of n for various values of f_c' are specified in AASHTO 10.38.1.3 (see Appendix A, Table A.14).

The effective width, b_e, of the concrete flange is arbitrarily set by AASHTO 10.38.3. For slabs symmetrical about the beam, the following requirements hold (AASHTO 10.38.3.1):

1. $b_e \not> L/4$
2. $b_e \not>$ center-to-center of girders
3. $b_e \not> 12t_{\text{slab}}$

For beams having the slab on one side only, the requirements are somewhat different (see AASHTO 10.38.3.2).

Note that these requirements vary somewhat from those for buildings specified in the AISC specifications [1989], for composite steel beams (allowable stress design), and in the ACI code [ACI 1995], for reinforced concrete T-beams. Although all specify requirements similar to items 1 and 2 above, the requirements for buildings do not specify item 3. Previous editions of AISC [1989] and ACI codes specified the third requirement as b_e not to exceed 16 times the slab thickness plus the web thickness, which is less conservative than item 3 above. Specification commentaries on composite beams suggest dropping this requirement so that the composite-beam requirements are in accord with both theoretical and experimental studies as well as with composite-beam codes in other countries.

Also note that the AASHTO criteria are conservative and give low values for the effective width. This is because the deck slab built integrally over several beams is also subjected to transverse bending between the beams, which reduces the effectiveness of the slab in carrying compression at points remote from the steel beam flange. Thus, some degree of uncertainty is involved in evaluating the precise value of the effective width. Considering the fact that the effective width varies with the type of loading, the spacing of beams, and the ratios t/h, L/b_w, and L/b_o, the AASHTO criteria for effective width appear to be much simplified. Compared to these criteria, the foreign specifications are much more restrictive. For example, the British CP117 specifications [BSI, 1972] require that whenever the actual width, b, exceeds $L/20$, the effective width be limited to

$$b_e = \frac{b}{\sqrt{1 + 12(2b/L)^2}} \tag{8.11}$$

but not less than $L/20$. The European Concrete Committee [Leve, 1961; Brendel, 1964] presents detailed procedures for determination of the effective width.

Effects of sustained loads

For the effects of sustained (long-term) loads, such as the composite portion of the dead load, the effects of plastic flow and creep are considered by increasing the value of the modular ratio to $3n$, three times the values referred to in the above paragraph (AASHTO 10.38.1.4) [Roll, 1971].

Stresses in composite section

The bending stresses in the composite section are calculated using the elastic theory, $f = Mc/I_c$, where I_c represents the moment of inertia of the composite section (i.e., the transformed section). The effects of creep are accounted for by a two-step stress computational procedure. Stresses due to sustained loads are computed with section properties based on the increased modular ratio, $3n$, whereas those due to transient loads (e.g., live load plus impact) are computed with section properties based on the modular ratio, n. The algebraic sum of the two stresses gives the total stresses in the beam (AASHTO 10.38.4.1).

The unit shear in the composite section is determined on the basis of the steel section alone. It is assumed that the entire external shear is resisted by the web only, and the steel flanges and the concrete slab do not contribute any shear resistance (AASHTO 10.38.5.2).

8.5.2.4 Requirements for cover plates

According to AASHTO 10.38.1.6, composite sections in simple spans, and the positive-moment regions of continuous spans, should be so proportioned that the neutral axis lies below the top surface of the steel beam. Concrete on the tension side of the neutral axis (as in the case of a composite beam in the negative-moment region of a continuous beam) is neglected, and only the longitudinal reinforcement in the slab is considered for computing resisting moments of the composite section. However, concrete on the tension side of the neutral axis can be considered for computing section properties to be used in deflection computations and for determining stiffness factors used in computing moments and shears.

When a nominal 7-in. or thicker slab is used compositely with a rolled section, its transformed area results in concentration of a large area in the compression flange, and the moment of inertia of the section is significantly increased. However, because the (composite) compression flange area becomes much larger than the tension flange area of the rolled section, the neutral axis moves much closer to the steel compression flange and much farther from the tension flange. As a result, the section modulus of the bottom flange does not increase quite in proportion to the increase in the moment of inertia, resulting in very high tensile stresses in the bottom flange. To achieve a more efficient section (i.e., to keep stresses in the bottom flange low), it is common practice to increase the area of the tension flange by welding a cover plate along the length of the steel beam. It has been found that the lightest and the shallowest steel sections with the largest cover plate offer the most economical design [Heins and Firmage, 1979; AISC Mkt., 1987].

Requirements for cover plates for rolled steel beams are specified in AASHTO 10.13. The following restrictions apply:

1. Moments in a beam vary along the span, and cover plates are required only in the regions of large moments (e.g., in the midspan region of a simple span or in the negative-moment region of a continuous span). Consequently, cover plates are provided only over the partial lengths of beams. However, partial-length cover plates are not permitted on flanges more than 0.8 in. thick for nonredundant load path structures[3] subjected to repetitive loadings that produce tension or reversal of stress in the beam.

   AASHTO 10.13.3 permits use of multiple cover plates to augment the area of a flange, with the total thickness of all cover plates limited to $2\frac{1}{2}$ times the flange thickness. However, this provision has been deleted from the LRFD specifications (6.10.9) [AASHTO, 1994a]. Consequently, *multiple cover plates should not be used.*

2. The maximum thickness of a cover plate is limited to twice the thickness of the flange to which the cover plate is attached.

   Note that steel plates are available in various widths and thicknesses in the following increments [AISC, 1989, 1994]:

   $\frac{1}{32}$-in. increments to $\frac{1}{2}$ in.

   $\frac{1}{16}$-in. increments from $\frac{1}{2}$ to 1 in.

---

[3]See Chapter 5, Sec. 5.3.2., for definition. Also refer to AASHTO 10.3.1, for examples of nonredundant load path structures.

$\frac{1}{8}$-in. increments from 1 to 3 in.

$\frac{1}{4}$-in. increments over 3 in.

The thickness selected for a cover plate should conform to the available market sizes.

3. The length of any cover plate added to a rolled beam should not be less than $(2d + 3)$ ft, where d is the depth of the beam, in ft. Note that in the LRFD specifications (6.10.9) [AASHTO, 1994a], this requirement has been reduced to $(d/6 + 3)$ ft.

    Cover plates may be narrower or wider than the width of the flange to which they are attached; this is generally a matter of designer's preference. Although no restrictions regarding their width are specified in the AASHTO specifications [AASHTO, 1992, 1994b], they are governed by good fabrication practices. If the cover plate is narrower, there should be enough room—at least equal to the weld size plus $\frac{1}{8}$ in.— to place longitudinal welds on each side. A cover plate wider than the flange should be at least 2 in. wider [Heins and Firmage, 1979].

4. Design for lengths of partial cover plates is covered by AASHTO 10.13.4. The basis of design is the allowable *fatigue stress* in the beam flange at the ends of the cover plates, and not the allowable stress without fatigue considerations.

    The theoretical cutoff point for a cover plate is defined by the stress *limit states*. Under the service load design method, the cutoff point is defined as a section where the stress in the flange without that cover plate equals the allowable service load stress, excluding fatigue considerations. Under the strength design criteria (i.e., the load factor design method), the cutoff point is defined as a section at which the flange strength without the cover plate equals the required strength for the design loads, excluding fatigue requirements.

    A partial-length cover plate must be extended beyond its theoretical cutoff point by a *terminal distance;* that is, it must extend to a section where the *stress range* (and not the total stress) in the beam flange is equal to the *allowable fatigue stress range* for the base metal adjacent to or connected by the weld metal.

    The length of the terminal distance is arbitrarily set by the specifications, based on how the *ends* of the cover plate are welded to the flange, as shown in Table 8.1.

    The minimum width at the ends of the tapered cover plates is required to be 3 in. All welds, including those in the terminal distance, are required to be continuous and to have a minimum size as specified in AASHTO 10.23.2.2. The weld connecting the cover plate to the flange in its terminal distance must be of sufficient size to develop a total stress of not less than the computed stress in the cover plate at its theoretical end.

    The fact that, in composite construction, some portion of the load is carried by the steel section alone makes the determination of the exact location of the theoretical cutoff point somewhat difficult. An approximate formula based on the premise that both cross sections (with and without the cover plate) of a composite beam are stressed to the allowable stress values (and thus, they are equal) is presented by Gaylord, Gaylord, and Stallmeyer [1992]. Figure 8.11a shows the moment diagram for a uniformly loaded, partially cover-plated beam. The moments at the midspan section (M) and those at the end of the cover plate (M') are given by

$$M = \frac{wL^2}{8} \qquad\qquad (8.12)$$

TABLE 8.1
Terminal distance for cover plates

Condition at end of cover plate	Length of terminal distance
Cover plates not welded across their ends	Two times the width of the cover plates
Cover plates welded across their ends	$1\frac{1}{2}$ times the width of cover plates

$$M' = \frac{w[L^2 - (L')^2]}{8} \tag{8.13}$$

Since $f = M/S_c$, the corresponding stresses, f and f', at the two sections are as follows: At the midspan,

$$f = \frac{wL^2}{8S_c} \tag{8.14}$$

and at the end of the cover plate,

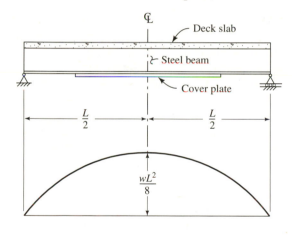

FIGURE 8.11a
Moment diagram for a uniformly loaded cover-plated beam.

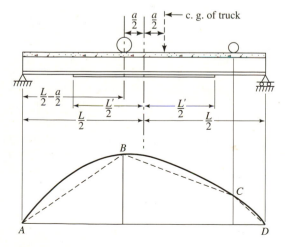

FIGURE 8.11b
Moment diagram for H20-truck loading on a cover-plated beam [Gaylord, Gaylord, and Stallmeyer, 1992].

$$f' = \frac{w[L^2 - (L')^2]}{8S'_c} \qquad (8.15)$$

where w = uniform load on beam
  L = span
  L' = length of the cover plate
  S_c = section modulus of the cover-plated composite section
  S'_c = section modulus of composite section without the cover plate

Equating $f = f'$ = allowable stress, we obtain

$$\frac{L'}{L} = \sqrt{1 - \frac{S'_c}{S_c}} \qquad (8.16)$$

Because Eq. 8.16 is derived for the case of a uniformly loaded beam for which the maximum moment occurs at midspan, it is not valid for beams that support moving loads, as in the present case. Therefore, this equation must be modified.

Positioning of truck loadings for maximum moment in the beam was discussed in Chapter 4. Figure 8.11b [Gaylord, Gaylord, and Stallmeyer, 1992] shows the position of a typical H-truck loading for maximum moment in the beam. The corresponding moment diagram, including the effects of the uniform dead load, is shown by $ABCD$. Segment AB is conservatively assumed to be a parabola with vertex at B, and Eq. 8.16 is used to determine the distance from B to the left end of the cover plate. The half-length $L'/2$ of the cover plate is obtained by substituting $(L/2 - a/2)$ for L in Eq. 8.16 and adding $a/2$ to the resulting expression [Porete, 1949]. Thus,

$$L' = L\sqrt{1 - \frac{S'_c}{S_c}}$$

$$\frac{L'}{2} = \frac{a}{2} + \left(\frac{L}{2} - \frac{a}{2}\right)\sqrt{1 - \frac{S'_c}{S_c}}$$

which yields

$$L' = a + (L - a)\sqrt{1 - \frac{S'_c}{S_c}} \qquad (8.17)$$

where a is the distance between the centroid of the group of point loads and the nearest point load. Values of a for H and HS loadings are given in Table 8.2. The

TABLE 8.2
Values of distance a

H20 truck loading		HS20 truck loading	
Span (ft)	a (ft)	Span (ft)	a (ft)
Less than 26.5	0	Less than 23.9	0
Greater than 26.5	2.8	Between 23.9 and 33.8	7
		Greater than 33.8	4.7

procedure involved in determining the cutoff point for the cover plate is one of trial and error. Knowing the approximate location of the theoretical cover plate cutoff point, the stresses at that point without the cover plate can be determined. If the controlling stresses (usually steel stress in the bottom flange) exceeds the allowable stress, the cutoff point is moved slightly, and stresses are recalculated. This computational cycle is repeated until the controlling stress equals the allowable stress.

8.5.2.5 Allowable fatigue stresses

The allowable fatigue stresses are given by AASHTO 10.3.1. The commonly built simple multibeam composite slab–stringer bridges fall in the category of redundant path structures [AASHTO, 1992, p. 188; ASCE–AASHTO, 1985; Frangopol and Nakib, 1991] for which the allowable fatigue stress range is given in AASHTO Table 10.3.1A. To select the appropriate allowable fatigue stress range from this table, first select from AASHTO Fig. 10.3.1C the stress category for the member being designed. This figure illustrates several examples of the type and location of various members and fasteners subject to repeated variations or reversals of stresses. Then make cross reference to AASHTO Table 10.3.1B to fit the description of design, and, finally, select the allowable fatigue stress range from AASHTO Table 10.3.1A. For partial-length welded cover plates (with or without welds across the ends), the stress category is E if the flange thickness is less than 0.8 in., or E′ if the flange thickness is greater than 0.8 in.

8.5.2.6 Methods of developing composite action

The term "composite action" implies that the concrete slab and the steel beam will act in unison, i.e., as a unit, with no slip at the interface. However, the natural bond that exists between the concrete slab and the steel beam is considered insufficient and unreliable for providing the shearing resistance essential to composite action. The required composite action between the concrete slab and the steel beam is therefore developed by means of mechanical anchorages, commonly referred to as *shear connectors,* welded to the top of the compression flange and embedded in the concrete slab. Because of the tendency of the slab to slip both vertically as well as horizontally, the shear connectors should be capable of preventing these slippages at the steel–concrete interface with extremely small deformation (AASHTO 10.38.2.1).

Many types of mechanical anchorages, such as spiral bars, channels, zees, angles, and studs (Fig. 8.12), have been developed to resist horizontal shear at the concrete–steel interface. However, usually for economic reasons, the most common types of shear connectors are (1) steel headed shear studs automatically end-welded to the top flanges of beams, and (2) channels fillet-welded transversely to the top flanges of beams. The allowable loads for both are specified in AASHTO 10.38.5.1. In design examples presented in this book, only headed shear studs have been used. These headed studs are actually round steel bars 2 to 4 in. long and $\frac{1}{2}$ to 1 in. in diameter, welded at one end to the flange of steel beams and upset at the other end to prevent vertical separation from the concrete slab. Fabrication of such beams is quick and fairly simple because the studs can be welded to beams by stud-welding by semi-skilled labor. Figure 8.13 shows typical steel bridge beams with headed shear studs and channel shear connectors.

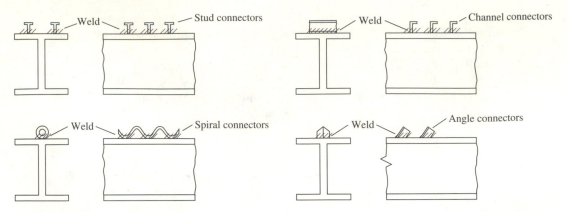

FIGURE 8.12
Various kinds of mechanical anchorages for resisting horizontal shear (i.e., developing composite action) at the concrete–steel interface in beams [McCormac, 1992].

The AASHTO specifications have dual criteria for the design of shear connectors: fatigue and ultimate strength criteria (10.38.5.1.1 and 10.38.5.1.2). The shear connectors are first designed for fatigue under service-load conditions to ensure serviceability and durability, and later they are checked to ensure that they can develop the ultimate strength of the section. These two design criteria are likely to result in different numbers of total shear connectors required; the larger number should be used to satisfy both criteria.

Design for fatigue. As discussed in Chapter 5, *fatigue* is a phenomenon or a process by which portions of a metal structure degrade or fail due to cyclic loading. Fatigue failure generally involves two stages: initiation of a crack and subsequent growth to failure. The number of loading cycles required for crack initiation depend on the material properties, the load range, and the stress concentration factor of the notch. Because the crack growth is independent of material strength, it is seldom possible to achieve greater fatigue life through material selection alone. Use of proper design methods, detailing, and fabrication procedures are of utmost importance and critical to maximizing the fatigue life of metal structures, including bridges.

Shear resistance considerations

A discussion on fatigue strength of shear connectors is provided by Slutter and Fisher [1966] and Toprac [1965b]. For fatigue considerations, the critical design parameter involved is the *range* of shear, V_r, due to live load and impact, not the total shear at a section. Since the dead load is permanent, the range of shear, V_r, is caused by live load and impact only. At a given section, the shear may be positive or negative, depending on the position of wheel loads on the span. The *range of shear, V_r,* is defined as the algebraic difference between the positive and negative shear at a section due to live load and impact, as the live load moves from one end of the span to the other. To obtain the maximum values of positive or negative live-load shears at a section, only the corresponding portions of the span, as indicated by the influence-line diagram, should

(a)

(b)

FIGURE 8.13
Typical steel bridge beams with (a) headed shear studs and
(b) channel shear connectors (Courtesy of United States Steel).

be loaded. Appropriate distribution and impact factors should be applied to both the positive and negative shears.

Note that, since the loaded lengths for the positive and negative shear are usually different, the impact factor, which depends on the loaded length L (to be used in the formula $I = 50/(L + 125)$), is also different for each shear. An exception to this is when the loaded length $L \leq 41.6$ ft, in which case $I = 0.3$.

The range of shear stress, S_r, is calculated from Eq. 8.18 (AASHTO Eq. 10.57):

$$S_r = \frac{V_r Q}{I} \tag{8.18}$$

where S_r = range of horizontal shear, in ksi, at the interface of the concrete slab and
the steel beam at the point in the span under consideration

V_r = range of shear due to live loads and impact, in kips, as defined earlier

Q = statical moment about the neutral axis of the composite section of the transformed compressive concrete area, or the area of reinforcement embedded in the concrete for negative moment, in in.[3]

I = moment of inertia of the transformed section in positive moment regions, or the moment of inertia provided by the steel beam, including or excluding (as necessary) the area of reinforcement embedded in concrete in the negative moment regions, in in.[4]

The allowable range of horizontal shear, Z_r, for an individual shear connector, is given by the following expressions: For channels (AASHTO Eq. 10.58),

$$Z_r = Bw \tag{8.19}$$

For welded studs, for $H/d \geq 4$ (AASHTO Eq. 10.59),

$$Z_r = \alpha d^2 \tag{8.20}$$

where w = length of a channel shear connector, in in.

H = height of stud, in in.

d = diameter of studs, in in.

and B and α are coefficients that depend on the cycles of loading, as shown in Table 8.3.

Studs are available with diameters in increments of $\frac{1}{8}$ in.; commonly used diameters are $\frac{3}{4}$, $\frac{7}{8}$, and 1 in. Their lengths have increments of $\frac{1}{2}$ in.

More than one shear connector may be placed transversely across the top flange of the steel section; they may be spaced at regular or variable intervals. For more than one welded shear stud along a transverse section of the beam, the allowable range of horizontal shear of all connectors is given by $\sum Z_r$. The pitch, p, of the shear studs along the length of beam can be calculated by dividing the allowable range of horizontal shear of all connectors at one transverse girder cross section ($\sum Z_r$) by the horizontal range of shear, S_r (AASHTO 10.38.5.1.1):

$$pS_r = \sum Z_r$$

from which

$$p = \frac{\sum Z_r}{S_r} \tag{8.21}$$

TABLE 8.3
Values of constants α and B

Number of cycles	α	B
100,000	13,000	4000
500,000	10,600	3000
2,000,000	7850	2400
Over 2,000,000	5500	2100

Thus, the larger the stud diameter, the larger its range of allowable horizontal shear, Z_r, and the larger the required spacing.

Spacing and positioning of shear studs

To prevent vertical and horizontal slippage between the concrete slab and the steel flange, certain penetration (in concrete) requirements and certain spacing requirements for shear connectors must be satisfied. Penetration of shear studs in concrete is specified by AASHTO 10.38.2.3. The clear depth of concrete cover over the tops of shear connectors should be at least 2 in., and the studs should penetrate concrete at least 2 in. above the bottom of the slab. The upset ends of shear studs prevent vertical separation between the concrete slab and the steel beam. The clear distance between the edge of a girder flange and the edge of the shear connectors should be at least 1.0 in., and the minimum center-to-center spacing of shear connectors should be at least four diameters (AASHTO 10.38.2.4). AASHTO 10.38.5.1 limits maximum spacing of shear studs to 24 in. within these constraints; more than one shear connector (headed studs) may be placed in a transverse cross section of the girder. The idea is to provide enough space around a shear stud to be occupied by concrete to develop composite action. Various aspects of shear-connector spacing are discussed by Lew [1970].

Design for ultimate strength. The ultimate strength of I-beam bridges is documented in a state-of-the-art report [ASCE–AASHTO, 1975], and is discussed by Ollgaard, Slutter, and Fisher [1971], and by Slutter and Fisher [1971]. AASHTO 10.38.5.1.2 requires that the number of shear studs provided for fatigue be checked to ensure they are adequate for the ultimate strength. This requirement assures the capability of developing full plastic stress distribution in the beam (Fig. 8.14). For ultimate strength considerations, the stress in concrete is assumed to be $0.85f_c'$, and the stress in steel is assumed to be F_y. Consistent with these assumptions, Fig. 8.13 shows two states of plastic stress distribution. In most practical cases, the neutral axis is located within the concrete slab, as shown in Fig. 8.14(a), in which case the entire steel cross

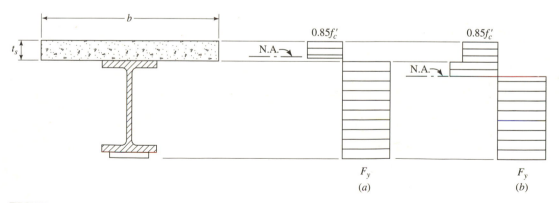

FIGURE 8.14
Stress distribution in a composite steel beam at the ultimate load conditions: (a) neutral axis in the concrete slab; (b) neutral axis outside the concrete slab.

section remains under a constant stress—F_y, the yield stress. Under this condition, the maximum force that can be developed in steel is equal to A_sF_y. Occasionally, the neutral axis will lie in or below the top flange of the beam, as shown in Fig. 8.14(b). In this case, the maximum compressive force that can be developed in concrete equals $0.85f_c'bt_s$,

where A_s = total area of steel section, including the cover plates
   F_y = specified minimum yield point of steel being used
   f_c' = 28-day compressive strength of concrete
   b = effective flange width of slab
   t_s = thickness of concrete slab

The maximum horizontal force in the beam cannot exceed the smaller of two values—A_sF_y, the maximum developable tensile force in the steel beam, or $0.85f_c'bt_s$, the maximum developable compression force in the concrete slab. Therefore, the ultimate strength of the shear connectors provided is governed by the smaller of these two forces.

The total number of shear connectors required to satisfy ultimate strength requirements depends on the type of span considered—simple, having only positive moment, or continuous, having both positive and negative moments. When a composite beam is loaded to the ultimate moment, equilibrium with respect to the concrete slab must be satisfied over the length, L, between the point of plastic moment and the point of zero moment. For a beam with positive moment only, the total number of shear connectors can be calculated from Eq. 8.22 (AASHTO Eq. 10.68):

$$N_1 = \frac{P}{\phi S_u} \tag{8.22}$$

where N_1 = number of shear connectors between the points of maximum positive moment and the adjacent end supports
   S_u = ultimate strength of the shear connector (defined later)
   ϕ = strength reduction factor
   P = force in the slab at points of maximum moment

The force, P, in the slab at points of maximum moment is taken as the smaller of P_1, the tensile strength of the steel section, including the cover plate, or P_2, the compression strength of the concrete slab. These values are given by (AASHTO Eqs. 10.61 and 10.62)

$$P_1 = A_sF_y \tag{8.23}$$

$$P_2 = 0.85f_c'bt_s \tag{8.24}$$

Similarly, the number of shear connectors, N_2, required between the points of maximum positive moment and the points adjacent to the maximum negative moment is given by (AASHTO Eq. 10.63)

$$N_2 = \frac{P + P_3}{\phi S_u} \tag{8.25}$$

where P_3 is the force in the slab at points of maximum negative moment and is computed from Eq. 8.26 (AASHTO Eq. 10.64):

$$P_3 = A_s^r F_y^{r*} \tag{8.26}$$

where A_s^r = total area of longitudinal reinforcing steel at the interior support within the effective flange width

F_y^{r*} = specified minimum yield point of reinforcing steel

The ultimate strength of a shear stud, with $H/d \geq 4$, is given by (AASHTO Eq. 10.66)

$$S_u = 0.4d^2 \sqrt{f_c' E_c} \tag{8.27}$$

where d = diameter of stud, in in.

E_c = modulus of elasticity of concrete, in psi

= $w_c^{1.5} 33 \sqrt{f_c'}$, w_c = weight of concrete = 145 lb/ft^3 for normal weight concrete

f_c' = 28-day compressive strength of concrete

The number of additional shear connectors, required at points of contraflexure when reinforcing steel is embedded in the concrete is not used in computing section properties for negative moments. This value, N_c, is computed from Eq. 8.28 (AASHTO Eq. 10.68):

$$N_c = \frac{A_r^s f_r}{Z_r} \tag{8.28}$$

where N_c = number of additional shear connectors for each beam at point of contraflexure

f_r = range of stress due to live load plus impact in the slab reinforcement over the support

Other terms appearing in the above equations were defined earlier.

These additional shear connectors are to be placed adjacent to the point of contraflexure within a distance equal to one-third the effective slab width, i.e., they should be placed on either side of this point or centered about it.

8.5.3 Economics of Noncomposite vs. Composite Superstructure

Economic considerations for steel bridge superstructures are discussed in several references [Bethlehem, 1967, 1968; Knight, 1984; Lorenz, 1983; Zahn, 1987; Keating, 1990; AISC, 1992; Guzek and Grzybowski, 1992; Gatti, 1994; Mistry, 1994]. In general, the economics of steel bridge superstructures is related to cost-effective span lengths. A few examples of typical girders and cost-effective span lengths are given in Table 8.4 [Mistry, 1994]. The cost of the substructure has an important bearing on the selection of the type of span layout. Shorter spans are cost-effective when the substructure cost is relatively small compared to the total cost of the structure. For substructures requiring costly foundation work, longer spans are cost-effective alternatives. Computer programs are available that determine the most cost-effective span arrangements.

The economics of noncomposite vs. composite construction depends on many factors and cannot be considered from the viewpoint of savings in material (weight) alone. The cost of erection and fabrication also becomes part of the cost of the completed

TABLE 8.4
Girder type and cost-effective span lengths [Mistry, 1994]

Type of girder	Cost-effective span length (ft)
Rolled beams	50–90
Plate girders	80–250
Box girders	150–250
Trusses	350–900
Cable-stayed	800–2000

superstructure. Thus, a least-weight design does not necessarily translate into a least-cost alternative. This is particularly true in the United States, where the high costs associated with fabrication and erection tend to increase the cost of the completed structure and may not offset savings in material costs.

Fabrication costs become a large part of the cost of the completed structure, so they should be kept at a minimum. Fabricated items include such components as flange cover plates, web stiffeners, studs for composite action, haunched girders, diaphragms, and expansion bearings. Fabrication costs are low for girders with parallel flanges compared to those for haunched girders (girders with nonparallel flanges and, hence, a nonprismatic beam). This is an important consideration for continuous spans. It is usually possible to build continuous and suspended-span bridges of normal span lengths with rolled beams, without any need for haunching. However, haunched girders (Fig. 8.15) may be required to provide for the necessary clearances under the bridge. Some designers may also prefer them for the sake of aesthetics, although their attractiveness is questionable. Methods of cost reduction through proper fabrication procedures and detailing are reported in the literature [Knight, 1984; AISC, 1992; Guzek and Grzybowski, 1992; Gatti, 1994; Mistry, 1994].

Girder (or stringer) spacing is one of the most important factors influencing the cost of steel beam bridge superstructures. Fabrication labor costs tend to be roughly proportional to the total length of the girders. Increased spacing results in a reduced number of girders and, hence, reduced total footage of girders, resulting in savings in fabrication costs. For example, for a multilane highway bridge, increasing the girder spacing from 7 ft 6 in. to 10 ft 8 in. would reduce the number of girders from 11 to 8, resulting in a potential savings of 8 to 13 percent in fabrication costs [Schilling, 1985]. A smaller number of girders also means savings in shipping, erection, and maintenance costs. Additional savings result from reducing the number of cross frames and bearings. Although a thicker slab, necessitated by wider girder spacing, would partially offset cost savings accruing from fewer girders, a minimum girder spacing of approximately 9 to 10 ft should be considered for an overall economical design.

For longer spans, the number of girders can be reduced by increasing spacing to as much as 20 ft. A combination of high-strength concrete and transverse prestressing (discussed in Ch. 7) can be advantageously used for the slab to span these wider spacings. Although 4000-psi concrete should be considered for conventional slabs, a 5000-psi or higher-strength concrete with transverse prestressing should be considered for girder spacings of 13 ft or wider [Schilling, 1985; Mistry, 1994].

Wider girder spacing can also be attained by using a *substringer framing system*. This system can actually be considered an intermediate step between the traditional

Algodones Interchange
Algodones, New Mexico

1984 Award of Merit Winner
Category: Grade Separation

FIGURE 8.15
A continuous bridge with haunched girders, the Algodones Interchange, Algodones, New Mexico
(Courtesy of AISC).

closely spaced girder layout and the widely spaced girder layout with transversely pre-stressed decks. The system involves placing a single rolled beam, referred to as a sub-stringer, typically a W24 section, midway between girders spaced at about 18 to 20 ft. This results in a slab span of about 9 to 10 ft, which requires a thickness of 8 or 9 in. The substringer is supported on cross frames placed at a maximum distance of 25 ft to conform to AASHTO 10.20.1. The cross frames typically form an inverted V supporting the substringer [Schilling, 1985].

Another important factor intertwined with cost considerations is the type of span arrangement. From this viewpoint, three types of slab–steel beam bridges may be recognized: simple spans, continuous spans, and cantilevered spans (i.e., continuous bridges with suspended spans). In a continuous beam arrangement, savings result primarily from eliminating bearings and expansion joints. For example, two simple spans would require four bearings, whereas a two-span continuous beam would require only three bearings. As the number of spans increases, the influence of continuity on the economics of construction is even greater. For example, three simple spans would require six bearings, whereas three continuous spans would require only four bearings.

Because of these complexities, it is difficult to calculate exact economical span lengths for various types of span arrangements; only rough estimates of economical span ranges can be made. A discussion on the relative economics of noncomposite vs. composite steel beam bridges can be found in several references [AISC Mkt., 1987; Elliot, 1990]. This discussion is summarized as follows:

- Generally, for simple spans up to about 40 ft and continuous spans up to about 60 ft, noncomposite construction with rolled wide-flange shapes is economical.
- Composite construction with rolled beams may be economical for simple spans in excess of 40 ft, or when the end span of a continuous beam exceeds 50 ft or the interior span of a continuous beam exceeds 65 ft.
- For spans up to 85 ft, rolled wide-flange shapes of A36 steel, designed to act compositely with the concrete slab, are economical.
- For simple spans exceeding 85 ft, rolled beams made from high-strength steels or plate girders should be considered.
- Unsymmetrical I-sections, such as rolled wide-flange beams with cover plates on the bottom flange, or welded girders with bottom flange plates heavier than the top flange plates, are generally economical for composite construction.
- For long-span superstructures, savings can be realized by using a partially cover-plated rolled beam section. This can be done by using a smaller rolled beam section than required for maximum moment, and adding a cover plate to the bottom flange (to enhance its moment of resistance) only in the region of maximum moment.
- *Hybrid girders,* built-up beams with stronger steel in one or both flanges than in the web, can be used to meet the need for large moment capacity without increasing the girder depth. The moment resisted by the web of a beam is a small part of the total moment of resistance of the beam, and since its shear strength depends on its slenderness ratio, it may be economical to fabricate a built-up beam with a web of lower-strength steel and flanges of higher-strength steel [Haaijer, 1961].

  A simple way of fabricating a hybrid girder would be to weld a plate of lower-strength steel to two WT sections made from higher-strength steel. Design of hybrid girders is covered by AASHTO 10.40 and 10.53. A discussion on hybrid girders can be found in several references [Haaijer, 1961; Frost and Schilling, 1964; Schilling, 1967; Carskadden, 1968; Schilling, 1968; Toprac and Murugesam, 1971; Salmon and Johnson, 1990; Dhillon, 1991].
- The load-factor design method (LFD, described later) is more cost-effective than the service load design method [CE, 1982; Knight, 1984; AISI, 1972; Schilling, 1985; Zahn, 1987]. According to the FHWA, LFD can produce cost savings of 5 to 12 percent in spans up to 200 ft and 12 to 20 percent in longer spans [Mistry, 1994].

8.6
DESIGN METHODS

Various structural design philosophies were discussed in Chapter 1. For the design of steel beam bridges, two methods are permitted by the specifications: the *service load design method,* also referred to as the *allowable stress design method* (formerly known as the working stress method), and the *load factor design method,* commonly referred to as the *strength design method* in the context of design of steel buildings. Both methods are covered in Chapter 10, Part C of the AASHTO specifications [AASHTO, 1992].

8.6.1 Service Load Design Method

Philosophically speaking, the service load design method deals with the behavior of a structure under service load conditions. The term "service load" is defined to include nominal dead load of the structure plus the live load, including impact, due to vehicles that are expected to use a bridge routinely. AASHTO 10.31 defines the service load design method as "a method for proportioning structural members using design loads and forces, allowable stresses, and design limitations for the appropriate material." Hence, the method is aptly called the allowable stress design method.

8.6.1.1 Allowable stresses

Allowable stresses to be used for designing concrete deck slab were discussed in Chapter 6; that discussion will not be repeated here. Allowable stresses for structural steel are given in AASHTO Table 10.32.1A, which is quite extensive and is excerpted in Appendix A (Table A.26). The allowable stresses for bending members are given in Table 8.5.

Because the AASHTO and ASTM designations for structural steels are not identical, their correspondence with one another, as specified in AASHTO Table 10.32.1A, should be carefully noted when specifying and ordering materials. This table lists two designations: AASHTO M270, which was first published in 1977 (*Interim Specification—Materials*), and the equivalent ASTM A709, which was initially published in 1974. As a matter of general practice, AASHTO prepares material specifications and revisions based on the *published* ASTM specifications; consequently, there is always a time lag pending AASHTO approval.

Footnote *h* in AASHTO Table 10.32.1A gives equivalents of the two designations, as well as their former equivalents. These equivalents are summarized in Table 8.6. These steels are available in grades 36, 50, 70, and 100; where enhanced atmospheric corrosion is desired, the letter "W" follows the grade. As is pointed out in footnote *e* of Table 10.32.1A, except for the mandatory notch toughness and weldability requirements, the ASTM designations are similar to the AASHTO designations. Steels that meet the AASHTO requirements are prequalified for use in welded bridges.

TABLE 8.5
Allowable stresses in bending members

Type of stress	Allowable stress	Values for A36 steel (psi)
Tension in extreme fibers of rolled-shaped girders and in built-up sections subject to bending—F_b	$0.55F_y$	20,000*
Compression in extreme fibers of rolled-shaped girders and in built-up sections subject to bending, with the compression flange continuously supported by embedment in concrete—F_b	$0.55F_y$	20,000*
Shear in girder webs—F_v	$0.33F_y$	12,000*

*Rounded-off values.

TABLE 8.6
AASHTO and equivalent ASTM designations of structural steels [Bethlehem, 1992]

AASSHTO M270 grade	Equiv. AASHTO grade	ASTM A709 grade	Equiv. ASTM grade	Min. yield	Min. T.S.	Availability	
						Plates	Shapes
36	M183	36	A36	36	58	to 4″ incl.	All groups
50	M223	50	A572	50	65	to 4″ incl.	All groups
50W	M222	50W	A588	50	70	to 4″ incl.	All groups
70W	M313	70W	A852	70	90	to 4″ incl.	Not applicable
100	M244	100	A514	100	110	to $2\frac{1}{2}$″ incl.	Not applicable
				90	100	OV $2\frac{1}{2}$ to 4″ incl.	Not applicable
100W	M244	100W	A514	100	110	to $2\frac{1}{2}$″ incl.	Not applicable
				90	100	OV $2\frac{1}{2}$ to 4″ incl.	Not applicable

8.6.2 Load Factor (Strength) Design Method

The introduction of the load factor method of design for steel highway bridges dates to the early 1930s, when the American Association of State Highway Officials (AASHO, as it was then known) produced specifications for designing bridges for a 100-percent overload. This was the first attempt to build overload capacities in highway bridges. This design philosophy permitted ordinary stresses for a combination of dead load, live load plus impact, and a 50-percent increase in the stresses for dead load plus $2(LL + I)$, whichever governed. This innovative design methodology was permitted only for a couple of years, followed by a whole generation of bridges that were built without any definite overload provisions. However, a study in the 1960s of about 150 bridges in the state of New York revealed that about 90 percent of these bridges, which were 50 to 70 years old at that time, could carry the then-permitted maximum legal load (a $35\frac{1}{2}$-ton truck), even though these bridges were designed for smaller loads [Moon and Maun, 1972]. This was a tacit recognition of the fact that steel members possessed ample reserve strength beyond the load resistance corresponding to a calculated first-yield stress. These observations spurred further research both in designing bridges with more effective (i.e., more economical) use of steel and in obtaining greater consistency in the maximum live-load carrying capacities of steel bridges [Vincent, 1969]. This research resulted in the development of a new design method known as the load factor design (LFD) method. A good discussion on this design method is provided by Hansell and Viest [1971].

The service load method was the method used to design steel bridges and most other bridges prior to 1971. In the 1971 interim AASHTO specifications, an alternate method of design, now called the load factor design, was introduced. The two main features that this method included were the use of plastic design principles for compact sections and a uniform live-load factor of safety for all span lengths. Initially slow to catch on since its introduction in 1969, it has steadily gained widespread acceptance, and about two-thirds of states in the United States design some or all of their bridges by LFD, resulting in cost savings.

As mentioned in Chapter 1, different load factors are applied in LFD. These load factors may be compared to the factors of safety used in the service load design method.

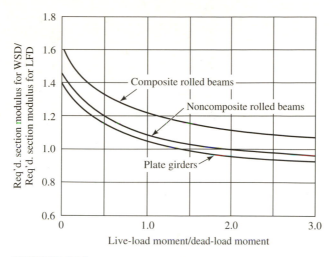

FIGURE 8.16
Comparison of service load and load factor design [Schilling, 1985].

In service load design, where the allowable stress in flexure is equal to $0.55 f_y$, a uniform factor of safety of 1.82 (1/0.55) is applied to both dead and live loads. But in LFD, the load factors are 1.3 for the dead load and 2.17 ($1.3 \times 5/3$) for the live load. The smaller load factor for dead loads is justified because dead load computations involve fewer uncertainties.

The economy achieved through applying these different but logical load factors in LFD is reflected in the design of beams and girders, as shown in Fig. 8.16 [Schilling, 1985]. For noncomposite rolled beams, when the ratio of live-load moment to dead-load moment, M_L/M_D, is 2, the service load method and the LFD method require the same section modulus. For longer spans, the M_L/M_D ratio decreases rapidly. For very long spans, this ratio approaches zero, and the working stress design requires a 45 percent larger section. A similar trend is seen for the composite section—the working stress design requires almost a 60 percent larger section for longer spans.

Economy in the plate girder design is also shown in Fig. 8.17. For an M_L/M_D ratio of 1.5, the section requirements are the same for both methods, whereas, for very long spans, the working stress method would require a 40 percent larger section modulus. Of course, for shorter spans, the M_L/M_D ratios are smaller, and LFD requires a relatively larger section modulus when this ratio is greater than 1.5, but this increase is rather modest.

Economy is also achieved in LFD through the larger web slenderness ratios (D/t_w) permitted for plate girders. For example, for longitudinally stiffened plate girders consisting of 36- and 50-ksi steels, LFD permits approximately 17 percent larger slenderness ratios (AASHTO 10.34.3.2.2 and 10.48.6.1). LFD also permits either wider spacing of transverse stiffeners for the same shear or higher shear for the same spacing of transverse stiffeners.

A comparison of savings in steel for several bridges attained through LFD over the conventional service load design method is presented in Figs. 8.17 [ENR, 1978a] and 8.18 [Beezone, 1972] and in Table 8.7 [Vincent, 1969]. In general, LFD permits

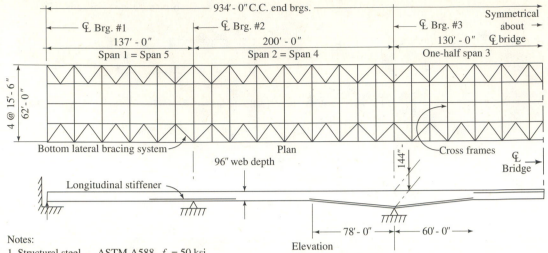

Notes:
1. Structural steel — ASTM A588, $f_y = 50$ ksi
2. Live load = HS20, Bikeway — 300 lb/ft, Sidewalk — 224 lb/ft
3. Stud shear connectors used throughout length of bridge

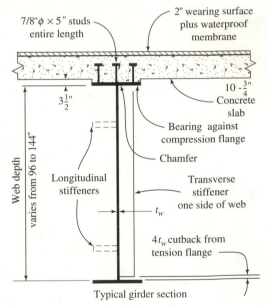

Typical girder section

Material Summary		
	Load factor design	Working stress design
Total weight of steel One girder Bridge	181 tons 1049 tons	206 tons 1181 tons
Unit weight of steel per square foot of deck	30.0 lb	33.7 lb
Number of $7/8''\phi \times 5''$ studs Per girder Per bridge	2133 10665	2031 10155

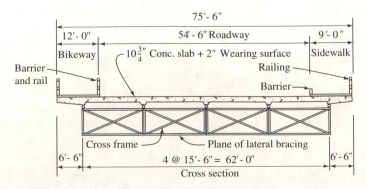

Cross section

FIGURE 8.17
Comparison of service load and load factor designs for a three-span plate girder bridge [ENR, 1978a].

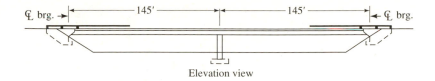

Elevation view

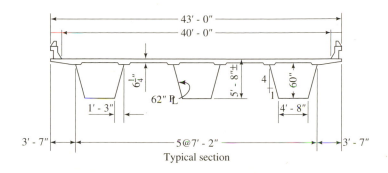

Typical section

Steel quantities	Working stress	Load factor
Webs	160,500 lb	137,800 lb
Top flanges (pos. moment)	58,500	38,900
Bottom flange (pos. moment)	85,800	77,700
Top flanges (neg. moment)	31,000	25,500
Bottom flange (neg. moment)	31,000	28,400
Bottom flange stiffener	2680	2280
Bearing stiffener (abutment)	800	800
Bearing stiffener (bent)	950	950
Intermediate stiffener	3560	4740
Shear connectors	15,370	15,370
Totals	390,160 lb	332,440 lb

FIGURE 8.18

Comparison of service load and load factor designs for a continuous two-span steel box girder bridge [Beezone, 1972].

bridge designs that are more economical than those designed by the service load design method. Savings increase with span lengths, typically 5 to 12 percent for spans up to 200 ft and 12 to 20 percent for longer spans [Schilling, 1985].

Conceptually, the strength design method for steel beam bridges is a *limit-states design,* analogous to the strength design of reinforced concrete members. It involves analyzing structures by methods of elastic analysis and proportioning structural members for multiples of design loads. These higher loads are obtained by multiplying the conventional design loads by certain factors called *load factors*; hence the term "load factor design," which is used synonymously with the "strength design method" specified in the AASHTO specifications [AASHTO, 1992].

AASHTO 10.42 refers to the load factor design method as an "alternate method for the design of simple and continuous beam girders of moderate length." The underlying idea is simply to preserve bridge safety under exceptionally heavy loading

TABLE 8.7
Summary of comparison between designs by the service load and the load factor design methods [Vincent, 1969]

Design no.	Span	Bridge type	Location	Steel type	Loading	Stringer spacing	*Weight of steel (lb)		Percent saving
							Conventional design	Load factor design	
Simple spans									
2	51'	Noncomp. rolled beam	Georgia	A36	H15-44	7' 4"	7020	6760	3.7
							7020	6760	3.7
3	65'	Noncomp. rolled beam	Georgia	A36	H15-44	7' 4"	12,804	12,012	6.2
							11,220	11,220	0.0
1	40'	Composite rolled beam w. cov. pl.	U.S.S. Report	A36	HS20-44	8' 4"	3811	3249	14.7
6	60'	Composite rolled beam w. cov. pl.	B.P.R. Stds.	A36	HS15-44	7' 4"	7059	5539	21.5
13	73' 4"	Composite rolled beam w. cov. pl.	West Virginia	A36	HS20-44	7' 7½"	13,140	11,320	13.8
4	81'	Composite rolled beam w. cov. pl.	Georgia	A36	H15-44	8' 0"	15,302	11,913	22.1
							13,133	11,261	14.2
5	80'	Composite welded girder	U.S.S. Report	A36	HS20-44	8' 4"	11,227	10,438	7.0
Two-span continuous									
7	70'–70'	Composite rolled beam w. cov. pls.	U.S.S. Report	A36	HS20-44	8' 4"	21,291	20,227	5.0
9	150'–150'	Noncomp. welded girder□	Summersville, W. Virginia	A441	H20-44 Truck HS15-44 Lane	23' 0"	•114,824	•102,673	10.6
19	100'–100'	Composite welded girder	U.S.S. Report	A36	HS20-44	8' 4"	30,861	27,964	9.4
14	118'–118'	Composite welded girder	Utah	A36	HS20-44	9' 3"	52,296	45,514	13.0
8	151'9"–120'9"	Composite	Georgia	A36 A441	HS20-44	7' 0"	•65,002	•55,655	14.4

Three-span continuous

	Type	Location	Span	Steel	Loading	Spacing			
15	Composite welded girder△	West Virginia	50'–85.5'–50'	A36	HS20-44	7' 5"	20,364	19,251	5.5
11	Composite welded girder△	U.S.S. Report	156'–200'–156'	A36	HS20-44	8' 4"	155,822	134,730	13.5

Five-span continuous—hinges in center span

	Type	Location	Span	Steel	Loading	Spacing			
12	Composite welded girder	San Mateo Creek, California	280'–360'–360'–360'–280'	A36 A441 A514	HS20-44	20' 0"	●1,494,849	●1,319,755	11.7

Weight A36 $\times$ 1.0

Weight A441 $\times \frac{31}{29}$

Weight A514 $\times \frac{45}{29}$

*Weight for one stringer including stiffeners. No diaphragms, bracing, or other details included.

●Steel weights expressed in terms of equivalent weight of A36:

□The conventional design for this bridge was redone in accordance with the 1965 AASHO specifications.

△The conventional design for this bridge was originally a noncomposite rolled beam. It was redesigned as a welded girder to afford a comparison with a welded girder design using the load factor design criteria.

conditions, i.e., under *maximum loads,* while ensuring performance, i.e., serviceability and durability, by controlling permanent deformations under *overloads,* by controlling deflections, and by providing adequate fatigue life under *service* loads. Under service load conditions, a bridge must demonstrate satisfactory performance, evidenced by acceptable deflection and adequate fatigue life. These performance criteria are referred to as the *service limit state* and the *fatigue limit state,* respectively, in the new LRFD specifications (6.5.2 and 6.5.3) [AASHTO, 1994a].

The term "overload" includes the nominal dead load of the bridge (as in the service load design method) plus live load, including impact, due to vehicles that are 1.67 ($\frac{5}{3}$) times as heavy as the service load vehicles. Under these loading conditions, a bridge must not deform permanently and cause objectionable riding qualities. This performance criterion is referred to as the "strength limit state" in the LRFD specifications (6.5.4) [AASHTO, 1994a].

The term "maximum load" is defined as the largest load that a bridge must be able to sustain. Maximum load is taken as 1.3 times the overload and has been selected to provide safety against failure rather than as load that a bridge is likely to experience. This criterion is referred to as an "extreme event limit state" in the LRFD specifications (6.5.5) [AASHTO, 1994a].

Designing a bridge by the load factor design method involves proportioning or designing members for multiples of design loads commonly referred to as factored loads. The three theoretical models of factored loads and related structural and performance requirements are described in Table 8.8 [Schilling, 1985; Haaijer, Carskadden, and Grubb, 1987, 1983].

The maximum load is defined as 1.3 times the overload because the maximum design load criteria are intended to ensure members of a highway bridge superstructure against any significant permanent damage that may be caused as a result of a few passages of exceptionally heavy vehicles in times of extreme emergency. The overload design criteria, on the other hand, are intended to ensure a member against permanent deformations that may be caused by occasional overweight vehicles and that may result in objectionable riding qualities of the superstructure. In both cases, it is assumed that these extra-heavy vehicles may be moving simultaneously in more than

TABLE 8.8
Load levels and structural-performance requirements [Haaijer, Carskadden, and Grubb, 1983]

Load category	Load level	Structural-performance requirement
Service load	$D + (L + I)$ Normal traffic (nominal dead load plus standard vehicles plus impact)	Provide adequate fatigue life and acceptable live-load deflection
Overload	$D + 5(L + I)/3$ Expected occasional overload (nominal dead load plus occasional heavy vehicles plus impact)	Control permanent deformations that otherwise could create objectionable riding quality*
Maximum load	$1.3[D + 5(L + I)/3]$ Hypothetical load chosen to ensure adequate strength, but not expected to be applied (1.3 times the overload)	Provide load resistance equal to or greater than maximum load, with the ability to sustain severe damage

*The autostress design imposes additional conditions regarding crack widths in the concrete slab to minimize rapid deterioration.

one lane. The service load criteria ensure that the live-load deflections and fatigue life (for the assumed fatigue loading) of a member are controlled within acceptable limits.

The philosophy behind the LFD method was presented in Chapter 1. Essentially, this design method involves three distinct steps, as specified in AASHTO 10.44:

1. Analysis of factored loads, referred to as the maximum design loads (e.g., moments, shears, etc., to be sustained by a stress-carrying member) in AASHTO 10.47:

$$\text{Maximum design load} = 1.3\left[D + \tfrac{5}{3}(L + I)\right] \qquad (8.29)$$

2. Design of steel beam sections to resist factored loads, i.e., loads computed by the above expression
3. Checking the service load behavior, controlling (a) permanent deformations under overloads, (b) fatigue characteristics under service loadings, and (c) live-load deflections under service loadings

The load factors are defined in AASHTO 3.22 (see Chapter 3, Tables 3.12 and 3.13). The overloads are defined in AASHTO 10.43.3, as the live loads that can be allowed—*infrequently*—on a structure without causing permanent damage. For design purposes, the maximum overload is taken as $5(L + I)/3$, and the total load under this condition is

$$\text{Overload} = D + \tfrac{5}{3}(L + I) \qquad (8.30)$$

The design stress in steel is taken as F_y, the yield point, or the yield strength, of steel.

According to AASHTO 10.44.3, the overload provision of the service load behavior is to be investigated according to AASHTO 10.57 through 10.59. The fatigue (AASHTO 10.58) and deflection (AASHTO 10.59) considerations referred to in items 3b and 3c in the list above are the same, in the context of service load behavior, for both the service load and the load factor design methods. Design for fatigue was discussed earlier, in Sec. 8.5.2. A discussion on deflection requirements and calculation methods was presented in Chapter 5.

The provisions for controlling permanent deformations under overloads are specified in AASHTO 10.57, and they differ for noncomposite and composite steel beams as follows:

Noncomposite beams

- The moment caused by $D + 5(L + I)/3$ should not exceed $0.8F_yS$.
- For beams designed for Group IA loading (see AASHTO 3.5 and Table 3.22.1A), the moment caused by $D + 2.2(L + I)$ should not exceed $0.8F_yS$.

Note that, according to the LRFD specifications [AASHTO, 1994a], noncomposite flexural members are not recommended, but they are permitted (AASHTO, 1994a, Commentary C6.10.10).

Composite beams

- The moment caused by $D + 5(L + I)/3$ should not exceed $0.95F_yS$.
- For beams designed for Group IA loading, the moment caused by $D + 2.2(L + I)$ should not exceed $0.95F_yS$.

8.6.2.1 Design assumptions

The load factor design method is based on the premise that both concrete and steel attain their maximum strengths under factor loads. The following design assumptions are stipulated in AASHTO 10.45:

- Strain in flexural members is directly proportional to the distance from the neutral axis.
- At factored loads, the stress in steel equals the yield strength of steel, F_y, and the compressive stress in concrete equals $0.85 f_c'$.
- The stress in steel below the yield strength, F_y, is computed as 29,000 ksi, or E, the modulus of elasticity of steel, multiplied by the steel strain, ϵ (based on Hooke's law); i.e., $f = \epsilon E$. For strains greater than those corresponding to the yield strength, F_y, the stress is assumed to be equal to F_y. This assumption also applies to the longitudinal steel reinforcement in the concrete deck in the region of negative moment when shear connectors are provided to ensure composite action in that region.
- Tensile strength of concrete is neglected in flexural calculations.

Design requirements for steel beams and girders by the load factor design method are covered in AASHTO 10.48 through 10.57. These requirements are briefly discussed, as follows, and then are appropriately referenced in design examples.

The term "compact section" will be used repeatedly in the context of the load factor design of steel beams. As defined by AASHTO 10.48.1, symmetrical I-shaped beams and girders with high resistance to local buckling and with proper bracing to resist lateral torsional buckling qualify as *compact sections*. Compact sections are characterized by their ability to form plastic hinges with an inelastic rotation capacity of three times the elastic rotation corresponding to the plastic moment. These compact sections are made from steels whose stress–strain diagram exhibits a yield plateau followed by a strain-hardening range (AASHTO 10.48.1.2). Steels that meet these requirements are AASHTO M270 Grades 36, 50, and 50W (ASTM A709 Grades 36, 50, and 50W; see Table 8.6).

Flexural strength. The maximum flexural strength, M_u, of compact sections can be computed on the premise that the entire cross section is subjected to uniform compressive or tensile stress equal to F_y (AASHTO Eq. 10.91)

$$M_u = F_y Z \tag{8.31}$$

where Z = the plastic section modulus of a compact section, and Z is always greater than the elastic section modulus, S. Methods of computing Z can be found in several references, such as Beedle [1958] and Vincent [1969]. Values of the plastic section modulus for various W-shapes are listed in the AISC manuals [1989, 1994].

The compactness requirements for steel beams for highway bridges have evolved from those used for steel buildings and are adopted from the AISC specifications [AISC, 1989]. The apparent differences between AASHTO and AISC specifications in the numerical coefficients of various equations defining the compactness requirements is due to the fact that the AASHTO equations use the yield strength of steel, F_y, in units of lb/in.^{2} rather than in units of kips/in.^{2} as is used in AISC [1989]. Differences in the notations used by AISC [1989, 1994] and AASHTO [1992] should be noted. A comprehensive discussion on this topic has been presented by Haaijer, Carskadden, and Grubb [1987].

Elements (flanges and webs) of symmetrical I-shaped beams and fabricated girders designed as compact sections must meet the following four requirements:

Projecting compression flange element

AISC [1989] limits the width–thickness ratio to $b'/t \leq 65/\sqrt{F_y}$, where F_y is the yield stress in ksi units. If psi units are adopted for F_y, then this relationship can be expressed as follows (AASHTO Eq. 10.92):

$$\frac{b'}{t} = \frac{65}{\sqrt{F_y}}$$

$$= \frac{65 \times \sqrt{1000}}{\sqrt{F_y \times 1000}}$$

$$= \frac{2055}{\sqrt{F_y}} \tag{8.32}$$

where b' = width of the projecting flange element = $\frac{1}{2}(b - t_w)$
  b = width of flange
  t = thickness of flange
  t_w = thickness of web

The preceding requirement applies to both noncomposite and composite beams and girders. However, AASHTO 10.50(c) stipulates additional width–thickness ratio requirements for composite beams and girders (AASHTO Eq. 10.121):

$$\frac{b'}{t} \leq \frac{2200}{\sqrt{1.3 f_{DL1}}} \tag{8.33}$$

where f_{DL1} is the top-flange compressive stress due to noncomposite dead load.

Web thickness

AISC [1989] limits the depth–thickness ratio to $d/t \leq 640/\sqrt{F_y}$, where F_y is the yield stress in ksi units, and d is the total depth of the section. This requirement was liberalized in AISC [1994] as $h_c/t_w \leq 640/\sqrt{F_y}$, where h_c is the depth of the web between the flanges. AASHTO specifications express the same parameter in terms of D/t, where $D = h_c$. Again, if psi units are adopted for F_y, and assuming that the actual depth of the web between the flanges, D, is about 95 percent of the total depth of the section, d (i.e., $D \approx 0.95d$), then this relationship can be expressed by Eq. 8.34 (AASHTO Eq. 10.93):

$$\frac{D}{t_w} = \frac{0.95 \times d}{t_w}$$

$$= \frac{0.95 \times 640}{\sqrt{F_y}}$$

$$= \frac{608 \times \sqrt{1000}}{\sqrt{F_y \times 1000}}$$

$$= \frac{19{,}230}{\sqrt{F_y}} \tag{8.34}$$

where D = clear distance between the flanges
$\qquad$ = $(d - 2t)$ for a W-section
$\quad d$ = total depth of the beam section

For frequently used steels, the requirements above are listed in Table 8.9. When both b'/t and D/t_w exceed 75 percent of the values given by Eqs. 8.32 and 8.34, the interaction equation, given by Eq. 8.35 (AASHTO Eq. 10.94) should be used:

$$\frac{D}{t_w} + 9.35\left(\frac{b'}{t}\right) \leq \frac{33{,}650}{\sqrt{F_{yf}}} \tag{8.35}$$

where F_{yf} = yield strength of compression flange, in psi.

In the case of composite beam design for continuous spans, the interaction equation (Eq. 8.35) must be modified. In the positive-moment region of a continuous beam, the depth of the neutral axis of a composite section, because of the presence of the large compression area provided by the slab, will generally be less than $D/2$. However, in the negative-moment region, the depth of the neutral axis may be greater than $D/2$. This is because, in this region, the area of longitudinal reinforcing tension steel in the slab, which is on the tension side of the beam, is considered (in conjunction with the cross-sectional area of the steel beam in tension) in computing the section properties of the composite section. Thus, according to AASHTO 10.50.2.1, when the depth of the neutral axis is greater than $D/2$, the interaction equation (Eq. 8.35) is modified by replacing D by $2D_{cp}$ (AASHTO Eqs. 10.93 and 10.94, modified):

$$\frac{2D_{cp}}{t_w} = \frac{19{,}230}{\sqrt{F_y}} \tag{8.36}$$

$$\frac{2D_{cp}}{t_w} + 9.35\left(\frac{b'}{t}\right) \leq \frac{33{,}650}{\sqrt{F_{yf}}} \tag{8.37}$$

where D_{cp} is the distance to the compression flange from the neutral axis for plastic bending.[4]

TABLE 8.9
Compactness requirements for steel beams for highway bridges

		F_y = 36,000 psi	F_y = 50,000 psi
b'/t		10.8	9.2
D/t_w		101	86
L_b/r_y	(when M_1/M_u = 0*)	100	72
L_b/r_y	(when M_1/M_u = 1*)	39	28

*For values of M_1/M_u other than 0 and 1, use AASHTO Eq. 10.95.

L_b = distance between the points of bracing of the compression flange
r_y = radius of gyration of the steel section with respect to the y-y axis
M_1 = smaller moment at the end of the unbraced segment of the beam
M_u = ultimate moment = $F_y Z$

---

[4]Plastic bending refers to a state of uniform stress distribution in the cross section of a composite beam when the compressive stress in concrete is $0.85 f_c'$, and the compressive or tensile stress in steel is F_y.

Although not explicitly stated in the guide specifications [AASHTO, 1991], the above requirement applies equally to unsymmetrical noncomposite beams in negative bending where the distance from the neutral axis to the compression flange exceeds $D/2$ [AASHTO, 1991].

The value of D_{cp} can be computed simply from statics, by equating the total force in tension (including that in the longitudinal reinforcing steel) to the total force in compression. An expression for computing D_{cp} is derived in the next section.

In the negative-moment region of a composite beam, the longitudinal reinforcing steel in the slab must, according to AASHTO 10.38.4.3 and 10.50.2.3, equal or exceed 1 percent of the cross-sectional area of the slab (within the effective slab width). Two-thirds of this required reinforcement is to be placed in the top layer of slab within the effective width. In this region, the placement of distribution steel according to AASHTO 3.24.10.2 ($A_s = 220/\sqrt{S}$, maximum 67 percent) is waived within the effective width. According to LRFD, Com. C6.10.1.2 [AASHTO, 1994A], 1 percent of the reinforcement with size not exceeding no. 6 is intended to provide a small enough reinforcement spacing to minimize slab cracking. Such reinforcement, with yield strength of at least 60 ksi, will remain elastic even when plastic hinges form in the negative-moment region (i.e., at the supports) of beams made from 50-ksi or lower-strength steels. This ensures that the cracks formed in the slab under the overload condition will close after the live load is removed.

Bracing intervals

The compression flange must be supported laterally, i.e., braced, at intervals not exceeding (AASHTO Eq. 10.95)

$$L_b = \left[\frac{3.6 - 2.2(M_1/M_u)}{F_y} \right] \times r_y \times 10^6 \tag{8.38}$$

where L_b = distance between the points of bracing of the compression flange
$\quad\quad\ r_y$ = radius of gyration of the steel section with respect to the y-y axis
$\quad\quad\ M_1$ = smaller moment at the end of the unbraced segment of the beam
$\quad\quad\ M_u$ = ultimate moment = $F_y Z$

The parameter M_1/M_u in Eq. 8.38 is subject to the following sign convention:

- M_1/M_u is *positive* when moments cause *single curvature* ($\smile$ or $\frown$) between the points of lateral bracings.
- M_1/M_u is *negative* when moments cause *reverse curvature* ($\sim$) between the points of lateral bracings.

The required lateral bracings that are provided should be capable of preventing the two phenomena that accompany lateral buckling of transversely loaded beams—lateral displacement and twisting. One of the commonly used methods to prevent both of these phenomena is to embed the compression flange of the beam to its full thickness in the concrete slab that it supports.

Maximum axial compression

The maximum axial compression is limited as given by Eq. 8.39 (AASHTO Eq. 10.96):

$$P \le 0.15 F_y A \tag{8.39}$$

where A is the cross-sectional area of the beam.

Requirements for designing beams that do not meet the stipulations above for braced compact sections are covered in AASHTO 10.48.2, 10.48.3, and 10.48.4.

The flexural strength of braced *noncompact* sections, i.e., sections that do not meet the above requirements, is computed as the strength at *first yield,* which is characterized by linear stress distribution, with yield stress, F_y, in the extreme fibers (AASHTO Eq. 10.97):

$$M_u = F_y S \tag{8.40}$$

The limitations for b'/t, D/t_w, and the bracing requirements for noncompact beams and girders for which Eq. 8.40 applies are given in AASHTO 10.48.2.

Shear strength. The shear capacity of rolled or fabricated I-shaped beams and fabricated girders depends on whether the web is unstiffened (e.g., in rolled sections) or stiffened (e.g., in plate girders), as specified in AASHTO 10.28.8.

For beams and girders with *unstiffened webs,* the shear capacity is limited by the plastic or buckling shear force, which is computed from Eq. 8.41 (AASHTO Eq. 10.112):

$$V_u = CV_P \tag{8.41}$$

For girders with *stiffened webs* and $(d_o/D) \leq 3$, the shear capacity is determined by including postbuckling resistance due to tension field action and is computed from Eq. 8.42 (AASHTO Eq. 10.113):

$$V_u = V_P \left[C + \frac{0.87(1 - C)}{\sqrt{1 + (d_o/D)^2}} \right] \tag{8.42}$$

where V_P is the plastic shear force, computed as follows (AASHTO Eq. 10.114):

$$V_P = 0.58F_y D t_w \tag{8.43}$$

The coefficient C in Eqs. 8.41 and 8.42 is equal to the buckling shear stress divided by the shear yield stress, whose value depends on the web depth–thickness ratio. The shear yield stress is determined as follows (Eqs. 8.45 and 8.46 match AASHTO Eqs. 10.115 and 10.116, respectively):

$$\frac{D}{t_w} < \frac{6000\sqrt{k}}{\sqrt{F_y}}, \qquad C = 1.0 \tag{8.44}$$

$$\frac{6000\sqrt{k}}{\sqrt{F_y}} \leq \frac{D}{t_w} \leq \frac{7500\sqrt{k}}{\sqrt{F_y}}, \qquad C = \frac{6000\sqrt{k}}{(D/t_w)\sqrt{F_y}} \tag{8.45}$$

$$\frac{D}{t_w} > \frac{7500\sqrt{k}}{\sqrt{F_y}}, \qquad C = \frac{4.5 \times 10^7 k}{(D/t_w)^2 F_y} \tag{8.46}$$

where D = clear, unsupported distance between the flanges
$\quad d_o$ = distance between transverse stiffeners
$\quad F_y$ = yield strength of the web plate
$\quad k = 5 + 5/(d_o/D)^2$
$\qquad$ = 5 for unstiffened beams and girders

Since $k = 5$ for unstiffened beams and girders (e.g., for rolled beams), the lower limits for D/t_w of steel sections with $F_y = 36$ and 50 ksi, for which $C = 1$ always, are given by Eqs. 8.47 and 8.48, respectively:

$$\frac{D}{t_w} < \frac{6000\sqrt{5}}{\sqrt{36,000}} = 70.7 \qquad \text{for } F_y = 36 \text{ ksi} \qquad (8.47)$$

$$\frac{D}{t_w} < \frac{6000\sqrt{5}}{\sqrt{50,000}} = 60.0 \qquad \text{for } F_y = 50 \text{ ksi} \qquad (8.48)$$

For these special cases, $V_u = 0.58F_yDt_w$. A study of the W-shapes listed in the AISC manual [AISC, 1989] indicates that all listed W-sections qualify for the lower limits of D/t_w.

Likewise, the upper limits of D/t_w for which AASHTO Eq. 10.112 can be used are

$$\frac{7500\sqrt{5}}{\sqrt{F_y}} = \frac{7500\sqrt{5}}{\sqrt{36,000}} = 106 \qquad \text{for } F_y = 36 \text{ ksi} \qquad (8.49)$$

$$\frac{7500\sqrt{5}}{\sqrt{50,000}} = \frac{7500\sqrt{5}}{\sqrt{50,000}} = 90 \qquad \text{for } F_y = 50 \text{ ksi} \qquad (8.50)$$

These limits would generally apply to plate girders.

When shear capacity is computed from AASHTO Eq. 10.113, and the girder panel is subjected to the simultaneous action of shear and bending such that the magnitude of the bending moment is greater than $0.75M_u$, the shear capacity, V, is computed from Eq. 8.51 (AASHTO Eq. 10.117):

$$V \le \left[2.2 - \left(\frac{1.6M}{M_u} \right) \right] V_u \qquad (8.51)$$

8.6.2.2 Moment capacity of a compact composite section

Application of ultimate strength concepts to structural design of composite steel sections evolved from recommendations made by the Joint ASCE–ACI Committee [1960], which are discussed in the literature [Viest, 1974; ASCE–AASHTO, 1975; Salmon and Johnson, 1990]. Although the allowable stress design has been in routine use for composite beams, this design has actually been based on the nominal-moment strength concepts. A discussion on the ultimate strength of a composite steel section can be found in several references, such as Hansell et al. [1978], Lorenz [1983], and Salmon and Johnson [1990].

Requirements for the load factor design of composite beams and girders are given in AASHTO 10.50. The b'/t ratio for the projecting top compression flange element of a composite beam should meet the requirement given by Eq. 8.33 to ensure flange stability prior to deck placement (AASHTO Eq. 10.121).

Additional requirements are as specified in AASHTO 10.50. When a steel beam, which is a part of a composite section, satisfies the above compactness criteria, the beam section is referred to as a *compact composite section*. The moment capacity (also referred to as the ultimate strength) of a compact composite section is computed on the premise that the entire section is under plastic stress distribution. This means that the concrete slab, which forms the top flange (in compression) of the composite section, is partly or wholly under a uniform maximum compressive stress equal to $0.85f_c'$, and the stress in the entire steel cross section equals the yield stress, F_y. The neutral axis consistent with the plastic stress distribution is called the *plastic neutral axis* (PNA).

Although the slab can participate in resisting positive moment, which causes compression in concrete, which concrete can resist, it cannot participate in resisting negative moment, which causes tensile stress in concrete, which concrete can resist very little. For this reason, the section properties of the same composite beam section are different in positive- and negative-moment regions of a continuous beam. Consequently, the moment capacity of a compact composite section is computed differently for positive- and negative-moment regions of a beam. Both cases are discussed as follows.

Moment capacity of compact composite section in the positive-moment region of a beam. In a composite beam under positive moment, the compression flange of the steel beam is embedded in the bottom of the supported slab, and it is considered to be continuously braced. Therefore, the compression flange is safe against buckling under service loads. Such beams qualify as compact sections when their webs qualify under AASHTO 10.48.1.1(b).

In general, the moment capacity of a beam's cross section equals the sum of moments about the PNA of all compressive and tensile forces acting on the cross section. The nature of the resultant forces, compressive or tensile, depends on the location of the PNA. Figure 8.19 shows the cross section of a compact composite beam, with plastic stress distribution, subjected to positive moment. The PNA may pass through the slab [Fig. 8.19(a)] or through the steel section [Fig. 8.19(b)]. It is assumed that the concrete in the slab is subjected to a uniform compressive stress equal to $0.85f_c'$, and that the top flange and the web above the PNA are subjected to their respective compressive yield strengths, which may differ from one another. On the tension side of the cross section (below the PNA), the web and the bottom flange are subjected to their respective tensile yield strengths, which may also differ.

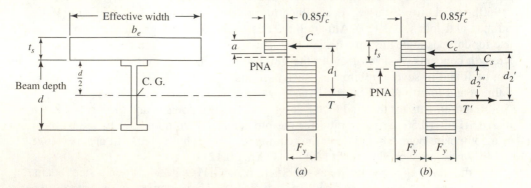

FIGURE 8.19

A compact composite cross section under plastic stress distribution: (*a*) PNA in slab; (*b*) PNA in web [Salmon and Johnson, 1990].

A comprehensive discussion on methods of determining the PNA of a composite section has been presented by Salmon and Johnson [1990]. The PNA may be located in the slab or in the steel section. In either case, the location of the PNA can be determined from the static equilibrium of forces. These two cases may be considered as follows:

PNA in the slab [Fig. 8.19(a)]

The compression stress resultant, C, is given by

$$C = 0.85 f_c' a b \tag{8.52}$$

The tensile stress resultant in the steel section, T, is

$$T = A_s F_y \tag{8.53}$$

The horizontal equilibrium of forces, $C = T$, yields $0.85 f_c' a b = A_s F_y$, from which

$$a = \frac{A_s F_y}{0.85 f_c' b} \tag{8.54}$$

where a = depth of compression block of concrete
b_e = effective width of slab
A_s = cross-sectional area of steel beam
F_y = specified yield strength of steel

PNA in the steel section [Fig. 8.19(b)]

In this case, the compression force resultant, C, consists of two components: C_c, the compressive force in the *entire* slab (of thickness t_s), which is subjected to a uniform compressive stress equal to $0.85 f_c'$, and C_s, the compressive force in the portion of the steel section (of unknown depth) above the PNA, which is subjected to specified yield stress in compression. Thus,

$$C_c = 0.85 f_c' t_s b \tag{8.55}$$
$$C_s = \text{area of steel in compression} \times F_y \tag{8.56}$$
$$C = C_c + C_s \tag{8.57}$$

For horizontal equilibrium, the total compressive force, C, must equal the total tensile force, T', in the steel portion of the section below the PNA,

$$T' = C_c + C_s \tag{8.58}$$

The tensile force, T', can also be expressed as the tensile strength of the entire steel section ($A_s F_y$) less the strength of the steel section in compression (C_s), i.e.,

$$T' = A_s F_y - C_s \tag{8.59}$$

Equating the values of T' from Eqs. 8.58 and 8.59 yields

$$C_s = \frac{A_s F_y - C_c}{2} \tag{8.60}$$

Whether the PNA is in the slab or in the steel section in a given situation can be easily ascertained by assuming that the PNA is located at the slab–flange interface. In such a case, the depth of the compression block equals the thickness of the slab, t_s, and the expression for the compression force, C_c, can be written by replacing a by t_s in the above expressions:

$$C_c = 0.85 f_c' t_s b \qquad (8.55)$$

Since the value of T cannot exceed $A_s F_y$, one may write

$$C_c \overset{>}{=} T$$

or
$$0.85 f_c' t_s b \overset{>}{=} A_s F_y \qquad (8.61)$$

If T is larger than C_c, it is obvious that the PNA is located in the web, and the difference $(T - C_c)$ must be provided by the compressive force in the steel portion of the section above the PNA.

Note that the compression force present in the longitudinal reinforcement in the slab has been neglected in the above formulations. However, compatibility of strains (consistent with $\epsilon_c = 0.003$) indicates that this reinforcement is stressed to its yield point, and the compression force in the longitudinal reinforcement, C_r, would be

$$C_r = (AF_y)_c \qquad (8.62)$$

where $(AF_y)_c$ is the product of the area and the yield point of reinforcement in the slab located above the PNA.

If the entire slab is under uniform compression, then the total compression force, C, will be

$$
\begin{aligned}
C &= C_c + C_r \\
&= 0.85 f_c' t_s b + (AF_y)_c \qquad (8.63)
\end{aligned}
$$

Principles and formulas presented in the preceding discussion can be used to determine the location of the PNA, from which the moment capacity of any composite section, referred to as nominal moment, M_n, can be computed as the moment of C–T couple,

$$M_n = C d_1 = T d_1 \qquad (8.64)$$

where $d_1 =$ lever arm. Again, note that AASHTO specifications do recognize the contribution of compression force present in the reinforcement in the compression zone of the concrete slab for computing the location of the PNA.

For purposes of design, the method of computing the moment capacity of a compact composite section is specified in AASHTO 10.50.1.1. The location of the PNA is determined by first computing the value of the maximum permissible compression resultant, C, as the smallest of the following three values:

1. The maximum developable compressive force in the concrete slab, including that in the longitudinal reinforcement (which, per AASHTO specifications, was not considered in the design of shear connectors in Sec. 8.4.2), given by Eq. 8.65 (AASHTO Eq. 10.122):

$$C = 0.85 f_c' b t_s + (AF_y)_c \qquad (8.65)$$

where $\quad b$ = effective width (b_e) of the slab

$\quad t_s$ = thickness of the slab

$\quad (AF_y)_c$ = product of the area and yield strength of that part of the longitudinal (parallel to stringer) reinforcement that is in compression

2. Maximum developable tensile force in steel, given by Eq. 8.66 (AASHTO Eq. 10.123):

$$C = (AF_y)_{bf} + (AF_y)_{tf} + (AF_y)_w \qquad (8.66)$$

$$= \sum AF_y \qquad (8.67)$$

where $(AF_y)_{bf}$ = product of the area of the bottom flange and its yield strength

$\quad (AF_y)_{tf}$ = product of the area of the top flange and its yield strength

$\quad (AF_y)_w$ = product of the area of the web and its yield strength

3. Ultimate resistance of shear connectors, given by Eq. 8.68 (AASHTO Eq. 10.124):

$$C = \sum Q_u \qquad (8.68)$$

where $\sum Q_u$ is the sum of the ultimate strengths of shear connectors between the section under consideration and the point of zero moment.

Once the value of the compressive force in the slab, C, is selected from one of the above three values, the value of the tensile stress resultant, which equals C, is automatically determined. The location of the PNA is then determined by investigating whether it lies in the slab or in the steel section. For example, if the value of C given by AASHTO Eq. 10.122 is greater than that given by AASHTO Eq. 10.123, it will indicate that the PNA lies in the slab; i.e., only a part of the slab is in compression. In such a case,

$$C = 0.85 f'_c ab + (AF_y)_c \qquad (8.69)$$

where a is the depth of the Whitney's rectangular stress block, which can be computed from Eq. 8.69 (rearranged) (AASHTO Eq. 10.125):

$$a = \frac{C - (AF_y)_c}{0.85 f'_c b} \qquad (8.70)$$

The PNA will be located at a distance $c = a/\beta_1$ from the top of the slab, where, according to AASHTO 8.16.2.7, $\beta_1 = 0.85$ for $f'_c \le 4000$ psi. For $f'_c > 4000$ psi,

$$\beta_1 = 0.85 - 0.05\left(\frac{f'_c - 1000}{1000}\right) \qquad (8.71)$$

but not less than 0.65. On the other hand, if the value of C given by AASHTO Eq. 10.122 is smaller than that given by AASHTO Eq. 10.123, this indicates that the PNA lies in the steel section. In such a case, the compressive force, C', in the steel section above the PNA (as derived earlier) is given by (AASHTO Eq. 10.126)

$$C' = \frac{\sum (AF_y) - C}{2} \qquad (8.72)$$

The PNA may be located in the flange or in the web. In either case, the location of the PNA may be determined by comparing values of C' and $(AF_y)_{tf}$ (the product of the area of the top flange and its specified yield stress, i.e., compression capacity of the flange), as follows:

1. When $C' = (AF_y)_{tf}$, the PNA lies at the underside of the top flange; i.e., $y = t_f$.
2. When $C' < (AF_y)_{tf}$, the PNA lies in the flange [Fig. 8.20(a)]. In such a case, if b_f is the width of the top flange, the value of C' is

$$C' = \text{Area of flange in compression} \times F_y$$
$$= b_f \overline{y} F_y \qquad (8.73)$$

from which

$$\overline{y} = \frac{C'}{b_f F_y} \qquad (8.74)$$

Multiplying the numerator and the denominator of the right-hand side of Eq. 8.74 by t_{tf} (the thickness of the top flange), and substituting $(AF_y)_{tf}$ for $b_f t_f F_y$, the resulting expression is (AASHTO Eq. 10.127)

$$\overline{y} = \frac{C'}{(AF_y)_{tf}} t_{tf} \qquad (8.75)$$

3. When $C' > (AF_y)_{tf}$, the PNA will be in the web [Fig. 8.20(b)]. In this case, the entire top flange and a portion of the web are subjected to the yield point. Thus, referring to Fig. 8.20(b),

$$C' = \text{compression force in top flange} + \text{compression force in web}$$
$$= (AF_y)_{tf} + (AF_y)_w \qquad (8.76)$$
$$= (AF_y)_{tf} + [(y - t_f)tF_y]_w$$

Equation 8.76 can be simplified as follows to determine y, the depth of the PNA below the top of the flange of the steel beam (AASHTO Eq. 10.128):

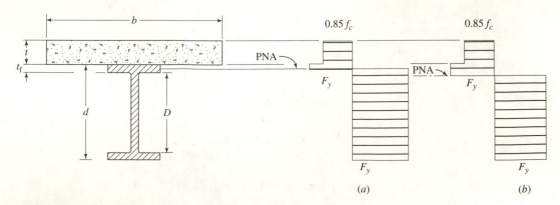

FIGURE 8.20
Determination of the depth of the steel portion of a composite section in compression under plastic stress distribution condition: (a) PNA in the flange; (b) PNA in the web.

$$\overline{y} = \frac{C' - (AF_y)_{tf} + t_f(tF_y)_w}{(tF_y)_w}$$

$$= t_f + \frac{C' - (AF_y)_{tf}}{(tF_y)_w}$$

$$= t_f + \left[\frac{C' - (AF_y)_{tf}}{D(tF_y)_w}\right]D$$

$$= t_f + \left[\frac{C' - (AF_y)_{tf}}{(AF_y)_w}\right]D \tag{8.77}$$

Moment capacity of compact composite section in the negative-moment region of a beam. In a continuous composite beam, a portion of the beam adjacent to the interior support is under negative moment, and the bottom flange of the steel section is in compression and remains unbraced. Such sections qualify as compact sections when their steel sections meet the compactness requirements of AASHTO 10.48.1.1, and when the stress–strain diagram of steel exhibits a yield plateau followed by a strain-hardening range (AASHTO 10.50.2.1).

The ultimate strength of continuous composite beams has been reported by Kubo and Galombos [1988], Hamada and Longworth [1976], Garcia and Daniels [1971], Johnson, Dalen, and Kemp [1967], and Daniels and Fisher [1967]. Because in the negative-moment region of the beam the concrete in the entire slab is in tension, the contribution of the slab is neglected altogether. However, the *longitudinal* reinforcement (which is assumed to have yielded) present in the slab is assumed to act compositely with the steel beam. The tensile force in this longitudinal reinforcement causes the PNA to shift toward the top flange (or toward the slab). Figure 8.21 shows a cross section of a composite steel beam in the negative-moment region of the beam. The PNA is assumed to be located at a distance of D_{cp} from the inside face of the compression (bottom) flange of the beam. The following notations are used in deriving the expression for D_{cp}:

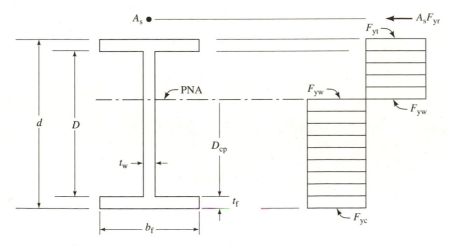

FIGURE 8.21
Composite beam cross section in the negative-moment region of a beam.

A_s = area of longitudinal reinforcing steel in tension, in.^{2}
A = area of steel beam, in.^{2}
A_{ft} = area of flange in tension, in.^{2}
A_{fc} = area of flange in compression, in.^{2}
A_{wt} = area of web in tension, in.^{2}
A_{wc} = area of web in compression, in.^{2}
D = distance between flanges, in.
D_{cp} = distance of PNA from the compression flange, in. (Fig. 8.21)
F_{yr} = specified minimum yield strength of reinforcement, lb/in.^{2}
F_{yt} = specified minimum yield strength of steel in tension, lb/in.^{2}
F_{yc} = specified minimum yield strength of steel in compression, lb/in.^{2}
F_{yw} = specified minimum yield strength of steel in web, lb/in.^{2}

Tensile force in longitudinal reinforcing steel $= A_s F_{yr}$
Tensile force in the top flange $= A_{ft} F_{yt}$
Tensile force in the web $= (D - D_{cp}) t_w F_{yw}$
Total tensile force $= A_s F_{yr} + A_{ft} F_{yt} + D t_w F_{yw} - D_{cp} t_w F_{yw}$

Compression force in flange $= A_{fc} F_{yc}$
Compression force in web $= D_{cp} t_w F_{yw}$
Total compression force $= A_{fc} F_{yc} + D_{cp} t_w F_{yw}$

Equating the total tension force with the total compression force,

$$A_s F_{yr} + A_{ft} F_{yt} + D_{tw} F_{yw} - D_{cp} t_w F_{yw} = A_{fc} F_{yc} + D_{cp} t_w F_{yw}$$

Substituting $t_w = A_w / D$ in the above expression yields

$$D_{cp} = \frac{D}{2 A_w F_{yw}} [A_s F_{yr} + A_{ft} F_{yt} + A_w F_{yw} - A_{fc} F_{yc}] \qquad (8.78)$$

Note that, for a rolled wide-flange steel beam, the minimum yield strengths are the same for flanges and web; i.e., $F_{yc} = F_{yt} = F_{yw} = F_y$, and $A_{ft} = A_{fc}$. Thus, Eq. 8.78 is simplified to

$$D_{cp} = 0.5 D \left[\frac{A_s}{A_w} \frac{F_{yr}}{F_y} + 1 \right] \qquad (8.79)$$

Application of Eq. 8.79 is demonstrated in Example 8.6.

When the steel section of a composite beam does not meet the compactness requirements as specified in AASHTO 10.50.1.1.2, the maximum flexural strength, M_u, of the section is taken as the moment at the first yielding (AASHTO 10.50.1.2.1); i.e., $M = F_y S$.

Examples 8.4 and 8.5 illustrate application of the load factor design principles for noncomposite and composite bridge superstructures. Design examples of load factor design used for continuous bridges are reported in the literature [AISC Mkt.,1987; AISI, 1972; Moon and Maun, 1972; Beezone, 1972; Breen, 1972; Gonulsen and Hsiong,

1972]. Typical details of the design by the load factor method of simple and continuous steel superstructures, both noncomposite and composite, and of various roadway widths and spans, can be found in design handbooks and manuals such as USS (1973). Typical standard plans for steel highway bridges can be found in the catalogs of various design organizations and in the publications of state and federal agencies, such as USDOT [1968] and USDOC [1990].

8.6.2.3 Limitations of the load factor design method

The current LFD provisions of AASHTO specifications [AASHTO, 1992], which are limited to beam and girder bridges, had been adopted in 1979 [Conway, 1989]. Experience and confidence gained through the design and performance of these bridges led to the use of LFD for long-span truss bridges, now covered by AASHTO's *Guide Specifications* [AASHTO, 1986]. The first application of LFD for designing a truss bridge, before any LFD procedure by AASHTO had been worked out for truss bridges, was the Greater New Orleans Bridge No. 2 over the Mississippi in New Orleans, built to carry business route U.S. 90 [ENR, 1978d]. As shown in Fig. 8.22, this three-span cantilever bridge, one of the largest truss bridges ever built, has a roadway width of 94 ft, and it consists of a 1575-ft main span (including a 750-ft suspended span) and unsymmetrical anchor spans of 850 and 590 ft [Conway, 1989]. Designed by the firm of Modjeski and Masters in Harrisburg, Pennsylvania, the construction on this bridge began in August 1980, and the bridge was opened to traffic on September 30, 1988 [Conway, 1989].

Compared to the service load design, application of LFD for the design of this bridge resulted in a savings of some 3000 tons of steel [CE, 1982; ENR, 1984; Conway, 1989]. The load factors used for this truss bridge were different from those permitted for beam girder bridges. Notable are the load factors of 1.5 and 2.0 for dead and live loads, respectively, compared to load factors of 1.3 and 2.17, respectively, for beam girder bridges [Conway, 1989; Modjeski and Masters, 1979; Kulicki, 1982].

Another important aspect of New Orleans Bridge No. 2 was the judicious use of different grades of steel for various structural members—chords, diagonals, hanger posts, bracings—to reduce the dead load and save costs. It was mentioned earlier in this chapter that material selection (i.e., the use of high-strength steel) is one of the most important considerations for achieving cost-effective designs, as this bridge demonstrates [CE, 1982; ENR, 1984]. The following structural steels were used in this project [Conway, 1989]:

ASTM type	Thickness	Minimum F_y (ksi)
A36	4 in. max	36
A588	Up to 4 in.	50
A572 Gr 50	Up to 2 in.	50
A572 Gr 60	Up to $1\frac{1}{4}$ in.	60
A514	Up to $2\frac{1}{2}$ in.	100
A514	Over $2\frac{1}{2}$ to 4 in.	90

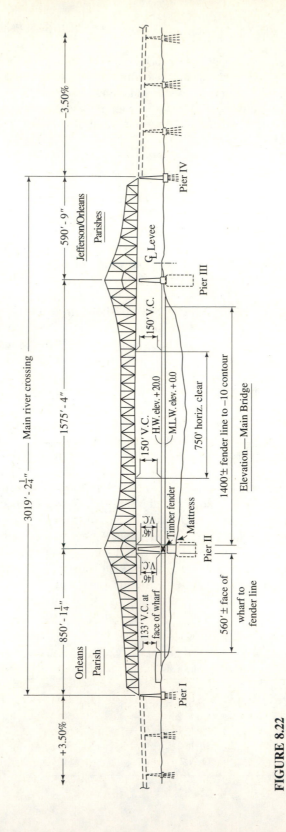

FIGURE 8.22
The Greater New Orleans Bridge No. 2 [Conway, 1989].

772

8.6.3 Alternative Load Factor Design Procedures for Steel Beam Bridges Using Braced Compact Sections

The two design methods discussed in the preceding paragraphs—the service load and the load factor design methods—have one thing in common: the member forces are computed based on the elastic analysis of structures, even though ductile behavior of steel has been known to engineers since the discovery of Hooke's Law in 1676. It was Gabor Kazinczy, a Hungarian researcher, who first experimentally recognized in 1914 that the ductility of steel permitted a redistribution of stresses in overloaded, statically indeterminate structures [Beedle, 1974; McCormac, 1992]. In the United States, *plastic theory* was introduced by A. Van den Broek who called it the *limit design* [Van den Broek, 1939, 1940]. The credit for the first plastic design in North America goes to D. T. Wright, and that for the first plastic design in the United States goes to W. A. Milek [Beedle, 1974]. Methods for plastic design of buildings have been discussed in many references, such as Neal [1950a], Beedle [1958], and ASCE–WRC [1971], and in many texts on the design of steel structures. However, all this development and the many advantages notwithstanding, plastic design philosophy has failed to gain widespread acceptance by the design profession.

Although the design methods for the plastic design of multistory frames were issued in 1965 [Beedle, 1974] and the required design specifications were formed [AISC, 1989], no recognized work had been done to apply these principles to the design of bridges until recently. In the United States, application of the principles of plastic design for bridges evolved from Haaijer's 1973 paper [Haaijer, 1973], which suggests that the *shakedown theory* be considered as a practical method of plastic analysis of steel structures subjected to variable, repeated loads.

Shakedown theory was initially developed in Europe in the 1920s. Gruning [1926] was the first to recognize that under variable repeated loads, a structure may fail due to a lack of deflection stability [ASCE–WRC, 1971]. Further extensive studies in this field were reported by Bleich [1932], Melan [1936], and Horne [1954]. The basic shakedown theorems were developed in the 1950s and 1960s [Neal, 1950a,b, 1951; Neal and Symonds, 1950, 1958; Symonds, 1950; Hodge, 1954; Gozum and Haaijer, 1955; Ghani, 1967]. Studies on the behavior of beams under moving loads were made by Davies [1965, 1967], Toridis and Wen [1966], Fukumoto and Yoshida [1969], and Eyre and Galambos [1970]. Eyre and Galambos [1969] have provided the literature survey on the subject.

The term "shakedown" relates to structural behavior under cyclic loading. Under repeated loading, a characteristic of bridges, it is possible for indefinite plastic flow to occur at load levels below the static collapse load [Neal, 1950a,b; Baker, Horne, and Heyman, 1956]. This can take the form of either alternating plasticity or a condition known as incremental collapse. *Alternating plasticity* refers to the state of member stresses when a plastic hinge is worked back and forth so that yield of the member's fibers occurs alternately in tension and compression. *Incremental collapse* refers to a gradual buildup of indefinitely large deformations. This happens when individual plastic hinges rotate at different stages of the variable repeated loading in such a way that if they were all to rotate simultaneously, they would cause a collapse mechanism. The limiting load above which one or the other of these two effects may take place is called the shakedown load. The *shakedown load* of a structure may lie anywhere between the yield load and the collapse load, and it can be considered to be the true failure load of the structure [Davies, 1967; ASCE–WRC, 1971].

Referring to incremental collapse, the failure is characterized by an increase in deflection during each cycle of loading, where the increments of deflection are in the same direction. After a few cycles of application of certain magnitudes of loads, the deflection has been found to "stabilize." When a structure reaches this state of stabilized deflection, it is said to have *shaken down,* and the corresponding set of loads is referred to as the *stabilizing load* or the *shakedown load.* The structure henceforth responds to this load elastically [ASCE–WRC, 1971].

Research in the past fifteen years by Haaijer, Carskadden, Grubb, and Schilling, carried out under the auspices of the American Iron and Steel Institute (Projects 51, 188, and 330), has shown that plastic design methods can be used to establish the strength of continuous prismatic compact beams, and these methods can be used for *maximum load* calculations [Haaijer, 1973, 1985; Carskadden, 1976, 1980; Grubb and Carskadden, 1979, 1981; Haaijer, Carskadden, and Grub, 1987; Schilling, 1989]. Recognizing that plastic redistribution takes place in continuous beams with braced compact sections, AASHTO, in 1985, approved the use of *Guide Specifications for Alternate Load Factor Design Procedures for Steel Beam Bridges Using Braced Compact Sections* [AASHTO, 1991]. Thus came a new method of inelastic analysis and design of bridges variously known as the *unified autostress method* (UAM), or *autostress design* (ASD), or *autostress load factor design* (ALF) method, which can be used for checking AASHTO *overload* and maximum loads. The autostress design method is incorporated in the new AASHTO–LRFD specifications, 6.10.11, "Inelastic Analysis Procedures" [AASHTO, 1994a]. Because the present research on plastic design has been limited to materials not exceeding $F_y = 50$ ksi, the ASD procedures are limited to materials that have an F_y of 50 ksi or less [AASHTO, 1991, 10.50A(1)]. For simple-span beams, the ASD and LFD methods may be viewed as identical.

The AASHTO–LRFD specifications permit two inelastic analytical methods: the *mechanism method* [ASCE–WRC, 1971] and the *unified autostress method* [Schilling, 1991]. A fundamental premise of plastic analysis is that when certain sections of a compact continuous steel beam reach their capacity consistent with uniform plastic stress distribution throughout the cross section (i.e., when $M_p = F_y Z$), the beam is said to have formed hinges at these locations, and it behaves as if it were loaded by constant moments, M_p, at these locations. When a sufficient number of hinges have formed, the beam behaves as a mechanism, loaded by plastic moments, M_p, at those locations. Because these moments form automatically as a result of plastic stress distribution in the beam's cross sections, rather than through external moments (such as in a prestressed beam), the design method using this concept is referred to as autostress design.

Haaijer, Carskadden, Grubb, and Schilling provide comprehensive discussions on the ASD Method [Haaijer, 1973; Haaijer, Carskadden, and Grubb, 1983, 1987; Schilling, 1991; Haaijer, Schilling, and Carskadden, 1979; Haaijer and Carskadden, 1980]. The ASD method simply extends the plastic design concept of mechanism formation permitted by LFD for simple-span bridges (AASHTO 10.48.1) to continuous bridges; thus, ASD is a logical extension of LFD permitted for simple spans to continuous spans. The ASD method recognizes the ability of continuous steel members to adjust automatically for the effects of local yielding caused by overload, as shown in Fig. 8.23. That is, after undergoing some permanent deflection at the support and several cycles of loading, the structure begins to behave elastically again as the loads are distributed to the other parts of the beam. This phenomenon is also referred to as *shakedown*. The deflections caused by the automoments are treated as dead-load deflections and negated by properly cambering the beam. The permanent deflections caused by positive bending are kept within the permitted limits by applying the limit state criteria of the LFD method (AASHTO 10.57).

The three load levels and the performance requirements considered in LFD (Table 8.8) are also considered in ASD. An additional performance requirement is imposed in ASD—to control cracking of concrete and to keep crack widths within acceptable limits at overloads. This requires the reinforcing bars to remain elastic under the overload condition. Because the ASD method is presently permitted only for steel yield strengths not exceeding 50 ksi, the elastic condition of reinforcing bars can be maintained by specifying 60-ksi bars. The necessary distribution of reinforcing bars for crack control was discussed in Chapter 6. The structural requirements in ASD, however, are based on the actual elastic–plastic behavior of steel beams; thus these requirements differ from those used in LFD.

According to plastic theory, a plastic hinge forms first at the location of the maximum moment. In a continuous beam, when the (negative) moments at interior supports are larger than the (positive) moments at the midspan, hinges first form at the supports. However, formation of hinges only at the interior supports is not sufficient to transform a beam into a mechanism because three hinges must be present in a beam to form a mechanism. Thus, an additional hinge is required somewhere between the supports of a beam. Together with the true hinges at the end supports, this additional hinge transforms the beam into a mechanism, rendering the beam incapable of taking

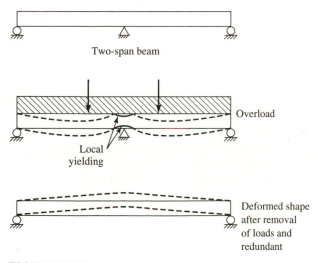

FIGURE 8.23
Plastic deformation in a two-span continuous beam in the negative-moment region over the support [Haaijer, 1985].

any additional loading. Likewise, the ASD method permits formation of hinges at the interior supports of a continuous beam. The ultimate load condition is assumed to have been reached when the maximum moment in each span reaches the plastic moment capacity, M_p, of the beam.

This represents the major difference between the ASD and the LFD approaches. The LFD method, which is based on *elastic analysis* principles, limits the load capacity of a beam to its plastic moment capacity, M_p, consistent with the maximum negative moment at the support. The ASD method, on the other hand, is based on *plastic analysis* principles, and the load capacity of the beam is based on the maximum negative moment at the support and the maximum positive moment near the midspan, both of which are consistent with the plastic moment capacity of the beam, M_p. In general, the ASD method results in a load-carrying capacity of a steel bridge that is considerably higher than that given by the LFD method. Typically, for a two-span, continuous, compact rolled beam bridge, the strength given by the ASD method is about 31 percent higher than that given by the LFD method [Schilling, 1985].

8.6.3.1 Mechanism strength

The ASD method uses the principle of plastic design to compute the resistance of a beam at the maximum load by the mechanism method, which requires the formation of a sufficient number of hinges in a span. The compactness requirements for a steel beam section capable of hinge formation were discussed in an earlier section. Sections with slenderness ratios of the flanges and web that are well below these requirements are termed *ultracompact* [AASHTO, 1991]. Slenderness requirements for ultracompact sections are based on the limitations imposed by the AISC specifications [AISC, 1989, Ch. N] for plastic design of beams and frames. "Ultracompact sections have sufficient inelastic rotation capacity at rotating hinges to allow a plastic mechanism analysis using the plastic moment, M_P, at the rotating hinges" [AASHTO, 1991]. The requirements for width–thickness ratios for ultracompact sections subject to plastic bending, according to AISC [1989], are as follows [Haaijer, Carskadden, and Grubb, 1987]:

Compression flange. For a flange of width b_f and having $F_y = 50$ ksi,

$$\frac{b_f}{2t_f} = 7\sqrt{\frac{50}{F_{yf}}} = \frac{49.5}{\sqrt{F_{yf}}} \tag{8.80}$$

where F_{yf} is the yield strength of the compression flange in ksi units. If F_{yf} is expressed in psi units, Eq. 8.80 can be expressed as

$$\frac{b'}{t} \leq \frac{(49.5)\sqrt{1000}}{\sqrt{F_{yf}}} = \frac{1565}{\sqrt{F_{yf}}} \tag{8.81}$$

As suggested by Haaijer, Carskadden, and Grubb [1987], rather than limit the maximum value of the flange slenderness according to the specified minimum yield point (as in the above expression), an effective yield point of the flange material, F_{yfe}, is defined by rewriting Eq. 8.81:

$$F_{yfe} = (1565)^2 \left(\frac{t}{b'}\right)^2 \leq F_{yf}$$

$$= (1565)^2 \left(\frac{E}{29,000,000}\right)\left(\frac{t}{b''}\right) \leq F_{fy} \tag{8.82}$$

$$= 0.0845E\left(\frac{t}{b'}\right) \leq F_{fy}$$

Note that the right side of Eq. 8.82 is now a function of the modulus of elasticity, E, but it is no longer a function of the material yield strength, F_y, and thus Eq. 8.82 can also be used for hybrid sections.

Web. Using AISCS Eq. N7.1,

$$\frac{d}{t} = \frac{412}{\sqrt{F_y}}\left(1 - 1.4\frac{P}{P_y}\right) \qquad \text{when } \frac{P}{P_y} \leq 0.27 \tag{8.83}$$

For a case of pure bending, $P = 0$, note that the depth, D, between the flanges is approximately equal to 95 percent of the total section depth, d (i.e., $D \approx 0.95d$). Thus, Eq. 8.83, with the minimum specified yield point of the web, F_{yw}, expressed in psi units, becomes

$$\frac{D}{t} \leq \frac{0.95d}{t} = \frac{0.95 \times 412 \times \sqrt{1000}}{\sqrt{F_{yw}}} = \frac{12,377}{\sqrt{F_{yw}}} \tag{8.84}$$

However, because the plastic web buckling is governed by the flange strain [AASHTO, 1991], the value of F_{yw} is limited to F_{yf}, and Eq. 8.84 is written as

$$\frac{D}{t_w} \leq \frac{0.95d}{t_w} = \frac{0.95 \times 412 \times \sqrt{1000}}{\sqrt{F_{yf}}} = \frac{12,377}{\sqrt{F_{yf}}} \tag{8.85}$$

According to the AASHTO guide specifications [AASHTO, 1991], when the distance from the neutral axis to the compression flange exceeds $D/2$, the web compactness requirements are modified by replacing D with the quantity $2D_{cp}$ in Eq. 8.85. Thus,

$$\frac{2D_{cp}}{t_w} = \frac{12,377}{\sqrt{F_{yf}}} \tag{8.86}$$

The value of the effective yield point of the web, F_{ywe}, is defined by rewriting Eq. 8.86 as follows:

$$F_{ywe} = (12,377)^2 \left(\frac{t_w}{2D_{cp}}\right)^2 \leq F_{yf}$$

$$= (12,377)^2 \left(\frac{E}{29 \times 10^6}\right)\left(\frac{t_w}{2D_{cp}}\right)^2 \leq F_{yf} \tag{8.87}$$

$$= 1.32E\left(\frac{t_w}{D_{cp}}\right)^2 \leq F_{yf}$$

Both of the above requirements are covered in the new Article 10.50A in AASHTO [1991].

If one or both of the ultracompact requirements are exceeded, the corresponding effective yield strength will be less than the yield strength of the compression flange; the effective plastic moment, M_{pe}, rather than the full plastic moment, M_p ($M_{pe} < M_p$), is used for the strength analysis at maximum loads. The procedure for computing effective plastic moment has been presented by Carskadden, Haaijer, and Grubb [1978], and Haaijer, Carskadden, and Grubb [1987, Appendix C]. The concept of the effective plastic moment, M_{pe}, is not covered in AASHTO 1992 or 1994b, but it is covered in AASHTO 1991, where it is defined as [AASHTO, 1991, Eq. 10.128a]

$$M_{pe} = R_f M_{pf} + R_w M_{pw} \tag{8.88}$$

where M_{pf} = flange component of plastic moment, including composite rebars
M_{pw} = web component of plastic moment
R_f = reduction factor for flange component = F_{yfe}/F_{yf}
R_w = reduction factor for web component = F_{ywe}/F_{yf}

Note that both F_{yfe} and F_{ywe} are limited to F_{yf} because the plastic flange and web buckling are controlled by flange strain. A discussion on effective plastic moment is provided by Carskadden, Haaijer, and Grubb [1978]. This and many other aspects of the development of the ASD method are discussed in the literature [Haaijer, 1985; Haaijer, Carskadden, and Grubb, 1980, 1987; Schilling, 1991]. As stated earlier, the autostress method is based on the classical shakedown theory, which indicates that, in a continuous span, small permanent (plastic) deformations that occur at the supports eventually stabilize after a few cycles of loading, and the structure begins to behave elastically again. This occurs because these plastic deformations occur only in the flange outer fibers, and they do not form a plastic hinge. That is, the moment in the negative-moment region reaches past M_y, the moment at first yield ($F_y S_x$), but it is less than M_p, the plastic moment capacity of the beam ($F_y Z$).

The ASD method can be considered an extension of the 10-percent redistribution (AASHTO 10.48.1.3) allowed in the LFD method. Various advantages of this method are reported in the literature [Haaijer, 1985; Schilling, 1985, 1991; Loveall, 1987]:

- Because the moment capacity (M_p) requirements are the same at both the interior support and near the midspan, the same beam cross section can be used for negative moments at the interior supports and for positive moments in the midspan region of a beam. This is a major advantage of ASD; it permits elimination of cover plates from the negative-moment region of a continuous span, resulting in savings in material and fabrication costs.
- Eliminating cover plates means also eliminating the terminal details, which have poor fatigue strengths. Terminal details have been the source of fatigue problems in older bridges and of additional costs in newer bridges.
- ASD will result in fewer splices and thinner flange plates when it is applied to welded sections.

Roeder and Eltvik [1985a,b] describe the load tests conducted in 1982 by the University of Washington on the three-span (50, 80, and 50 ft), continuous, composite, single-lane Whitechuck River Bridge in the Mount Baker, Snoqualmie National

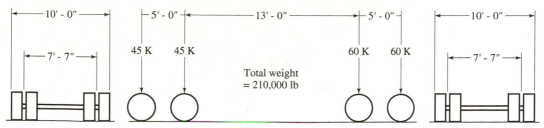

Skagit BU-99 yarder and T-110 tower

FIGURE 8.24
Overload vehicle used in designing the Whitechuck River Bridge [Haaijer, Carskadden, and Grubb, 1987].

Forest near Darrington, Washington, the first bridge ever designed by ASD. Details of the overload vehicle used for designing this bridge are shown in Fig. 8.24; the bridge and its cross section are shown in Fig. 8.25 [Haaijer, Carskadden, and Grubb, 1987]. The bridge is reported to have performed as predicted, without any signs of distress during or after the tests.

8.6.3.2 Design of shear connectors

To ensure serviceability and durability, AASHTO specifications recommend design of shear connectors based on the fatigue under service load conditions. Therefore, the procedure in ASD for designing shear connectors remains identical to that explained earlier in the context of service load design method. This procedure is illustrated in Example 8.3.

Recognizing the advantages and cost savings of autostress design, bridge design engineers across the United States have taken note of ASD. Presently, ASD applies only to rolled beam bridges and is used only in a very few states. One example of ASD is an 872-ft-long, eight-span (one 100, six 112, and one 100 ft) continuous bridge designed in 1987 by the Tennessee Department of Transportation. W36 × 170 sections of AASHTO M270 grade 50 steel were used for the superstructure of this bridge, with no cover plates in the negative-moment regions over the piers [Loveall, 1987]. Also in Tennessee, a four-span (101, 128, 128, and 101 ft) continuous bridge that carries Route 42 over the Wolf River was completed and opened to traffic in June 1989. The 44-ft-wide superstructure of this bridge consists of six W36 × 194 sections of AASHTO M270 grade 50 (ASTM A790 grade 50) steel. The use of autostress procedure permitted elimination of cover plates in the negative-moment region over the piers. This final design was the most cost-effective, outbidding three alternative designs: a precast prestressed concrete bridge, a welded plate girder bridge designed by LFD, and a cover-plated rolled beam bridge design by LFD [AISC, 1991].

Research continues on both rolled beam and plate girder bridges [Schilling, 1985; Wasserman, 1987] so that ASD can be extended to the design of plate girder bridges. Example 8.6 applies this method for designing a two-span highway bridge using rolled steel sections.

(a)

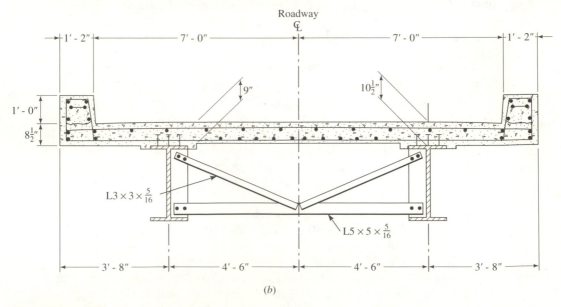

(b)

FIGURE 8.25

(a) The three-span continuous composite Whitechuck River Bridge in Mount Baker, Snoqualmie National Forest, Washington (Courtesy: AISC, 1984). (b) Cross section of the bridge [Haaijer, Carskadden, and Grubb, 1987].

8.7
DESIGN OF CONTINUOUS STEEL BEAM BRIDGES

8.7.1 Economic Considerations

The preceding paragraphs focused on simple-span noncomposite and composite steel beam bridges, which have been built in the span range of 40 to 110 ft. When general beam spacing guides can be followed, these bridges can be built economically with rolled wide-flange beams in the span range of 80 to 90 ft. For longer spans, instead of building several single-span structures, continuity in beams should be considered as an economical alternative. A discussion on the advantages and disadvantages of continuous bridges was presented in Chapter 7. A discussion on economic considerations for slab–steel beam bridges can be found in several references [Knight, 1984; Schilling, 1985; AISC Mkt., 1987].

A continuous beam bridge can be noncomposite, composite, or a combination of both. For example, some of the shorter spans of a continuous span can be noncomposite, while the longer spans are composite. This is so because the added cost of shear connectors for the composite span may be greater than the material savings of the shorter spans. Of course, a noncomposite span would require a heavier beam than a composite or a continuous span. Figure 8.26 shows the steel weight–span relationship for continuous noncomposite and composite steel superstructures.

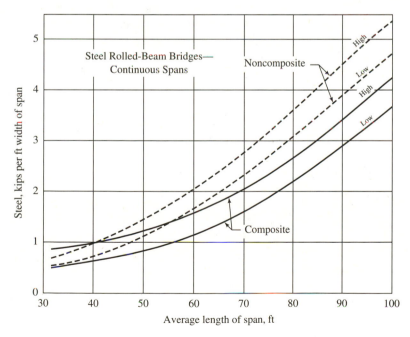

FIGURE 8.26
Steel weight–span relationships for continuous rolled steel beam bridges [USDOC, 1990].

In a continuous beam arrangement, initial savings result primarily from the elimination of bearings and expansion joints. For example, two simple spans would require four bearings, whereas a two-span continuous beam would require only three. As the number of spans increases, the influence of continuity on the economics of construction is even greater. For example, three simple spans would require six bearings, whereas three continuous spans would require only four, and so on. Joints and bearings are costly to buy and install, and any reduction in their numbers results in potential savings.

Elimination of joints, a result of providing continuity, also significantly reduces the life-cycle costs of a bridge. It is customary to provide expansion joints in the deck, at abutments, and at other locations in the deck as needed, to permit longitudinal movements due to deflections and temperature changes (AASHTO 10.30.4). Assuming the coefficient of expansion of steel is 6.5×10^{-6} in./in./°F, a temperature change of 100°F would cause a deck movement of 0.78 in. per 100 ft of span ($6.5 \times 10^{-6} \times 100 \times 100 \times 12$). The temperature range for which provision should be made for expansion and contraction of a bridge superstructure depends on many variables, such as the geographical location and the type of the bridge superstructure. This range is determined by jurisdictional authorities. For example, the Tennessee Department of Transportation uses a temperature range of 120 °F (i.e., 0–120°F) for steel beam superstructures, and a range of 70°F (i.e., 20°–90°F) for concrete superstructures. Based on these specifications, in a 400-ft continuous steel beam bridge, provision must be made for a total movement of 3.74 in. [Wasserman, 1987].

A variety of expansion joints are used in practice, several of which are shown in Fig. 8.27 [NCHRP, 1989; CONC, 1994]. All of these joints have one thing in common: none of them is perfect. Experience has shown that the most frequently encountered corrosion problems in steel beam bridges originate from leaking expansion joints and seals. Leaky joints permit thawing snow and ice mixed with deicing chemicals from the roadway surface to leak and flow down to the flanges and webs of the steel girders, to the bearings, and to the pier caps below [NCHRP, 1989; Brinckerhoff, 1989]. In the course of time, these joints become clogged with accumulated debris, and thus they become inoperative. Based on reports [Lee and Sarsam, 1972] of successful performance of many older highway bridges either constructed without joints or performing with inoperative joints, several states have elected to design and build short and moderate bridges without joints. In 1980, the FHWA recommended that bridges with overall lengths less than those listed in the following table be constructed as continuous and, if unrestrained, have integral abutments. It also recommended that greater span lengths be used, if experience indicated such designs to be satisfactory [FHWA, 1980b]:

Bridge Type	Maximum length for which continuous design is recommended with integral abutments (ft)
Steel	300
Cast-in-place concrete	500
Pre- or post-tensioned concrete	600

As a result, the practice of building *jointless bridges,* also referred to as *integral abutment structures* (Fig. 8.28) [Schilling, 1985; Wasserman, 1987], is becoming

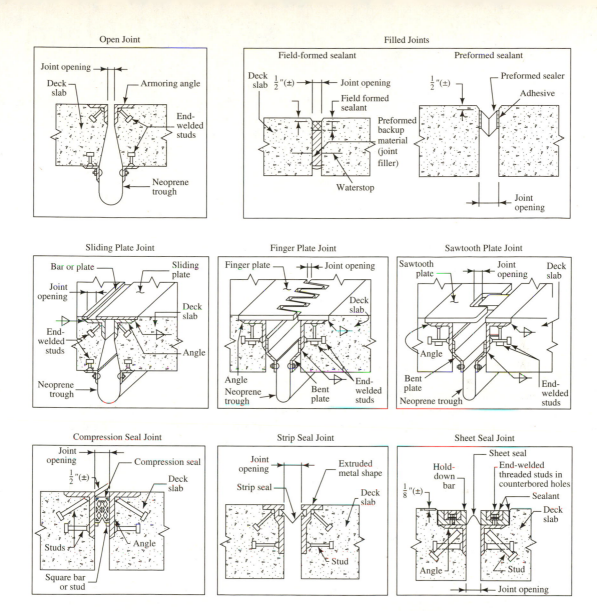

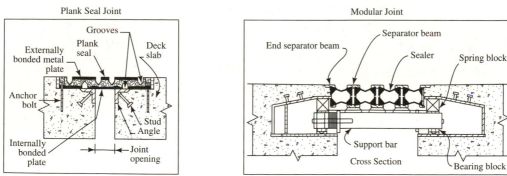

FIGURE 8.27
Various kinds of expansion joints [NCHRP, 1989].

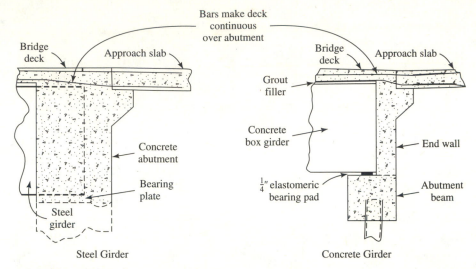

FIGURE 8.28
Integral abutments [Wasserman, 1987].

widespread. Many states—California, Colorado, Idaho, Iowa, Kansas, Missouri, Ne-braska, North Dakota, Ohio, Pennsylvania, South Dakota, Tennessee, Virginia, and Wisconsin—have used jointless bridges [Schilling, 1985]. In Ohio, jointless bridges are built up to 300 ft in overall length, and in Tennessee, bridges have been built as long as 400 ft with no joints, even at the abutments [Wasserman, 1987; Montgomery, Gorman, and Alpago, 1992]. The Tennessee Department of Transportation, the leader in the field, has built bridges up to 2000 ft long with joints only at the abutments; it does not use expansion joints unless they are deemed absolutely necessary [Loveall, 1985; Montgomery, Gorman, and Alpago, 1992; TennDOT, 1986; Mistry, 1994]. A twelve-span continuous prestressed concrete bridge with a total length of 1635 ft 9 in. between the centers of bearings was built over the North Branch Susquehanna River in Pennsyl-vania in 1992. This bridge, known as the Mifflinville River Bridge, has an 8-in.-thick slab and a 40-ft width between the curbs, and has joints at abutments only. However, integral abutment designs are not recommended for bridges with skews exceeding 30° because of serviceability problems with such bridges in the past.

An important consideration in a continuous-beam design is to minimize the number of splices by procuring the maximum available beam lengths, usually in the range of 100 to 120 ft. However, girder lengths should be limited to 120 ft for easy and cost-effective transportability and handling [AISC, 1992].

Greater overload capacity is another significant advantage offered by a continu-ous bridge girder. Failure does not necessarily occur if overloads cause yielding at one point in a span or at supports, for the presence of continuity enables moments to be redistributed to other parts of the girder that are not overstressed.

Lesser weight, greater stiffness, smaller deflection, and low depth–span ratios are some additional advantages offered by continuous-span bridges. But all these advan-tages notwithstanding, there are some shortcomings. These include complex fabrication and erection procedures and additional field splices, all of which increase costs.

8.7.2 Analytical and Design Considerations

For the sake of economy, composite construction should generally be considered for continuous spans greater than 65 ft. Composite construction can be used throughout the span or only in the positive-moment areas; the costs in both cases are about the same [AISC Mkt., 1987].

The design of a girder segment in the positive-moment region is similar to that of a simple-span composite girder, but design in the negative-moment region differs from the simple-span composite design in many respects. The major difference occurs in the cross-sectional properties of the beam in the positive- and negative-moment regions. In the positive-moment region, the deck slab is in compression and, with its effective width, forms a part of the top flange of the composite beam cross section, where it participates in resisting moments imposed by the superimposed dead load and the live load. But in the negative-moment region, the same slab is in tension. Because of concrete's inability to resist any tension, the slab is assumed not to participate in resisting any moments, and its presence is ignored in computing section properties of the composite beam, except that the *longitudinal* steel reinforcement (parallel to the stringer) must be added to the slab to resist tension in the concrete caused by composite action. AASHTO 10.38.4.3 specifies a minimum longitudinal reinforcement, including the longitudinal distribution reinforcement, of not less than 1 percent of the cross-sectional area of the concrete slab.

In both simple and continuous beams, the maximum moments and shears at critical points must be known in order to determine the cutoff points for reinforcing bars in reinforced concrete beams and the lengths of cover plates in steel beams. The presence of moving loads renders analysis of a continuous structure more difficult than that of a simple structure. The maximum moment due to live load at any section in a simple span is always positive. But in a continuous beam, the maximum live-load moment at a section, depending on the number of spans and the position of the live load, may be positive or negative, causing stress reversal. As a result, designing for fatigue becomes an important consideration in the design of a continuous beam. Also, continuous-beam design is governed by maximum positive-moment in the midspan region and by the maximum negative moment in the support region. The sum of dead-load and live-load moments is usually greater at the support than at the midspan.

Whereas in a simple span the maximum dead-load moment occurs at midspan and is always positive, the maximum moment in a continuous beam may occur at the support and is always negative. In general, the negative moment decreases rapidly with distance from the support, the inflection point being near the quarter point of the span from the support. For the common two- or three-span continuous beams, dead-load moments can be conveniently computed by elastic analysis methods such as the three-moment equation or the moment distribution method. Figure 8.29 shows shear and moment diagrams for a two-span continuous beam, where spans are the same length, with constant moment of inertia. For this beam, moments (M_x) and shears (V_x) at a distance x from the left support due to uniform dead loads may be computed from Eqs. 8.89 and 8.90:

$$M_x = \left(\frac{3wL}{8}\right)x - \frac{wx^2}{2} \tag{8.89}$$

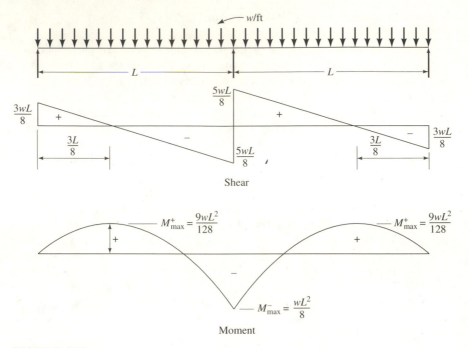

FIGURE 8.29
Shear and moment diagrams, due to dead load, for a two-span continuous beam.

$$V_x = \frac{3wL}{8} - wx \qquad (8.90)$$

where w = uniform load on the beam
$\frac{3}{8}wL$ = reaction at the end support

Unfortunately, computation of maximum moment and shear at a given point in a continuous beam due to live load is not simple and straightforward; it depends on many variables, such as the total number of spans, the lengths of spans, the position of wheel loads on the span (or spans), the type of loading (truck or lane loading), and whether maximum positive or maximum negative moment (or shear) is the quantity of interest. For example, maximum positive moment in a span under about 110 ft is governed by the truck loading, whereas for longer spans, it is governed by lane loading. On the other hand, maximum negative moment is governed by lane loading, except for spans less than about 45 ft, in which case it may be governed by truck loading.

Careful consideration should be given to the type of loading—truck or lane loading—and the manner of loading—i.e., only one span loaded, or more than one span loaded, depending on the number of spans in a structure—that will cause maximum positive or negative live-load moment at a given section of the girder. Accordingly, the placement of live load on continuous spans is governed by AASHTO specifications [AASHTO, 1992] as follows:

1. Article 3.11.4 requires that, on both simple and continuous spans, the type of loading used—truck or lane—should be such that it produces maximum stress. For contin-

uous spans, the standard lane load, including impact, rather than the standard truck loading, governs critical negative moment at the support.

2. Article 3.11.4.2 requires that, for the design of continuous spans, the lane loading may be continuous or discontinuous (as necessary) to cause maximum live-load moment. However, if truck loading is used to determine the maximum live-load moment, only one standard H or HS truck per lane is permitted to be loaded on any one span.

3. Article 3.11.3 requires that, in the design of continuous spans, for determination of maximum negative moment due to lane load, a second equal-weight concentrated load (e.g., an 18-kip load for an HS20 lane loading) should be placed in one other span in series in such a position as to produce the maximum effect. These positions are defined, for both spans, by the locations where the ordinates of influence line for the negative moment are the greatest. For maximum positive moment, however, only one concentrated load per lane is permitted, combined with as many spans loaded uniformly as are required to produce maximum moment.

A good discussion on maximum positive and negative moments and shears in continuous beams is provided by Elliot [1990]. When maximum positive or negative moments are governed by truck loading, the relative positions of wheel loads with respect to the section (i.e., with smaller loads to the left or the right of the section) should be carefully considered. In general, in a continuous beam, where the end span length varies from 75 to 100 percent of that of the adjacent span, the maximum positive moment occurs at a point between $0.35L$ and $0.45L$ from the nearest discontinuous end; for practical purposes, this distance may be considered as $0.4L$. Though not always true, the maximum moment due to two or more moving-point loads (wheel loads) generally occurs when the heaviest load is at the section. Thus, the maximum positive moment in the end span may be determined by placing the heavy wheel load at $0.4L$ from the discontinuous end. Uncertainty regarding the proper position of wheel loads (i.e., the 4-kip load positioned to the left of the $0.4L$ point or to its right) can be avoided by placing the 4-kip load over the smaller influence-line ordinate, as illustrated in Example 8.6.

For maximum negative moment in a span, the relative position of the truck's wheel loads (i.e., a truck moving from left to right, or from right to left) depends on which span is under consideration, e.g., the end or the interior span. Such positions can be determined from influence lines. A reasonably acceptable value of maximum negative moment in a span can be determined by loading the span adjacent to the one under consideration, placing the centroid of the heavy wheels at $0.4L$ from the common support. For example, for maximum negative moment in span 1, wheel loads should be placed as shown in Fig. 8.30(a), whereas for maximum negative moment in span 2, wheel loads should be placed as shown in Fig. 8.30(b) [Elliot, 1990].

The total maximum moment and shear at a point is obtained by summing up the effects of dead load and live load. For computing maximum moments and shears due to live load at various sections of a continuous beam, a good working knowledge of influence lines for maximum moments and shears at various points in a beam, both simple and continuous, is required. A good discussion on influence lines for continuous beams is provided by Kinney [1957].

It is common practice to compute maximum moment and shear values at *tenth points* (i.e., every one-tenth of the span) of a beam and plot them on a graph, resulting

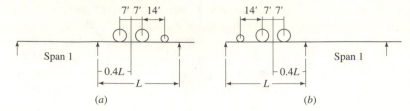

FIGURE 8.30

Approximate maximum negative moment in continuous beams. Position of wheel loads for (*a*) maximum negative moment in span 1, and (*b*) maximum negative moment in span 2.

in composite curves, commonly referred to as *envelopes*, which approximate parabolic shapes. Moment envelopes differ for maximum positive and negative moments in a continuous beam. Methods of determining moment and shear envelopes are presented by Lay [1974] and Elliot [1990].

Maximum values of shear at various points on a beam due to live load are also obtained from influence lines. Maximum shear at a point on a beam, simple or continuous, may be caused by truck or lane loading. The span lengths in Table 8.10 may be used as approximate limits up to which the maximum shear is produced by HS20 truck loading; for longer spans, the lane loading governs [Elliot, 1990].

The total maximum shears at various points on a beam are obtained by adding shears due to dead and live loads; from these shear values at various points, shear envelopes can be drawn.

Determination of ordinates for moment and shear envelopes is a tedious task that can be expedited by design aids (charts and tables) described in the next section. Computations for moment and shear envelopes for a two-span (two 100 ft) continuous beam are illustrated in Example 8.6.

The impact factor for a continuous span is computed from the same formula used for the simple spans. However, because one or more spans can be loaded in certain combinations (depending on the number of spans) to produce maximum positive or negative moments, the span length, L, to be used in the formula for impact factor should be chosen as specified in AASHTO 3.8.2.2(e). For positive moment, L is the actual span length that should be loaded to achieve maximum load effects. For negative moments, however, L is taken as the average of the two adjacent loaded spans (Fig. 3.12, Chapter 3).

TABLE 8.10

Approximate maximum span length for which maximum shear is governed by HS20 truck loading

Location for maximum shear	Span length (ft)
Shear and reaction at the end support	140
Shear at left of first interior support	110
Shear at right of first interior support	110
Reaction at the first interior support	58

The distribution factor is computed the same way it is for a simple-span bridge.

Ends of continuous beams usually are simply supported. The maximum positive and negative moments in various spans of a continuous beam depend on the relative lengths of the interior and exterior spans. For composite continuous construction, the minimum span is considered to be about 60 ft, the maximum intermediate span is in the 100-ft range, and a maximum end span is in the 90-ft range [AISC Mkt., 1987]. The span ratios for various spans should be chosen so that the design moments in the adjacent spans are nearly equal. This permits duplication of sections, an important consideration resulting in significant cost savings. The most advantageous ratios for length of interior to exterior spans are approximately 1.33 for interior spans less than about 60 ft, 1.30 for interior spans between 60 to 110 ft, and about 1.25 for longer spans [Elliot, 1990].

8.8
DESIGN AIDS

Except for noncomposite bridges, design calculations for bridges tend to be very time-intensive and mundane. Several trial designs must be made for preliminary designs before a final design is selected. Selecting reinforcing bars for the deck, selecting the proper size (i.e., width and thickness) and length for the cover plate for a partially coverplated composite beam, computing the moment of inertia of the noncomposite and composite section, and computing the moments and shears at tenth points of a simple or a continuous beam (required for moment and shear envelopes) are only some of the design tasks that require tremendous time and effort. Fortunately, for many such tasks, design aids are available for computational efficiency. A few examples of design aids that can be used for the service load design follow. Most design offices use these or other similar design aids for quick preliminary designs that are followed by detailed calculations. Computers, of course, have made design tasks less mundane and more efficient.

Figure 8.31 shows a typical reinforced concrete deck panel and the accompanying bar chart to facilitate quick selection of deck reinforcement [PennDOT, 1970]. Figure 8.32 shows an economy graph for A36 steel W-shaped beams for various spans and beam spacings for composite steel beams. For a given span and beam spacing, a suitable beam size can be selected from this graph for a preliminary design. Alternatively, for a given span and beam size, maximum permissible beam spacing can be determined. Figure 8.33 shows, for various dead loads, a relationship between the span, girder spacing, and cover-plated composite A36-steel beam. Figures 8.32 and 8.33 show graphs for only a few selected W-shapes and steel strength; similar graphs are available for most beam sizes that can be used for highway bridges [PennDot, 1970]. Figure 8.34 shows graphs from which moments of inertia of composite cover-plated W-shaped beams can be read.

Many tables and charts are available for determining ordinates for plotting moment and shear envelopes for continuous beams. For example, references such as Anger [1956], Anger and Tramm [1965], and AISC [1966] provide influence-line coefficients for determining support reactions, moments, and shears at various sections of a continuous beam; use of the tables from AISC [1966] is illustrated in Example 8.6. Elliot

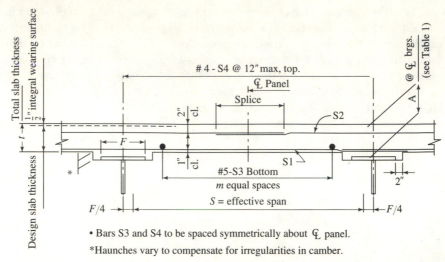

• Bars S3 and S4 to be spaced symmetrically about ₵ panel.

*Haunches vary to compensate for irregularities in camber.

Typical Slab Panel

S	t	Bars S1 and S2	Bars S3	
			m	Spacing
4'-7"	$7\frac{1}{2}''$	#5 @ 8" = 0.47 in.²	3	11"
4'-11"	$7\frac{1}{2}''$	#5 @ $7\frac{1}{2}''$ = 0.50 in.²	4	11"
5'-3"	$7\frac{1}{2}''$	#5 @ 7" = 0.53 in.²	4	10"
5'-5"	$7\frac{1}{2}''$	#5 @ $6\frac{1}{2}''$ = 0.57 in.²	5	9"
5'-7"	$7\frac{1}{2}$	#5 @ 6" = 0.62 in.²	5	9"
5'-10"	8"	#5 @ 7" = 0.53 in.²	5	10"
6'-4"	8"	#5 @ $6\frac{1}{2}''$ = 0.57 in.²	6	9"
6'-7"	8"	#5 @ 6" = 0.62 in.²	7	9"
6'-10"	8"	#5 @ $5\frac{1}{2}''$ = 0.68 in.²	8	8"
7'-0"	$8\frac{1}{2}$	#5 @ $6\frac{1}{2}''$ = 0.57 in.²	7	9"
7'-7"	$8\frac{1}{2}$	#5 @ 6" = 0.62 in.²	8	9"
7'-11"	$8\frac{1}{2}$	#5 @ $5\frac{1}{2}''$ = 0.68 in.²	9	$8\frac{1}{2}''$

Table 1		
Camber	A	
Up to $1\frac{1}{2}''$	$t + \frac{1}{2}''$	
Over $1\frac{1}{2}''$ to 3"	$t + \frac{3}{4}$	
Over 3"	$t + 1''$	

Variation in flange thickness is not included in "A".

"A" shall be modified for a concave (sag) vertical curve.

S = max. normal effective span permitted for given
   reinforcement bars S1 and S2.

Slab Reinforcement

FIGURE 8.31
Bar chart for reinforced concrete deck slab supported over steel stringers [PennDOT, 1970].

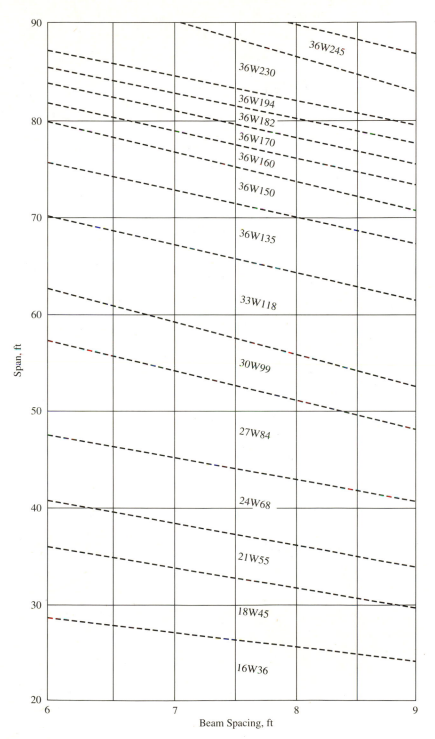

FIGURE 8.32
Economy graph for composite A36-steel W-shaped beams [PennDOT, 1970].

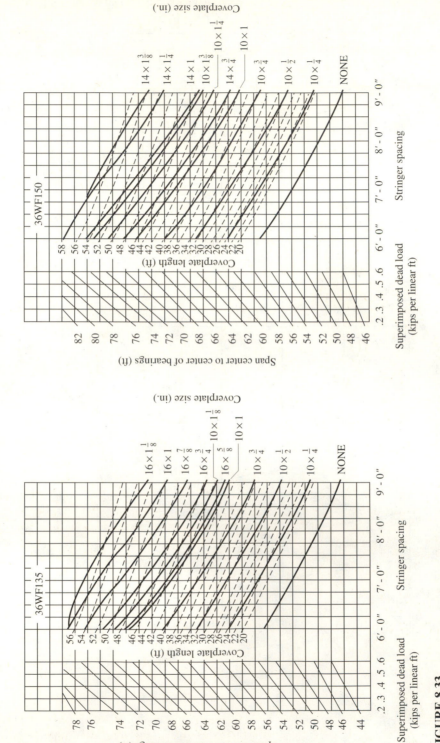

FIGURE 8.33
Span–girder spacing for composite cover-plated beams [PennDOT, 1970].

792

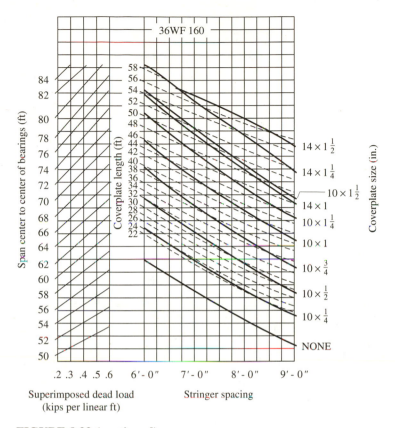

FIGURE 8.33 (continued)

[1990] provides tables for positive and negative moments for various span lengths and provides end conditions from which the ordinates required for moment envelopes can be computed.

Figures 8.35 to 8.37, from CALTRANS [1993], show nondimensional envelopes that can be used for computing maximum moment envelopes for specific types of continuous beams. Fig. 8.35 can be used for a two-span continuous beam (equal spans), Fig. 8.36 for a three-span continuous beam (equal spans), and Fig. 8.37 for maximum positive and negative moments in the interior span of a continuous beam. Many such curves are also available for four- and five-span continuous beams [CALTRANS, 1993].

8.9
DESIGN EXAMPLES

In the remainder of this chapter, six design examples of slab–steel beam superstructure are presented. In each case, pertinent AASHTO specifications are cited throughout the calculations.

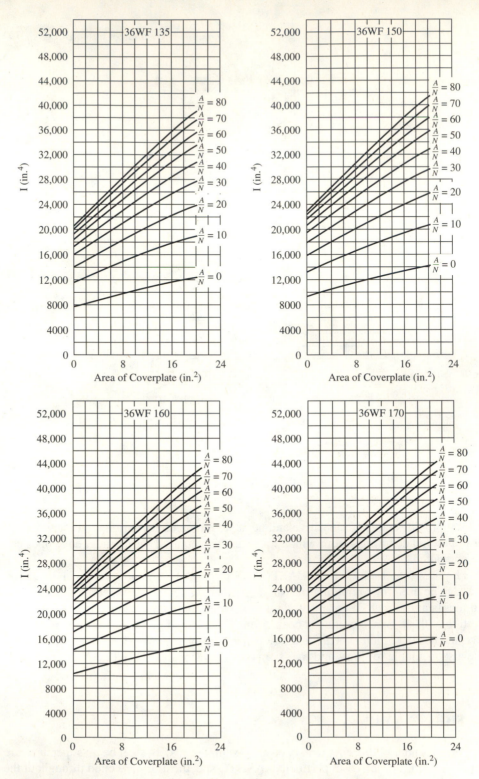

FIGURE 8.34

Moments of inertia for composite cover-plated W-shaped beams [PennDOT, 1970].

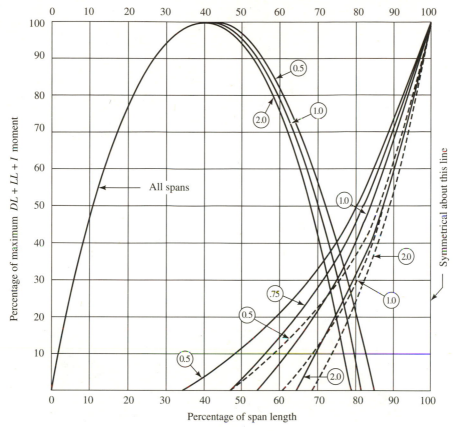

Ratio of $\dfrac{DL \text{ moment}}{LL+I \text{ moment}}$ is shown thus: $\boxed{1.0}$

This chart can be used for a two-span continuous structure in which the ends and center are simply supported. It may be used for a structure in which the center bent is fixed with the girders; however, bar lengths will be slightly longer than required.

Solid lines ———— 50′ spans
Dashed lines – – – – 100′ spans

FIGURE 8.35
Moment envelope for two-span continuous beam with equal spans [CALTRANS, 1993].

Example 8.1 presents the design of a 50-ft-span noncomposite slab–steel beam bridge by the service load design method using A36-steel rolled W-shaped beams. Example 8.2 presents the design of the same bridge in Example 8.1, using high-strength (A572 grade 50) steel instead of A36 steel, resulting in cost savings. Example 8.3 presents the design of a 70-ft-span composite slab–steel beam bridge by the service load method of design. In both Examples 8.1 and 8.3, complete designs of the interior as well as exterior stringers are presented. Section properties of rolled beam sections, and the values of their elastic section modulus used in these examples, are taken from

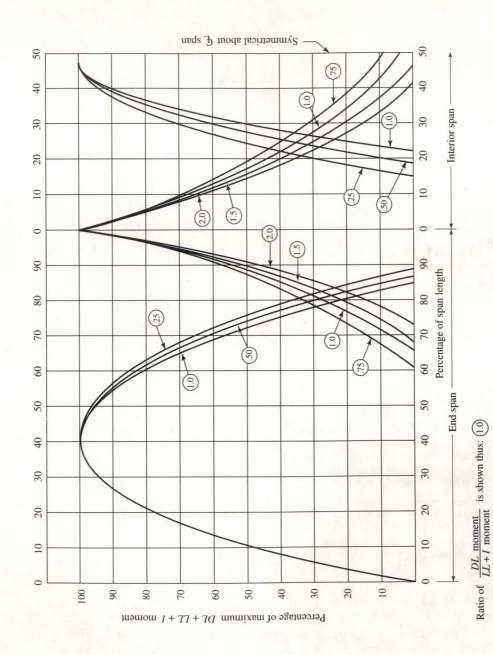

FIGURE 8.36
Moment envelope for three-span continuous beam (equal spans) [CALTRANS, 1993].

Ratio of $\dfrac{DL \text{ moment}}{LL + I \text{ moment}}$ is shown thus: (1.0)

Live load = H20-S16-44

796

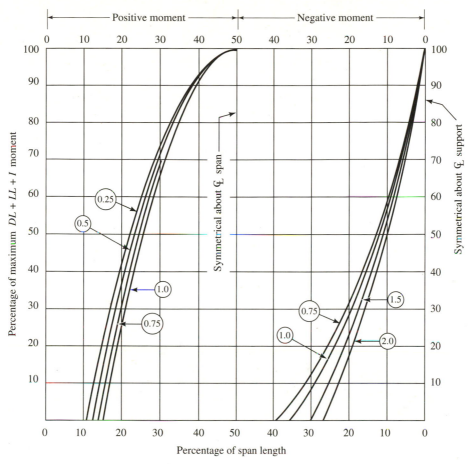

Notes: Use for continuous structures with approximately equal spans, or use adjacent to $\frac{3}{4}$ length simply supported end span.

Ratio of $\dfrac{DL\ \text{moment}}{LL + I\ \text{moment}}$ is shown thus: (1.0)

AASHO 1944, and subsequent revisions

LL H20-S16-44

Use of chart: Calculate max. negative $DL + LL + IM$ at support by conventional methods. Call this total 100%. Find ratio $DLM/(LL + IM)$ using max. M values at support. To find max. neg. M at other points in span, read percentage from proper ratio curve and multiply max. neg. M at support by this percentage. Calculate max. positive $DL + LL + IM$ at $\mathcal{C}$ span, and continue as above, referring all values to $\mathcal{C}$ span.

FIGURE 8.37
Moment envelope for the interior span of a continuous beam [CALTRANS, 1993].

AISC, Part 1, whereas the values of the plastic section modulus, Z, are taken from AISC Part 2 (see "Plastic Design Selection Table") [AISC, 1989].

In Example 8.3, the computations for composite design are rather long and time-intensive. In general, computations for the exterior stringer are similar to those for the interior stringer (both carry different loads). For computational efficiency, however, the various values of forces, stresses, etc., for the exterior stringer have been computed from proportions of those computed for the interior stringer, since the same section has been used for both.

Examples 8.4 and 8.5 present the design of the bridge superstructures of Examples 8.1 and 8.3, respectively, by the load factor design method. Note that, in each example, all computations of the service load method of design are required as a check for the service load behavior. Therefore, only supplementary calculations, which deal with the factored loads, are presented in Examples 8.4 and 8.5.

Example 8.6 presents the design of the interior beam of a two-span continuous bridge by the alternative load factor design (ALFD) procedure known as the autostress design procedure, using braced compact sections. Specifications pertinent to this design procedure are given in AASHTO [1991]. In all examples, wherever welding is involved, weld metal should conform to the *Bridge Welding Code* [ANSI/AASHTO/AWS, 1995] as required by AASHTO 10.2.5.

As explained in Chapters 3, 6, and 7, for concrete decks, it is a general practice to provide for the addition of a bituminous wearing surface—25 to 35 lb/ft² of the deck area—at some future time. Some design organizations provide for an *additional* future wearing surface since the original bituminous material is not always stripped off before the new surface is added. In examples in this book, for illustrative purposes, a wearing surface weighing 25 lb/ft² has been considered as a part of the dead load; however, no provision has been made for the additional dead load for the future wearing surface.

8.9.1 Simple-Span Slab–Steel Beam Bridge Design

EXAMPLE 8.1. DESIGN OF A NONCOMPOSITE SLAB–STRINGER BRIDGE. Make a preliminary design of a two-lane slab–stringer bridge for an effective span of 50 ft to carry an HS20-44 loading. The roadway width is to be 26 ft (two lanes of 13 ft each). Assume $f_c' = 4000$ psi, and use grade 40 reinforcement for the concrete slab and A36 steel for the stringers.

Solution. As a first step, a minimum slab thickness of $7\frac{1}{2}$ in. and stringer spacings of 7 ft center-to-center are selected *arbitrarily*. This results in the superstructure having five stringers. For illustrative purposes, a standard curb-parapet, as discussed in Chapter 3, is provided in this example, although other types could be used at the discretion of the designer. A typical cross section of the bridge is shown in Fig. E8.1a.

Also, the flange width of stringers is assumed to be 12 in. (a convenient number for calculations); this dimension is required to compute the effective span of slab, and it will be verified later.

The design of the superstructure for this bridge involves calculations for three basic components— the slab, stringers, and bearings. The exterior and the interior stringers are designed separately because they carry different dead and live loads. Consequently, the same design quantities must be computed separately for the exterior and the interior stringers.

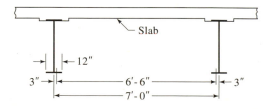

FIGURE E8.1a
Typical cross section of the superstructure in Example 8.1.

The intermediate and end diaphragms will be provided per AASHTO 10.20.1. The design of bearings is not covered in this example.

The design of the slab presented in this example follows the service load method for illustrative purposes, although the load factor method could also have been used. For the latter method of slab design, readers may refer to examples in Chapters 6 and 7.

Design of slab. Compute the effective span, S, per AASHTO 3.24.1.2(b):

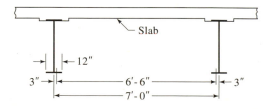

Effective span, S = center-to-center of stringers $- \frac{1}{2} \times$ flange width

$$= 7.0 - \tfrac{1}{2} \times 1 = 6.5 \text{ ft}$$

Self weight of slab $= (7.5/12) \times 0.15 = 0.094 \text{ k/ft}^2$

Weight of wearing surface $= 0.025 \text{ k/ft}^2$

Total dead load $= w = 0.119 \text{ k/ft}^2$

$$M_D = \pm \frac{wS^2}{10}$$

$$= \pm \frac{0.119 \times (6.5)^2}{10}$$

$$= \pm 0.50 \text{ k-ft}$$

Compute live-load moment per AASHTO 3.24.3.1 Case A:

$$M_L = \left(\frac{S + 2}{32}\right) P_{20}$$

$$= \left(\frac{6.5 + 2}{32}\right) \times 16$$

$$= 4.25 \text{ k-ft}$$

For a slab spanning over three or more supports,

$$M_L = 0.8 M_L = 0.8 \times 4.25 = 3.4 \text{ k-ft/ft}$$

The impact factor is 0.3, so

$$M_{L+I} = 3.4 \times (1 + 0.3) = 4.42 \text{ k-ft/ft}$$

$$M_{\text{design}} = 0.50 + 4.42 \qquad = 4.92 \text{ k-ft/ft}$$

Calculate the required depth d. From Table A16 (Appendix A), for $n = 8$, $f_c = 1600$ psi, and $f_s = 16,000$ psi, $R = 272$ psi.

$$Rbd^2 = m$$

$$272bd^2 = 4.92 \times 12,000$$

$$d = \sqrt{\frac{4.92 \times 12,000}{272 \times 12}} = 4.25 \text{ in.}$$

Assuming #6 bar for the main reinforcement, the depth provided is

$$d = 7.5 - 2 - \tfrac{1}{2} \times 0.75 = 5.125 \text{ in.}$$

$$A_s = \frac{M}{f_s jd} = \frac{4.92 \times 12}{20 \times 0.87 \times 5.125} = 0.66 \text{ in.}^2$$

Provide #6 @ $7\frac{1}{2}$ in. o.c., perpendicular to the stringers, both at the top and the bottom.

$$A_s = 0.71 \text{ in.}^2 > 0.66 \text{ in.}^2, \text{ OK (Table A.19, Appendix A)}$$

Distribution of steel (at bottom of slab). For main reinforcement perpendicular to traffic, the required amount of steel distribution is expressed as a percentage of the main reinforcement required for positive moment, per AASHTO 3.24.10.2:

$$\text{Percentage of steel reinforcement} = \frac{220}{\sqrt{S}} = \frac{220}{\sqrt{6.5}} = 86.3\% > 67\% \text{ (maximum)}$$

Therefore, $A_s = 0.71 \times 0.67 = 0.48$ in.^{2} Provide #5 @ $7\frac{1}{2}$ in., parallel to stringers, above the bottom main reinforcement: $A_s = 0.49$ in.$^2 > 0.48$ in.^{2}, OK (Table A.19, Appendix A).

Per AASHTO 3.24.10.3, the distribution reinforcement computed above should be placed in the middle half of the slab span, and not less than 50 percent of the specified amount should be placed in the outer quarters of the span.

Temperature steel (at top of slab): AASHTO 8.20. Provide $\frac{1}{8}$ in^2/ft width in each direction at the top of the slab, maximum spacing not to exceed three times the slab thickness, or 18 in. Provide #4 @ 18 in.: $A_s = 0.133$ in.^{2}/ft > 0.125 in.^{2}/ft, OK.

Shear and bond. Per AASHTO 3.24.4, a slab designed according to the service load method is deemed to be satisfactory for shear and bond requirements.

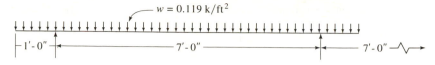

FIGURE E8.1b

Design of stringers

Exterior stringer—bending moment. For computing moments due to the dead load of the deck (i.e., the slab and the wearing surface), it is assumed that the deck is simply supported on the exterior and on the adjacent interior stringer (Fig. E8.1b). The load on the exterior beam is computed by taking moments about the interior stringer.

$$\text{Dead load from the deck} = 119 \text{ lb/ft}^2 \text{ (from previous calculations)}$$

The dead load transferred from the deck to the exterior stringer is computed by the lever rule method:

$$w = (0.119 \times 8) \times \tfrac{4}{7} = 0.54 \text{ k/ft}$$

The dead load from parapets is distributed equally to all stringers, per AASHTO 3.23.2.3.1.1.

$$\text{Parapet load (including railings)} = w_p = (2 \times 0.5)/5 = 0.2 \text{ k/ft}$$

$$\text{Self-weight of stringer (assumed)} = 0.16 \text{ k/ft}$$

$$\text{Total load} = 0.54 + 0.2 + 0.16 = 0.90 \text{ k/ft}$$

$$\text{Moment due to the dead loads} = M_D = \tfrac{1}{8}wL^2 = \tfrac{1}{8} \times 0.90 \times (50)^2 = 281 \text{ k-ft}$$

To compute the live load on the exterior stringer, the wheel load is positioned 2 ft inside the curb, as shown in Fig. 3.6 (per AASHTO Fig. 3.7.6A). This places the outside wheel load, P, of the truck at 3 ft from the exterior stringer (Fig. E8.1c), and the live load on this stringer is computed per AASHTO 3.23.2.3.1.2.

$$\text{Wheel load on exterior stringer} = \tfrac{4}{7}P = 0.57P$$

However, for a deck supported on four or more steel stringers, the wheel load factor should not be less than that specified in AASHTO 3.23.2.3.1.5. In this example, the deck is supported by five stringers. The spacing, S, of stringers is 7.0 ft. Therefore,

$$\text{Wheel load factor} = \frac{S}{(4.0 + 0.25S)} = 1.22 > 0.57$$

The larger value of the wheel load factor, 1.22, governs.

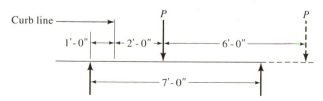

FIGURE E8.1c

The maximum moment per lane due to the live load (HS20 loading) is obtained from Table A.6 (Appendix A) for $L = 50$ ft: $M_L = 628$ k-ft.

$$\text{Maximum live-load moment in exterior stringer} = \tfrac{1}{2} \times 628 \times 1.22$$
$$= 383 \text{ k-ft}$$

$$\text{Impact factor} = I = \frac{50}{L + 125} = \frac{50}{50 + 125} = 0.286$$

The live-load moment, including impact, is

$$M_{L+I} = 383 \times (1 + 0.286) = 493 \text{ k-ft}$$

The total design moment, M_{design}, is $281 + 493 = 774$ k-ft.

Exterior stringer—shear

$$W_D = 0.9 \text{ k/ft}$$
$$V_D = \tfrac{1}{2}wL = \tfrac{1}{2} \times 0.9 \times 50 = 22.5 \text{ kips}$$

Maximum shear due to live load is computed as a reaction in the exterior stringer when the wheel loads are positioned per AASHTO 3.23.3. Fractions of wheel loads so obtained are placed on the stringer, with the rear wheel load on the support, as shown in Fig. E8.1d.

For the wheel load near the support, the fraction of wheel load distributed to the exterior stringer is (by the lever rule method) $P \times \tfrac{4}{7} = 0.57P$. For wheel loads away from the support, the fraction of wheel load is $1.22P$, as computed earlier for the moment. Assume $P = 16$ kips.

$$V_L = 0.57P + \left(P \times \frac{36}{50} + \frac{P}{4} \times \frac{22}{50}\right) \times 1.22$$

$$= 1.58 \times 16 = 25.3 \text{ kips}$$

The live-load shear, including the impact, is

$$V_{L+I} = 25.3 \times (1 + 0.286) = 32.5 \text{ kips}$$

The total design shear is

$$V_{\text{design}} = 22.5 + 32.5 = 55.0 \text{ kips}$$

AASHTO 3.23.2.3.1.4 requires that the capacity of the exterior stringer be no smaller than that of the interior stringers. Therefore, the moment and shear in the interior stringers are computed next. The larger values of moment and shear will be used to size the stringers.

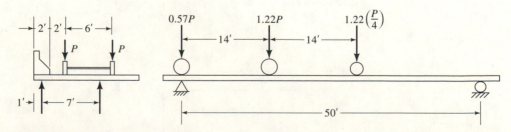

FIGURE E8.1d

Interior stringer—bending moment. Dead load on the interior stringer is computed on the basis of the tributary width. The load due to the parapet is distributed to all stringers equally.

$$\text{Dead load due to slab and wearing surface} = 0.119 \times 7 \text{ k/ft}$$

$$= 0.83 \text{ k/ft}$$

$$\text{Dead load due to parapet} = (2 \times 0.5)/5 = 0.20 \text{ k/ft}$$

$$\text{Self-weight of stringer (assumed)} = 0.16 \text{ k/ft}$$

$$\text{Total dead load} = 1.19 \text{ k/ft}$$

$$M_D = \tfrac{1}{8} w L^2 = \tfrac{1}{8} \times 1.19 \times (50)^2 = 372 \text{ k-ft}$$

The live-load moment in the interior stringers is computed according to AASHTO 3.23.2.2. For a bridge deck carrying two or more lanes and with average stringer spacing, $S < 14$ ft,

Live-load distribution factor $= S/5.5 = 1.27$ (Table A.7, Appendix A)
Live-load moment in the stringer (per lane moment) $= 628$ k-ft
Live-load moment in stringer $= \tfrac{1}{2} \times 628 \times 1.27 = 399$ k-ft
Impact factor, $I = 0.286$
$M_{L+I} = 399 \times (1 + 0.286) = 513$ k-ft

Total moment $= M_{\text{design}} = 372 + 513 = 885$ k-ft

Interior stringer—shear

$$V_D = \tfrac{1}{2} w L = \tfrac{1}{2} \times 1.19 \times 50 = 29.8 \text{ k}$$

Shear due to the live load is computed in the same manner as for the exterior stringer. As explained in Chapter 4, for wheel loads *near* the end of the interior stringer, three cases (Fig. 4.17c) must be considered to establish the maximum distribution factor for shear. It was established that, for $6 \le S \le 8$ ft (Fig. 4.17(c)(ii), redrawn as Fig. E8.1e), Eq. 4.4c gives the maximum value of shear. Thus,

$$R = P\left(3 - \frac{10}{S}\right) \tag{4.4c}$$

$$= P\left(3 - \frac{10}{7}\right)$$

$$= 1.57P$$

The wheel load distribution factor for the wheels *away* from the end of the interior stringer is taken as the same as that for the live-load distribution factor for the moment, i.e., 1.27 (computed earlier). The maximum live-load shear is computed as a reaction in

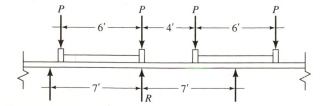

FIGURE E8.1e

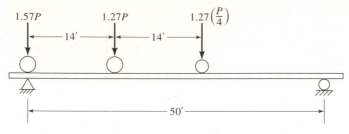

FIGURE E8.1f

the stringer when the equivalent wheel loads are positioned as shown in Fig. E8.1f. With $P = 16$ kips,

$$V_L = 1.57P + 1.27\left(P \times \frac{36}{50} + \frac{P}{4} \times \frac{22}{50}\right)$$

$$= 2.6241P$$

$$= 2.6242 \times 16$$

$$= 42 \text{ kips}$$

With impact,

$$V_{L+I} = 42.0(1 + 0.286) = 54.0 \text{ kips}$$

Total design shear is

$$V_{\text{design}} = 29.8 + 54.0 = 83.8 \text{ kips}$$

Note that the design moment and shear for the interior stringers ($M = 885$ k-ft, $V = 83.8$ kips) are greater than the corresponding values for the exterior stringers ($M = 774$ k-ft, $V = 55$ kips). Hence, the stringers will be designed for $M = 885$ k-ft and $V = 83.8$ kips.

The compression flanges of stringers will be embedded in concrete such that they are fully restrained, and the allowable stress in steel is $f_s = 20,000$ psi $= 20$ ksi (Table 8.5). The required section modulus for the steel stringer is

$$S_{\text{reqd}} = \frac{885 \times 12}{20.0} = 531 \text{ in.}^3$$

Provide W36×160, $S_x = 542$ in.$^3 \geq 531$ in.^{3}, OK. Note that the self-weight of the stringer, 160 lb/ft, is the same as that assumed in the design computations. Therefore, the design does not need to be revised.

Check the depth-span ratio: AASHTO 10.5.1. With a 36-in. beam, the ratio of the depth of the steel beam to the span is 3:50 $= 1:16.7 > 1:25$, OK.

Check shear stress:

$$f_v = \frac{V}{dt_w} = \frac{83.8}{36.01 \times 0.65} = 3.58 \text{ ksi} < 12 \text{ ksi, OK}$$

Therefore, provide W36 × 160 for both the exterior as well as the interior stringers.

Deflection. Methods of computing deflections due to live load were discussed in Chapter 5. For simplicity, assume that the maximum deflection occurs at the midspan when the

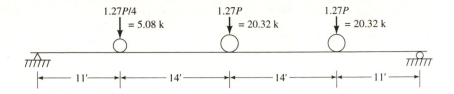

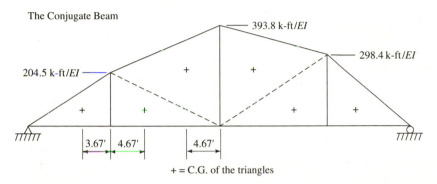

FIGURE E8.1g

HS20 truck is so positioned that its middle axle (16 kip-load) is at the midspan, as shown in Fig. E8.1g. Under this assumption, live-load deflection is computed by the conjugate beam method as follows.

The M/EI diagram is drawn as the load on the conjugate beam. Compute the reaction in the conjugate beam.

$$R = \tfrac{1}{50} \times \frac{1}{2EI}[204.5 \times 11 \times 42.67 + 204.5 \times 14 \times 34.33$$
$$+ \ 393.8 \times 14 \times 29.67 + 393.8 \times 14 \times 20.33$$
$$+ \ 298.4 \times 14 \times 15.67 + 298.4 \times 11 \times 7.33]$$

$$= (5955 \text{ k-ft}^2)/EI$$

$$EI\Delta_{L,\text{midspan}} = 5595 \times 25 - \tfrac{1}{2}(204.5 \times 11 \times 17.67 + 204.5 \times 14$$
$$\times 9.33 + 393.8 \times 14 \times 4.67)$$

$$= 93{,}771 \text{ ft}^3\text{-kips}$$

$$\Delta_L = \frac{93{,}771 \times 12^3}{29{,}000 \times 9750} = 0.57 \text{ in.}$$

$$\Delta_{L+I} = 0.57 \times (1 + 0.286) = 0.74 \text{ in.}$$

$$\frac{L}{800} = \frac{50 \times 12}{800} = 0.75 \text{ in.} > 0.74 \text{ in., OK.}$$

Alternatively, the live-load deflection can be computed from Eq. (5.12), as discussed in Chapter 5, where I_c has been replaced by I_s:

$$\Delta_{L+I} = \frac{P_T}{90I_s}(L^3 - 555L + 4780)(1 + I)(DF) \text{ in.}$$

where P_T = weight of one front wheel × no. of wheels per trucks × no. of truck lanes, kips

I_s = moment of inertia of one stringer × no. of stringers, in.[4]

L = span, ft

I = impact factor

DF = distribution factor

Substituting

$P_T = 4 \times 2 \times 2 = 16$ kips

$I_s = 9750 \times 5 = 48,750$ in.[4]

$L = 50$ ft

$I = 0.286$

$DF = 1.27$

$$\Delta_{L+I} = \frac{16}{90 \times 48,750}(50^3 - 555 \times 50 + 4780) \times 1.286 \times 1.27$$

$$= 0.60 \text{ in.}$$

The small difference between the values of deflection computed by the two methods can be attributed to approximations involved in the two methods.

Diaphragms: AASHTO 10.21.1. Provide C15 × 33.9 for diaphragms at ends and at midspan, spaced at 25 ft. The stress due to wind loading, when top flanges of stringers are continuously supported, is computed according to AASHTO 10.20.2. The maximum induced stress, F, in the bottom flange of each girder in the system can be computed from Eq. 8.5:

$$F = RF_{cb} \qquad \text{(AASHTO Eq. 10.5)} \qquad (8.5)$$

In the absence of the bottom lateral bracings, the values of R, F_{cb}, and M_{cb} are

$$R = [0.2272L - 11]S_d^{-2/3} \qquad \text{(AASHTO Eq. 10.6)} \qquad (8.6)$$

$$F_{cb} = \frac{72M_{cb}}{t_f b_f^2} \text{ psi} \qquad \text{(AASHTO Eq. 10.8)} \qquad (8.4)$$

$$M_{cb} = 0.08WS_d^2 \text{ ft-lb} \qquad \text{(AASHTO Eq. 10.9)} \qquad (8.3)$$

where W = wind loading along the exterior flange, lb/ft, $\not<$ 150 lb/ft

S_d = diaphragm spacing, ft

L = span length, ft

t_f = thickness of flange (of the exterior stringer)

b_f = width of (exterior) flange

Per AASHTO 3.15.2.1.1, for a 0° angle of skew, the lateral load on the girder is 50 lb/ft^2. The height, in elevation, exposed to wind loads, extends from the bottom of the exterior stringer to the top of the parapet (Fig. E8.1h):

Thickness of bottom flange of W36 × 160 = 1.02 in.

Depth of W36 × 160 between flanges = 33.97 in.

Haunch = 2.0 in.

Deck slab = 7.5 in.

Height of parapet (2 ft 8 in.) = 32.0 in.

Total height = 72.49 in. = 6.04 ft

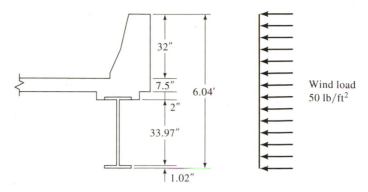

FIGURE E8.1h

Wind load on the stringer $= 50 \times 6.04 = 302$ lb/ft > 300 lb/ft, OK.
Wind load on the bottom flange $= W = \frac{1}{2} \times 302 = 151$ lb/ft.

In the absence of the diaphragms, the moment in the bottom flange is

$$M = \tfrac{1}{8}WL^2 = \tfrac{1}{8} \times 0.151 \times (50)^2 = 47.2 \text{ k-ft}$$

For a W36 $\times$ 160, $t_f = 1.02$ in., $b_f = 12$ in., and the section modulus of the bottom flange is

$$S_{\text{bot.fl.}} = \frac{t_f b_f^2}{6} = \frac{1.02 \times (12)^2}{6} = 24.48 \text{ in.}^3$$

The flange stress, f_w, due to wind load is

$$f_w = \frac{47.2 \times 12}{24.48} = 23.14 \text{ ksi} > f_{b,\text{ allowable}} = 20 \text{ ksi}$$

With diaphragm spacing of 25 ft, i.e., $S_d = 25$ ft, the moment and the stress in the bottom flange are computed as

$$M_{\text{cb}} = 0.08WS_d^2 = 0.08 \times 0.151 \times 25^2 = 7.55 \text{ k-ft}$$

$$F_{\text{cb}} = \frac{M}{S} = \frac{7.55 \times 12}{24.48} = 3.7 \text{ ksi}$$

Assuming that lateral bracings are not provided,

$$R = [0.2272L - 11]S_d^{-2/3}$$
$$= [0.2272 \times 50 - 11] \times (25)^{-2/3}$$
$$= 0.0421$$
$$F = RF_{\text{cb}} = 0.0421 \times 3.70$$
$$= 0.15 \text{ ksi (very small)}$$

Bending stress in the exterior stringer due to dead and live load, where $M = 774$ k-ft and $S = 542$ in.^{3}, is

$$f_b = \frac{M}{S} = \frac{774 \times 12}{542} = 17.14 \text{ ksi}$$

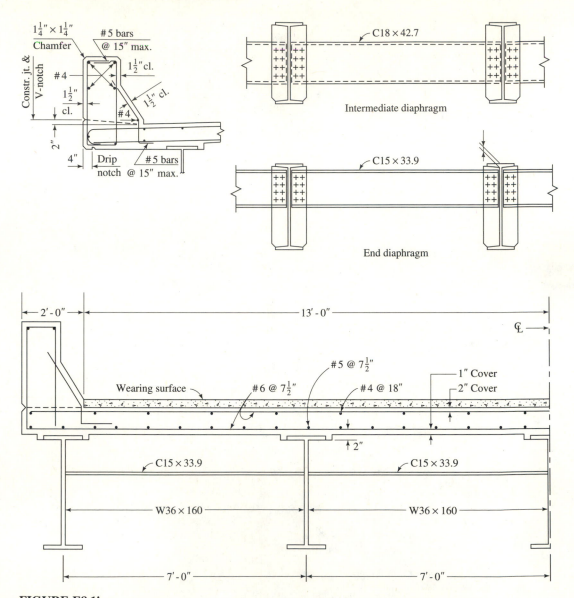

FIGURE E8.1i
Typical bridge cross section.

Total stress in the flange $= 17.14 + 0.15 = 17.29$ ksi < 20.0 ksi, OK. Hence, lateral bracings are not required for the bottom flange of the exterior stringer. A typical cross section of the bridge is shown in Fig. E8.1i.

EXAMPLE 8.2. NONCOMPOSITE STEEL BEAM BRIDGE USING HIGH-STRENGTH STEEL. Redesign the bridge superstructure of Example 8.1 using A572 grade 50 steel and estimate the savings in cost compared to the design of Example 8.1, in which A36 steel was used.

Solution. From Example 8.1, it is known that the interior stringer governs the design. The maximum moment was computed to be 885 k-ft.

For A572 grade 50 steel, $F_{\text{allow}} = 27$ ksi (Table A.26, Appendix A). Hence,

$$S_{\text{reqd}} = (885 \times 12)/27 = 393 \text{ in.}^3$$

(compared to 531 in.^{3} for A36 steel)

Try W33 × 130, for which $S = 406$ in.^{3} > 393 in.^{3} (required), OK.

Check deflection. The moment of inertia of W33 × 130 is $I_x = 6710$ in.^{4}

The deflection due to live load plus impact can be computed from the proportion to deflection (0.6 in.) of W36 × 160 ($I_x = 9750$ in.^{4}) computed in Example 8.1.

$$\Delta_{L+I} = 0.06 \times \frac{9750}{6710} = 0.87 \text{ in.} > \frac{L}{800} = 0.75 \text{ in., NG}$$

Therefore, revise the beam size to satisfy deflection limitations. Compute I_{reqd} from Eq. 5.12 to limit deflection due to live load plus impact to 0.75 in. ($L/800$).

$$\Delta_{L+I} = \frac{P_T}{90I}[L^3 - 555L + 4780] \times DF \times (1 + I)$$

$$= \frac{4 \times 2 \times 2}{90 \times 5I}[50^3 - 555 \times 50 + 4780] \times 1.27 \times 1.286$$

$$= \frac{5925}{I} = 0.75 \text{ in.}$$

$$I = 7900 \text{ in.}^4$$

Try W36 × 135. Its section properties are $I_x = 7800$ in.^{4} < $I_{\text{reqd}} = 7900$ in.^{4}, $S = 439$ in.^{3} > $S_{\text{reqd}} = 393$ in.^{3}, OK.

Compute the deflection of W36 × 135 due to live load plus impact:

$$\Delta_{L+I} = 0.75 \times \frac{7900}{7800} = 0.76 \text{ in.} \approx 0.75 \text{ in., OK.}$$

Thus, actual deflection due to live load plus impact is only 1.3 percent above the allowable deflection, which is very small. Therefore, use W36 × 135.

For a 50-ft span, it is assumed that five 52-ft beams would be required. Savings are achieved because the cost per foot of the heavier A36 steel beam (W36 × 160) is greater than that of the lighter A572 grade 50 steel beam (W36 × 135.) A cost comparison is made based on the cost of five stringers as follows:

Cost comparison

	Section required	Cost per ft (Bethlehem, 1990c)	Weight savings		Cost savings	
			percent	tons	percent	dollars
A36	W36×160	$39.20				
A572 grade 50	W36×135	$35.78	6.5	15.7	8.7	889

The preceding table shows that the use of high-strength steel results in a weight savings of 6.5 percent and a cost savings of 8.7 percent. The savings would be higher if four stringers were used instead of five, by increasing their spacings. This would require a slightly thicker slab, but the increased cost of the slab is likely to be more than offset by the savings in the cost of steel.

EXAMPLE 8.3. DESIGN OF A COMPOSITE SLAB–STRINGER BRIDGE. A preliminary design is required for a composite slab–stringer bridge with a clear span of 70 ft and having a clear roadway width of 28 ft. Provide a standard parapet and railing and a 3-ft-wide sidewalk on each side. A minimum slab thickness of $7\frac{1}{2}$ in. is required, and construction is unshored. Use the following data:

> Loading: HS 20-44 and 2×10^6 cycles of loading
> $f_c' = 3500$ psi, grade 40 steel reinforcement for the deck slab
> A36 for stringers
> $\frac{3}{4} \times 4$-in.-high headed shear studs for composite action

Solution. The first step is to assume a typical bridge section, as shown in Fig. E8.3a. A stringer spacing of 7 ft 6 in., with W36 × 135 steel stringers, has been selected arbitrarily so that the length of overhang of the deck slab on each side is equal to half the stringer spacing (although it is not necessary). Also, a $7\frac{1}{2}$-in. slab would be adequate for a stringer spacing of 7 ft 6 in., as demonstrated in Example 8.1. Obviously, a larger stringer spacing could have been selected, which might be even more economical in spite of the thicker slab (see Fig. 8.31) that would be required.

The design calculations for the deck slab are identical to those presented in Example 8.1, and they are not repeated here. The reinforcement requirements are also identical: #6 @ $7\frac{1}{2}$-in. o.c. for the main reinforcement (at top and bottom, perpendicular to stringers), #5 @ $7\frac{1}{2}$-in. o.c for distribution steel (bottom of slab), and #4 @ 18-in. o.c. for temperature steel (both top and bottom, parallel to stringers).

Both the exterior and the interior stringers are designed separately since they have to carry different loads. In general, identical design quantities have to be computed for both stringers. As defined in the problem statement, unshored construction is used, meaning that the weight of the wet concrete of the deck slab will be supported by steel stringers alone (without the benefit of composite action). After the deck hardens, shores will be removed and the superimposed dead load and the live load will be carried by the composite section of the beams. Calculations for the dead loads are made in two steps. Step one involves the dead load to be carried by the steel stringer alone, referred to as *dead load 1* (DL1), which

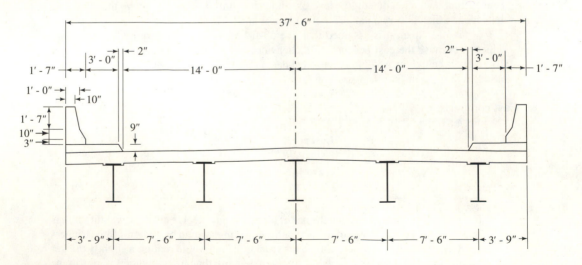

FIGURE E8.3a
Typical bridge section for Example 8.3.

consists of the self-weight of the stringer (including the cover plate, if any), the diaphragms, and the weight of the slab and the formwork on which it will be poured. Step two involves the dead load to be carried by the composite section, referred to as *dead load 2* (DL2); this consists of the superimposed load—the dead load due to the sidewalk, parapet, curb and railing, wearing surface, etc.—which is equally distributed to all stringers.

As discussed earlier, a cover plate $14 \times 1\frac{1}{2}$ in., 2 in. wider than the 12-in.-wide bottom flange of W36 × 135, has been selected in this example to satisfy the AASHTO requirements. Also, a 2×12-in. haunch has been used for DL1 calculations, although only a 1-in. haunch has been used for section properties (conservative).

Design of the interior stringers

Dead load. DL1 is the dead load for the *noncomposite* section:

$$\text{Self-weight of stringer (including diaphragms)} = 0.150 \text{ k/ft}$$

$$\text{Weight of slab} = 7.5 \times (7.5/12) \times 0.15 = 0.703 \text{ k/ft}$$

$$\text{Weight of 1} \times \text{12-in. haunch} = \tfrac{1}{12} \times 2 \times 0.15 = 0.025 \text{ k/ft}$$

$$\text{Weight of } 14 \times 1\tfrac{1}{2}\text{-in. cover plate at 72 lb/ft} = 0.072 \text{ k/ft}$$

$$\text{Total dead load 1, } w_{\text{DL1}} = 0.95 \text{ k/ft}$$

Dead load moment $M_{\text{DL1}} = \frac{1}{8} w_{\text{DL1}} L^2 = \frac{1}{8} \times 0.95 \times (71)^2 = 599$ k-ft

DL2 is the dead load for the *composite* section:

Dead load due to the weight of the parapet curb and railing (distributed equally to all five stringers) is $2 \times 0.5/5 = 0.20$ k/ft.

The average width of the sidewalk is 56 in. The thickness of the sidewalk is kept at 9 in. The dead load due to the weight of the sidewalk is distributed equally to all five stringers. Thus,

$$DL_{\text{sidewalk}} = \frac{2 \times (56 \times 9) \times 0.15}{144} \times \frac{1}{5} = 0.210 \text{ k/ft}$$

Dead load due to the wearing surface (25 psf) $= 0.025 \times 7.5 = 0.188$ k/ft.

$$\text{Total dead load 2, } w_{\text{DL2}} = 0.20 + 0.21 + 0.188 = 0.598 \text{ k/ft}$$

$$\text{Dead-load moment, } M_{\text{DL2}} = \tfrac{1}{8} w_{\text{DL2}} L^2 = \tfrac{1}{8} \times 0.598 \times (71)^2 = 377 \text{ k-ft}$$

$$\text{Total dead-load moment, } M_D = 600 + 377 = 977 \text{ k-ft}$$

Live load. Assume 1-ft bearing at each end. Therefore, the effective span $= 70 + \frac{1}{2}(1+1) = 71$ ft. From Table A.6 (Appendix A), for $L = 71$ ft, by interpolation,

$$M_L = 985.6 + \frac{(1075.1 - 985.6) \times 1}{5}$$

$$= 1003.5 \text{ k-ft}$$

The live-load distribution factor, DF, is

$$DF = \frac{S}{5.5} = \frac{7.5}{5.5} = 1.364$$

(Table A.7, Appendix A). Hence, the live-load moment in the stringer is

$$M_L = \tfrac{1}{2} \times 1003.5 \times 1.364 = 684 \text{ k-ft}$$

The impact factor, I, is

$$I = \frac{50}{L + 125}$$

$$= \frac{50}{71 + 125}$$

$$= 0.255$$

Therefore, total live-load moment, including impact, is

$$M_{L+I} = 684 \times (1 + 0.255) = 858 \text{ k-ft}$$

Section properties: Noncomposite section.   After some preliminary calculations, a W36×135 is selected as a trial size for the interior stringer. Its section properties are: $A = 39.7$ in.^{2}, $d = 35.55$ in., $b_f = 11.9$ in., $t_f = 0.79$ in., $t_w = 0.6$ in., $I_x = 7800$ in.^{4}, and $S_x = 439$ in.^{3}.

This section satisfies depth-to-span ratios specified by AASHTO 10.5.2:

$$\frac{\text{Overall girder depth}}{\text{Span}} = \frac{35.5 + 7.5}{71 \times 12} = \frac{1}{19.8} > \frac{1}{25}, \text{ OK}$$

$$\frac{\text{Depth of steel girder}}{\text{Span}} = \frac{35.5}{71 \times 12} = \frac{1}{24} > \frac{1}{30}, \text{ OK}$$

A partial-length cover plate is provided at the bottom flange of W36 × 135. AASHTO 10.13.3 permits the maximum thickness of the cover plate to be up to two times the flange thickness. In the present case, the thickness of the cover is limited to 2×0.79, or 1.58 in. Therefore, a cover plate $14 \times 1\frac{1}{2}$ in. is tried initially. Note that the 14-in. width of the cover plate is 2 in. wider than the width of the flange (11.9 in.) of W36 × 135. Also note that both steel components—the W36 × 135 and the $14 \times 1\frac{1}{2}$ in. cover plate—satisfy AASHTO 10.8.1, which limits the minimum thickness of metal to $\frac{5}{16}$ in.

The section properties of the noncomposite section with the cover plate, and of the composite steel section with and without the cover plate, are computed next. These different section properties are required to compute flexural stresses in the beam at different stages of loading (DL1, DL2, live load, etc.). For the composite section, the value of the modular ratio, $n = 9$ for $f_c' = 2900$–3500 psi, is selected per AASHTO 10.38.1.3. Note also that AASHTO 10.38.1.4 requires that to consider the effect of creep in composite girders that have dead loads (i.e., sustained loads) acting on the composite section, stresses and horizontal shears must be computed on the basis of the composite section with three times the value of n stated above—i.e., $9 \times 3 = 27$ in the present case. Accordingly, two sets of section properties are computed for the composite section, with and without the cover plate—one set with $n = 9$, and one with $n = 27$. Thus, including the section properties of the noncomposite section, a total of five sets of section properties are computed.

Noncomposite section with cover plate (see Fig. E8.3b)

$$\overline{y_t} = \frac{\sum AY}{\sum A}$$

$$= \frac{39.7 \times 17.775 + 21.0 \times 36.3}{39.7 + 21.0}$$

$$= \frac{1468}{60.7}$$

$$= 24.18 \text{ in.}$$

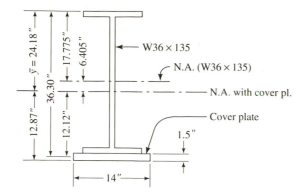

FIGURE E8.3b
Noncomposite section with cover plate.

$$I = 7800 + 39.7 \times (6.405)^2 + 21.0 \times (12.12)^2 + 14 \times 1.5^3/12$$
$$= 12,517 \text{ in.}^4$$

The section moduli at the top (S_{ts}) and bottom (S_{bs}) of the steel section are

$$S_{ts} = \frac{12,517}{24.18} = 518 \text{ in.}^3$$

$$S_{bs} = \frac{12,517}{12.87} = 973 \text{ in.}^3$$

Composite section ($n = 9$) with cover plate (see Fig. E8.3c). The effective width of the flange of the composite section is as follows: With 1-ft bearings at each end, the effective span is $L = 71$ ft. Per AASHTO 10.38.3.1, the effective flange width, b_e, should be the least of the following:

- $\frac{1}{4}L = \frac{1}{4} \times 71 = 17.75$ ft
- Center-to-center distance of stringers = 7.5 ft
- Twelve times the slab thickness = $12 \times 7.5 = 7.5$ ft

Therefore, $b_e = 7.5$ ft = 90 in.

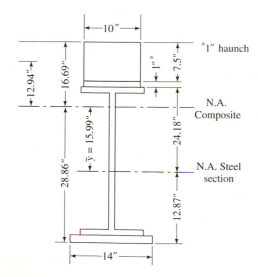

FIGURE E8.3c
Composite section with cover plate ($n = 9$).

This effective width will be used to compute the section properties of the composite section. The transformed width of the slab is $b_{tr} = b_e/n = \frac{90}{9} = 10$ in.

$$\bar{y} = \frac{75 \times (7.5/2 + 25.18)}{75 + 60.7} = 15.99 \text{ in.}$$

$$I = [12{,}517 + 60.7 \times 15.99^2] + 75 \times 12.94^2 + 10.0 \times 7.5^3/12$$
$$= 40{,}947 \text{ in.}^4$$

The section moduli at the top of the concrete slab (S_{tc}) and at the top and bottom of the steel section are

$$S_{tc} = \frac{40{,}947}{16.69} = 2453 \text{ in.}^3$$

$$S_{ts} = \frac{40{,}947}{(16.69 - 8.5)} = 5000 \text{ in.}^3$$

$$S_{bs} = \frac{40{,}947}{28.86} = 1419 \text{ in.}^3$$

Composite section ($n = 9$) *without cover plate* (see Fig. E8.3d)

$$\bar{y} = \frac{75 \times (7.5/2 + 18.775)}{75 + 39.7} = 14.73 \text{ in.}$$

$$I = 7800 + 39.7 \times 14.73^2 + 75 \times 7.8^2 + 10.0 \times 7.5^3/12$$
$$= 21{,}329 \text{ in.}^4$$

The various section moduli are

$$S_{tc} = \frac{21{,}329}{11.55} = 1847 \text{ in.}^3$$

$$S_{ts} = \frac{21{,}329}{11.55 - 8.5} = 6993 \text{ in.}^3$$

$$S_{bs} = \frac{21{,}329}{32.5} = 656 \text{ in.}^3$$

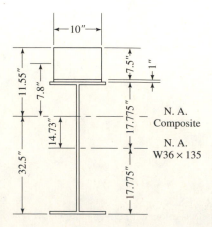

FIGURE E8.3d
Composite section with cover plate ($n = 9$).

Composite section ($n = 27$) *with the cover plate* (see Fig. E8.3e)

$$\bar{y} = \frac{25.0 \times (7.5/2 + 25.18)}{25.0 + 60.7} = 8.44 \text{ in.}$$

$$I = 12,513 + 60.7 \times 8.44^2 + 25.0 \times 20.49^2 + 3.33 \times 7.5^3/12$$
$$= 27,450 \text{ in.}^4$$

The various section moduli are

$$S_{tc} = \frac{27,450}{24.24} = 1132 \text{ in.}^3$$

$$S_{ts} = \frac{27,450}{24.24 - 8.5} = 1744 \text{ in.}^3$$

$$S_{bs} = \frac{27,450}{21.31} = 1288 \text{ in.}^3$$

Composite section ($n = 27$) *without cover plate* (see Fig. E8.3f)

$$\bar{y} = \frac{25.0 \times (7.5/2 + 18.775)}{25.0 + 39.7} = 8.7 \text{ in.}$$

$$I = 7800 + 39.7 \times 8.72^2 + 25.0 \times 13.82^2 + 3.33 \times 7.5^3/12$$
$$= 15,697 \text{ in.}^4$$

The various section moduli are

$$S_{tc} = \frac{15,697}{17.57} = 893 \text{ in.}^3$$

$$S_{ts} = \frac{15,697}{17.57 - 8.5} = 1731 \text{ in.}^3$$

$$S_{bs} = \frac{15,697}{26.48} = 593 \text{ in.}^3$$

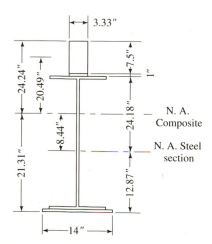

FIGURE E8.3e
Composite section with cover plate ($n = 27$).

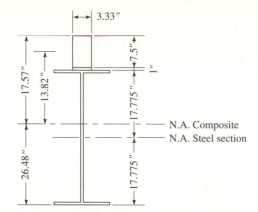

FIGURE E8.3f
Composite section without cover plate
($n = 27$).

Stresses. The section properties computed above will be used to compute stresses. The following notations are used:

f_{bs} = stress in the bottom fibers of steel section
f_{ts} = stress in the top fibers of steel section
f_{tc} = stress in the top fibers of concrete
f_c = transformed stress in the top fibers of concrete

Stress due to dead load on noncomposite section

$$M_{DL1} = 599 \text{ k-ft}$$

$$f_{bs} = \frac{599 \times 12}{973} = 7.4 \text{ ksi}$$

$$f_{ts} = \frac{599 \times 12}{518} = 13.90 \text{ ksi}$$

Stress due to dead load on composite section ($n = 27$) AASHTO 10.38.1.4

$$M_{DL2} = 377 \text{ k-ft}$$

$$f_{bs} = \frac{377 \times 12}{1288} = 3.51 \text{ ksi}$$

$$f_{ts} = \frac{377 \times 12}{1744} = 2.59 \text{ ksi}$$

$$f_{tc} = \frac{377 \times 12}{1132} = 4.0 \text{ ksi}$$

$$f_c = \frac{4.0}{n} = \frac{4.0}{27} = 0.148 \text{ ksi}$$

Stress due to live load and impact on composite section ($n = 9$)

$$M_{L+I} = 858 \text{ k-ft}$$

$$f_{bs} = \frac{858 \times 12}{1419} = 7.26 \text{ ksi}$$

$$f_{ts} = \frac{858 \times 12}{5000} = 2.06 \text{ ksi}$$

$$f_{tc} = \frac{858 \times 12}{2453} = 4.20 \text{ ksi}$$

$$f_c = \frac{4.20}{n} = \frac{4.20}{9} = 0.467 \text{ ksi}$$

Total stresses

$$f_{bs} = 7.40 + 3.51 + 7.26 = 18.17 \text{ ksi} < 20 \text{ ksi, OK}$$

$$f_{ts} = 13.90 + 2.59 + 2.06 = 18.55 \text{ ksi} < 20 \text{ ksi, OK}$$

$$f_c = 0.148 + 0.467 = 0.62 \text{ ksi} < 1.4 \text{ ksi, OK}$$

Thus, all stresses are within the allowable limits. Note that steel stresses are quite close to the allowable stress of 20 ksi, which indicates that a smaller steel section would not be much more economical. Use W36 × 135 with a 14 × $1\frac{1}{2}$-in. partial-length cover plate and a $7\frac{1}{2}$-in.-thick concrete slab.

Cutoff point for cover plate. Stresses are computed at any section of the beam to determine the point on the span where the cover plate is no longer required. Figure E8.3g shows the influence line (IL) for the moment for a section at a distance x from the left support ($x \leq L/2$). Moments due to various stages of loadings are computed from this influence line.

$$M_{DL1} = w_{DL1} \cdot \frac{x(L - x)}{2} = 0.95 \left[\frac{x(71 - x)}{2} \right] = -0.475x^2 + 33.725x$$

$$M_{DL2} = w_{DL2} \cdot \frac{x(L - x)}{2} = 0.598 \cdot \frac{x(71 - x)}{2} = -0.299x^2 + 21.229x$$

$$M_{L+I} = \left[P \cdot \frac{x(L - x)}{L} + P \cdot \frac{x(L - x - a)}{L} + \frac{P}{4} \cdot \frac{x(L - x - 2a)}{L} \right] (DF)(1 + I)$$

$$= \left[16 \cdot \frac{x(71 - x)}{71} + 16 \cdot \frac{x(57 - x)}{71} + 4 \cdot \frac{x(43 - x)}{71} \right] (1.364)(1.25)$$

$$= -0.868x^2 + 53.525x$$

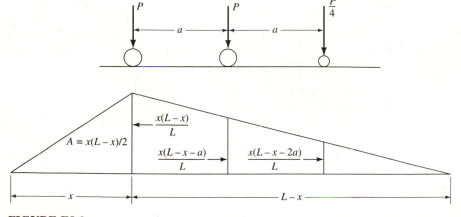

FIGURE E8.3g
Influence line for the moment for a section at distance x from the left support.

For a section without a cover plate, flexural stresses due to various loadings are obtained by dividing moments by the appropriate values of section moduli. The total flexural stress is limited to 20 ksi. The section modulus of W36 × 135, S_x, equals 439 in.^{3}. Thus,

$$f_{bs} = \frac{(-0.475x^2 + 33.725x) \times 12}{439} + \frac{(-0.299x^2 + 21.229x) \times 12}{593}$$
$$+ \frac{(-0.868x^2 + 53.525x) \times 12}{656}$$
$$= -0.0349x^2 + 2.331x \le 20 \text{ ksi}$$

A factor of 12 has been used as a multiplier in the above expression for converting moments into k-in. units. Solving the quadratic equation for x yields

$$0.0349x^2 - 2.331x + 20 = 0$$

$$x = 10.24 \text{ ft (or 56 ft—rejected)}$$

This distance, $x = 56$ ft, is rejected because the IL diagram drawn for these computations will not be valid for this value of x. That is, theoretically, the cover plate can be cut off at 10.24 ft from the support. However, AASHTO 10.13.4 mandates that the cover plate be extended by a certain terminal distance beyond the theoretical cutoff point (discussed earlier). The cover plate in the present case will be welded across the end (at the designer's discretion) for which the terminal distance is $1\frac{1}{2}$ times its width. Hence, extend the cover plate beyond its theoretical cutoff point by 1.5 × 14 = 21 in. or 1.75 ft, which locates the actual cutoff point at 10.24 − 1.75 = 8.49 ft. This may be rounded off to 8 ft from the centerline of the support.

Fatigue strength of cover plate. The other criterion governing the cutoff point for the cover plate is its fatigue strength. As discussed earlier, AASHTO 10.13.4 requires that a partial-length cover plate be extended beyond the theoretical end by the terminal distance, or it should extend to a section where the stress range in the beam flange is equal to the allowable fatigue stress range for base metal adjacent to or connected by fillet welds. The location of this section is determined as follows.

This bridge is classified as a *redundant path structure,* and the allowable fatigue stress is selected from Table A.10 (Appendix A) (AASHTO Table 10.3.1A). The allowable fatigue stress depends on the number of maximum stress cycles for the beam and on the type of weld detail provided for the cover plate–to–flange weld. A decision regarding the maximum stress cycles for the life of the bridge should be made at this stage. This bridge is to be designed for a lifetime of 2×10^6 maximum stress cycles, which corresponds to 110 maximum stress cycles per day for a 50-year life, or 73 maximum stress cycles per day for a 75-year life. The cover plate–to–flange weld detail in the present case corresponds to category *E* as described in Table A.12 (Appendix A) and in AASHTO Table 10.3.1B (built-up members, where base metal at the ends of partial-length welded cover plates is wider than the flange, without welds across the ends, Illustrative Example 7). The corresponding maximum permissible fatigue stress range for this case is 8.0 ksi. The stress range is caused by live load plus impact only. The moment due to the live load plus impact was computed earlier to be

$$M_{L+I} = -0.868x^2 + 53.525x$$

The corresponding stress in the bottom fibers of the steel section (i.e., the fibers in tension) is equated to 8 ksi to determine the value of x:

$$f_{bs} = \frac{(-0.868x^2 + 53.525x)12}{656} \le 8.0 \text{ ksi}$$

The above expression is simplified to

$$-0.0159x^2 + 0.979x - 8.0 \leq 0$$

or

$$x^2 - 61.57x + 503.14 \leq 0$$

which yields $x = 9.7$ ft (or 51.9 ft—rejected).

The compressive stress in the top fibers of the steel section is equated to 20 ksi:

$$f_{ts} = \frac{(-0.475x^2 + 33.725x)12}{517} + \frac{(-0.299x^2 + 21.229x)12}{1731}$$

$$+ \frac{(-0.868x^2 + 53.525x)12}{6993}$$

$$= -0.0146x^2 + 1.0218x \leq 20 \text{ ksi}$$

The above expression is simplified to

$$-0.0146x^2 + 1.0218x - 20 \leq 0$$

or

$$x^2 - 70x + 1370 \leq 0$$

The above equation has no real roots. The stress in the top concrete fibers, which is due to DL2 and live load plus impact, is equated to 1.4 ksi $(= 0.4f_c' = 0.4 \times 3500 \text{ psi})$:

$$f_c = \left[\frac{(-0.299x^2 + 21.229x)}{893 \times 27} + \frac{(-0.868x^2 + 53.525x)}{1847 \times 9} \right] 12 \leq 1.4$$

This equation is simplified to

$$-0.000775x^2 + 0.049x - 1.4 \leq 0$$

or

$$x^2 - 63.22x + 1806 \leq 0$$

The above equation has no real roots.

Thus, the cover plate can be cut off at 9.74 ft from the centerline of the supports. However, as noted earlier, the terminal distance requirement dictates that the cutoff point be 8.0 ft (less than 9.74 ft) from the centerline of the support. Thus, this distance governs the location of the cutoff point for the cover plate.

End shear. The distribution factor for the rear axle (near the support) will be determined as explained in Chapter 4 and illustrated in Example 8.1. For the stringer spacing, S, between 6 and 8 ft, the DF is given by Eq. 4.4c; the corresponding wheel load positions are shown in Fig. E8.3h:

$$R = P\left(3 - \frac{10}{S}\right) \tag{4.4c}$$

$$= P\left(3 - \frac{10}{7.5}\right)$$

$$= 1.667P$$

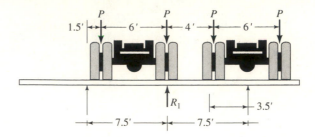

FIGURE E8.3h

The distribution factor for the other two axles is the same as that for the moment—1.364 (computed earlier). The wheel loads of the HS truck are placed as shown in Fig. E8.3i to compute the maximum beam shear. With $P = 16$ kips,

$$V_L = 1.667P + 1.364P\left(\frac{57}{71}\right) + 1.364\left(\frac{P}{4}\right)\left(\frac{43}{71}\right)$$

$$= 47.5 \text{ kips}$$

$$V_{L+I} = 47.5 \times 1.255 = 59.6 \text{ kips}$$

$$V_D = \tfrac{1}{2}(0.95 + 0.598)71 = 55 \text{ kips}$$

$$V_{\text{Total}} = 59.6 + 55 = 114.6 \text{ kips}$$

$$f_v = \frac{V}{dt_w} = \frac{114.6}{35.55 \times 0.6} = 5.3 \text{ ksi} < F_v = 12.0 \text{ ksi, OK}$$

Therefore, stiffeners are not required.

Shear connectors ($\frac{3}{4} \times$ 4-in. studs). Shear connectors are to be designed for both fatigue and strength considerations, per AASHTO 10.38.5. A common practice is to use $\frac{3}{4} \times$ 4-in.-headed studs in single or multiple rows, as necessary. The pitch of shear studs is computed first to satisfy fatigue requirements, and then the total number of studs is checked next to satisfy the strength requirements.

Fatigue. Calculate the number and spacing of shear studs along the span. The number and spacing of studs depend on the *range* of shear at the section under consideration. Since shear due to dead loads is constant, the range of shear at a section in a beam depends on the variation of shear due to live load plus impact at that point, which is determined from influence lines for shear. It is common practice to determine shear stud requirements at the support and at several other points (usually at tenth points) along span, and to provide a

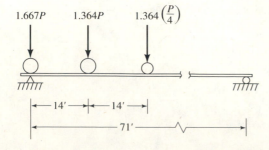

FIGURE E8.3i
Position of HS truck for maximum shear at support.

sufficient number of studs to satisfy the fatigue requirements. In this example, shear stud spacing will be calculated at the support and at every 10 ft from the support to the midspan.

1. *Shear stress at supports.* Horizontal shear stress at the interface of the concrete slab and the steel section is computed from Eq. 8.18 (per AASHTO 10.38.5.1, Eq. 10.57):

$$S_r = \frac{V_r Q}{I} \tag{8.18}$$

The terms in Eq. 8.18 are defined in AASHTO 10.38.5.1.1.

$$\text{Range of shear force} = V_r = V_{L+I} = 59.6 \text{ kips}$$

The beam section at the support consists of the steel section without the cover plate. Therefore,

$$Q \text{ (without the cover plate)} = 75 \times 7.8 = 585 \text{ in.}^3$$

$$S_r = \frac{59.6 \times 1000 \times 585}{21,329} = 1635 \text{ lb/in.}$$

Try three studs per transverse row. The pitch, p, of shear studs will be computed from Eq. 8.21:

$$p = \frac{\sum Z_r}{S_r} \tag{8.21}$$

where $Z_r = \alpha d^2$ (Eq. 8.20, AASHTO Eq. 10.59)
  d = diameter of the stud

For 2,000,000 cycles, $\alpha = 7850$ (Table 8.3), which gives

$$Z_r = \alpha d^2 = 7850 \times 0.75^2 = 4416 \text{ lb}$$

Therefore, the pitch of shear studs is

$$p = \frac{\sum Z_r}{S_r} = \frac{3 \times 4416}{1635} = 8.1 \text{ in., rounded off to 8.0 in.}$$

2. *Shear stress at 10 ft from the supports.* Maximum shear force at 10 ft from the left support is computed from the influence line for shear at $x = 10$ ft (Fig. E8.3j). For maximum positive shear, the loaded length of the beam is $71 - 10 = 61$ ft, for which the impact factor, I, is

$$I = \frac{50}{L + 125} = \frac{50}{61 + 125} = 0.269$$

$$V_{\max}^+ = [16 \times (0.859 + 0.662) + 4 \times 0.465] \times 1.269 = 33.24 \text{ kips}$$

For the maximum negative shear, the loaded length of the span is 10 ft, for which the impact factor, I, is 0.3. Therefore,

$$V_{\max}^- = [16 \times (-0.141)] \times 1.3 = -2.93 \text{ kips}$$

The range of shear, V_r, is the algebraic difference of $V_{\max}^+$ and $V_{\max}^-$ multiplied by the distribution factor, 1.364:

$$V_{r(10')} = [33.24 - (-2.93)] \times 1.364 = 49.34 \text{ kips}$$

where 1.364 is the DF.

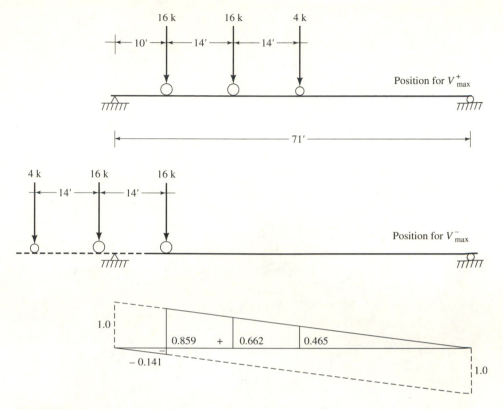

FIGURE E8.3j
Influence line for maximum shear at 10 ft from the left support, and position of HS truck for maximum positive and negative shear.

At 10 ft from the support, the beam section consists of the cover-plated W-section. Therefore, $Q = 75 \times 12.94 = 970.5$ in.^{3}. The range of shear stress and the required pitch of studs are

$$S_r = \frac{V_r Q}{I} = \frac{49.34 \times 970.5 \times 1000}{40,947} = 1168.5 \text{ lb/in.}$$

$$p = \frac{\sum Z_r}{S_r} = \frac{3 \times 4416}{1168.5} = 11.34 \text{ in., rounded off to 11 in.}$$

3. *Shear stress at 20 ft from supports.* The loaded length of the span for maximum positive shear at 20 ft from the left support is $71 - 20 = 51$ ft, for which the impact factor is

$$I = \frac{50}{L + 125} = \frac{50}{51 + 125} = 0.284$$

The IL for shear at 20 ft from the left support is shown in Fig. E8.3k.

$$V^+_{max} = (16 \times 0.718 + 16 \times 0.521 + 4 \times 0.324) \times 1.284 = 27.12 \text{ kips}$$

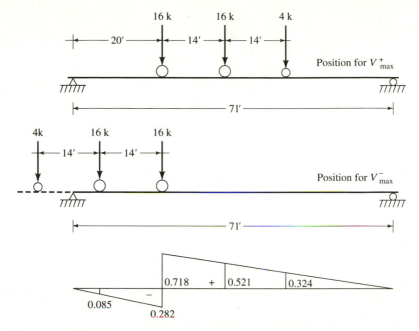

FIGURE E8.3k
Influence line for maximum shear at 20 ft from the left support, and the
position of the HS truck for maximum positive and negative shear.

For maximum negative shear, the loaded length of the span is 20 ft, for which I is 0.3.
Therefore,

$$V^-_{max} = [16 \times (-0.085 - 0.282)] \times 1.3 = -7.63 \text{ kips}$$

$$V_{r(20')} = [27.12 - (-7.63)] \times 1.364 = 47.40 \text{ kips}$$

where 1.364 is the DF.

The value of Q remains the same as that at $x = 10$ ft. Thus,

$$S_r = \frac{V_r Q}{I} = \frac{47.4 \times 970.5 \times 1000}{40,947} = 1123.4 \text{ lb/in.}$$

$$p = \frac{\sum Z_r}{S_r} = \frac{3 \times 4416}{1123.4} = 11.8 \text{ in.}$$

4. *Shear stress at 30 ft from the left support.* The loaded length of the span for maximum positive shear at 30 ft from the left support is $71 - 30 = 41$ ft. The impact factor for all spans 41 ft and under is 0.3. The IL for shear at 30 ft from the left support is shown in Fig. E8.3l.

$$V^+_{max} = [16 \times (0.577 + 0.38) + 4 \times 0.183] \times 1.3 = 20.86 \text{ kips}$$

$$V^-_{max} = [16 \times (-0.225 - 0.423) + 4 \times (-0.028)] \times 1.3 = 13.62 \text{ kips}$$

$$V_{r(30')} = [20.86 - (-13.62)] \times 1.364 = 47.03 \text{ kips}$$

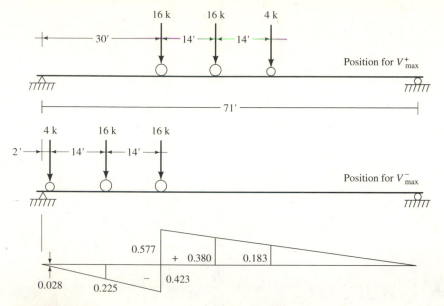

FIGURE E8.3l
Influence line for maximum shear at 30 ft from the left support, and the position of the HS truck for maximum positive and negative shear.

where 1.364 is the DF. The value of Q remains the same as before. Therefore,

$$S_r = \frac{V_r Q}{I} = \frac{47.03 \times 970.3 \times 1000}{40,947} = 1114.4 \text{ lb/in.}$$

$$p = \frac{\sum Z_r}{S_r} = \frac{3 \times 4416}{1114.4} = 11.89 \text{ in.}$$

5. *Shear stress at midspan (35.5 ft from the support).* The impact and the distribution factors are, respectively, 0.3 and 1.364, as before. The IL for shear at 35.5 ft from the left support is shown in Fig. E8.3m. Thus,

$$V_{max}^+ = [16 \times (0.500 + 0.303) + 4 \times 0.106] \times 1.3 = 17.25 \text{ kips}$$

$$V_{max}^- = [16 \times (-0.303 - 0.500) + 4 \times (-0.106)] \times 1.3 = 17.25 \text{ kips}$$

$$V_{r(35.5')} = [17.25 - (-17.25)] \times 1.364 = 47.06 \text{ kips}$$

The value of Q is still the same as before. Thus,

$$S_r = \frac{V_r Q}{I} = \frac{47.06 \times 970.3 \times 1000}{40,947} = 1115 \text{ lb/in.}$$

$$p = \frac{\sum Z_r}{S_r} = \frac{3 \times 4416}{1115} = 11.88 \text{ in.}$$

Figure E8.3n shows the plot of the pitch requirements for the half-span of the beam; the other half is symmetrical about its centerline. AASHTO 10.38.2.4 limits the minimum pitch to 4 in., and 10.38.5.1 limits the maximum pitch to 24 in. Hence, use the following

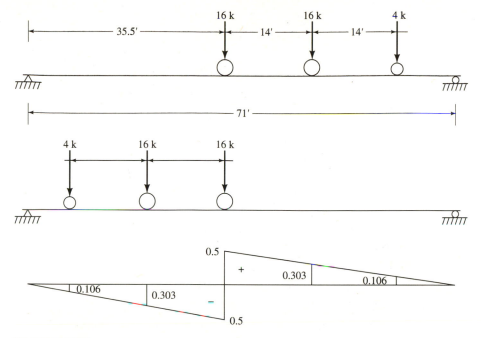

FIGURE E8.3m

Influence line for maximum shear at 35.5 ft from the left support (midspan), and the position of the HS truck for maximum positive and negative shear.

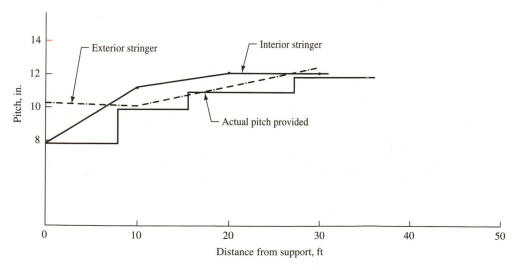

FIGURE E8.3n

Pitch of shear studs for the interior stringer.

spacings between the support and the centerline of the beam:

First-row studs at 2 in. from support = 0 ft 2 in.

11 spacings at 8 in. = 7 ft 4 in.

9 spacings at 10 in. = 7 ft 6 in.

12 spacings at 11 in. = 11 ft 0 in.

$9\frac{1}{2}$ spacings at 12 in. = 9 ft 6 in.

Total distance = 35 ft 6 in.

Total number of studs = $(1 + 11 + 9 + 12 + 9) \times 3$ studs/row

= 126 for half span

Note that the actual pitch has been provided so that it also satisfies, as discussed later, the pitch requirements for the exterior stringer.

Check for strength requirements. The strength requirements for composite beams are covered by AASHTO 10.38.5.1.2, which mandates that the number of shear connectors equal or exceed the number given by Eq. 8.22.

$$N_1 = P/\phi S_u \qquad \text{(AASHTO Eq. 10.60)} \qquad (8.22)$$

ϕ = reduction factor = 0.85
P = force in deck slab

The force P in the deck slab is to be taken as the smaller of P_1, the tensile strength of the steel beam at yield (Eq. 8.23), or P_2, the compression strength of the slab (Eq. 8.24). The values of P_1, P_2, and the total number of studs, N, based on the smaller of P_1 or P_2, are computed as follows:

$P_1 = A_s F_y = 60.7 \times 36 = 2185$ kips

$P_2 = 0.85 f_c' b t_s = 0.85 \times 3.5 \times 90 \times 7.5 = 2008$ kips < 2185 kips

Therefore, the smaller value, $P_2 = 2008$ kips, governs.

$E_c = 33 w^{1.5} \sqrt{f_c'} = 33 \times (145)^{1.5} \times \sqrt{3500} = 3.41 \times 10^6$ lb/in.²

$S_u = 0.4 d^2 \sqrt{f_c' E_c} = 0.4 \times (0.75)^2 \times \sqrt{3500 \times 3.41 \times 10^6} = 24{,}581$ lb

$N = \dfrac{P}{\phi S_u} = \dfrac{2008 \times 1000}{0.85 \times 24{,}581} = 96$ studs < 126 studs provided, OK

Therefore, use the pitch of shear studs as shown in Fig. E8.3n.

Welding of cover plate

1. *Strength.* Consider the shear stress at the end of the cover plate, i.e., 8.0 ft from the support. The shear at this section is computed from the influence line for shear at that section (Fig. E8.3o).

Shear due to dead load on steel section alone

$$w_{\text{DL1}} = 0.95 \text{ k/ft}$$

$$V_{d(\text{NC})} = 0.95 \times \left(\tfrac{1}{2} \times 0.887 \times 63.0 - \tfrac{1}{2} \times 0.113 \times 8.0\right) = 26.11 \text{ kips}$$

Compute the shear per unit length (referred to as *shear flow* in texts on strength of materials), $f_v = VQ/I$, where $Q = 21.0 \times 12.12 = 254.5$ in.³

$$f_{v,d(\text{NC})} = \frac{VQ}{I} = \frac{26.11 \times 254.5}{12{,}513} = 0.53 \text{ k/in.}$$

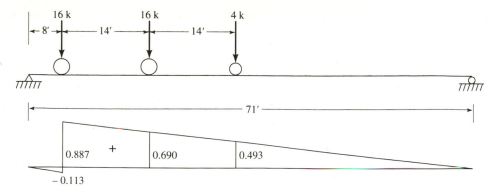

FIGURE E8.3o

Influence line for maximum shear at 8 ft from support, and the position of the HS truck for maximum shear.

Shear due to dead load on composite section

$(n = 27)$

$$w_{DL2} = 0.598 \text{ k/ft}$$

$$V_{d(C)} = 0.598 \times (\tfrac{1}{2} \times 0.887 \times 63.0 - \tfrac{1}{2} \times 0.113 \times 8.0) = 16.44 \text{ kips}$$

$$Q = 21.0 \times (21.31 - \tfrac{1}{2} \times 1.5) = 431.8 \text{ in.}^3$$

$$f_{v,d(C)} = \frac{VQ}{I} = \frac{16.44 \times 431.8}{27,450} = 0.26 \text{ k/in.}$$

Shear due to live load on composite section $(n = 9)$.
Where the impact factor for a loaded length of $71 - 8 = 63$ ft is

$$I = \frac{50}{L + 125} = \frac{50}{63 + 125} = 0.266$$

$$V_{L+I} = 16 \times (0.887 + 0.690 + \tfrac{1}{4} \times 0.493) \times 1.364 \times 1.266 = 47.0 \text{ kips}$$

where 1.364 is the DF.

$$Q = 21.0 \times (28.86 - \tfrac{1}{2} \times 1.5) = 590.3 \text{ in.}^3$$

$$f_{v,L+I} = \frac{VQ}{I} = \frac{47.0 \times 590.3}{40,947} = 0.68 \text{ k/in.}$$

Total shear stress $= 0.53 + 0.26 + 0.68 = 1.47$ k/in.

Because the unit shear is so small (1.46 k/in.), try the minimum allowable weld size. AASHTO 10.32.2.2 specifies that, for the base metal thickness of the thicker part joined ($1\tfrac{1}{2}$-in.-thick cover plate in the present case), the minimum weld thickness is $\tfrac{5}{16}$ in. Also, the weld size should not exceed the thickness of the thinner part joined (0.79-in.-thick flange of W36 × 135 in the present case). Thus, a $\tfrac{5}{16}$-in.-thick weld can be used.

$$\text{Stress on two lines of weld} = \frac{1.47}{2 \times 5/16 \times 0.707} = 3.33 \text{ ksi}$$

Per AASHTO 10.32.2, the maximum allowable stress in the fillet weld $= 0.27F_u = 0.27 \times 58 = 15.66$ ksi > 3.33 ksi, OK.

2. *Check for fatigue.* The shear due to live load *plus* impact at 8 ft from the support was computed earlier to be 47.0 kips. The range of shear due to live load plus impact, with $I = 0.3$ and $DF = 1.364$, is

$$V_{r,L+I} = 47.0 - (-4 \times 0.113) \times 1.364 \times 1.3 = 47.8 \text{ kips}$$

The range of unit shear is

$$S_r = \frac{V_r Q}{I} = \frac{47.8 \times 590.3}{40,947} = 0.69 \text{ k/in.}$$

$$\text{Stress on two lines of } \frac{5}{16}\text{-in. weld} = \frac{0.69}{2 \times 5/16 \times 0.707} = 1.56 \text{ ksi}$$

The applicable fatigue stress category for a fillet-welded cover plate corresponds to stress category E, Illustrative Example 7, as specified in Table A.12 (Appendix A) (AASHTO Table 10.3.1B: "Built-up members"). The value of allowable range of shear stress is read from Table A.10 (Appendix A) (AASHTO Table 10.3.1A) for stress category E at 2,000,000 cycles: 8 ksi > 1.56 ksi, OK.

3. *Development length of cover plate.* Per Table A.26 (Appendix A) (AASHTO Table 10.32.1A), the allowable stress in flexural tension is 20 ksi. Therefore,

$$\text{Strength of cover plate} = A_{\text{cov. pl.}} \times \text{allowable stress}$$

$$= 14 \times 1.5 \times 20 = 420 \text{ kips}$$

$$\text{Strength of two } \tfrac{5}{16}\text{-in. fillet welds} = 2 \times \tfrac{5}{16} \times 0.707 \times 15.66$$

$$= 6.92 \text{ k/in.}$$

$$\text{Required development length} = \frac{420}{6.92} = 60.7 \text{ in.}$$

i.e., a weld length of 60.7 in. is required to resist shear. However, the actual weld is continuous along the cover plate. With the cutoff point at 8 ft from the support, the actual length provided $= 71 - 2 \times 8 = 55$ ft.

Per AASHTO 10.13.1, the minimum permissible length of the cover plate is $2d + 3$ ft. For a W36 × 135 beam, $2d + 3 = 2 \times (35.55/12) + 3 = 9$ ft. Thus, the length of the weld provided is more than adequate.

Exterior stringers

Dead load. The dead load due to the weight of the deck slab will be computed by considering a portion of the deck as a simple span with an overhang supported by the exterior and adjacent interior stringers, as shown in Fig. E8.3p. The corresponding reaction in the exterior

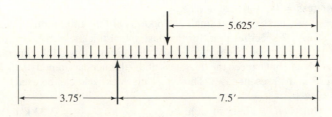

FIGURE E8.3p
Exterior and adjacent interior stringers supporting a portion of the deck slab.

stringer due to a uniform load w on the span is

$$w_1 = w \times 11.25 \times \frac{5.625}{7.5} = 8.44w$$

Dead load due to the $7\frac{1}{2}$-in. deck slab on the noncomposite section $= \left(\frac{7.5}{12} \times 0.15\right) \times 8.44 = 0.79 \text{ k/ft}$

Self-weight of the stringer (try W36 ×135, same as that used for the interior stringer) $= 0.135 \text{ k/ft}$

Dead load due to $14 \times 1\frac{1}{2}$-in. cover plate $= 0.072 \text{ k/ft}$

Dead load on noncomposite section $= 0.79 + 0.135 + 0.072$

$$= 0.997 \text{ k/ft} \approx 1.0 \text{ k/ft}$$

$$M_{D(NC)} = \tfrac{1}{8} \times wL^2 = \tfrac{1}{8} \times 1.0 \times (71)^2 = 630 \text{ k-ft}$$

The following dead loads are taken from the design of the interior stringer:

Dead load of parapets on exterior stringer $= 0.20 \text{ k/ft}$

Dead load due to railings on exterior stringer $= 0.008 \text{ k/ft}$

Dead load due to sidewalk $= 0.210 \text{ k/ft}$

Total $= 0.418 \text{ k/ft}$

The dead load due to the wearing surface on the entire 28-ft-wide roadway is distributed equally to all stringers. Therefore,

Dead load due to the wearing surface $= 0.025 \times 28/5 = 0.140 \text{ k/ft}$

Additional dead load on composite section $= (0.418 + 0.140)$

$$= 0.558 \text{ k/ft}$$

$$M_{D(C)} = wL^2/8 = 0.558 \times (71)^2/8 = 352 \text{ k-ft}$$

The live load on the sidewalk is computed per AASHTO 3.14.1.1: $w = 85$ lb/ft^2, and is positioned as shown in Fig. E8.3q. The portion of load distributed to the exterior stringer is computed as the reaction in the beam treating the deck as simply supported on the exterior and the interior stringers. The centroid of the sidewalk live load is located at 8.17 ft from the interior stringer:

$$\text{Sidewalk load} = (0.085 \times 3) \times \frac{8.17}{7.5} = 0.28 \text{ k/ft}$$

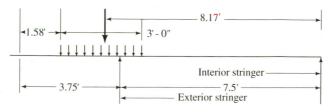

FIGURE E8.3q
Position of the sidewalk live load.

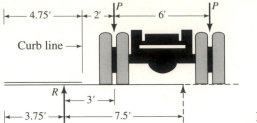

FIGURE E8.3r

The corresponding moment is

$$M_s = \tfrac{1}{8} \times wL^2 = \tfrac{1}{8} \times 0.28 \times (71)^2 = 176 \text{ k-ft}$$

Live load. The distribution factor for the exterior stringer is computed by two methods, per AASHTO 3.23.2.3.1, and the larger value is used for design.

First method, per AASHTO 3.23.2.3.1.2. The position of the HS truck is as shown in Fig. E8.3r. The load in the exterior stringer is the reaction of the wheel load obtained by assuming the flooring acts as a simple span between stringers. The reaction, R, is

$$R = P \times \frac{4.5}{7.5} = 0.60P$$

Second method, per AASHTO 3.23.2.3.1.5. For a slab supported by four or more stringers spaced more than 6 ft apart,

$$\text{Distribution factor} = \frac{S}{4.0 + 0.25S} = \frac{7.5}{4.0 + 0.25 \times 7.5} = 1.277 > 0.60$$

Therefore, the distribution factor = 1.277 (> 0.60). For $L = 71$ ft, the maximum moment per lane = 1003.5 k-ft.

$$M_L \text{ for wheel load} = \tfrac{1}{2} \times 1003.5 \times 1.277 = 641 \text{ k-ft}$$

Impact factor, $I = 0.255$, the same as that for the interior stringer.

$$M_{L+I} = 641 \times (1 + 0.255) = 804 \text{ k-ft}$$

Effective width of flange

$$b_e = \tfrac{1}{2} \times \text{interior flange width} + \text{cantilever slab}$$

$$= \tfrac{1}{2} \times 7.5 + 3.75$$

$$= 7.5 \text{ ft} = 90 \text{ in., the same as that for the interior stringer}$$

Section properties. Try the W36 × 135 with a 14 × 1½-in. cover plate—the same cover plate used for the interior stringer. Therefore, the section properties of both the steel (noncomposite) and the composite sections also remain the same as those for the interior stringer. This also satisfies AASHTO 3.23.2.3.1.4, which requires that "in no case shall an exterior stringer have less carrying capacity than an interior stringer." However, stress due to all kinds of loadings at various stages of construction must be checked.

Stresses. Stresses in the noncomposite and composite sections are checked as follows, where the section properties and notations from previous computations for the interior stringer have been used.

Stress due to dead load on noncomposite section

$$M_{D(NC)} = 630 \text{ k-ft}$$

$$f_{bs} = \frac{630 \times 12}{973} = 7.78 \text{ ksi}$$

$$f_{ts} = \frac{630 \times 12}{518} = 14.62 \text{ ksi}$$

Stress due to dead load on composite section

$$M_{D(C)} = 352 \text{ k-ft}$$

$$f_{bs} = \frac{352 \times 12}{1288} = 3.28 \text{ ksi}$$

$$f_{ts} = \frac{352 \times 12}{1744} = 2.42 \text{ ksi}$$

$$f_{tc} = \frac{352 \times 12}{1132} = 3.73 \text{ ksi}$$

$$f_c = \frac{f_{tc}}{n} = \frac{3.73}{27} = 0.14 \text{ ksi}$$

Stress due to sidewalk live load

$$M_{s(C)} = 176 \text{ k-ft}$$

$$f_{bs} = \frac{176 \times 12}{1419} = 1.49 \text{ ksi}$$

$$f_{ts} = \frac{176 \times 12}{5000} = 0.42 \text{ ksi}$$

$$f_{tc} = \frac{176 \times 12}{2438} = 0.87 \text{ ksi}$$

$$f_c = \frac{f_{tc}}{n} = \frac{0.87}{9} = 0.10 \text{ ksi}$$

Stress due to truck load including impact

$$M_{L+I} = 804 \text{ k-ft}$$

$$f_{bs} = \frac{804 \times 12}{1419} = 6.80 \text{ ksi}$$

$$f_{ts} = \frac{804 \times 12}{5000} = 1.93 \text{ ksi}$$

$$f_{tc} = \frac{804 \times 12}{2438} = 3.96 \text{ ksi}$$

$$f_c = \frac{3.96}{9} = 0.44 \text{ ksi}$$

Combined stresses. The allowable stresses in the exterior stringer are 25 percent higher when sidewalk live load is also considered in conjunction with dead load, traffic live load, and impact (AASHTO 2.23.2.3.1.3). Therefore, the combined stresses due to loads with and without the sidewalk live load are checked separately. Note that the allowable stress in the exterior stringer is increased by 25 percent for the combination of dead load, sidewalk live load, traffic live load, and impact. However, no increase is permitted for the allowable concrete stress.

1. *Stresses due to all loads, including the sidewalk live load*

$$f_{bs} = 7.78 + 3.28 + 1.49 + 6.80 = 19.35 < 1.25 \times 20 = 25 \text{ ksi}$$

$$f_{ts} = 14.62 + 2.42 + 0.42 + 1.93 = 19.39 < 1.25 \times 20 = 25 \text{ ksi}$$

$$f_c = 0.14 + 0.10 + 0.44 = 0.68 < 1.40 \text{ ksi}$$

2. *Stresses due to all loads, excluding the sidewalk loads*

$$f_{bs} = 7.78 + 3.28 + 6.80 = 17.86 < 20 \text{ ksi, OK}$$

$$f_{ts} = 14.62 + 2.42 + 1.93 = 18.97 < 20 \text{ ksi, OK}$$

$$f_c = 0.14 + 0.44 = 0.58 < 1.4 \text{ ksi, OK}$$

All stresses are within the allowable limits. Therefore, use W36 × 135 with 14 × 1$\frac{1}{2}$-in. cover plate (on the bottom flange) for the exterior stringer, composite with 7$\frac{1}{2}$-in. slab. Also, use the same length of cover plate used for the interior stringer, the same pitch for shear connectors, the same number of shear connectors, and the same size of fillet welds. This ensures that the exterior stringer has the same capacity as the interior stringer, as required per AASHTO 3.23.2.3.1.4.

Check for stresses in cover plate at 8 ft from support. Moments due to various loading conditions are computed from the influence line (Fig. E8.3s) for the moment at 8 ft from the support, which is the cutoff point of the cover plate. The DF and I are 1.277 and 0.255, respectively.

$$M_{D(NC)} = \tfrac{1}{2} \times 0.997 \times 7.10 \times 71 = 251.3 \text{ k-ft}$$

$$M_{D(C)} = \tfrac{1}{2} \times 0.558 \times 7.10 \times 71 = 140.6 \text{ k-ft}$$

$$M_{SW} = \tfrac{1}{2} \times 0.28 \times 7.10 \times 71 = 70.6 \text{ k-ft}$$

$$M_{L+I} = [16(7.10 + 5.52) + 4 \times 3.94] \times 1.277 \times 1.255 = 349 \text{ k-ft}$$

1. *Stresses with sidewalk loading*

$$f_{bs} = \left[\frac{251.3}{973} + \frac{140.6}{593} + \frac{70.6}{656} + \frac{349}{656} \right] \times 12 = 13.62 \text{ ksi} < 25 \text{ ksi, OK}$$

$$f_{ts} = \left[\frac{251.3}{518} + \frac{140.6}{1731} + \frac{70.6}{6993} + \frac{349}{6993} \right] \times 12 = 7.52 \text{ ksi} < 25 \text{ ksi, OK}$$

$$f_c = \left[\frac{140.6}{893 \times 27} + \frac{70.6}{1847 \times 9} + \frac{349}{1847 \times 9} \right] \times 12 = 0.37 \text{ ksi} < 1.4 \text{ ksi, OK}$$

2. *Fatigue strength of cover plate.*

The fatigue stress range, F_{sr}, was established to be 8 ksi for the interior stringer. For the exterior stringer, an overstress of 25 percent will be permitted in the presence of the sidewalk live load in combination with other dead and live loads.

$$f_{b,F(pl.)} = \left[\frac{70.6}{656} + \frac{349}{656} \right] \times 12 = 7.68 \text{ ksi} < 1.25 \times 8 = 10.0 \text{ ksi, OK}$$

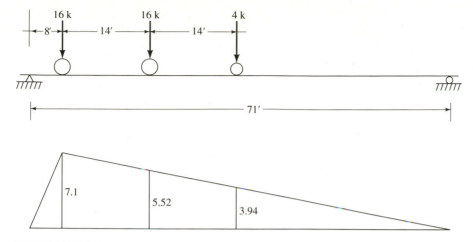

FIGURE E8.3s
Influence lines for moment at 8 ft from support.

3. *Stresses without sidewalk loading*

$$f_{bs} = \left[\frac{251.3}{973} + \frac{140.6}{593} + \frac{349}{656} \right] \times 12 = 12.33 \text{ ksi} < 20 \text{ ksi, OK}$$

$$f_{ts} = \left[\frac{251.3}{518} + \frac{140.6}{1731} + \frac{349}{6993} \right] \times 12 = 7.40 \text{ ksi} < 20 \text{ ksi, OK}$$

$$f_c = \left[\frac{140.6}{893 \times 27} + \frac{349}{1847 \times 9} \right] \times 12 = 0.38 \text{ ksi} < 1.4 \text{ ksi, OK}$$

4. *Fatigue strength of cover plate*

$$f_{b,F(\text{pl.})} = \tfrac{349}{656} \times 12 = 6.38 \text{ ksi} < 8.0 \text{ ksi, OK}$$

Therefore, the same cutoff point for the cover plate (8 ft from the support) that was used for the interior stringers will be adequate for the exterior stringers.

End shear
Shears due to various dead loads

$$V_{D(\text{NC})} = \tfrac{1}{2} \times 0.997 \times 71 = 35.4 \text{ kips}$$

$$V_{D(\text{C})} = \tfrac{1}{2} \times 0.558 \times 71 = 19.8 \text{ kips}$$

$$V_{\text{SW}} = \tfrac{1}{2} \times 0.28 \times 71 = 9.9 \text{ kips}$$

Shear due to live load. The transverse and longitudinal positions of wheel loads for maximum shear in the exterior stringer, per AASHTO Fig. 3.7.7A (see Fig. 3.6 in this book) are shown in Fig. E8.3t.

The distribution factor for wheel loads at ends is $DF = (4.5/7.5)P = 0.60P$. The distribution factor for wheel loads at other positions is the same as that for the moment—$DF = 1.277$. The impact factor is $I = 0.255$, the same as that for the interior stringer.

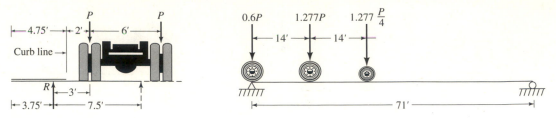

FIGURE E8.3t
Critical transverse position of wheel loads for maximum shear in the exterior stringer.

Therefore, shear due to live load plus impact is

$$V_{L+I} = \left[16 \times 0.6 + \left(1.277 \times 16 \times \tfrac{57}{71} \right) + \left(1.277 \times 4 \times \tfrac{43}{71} \right) \right] \times 1.255 = 36.5 \text{ kips}$$

Total shears are as follows:

With sidewalk load, $V = 35.4 + 19.8 + 9.9 + 36.5 = 100.6$ kips

Without sidewalk load, $V = 35.4 + 19.8 + 36.5$ $= 90.7$ kips

The corresponding shear stresses are

$$f_{v,\text{sw}} = \frac{100.6}{35.55 \times 0.6} = 4.72 \text{ ksi} < 1.25 \times 12 = 15 \text{ ksi, OK}$$

$$f_v = \frac{90.7}{35.55 \times 0.6} = 4.25 \text{ ksi} < 12 \text{ ksi, OK}$$

where $f_{v,\text{sw}}$ = shear stress due to loads, including the sidewalk loading
f_v = shear stress due to loads, without the sidewalk loading

Pitch of shear connectors. Pitches of shear connectors for the exterior stringer are computed for shear at the same distances from the support used for the interior stringer. Therefore, the influence-line diagrams for shear at various sections of the interior stringer can be used for the corresponding sections of the exterior stringer. Also, the range of shears due to live load plus impact at various sections of both the interior and the exterior stringers, *except for the distribution factor,* are identical. For computational expediency, therefore, the values of range of shear for the interior stringer due to live load plus impact, but without the distribution factor, are also used for the exterior stringer. These values are then multiplied by the distribution factor for the exterior stringer.

We will use $\frac{3}{4} \times 4$-in. headed studs, three studs per row, as were used for the interior stringer. The pitch of the studs can be computed in a manner similar to that used for the interior stringer. However, since the only variable that is different in the case of the exterior stringer is the range of shear, pitches at various sections of the exterior stringer are computed by the proportion of the pitches for the interior stringer at the same section. This method simply makes computations convenient and expedient. The range of shear and the corresponding pitches for the interior stringer (computed earlier) are used in the following computations.

1. *Shear and pitch at support.* Loaded length of span = 71 ft.

$$V_{\text{SW}} = 9.9 \text{ kips (computed above)}$$

$$V_{L+I} = 36.5 \text{ kips (computed above)}$$

Range of shear without sidewalk live load, $V_r = 36.5$ kips

Range of shear with sidewalk live load, $V_{r,SW} = 36.5 + 9.9 = 46.4$ kips

For the interior stringer, $V_r = 59.6$ kips, and pitch $= 8.1$ in. Therefore, by proportion

$$\text{Without sidewalk live load, pitch} = 8.1 \times \frac{59.6}{36.5} = 13.2 \text{ in.}$$

$$\text{With sidewalk live load, pitch} = 8.1 \times \frac{59.6}{46.4} = 10.4 \text{ in.}$$

2. Shear and pitch at 10 ft from support. Loaded length $= 71 - 10 = 61$ ft. Referring to Fig. E8.3j,

$$V_{SW} = 0.28 \times \tfrac{1}{2} \times 0.859 \times 61 = 7.34 \text{ kips}$$

For the interior stringer, the maximum shear due to live load plus impact is

$$V_{max}^+ = 33.24 \text{ kips}, \qquad V_{max}^- = -2.93 \text{ kips}$$

Therefore, for the exterior stringer, for which the distribution factor is 1.277,

$$V_{L+I} = [33.24 - (-2.93)] \times 1.277 = 46.19 \text{ kips}$$

Without sidewalk live load, $V_r = 46.19$ kips

With sidewalk live load, $V_r = 7.34 + 46.19 = 53.53$ kips

$$\text{Without sidewalk live load, pitch} = 11.04 \times \frac{49.34}{46.19} = 11.8 \text{ in.}$$

$$\text{With sidewalk live load, pitch} = 11.04 \times \frac{49.34}{53.53} = 10.2 \text{ in.}$$

3. Shear and pitch at 20 ft from support. Loaded length $= 71 - 20 = 51$ ft. Referring to Fig. E8.3k,

$$V_{SW} = 0.28 \times \tfrac{1}{2} \times 0.718 \times 51 = 5.13 \text{ kips}$$

For the interior stringer, the maximum shear due to live load plus impact is

$$V_{max}^+ = 27.12 \text{ kips}, \qquad V_{max}^- = -7.63 \text{ kips}$$

Therefore, for the exterior stringer,

$$V_{L+I} = [27.12 - (-7.63)] \times 1.277 = 44.38 \text{ kips}$$

Without sidewalk live load, $V_r = 44.38$ kips

With sidewalk live load, $V_{r,SW} = 5.13 + 44.38 = 49.51$ kips

$$\text{Without sidewalk live load, pitch} = 11.5 \times \frac{47.4}{44.38} = 12.38 \text{ in.}$$

$$\text{With sidewalk live load, pitch} = 11.5 \times \frac{47.4}{49.51} = 11.01 \text{ in.}$$

4. Shear and pitch at 30 ft from support. Loaded length $= 71 - 30 = 41$ ft. Referring to Fig. E8.3l,

$$V_{SW} = 0.28 \times \tfrac{1}{2} \times 0.577 \times 41 = 3.31 \text{ kips}$$

For the interior stringer, the maximum shear due to live load plus impact is

$$V_{max}^+ = 20.86 \text{ kips}, \qquad V_{max}^- = -13.62 \text{ kips}$$

Therefore, for the exterior stringer,

$$V_{L+I} = [20.86 - (-13.62)] \times 1.277 = 44.03 \text{ kips}$$

Without sidewalk live load, $V_r = 44.03$ kips

With sidewalk live load, $V_{r,SW} = 3.31 + 44.03 = 47.34$ kips

Without sidewalk live load, pitch $= 11.59 \times \dfrac{47.03}{44.03} = 12.38$ in.

With sidewalk live load, pitch $= 11.59 \times \dfrac{47.03}{47.34} = 11.51$ in.

5. *Shear and pitch at midspan.* Loaded length $= \frac{1}{2} \times 71 = 35.5$ ft. Referring to Fig. E8.3m,

$$V_{SW} = 0.28 \times \tfrac{1}{2} \times 0.5 \times 35.5 = 2.49 \text{ kips}$$

For the interior stringer, the maximum shear due to live load plus impact is

$$V_{max}^+ = 17.25 \text{ kips}, \qquad V_{max}^- = -17.25 \text{ kips}$$

Therefore, for the exterior stringer,

$$V_{L+I} = [17.25 - (-17.25)] \times 1.277 = 44.06 \text{ kips}$$

Without sidewalk live load, $V_r = 44.06$ kips

With sidewalk live load, $V_{r,SW} = 2.49 + 44.06 = 46.55$ kips

Without sidewalk live load, pitch $= 11.58 \times \dfrac{47.06}{44.06} = 12.37$ in.

With sidewalk live load, pitch $= 11.58 \times \dfrac{47.06}{46.55} = 11.71$ in.

Note that the pitch of shear connectors is larger for shear *without* the sidewalk live load than for shear *with* the sidewalk live load. Also note that these pitches are close to those computed earlier for the interior stringer, as shown in the following table:

Pitch for shear connectors for the interior and exterior stringers

	Location of section from support				
	At support	10 ft	20 ft	30 ft	At midspan
	Pitch of shear connectors (in.)				
Interior stringer	8.1	11.0	11.5	11.6	11.6
Exterior stringer with sidewalk live load	10.4	10.2	11.0	11.5	11.7

A plot of the distance from support vs. the pitch is shown in Fig. E8.3n. As mentioned earlier, the following actual pitch has been selected such that it satisfies pitch requirements for both the exterior as well as the interior stringers:

$$1 \text{ at 2 in. from support} = \quad 0 \text{ ft 2 in.}$$

$$11 \text{ spaced at 8 in. from support} = \quad 7 \text{ ft 4 in.}$$

$$9 \text{ spaced at 10 in. from support} = \quad 7 \text{ ft 6 in.}$$

$$12 \text{ spaced at 11 in. from support} = \quad 11 \text{ ft 0 in.}$$

$$9\tfrac{1}{2} \text{ spaced at 12 in. from support} = \quad 9 \text{ ft 6 in.}$$

$$\text{Total 126 studs} \; = 35 \text{ ft 6 in.} = \text{Half span}$$

Note that the same pitches are also provided for the interior stringer.

Check for strength. The strength requirement for shear connectors for the exterior stringer is identical to that for interior stringers. Therefore, the pitches, which are the same as for the interior stringers, are adequate for the exterior stringers.

Development length of cover plate. Analysis for the development length of the cover plate for the exterior stringer is identical to that for the interior stringer. Therefore, the development length requirement is satisfied.

Welding of cover plate (8 ft from support). For the interior stringer, shear stress in the cover plate at 8 ft from the support due to loads on the noncomposite and composite sections were computed earlier. For the exterior stringer, the section properties are the same as those for the interior stringer. It is expedient to compute shear stresses for the exterior stringer from proportions of stresses due to similar loads on the interior stringer. For shear stress due to live load plus impact, the shear stress is proportioned with respect to proper distribution factors (1.364 for the interior stringer, 1.277 for the exterior stringer).

$$f_{v,D(NC)} = 0.55 \times \frac{0.997}{0.95} = 0.58 \text{ k/in.}^2$$

$$f_{v,D(C)} = 0.29 \times \frac{0.558}{0.598} = 0.27 \text{ k/in.}^2$$

$$f_{v(L+I)} = 0.69 \times \frac{1.277}{1.364} = 0.65 \text{ k/in.}^2$$

$$\text{Total shear stress} = 1.52 \text{ k/in.}^2$$

The loaded length of span $= 71 - 8 = 63$ ft. Referring to Fig. E8.3o, the shear due to sidewalk live load is

$$V_{SW} = 0.28 \times (\tfrac{1}{2} \times 0.887 \times 63) = 7.82 \text{ kips}$$

$$Q = 590.3 \text{ in.}^3$$

$$f_{vs} = \frac{7.82 \times 590.3}{40,947} = 0.11 \text{ k/in.}^2$$

Shear stress due to loads including the sidewalk live load is

$$f_{v,SW} = 1.52 + 0.11 = 1.63 \text{ ksi}$$

With two lines of $\frac{5}{16}$-in. fillet weld, stresses in the weld are

$$\text{Without sidewalk live load, } f_v = \frac{1.52}{2 \times 5/16 \times 0.707} = 3.44 \text{ ksi}$$

$$\text{With sidewalk live load, } f_{v,SW} = \frac{1.63}{2 \times 5/16 \times 0.707} = 3.69 \text{ ksi}$$

In both cases, the weld stresses are below the allowable stress (15.66 ksi). Hence, two $\frac{5}{16}$-in. welds are adequate.

Fatigue. The range of shear due to live load plus impact is computed from the proportion of that for the interior stringer, in the ratio of their distribution factors. The following values for the interior stringer were computed earlier at 8 ft from the support:

$$V_{L+I} = 47.0 \text{ kips}$$

The distribution factors are

$$\text{For interior stringer, } DF = 1.364$$

$$\text{For exterior stringer, } DF = 1.277$$

Again, referring to Fig. E8.3o,

$$V_{rL+I} = 47.0 \times \frac{1.277}{1.364} - (-4 \times 0.113) \times 1.277 \times 1.266 = 44.73 \text{ kips}$$

Due to sidewalk live load,

$$V_{SW} = 0.28[0.887 \times \tfrac{63}{2} - (-0.113) \times \tfrac{8}{2}] = 7.95 \text{ kips}$$

With sidewalk live load, $V_{r,SW} = 44.73 + 7.95 = 52.68$ kips

Shear stresses, without and with the sidewalk live load, are

$$f_{vr} = \frac{44.73 \times 590.3}{40,947} = 0.64 \text{ ksi}$$

$$f_{vr,SW} = \frac{52.68 \times 590.3}{40,947} = 0.76 \text{ ksi}$$

With two $\frac{5}{16}$-in. welds, the corresponding weld stresses are

$$\text{Without sidewalk live load, } f_{vw} = \frac{0.64}{2 \times 5/16 \times 0.707} = 1.45 \text{ ksi}$$

$$\text{With sidewalk live load, } f_{vw,SW} = \frac{0.76}{2 \times 5/16 \times 0.707} = 1.72 \text{ ksi}$$

Both weld stresses are less than the allowable value of 8 ksi. Hence, the strength of welds is adequate.

Diaphragms. Provide W24 $\times$ 55 diaphragms at $\frac{1}{3} \times 71 = 23$ ft 8 in. from each support and at each end. This satisfies AASHTO 10.20.1, which requires that diaphragms be provided at each end and at intervals not exceeding 25 ft. The minimum required depth of the diaphragm is

$$\tfrac{1}{2} \times \text{girder depth} = \tfrac{1}{2} \times (35.55 + 1.5) = 18.5 \text{ in.}$$

Depth of W24 $\times$ 55 = 23.57 in. > 18.5 in., OK

Wind bracings. As illustrated in Example 8.1, wind loads would be small for this bridge and, therefore, wind bracings are not required. For illustrative purposes only, the following computations are provided.

Height from bottom of slab to top of parapet	$= 48.5$ in.
Haunch	$= 2.0$ in.
Depth of W36 × 135 between flanges $= 35.55 - 2 \times 0.79 =$	33.97 in.
Depth of bottom flange	$= 0.79$ in.
Cover plate $1\frac{1}{2}$-in. thick	$= 1.5$ in.

Total height in elevation $= 86.76$ in. $= 7.23$ ft

Wind load on exterior girder $= 50 \times 7.23$ (Fig. E8.3u)

$= 362$ lb/ft > 300 lb/ft, OK

Wind load on the bottom flange, W $= \frac{1}{2} \times 362 = 181$ lb/ft

Diaphragm spacing, S_d $= 23.67$ ft

Moment due to wind load, $M_{cb} = 0.08WS_d^2 = 0.08 \times 0.181 \times (23.67)^2 = 8.11$ k-ft

The bottom flange of the beam consists of two plates: 11.90 × 0.79 (rolled) and the cover plate, 14 × 1.5. For computational purposes, the bottom flange is assumed to be 12 in. wide and $1.5 + 0.79 = 2.29$ in. thick, with the section modulus

$$S = \frac{t_f b_f^2}{6} = \frac{2.29 \times (12)^2}{6} = 54.96 \text{ in.}^3$$

The bending stress due to M_{cb} is

$$f_{cb} = \frac{M}{S} = \frac{8.11 \times 12}{54.96} = 1.77 \text{ ksi}$$

Assuming that lateral bracings are not provided,

$$R = \frac{(0.2272L - 11)}{(S_D)^{2/3}} = \frac{[(0.2272)(71) - 11]}{(23.67)^{2/3}} = 0.622$$

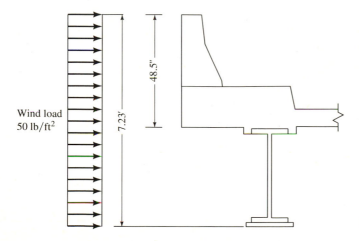

Wind load
50 lb/ft²

FIGURE E8.3u

The stress in the bottom flange due to wind load is

$$F = R f_{cb} = 0.622 \times 1.77 = 1.10 \text{ ksi}$$

Maximum stress in the exterior stringer due to dead and live load plus impact was computed to be 17.78 ksi. Therefore, the total stress in the bottom flange is

$$f_{bs} = 17.78 + 1.10 = 18.88 \text{ ksi} < 20.0 \text{ ksi, OK}$$

Typical details of the superstructure (slab and stringers) are shown in Fig. E8.3v.

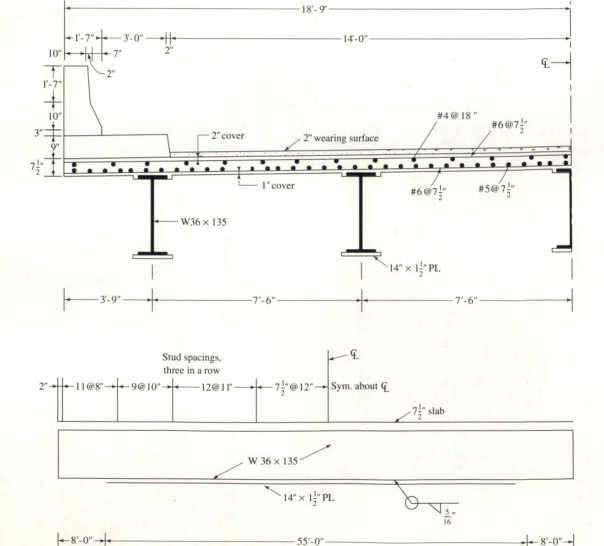

FIGURE E8.3v
Typical details of the superstructure.

EXAMPLE 8.4. LOAD FACTOR DESIGN OF THE SUPERSTRUCTURE OF EXAMPLE 8.1. It was explained in Section 8.6.2 that the criteria for service load behavior in the load factor design are the same as those for the service load design method. Therefore, in this example, only supplementary calculations pertaining to the load factor design are presented.

Check for maximum moments (AASHTO 10.48.1). First, the steel section required on the basis of load factor design will be selected as governed by the maximum loads. The service loads are $M_D = 372$ k-ft and $M_{L+I} = 513$ k-ft. Thus, the maximum loads are

$$M_{\max} = 1.3\left[D + \tfrac{5}{3}(L + I)\right] \tag{8.29}$$

$$= 1.3\left[372 + \tfrac{5}{3}(513)\right]$$

$$= 1595 \text{ k-ft, OK}$$

The plastic section modulus, Z, required is

$$Z = \frac{M_u}{F_y} = \frac{1595 \times 12}{36} = 532 \text{ in.}^3$$

From AISC [1989] ("Plastic Design Selection Table," p. 2-19), the most economical section is found to be W40 × 149 ($Z = 597$ in.^{3}). Check that this section meets the compactness requirements (AASHTO 10.48.4.4): The section properties of W40 × 149 are

$$d = 38.20 \text{ in.} \qquad b_f = 11.81 \text{ in.} \qquad S_x = 512 \text{ in.}^3 \qquad I = 9780 \text{ in.}^4$$

$$t_w = 0.63 \text{ in.} \qquad t_f = 0.83 \text{ in.} \qquad Z = 597 \text{ in.}^3$$

Check the slenderness ratio, b'/t, of the projecting compression flange element:

$$\frac{b'}{t} = \frac{1/2 \times (11.81 - 2 \times 0.63)}{0.83} = 6.36 < 10.8, \text{ OK} \qquad \text{(see Table 8.9)}$$

Check the slenderness ratio, D/t_w, for the web:

$$\frac{D}{t_w} = \frac{38.20 - 2 \times 0.83}{0.63} = 58.0 < 101, \text{ OK} \qquad \text{(see Table 8.9)}$$

By inspection, note that both b'/t and D/t_w ratios are less than 75 percent of their respective maximum permitted values. Therefore, a check by the interaction formula (AASHTO Eq. 10.94) is not required. Thus, W40 × 149 qualifies as a compact section, and its maximum strength is

$$M_u = F_y Z \tag{8.31}$$

$$= 36 \times \tfrac{597}{12}$$

$$= 1791 \text{ k-ft} > M_{\max} = 1595 \text{ k-ft, OK}$$

Note that maximum loads are only 89 percent of the capacity of the section.

Check for overloads (AASHTO 10.57)

$$0.8F_y S = 0.8 \times 36 \times \tfrac{512}{12} = 1229 \text{ k-ft}$$

$$\text{Overloads} = D + 5(L + I)/3 \tag{8.30}$$

$$= 372 + 5 \times \tfrac{513}{3}$$

$$= 1227 \text{ k-ft} < 1229 \text{ k-ft, OK}$$

The overloads are just under 100 percent of the overload capacity of the beam. Therefore, provide W40 × 149 for both interior and exterior stringers.

Since the top flange will be embedded in the bottom of the concrete slab (and thus continuously braced), lateral bracing of the compression flange is not a consideration in this example.

Check for shear (AASHTO 10.48.8)

$$V_u = CV_p \qquad \text{(AASHTO Eq. 10.112)} \qquad (8.41)$$

The buckling coefficient is $k = 5$ for rolled beams (unstiffened beams).

$$D/t_w = 58 \qquad \text{(computed above)}$$

$$\frac{6000\sqrt{k}}{\sqrt{F_y}} = \frac{6000 \times \sqrt{5}}{\sqrt{36,000}} = 70.71 > \frac{D}{t_w} = 58$$

Hence, $C = 1$.

$$V_p = 0.85F_y Dt_w \qquad (8.43)$$

$$= 0.85 \times 36 \times (38.20 - 2 \times 0.83) \times 0.63$$

$$= 704.4 \text{ kips}$$

$$V_u = CV_p = 1 \times 704.4 = 704.4 \text{ kips}$$

Shears under service load condition were computed to be $V_D = 29.8$ kips and $V_{L+I} = 54$ kips. Therefore, shear under maximum loads is

$$V_{\max} = 1.3\left[D + \tfrac{5}{3}(L + I)\right]$$

$$= 1.3\left[29.8 + \tfrac{5}{3} \times 54\right]$$

$$= 155.74 \text{ kips} < V_u = 704.4 \text{ kips, OK}$$

Deflection. Deflection is computed in exactly the same manner as in Example 8.1, in which W36 × 160 was used ($I_x = 9750$ in.[4]). Deflection of the W40 × 149 beam with its greater moment of inertia ($I_x = 9780$ in.[4]) would obviously be smaller than that of W36 × 160 and, hence, it would be acceptable.

Thus, according to the load factor design, a W40 × 149 beam can be used, whereas, according to the service load design, a W36 × 160 beam is required; the load factor design results in savings of 7 percent in the weight of steel.

Discussion: Alternative design. According to the AISC manual footnote, p. 1-10, [AISC, 1989], a W40 × 149 beam is not available from domestic producers and is available only from some producers, thus presenting a potential material procurement problem. The next most economical section available is a W36 × 160 beam [AISC, 1989, p. 2-19] with a plastic section modulus of $Z = 597$ in.[3] This section was selected for the service load design in Example 8.1, and will also qualify under the provisions of the load factor design, as shown by the following calculations:

Check for maximum loads. Check that the section is compact. The section properties of W36 × 160 are

$$d = 36.01 \text{ in.} \qquad b_f = 12.0 \text{ in.} \qquad S_x = 542 \text{ in.}^3$$

$$t_w = 0.65 \text{ in.} \qquad t_f = 1.02 \text{ in.} \qquad Z = 624 \text{ in.}^3$$

Check the slenderness ratio, b'/t, of the projecting compression flange element:

$$\frac{b'}{t} = \frac{\frac{1}{2} \times (12.00 - 0.65)}{1.02} = 5.56 < 10.8, \text{ OK (see Table 8.9)}$$

Check the slenderness ratio, D/t_w for the web:

$$\frac{D}{t_w} = \frac{36.01 - 2 \times 1.02}{0.65} = 52.26 < 101, \text{ OK (see Table 8.9)}$$

By inspection, note that both b'/t and D/t_w ratios are less than 75 percent of their respective maximum permitted values. Therefore, a check by the interaction formula (AASHTO Eq. 10.94) is not required. Thus, W36×160 qualifies as a compact section, and its maximum strength is

$$M_u = F_y Z \tag{8.31}$$

$$= 36 \times 624/12$$

$$= 1872 \text{ k-ft} > M_{max} = 1595 \text{ k-ft}$$

Maximum loads are only 85 percent of the capacity of the section.

Check for overloads (AASHTO 10.57.1*)

$$0.8 F_y S = 0.8 \times 36 \times 542/12 = 1301 \text{ k-ft}$$

$${}^*\text{Overloads} = D + \tfrac{5}{3}[L + I] \tag{8.30}$$

$$= 372 + \tfrac{5}{3} \times 513$$

$$= 1227 \text{ kips} < 1301 \text{ kips, OK}$$

Overloads are 94 percent of the overload capacity of the beam. Note that a lighter section would not be adequate in this situation. (*$\beta = \tfrac{5}{3}$ for Group I loading, considered here. See Table 3.12. Group IA, for which $\beta = 2.2$, is applicable for loadings less than H20 (AASHTO 3.5.1) and is not considered here.)

Check for shear

$$V_p = 0.85 F_y D t_w \tag{8.43}$$

$$= 0.85 \times 36 \times (36.01 - 2 \times 1.02) \times 0.65$$

$$= 675.7 \text{ kips} > V_{max} = 155.74 \text{ kips, OK}$$

EXAMPLE 8.5. LOAD FACTOR DESIGN OF SUPERSTRUCTURE OF EXAMPLE 8.3. Supplementary computations pertaining to the load factor design are presented as follows. Computations for fatigue design and deflections remain the same as for the service load design presented in Example 8.3.

Check for maximum loads. Compute the maximum strength of the beam section. The design is governed by loads on the interior stringer, for which a W36×135 beam with a $14 \times 1\frac{1}{2}$-in. cover plate (partial) was selected, resulting in an unsymmetrical section. The same section was adopted for the exterior stringer as well.

Check that the section is compact. The section properties of W36 × 135 are

$$d = 35.55 \text{ in.} \qquad b_f = 11.95 \text{ in.} \qquad S_x = 439 \text{ in.}^3$$

$$t_w = 0.60 \text{ in.} \qquad t_f = 0.79 \text{ in.} \qquad Z = 509 \text{ in.}^3$$

Check the slenderness ratio, b'/t, of the projecting compression flange element per AASHTO 10.50(c). The dead load stress in the top compression flange due to DL1 was computed to be 13.90 ksi.

$$\frac{b'}{t} = \frac{1/2 \times (12.01 - 0.65)}{1.02} = 5.56$$

$$\frac{2200}{\sqrt{1.3 \times f_{\text{DL1}}}} = \frac{2200}{\sqrt{1.3 \times 19,300}} = 13.89 > \frac{b'}{t} = 5.56, \text{ OK}$$

Check the slenderness ratio, D/t_w, for the web, from Eq. 8.34, per AASHTO 10.50.1.1.2 and 10.48.1.1(b):

$$\frac{2D_{\text{cp}}}{t_w} \leq \frac{19,230}{\sqrt{36,000}} = 101 \qquad \text{(see Table 8.9)}$$

where D_{cp} is the depth of the compression flange in the plastic bending. To determine D_{cp}, the PNA (plastic neutral axis) should be located.

With concrete strength $f'c = 4.0$ ksi and $F_y = 36$ ksi, the maximum compressive strength of the slab, P_2, and the plastic force developable in the steel section, P_1, were computed earlier in Example 8.3 for determining the number of shear studs. These values are

$$P_1 = \sum A_s F_y = 2185 \text{ kips}$$

$$P_2 = 0.85 f'_c b t_s = 2008 \text{ kips}$$

Since $P_1 > P_2$, the PNA lies in the steel section, and using the notation of AASHTO 10.50.1.1.1, $C = 2008$ kips. Thus, the top portion of the steel section will be subjected to the compressive force C' to be computed from Eq. 8.72 (AASHTO Eq. 10.126):

$$C' = \frac{\sum (AF_y) - C}{2}$$

$$= \frac{2185 - 2008}{2} = 177 \text{ kips}$$

The plastic force developable in the top flange is

$$C_{\text{tf}} = (AF_y) = b_f t_f F_y = 11.95 \times 0.79 \times 36 = 340 \text{ kips} > C'$$

Therefore, the PNA lies in the top flange (Fig. E8.5a), and is located below the top of the top flange at a distance given by Eq. 8.75 (AASHTO Eq. 10.127),

$$\bar{y} = \frac{C'}{(AF_y)_{\text{tf}}} t_{\text{tf}}$$

$$= \frac{177}{340}(0.79) = 0.41 \text{ in.}$$

Therefore, $D_{\text{cp}} = 0.41$ in. Note that, because the flange stress would be limited to the specified yield stress, $F_y = 36$ ksi, AASHTO Interim 1994, Eq. 10.128a need not be checked.

Check the compact section requirements for the web. For composite sections, web compactness is defined by the ratio $2D_{\text{cp}}/t_w$ instead of D/t_w (AASHTO Interim 1994, 10.50.1.1.2).

$$\frac{2D_{\text{cp}}}{t_w} = \frac{2 \times 0.41}{0.60} = 1.37 < 101, \text{ OK} \qquad \text{(see Table 8.9)}$$

The compression flange is adequately (continuously) braced by its embedment in the bottom of the slab. Thus, all compactness requirements are satisfied, and the girder section, con-

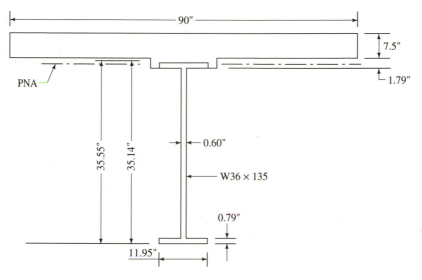

FIGURE E8.5a

sisting of the W36 × 135 beam and the $7\frac{1}{2}$-in.-thick slab, qualifies as a compact composite section. The flexural strength of the composite section is computed as the first moment of all forces about the PNA, taking all forces and moment arms as positive quantities. Thus,

$$
\begin{aligned}
M_u = &\, [0.85(4)(90)(4.955) + 11.95(0.41)^2(\tfrac{1}{2})(36) \\
&+ 11.95(0.79 - 0.41)^2(\tfrac{1}{2})(36) + 33.97(0.60)(17.365)(36) \\
&+ 11.95(0.79)(34.745)(36) + 14(1.5)(35.89)(36)]/12 \\
= &\, 4438.9 \text{ k-ft}
\end{aligned}
$$

The service loads are

$$M_D = 976 \text{ k-ft}$$

$$M_{L+I} = 858 \text{ k-ft}$$

Therefore, the maximum loads are (see Table 3.12)

$$
\begin{aligned}
M_{\max} &= 1.3\left[D + \tfrac{5}{3}(L + I)\right] & (8.29)\\
&= 1.3\left[976 + \tfrac{5}{3}(858)\right] \\
&= 3128 \text{ k-ft} < M_u = 4338.9 \text{ k-ft, OK}
\end{aligned}
$$

Maximum loads are only 70.5 percent of the capacity of the composite section.

Check for overloads (AASHTO 10.57.2)

$$0.95F_y S = 0.95 \times 36 \times \tfrac{972}{12} = 2770.2 \text{ k-ft}$$

$$
\begin{aligned}
\text{Overloads} &= D + \tfrac{5}{3}(L + I) & (8.30)\\
&= 976 + \tfrac{5}{3} \times 858 \\
&= 2406 \text{ k-ft} < 2770.2 \text{ k-ft, OK}
\end{aligned}
$$

Check shear (AASHTO 10.48.8)

$$V_u = CV_p \qquad \text{(AASHTO Eq. 10.112)} \qquad (8.41)$$

$$\frac{D}{t_w} = \frac{35.55 - 2 \times 0.79}{0.60} = 56.6$$

The buckling coefficient is $k = 5$ for rolled beams (unstiffened beams). From Eq. 8.37,

$$\frac{6000\sqrt{k}}{\sqrt{F_y}} = \frac{6000 \times \sqrt{5}}{\sqrt{36,000}} = 70.7 > \frac{D}{t_w} = 56.6$$

Hence, $C = 1$.

$$V_p = 0.85F_y Dt_w \qquad (8.43)$$
$$= 0.85 \times 36 \times (35.55 - 2 \times 0.79) \times 0.60$$
$$= 623.7 \text{ kips}$$

$$V_u = CV_p = 1 \times 623.7 = 623.7 \text{ kips}$$

Shears under service load conditions were computed to be $V_D = 53.5$ kips and $V_{L+I} = 59.6$ kips. Therefore, shear under maximum load is

$$V_{\max} = 1.3\left[D + \tfrac{5}{3}(L + I)\right]$$
$$= 1.3\left[53.5 + \tfrac{5}{3} \times 59.6\right]$$
$$= 198.7 \text{ kips} < V_u = 623.7 \text{ kips, OK}$$

Check deflection. Deflection computations remain the same as in Example 8.3.

8.9.2 Continuous Slab–Steel Beam Bridge Design

This example is excerpted partly (beginning with "Design of stringers") from AASHTO [1991] *Guide Specifications for Alternate Load Factor Design Procedures for Steel Beam Bridges Using Braced Compact Sections,* copyright 1991 by the American Association of State Highway and Transportation Officials, Washington, D.C. Used by permission. The longhand calculations for determining maximum moments and shears, as well as those values at tenth-points of span, have been provided by the author. These calculations are not provided in AASHTO's example. This example, excerpted from AASHTO, 1991, is based on the 1989 AASHTO specifications. However, it has been annotated by the author, with necessary changes to reflect the current AASHTO practice in accordance with the 1992 [AASHTO, 1992] and 1994 interim AASHTO specifications [AASHTO, 1994b]. Readers should review and become familiar with the concepts of plastic design of steel structures before following this example.

EXAMPLE 8.6. Design an interior beam for a two-span (100 and 100 ft) continuous composite steel beam bridge for HS-20 loading with a clear roadway width of 28 ft. The following data are given:

Structural steel:	AASHTO M270 Grade 50W
	(ASTM A709 Grade 50W), with $F_y = 50,000$ psi
Concrete:	$f_c' = 4000$ psi
Slab reinforcement:	ASTM A615, Grade 60 with $F_y = 60,000$ psi

Loading conditions

Case 1:	Weight of girder and slab (DL_1) supported by steel girder alone
Case 2:	Superimposed dead load (DL_2) (curbs and railings) supported by the composite section
Case 3:	Live load plus impact ($L + I$) supported by the composite action
Loading combinations:	Combination A = Case 1 + Case 2 + Case 3
Stress cycles for fatigue:	500,000 cycles of truck loading
	100,000 cycles of lane loading

Calculations. Figure E8.6a shows the typical cross section of the bridge to be designed. The slab thickness is assumed to be 7 in., supported by four W36 × 170 steel stringers. A stringer spacing of 8 ft 4 in. results in an overhang width of 4 ft 2 in., which is half of the stringer spacing. The top flange of the steel beam is embedded in the slab by providing a 2-in. haunch, which qualifies the beam as continuously braced and prevents lateral buckling.

Design for dead loads. Computations for the design of the deck slab are similar to those presented in Examples 8.1 and 8.2, and they are not repeated here. With W36×170 stringers, the initial dead load (DL1) consists of an estimated 230 lb/ft for beam and framing details, plus the self-weight of a 7-in.-thick slab. No future wearing surface is anticipated for this bridge; consequently, none is considered in design. The dead load carried by the composite section (DL2) consists of the weight of the curbs and railings, which is distributed equally to all four stringers. Thus, we arrive at the following dead loads:

Dead load carried by steel beam alone, DL1

$$\text{Self-weight of slab} = \tfrac{7}{12} \times 8.33 \times 0.15 = 0.73$$

$$\text{Steel girder, framing, and concrete haunch} = 0.23 \text{ (estimated)}$$

$$\text{DL1 per girder} = 0.96 \text{ k/ft}$$

Dead load carried by composite section, DL2

$$\text{Curbs and railings, DL2} = 0.660 \text{ k/ft}$$

$$\text{DL2 per girder} = \frac{0.660}{4} = 0.165 \text{ k/ft}$$

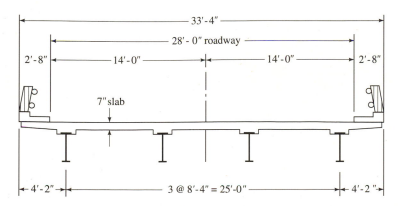

FIGURE E8.6a
Typical section of bridge superstructure.

Design for live load

$$\text{Live load distribution factor} = \frac{S}{5.5}$$

$$= \frac{8.33}{5.5} = 1.51 \text{ for wheels} = 0.755 \text{ for axles}$$

$$\text{Impact factor} = \frac{50}{L + 125} = \frac{50}{100 + 125} = 0.222$$

Design for moments and shears at tenth-points of span. It is customary to compute moments and shears at tenth-points of the span for design purposes. For both dead loads, DL1 and DL2, and the live load, the maximum moment and shear envelopes are computed by any of the convenient methods available [Anger, 1956; Anger and Tramm, 1965; AISC, 1966; Elliot, 1990]. They can also be determined from the influence lines, as explained in such references as Kinney [1957] and Lay [1974]. Alternatively, for a two-span continuous beam with equal spans and with constant moment of inertia, the moments, M_x, and shears, V_x, at a distance x from the left support due to dead loads may simply be computed from the following expressions:

$$M_x = \left(\frac{3wL}{8}\right)x - \frac{wx^2}{2}, \qquad 0 \le x \le L \tag{8.89}$$

$$V_x = \frac{3wl}{8} - wx, \qquad 0 \le x \le L \tag{8.90}$$

where $w = $ uniform load on the beam
$\frac{3}{8}wL = $ reaction at the end support

With $L = 100$ ft, the above expressions simplify to

$$M_x = 37.5wx - 0.5wx^2$$

$$V_x = 37.5w - wx$$

Moments and shears due to both dead loads DL1 and DL2 computed from the above expressions for every tenth-point of the span are shown in the following table:

Moment and shear at tenth-points of span due to DL1 and DL2

Location	Moment due to dead load ($M_x = 37.5wx - 0.5wx^2$)		Shear due to dead load ($V_x = 37.5w - wx$)	
	DL1	DL2	DL1	DL2
At support	0	0	35.9	6.2
0.1L	311	54	26.3	4.5
0.2L	528	91	16.7	2.9
0.3L	649	111	7.1	1.2
0.4L	672	116	−2.5	−2.5
0.5L	599	103	−121.0	−2.1
0.6L	432	74	−222.0	−3.7
0.7L	169	29	−31.3	−5.4
0.8L	−192	−33	−40.9	−7.0
0.9L	−641	−111	−50.5	−8.7
1.0L	−1200	−206	−59.9	−10.3

Values in the above table can be readily verified. For example, at 40 ft from the left support, $x = 40$ ft, and $w_{DL1} = 0.96$ k/ft, we have

$$M_{40} = 37.5 \times 0.96 \times 40 - 0.96 \times (40)^2/2 = 672 \text{ k-ft}$$

$$V_{40} = 37.5 \times 0.96 - 0.96 \times 40 = -2.4 \text{ kips}$$

$$V_o = 37.5 \times 0.96 = 36.0 \text{ kips (at left support)}$$

Maximum negative moment and shear, which occur at the interior support, are

$$M_{max}^- = -\frac{wL^2}{8} = -\frac{0.96 \times 100^2}{8} = -1200 \text{ k-ft}$$

$$V_{max}^- = -\frac{5wL}{8} = -\frac{5 \times 0.96 \times 100}{8} = -60 \text{ kips}$$

Moments and shears due to live load. Reactions, moments, and shears at tenth-points of a span are computed from the influence coefficients, as explained in AISC [1966] for a two-span continuous beam with $N = 1$ (i.e., for equal spans). The influence coefficients, excerpted from AISC [1966] with permission from the American Institute of Steel Construction, are shown in Tables 8.11 and 8.12. Values given in any one row of these tables are ordinates to the bending moment diagram produced by a unit load placed at the load point, which is shown at the left end of the table in the same row. Values in any one column of this table are ordinates to the influence line for the point under which they are tabulated.

Moments due to live load. Note that the values of the influence coefficients tabulated in Tables 8.10 and 8.11 are for every tenth point only. Values of any other point can be computed by interpolation. Moments and shears obtained from these influence coefficients are those due to the axle loads of HS20-44 loading. Therefore, these values must be multiplied by the appropriate distribution and impact factors to obtain moments and shears in a beam or a girder.

To develop a clear understanding of the use of these tables, moments due to live load at 10 and 20 ft from the left support are computed as follows.

1. *Live-load moment at 10 ft from left support.* The influence line for maximum moment at 10 ft from the left support is shown in Fig. E8.6b, which also shows the position of HS20 truck loading for maximum moment at that point.

The following tabulated values of influence coefficients (IC) are obtained from Table 8.11 (column under "0.1 span"):

$$IC_{0.1L} = 0.0875$$

$$IC_{0.2L} = 0.0752$$

$$IC_{0.3L} = 0.0632$$

$$IC_{0.4L} = 0.0516$$

The influence coefficients for $x = 24$ ft and 38 ft from the left support (positions of the axle loads) are computed by interpolation:

$$IC_{0.24L} = 0.0752 - \tfrac{4}{10} \times (0.0752 - 0.0632) = 0.0704$$

$$IC_{0.38L} = 0.0632 - \tfrac{8}{10} \times (0.0632 - 0.0516) = 0.05392$$

These moment coefficients are multiplied by the corresponding wheel loads:

$$\sum(\text{Load} \times IC) = 16 \times (0.0875 + 0.0704) + 4 \times (0.05392) = 2.74208$$

TABLE 8.11

Influence coefficients—moments at tenth-points [AISC, 1966]

Moments/PL*

Columns A through B are **Span 1**; columns after B through C are **Span 2**.

Unit load at	A	0.1	0.2	0.3	0.4	0.5	0.6	0.7	0.8	0.9	B	0.1	0.2	0.3	0.4	0.5	0.6	0.7	0.8	0.9	C
Span 1																					
A	0	0	0	0	0	0	0	0	0	0	0	0	0	0	0	0	0	0	0	0	0
0.1	0	0.0875	0.0751	0.0626	0.0501	0.0376	0.0252	0.0127	0.0002	−0.0123	−0.0248	−0.0223	−0.0198	−0.0173	−0.0149	−0.0124	−0.0099	−0.0074	−0.0050	−0.0025	0
0.2	0	0.0752	0.1504	0.1256	0.1008	0.0760	0.0512	0.0264	0.0016	−0.0232	−0.0480	−0.0432	−0.0384	−0.0336	−0.0288	−0.0240	−0.0192	−0.0144	−0.0096	−0.0048	0
0.3	0	0.0632	0.1264	0.1895	0.1527	0.1159	0.0791	0.0422	0.0054	−0.0314	−0.0683	−0.0614	−0.0546	−0.0478	−0.0410	−0.0341	−0.0273	−0.0205	−0.0137	−0.0068	0
0.4	0	0.0516	0.1032	0.1548	0.2064	0.1580	0.1096	0.0612	0.0128	−0.0356	−0.0840	−0.0756	−0.0672	−0.0588	−0.0504	−0.0420	−0.0336	−0.0252	−0.0168	−0.0084	0
0.5	0	0.0406	0.0813	0.1219	0.1625	0.2031	0.1438	0.0844	0.0250	−0.0344	−0.0938	−0.0844	−0.0750	−0.0656	−0.0563	−0.0469	−0.0375	−0.0281	−0.0188	−0.0094	0
0.6	0	0.0304	0.0608	0.0912	0.1216	0.1520	0.1824	0.1128	0.0432	−0.0264	−0.0960	−0.0864	−0.0768	−0.0672	−0.0576	−0.0480	−0.0384	−0.0288	−0.0192	−0.0096	0
0.7	0	0.0211	0.0422	0.0632	0.0843	0.1054	0.1265	0.1475	0.0686	−0.0103	−0.0893	−0.0803	−0.0714	−0.0625	−0.0536	−0.0446	−0.0357	−0.0268	−0.0179	−0.0089	0
0.8	0	0.0128	0.0256	0.0384	0.0512	0.0640	0.0768	0.0896	0.1024	0.0152	−0.0720	−0.0648	−0.0576	−0.0504	−0.0432	−0.0360	−0.0288	−0.0216	−0.0144	−0.0072	0
0.9	0	0.0057	0.0115	0.0172	0.0229	0.0286	0.0344	0.0401	0.0458	0.0515	−0.0428	−0.0385	−0.0324	−0.0299	−0.0257	−0.0214	−0.0171	−0.0128	−0.0086	−0.0043	0
B	0	0	0	0	0	0	0	0	0	0	0	0	0	0	0	0	0	0	0	0	0
Span 2																					
0.1	0	−0.0043	−0.0086	−0.0128	−0.0171	−0.0214	−0.0257	−0.0299	−0.0342	−0.0385	−0.0428	0.0515	0.0458	0.0401	0.0344	0.0286	0.0229	0.0172	0.0115	0.0057	0
0.2	0	−0.0072	−0.0144	−0.0216	−0.0288	−0.0360	−0.0432	−0.0504	−0.0576	−0.0648	−0.0720	0.0152	0.1024	0.0896	0.0768	0.0640	0.0512	0.0384	0.0256	0.0128	0
0.3	0	−0.0089	−0.0179	−0.0268	−0.0357	−0.0446	−0.0536	−0.0625	−0.0714	−0.0803	−0.0893	−0.0103	0.0686	0.1475	0.1265	0.1054	0.0843	0.0632	0.0422	0.0211	0
0.4	0	−0.0096	−0.0192	−0.0288	−0.0384	−0.0480	−0.0576	−0.0672	−0.0768	−0.0864	−0.0960	−0.0264	0.0432	0.1128	0.1824	0.1520	0.1216	0.0912	0.0608	0.0304	0
0.5	0	−0.0094	−0.0188	−0.0281	−0.0375	−0.0469	−0.0563	−0.0656	−0.0750	−0.0844	−0.0938	−0.0344	0.0250	0.0844	0.1438	0.2031	0.1625	0.1219	0.0813	0.0406	0
0.6	0	−0.0084	−0.0168	−0.0252	−0.0336	−0.0420	−0.0504	−0.0588	−0.0672	−0.0756	−0.0840	−0.0356	0.0128	0.0612	0.1096	0.1580	0.2064	0.1548	0.1032	0.0516	0
0.7	0	−0.0068	−0.0137	−0.0205	−0.0273	−0.0341	−0.0410	−0.0478	−0.0546	−0.0614	−0.0683	−0.0314	0.0054	0.0422	0.0791	0.1159	0.1527	0.1895	0.1264	0.0632	0
0.8	0	−0.0048	−0.0096	−0.0144	−0.0192	−0.0240	−0.0288	−0.0336	−0.0384	−0.0432	−0.0480	−0.0232	0.0016	0.0264	0.0512	0.0760	0.1008	0.1256	0.1504	0.0751	0
0.9	0	−0.0025	−0.0050	−0.0074	−0.0099	−0.0124	−0.0149	−0.0173	−0.0198	−0.0223	−0.0248	−0.0123	0.0002	0.0127	0.0252	0.0376	0.0501	0.0626	0.0751	0.0875	0
C	0	0	0	0	0	0	0	0	0	0	0	0	0	0	0	0	0	0	0	0	0
+ Area	0	0.0388	0.0675	0.0863	0.0950	0.0938	0.0825	0.0613	0.0300	0.0061	0	0.0061	0.0300	0.0613	0.0825	0.0938	0.0950	0.0863	0.0675	0.0388	0
− Area	0	−0.0063	−0.0125	−0.0188	−0.0250	−0.0313	−0.0375	−0.0438	−0.0500	−0.0736	−0.1250	−0.0736	−0.0500	−0.0438	−0.0375	−0.0313	−0.0250	−0.0188	−0.0125	−0.0063	0
Total area	0	0.0325	0.0550	0.0675	0.0700	0.0625	0.0450	0.0175	−0.0200	−0.0675	−0.1250	−0.0675	−0.0200	0.0175	0.0450	0.0625	0.0700	0.0675	0.0550	0.0325	0

*where P = wheel load (kips)

L = span length (ft)

TABLE 8.12

Influence coefficients—reactions and shears [AISC, 1966]

Unit load at		R_A	R_B	R_C	V_{AB}	V_{BA}	V_{BC}	V_{CB}
		Reactions/P^*			Shears/P^*			
Span 1	A	1.0	0	0	1.0	0	0	0
	0.1	0.8753	0.1495	−0.0248	0.8753	−0.1247	0.0248	0.0248
	0.2	0.7520	0.2960	−0.0480	0.7520	−0.2480	0.0480	0.0480
	0.3	0.6318	0.4365	−0.0683	0.6318	−0.3682	0.0683	0.0683
	0.4	0.5160	0.5680	−0.0840	0.5160	−0.4840	0.0840	0.0840
	0.5	0.4063	0.6875	−0.0938	0.4063	−0.5937	0.0938	0.0938
	0.6	0.3040	0.7920	−0.0960	0.3040	−0.6960	0.0960	0.0960
	0.7	0.2108	0.8785	−0.0893	0.2108	−0.7892	0.0893	0.0893
	0.8	0.1280	0.9440	−0.0720	0.1280	−0.8720	0.0720	0.0720
	0.9	0.0573	0.9855	−0.0428	0.0573	−0.9427	0.0428	0.0428
Span 2	B	0	1.0	0	0	−1.0 / 0	0 / 1.0	0
	0.1	−0.0428	0.9855	0.0573	−0.0428	−0.0428	0.9427	−0.0573
	0.2	−0.0720	0.9440	0.1280	−0.0720	−0.0720	0.8720	−0.1280
	0.3	−0.0893	0.8785	0.2108	−0.0893	−0.0893	0.7892	−0.2108
	0.4	−0.0960	0.7920	0.3040	−0.0960	−0.0960	0.6960	−0.3040
	0.5	−0.0938	0.6875	0.4063	−0.0938	−0.0938	0.5937	−0.4063
	0.6	−0.0840	0.5680	0.5160	−0.0840	−0.0840	0.4840	−0.5160
	0.7	−0.0683	0.4365	0.6318	−0.0683	−0.0683	0.3682	−0.6318
	0.8	−0.0480	0.2960	0.7520	−0.0480	−0.0480	0.2480	−0.7520
	0.9	−0.0248	0.1495	0.8753	−0.0248	−0.0248	0.1247	−0.8753
	C	0	0	1.0	0	0	0	−1.0
+ Area		0.4375	1.2500	0.4375	0.4375	0	0.6250	0.0625
− Area		−0.0625	0	−0.0625	−0.0625	−0.6250	0	−0.4375
Total area		0.3750	1.2500	0.3750	0.3750	−0.6250	0.6250	−0.3750

*where P = wheelload (kips)

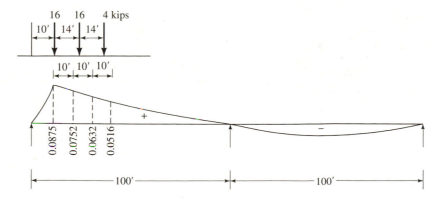

FIGURE E8.6b

Influence line for maximum moment at x = 10 ft from left support.

Then, for $L = 100$ ft, the moment due to live load plus impact is obtained by multiplying the above quantity by 100, the distribution factor (1.51), and the impact factor (1.222). Thus,

$$M_{L+I} = 2.7408 \times 100 \times 1.51 \times 1.222 = 506 \text{ k-ft}$$

The slight difference in the computed value (506 k-ft) and the plotted value (504 k-ft) is due to the rounding-off errors.

2. *Live-load moment at 20 ft from left support.* The influence line for maximum moment at 20 ft from the left support is shown in Fig. E8.6c, which also shows the position of HS20 truck loading for maximum moment at that point. The tabulated values of influence coefficients are obtained from Table 8.11 (column under "0.2 span"):

$$IC_{0.2L} = 0.1504$$

$$IC_{0.3L} = 0.1264$$

$$IC_{0.4L} = 0.1032$$

$$IC_{0.5L} = 0.0813$$

Influence coefficients for $x = 34$ ft and 48 ft from the left support are computed by interpolation:

$$IC_{0.34L} = 0.1264 - \tfrac{4}{10} \times (0.1264 - 0.1032) = 0.11712$$

$$IC_{0.48L} = 0.1032 - \tfrac{8}{10} \times (0.1032 - 0.0813) = 0.08568$$

These moment coefficients are multiplied by the corresponding wheel loads:

$$\sum(\text{Load} \times IC) = 16 \times (0.1504 + 0.11712) + 4 \times (0.08568) = 4.62304$$

Then, for $L = 100$ ft, the moment due to live load plus impact is obtained by multiplying the above quantity by 100, the distribution factor (1.51), and the impact factor (1.222). Thus,

$$M_{L+I} = 4.62304 \times 100 \times 1.51 \times 1.222 = 853 \text{ k-ft}$$

3. *Live load moment at 40 ft from left support.* Computation of the positive moment at this point is of special interest because the causative position of wheel loads, i.e., the truck moving from left to right (position 1) or from right to left (position 2), for maximum moment

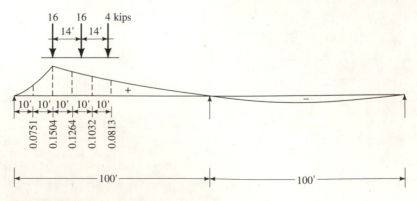

FIGURE E8.6c
Influence line for maximum moment at $x = 20$ ft from the left support.

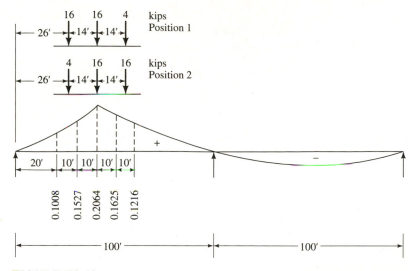

FIGURE E8.6d

Influence line for maximum moment at $x = 40$ ft from the left support.

must be determined first. The influence line for the maximum moment at 40 ft from the left support is shown in Fig. E8.6d, which also shows the positions of HS20 truck loading for maximum moment at that point. The tabulated values of influence coefficients (IC) are obtained from Table 8.11 (column under "0.4 span"):

$$IC_{0.2L} = 0.1008$$

$$IC_{0.3L} = 0.1527$$

$$IC_{0.4L} = 0.2064$$

$$IC_{0.5L} = 0.1625$$

$$IC_{0.6L} = 0.1216$$

Influence coefficients for $x = 26$ ft and 54 ft from the left support are computed by interpolation:

$$IC_{0.26L} = 0.1008 + 0.6 \times (0.1527 - 0.1008) = 0.1319$$

$$IC_{0.54L} = 0.1216 + 0.6 \times (0.1625 - 0.1216) = 0.1461$$

Since the influence line coefficient is greater at $0.54L$ than at $0.26L$, the truck should be placed in position 2 for maximum moment. These moment coefficients are multiplied by the corresponding wheel loads:

$$\sum(\text{Load} \times IC) = 16 \times (0.2064 + 0.1461) + 4 \times 0.1319 = 6.1676$$

Then, for $L = 100$ ft, the moment due to live load plus impact is obtained by multiplying the above quantity by 100, the distribution factor (1.51), and the impact factor (1.222). Thus,

$$M_{L+I} = 6.1676 \times 100 \times 1.51 \times 1.222 = 1138 \text{ k-ft}$$

Moments for other tenth-points along the span can be computed in a similar manner.

Maximum positive moment. Table 2.0 of AISC [1966] lists the maximum positive and negative moments for various span lengths for two-span continuous beams due to HS20-44 loading. For the total span length of 200 ft (each span length is 100 ft), the maximum positive moment is listed as 1233.9 k-ft, occurring at 41.5 ft from the left support. Therefore, the maximum positive moment is computed to be

$$M_{\text{max, pos}} = \tfrac{1}{2}[1233.9 \times \text{Distribution factor} \times \text{Impact factor}$$
$$= \tfrac{1}{2} \times 1233.9 \times 1.51 \times 1.222$$
$$= 1138 \text{ k-ft}$$

which is the same (approximated as 1136 k-ft in Fig. E8.6f) as the maximum positive moment at 40 ft (0.4L) from the left support, computed earlier.

Moment at the interior support. The moment at the interior support is listed in Table 2.0 of AISC [1966] as −1146.4 k-ft. The maximum negative moment at the interior support, therefore, is

$$M_{\text{max, neg.}} = \tfrac{1}{2}(-1146.4) \times \text{Distribution factor} \times \text{Impact factor}$$
$$= \tfrac{1}{2} \times (-1146.4) \times 1.51 \times 1.222$$
$$= -1058 \text{ k-ft (shown as } -1056 \text{ k-ft in Fig. E8.6f)}$$

Note that, as indicated in AISC [1966], the maximum negative moment at the interior support is caused by lane loading.

Shear due to live load. Shear due to live load at tenth-points can be computed from the influence coefficients as follows:

Reaction at the left support (maximum shear at left support). The influence line for the reaction at the left support is shown in Fig. E8.6e. The following tabulated values of the

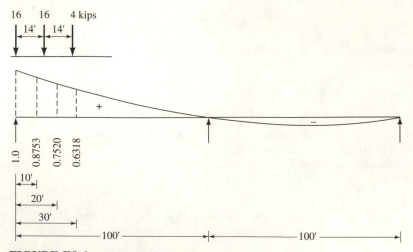

FIGURE E8.6e
Influence line for maximum reaction at left support.

influence coefficients are obtained from Table 8.12:

$$IC_{0L} = 1.0 \qquad IC_{0.2L} = 0.7520$$

$$IC_{0.1L} = 0.8753 \qquad IC_{0.3L} = 0.6318$$

By interpolation,

$$IC_{0.14L} = 0.8753 - \tfrac{4}{10} \times (0.8753 - 0.7520) = 0.82598$$

$$IC_{0.28L} = 0.7520 - \tfrac{8}{10} \times (0.7520 - 0.6318) = 0.65584$$

$$\sum (\text{Load} \times IC) = 16(1.0 + 0.82598) + 4 \times 0.65584 = 31.84 \text{ kips}$$

The shear due to live load plus impact is obtained by multiplying the above value by the distribution factor (1.51) and the impact factor (1.222). Thus,

$$V_{L+I} = 31.84 \times 1.51 \times 1.222 = 58.75 \text{ kips}$$

The maximum moment and shear curves are shown in Fig. E8.6f.

Design of stringer section. In the positive-moment region, the compression flange of the stringer is embedded in the concrete slab through a haunch, which ensures a continuous lateral support. Therefore, only two compactness criteria—the depth-thickness ratio of the web and the shear capacity—apply to the compression flange. However, in the negative-moment region, the bottom flange is in compression and laterally unsupported. Consequently, all compactness criteria must be investigated.

The section properties of a W36 × 170 are:

$$A = 50.0 \text{ in.}^2 \qquad d = 36.17 \text{ in.} \qquad t_w = 0.68 \text{ in.} \qquad b_f = 12.03 \text{ in.}$$

$$t_f = 1.10 \text{ in.} \qquad d/t_w = 53.2 \qquad I_x = 10{,}500 \text{ in.}^4 \qquad S_x = 580 \text{ in.}^3$$

$$r_x = 14.5 \text{ in.} \qquad I_y = 320 \text{ in.}^4 \qquad S_y = 53.2 \text{ in.}^3 \qquad r_y = 2.53 \text{ in.}$$

$$Z_x = 668 \text{ in.}^3$$

Check the actual width-thickness ratio of the projecting compression flange element (the bottom flange in the negative-moment region) per AASHTO Eq. 10.92:

$$\frac{b'}{t} = \frac{\tfrac{1}{2} \times (12.03 - 0.68)}{1.10} = 5.16$$

The allowable width-thickness ratio is given by Eq. 8.32:

$$\frac{b'}{t} \leq \frac{2055}{\sqrt{50{,}000}} = 9.2 > 5.16, \text{ OK}$$

Check the width-thickness ratio of the web from Eq. 8.34 (per AASHTO Eq. 10.93, with D replaced by $2D_{cp}$): Because the longitudinal reinforcing steel in tension over the negative-moment region is considered in computing section properties, the distance from the neutral axis to the compression flange exceeds $D/2$ in this region. Thus, the web compact section requirements must be modified by replacing D by $2D_{cp}$, where D_{cp} is the distance to the compression flange from the neutral axis for plastic bending (AASHTO 10.50.2.1).

The slab contains fourteen #6 longitudinal bars ($A_s = 6.16 \text{ in.}^2$) at 6-in. o.c. According to AASHTO 10.38.4.3, in the negative-moment regions of continuous spans, the minimum longitudinal reinforcement must equal or exceed 1 percent of the cross-sectional area of the

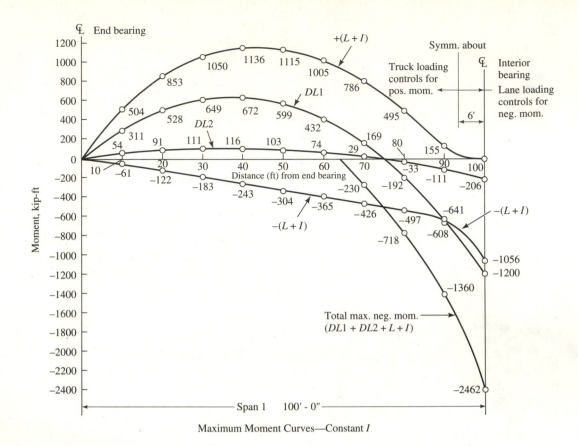

Maximum Moment Curves—Constant I

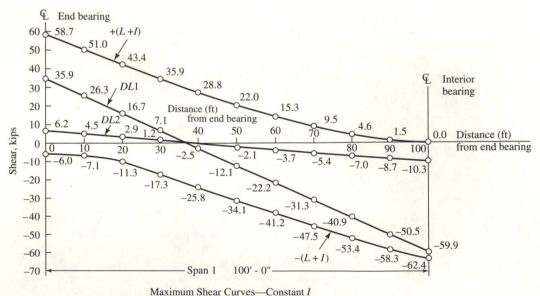

Maximum Shear Curves—Constant I

FIGURE E8.6f
Maximum moment and shear curves.

slab within the effective width. The effective width of slab is the least of the following:

- $\frac{1}{4}L = \frac{1}{4} \times 100 = 25$ ft
- Center-to-center of stringers = 8.33 ft
- 12× slab thickness = $12 \times 7/12 = 7$ ft (governs)

$$A_{s,min} = 0.01 \times (7 \times 12) \times 7 = 5.88 \text{ in.}^2 < 6.16 \text{ in.}^2, \text{ OK}$$

The reinforcing steel is placed 3.3 in. above the bottom of the slab. With a concrete haunch of 2 in. and the flange thickness of 1.1 in., the longitudinal steel is positioned at 4.2 in. from the top of the top flange. The cross section of the beam in the negative-moment region is shown in Fig. E8.6g.

Because of the presence of the longitudinal reinforcement above the top flange (which is in tension) of the stringer, the neutral axis of the plastic section is not at the centroid of the steel section. The shift in the neutral axis is computed considering the equilibrium of forces in a fully yielded cross section. Assume that the steel beam has reached its yield strength, $F_y = 50,000$ psi, and the reinforcement has reached its yield strength, $F_y = 60,000$ psi.

$$\text{Tensile force in reinforcing steel} = 6.16 \times 60,000 = 369,000 \text{ lbs}$$

$$\text{Tensile force in steel section} = \text{steel area in tension} \times F_y$$

$$\text{Half the cross-sectional area of steel beam} = \frac{1}{2} \times 50 = 25 \text{ in.}^2$$

$$\text{Distance between flanges} = d - 2t_f$$
$$= 36.17 - 2 \times 1.10 = 33.97 \text{ in.}$$

$$\text{Net area of steel in tension} = 25 - (D_{cp} - \frac{1}{2} \times 33.97) \times 0.68$$
$$= 13.45 + 0.68D_{cp}$$

$$\text{Tension force in steel} = (36.55 + 0.68D_{cp}) \times 50,000$$
$$= 1,827,500 - 34,000D_{cp}$$

$$\text{Total tension} = 369,000 + 1,827,500 - 34,000D_{cp}$$
$$= 2,197,100 - 34,000D_{cp}$$

$$\text{Force in compression} = (25 - 13.45 + 0.68D_{cp}) \times 50,000$$
$$= 672,500 + 34,000D_{cp}$$

Equating tensile and compressive forces,

$$2,197,100 - 34,000D_{cp} = 672,500 + 34,000D_{cp}$$

$$D_{cp} = 22.42 \text{ in.}$$

Alternatively, D_{cp} can be computed from Eq. 8.79, which was derived in Sec. 8.6.2.2:

$$D = 33.97 \text{ in.}$$

$$A_s = 6.16 \text{ in.}^2$$

$$A_w = Dt_w = 33.97 \times 0.68 = 23.1 \text{ in.}^2$$

$$D_{cp} = 0.5D \left[\frac{A_s}{A_w} \frac{F_{yr}}{F_y} + 1 \right] = 22.42 \text{ in.}$$

The allowable depth-thickness ratio is given by Eq. 8.34 by substituting $2D_{cp}$ for D:

$$\frac{2D_{cp}}{t_w} = \frac{19,300}{\sqrt{50,000}} = 86.0$$

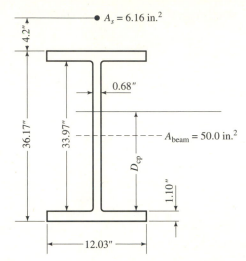

FIGURE E8.6g
Cross section of stringer in the negative-moment region.

The actual depth-thickness ratio is

$$\frac{2D_{cp}}{t_w} = \frac{2(22.42)}{0.68} = 65.9 < 86.0, \text{ OK}$$

Determine if the interaction check is required as given by Eq. 8.35 (per AASHTO Eq. 10.94, with D replaced by $2D_{cp}$). This check is required if *both* b'/t and $2D_{cp}/t_w$ exceed 75 percent of the limits permitted by AASHTO Eqs. 10.92 and 10.93, respectively. This check is not required if only one of the above ratios exceeds 75 percent of the permitted limit.

$$\frac{(b'/t)_{\text{actual}}}{(b'/t)_{\text{allow}}} = \frac{5.16}{9.2} = 0.56 < 0.75$$

$$\frac{(2D_{cp}/t_w)_{\text{actual}}}{(2D_{cp}/t_w)_{\text{allow}}} = \frac{65.9}{86.0} = 0.77 > 0.75$$

Since only one ratio exceeds 75 percent of the permitted limit, the check of the interaction is not required.

Cross frames must be placed at supports, and intermediate cross frames must be provided in all bays spaced at intervals not to exceed 25 ft (AASHTO 10.20.1). In the positive-moment region, the concrete slab provides continuous lateral bracing for the top flange of the steel beam, which is in compression. In the negative-moment region, however, the bottom flange is in compression. The required bracing distance adjacent to the pier section will be determined in subsequent calculations. The layout of the remaining cross frames will also be determined later. Therefore, the section qualifies as a braced compact section.

Section properties. Because the concrete slab participates in resisting compression in the positive-moment region but does not participate in resisting tension in the negative-moment region, the section properties in the two regions differ and are computed separately. Both the elastic and the plastic section properties are computed.

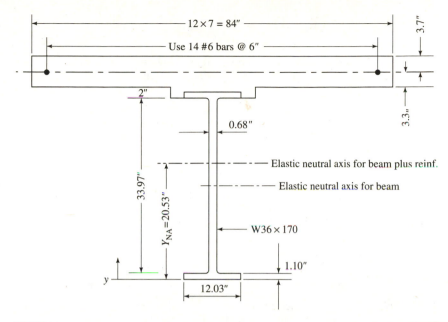

FIGURE E8.6h
Beam cross section in the negative-moment region.

Maximum negative-moment region: elastic section properties. At the interior support, the cross section (Fig. E8.6h) consists of a W36 × 170 beam and fourteen #6 reinforcing bars placed 4.2 in. above the top flange of the steel beam (3.3 in. above the bottom of the slab), which is in tension. The elastic properties are computed in the following table.

Elastic properties of section in negative-moment region

Material	A (in.²)	y (in.)	Ay (in.³)	d (in.)	Ad^2 (in.⁴)	I_o (in.⁴)	I (in.⁴)
W36 × 170	50.0	18.085	904.25	2.445	298.9	10,500	10,799
Rebars (fourteen # 6)	6.16	40.37	248.68	19.84	2424.7		2425
Total	56.16		1152.93			I_{NA} =	13,224

$$y_{NA} = \frac{1152.93}{56.16} = 20.53 \text{ in.}$$

$$d_{reinf} = 36.17 + 4.2 - 20.53 = 19.84 \text{ in.}$$

$$d_{top \, of \, steel} = 36.17 - 20.53 = 15.64 \text{ in.}$$

$$S_{reinf} = \frac{13,224}{19.84} = 666.6 \text{ in.}^3$$

$$S_{top \, of \, steel} = \frac{13,224}{15.64} = 845.5 \text{ in.}^3$$

$$S_{\text{bottom of steel}} = \frac{13,224}{20.53} = 644.1 \text{ in.}^3$$

Plastic section properties. The entire cross section is assumed to have yielded. The cross section of the beam with plastic stress distribution is shown in Fig. E8.6i. D_{cp}, the depth of the plastic neutral axis from the inside face of the bottom flange, was computed earlier as 22.42 in.

Tensile force in reinforcing bars = 369.6 kips (computed earlier)

Tensile force in top flange = $12.03 \times 1.1 \times 50 = 661.65$ kips

Tensile force in web = $(33.97 - 22.42) \times 0.68 \times 50 = 392.7$ kips

Total tensile force = $369.6 + 661.65 + 392.7 = 1423.95$ kips

Compressive force in bottom flange = $12.03 \times 1.1 \times 50 = 661.65$ kips

Compressive force in web = $22.42 \times 0.68 \times 50 = 762.3$ kips

Total compressive force = $661.65 + 762.3 = 1423.95$ kips

Total tensile force = Total compressive force (checks).

The plastic moment of the section is obtained by taking moments of tensile and compressive forces in various elements about the plastic neutral axis. Thus,

$$M_{p,\text{ rebars}} = 369.6 \times 16.85 = 6227.8 \text{ k-in.}$$

$$M_{p,\text{ flange}} = 661.65 \times (12.1 + 22.97) = 23,204.1 \text{ k-in.}$$

$$M_{p,\text{ web}} = 392.7 \times 5.775 + 762.3 \times 11.21 = 10,813.2 \text{ k-in.}$$

$$\sum M_p = 40,245.1 \text{ k-in.}$$
$$= 3353.8 \text{ k-ft}$$

Note that fillets (at the junction of flanges and the web) have been conservatively neglected in the above computations.

Maximum positive-moment region: elastic section properties

Steel section only

$$Z_x = 668 \text{ in.}^3$$

$$M_P = F_y Z_x = 668 \times \frac{50}{12} = 2783.3 \text{ k-ft}$$

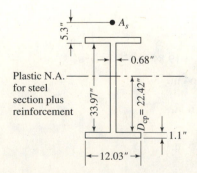

FIGURE E8.6i
Beam cross section with plastic stress distribution.

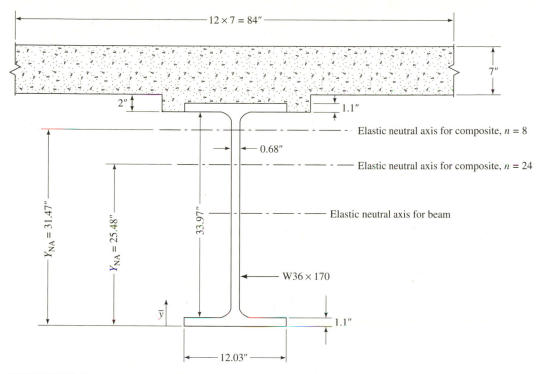

FIGURE E8.6j

Cross section of composite beam in the positive-moment region.

Composite section. For the composite section, two sets of elastic section properties must be computed—one with $n = 8$ and the other with $3n = 24$. The latter value is used for computing stresses and deflections due to sustained loads.

The beam cross section in the positive-moment region is shown in Fig. E8.6j. Various parameters for elastic section properties using $n = 8$ are shown in the following table.

Elastic properties of section in positive-moment region: $n = 8$, 40 ft from end bearing

Material	A (in.²)	y (in.)	Ay (in.³)	d (in.)	Ad^2 (in.⁴)	I_o (in.⁴)	I (in.⁴)
W36 × 170	50.0	18.085	904.3	13.385	8958	10,500	19,458
Concrete (84 × 7/8)	73.5	40.57	2982	9.10	6087	300	6387
Total	123.5		3886.3			I_{NA} = 25,845

$$y_{NA} = \frac{3886.3}{123.5} = 31.47 \text{ in.}$$

$$d_{\text{top of slab}} = (36.17 - 1.1) + 2 + 7 - 31.47 = 12.6 \text{ in.}$$

$$d_{\text{top of steel}} = 36.17 - 31.47 = 4.70 \text{ in.}$$

$$S_{\text{top of slab}} = \frac{25,845}{12.6} = 2051.1 \text{ in.}^3$$

$$S_{\text{top of steel}} = \frac{25{,}845}{4.7} = 5498.8 \text{ in.}^3$$

$$S_{\text{bottom of steel}} = \frac{25{,}845}{31.47} = 821.2 \text{ in.}^3$$

Various parameters for elastic section properties using $3n = 24$ are shown in the following table. Refer again to Fig. E8.6k.

Elastic properties of section in positive-moment region: $3n = 24$, 40 ft from end bearing

Material	A (in.^{2})	y (in.)	Ay (in.^{3})	d (in.)	Ad^2 (in.^{4})	I_o (in.^{4})	I (in.^{4})
W36 × 170	50.0	18.085	904.25	7.395	2734.3	10,500	13,234
Concrete (84 × 7/24)	24.5	40.57	903.97	15.09	5578.8	100	5679
Total	74.5		1898.22			$I_{\text{NA}} =$	18,913

$$y_{\text{NA}} = \frac{1898.3}{74.5} = 25.48 \text{ in.}$$

$$d_{\text{top of slab}} = (36.17 - 1.1) + 2 + 7 - 25.48 = 18.59 \text{ in.}$$

$$d_{\text{top of steel}} = 36.17 - 25.48 = 10.69 \text{ in.}$$

$$S_{\text{top of slab}} = \frac{18{,}913}{18.59} = 1017.4 \text{ in.}^3$$

$$S_{\text{top of steel}} = \frac{18{,}913}{10.69} = 1769.2 \text{ in.}^3$$

$$S_{\text{bottom of steel}} = \frac{18{,}913}{25.48} = 742.3 \text{ in.}^3$$

Plastic moment capacity of composite section, M_p. It was pointed out earlier that W36 × 170 with a concrete slab qualifies as a compact composite section. Therefore, the plastic moment capacity of the section, M_p, can be computed as discussed in section 8.6.2.2. The first step is to determine whether the PNA lies in the slab or the steel section. For simplicity, assume that the PNA lies at the slab–flange interface of the section, and check whether the compressive force in the slab is equal to the tensile force in the steel section; i.e.,

$$\text{Compression force} \gtreqqless \text{tension force}$$

$$0.85 f_c' b t_s + (AF_y c) \gtreqqless AF_y$$

$$0.85 \times 4.0 \times 84 \times 7 + 6.16 \times 60 \gtreqqless 50.0 \times 50.0$$

$$2368.8 < 2500 \text{ kips}$$

This means that the PNA lies in the steel section, which must furnish a compressive force, C', given by Eq. 8.72:

$$C' = \frac{\sum(AF_y) - C}{2} = \frac{2500 - 2368.8}{2} = 65.6 \text{ kips} \tag{8.72}$$

Next, determine whether the PNA lies within the flange or in the web. If the PNA lies at the underside of the top flange, the compression force furnished is

$$(AF_y)_{\text{top flange}} = 12.03 \times 1.1 \times 50 = 661.65 \text{ kips}$$

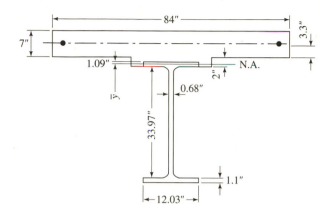

FIGURE E8.6k

This means that the PNA lies within the flange (Fig. E8.6k), and, from Eq. 8.75,

$$\bar{y} = \frac{C'}{(AF_y)_{tf}} t_{tf} \qquad (8.75)$$

$$= \frac{65.6}{661.65}(1.1)$$

$$= 0.109 \text{ in. from the top of the steel section}$$

The plastic moment capacity, M_p, is computed by taking moments of all compressive and tensile forces about the PNA. Thus,

$$
\begin{aligned}
M_p = {} & [(0.85 \times 4 \times 84 \times 7 \times 4.509) + 6.16 \times 60 \times 4.309 \\
& + \tfrac{1}{2} \times 12.03 \times (0.109)^2 \times 50 + \tfrac{1}{2} \times 12.03 \times (1.1 - 0.019)^2 \times 50 \\
& + 0.68 \times 33.97 \times 50 \times 17.976 + 12.03 \times 1.1 \times 50 \times 35.511]/12 \\
= {} & 4597.0 \text{ k-ft}
\end{aligned}
$$

Note that, in the above computations, the contribution of forces in the fillets of the steel section have been neglected.

Design for maximum loads

Step 1. Check to determine if the first hinge is formed at the pier. Because the yield stress of the steel section is 50 ksi, the maximum strength of the compact composite section can be computed on the basis of plastic analysis using the autostress procedures (permitted only for steel of 50 ksi or below). For sections in negative bending that are composite with slab reinforcement, an effective plastic moment, M_{pe}, is determined if plastic rotations are required. If a composite section reaches the plastic moment capacity, M_p, in the positive-moment region, no further rotations are permitted.

The effective plastic moment, M_{pe}, accounts for the effects of local web or flange buckling as a section undergoes plastic rotations. In plastic mechanism analysis, the section at the first hinge to form must have adequate inelastic rotation capacity (at a given moment), as the load redistributes. The effective plastic moment is a reduced plastic moment at which a section can be considered to have adequate rotation capacity.

For the pier section,

$$M_u = M_{pe} = R_f M_{pf} + R_w M_{pw}$$

where $R_f = F_{yfe}/F_{yf}$
$R_w = F_{ywe}/F_{yf}$

Compute the effective yield strength of the compression flange:

$$F_{yfe} = 0.0845E(t/b')^2 \leq F_{yf}$$
$$= 0.0845(29,000,000)(1.10/5.675)^2$$
$$= 92,068 \text{ psi} > 50,000 \text{ psi}$$

Therefore, $F_{yfe} = 50,000$ psi governs.
Compute the effective yield strength of the web:

$$F_{ywe} = 1.32E(t_w/D_{cp})^2 \leq F_{yf}$$
$$= 1.32(29,000,000)(0.68/22.42)^2$$
$$= 35,214 \text{ psi} < 50,000 \text{ psi}$$

Therefore, $F_{ywe} = 35,214$ psi governs.

$$R_f = \frac{50,000}{50,000} = 1.0$$

$$R_w = \frac{35,214}{50,000} = 0.704$$

The flange and the web components of the plastic moment for the maximum negative section were computed earlier as

$$M_{pf} = -2452.7 \text{ k-ft}$$
$$M_{pw} = -901.1 \text{ k-ft}$$
$$\overline{\text{Total} = -3353.8 \text{ k-ft}}$$

The effective plastic moment is

$$M_{pe} = 1.0 \times (-901.1) + 0.704 \times (-2452.7) = -3087.1 \text{ k-ft}$$

$$\frac{M_{pe}}{M_p} = \frac{3087.1}{3353.8} = 0.92$$

That is, M_{pe} is 92 percent of M_p of the negative-moment section.

For the plastic mechanism analysis, assume that the section is elastic–perfectly plastic for M_{pe} at the interior support (pier), and elastic up to M_p at the positive-moment section (possible hinge locations). Estimate where the first hinge may form under the maximum design load by looking at the elastic moment envelopes.

At the pier, the maximum moment is

$$M_{max} = 1.3 \left[D + \tfrac{5}{3}(L + I) \right] \qquad (8.29)$$

$$= 1.3 \left[-1200 + (-206) + \tfrac{5}{3}(-1056) \right]$$

$$= -4115.8 \text{ k-ft}$$

At the location of maximum positive moment ($0.4L$), the maximum moment is

$$M_{max} = 1.3 \left[672 + 116 + \tfrac{5}{3}(1136) \right] = 3485.7 \text{ k-ft}$$

Because the elastic moment at the pier is greater than M_{pe} and the maximum positive moment is less than M_p, a hinge is formed first at the pier. If the hinge were to form first at the maximum-moment section ($M_{0.4L} > M_p$; $M_{pier} < M_{pe}$), no further rotation would be permitted, and the limit state would be reached.

Since the hinge is formed first at the pier, plastic rotation may be required (the load would distribute to the positive-moment section). Therefore, we must ensure that the maximum positive moment does not exceed the plastic moment.

To check for a mechanism, assume that a hinge, which rotates at the constant moment M_{pe}, forms at the pier. The critical positive moment under the maximum design loads is then computed for a simple beam with an end moment at the pier equal to M_{pe}, and with the assumption that the rest of the structure remains elastic. This critical positive moment is then compared with M_p, which, if found to be greater than M_p, will indicate an unsatisfactory design.

Step 2. Locate the position of the hinge in the positive-moment region of the beam. Because the location of a hinge in the positive-moment region of a beam depends on the type of loading (e.g., concentrated load or distributed loads), the hinge location must be investigated for both types of loadings—truck as well as lane—based on the principles of plastic analysis. For this analysis, assume that the beam is subjected to a constant (known) moment, M_{pe}, at the right support, and hence, is statically determinate.

Truck loading. It is assumed here that the minimum rear-axle spacing (14 ft) governs the moment. The maximum loads are

$$D_{max} = \text{Load factor} \times \text{service dead load}$$
$$= 1.3(0.960 + 0.165) = 1.463 \text{ k/ft}$$

$$(L + I)_{max} = \text{Load factor} \times \text{service live load}$$
$$= \text{Load factor} \times \text{wheel load} \times \text{distribution factor} \times \text{impact factor}$$
$$= \text{Load factor} \times \text{distribution factor} \times \text{impact factor} \times \text{wheel load}$$
$$= \left(1.3 \times \tfrac{5}{3}\right) \times 1.51 \times 1.222 \times \text{wheel load}$$
$$= 4 \times \text{wheel load} = F \times \text{wheel load}$$

where $F = (\text{Load factor})(\text{distribution factor})(\text{impact factor}) = 4$

For simplicity, it is also assumed here that the maximum positive moment occurs under the middle axle of the truck, located at an unknown distance, x, from the left support (Fig. E8.6l). The moment under the middle wheel load is

$$M_x = \frac{x}{100}(-3087.1) + \frac{1.463x}{2}(100 - x)$$

$$+ \left[4.0\frac{(x - 14)(100 - x)}{100} + 16.0\frac{x(100 - x)}{100} + 16.0\frac{(86 - x)x}{100}\right](F)$$

$$= -2.172x^2 + 179.6x - 224$$

For the maximum value of M_x, set $dM_x/dx = 0$. Thus, $-4.344x + 179.6 = 0$, which yields $x = 41.34$ ft from the abutment. Substituting x for M_x in the above expression yields

$$M_x = -2.172(41.34)^2 + 179.6(41.34) - 224$$
$$= 3488.7 \text{ k-ft} < M_p = 4597.0 \text{ k-ft}$$

This moment is $3488.7/4597 = 0.759$, which is approximately 76 percent of M_p.

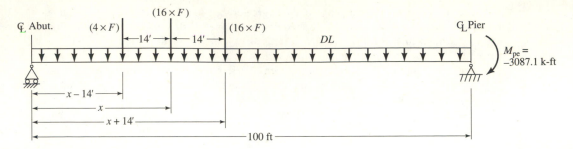

FIGURE E8.6l

Location of hinge in the positive-moment region due to dead load plus truck loading.

Since $M_x < M_p$, a mechanism will not form in the positive-moment region under the maximum load condition when it is caused by truck loading.

It was originally assumed that a hinge forms at the pier. Therefore, a check should be made to determine if a hinge actually does form at the pier with the truck in the position determined above. Use the beam influence line to determine the elastic live-load moment at the pier. Any convenient method (as explained earlier) can be used to determine the influence line.

$$M_{DL} = 1.3[-1200 + (-206.0)] = -1827.8 \text{ k-ft}$$

$$M_{LL+I} = (4.0 \times F)(-6.29) + (16 \times F)(-8.53) + (16 \times F)(-9.50)$$
$$= -1254.6 \text{ k-ft}$$

$$M_{DL} + M_{(LL+I)} = -1827.8 + (-1254.6)$$
$$= -3082.4 \text{ k-ft} < M_{pe}$$

Since the elastic maximum design load moment (with the truck in position for the critical positive moment) does not exceed M_{pe}, a hinge did not form at the pier as assumed. Therefore, the structure remains elastic for this loading case. It was previously shown that the elastic maximum design load moment at $0.4L$ for this loading case (3485.7 k-ft) does not exceed M_p; therefore, the limit state is satisfied.

Now, investigate for a mechanism under dead load plus HS20 lane load. The location of the concentrated load portion (18 kips) of the lane load will be determined in the same manner as for the truck load. Assume that the critical positive moment is directly under the

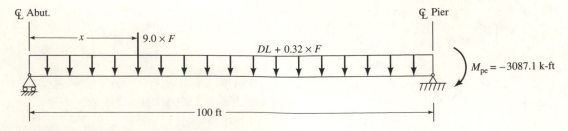

FIGURE E8.6m

Location of hinge in the positive-moment region due to dead load and lane loading.

concentrated load (Fig. E8.6m). Use superposition, as before.

$$M_x = \frac{x}{100}(-3087.1) + \frac{(1.463 + 0.32F)}{2}(100 - x) + \frac{9F(100 - x)x}{100}$$
$$= -1.7315x^2 + 142.28x$$

Find the location of the concentrated load for the maximum M_x by setting dM_x/dx to zero.

$$\frac{dM_x}{dx} = -3.463x + 142.28 = 0$$

which yields $\qquad\qquad x = 41.1$ ft from the abutment

Substitute the value of x in the above expression to find the maximum M_x:

$$M_x = -1.7315(41.1)^2 + 142.28(41.1) = 2922.8 \text{ k-ft}$$

This moment is $2922.8/4597.0 = 0.636$, which is approximately 64 percent of M_p. Since M_x is less than $M_p = 4597.0$ k-ft, a mechanism will not form under maximum design load (considering the lane load).

Check whether the hinge actually forms at the pier with concentrated load (18 kips) in the position determined above. (Note: It is assumed that the uniform live load is also in the adjacent span and that a second concentrated load (18 kips) is in the adjacent span placed at the position for the critical pier moment.)

$$M_{DL} = -1827.8 \text{ k-ft}$$

$$M_{LL+I} = 2(9F)(-8.507) + 2(0.32F)(-623.4)$$
$$= -2208.4 \text{ k-ft}$$

$$M_{DL} + M_{LL+I} = -1827.8 + (-2208.4)$$
$$= -4036.2 \text{ k-ft} > M_{pe}$$

Since the elastic maximum design load moment at the pier (with the concentrated load in position for the critical positive moment) is greater than M_{pe}, a hinge forms as assumed, and the preceding calculation is valid. Because the margin over M_{pe} is greater than that for truck loading, lane loading governs the hinge rotation at the maximum design load. It was shown earlier that a hinge does not form in positive bending; thus, the design is satisfactory for the maximum design lane load.

The rolled beam satisfies the strength limit state at the maximum design load. The maximum positive moment due to the maximum design load is only 76 percent of the plastic moment for truck loading and only 64 percent for lane loading. The bridge therefore has significant excess strength. Therefore, permanent deformation limitations at overload govern the design.

Check shear. First, the maximum shear at the maximum design load is computed. The maximum shear occurs at the interior pier. Assume that the lane loading governs the shear at the interior pier. According to AASHTO 3.7.1.3, a heavier concentrated load equal to 13.0 kips ($\frac{1}{2} \times 26$ kips) shall be used with the uniform lane loading when computing shear. Also assume that a hinge forms at the interior pier under the lane loading, as shown earlier. The hinge is assumed to rotate at a constant moment equal to M_{pe}.

According to AASHTO 3.23.1, when reactions are calculated, the distribution factor for a wheel load directly over a support is computed assuming the flooring acts as a simple span between stringers:

$$DF_{reactions} = \frac{4.33 + 8.33 + 2.33}{8.33} = 1.80 \text{ wheels}$$

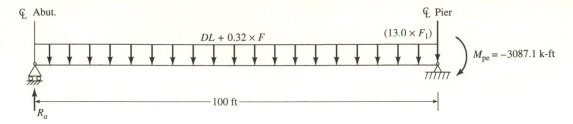

FIGURE E8.6n

$$F_1 = \text{(Load factor)(distribution factor)(impact)}$$
$$= (1.3 \times \tfrac{5}{3})(1.80)(1.222) = 4.77$$

$$F = 4.0, \text{ as computed before}$$

From statics, R_a is computed as follows (refer to Fig. E8.6n):

$$-3087.1 - 100R_a + (1.463 + 0.32F)(100)(50) = 0$$
$$R_a = 106.3 \text{ kips}$$

The maximum shear at the interior pier is then computed as

$$V = 106.3 - (1.463 + 0.32F)(100) - (13.0 \times F_1)$$
$$= -230.0 \text{ kips}$$

Check that a hinge does form, as assumed, at the interior pier for the loading shown in Fig. E8.6o.

$$M_{DL} = -1827.8 \text{ k-ft}$$
$$M_{LL+I} = 2(0.32F)(-623.4) = -1594.9 \text{ k-ft}$$
$$M_{DL} + M_{LL+I} = -3423.7 \text{ k-ft} > M_{pe}$$

Since the elastic maximum design load moment at the pier for the above loading is greater than M_{pe}, a hinge forms as assumed, and the preceding calculation is valid. A similar computation for truck loading showed that it does not govern the shear at the interior pier.

According to AASHTO 10.48.8, the shear capacity of an unstiffened beam is equal to

$$V_u = CV_p \tag{8.41}$$

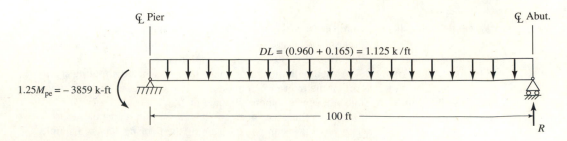

FIGURE E8.6o
Check for uplift.

The plastic shear force, V_p, is equal to

$$V_p = 0.58F_y Dt_w \qquad (8.43)$$
$$= 0.58(50)(33.97)(0.68)$$
$$= 669.9 \text{ kips}$$

The constant C is equal to the buckling shear stress divided by the shear yield stress, and C depends on the web slenderness and the shear buckling coefficient, k. k is taken as 5.0 for unstiffened beams. From Eq. 8.44,

$$\frac{6000\sqrt{k}}{\sqrt{F_y}} = \frac{6000\sqrt{5}}{\sqrt{50,000}} = 60$$

$$\frac{D}{t_w} = \frac{33.97}{0.68} = 50 < 60$$

Therefore, $C = 1.0$, and $V_u = V_p = 669.9$ kips > 230.0 kips. Thus, the shear is OK.

Check uplift. According to AASHTO 3.17, the beam must be investigated for uplift under a loading equal to $[D + 2(L + I)]$. Since a truck in one span is the worst case for uplift, place twice the maximum design load truck (i.e., $2(L + I)$) in the left span at the position for the worst negative moment at the pier.

Check whether a hinge forms by loading the influence line. From the moment envelope (see Fig. E8.6g), and using $M_{DL1} = -1200$ k-ft and $M_{DL2} = -206$ k-ft,

$$M_{DL} = -1200 + (-206) = -1406 \text{ k-ft}$$

$$M_{LL+I} = (8F)(-8.235) + (32F)(-9.600) + (32F)(-8.985)$$
$$= -2642 \text{ k-ft}$$

$$M_{DL} + M_{LL+I} = -1406 + (-2642)$$
$$= -4048 \text{ k-ft} > M_{pe}$$

Therefore, a hinge forms at the pier under this loading. This is the worst case for uplift.

Investigate the right span with the truck in the left span only and a hinge at the pier rotating at $1.25 M_{pe}$. The factor of 1.25 accounts for the fact that the section will actually exceed M_{pe} during hinge rotation, which increases the potential for uplift.

Determine whether the dead load prevents uplift at the abutment. Because the beam is now statically determinate and assumed to be elastic except right at the pier, the reaction, R, is determined from statics. Refer to Fig. E8.6o.

$$\sum M_{pier} = 0$$

$$100R + 3859 - \frac{1.125(100)^2}{2} = 0$$

$$R = 17.7 \text{ kips (upward)}$$

Therefore, no tiedown is required at the abutments to prevent uplift.

Check lateral bracing. The required bracing distance of the compression flange adjacent to the piers is given by Eq. 8.38:

$$L_b = \frac{[3.6 - 2.2(M_1/M_2)] \times 10^6}{F_y} \times r_y$$

It was shown earlier that lane loading governed the hinge formation at maximum load and that a hinge formed at the pier with the concentrated-load portion of the lane load in the position for the critical positive moment. Therefore, M at the brace point will be computed for a simple beam under lane load with an end moment equal to M_{pe}. Because the structure is statically determinate and assumed to be elastic (except right at the pier), M can be computed from statics.

First, the reaction, R_a, at the abutment is determined by taking moments about the pier section (Fig. E8.6p):

$$3087.1 + 100R_a - (1.463 + 0.32F)(100)(50) - 9F(100 - 41.1) = 0$$

$$R_a = 127.5 \text{ kips}$$

A trial-and-error procedure is now required to determine L_b. After several trials, assume $L_b = 11.5$ ft. The moment, M, at $L_b = 11.5$ ft from the pier is determined from statics as

$$M = 127.5(100 - 11.5) - \frac{(1.463 + 0.32F)(100 - 11.5)^2}{2} - 9F(100 - 11.5 - 41.1)$$

$$= -1164.6 \text{ k-ft} = M_1$$

For the W36 × 170 rolled beam, $r_y = 2.53$ in. Therefore, since $M_u = M_{pe}$ at the brace location at the pier,

$$L_b = \frac{[3.6 - 2.2(-1164.6)/(-3087.1)] \times 10^6}{50,000 \times 12} \times 2.53$$

$$= 11.7 \text{ ft}$$

Since the computed L_b is slightly larger than the assumed L_b (11.5 ft), the assumed value is conservative. Therefore, the first brace is located 11 ft 6 in. from the pier. Though not shown here, a similar check should also be made for truck loading.

Cross frames must also be placed at the supports, and intermediate cross frames must be provided in all bays spaced at intervals not exceeding 25 feet. Therefore, use the cross-frame spacing shown in Fig. E8.6q. Bent-plate channel diaphragms with a depth equal to at least half the web depth are recommended. Diaphragms adjacent to the interior pier should be placed lower on the web near the compression flange.

The distance to the next brace (15.5 ft) in the negative-moment region exceeds the bracing requirement given above. L_b in this region may be checked according to the provisions in AASHTO 10.48.4.1 (not illustrated here).

Bearing stiffeners. In the autostress procedures, a bearing stiffener is required at the location of a rotating plastic hinge (the pier section).

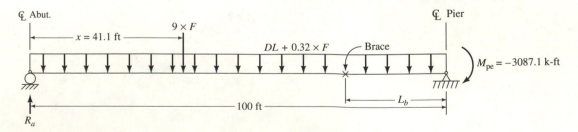

FIGURE E8.6p
Check for lateral bracing.

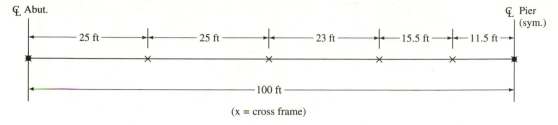

FIGURE E8.6q
Cross-frame spacing.

The load factor design provisions of AASHTO [1992] (10.48.7), require that bearing stiffeners be designed in accordance with Article 10.33.2, for rolled beams, and Article 10.34.6, for welded girders. According to these specifications, bearing stiffeners preferably should be made of plates and should satisfy the following requirements:

- Bearing stiffeners should extend as nearly as practicable to the outer edges of the flange.
- The plates should be placed on both sides of the web.
- The stiffeners should be designed as columns. For stiffeners composed of a pair of plates, the column section should be assumed to comprise those plates plus a centrally located strip of web with width not exceeding 18 times the web thickness.
- The connection of stiffeners to the web should be capable of transmitting the entire reaction to the bearings.
- The stiffeners should be either ground to fit against the flange through which they receive their reaction, or attached to the flange by full-penetration groove welds.
- Only the portion of the stiffeners outside the flange-to-web plate welds or fillets should be considered effective in bearing.
- The thickness of the stiffener plates should be at least

$$t = \frac{b'}{12} \sqrt{\frac{F_y}{33,000}} \qquad \text{(AASHTO Eq. 10.34)}$$

AASHTO 10.54 contains load factor design provisions for compression members. Presumably, these provisions apply to the design of bearing stiffeners as columns, whereas the bearing pressure is limited by the allowable stress in bearing. The total end reaction transmitted to the bearings and caused by the maximum design loads, therefore, should not exceed the maximum strength of the bearing stiffeners as a column. According to AASHTO 10.54.1, the maximum strength may be computed from

$$P_u = 0.85A_sF_{cr} \qquad \text{(AASHTO Eq. 10.150)}$$

where A_s = gross effective areas of the column cross section
F_{cr} = critical stress

Critical stress is determined from whichever of the following formulas is appropriate. For $KL_c/r \leq \sqrt{2\pi^2E/F_y}$,

$$F_{cr} = F_y \left[1 - \frac{F_y}{4\pi^2E} \left(\frac{KL_c}{r}\right)\right] \qquad \text{(AASHTO Eq. 10.151)}$$

Or for $KL_c/r > \sqrt{2\pi^2E/F_y}$,

$$F_{cr} = \frac{\pi^2E}{(KL_c/r)^2} \qquad \text{(AASHTO Eq. 10.153)}$$

where K = effective length factor, which may be taken as unity for bearing stiffeners [AASHTO, 1991]

L_c = length of member between points of support, in.

   = D (height of web) for bearing stiffeners

r = radius of gyration of the column section in the plane of buckling, in.

Interior reaction. Earlier, the maximum shear at the interior pier under the maximum design load lane loading (using a 13.0-kip concentrated load) was computed to be 230.0 kips. The same loading is also critical for the interior pier reaction. Therefore, the reaction at the interior pier is computed as

$$R_b = 2(230.0) - (13.0 \times F_1) = 398.0 \text{ kips}$$

Try two $5\frac{1}{4}$-in. plates. The minimum thickness required is

$$t = \frac{5.25}{12} \sqrt{\frac{50,000}{33,000}} = 0.54 \text{ in.}$$

Use $\frac{5}{8} \times 5\frac{1}{4}$-in. stiffeners at the pier.

The equivalent column consists of two stiffener plates and a length of web equal to eighteen times the web thickness: $L_w = 18(0.68) = 12.24$ in. (Fig. E8.6r).

$$A_{\text{col}} = 2(5.25)(0.625) + 12.24(0.68) = 14.9 \text{ in.}^2$$

$$I_{\text{col}} = \left(\frac{1}{12}\right)(0.625)(5.25 + 0.68 + 5.25)^3 = 72.8 \text{ in.}^4$$

$$r_{\text{col}} = \sqrt{\frac{I_{\text{col}}}{A_{\text{col}}}} = \sqrt{\frac{72.8}{14.9}} = 2.21 \text{ in.}$$

$$\frac{KL_{\text{col}}}{r_{\text{col}}} = \frac{D}{r_{\text{col}}} = \frac{33.97}{2.21} = 15.4$$

$$\sqrt{\frac{2\pi^2 E}{F_y}} = 107.0 > 15.4$$

Therefore, AASHTO Eq. 10.151 applies:

$$F_{\text{cr}} = F_y \left[1 - \frac{F_y}{4\pi^2 E} \left(\frac{D}{r_{\text{col}}} \right)^2 \right] = 50 \left[1 - \frac{50}{4\pi^2 (29,000)} (15.4)^2 \right]$$

$$= 49.5 \text{ ksi}$$

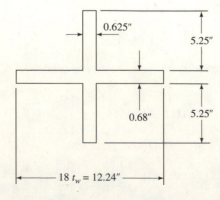

FIGURE E8.6r
Equivalent column (bearing stiffener).

The capacity of the equivalent column is obtained from AASHTO Eq. 10.150:

$$P_u = 0.85 A_{col} F_{cr}$$
$$= 0.85(14.9)(49.5)$$
$$= 626.9 \text{ kips} > 398.0 \text{ kips}$$

Check the bearing stress. Allow $\frac{1}{2}$ in. to clear the web-to-flange fillet. The service load reaction at the interior pier is computed to be 232.4 kips. Therefore,

$$\text{Bearing stress} = \frac{232.4}{(5.25 - 0.5)(0.625)(2)}$$
$$= 39.1 \text{ ksi} < 40 \text{ ksi (allowable), OK}$$

End reaction. At the abutments, bearing stiffeners are not required for rolled beams if the elastic web shearing stress does not exceed 75 percent of the allowable shearing stress (AASHTO 10.33.2). At the abutments, the elastic reactions (from the shear envelope) due to dead loads, live load, and impact are as follows:

$$R_{DL1} = 35.9 \text{ kips}$$
$$R_{DL2} = 6.2 \text{ kips}$$
$$R_{L+I} = \underline{58.7 \text{ kips}}$$
$$\text{Total} \quad R = 100.8 \text{ kips}$$

The shear stress in the web is

$$f_v = \frac{R}{d t_w} = \frac{100.8}{36.17(0.68)} = 4.1 \text{ ksi}$$

$$F_v = 17.0 \times 0.75 = 12.75 \text{ ksi} > 4.1 \text{ ksi, OK}$$

Therefore, stiffeners are not required at the abutments.

For compact welded beams, bearing stiffeners generally are required at the abutments. The reactions at the abutments are computed assuming a hinge rotating at M_{pe} forms at the pier, with the live loading in the position for the maximum abutment reaction (i.e., at least one concentrated load is directly over the abutment). The distribution factor for reactions—computed assuming the flooring to act as a simple span between stringers—is applied to the concentrated load directly over the abutment. To validate the computation, a check should again be made to determine if a hinge does form at the pier with the live load in this position.

In addition, because of the yielding that occurs at the interior pier under the maximum design load, positive residual automoments are formed that remain in the beam after the live load is removed. These moments result in self-equilibrating residual reaction forces that increase the end reactions at the abutments. These additional residual end reactions are a result of the plastic rotation that occurs at the interior pier. These residual reactions could be accounted for when computing the final end reactions.

Design for overloads. Autostress procedures require that the elastic overload moments be redistributed to account for inelastic rotation at pier sections. In establishing the required camber, the permanent deflections resulting from the automoments that are formed are treated as additional dead load deflections. These deformations stabilize after a few passages of the overload vehicle (shakedown).

Because the bridge is built using unshored construction, determine if the noncomposite dead load, DL1 = 0.960 k/ft, causes any inelastic rotation, resulting in automoments in the noncomposite section.

The elastic moment at the pier due to DL1 is −1200 k-ft. Determine the ratio of this moment to the plastic moment of the steel beam alone.

$$\frac{M}{M_p} = \frac{M}{F_y Z} = \frac{-1200(12)}{-50(668)} = 0.43$$

The inelastic rotation curve for the noncomposite section (Fig. E8.6s) indicates that no inelastic rotation, θ_P, occurs in the steel beam alone for M/M_p less than 0.6. Thus, DL1 causes no automoment in the noncomposite section.

Next, determine the inelastic rotation and automoment in the composite section. It is first assumed that no inelastic rotation occurs in the composite section at the pier until the DL1 moment is exceeded. This occurs at

$$\frac{M}{M_p} = \frac{-1200.0}{-3353.8} = 0.36$$

M_p is the plastic moment of the steel beam plus composite reinforcing bars. Thus, as shown in Fig. E8.6s, the vertical axis is shifted so that inelastic rotation of the composite section starts at $M/M_p = 0.36$. The DL1 moment is considered to be *locked in* the composite beam.

The total elastic overload moment at the pier is equal to

$$M = -1200 + (-206) + \tfrac{5}{3}(-1056) = -3166 \text{ k-ft}$$

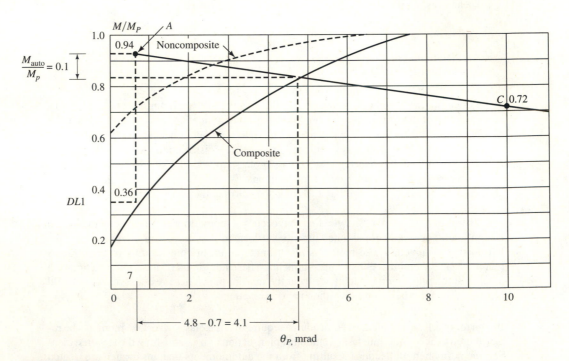

FIGURE E8.6s
Design for overloads: beam-line computation.

The ratio of this moment to the plastic moment of the steel beam plus composite reinforcing bars is

$$\frac{M}{M_p} = \frac{-3166.0}{-3353.8} = 0.94$$

This value is plotted as point A on the graph in Fig. E8.6s.

Point B on the abscissa of the graph (not shown in Fig. E8.6s) is equal to the total rotation at the pier due to the elastic overload moment, assuming there is a free hinge at the pier and the rest of the structure is elastic. AASHTO HS20 lane loading plus impact governs the elastic overload live-load moment at the pier. The pier rotation can, therefore, be estimated from the formula for the elastic end rotation of a simple beam under uniform and concentrated loads. The transformed ($n = 8$) composite moment of inertia is used and is assumed constant throughout this illustration for simplicity.

$$DL = 0.960 + 0.165 = 1.125 \text{ k/ft}$$

$$F = \text{(Load factor)(distribution factor)(impact)}$$

$$= \left(\tfrac{5}{3}\right)(1.51)(1.222)$$

$$= 3.075$$

Superposition is valid since the structure is assumed to be elastic except right at the pier. So the rotation, θ, at the end of a simple beam under uniform and concentrated loads is as follows (refer to Fig. E8.6t):

$$\theta = \frac{WL^3}{24EI} + \frac{Pab(L + a)}{6LEI}$$

The total rotation at the pier, θ_P, is equal to twice the end rotation because of the equal contributions from both spans.

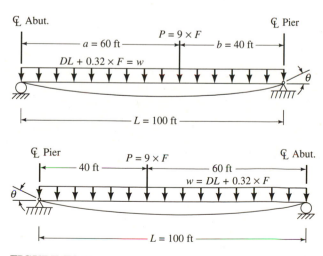

FIGURE E8.6t
Computation of point B.

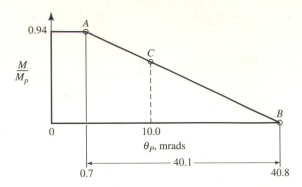

FIGURE E8.6u
Computation of point C.

$$\theta_P = \frac{WL^3}{12EI} + \frac{Pab(L+a)}{3EIL}$$

$$= \frac{(1.125 + 0.32 \times 3.075)(100)^3(144)}{12(29,000)(25844.4)}$$

$$+ \frac{(9 \times 3.075)(60)(100+60)(144)}{3(100)(29,000)(25844.4)}$$

$$= 40.1 \times 10^{-3} \text{ radians} = 40.1 \text{ mrads*}$$

(*1 mrad is a slope of approximately $\frac{1}{8}$-in. in 10 ft.)

As discussed in the commentary [AASHTO, 1991, Appendix A], a more accurate analysis that assumes the concrete on the tension side of the neutral axis is not fully effective should be used to compute the beam-line coordinates (points A and B).

Because point B is off the scale on the graph (Fig. E8.6s), determine the slope of the beam line between points A and B.

Compute the ordinate of a point C at $\theta_P = 10.0$ mrads (Fig. E8.6u).

$$\frac{M_C}{M_A} = \frac{30.8}{40.1}, \qquad M_c = \frac{30.8}{40.1}(0.94) = 0.72$$

Point C is plotted on the graph and the beam line is drawn between points A and C. The automoment is equal to the elastic moment minus the moment at the intersection of the beam line and the inelastic rotation curve for the composite section. From the graph in Fig. E8.6s,

$$\frac{M_{\text{auto}}}{M_p} = 0.1$$

Thus, the automoment at the pier is equal to

$$M_{\text{auto}} = 0.1M_p = 0.1(3353.8) = 335.4 \text{ k-ft}$$

From the graph (Fig. E8.6s), the plastic rotation at the pier at overload is approximately 4.1 mrads. The deflections due to this rotation will be included in the dead-load camber. The actual negative overload moment at the pier is

$$M_o = -3166 + 335.4 = -2830.6 \text{ k-ft}$$

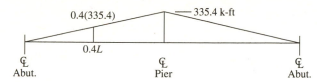

FIGURE E8.6v
Automoment diagram.

The automoment diagram is linear as shown in Fig. E8.6v. Thus, the automoment results in the increase in the maximum positive moment (at $0.4L$) equal to

$$0.4(335.4) = 134.2 \text{ k-ft}$$

This moment will be applied to the transformed ($3n = 24$) composite section in computing the stress in positive bending, since the automoment is considered to be a long-term loading condition.

The maximum stress in positive bending (at $0.4L$) at overload is equal to

$$f_b = (12)\left[\frac{672.0}{580.0} + \frac{116.0 + 134.2}{742.3} + \frac{(5/3) \times 1136}{821.2}\right]$$

$$= 45.6 \text{ ksi} = 0.91F_y < 0.95F_y, \qquad \text{OK}$$

where $F_y = 50$ ksi. Therefore, the rolled beam satisfies the alternate load factor design limit states at overload.

Check concrete cracking. To limit concrete cracking, it is suggested in the autostress procedures that the stress in the reinforcing bars in negative bending at overload be limited to the yield stress of the reinforcing bar. The effects of local yielding elsewhere in the cross section (bottom flange) should be taken into account.

For this computation, the elastic overload moment at the pier will be used to compute the stress in the reinforcing bars. The actual negative overload moment at the pier will be less because of the automoment, but the stress in the reinforcing bars may be higher because of the yielding that occurs in the bottom flange. Therefore, the higher elastic moment will be used to try to account for the effects of local yielding.

The elastic overload moment at the pier due to composite dead load (*DL2*) and live load is $M = -206 + \frac{5}{3}(-1056) = -1966$ k-ft. The stress in the reinforcing bars is therefore

$$f_r = \frac{M}{S_{\text{reinf}}} = \frac{1966(12)}{666.5} = 35.4 \text{ ksi} < 60.0 \text{ ksi}, \qquad \text{OK}$$

A more refined analysis can be made to show that yielding of the compression flanges does not cause an increase in the rebar stress above its yield point.

Furthermore, it is suggested in the autostress procedures that the reinforcement be distributed in accordance with AASHTO 8.16.8.4. According to Article 8.16.8.4, the bar sizes and spacing at maximum positive and negative moment sections shall be chosen so that the calculated stress in the reinforcement at service load, f_s, in ksi, does not exceed the value computed from AASHTO Eq. 8.61:

$$f_s = \frac{Z}{(d_c A)^{1/3}} \leq 0.60 f_y$$

where A = effective tension area, in square inches of concrete surrounding the flexural tension reinforcement and having the same centroid as that of the reinforcement,
  divided by the number of bars or wires. When the flexural reinforcement consists of several bar or wire sizes, the number of bars or wires shall be computed
  as the total area of reinforcement divided by the area of the largest bar or wire
  used (see discussion in Chapter 6).

d_c = thickness of concrete cover, in in., measured from the extreme tension fiber to
  the center of the closest bar or wire.

The quantity Z shall not exceed 170 kips per inch for members in moderate exposure conditions and 130 kips per inch for members in severe exposure conditions (AASHTO 8.16.8.4).
AASHTO Eq. 8.61 may be rewritten as

$$Z = f_s(d_c A)^{1/3}$$

The service load stress in the reinforcement over the pier due to the composite dead
load and live load is as follows:

$$M = -206 + (-1056) = -1262 \text{ k-ft}$$

$$f_s = \frac{M}{S_{\text{reinf}}} = \frac{1262(12)}{666.5} = 22.7 \text{ ksi} < 0.6 f_y = 36 \text{ ksi}$$

With $d_c = 3.70$ in. and $b_e = 84$ in., the effective tension area of the concrete surrounding the flexural tension reinforcement within the effective width is conservatively taken as
$2d_c b_e = 2(3.70)(84.0) = 621.6$ in.^{2} Therefore, with a total of fourteen bars, A within the
effective width is

$$A = \frac{621.6}{14} = 44.4 \text{ in.}^2$$

Z is computed as

$$Z = (22.7)[(3.7)(44.4)]^{1/3} = 124.3 \text{ kips/in.}$$

Since the computed Z value does not exceed the value of 130 kips/in. for severe exposure
conditions or 170 kips/in. for moderate exposure conditions (AASHTO 8.16.8.4), the distribution of reinforcement in negative bending is satisfactory for crack control.

Design for service loads

Deflection due to live load plus impact. According to AASHTO 10.6, live load for deflection
consists of truck loading distributed equally to the four stringers (when the cross bracing is
sufficient in strength to ensure lateral distribution of the loads). Equation 5.15 (Chapter 5)
will be used to compute the maximum live-load deflection at the 0.4 point of each span due
to HS truck loading. The composite ($n = 8$) moment of inertia is used and is assumed to be
constant throughout the span:

$$\Delta = \frac{300}{E_s I}[P_T(L^3 + 3.89L^2 - 680L + 5910) - 0.32M_R L^2] \tag{5.15}$$

where P_T = weight of front truck wheel $\times$ distribution factor, plus impact, kips
  I = moment of inertia of midspan section, in.^{4}
  L = span length, ft
  M_R = bending moment due to live load plus impact at the interior support, kip-ft

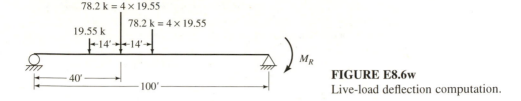

FIGURE E8.6w
Live-load deflection computation.

Assume that two lanes of live load (four wheels abreast) plus 22 percent impact are equally distributed over four stringers.

$$P_T = 4 \times 4 \times 1.222 = 19.55 \text{ kips}$$

$$I = 4 \times 25,844.4 = 103,378 \text{ in.}^4$$

The moment M_R at the interior support is computed from influence coefficients, which can be determined in several different ways. Referring to Fig. E8.6w,

$$M_R = 19.55(-6.018) + 78.2(-8.40) + 78.2(-9.468)$$

$$= -1515 \text{ k-ft}$$

where the parenthetical numbers are obtained by interpolating the appropriate *IL* coefficients under column B (Table 8.11) and multiplying them by 100 ft.

The maximum live-load deflection therefore is

$$\Delta = \frac{300}{29,000(103,378)}$$

$$\times \{19.55[(100)^3 + 3.89(100)^2 - 680(100) + 5910]$$

$$- 0.32(1515)(100)^2\}$$

$$= 1.43 \text{ in.}$$

The ratio of live-load deflection to span is

$$\frac{1.43}{100 \times 12} = \frac{1}{839} < \frac{1}{800} \qquad \text{OK}$$

Check fatigue stresses. Fatigue stresses will be checked for the service load conditions. *Reinforcing steel* (stress range limited to 20 ksi). The variation of moment occurs only due to live load plus impact. At the pier, from the moment envelope (Fig. E8.6f),

$$M_{L+I} = 1056 \text{ k-ft}$$

At the maximum negative moment section (i.e., at the pier), the elastic section modulus, S_{reinf}, was computed to be 666.5 in.^{3} Therefore, the stress range in the reinforcement is

$$f_{\text{sr}} = \frac{(1056 + 0)}{666.5} = 19.0 \text{ ksi} < 20.0 \text{ ksi}, \qquad \text{OK}$$

Fatigue at stud welds. Fatigue must be investigated for the base metal adjacent to stud shear connectors on the tension flange. Tensile stress in the top flange adjacent to the stud shear connector falls into AASHTO fatigue stress category C (Table A.12, Appendix A, illustrative example 18). From Table A.10 (Appendix A), for 500,000 cycles (truck loading), the allowable stress range is 21 ksi for redundant load path structures. For 100,000 cycles (lane loading), the allowable stress range is 35.5 ksi for redundant load path structures. The stress ranges at the pier sections are calculated as follows:

For truck loading,

$$\text{Range of moment} = 613 \text{ k-ft}$$

$$S_{x, \text{ top of steel}} = 845.5 \text{ in.}^3$$

Therefore, the stress range is

$$f_{sr} = \frac{(613 - 0) \times 12}{845.5} = 8.7 \text{ ksi} < 21.0 \text{ ksi}, \qquad \text{OK}$$

For lane loading,

$$\text{Range of moment} = 1056 \text{ k-ft (Fig. E8.6f)}$$

Therefore, the stress range is

$$f_{sr} = \frac{(1056 - 0) \times 12}{845.5} = 15.0 \text{ ksi} < 35.5 \text{ ksi}, \qquad \text{OK}$$

For truck loading at 0.7L (Fig. E8.6f),

$$f_{sr} = \frac{(786.0 + 426.0) \times 12}{845.5} = 17.2 \text{ ksi} < 21.0 \text{ ksi}, \qquad \text{OK}$$

For lane loading at 0.7L,

$$f_{sr} = \frac{(607.0 + 369.4) \times 12}{845.5} = 13.9 \text{ ksi} < 35.5 \text{ ksi}, \qquad \text{OK}$$

Bearing stiffener welds. The welds at the top and bottom of the bearing stiffeners also fall into AASHTO fatigue category C (Table A.12, Appendix A). The allowable stresses are the same as those for the stud shear connectors.

For truck loading, for the bearing stiffeners at the pier,

$$f_{sr} = \frac{(613.0 - 0) \times 12}{909.5} = 8.1 \text{ ksi} < 21.0 \text{ ksi}, \qquad \text{OK}$$

For lane loading, for the bearing stiffeners at the pier (Fig. E8.6g),

$$f_{sr} = \frac{(1056 - 0) \times 12}{909.5} = 13.9 = \text{ ksi} < 35.5 \text{ ksi}, \qquad \text{OK}$$

Diaphragm connection plate welds. The diaphragm connection plates must be rigidly connected to the top and bottom flanges. The diaphragm nearest the point of maximum stress is located at 0.5L. The stress range at the tension flange is computed as follows:

For lane loading,

$$f_{sr} = \frac{[1115 - (-211)] \times 12}{851.1} = 15.7 \text{ ksi} < 35.5 \text{ ksi}, \qquad \text{OK}$$

For truck loading (Fig. E8.6g),

$$f_{sr} = \frac{[1115 - (-304)] \times 12}{851.0} = 20.0 \text{ ksi} < 21.0 \text{ ksi}$$

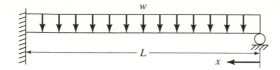

FIGURE E8.6x
Beam loading for dead load deflections.

The rolled beam thus satisfies the live-load deflection and fatigue limit states at service load. The diaphragm at 11.5 ft from the pier (L_b, computed earlier) shall be placed near the compression flange. The diaphragms will be bent-plate channels with a depth equal to at least half the web depth.

All other connection plate welds are satisfactory, by inspection.

Check flange stability prior to concrete deck placement. According to AASHTO 10.50(c), the ratio of the projecting top-compression flange width to the thickness shall not exceed that given by Eq. 8.33:

$$\frac{b'}{t} = \frac{2200}{\sqrt{1.3 f_{DL1}}}$$

where f_{DL1} is the top-flange compressive stress due to noncomposite dead load. At the section of maximum positive moment, $M_{DL1} = 672$ k-ft (Fig. E8.6f):

$$f_{DL1} = \frac{672.0(12)}{580.0} = 13.9 \text{ ksi} < 20 \text{ ksi}, \qquad \text{OK}$$

$$\frac{2200}{\sqrt{1.3(13,900)}} = 16.4 > \frac{b'}{t} = 5.16 \text{ (computed earlier)}, \qquad \text{OK}$$

Dead-load camber. The dead-load camber will now be calculated and will include deflections due to the automoments. The moment of inertia at midspan is assumed constant throughout the span in these calculations. For DL1 and DL2, both spans are symmetrical about the interior support. Hence, the beam may be analyzed by considering only one span, as follows. Referring to Fig. E8.6x,

$$\Delta = \frac{wx}{48EI}(L^3 - 3Lx^2 + 2x^3)$$

For the automoments, referring to Fig. E8.6y,

$$\Delta = \frac{Mx}{6EIL}(L^2 - x^2)$$

where M is the automoment at the pier.

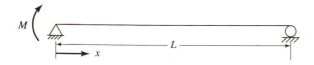

FIGURE E8.6y
Beam loading for automoments.

Deflections due to DL1, DL2, and automoment are shown in the following table.

Deflections due to various loadings

Loading	Deflections at, (in.)				
	0.2L (x = 20 ft)	0.4L (x = 40 ft)	0.6L (x = 60 ft)	0.75L (x = 75 ft)	0.9L (x = 90 ft)
DL1	2.03	2.94	2.40	1.33	0.29
DL2	0.194	0.281	0.229	0.127	0.027
Automoment	0.338	0.592	0.676	0.578	0.301
Total*	2.562	3.813	3.305	2.035	0.618

*Total camber will be opposite to these deflection values.

The camber will be the opposite of the computed deflections, as shown below. The following values have been used to compute deflections due to various loadings. For computing deflections due to long-term loading (DL2 and automoment M), use the moment of inertia of the composite section, with $3n = 24$.

Noncomposite dead load, DL1: $I = 15{,}500$ in.^{4} $w_{DL1} = 0.960$ k/ft
Composite dead load, DL2: $I = 18{,}913.1$ in.^{4} $w_{DL2} = 0.165$ k/ft
Automoment, M: $I = 18{,}913.1$ in.^{4} $M = 335.4$ k-ft

The camber diagram is shown in Fig. E8.6z.

Check for wind loads. According to AASHTO 3.15 and 10.21.2, a horizontal wind force of 50 lb/ft^2 is applied to the area of the superstructure exposed in elevation. Half of this force is applied in the plane of each flange. Also, the total wind force is not less than 300 lb/ft. Stresses and moments due to the wind load are computed per AASHTO 10.20.2.1, and the stresses and moments are factored according to Sec. 3.22.

The strength of the beam under Group II and Group III loading combinations (see Table 3.12, Load factor design, Chapter 3) will be determined from a plastic mechanism analysis:

Group II: $1.3[D + W]$

Group III: $1.3[D + (L + I) + 0.3W]$

In addition, the total stress (including the stress due to the automoment) on the composite section in positive bending will be checked against the limit state of $0.95Fy$, for the

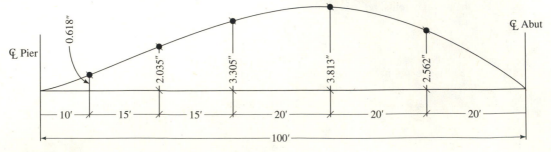

FIGURE E8.6z
Camber diagram.

following load combinations per Article 10.57.2.2 [AASHTO, 1991]:

$$[D + W]$$

$$[D + (L + I) + 0.3W]$$

In both instances, the wind acting on the live load will be neglected since that portion of the wind is assumed to be carried by the slab, not by the bottom flange.

Group II loading—mechanism strength (maximum load). To check the strength under $1.3[D + W]$, first determine if a hinge forms anywhere in the beam under $1.3D$, assuming the section is elastic–perfectly plastic for M_{pe} at the interior pier, and elastic up to M_p at the maximum positive moment section (possible hinge locations).

The factored wind-load moment, $1.3W$, is assumed to be resisted laterally by the bottom flange. This effectively reduces the amount of bottom-flange area that is available to resist $1.3D$. Therefore, M_{pe} is reduced at the interior pier, and M_p is reduced at the maximum positive moment section. To compute the reduced M_{pe} and M_p, the area of the bottom flange required to resist the factored wind-load moment will be determined conservatively, assuming the bottom flange has fully yielded.

First, the wind-load moment is computed at the interior pier. Assuming the parapets are 32 in. high, the height of the exposed fascia of the bridge is computed from Fig. E8.6k by adding 32 in. to the depth of the cross section:

$$\text{Height of fascia} = (1.10 + 33.97 + 2.0 + 7.0 + 32.0)/12 = 6.3 \text{ ft}$$

Therefore, the total wind load at 50 lb/ft^2 is computed to be

$$W = \frac{50}{1000} \times 6.3 = 0.315 \text{ k/ft} > 0.3 \text{ k/ft}, \qquad \text{OK}$$

The wind load applied to the bottom flange is equal to $0.315/2 = 0.158$ k/ft. The wind-load moment is determined from Eq. 8.6 (AASHTO 10.20.2.1). Assume there is no bottom lateral bracing.

$$R = [0.2272L - 11]S_d^{-2/3}$$

For a diaphragm spacing, $S_d = 11.5$ ft, adjacent to the interior pier,

$$R = [0.2272(100) - 11](11.5)^{-2/3} = 2.3$$

$$M_{cb} = 0.08WS_d^2 \qquad\qquad (8.3)$$

$$= 0.08(0.158)(11.5)^2 = 1.67 \text{ k-ft}$$

The wind-load moment, M_w, is equal to

$$M_w = RM_{cb} = (2.30)(1.67) = 3.84 \text{ k-ft}$$

$$1.3M_w = 1.3(3.84) = 4.99 \text{ k-ft}$$

The area of the bottom flange required to resist the factored wind-load moment is determined assuming the flange has fully yielded. Under the action of wind loading, the bottom flange bends in a horizontal plane, subjecting one side of the flange (of width x) to compression and the other side (of width x) to tension, as shown in Fig. E8.6aa. Thus, these areas, which are under compression and tension, are each equal to xt_f, subjected to a stress equal to F_y. Referring to Fig. E8.6aa,

$$\text{Compressive force} = \text{tensile force} = xt_fF_y$$

$$\text{Lever arm} = b_f - x = 12.03 - x$$

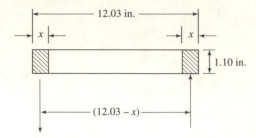

FIGURE E8.6aa
Bottom flange.

Therefore,

$$F_y(x)(1.10)(12.03 - x) = 4.99(12)$$

Substituting the yield strength $F_y = 50$ ksi in the above expression gives

$$661.65x - 55x^2 = 59.9$$

which yields

$$x = 0.091 \text{ in.}$$

Alternatively, x may be computed from the following formula:

$$x = \frac{b_f}{2} - \frac{\sqrt{(b_f t_f F_{yb})^2 - 4t_f F_{yb} M_w}}{2t_f F_{yb}} \le \frac{b_f}{2}$$

where b_f = bottom-flange width
$\quad\quad t_f$ = bottom-flange thickness
$\quad\quad F_{yb}$ = specified minimum yield stress of the bottom flange

Thus, $2(0.091)(1.10) = 0.2$ in.^{2} of the bottom flange of the composite interior-pier rolled section is required to resist the factored wind-load moment. The remaining bottom-flange area, equal to $(12.03 - 0.091 - 0.091 = 11.848) \times 1.10 = 13.03$ in.^{2}, is available to resist the pier moment due to the factored dead load, $1.3D$. Using the procedure demonstrated earlier, the reduced effective plastic moment of the composite interior-pier section with an 11.848×1.10 in. bottom flange is computed to be

$$(M_{pe})_{red} = -3004.4 \text{ k-ft}$$

which is

$$\frac{-3004.4}{-3087.1} = 0.973, \quad\quad \text{or 93.7 percent of } M_{pe}$$

At the maximum positive moment section, $S_d = 25.0$ ft,

$$R = [10.2272(100) - 11](25)^{-2/3} = 1.37$$

$$M_{cb} = 0.08(0.158)(25)^2 = 7.9 \text{ k-ft}$$

The wind-load moment, M_w, is computed to be

$$M_w = RM_{cb} = (1.37)(7.9) = 10.8 \text{ k-ft}$$

$$1.3M_w = 1.3(10.8) = 14.04 \text{ k-ft}$$

The area of the bottom flange required to resist the factored wind-load moment is again determined assuming the flange has fully yielded.

$$F_y(x)(1.10)(12.03 - x) = 14.04(12)$$

Substitution of the yield strength $F_y = 50$ ksi in the above expression gives

$$661.65x - 55x^2 = 168.5$$

$$x = 0.260 \text{ in.}$$

Thus, $2(0.260)(1.10) = 0.572$ in.^{2} of the bottom flange of the composite rolled section is required to resist the factored wind-load moment. The remaining bottom-flange area, equal to $(12.03 - 0.260 - 0.260 = 11.51) \times 1.10 = 12.66$ in.^{2}, is available to resist the maximum positive moment due to $1.3D$. Again, using the procedure presented earlier, the reduced plastic moment, $(M_p)_{\text{red}}$, of the composite rolled section, with an 11.51×1.10-in. bottom flange, is computed to be

$$(M_p)_{\text{red}} = 4512.3 \text{ k-ft}$$

which is

$$\frac{4512.3}{4597.0} = 0.9816 \qquad \text{or 98.2 percent of } M_{\text{pe}} \text{ in positive bending}$$

Now, determine if a hinge forms anywhere in the beam under $1.3D$, assuming the section is elastic–perfectly plastic for $(M_{\text{pe}})_{\text{red}}$ at the interior pier, and elastic up to $(M_p)_{\text{red}}$ at the maximum positive moment section. The check will be made by looking at the elastic factored dead-load moments. At the interior pier, from Fig. E8.6g,

$$M_{\text{DL1}} + M_{\text{DL2}} = 1.3[-1200 + (-206)] = -1827.8 \text{ k-ft} < (M_{\text{pe}})_{\text{red}}$$

At the maximum positive moment section ($0.4L$),

$$M_{\text{DL1}} + M_{\text{DL2}} = 1.3[672 + 116] = 1024.4 \text{ k-ft} < (M_p)_{\text{red}}$$

Therefore, a hinge does not form anywhere in the beam under $1.3D$. The beam is satisfactory for strength under $1.3(D + W)$.

Group II loading—permanent deformations (overload). The total stress on the maximum positive moment section under $D + W$, including the stress due to the automoment at the section (at $0.4L$), will also be checked against the limit state of $0.95F_y$. The total dead-load stress in the bottom flange (including the stress due to the automoment) at this section (at $0.4L$) is equal to

$$F_{\text{DL}} = (12)\left[\frac{672}{580.0} + \frac{116 + 0.4(335.4)}{742.3}\right] = 17.95 \text{ ksi}$$

where $M_{\text{auto}} = 335.4$ k-ft at the pier, computed earlier, so that the automoment at $0.4L$ from the pier, $M_{\text{auto, } 0.4L}$, equals $0.4(335.4)$ k-ft. The wind load stress in the bottom flange at this section is computed from AASHTO Eq. 10.8 as follows:

$$F_{\text{cb}} = \frac{72M_{\text{cb}}}{t_f b_f^2}$$

$$= \frac{72(12)}{(1.1)(12.03)^2}$$

$$= 3.57 \text{ ksi}$$

$$F_w = RF_{\text{cb}} = (1.37)(3.57) = 4.89 \text{ ksi}$$

Check the combined flange-tip stresses:

$$(F_{DL} + F_w) = 17.95 + 4.89 = 22.84 \text{ ksi} < 0.95(50) = 47.5 \text{ ksi}, \qquad \text{OK}$$

Therefore, bottom lateral bracing is not required for dead load plus wind loading, $D + L$.

Group III loading—mechanism strength (maximum load). Next, strength will be checked under Load Factor Design Group III Loading, $1.3[D + (L + I) + 0.3W]$. Lane loading will be considered first. Determine if a hinge forms anywhere in the beam under $1.3[D + (L + I)]$, considering lane loading and assuming the section is elastic–perfectly plastic for M_{pe} at the interior pier and elastic up to M_p at the maximum positive moment section (possible hinge locations).

The methodology used is the same as that for $1.3[D + W]$. The factored wind-load moment, $1.3(0.3W)$, is again assumed to be resisted laterally by the bottom flange, which effectively reduces the bottom-flange area available to resist $1.3[D + (L + I)]$. Therefore, $(M_{pe})_{red}$ and $(M_p)_{red}$ must be computed. The factored wind-load moment in the bottom flange at the interior pier is computed to be

$$1.3(0.3M_w) = 1.3(0.3)(3.84) = 1.50 \text{ k-ft}$$

Assuming the flange has fully yielded, and referring to Fig. E8.6aa,

$$F_y(x)(1.10)(12.03 - x) = 1.50(12)$$

Substituting the yield strength $F_y = 50$ ksi in the above expression gives

$$661.65x - 5x^2 = 18.0$$

which yields

$$x = 0.077 \text{ in.}$$

Thus, $2(0.077)(1.10) = 0.169$ in.^{2} of the bottom flange of the composite rolled section is required to resist the factored wind-load moment. The remaining bottom-flange area, equal to $(12.03 - 0.077 - 0.077) \times (1.10) = 13.06$ in.^{2}, is available to resist the pier moment due to $1.3[D + (L + I)]$. Using the procedure demonstrated earlier, the reduced plastic moment, $(M_p)_{red}$, of the composite rolled section with an 11.876×1.10-in. bottom flange is computed to be

$$(M_p)_{red} = 4571.9 \text{ k-ft}$$

which is

$$\frac{4571.9}{4597.0} = 0.9945 \qquad \text{or} \qquad 99.5 \text{ percent of } M_p \text{ in positive bending}$$

Next, determine whether a hinge forms anywhere in the beam under $1.3[D + (L + I)]$, assuming the section is elastic–perfectly plastic for $(M_p)_{red}$ at the maximum positive moment section. The check is made by looking at the elastic moments, considering lane loading. Referring to Fig. E8.6g, at the interior pier,

$$1.3(M_{DL1} + M_{DL2} + M_{L+I}) = 1.3[-1200 + (-206) + (-1056)] = -3200.6 \text{ k-ft} > (M_p)_{red}$$

At the maximum positive moment section $(0.4L)$ from the left support,

$$1.3(M_{DL1} + M_{DL2} + M_{L+I}) = 1.3(672 + 116 + 1136) = 2501.2 \text{ k-ft} < (M_p)_{red}$$

Because the elastic moment at the pier is greater than $(M_p)_{red}$ and the maximum elastic positive moment is less than $(M_p)_{red}$, a hinge forms first at the pier. If the hinge were to

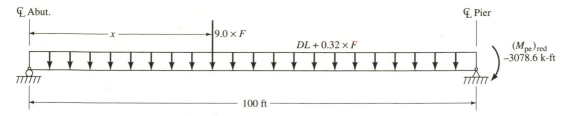

FIGURE E8.6bb
Mechanism strength with maximum load, Group-III loading.

form first at the maximum positive moment section $[M_{0.4L} > (M_p)_{red}; M_{pier} < (M_{pe})_{red}]$, no further rotation would be permitted, and the limit state would be reached.

Since the hinge forms first at the pier, plastic rotation may be required as the load distributes to the positive moment section. Assume that the interior-pier section rotates inelastically at the constant moment, $(M_{pe})_{red}$. The positive moment under $1.3[D + (L + I)]$ will therefore be computed for a simple beam with an end moment equal to $(M_{pe})_{red}$. It is assumed that the rest of the structure remains elastic. If the computed positive moment is less than $(M_p)_{red}$, then a mechanism will not form under the combined loading, and the beam would be satisfactory for strength without bottom lateral bracing.

$$1.3DL = 1.3(0.960 + 0.165) = 1.463 \text{ k-ft}$$

$$F = \text{(load factor)(distribution factor)(impact)}$$

$$= 1.3(1.51)(1.222) = 2.40$$

It is assumed that the critical positive moment occurs directly under the concentrated load. Above $(M_{pe})_{red}$, the beam acts as if it were fully elastic, where $(M_{pe})_{red}$ is similar to an applied constant moment. Therefore, the moment under the concentrated load due to DL, the lane loading, and $(M_{pe})_{red}$ is computed as (refer to Fig. E8.6bb)

$$M_x = \frac{x}{100}(-3078.6) + \left(\frac{(1.463 + 0.32F)}{2}\right)(100 - x) + \frac{9F(100 - x)}{100}$$

$$= -1.3315x^2 + 102.36x$$

Find the location of the concentrated load for the maximum M_x by setting $dM_x/dx = 0$:

$$\frac{dM_x}{dx} = -2.663x + 102.36 = 0$$

from which $x = 38.4$ ft from the abutment. Substituting $x = 38.4$ into the above expression of find the maximum value of M_x yields

$$M_x = -1.3315(38.4)^2 + 102.36(38.4) = 1967.2 \text{ k-ft} < (M_p)_{red}$$

We originally assumed that a hinge formed at the pier. Therefore, a check should be made, under both the truck *and* the lane loading conditions, to determine if a hinge actually does form at the pier with the concentrated load in the position determined above. Use the beam influence line to determine the elastic live-load moment at the pier. Any convenient method can be used to determine the influence line.

For lane-loading conditions, assume, per AASHTO 3.11.3, that the uniform live load is also present in the adjacent span, and that a second concentrated load (18 kips) is in the adjacent span placed at the position for the critical pier moment.

$$M_{\text{DL}} = 1.3[-1200 + (-206)] = -1827.8 \text{ k-ft}$$
$$M_{L+I} = 2(\tfrac{1}{2} \times 18.0 \times F)(-8.15) + 2(0.32 \times F)(-623.4) = 1309.6 \text{ k-ft}$$
$$M_{\text{DL}} + M_{L+I} = -3137.4 \text{ k-ft} > (M_{\text{pe}})_{\text{red}}$$

Since the elastic moment at the pier (with the concentrated load in position for the critical positive moment) is greater than $(M_{\text{pe}})_{\text{red}}$, a hinge forms as assumed under $1.3[D + (L+I)]$, and the preceding computation is valid. Therefore, the beam is satisfactory for strength under $1.3[D + (L+I) + 0.3W]$ for *lane* loading.

Strength will now be checked under $1.3[D+(L+I)+0.3W]$, for *truck* loading. Separate calculations similar to those illustrated above, using $(M_{\text{pe}})_{\text{red}}$ and $(M_p)_{\text{red}}$, show that a hinge does not form anywhere in the beam under $1.3[D + (L+I)]$, considering truck loading. Therefore, the beam is satisfactory for strength under $1.3[D + (L+I) + 0.3W]$ for truck loading.

Group III loading—permanent deformations (overload). Finally, the total stress on the maximum positive moment section under $[D + (L+I) + 0.3W]$, including the stress due to the automoment at that section, will be checked against the limit state of $0.95F_y$. The total dead-load stress in the bottom flange (including the stress due to the automoment) was earlier computed to be

$$F_{\text{DL}} = 17.95 \text{ ksi}$$

The live-load stress in the bottom flange at this section is computed to be (truck loading governs)

$$F_{\text{LL}} = \frac{1136(12)}{821.2} = 16.6 \text{ ksi}$$

The wind-load stress in the bottom flange at this section was earlier computed to be

$$F_w = 4.89 \text{ ksi}$$

Checking the combined flange-tip stresses,

$$(F_{\text{DL}} + F_{\text{LL}} + 0.3F_w) = [17.95 + 16.6 + 0.3(4.89)]$$
$$= 36.02 \text{ ksi} < 0.95(50) = 47.5 \text{ ksi}$$

Therefore, bottom lateral bracing is not required for dead load plus live load plus wind load.

Though not illustrated here, a separate check of the wind load combined with the non-composite dead load (DL1) alone, during the construction phase prior to hardening of the concrete slab, may indicate a need for temporary bracing of the top flange.

Other design calculations. The design of shear connectors and splices is identical to current procedures for load factor design and is not presented here. A detailed design procedure for shear connectors is presented in Example 8.3. Several examples can be found in references such as AISC Mkt. [1987].

Exterior stringer. Generally, when using the specified AASHTO live-load lateral distribution factors, the live load applied to an outer stringer of a bridge designed for two or more lanes of traffic will be slightly less than that for an interior stringer. If stringers are positioned under the roadway to give equal dead loads to interior and exterior stringers, often only the interior stringer need be designed—the same beam section may be used for the exterior stringer (unless the wind loading combinations should govern the design of the exterior stringer combinations).

Various details of the bridge superstructure are shown in Fig. E8.6cc.

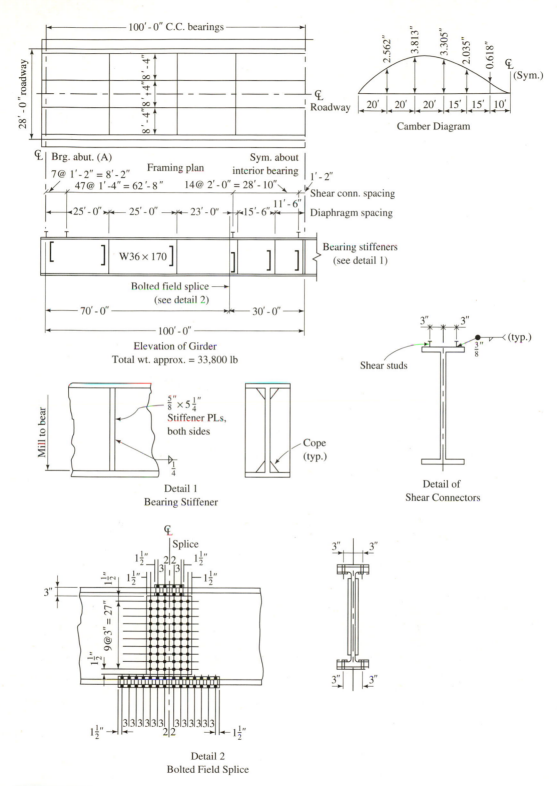

FIGURE E8.6cc
Details of bridge superstructure.

8.10
NEW DEVELOPMENTS

8.10.1 Steel-Free Concrete Bridge Deck

The design of concrete decks, adequately reinforced for flexure, was discussed in Chapters 6 and 7 and also in this chapter. Bridge decks are universally designed in this manner, and they have been performing satisfactorily from the viewpoint of strength and stiffness. As a result, the conventional method of design based on pure flexural behavior continues to be used. However, extensive research [Bakht and Agarwal, 1995; Newhook and Mufti, 1996; Newhook, Mufti, and Wegner, 1995] undertaken by the Ministry of Transportation in Ontario, Canada, during the past twenty years has concluded that [Mufti, Bakht, and Jaeger, 1996]

- Concrete deck slabs, instead of being in pure flexure, develop an internal arching action under loads.
- Because of this arching action, the deck slabs fail under concentrated loads in a punching shear mode.
- The load corresponding to the punching shear mode failure is much higher than that corresponding to the purely flexural mode.

Several field and laboratory tests [Selvadurai, 1995; Selvadurai and Bakht, 1995; Bakht and Mufti, 1996] revealed that concrete deck slabs with only nominal steel reinforcement have more than adequate strength and stiffness to safely sustain the present-day heavy vehicular loads. In the absence of conventional flexural reinforcement in the slab, the source of the strength and stiffness of the deck slab was ascribed to the presence of the arching action in the slab. Consequently, it was concluded that the internal arching action of the deck slabs of slab–girder bridges could be harnessed by connecting the slab to the girders by shear connectors and by using transverse confinement of the slab [Bakht and Mufti, 1996].

As a result of the Ontario research program, an innovative superstructure design for slab–girder bridges has been developed in Ontario, Canada. Essentially, the system consists of

- Fiber-reinforced concrete slab. The synthetic fibers, randomly mixed with concrete, are an inexpensive, low-modulus type, such as polypropylene. Because of their low modulus, these fibers do not increase the tensile strength of concrete significantly. However, they help control temperature- and shrinkage-induced cracks during the curing period.
- Transverse steel straps, welded to the adjacent steel girders. These straps provide the transverse confinement of the slab, and are spaced not exceeding half the spacing of the girders.
- Steel girders with shear connectors to develop composite action with the fiber-reinforced deck slab.

As pointed out in Chapter 2, a significant advantage of the fiber-reinforced concrete deck slab is enhanced durability, since the fibers are practically inert to the effects of deicing chemicals. Also, the absence of conventional steel reinforcement for flexure eliminates the corrosion problem commonly associated with concrete slabs.

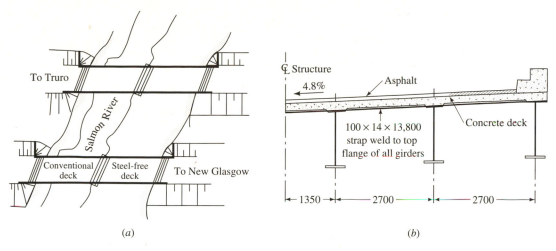

(a)   (b)

FIGURE 8.38
The Salmon River Bridge, Canada: (*a*) Plan view, (*b*) the steel-free bridge deck (dimensions in mm). The sloped top flanges of the primary girders run parallel to the top deck surface of the bridge [Newhook and Mufti, 1996].

The first known fiber-reinforced concrete (FRC) deck slab without any conventional flexural reinforcement was constructed on the Trans-Canadian Highway 104 and opened to traffic on December 5, 1995. Known as the Salmon River Bridge, its superstructure consists of two separate sections, one eastbound and one westbound. Each section consists of two simple spans, 102.4 ft each. To compare the actual service performance of the two types of decks, each section has one span with the conventional flexural steel reinforcement and one span with a steel-free deck. To gain valuable in-service data, the steel-free deck of the bridge is monitored for field performance. The monitoring system consists of a combination of conventional electronic resistance foil gauges and Bragg grating–type fiber optic sensors [Newhook and Mufti, 1996].

A plan view and a partial cross section of the Salmon River Bridge are shown in Fig. 8.38. The 8-in.-thick steel-free deck of each section is poured from 5000-psi concrete and made composite with steel girders by shear connectors. Devoid of any conventional flexural reinforcement, the concrete of the steel-free deck slab contains 0.55 percent by volume of polypropylene fibers. The transverse confinement of the slab is provided by the 4 × 0.55-in. transverse straps of uncoated weathering steel spaced at 3.94 ft (1.2 m) o.c. and welded to the adjacent plate girders. These steel straps represent only a 0.5 percent effective steel ratio compared with the 1.2 percent of steel reinforcement required for the conventional design of a deck slab according to OHBDC (1995). The six steel girders, which comprise the main load-carrying system of the superstructure, are spaced 8.86 ft apart from each other and 59 in. deep, and their top flanges are sloped at 4.8 percent to match the cross slope of the deck, instead of being welded perpendicular to the web. The key parameters for both deck designs (conventionally reinforced and steel-free) are summarized in Table 8.13. Design and construction of this bridge are discussed by Newhook et al. [1996], and by Newhook and Mufti [1996].

TABLE 8.13
General design details of Salmon River Bridge [Newhook and Mufti, 1996]

Item	Conventional design	Steel-free design
Girder spacing	8.86 ft	8.86 ft
Slab thickness	8 in.	8 in.
Concrete strength	5000 psi	5000 psi
Steel reinforcement	1.9%	0%
Steel straps	0%	0.5%

8.10.2 Proposed Canadian Highway Bridge Design Code Provisions

Note that the proposed Canadian Highway Bridge Design Code (CHBDC), a new code to be published in 1997, has a section on fiber-reinforced structures. The final draft of this CHBDC [CHBDC, 1996a,b] permits the design of FRC deck slabs, with certain limitations on the minimum axial stiffness of the transverse straps. The empirical method for designing steel-free slabs proposed in the draft applies to composite slab–girder bridges in which the girder spacing does not exceed 3.7 m (approximately 12 ft). The code calls for a minimum deck slab thickness of 175 mm (approximately 7 in.) or $S/15$, where S is the girder spacing in mm. The concrete for the deck slab is to have a minimum strength of 30 MPa (4350 psi). The low-modulus synthetic fibers (acrylic, nylon, polyethylene, polypropylene, or vinylon), to be randomly mixed with the concrete for the control of thermal and shrinkage cracks, are to have a minimum fiber volume fraction of 0.005 but not to exceed 0.01. The flanges of the girders supporting the steel-free deck slab are to be connected by steel straps having an axial stiffness of not less than 270 MN/m per meter length of the deck slab in the direction of the bridge span. The spacing of the steel straps is not to exceed half the girder spacing [Mufti, Bakht, and Jaeger, 1996].

8.11
BRIDGE DECK PANELS

With an increasing number of deteriorating bridges in the United States, compounded by budget constraints, rehabilitation, rather than replacement, of the old bridges has become more common. In many cases, the main component of the rehabilitation project is the replacement of the deteriorated concrete decks (discussed in Chapter 10). In old bridges, the replacement decks usually are required to be lighter so that the live-load capacity of the bridge can be increased.

To minimize the disruption to traffic, this work is generally done at night. Also, the work is required to be completed in the least amount of time, to cut cost. Prefabricated deck panels are often used as a cost-effective alternative to replace the existing deck slab.

Depending on the job requirements, these deck panels can be designed in several ways. For example, they can be designed as orthotropic steel deck panels, as was used for the replacement of the George Washington Bridge deck [Fasullo and Han, 1977].

Alternatively, they can be open or filled steel deck panels, or full-depth precast and precast prestressed concrete deck panels. All types have been used in the rehabilitation of many bridges.

8.11.1 Steel Deck Panels

A typical steel deck panel is shown in Fig. 8.39. Essentially, the panel consists of a system of three steel bars:

- The main bearing bars that span transversely between, and are supported on, the adjacent beams or girders
- The distribution bars placed perpendicular to and supported by the main bearing bars. These bars are oriented parallel to the beams supporting the panel. They distribute loads across several main bearing bars.
- Tertiary bars that are parallel to the main bearing bars. They are welded into the slots of the distribution bars. These bars extend into the reinforced concrete component of the deck. Their purpose is to provide horizontal shear transfer, assuring full composite action between the steel grid and the concrete (if the panel is filled with concrete).

Steel deck panels are available in several configurations. They can be open, i.e., without concrete fill, or filled, i.e., filled with concrete. Depending on the job requirements, the concrete component of the steel grid panels can be precast before the modules are placed on the girders, or it can be cast in place. The concrete depth in the panels is typically 3 to 5 in. Composite action with the supporting girders can be achieved with cast-in-place concrete poured full depth over the girders. An extensive testing of the steel deck panels was conducted in the 1980s at West Virginia University in Morgantown, West Virginia [GangaRao, Seifert, and Kevork, 1988].

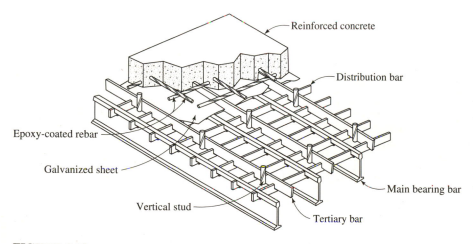

FIGURE 8.39

Typical steel bridge deck panel. Thickness of concrete and bar sizes may vary depending on the job requirements [EBDI, 1996].

Deck panels are generally patented items, such as the Exodermic Bridge Deck [EBDI, 1996], that are supplied by vendors for specific projects. Several examples of recent application of these deck panels are reported in the literature [Bettigole, 1992; EXONEWS, 1994a, 1994b, 1995, 1996a,b]. A recent example is the deck replacement of New York's 16,000-ft-long, seven-lane Tappan Zee Bridge, which carries the New York State Thruway over the Hudson River with average daily traffic of 115,000 vehicles [EXONEWS, 1995]. Other examples are the redecking of the Hudson River Bridge on Route 378, between Troy and Menands in the state of New York [EXONEWS, 1996a], and new bascule bridges to be built in Green Bay, Wisconsin, and in Ft. Lauderdale, Florida [EXONEWS, 1996b].

Note that because they are lightweight and are easily and rapidly installed, steel deck panels were originally envisioned only for bridge deck rehabilitation work. However, for these same reasons, deck panels are being specified more and more as viable cost-cutting alternatives for new construction.

8.11.2 Precast and Precast Prestressed Concrete Deck Panels

Use of precast prestressed concrete form panels to support fresh concrete of the deck was discussed in Chapter 7. With advancement in precasting technology, a similar product, but one that can be used for the full depth of the deck, has been used since the 1970s [Barker, 1975; Kluge and Sawyer, 1975; Taly, 1976; Taly and GangaRao, 1979] for rehabilitation of existing bridges [Knudsen, 1980; Lutz and Scalia, 1984] as well as for new bridges [Issa et al., 1995a], in both the United States and in Canada.

In this type of construction, the entire bridge deck is constructed from precast concrete; with the exception of connections, shear keys, and slab closures, no additional field-cast concrete acting structurally is involved. Composite construction is also possible with these full-depth panels. Major advantages offered by this type of construction are as follows [Issa et al., 1995a]:

- Superior quality results from in-plant prefabrication that provides enhanced durability.
- Prefabrication of deck panels can significantly reduce the time for new deck construction as well as the out-of-service time required for bridge repairs and replacement.
- Cost savings result from reduced field labor and reduced traffic delays.
- This construction method applies to all requirements of repairs and replacements as well as to new construction.
- This type of construction is very suitable for the systems approach [Taly, 1976].

Various aspects of design and recommended practices for the precast and precast prestressed concrete composite bridge panels are reported in references [USS, 1981; PCIJ, 1987, 1988] and have also been discussed by others [Slavis, 1982, 1983; Berger, 1983; Fagundo et al., 1985; Biswas, 1986]. Issa et al. [1995a] have provided a state-of-the-art report that discusses the use of these panels for several bridges with steel girders. Both types of panels have been used for all types of bridges, including suspension, cable-stayed, truss, and girder bridges.

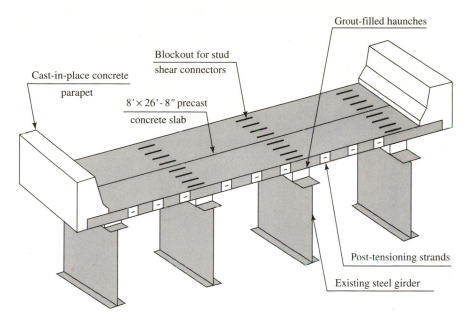

FIGURE 8.40
Typical section of precast concrete slab—used for Bridge 03200, Connecticut Department of Transportation [Issa et al., 1995a].

Typically, these panels are precast in widths equal to full bridge widths, 5 to 12 ft long (parallel to the longitudinal axis of the bridge), and are 6 in. to 10 in. thick (Fig. 8.40). Panels of varying depths (thicker at the centerline of the bridge and thinner near the curb line) have also been used. The panels can be made from normal-weight or lightweight concrete. The transverse joints between the adjacent panels, referred to as shear keys, are female-to-female type or tongue-and-groove type joints (Fig. 8.41).

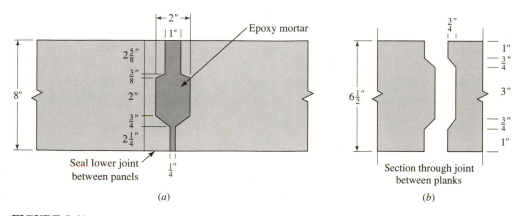

FIGURE 8.41
Typical shear keys between the adjacent deck panels: (*a*) female-to-female type; (*b*) tongue-and-groove type (Issa et al., 1995a).

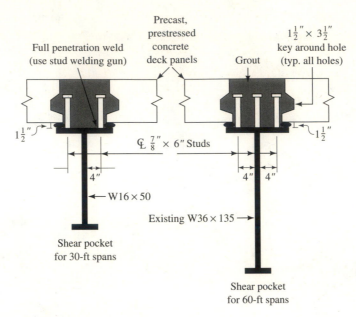

FIGURE 8.42
Typical shear connector details. Those shown have been used for the Dalton Highway Bridge rehabilitation in Alaska [Issa, et al., 1995a].

After installation, these joints are filled with high-strength, nonshrink grout or with epoxy mortar. The purpose of these shear keys is to provide interaction between the adjacent panels in resisting vertical shear. Longitudinal post-tensioning may be provided to give sufficient compression to keep the transverse joints between panels closed. To develop composite action between the precast panels and the steel beams (i.e., to resist the horizontal shear), headed shear studs are welded to the top flanges of steel beams, and shear connector blockouts are provided in the precast panels whose positions match the positions of shear studs on the beams (Fig. 8.42). After panels are placed in the proper positions, these blockouts are filled with the nonshrink grout.

An important component of this panelized construction is the joints between the adjacent panels and those provided for the shear connector blockouts; the long-term bridge deck performance is manifested in the behavior of these joints. A report by Issa et al. [1995b] on performance of such bridge decks has revealed that these joints are not without problems.

REFERENCES

AASHTO. (1986). *Guide Specifications for Strength Design of Truss Bridges (Load Factor Design)*, AASHTO, Washington, DC.

———. (1991). *Guide Specifications for Alternate Load-Factor Design Procedures for Steel Beam Bridges Using Braced Compact Sections*, AASHTO, Washington, DC.

———. (1992). *Standard Specifications for Highway Bridges*, 15th ed., AASHTO, Washington, DC.

———. (1993). *Guide Specifications for Horizontally Curved Highway Bridges,* AASHTO, Washington, DC.

———. (1994a). *LFRD Bridge Design Specifications, Customary U.S. Units,* 1st ed., AASHTO, Washington, DC.

———. (1994b). *Interim Specifications—Bridges—1994,* AASHTO, Washington, DC.

Abdel-Sayed, G. (1969a). "Effective Width of Steel Deck-Plate in Bridges," *ASCE J. Struct. Div.,* 95(7), pp. 1459–1474.

———. (1969b). "Effective Width of Thin Plates in Compression," *ASCE J. Struct. Div.,* 95(10), pp. 1459–1474.

ACI. (1989). *Building Code Requirements for Reinforced Concrete,* ACI 318-89/ACI318R-89 (Revised 1992), American Concrete Institute, Detroit, MI.

———. (1995). *Building Code Requirements for Reinforced Concrete,* ACI 318-95/ACI318R-95 (1995), ACI, Detroit, MI.

Adekola, A. O. (1968). "Effective Widths of Composite Beams of Steel and Concrete," *Structural Engineer,* 49(9), September.

AISC. (1966). *Moments, Shears, and Reactions for Continuous Highway Bridges,* AISC, New York.

———. (1994). *Manual of Steel Construction: Load and Resistance Factor Design,* Vol. 1, 1st ed., AISC, Chicago.

———. (1989). *Manual of Steel Construction: Allowable Stress Design,* 9th ed., AISC, Chicago.

———. (1991). "Rolled Structural Beams Solve Bridge Design Challenge," *AISC Brief Case,* 1(5), August.

———. (1992). "What Design Engineers Can Do to Reduce Bridge Fabrication Costs: A Compilation of Comments from Experienced Fabricators and Detailers across the Country," *AISC Modern Steel Constr.,* 34(9), September, pp. 28–36.

AISC. Mkt. (1978). *Steel/Concrete Composite Box-Girder Bridges: A Construction Manual,* U.S. Steel Corp., AISC Marketing, Inc., Pittsburgh, PA.

———. (1987). *Highway Structures Design Handbook,* Vol. 2, U.S. Steel Corp., AISC Marketing, Inc., Pittsburgh, PA.

AISI. (1972). *Four Design Examples—Load Factor Design of Steel Highway Bridges,* Pub. No. P123(PS010), AISI, New York, March.

———. (1982). *Performance of Weathering Steel in Highway Bridges,* AISI, First Phase Report of Task Group on Weathering Steel Bridges, AISI, Washington, DC.

Albrecht, P., and Naeemi, A. H. (1984). *The Performance of Weathering Steel in Bridges,* National Cooperative Hwy. Res. Prog., Report No. 272, Transportation Research Board, National Research Council, Washington, DC, June.

Anger, G., and Tramm, K. (1965). *Deflection Ordinates for Single-Span and Continuous Beams,* trans. from German by C. V. Amerongen, Frederick Unger, New York.

Anger, G., (1956). *Ten-Division Influence Lines for Continuous Beams,* Frederick Unger, New York.

ANSI/AASHTO/AWS. (1995). *Bridge Welding Code D1.5-95,* AASHTO, Washington, DC.

ARBED. (year unknown). *Short-Span Composite Bridges,* ARBED, Arbed-Tcom/S, ed. Ref.: B 3.3 VEBR-E, Germany.

ASCE. (1960). "Tentative Recommendations for the Design and Construction of Composite Beams and Girders for Buildings," *ASCE Proc. J. Struct. Div.,* 86(ST12), December, pp. 73–92.

———. (1984a). *Specifications for the Design and Construction of Composite Slabs,* ASCE Technical Council on Codes and Standards, New York.

———. (1984b). *Commentary on Specifications for the Design and Construction of Composite Slabs,* ASCE Technical Council on Codes and Standards, New York.

ASCE–AASHO. (1968). "Development and Use of Prestressed Steel Flexural Members," Report by Subcommittee 3 of the Joint ASCE–AASHO Committee on Steel Flexural Members, *ASCE J. Struct. Div.,* 94(ST9), September, pp. 2033-2060.

ASCE–AASHTO. (1975). "State-of-the-Art Report on Ultimate Strength of I-Beam Bridge Systems." Subcommittee on Ultimate Strength, Joint ASCE-AASHTO Task Committee on Metals, Structural Division, *ASCE, J. Struct. Div.,* 101(ST5), May, pp. 1085–1096.

———. (1985). Task Committee on Redundancy of Flexural Systems of ASCE–AASHTO Committee on Flexural Members of the Committee on Metals of the Structural Division, "State-of-the-Art Report on Redundant Bridge Systems," *ASCE J. Str. Eng.,* 3(12).

ASCE–ACI. (1960). Joint ASCE-ACI Committee on Composite Construction, "Tentative Recommendations for the Design and Construction of Composite Beams and Girders for Buildings," *ASCE J. Struct. Div.,* 86(ST12), December, pp. 73–92.

ASCE–WRC. (1971). *Plastic Design in Steel, A Guide and Commentary,* 2nd ed., ASCE Manuals and Reports on Engineering Practice, No. 41, Joint Committee of the Welding Research Council and the American Society of Civil Engineers, published by the ASCE, New York.

ASM. (1978). *Atmospheric Corrosion,* American Society for Metals, Metals Park, OH.

ASTM. (1988). *Standard Specification for General Requirements for Rolled Steel Plates, Shapes, Sheet Piling and Bars for Structural Use,* A6/A6M, ASTM, Philadelphia, PA.

Aulthouse, F. D. (1989). *Economics of Weathering Steel in Highway Structures,* FHWA Pub. FHWA-TS-89-016, Federal Highway Administration Forum on Weathering Steels for Highway Bridges, Alexandria, VA, June.

Baes, L., and Lipski, A. (1958). *Preflex Beam Principles, Notes on Calculation and Descriptive Notes,* Sections I, II, and III, Preflex, S. A., Brussels, June 1953, May 1954, April 1958.

Baker, J. F., Horne, M. R., and Heyman, J. (1956). *The Steel Skeleton,* Vol. 2, Cambridge University Press, Cambridge, England.

Bakht, B., and Agarwal, A. C. (1995). "Deck Slabs of Skew Girder Bridges," *Canadian J. Civ. Eng.,* 22(3).

Bakht, B., and Jaeger, J. (1985). *Bridge Analysis Simplified,* McGraw-Hill Companies, Inc., New York.

Bakht, B., and Mufti, A. A. (1996). "FRC Deck Slabs without Tensile Reinforcement," *Concrete Intl.,* February, 18(2), pp. 50–55.

Bares, R., and Massonet, C. (1968). *Analysis of Beam Grids and Orthotropic Plates,* Frederic Unger, New York.

Barker, J. M. (1975). "Research Application and Experience with Precast Prestressed Bridge Deck Panels," *PCI J.,* 20(6), November–December, pp. 66–85.

Beedle, L. S. (1958). *Plastic Design of Steel Frames,* John Wiley & Sons, New York.

———. (1974). "Introduction," in Lambert Tall, ed., *Structural Steel Design,* 2nd ed., Ronald Press, New York, pp. 3–33.

Beezone, A. P. (1972). "A Comparison of Working Stress and Load Factor Design for a Composite Box Girder Design," *Four Design Examples—Load Factor Design of Steel Highway Bridges,* Publication no. P123(PS010), AISI, New York, March, pp. 4-1–4-50.

Bellenoit, J. R., Yen, B. T., and Fisher, J. W. (1984). "Stresses in Hanger Plates of Suspended Bridge Girders," *Trans. Res. Rec.,* 2(950), pp. 20–23.

Berger, R. H. (1983). "Full-Depth Modular Precast Prestressed Bridge Decks," *Trans. Res. Rec. 903, Bridge and Culverts,* Transportation Research Board, Washington, DC., pp. 52–59.

Bethlehem. (1967). *Economics of Simple-Span Highway Bridges,* Bethlehem Steel Corp., Bethlehem, PA.

———. (1968). *Bridge Design Aids, Guidelines for Economical Bridge Girder Design,* Bethlehem Steel Corp., Bethlehem, PA.

———. (1988). "Suggested Guidelines for Improving Performance of Weathering Steel Bridges," Tech. Bull. TB-301, Bethlehem Steel Corp., Bethlehem, PA, January.

———. (1990a). "Uncoated Weathering Steel Structures," Tech. Bull. TB-307, Bethlehem Steel Corp., Bethlehem, PA, February.

———. (1990b). "Standard Steels for Buildings and Bridge Construction," Tech. Bull. TB-302 A, Bethlehem Steel Corp., Bethlehem, PA, October.

———. (1990c). "Cost per Foot of Wide-Flange and Standard Structural Shapes," Tech. Bull. TB-300 B, Bethlehem Steel Corp., Bethlehem, PA, November.

———. (1992). "ASTM A709 and AASHTO M270 Steels for Bridge Construction," Tech. Bull. TB-311, Bethlehem Steel Corp., Bethlehem, PA, June.

———. (1993). *Weathering Steel,* Booklet no. 3791, Bethlehem Steel Corp., Bethlehem, PA, May.

Bettigole, N. H. (1992). "Exodermic Decks Offer Design Alternative," *Roads and Bridges,* 30(4), April, pp. 36–37.

Biswas, M. (1986). "Precast Bridge Deck Design Systems," *PCI J.,* 31(2), March–April, pp. 40–94.

Bleich, H. (1932). "Uber die Bemessung Statisch Unbestimmter Stahl-Tragwerke unter Beruck-sichtigung Elastisch-Plastischen Baustoff (The Design of Statically Indeterminate Steel Frames Considering the Elastic-Plastic Behavior of the Material)," *Bauingenieur,* 13, p. 261 (in German).

Breen, F. L. (1972). "Load Factor Design of W Beams," *Four Design Examples—Load Factor Design of Steel Highway Bridges,* Pub. no. P123(PS010), AISI, New York, pp. 1–14, 1-1E–1-16E, 1-1EA–1-6EA.

Brendel, G. (1964). "Strength of the Compression Slab of T-Beams Subject to Simple Bending," *ACI J. Proc.,* 61(1), January, pp. 57–76.

Brinckerhoff, P. (1989). *Bridge Inspection and Rehabilitation,* John Wiley & Sons, New York.

Brockenbrough, R. L. (1983). "Considerations in the Design of Bolted Joints for Weathering Steel," *AISC Eng. J.,* 20(1), pp. 40–45.

BSI. (1972). "Beams for Bridges," *Composite Construction in Structural Steel and Concrete,* British Standard Code of Practice, CP117, Part 2, British Standard Institution, London.

CALTRANS. (1993). "Bridge Design Aids," in *Bridge Planning and Design Manual,* State of California Department of Transportation, Sacramento.

Carpentier, L. (1962). "It's Been Done Before," *Eng. News-Record,* March 15, p. 12.

Carskadden, P. S. (1968). "Shear Buckling of Unstiffened Hybrid Beams," *ASCE J. Struct. Div.,* 94(ST8), August, pp. 1965–1990.

———. (1976). *Autostress Design of Highway Bridges, Phase I: Design Procedure and Example Design,* Project 188, AISI, Washington, DC, March 8.

———. (1980). *Autostress Design of Highway Bridges, Phase 3: Interior Support Model Test,* Project 188, AISI, Washington, DC, February 11.

Carskadden, P. S., Haaijer, G., and Grubb, M. A. (1978). "Computing the Effective Plastic Moment," *AISC Eng. J.,* 19(1), pp. 12–15.

CE. (1982). "Bridge Superstructure Cost Cut 10 Percent by Load-Factor Design," *ASCE Civ. Eng.,* July.

———. (1996). "New Aluminum Decks Cut Loads, Add Life," *ASCE Civ. Eng.,* August, p. 12.

Chapman, J. C. (1964). "Composite Construction in Steel and Concrete—Behavior of Composite Beams," *Struct. Engineer,* 42(4), pp. 115–125.

CHBDC. (1996a). *Canadian Highway Bridge Design Code—Section 16, Fibre-Reinforced Structures,* final draft, July 6, 1996.

———. (1996b). "Design Provisions for Fibre-Reinforced Structures in Canadian Highway Bridge Design Code," Canadian Highway Bridge Design Code Technical Subcommittee no. 16, *Proc. 2nd Intl. Conf. Advanced Composite Materials in Bridges and Structures,* Montreal, Aug. 12–14, pp. 391–406.

Chwalla, E. (1936). "Die Formeln zur Berechung der Vollmittragenden Breite Dunner Gurtung Rippenplatten," *Der Stahlbau,* Berlin, 9(10), pp. 73–78 (in German).

Cheung, M. S., and Chan, M. Y. T. (1978). "Finite-Strip Evaluation of Effective Flange Width of Bridge Girders," *Canadian J. Civ. Eng.,* 5(2), pp. 174–185.

CONC. (1994). "Raising Bridge Deck Joints during Overlay Repair," *Concrete Repair Digest,* October/November, 6(5), pp. 284–290.

Conway, W. B. (1989). "Greater New Orleans Bridge No. 2," paper presented to AASHTO Subcommittee on Bridges and Structures, *Proc. AASHTO Subcommittee on Bridges and Structures,* AASHTO, Washington, DC.

Cosaboom, B., Mehalchick, G., and Zoccola, J. C. (1979). *Bridge Construction with Unpainted High-Strength Low-Alloy Steel: Eight-Year Progress Report,* Report no. 79-001-7799, New Jersey Department of Transportation, Trenton, February.

Culp, J. D., and Tinklenberg, G. L. (1980). *Interim Report on Effects of Corrosion on Bridges of Unpainted A588 Steel and Painted Steel Types,* Research Report no. R-1142, Michigan Department of Transportation, Lansing, June.

Daniels, J. H, and Fisher, J. W. (1967). *Static Behavior of Continuous Composite Beams,* Fritz Eng. Lab. report no. 324.2, Lehigh University, Bethlehem, PA, March.

Davies, J. M. (1965). "The Stability of Plane Frameworks under Static and Repeated Loading," PhD thesis, University of Manchester, England.

———. (1967). "Collapse and Shakedown Loads of Plane Frame Works," *ASCE J. Str. Div.,* 93(ST3), June, pp. 35–50.

Dhillon, B. S. (1991). "Optimum Design of Composite Hybrid Plate Girders," *ASCE J. Struct. Eng.,* 117(7), July, pp. 2088–2098.

Dischinger, F., and Mehmel, A. (1955). "Massivbau Taschenbuch fur Bauingenieure," Springer Verlag, Berlin.

DOT, UK. (1981). *The Use of Weathering Steel for Highway Structures,* Department of Transport Standard BD/7/81, London.

EBDI. (1996). "Exodermic Bridge Deck," *Exodermic Bridge Handbook,* Exodermic Bridge Deck Institute, Scarsdale, NY.

Elliot, A. L. (1990). "Steel and Concrete Bridges," in E. H. Gaylord and C. N. Gaylord, eds., *Structural Engineering Handbook,* 3rd ed., McGraw-Hill Companies, Inc., New York.

ENR. (1961). "Prestressing Steel Stringers Reduce Bridge Weight by 25 Percent," *Eng. News-Record,* October 19, pp. 32–33.

———. (1978a). "One Example of Highway Bridge Design Using Both the Load Factor Method and the Working Stress Provisions of AASHTO Specifications," *Eng. News-Record,* March 16, p. 9.

———. (1978b). "Cable Corrosion Forces Bridge Reconstruction," *Eng. News-Record,* November 2, p. 19.

———. (1978c). "Corrosion Forces Bridge Cable Repair," *Eng. News-Record,* May 18, p. 41.

———. (1978d). "New Mississippi River Bridge Goes Forward," *Eng. News-Record,* October 26, p. 15.

———. (1982a). "Bridge Design Cuts Weight," *Eng. News-Record,* July 22, p. 13.

———. (1982b). "Steel Design Sweeps Bid," *Eng. News-Record,* September 2, p. 12.

———. (1983). "Prestressed Steel Bridge a Winner," *Eng. News-Record,* December 22, pp. 48–49.

———. (1984). "Reaching to the Crescent City," *Eng. News-Record,* April 26, pp. 30–32.

EXONEWS. (1994a). "Tappan Zee Bridge Deck Repairs Use Exodermic Panels," *Exo News,* Exodermic Bridge Deck Institute, Westwood, NJ, winter 1994/95, p. 1.

———. (1994b). "Nighttime Deck Replacement Using Precast Exodermic Panels," *Exo News,* Exodermic Bridge Deck Institute, Westwood, NJ, winter 1994, p. 1.

———. (1995). "Exodermic Decks in New Construction," *Exo News,* Exodermic Bridge Deck Institute, Westwood, NJ, summer 1995, p. 2.

———. (1996a). "Hudson River Bridge Redecked at Night," *Exo News,* Exodermic Bridge Deck Institute, Westwood, NJ, winter/spring 1996, p. 1.

———. (1996b). "New Bascule Bridges to Use Exodermic Decks," *Exo News,* Exodermic Bridge Deck Institute, Westwood, NJ, winter/spring 1996, p. 1.

Eyre, D. G., and Galambos, T. V. (1969). *Variable Repeated Loading—A Literature Survey,* Bull. no. 142, Welding Research Council, July.

Eyre, D. G., and Galambos, T. V. (1970). "Shakedown Tests on Steel Bars and Frames," *ASCE J. Str. Div.,* 96(ST7), July, pp. 1287–1304.

Fagundo, F. E., Tabatabai, H., Soongs-wang, K., Richardson, J. M., and Callis, E. G. (1985). "Precast Panel Composite Bridge Decks," *Concrete Intl.,* 7(5), May, pp. 59–65.

Fasullo, E. J., and Hahn, D. M. (1977). "George Washington Bridge Redecked with Prefabricated Panels and No Delay," *ASCE Civ. Eng.,* December, pp. 57–61.

FHWA. (1980a). *Proposed Design Specifications for Steel Box Girder Bridges,* FHWA report no. FHWA-TS-80-205, Federal Highway Administration, Washington, DC.

———. (1980b). *Integral, No-Joint Structures and Required Provisions for Movement,* FHWA Technical Advisory T 5140.13, Federal Highway Administration, Washington, DC, June 28.

———. (1989). *Technical Advisory on Uncoated Weathering Steel in Structures,* FHWA Technical Advisory, Federal Highway Administration, Washington, DC, October 3.

Finn, E. V. (1964). "The Use of Prestressed Steel in Elevated Roadway," *Struct. Engineer,* 42(1), January.

Fisher, J. W. (1970). "Design of Composite Beams with Formed Metal Deck," *AISC Eng. J.,* 7(3), July, pp. 88–96.

———. (1984). *Fatigue and Fracture in Steel Bridges—Case Studies,* John Wiley & Sons, New York.

Francis, A. J. (1980). *Introducing Structures,* Pergamon Press, New York, pp. 139–140.

Frangopol, D. M., and Nakib, R. (1991). "Redundancy in Highway Bridges," *AISC Eng. J.,* 1st qtr., pp. 45–50.

Frost, R. W., and Schilling, C. G. (1964). "Behavior of Hybrid Beams Subjected to Static Loads," *ASCE J. Struct. Div.,* 90(ST3), June, pp. 55–88.

Fukumoto, Y., and Yoshida, H. (1969). "Deflection Stability of Beams under Repeated Loads," Proc. paper 6668, *ASCE J. Struct. Div.,* 95(ST7), July, p. 1443.

GangaRao, H. V. S., Seifert, W., and Kevork, H. (1988). *Behavior and Design of Open Steel Grid Decks for Highway Bridges,* Final report, Vol. 1, Civil Engineering Dept., West Virginia University, Morgantown.

Garcia, I., and J. H. Daniels (1971). *Negative Moment Behavior of Composite Beams,* Fritz Eng. Lab. report no. 359.4, Lehigh University, Bethlehem, PA.

Gatti, W. (1994). "Economical Steel Bridge Details," *AISC Modern Steel Constr.,* 34(9), September, pp. 24–29.

Gaylord, E. H., and Gaylord, C. N., eds. (1990). *Structural Engineering Handbook,* 3rd ed., McGraw-Hill Companies, Inc., New York.

Gaylord, E. H., Gaylord, C. N., and Stallmeyer, J. E. (1992). *Design of Steel Structures,* 3rd ed., McGraw-Hill Companies, Inc., New York.

Ghani, A. F. M. R. (1967). "Shakedown Analysis of Nonprismatic Beams," *ASCE J. Struct. Div.,* 93(ST6), Proc. paper 5643, December, p. 25.

Girkmann, K. (1954). *Flachentragwerke,* 3rd ed., Springer Verlag, Vienna, pp. 171–177.

Goldstein, H. (1996). "Focus on Structures: Tappan Zee Set for Inverset," *ASCE Civ. Eng.,* September, pp. 12A–13A.

Gonulsen, Y. I., and Hsiong, W. (1972). "Two-Span Continuous Composite Welded Girder Highway Bridge," in *Four Design Examples—Load Factor Design of Steel Highway*

Bridges, Pub. no. P123(PS010), American Iron and Steel Institute, New York, pp. 3-1–3-35, 3-1A–3-5A.

Gozum, A. T., and Haaijer, G. (1955). "Deflection Stability of Continuous Beams," Report no. 205G.1, Fritz Eng. Lab., Lehigh University, Bethlehem, PA.

Grant, J. A., Fisher, J. W., and Slutter, R. O. (1977). "Composite Beams with Formed Steel Deck," *AISC Eng. J.,* 14(1), pp. 24–43.

Grubb, M. A., and Carskadden, P. S. (1979). *Autostress Design of Highway Bridges, Phase 3: Initial Moment-Rotation Tests,* Project 188, AISI, Washington, DC, April 18.

———. (1981). *Autostress Design of Highway Bridges, Phase 3: Moment-Rotation Requirements,* Project 188, AISI, Washington, DC, July 6.

Gruning, M. (1926). *Die Tragfahigkeit Statisch Unbestimmter Trag-Werke aus Stahl bei Beliebig Haufig Wiederholter Belastung (The Carrying Capacity of Statically Indeterminate Steel Frames Subjected to Arbitrarily Repeated Loading),* Julius Springer, Berlin (in German).

Guzek, T. P., and Grzybowski, J. R. (1992). "Reducing Bridge Costs," *AISC Modern Steel Constr.,* 34(9), September, pp. 24–27.

Haaijer, G. (1961). "Economy of High-Strength Steel Structural Members," *ASCE J. Struct. Div.,* 87(ST12), December, pp. 1–23.

———. (1973). "Autostress Design of Steel Structures," *ASCE Natl. Str. Engr. Meeting,* Preprint no. 1930, San Francisco, April 9-13.

———. (1985). "Advances in Short-Span Steel Bridges," *ASCE Civ. Eng.,* November 1985, pp. 45–47. Presented at the 1985 *Intl. Eng. Symp.,* Chicago, May.

Haaijer, G., and Carskadden, P. S. (1980). "Autostress Design of Continuous Steel Bridge Members," *Proc. Canadian Str. Engr. Conf.,* Canadian Steel Industries Construction Council, Montreal, Canada, February, pp. 1–20.

Haaijer, G., Carskadden, P. S., and Grubb, M. A. (1980). "Plastic Design with Noncompact Section Including Composite Bridge Members," *Proc. Structural Stability Research Council,* Lehigh University, Bethlehem, PA, pp. 29–31.

———. (1983). "Autostress Design of Steel Bridges," *ASCE J. Struct. Eng.,* 109(ST1), January, pp. 188–199.

———. (1987). *Suggested Autostress Procedures for Load and Resistance Factor Design of Steel Beam Bridges,* Bull. no. 29, AISI, Washington, DC, April.

Haaijer, G., Schilling, C. G., and Carskadden, P. S. (1983). "Limit-State Criteria for Load Factor Design of Steel Bridges," *Engineering Struct.,* Surrey, England, 5(1), pp. 26–30.

———. (1979). *Bridge Design Procedures Based on Performance Requirements,* Trans. Res. Rec. 711, Transportation Research Board, Washington, DC.

Hacker, J. C. (1957). "A Simplified Design of Composite Bridge Structures," *ASCE J. Struct. Div.,* 93(ST11), Paper no. 1432, November.

Hall, D. H. (1971). *Orthotropic Bridges–PD-2032,* Bethlehem Steel Corp., Bethlehem, PA, March.

Hamada, S., and Longworth, J. (1976). "Ultimate Strength of Continuous Composite Beams," *ASCE J. Struct. Div.,* 102(ST7), July, pp. 1463–1478.

Hambly, E. C. (1991). *Bridge Deck Behavior,* Halstead Press, John Wiley & Sons, New York.

Hansell, W. C., Galambos, T. V., Ravindra, M. K., and Viest, I. M. (1978). "Composite Beam Criteria in LRFD," *ASCE J. Struct. Div.,* 104(ST9), September 1978, pp. 1409–1426; *Discussion,* 106(ST2), February, 1980, pp. 571–572.

Hansell, W. C., and Viest, I. M. (1971). "Load Factor Design of Highway Bridges," *AISC Eng. J.,* 8(4), pp. 113–123.

Hedefine, A. (1972). "Beam and Girder Bridges," Section 11, *Structural Steel Designer's Handbook,* F. S. Merritt, ed., McGraw-Hill Companies, Inc., New York.

Heins, C. P., and Fan, H. M. (1976). "Effective Composite Beam Width at Ultimate Load," *ASCE J. Struct. Div.,* 102(ST11), November, pp. 2163–2179.

Heins, C. P., and Firmage, D. A. (1979). *Design of Modern Steel Highway Bridges,* John Wiley & Sons, New York.

Hoadley, P. G. (1963). "Behavior of Prestressed Composite Steel Beams," *ASCE J. Struct. Div.,* 89(ST3), June, pp. 21–34.

Hodge, P. G., Jr. (1954). "Shakedown of Elastic-Plastic Structures," in W. R. Osgood, ed. *Residual Stress in Metals and Metal Construction,* Reinhold, New York.

Hooper, I., Gruble, M. A., and Viest, I. M. (1990). "Design of Composite Members," Section 1A in E. H. Gaylord and C. N. Gaylord, eds., *Structural Engineering Handbook,* McGraw-Hill Companies, Inc., New York.

Horne, M. R. (1954). "The Effect of Variable Repeated Loads in Building Structures Designed by the Plastic Theory," *Proc. IABSE,* 14, p. 53.

Issa, M. A., Idris, A.-T., Kaspar, I. I., and Khayyat, S. Y. (1995a). "Full-Depth Precast, and Precast Prestressed Concrete Bridge Deck Panels," *PCI J.,* 40(1), January–February, pp. 59–80.

Issa, M. A., Yousif, A. A., Issa, M. A., Kaspar, I. I., and Khayyat, S. Y. (1995b). "Field Performance of Full-Depth Precast Concrete Panels in Bridge Deck Reconstruction," *PCI J.,* 40(3), May–June, pp. 82–108.

Johnson, J. E., and Lewis, A. D. M. (1966). "Structural Behavior in a Gypsum Roof-Deck System," *ASCE J. Struct. Div.,* 92(ST12), December, pp. 283–296.

Johnson, R. P., and Buckby, R. J. (1986). *Composite Structures of Steel and Concrete,* Vol. 2, *Bridges,* 2nd ed., William Collins Sons & Co., London.

Johnson, R. P., Dalen, K. V., and Kemp, A. R. (1967). "Ultimate Strength of Continuous Composite Beams," *Proc. Conf. Struct. Steelwork,* British Constructional Steel Association, November.

Johnston, B. G., Lin, F. Y., and Galambos, T. V. (1986). *Basic Steel Design,* Prentice Hall, Englewood Cliffs, NJ.

Karpenco, G. V., and Vasilenko, I. I. (1985). *Stress Corrosion Cracking of Steels,* Freund Publishing, Tel Aviv.

Kayser, J. R. (1988). *The Effects of Corrosion on the Reliability of Steel Girder Bridges,* PhD thesis, Department of Civil Engineering, University of Michigan at Ann Arbor.

Kayser, J. R., and Nowak, A. S. (1987). "Evaluation of Corroded Steel Bridges," *ASCE Bridges and Transmission Line Structures,* pp. 35–46.

———. (1989). "Capacity Loss Due to Corrosion in Steel-Girder Bridges," *ASCE J. Struct. Eng.,* 115(6), June, pp. 1525–1537.

Keating, P. B., ed. (1990). *Economical and Fatigue-Resistant Steel Bridge Details,* Pub. no. FHWA-H1-90-043, U.S. Department of Transportation, McLean, VA, October.

Ketchek, K. (1963). "Design of Composite Beams for Highway Bridges," *ASCE Civ. Eng.,* July, pp. 60–61.

Kinney, J. S. (1957). *Indeterminate Structural Analysis,* Addison Wesley, Reading, MA.

Kluge, R. W., and Sawyer, H. A. (1975). "Interacting Pretensioned Concrete Form Panels for Bridge Decks," *PCI J.,* 20(3), May–June, pp. 34–61.

Knapp, N. P. (1994). Personal communication with N. P. Knapp, Director, State of Louisiana Department of Transportation and Development, Bridges and Structures Division, Baton Rouge, June 29.

Knight, R. P. (1984). "Economical Steel Plate Girder Bridges," *AISC Eng. J.,* pp. 89–93; also presented at Natnl. Bridge Conf., Pittsburgh, PA, June 1, 1983.

Knowles, P. R. (1973). *Composite Steel and Concrete Construction,* John Wiley & Sons, London.

Knudsen, C. V. (1980). "Re-Decking of a Bridge with Precast Concrete," *ASCE Civ. Eng.,* April, pp. 75–77.

Komp, M. E. (1983). "Atmospheric Ratings of Weathering Steels—Calculations and Significance," *Materials Performance,* 26(7), pp. 42–44.

Ku, C. Y. (1986). *Deflection of Beams for All Spans and Cross Sections,* McGraw-Hill Companies, Inc., New York.

Kubo, M., and Galambos, T. (1988). "Plastic Collapse Load of Continuous Composite Plate Girders," *AISC Eng. J.,* 25(4), pp. 145–155.

Kulicki, J. (1982). "Development of Proposed Specifications for Strength Design Criteria of Truss Bridges," *ASCE Struct. Congress '82,* October.

Kulkarni, S. R. (1994). Personal communication with S. R. Kulkarni, State of Michigan Department of Transportation, Lansing, June 22.

Kuzmanovic, B. O., and Willems, N. (1983). *Steel Design for Structural Engineers,* 2nd ed., Prentice Hall, Englewood Cliffs, NJ.

Lay, M. G. (1974). "Bridges," in *Structural Steel Design,* 2nd ed., Lambert Tall, ed., Ronald Press, New York, pp. 94–143.

Lee, H. W., and Sarsam, M. B. (1972). *Analysis of Integral Abutment Bridges,* Department of Civil Engineering, South Dakota State University, Brookings, July.

Lee J. A. N. (1962). "Effective Width of T-Beams," *Struct. Engineer,* 40(1), pp. 21–27.

Leve, F. (1961). "Work of the European Concrete Committee," *ACI J. Proc.,* 573, March, pp. 1049–1054.

Levine, L., and McLoughlin, J. (1967). "Prestressed Steel Stringers Solve Bridge Clearance Problems," *ASCE Civ. Eng.,* April, pp. 42–43.

Lew, H. S. (1970). *Effect of Shear Connector Spacing on the Ultimate Strength of Steel–Concrete Composite Beams,* National Bureau of Standards report no. 10, 246, U.S. Department of Commerce, Washington, DC, August.

Lorenz, R. F. (1983). "Some Economic Considerations for Composite Floor Beams," *AISC Eng. J.,* 20(2), pp. 78–81.

———. (1988). "Understanding Composite Beam Design Methods Using LRFD," *AISC Eng. J.,* 25(1), pp. 35–38.

Loveall, C. L. (1985). "Jointless Bridge Decks," *ASCE Civ. Eng.,* November, pp. 64–67.

———. (1987). "Advances in Bridge Design and Construction," *AISC Modern Steel Constr.,* 27(2), February, pp. 31–34.

Loveys, P. C. (1963). *Orthotropic Steel Plate Deck Bridges,* Canadian Institute of Steel Construction, November.

Lutz, J. G., and Scalia, D. J. (1984). "Deck Widening of Woodrow Wilson Memorial Bridge," *PCI J.* 29(3), May–June, pp. 74–93.

Magnel, G. (1950). "Prestressed Steel Structures," *Struct. Engineer,* 28(11), November.

McCrum, R. L., Reincke, J. W., and Lay, J. W. (1984). *Evaluation of Calcium Magnesium Acetate (CMA) as a Deicing Agent: Corrosion Phase—A Comparative Evaluation of the Effects of CMA vs. Salt (NaCl) on Highway Metals (Three-Month Exposure),* Research report no. R-1258, Michigan Department of Transportation, Lansing, November.

McGarraugh, J. B., and Baldwin, J. W. (1971). "Lightweight Concrete-on-Steel Composite Beams," *AISC Eng. J.,* 8(3), July, pp. 90–98.

McGuire, W. (1968). *Steel Structures,* Prentice Hall, Englewood Cliffs, NJ.

McMormac, J. (1992). *Structural Steel Design, ASD Method,* 4th ed., HarperCollins, New York.

Melan, E. (1936). "Theorie Statisch Unbestimmter System Aus Ideal Plastischen Baustoff (The Theory of Statically Indeterminate Systems Made of Ideally Plastic Material)," *Sitzber. Akad. Wiss.,* 145(IIa), p. 195 (in German).

Merritt, F. S., ed. (1972). *Structural Steel Designer's Handbook,* McGraw-Hill Companies, Inc., New York.

Metzer, W. (1929). "Die Mittragende Breite," *Luftfahrtforschung,* 4, pp. 1–20 (in German).

MIDOT. (1985). *Current Status Report—Effects of Corrosion on Unpainted Weathering Steel Bridges,* Testing and Research Division, Research Laboratory Section, Michigan Department of Transportation, Lansing.

Miller, A. B. (1929). *The Effective Width of a Plate Supported by a Beam,* Selected engineering papers, no. 83, The Institute of Civil Engineers, London.

Mistry, V. (1994). "Economical Bridge Design," Federal Highway Administration Guidelines, *AISC Modern Steel Constr.,* 34(3), March, pp. 42–47.

Modjeski and Masters. (1979). *Load Factor Design Applied to Truss Members with Application to the Design of Greater New Orleans Bridge No. 2,* Modjeski and Masters, Harrisburg, PA, October.

Moffatt, K. R., and Dowling, P. J. (1975). "Shear Lag in Steel Box Girders," *Struct. Engineer,* 53(10), pp. 439–448.

Montens, S., and O'Hagan, D. (1992). "Bringing Bridge Design into the Next Century: The Construction of the Roize Bridge," *AISC Modern Steel Constr.,* 32(9), September, pp. 53–54.

Montgomery, J. M., Gorman, C. D., and Alpago, P. E. (1992). "Short-Span Bridge Design in the 1990s," *AISC Modern Steel Constr.,* June, pp. 32–36.

Moon, T. J., and Maun, V. P. (1972). "Design of a Three-Span Noncomposite Plate Girder Using the Tentative Criteria for Load Factor Design of Steel Highway Bridges," *Four Design Examples—Load Factor Design of Steel Highway Bridges,* Pub. no. P123(PS010), AISI, New York, March, pp. 2-1–2-24.

Mufti, A. A., Bakht, B., and Jaeger, L. G. (1996). *Bridge Superstructures—New Developments,* National Book Foundation, Islamabad, Pakistan.

Muller, J. M. (1993). "Bridge to the Future," *ASCE Civ. Eng.,* January, pp. 40–43.

Muller, J. M., and Lockwood, J. D. (1992). "Innovations in Composite Bridge Structures," *AISC Modern Steel Constr.,* 32(9), September, pp. 47–52.

Nakai, H., and Yoo, C. H. (1988). *Analysis and Design of Curved Steel Bridges,* McGraw-Hill Companies, Inc., New York.

NCHRP. (1989). *Bridge Deck Joints,* Synthesis of Highway Practice Report no. 141, National Cooperative Highway Research Program (NCHRP), Washington, DC.

Neal, B. G. (1950a). *The Plastic Methods of Structural Analysis,* Chapman and Hall, London.

———. (1950b). "Plastic Collapse and Shakedown Theorems for Structures of Strain-Hardening Material," *J. Aeronautical Science,* 117, p. 297.

———. (1951). "The Behavior of Framed Structures under Repeated Loading," *Quarterly J. Mechanics and Applied Mathematics,* 4, p. 78.

Neal, B. G., and Symonds, P. S. (1950). "A Method for Calculating the Failure Load for a Framed Structure Subjected to Fluctuating Loads," *J. Inst. Civ. Eng.,* 35, p. 186.

———. (1958). "Cyclic Loading of Portal Frames—Theory and Tests," *Proc. IABSE,* 18, p. 171.

Newhook, J. P., and Mufti, A. A. (1996). "A Reinforcing Steel-Free Concrete Deck Slab for the Salmon River Bridge," *Concrete Intl.,* 18(6), June.

Newhook, J. P., Mufti A. A., Jaeger, L. G., MacDonnell, R. E., and Hamilton, D. (1966). "Steel-Free Concrete Bridge Deck—the Salmon River Project: Design and Construction," *Proc. Canadian Soc. Civ. Eng. (CSEC) Annual Eng. Conf.,* Edmonton.

Newhook, J. P., Mufti, A. A., and Wegner, L. D. (1995). "Fiber-Reinforced Concrete Deck Slabs without Steel Reinforcement: Half-Scale Testing and Mathematical Formulation," Research Report no. 1-1995, Nova Scotia CAD/CAM Centre, Halifax, Canada.

NJDOT. (1968). *Unpainted Low-Alloy Steels for Use in the Construction of Highway Bridges,* Bureau of Structures and Materials, Division of Research and Evaluation, New Jersey Department of Transportation, Trenton, September.

OHBDC. (1995). *Ontario Highway Bridge Code, Addendum 1995,* Ministry of Transportation of Ontario.

Ollgaard, J. G., Slutter, R. G., and Fisher, J. W. (1971). "Shear Strength of Stud Shear Connections in Lightweight Concrete and Normal-Weight Concrete," *AISC Eng. J.,* 8(2), April, pp. 55–64

PCIJ (1987). "Precast Prestressed Concrete Bridge Deck Panels," PCI Committee on Bridges, *PCI J.,* 32(2), March–April, pp. 26–45.

———. (1988). "Recommended Practice for Precast Concrete Composite Bridge Deck Panels," Special Report, *PCI J.,* 33(2), March–April, pp. 67–109.

PennDOT. (1970). *Standard for Bridge Design, Reinforced Concrete, and Steel Structures,* BD-100 series, Pennsylvania Department of Transportation, Harrisburg, September.

———. (1993). *Design Manual Part 4,* vol. 1 of 3 vols., *Structures, Procedures, Design Plans, Presentations,* PDT pub. no. 15, Pennsylvania Dept. of Transportation, Harrisburg, August.

Porete. (1949). *Alpha Composite Construction Engineering Handbook,* Porete Manufacturing Company, North Arlington, NJ.

Reagan, R. S., and Krahl, N. W. (1967). "Behavior of Prestressed Composite Beams," *ASCE J. Struct. Div.,* 93(ST6), Proc. paper 5663, December, pp. 87–108.

Roeder, C. W., and Eltvik, L. (1985a). "Autostress Design Criteria—Load Test of the Whitechuck River Bridge," Final report, Federal Highway Administration project DTFH 61-81-C00114, University of Washington, Seattle, January.

———. (1985b). "An Experimental Evaluation of Autostress Design," Trans. res. rec. 1044, Transportation Research Board, Washington, DC.

Roll, F. (1971). "Effects of Differential Shrinkage and Creep on a Composite Steel–Concrete Structure," in *Designing for Effects of Creep, Shrinkage, Temperature in Concrete Structures,* American Concrete Institute, ACI SP-27, Detroit, MI, pp. 187–214.

Ruesch, H. (1953). "Die Mitwirkende Plattenbreite bei Plattenbalken," *Der Stahlbau,* Berlin, 10 (in German).

Salmon, C. G., and Johnson, J. E. (1990). *Steel Structures—Design and Behavior,* 3rd ed., HarperCollins, New York.

Sattler, K. (1961). "Composite Construction in Theory and Practice," *Struct. Engineer,* 39(4), April, pp. 122–144.

Schilling, C. G. (1967). "Web Crippling Tests on Hybrid Girders," *ASCE J. Struct. Div.,* 93(ST1), February, pp. 59–70.

———. (1968). "Design of Hybrid Steel Beams," Report of Subcommittee on Hybrid Beams and Girders, Joint ASCE–AASHO Committee on Flexural Members, *ASCE J. Struct. Div.,* 94(ST6), June, pp. 1397–1426.

———. (1985). *Steel Bridges: The Best of Current Practice,* AISC pub. no. G-446-2/1/85, AISC, Chicago.

———. (1989). *A Unified Autostress Method,* Report on project 51, AISI, Washington, DC.

———. (1991). "Unified Autostress Method," *AISC Eng. J.,* 28(4), pp. 169–176.

Seim, C. (1983). "Steel Beats Concrete for Idaho Bridge," *ASCE Civ. Eng.,* August, pp. 28–32.

Selvadurai, A. P. S. (1995). *Structural Behavior under Moving Loads, Phase I: Fibre-Reinforced Concrete Decks,* Final report on Ontario Joint Transportation Research Programme, Submitted to Ministry of Transportation, Quality and Standards Division, Research and Development, Downsview, Canada, February.

Selvadurai, A. P. S., and Bakht, B. (1995). "Simulation of Rolling Wheel Loads on an FRC Deck Slab," *Proc. 2nd University–Industry Workshop on FRC,* Toronto, pp. 273–287.

Slavis, C. (1982). "Precast Concrete Deck Modules for Bridge Deck Reconstruction," *PCI J.,* 28(4), July–August, pp. 120–135.

———. (1983). "Precast Concrete Deck Modules for Bridge Deck Reconstruction," *Transp. Res. Rec. 871, Segmental and System Bridge Construction: Concrete Box Girder and Steel Design,* Transportation Research Board, Washington, DC., pp. 30–33.

Slutter, R. G. (1974). "Composite Steel–Concrete Members," in Lambert Tall, ed., *Structural Steel Design,* 2nd ed., Ronald Press Co., New York.

Slutter, R. G., and Driscoll, G. C. (1965). "Flexural Strength of Steel–Concrete Composite Beams," part 1, paper no. 4294, *ASCE J. Struct. Div.,* 91(ST2), April, pp. 71–99.

Slutter, R. G., and Fisher, J. W. (1966). *Fatigue Strength of Shear Connectors,* National Research Council, Highway Research Board, Hwy. Res. Rec. no. 147, pp. 65–88.

———. (1971). "The Strength of Stud Shear Connectors in Lightweight and Normal-Weight Concrete," *AISC Eng. J.,* 8(2), April, pp. 55–64.

Spaans, L. (1994). "Post-Tensioning Cuts Steel Bridge Costs," *AISC Modern Steel Constr.,* 34(9), September, pp. 38–43.

Steel Constr. (1961). "Prestressed Steel Beams Replace Concrete," *Steel Constr. Digest,* 18(2), p. 10.

Steinman, D. B., and Watson, S. R. (1957). *Bridges and Their Builders,* Dover, New York.

Symonds, P. S. (1950). "The Basic Theorems in the Plastic Theory of Structures," in "Readers Forum," *J. Aeronautical Science,* 17(10), October, pp. 669–670.

Tall, L., ed. (1974). *Structural Steel Design,* Ronald Press, New York.

Taly, N. (1976). *Development of Short-Span Bridge Systems,* PhD dissertation, West Virginia University, Morgantown, December.

Taly, N., and GangaRao, H. V. S. (1974). "Development of Standardized Short-Span Bridges," Meeting preprint 2407, *ASCE Annual and Natnl. Environmental Eng. Conv.,* Kansas City, MO, October 21–25.

———. (1979). "Prefabricated Press-Formed Steel T-Box Girder Bridge System," *AISC Eng. J.,* 16(3), pp. 75–83.

TennDOT. (1986). *Structural Memorandum No. 45,* Division of Structures, Tennessee Department of Transportation, Nashville, January.

Timoshenko, S. (1953). *History of Strength of Materials,* McGraw-Hill Companies, Inc., New York.

Timoshenko, S., and Goodier, J. N. (1951). *Theory of Elasticity,* McGraw-Hill Companies, Inc., New York, pp. 262–268.

Toprac, A. A. (1965a). "Strength of Three New Types of Composite Beams," *AISC Eng. J.,* 2(1), January, pp. 21–30.

———. (1965b). "Fatigue Strength of $\frac{3}{4}$-in. Stud Shear Connectors," National Research Council, Highway Research Board, Rec. 103, pp. 53–77.

Toprac, A. A., and Murugesam, N. (1971). "Fatigue Strength of Hybrid Plate Girders," *ASCE J. Struct. Div.,* 97(ST4), April, pp. 1203–1225.

Toridis, T. G., and Wen, R. K. (1966). "Inelastic Response of Beams to Moving Loads," *ASCE J. Eng. Mech. Div.,* 92(EM6), Proc. paper 5028, December, p. 1443.

Troitsky, M. S. (1967). *Orthotropic Bridges: Theory and Design,* James F. Lincoln Arc Welding Foundation, Cleveland, OH.

———. (1988). *Prestressed Steel Structures—Theory and Design,* James F. Lincoln Arc Welding Foundation, Cleveland, OH.

———. (1990). *Prestressed Steel Bridges,* Van Nostrand Reinhold, Florence, KY.

Troitsky, M. S., Zielinski, Z. A., and Rabbani, N. F. (1989). "Prestressed-Steel Continuous-Span Girders," *ASCE J. Str. Eng.,* 115(6), June, pp. 1357–1370.

Uhlig, H. H., ed. (1948). *Corrosion Handbook,* John Wiley & Sons, New York.

U.S. DOC. (1990). *Catalog of Highway Bridge Plans,* U.S. Department of Commerce, Bureau of Public Roads, Washington, DC.

U.S. DOT. (1968). *Standard Plans for Highway Bridges,* vol. 2: *Structural Steel Superstructure,* U.S. Department of Transportation, Federal Highway Administration, Bureau of Public Roads, Washington, DC.

USS. (1973). *Short-Span Bridges: Load Factor Design,* U.S. Steel Corp., Pub. no. ADUSS 88-5732-01, Pittsburgh, PA, September.

———. (1981). *Precast Slabs for Composite Bridge Decking—State-of-the-Art Report,* U. S. Steel Corp., Pittsburgh, November.

Vallenilla, C. R., and Bjorhovde, R. (1985). "Effective Width Criteria for Composite Beams," *AISC Eng. J.,* 22(4), pp. 169–175.

Van den Broek, A. (1939). "Theory of Limit Design," *Proc. ASCE,* 65, February, pp. 193–216.

———. (1940). "Theory of Limit Design," *Trans. ASCE,* 105, pp. 638–730.

Viest, I. A. (1974). "Composite Steel-Concrete Construction," Report of the Subcommittee on the State-of-the-Art Survey of the Task Committee on Composite Construction of the Committee on Metals of the Structural Division, *ASCE J. Struct. Div.,* 100(ST5), May, pp. 1085–1139.

Viest, I. M. (1960). "Review of Research on Composite Steel–Concrete Beams," paper no. 2621, *Proc. ASCE J. Struct. Div.,* 8(ST6), June, pp. 23–51.

Viest, I. M., Fountain, R. S., and Seiss, C. P. (1957). "Development of the New AASHTO Specifications for Composite Steel and Concrete Bridges," *Natnl. Res. Council, Hwy. Res. Board, Bull.,* January, pp. 1–17.

Viest, I. M., Fountain, R. S., and Singleton R. C. (1958). *Composite Construction in Steel and Concrete for Bridges and Buildings,* McGraw-Hill Companies, Inc., New York.

Vincent, G. S. (1969). *Steel Research for Construction—Tentative Criteria for Load-Factor Design of Steel Highway Bridges,* Bull. no. 15, AISI, New York, March.

Vitols, V., Clifton, R. J., and Au, T. (1963). "Analysis of Composite Beam Bridges by Orthotropic Plate Theory," *Proc. ASCE J. Struct. Div.,* 89(ST4), part 1, paper 3584, August, pp. 71–94.

von Karman, T. (1924). "Die Mittragende Breitte," *August-Foppel-Festschrift* (in German). Also, *Collected Works of Theodore von Karman,* vol. II, p. 176.

Wasserman, E. (1987). "Jointless Bridge Decks," *AISC Eng. J.,* 24(3), pp. 93–100.

Weaver, D. L., and Bonasso, S. M. (1994). "Exploring New Bridge Designs," *AISC Modern Steel Constr.,* 34(9), September, pp. 50–53.

Wolchuck, R. (1963). *Design Manual for Orthotropic Steel Plate Deck Bridges,* AISC, New York.

———. (1990). "Box Girders," in "Steel-Plate Deck Bridges," Section 19, in *Structural Engineering Handbook,* E. H. Gaylord and C. N. Gaylord, eds., 3rd ed., McGraw-Hill Companies, Inc., New York, pp. 19-1–19-28.

Wright, R. N., and Walker, W. H. (1971). *Criteria for Deflection of Steel Bridges,* AISI Bull. no. 19, November.

———. (1972). "Vibration and Deflection of Steel Bridges," *AISC Eng. J.,* 9(1), January, pp. 20–31.

Yura, J. A., Frank, K. H., and Polyzois, D. (1978). *High-Strength Bolts for Bridges,* PMFSEL Report no. 87-3, University of Texas at Austin, May.

Zahn, M. C. (1987). "The Economics of LRFD in Composite Floor Beams," *AISC Eng. J.,* 24(2), pp. 87–92.

Zoccola, J. C. (1976). *Eight-Year Corrosion Test Report—Eight Mile Road Interchange,* Report no. 1801-1e, TZ-34-75019, Bethlehem Steel Corp., Bethlehem, PA, April.

Zoccola, J. C., Permoda, A. J., Oehler, L. T., and Horton, J. B. (1976). "Performance of Mayari R Weathering Steel (ASTM 242) in Bridges at the Eight-Mile Road and John Lodge Expressway in Detroit, Michigan," Bethlehem Steel Corp., Bethlehem, PA, April.

CHAPTER 9

Plate Girder Bridges

9.1
INTRODUCTION

Plate girders may be defined as structural members that resist loads primarily in flexure and shear. Although shaped similarly to the commonly used *hot-rolled* wide-flange steel beams (I-shaped), plate girders differ from them in that they are *fabricated* from plates[1] or other elements (angles, structural Ts) that are joined together to form I-shapes. They are characterized by slender webs, which are usually (but not necessarily) deeper than those of the deepest available rolled W shapes. Webs of plate girders generally are too thin to develop the required resistance to shear and buckling that they must endure under loads and during handling, transportation, and erection. To overcome these potential deficiencies, web stiffening is usually a requisite remedy. By contrast, rolled beams are produced with relatively thick webs that provide adequate resistance to shear and buckling, usually without stiffeners.

From a design perspective, a plate girder can be defined as a beam-type member with a plane of symmetry in the plane of the web, having equal or unequal flanges, and a single thin-walled web that will be limited by buckling either in flexure or shear [Cooper, Galambos, and Ravindra, 1978]. This definition permits separation of beam- and girder-type members through a limiting depth-to-thickness ratio for the web. Accordingly, the AISC–ASD [1989] defines plate girders as built-up beams and distinguishes them from the conventional steel beams (rolled shapes) with respect to the depth-to-thickness ratio for the web (h/t_w): girders with h/t_w exceeding $760/\sqrt{F_b}$

---

[1] AASHTO–LRFD [1994, p. 6-3] defines a plate as a flat-rolled steel product having thickness greater than $\frac{1}{4}$ in. The AISC [1989, p. 1-105] defines plates as rolled steel products that comply with the following width and thickness classifications: over 8 in. to 48 in. in width, 0.230 in. and over in thickness; over 48 in. in width, 0.180 in. and over in thickness.

according to the AISC–ASD specification [1989], and with h/t_w exceeding $970/\sqrt{F_y}$ according to the AISC–LRFD [1986] specification are classified as plate girders, where

h = height (or depth) of web between flanges
t_w = thickness of web
F_b = allowable bending stress, psi
F_y = yield strength for the web, psi

No such distinction is provided by the AASHTO specifications.

From a structural standpoint, plate girders offer an alternative when the required flexural capacity exceeds that of the deepest available rolled sections. Because of their high flexural capacity, plate girders can be used for longer-span bridges than are possible with the rolled steel beams. More important, with plate girders a variety of superstructure layout schemes of supporting the deck are possible, in addition to the conventional scheme of supporting a deck transversely on rolled or coverplated W-shape beams as discussed in Chapter 8. Several such schemes are discussed later in this chapter.

9.2
HISTORICAL BACKGROUND

Plate girder bridges enjoyed an auspicious early history, which can be traced to mid-nineteenth century England, where iron-plate girders of I-section were commonly used for bridges of small spans. However, for larger structures, other kinds of structures were needed for carrying railroad trains. The long-span suspension bridges already existed, but they were considered unsuitable (because of their great pliability under heavy moving loads) for railroad traffic. A search for a more rigid structure for the Britannia Bridge over the Menai Straits, England, led to the development of tubular structures, fabricated from thin wrought-iron plates, with webs stiffened to prevent buckling.

The famed four-span (230, 460, 460, and 230 ft) Britannia Bridge, built over the Menai Straits, England, from 1846 to 1850 by Robert Stephenson (1803–1858) was completed on March 5, 1850 [Gies, 1963]. Built a few hundred yards from Telford's old suspension bridge of 1826, it consists of two separated parallel rectangular tubes, each carrying a railroad track that passes *through* the tube (Figure 1.21, Chapter 1). Fabricated from some two million rivets and wrought-iron plates of the order 2×8 ft, with thicknesses up to $\frac{3}{4}$ in., the webs of these tubes are stiffened with T-irons spaced about 24 in. on centers, which also serve as splices. The Conway Bridge,[2] a low-level bridge over the Conway River in northern Wales, consisting of two adjacent parallel 400-ft-span tubular structures, built simultaneously but whose completion in January 1849 preceded that of the Britannia Bridge, served as a prototype of the Britannia Bridge, with

---

[2]Both the Britannia and the Conway bridges are of tubular type, built about 15 miles apart on the London-to-Dublin rail route. The construction of the Conway Bridge overlapped but preceded that of the Britannia Bridge. Construction of the Conway Bridge began in April 1847, and the first train passed through the first tube a year later in April 1848. The first tube of the Britannia Bridge was opened to traffic in March 1850, and the second one in October 1850 [Rosenberg and Vincenti, 1978, p. 82]. The largest of the Britannia's tube spanning 460 ft measures 30 ft tall and 14 ft 8 in. wide, and weighs 1400 tons [Fairbairn, 1849, pp. 184–185; Rosenberg and Vincenti, 1978, p. 89].

respect to the design, fabrication, and erection practices [Fairbairn, 1849, 1854; Clark, 1850; Tyrell, 1911; Rosenberg and Vincenti, 1978; O'Connor, 1971].

The designs of the Conway and the Britannia bridges were based on extensive model tests[3] by William Fairbairn (1789–1874), an experienced and well-known iron shipbuilder, and experimental and analytical studies[4] by Eaton Hodgkinson (1789–1861) [Clark, 1850; Timoshenko, 1953]. The tubular girders used for the Conway and Britannia bridges, and later patented[5] by Fairbairn, have a unique place in the history of structural engineering, for they and a very few others were the first[6] and the last[7] such girder forms to be used for bridges. Through their use the postbuckling phenomenon of wave formation in the vertical sides of the tube girders was recognized, which eventually resulted in Fairbairn developing the method of stabilizing the webs of plate girders with stiffeners. Fairbairn's tests were the first to draw engineers' attention to the importance of the stability question in designing compressed iron plates and shells [Timoshenko, 1953, p. 193]. The Britannia remained the longest railway bridge in the world until the construction of Roebling's double-deck,[8] 821-ft-span Niagara Suspension Bridge in March 1855 [Steinman and Watson, 1957]. Significantly, the tubular-bridge experience of the Britannia and Conway bridges, the associated technology, and the unprecedented advancements in the understanding of the use of wrought

---

[3]Conducted at Milwall, England, the test involved a one-sixth scale specimen, having a span of 75 ft. Because of the prohibitive cost of building more than one model, Fairbairn proceeded solely by trial-and-error: after the failure of one test, the tube was repaired, strengthened against the observed failure, and tested again [Rosenberg and Vincenti, 1978, p. 25]. "As a result of these tests, it was concluded that the friction produced between the plates of a joint by the rivets was sufficient to resist shearing forces and that the deflection is the result of elastic deformation alone" [Timoshenko, 1953, p. 160]. Fairbairn was the first to conduct experiments with buckling of tubes [Timoshenko and Gere, 1961, p. 468].

[4]Hodgkinson's tests, which began in January 1846 and were conducted in Manchester, England, were "the first experimental study of the buckling of compressed plates and of thin-walled tubes" [Timoshenko, 1953, p. 107]. These tests included 40 plates, 29 rectangular tubes, and 37 circular tubes—all tested in compression—as well as 30 tests on plain (noncellular) rectangular tubes as beams in bending. Through these tests, he made a systematic parametric study of tubular structures exploring the effects of changes in length, width, plate thickness, etc. [Rosenberg and Vincenti, 1978, p. 29]. This work provided the basic source of knowledge on the buckling of thin-walled structures. The theoretical study of the problem of stability of compressed plates did not begin until 1891 when G. H. Bryan gave the formula for calculating the value of the critical buckling stress for a compressed rectangular plate with simply supported edges [Timoshenko, 1953, p. 299].

[5]Patent No. 11,401 dated October 8, 1846 [Rosenberg and Vincenti, 1978, p. 92].

[6]According to Edwin Clark, Robert Stephenson's assistant, even before the completion of the large tubes of the Britannia and Conway bridges, Stephenson in 1846–1847 built a 60-ft girder bridge of this type, which according to Clark "was indeed the first application of hollow wrought iron girders to the construction of bridges" [Clark, 1850, p. 524].

[7]Stephenson built four more bridges using tubular structures: the Brotherton Bridge across the River Aire on the York and North Midland Railway, two bridges in lower Egypt (one of them across the Nile), and a bridge across the St. Lawrence River at Montreal [Smiles, 1868, p. 475].

[8]This was the first suspension bridge in the world to carry trains. The upper deck was 24 ft wide to carry single-track railroad traffic, and the lower 15 ft wide to carry roadway traffic, connected together on each side by 20-ft-deep trusses. Having served for 42 years through many successive repairs and retrofittings, this bridge was dismantled in 1897 and replaced by a 550-ft-span steel arch bridge to suit the present-day heavy traffic [Hopkins, 1970, pp. 218–219; Steinman and Watson, 1957, p. 219].

iron marked a turning point in the history of structural engineering. These bridges were symbols of the innovative use of wrought iron, then known as a material of great malleability and superior strength, in bridge building. By 1840, just 10 years before the completion of these bridges, cast iron was firmly established as the modern structural material, both for buildings and bridges. Wrought iron, a material much stronger in tension than cast iron,[9] was rare and virtually unheard of. By the end of 1850 (after the completion of the Britannia and Conway bridges), however, wrought iron had become a preferred and dominant structural material[10] for bridges, and the use of cast iron as bridge-building material had become obsolete [Sutherland, 1963].

Although the tubular cross sections were especially suitable for the long-span Britannia and Conway bridges, Isambard Kingdom Brunel[11] (1806–1859), an English shipbuilder and bridge builder, reasoned that, for shorter spans, the web could be easily and efficiently provided by a single vertical web. Because a rolled section was rarely more than 10 inches deep then [Sealy, 1976], for any considerable span, a beam had to be built from plates and angles (Fig. 9.1). This was the evolution of the thin-walled plate girder. Brunel's experience with wrought iron used in ship hulls for framing, as well as for plating, played an important role in the development of wrought iron I-beams [Jewett [1967]; Timoshenko, 1953; Hopkins, 1970]. His plate girders gained widespread acceptance for use for medium-span bridges[12] because tests[13] on them gave very favorable results [Timoshenko, 1953]. Figure 9.2 shows the Windsor Bridge over the Thames at Windsor, England, a bowstring trussed bridge spanning 187 ft with a rise of 25 ft [Tyrell, 1911],[14] one of the notable bridges using plate girders designed by Brunel in 1849. Soon the plate girders were used for replacing the early iron bridges and timber trestles. Today, plate girder bridges fill the gap between economic spans for rolled beam and truss highway bridges, and along with prestressed concrete bridges, they offer competitive alternatives for highway bridges in the medium-span range.

---

[9]Singer [1962] lists tensile strengths of gray cast iron and wrought, respectively, as 20 ksi and 50 ksi. Pig iron, which melts at a relatively low temperature (about 2200° F) can be easily cast into molds, hence alternatively called *cast* iron. It contains 2 to 5 percent carbon alloyed with the iron and is the direct result of the smelting of iron in a blast furnace. By contrast, wrought iron has a higher melting point (about 2700° F), contains less than 0.1 percent of alloyed carbon (plus 1 to 2 percent of mechanically mixed impurities called *slag*). When red-hot, wrought iron becomes malleable and can be hammered or rolled into shapes, a property not possessed by cast iron [Rosenberg and Vincenti, 1978, pp. 81–82].

[10]Tyrell, p. 195. The first wrought-iron girder bridge spanning only $31\frac{1}{2}$ ft was built by A. Thompson in 1841, to carry a highway over the Pollock and Govan railroad near Glasgow, England. It was $25\frac{1}{2}$ ft wide, with six lines of girders.

[11]Brunel is also credited with evolving the torsionally stiff "Delta" (∇) cross section, which he first used in 1849 for the tied arch bridge at Windsor, England [Hopkins, 1970, p. 135].

[12]In reference to girder bridges, Fairbairn reportedly stated that up to 1870, he and his company alone had built "nearly one thousand bridges, some of them of large spans varying from 40 to 300 feet" [Pole, 1877, p. 213].

[13]Brunel carried out large-scale experiments in the early 1840s on the strength of plate girders (single-web section or I-section), and used novel forms of compression flange including the tube and variants thereon [Charlton, 1976; Rolt, 1957; Clark, 1850, pp. 437–441]. Further experiments with plate girders were conducted by M. Houbotte, a Belgian engineer, and by W. E. Lilly [Timoshenko and Gere, 1961, p. 433].

[14]See Tyrell, 1911, p. 166.

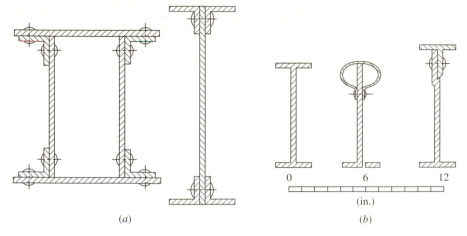

(a)   *(b)*

FIGURE 9.1
Examples of early wrought-iron plate girders [Fairbairn, 1854].

FIGURE 9.2
The Windsor Bridge, a bowstring trussed bridge using plate girders, designed by Brunel in 1849 [Sealey, 1976].

9.3
PLATE GIRDERS AND BRIDGE SUPERSTRUCTURES

9.3.1   Cross Sections of Plate Girders

Several cross sections of plate girders are shown in Fig. 9.3. Since its evolution as a flexural member that can be fabricated from plates, angles, or Ts (acting as flanges) attached to a plate (acting as a web) forming an I-shape, a few other innovative ways have been used to arrange material more efficiently in the girder's cross section.

Tubular compression flanges for rolled I-beams, recognized for their torsional rigidity, were suggested since their early development as shown in Fig. 9.1. They were proposed in Germany by Dornen [1951], mainly for having a reduced web depth. However, he did not emphasize the resulting increased stability of flange, an important advantage.

Figure 9.4(*a*), (*b*) shows cross sections of the *delta* girder—so called because of the characteristic ∇ (delta) shape of one (compression) or both flanges. It is essentially a plate girder with boxed (or tubular) flanges, formed from two short inclined plates welded to the web and each flange (or only to compression flange). By providing support to the tips of the compression flange, the inclined plates permit higher width-to-thickness ratio for the flange. They also act as longitudinal stiffeners supporting the web, thus obviating the need for transverse stiffeners. In general, these plates increase torsional stiffness of the girder as a whole, thereby enhancing its lateral buckling resistance, as well as the local buckling resistance of both the flange and the web [Johnston, 1966]. The improvement in the buckling strength may not be an important factor once the bridge is completed, and the deck provides the required lateral stability. However, these shapes may be most useful for applications requiring large unsupported lengths during handling and erection. A discussion on the performance and tests to failure of delta girders has been provided by Hadley [1961a,b].

Alternatively, tubular flanges can be formed using large angles or semicircular elements welded to the end (or ends) of the web (Fig. 9.4(*c*),(*d*)). Tests by Massonet, Mas, and Maus [1962] on the tubular type of plate girders showed their superior behavior even with depth-thickness ratio as high as 500.

Evidently, plate girders with tubular flanges would be costly because of the great deal of welding associated with their fabrication. A discussion on the buckling of slender beams with tubular flanges has been provided by O'Connor, Goldsmith, and Ryall [1965]. Tests to failure of this type of girder have been reported by Hadley [1962, 1964].

Unlike their predecessors, which were fabricated by riveting, the components of modern plate girders—flanges, web, and stiffeners—are joined by welding and bolting, a practice that began in the early 1950s. Today, most plate girders are shop-welded and field-spliced by high-strength bolts. Welding,[15] which began to be widely used

---

[15] According to Winterton [1962a,b], *forge welding*—man's first process to join pieces of metal together—was known to Egyptians as early as 3000 B.C. The process was used to hammer gold foils into the base copper of art objects. Sir Humphrey Davy is credited to have discovered *electric arc* in 1801, but no attempts were made for its practical use until 1881 [Morris, 1954]. While electric arc welds of one type or another were formed by several Europeans in the 1880s, in the United States, the first patent for arc welding was issued to Charles Coffin in 1892 [*The Iron Age*, 1955; Winterton, 1962a,b]. The first all-welded bridge was built in the United States in 1928, and the first one in England shortly after [Hopkins, 1970].

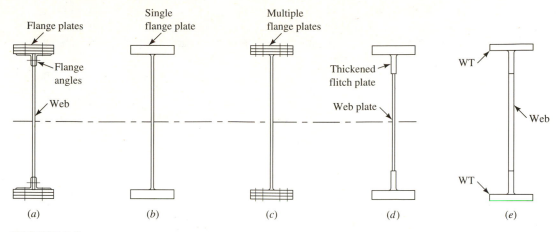

FIGURE 9.3
Cross sections of conventional plate girders: (*a*) riveted or bolted; (*b*) welded; (*c*) part bolted and part welded; (*d*) welded with flitch plates; (*e*) WT sections welded to a plate.

in the 1950s, has also significantly simplified the fabrication of plate girders. Before the advent of welding, the flanges of plate girders usually consisted of four angles, with a pair riveted to each end of the web (Fig. 9.1(*a*)). Cover plates were riveted to the outstanding legs of these angles to augment the flange area when necessary. By contrast, the modern plate girder merely consists of an assembly of plate elements—two flanges

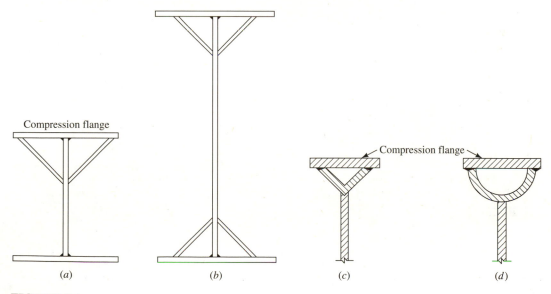

FIGURE 9.4
Delta girders: (*a*) ∇-shaped compression flange formed from plates; (*b*) both ∇-shaped flanges formed from plates; (*c*) ∇-shaped flange formed from large angles; (*d*) tubular flange formed from semicircular element.

and a web—welded together to form an I-shaped beam. Similarly, the pre-welding era plate girders used angles for stiffeners that were riveted or bolted to webs, whereas the modern plate girders use plates (or bars) for stiffeners that are welded to the web, or sometimes to both the web and the flange.

A significant advantage offered by a plate girder is the discretion a designer can have in proportioning flanges and web to achieve maximum economy through more efficient arrangement of material than is possible with rolled beams. For example, flanges can comprise a series of plates of varying thicknesses or widths, proportioned to variation in the moment capacity required in various segments of a plate girder. These different segments of plates can be joined end to end by full-penetration butt welds (AASHTO 10.34.2.1.1). When flange plates of *different widths* are spliced by butt-welding, AASHTO 10.18.5.5 requires a uniform transition conforming to Fig. 9.5 [AASHTO 1992], except that for M270 Grades 100/100W steels only, the 2'-0" radius transition (Fig. 9.5(a)) is required. A butt weld splice joining plates of

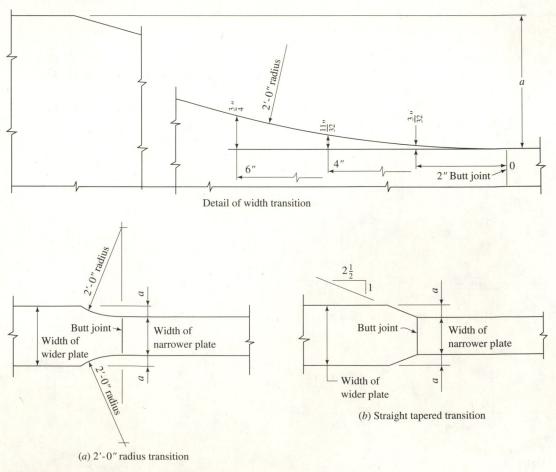

Detail of width transition

(a) 2'-0" radius transition

(b) Straight tapered transition

FIGURE 9.5
Required transitions for butt-welded flange plates of different widths.

different *thicknesses* is required to have a uniform slope between the offset surfaces of not more than 1 in $2\frac{1}{2}$ with respect to the surface of either part.

Because a plate girder is fabricated from individual elements that constitute its flanges and the web, a designer has the freedom of designing it with flanges and web from the same or different grades of steel. In some cases, it may be economical to design a plate girder using high-strength steel in conjunction with a lower-strength steel such as conventional A36 steel [Haaijer, 1961; Schilling, 1968]. In general, higher-strength steel can be used in a structure for the more severely stressed components—higher-strength steel where stresses are higher, and lower-strength steel where stresses are lower, resulting in what are referred to as *hybrid structures*. Essentially, *hybrid girders* consist of flanges and webs fabricated from steels of different grades and provide variable material strength in accordance with stresses. In a beam, flexural stresses are maximum in the flange and relatively low in the web, or stated otherwise, the web contributes only a small portion of the flexural capacity of the beam. Consequently, a beam with one or both flanges made from a higher-grade steel than the web may be more economical than the conventional beam with flanges and web of the same grade steel. AASHTO [1992, 1994], AISC–ASD [1989], and AISC–LRFD specifications [1986] narrowly define a hybrid girder as a fabricated steel beam having web of lower minimum specified yield strength than that of one or both flanges; others [Beedle, 1991] define it broadly as one composed of flanges and web of steels of different yield strengths. Whenever the maximum flange stress is less than or equal to the web steel yield stress, the girder is considered *homogeneous*.

Special precautions must be taken in a fabrication shop in order to properly identify individual pieces of different-grade steels to be used for a hybrid girder to prevent a mix-up. AASHTO, Div. II, Construction, Art. 11.4.1 requires that each piece of steel, other than Grade 36 steel, be clearly identifiable, either by writing the material specification on the piece or using the identification color code as shown in Table 9.1.

Hybrid plate girders can be formed in many ways. They can be formed by welding WT of higher-grade (e.g., 50-ksi) steel to web of lower-grade (e.g., A36) steel (Fig. 9.6(*a*)). This concept is analogous to glued-laminated wood beams, which are fabricated from outer laminations of superior-grade wood compared to the inner laminations. Alternatively, they may be fabricated from plates of different-strength steels suitably placed along the span (Fig. 9.6(*b*)). For example, higher-strength materials can be placed at locations of higher moments or shear (e.g., in the negative-moment region of a continuous beam) to achieve a uniform girder depth instead of a haunched girder. Figure 9.6(*c*) shows details of the typical profile of plate girders used for the three-span (260, 350, and 260 ft) continuous Whisky Creek Bridge in Shasta County, California [Elliot,

TABLE 9.1
Identification color codes [AASHTO, 1992]

Grade of steel	Color code
Grade 50	Green and yellow
Grade 50W	Blue and yellow
Grade 70W	Blue and orange
Grade 100	Red
Grade 100W	Red and orange

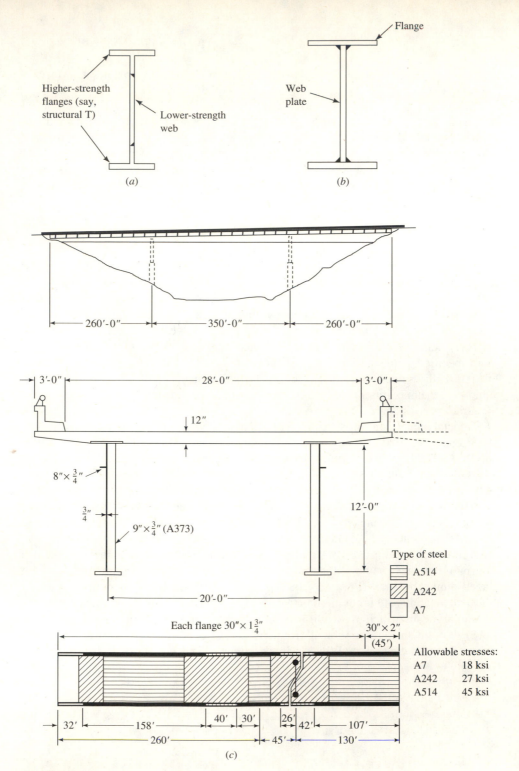

FIGURE 9.6
Hybrid girders: (*a, b*) cross sections; (*c*) details of Whisky Creek Bridge, California.

918

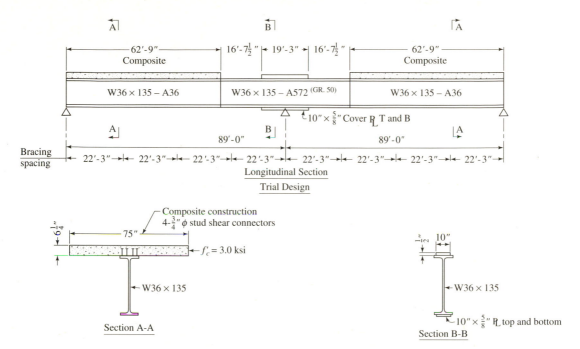

FIGURE 9.7
Use of rolled beams of different-grade steels along a bridge span.

1960, 1962; Errera, 1974; Hollister and Sunbury, 1960]. For this bridge, steels of three different yield strengths (A7, A242, and A514 steel) have been used to achieve a uniform depth for the entire bridge. It is also possible to use rolled beam segments of steels of different yield strengths, welded together, to maintain a uniform girder depth for the entire bridge (Fig. 9.7) [Breen, 1972].

Construction with hybrid girders can be both noncomposite or composite, design provisions for which are covered in AASHTO 10.40 (service load design) and AASHTO 10.53 (load factor design). Design of hybrid girders is beyond the scope of this text and will not be discussed further. A discussion on this subject can be found in the literature [Haaijer, 1961; Toprac, 1963; Frost and Schilling, 1964; Schilling, 1967; Lew and Toprac, 1967; Carskadden, 1968; Toprac and Natrajan, 1971; Salmon and Johnston, 1990; Dhillan, 1991; Gaylord, Gaylord, and Stallmeyer, 1992]. A state-of-the-art report and general design recommendations for hybrid girders can be found in the ASCE–AASHO Joint Committee Report [1968].

Design of plate girders involves some departure from that of rolled W-shaped beams because the latter are generally proportioned with relatively compact webs and flanges and are unaffected with respect to local and shear buckling. In contrast, the freedom afforded in material selection in a plate girder design makes buckling a controlling design criterion for webs.

Historically, it may be noted that the first fasteners to be used were ordinary bolts (or so-called *unfinished bolts*) because cast iron, the first iron material used in iron structures, was too brittle for riveting. With the advent of wrought iron in the 1840s, which replaced cast iron, riveting became a widely used connection technique. Rivets were recognized to be superior to the ordinary bolts then in use because of the higher clamping forces developed between the connected parts while considerable friction between the fraying surfaces also existed. Also, deformations of joints using ordinary bolts are larger and require more bolts per joint as compared with the number of rivets. Introduction of electric arc welding in 1881 brought about a new fabrication technique that revolutionized the connection design. At a much later date, high-strength bolts were developed. The year 1949 marked the issuance of the first specifications for high-strength bolts that replaced the use of common bolts [Beedle, 1974]. Interestingly, the high-strength bolts were first used to replace rivets that had worked loose in an ore bridge. Demonstrated by their performance (tightness) over several years of operations and the increased clamping force provided by them that was beneficial for the fatigue strength of joints, use of high-strength bolts became a common practice, especially for field joints [Kuzmanowic and Willems, 1983]. Riveting is now practically obsolete as a fabrication technique for steel structures in the United States. A comprehensive discussion on riveted plate girders can be found in the literature [Shedd, 1934; Gaylord, Gaylord, and Stallmeyer, 1957].

9.3.2 Components of a Plate Girder

A detailed discussion on several aspects of steel beam bridges is presented in Chapter 8. Many aspects of steel beam bridges discussed in that chapter (advantages and disadvantages, noncomposite and composite design, corrosion problem, the service load and the load factor design principles, the design of continuous steel beam bridges, economic considerations, etc.) are valid for plate girder bridges as well, and will not be repeated here. A thorough reading of Chapter 8 is highly recommended to get a good understanding of material presented in this chapter.

It is helpful to understand the terminology associated with various components of a plate girder (Fig. 9.8) as well as functions of these components. While discretion

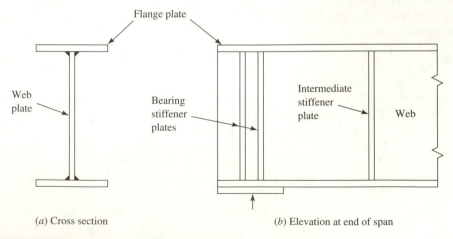

(a) Cross section   (b) Elevation at end of span

FIGURE 9.8
Components of a plate girder.

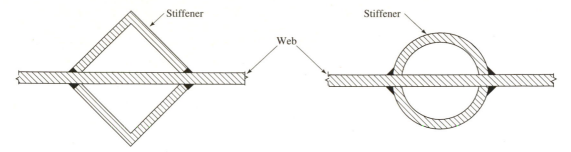

FIGURE 9.9
Tubular stiffeners.

afforded the designers in proportioning components (flanges and web) of a plate girder is a definite advantage from the viewpoint of economics, it also encourages them to choose narrow flanges and thin, deep webs (to have large moments of inertia). This results in noncompact, light, slender members (least-weight approach, naturally), with both the flange and the web ending up having large *width-to-thickness ratios*. It should be realized, however, that the presence of the compressive stresses in the plane of these elements causes them to be highly susceptible to buckling. The maximum strength of a plate girder as a whole can be realized only if the component plates do not buckle locally, because local buckling can cause premature failure of the entire plate girder, or at least impair its load-carrying capacity resulting from nonuniform stress distribution caused by buckling. To prevent this buckling tendency, slender webs usually need to be *stiffened*. Therefore, transverse or longitudinal stiffeners, or a combination of both, play an important role in the design of plate girders. Stiffening requirements for plate girders are dictated by the slenderness ratio (D/t_w = web depth/web thickness) of the web. As mentioned, the idea of web stiffeners grew from the wrought-iron tubed girders adopted for the English railway bridges, first introduced by Fairbairn [Timoshenko, 1953]. The current trend, however, is to opt for unstiffened webs for the sake of economy.

A *stiffener* is simply a member, usually an angle (used in older riveted or bolted plate girders), or more generally a plate (i.e., a rectangular bar in modern welded girders), attached to the web of a beam or girder to distribute load, to transfer shear, or to prevent buckling. Tubular stiffeners (Fig. 9.9) were suggested by Bornscheuer [1947], who showed that they were much superior to the conventional type because of their high torsional rigidity. They also provide greater bending stiffness vertically and thus induce a more favorable orientation of the tension field [Johnston, 1966]. However, fabrication of girders with tubular stiffeners would likely be more costly than girders with conventional stiffeners.

Stiffeners may be *vertical* (oriented in the direction of the applied loads), in which case they are called *transverse* stiffeners; or they may be *horizontal* (parallel to the girder flanges[16] and the longitudinal axis of the girder), in which case they are called

---

[16]A deep haunched girder may require multiple longitudinal stiffeners. In such a case, the top longitudinal stiffener will be parallel to the top flange of the girder, the bottom one parallel to the bottom flange, and the intermediate longitudinal stiffeners may be positioned at an angle to the horizontal.

longitudinal stiffeners. A web may be stiffened with transverse stiffeners only or with both transverse *and* longitudinal stiffeners (single or multiple), depending on the proportions of the web and applicable specifications. From the viewpoint of web buckling, the most effective way of stiffening web plates subjected to bending is a longitudinal (or horizontal) stiffener. In general, web plates of deep girders are too thin to develop a sufficiently high buckling strength for an economical design of the web without providing stiffeners. The main reason for using longitudinal stiffeners is to take advantage of thinner web permitted by AASHTO specifications if longitudinal stiffeners are used. Other reasons for using longitudinal stiffeners are to prevent lateral deflection of the web and to improve fatigue life due to reduced lateral deflections [Yen and Mueller, 1966]. Some designers opine that they improve aesthetics when placed on the fascia girders of a plate girder bridge. Longitudinal stiffeners are generally used only for long-span continuous-plate girder bridges when the girder depth exceeds about 7 ft [ASCE–AASHTO, 1978]. Because of the fabrication costs involved, they are used only when absolutely necessary. Studies at Bethlehem Corporation have concluded that, to be economical, longitudinal stiffeners should not be considered for span lengths of less than 300 ft [Knight, 1984; Guzek and Grzybowski, 1992].

Vertical (or transverse) stiffeners can be *intermediate* (or nonbearing) stiffeners or *bearing* stiffeners. Intermediate stiffeners are transverse stiffeners that are placed perpendicular to the compression flange at various intervals along the span. The stiffener spacings may be the same or increase progressively with distance from support to midspan. The segment of plate girder between two adjacent vertical stiffeners is called a *panel;* the one between the end stiffener and the adjacent intermediate stiffener is referred to as the *end panel.* A stiffened web panel divided by one or more longitudinal stiffeners results in two or more *subpanels.* That is, a subpanel is a segment of the plate girder bounded by two adjacent transverse stiffeners, a longitudinal stiffener, and the flange, or by two adjacent transverse stiffeners and two adjacent longitudinal stiffeners in the case of a web having multiple longitudinal stiffeners (Fig. 9.8).

The *end stiffeners* are the bearing (transverse) stiffeners that are placed at the ends of plate girders. Referred to as *bearing stiffeners*, their purpose is to distribute reactions to the full depth of the web without putting all the load on the flange connections. The bearing stiffeners participate integrally with certain portions of the web (extending on both sides of the stiffeners, discussed later) and act as a column in transmitting reactions to the supports of the plate girder. An intermediate stiffener can also be a bearing stiffener used to transmit a concentrated load on the plate girder. A web without any stiffeners is referred to as *unstiffened;* otherwise it is *stiffened.* All plate girders, stiffened or unstiffened, are provided with bearing stiffeners and intermediate stiffeners at diaphragm or cross frame locations.

With the exception of the bearing stiffeners—which, according to AASHTO 10.34.6.1, must be provided in pairs (i.e., on both sides of the web)—a designer has the option of providing both transverse and longitudinal stiffeners on one side of the web only or on both sides of the web. For the sake of economy and convenience in fabrication, however, they are placed on one side of the web only. When provided only on one side of the web, they are generally placed on the inside face of the web for improved aesthetics, and they are sometimes referred to as *internal stiffeners.* When placed on the same side of the web, the transverse and the longitudinal stiffen-

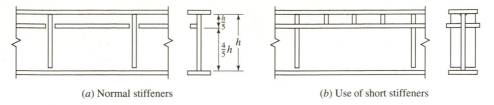

(*a*) Normal stiffeners   (*b*) Use of short stiffeners

FIGURE 9.10
Various schemes for stiffener arrangements.

ers intersect each other, and several schemes of stiffener arrangements are possible, as shown in Fig. 9.10. For example, the transverse stiffeners can be placed on one side of the web and the longitudinal stiffeners can be placed on the other side, without any interruption by the transverse stiffeners, a convenient and cost-effective scheme for fabrication. Alternatively, the transverse stiffeners are continuous for the full depth of the web, and the longitudinal stiffeners, which need not be continuous, are cut to fit in between the adjacent transverse stiffeners, as permitted under AASHTO 10.34.5.4. Yet another scheme is to use short transverse stiffeners in the smaller subpanels (positioned between the compression flange and the continuous longitudinal stiffener).

Girder webs that are transversely stiffened only at the diaphragm connections are referred to as *unstiffened*. A *nominally stiffened* web is defined as one having a thickness $\frac{1}{16}$ in. less than the unstiffened web. The thinnest web allowed by AASHTO with a maximum number of transverse stiffeners is defined as "fully stiffened" [Knight, 1984]. The minimum metal thickness permitted by AASHTO 10.8.1 is $\frac{5}{16}$ in., except that the minimum permitted thickness is 0.23 in. for rolled beams and channels and $\frac{3}{16}$ in. for closed ribs in *orthotropic* decks. The mandatory requirements for the minimum steel thickness are presumably meant to protect against corrosion and ensure a satisfactory handling of material during construction and shipping. Certain jurisdictions may impose somewhat stricter requirements for the minimum metal thicknesses. For example, the Pennsylvania Department of Transportation requires minimum thickness for girder flanges to be $\frac{3}{4}$ in. "unless the fabricator can demonstrate the ability to satisfactorily fabricate and erect plate girders with thinner flange plates" [PennDOT, 1994].

9.3.3 Schematics of Layout of Plate Girders for Highway Bridge Superstructures

The layout of plate girders for a highway bridge superstructure varies from a simple conventional type to one with a secondary system of stringers. Suitability of a particular type of layout depends on several factors, such as the span and width of the bridge and the site condition. Some common forms of layouts for girders, from the standpoint of load path, are described as follows. In all cases, the girders can be simple or continuous and can have noncomposite or composite construction.

Figure 9.11 shows cross sections of superstructures with the conventional layout of plate girders, which consist of several equally spaced girders laid parallel to each other, supporting a reinforced concrete deck. This type of layout is the simplest and is similar to the conventional steel superstructure, which consists of several equally

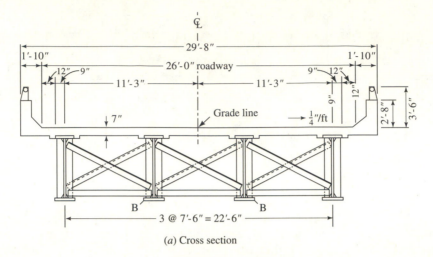

(*a*) Cross section

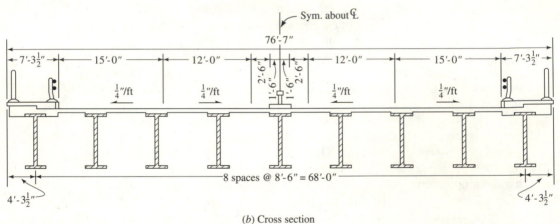

(*b*) Cross section

FIGURE 9.11
Conventional layout of plate girders for a highway bridge superstructure: (*a*) a two-span bridge; (*b*) a
four-span bridge (cross-bracings not shown).

spaced stringers (wide flange beams) as discussed in Chapter 8. The load path is also
similar to that for a superstructure with stringers, and moments and shears in girders
are computed in a similar manner.

Figure 9.12 shows a layout that consists of several transverse members referred
to as floor beams, each of which is end supported by two widely spaced plate girders.
It differs from the layout of Fig. 9.11 in that the deck is supported on the floor beams,
and not directly on the girders, resulting in a different load path. The deck spans between the floor beams, so that the main slab reinforcement is parallel to the traffic (and
perpendicular to floor beams). The live-load moments in the slab and in the floor beam
are calculated, respectively, according to AASHTO 3.24.3.2 and 3.23.3 (discussed in
Chapter 4). The floor beams transmit all loads (dead and live) to the girders through the
end connections between them and the two girders. Consequently, regardless of whether

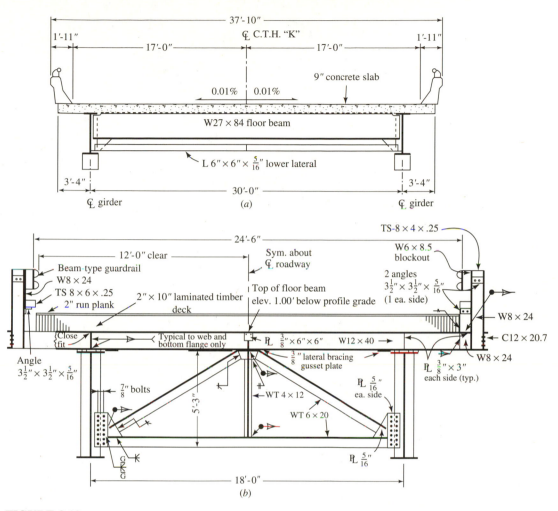

FIGURE 9.12

Plate girders supporting floor beams, which, in turn, support the deck: (*a*) concrete deck; (*b*) laminated timber deck.

the truck or the lane loading governs for the bridge span, the effect on the girder is that of concentrated loads applied at the panel points of the girders.

Figure 9.13 shows yet another layout in which the live loads are not directly applied to the girder but are transmitted by a stringer and floor-beam system to the two main girders. Typically, the deck is supported on several parallel, equally spaced stringers (oriented parallel to traffic), which, in turn, are supported on the floor beams. The floor beams are end supported on two girders, which are oriented parallel to the stringers (and to the traffic). Obviously, the load path in this layout differs from that for the layouts shown in Figs. 9.11 and 9.12. The stringers may be framed directly into the floor beams (Fig. 9.13(*a*)), or they may be supported on the top flange of the floor beams (Fig. 9.13(*b*)).

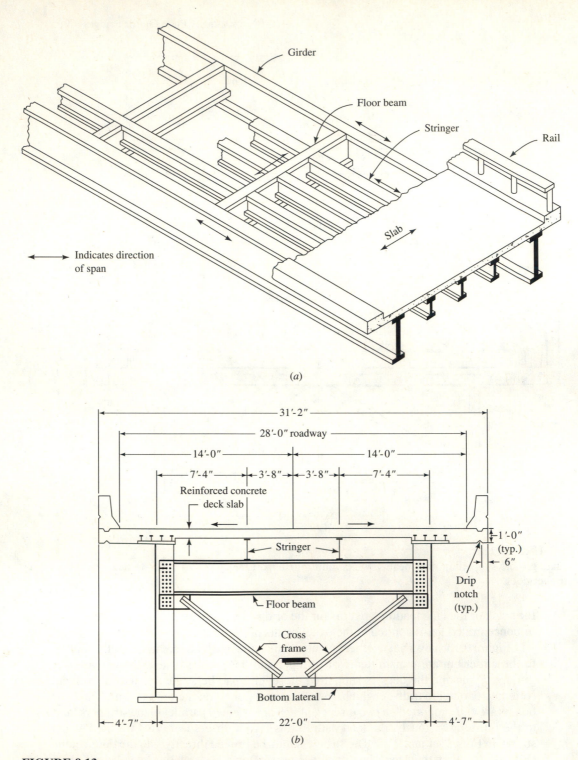

FIGURE 9.13
Stringer–floor beam–girder system: (*a*) stringers framed directly into the floor beams; (*b*) stringers supported on the top flange of the floor beams.

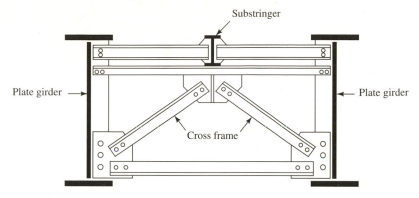

FIGURE 9.14
Plate girder with substringers.

Figure 9.14 shows a *substringer* framing system, which can permit a wider girder spacing with conventional slab design. Adaptable to longer-span girder bridges, this system can be considered as an intermediate step between the conventional closely spaced girder systems and widely spaced girders with floor beams. Typically, the girders are spaced about 18 to 20 ft apart, and a single rolled-beam stringer is placed midway between them. This arrangement permits an 8- or 9-in.-thick slab having a span of 9 or 10 ft. The substringer is typically a W24 beam, supported on cross frames placed at a maximum distance of 25 ft as permitted by AASHTO (the maximum permissible distance between the diaphragms). The cross frame typically consists of diagonals forming an inverted $\vee$ supporting the substringer [Schilling, 1985].

9.3.4 Some Notable Plate Girder Highway Bridges

Plate girder bridges were alluded to in Chapters 1 and 8. They can be noncomposite or composite. Generally speaking, the economic competitiveness of a plate girder bridge depends on many factors, such as whether the bridge is simple or continuous, whether it is composite or noncomposite, and the maximum transportable lengths of girder segments. For highway bridges, plate girder bridges can be economical in ranges of 80 to 150 ft, and they are often competitive for longer spans. Composite plate girders have been used for bridges with spans in ranges of 60 to 100 ft. Continuous plate girder bridges with spans exceeding 950 ft have been built [Gaylord, Gaylord, and Stallmeyer, 1992]. Where loads are extremely heavy, as in the case of railroad bridges, plate girders can be competitive for spans as low as 45 ft, although they are generally economical for spans in ranges of 50 to 130 ft [McCormac, 1992]. Brief descriptions of a few notable plate girders are presented in the following paragraphs.

9.3.4.1 Sava I Bridge, Belgrade, former Yugoslavia

Figure 1.28 (Chapter 1) shows the three-span (246, 856, and 246 ft), continuous Sava I Bridge in the former Yugoslavia, the world's second longest plate girder bridge, built in 1956 to replace a suspension bridge that was destroyed in World War II. It carries a 39 ft 4 in. roadway and two 9 ft 10 in. sidewalks over two plate girders spaced at 39.7 ft centers. Built with an orthotropic deck, this bridge combines both riveted and welded construction, and is a double box girder in cross section with depths varying from 15 ft 8 in. at the abutment to 14 ft 9 in. at the midspan to 31 ft 6 in. at the piers. The web, a mere $\frac{9}{16}$ in. thick, has a depth-to-thickness ratio varying between 690 and 320. It is stiffened by vertical stiffeners spaced 30 ft apart and four to seven rows of longitudinal stiffeners spaced about 2 ft 6 in. apart and placed in the web's compression zone. The riveted bottom flange of the girder consists of 2Ls $9.8 \times 9.8 \times 0.79$ in., 2 PL 17.7×0.31 in., and 1 to 10 plates 47.2 in. $\times$ 0.79 in., with a maximum flange cross-sectional area of approximately 390 in.[2] [ENR, 1956; Schafer, 1957; AISC, 1963; Troitsky, 1967; O'Connor, 1971].

The deck of this bridge is formed by stiffened steel plate varying in thickness from $\frac{7}{16}$ in. to 1 in. Significantly, design of this steel plate deck was based, for the first time, on the ultimate strength principles rather than on the conventional allowable stress design principles.

9.3.4.2 Wiesbaden-Schierstein Bridge, Germany

This 14-span (152, 171, 230, 558, 4×230, 279, 673, 279, 230, 197, and 180 ft) plate girder bridge has an orthotropic deck that carries a 65 ft 7 in. roadway and a 6 ft 8 in. sidewalk on each side of the roadway (Fig. 9.15). The girder depth varies from 14 ft 7 in. to 24 ft 5 in. The 0.47-in. web, having a maximum depth-to-thickness ratio of 600, terminates into and is butt-welded to a 19.7×0.79 in. vertical *flitch plate,* which, in turn, is welded to a 4 ft 11 in. $\times$ 0.59 in. bottom flange plate. This flange plate is additionally reinforced by up to eleven 4 ft 11 in. $\times$ 0.59 in. cover plates by means of edge welds and rivets. The web is internally stiffened, both vertically and longitudinally, the longitudinal stiffeners being typically spaced at 25.6 in. in the web's compression zone (excluding the flitch plate portion) [Weitz, 1960; O'Connor, 1971].

9.3.4.3 La Louviere Bridge, Belgium

Built near La Louviere, south of Brussels, over the Charleroi-Brussels Canal in Belgium, this three-span (164, 358, and 164 ft) bridge (Fig. 9.16) carries the Wallonia Expressway, which has two roadways (53 and 71 ft wide) and two sidewalks (4 ft 6 in. each). Its superstructure consists of multiple parallel plate girders, which support a reinforced concrete composite deck that consists of 4-in. cast-in-place concrete over $3\frac{1}{2}$-in.-thick precast concrete slabs spanning 10 ft 3 in. or 13 ft 3 in. With transverse stiffeners and the cross frames between the girders located at approximately every 23 ft 6 in., the webs of the girders are from 0.47 to 0.59 in. thick, and longitudinally stiffened, with two to five longitudinal stiffeners. The layout of the longitudinal stiffeners matches the profile of the curved bottom flange of girders [Laviolette, 1968].

9.3.4.4 Yakima River Bridge, United States

This three-span (75, 240, and 75 ft) bridge is built over the Yakima River, Washington. The salient feature of this bridge is the two parallel delta girders (Fig. 9.17), which support a composite reinforced concrete deck. The girders are 4 ft 8 in. deep at the abutment, 6 ft 2 in. at the midspan, and 8 ft 5 in. over the piers. The inclined plates, welded to the web and the tips of both top and the bottom flanges, are 28 in. $\times \frac{5}{16}$ in., and the flanges are 36 in. $\times 2\frac{1}{4}$ in. to $36 \times \frac{3}{8}$ in. [Hadley, 1962, 1963].

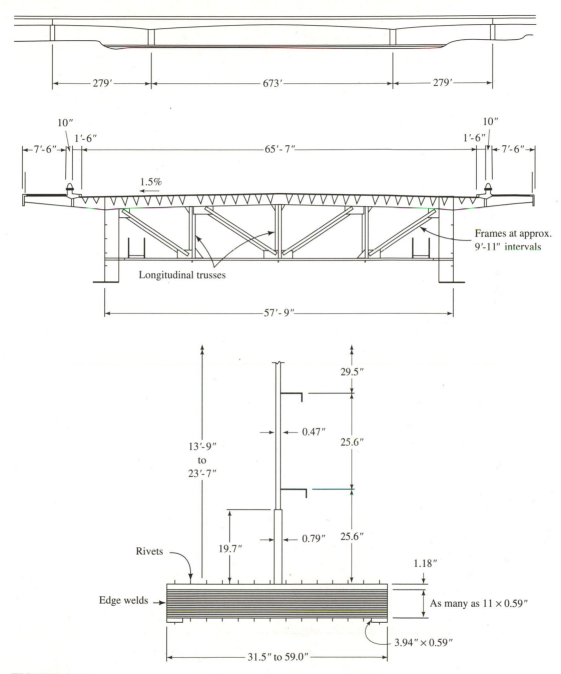

FIGURE 9.15
Wiesbaden-Schierstein Bridge, Germany.

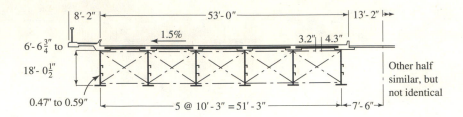

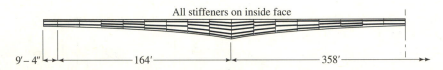

FIGURE 9.16
La Louviere Bridge, Belgium.

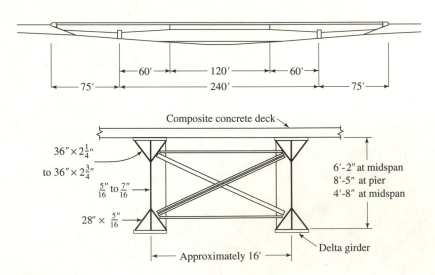

FIGURE 9.17
Yakima River Bridge, Washington State.

9.3.4.5 Whisky Creek Bridge, California

This cantilever–suspended span structure (Fig. 9.6), built over the Whisky Creek, California, in 1960 and 1961, has a unique place in the history of plate girders in the United States as being one of the first for which high-strength steels of several grades were used. The girders of the end spans of this three-span (260, 350, and 260 ft) bridge cantilever 45 ft into the main span to support a suspended span of 260 ft. A constant depth of 12 ft was required for these girders to limit the deflection to $L/800$ for the 350-ft main span, and $L/300$ for the cantilever span. The $\frac{3}{4}$-in. web has a depth-to-thickness ratio of 192. The web is transversely stiffened internally and longitudinally stiffened on the outside with a single longitudinal stiffener.

The three steel grades and the corresponding allowable stresses used for fabricating these girders were as follows [O'Connor, 1971; Errera, 1974]:

Steel grade	Allowable stress
A7	18 ksi
A242	27 ksi
A514	45 ksi

The use of these multiple grades of steel enabled designers to achieve a constant cross section of flange at $30 \times 1\frac{3}{4}$ in., except for an increase to 30×2 in. over the central 90-ft segment of the main span [Elliot, 1960, 1962; Hollister and Sunbury, 1969].

In the United States, many continuous plate girder bridges with main spans exceeding 400 ft have been built. The three-span Veterans Memorial Bridge, Ottawa, Illinois, with a main span of 510 ft, was built in 1984 [Robinson, 1984]. Until about the mid-twentieth century, steel and reinforced concrete bridges formed an all too familiar sight on the American landscape. With the advent of prestressed concrete, however, the competitive edge of steel beam bridges (because of their high life-cycle costs) declined significantly, and they have lost their appeal. Nevertheless, composite welded plate girder bridges, the most common type of steel bridge in use today, are still found to be competitive in the span range of 100 to 450 ft [Schilling, 1985]. A description of a few pre-1970 bridges has been provided by O'Connor [1971].

Although the common perception of plate girder bridges is a superstructure with a system of plate girders supporting a deck, they have been successfully used for orthotropic decks of long-span bridges. The Cologne-Muelheim Bridge, Germany, a suspension bridge (279, 1033, and 279ft) built in 1951 to replace a self-anchored suspension bridge destroyed during World War II, is an excellent example of application of plate girders to be used as stiffening girders for the suspension bridge. Considered as the longest plate girders in the world, they support an orthotropic deck that consists of a stiffened $\frac{1}{2}$-in.-thick steel plate deck, except near the pylons, where it is $\frac{5}{8}$ in. thick. The 11-ft-deep plate girders, suspended from the hangers, which transfer their load to the suspension cables above, are of riveted construction and have a $\frac{9}{16}$-in. web, which is stiffened with longitudinal stiffeners of bulb shapes spaced at 12-in. centers [Leonhardt and Pelikan, 1951; Schussler and Pelikan, 1951; Troitsky, 1967].

9.4
BEHAVIOR OF PLATE GIRDERS UNDER LOADS

9.4.1 Buckling Problems Associated with Plate Girders

Since the introduction of plate girders for bridges by Brunel in the 1850s, many experimental studies have been made to understand their behavior under loads and determine their strength. Some of the early tests include tests on models of plate girders measuring 5 ft 3 in. long and $9\frac{1}{2}$ in. deep conducted by Lilly [1908], tests on large size plate girders made by F. E. Turneaure [1898, 1907], and a series of tests on rolled I-beams and built-up plate girders made by Moore and Wilson [1913, 1916]. An extensive series of tests of plate girders with thin webs conducted at the Institute of Technology, Stockholm [Wastland and Bergman, 1947], showed that because of various imperfections present in the web plates, they buckle at a very small load, and in most cases the behavior of the web plates was similar. From 1950 to 1960, an extensive testing of plate girders conducted at Lehigh University by Basler [1961a,b,c], and Basler and Thurlimann [1959, 1961] led to the conclusions that (1) the theoretical critical load of plane web plates bore no direct relation to the ultimate load, (2) the ratio of the ultimate load to the theoretical critical load increased with the slenderness ratio, and (3) the load-bearing capacity of the web is not exhausted until yielding begins in a comparatively large portion of the web [Timoshenko and Gere, 1961, p. 434].

Ever since the advent of plate girders, it has been recognized that beam action alone is not responsible for carrying shear in the web. Investigations showed early on that the ultimate strength of a plate girder is *not* controlled by web buckling because of the *postbuckling strength* that develops *after* elastic buckling of the web occurs. This behavior of plate girders was first discovered during Fairbairn's model tests for the Britannia Bridge. D. J. Jourawski (1821–1891), a Russian engineer and contemporary of Fairbairn who also investigated the design of the Britannia Bridge, concluded (with consideration of latticed trusses) that the buckling of the sides of the tubular bridge was caused by compressive stresses acting in the sides at an angle of 45° to the longitudinal axis of the girder, and recommended placing stiffeners in the direction of the maximum compressive stress [Timoshenko, 1953].[17] This was perhaps the first tacit recognition of the phenomenon that later came to be known as "tension-field action" (discussed later). Toward the end of the nineteenth century, the problem of web stiffening was the focus of attention by many researchers [Beach, 1898, 1899; Wilson, 1898; Turneaure, 1898; Turner and Shinner, 1898]. Observation of wave formation in the web at an angle of 45° with the longitudinal axis of a girder in various experimental studies firmly established the concept of tension-field action, which is now a basis of plate girder design. Consequently, the mechanics of load transmission in a transversely loaded plate girder with stiffeners can be explained as follows [Timoshenko and Gere, 1961, p. 434]:

1. If the transverse load is not sufficiently large to cause a wave formation, the web transmits shear to the bearings by working in shear. This is referred to as *beam action*.

2. If the wave formation does occur as result of larger loads, a portion of the total shear is transmitted to the bearings through the shearing action in the web through beam action, and the remainder is transmitted as in a truss, in which the web acts as a series of ties and the stiffeners as struts. This latter action is known as the tension-field action and occurs only after the onset of buckling in the web. The magnitude of the load that can cause wave formation depends on the thickness of the web and the spacing of stiffeners.

---

[17]"To prove his point, he made some very interesting experiments with models which were made of thick paper reinforced by cardboard stiffeners.... Using his paper models, Jourawski measures the deformation in the plane of the web near the neutral axis and shows that the largest compressive strain there is in the 45-degree direction (with respect to the vertical). He was also able to study the direction of waves which were formed during buckling of the sides" [Timoshenko, 1953, pp. 162–163].

To understand the behavior of stiffened plate girders and formulate design criteria, an extensive investigation of welded plate girders was conducted by Konrad Basler and Bruno Thurlimann at Lehigh University, Pennsylvania, during the years 1957 to 1960. The details of the tests and the related theoretical considerations pertaining to these tests are reported in the literature [Basler 1961a,b; Basler and Thurlimann, 1959, 1961; Basler et al., 1960]. The theoretical model that evolved from this research to predict the bending strength of plate girders is referred to as the *Basler-Thurlimann model* (discussed later) and formed the basis of the current design practices for designing plate girders in the United States. Other theoretical models for predicting the bending strength of plate girders have been reported in the literature [Holgund, 1973; Fujii, 1968] and are not discussed here. Chern and Ostapenko [1970a,b] have studied the strength of unsymmetrical plate girders. A summary of theory and design of plate girders (with numerous references) can be found in references such as Cooper [1974], ASCE–AASHTO [1978], SSRC, [1988], Evans [1983], and various handbooks [Gaylord and Gaylord, 1990; Merrit, 1992]. General discussion on design of plate girders, albeit mostly for buildings, can be found in several texts on structural steel design [Kuzmanowic and Willems, 1983; Cooper and Chen, 1985; Salmon and Johnson, 1990; Gaylord, Gaylord, and Stallmeyer, 1992; McCormac, 1992].

9.4.2 Tension Field Action in a Plate Girder

Figure 9.18a shows the shear buckling of a plate girder web as observed in a test at the Fritz Engineering Laboratory at Lehigh University. The right half of the web is stiffened with vertical as well as diagonal stiffeners, and it remained unbuckled under loads. On the other hand, the left half of the web is unstiffened and buckled in the direction of principal compression, as indicated by formation of waves (or wrinkles) in the direction of principal tension. Similarly, Fig. 9.18b shows the shear buckling of the stiffened web of a cantilevered aluminum plate girder. In spite of the web having buckled, the girders have not collapsed and still have some load-carrying capacity. The mechanism by which the buckled web offers resistance to loads is referred to as tension-field action and can be analogized to the force-resisting mechanism in a Pratt truss, in which the diagonals resist tension and the verticals resist compression (Fig. 9.19) [Basler, 1961a]. In a plate girder, each panel, bounded by two adjacent transverse (intermediate) stiffeners, acts like a panel of a Pratt truss. After the plate buckles, a Pratt truss-like force-resisting mechanism develops in the plate girder. The web, through the *membrane action*, acts as diagonal tension members between the transverse stiffeners, while the transverse stiffeners act as the compression members to resist the vertical component of the diagonal tension in the web. Thus, the intermediate transverse stiffeners, which are assumed to carry no load before onset of web buckling, carry compression (similar to the verticals in the Pratt truss) after the onset of web buckling. The horizontal component of diagonal tension (membrane action in the plate) is assumed to be resisted by the flange in the adjacent panel. As first pointed out by Basler [1961a], the development of the tension field (or the truss action) raises the shear strength from that based on buckling (Fig. 9.20(*a–d*)) to approach a condition corresponding to shear yield in a classical beam theory (Fig. 9.20(*a*), (*b*), (*e*)). Of course, under this condition, the compression buckling

FIGURE 9.18a
Shear buckling of plate-girder web. (Fritz Engineering Laboratory, Lehigh University, Bethlehem, PA.)

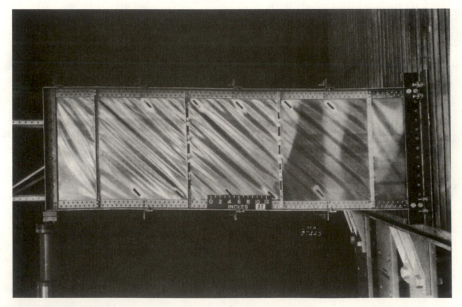

FIGURE 9.18b
Shear buckling of aluminum-beam web. (National Aeronautics and Space Administration.)

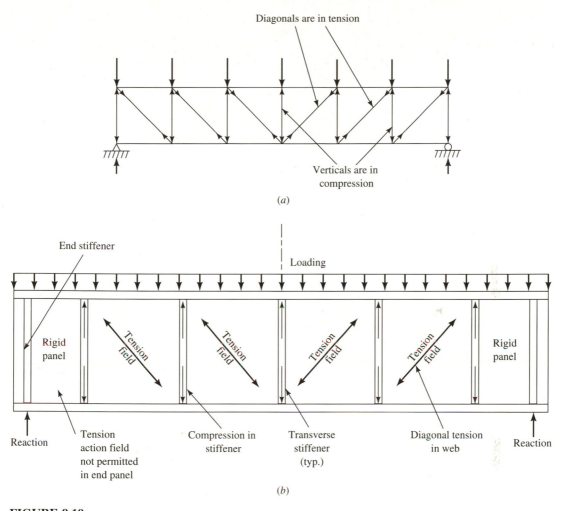

Diagonals are in tension

Verticals are in compression

(a)

End stiffener

Loading

Rigid panel

Tension field

Tension field

Tension field

Tension field

Rigid panel

Reaction

Tension action field not permitted in end panel

Compression in stiffener

Transverse stiffener (typ.)

Diagonal tension in web

Reaction

(b)

FIGURE 9.19

Tension-field action: (*a*) a Pratt truss under load; (*b*) analogy to the tension-field action in a plate girder.

of the web may lead to some waviness in the web, indicating the presence of the tension field (indicated by buckling of the web perpendicular to the direction of the waves), but this is not an indication of failure. The net result, as a consequence of tension-field action, is that a transversely stiffened plate girder can carry probably two or three times the load initiating web buckling before collapse occurs [McCormac, 1992].

The general nature of distribution of the tension field that develops in a transversely stiffened plate girder is shown in Fig. 9.21(*a*). Such a stress distribution has been experimentally verified by Basler et al. [1960]; Clark and Sharp [1971]; and Steinhardt and Schroter [1971]. In a Pratt truss–like action, the horizontal and vertical components of the tension field in a girder are anchored, respectively, by the flanges and stiffeners. The resulting lateral load on the flanges causes them to bend inward, as shown in Fig. 9.21(*b*).

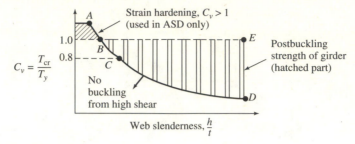

FIGURE 9.20
Shear capacity available considering postbuckling strength
[Adapted from Salmon and Johnson, 1990, p. 483].

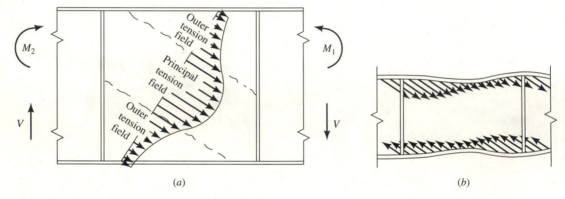

FIGURE 9.21
Tension-field action: (*a*) stress distribution in the web due to tension field; (*b*) action of tension field on flanges [Johnston, 1976].

When a longitudinal stiffener is provided between the two adjacent transverse stiffeners, the panel containing the longitudinal stiffener is divided into two subpanels. In such a case, the longitudinal stiffener must have the minimum area to anchor the tension-field force.

9.5
BUCKLING CONSIDERATIONS FOR DESIGN OF PLATE GIRDERS

9.5.1 Problem of Buckling of Plates under Compression

Theory of buckling of rectangular plates under compressive loads is germane to theory and design of plate girders because the latter is essentially based on the former. Flanges can be modeled as long plates under uniform compression with one long edge assumed simply supported and the other long edge free. Webs can be modeled as long plates under compression with the two near edges as simply supported. Phenomena such as local buckling of flanges and webs of open and closed sections of thin-walled beams are really forms of plate buckling phenomena.

The compression (on the edge of the plate) may be uniform, as in the flange of an I-beam, or nonuniform, as in the web of an I-beam. In classical plate theory, such plate elements are classified as either *unstiffened* or *stiffened.* Unstiffened plate elements are defined as those that are supported along one edge and free along the other edge parallel to the direction of compressive stress. Examples of unstiffened plates are the flanges of I-, channel-, and Z-sections, the flange and the web of a T-section, and the legs of an L-section. Stiffened elements are those that are supported along both edges parallel to the direction of the compressive stress. Examples of stiffened elements are the web of an I-section, the flanges and webs of a box-section, and the flange of a delta-section. Both examples are shown in Fig. 9.22. A critical design parameter for these elements is the width-to-thickness ratio, commonly expressed as the b/t ratio.

The conditions of support at the edges for both unstiffened and stiffened elements are assumed, ideally, as *simply supported*, *clamped* (fixed), or *free.* Of course, in practice, the actual edge support conditions are not ideal, except that of the free edge. These edge restraint conditions have significant influence on the buckling characteristics of the plate as indicated by value of the plate buckling coefficient, k (discussed later).

Buckling strength of a plate element under edge compression depends, among other factors, on its *aspect ratio,* which is defined as the ratio of its length to its width. For the flange element, the aspect ratio would be its length divided by its width (a/b), whereas for the web, the aspect ratio would be its length divided by its depth (a/h). Likewise, the aspect ratio of a transversely stiffened panel would be the ratio of distance between the adjacent transverse stiffeners and the web depth (a/h), where a is the distance between the adjacent stiffeners.

A comprehensive history of theory of plates has been presented by Timoshenko [1953] and Todhunter and Pearson [1960]; a brief history of development of various plate theories has been provided by Szilard [1974].

Historically, the first mathematical approach to the problem of deflection of elastic surfaces is due to Leonhard Euler (1707–1783), who gave the following differential equation to describe the vibration of a perfectly flexible membrane, which he assumed

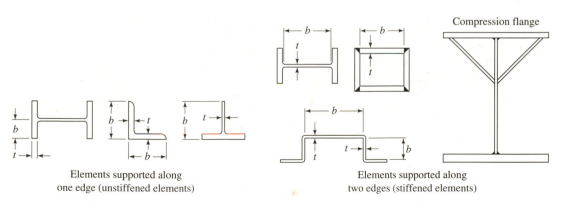

Elements supported along
one edge (unstiffened elements)

Elements supported along
two edges (stiffened elements)

FIGURE 9.22
Unstiffened and stiffened elements.

to be composed of two systems of stretched strings perpendicular to each other [Euler, 1766; Timoshenko, 1953, p. 119]:

$$\frac{\partial^2 w}{\partial t^2} = A\frac{\partial^2 w}{\partial x^2} + B\frac{\partial^2 w}{\partial y^2} \tag{9.1}$$

where w = deflection and A and B are constants.

Later, extending Euler's notion, Jacques Bernoulli (1759–1789) used the gridwork analogy and gave the following differential equation as an approximate solution for the analysis of plates [Timoshenko, 1953, p. 119]:

$$D\left(\frac{\partial^4 w}{\partial x^4} + \frac{\partial^4 w}{\partial y^4}\right) = q \tag{9.2}$$

where D = flexural rigidity of the plate
  q = intensity of the lateral load

Great interest in vibration of plates was aroused in the early nineteenth century by the German physicist E. F. F. Chladni's work in acoustics, and especially by his experiments with sound produced by vibrating plates [Timoshenko, 1953; Todhunter and Pearson, 1960]. The French mathematician Sophie Germain (1776–1831), using the calculus of variations, obtained the differential equation for the vibrating plates. However, she neglected the strain energy of the plate due to the warping of the middle surface of the plate. This error was noted by J. L. Lagrange (1736–1813), who became the first to give, in 1811, the following differential equation for the theory of plate vibration [Timoshenko, 1953, p. 120; Bulson, 1969]:

$$k\left(\frac{\partial^4 w}{\partial x^4} + 2\frac{\partial^4 w}{\partial x^2 \partial y^2} + \frac{\partial^4 w}{\partial y^4}\right) + \frac{\partial^2 w}{\partial t^2} = 0 \tag{9.3}$$

Further attempts to improve the theory of plates were made by S. D. Poisson (1781–1840). However, the credit for giving the first satisfactory theory of bending of plates is given to Louis Marie Henry Navier (1785–1836), the great engineer-mathematician, who gave the following differential equation in 1820 [Navier, 1823; Timoshenko, 1953, p. 121]:

$$D\left(\frac{\partial^4 w}{\partial x^4} + 2\frac{\partial^4 w}{\partial x^2 \partial y^2} + \frac{\partial^4 w}{\partial y^4}\right) = q \tag{9.4}$$

where q = intensity of load perpendicular to the middle plane of the plate
  D = flexural rigidity of the plate[18]
  $= EI/(1 - v^2)$
  w = deflection perpendicular to the plane of the plate, measured positive downward.

---

[18]In classical books [Bleich, 1952; Timoshenko and Gere, 1961] and others [Bulson, 1969; Donnell, 1976] dealing with the topic of stability of plates, the symbol D has been used to denote the rigidity of the plate. However, in AASHTO specifications [AASHTO 1992, 1994], the symbol D has been used to denote the depth of the web between flanges, which is also followed in this book for the sake of conformity.

In Eq. 9.4, the quantity D, the *flexural rigidity of a plate*, is analogous to the *flexural stiffness, EI,* of a beam.

Navier was also the first to correctly formulate (in 1823) the following differential equation for the buckled surface of a plate under the action of compressive forces T uniformly distributed along the boundary of the plate [Timoshenko, 1953, p. 122]:

$$D\left(\frac{\partial^4 w}{\partial x^4} + 2\frac{\partial^4 w}{\partial x^2 \partial y^2} + \frac{\partial^4 w}{\partial y^4}\right) + T\left(\frac{\partial^2 w}{\partial x^2} + \frac{\partial^2 w}{\partial y^2}\right) = 0 \qquad (9.5)$$

Navier applied Eq. 9.5 to the problem of a rectangular plate supported at four corners, which he failed to solve. Later, B. de Saint Venant (1797–1886), a student of Navier, gave the following correct differential equation for the deflection of a thin plate under the action of forces N_x and N_y in its middle plane, in the x and y directions, respectively (Fig. 9.23), and a lateral load q, with the assumption that the deflection w

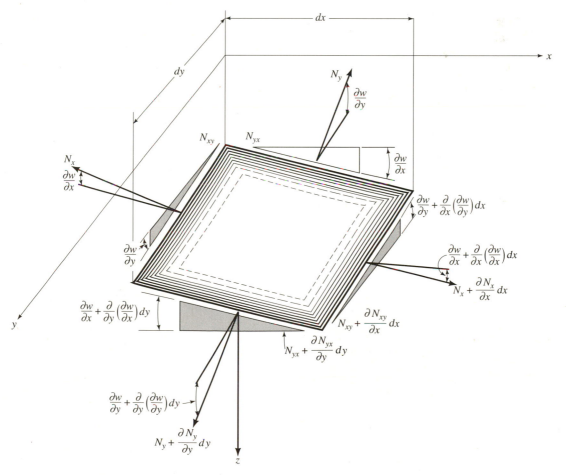

FIGURE 9.23
Forces acting in the middle plane of a plate.

is small in comparison to the thickness t of the plate [Timoshenko and Gere, 1961, p. 334]:

$$\frac{\partial^4 w}{\partial x^4} + 2\frac{\partial^4 w}{\partial x^2 \partial y^2} + \frac{\partial^4 w}{\partial y^4} = \frac{1}{D}\left(q + N_x\frac{\partial^2 w}{\partial x^2} + N_y\frac{\partial^2 w}{\partial y^2} + 2N_{xy}\frac{\partial^2 w}{\partial x\partial y}\right) \quad (9.6)$$

Buckling of plates can be investigated by assuming $q = 0$ in Eq. 9.6 [Timoshenko and Gere, 1961, p. 348]:

$$\frac{\partial^4 w}{\partial x^4} + 2\frac{\partial^4 w}{\partial x^2 \partial y^2} + \frac{\partial^4 w}{\partial y^4} = \frac{1}{D}\left(N_x\frac{\partial^2 w}{\partial x^2} + N_y\frac{\partial^2 w}{\partial y^2} + 2N_{xy}\frac{\partial^2 w}{\partial x\partial y}\right) \quad (9.7)$$

Alternatively, Eq. 9.7 can be expressed as

$$\nabla^4 w = \frac{1}{D}\left(N_x\frac{\partial^2 w}{\partial x^2} + N_y\frac{\partial^2 w}{\partial y^2} + 2N_{xy}\frac{\partial^2 w}{\partial x\partial y}\right) \quad (9.8)$$

Equation 9.7 can be expressed in terms of stresses that are obtained by dividing forces by the plate thickness, t [Bleich, 1952, p. 306]:

$$\left(\frac{\partial^4 w}{\partial x^4} + 2\frac{\partial^4 w}{\partial x^2\partial y^2} + \frac{\partial^4 w}{\partial y^4}\right) + \frac{t}{D}\left(\sigma_x\frac{\partial^2 w}{\partial x^2} + \sigma_y\frac{\partial^2 w}{\partial y^2} + 2\tau_{xy}\frac{\partial^2 w}{\partial x\partial y}\right) = 0 \quad (9.9)$$

where σ_x ($= N_x/t$) and σ_y ($= N_y/t$) are, respectively, the normal stresses in the direction of the x or y axis, and τ_{xy} ($= N_{xy}/t$) is the shear stress in a section perpendicular to the plane of the plate cut parallel to the x or y axis, all stresses being due to forces acting on the boundary of the plate. For a rectangular plate loaded in its middle plane in the x direction (i.e., at edges b) only, σ_x becomes constant, and σ_y and τ_{xy} vanish. The solution for this simplest case (a rectangular plate, uniformly compressed in one direction, loaded at the edges b, with simply supported edges) was given by G. H. Bryan in 1891 [Bryan, 1891; Timoshenko and Gere, 1961, p. 351][19] as follows:

$$\left(\frac{\partial^4 w}{\partial x^4} + 2\frac{\partial^4 w}{\partial x^2\partial y^2} + \frac{\partial^4 w}{\partial y^4}\right) + \frac{\sigma_x t}{D}\frac{\partial^2 w}{\partial x^2} = 0 \quad (9.10)$$

where E = modulus of elasticity
   v = Poisson's ratio
   t = thickness of plate
   w = lateral deflection
   σ_x = edge compression

Equation 9.10 is a homogeneous differential equation that is commonly used in dealing with various problems of instability of compressed plates. The solution of this problem is similar to that of the instability of a column described by Eq. 9.11:

$$EI\frac{d^2 y}{dx^2} + Py = 0 \quad (9.11)$$

---

[19] As pointed out by Bleich, "Bryan was not only the first to treat the stability problem of the plates, but the importance of his classic paper lies in the fact that he was the first to apply the energy criterion of stability to the solution of a buckling problem" [Bleich, 1952, p. 303].

It is important to note that Eq. 9.10 is valid only in the elastic range for which Hooke's law is valid and must be modified when σ_x exceeds the proportional limit.

More than 15 years later, H. Reissner [1909], J. Boobnov [1914], and S. Timoshenko [1915, 1935] gave solutions for the plate buckling problem with other boundary conditions. Timoshenko was the first to present a practical solution of the stability problem of rectangular plates in shear by applying the energy method [Bleich, 1952]. The treatment of the *inelastic* buckling of plates was first presented by F. Bleich in 1924 [Bleich, 1924]. This was followed by more work of Ros and Eichenger [1932], Bijlaard [1940–1941, 1947], and Ilyushin [1947].

Early experiments on built-up I-beams were carried out in Belgium by Houbotte in the 1850s. By applying a concentrated load at the middle of a built-up I-beam, he found that in all cases failure occurred due to local buckling of the web near the point of application of the load,[20] a phenomenon now known as *elastic buckling*. However, it was not until 1935 that, as a result of experimental research, two types of failures were recognized corresponding to this case: *plate buckling* in webs with large depth-thickness ratios (typically used in plate girders), and *plate crippling* resulting from local yielding. Plate crippling was introduced by the AISC as a design criterion in 1936; current AISC specifications consider both types of buckling as the design criteria [Ostapenko, 1974].

Initially, the design of plate girders was based, to a great extent, on empirical rules that were based on experience. However, investigations since their introduction in the 1850s have shown that their ultimate strength is significantly influenced by buckling of the web. "The problem of determining web thickness and stiffening of the web is essentially a stability problem" [Timoshenko and Gere, 1961, p. 431], i.e., it is basically related to the stability (or the lack of it) of the web. The load-carrying capacity of a plate girder may be significantly influenced by the web as a result of (1) buckling due to bending in the plane of the web, which will reduce its moment-carrying capacity in the elastic range; and (2) buckling of the compression flange in the vertical direction, which may occur due to inadequate stiffness of the web, and buckling due to shear.

To understand the rationale behind design criteria for plate girders, it is instructive to review the theory of buckling of plates, which forms the basis for the width-to-thickness ratios for flanges and webs of plate girders. This subject is covered extensively in the literature [Bleich, 1952; Timoshenko and Gere, 1961; Bulson, 1969; Szilard, 1974; Troitsky, 1976; Bazant and Cedolin, 1991]. Nevertheless, a short discussion on the phenomenon of plate buckling is presented here to serve as analytical basis for specifications for design of plate girders.

Figure 9.24(a) shows buckled configuration of a perfectly flat[21] rectangular plate with all edges simply supported and uniaxially compressed by a uniformly distributed load in the plane of the plate. Up to a certain load, the plate remains compressed in its own plane. However, as the load increases and reaches a critical value, the plane state of plate deformation becomes unstable. Further increase in load causes the plate

---

[20]Houbotte, a Belgian engineer, tested two centrally loaded plate girders: 1.5 m in span, 0.5-cm thick web without any stiffeners, and 30 and 49 cm in depth. Both girders failed by buckling of web. The deeper girder failed at smaller load even though its section modulus was twice as great as that of the smaller girder [Timoshenko and Gere, 1961, p. 433].

[21]In all practical cases, some initial out-of-straightness exists; however, the case of an initially perfectly flat plate is considered as basis for theoretical development of the formula and design.

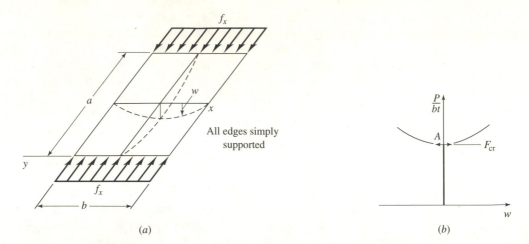

FIGURE 9.24

(*a*) Buckling of a uniformly compressed plate; (*b*) lateral deflection of a buckled plate.

to deflect laterally, resulting in out-of-plane configuration. This phenomenon is referred to as buckling of the plate, and the causative load is called the buckling, or critical, load. Although this lateral deflection of the compressed plate is highly undesirable, it does not necessarily imply failure of the plate, because plates are known to possess postbuckling strength due to the tension-field action that develops following the onset of buckling.

The buckling stress is equal to *P/bt*, where *P* is the buckling load and *b* and *t* are the width and the thickness, respectively, of the plate. The plate may buckle in either direction, as shown in Fig. 9.24(*b*). The buckled configuration of this plate is defined by Eq. 9.10 and represents an *eigenvalue problem*. For use in design, we need to determine the deflection function *w* (referred to as *eigenfunction*) and the corresponding value of σ_x (referred to as *eigenvalue*) that will satisfy this equation at the boundaries and over the whole loaded plate. Obviously, one solution of the equation is given by $w = 0$, which corresponds to $\sigma_x = 0$, known as the *trivial solution*. The other solutions, referred to as *nontrivial solutions*, correspond to nonzero values of σ_x, for which $w \neq 0$. These values of σ_x are referred to as the *characteristic values, σ_c*. Stated otherwise, if the value of σ_x is different from the characteristic values σ_c, Eq. 9.10 is satisfied only by the solution $w = 0$, the trivial solution. Physically speaking, as the value of σ_x is increased from zero to the *lowest* characteristic value of σ_c, a state of equilibrium is reached such that the plate (or for that matter, an axially loaded column) can be in either a straight or a slightly deflected configuration—a state of equilibrium referred to as *bifurcation* (Fig. 9.24(*b*)). The deflection of the perfectly flat plate can occur in either direction. Determination of σ_c involves simply the determination of the characteristic value of σ_x in Eq. 9.10.

For the case of a rectangular simply supported plate, function *w* can be expressed by the Fourier double sine series [Timoshenko and Gere, 1961, p. 351]:

$$w = w(x, y) = \sum_{m=1}^{\infty} \sum_{n=1}^{\infty} A_{mn} \sin \frac{m\pi x}{a} \sin \frac{n\pi y}{b} \tag{9.12}$$

where A_{mn} are the unknown coefficients representing generalized displacements. Note that this function satisfies the kinematic boundary conditions of zero deflection and the static boundary condition of zero moment at $x = 0$ and $x = a$ and at $y = 0$ and $y = b$. Substitution of the appropriate partial derivatives of this equation in Eq. 9.10 yields

$$\left[\left(\frac{m\pi}{a}\right)^2 + 2\left(\frac{m\pi}{a}\right)^2\left(\frac{n\pi}{b}\right)^2 + \left(\frac{n\pi}{b}\right)^4 - \frac{\sigma t}{D}\left(\frac{m\pi}{a}\right)^4\right]w = 0 \qquad (9.13)$$

Equation 9.13 has two possible solutions: either $w = 0$, or the term in the bracket is zero. As mentioned earlier, $w = 0$ represents the trivial solution, corresponding to which $\sigma_c = 0$ (i.e., plate is unstressed) and, consequently, is of no interest. The nontrivial solution is obtained by setting the bracketed term equal to zero:

$$\left[\left(\frac{m\pi}{a}\right)^2 + 2\left(\frac{m\pi}{a}\right)^2\left(\frac{n\pi}{b}\right)^2 + \left(\frac{n\pi}{b}\right)^4 - \frac{\sigma_x t}{D}\left(\frac{m\pi}{a}\right)^4\right] = 0 \qquad (9.14)$$

which yields

$$\sigma_x = \frac{\pi^2 D}{t}\left[\left(\frac{m}{a}\right)^2 + 2\left(\frac{n}{b}\right)^2 + \left(\frac{a}{m}\right)^2\left(\frac{n}{b}\right)^4\right] \qquad (9.15)$$

In Eq. 9.15, we substitute

$$D = \frac{EI}{(1 - \nu^2)} = \frac{Et^3}{12(1 - \nu^2)} \qquad (9.16)$$

where $I = t_3/12$ for a plate strip of unit width. The resulting expression is

$$\sigma_x = \frac{\pi^2 E}{12(1 - \nu^2)}\left(\frac{t}{b}\right)^2\left[\left(\frac{mb}{a}\right)^2 + 2n^2 + n^4\left(\frac{a}{mb}\right)^2\right]$$
$$= \left[\frac{mb}{a} + \frac{a}{mb}n^2\right]^2 \frac{\pi^2 E}{12(1 - \nu^2)}\left(\frac{t}{b}\right)^2 \qquad (9.17)$$

The bracketed quantity in Eq. 9.17 is called the *plate buckling coefficient k*:

$$k = \left[\frac{mb}{a} + \frac{a}{mb}n^2\right]^2 \qquad (9.18)$$

In Eqs. 9.17 and 9.18, m and n are the numbers of sine half-waves in the x and y directions, respectively. For each set of values of m and n, there exists a corresponding buckling stress and a buckled configuration. Figure 9.25 shows examples of buckled configuration of the plate with arbitrarily selected pairs of m and n values.

Equation 9.17 is the required solution to determine the characteristic values of the parameter σ_c. Of the various possible characteristic values that will satisfy Eq. 9.17, the one of primary interest is the smallest value of σ_c that evidently corresponds to the smallest value of the buckling coefficient k. An examination of Eq. 9.18 readily shows that the smallest value of k corresponds to $n = 1$ (because n^2 occurs in the numerator). Physically, this means that the buckled configuration of the plate is such that one half-wave is formed across the width b of the plate (Fig. 9.25(a)). Substituting $n = 1$ in

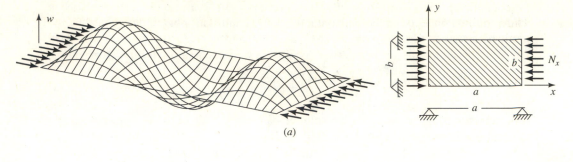

(a)

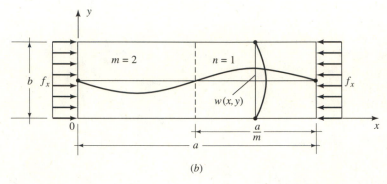

(b)

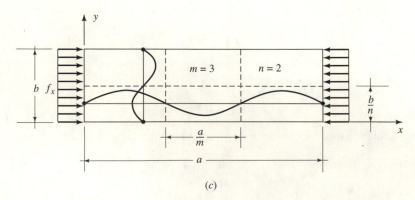

(c)

FIGURE 9.25
Buckled configurations of a uniaxially compressed (at two opposite edges) rectangular plate simply supported on all four edges corresponding to (a) $m = 3, n = 1$; (b) $m = 2, n = 1$; (c) $m = 3, n = 2$.

Eq. 9.18 yields

$$k = \left(\frac{mb}{a} + \frac{a}{mb}\right)^2 \tag{9.19}$$

The value of the critical stress for $m = 1$, which corresponds to one half-wave in the direction of stress, is given by

$$\sigma_c = \frac{\pi^2 E}{12(1 - \nu^2)}\left(\frac{t}{b}\right)^2\left(\frac{b}{a} + \frac{a}{b}\right)^2 \tag{9.20}$$

Equation 9.20 shows the dependence of the critical stress on the aspect ratio a/b. The minimum value of the parenthetical expression can be determined by equating the partial derivative of a/b (or b/a) to zero:

$$\frac{\partial}{\partial b}\left(\frac{b}{a} + \frac{a}{b}\right)^2 = 2\left(\frac{b}{a} + \frac{a}{b}\right)\left(\frac{1}{a} - \frac{a}{b^2}\right) = 0 \tag{9.21}$$

For Eq. 9.21 to be valid, the second parenthetical expression should be equal to zero, which yields $a = b$, meaning that the critical stress given by Eq. 9.20 reaches its minimum value when a plate is a square, and for which the critical stress would be

$$\sigma_c = \frac{4\pi^2 E}{12(1 - \nu^2)}\left(\frac{t}{b}\right)^2 \tag{9.22}$$

However, plate elements used for girders (such as flanges and webs) are relatively long and narrow, not square. Critical stress for such elements can be studied by examining Eq. 9.19, which clearly shows the dependence of k on both m and the a/b ratios. We wish to determine the smallest value of m for which the characteristic value σ_c will be smallest. This is obtained by minimizing k in Eq. 9.19 with respect to m, through partial differentiation:

$$\frac{\partial}{\partial m}\left(\frac{mb}{a} + \frac{a}{mb}\right)^2 = 0 \tag{9.23}$$

Solution of Eq. 9.23 is given by

$$2\left(\frac{mb}{a} + \frac{a}{bm}\right)\left(\frac{b}{a} - \frac{a}{bm^2}\right) = 0 \tag{9.24}$$

For Eq. 9.24 to be valid, we must have

$$\frac{b}{a} - \frac{a}{bm^2} = 0 \quad\text{or}\quad m = \frac{a}{b} \tag{9.25}$$

Substitution of $n = 1$ and $m = a/b$ in Eq. 9.18 yields

$$k_{\min} = 4 \tag{9.26}$$

Equation 9.25 can also be expressed as

$$\frac{a}{m} = b \tag{9.27}$$

The physical interpretation of Eq. 9.27 is that a long plate of length a (measured in the direction of edge compressive stress σ_c) and width b will buckle into m half-waves of length b.

Evidently, the value of the buckling coefficient k depends on the aspect ratio a/b. Figure 9.26 shows the dependence of k on the value of a/b for various values of m. Referring to the curve for $m = 1$, it is seen that k is large for small values of a/b and decreases as a/b increases until $a/b = 1$ (i.e., $a = b$) when k reaches its minimum value of 4. The value of k increases again as a/b increases. For $m = 2$, Eq. 9.19 yields

$$k = \left(\frac{2b}{a} + \frac{a}{2b}\right)^2 \tag{9.28}$$

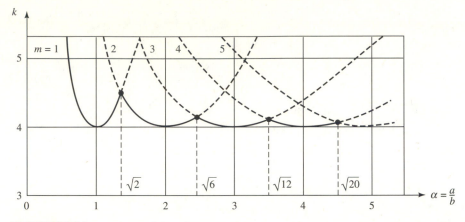

FIGURE 9.26
Buckling coefficients for a uniaxially compressed rectangular plate simply supported on all four edges.

which gives $k_{min} = 4$ when $a/b = 2$ (i.e., a plate of aspect ratio 2 buckles in two square half-waves). Again, referring to the curve for $m = 2$ in Fig. 9.26, it is seen that the value of k is higher than 4 for $a/b \neq 2$. Proceeding in a similar way, curves for $m = 3, 4, 5$, etc. can be plotted as shown in Fig. 9.26. From these curves, the critical load and the number of half-waves for any aspect ratio a/b can be determined. In each case, it turns out that $k_{min} = 4$ and corresponds to the aspect ratios having *integer* values ($a/b = 1, 2, 3, \ldots$).

In Fig. 9.26, the portions of the curves defining the critical values of the load are shown by full lines. Beginning from the intersection of the curves $m = 1$ and $m = 2$, the latter curve has the smallest ordinates, meaning that the plate buckles in two half-waves. This buckled configuration holds until the intersection of the curves $m = 2$ and $m = 3$; from this point on the plate buckles in three half-waves, and so on.

Figure 9.26 shows also that the value of the buckling coefficient k is somewhat greater than the minimum value of 4 for the noninteger values of the aspect ratios. Values of these higher ordinates can be computed by equating the values of the ordinates corresponding to m and $(m + 1)$. Substitution in Eq. 9.19 yields

$$\frac{mb}{a} + \frac{a}{mb} = \frac{(m + 1)b}{a} + \frac{a}{(m + 1)b} \tag{9.29}$$

The solution of Eq. 9.29 is

$$\frac{a}{b} = \sqrt{m(m + 1)} \tag{9.30}$$

Substitution for a/b from Eq. 9.30 in Eq. 9.19 yields

$$k = \left(\frac{m}{\sqrt{m(m + 1)}} + \frac{\sqrt{m(m + 1)}}{m}\right)^2$$

$$= \left(\sqrt{\frac{m}{m + 1}} + \sqrt{\frac{m + 1}{m}}\right)^2 \tag{9.31}$$

TABLE 9.2
Values of k for noninteger values of aspect ratio a/b

m	1	2	3	4	5	10	15	20
a/b*	1.41	2.45	3.46	4.47	5.48	10.49	15.49	20.49
k	4.50	4.167	4.083	4.05	4.03	4.01	4.004	4.002

*Computed from Eq. 9.30 and rounded off to two decimal places.

For all integer values of m ($= 1, 2, 3, \ldots$), the values of the aspect ratios a/b, and the corresponding values of the plate buckling coefficient k, can be computed from Eq. 9.30 and Eq. 9.31, respectively:

$$m = 1 \qquad a/b = \sqrt{2} \qquad k = \left(\sqrt{\tfrac{1}{2}} + \sqrt{\tfrac{2}{1}}\right)^2 = 4.5$$

$$m = 2 \qquad a/b = \sqrt{6} \qquad k = \left(\sqrt{\tfrac{2}{3}} + \sqrt{\tfrac{3}{2}}\right)^2 = 4.167$$

and so on. Values of k for various noninteger values of a/b corresponding to the intersections of various m curves (Fig. 9.26) are shown in Table 9.2. It is noted that values of k rapidly approach $k_{\min}$ ($= 4$) as the plate length a increases. Therefore, $k = 4$ may be considered as valid for all values of a/b ratios and may be used as the basis for designing practical girders and columns, which are commonly assembled from long and narrow rectangular plate elements.

In a physical sense, Eq. 9.31 is interpreted to mean that at $a/b = \sqrt{2} = 1.41$, the buckled configuration has a transition from one to two half-waves; at $a/b = \sqrt{6} = 2.45$, the buckled configuration has a transition from two to three half-waves; and so on. It is also evident that the number of half-waves increases with the aspect ratio a/b. For very long plates, m is a large number so that

$$\frac{a}{b} = \sqrt{m(m + 1)} \approx m \tag{9.32}$$

The physical interpretation of Eq. 9.32 is that a very long plate buckles in half-waves whose lengths approach the width of the plate. It follows, then, that a long plate, simply supported on all four edges, and uniformly compressed along the shorter sides, on buckling, subdivides itself approximately (because a/b may not necessarily be an integer value) into squares (Fig. 9.27).

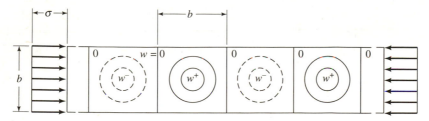

FIGURE 9.27
Buckled pattern of a uniaxially compressed long plate.

At this point, it is instructive to compare and understand the differences between the buckling behavior of simply supported plates and that of the axially loaded simply supported columns for which the critical load is given by Eq. 9.33:

$$P_{cr} = \frac{\pi^2 EI}{L^2} \tag{9.33}$$

Because of familiarity with the column buckling behavior, one might intuitively infer that an axially loaded long plate will also buckle similar to a long column. However, the preceding discussion shows that such is *not* the case. A simply supported long slender column, regardless of its length, buckles into *one* half-wave of length L (corresponding to $m = 1$ for a plate). Although the critical load is inversely proportional to L^2, it is independent of the width of the column. By contrast, because of the supports along the unloaded edges, a plate buckles into multiple half-waves the lengths of which approach the width of the plate. The critical stress in a simply supported plate is inversely proportional to b^2 and independent of its length $a (= L)$.

It can be seen that σ_c as a function of the aspect ratio a/b always has a positive curvature, and the minimum value of σ_c occurs when $a/b = m$, for which the critical stress is given by Eq. 9.22.

In general, substitution for k from Eq. 9.18 in Eq. 9.17 yields

$$\sigma_c = k \frac{\pi^2 E}{12(1 - \nu^2)} \left(\frac{t}{b} \right)^2 \tag{9.34}$$

Equation 9.34 is the fundamental equation used to define slenderness ratios (width-to-thickness ratio for the flange, or the depth-to-thickness ratio for the web) of the plate elements that constitute a plate girder. From a design standpoint, the critical (or the buckling) stress, σ_c, should be considered a danger signal; the designer must control the loading so that the stresses caused are below the critical stress level.

For use in design, Eq. 9.34 can be expressed as

$$\frac{b}{t} = \sqrt{\frac{k \pi^2 E}{12(1 - \nu^2) \sigma_c}} \tag{9.35}$$

The buckling coefficient k in Eq. 9.35 must be evaluated for each particular case of plate geometry (aspect ratio a/b), boundary conditions (fixed, simple, or free at the edges), and edge loading. As derived earlier, for long and narrow plates (i.e., $a \gg b$), $k = 4$, and for wide and short plates (i.e., $b \gg a$), $k = 1$. Also, depending on the loading conditions, σ_c can be either a critical compressive stress due to bending or a critical shear stress. Figure 9.28 shows the buckling coefficient k as a function of the aspect ratio a/b for various boundary conditions of edge-compressed rectangular plates as obtained by Lundquist and Stowell [1942]. The values of the buckling coefficient k for various loading and boundary conditions are presented in the form of charts and tables in several references, such as Lundquist and Stowell [1942], Kloppel and Scheer [1960], Kloppel and Moller [1968], and Brockenbrough and Johnston [1974].

It should be noted that Eq. 9.34 is valid within the range of elastic loading conditions only for which Hooke's law is valid. Bleich [1952, p. 322, Eq. 638a] has shown

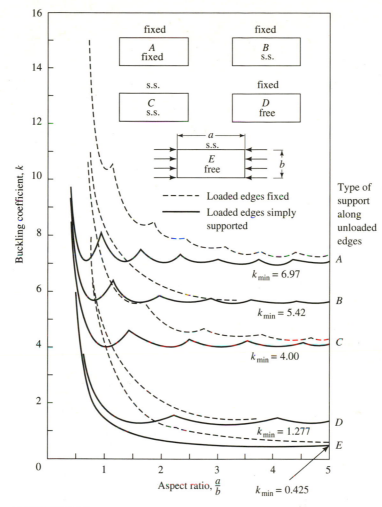

FIGURE 9.28

Plate buckling coefficients k for uniformly compressed rectangular plates with various boundary conditions [Gerard and Becker, 1957].

that the critical stress in the inelastic range is given by Eq. 9.36:

$$\sigma_c = \frac{\pi^2 E \sqrt{\tau}}{12(1 - \nu^2)} \left(\frac{t}{b}\right)^2 k \tag{9.36}$$

where $\tau = \dfrac{E_t}{E}$

  E_t = the tangent modulus

Equation 9.36 can be written in simplified form as

$$\sigma_c = k \frac{\pi^2 \sqrt{E E_t}}{12(1 - \nu^2)} \left(\frac{t}{b}\right)^2 \tag{9.37}$$

9.5.2 Local Buckling of Flange

9.5.2.1 General considerations

A plate girder may be characterized as an assemblage of plate elements that are susceptible to the weakening effects of plate buckling. In general, buckling can be characterized as an out-of-plane deformation that affects both the flange and the web of a plate girder. Local buckling refers to the wave formations that develop in plate elements, such as flanges, webs, and outstanding legs of angles, when subjected to compression. The general formulation of the plate buckling problem is presented in Sec. 9.4.1.

The out-of-plane displacements of a compressed plate (plate buckles) can be seen in the form of waves, longitudinal as well as transverse. A flange plate is essentially a uniformly compressed long narrow plate that, on buckling, develops waves like any conventional plate. However, because the wavelength of the flange buckle is usually considerably smaller than the length of the member itself, this form of buckling is referred to as *local buckling*. Physically, local buckling of an element of a cross section simply means that the cross-sectional shape has been sufficiently deformed and, as a potential consequence, the stress distribution may become nonuniform, rendering it incapable of carrying the load to its capacity.

A plate element may be subjected to in-plane compressive stress due to direct compression, bending, shear, or a combination of these forces. For a member to satisfactorily carry compressive stresses, it is necessary to maintain the integrity of its cross section until the overall buckling of the member occurs or the material reaches the yield stress. Obviously, for a member to be able to carry the design load satisfactorily, local buckling of its constituent plates must be avoided. Consequently, understanding the local buckling behavior of plate assemblies is necessary to accurately predict the compressive strength of plate assemblies.

Research has indicated that plates can carry additional loads well beyond the theoretical buckling loads. This additional margin of strength is called the postbuckling strength of the plate. It exists due to redistribution of the axial compressive stresses and, to a lesser extent, the membrane tension of the plate in both the longitudinal and the transverse directions [Galambos, 1988].

Both the critical loads and the postbuckling strength of a plate assembly depend on the nature of connectivity (boundary conditions) between the constituent plates. An edge of a plate element may be in some way connected to another plate, or it may be free. For example, the flange of a plate girder is connected to the web along the flange's centerline while both edges are free. By contrast, the web of a plate girder is connected to the flanges along both of its longitudinal edges. The connection between the two plates can be assumed to be simply supported or clamped (fixed).

Conservatively, a lower bound of the critical stress can be determined by assuming the connected edge as simply supported and the unconnected edge as free. In reality, however, the connected edges are not simply supported and, in fact, do get some degree of restraint from the adjacent elements. Consequently, the smallest value of critical stress for any particular plate element, which is based on the assumption of a simply supported condition at the connection, will usually be less than the actual compressive strength of the plate element.

9.5.2.2 Limiting *b/t* ratio for flange in the elastic range

For design purposes, the limit states or the desired performance can be defined, and Eq. 9.35 can be used to obtain the required values of *b/t* ratios. For example, in the elastic range, a limit may be prescribed requiring the flange stress to reach the yield stress without buckling, i.e.,

$$(F_{cr})_{\text{plate}} \geq F_y \tag{9.38}$$

Eq. 9.35 can be used to establish such a condition by writing

$$F_{cr} = \frac{k\pi^2 E}{12(1 - \nu^2)(b/t)^2} \geq F_y \tag{9.39}$$

A dimensionless representation of the plate strength in edge compression can be made by normalizing Eq. 9.39 by dividing both sides by F_y:

$$\frac{F_{cr}}{F_y} = \frac{k\pi^2 E}{12(1 - \nu^2)(b/t)^2 F_y} \tag{9.40}$$

By introducing the plate slenderness function (or the plate slenderness parameter[22]) λ_c, which is defined as

$$\lambda^2 = \frac{F_y}{F_{cr}} \tag{9.41}$$

Equation 9.40 can be expressed as

$$\lambda_c = \sqrt{\frac{F_y}{F_{cr}}} = \frac{b}{t} \sqrt{\frac{F_y}{E} \frac{12(1 - \nu^2)}{k\pi^2}} \tag{9.42}$$

A plot of F_{cr}/F_y versus λ_c is shown in Fig. 9.29, which is based on the test results of various investigators [von Karman, Sechler, and Donnell, 1932; Frankland, 1940; Stowell et al., 1952; Bleich, 1952; Gerard, 1957; Kollbrunner and Meister, 1958; Timoshenko and Gere, 1961; Jombock and Clark, 1962; Ueda, 1962; and Dwight and Ratcliffe, 1967]. Because of the differences in the material properties and edge conditions involved in various tests, the results are plotted in this figure nondimensionally for a meaningful comparison of results. It must be noted that the quantity under the radical sign on the right-hand side of Eq. 9.42 is constant for a given material and edge condition. Therefore, the curve shown in Fig. 9.29 gives the relationship between F_{cr} (or F_u) and *b/t* ratio. Note that curve *a* represents the theoretical buckling curve (analogous to the Euler column curve), and curves *b* and *c* represent the theoretical buckling curves in the strain-hardening range for plates supported at both edges and at one edge, respectively [Haaijer, 1957; Haaijer and Thurlimann, 1959; Ostapenko, 1974]. The available test, if plotted, would fall approximately in the shaded zones surrounding the theoretical curve.

---

[22]AISC–LRFD [1986, pp. 6–39] has introduced λ_c as the slenderness parameter (instead of KL/r) for design of columns.

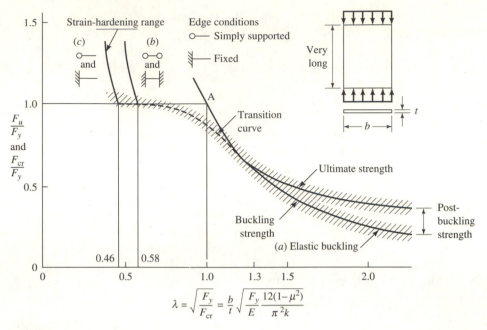

FIGURE 9.29

Test results—plate buckling curve [Ostapenko, 1974].

The design condition (or the limit state) of preventing the elastic buckling before the flange reaches the yield stress is given by point A, the intersection of the horizontal line corresponding to $F_{cr}/F_y = 1.0$ in Fig. 9.29 with the elastic buckling parabola. Tests have shown that for low b/t ratios, strain hardening can be achieved without buckling of the flange, whereas for high b/t ratios, plate buckling occurs before the flange reaches the yield stress. For the intermediate values of b/t ratios, the plate behavior is influenced by presence of the residual stresses and geometrical imperfections, resulting in inelastic buckling of the plate shown by the transition curve. It is known that point A in Fig. 9.29, lying above the transition curve, overestimates the actual strength of the plate, whereas for large b/t ratios the elastic buckling parabola underestimates the actual plate strength. Note also the divergence of the curves for elastic buckling and the ultimate strength for values of $\lambda_c > 1.3$; the ordinates between the two curves represent the postbuckling strength.

A reduced value of $\lambda_c = 0.7$ is taken to minimize the deviation between F_y and the transition curve, which accounts for the residual stress and imperfections in the plate geometry [Salmon and Johnson, 1990]. This is also approximately the point where the transition curve reaches the straight line (point B in Fig. 9.30) and is between $\frac{2}{3}$ and $\frac{3}{4}$, which have been used by various specifications [Ostapenko, 1974]. Substitution of $\lambda_c = 0.7$ in Eq. 9.42 yields

$$\frac{b}{t} \sqrt{\frac{F_y}{E} \frac{12(1 - \nu^2)}{k\pi^2}} = 0.7 \qquad (9.43)$$

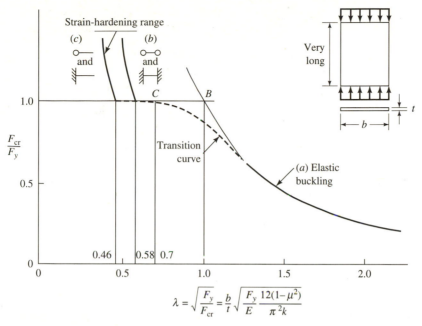

FIGURE 9.30
Plate buckling curve [Ostapenko, 1974].

Substitution of $E = 29{,}000$ ksi and $\nu = 0.3$ in Eq. 9.43 yields

$$\frac{b}{t} = 114\sqrt{\frac{k}{F_{y,\,ksi}}} \tag{9.44}$$

To establish the numerical values of the b/t ratios for design of flange, the value of the buckling coefficient k, which depends on the degree of the restraint offered by the web (i.e., the boundary condition between the flange and the web), must be established. A flange is supported by the web (through the welds) along its centerline, a boundary condition considered midway between "clamped" and "simply supported," the minimum k values for which are 1.227 and 0.425, respectively (Fig. 9.28). For such a boundary condition, $k = 0.7$ has been considered as the lowest value occurring in the practical members [Ostapenko, 1974], substitution of which in Eq. 9.44 yields

$$\frac{b}{t} = \frac{95}{\sqrt{F_{y,\,ksi}}} \tag{9.45}$$

which is the limiting b/t ratio specified in AISC [1989] for flanges of noncompact welded I-shaped beams in flexure.

   It has been determined that for the flange to reach the strain-hardening range without buckling, the value of λ_c in Eq. 9.42 should be restricted to 0.46, which yields

$$\frac{b}{t} = 74.5\sqrt{\frac{k}{F_{y,\,ksi}}} \tag{9.46}$$

With $k = 0.425$, the least value of the buckling coefficient for an unstiffened element (corresponding to the boundary condition defined by one edge simply supported and the other edge free, as in Fig. 9.28), the b/t ratio is given by

$$\frac{b}{t} \leq \frac{48.5}{\sqrt{F_{y,\,ksi}}} \tag{9.47}$$

Equation 9.47 is considered overly conservative for the following reasons [Salmon and Johnson, 1990]:

1. The residual stresses disappear in the inelastic range.
2. The material imperfections have minimal effects on the behavior in the inelastic range.
3. The strain at the onset of strain hardening is 15 to 20 times the yield strain (ϵ_y), whereas the limiting value of λ_c used in both the AISC [1989] and AISC [1986] specifications is one that corresponds to the plastic strain of 7 to 9 times ϵ_y, about one-half the strain necessary to reach strain hardening.

Consequently, the limiting value of the b/t ratio is taken as

$$\frac{b}{t} \leq \frac{65}{\sqrt{F_{y,\,ksi}}} \tag{9.48}$$

The value of F_y in Eq. 9.48 may be expressed in units of psi to read

$$\frac{b}{t} \leq \frac{2055}{\sqrt{F_{y,\,psi}}} \tag{9.49}$$

which is the limiting b/t ratio specified in AASHTO 10.48.1.1 (Eq. 10.92) for load factor design.

Equation 9.48 can be normalized with respect to E and expressed as

$$\frac{b}{t} \leq 65\sqrt{\frac{E}{EF_y}} \tag{9.50}$$

Substitution of $E = 29,000$ ksi in the denominator of Eq. 9.50 yields

$$\frac{b}{t} \leq 0.382\sqrt{\frac{E}{F_y}} \tag{9.51}$$

which is the same the as AASHTO–LRFD Eq. 6.10.5.2.3c-1 [AASHTO, 1994].

9.5.2.3 Limiting b/t ratio for flange based on postbuckling strength

Plates with large b/t ratios exhibit postbuckling strength, as shown in Fig. 9.29. A summary of the analytical work on the b/t ratios in the inelastic range for I-shaped girders can be found in the literature [ASCE-WRC, 1971] wherein approaches by Haaijer [1957] and Lay [1965] are discussed. Essentially, the problem is treated as one of classical buckling with bifurcation of the equilibrium position. The physical model used in both analyses is shown in Fig. 9.31, which consists of a uniformly compressed plate element of width b and thickness t, restrained in some way at the flange-web juncture.

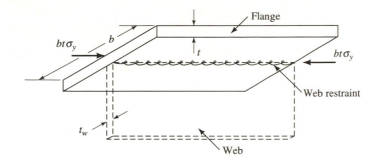

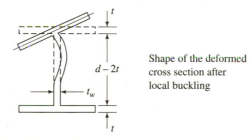

Shape of the deformed
cross section after
local buckling

FIGURE 9.31
Compression flange local-buckling model [ASCE–WRC, 1971].

The cross-sectional shape before and after the attainment of the critical load (i.e., buckling) assumed in the model is also shown in Fig. 9.31. Only the effect of local buckling has been shown in this model; the effect of lateral buckling has been omitted for clarity.

The work of Haaijer [1957] shows two possible ways of treating the problem of local buckling of the flange. In both approaches it is assumed that the material has been strained uniformly to a strain level equal to ϵ_{st}, with a strain-hardening modulus equal to E_{st}. Figure 9.32 shows partial strain-hardening ranges of various grades of steel. Figures 9.33 and 9.34 show the idealized stress-strain curves for four steels and the three approaches used in determining E_{st}, which have been described by Beedle and Tall [1960], Desai [1969a,b], and Johnston [1966], and are briefly described in ASCE–WRC [1971]. Of the three values of E_{st} (E_{st1}, E_{st2}, and E_{st3}) determined from tests, values of E_{st2} are used as the basis for calculations because they exhibit the least scatter of the test values, and they also define the average slope of the test values into which most steel members are strain-hardened.

In the strain-hardening range, the material remains homogeneous, but because of the yielding process, Haaijer [1957] assumes the material to be orthotropic. Lay [1965] treats the problem as one of torsional buckling of a restrained rectangular plate.

For the limiting case of a plate with one edge hinged and the other edge free, Haaijer's solution [Haaijer, 1959, p. 122, Eq. 12] is

$$\sigma_c = \left(\frac{t}{b}\right)^2 \left[\frac{\pi D_x}{12}\left(\frac{b}{L}\right)^2 + G_t\right] \tag{9.52}$$

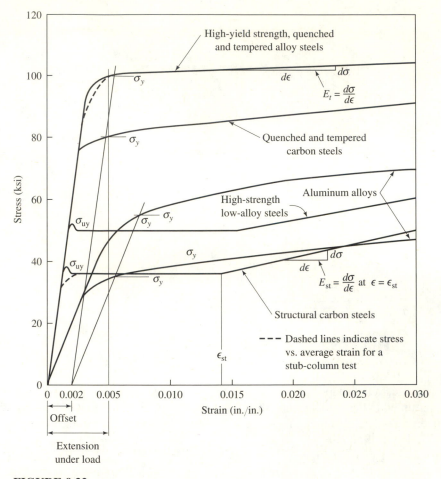

FIGURE 9.32
Partial $\sigma-\epsilon$ curves for various steels showing partial strain-hardening range. The complete curves plotted to the same scale would occupy a horizontal space 20 to 30 times that available on the drawing [Galambos, 1988].

where L = length of the plate
$D_x = E_x/(1 - \nu_x \nu_y)$
ν_x = Poisson's ratio, coefficient of dilatation for stress in the x direction
ν_y = Poisson's ratio, coefficient of dilatation for stress in the y direction
G_t = tangent modulus in shear

For a long plate, the first term within the bracket is neglected so that Eq. 9.52 reduces to

$$\sigma_c = \left(\frac{t}{b}\right)^2 G_t \tag{9.53}$$

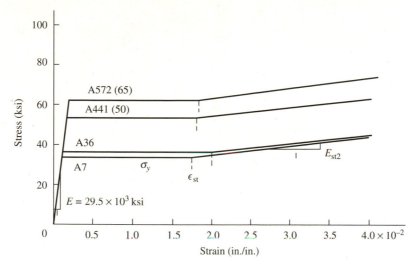

FIGURE 9.33
Idealized stress-strain curves for four structural steels [ASCE–WRC, 1971].

Using the AASHTO [1992] notation, Eq. 9.53 can be expressed as

$$\frac{b'}{t} = \sqrt{\frac{G_{st}}{F_y}} \qquad (9.54)$$

where $G_{st} = G_t$ = strain-hardening modulus in shear
  b' = half flange width or the width of the outstanding leg of the flange angle
  F_y = yield strength of the flange = limiting value of σ_c

Several possible approaches to obtain values of G_{st} have been proposed [Bijlaard, 1947; Haaijer, 1957; Lay, 1965]. According to Lay [1965, p. 106, Eq. 20],

$$\frac{G'}{G_e} = \frac{2}{1 + h/[4(1 + \nu)]} \qquad (9.55)$$

where G' = shear modulus in the yielded zone
   = G_{st}
  G_e = elastic shear modulus
   = G
   h = ratio of Young's modulus to strain-hardening modulus
   = E/E_{st}

With this notation, Eq. 9.55 can be rewritten as [Adams, 1966]

$$\frac{G_{st}}{G} = \frac{2}{1 + E/[4E_{st}(1 + \nu)]} \qquad (9.56)$$

Steel	σ_y (ksi)	ϵ_{st} (in./in.)	Average static values of		
				E_{st2} (ksi)	
			Tension	Compression	
A7	34.1	0.0177	570*	−700*	
A36	37.1	0.0203	450	—	
A441(50)	53.3	0.0183	650	810	
A572(65)	62.1	0.0186	550	820	

*Value determined by a method that approximates to E_{st2}.

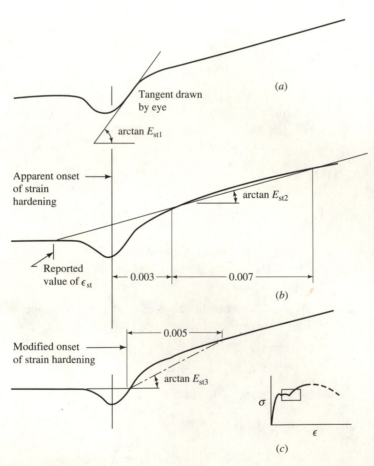

FIGURE 9.34
Various methods used in determining E_{st} [ASCE–WRC, 1971].

With $G = 11,200$ ksi, $E = 29,000$ ksi, $E_{st} = 800$ ksi (Fig. 9.33), and $\nu = 0.3$, Eq. 9.56 yields $G_{st} = 2810$ ksi. Substitution of the rounded-off value of $E_{st} = 2800$ ksi (as suggested in ASCE–WRC [1971]) in Eq. 9.54 yields

$$\frac{b'}{t} = \sqrt{\frac{2800}{F_y}} = \frac{52.915}{\sqrt{F_{y,\text{ksi}}}} = \frac{1673}{\sqrt{F_{y,\text{ psi}}}} \tag{9.57}$$

AASHTO 10.34.2.2.2 gives the following value of the b'/t ratio in terms of the bending stress f_b considered as the limit of the critical stress:

$$\frac{b'}{t} = \frac{1625}{\sqrt{f_{b,\text{psi}}}} \tag{9.58}$$

As pointed out by Lay [1965], Eq. 9.58 can also be obtained from the following equation as suggested by Bleich [1956]:

$$P = \frac{G_{st}K_T}{r_0^2} \tag{9.59}$$

where $P = btF_y$
$K_T = \frac{1}{3}bt^3$ and
r_0^2 = torsional buckling parameter
$= b^2/12$

Substitution of these values in Eq. 9.59 results in

$$\frac{b}{t} = 2\sqrt{\frac{G_{st}}{F_y}} \quad \text{or} \quad \frac{b'}{t} = \sqrt{\frac{G_{st}}{F_y}} \tag{9.60}$$

Lay's solution for the critical flange force that considers torsional buckling is [Lay, 1965, p. 109, Eq. 27]

$$P = \frac{1}{r_0^2}\left[G'K_T + \left(\frac{n\pi}{L}\right)^2 E'I_w + k\left(\frac{L}{n\pi}\right)^2\right] \tag{9.61}$$

where $P = \sigma_{cr}bt$
σ_{cr} = critical flange stress
n = an integer
L/n = half-wavelength of the buckle
K_T = St. Venant torsion constant
$= \frac{1}{3}bt^3$
E' = Young's modulus in the yielded zone
$= E_{st}$
k = spring constant of rotational spring representing torsional resistance of the web

$$K_T = \text{St. Venant torsion constant} = \frac{1}{3}bt^3 \tag{9.62}$$

and, from thick plate considerations,

$$I_w = \text{warping constant} = \frac{7}{16}\left(\frac{b^3 t^3}{144}\right) \tag{9.63}$$

For analytical simplicity, it is assumed that the web is fully yielded under the longitudinal stresses. This, however, is only approximately correct because the condition of full plasticity cannot be achieved in reality [Lay, 1965, p. 109]. Under this condition, in the derivation of G', the shear stress could be replaced by any transverse stress without altering the solution. Under this assumption, k may be estimated from Eq. 9.64 in which the relationship $t_w(d - 2t) = A_w$ (area of web) has been substituted [Lay, 1965]:

$$
\begin{aligned}
k &= \left(\frac{4G'}{d - 2t}\right)\frac{t_w^3}{12} \\[2mm]
&= \frac{G' t_w^3}{3(d - 2t)} \\[2mm]
&= \frac{G_{st} t_w^4}{3 t_w(d - 2t)} \\[2mm]
&= \frac{G_{st} t_w^4}{3 A_w}
\end{aligned} \tag{9.64}
$$

Substitution in Eq. 9.64 for G_{st} from Eq. 9.56 yields

$$k = \frac{2G}{1 + E/[4E_{st}(1 + \nu)]}\left(\frac{t_w^4}{3A_w}\right) \tag{9.65}$$

from which one obtains

$$
\begin{aligned}
\frac{1}{k} &= \left[\frac{1 + E/[4E_{st}(1 + \nu)]}{2G}\right]\left(\frac{3A_w}{t_w^4}\right) \\[2mm]
&= \left[\frac{4E_{st}(1 + \nu) + E}{4E_{st} \times 2G(1 + \nu)}\right]\left(\frac{3A_w}{t_w^4}\right)
\end{aligned} \tag{9.66}
$$

Substitution of $2G(1 + \nu) = E$ in Eq. 9.66 yields

$$
\begin{aligned}
\frac{1}{k} &= \left[\frac{4E_{st}(1 + \nu) + E}{4E_{st}E}\right]\left(\frac{3A_w}{t_w^4}\right) \\[2mm]
&= \frac{1}{E_{st}}\left[\frac{1 + \nu}{(E/E_{st})} + \frac{1}{4}\right]\left(\frac{3A_w}{t_w^4}\right)
\end{aligned} \tag{9.67}
$$

In Eq. 9.61, the value of n, an integer, is that value which gives the minimum value of $P = bt\sigma_y$. A first estimate of n, assuming that it varies continuously, can be found by minimizing Eq. 9.61 with respect to n so that $\partial P/\partial n = 0$. Partial differentiation of Eq. 9.61 yields

$$2n\frac{\pi^2}{L^2}E'I_w - \frac{2kL^2}{\pi^2 n^3} = 0$$

$$\left(\frac{L}{n\pi}\right)^4 = \frac{E'I_w}{k} \tag{9.68}$$

$$\frac{L}{n\pi} = \sqrt[4]{\frac{E'I_w}{k}}$$

Equation 9.68 can be further simplified by substituting for I_w and $1/k$ from Eq. 9.63 and Eq. 9.67, respectively:

$$\frac{L}{n\pi} = \left[E_{st}\frac{7}{16}\left(\frac{b^3 t^3}{144}\right)\frac{1}{E_{st}}\left(\frac{1+\nu}{E/E_{st}} + \frac{1}{4}\right)\left(\frac{3A_w}{t_w^4}\right)\right]^{1/4}$$

$$= \frac{b}{4}\left[\frac{t}{t_w}\left(\frac{A_w}{A_f}\right)^{1/4}\right]\left[\frac{7}{3}\left(\frac{1+\nu}{E/E_{st}} + \frac{1}{4}\right)\right]^{1/4} \tag{9.69}$$

Note that $bt = A_f$ (area of flange) has been substituted in deriving Eq. 9.69. With $\nu = 0.3$, $E = 29,000$ ksi, and $E_{st} = 800$ ksi, the second parenthetical expression in Eq. 9.69 yields

$$\frac{1+\nu}{E/E_{st}} = \frac{1+0.3}{(29,000/800)} = 0.036 \tag{9.70}$$

which is very small and may be neglected to get an approximate value of the wavelength of the buckle. Thus, Eq. 9.69 can be closely approximated by

$$\frac{L}{nb} = \frac{\pi}{4}\left[\frac{t}{t_w}\left(\frac{A_w}{A_f}\right)^{1/4}\right]\left(\frac{7}{12}\right)^{1/4}$$

$$= \frac{\pi t}{4t_w}\left(\frac{7A_w}{12A_f}\right)^{1/4} \tag{9.71}$$

$$= 0.713\left(\frac{t}{t_w}\right)\left(\frac{A_w}{A_f}\right)^{1/4}$$

Equation 9.71 gives the half-wavelength of the local buckle and is basic to determining the onset of local buckling in beams and beam-columns under moment gradient as discussed later. Measurements of L/nb by Haaijer [1957] from tests on nine 8-in.-wide and 10-in.-wide flange beams gave values that were in close agreement to those predicted by Eq. 9.71 [Lay, 1965, p. 110, Table 1].

Substitution of Eq. 9.68 in Eq. 9.61 yields

$$P = \frac{1}{r_0^2}\left[G'K_T + \left(\sqrt{\frac{k}{E'I_w}}\right)E'I_w + k\sqrt{\frac{E'I_w}{k}}\right]$$

$$= \frac{1}{r_0^2}\left[G'K_T + 2\sqrt{kE'I_w}\right] \tag{9.72}$$

Substitution in Eq. 9.72 of $P = bt\sigma_y$, $h = E/E_{st}$, values of K_T (as previously defined), and k and I_w (from Eq. 9.62 and Eq. 9.63, respectively) yields

$$\left(\frac{b}{2t}\right)^2 = \frac{1}{\sigma_y}\left[G' + 0.381\left(\frac{E}{h}\right)\left(\frac{t_w}{t}\right)^2 \sqrt{\frac{A_f}{A_w}}\right] \tag{9.73}$$

Introducing in Eq. 9.73 the notation $\sigma_y = F_y$ and $G' = G_{st}$, we obtain

$$\frac{b}{t} = 2\sqrt{\frac{G_{st}}{F_y} + 0.381\left(\frac{E_{st}}{E}\right)\left(\frac{t_w}{t}\right)^2\left(\frac{A_f}{A_w}\right)^{1/2}} \tag{9.74}$$

In Eq. 9.74, the first term under the radical sign, G_{st}/F_y, is the same as in Eq. 9.54, and the second term represents the contribution of the restraint to torsional buckling offered by the web. According to Lay, local buckling commences at the onset of strain-hardening when the b/t ratio is equal to the limiting ratio given by Eq. 9.74 if a length of flange equal to the full wavelength has become yielded. Lay [1965, p. 112] estimated that, for most sections, the increase in the allowable ratio resulting from web restraint fell between 2 percent and 3.2 percent and was therefore insignificant. Thus, if the second term under the radical sign in Eq. 9.74 is neglected,

$$\frac{b'}{t} = \frac{b}{2t} \tag{9.75}$$
$$= \sqrt{\frac{G_{st}}{F_y}}$$

On the other hand, if an average value of the second term is taken as 3 percent of the first term (as suggested in ASCE–WRC [1971]), Eq. 9.74 can be written as

$$\frac{b}{t} = 2\sqrt{\frac{1.03G_{st}}{F_y}} \tag{9.76}$$

Substitution for G_{st} in Eq. 9.76 from Eq. 9.56 yields

$$\frac{b}{t} = 2\sqrt{\frac{2.06G}{F_y[1 + E/[4E_{st}(1 + \nu)]]}} \tag{9.77}$$

Substituting $E = 29{,}000$ ksi and $G = 11{,}200$ ksi so that $G = E/2.6$ and $\nu = 0.3$, Eq. 9.77 is simplified to

$$\frac{b}{t} = \frac{1.78}{\sqrt{F_y/E}}\sqrt{\frac{1}{1 + E/5.2E_{st}}} \tag{9.78}$$

Lay and Galambos [1964, 1967] have theorized that local buckling of wide-flange beams would normally occur when they are loaded into the inelastic range with a bending moment that varies along the length of the beam, a condition referred to as the *moment gradient.* Under this condition of loading, the stress in the flange would increase from F_y at the commencement of yielding (corresponding to $M_y = F_y S$) to a greater stress corresponding to the maximum moment M_0 when the material is in the strain-hardening range. This loading condition for a centrally loaded beam is shown in Fig. 9.35.

According to Lay and Galambos [1964], the maximum expected value of M_0 resulting from strain-hardening is taken as [Lay, 1965, Eq. 39]

$$M_0 = \frac{1}{2}\left(1 + \frac{\sigma_u}{\sigma_y}\right)M_p \tag{9.79}$$

where σ_u = the ultimate strength of steel
       M_p = plastic moment capacity

The average stress, σ_y^*, in the locally buckled segment of the flange is taken as [Lay, 1965, Eq. 40]

$$\sigma_y^* = \frac{1}{4}\left(3 + \frac{\sigma_u}{\sigma_y}\right)\sigma_y$$

$$= \frac{1}{4}\left(3 + \frac{F_u}{F_y}\right) \tag{9.80}$$

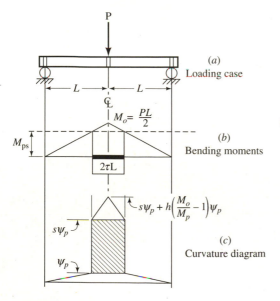

(a) Loading case

(b) Bending moments

$M_o = \dfrac{PL}{2}$

$2\tau L$

$-s\psi_p + h\left(\dfrac{M_o}{M_p} - 1\right)\psi_p$

$s\psi_p$

ψ_p

(c) Curvature diagram

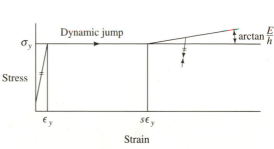

Discontinuous stress-strain curve

τ = ratio of yielded length of span to total length
s = ratio of strain at strain hardening to yield strain
$h = \dfrac{E}{E_{st}}$

FIGURE 9.35
Beam under moment gradient [Lay and Galambos, 1967].

Substitution of σ_y^* from Eq. 9.80 in Eq. 9.76 yields

$$\frac{b}{t} = \frac{1.78}{\sqrt{F_y/E}} \sqrt{\frac{1}{\frac{1}{4}(3 + F_u/F_y)(1 + E/5.2E_{\text{st}})}}$$

$$= 3.56 \sqrt{\frac{E}{F_y}} \left(\sqrt{\frac{1}{(3 + F_u/F_y)(1 + E/5.2E_{\text{st}})}} \right) \tag{9.81}$$

With $E_{\text{st}} = 800$ ksi and $E = 29{,}000$ ksi, Eq. 9.81 gives the following b/t ratios:

$$\text{A36 steel, } F_y = 36 \text{ ksi, } F_u = 58 \text{ ksi, } \frac{b}{t} = \frac{3162}{\sqrt{f_y}}$$

$$\text{A572(50) steel, } F_y = 50 \text{ ksi, } F_u = 65 \text{ ksi, } \frac{b}{t} = \frac{3275}{\sqrt{F_y}} \tag{9.82}$$

AASHTO 10.34.2.1.3 specifies b/t ratios in terms of the calculated maximum compressive bending stress f_b:

$$\frac{b}{t} = \frac{3250}{\sqrt{f_{b,\text{psi}}}} \tag{9.83}$$

The compression flange can be assumed as a long plate hinged at the flange-web juncture that is subjected to pure uniform edge compression at its ends (Fig. 9.36). The requirement to achieve yield stress without local buckling (i.e., sudden movement of flange into the web) of the compression flange is

$$F_{\text{cr}} = \frac{k\pi^2 E}{12(1 - \nu^2)(b/t)^2} \geq F_y \tag{9.84}$$

For design purposes, Eq. 9.84 can be rearranged to read

$$\frac{b}{t} \leq \sqrt{\frac{k\pi^2 E}{12(1 - \nu^2)F_{\text{cr}}}} \tag{9.85}$$

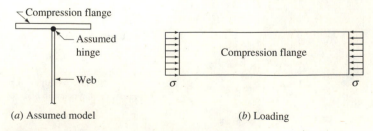

(a) Assumed model

(b) Loading

FIGURE 9.36
Model of the compression flange of a W-beam.

Substituting $E = 29 \times 10^6$ psi, $\nu = 0.3$, and limiting F_{cr} to F_y, Eq. 9.85 can be expressed as

$$\frac{b}{t} \leq 5120 \sqrt{\frac{k}{F_{y,\text{psi}}}} \tag{9.86}$$

Assuming 1.25 as a factor of safety under the service load design criteria so that $F_{cr} = 1.25 f_b$ and $k = 0.425$ for the hinged condition, Eq. 9.85 becomes

$$\frac{b}{t} = \frac{2985}{\sqrt{f_{b,\text{psi}}}} \tag{9.87}$$

AASHTO 10.34.2.1.3 permits

$$\frac{b}{t} = \frac{3250}{\sqrt{f_{b,\text{psi}}}} \not> 24 \tag{9.88}$$

An upper limit of 24 is obtained by substituting $f_b = 0.55 F_y = 18,000$ psi in Eq. 9.88. It is instructive to note that the ultimate load of a test girder built with a b/t ratio $= 24$ exceeded the computed flange buckling stress by about 10 percent as reported by Basler and Thurlimann [1961]. However, the attainment of the ultimate load was accompanied by large distortions that impaired the serviceability of the girder. It may be noted that most slender flanged U.S. rolled section is W6 $\times$ 15, which has a b/t ratio of only 23.

The AASHTO–LRFD 6.10.5.2.3C [AASHTO, 1994] specifies the width-thickness ratio for the compression flange as

$$\frac{b_f}{2t_f} \leq 0.382 \sqrt{\frac{E}{F_{yc}}} \tag{9.89}$$

where b_f = width of the compression flange
$\qquad F_{yc}$ = specified minimum yield strength of the compression flange

Equation 9.89 has been presented somewhat differently in the context of load factor design in the 1992 AASHTO specifications. Substitution of $E = 29 \times 10^6$ psi in Eq. 9.89 results in

$$\frac{b_f}{2t_f} \leq \frac{2057}{\sqrt{F_y}} \tag{9.90}$$

The numerator in Eq. 9.90 has been rounded off to 2055, resulting in AASHTO Eq. 10.92 [AASHTO, 1992] specified for the load factor design:

$$\frac{b'}{t} \leq \frac{2055}{\sqrt{F_{y,\text{psi}}}} \tag{9.91}$$

where b' = width of the projecting element
$\qquad t$ = flange thickness

In general, in designing the flange of a plate girder, a designer is faced with a paradox. The compression flange should be made as wide as possible to increase its lateral stability and lateral buckling strength. However, if this is done in excess, torsional buckling of the flange plate will replace the lateral buckling at a lower ultimate stress [Basler and Thurlimann, 1961].

9.5.2.4 Limiting slenderness ratios for the flange plates: AASHTO specifications [AASHTO, 1992]

Replacing σ_c with F_{cr}, Eq. 9.35 can be conveniently written as

$$\left(\frac{b}{t}\right)^2 = k\frac{\pi^2 E}{12(1 - \nu^2)F_{cr}} \tag{9.92}$$

Substitution of $\nu = 0.3$ and $k = 0.425$ (for the boundary condition defined as one edge simply supported and the other free, as applied to the half flange width) in Eq. 9.92 yields

$$\frac{b}{t} = 0.62\sqrt{\frac{E}{F_{cr}}} \tag{9.93}$$

Similarly, for the case of both edges simply supported, $k = 4$, which, when substituted in Eq. 9.92, yields

$$\frac{b}{t} = 1.901\sqrt{\frac{E}{F_{cr}}} \tag{9.94}$$

In the AASHTO–LRFD specifications [AASHTO, 1994], with F_y as the upper limit for the buckling stress F_{cr}, the requirement for the b/t ratio is specified as

$$\frac{b}{t} \leq k\sqrt{\frac{E}{F_y}} \tag{9.95}$$

Values of k for use in conjunction with Eq. 9.95 are shown in Table 9.3. These values have been modified to reflect the effects of residual stresses, initial imperfections, and actual—as opposed to ideal—support conditions.

For the service load design, the requirements for b/t ratios for flanges of plate girders are given by Eqs. 9.96, 9.97, and 9.98 (AASHTO 10.34.2, Eqs. 10.19, 10.20, and 10.21) [AASHTO, 1992]. For bolted girders, the width-to-thickness ratio refers to the outstanding leg of the flange angles in compression.

$$\text{For welded girders, } \frac{b}{t} = \frac{3250}{\sqrt{f_{b,\text{psi}}}} \not> 24 \tag{9.96}$$

$$\text{For bolted girders, } \frac{b'}{t} = \frac{1625}{\sqrt{f_{b,\text{psi}}}} \not> 12 \tag{9.97}$$

$$\text{For composite girders, } \frac{b}{t} = \frac{3860}{\sqrt{f_{\text{dl, psi}}}} \tag{9.98}$$

where b = width of the flange plate in compression
  b' = width of the outstanding leg of the angle used for compression flange of the bolted girder

TABLE 9.3
Limiting width-thickness ratios (AASHTO–LRFD, 1994)

Plates supported along one edge	k	b
Flanges and projecting legs or plates	0.56	Half-width of I-sections
		Full-flange width of channels
		Distance between free edge and first line of bolts or welds in plates
		Full width of an outstanding leg for pairs of angles in continuous contact
Stems of rolled T	0.75	Full-depth of T
Other projecting elements	0.45	Full-width of outstanding leg for single-angle strut or double-angle strut with separator
		Full projecting width for others

Plates supported along two edges	k	b
Box flanges and cover plates	1.40	Clear distance between webs minus inside corner radius on each side for box flanges
		Distance between lines of welds or bolts for flange cover plates
Webs and other plate elements	1.49	Clear distance between flanges minus fillet radii for webs of rolled beams
		Clear distance between edge supports for all others
Perforated cover plates		Clear distance between edge supports

t = thickness of flange (or the outstanding leg of angle)
f_b = calculated maximum bending stress
f_{dl} = top flange compressive stress due to noncomposite dead load

9.5.3 Buckling of Web

9.5.3.1 Limiting D/t ratios for web

The possibility of web buckling arises in a transversely loaded plate girder because one of the principal stresses in the web is compressive (since the web is partly in tension).

Although buckling of the web of a plate girder does not imply an immediate failure of the girder, the geometric parameters of the web—the depth D between flanges, the thickness t_w, and the spacing d between the transverse stiffeners (when used)—are so chosen that this possibility is eliminated. According to the SSRC Guide [Galambos, 1988, p. 190], four limiting values of the web slenderness (D/t_w) must be established to preclude the possibility of bend buckling:

1. D/t_w limiting values for a web without a longitudinal stiffener
2. D/t_w limiting values for a web with a longitudinal stiffener
3. D/t_w limiting values for a web without transverse stiffeners
4. D/t_w limiting values for a web with transverse stiffeners

From the perspective of load and resistance factor design, these limits can be chosen so that the limiting values of buckling stresses (flexural or shear) are not exceeded. From the service load design perspective, these limits are so chosen that a desired factor of safety is provided. The limiting values of the D/t_w values from both perspectives are discussed in the following paragraphs.

Denoting the depth of web as D, Eq. 9.92 can be expressed as

$$F_{cr} = k \frac{\pi^2 E}{12(1 - \nu^2)} \left(\frac{t_w}{D} \right)^2 \tag{9.99}$$

Figure 9.37 shows a typical buckling pattern of a web initiated by bending of a plate girder (hence the term *bend buckling*), which is somewhat different than the buckling of uniformly edge-compressed plates in that the out-of-plane deformation in the tensile zone of the web is zero (shown by $w = 0$). Beam webs bend buckle in a single half-wave transversely (i.e., depthwise) and in multiple half-waves longitudinally (i.e., lengthwise).

Critical stress for a plate in bending in the plane of the plate can be calculated from Eq. 9.34 using the bend-buckling coefficient k_b instead of k. The mathematical treatment of the problem of buckling of simply supported plates under combined

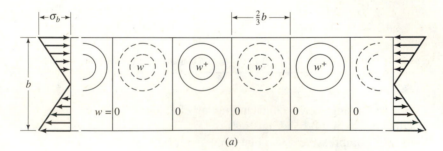

(a)

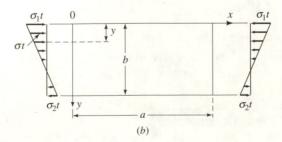

(b)

FIGURE 9.37
Bend buckling of a web: (*a*) buckled configuration; (*b*) general state of stress distribution in web.

bending and shear,[23] and the method of determining k_b, has been given by Timoshenko [1961, pp. 373–379]. The value of k_b, similar to that of k in Eq. 9.34, depends on the boundary conditions at the web-flange junctures and the aspect ratio. As shown in Fig. 9.37, the web plate buckles in multiple waves, the lengths of which approach $\frac{2}{3}b$ for a simply supported plate. Therefore, the value of k_b is much higher than the buckling coefficients k in other loading cases. Values of k_b for plates simply supported along the loaded edges, and having various degrees of restraints along the two unloaded edges, as obtained by Shuette and McCulloch [1947], are shown in Fig. 9.38. Each curve represents a specific boundary condition, varying from simply supported edges (defined by $\epsilon = 0$) to fixed or clamped edges (defined by $\epsilon = \infty$). ϵ is defined as the ratio of edge moment to edge slope.

Referring to Fig. 9.37(b), compressive stress at distance y from the upper edge of the web can be expressed as [Bleich, 1952, p. 399]

$$\sigma = \sigma_1 \left(1 - \frac{\xi y}{b}\right) \tag{9.100}$$

where

$$\xi = \frac{\sigma_1 - \sigma_2}{\sigma_1} \tag{9.101}$$

In Eq. 9.100, the parameter ξ (xi) is introduced to express a relationship between the compressive stress σ_1 and tensile stress σ_2 at the opposite edges of the web due to imposed loads. $\xi = 0$ indicates a uniformly distributed compressive stress, whereas $\xi = 2$ indicates the case of pure bending ($\sigma_1 = -\sigma_2$). The intermediate values, $0 < \xi < 2$, indicate combined bending and compression. The condition $\xi > 2$ indicates combined bending and tension. Table 9.4 gives the plate buckling factors k_b for simply supported plates in nonuniform longitudinal compression for a few values of ξ (i.e., types of stress distribution) and the aspect ratio α ($= a/b$) [Bleich, 1952].

Figure 9.38 and Table 9.4 show that for the case of pure bending of simply supported rectangular plates, $k_{min} = 23.9$, which occurs at $\alpha = \frac{2}{3}$ for $\xi = 2$. It follows, therefore, that a very long plate buckles in half-waves of length $2b/3$ in the case of pure bending. Table 9.4 shows also that $k_{min} = 4$, which occurs at $\alpha = 1$ for $\xi = 0$, a case of pure compression (discussed earlier).

The web of a plate girder is usually assumed hinged at its junctures with flanges so that $k_b = 23.9$. Substitution of $k = k_b = 23.9$ as a limiting value, $E = 30,000$ ksi, and $\nu = 0.3$ in Eq. 9.34 yields

$$F_{b,cr} = \frac{648,032}{(D/t_w)^2} \approx \frac{650,000}{(D/t_w)^2} \text{ ksi} \tag{9.102}$$

Tests have indicated that because of the postbuckling strength of the web, a plate girder will not fail on buckling of the web. Under service load design criteria, this

---

[23]The case of pure bending is a special case of this general loading condition.

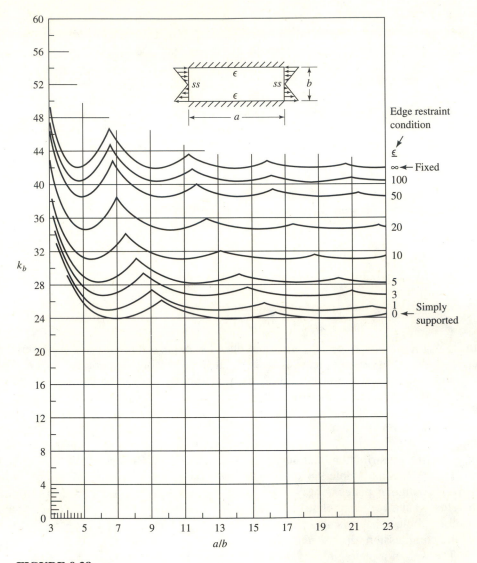

FIGURE 9.38
Bend-buckling coefficients, k_b, as a function of aspect ratios, for rectangular plates having various degrees of end restraints [Gerard, 1962, p. 63].

postbuckling strength is utilized by adopting limiting slenderness ratios that inherently provide a low factor of safety (1.25) for bending stress, i.e., $F_{cr} = 1.25 F_b$ [SSRC, 1988]. Substituting for F_{cr} in Eq. 9.102, we obtain the limiting D/t_w ratio:

$$1.25 F_b = \frac{650,000}{(D/t_w)^2}$$

TABLE 9.4
Plate buckling factors k for simply supported plates in nonuniform compression [Bleich, 1952]

Type of stress distribution	$\alpha = a/b$							
	0.4	0.5	0.6	0.667	0.75	0.8	1.0	1.5
$\sigma_2 = -\sigma_1$	29.1	25.6	24.1	23.9	24.1	24.4	25.6	24.1
$\sigma_2 = -\dfrac{2\sigma_1}{3}$	23.6	...	17.7	...	15.7	16.4	16.9	15.7
$\sigma_2 = -\dfrac{\sigma_1}{3}$	18.7	...	12.9	...	11.5	11.2	11.0	11.5
$\sigma_2 = 0$	15.1	...	9.7	...	8.4	8.1	7.8	8.4
$\sigma_2 = \dfrac{\sigma_1}{3}$	10.8	...	7.1	...	6.1	6.0	5.8	6.1
$\sigma_2 = \sigma_1$	8.4	...	5.2	...	4.3	4.2	4.0	4.3

which gives

$$\frac{d}{t_w} = \sqrt{\frac{650{,}000}{1.25 F_{b,\text{ksi}}}} = \frac{22{,}800}{\sqrt{f_{b,\text{psi}}}} \tag{9.103}$$

Equation 9.103 is the same as AASHTO Eq. 10.23 with the numerator rounded off to 23,000 and expressed as

$$t_w = \frac{D\sqrt{f_{b,\text{psi}}}}{23{,}000} \tag{9.104}$$

Note that in Eq. 104, f_b = calculated bending stress.

A minimum value of the D/t_w ratio can be calculated on the basis of certain minimum values of F_{cr} and E. For example, according to Timoshenko and Gere [1961, pp. 436–437], for a steel with $F_y = 34{,}000$ psi, $f_b = 16{,}000$ psi, $E = 30 \times 10^6$, and $\nu = 0.3$, and a factor of safety of 1.5 for buckling stress has been used. It has been assumed that the maximum bending stress of 16,000 psi is obtained by deducting 15 percent of the area for the rivet holes. Substitution of these values in Eq. 9.99 yields

$$\frac{D}{t_w} = \sqrt{23.9\,\frac{\pi^2 E}{12(1 - \nu^2)(16{,}000)(0.85)(1.5)}} = 180 \tag{9.105}$$

Since, according to AASHTO [1992], $F_b = 0.55F_y$ and the minimum value of $F_y = 33$ ksi (used for the A7 steel girders used in the Lehigh University tests), Eq. 9.104 gives the maximun value of D/t_w for webs as specified in AASHTO 10.34.3.1:

$$\left(\frac{D}{t_w}\right)_{max} = \frac{23,000}{\sqrt{0.55 \times 33,000}} = 170.7 \approx 170 \tag{9.106}$$

For webs with one longitudinal stiffener at $D/5$ from the compression flange, it has been shown that $k = 129$ [Bleich, 1952]. Substituting $k = 129$ instead of 23.9 in Eq. 9.99, one obtains

$$F_{b,cr} = \frac{3.5 \times 10^6}{(D/t_w)^2}$$

so that

$$1.25F_b = \frac{3.5 \times 10^6}{(D/t_w)^2}$$

which gives

$$\frac{D}{t_w} = \sqrt{\frac{3.5 \times 10^6}{1.25F_{b,psi}}} = \frac{52,915}{\sqrt{F_{b,psi}}} \tag{9.107}$$

However, AASHTO 10.34.3.1 limits the maximun D/t_w ratio for a web with one longitudinal stiffner as (AASHTO Eq. 10.24)

$$\left(\frac{d}{t_w}\right)_{max} = \frac{46,000}{\sqrt{F_{b,psi}}} \tag{9.108}$$

In general, for $F_y = 33$ ksi and $F_b = 0.55F_y$, Eq. 9.108 can be expressed to give the upper limit of the D/t_w ratio as (AASHTO 10.34.3.2.1)

$$\left(\frac{D}{t_w}\right)_{max} = \frac{46,000}{\sqrt{0.55 \times 33,000}} = 341 \approx 340 \tag{9.109}$$

9.5.3.2 Postbuckling bending strength of plate girder webs

Although the flexural stress distribution in the cross section of a plate girder under elastic conditions is linear as given by Navier-Bernoulli theory (or the conventional beam theory, i.e., $f = MC/I$), it is nonlinear when the girder reaches the state of first yielding. Both types of stress distribution are shown in Fig. 9.39.

Essentially, what happens is that as the extreme fibers of the compression flange reach the yield stress, the web experiences out-of-plane deformation (or lateral deflection). Because in all practical girders, webs are not perfectly plane, and in fact do possess some initial out-of-straightness characteristic (or waviness), the lateral deflection initiates at an early stage of loading and continues to increase with increases in loading. The lateral deflection increases rapidly as the flange flexural stress reaches the yield stress level. Consequently, the compressed portion of the web is unable to carry the stress predicted by the conventional beam theory (linear distribution), and the stress

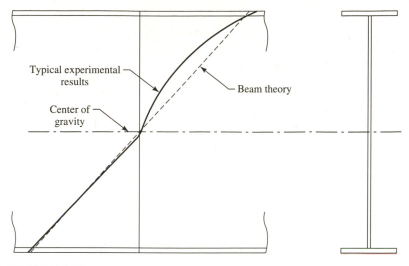

FIGURE 9.39
Theoretical and experimental flexural stress distribution in a plate girder at first yielding.

distribution becomes nonlinear, a behavior that has been amply demonstrated by tests [Basler et al., 1960; Basler and Thurlimann, 1961].

Furthermore, the flexural stress in the laterally deflected web is smaller than that predicted by the beam theory, and the stress in the flange is larger than that predicted by the beam theory. This redistribution of stresses led to the assumption that the contribution of the compressed portion of the web can be disregarded, except that of a small portion near its juncture with the compression flange, referred to as the *effective web*. Basler and Thurlimann [1961] have shown that the depth of this effective portion of the web can be taken as $30t_w$ from the extreme fibers of the compression flange, as shown in Fig. 9.40(*b*). Analytically, with the remainder of the web in compression disregarded, the compression flange, together with the effective web ($30t_w$), can be treated as an isolated column. Such a column has three degrees of freedom with respect to buckling: lateral, torsional, and vertical (Fig. 9.39(*c*)). This analytical model of the plate girder is referred to as the *Basler-Thurlimann* model. The buckling of the web is also accompanied by *vertical buckling* of the compression flange, as shown in Fig. 9.41, a photographic view of a Lehigh test girder [Basler et al., 1960].

When a girder is subjected to bending, the curvature of the flanges causes the web to experience compressive forces, which can be calculated from the free-body diagram of a bent portion of a plate girder. Referring to Fig. 9.42,

$$\text{Compressive force in flange } = \sigma_f A_f$$

From Hooke's law,

$$\text{Deformation over a length } dx \text{ of flange } = \epsilon_f \, dx$$

where ϵ_f = unit strain in compression flange. From the geometry of the bent girder, since $d\theta$ is very small,

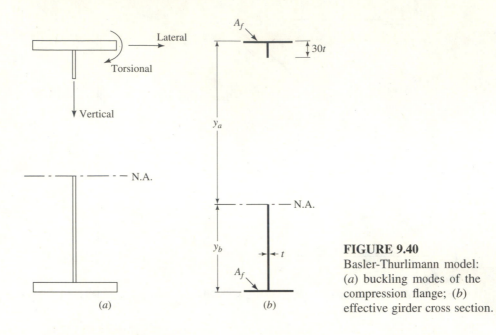

FIGURE 9.40
Basler-Thurlimann model:
(*a*) buckling modes of the
compression flange; (*b*)
effective girder cross section.

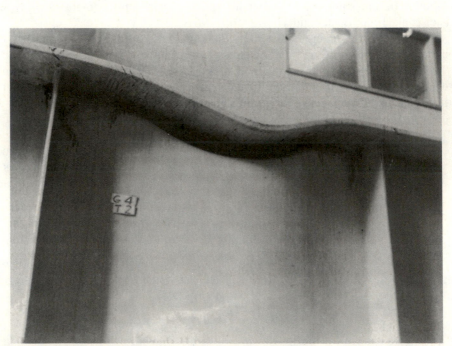

FIGURE 9.41
Vertical buckling of compression flange of a Lehigh test girder [Basler et al., 1960].

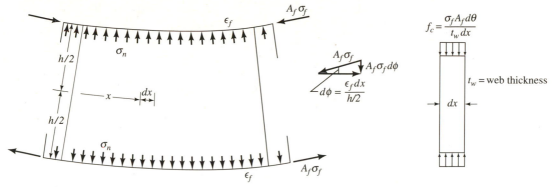

FIGURE 9.42
Forces due to vertical buckling of compression flange.

$$\frac{\epsilon_f \, dx}{h/2} = \tan(d\theta) = d\theta$$

so that

$$d\theta = \frac{2\epsilon_f}{h} \, dx \tag{9.110}$$

The vertical component of the compression flange force, F_c, is given by

$$F_c = \sigma_f A_f \sin(d\theta) = \sigma_f A_f \, d\theta \tag{9.111}$$

Substitution for $d\theta$ from Eq. 9.110 yields

$$F_c = \sigma_f A_f \frac{2\epsilon_f}{h} \, dx = \frac{2\sigma_f A_f \epsilon_f}{A_w} \tag{9.112}$$

The force F_c given by Eq. 9.112 is assumed to act on a hypothetical column (a vertical segment of web dx wide and t_w thick and simply supported at the flanges) of height h and cross-sectional area $t_w \, dx$. The compressive stress f_c in this hypothetical column is

$$f_c = \frac{F_c}{t_w \, dx} = \frac{2\sigma_f A_f \epsilon_f}{t_w h} = \frac{2\sigma_f A_f \epsilon_f}{A_w} \tag{9.113}$$

It was shown earlier that the critical buckling stress is given by Eq. 9.34. Substitution of $t = t_w$ (web thickness), $b = h$ (depth of web between flanges), and $k = 1$ (for the hypothetical column, a plate free along the edges parallel to loading and simply supported at its junctures with flanges) in Eq. 9.34 yields

$$F_{cr} = \frac{\pi^2 E}{12(1 - \nu^2)(h/t_w)^2} \tag{9.114}$$

Equating f_c from Eq. 9.113 to F_{cr} from Eq. 9.114 yields

$$\frac{2\sigma_f A_f \epsilon_f}{t_w h} = \frac{\pi^2 E}{12(1 - \nu^2)(h/t_w)^2} \tag{9.115}$$

from which

$$\frac{h}{t_w} = \sqrt{\frac{\pi^2 E}{24(1 - \nu^2)(A_w/A_f)(1/\sigma_f \epsilon_f)}} \qquad (9.116)$$

A few assumptions have been made to simplify the analysis. Basler and Thurli-mann [1961] rationalized that, in general, the ratio of web area to the flange area, A_w/A_f, for practical girders varies between 0.5 and 2.0. The flange stress σ_f must reach the flange yield stress F_{yf} to achieve full strength of the flange. They also assumed that the residual stress F_r in the flange varied linearly, maximum compressive at the flange tips to maximum tensile at the juncture with the web (Fig. 9.43). Combining the resid-ual stress with the yield stress caused by bending, the maximum stress in the flange is $F_r + F_{yf}$, and the corresponding strain (from Hooke's law) is

$$\epsilon_f = \frac{(F_r + F_{yf})}{E} \qquad (9.117)$$

Substitution for ϵ_f from Eq. 9.117 and $\sigma_f = F_{yf}$ in Eq. 9.116 yields

$$\frac{h}{t_w} = \frac{0.48E}{\sqrt{F_{yf}(F_{yf} + F_r)}} \qquad (9.118)$$

The value of the residual stress F_r is usually taken as 16.5 ksi, so that

$$\frac{h}{t_w} = \frac{0.48E}{\sqrt{F_{yf}(F_{yf} + 16.5)}} \qquad (9.119)$$

With $E = 29,000$ ksi, Eq. 9.119 yields

$$\frac{h}{t_w} = \frac{13,920}{\sqrt{F_{yf}(F_{yf} + 16.5)}} \qquad (9.120)$$

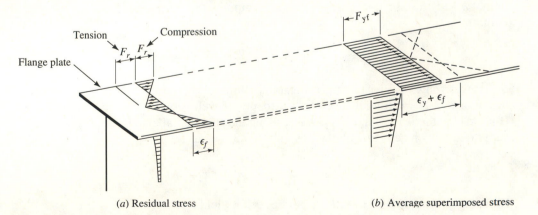

(a) Residual stress   (b) Average superimposed stress

FIGURE 9.43
Distribution of the residual stress in the flange.

AISC–LRFD [AISC, 1986] uses Eq. 9.120, with the numerator rounded off to 14,000, and expressed as

$$\frac{h}{t_w} = \frac{14{,}000}{\sqrt{F_{yf}(F_{yf} + 16.5)}} \qquad (9.121)$$

It was stated earlier that redistribution of flexural stresses from the compression portion of the web to the compression flange results in increased stress in the compression flange. From a design standpoint, this requires that the allowable stress in the flange be reduced somewhat.

Based on tests on A7 steel girders ($F_y = 33$ ksi), Basler and Thurlimann [1961] showed that the resistance moment of a plate girder depends on the web slenderness ratio h/t_w and the ratio of web to flange areas, A_w/A_f. Figure 9.44 shows, for various A_w/A_f ratios, the relationship between the ultimate moment (i.e., nominal moment) M_u (expressed nondimensionally on the y-axis in terms of M_y) and the h/t_w ratios. Basler and Thurlimann [1961] suggested the general equation for these lines in the following form:

$$\frac{M_u}{M_y} = 1 - C(\beta - \beta_0) \qquad (9.122)$$

where C = slope of any of the lines in Fig. 9.44
     $\beta = h/t_w$ ratio
     β_0 = intersecting abscissa of M_u/M_y = one and the same line

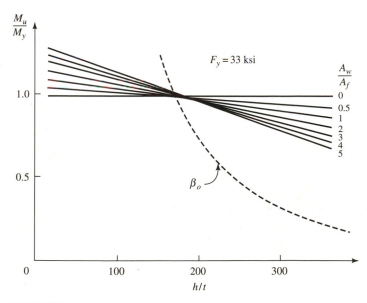

FIGURE 9.44
Influence of h/t_w and A_w/A_f on the nominal moment capacity of a plate girder [Cooper, 1967].

β_0 is defined as the slenderness ratio at which, according to the plate buckling theory, web buckling would occur when the applied moment reached M_y. Alternatively, β_0 can be defined as the highest slenderness ratio for which a linear stress distribution can be developed according to beam theory.

The general relationship between the ultimate moment and the web slenderness ratio can be summarized as follows [Cooper, 1967]:

$$\text{for} \quad \beta = \beta_A, \quad \frac{M_u}{M_y} = \frac{M_p}{M_y}$$

$$\text{for} \quad \beta_A \leq \beta \leq \beta_0, \quad \frac{M_p}{M_y} \geq \frac{M_u}{M_y}$$

$$\text{for} \quad \beta = \beta_0, \quad \frac{M_u}{M_y} = 1 \qquad (9.123)$$

$$\text{for} \quad \beta > \beta_0, \quad \frac{M_u}{M_y} < 1$$

where β_A = highest slenderness ratio for which the plastic moment M_p can be developed. As shown in Fig. 9.45, for F_{yf} = 33 ksi (= yield strength of the steel of test girders), $M_u = M_p$ at β_A = 53, $M_u = M_y$ at β_0 = 170, and $M_u = M_y$ of the reduced section of β_B = 360. The corresponding stress distributions are shown in circles in Fig. 9.45.

Because most girders are built in the range of $A_w/A_f < 2$, the value of coefficient C was suggested to be [Basler and Thurlimann, 1961]

$$C = 0.0005 \frac{A_w}{A_f} \qquad (9.124)$$

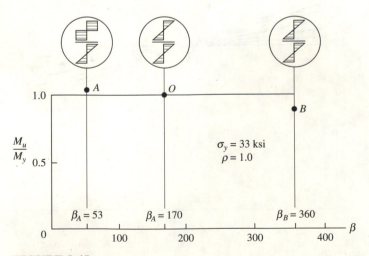

FIGURE 9.45
Nominal bending moment versus web slenderness ratio [Cooper, 1967].

which, when substituted in Eq. 9.122, yields

$$M_u = M_y \left[1 - 0.0005 \frac{A_w}{A_f} (\beta - \beta_0) \right] \tag{9.125}$$

Equation 9.125 can be expressed in terms of stresses by assuming that the nominal moment M_u can be computed on the basis of the section modulus concept, i.e., $M_u = F_u S_x$. Because, by definition, $M_y = F_y S_x$, Eq. 9.125 can be written as

$$F_u = F_y \left[1 - 0.0005 \frac{A_w}{A_f} (\beta - \beta_0) \right] \tag{9.126}$$

Equation 9.126 is written based on the assumption that the resistance moment of the flange will not be influenced by the flange instability. To incorporate the influence of lateral or torsional buckling, F_y in Eq. 9.126 can be replaced by F_{cr}:

$$F_u = F_{cr} \left[1 - 0.0005 \frac{A_w}{A_f} (\beta - \beta_0) \right] \tag{9.127}$$

Equation 9.127 is to be used only for the range of web slenderness ratios $\beta > \beta_0$, i.e., only in the postbuckling range where the linear flexural stress distribution would be invalid. In the postbuckling range, the computed bending stress is greater than the critical stress, F_{cr}. The value of β_0, i.e., the upper limit of the web slenderness ratio h/t_w beyond which Eq. 9.127 is to be used, depends on the boundary conditions of the web at its junctures with the flanges. As pointed out earlier, in the absence of any flange restraint, the plate buckling coefficient $k = 23.9$ [Timoshenko and Gere, 1961, p. 436] so that

$$F_b = F_{cr} = \frac{(23.9)\pi^2 E}{12(1 - \nu^2)(h/t_w)^2} \tag{9.128}$$

from which

$$\frac{h}{t_w} = 4.6 \sqrt{\frac{E}{F_{cr}}} \tag{9.129}$$

For the case of full flange restraint, $k = 39.6$ [Bleich, 1952, p. 402, Table 35], so that

$$F_b = F_{cr} = \frac{(39.6)\pi^2 E}{12(1 - \nu^2)(h/t_w)^2} \tag{9.130}$$

which yields

$$\frac{h}{t_w} = 6.0 \sqrt{\frac{E}{F_{cr}}} \tag{9.131}$$

However, tests on plate girders [Basler and Thurlimann, 1961] indicated that the deformation of the web of a plate girder is restrained to some degree by the flanges and is considerably smaller than would be expected for a simply supported plate. Conservatively speaking, the restraint provided by flanges in welded girders increases the theoretical buckling load by about 30 percent [Vincent, 1969]. Thus, assuming a condition of partial restraint in practical girders, Basler and Thurlimann [1961] suggested an intermediate value of h/t_w (or β_0):

$$\beta_0 = 5.7 \sqrt{\frac{E}{F_{cr}}} \qquad (9.132)$$

which gives $\beta_0 = 170$ when $F_y = 33$ ksi. Substitution for β_0 from Eq. 9.132 in Eq. 9.127 yields

$$F_u = F_y \left[1 - 0.0005 \frac{A_w}{A_f} \left(\frac{h}{t_w} \beta - 5.7 \sqrt{\frac{E}{F_{cr}}} \right) \right] \qquad (9.133)$$

Or, substituting $E = 29{,}000$ ksi in Eq. 9.133, one obtains

$$F_u = F_y \left[1 - 0.0005 \frac{A_w}{A_f} \left(\frac{h}{t_w} - \frac{970}{\sqrt{F_{cr}}} \right) \right] \qquad (9.134)$$

Note that the bracketed term in Eq. 9.134 is the same as the bending stress reduction parameter for a plate girder, R_{PG}, in AISC–LRFD Eq. A-G2-3 (Appendix G) [AISC, 1986] and may be considered as a factor to account for the reduced resistance moment of web due to bend buckling as a result of being "slender."

Equation 9.134 can be applied for service load design by limiting F_{cr} to $F_y = 1.65F_b$ and by dividing both F_u and F_y by the factor of safety 1.65. Expressing $F_u/1.65 = F'_b$, and $F_y/1.65 = 0.6F_y$ = maximum allowable bending stress F_b (AISC specifications), Eq. 9.134 can be expressed as

$$\begin{aligned} F'_b &= 0.6M_y \left[1 - 0005 \frac{A_w}{A_f} \left(\frac{h}{t_w} - \frac{970}{\sqrt{1.65F_b}} \right) \right] \\ &= F_b \left[1 - 0.0005 \frac{A_w}{A_f} \left(\frac{h}{t_w} - \frac{760}{\sqrt{F_b}} \right) \right] \end{aligned} \qquad (9.135)$$

Equation 9.135 is AISC–ASD Eq. G2-1 [AISC, 1989], in which the value of the bending stress reduction parameter R_{PG} is given by the bracketed term. Philosophically, Eq. 9.135 states that the more slender the web, the larger will be the reduction in the contribution of the web to the maximum strength of the girder.

In plate girders for bridges, longitudinal stiffeners are often used in conjunction with a slender web to increase the nominal moment capacity. For a web (in pure bending) reinforced by a longitudinal stiffener located at $h/5$ from the compression edge of the plate, Dubas [1948] has shown that the value of k can be taken as 129 [Bleich, 1952, p. 423]. The critical stress for such a plate can be calculated from Eq. 9.34 by substituting $E = 29{,}000$ ksi and $\nu = 0.3$:

$$F_{cr} = \frac{3{,}381{,}150}{(h/t)^2} \qquad (9.136)$$

Assuming $F_{cr} = F_y = 36$ ksi, Eq. 9.136 yields

$$\frac{h}{t} = \sqrt{\frac{3,381,150}{36}} = 306 \tag{9.137}$$

which is shown by point B in Fig. 9.45. From this plot, one may observe that plate girders with large h/t_w ratios, but without a longitudinal stiffener, can develop almost as much resistance moment as the same girder with a longitudinal stiffener, leading to the conclusion that a longitudinal stiffener offers no or little advantage. However, tests by various researchers, such as Yen and Mueller [1966] and Lew and Toprac [1967], have shown that the fatigue life of longitudinally unstiffened girders with large h/t_w ratios is shorter than that of the stiffened girders. Their test results are summarized in Fig. 9.46, which shows that all plate girders with $D/t_w < 200$ had relatively flat web plate and survived 2,000,000 or more cycles. According to Mueller and Yen [1968], several girders with $D/t_w > 200$ suffered fatigue failure at less than 2,000,000 cycles due to excessive lateral web deflection. Because fatigue is not a concern in buildings (since loads are static), no provision is made to reflect this behavior in the AISC specifications. But, on account of moving loads, fatigue *is* a (paramount) design factor for bridges. Consequently, web slenderness for girders without longitudinal stiffeners must be limited to preclude the possibility of fatigue failure, and, to this end, $D/t_w = 200$ may be considered as a threshold value.

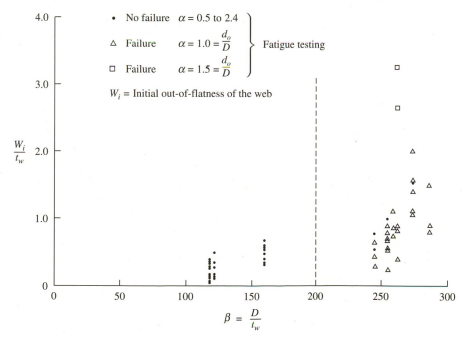

FIGURE 9.46
Fatigue tests of longitudinally stiffened girders [Vincent, 1969].

Using the AASHTO notations ($h = D$), and psi units, Eq. 9.135 can be written as [Vincent, 1969]

$$F = F_y \left[1 - 0.0005 \frac{A_w}{A_f} \left(\frac{h}{t_w} - \frac{31,000}{\sqrt{F_{y,\text{psi}}}} \right) \right] \qquad (9.138)$$

where the numerator 31,000 has been rounded off from the actual value of 30,674.

It is instructive to note that Eq. 9.138, which gives the reduced value of the permitted flange stress for girders with slender webs, would not have to be used if $D/t_w \leq 30{,}674/\sqrt{F_y}$ (actual value). Denoting the depth of the compression portion of the web as D_c ($= D/2$ for a monosymmetric girder), this limit can be expressed as

$$\frac{D_c}{t_w} \leq \frac{15,400}{\sqrt{F_y}} \qquad (9.139)$$

which is AASHTO Eq. 10.99 [AASHTO, 1992] for braced noncompact sections. Note that the numerator 15,400 has been rounded off from the actual value of $\frac{1}{2} \times 30{,}674 = 15{,}337$. Similarly, according to AASHTO 10.48.5.1, plate girders with transverse stiffeners, but without a longitudinal stiffener, must meet the requirement

$$\frac{D}{t_w} = \frac{36,500}{\sqrt{F_{y,\text{psi}}}} \qquad (9.140)$$

which is AASHTO Eq. 10.103 [AASHTO, 1992] for load factor design. For A36 steel, whose yield strength $F_y = 36$ ksi is the smallest of yield strengths of structural steels, Eq. 9.140 gives $D/t_w = 192 < 200$, the threshold value of the D/t_w ratio to preclude the possibility of fatigue failure. However, if a longitudinal stiffener is provided, located at $D/5$ from the compression edge of the web, the governing requirement is

$$\frac{D}{t_w} = \frac{73,000}{\sqrt{F_{y,\text{psi}}}} \qquad (9.141)$$

which is AASHTO Eq. 10.108 [AASHTO, 1992].

In general, the values of D/t_w ratios for webs of plate girders for highway bridges have been kept below the limit for which the reduced contribution of resistance moment of the web is not a consideration. Consequently, there is no formula similar to Eq. 9.135 in the AASHTO specifications.

9.5.4 Strength of Plate Girder Webs in Shear

9.5.4.1 Buckling of rectangular plates under the action of shearing stresses

As pointed out earlier, shear is seldom a determining factor in design of rolled beams because of their relatively thick webs. However, the relatively larger web slenderness ratio (h/t_w) used in designing a plate girder significantly influences its postbuckling strength and, thus, shear strength of web forms an important design parameter.

Theoretical expressions for the buckling strength of the web of a plate girder under shear are based on the assumption of a perfectly flat rectangular plate simply supported on all four edges. For analytical purposes, as before, a rectangular plate of length a, width b, and thickness t is considered. In a plate girder without any stiffeners, such a plate is represented by the web, which is assumed simply supported at its junctures with the flanges. In the case of a stiffened web, the assumed "simple support" boundary conditions are provided at the edges of the plate by the flanges or a flange and the longitudinal stiffener, and the two adjacent transverse stiffeners.

Figure 9.47 shows the stress distribution for the general case of a web under combined bending and shear. The plate is subjected to distributed shear forces $\tau_{xy}t$ along all edges, along with the longitudinal forces σt due to flexure. However, near the end of simply supported beams, flexural stresses are very small, and as a matter of simplification, may be neglected. The general problem of stability under combined bending and shear is discussed later. The stability of web under pure shear is discussed in this section.

It should be noted that the state of shear forces shown in Fig. 9.47 is approximate. It is known that the distribution of shear stresses along the vertical edges ($x = 0$ and $x = a$) is parabolic, and generally the shear stresses also vary along the longitudinal edges of the plate. Also, since in a practical plate girder the moment varies along the span, the assumption of σ_x as a constant longitudinal stress between $x = 0$ and $x = a$ has been made as a simplification for analytical purposes [Bleich, 1952].

Timoshenko is credited to be the first to develop a practical solution of rectangular plates in shear by applying the principle of stationary potential energy[24] [Timoshenko, 1915, 1921]. He also used that method to determine critical stresses for simply supported rectangular plates under bending and compressive stresses, and extended the use of the method to the case of combined bending and shear [Timoshenko, 1935].

A web in the state of "pure shear" is characterized by edge shear stresses (Fig. 9.48), which are equivalent to tension and compression stresses, equal in magnitude to the shear stresses, and inclined at 45°. Instability is caused by the compression stress, which is countered by the presence of the tension stress. Under this state of stress, the buckling mode is composed of multiple waveforms, which are skewed with respect to the edges (i.e., the nodal lines are not straight), and have a half-wavelength equal to $1.25b$ for long, simply supported plates (Fig. 9.49) [Gerard, 1962].

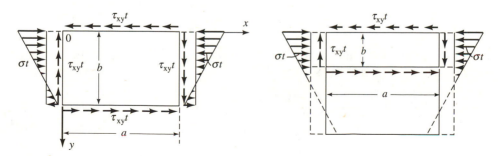

FIGURE 9.47
A rectangular plate under flexure and shear.

---

[24]A discussion on this subject has been provided by Bleich [1952, pp. 69–81] and Hoff [1956, pp. 121–173].

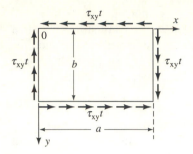

FIGURE 9.48
Web in a state of pure shear.

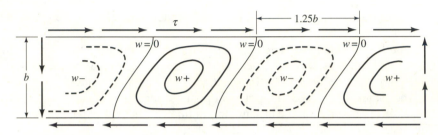

FIGURE 9.49
Buckled configuration of a rectangular simply supported in shear.

Equation 9.9 (discussed earlier) is the fundamental differential equation used to describe the deflected shape of the plate. The exact solution of Eq. 9.9 that defines the buckling problem for a plate of finite length a is not known; the approximate solution using the theorem of stationary potential energy has been provided by Timoshenko [1961] and discussed by Bleich [1952]. The boundary conditions at the plate's supported edges are satisfied by taking for deflection surface of the buckled plate the previously used function (Eq. 9.12) in the form of Fourier double-sine series. The resulting solution for the critical shear stress is given by

$$\tau_c = k_s \frac{\pi^2 E}{12(1 - \nu^2)} \left(\frac{t}{b}\right)^2 \tag{9.142}$$

where k_s is the plate factor or the buckling coefficient for shear. It may be noted that Eq. 9.142 has the same form as Eq. 9.34. The value of k_s has been given by Stein and Neff [1947] as a function of aspect ratio:

$$k_s = \frac{9\pi^2}{32} \frac{(1 + \alpha^2)^2}{\alpha^3} \tag{9.143}$$

where $\alpha = a/b$, the aspect ratio. The influence of a/b on the values of k_s for rectangular plates with simply supported and clamped edges, based on the works of Stein and Neff [1947] and Budiansky and Connor [1948], is shown in Fig. 9.50.

It has been pointed out that the value of k_s given by Eq. 9.143 is approximate; the error is about 15 percent for $\alpha = 1$ (square plates) and is even larger for $\alpha > 1$

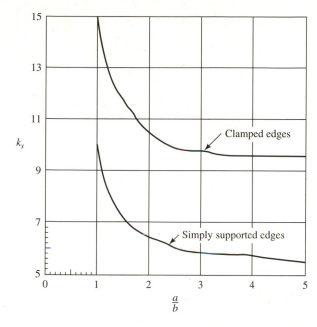

FIGURE 9.50
Plate buckling coefficients for shear.

[Timoshenko and Gere, 1961; Bleich, 1952]. Solutions with better approximation (Eq. 9.144) were given by Timoshenko [1910], Bergmen and Reissner [1932], and Seidel [1933]:

$$k_s = 4.00 + \frac{5.34}{\alpha^2} \quad \text{for } \alpha \leq 1$$

$$k_s = 5.34 + \frac{4.00}{\alpha^2} \quad \text{for } \alpha \geq 1 \tag{9.144}$$

The exact value of $k_s = 5.34$ for $\alpha = \infty$ (very long simply supported rectangular plate) and $k_s = 9.34$ for $\alpha = 1$ (a simply supported square plate) are due to Skan and Southwell [1924] and Seydel [1933]. The best values for other ratios are given by Stein and Neff [1947]. As shown in Fig. 9.51, a parabolic curve given by

$$k_s = 5.35 + \frac{4}{\alpha^2} \tag{9.145}$$

can be taken to give approximate values of k_s for other proportions of the plate [Timoshenko and Gere, 1961]. Nevertheless, by comparison with their data, Bleich [1952] showed that the value of k_s given by Eq. 9.146 (which is valid for $\alpha > 1$) can be used as a closer approximation for design purposes, and that the same equation could be used for the cases of $\alpha < 1$ by selecting the dimension a as always the larger dimension, as shown in Fig. 9.52.

$$k_s = 5.34 + \frac{4}{\alpha^2} \tag{9.146}$$

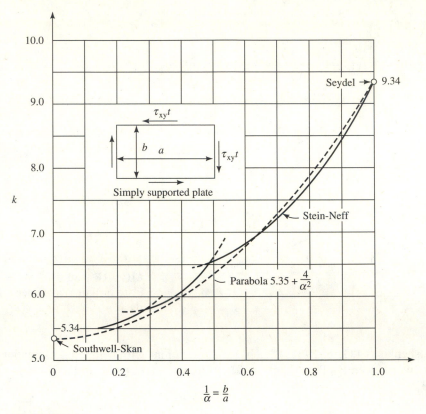

FIGURE 9.51
Shear buckling coefficient k_s for various values of a/b. [Adapted from Bleich, 1953, p. 394.]

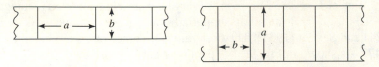

FIGURE 9.52
The dimension a selected as the larger dimension regardless of the orientation.

Equation 9.144 formed the basis of design of stiffened plate girders for buildings according to the AISC specifications [AISC, 1989] and for highway bridges according to the earlier versions of the AASHTO specifications. For design purposes, further simplification of Eq. 9.144 has been suggested by Vincent [1969] as

$$k_s = 5 + \frac{5}{(d_o/D)^2} \tag{9.147}$$

where d_o = spacing of intermediate stiffeners ($= a$)
$\quad\quad D$ = unsupported depth of web plate between flanges ($= b$)
$\quad\quad \alpha = d_o/D$

A plot of k_s values given by Eqs. 9.144 and 9.147 is shown in Fig. 9.53; the closeness between the two curves is apparent. A numerical comparison of k_s values for values of aspect ratio a/b (or a/h, where $b = h$) varying between 0.2 and 3.0 (recommended practical limits) by Eqs. 9.144 and 9.147 has been provided by Salmon and Johnson [1990, p. 678], which shows the validity of Eq. 9.147 as an acceptable single equation for design purposes within the accuracy that the theoretical elastic buckling solution agrees with a real plate girder. Equation 9.147 now forms the basis of design for the stiffened plate girders for buildings [AISC, 1986] and highway bridges [AASHTO, 1992, 1994]. In AASHTO [1992] and AASHTO [1994], Eq. 9.147 is stated as Eq. 10.27B and implied in Eq. 6.10.7.2-1, respectively.

9.5.4.2 Inelastic design for webs in shear

The shear provisions of AASHTO 10.34.4 [AASHTO, 1992] are based on the elastic behavior of plate girders. As pointed out by Basler [1961a], based on the Mises' yield condition, the shear yield stress F_{vy} equals $F_y/\sqrt{3}$. With a factor of safety of 1.75 [Gaylord, Gaylord, and Stallmeyer, 1992] the maximum allowable shear stress is obtained as

$$F_v = \frac{F_y}{\sqrt{3}}\left(\frac{1}{1.75}\right) \approx \frac{F_y}{3} \tag{9.148}$$

where F_{vy} = yield stress in shear.

The critical shear stress can be obtained by substituting $k_s = 5.34$, $E = 29,000$ ksi, and $\nu = 0.3$ in Eq. 9.142:[25]

$$\tau_c = \frac{139,000}{(b/t)^2} \tag{9.149}$$

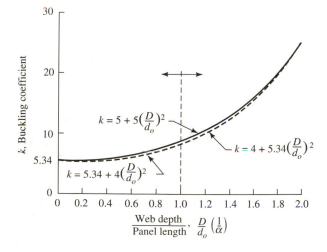

FIGURE 9.53
Comparison of values of k_s from Eqs. 9.144 and 9.147. ($\alpha = a/b = d_o/D$ per AASHTO notation) [From Vincent, 1969].

---

[25] The numerator in Eq. 9.149 has been conservatively rounded off from 139,964 to 139,000.

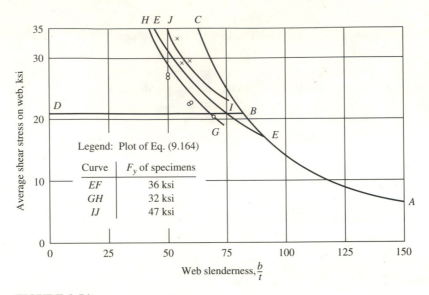

FIGURE 9.54
Average shear stress on web versus b/t ratios. [Adapted from Gaylord, Gaylord, and Stallmeyer, 1992].

Plot of Eq. 9.149 is shown in Fig. 9.54 by line ABC [Gaylord, Gaylord, and Stallmeyer, 1992], which gives $b/t = 82$ corresponding to $\tau_c = 21$ ksi($= F_y/\sqrt{3}$) for A36 steel (shown by line DB). Therefore, the curve DBA shows the behavior of an ideal web. However, tests by Lyse and Godfrey [1935] on welded steel beams with b/t ratios in the range of 50 to 70 have shown that for small b/t ratios, the webs can strain harden. Their test data for various specimens with average yield stresses ranging from 32 to 47 ksi are shown in Fig. 9.54. The allowable shear stresses for design can be taken as those which can be defined by the (lower bound) envelope $DIEA$, which can be expressed as follows:

$$F_v = F_{vy} \quad \text{for} \quad 0 < \frac{b}{t} \leq 144\sqrt{\frac{k_s}{F_{vy}}} \tag{9.150}$$

$$F_v = \frac{144}{(b/t)}\sqrt{k_s F_{vy}} \quad \text{for} \quad 144\sqrt{\frac{k_s}{F_{vy}}} \leq \frac{b}{t} \leq 181\sqrt{\frac{k_s}{F_{vy}}} \tag{9.151}$$

$$F_v = \frac{26{,}000 k_s}{(b/t)^2} \quad \text{for} \quad \frac{b}{t} > 181\sqrt{\frac{k_s}{F_{vy}}} \tag{9.152}$$

Equations 9.150 through 9.152 form the basis of design provisions for shear as specified in various specifications [Gaylord, Gaylord, and Stallmeyer, 1992]. The AASHTO specification [AASHTO, 1992] does not recognize the inelastic behavior represented by Eq. (9.151), and the allowable stresses are given by the curve $DBEA$ in Fig. 9.54.

For practical plate girders, the ratio b/t is usually large so that $k_s = 5$ in Eqs. 9.150 through 9.152. With a value of $F_{vy} = F_y/\sqrt{3}$ and a factor of safety of 1.75, we obtain

$$F_v = \frac{(26,000)(5)(1000)}{(b/t)^2(1.75)} = \frac{7.43(10^7)}{(b/t)^2} \tag{9.153}$$

for

$$\frac{b}{t} = 181\sqrt{\frac{k_s}{F_{vy}}} = 181\sqrt{\frac{5(1000)}{(F_y/\sqrt{3})(1000)}} = \frac{16,844}{\sqrt{F_{y,\text{psi}}}} \tag{9.154}$$

Equations 9.153 and 9.154 are similar to AASHTO Eq. 10.26:

$$F_v = \frac{7.33 \times 10^7}{(D/t_w)^2} \tag{9.155}$$

where b and t have been replaced by D and t_w, respectively (AASHTO notation).

At this point, it should be noted that Eq. 9.155 does not recognize the increase in shear buckling strength of web due to the presence of the transverse stiffeners, although their requirements (AASHTO 10.34.4.2) are based on the postbuckling shear strength of web.

For design purposes, it is convenient to define the web buckling coefficient C (also expressed as C_v in some design specifications, such as AISC [1989]) as a ratio of the critical buckling shear stress τ_{cr} (or τ_c) as given by Eq. 9.142 to yield shear stress τ_y:

$$C = \frac{\tau_{cr}}{\tau_y} = \frac{\pi^2 E k_s}{\tau_y(12)(1 - \nu^2)(b/t)^2} \tag{9.156}$$

so that

$$\tau_{cr} = C\tau_y \tag{9.157}$$

Substitution of $E = 29,000$ ksi, $\nu = 0.3$, and $\tau_y = F_y/\sqrt{3}$ in Eq. 9.156 yields

$$\begin{aligned}
C &= \frac{\pi^2(29,000)k_s}{(F_y/\sqrt{3})(12)(1 - 0.09)(h/t_w)^2} \\
&= \frac{45,398k_s}{(h/t_w)^2 F_y} \\
&\approx \frac{45,000k_s}{(h/t_w)^2 F_{y,\text{ksi}}}
\end{aligned} \tag{9.158}$$

where k_s and b/t have been replaced by k and h/t_w (to conform to AISC notation). Equation 9.158 gives the value of the coefficient C_v in AISC-ASD-F4 [AISC, 1989].

Often, the value of $\tau_y = F_y/\sqrt{3}$ is approximated as $0.6F_y$ (and sometimes more accurately as $0.58F_y$) which, when substituted in Eq. 9.158, yields

$$\begin{aligned}
C &= \frac{43,684k_s}{(h/t_w)^2 F_y} \\
&\approx \frac{44,000k_s}{(h/t_w)^2 F_{y,\text{ksi}}}
\end{aligned} \tag{9.159}$$

which is the value of C_v in AISC [1986, Appendix G].

It is reiterated that the preceding discussion relates to the design criteria for shear under elastic conditions. However, due to the presence of the residual stresses and imperfections, for all compression elements made of mild steel having a range of low slenderness ratios, the actual failure stress exceeds the yield stress. As pointed out by Basler [1961a], this is due to the fact that yielding is confined to slip bands, while the steel outside the slip bands remains below the yield stress level. On further increasing the load, the steel within the slip bands begins to strain harden, while the steel next to these bands is on the verge of yielding. For these stress conditions, Basler [1961a] theorized that a relationship of the form given by Eq. 9.160 exists above the proportional limit with C_{in} and the exponent n to be determined:

$$\tau_{cr,\,in} = C_{in}\tau_{cri}^{n} \tag{9.160}$$

where $\tau_{cr,\,in}$ = critical shear stress in the inelastic range
τ_{cri} = ideal critical shear in the elastic range
C_{in} = web buckling coefficient in the inelastic range

Reasoning that the ideal critical shear stress (elastic) τ_{cri} and the actual critical shear stress have to be equal at the proportional limit, τ_{pr}, Basler proposed that

$$C_{in} = \tau_{pr}^{(1-n)} \tag{9.161}$$

From curve fitting for the Lyse-Godfrey test data,[26] Basler determined that, for $\tau_{pr} = 0.8\tau_y$, 0.5 was the best choice for the exponent n. With $n = 0.5$, Eq. 9.161 yields

$$C_{in} = \sqrt{\tau_{pr}} \tag{9.162}$$

which, when substituted in Eq. 9.160, yields

$$\tau_{cr,\,in} = \sqrt{\tau_{cr}\tau_{cri}} \tag{9.163}$$

Equation 9.163[27] affords a much more realistic estimate of the shear strength of web in the inelastic and strain-hardening range. The value of the web buckling coefficient C in this range can be obtained by dividing the value of $\tau_{cr,\,in}$ from Eq. 9.163 by τ_y. The value of the proportional limit shear stress τ_{pr} is taken as $0.8\tau_y$ [Basler, 1961a; SSRC, 1988, p. 195]. Thus,

$$\tau_{cri} = \sqrt{0.8\tau_{cr}\tau_{yw}}, \quad 0.8\tau_y \le \tau_{cr} \le 1.25\tau_y \tag{9.164}$$

and

$$\begin{aligned}
C_{in} = \frac{\tau_{cr,\,in}}{\tau_y} &= \frac{1}{\tau_y}\sqrt{\tau_{pr}\tau_{cri}} \\
&= \frac{1}{\tau_y}\sqrt{0.8\tau_y\tau_{cri}} \\
&= \sqrt{\frac{0.8\tau_{cri}}{\tau_y}}
\end{aligned} \tag{9.165}$$

---

[26]Given in Lyse and Godfrey [1935] and summarized by Basler [1961a].

[27]Same as Basler's Eq. 18 [Basler, 1961a, p. 702].

The value of τ_{cri}, the ideal elastic critical shear stress, is obtained by equating Eqs. 9.157 and 9.158:

$$\tau_{\text{cri}} = \tau_{\text{cr}} = C_{\text{elastic}}\tau_y = \left[\frac{45,000k_s}{(h/t_w)^2 F_y}\right]\tau_y \qquad (9.166)$$

Substitution for τ_{cri} from Eq. 9.166 in Eq. 9.165 yields

$$\begin{aligned} C_{\text{in}} &= \sqrt{(0.8)\frac{45,000k_s}{(h/t_w)^2 F_y}} \\ &= \frac{190}{(h/t_w)}\sqrt{\frac{k_s}{F_y}} \end{aligned} \qquad (9.167)$$

which is the value of C specified in AISC-ASD-F4 [AISC, 1989].

9.5.5 Shear Contribution from Tension-Field Action

The preceding discussion focused on the strength of shear-resistant webs, assuming that the beam web, made of material that is elastic-plastic, is plane, perfectly flexible, and incapable of resisting diagonal compressive stresses. This model predicts the shear capacity of a plate girder that corresponds to the beam-action strength. However, tests have shown that girder webs do resist some *diagonal compressive* stresses after buckling, which is followed by stress redistribution and development of diagonal tension, resulting in considerable postbuckling strength. In general, as the applied loading is increased, a stage is reached when the web buckles and loses its ability to carry any additional compressive load. Before buckling, the shear stress in the web can be computed by the conventional beam shear formula: $\tau = VQ/It$. If the web is subjected to shear loadings only, the state of stress in a small element in the web can be represented by equal tensile and compressive stresses, as shown in Fig. 9.55(a). At buckling, the critical shear stress τ_{cr} ($= \tau_c$) in the web can be computed from Eq. 9.142. While the web is in the buckled state, a new load-carrying mechanism—the so-called tension-field action (discussed in Sec. 9.4.2)—is developed within an inclined narrow band of the web whereby any additional shear loading is supported by an inclined tensile membrane field σ_t (Fig. 9.55(b)). In test girders, this is evidenced by formation of buckles in a waveform parallel to the tensile direction, as shown in Figs. 9.17 and 9.18. This membrane stress field is anchored against the top and bottom flanges and against the adjacent members on either side of the web. The shear stress carried by the tension field action equals $(\tau - \tau_{\text{cr}})$ where τ is the total shear stress in the web before collapse. With further increase in the applied loading, the tensile membrane stress σ_t in the web continues to increase, exerting a greater pull on the flanges. Finally, the membrane stress in the web reaches the yield stress σ_y of the web material, followed by, according to some researchers, formation of plastic hinges in both flanges, as shown in Fig. 9.55(c). Consequently, a *panel mechanism* is formed, resulting in the collapse of the girder. This failure mode was first postulated by Rockey, Porter, and Evans [Rockey et al., 1974; Porter et al., 1975]. Even without transverse stiffeners, the web of a plate girder can

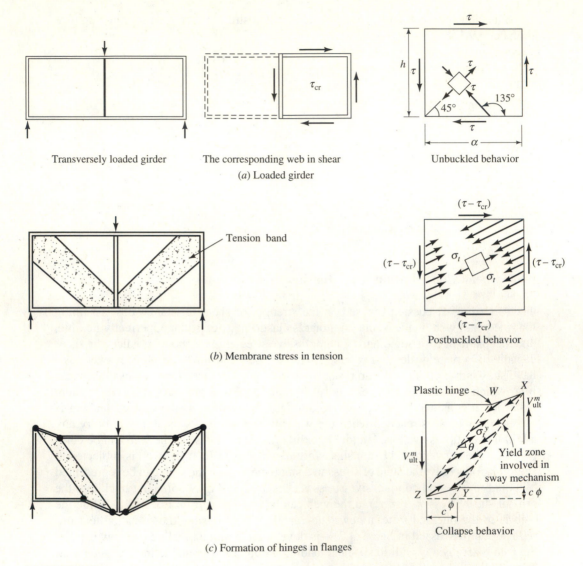

FIGURE 9.55
Behavior of a plate girder web in shear.

develop a shear stress at the ultimate load that is several times the shear-buckling stress [SSRC, 1988].

In recognition of the presence of the tension-field action, webs can be characterized as acting in intermediate stage between shear-resistant webs and pure tension-field webs. Stated differently, in plate girders with thin webs, neither a pure beam action nor a pure tension-field action occurs alone. Such beams are referred to as *semi-tension-field beams, partial tension-field beams,* or *incompletely developed diagonal tension-field beams* [Peery and Azar, 1982].

A tension field is simply a *membrane stress field*, the presence of which develops ultimate shear strength of plate girder that is several times the buckling shear strength. Its contribution toward the ultimate strength of thin plates in shear was recognized as early as 1886 by Wilson [1886, 1898]. According to Basler [1961a], a mathematical formulation of the effect of a tension field or truss action (which sets in after the web loses its stiffness due to buckling) was presented by Rode [1916]—he may have been the first—in his dissertation in a chapter dealing with webs of plate girders. He proposed to evaluate its influence by considering a tension diagonal of a width equal to 80 times the web thickness. However, it was the development of aeronautical science that gave an impetus to the study of the shear-carrying capacity of membrane-like structures such as aircraft. Their paramount design requirement—minimize the weight of the structure— led to designs involving extremely thin webs and ultimately resulted in the application of the phenomenon of tension-field action.

The credit of first publishing the theory of pure tension-field beams is given to Wagner [1929, 1931], who discussed theoretically the load-carrying capacity of thin webs by neglecting their flexural rigidity (i.e., neglecting beam action completely). His results (the strength of a panel in pure shear), known as the *diagonal tension-field theory,* are based on assuming webs as membranes in uniform stress field, resistant only to tension. He assumed plate girders as having infinitely stiff flanges (and therefore formation of plastic hinges was precluded) and very thin webs. Since then, many investigators have studied the problem of semi-tension-field beams. Kromm and Marguerre [1937] presented the general solution of the problem, taking into account the membrane and bending stresses. Levy, Fienup, and Wooley [1945, 1946] studied the problem of web plates of girders having transverse stiffeners forming square panels. Lahde and Wagner [1936] published empirical data in 1936 that were based on the strain measurement of buckled rectangular sheets. An extensive test program was conducted by NACA under the direction of Paul Kuhn. Strain measurements in the vertical stiffeners of a large number of beams were made by Kuhn, Peterson, and Levin [1952] and Kuhn and Peterson [1947], who derived empirical equations from these measurements. However, all these pioneering studies were directed toward the design of aircraft and had little bearing on the problems encountered in the design of steel plate girders for buildings and bridges. A discussion on semi-tension-field beams as used in aircraft structures has been presented by Peery and Azar [1982].

Although the Wagner analysis was found to be adequate for aircraft, it was not considered applicable for plate girders of the type used in civil engineering structures. This thinking was based on several assumptions:

1. There are significant differences in proportions of the plate girders used in aircraft and civil engineering structures.
2. The flanges of civil engineering structures are usually much less rigid than those of aircraft girders. Consequently, significant distortions can occur under the action of the forces imposed on the flanges by the tension stress field that influence the tension stress field (magnitude and direction) developed in the web.
3. Aircraft are built of aluminum alloys whose modulus of elasticity and, hence, web buckling stresses are lower than for steel structures.
4. With a continuous skin, such as around the fuselage or wing of an aircraft, the boundary conditions are much more favorable for membrane action to develop in aircraft

girders than in a conventionally welded plate girder, where no angle sections be-tween the web and flanges are provided, which could provide a certain degree of rigidity [Basler, 1961a].

Basler and Thurlimann were the first, in the late 1950s, to establish a theory [Basler and Thurlimann, 1959, 1960a,b, 1961] that now forms the basis of design specifications for plate girders for buildings and bridges in the United States. In contrast to Wagner's assumption of infinitely rigid flanges, they conservatively assumed the girder flanges to be very flexible and, therefore, incapable of supporting the loads imposed on them by the web's tension stress field, so that the membrane stress field would anchor against the vertical edges of the panel only.

In between these two extreme assumptions—very rigid flanges to very flexible flanges—several researchers have provided models for determining the shear strength of plate girders. These models considered that the rigidity of flanges was significant and had great influence on the ultimate strength of girders. Also, the assumption of flanges not being infinitely stiff permitted formation of plastic hinges in them. Since 1960, many variations of the postbuckling tension field have been developed following the Basler-Thurlimann model. These include Takeuchi [1964], Fujii [1968, 1971], Komatsu [1971], Chern and Ostapenko [1969], Sharp and Clark [1971], Steinhardt and Schroter [1971], Hoglund [1971a,b], Calladine [1973], and Porter, Rockey, and Evans [1975]. The main characteristics of these models are shown in Table 9.5 and summarized in the literature [Thurlimann, 1963; AISC–AASHTO, 1978; SSRC, 1988]. These various models differ in many respects, primarily in the nature of distribution of the tension-field stresses, the positions of plastic hinges if they are involved in the solution, and the edge conditions assumed in computing the shear buckling stress.

Takeuchi [1964] is reported to have been the first to consider the effect of flange rigidity on the yield zone of the web [SSRC, 1988]. He assumed the location of boundaries of the tension field at distances c_1 and c_2 (Table 9.5) from the diagonally opposite corners of a panel. These distances were assumed proportional to the respective flange rigidity I_{f1} and I_{f2} and were chosen to maximize the shear strength. However, this model did not correlate well with the test results. An improved model was suggested by Rockey and Skaloud [1968], who established that the collapse mode of a plate girder involved formation of plastic hinges in both flanges. Later, Rockey, Porter, and Evans [1974] proposed a more general applicable mechanism (panel mechanism, Fig. 9.55(c), the accuracy of which was established by them after comparison with results of 58 tests obtained from many different sources. These comparisons are summarized by Rockey, Evans, and Porter [1978]. In any case, the general hypothesis of all failure modes is that a plate girder follows beam theory until the web buckles. After buckling, tension field develops in a narrow band of the web, inclined at an angle to the flange. At some point plastic hinges are formed in both flanges triggering the collapse of the plate girder. Plastic hinges have also been observed in other tests [Moriwaki and Fujino, 1976]. Consequently, both tension-field action and frame action are considered in analysis. In all models except the Fujii and Herzog models, the shear-buckling strength is added to the vertical component of the tension field to obtain the contribution of the web to the shear strength of the girder panel [SSRC, 1988]. The following discussion examines the Basler-Thurlimann model in some detail because it forms the basis of the AASHTO design criteria. It is also one of the simplest to use.

TABLE 9.5
Various tension-field theories [SSRC, 1988]

Investigator	Mechanism	Web buckling edge support	Unequal flanges	Longitudinal Stiffener	Shear and moment
Basler (1963-a)		S S S (θ)	Immaterial	Yes, Cooper (1965)	Yes
Takeuchi (1964)	(c_1, c_2)	S S S	Yes	No	No
Fujii (1968, 1971)	($\frac{d}{2}$, $\frac{d}{2}$)	S F F S	Yes	Yes	Yes
Komatsu (1971)	(c, c)	S F F S	No	Yes, at mid-depth	No
Chem and Ostapenko (1969)		S F F S	Yes	Yes	Yes
Porter et al. (1975)	(c, A, D, B, θ, C, c)	S S S	Yes	Yes	Yes
Hoglund (1971a,b)	(c, δ, c)	S S S	No	No	Yes
Herzog (1974a,b)	(c, $\frac{h}{2}$, c)	Web buckling component neglected	Yes, in evaluating c	Yes	Yes
Sharp and Clark (1971)		S $F/2$ $F/2$ S	No	No	No
Steinhardt and Schroter (1971)		S S S	Yes	Yes	Yes

9.5.6 Basler's Tension-Field Model

It should be recognized at the outset that the tension-field model is valid only for transversely stiffened webs, with or without longitudinal stiffeners. Consequently, tension-field action is discussed with regard to the membrane stresses in the panel of a plate girder bounded by top and bottom flanges and the two adjacent transverse stiffeners (on the sides). When longitudinal stiffeners are also provided, tension-field action can be considered in subpanels whose boundaries are formed by a flange and the longitudinal stiffener and a pair of adjacent transverse stiffeners.

The stress distribution in a panel's tension field is highly influenced by its boundary conditions. If the boundary members, which act as anchors for the tension stress field, were infinitely stiff, the tension field stresses in the panel would be uniform. However, in a conventionally welded plate girder, the support conditions along the horizontal and the vertical boundaries of a panel are very different from each other.

It is assumed that the flexural stiffness of flanges in the plane of the web is small and ineffective in resisting vertical stresses at its juncture with the web. Such flanges are therefore ineffective as anchors for a tension stress field. On the other hand, at the web–transverse stiffener juncture, the stiffeners are sufficiently stiff to keep the web straight and prevent it from buckling, and, consequently, the tension strips can effectively transmit the vertical component of tension-field stresses in the transverse stiffeners. Because of these differences in the panel's boundary conditions, it is assumed that only a partial tension stress field is developed. This stress field consists of fields of small tension-field stresses in the web near the two flanges (referred to as the *outer tension fields*) and a field of pronounced tension-field stresses in the remainder of the web (referred to as the *principal tension field*). The general distribution of the tension field consistent with this assumption is shown in Fig. 9.21(a) and has been verified experimentally by several researchers [Basler et al., 1960; Clark and Sharp, 1971; Steinhardt and Schroder, 1971; Evans and Tang, 1981]. However, unlike other models, no formation of hinges in the flanges is assumed (as shown in Fig. 9.55(c)) in the Basler model.

For simplicity in developing an analytical model, the presence of the smaller membrane stresses in the outer tension fields is ignored, and only the principal tension field stresses (assumed uniform) extending over a bandwidth s, and inclined at an angle θ with the horizontal (Fig. 9.56), are considered in the Basler model. Note that the tension-field angle θ is smaller than the angle between the diagonal of the panel and the horizontal.

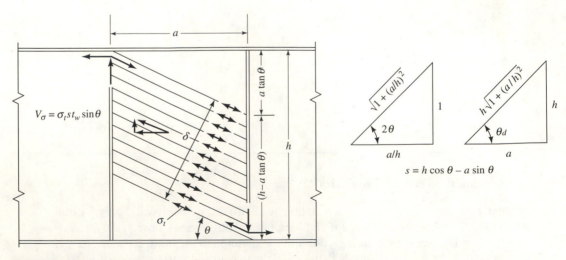

FIGURE 9.56
Tension-field forces in a plate girder panel.

Referring to Fig. 9.56, which shows the forces arising from the tension field in a panel, the contribution of the tension field toward the shear strength of web can be evaluated by considering a section through the web. Let

s = bandwidth
σ_t = membrane tensile stress (or the tension-field stress)
θ = angle between the direction of tension-field stress and the horizontal

The tension-field stress resultant is then $\sigma_t s t_w$.

The tension-field force V_{tf}, developed by compression in the stiffener, is given by

$$V_{tf} = \sigma_t s t_w \sin \theta \tag{9.168}$$

From the geometry of the panel, the bandwidth s is given by

$$s = h \cos \theta - a \sin \theta$$

Substitution of the value of the bandwidth in Eq. 9.168 yields

$$
\begin{aligned}
V_{tf} &= \sigma_t t_w (h \cos \theta - a \sin \theta) \sin \theta \\
&= \sigma_t t_w (h \cos \theta \sin \theta - a \sin^2 \theta) \\
&= \sigma_t t_w \left[\frac{h}{2} \sin 2\theta - \frac{a}{2}(1 - \cos 2\theta) \right]
\end{aligned}
\tag{9.169}
$$

In Eq. 9.169, the angle of inclination of the membrane tensile stress, θ, is unknown. Its value corresponding to the maximum value of V_{tf} can be determined by differentiating with respect to θ and setting

$$\frac{d}{d\theta}(V_{tf}) = 0 \tag{9.170}$$

Thus, differentiating both sides of Eq. 9.169, we obtain

$$\frac{d}{d\theta}(V_{tf}) = \sigma_t t_w (h \cos 2\theta - a \sin 2\theta) = 0 \tag{9.171}$$

Because $\sigma_t t_w$ cannot be zero, it follows that

$$h \cos 2\theta - a \sin 2\theta = 0 \tag{9.172}$$

from which

$$\tan 2\theta = \frac{h}{a} = \frac{1}{(a/h)} \tag{9.173}$$

Angle 2θ can be defined by the geometry of the panel as shown in Fig. 9.56:

$$
\begin{aligned}
\sin 2\theta &= \frac{1}{\sqrt{1 + (a/h)^2}} = \sin \theta_d \\
\cos 2\theta &= \frac{a/h}{\sqrt{1 + (a/h)^2}} = \cos \theta_d
\end{aligned}
\tag{9.174}
$$

Also, noting that $\tan \theta_d = h/a$, we obtain $\theta_d = 2\theta$ (or $\theta = \theta_d/2$), where θ_d = angle between the panel diagonal and the flange, i.e., the tension-field angle θ equals one-half the angle between the flange and the panel diagonal. Because the maximum value of 2θ cannot exceed $90°$, it is obvious that the tension-field angle θ will vary between a maximum approaching $45°$ (for extremely close stiffeners) to a minimum of $0°$ for unstiffened webs (i.e., no tension field).

The maximum value of V_{tf} corresponding to this value of θ can be obtained by substitution in Eq. 9.169:

$$
\begin{aligned}
V_{tf} &= \sigma_t t_w \left[\frac{h}{2} \frac{1}{\sqrt{1 + (a/h)^2}} - \frac{a}{2} \left(1 - \frac{a/h}{\sqrt{1 + (a/h)^2}} \right) \right] \\
&= \frac{1}{2} \sigma_t t_w h \left[\frac{1 - (a/h)\sqrt{1 + (a/h)^2} + (a/h)^2}{\sqrt{1 + (a/h)^2}} \right] \\
&= \frac{1}{2} \sigma_t t_w h \left[\sqrt{1 + (a/h)^2} - a/h \right]
\end{aligned}
\tag{9.175}
$$

Alternatively, V_{tf} can be expressed in terms of the angle of the panel diagonal θ_d by substituting $2\theta = \theta_d$ in Eq. 9.169:

$$
\begin{aligned}
V_{tf} &= \sigma_t t_w \left[\frac{h}{2} \sin \theta_d - \frac{a}{2}(1 - \cos \theta_d) \right] \\
&= \frac{1}{2} \sigma_t h t_w \left[\sin \theta_d - \frac{a}{h}(1 - \cos \theta_d) \right] \\
&= \frac{1}{2} \sigma_t h t_w \left[\sin \theta_d - \cot \theta_d (1 - \cos \theta_d) \right] \\
&= \frac{1}{2} \sigma_t h t_w \left[\frac{1 - \cos \theta_d}{\sin \theta_d} \right]
\end{aligned}
\tag{9.176}
$$

As pointed out earlier, Eq. 9.175 takes into account the tension-field force only in the principal (or primary) tension field, and that tension-field forces in the outer tension fields have been ignored (because of the uncertain state of stress distribution). Therefore, Eq. 9.175 (or Eq. 9.176) is not practical for use in design. Basler's model (Fig. 9.57) suggests an alternative approach to this problem.

Referring to Fig. 9.57, a section is cut along the longitudinal axis of the plate girder with equally spaced transverse stiffeners. To evaluate the shear strength contribution of the tension field, equilibrium of a free body below this longitudinal section, bounded by the centerlines of the adjacent panels, and containing a centrally located transverse stiffener, is considered. The width of the web in this free body, measured perpendicular to the tension-field stresses, equals $a \sin \theta$, and the resultant tension-field force equals $\sigma_t t_w a \sin \theta$. The horizontal equilibrium of this free body yields

$$
\Delta F_f + F_f - F_f - (\sigma_t t_w a \sin \theta) \cos \theta = 0
\tag{9.177}
$$

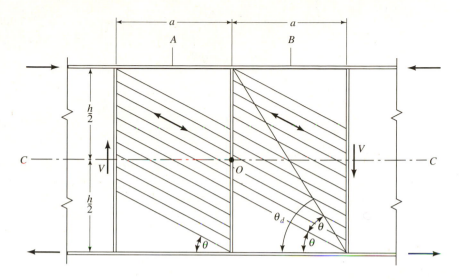

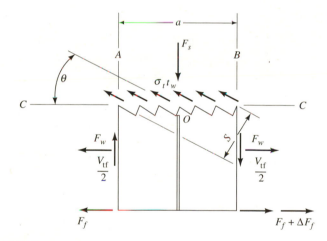

FIGURE 9.57
Basler's tension-field model.

where ΔF_f = tension force in the flange. Equation 9.177 yields

$$\Delta F_f = \sigma_t t_w a \sin\theta \cos\theta$$
$$= \tfrac{1}{2}\sigma_s t_w a \sin 2\theta \qquad (9.178)$$

Also, the moment equilibrium about point O yields

$$\Delta F_f \frac{h}{2} - 2\left(\frac{V_{tf}}{2}\frac{a}{2}\right) = 0$$

from which

$$\Delta F_f = \frac{v_{tf} a}{2} \qquad (9.179)$$

Substitution of ΔF_f from Eq. 9.178 and for $\sin 2\theta$ from Eq. 9.174 in Eq. 9.179 yields

$$\frac{V_{\text{tf}}a}{h} = \frac{1}{2}\sigma_t t_w a \sin 2\theta$$

whence

$$V_{\text{tf}} = \frac{1}{2}\sigma_t A_w \left(\frac{1}{\sqrt{1 + (a/h)^2}}\right) \tag{9.180}$$

where $ht_w = A_w$, area of web. Equation 9.180 gives the required value of shear contribution of tension stress field in the web.

When the tension field develops in the web of a transversely stiffened plate girder, the transverse stiffeners are stressed similar to the struts in a Pratt truss. The compressive force F_s in the transverse stiffener is obtained by considering the vertical equilibrium of the free body in Fig. 9.57:

$$F_s - (\sigma_t t_w a \sin\theta)\sin\theta = 0 \tag{9.181}$$

which, with the value of $\cos 2\theta$ substituted from Eq. 9.174, yields

$$\begin{aligned} F_s &= \sigma_t t_w a \sin^2\theta \\ &= \tfrac{1}{2}\sigma_t t_w a(1 - \cos 2\theta) \\ &= \frac{1}{2}\sigma_t t_w a\left[1 - \frac{a/h}{\sqrt{1 + (a/h)^2}}\right] \end{aligned} \tag{9.182}$$

Equation 9.182 is the Basler formula for calculating the contribution from the tension field to the shear strength of the web. However, it should be noted, as pointed out first by Gaylord [Basler, 1961a], and later by Fujii [1968a] and Selberg [1973], that Eq. 9.182 gives the shear strength of the web based on the *complete* tension field, not based on the *partial* (or limited) tension field as assumed by Basler. The correct expression for shear strength due to the tension field in the limited band assumed by Basler is [SSRC, 1988, p. 195]

$$\tau_u = \tau_{\text{cr}} + \left[\sigma_{\text{yw}}\left(1 - \frac{\tau_{\text{cr}}}{\tau_y}\right)\right]\frac{\sin\theta_d}{2 + \cos\theta_d} \tag{9.183}$$

where the quantity in brackets is the value of the tension-field stress σ_t.

At failure, the web is subjected to a state of combined stresses: normal stress σ_t and the critical shear stress τ_{cr}. Figure 9.58 shows an element located at the neutral axis of a plate girder (so that the flexural stress is zero) subjected to a state of pure shear τ_{cr}, in addition to the tension-field stress σ_t acting at an angle θ with the horizontal as previously discussed. Basler's model for the failure criteria assumes that the critical shear stress τ_{cr} remains constant as the load increases from the buckling load to the ultimate load, and the principle of superposition is valid. At buckling, the principal stresses resulting from the state of pure shear are each equal to τ_{cr}-tensile and -compressive, acting at angles of 45° and 135° as shown in Fig. 9.58. For analytical simplicity, Basler assumed conservatively that angle $\theta = 45°$, so that σ_t and τ_{cr} would be additive, and the

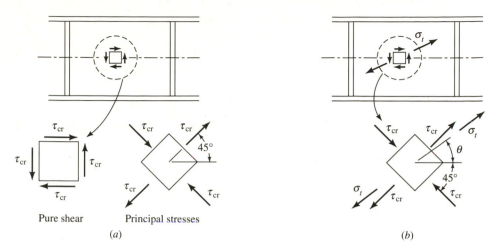

FIGURE 9.58

States of stresses in the web: (*a*) critical shear stress; (*b*) at the ultimate load.

principal of superposition could be used.[28] Based on this assumption, the combined state of stress in the element is shown in Fig. 9.59.

Basler applied the Huber–von Mises–Hencky yield criterion (also referred to as the *energy of distortion theory,* or the *Mises yield criterion for plane stress* [Seely and Smith, 1952]) to determine the stress at failure under the combined state of stress. The relationship between the principal stresses σ_1 and σ_2 is given by an ellipse, as shown in Fig. 9.59, and can be expressed as

$$\sigma_1^2 - \sigma_1\sigma_2 + \sigma_2^2 = F_y^2 \tag{9.184}$$

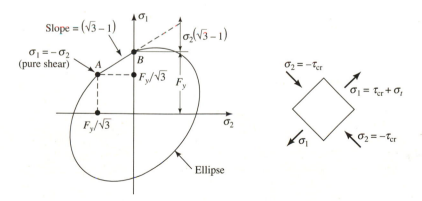

FIGURE 9.59

Huber–von Mises–Hencky yield criterion for shear failure in web [Salmon and Johnson, 1990].

---

[28]It was pointed out earlier that the maximum value of θ will approach 45° but will always be less than 45°.

In Fig. 9.59, point A represents the case of shear alone and point B represents the case of tension alone. Basler assumed that the straight line $\sigma_1 = \sigma_y + (\sqrt{3} - 1)\sigma_2$ passing through points A and B represented a fair approximation of the yield condition. Using the notation $\sigma_y = F_y$, this relationship can be expressed as

$$\sigma_1 = F_y + (\sqrt{3} - 1)\sigma_2 \tag{9.185}$$

With $\theta \approx 45°$, $\sigma_1 = \tau_{cr} + \sigma_t$, and $\sigma_2 = -\tau_{cr}$, Eq. 9.185 yields

$$\tau_{cr} + \sigma_t = F_y + (\sqrt{3} - 1)(-\tau_{cr})$$

from which

$$\sigma_t = F_y - \sqrt{3}\tau_{cr}$$

and

$$\frac{\sigma_t}{F_y} = 1 - \frac{\tau_{cr}}{(F_y/\sqrt{3})} \tag{9.186}$$

Substituting $F_y/\sqrt{3} = \tau_y$, and $\tau_{cr}/\tau_y = C$ (from Eq. 9.156) in Eq. 9.186, we obtain

$$\frac{\sigma_t}{F_y} = 1 - C \tag{9.187}$$

or

$$\sigma_t = (1 - C)F_y$$

The compressive force in the transverse stiffener given by Eq. 9.182 can now be expressed in terms of the aspect ratio a/h, the yield strength of the web material F_{yw}, and the web thickness t_w, by substituting for σ_t from Eq. 9.187:

$$
\begin{aligned}
F_s &= \frac{1}{2}\sigma_t t_w a \left[1 - \frac{a/h}{\sqrt{1 + (a/h)^2}} \right] \\
&= \frac{1}{2}(1 - C)F_{yw}t_w a \left[1 - \frac{a/h}{\sqrt{1 + (a/h)^2}} \right] \\
&= \frac{1}{2}(1 - C)F_{yw}t_w h \left[\frac{a}{h} - \frac{(a/h)^2}{\sqrt{1 + (a/h)^2}} \right]
\end{aligned}
\tag{9.188}
$$

where $F_y = F_{yw}$ = yield strength of web. Using the AASHTO notation $d_o/D = a/h$ (d_o = spacing of stiffeners), Eq. 9.188 becomes

$$F_s = \frac{1}{2}(1 - C)F_{yw}t_w D \left[\frac{d_o}{D} - \frac{(d_o/D)^2}{\sqrt{1 + (d_o/D)^2}} \right] \tag{9.189}$$

As pointed out by Vincent [1969], for practical girders, the aspect ratio d_o/D varies between $\frac{1}{3}$ and 1.5, which correspond to the variation in the bracketed quantity in Eq. 9.189 between 0.21 and 0.3. Using the larger value of 0.3, Eq. 9.189 simplifies to

$$F_s = 0.15(1 - C)F_{yw}t_wD \tag{9.190}$$

For design purposes, Eq. 9.190 has been modified in two respects. First, as suggested by Vincent [1969], the force in the transverse stiffener is reduced by V/V_u, the ratio of design shear to the shear strength, to reflect the condition when the tension field is not fully developed:

$$F_s = 0.15(1 - C)F_{yw}t_wD\frac{V}{V_u} \tag{9.191}$$

Second, it is logical to assume that a certain area A_w of web in the vicinity of transverse stiffeners participates (in conjunction with the stiffeners) in resisting the force F_s. The area of transverse stiffeners required, A_{st}, can be obtained by assuming plastic stress distribution in the transverse stiffener as suggested by Basler [1961a] and modified by Vincent [1969] (Fig. 9.60):

$$\begin{aligned} F_s &= A_wF_{yw} + A_1F_{yst} - (A_1 - A)F_{yst} \\ &= A_wF_{yw} + (2A_1 - A)F_{yst} \end{aligned} \tag{9.192}$$

where A_w = area of web tributary to stiffeners
          A = area of stiffeners
            = bt_s
         A_1 = partial area stiffeners at yield in compression
            = xt_s
   $A - A_1$ = partial area of stiffeners in tension
            = $(b - x)t_s$
         t_s = thickness of transverse stiffener

The plastic stress distribution shown in Fig. 9.60 is based on the assumption that, at the incipient web buckling, the transverse stiffener would yield in axial compression if it were placed in pairs (i.e., symmetrical with respect to the middle plane of the web).

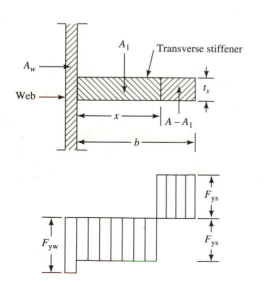

FIGURE 9.60
Plastic stress distribution in a transverse stiffener at failure.

If the stiffener were placed on one side only, the web buckling would induce bending in the stiffener, causing it to yield partially in compression and partially in tension. Equating the two values of F_s from Eqs. 9.191 and 9.192, we have

$$A_w F_{yw} + (2A_1 - A)F_{yst} = 0.15(1 - C)F_{yw}t_w D\frac{V}{V_u}$$

from which

$$A\left(\frac{2A_1 - A}{A}\right)F_{yst} = \left[0.15(1 - C)t_w D\frac{V}{V_u} - A_w\right]F_{yw}$$

and

$$A = \left[0.15(1 - C)t_w D\left(\frac{V}{V_u}\right) - A_w\right]\frac{F_{yw}}{F_{st}}\frac{1}{[2(A_1/A) - 1]} \qquad (9.193)$$

$$= \left[0.15(1 - C)t_w D\frac{V}{V_u} - A_w\right]YB$$

where Y is the ratio of the web yield stress to the stiffener yield stress, F_{yw}/F_{yst}, and B is a coefficient defined as

$$B = \frac{1}{2(A_1/A) - 1} \qquad (9.194)$$

As pointed out by Basler [1961a], the value of B depends on whether the transverse stiffeners are placed symmetrically (i.e., on both sides) or eccentrically (i.e., on one side only) with respect to the middle plane of web. With two symmetrical stiffeners, there is no bending (of stiffeners) involved, in which case the entire stiffener area is in compression and $A_1 = A$; for this case, $B = 1.0$. For the case of a one-sided plate stiffener, the value of B can be computed by considering the moment equilibrium of compressive and tensile forces in the stiffener at yield (i.e., at failure):

Compressive force in stiffener area A_1, $C = A_1 F_{yst}$
Tensile force in stiffener area $(A - A_1)$, $T = (A - A_1)F_{yst}$

Taking the moment of these forces about the face of the web, and dividing throughout by F_{yst}, one obtains

$$A_1\frac{x}{2} - (A - A_1)\left(\frac{b - x}{2} + x\right) = 0$$

which simplifies to

$$x^2 - \frac{b^2}{2} = 0$$

or

$$x = \frac{b}{\sqrt{2}} \qquad (9.195)$$

Referring to Fig. 9.60, we have

$$A = bt_s$$

$$A_1 = xt_s \tag{9.196}$$

$$= \frac{bt_s}{\sqrt{2}}$$

Substitution of the values of A and A_1 from Eq. 9.196 in Eq. 9.194 yields

$$B = \frac{1}{[2(A_1/A) - 1]} = \frac{1}{2[(bt_s/\sqrt{2})/bt_s] - 1} = \frac{1}{\sqrt{2} - 1} = 2.4 \tag{9.197}$$

When the transverse stiffener is a single angle, in which case the centroid of cross section (of the angle) is much closer to the middle plane of the web than that of a single plate stiffener, B is estimated to be 1.8. These three values ($B = 1.0, 2.4$, and 1.8) are specified in AASHTO 10.34.4.7 [AASHTO, 1992], and in AASHTO–LRFD 6.10.8.1.4 [AASHTO, 1994]. Also, in view of the scant information available about the width of the web tributary to stiffeners, it was assumed that

$$A_w = \frac{18t_w^2}{B} \tag{9.198}$$

Substitution for A_w in Eq. 9.193 yields

$$A = \left[0.15(1 - C)t_w D \frac{V}{V_u} - \frac{18t_w^2}{B} \right] YB$$

$$= \left[0.15BDt_w(1 - C)\frac{V}{V_u} - 18t_w^2 \right] Y \tag{9.199}$$

which is AASHTO Eq. 10.105 [AASHTO, 1992] for the load factor design. Also, using the AASHTO notation [AASHTO, 1992], and substituting $V/V_u = f_v/F_v$ for the service load design, Eq. 9.199 becomes

$$A_{st} = \left[0.15Dt_w(1 - c)\frac{f_v}{F_v} - 18t_w^2 \right] \tag{9.200}$$

Equation 9.200 is the same as AASHTO Eq. 10.31a [AASHTO, 1992]. Or, using the AASHTO–LRFD [AASHTO, 1994] notation, Eq. 9.200 can be expressed as

$$A_s \geq \left[0.15BDt_w(1.0 - C)\frac{V_u}{V_r} - 18.0t_w^2 \right] \left(\frac{F_{yw}}{F_{ys}} \right) \tag{9.201}$$

which is AASHTO–LRFD Eq. 6.10.8.1.4-1 [AASHTO, 1994]. In this equation,

$V_r = \phi V_n$, where V_n = nominal shear strength of girder
$F_{ys} = F_{y,st}$ = stiffener yield strength

In addition to the strength requirements given by Eqs. 9.199 through 9.201, the stiffeners must also be sufficiently stiff to preserve the straight boundaries that are assumed in computing the shear buckling of plate girder webs. An approximate solution by the energy method for determining the stiffness of the transverse stiffeners[29] was given by Timoshenko [1915]. His theory was later extended by Wang [1947] for a plate stiffened by any number of transverse stiffeners; Wang also gave diagrams for plates with three and four transverse stiffeners. A solution to this problem has been given by Stein and Fralich [1949] for the case of an infinitely long web with simply supported edges and equally spaced transverse stiffeners. Their theoretical results, obtained by the *Lagrangian multiplier method*[30] for three equal spacings ($D/d_o = 1, 2,$ and 5), are in fair agreement with the tests on 20 specimens. Based on these results, Bleich [1952] developed a formula for the stiffness required of a transverse stiffener, which can be put in the following form [SSRC, 1988]:

$$I = 2.5Dt_w^3\left(\frac{D}{d_o} - 0.7\frac{d_o}{D}\right), \qquad d_o \le D \qquad (9.202)$$

where I = moment of inertia of the stiffener with respect to the middle plane of the web. The AASHTO specification uses the coefficient of d_o/D in the parentheses as 0.8 instead of 0.7 so that

$$\begin{aligned} I &= 2.5Dt_w^3\left(\frac{D}{d_o} - 0.8\frac{d_o}{D}\right) \\ &= d_o t_w^3\left[2.5\left(\frac{D}{d_o}\right)^2 - 2\right] \\ &= d_o t_w^3 J \end{aligned} \qquad (9.203)$$

where

$$J = 2.5\left(\frac{D}{d_o}\right)^2 - 2 \ge 0.5 \qquad (9.204)$$

Equations 9.203 and 9.204 are the same as AASHTO Eqs. 10.30 and Eq. 10.31, respectively [AASHTO, 1992]. The same equations are also used in AASHTO–LRFD specifications [AASHTO, 1994], as Eqs. 6.10.8.1.3-1 and -2, respectively.

In regard to the stiffener area requirement, it should be noted that if a negative value is obtained from Eq. 9.200, AASHTO 10.34.4.7 [AASHTO, 1992] requires that the transverse stiffeners need only satisfy the moment of inertia requirement of Eq. 9.203 and the following additional requirements:

1. The width of a plate or the outstanding leg of an angle intermediate stiffener must be not less than 2 in. *plus* one-thirtieth of the depth of the girder—preferably not less than one-fourth the full width of the girder flange.
2. The thickness of a plate or the outstanding leg of an angle intermediate stiffener must be not less than one-sixteenth of its width.

Buckling of transversely stiffened plates has been discussed by Klitchieff [1949] who has provided recommendations for rigidity of stiffeners.

The postbuckling shear strength V_n of a plate girder is computed as the sum of the beam shear strength V_{cr} and the tension-field strength action V_{tf}:

---

[29]The problem involved shear strength of plates with one and two transverse stiffeners.
[30]See Bleich [1952], p. 78, for a discussion of this method.

$$V_n = V_{cr} + V_{tf} \tag{9.205}$$
$$= \tau_{cr}A_w + V_{tf}$$

Values of τ_{cr} and V_{tf} are given by Eqs. 9.157 and 9.180, respectively, which, when substituted in Eq. 9.205, and using the AASHTO notation ($h = D$, $a = d_o$, $a/h = d_o/D$, and $A_w = ht_w = Dt_w$), yield

$$V_n = C\tau_y A_w + \frac{1}{2}\sigma_t Dt_w \left(\frac{1}{\sqrt{1 + (d_o/D)^2}} \right) \tag{9.206}$$

With substitution in Eq. 9.206 of $\sigma_t = (1 - C)F_{yw}$ from Eq. 9.187 and $\tau_y = F_{yw}/\sqrt{3}$, we have

$$\begin{aligned} V_n &= CDt_w \frac{F_{yw}}{\sqrt{3}} + \frac{1}{2}Dt_w \left[\frac{(1 - C)F_{yw}}{\sqrt{1 + (d_o/D)^2}} \right] \\ &= \frac{F_{yw}}{\sqrt{3}}Dt_w \left[C + \frac{0.87(1 - C)}{\sqrt{1 + (d_o/D)^2}} \right] \\ &= V_p \left[C + \frac{0.87(1 - C)}{\sqrt{1 + (d_o/D)^2}} \right] \end{aligned} \tag{9.207}$$

where

$$V_p = Dt_w \left(\frac{F_{yw}}{\sqrt{3}} \right) = 0.58F_{yw}Dt_w \tag{9.208}$$

V_P is defined as the shear yield strength of web (AASHTO Eq. 10.114 and AASHTO–LRFD 6.10.7.3.3a-4).

Equation 9.207[31] is the same as AASHTO Eq. 10.113 [AASHTO, 1992] for the load factor design and AASHTO–LRFD Eq. 6.10.7.3.3a-1 [AASHTO, 1994] for load and resistance factor design. For service load design, Eq. 9.207 is expressed in terms of the allowable shear stress F_v obtained by dividing throughout by the web area $A_w = Dt_w$ and a factor of safety of 1.75. Using the approximation $1.75\sqrt{3} \approx 3$, one obtains

$$\frac{V_n}{Dt_w(1.75)} = \frac{F_{yw}}{1.75\sqrt{3}} \left[C + \frac{0.87(1 - C)}{\sqrt{1 + (d_o/D)^2}} \right] \tag{9.209}$$

from which

$$F_v = \frac{F_y}{3} \left[C + \frac{0.87(1 - C)}{\sqrt{1 + (d_o/D)^2}} \right] \tag{9.210}$$

Equation 9.210 is the same as AASHTO Eq. 10.26.

---

[31]With different notation, this equation is the same as Basler's Eq. 14 [Basler, 1961a, p. 691].

It is instructive to note that the same set of web buckling coefficients C (see next paragraph) is used for computing the *allowable* shear (service load design) or the *nominal* shear strength (load factor design) of a plate girder according to the AASHTO specifications. This is because the phenomenon of buckling is independent of the yield strength of the material. The only difference is in the value of the *permitted* shear stress. For the load factor design, the permitted shear stress is $F_y/\sqrt{3}$ ($= 0.58F_y$), whereas for the service load design, it is $\frac{1}{3}F_y = (F_y/\sqrt{3})/\sqrt{3}$, the multiplier to the bracketed term in Eq. 9.210.

The values of the web buckling coefficient C in Eqs. 9.207 through 9.210 are the same as those given by Basler [1961a, p. 704, Eq. 19d]. As defined by Eq. 9.156, coefficient C is the ratio of the critical buckling shear stress to yield shear stress:

$$C = \frac{\tau_{cr}}{\tau_y} = \frac{\pi^2 E k}{\tau_y (12)(1 - v^2)(D/t_w)} \tag{9.211}$$

where the web slenderness ratio h/t_w has been replaced by D/t_w (AASHTO notation). Substitution of $\tau_y = F_y/\sqrt{3}$, $E = 29 \times 10^6$ psi, and $v = 0.3$ in Eq. 9.211 yields

$$C = \frac{45,397,897k}{(D/t_w)^2 F_{y,\text{psi}}} \approx \frac{(4.5 \times 10^7)k}{(D/t_w)^2 F_{y,\text{psi}}} \tag{9.212}$$

and is applicable for the case $C \le 0.8$. The web slenderness ratio corresponding to $C = 0.8$ is

$$\frac{D}{t_w} = \sqrt{\frac{4.5 \times 10^7 k}{(C = 0.8)F_{y,\text{psi}}}} = 7500 \sqrt{\frac{k}{F_{y,\text{psi}}}} \tag{9.213}$$

For values of $C > 0.8$,

$$C = \frac{\tau_{cr}}{\tau_y} = \sqrt{\frac{0.8\pi^2\sqrt{3}E}{12(1 - v^2)F_{y,\text{psi}}} \frac{k}{(D/t_w)^2}}$$

$$= \frac{6026}{(d/t_w)}\sqrt{\frac{k}{F_{y,\text{psi}}}} \approx \frac{6000}{(d/t_w)}\sqrt{\frac{k}{F_{y,\text{psi}}}} \tag{9.214}$$

For design purposes, the values of C given by Eqs. 9.212 through 9.214 are specified for a range of web slenderness ratios to be used in conjunction with Eqs. 9.207 and 9.210 as follows (AASHTO Eq. 10.27, 10.27A, 10.27B, 10.115, and 10.116) [AASHTO, 1992]:

$$C = 1.0 \quad \text{for} \quad \frac{D}{t_w} < 6000 \sqrt{\frac{k}{F_{y,\text{psi}}}} \tag{9.215}$$

$$C = \frac{6000}{(D/t_w)}\sqrt{\frac{k}{F_{y,\text{psi}}}} \quad \text{for} \quad 6000\sqrt{\frac{k}{F_{y,\text{psi}}}} \le \frac{D}{t_w} \le 7500\sqrt{\frac{k}{F_{y,\text{psi}}}} \tag{9.216}$$

$$C = \frac{(4.5 \times 10^7)k}{(d/t_w)^2 F_{y,\text{psi}}} \quad \text{for} \quad \frac{D}{t_w} > 7500\sqrt{\frac{k}{F_{y,\text{psi}}}} \tag{9.217}$$

In AASHTO–LRFD specification [AASHTO, 1994], equations identical to Eqs. 9.215 through 9.217 have been specified (with F_y in ksi units), except that those equations have been normalized with respect to the modulus of elasticity E of steel (29,000 ksi). Thus, multiplying Eqs. 9.215 through 9.217 by $(\sqrt{E/29,000})^{1/2}$ or $(E/29,000)$ as appropriate, one obtains AASHTO–LRFD Eqs. 6.10.7.3.3a-5 through 6.10.7.3.3a-7:

$$C = 1.0 \quad \text{for} \quad \frac{D}{t_w} < 1.10 \sqrt{\frac{Ek}{F_{yw,ksi}}} \tag{9.218}$$

$$C = \frac{1.10}{(D/t_w)} \sqrt{\frac{Ek}{F_{yw,ksi}}} \quad \text{for} \quad 1.10 \sqrt{\frac{Ek}{F_{yw,ksi}}} \le \frac{D}{t_w} \le 1.38 \sqrt{\frac{Ek}{F_{yw,ksi}}} \tag{9.219}$$

$$C = \frac{1.52}{(D/t_w)^2} \frac{Ek}{F_{yw}} \quad \text{for} \quad \frac{D}{t_w} > 1.38 \sqrt{\frac{Ek}{F_{yw,ksi}}} \tag{9.220}$$

It is reiterated that in Eqs. 9.215 through 9.220, the value of the plate buckling coefficient k is given by Eq. 9.147.

In summary, the behavior and the shear strength of a transversely stiffened girder (Eqs. 9.207 and 9.210) are significantly influenced by the panel size d_o/D and the web buckling coefficient C, which, in turn, depends on the web slenderness ratio D/t_w (Eqs. 9.215 through 9.220). Thus, the dependence of the shear strength on the panel size (i.e., the spacing of transverse stiffeners d_o) and the web slenderness ratio (D/t_w) is established. Two additional requirements for the panel size are specified. The first of these, selected somewhat arbitrarily, limits the panel size for the cases where shear stresses are small. The dual requirements, introduced for practical reasons (to facilitate fabrication, handling, and erection) are (AASHTO 10.34.4.2) [AASHTO, 1992]

$$\frac{d_o}{D} \le \left(\frac{260}{D/t_w}\right)^2 \tag{9.221}$$

$$\frac{d_o}{D} \le 3$$

Although the preceding discussion focuses attention on the shear strength of a plate girder as given by Eq. 9.205, it is instructive to express the shear stress in the web at the ultimate conditions. Dividing Eq. 9.180 throughout by the web area $(A_w = ht_w)$, we obtain the shear stress τ_{tf} due to the tension field:

$$\tau_{tf} = \frac{V_{tf}}{ht_w} = \frac{1}{2}\sigma_t \left[\frac{1}{\sqrt{1 + (a/h)^2}} \right] \tag{9.222}$$

Alternatively, expressing the bracketed term in Eq. 9.222 as $\sin \theta_d$ from Eq. 9.174, we have

$$\tau_{tf} = \tfrac{1}{2}\sigma_t \sin \theta_d \tag{9.223}$$

The shear stress at the ultimate conditions is given by the sum of the critical stress τ_{cr} and the shear stress due to the tension field τ_{tf}:

$$\tau_u = \tau_{cr} + \tau_{tf}$$
$$= \tau_{cr} + \tfrac{1}{2}\sigma_t \sin \theta_d \tag{9.224}$$

Combining the critical shear stress τ_{cr} and the tension field shear stress τ_{tf}, and substituting in Mises' yield condition (Eq. 9.184), gives[32] [SSRC, 1988]

$$\sigma_t = -\tfrac{3}{2}\tau_{cr}\sin 2\theta + \sqrt{F_{yw}^2 + (\tfrac{9}{4}\sin^2 2\theta - 3)\tau_{cr}^2} \tag{9.225}$$

where θ = the angle between the tensile membrane stress σ_t and the horizontal. With Basler's assumption that τ_{cr} and τ_{tf} act in the same direction (at 45°) so that they are additive, the resulting combination of the principal stresses in a linear approximation of Mises' yield condition gives

$$\sigma_t = F_{yw}\left(1 - \frac{\tau_{cr}}{\tau_{yw}}\right) \tag{9.226}$$

Substitution of Eq. 9.226 in Eq. 9.224 gives

$$\tau_u = \tau_{cr} + \frac{1}{2}F_{yw}\left(1 - \frac{\tau_{cr}}{\tau_{yw}}\right)\sin \theta_d$$
$$= \tau_{cr} + \frac{1}{2}(F_{yw} - \sqrt{3}\tau_{cr})\sin \theta_d \tag{9.227a}$$

where the value of τ_{cr} is obtained from Eq. 9.142, and F_{yw} and τ_{yw} ($= F_{yw}/\sqrt{3}$) are the web yield stresses in tension and shear, respectively. It is to be noted that according to Basler's assumption that inelastic buckling will occur when $\tau_{cr} > 0.8\tau_{yw}$, the value of τ_{cr} in Eq. 9.226 is to be replaced by τ_{cri} given by Eq. 9.164 [SSRC, 1988, p. 195]. The resulting equation is

$$\tau_u = \tau_{cri} + \frac{1}{2}F_{yw}\left(1 - \frac{\tau_{cri}}{\tau_{yw}}\right)\sin \theta_d \tag{9.227b}$$

Of course, when $\tau_{cri} = \tau_{yw}$ ($= F_y/\sqrt{3}$), the parenthetical term in Eq. 9.227b becomes zero, and the equation reduces to

$$\tau_u = \tau_{cri} \tag{9.227c}$$

A careful examination of Eq. 9.227 leads to the following observations:

1. If transverse stiffeners are not provided ($a \gg h$), then a/h approaches infinity (condition of an unstiffened web) and $\sin \theta_d$ (Eq. 9.174) becomes zero, so that Eq. 9.227a becomes $\tau_u = \tau_{cr}$ and there is no contribution from the tension-field action, and therefore no postbuckling strength.
2. The significance of Eq. 9.227c is that the panel yields in shear, without any tension field being developed, and the shear strength of the panel is limited by τ_{cri}.

It should be realized that thick webs (small h/t_w ratios) will have values of τ_{cr} well in excess of τ_{yw} ($= F_y/\sqrt{3}$) in which case the web will yield and the tension-field action will not develop.

---

[32]This equation is the same as Basler's Eq. 11 [1961a].

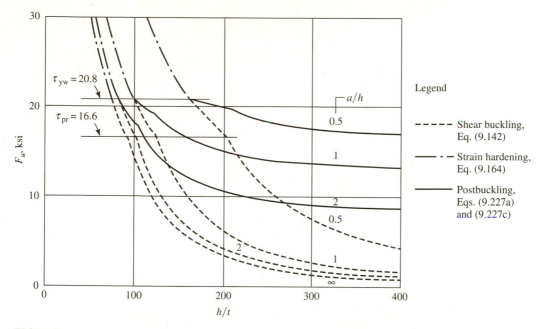

FIGURE 9.61
Comparison of the critical shear and the postbuckling stress for girder webs with various slenderness ratios and panel sizes [Gaylord, Gaylord, and Stallmeyer, 1992].

9.5.7 Comparison of Critical Shear and Tension-Field Stress

In the design of plate girders with *slender* webs, it is important to recognize that the critical shear stress τ_{cr} is smaller than the tension-field stress σ_t. The difference between the two values increases with increase in the web slenderness ratio. As pointed out earlier, these two stresses also depend on the panel size (i.e., the aspect ratio a/h or d_o/D); the smaller the panel size (close stiffener spacing), the larger the postbuckling stress, and hence the postbuckling strength. A comparison of the critical shear stress and the postbuckling stress (which includes the tension-field stress) for four panel sizes is shown in Fig. 9.61. As shown by the dashed curves in this figure, the critical shear stress for webs having panel size below 1 is very small. For the larger panel sizes, the critical shear stress fast approaches the value of the critical shear stress for an unstiffened web. Example 9.1 illustrates the computations for the two kinds of stresses for three different plate girder panel sizes, using the basic equations derived in the preceding paragraphs. Example 9.2 illustrates the use of the AASHTO equations for the same plate girder panels as used in Example 9.1. Example 9.3 illustrates computations for the allowable shear for the girder panel.

> **EXAMPLE 9.1.** Determine the critical and the tension-field stresses and the nominal shear strength of a plate girder panel of a highway bridge, made from a 0.5-in.-thick web (A36 steel), having a web slenderness ratio (D/t_w) of 300, and the aspect ratios as (a) 0.5, (b) 1.0, and (c) 2.0.

Solution. For all cases, $D/t_w = 300$. With $t_w = 0.5$ in.,

$$D = 300t_w = (300)(0.5) = 150 \text{ in.}$$
$$A_w = Dt_w = (150)(0.5) = 75 \text{ in.}^2$$

From Eq. 9.142, the critical shear stress is

$$\begin{aligned}
\tau_{cr} &= \frac{k\pi^2 E}{12(1 - v^2)(D/t_w)^2} \\
&= \frac{k(\pi^2)(29,000)}{(12)(1 - 0.09)(300)^2} \\
&= (0.2912)k \text{ ksi}
\end{aligned}$$

The web shear yield stress and the proportional shear stress are

$$\tau_{yw} = \frac{F_{yw}}{\sqrt{3}} = \frac{36}{\sqrt{3}} = 20.78 \text{ ksi}$$

$$\tau_{pr} = 0.8\tau_{yw} = (0.8)(20.78) = 16.62 \text{ ksi}$$

Aspect ratio, $\alpha = d_o/D = 0.5$. From Eq. 9.147, the plate buckling coefficient is

$$k = 5.0 + \frac{5}{\alpha^2} = 5.0 + \frac{5}{(0.5)^2} = 25$$

Therefore, the critical (or the buckling) shear stress is

$$\tau_{cr} = (0.2912)k = 0.2912 \times 25 = 7.28 \text{ ksi}$$

From Eq. 9.226, the tension-field stress is

$$\begin{aligned}
\sigma_t &= F_{yw}\left(1 - \frac{\tau_{cr}}{\tau_{yw}}\right) \\
&= (36)\left(1 - \frac{7.28}{20.78}\right) \\
&= 23.4 \text{ ksi}
\end{aligned}$$

From Eq. 9.174,

$$\sin\theta_d = \frac{1}{\sqrt{1 + \alpha^2}} = \frac{1}{\sqrt{1 + (0.5)^2}} = 0.8944$$

From Eq. 9.227, the ultimate shear stress is

$$\begin{aligned}
\tau_u &= \tau_{cr} + \tfrac{1}{2}[F_{yw} - \tau_{cr}(\sqrt{3})]\sin\theta_d \\
&= 7.28 + \tfrac{1}{2}[36 - (7.28)(\sqrt{3})](0.8944) \\
&= 17.74 \text{ ksi} > \tau_{pr} = 16.62 \text{ ksi}
\end{aligned}$$

Therefore, use Eq. 9.227b. From Eq. 9.164, we have

$$\tau_{cri} = \sqrt{0.8\tau_{cr}\tau_{yw}} = \sqrt{(0.8)(7.28)(20.78)} = 11.00 \text{ ksi} < \tau_{yw} = 20.78 \text{ ksi}$$

The ultimate shear stress is

$$\begin{aligned}
\tau_u &= \tau_{cri} + \tfrac{1}{2}(F_{yw} - \tau_{cri} \times \sqrt{3})\sin\theta_d \\
&= 11.00 + \tfrac{1}{2} \times (36 - 11.0 \times \sqrt{3}) \\
&= 18.58 \text{ ksi}
\end{aligned}$$

The nominal shear strength is

$$V_n = \tau_u A_w = 18.58 \times 75 = 1394 \text{ kips}$$

It is noted that the postbuckling shear strength is almost 2.6 times ($\approx 18.58/7.28$) the critical shear strength.

Aspect ratio $\alpha = d_o/D = 1.0$

$$k = 5 + \frac{5}{(1)^2} = 10$$

$$\tau_{cr} = (0.2912)k = 0.2912 \times 10 = 2.91$$

The tension-field stress is

$$\sigma_t = F_{yw}\left(1 - \frac{\tau_{cr}}{\tau_{yw}}\right) = (36)\left(1 - \frac{2.91}{20.78}\right) = 30.96 \text{ ksi}$$

$$\sin\theta_d = \frac{1}{\sqrt{1 + \alpha^2}} = \frac{1}{\sqrt{1 + 1}} = 0.707$$

The ultimate shear stress is

$$\begin{aligned}
\tau_u &= \tau_{cr} + \tfrac{1}{2}[(F_{yw} - (\tau_{cr})(\sqrt{3})]\sin\theta_d \\
&= 2.91 + \tfrac{1}{2}[36 - (2.91)(\sqrt{3})](0.707) \\
&= 2.91 + 10.94 \\
&= 13.85 \text{ ksi}
\end{aligned}$$

Therefore, the nominal shear strength is

$$V_n = \tau_u A_w = 13.85 \times 75 = 1039 \text{ kips}$$

It is noted that the postbuckling shear strength is almost 4.8 times ($\approx 13.85/2.91$) the critical shear strength.

Aspect ratio $\alpha = d_o/D = 2.0$

$$k = 5 + \frac{5}{(2)^2} = 6.25$$

$$\tau_{cr} = (0.2912)k = 0.2912 \times 6.25 = 1.82$$

The tension-field stress is

$$\sigma_t = F_{yw}\left(1 - \frac{\tau_{cr}}{\tau_{yw}}\right) = (36)\left(1 - \frac{1.82}{20.78}\right) = 32.85 \text{ ksi}$$

$$\sin\theta_d = \frac{1}{\sqrt{1 + \alpha^2}} = \frac{1}{\sqrt{1 + (2)^2}} = 0.4472$$

The ultimate shear stress is

$$\begin{aligned}
\tau_u &= \tau_{cr} + \tfrac{1}{2}[(F_{yw} - (\tau_{cr})(\sqrt{3})]\sin\theta_d \\
&= 1.82 + \tfrac{1}{2}[36 - (1.82)(\sqrt{3})] \times 0.4472 \\
&= 9.16 \text{ ksi} < \tau_{pr} = 16.62 \text{ ksi}
\end{aligned}$$

TABLE E9.1
Comparison of shear strengths

Shear strength	$\alpha = 0.5$	$\alpha = 1.0$	$\alpha = 2.0$
	$D/t_w = 300, t_w = 0.5$ in.		
Critical shear strength, V_{cr}	546	218	137
Postbuckling shear strength, V_n	1394	1039	687
Ratio of postbuckling to critical shear strength	2.55	4.77	5.01

Therefore, the nominal shear strength is

$$V_n = \tau_u A_w = (9.16)(75) = 687 \text{ kips}$$

It is noted that the postbuckling shear strength is 5 times ($\approx 9.16/1.82$) the critical shear strength.

Comments. The values of the critical and the postbuckling shear stresses computed in Example 9.1 for various aspect ratios can be seen in Fig. 9.61. A comparison of the critical and the postbuckling shear strengths of the panel with the three panel sizes in this example is shown in Table E9.1.

EXAMPLE 9.2. For the plate girder panels of Example 9.1, compute the nominal shear strength using the 1992 AASHTO specifications.

Solution. The nominal shear strength is obtained from Eq. 9.207 (AASHTO Eq. 10.113). For all cases,

$$D/t_w = 300, \ D = (300)(t_w) = 300 \times 0.5 = 150 \text{ in.}$$

$$A_w = Dt_w = (150)(0.5) = 75 \text{ in.}^2$$

From Eq. 9.208 (AASHTO Eq. 10.114), we have

$$V_P = 0.58 F_y Dt_w = (0.58)(36)(75) = 1566 \text{ kips}$$

Ranges of D/t_w to determine the web buckling coefficient C are obtained from Eqs. 9.215 through 9.217 (AASHTO Eqs. 10.115 and 10.116):

$$\frac{6000\sqrt{k}}{\sqrt{F_y}} = \frac{6000\sqrt{k}}{\sqrt{36,000}} = 31.623\sqrt{k}$$

$$\frac{7500\sqrt{k}}{\sqrt{F_y}} = \frac{7500\sqrt{k}}{\sqrt{36,000}} = 47.434\sqrt{k}$$

From Eq. 9.217 (AASHTO Eq. 10.116), for $D/t_w > 7500\sqrt{k}/\sqrt{F_y}$

$$C = \frac{(4.5)(10^7)(k)}{(D/t_w)^2 F_y} = \frac{(4.5 \times 10^7)k}{(300)^2(36,000)} = 0.0139k$$

$\alpha = 0.5, k = 25$ (from Example 9.1)

$$31.623\sqrt{k} = (31.623)(\sqrt{25}) = 158.11 < \frac{D}{t_w} = 300$$

$$47.434\sqrt{k} = (47.434)(\sqrt{25}) = 237.17 < \frac{D}{t_w} = 300$$

Therefore, C is to be obtained from Eq. 9.217 (AASHTO Eq. 10.116):

$$C = 0.0139k = 0.0139 \times 25 = 0.35$$

$$\left[C + \frac{0.87(1 - C)}{\sqrt{1 + (d_o/D)^2}} \right] = \left[0.35 + \frac{(0.87)(1 - 0.35)}{\sqrt{1 + (0.5)^2}} \right] = 0.856$$

Therefore, the nominal strength is (Eq. 9.207 or AASHTO Eq. 10.113)

$$V_n = (0.856)V_P = (0.856)(1566) = 1340 \text{ kips}$$

which is a little smaller than 1394 kips obtained in Example 9.1 for aspect ratio 0.5. Note that the value of the web buckling coefficient, C, by definition (Eq. 9.211), is

$$C = \frac{\tau_{cr}}{\tau_{yw}} = \frac{7.28}{36/\sqrt{3}} = 0.35 \qquad \text{as computed above}$$

$\alpha = 1.0, k = 10$ (from Example 9.1)

$$31.623\sqrt{k} = (31.623)(\sqrt{10}) = 100 < \frac{D}{t_w} = 300$$

$$47.434\sqrt{k} = (47.434)(\sqrt{10}) = 150 < \frac{D}{t_w} = 300$$

Therefore, C is to be obtained from Eq. 9.217 (AASHTO Eq. 10.116):

$$C = 0.0139k = (0.0139)(10) = 0.14$$

$$\left[C + \frac{0.87(1 - C)}{\sqrt{1 + (d_o/D)^2}} \right] = \left[0.14 + \frac{(0.87)(1 - 0.14)}{\sqrt{1 + (1)^2}} \right] = 0.669$$

Therefore, the nominal strength is

$$V_n = (0.669)V_P = (0.669)(1566) = 1048 \text{ kips}$$

which is very close to 1039 kips obtained in Example 9.1 for aspect ratio 1.0. Note that the value of the web buckling coefficient, C, by definition (Eq. 9.211), is

$$C = \frac{\tau_{cr}}{\tau_{yw}} = \frac{2.91}{36/\sqrt{3}} = 0.14 \qquad \text{as computed above}$$

$\alpha = 2.0, k = 6.25$ (from Example 9.1)

$$(31.623)\sqrt{k} = (31.623)(\sqrt{6.25}) = 79.1 < \frac{D}{t_w} = 300$$

$$(47.434)\sqrt{k} = (47.434)(\sqrt{10}) = 118.6 < \frac{D}{t_w} = 300$$

Therefore, C is to be obtained from Eq. 9.217 (AASHTO Eq. 10.116):

$$C = 0.0139k = (0.0139)(6.25) = 0.087$$

$$\left[C + \frac{0.87(1 - C)}{\sqrt{1 + (d_o/D)^2}} \right] = \left[0.087 + \left(\frac{(0.87)(1 - 0.087)}{\sqrt{1 + (2)^2}} \right) \right] = 0.442$$

Therefore, the nominal strength is

$$V_n = (0.442)V_P = (0.442)(1566) = 697 \text{ kips}$$

which is very close to 687 kips obtained in Example 9.1 for aspect ratio 2.0. Note that the value of the web buckling coefficient C, by definition (Eq. 9.211), is

$$C = \frac{\tau_{cr}}{\tau_{yw}} = \frac{1.82}{(36/\sqrt{3})} = 0.087 \qquad \text{as computed above}$$

EXAMPLE 9.3. Calculate the allowable shear for the panels of the plate girder in Example 9.1 according to the 1992 AASHTO specifications.

Solution. The allowable shear stress is given by Eq. 9.210 (AASHTO Eq. 10.26):

$$F_v = \frac{F_y}{3}\left[C + \frac{0.87(1 - C)}{\sqrt{1 + (d_o/D)^2}}\right]$$

The values of the web buckling coefficients C are calculated from Eqs. 9.215 through 9.217 (AASHTO Eqs. 10.27 and 10.27A), which are the same as for the load factor design (AASHTO Eqs. 10.115 and 10.116) used for Example 9.2, and so the bracketed quantities in Eq. 9.210 remain the same as in the previous example. Using those values, we have the following.

$\alpha = 0.5$

$$F_v = \left(\frac{F_y}{3}\right)(0.856) = \left(\frac{36}{3}\right)(0.856) = 10.27 \text{ ksi}$$

$$V = F_v A_w = (10.27)(75) = 770 \text{ kips}$$

$\alpha = 1.0$

$$F_v = \left(\frac{F_y}{3}\right)(0.669) = \left(\frac{36}{3}\right)(0.669) = 8.03 \text{ ksi}$$

$$V = F_v A_w = (8.03)(75) = 602 \text{ kips}$$

$\alpha = 2.0$

$$F_v = \left(\frac{F_y}{3}\right)(0.442) = \left(\frac{36}{3}\right)(0.442) = 5.30 \text{ ksi}$$

$$V = F_v A_w = (5.30)(75) = 398 \text{ kips}$$

9.5.8 Ultimate Shear Capacity of Plate Girders with Web Openings

9.5.8.1 General considerations

Often it is found necessary to provide openings in the webs of plate and box girders for carrying utility conduits and for providing access for inspection. The opening, usually circular or rectangular, may be concentric or eccentric with respect to the longitudinal axis of the web or the panel of a plate girder (Fig. 9.62). The presence of an opening in the web of a girder will alter the stress distribution in the member and its collapse behavior, and result in loss of strength. This was determined by twelve tests conducted by Hoglund [1971c] on four simply supported statically loaded plate girders containing both rectangular and circular holes. The webs, having slenderness ratios between 200 and 300, were, in keeping with the Swedish practice, unstiffened. These tests showed that the girders having openings in the high-shear zones failed at loads considerably lower than those that had openings in the high-moment zones. To develop the required girder strength, these openings therefore require extra reinforcing around their perimeter such as stiffeners or thickening of the plate material.

Although the literature is replete with discussion on shear strength of unstiffened and stiffened webs, relatively little has been done in terms of developing analytical tools to calculate the shear strength of webs with holes and cutouts of various configurations (round, elliptical, rectangular, etc.). Analysis and design of perforated webs can be classified into two categories: thick webs, which are commonly encountered in the hot-rolled wide-flange beams, and thin webs, which usually form part of plate and box girders. The available analytical methods have generally focused on the shear strength of thick perforated webs with D/t_w ratios in the range of 50 to 80, and have been reviewed by Redwood [1983]. Mathematical models for the analysis and design of thick perforated plates are mostly based on plastic design philosophy [Redwood, 1972; Redwood and Shrivastava, 1980]. However, these methods are not applicable to the thin

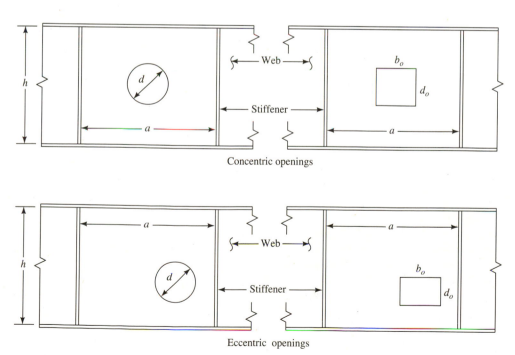

FIGURE 9.62
Plate girders with web openings.

webs used for plate and box girders, whose slenderness ratios typically vary between 300 and 350 and which invariably buckle before the collapse of the girder.

Needless to say, the presence of openings in a web complicates the analysis for strength of webs. The value of the critical shear stress τ_c is reduced in both the elastic and the postbuckling range. It has been suggested [Narayanan and Der-Avanessian, 1982a] that the critical shear stress in a web subjected to a state of pure shear may be calculated by an expression similar to Eq. 9.142:

$$(\tau_c)_{\text{red}} = k_0 \frac{\pi^2 E}{12(1 - v^2)} \left(\frac{t_w}{h}\right)^2 \tag{9.228}$$

where k_0 is the shear buckling coefficient for a plate with a circular opening whose value is given by

$$k_0 = k_s \left(1 - \frac{d}{h}\right) \tag{9.229}$$

where d and h are the diameter of the opening and the height of the web, respectively. In Eq. 9.229, the value of k_s is given by Eq. 9.145 for a plate simply supported on all four sides. For a plate with all four edges clamped (or fixed), the value of k_s, for $\alpha > 1$, is given approximately by [Bleich, 1952]

$$k_s = 8.98 + \frac{5.60}{\alpha^2} \tag{9.230}$$

Thus, in the elastic range, the reduced value of the critical shear stress for a plate with a circular opening can be obtained from the following approximate relationship:

$$(\tau_c)_{\text{red}} = k_s \left(1 - \frac{d}{h}\right) \frac{\pi^2 E}{12(1 - v^2)} \left(\frac{t_w}{h}\right)^2 \tag{9.231}$$

It is theorized that the presence of an opening in the web results in significant increase in the relative stiffness of the flange in comparison to that of the web, so that the boundary conditions approach clamped supports. Consequently, it has been suggested [Narayanan and Der-Avanessian, 1981a] that the value of k_s in Eq. 9.229 should be that for a plate with clamped edges (Eq. 9.230).

Based on the collapse mechanism (shear sway) model of Rockey, Porter, and Evans [1974] shown in Fig. 9.55, a method of computing the nominal shear strength of a plate girder with web openings has been suggested by Narayanan [1983]. The Rockey-Porter-Evans model gives the nominal shear strength V_n as the sum of three components: the critical load on the web, the contribution from the tension field action, and the contribution from the flanges when the collapse is imminent. It assumes that the tensile membrane stress, together with the critical shear stress, causes yielding of the flanges, and failure occurs when two hinges are formed in each flange to produce a combined mechanism that includes the yield zone $WXYZ$ (Fig. 9.55(c)). On the formation of hinges in the flanges, their moment capacity is equal to their plastic moment capacity, M_{pf}. Thus, for a girder *without* the web openings, the ultimate shear strength is obtained by adding the contribution of the flange stiffness to the load taken by the web [Narayanan, 1983, Eq. 1.4]:

$$V_u = \tau_{cr} A_w + \sigma_t A_w \left[\frac{c}{h} + \cot\theta - \cot\theta_d \right] \sin^2\theta + \frac{4M_{pf}}{c} \qquad (9.232)$$

where θ = angle of inclination of the membrane tensile stress
θ_d = angle between the panel diagonal and the flange
c = distance of the hinge locations as shown in Fig. 9.55(c)
M_{pf} = plastic moment capacity of the flange plates given by (for each flange)

$$M_{pf} = \left(\frac{b_f t_f^2}{4} \right) \sigma_{yf} \qquad (9.233)$$

where σ_{yf} and $b_f t_f^2/4$ are the yield strength and the plastic section modulus of the flange, respectively. The flange is assumed to act with an effective width of web b_e [SSRC, 1988, Eq. 6.15]:

$$b_e = 30t \left(1 - \frac{\tau_{cr}}{\tau_{yw}} \right), \qquad \frac{\tau_{cr}}{\tau_{yw}} \le 0.5 \qquad (9.234)$$

In Eq. 9.232, the middle term is the contribution of the tension-field force. The distance c (Fig. 9.55(c)) is given by

$$c = \frac{2}{\sin\theta} \sqrt{\frac{M_{pf}}{\sigma_t t_w}}, \qquad 0 \le c \le a \qquad (9.235)$$

and the value of the membrane tensile stress σ_t is to be computed from Eq. 9.225. It is interesting to note that if flanges cannot develop moment, then $M_{pf} = 0$, which gives $c = 0$ (from Eq. 9.235). Substitution of these values in Eq. 9.232 yields

$$V_n = \tau_{cr} A_w + \sigma_t A_w (\cot\theta - \cot\theta_d) \sin^2\theta \qquad (9.236)$$

The maximum value of V_n can be obtained by differentiating with respect to θ, the resulting expression being the true Basler's solution (Eq. 9.183).

9.5.8.2 Web with circular holes

An extensive investigation of thin webs with slenderness ratios in the range 200 to 350 and containing circular and rectangular holes was carried out at University College, Cardiff, England. The specimens varied in web slenderness, flange stiffness, and the size of the openings and were subjected to shear loading. Based on the ultimate load tests on 20 panels containing centrally placed holes, Narayanan and Rockey [1981] determined the following:

1. The ultimate shear strength of webs dropped almost linearly with the increase in the diameter of the opening.
2. The failure mechanism observed in girders with web holes was similar to that observed in girders with no web holes (Fig. 9.55), the only difference being in the position of the hinges.
3. The position and the diameter of the hole relative to the panel size have significant influence on the ultimate shear strength of girders with circular web holes. Eccentrically located small-diameter holes having $d \le 0.25h$ do not reduce the ultimate

shear strength of the girder appreciably, but for webs with larger holes, the ultimate shear strength is reduced significantly.

Based on the test results of this investigation, Narayanan and Rockey [1981] suggested an approximate method for computing the ultimate shear strength of a plate girder with circular web holes. It was theorized that if the diameter d of the hole extended the full depth of the web h, the failure would be essentially due to the *Vierendeel mechanism,* with hinges formed at the centers of both flanges (Fig. 9.63). The load corresponding to this mechanism is defined as the *Vierendeel load.* The proposed method consists of linearly interpolating between the value of the ultimate shear strength V_n given by Eq. 9.232 and the Vierendeel load V_v given by

$$V_V = \frac{8M_{pf}}{a} \tag{9.237}$$

where a = clear width of web plate between the stiffeners. Then, the ultimate shear strength of a girder with web having a circular hole of diameter d smaller than the web depth h can be approximately expressed as

$$V_{ult} = V_V + \left[\frac{V_n - V_V}{h}\right](h - d) \tag{9.238}$$

Although Eq. 9.238 is empiric, the ultimate shear strength predicted by this equation is reported to be in fair agreement with the test results [Narayanan and Rockey, 1981].

The position of the hole relative to the panel has significant influence on the ultimate shear strength in that the hole may interfere with the spread of the tension field in the web, which is included in Eq. 9.238. In general, two cases can be considered: concentric

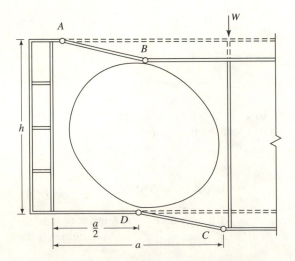

Note: Two hinges are formed at the center of the flanges when the diameter of the hole is nearly equal to the depth.

FIGURE 9.63
Vierendeel failure mechanism in a plate girder [Narayanan, 1983].

hole (Fig. 9.64(*a*)), and eccentric hole. In the latter case, the hole may be small (Fig. 9.64(*b*)) or large (Fig. 9.64(*c*)).

In the case of a concentric hole it has been observed that two tension bands—one above and the other below the opening—are formed. The free-body diagram in Fig. 9.65 shows the position of the hinges and forces due to the membrane tension field. The web area (or the band) containing the hole is assumed to be free of the membrane stresses. The vertical components of the two membrane tensile forces (F_s in each band) can be expressed as

$$2F_s = \sigma_t tw[2c \sin \theta + (h - a \tan \theta) \cos \theta - d] \qquad (9.239)$$

where the quantity in brackets is the total net width of the two tension bands (measured normal to the direction of the membrane stresses). The membrane stress σ_t is evaluated by applying Mises' yield criterion as before, except that the critical stress is the reduced value given by Eq. 9.231:

$$\sigma_t = -\tfrac{3}{2}(\tau_{cr})_{red} \sin 2\theta + \sqrt{F_{yw}^2 + (\tau_{cr})_{red}^2(\tfrac{9}{4} \sin^2 2\theta - 3)} \qquad (9.240)$$

The ultimate shear capacity is obtained from the vertical equilibrium of the free body:

$$V_u = (V_{cr})_{red} + 2F_s \sin \theta \qquad (9.241)$$

With substitution for F_s and σ_t from Eqs. 9.239 and 9.240, respectively, Eq. 9.241 becomes

$$\begin{aligned} V_u = {}&2c\sigma_t t_w \sin^2 \theta + \sigma_t A_w(\cot \theta - \cot \theta_d) \sin^2 \theta \\ &- \sigma_t t_w d \sin \theta + (\tau_{cr})_{red} A_w \end{aligned} \qquad (9.242)$$

Eq. 9.242 is suggested to be valid for all circular openings having $d \le (h \cos \theta - a \sin \theta)$ and covers all practical ranges of the hole diameters. For girders with larger holes, a separate method has been suggested by Narayanan and Der-Avanessian [1981a].

It should be noted that when the hole diameter $d = 0$, Eq. 9.242 reduces to the solution for a web without a hole (Eq. 9.238). In the case of a web with a small eccentrically placed hole (Fig. 9.63*b*), such that the hole does not interfere with the idealized tension band, V_u can be obtained from Eq. 9.242 by deleting the term containing the hole diameter d, the resulting equation being Eq. 9.238. Its validity is limited to the case when the spread of the tension field in the tension flange, g, is greater than the hinge distance c, where g is given by [Narayanan, 1983]

$$g = a - \frac{d}{2}\left(\cot \frac{\theta}{2} + 1\right) \qquad (9.243)$$

When the diameter of the hole is large enough to interfere with the idealized tension band (Fig. 9.64(*c*)), the hinge distances in the compression flange (C_c) and the tension flange (C_t) are not equal. Based on tests, it has been determined that there is no change in the location of the hinge in the compression flange (i.e., $c_t = c$). However, the hinge in the tension flange forms below the vertical diameter of the hole so that

$$c_t = a - \frac{d}{2} \qquad (9.244)$$

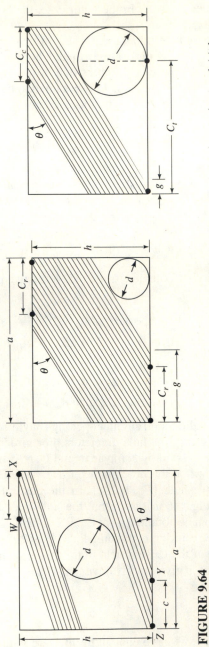

FIGURE 9.64
Tension field action in a web with circular openings: (*a*) concentric opening; (*b*) small eccentric opening; and (*c*) large eccentric opening [Narayanan, 1983].

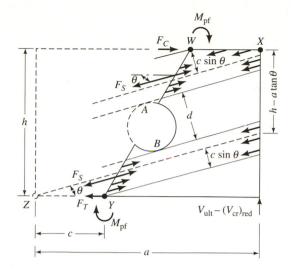

FIGURE 9.65

Free-body diagram showing membrane tensile forces in the two tension bands in a web with a circular hole [Narayanan, 1983].

For this case, it has been shown that the ultimate shear strength of the girder can be obtained from Eq. 9.245, which is valid for the case of $g < C_c$ [Narayanan, 1983]:

$$
\begin{aligned}
V_u = {} & (\tau_{cr})_{red} A_w + 0.5\sigma_t t_w \sin^2\theta \left[C_c - a + \frac{d}{2}\left(\cot\frac{\theta}{2} + 1 \right) \right] \\
& + \sigma_t t_w \left[h\cot\theta - \frac{d}{2}\left(\cot\frac{\theta}{2} + 1 \right) \right] \sin^2\theta + 2M_{pf}\left(\frac{C_c + c_t}{C_c C_t} \right)
\end{aligned}
\tag{9.245}
$$

9.5.8.3 Web with square and rectangular openings

For square plates having square or rectangular openings (Fig. 9.65), Shanmugam and Narayanan [1982] and Narayanan and Der-Avanessian [1982a] have suggested the following approximate formula to obtain the elastic critical stress:

$$
(\tau_{cr})_{red} = \frac{k_s \pi^2 E}{12(1 - v^2)} \left(\frac{t_w}{d} \right) \left[1 - \alpha_r \sqrt{\frac{A_c}{A}} \right]
\tag{9.246}
$$

where k_s = the plate buckling coefficient given by Eq. 9.230
    A = total area of plate including the opening
      = bd
    A_c = area of the opening
      = $b_o d_o$ (Fig. 9.66(a))
    α_r = a coefficient that depends on the boundary conditions of the plate
      = 1.25 for clamped edges

Note that even though Eq. 9.246 gives an approximate solution, the magnitude of approximation is very small because the elastic critical load forms only a small part of the ultimate load.

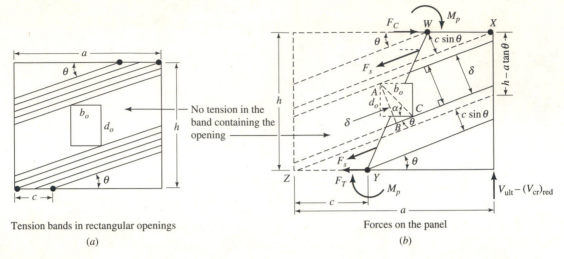

Tension bands in rectangular openings

(a)

Forces on the panel

(b)

FIGURE 9.66

A square plate with rectangular opening: (*a*) geometry of the plate; (*b*) free-body diagram [Narayanan, 1983].

Similar to the case of a plate with circular holes, four hinges—two in each flange—are formed when the collapse is imminent. Membrane tensile stresses are developed in the web in the form of two tension bands—one above and the other below the opening, as shown in Fig. 9.66(*a*)—whereas the band containing the opening is assumed to be free of the membrane stresses. Figure 9.66(*b*) shows the free-body diagram to the right of WY, along with the forces acting on the panel at this stage, and the hinges formed at W, X, Y, and Z. Because there are no membrane forces across AB (δ, the dimension perpendicular to the stress-free band containing the opening), the length δ may be considered as equivalent to the diameter of an imaginary central circular hole. From the geometry of the panel and the opening,

$$AC = \sqrt{b_o^2 + d_o^2}$$

$$\frac{AB}{AC} = \sin(\alpha + \theta) \tag{9.247}$$

$$\delta = AB = AC \sin(\alpha + \theta)$$
$$= \sqrt{b_o^2 + d_o^2} \sin(\alpha + \theta)$$

The total net width of the two tension bands (measured normal to the direction of the membrane stresses) is

$$\text{Net width of bands} = 2c \sin\theta + (h - a\tan\theta)\cos\theta - \delta \tag{9.248}$$

From the free-body diagram (Fig. 9.66(*b*)), the resultant $2F_s$ of the membrane tensile stresses (F_s in each band) can be expressed as

$$2F_s = \sigma_t \text{ (area of the web normal to the membrane stresses)}$$
$$= \sigma_t t_w [2c \sin \theta + (h - a \tan \theta) \cos \theta - \delta] \tag{9.249}$$

The vertical equilibrium of the free body yields

$$2F_s \sin \theta = V_u - (V_{cr})_{red}$$

from which

$$V_u = (V_{cr})_{red} + 2F_s \sin \theta \tag{9.250}$$

Substitution for F_s from Eq. 9.249 in Eq. 9.250 yields

$$V_u = (\tau_{cr})_{red} A_w + \sigma_t [2ct_w + A_w(\cot \theta - \cot \theta_d)] \sin^2 \theta$$
$$- \sigma_t t_w \sqrt{b_o^2 + d_o^2} \sin(\alpha + \theta) \sin \theta \tag{9.251}$$

which is valid for all depths of the rectangular openings except those given by $d_o > [h - (a + b_o)]$, which are unlikely to be encountered in practice.

9.5.8.4 Shear strength of webs containing reinforced openings

The presence of a web opening, depending on its size and location, may result in loss of shear strength of a plate girder, which may be unacceptable. In such cases, the openings are reinforced or stiffened around their boundaries, to restore the web to its capacity without the openings.

Commonly used reinforcement schemes involve the use of bars completely around the openings or the use of both horizontal and vertical bars. In the case of a web with a circular hole, the reinforcement is usually in the form of a ring around the hole (Fig. 9.67(a)). When the reinforcement is provided in the form of bars, e.g., to reinforce a rectangular opening, the horizontal bars, placed symmetrically above and below the opening (Fig. 9.67(b)) and welded to both faces of the web, are fully effective. Vertical bars or bars around the periphery of the opening are unnecessary and are not cost-effective. A discussion on the evaluation of the ultimate shear strength of plate girders with reinforced holes, based on the same principles as the strength of unreinforced webs, has been provided by Narayanan [1983].

The preceding discussion presents a brief summary of a basic approach to the problem of the ultimate shear strength of plate girders with web holes. For an in-depth study of this problem, refer to the work of Bowers [1966a,b, 1968], Rockey, Anderson, and Cheung [1967], Frost and Leffler [1971], Hoglund [1971], Mandel et al. [1971], Cooper and Snell [1972], ASCE [1973], Chan and Redwood [1974], Wang, Snell, and Cooper [1974], Larson and Shah [1976], Cooper, Snell, and Knostman [1977], Redwood, Baranda, and Daly [1978], Redwood and Uenoya [1979], Dougherty [1980], Narayanan [1980], Redwood and Shrivastava [1980], Narayanan and Der-Avanessian [1981a,b, 1982a,b], Narayanan and Rockey [1981], Redwood [1983] and Cooper and Roychowdbury, [1990]. Design tables for rectangular holes have been provided by Redwood [1972]. A design example has been presented by Kussman and Cooper [1976]. A discussion and examples, with a bibliography, on design of both noncomposite and composite girders using rolled W-shapes have been provided by Darwin [1990].

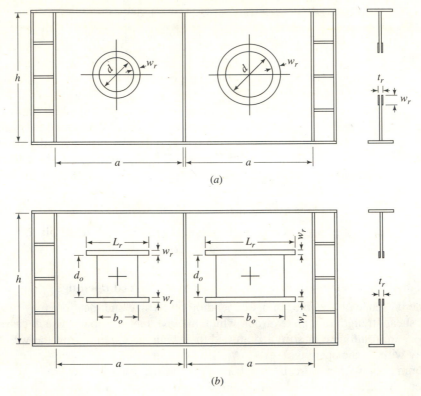

FIGURE 9.67
Reinforcement for web openings: (*a*) ring around circular holes; (*b*) horizontal bars for rectangular openings.

9.5.8.5 Influence of web openings on deflection

The influence of an opening on the deflection of a girder is a function of size, shape, and the location of the opening. In general, the presence of an opening in a girder's web results in reduced stiffness in the region of the opening and tends to increase the deflection. The effect of a single opening is small; however, multiple openings can increase the deflection appreciably.

According to a summary provided by Darwin [1990], circular openings have less effect on deflection than rectangular openings. The deflection caused by the opening increases with its size and closeness to the support. According to Donahey [1987] and Redwood [1983], rectangular openings with a depth d_o up to 50 percent of beam depth h, and circular openings with diameter d up to 60 percent of the depth h, cause little additional deflection. Procedures for computing deflections of girders with web openings have been discussed by McMormic [1972], ASCE [1973], and Dougherty [1980], among others. Donahey and Darwin [1986] and Donahey [1987] have discussed methods to compute deflection of composite members with perforated webs. A summary of these methods has been provided by Darwin [1990].

9.5.9 Special Cases

Heretofore, the discussion has focused on the shear strength of conventional plate girders, i.e., prismatic girders with vertical stiffeners. Exceptions to these are girders with different arrangements of stiffeners and girder geometry. Yonezawa et al. [1978] have proposed an ultimate strength theory for girders with webs having both vertical and diagonal stiffeners (placed between the adjacent vertical stiffeners). With this type of stiffener arrangement, the nominal shear strength of the girder is assumed to consist of three components: the critical (beam) shear force V_{cr} taken by the diagonally stiffened web, the shear force V_{tf} contributed by the tension-field action, and the shear force V_s taken by the diagonal stiffener. The buckling coefficient k_s is evaluated for the case of a plate with diagonal stiffener under shear.

Often, tapered girders are required for long continuous spans. Shear buckling of simply supported plates of variable depth has been investigated by El Gaaly [1973], who has provided charts for buckling coefficients based on the finite analysis. A method for estimating the nominal shear strength of girders with small tapers has been proposed by Falby and Lee [1976]. The method is somewhat approximate in that it does not take into account the effect on shear of the axial force in the inclined flange. This drawback has been eliminated by Davies and Mandel [1979], who have extended Rockey's tension-field model [Rockey, Porter, and Evans, 1974; Porter, Rockey, and Evans, 1975] to the case of tapered web girders. Their theory takes into account the influence of the axial force in the inclined flange and is not restricted to small tapers. Interested readers should refer to the cited references.

9.6
STRENGTH UNDER COMBINED BENDING AND SHEAR

Heretofore, we have discussed the behavior of plate girders under the separate actions of bending and shear. However, a common loading condition of plate girders involves a combination of both bending and shear. In general, a plate girder (and for that matter any flexural member) can be loaded in bending alone, but not to shear alone. This becomes obvious when one considers the fundamental relationship between shear and moment—shear is simply the rate of change of moment ($V = dM/dx$). In a practical plate girder, the various web panels will be subjected to different combinations of bending and shearing forces. In simply supported plate girders, the panels near the supports will be subjected primarily to shear (because moment is very small), whereas those near the midspan will be subjected to a combination of both bending and shear.

The problems of rectangular plates under the action of combined bending and shear were studied by Stein [1934], who gave tables showing the interaction between critical longitudinal stresses σ_c and critical shear stresses τ_c. Stowell and Schwartz [1943] and Batdorf and Stein [1947] examined the problems of plates under combined shear and uniform longitudinal stress. The problems of stiffened plates were studied by Timoshenko [1915, 1921].

In the case of plate girders with very slender webs, slight out-of-plane deflections of web (characterized as "bend buckling") result in transfer of flexural resistance from the web to the flanges. However, the shear-carrying capacity of the web, mostly contributed by the tension field, remains undiminished. When the webs are stocky, the possibility of bend buckling is precluded, but a combination of high web shear and bending may cause the webs to yield adjacent to the flanges, thus losing the webs' contribution to the girder's flexural capacity. As a result, a part of the web's share of bending moment must be resisted by the flanges. Consideration of girder strength under combined bending and shear thus results from the fact that in the presence of relatively high shear and moment, the full shear strength, V_u, and the full flexural strength, M_u, cannot be realized simultaneously. To define the girder strength under these conditions, an interaction diagram is used.

The interaction diagram described in the following paragraphs is based on empirical interaction equations, "determined arbitrarily but based on possible premises and agreeing reasonably well with test results" [Cooper, Galambos, and Ravindra, 1978]. It should be noted that there is no analytical basis for the interaction equations, and few test results are available. Initially, the interaction equations for plate girders were developed by Basler [1961b] based on tests conducted at Lehigh University. Later, Herzog [1974b] conducted 52 tests on plate girders to study their ultimate static strength, but most of these fall into the category where shear predominates.

Reference is made to Fig. 9.68 for discussing the interaction diagram. The following notations are introduced:

A_f = area of each flange

h = height of web

= the approximate distance between the centroids of flanges

M_f = moment carried by flanges when fully yielded

= $A_f F_y h$

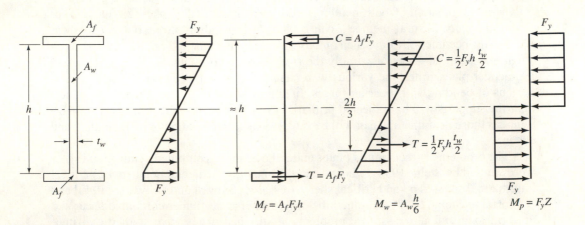

FIGURE 9.68
Plastic-elastic stress distribution in a plate girder at yield moment M_y and M_p.

Assuming the flanges to be at yield, and linear flexural stress distribution over the girder's cross section, the moment carried by the web is given by

$$M_w = F_y S_w = \frac{F_y A_w h}{6} \tag{9.252}$$

where S_w = section modulus of the web = $t_w h^2/6 = A_w h/6$. For the purpose of this discussion, the nominal moment M_n equals the yield moment, M_y, defined as the moment that will cause yielding at the centroid of the compression flange. Thus,

$$
\begin{aligned}
M_n &= M_y \\
&= M_f + M_w \\
&= A_f h F_y + \frac{F_y A_w h}{6} \\
&= F_y \left(A_f + \frac{A_w}{6} \right) h \\
&= A_f F_y h \left(1 + \frac{1}{6} \frac{A_w}{A_f} \right)
\end{aligned}
\tag{9.253}
$$

When the web has fully yielded in shear, it cannot resist any moment and the entire flexural resistance is provided by the flanges. This condition can be described as

$$
\begin{aligned}
V &= V_y = A_w F_{vy} \\
0 &\le M_f \le A_f F_y h
\end{aligned}
\tag{9.254}
$$

The plastic moment, M_p, is defined as the moment capacity of the fully yielded cross section. Thus,

$$M_p = F_y Z > M_y \tag{9.255}$$

The desired interaction diagram can be plotted by considering yielding of the flanges and the web under high moment and shear. It is based on the following hypotheses:

1. When the moment is high, stresses in entire flanges and the adjacent portions of the web reach yield level. This condition is described by Eq. 9.253.
2. When the shear is high, the middle portion of the web yields in shear and loses its ability to carry any moment, and therefore all moment must be carried by the flanges. This condition is described by Eq. 9.254.
3. In another situation, only the flanges are assumed to have yielded, whereas normal stresses σ ($< F_y$) and shearing stresses τ ($< \tau_y$) act over the entire web depth and are interrelated by the Hencky–von Mises yield criterion [Basler, 1961b]:

$$\sigma^2 + 3\tau^2 = \sigma_y^2 \tag{9.256}$$

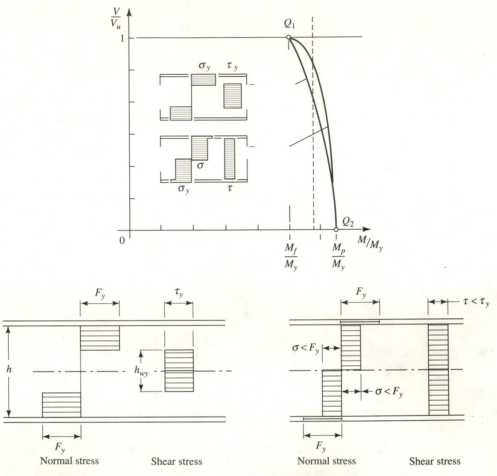

FIGURE 9.69

Basler's interaction diagram [Basler, 1961b].

The states of stresses corresponding to items (1) and (2) are shown in Basler's interaction diagram (Fig. 9.69). In the interaction diagram, both the applied shear force V and the applied moment M are nondimensionalized by dividing by V_n and M_n, respectively. Thus, M/M_n is plotted as the abscissa and V/V_n as the ordinate of the interaction diagram. To plot the interaction diagram, the following possible loading conditions should be recognized:

1. When $M = 0$, V can be as large as V_n, which is given by[33]

$$V_n = ht_w F_y \approx A_w F_y \tag{9.257}$$

---

[33]The discussion presented here is based on Basler's work [1961b]. His notations V_u to denote the nominal shear strength and M_u to denote the flexural strength have been changed to V_n and M_n, respectively.

2. When $M = M_f$, V can still be as large as V_n, because V_n is assumed to be carried by web only.
3. When $V = 0$, M can be as large as M_p as given by Eq. 9.255.

In Fig. 9.69, condition 1 is represented by $V/V_n = 1$, corresponding to $M/M_n = 0$. Condition 2 is represented by point Q_1, whose coordinates are $(M_f/M_n, 1.0)$. Thus, the horizontal line through $V/V_n = 1.0$ on the y-axis and the point $(M_f/M_n, 1.0)$ represent the first two loading conditions. The third loading condition—that the moment of resistance, in the absence of shear (i.e., $V = 0$), can be as large as the plastic moment M_p—is given by point Q_2 on the abscissa, whose coordinates are $(M_p/M_n, 0)$.

In the presence of some moment, only a central portion of the web having depth equal to h_{wy} is assumed to have yielded in shear as shown in Fig. 9.69, so that the corresponding nominal shear strength is

$$V'_n = h_{wy}t_w\tau_y \tag{9.258}$$

Dividing Eq. 9.257 by Eq. 9.258 yields the value of h_{wy} as

$$h_{wy} = \left(\frac{V'_n}{V_n}\right)h \tag{9.259}$$

According to the aforestated hypothesis, the central portion of the web having area equal to $t_f h_{wy}$, having yielded in shear, cannot resist any moment. Therefore, the nominal moment strength M'_n corresponding to this condition is given by

$$M'_n = A_f F_y h + \left(t_w\frac{h}{2}\right)F_y\left(\frac{h}{2}\right) - t_w\left(\frac{h_{wy}}{2}\right)F_y\left(\frac{h_{wy}}{2}\right)$$
$$= F_y h\left[A_f + \frac{1}{4}A_w - \frac{1}{4h}t_w h_{wy}^2\right] \tag{9.260}$$

Substitution for h_{wy} from Eq. 9.259 yields

$$M'_n = F_y h\left[A_f + \frac{A_w}{4} - \frac{t_w h^2}{4h}\left(\frac{V'_n}{V_n}\right)^2\right]$$
$$= F_y h\left[A_f + \frac{A_w}{4} - \frac{A_w}{4}\left(\frac{V'_n}{V_n}\right)^2\right] \tag{9.261}$$
$$= A_f F_y h\left[1 + \frac{A_w}{4A_f}\left(1 - \left(\frac{V'_n}{V_n}\right)^2\right)\right]$$

From Eq. 9.253, we have

$$F_y A_f h = \frac{M_y}{1 + \frac{1}{6}(A_w/A_f)} \tag{9.262}$$

which gives

$$\frac{A_f F_y h}{M_y} = \frac{1}{1 + \frac{1}{6}(A_w/A_f)} \tag{9.263}$$

Substitution in Eq. 9.261 for $A_f F_y h$ from Eq. 9.262 yields

$$M'_n = M_y \frac{1 + \frac{1}{4}(A_w/A_f)[1 - (V'_n/V_n)^2]}{1 + \frac{1}{6}(A_w/A_f)} \tag{9.264}$$

Dividing both sides of Eq. 9.264 by the section modulus, and expressing

$$\frac{V'_n}{V_n} = \frac{ht_w \tau}{ht_w \tau_u} = \frac{\tau}{\tau_u} \tag{9.265}$$

we obtain the following equation:

$$f = F_y \left(\frac{1 + \frac{1}{4}(A_w/A_f)[1 - (\tau/\tau_u)^2]}{1 + \frac{1}{6}(A_w/A_f)} \right) \tag{9.266}$$

Equation 9.266 (same as Basler's Eq. 5c [Basler, 1961b]) shows that the nature of the curve between points Q_1 and Q_2 depends on the ratio of the web area to the flange area, A_w/A_f. Figure 9.70 shows interaction curves for values of the ratio $A_w/A_f = 2.0, 1.5, 1.0, 0.5,$ and 0, where $A_w/A_f = 2.0$ is considered as the upper limit for practical girders. All curves are assumed to be parabolas with vertices on the x-axis and are assumed to have a common point of intersection at $V/V_n = 1/\sqrt{3}$. For clarity, Fig. 9.70 shows the interaction curve for $A_w/A_f = 2.0$. Values of M/M_n on the abscissa

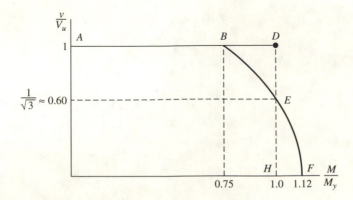

FIGURE 9.70
Interaction diagram for combined bending and shear for $A_w/A_f = 2.0$.

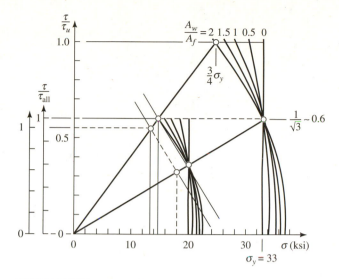

FIGURE 9.71
Interaction diagram showing failure and the allowable stresses [Basler, 1961b].

for corresponding values of V'_n/V_n can be obtained from Eqs. 9.263 and 9.264. When the entire web has yielded, Eq. 9.263 gives

$$\frac{M = A_f F_y h}{M_n} = \frac{1}{1 + \left(\frac{1}{6}\right)(2)} = 0.75$$

When the shear is zero, V'_n vanishes from Eq. 9.264, so that

$$\frac{M'_n}{M_n} = \frac{1 + \left(\frac{1}{4}\right)(2)}{1 + \left(\frac{1}{6}\right)(2)} = 1.12$$

Because V and V_n are proportional to τ and τ_u, respectively, the point $V/V_n = 1/\sqrt{3}$ also represents the point $\tau/\tau_u = 1/\sqrt{3}$. Figure 9.71 shows that for $\tau/\tau_u = 1/\sqrt{3} = 0.577$ (or approximately 0.6), $f_b = F_y$. For values higher than $\tau/\tau_u = 0.6$, the moment strength decreases.

The interaction diagrams adopted by AISC and AASHTO are based on Basler's work [Cooper, Galambos, and Ravindra, 1978; Vincent, 1969] with the ratio $A_w/A_f = 2.0$, except that a straight-line variation instead of the parabolic variation has been assumed. The validity of this assumption has been supported by tests [SSRC, 1988]. Figure 9.72 shows the interaction diagram for $A_W/A_f = 2.0$. The slope of line BE is -0.625 ($= -0.25/0.4$), which gives the equation of this straight line as

$$\frac{M'_n}{M_n} = 1 - 0.625 \left(\frac{V'_n}{V_n} - 0.6\right) \le 1.0$$

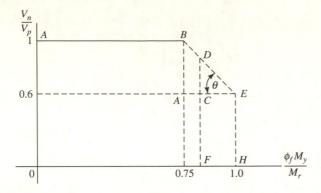

FIGURE 9.72
Interaction diagram for combined bending and shear.

or

$$\frac{M'_n}{M_n} = 1.375 - 0.625\left(\frac{V'_n}{V_n}\right) \tag{9.267}$$

Alternatively, Eq. 9.267 can be expressed as

$$\frac{V'_n}{V_n} = 2.2 - \left(\frac{1.6M'_n}{M_n}\right) \tag{9.268}$$

Using the AASHTO notation, Eq. 9.267 can be written as

$$\frac{V}{V_u} = 2.2 - \left(\frac{1.6M}{M_u}\right) \tag{9.269}$$

which is AASHTO Eq. 10.117 for load factor design and is to be used when a girder panel is subjected to combined bending and shear with $M > 0.75M_u$ (AASHTO 10.48.8.2).

For service load design, the desired expression for interaction diagram can be obtained by dividing Eq. 9.268 by the factor of safety 1.83 [Basler, 1961b]. Replacing M'_n/M_n by M/M_y ($= F_s/F_y$), and V'_n/V_n by V/V_n ($= f_v/F_v$), we obtain

$$\frac{F_s}{F_y} = \frac{1}{1.83}\left[1.375 - 0.625\left(\frac{f_v}{F_v}\right)\right]$$

$$= \left[0.751 - 0.341\left(\frac{f_v}{F_v}\right)\right] \tag{9.270a}$$

where F_s is the allowable bending stress. Equation 9.270a appears, in a slightly modified form, as Eq. 10.29 in AASHTO [1992]:

$$F_s = \left[0.754 - 0.34\left(\frac{f_v}{F_v}\right)\right]F_y \tag{9.270b}$$

Equation 9.270b applies when the ratio of actual shear stress, f_v, to the allowable shear stress, F_v, exceeds 0.6 (i.e., when $f_v/F_v \geq 0.6$).

It is instructive to note that the previously discussed interaction curve also forms the basis for the shear strength of plate girders in the AASHTO–LRFD specifications [AASHTO, 1994]. Referring to Fig. 9.72:

$$\tan\theta = \frac{AB}{AE} = \frac{0.4}{M_r - 0.75\phi_f M_y}$$

$$CD = CE\tan\theta = (M_r - M_u) \times \left(\frac{0.4}{M_r - 0.75\phi_f M_y}\right) \qquad (9.271)$$

$$FD = 0.6 + CD$$

$$= 0.6 + 0.4\left(\frac{M_r - M_u}{M_r - 0.75\phi_f M_y}\right)$$

Thus, when $M = M_u$, the maximum ratio of V_n/V_p is given by the ordinate FD, defined as the *shear interaction factor, R,* in the AASHTO–LRFD specifications [AASHTO, 1994, Eq. 6.10.7.3.3a-3]:

$$R = 0.6 + 0.4\left(\frac{M_r - M_u}{M_r - 0.75\phi_f M_y}\right) \qquad (9.272)$$

where

$$
\begin{aligned}
M_r &= \text{factored flexural resistance} \\
&= \phi_f M_n
\end{aligned}
\qquad (9.273)
$$

which is AASHTO–LRFD Eq. 6.10.2.1-2, ϕ_f being the resistance factor for flexure.

Recall that the nominal shear strength of the web was expressed as

$$V_n = V_p\left[C + \frac{0.87(1-C)}{\sqrt{1 + (d_o/D)^2}}\right] \qquad \text{(9.207 repeated)}$$

Thus, for the case of combined bending and shear, when $M_u > 0.5\phi_f M_p$, the nominal strength can be expressed by modifying Eq. 9.207 as

$$V_n = RV_p\left[C + \frac{0.87(1-C)}{\sqrt{1 + (d_o/D)^2}}\right] \qquad (9.274)$$

which is AASHTO–LRFD Eq. 6.10.7.3.3a-2 [AASHTO, 1994], and where R is given by Eq. 9.272.

In conclusion, it is reiterated that Basler's interaction diagram is based on the assumption that $M \leq M_y$ and $A_w/A_f = 2.0$. This was done to simplify design procedures. Had these assumptions not been made, the correlation of Basler's test points would be even better, as shown in Fig. 4 of Basler's work [Basler, 1961b].

In addition to Basler's model, several researchers have suggested other interaction diagrams for the case of combined bending and shear. A trilinear interaction diagram has been proposed by Herzog [1974a,b]. Fujii [1971] has discussed the case of a flange with no flexural resistance. A model by Chern and Ostapenko [1969, 1970a,b, 1971] assumes that the ultimate capacity of the girder will be governed by failure of the web, instability of the compression flange, or yielding of the tension flange. Yet other models have been proposed by Rockey [1971a,b], Rockey and Skaloud [1972], Rockey, Evans, and Porter [1973], and Porter, Rockey, and Evans [1975] for predicting the strength of girders without longitudinal stiffeners, under combined bending and shear. A brief summary of these models can be found in the SSRC Guide [SSRC, 1988]. A model based on plastic analysis, using the width of an effective resisting part in the web plate after buckling under pure bending, has been presented by Akita and Fujii [1966a,b] and Fujii [1967]. Wolchuck and Mayrbaurl [1980] and Wolchuck [1981] have proposed a practical method for designing webs subjected to simultaneous bending, axial stress, and shear. Herzog [1974a] has proposed a simple formula for the ultimate strength based on statistical data analysis [Owen, Rockey, and Skaloud, 1970]. An analytical procedure for estimating the ultimate strength of transversely stiffened plate girders under combined bending and shear, based on plastic analysis, has been proposed by Komatsu et al. [1984], who have considered the influence of residual stress, distance between the lateral supports, and the web aspect ratio, the three factors not considered by other researchers.

9.7
PLATE GIRDERS WITH STIFFENERS

9.7.1 General Considerations

In general, the problem of the strength of stiffened plate girders has two components to be considered: determination of the buckling load and determination of the ultimate load. In contrast with the behavior of the unstiffened plate beyond the critical load, the mathematical treatment of the problem of the stiffened plates is too complex. This is because of the large difference between the stiffness of the unstiffened plate and increased stiffness in the vicinity of the stiffener. Based on the test results, Lundquist concluded that a good approximate solution could be obtained by considering an effective portion of the plate as a part of the stiffener. An extensive mathematical treatment of the general problem of the stability of stiffened plates was given by Barbre [1936, 1937].

Historically speaking, Timoshenko [1915] was the first to study the complex behavior of stiffened rectangular plates supported on all four edges, and particularly the problem of minimum stiffness of stiffeners required to restrict buckling in a stiffened plate to plating between the stiffeners [Bleich, 1952, p. 358]. By applying his strain energy method, he obtained solutions for rectangular plates, stiffened longitudinally or transversely, and provided the first numerical tables[34] for designing stiffened plates [Timoshenko, 1921]. Timoshenko's theory was extended by Wang [1947] to the problem of plates reinforced by any number of transverse stiffeners. An exact solution of the problem of longitudinally or transversely stiffened plates under uniformly distributed stresses on two opposite edges was published by Lokshin [1935], who derived the sta-

---

[34]See Timoshenko and Gere [1961, pp. 394–408].

bility conditions for plates having any number of equidistant stiffeners. The problem of stability of webs of plate girders in combined bending and shear has been treated by Milosavljevitch [1947], who used the following differential equation,[35] which he solved by a series method:

$$D\left(\frac{\partial^4 w}{\partial x^4} + 2\frac{\partial^4 w}{\partial x^2 \partial y^2} + \frac{\partial^4 w}{\partial y^4}\right) = q - \sigma_1 t\left(1 - \xi\frac{y}{b}\right)\frac{\partial^4 w}{\partial x^2} - 2\tau_{xy}t\frac{\partial^2 w}{\partial x \partial y} \quad (9.275)$$

where $D = EI/(1 - v_2)$
$\quad \xi$ = a coefficient defining longitudinal stress distribution
$\quad = \sigma_1(1 - \xi y/b)$

$\xi = 0$ for uniformly compressive stress, $\xi = 2$ for pure bending, and $0 < \xi < 2$ for the case of combined bending and shear.

The plate has linearly distributed longitudinal stresses at the ends and uniform shearing stresses at the edges. Milosavljevitch [1947] includes the numerical solution for plates with two transverse stiffeners at the third points and a longitudinal stiffener at $b/4$ (Fig. 9.73) from the compression edge and provides tables for routine calculations for plates in pure bending and combined bending and shear.

Many other researchers have suggested methods to evaluate the strength of stiffened plates. A summary of the early work on the stability and strength of stiffened plates has been given by Bleich [1952]. A historical survey of bibliography on stiffened plates has been provided by D'Apice, Fielding, and Cooper [1966]. Rockey [1957, 1958], Rockey and Legget [1962], and Rockey and Cook [1965a,b] have suggested methods to design and evaluate the strength of plate girders stiffened with a variety of combinations of transverse and longitudinal stiffeners. Mathematical treatment of simply

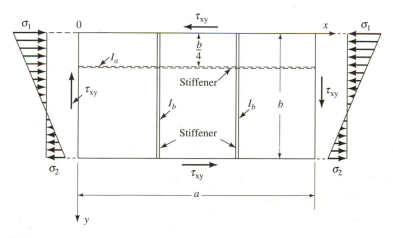

FIGURE 9.73
Rectangular plate under bending and shear, reinforced by transverse stiffeners at third points and one longitudinal stiffener at $b/4$ from the compression edge.

---

[35] See Bleich [1952, p. 424].

supported rectangular plates with longitudinal stiffeners has been provided by Timoshenko [1961, p. 394] and Bleich [1952, p. 418].

It should be recognized at the outset that the web of a plate girder can be (1) unstiffened, (2) transversely stiffened only, (3) longitudinally stiffened only, or (4) both transversely and longitudinally stiffened. Strengths of both unstiffened plate girders and girders with transverse stiffeners only are discussed in Sec. 9.5.4. Strengths of girders with only longitudinal stiffeners and with both transverse and longitudinal stiffeners will be discussed next.

9.7.2 Plate Girder with Longitudinal Stiffeners

9.7.2.1 Advantages of longitudinal stiffeners

It has been shown analytically that transverse stiffeners alone contribute little to the buckling strength of a plate unless they are spaced much closer than the width of the plate. The critical stress of the plate will increase significantly only if spacing of the transverse stiffeners is much smaller than the width of the plate. As discussed earlier, a longitudinally compressed rectangular plate of large aspect ratio, supported on all four edges, buckles in several half-waves whose lengths depend on the boundary conditions of its edges. Because of the inherent postbuckling strength, the web's initial buckling does not indicate failure of the plate girder. Investigations have shown that the bend-buckling resistance of a plate girder web can be considerably enhanced if longitudinal stiffeners are provided. A longitudinal stiffener essentially forces the web to buckle in a higher mode (i.e., $n \geq 2$) by forming a nodal line in the buckled configuration, with waves much shorter than those of the unstiffened plate [Bleich, 1952]. Providing longitudinal stiffeners, in addition to the transverse stiffeners, is a much more effective way of increasing the buckling strength of a plate. "These stiffeners not only carry a portion of the compressive load, but subdivide the plate into smaller panels, thus increasing considerably the critical stress at which the plate will buckle" [Bleich, 1952, p. 358]. Stated simply, transverse and longitudinal stiffeners together compartmentalize a web into several subpanels whose combined buckling strength is much higher than that of the unstiffened web as a whole.

The primary function of the longitudinal stiffeners is to minimize lateral deflection of the web (i.e., prevent bend buckling). Static tests of large plate girders with $D/t_w > 400$ [Cooper, 1967] have amply demonstrated the effectiveness of longitudinal stiffeners in reducing the lateral (or out-of-plane) web deflections.

From the viewpoint of flexural strength, the presence of a properly designed longitudinal stiffener increases the maximum allowable D/t_w ratio for the web, required to develop the yield stress flexural capacity of the girder without buckling, from 170 to about 400 for mild steel [ASCE–AASHTO, 1978]. An adequately designed longitudinal stiffener located at $D/5$ from the compression flange can eliminate the loss in strength due to flexural buckling for webs having overall slenderness ratios up to 450 [Cooper, 1967]. More significantly, as a consequence of controlled web deflection, stress redistribution from the web to the compression flange is also controlled or prevented. Thus, these tests concluded that within this range of web slenderness ratios, ordinary linear beam theory ($f = Mc/I$) can be used to predict stresses in the compression flange, and the ultimate flexural capacity of the girder can be computed using the critical stress for lateral or torsional buckling for the compression flange of the girder [ASCE–AASHTO, 1978]. Stated otherwise, placement of a longitudinal stiffener in the compression zone of the web enables the web to be fully effective in resisting bending stresses.

Because the presence of a longitudinal stiffener increases the resistance of the web to the out-of-plane bending, a premature vertical buckling of the compression flange is also prevented. Consequently, the flexural strength of the girder is increased. A method of predicting such an increase has been proposed by Cooper [1967] and has been verified by tests to be about 14 percent [Cooper, 1967] to about 26 percent [Longbottom and Heymen, 1956]. In general, however, the increase in the flexural capacity of a girder due to control or prevention of out-of-plane bending of the web is relatively small because the contribution of web to the overall flexural capacity of a girder is small to begin with.

Another advantage of providing longitudinal stiffeners is the improved fatigue resistance of plate girders [ASCE–AASHTO, 1978; SSRC, 1988] as demonstrated by tests of Yen and Mueller [Yen and Muller, 1966]. They have attributed the improved fatigue strength to reduced web deflection under cyclic loading. This reduced lateral deflection reduces the fatigue cracking in the flange-to-web welds due to oil canning of the web [ASCE–AASHTO, 1978]. Effectiveness of longitudinal stiffeners in preventing fatigue cracking of the webs of hybrid girders has been verified by tests [Toprac, 1963].

The advantages of longitudinal stiffeners notwithstanding, there is a drawback. Providing longitudinal stiffeners can also cause fatigue problems. The weld toe at the end of a longitudinal stiffener is considered a severe stress raiser and is classified as a *Category E detail* for the purposes of allowable fatigue stress [AASHTO, 1992, 1994].[36] Consequently, the longitudinal stiffener must be terminated in the region of low stress range [ASCE–AASHTO, 1978].

9.7.2.2 Strength of longitudinally stiffened girders

Location of the longitudinal stiffener. A longitudinal stiffener at the neutral axis of a web is relatively ineffective in improving the stability of web plates in pure bending. A stiffener located at the neutral axis of a web can increase its buckling strength to the order of only 50 percent of that of the unstiffened plate in the elastic range, and the increase is more modest in the inelastic range. However, the buckling strength increases substantially when the longitudinal stiffener is placed between the compression flange and the neutral axis [Bleich, 1952, p. 420].

Both the shear and flexural strength are increased by the presence of a properly designed longitudinal stiffener; its location is a key component that affects both. The influence of the location of the longitudinal stiffener in the compression zone of the web was studied by Chwalla [1936], who gave the numerical results for a plate of aspect ratio $\alpha = 0.8$, reinforced by a longitudinal stiffener located at $h/4$ from the compression flange. More detailed studies were made by Massonet [1940–1941].

---

[36]See AASHTO [1992, p. 192, Illustrative Example 7] and AASHTO–LRFD [1994, p. 6-26, Illustrative Example 7].

For a longitudinal stiffener to effectively control web deflections and prevent stress redistribution from the web to the compression flange, its desirable location is somewhere between the neutral axis and the compression flange. Theoretical and experimental studies have shown that the optimum location of one longitudinal stiffener is $0.2h$ from the compression flange for bending and $0.5h$ for shear [SSRC, 1988]. Tests by Cooper [1967] have shown that a longitudinal stiffener placed at $0.2h$ can effectively control lateral web deflection under bending. Because shear is always accompanied by moment, a longitudinal stiffener, regardless of its location, reduces web deflection due to shear.

The optimum location of a longitudinal stiffener is influenced, to some degree, by the flange restraint conditions. If the unloaded edges of the web are assumed to be restrained from both lateral deflection and rotation by the flanges, the optimum stiffener location has been found to be at $0.22h$ from the compression flange. However, if the unloaded edges are assumed to be simply supported, the optimum location has been found to be only slightly closer to the compression flange—$0.2h$ (instead of $0.22h$) from the compression flange [Dubas, 1948].

In bridge design practice, $0.2h$ (or $D/5$, $h = D = $ unsupported distance between the two flanges in inches) has been adopted (to maintain flexural efficiency) as the standard distance for a longitudinal stiffener, regardless of the end conditions of the web (i.e., fully restrained or simply supported at their junctures with flanges). This has been adopted nearly universally by the design specifications as the standard location for a longitudinal stiffener [ASCE–AASHTO, 1978]. AASHTO 10.34.5.1 defines distance $D/5$ as the distance from the compression edge of the web (i.e., measured from the inner surface or leg of the compression flange element) to the centerline of the plate stiffener or the gage line of the angle stiffener (if used). In the AASHTO–LRFD specifications [AASHTO, 1994] this distance has been defined as $2D_c/5$ (instead of $D/5$), where D_c is the depth of the web in compression.

It is important to note that the criteria for location of the stiffener are based on the elastic buckling considerations. The longitudinal stiffener may be more effective in contributing to the ultimate strength of the plate girder under combined bending and shear if placed somewhere between $D/5$ and $D/2$ from the compression edge of the web [ASCE–AASHTO, 1978].

Strength increase due to a longitudinal stiffener. From a design standpoint, the chief advantage derived from providing a longitudinal stiffener is a slender and economical web. AASHTO specifications [AASHTO, 1992] permit a 50 percent reduction in the web thickness when a longitudinal stiffener is provided at $0.2D$ from the compression edge of the web. This is because the presence of the longitudinal stiffener increases the buckling strength of the plate girder.

The location of the longitudinal stiffener has a significant influence on the increase of the buckling strength. According to Bleich [1952], the increase in the buckling strength that can be obtained by a longitudinal stiffener at the centerline of the web amounts to only 50 percent of the strength of the unstiffened plate in the elastic range and is even smaller in the inelastic range. The presence of a longitudinal stiffener midway between the neutral axis and the compressive edge of the web increases the value of the buckling coefficient k (in Eq. 9.34) to 101 for simply supported edges as compared to 23.9 for a longitudinally unstiffened web. According to Dubas

[1948],[37] for a web with a longitudinal stiffener at $D/5$ from the compressive edge of the web, the optimum location, $k = 129$ as shown in Fig. 9.74 [Bleich, 1952], which is the minimum buckling coefficient for a longitudinally stiffened plate [Rockey and Leggett, 1962]. This means a more than fivefold increase in the elastic critical bending strips as compared to that for a longitudinally unstiffened girder. The minimum web thickness (for service load design), with and without longitudinal stiffeners, is given by Eqs. 9.104 and 9.108, respectively (AASHTO Eqs. 10.23 and 10.24, respectively). The corresponding expressions for the load factor design are given by Eqs. 9.140 and 9.141, respectively (AASHTO Eqs. 10.103 and 10.108, respectively). A summary of these requirements is provided in Tables 9.6 through 9.8.

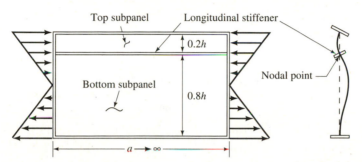

Bend-buckling of a plate reinforced with a longitudinal
stiffener at $0.2h$ from the compression flange

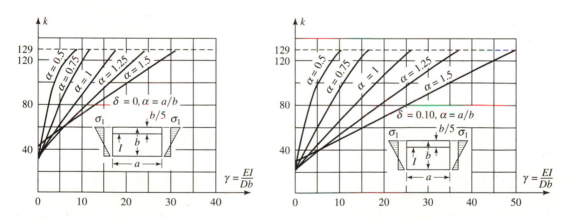

$b = h$ = clear depth of web, D = flexural rigidity of plate, I = moment of inertia of stiffener,
$\delta = A_{st}/A_w$, and γ = ratio of flexural rigidity of stiffener to that of the plate

FIGURE 9.74
Influence of one longitudinal stiffener on the plate buckling coefficient, k, for various aspect ratios [Bleich, 1952].

---

[37] A summary of Dubas's work on the influence of the longitudinal stiffener location has been provided by Bleich [1952, pp. 422–423]. Charts in Fig. 9.75 are due to Dubas [1948], who derived them by a method of successive approximations.

TABLE 9.6
Influence of longitudinal stiffening on web thickness*

Design methods	With longitudinal stiffeners		Without longitudinal stiffeners	
	Minimum web thickness, t_w	AASHTO Art.	Minimum web thickness, t_w	AASHTO Art.
Service load design	$\dfrac{D\sqrt{f_{b,\text{psi}}}}{46,000}$ but $\geq D/340$	10.34.3.2.1	$\dfrac{D\sqrt{f_{b,\text{psi}}}}{23,000}$ but $\geq D/170$	10.34.3.1.1
Load factor design	$\dfrac{D\sqrt{F_{y,\text{psi}}}}{73,000}$	10.48.6.1	$\dfrac{D\sqrt{F_{y,\text{psi}}}}{36,500}$	10.48.5.1

*D = depth of web between flanges, t_w = web thickness.

TABLE 9.7
Minimum thickness of web plates (service load design)

Yield strength, $F_{y,\text{psi}}$	Minimum web thickness, t_w	
	Longitudinally unstiffened, $t_w = \dfrac{D\sqrt{f_b}}{23,000} \geq \dfrac{D}{170}$	Longitudinally stiffened, $t_w = \dfrac{D\sqrt{f_b}}{46,000} \geq \dfrac{D}{340}$
36,000	$D/165$	$D/330$
50,000	$D/140$	$D/280$
70,000	$D/115$	$D/230$
90,000	$D/105$	$D/210$
100,000	$D/100$	$D/200$

TABLE 9.8
Minimum thickness of web plates (load factor design)

Yield strength, $F_{y,\text{psi}}$	Minimum web thickness, t_w	
	Longitudinally unstiffened, $t_w = \dfrac{D\sqrt{F_{y,\text{psi}}}}{36,500}$	Longitudinally stiffened, $t_w = \dfrac{D\sqrt{F_{y,\text{psi}}}}{73,000}$
36,000	$D/192$	$D/385$
50,000	$D/163$	$D/326$
70,000	$D/138$	$D/276$
90,000	$D/122$	$D/243$
100,000	$D/115$	$D/231$

A web may have no, one, or multiple *longitudinal* stiffeners. They may be provided on one or (rarely) both sides of the web and are economical for deep webs. According to the ASCE–AASHTO Joint Committee Report [ASCE–AASHTO, 1978, p. 712], "longitudinal stiffeners are not used unless the girder depth exceeds 7 ft. Since using stiffeners increases fabrication costs, many engineers try to avoid them." Economic considerations for plate girders are discussed later.

Design of longitudinal stiffeners. The primary function of the longitudinal stiffeners is to control bend buckling by minimizing lateral deflection of the web plate as the girder bends vertically. To perform this function efficiently, a longitudinal stiffener must meet the following four requirements [Cooper, 1967; Vincent, 1969; ASCE–AASHTO, 1978; SSRC, 1988]:

1. Because the resistance to bend buckling of the web is increased as a consequence of higher buckling mode owing to the presence of a longitudinal stiffener, it should be sufficiently stiff to maintain a longitudinal node (i.e., to maintain straightness) in the buckled web.
2. A longitudinal stiffener placed at the neutral axis of the web does not carry any compression. But when it is positioned in the compression zone of the web (optimally at $0.2D$ for a single longitudinal stiffener), it is required to resist a certain amount of axial compression. Thus, a longitudinal stiffener acts as a beam-column. When transverse stiffeners are also provided, the longitudinal stiffener should be sufficiently stiff to act as a beam supported between the intermediate transverse stiffeners. Therefore, the efficiency of a longitudinal stiffener depends on its cross-sectional area, its moment of inertia, and its position (distance from the compression flange). AASHTO 10.34.5.3 limits the permitted stress in a longitudinal stiffener to the basic allowable bending stress.
3. It must have maximum width-to-thickness ratio to avoid local buckling.
4. It must have a certain minimum cross-sectional area to anchor the tension-field forces developed in the subpanels.

To satisfy these requirements, both the area of cross section and the moment of inertia enter into the design of longitudinal stiffeners. The longitudinal stiffener behaves as a beam-column whose strength is governed by spacing of the transverse stiffeners. The value of the buckling coefficient $k = 129$ (used in determining D/t_w ratios for the longitudinally stiffened web) is dependent on the various previously stated factors. The basis of the formulas in AASHTO specifications [AASHTO, 1992] for designing a longitudinal stiffener is that it provide a nodal point in the buckled web by resisting local and overall stiffener buckling. The AASHTO requirement for the minimum moment of inertia for the longitudinal stiffener is based on the conservative assumption that the ratio of stiffener area to web area is $\frac{1}{20}$, as suggested by Erickson and VanEenam [1957]. The following AASHTO formula is derived from the work of Moisseiff and Lienhard [1941]:

$$I \nleq Dt_w^3 \left[2.4 \left(\frac{d_o}{D} \right)^2 - 0.13 \right] \tag{9.276}$$

where I = minimum moment of inertia of the longitudinal stiffener about its edge in contact with the web

D = unsupported distance between flanges

t_w = web thickness

d_o = actual distance between transverse stiffeners

Equation 9.276 is the same as AASHTO Eqs. 10.32 and 10.109 for the service load and the load factor design, respectively. The same equation has also been adopted as Eq. 6.10.8.3.3-1 in AASHTO–LRFD [AASHTO, 1994].

To ensure adequate stiffness against local buckling, the longitudinal stiffener should also meet certain limitations of the b'/t_s requirement. These can be determined on the same basis as the b'/t ratio for the outstanding legs of flange angles in compression as given by AASHTO Eq. 10.21 (discussed earlier):

$$\frac{b'}{t} = \frac{1625}{\sqrt{f_{b,\mathrm{psi}}}} \tag{9.58}$$

Based on the linear flexural stress distribution in the girder, stress in the web at $D/5$ (location of the longitudinal stiffener) from the compression flange, i.e., at $0.3D$ from the neutral axis, would be $0.60\,f_b$, where f_b = stress in the extreme compression fibers (Fig. 9.75). Substituting $0.60\,f_b$ in place of f_b in Eq. 9.58 yields

$$\frac{b'}{t} = \frac{1625}{\sqrt{0.60\,f_b}}$$

$$= \frac{2100}{\sqrt{f_{b,\mathrm{psi}}}} \tag{9.277}$$

AASHTO [1992] permits the following b'/t ratios

$$\text{Service load design}: \quad \frac{b'}{t} = \frac{2250}{\sqrt{f_{b,\mathrm{psi}}}} \tag{9.278a}$$

$$\text{Load factor design}: \quad \frac{b'}{t} = \frac{2600}{\sqrt{F_{y,\mathrm{psi}}}} \tag{9.278b}$$

as specified by AASHTO Eqs. 10.33 and 10.104, respectively [AASHTO, 1992]. It should be noted that AASHTO 10.8.1 [AASHTO, 1992] requires the minimum metal thickness to be at least $\frac{5}{16}$ in. As a matter of good design practice, usually a thickness of $\frac{3}{8}$ in. is used as a practical minimum.

As pointed out in ASCE–AASHTO [1978], the preceding formulas are based on a linear buckling analysis, and they provide for resisting capacity up to web buckling. For developing the ultimate strength of longitudinally stiffened girders, the stiffness of the longitudinal stiffener must be increased above the elastic buckling value. According to Massonet [1960], and verified by other researchers [Cooper, 1967; Dubas, 1971; Rockey, 1971a,b,c], the stiffness required to develop the elastic buckling critical load should be multiplied by a factor ranging from 3 for a stiffener located at $D/2$ of a panel to 7 for one located at $D/5$ from the compression flange.

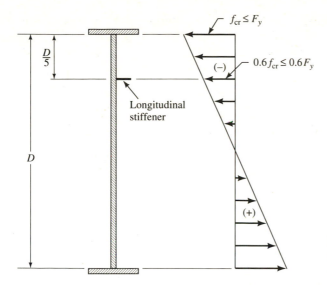

FIGURE 9.75
Linear distribution of flexural stress in a plate girder.

An expression for the required stiffness of the longitudinal stiffener (placed at $D/5$ from the compression flange) corresponding to the flexural stress equal to the critical stress in the extreme fibers of the girder (Fig. 9.75) can be computed on the basis of the flexural buckling stress in the flange. According to the SSRC guide [SSRC, 1988, Eqs. 3.5 and 3.7], the flexural buckling stress can be approximated by[38]

$$\frac{F_{cr}}{F_y} = 1 - \frac{\lambda_c^2}{4} \qquad \text{for } \lambda \leq \sqrt{2} \tag{9.279}$$

where

$$\lambda_c = \frac{KL}{r}\frac{1}{\pi}\sqrt{\frac{F_y}{E}} \tag{9.280}$$

In Eq. 9.280, λ_c is defined as the column slenderness parameter [AISC–LRFD, 1994, p. 6-47, Eq. E2-4].

Assuming linear flexural stress distribution in the girder and the extreme fiber stress $f_{cr} \leq F_y$, the corresponding compressive stress at $D/5$ from the compression flange (or $0.3D$ from the neutral axis) would be $0.60F_y$. The longitudinal stiffener must be stiff enough to resist this compressive stress as a column whose effective length is taken as the distance between a pair of adjacent stiffeners, d_o (d_o/D = aspect ratio). Assuming partially restrained end conditions, for which the effective length factor $K = 0.7$ [Vincent, 1969, p. 33], we have

$$\frac{KL}{r} = \frac{0.7d_o}{r} \tag{9.281}$$

---

[38]The SSRC guide [SSRC, 1988, p. 32] uses the symbols σ_{cr} and σ_y, respectively, for F_{cr} and F_y. These latter symbols are followed in this book in order to maintain conformity with the AASHTO specifications.

It is assumed that the eccentricity of the load and initial out-of-straightness cause a 20 percent increase in stress at the stiffener location (i.e., $f_{b,\text{stiffener}} = 1.2 \times 0.60 F_y$) [Vincent, 1969; AASHTO–LRFD, 1994]. Substitution of these values in Eq. 9.280 yields

$$\left(\frac{1.2 \times 0.60 F_y}{F_y}\right) = 1 - \frac{F_y}{4\pi^2 E}\left(\frac{0.7 d_o}{r}\right)^2$$

from which

$$r^2 = \frac{(0.7 d_o)^2 F_y}{0.28 \times 4\pi^2 E}$$

or

$$r = \frac{0.7 d_o \sqrt{F_y}}{\sqrt{0.28(4\pi^2 E)}}$$

$$= \frac{d_o \sqrt{F_{y,\text{psi}}}}{25,600} \tag{9.282}$$

In derivation of Eq. 9.282, $E = 29,000$ ksi has been substituted to obtain a simple expression for design purposes, and the number in the denominator has been rounded off from 25,578 to 25,600. Equation 9.282 forms the basis of AASHTO Eq. 10.110 [AASHTO, 1992] specified for the load factor design, which is similar (but with the denominator as 23,000):

$$r = \frac{d_o \sqrt{F_y}}{23,000} \tag{9.283}$$

An alternative form of Eq. 9.283 can be written by normalizing with the modulus of elasticity, E, as follows:

$$r = \frac{d_o \sqrt{F_{yc,\text{psi}}}}{23,000}$$

$$= \frac{d_o \sqrt{F_{yc,\text{ksi}} \times 1000}}{23,000}$$

$$= \frac{d_o \sqrt{F_{yc,\text{ksi}} \times 1000 \times \dfrac{(E = 29,000)}{E_{\text{ksi}}}}}{23,000} \tag{9.284}$$

$$= \frac{d_o \sqrt{\dfrac{29 F_{yc}}{E}}}{23}$$

$$= 0.234 d_o \sqrt{\frac{F_{yc}}{E}}$$

where F_{yc} is the specified minimum yield strength of the adjacent compression flange. Equation 9.284 is AASHTO–LRFD Eq. 6.10.8.3.3-2 [AASHTO–LRFD, 1994].

The longitudinal stiffener essentially serves as a horizontal column just as the compression flange does. Because it must function as a column in conjunction with the web, it is obvious that a portion of the web in the vicinity of both sides of the stiffener would participate structurally with the longitudinal stiffener column. Strain measurements reported by Massonet [1960] have shown a mean effective width of $20t_w$ as participating with the longitudinal stiffener. Both the current [AASHTO, 1992] and the AASHTO–LRFD specifications [AASHTO–LRFD, 1994] permit a centrally located strip of the web to the maximum of $18t_w$ to be considered as part of the longitudinal stiffener column, based on the design practice in vogue [Vincent, 1969]. A similar approach has been adopted in the British specification [BSI, 1982] which permits an effective width of web plate of $16t_w$ on each side of the stiffener (as compared to AASHTO's $9t_w$). This design procedure has been discussed by Chatterjee [1981].

A longitudinal stiffener meeting the discussed requirements is considered to have sufficient cross-sectional area required to anchor the tension field that is likely to develop in the subpanels in the postbuckling range. Consequently, no additional requirements are specified for the cross-sectional area of the longitudinal stiffener [Vincent, 1969, p. 33].

It is to be noted that even though the design requirements in both AISC specifications [1989, 1994] and AASHTO specifications [1992, 1994] are based on the same general criteria, the AISC specifications do not recognize the contribution of longitudinal stiffeners to the postbuckling strength of webs.

9.7.2.3 Longitudinally and transversely stiffened girders

It was pointed out earlier that in a transversely stiffened web, introduction of a longitudinal stiffener divides a panel (bounded by two adjacent transverse stiffeners) into two subpanels. With properly designed longitudinal and transverse stiffeners, each subpanel develops a tension field, after buckling, independently of the other [Cooper, 1967]. Each subpanel also develops its own shear carrying capacity, which is equal to the sum of its beam-action shear at buckling and the vertical component of its tension field. The shear capacity of the entire panel with the longitudinal stiffener is taken as the sum of shear capacities of the subpanels. The optimum location of a longitudinal stiffener to increase resistance to shear buckling is at the mid-depth of the web. In this case, the two subpanels buckle simultaneously, and the increase in the critical stress can be substantial. However, as discussed earlier, the optimum location of the longitudinal stiffener to prevent bend buckling of the web (which is its primary purpose) is at $D/5$. In this case, the larger subpanel buckles first, and at a smaller critical stress than for the stiffener at mid-depth. As shown in Fig. 9.76, the contribution of the longitudinal stiffener placed at $D/5$ is relatively small and is neglected in computing the shear strength of the plate girder [Vincent, 1969]. This conservatism also leads to a simplified design procedure. A comprehensive discussion on this topic has been reported in the literature [Cooper, 1967; ASCE–AASHTO, 1978; SSRC, 1988].

When both transverse and longitudinal stiffeners are provided, a function of the transverse stiffeners is to support the longitudinal stiffener as it forces a horizontal node in the bend-buckling configuration of the web. Cooper [1967, p. 433, Eq. 14] has shown that the relationship between the section moduli of the two types of stiffeners can be

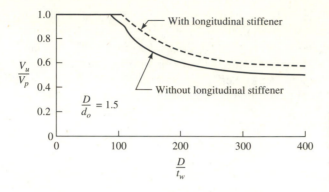

FIGURE 9.76

Influence of longitudinal stiffener (at $0.2h$ from the compression flange) on the shear strength of web [Vincent, 1969].

expressed as

$$S_T = \frac{S_L}{\alpha} \tag{9.285a}$$

where α = the aspect ratio = d_o/D
 S_T = section modulus of the transverse stiffener
 S_L = section modulus of the longitudinal stiffener at $D/5$
 D = total panel depth (clear distance between flange components)
 d_o = spacing of transverse stiffeners

However, this requirement has been considerably reduced in the load factor design provisions [AASHTO, 1992], which specify a minimum section modulus of the transverse stiffener given by Eq. 9.285b:

$$S_s \not< \frac{1}{3}\left(\frac{D}{d_o}\right)S_t \tag{9.285b}$$

which is AASHTO Eq. 10.111 [AASHTO, 1992]. In the AASHTO–LRFD [1994] specifications, Eq. 9.285b has been expressed in terms of the flexural rigidities of transverse and longitudinal stiffeners, I_t and I_l. Noting that

$$S_T = \frac{I_t}{b_t/2} \quad \text{and} \quad S_L = \frac{I_l}{b_l/2}$$

where b_t and b_l are the widths of the transverse and the longitudinal stiffeners, respectively. Equation 9.285b can be expressed as

$$I_t \geq \left(\frac{b_t}{b_l}\right)\left(\frac{D}{3d_o}\right)I_l \tag{9.285c}$$

which is AASHTO–LRFD Eq. 6.10.8.1.3-3 [AASHTO–LRFD, 1994]. Additionally, it is also required (when using load factor design) that for designing transverse stiffeners containing the longitudinal stiffener, the maximum subpanel depth ($0.8D$ when a longitudinal stiffener is provided at $0.2D$), rather than the full panel depth D, be used in conjunction with Eqs. 9.202 and 9.204 (AASHTO, 1992, Eqs. 10.105 and 10.107, respectively).

According to AASHTO 10.34.5.4, the longitudinal stiffeners may be not continuous and may be cut at their intersection with the transverse stiffeners. They are usually placed on only one side of the web. It can be shown that use of a one-sided stiffener requires only 63 percent of the area required for a two-sided stiffener when only the stiffener moment of inertia is considered [Cooper, 1974]. Thus, it is economical to provide a longitudinal stiffener on one side only.

9.7.2.4 Plate girders with multiple longitudinal stiffeners

The existing AASHTO provisions for transverse and longitudinal stiffeners are intended for plate girders for moderate-span bridges and are not adequate for long-span bridges, which require plate girders with very deep webs. Webs as deep as 40 ft have been used for long-span bridges in which haunched girders have been used.

For webs with extremely high slenderness ratios ($D/t_w \gg 450$), a single longitudinal stiffener is found to be rather inadequate to control or prevent web deflections in the entire region between the neutral axis and the compression flange, thus limiting the ultimate strength of the girder. The ultimate strength of a deep plate girder can be increased, either by providing a thicker web, by reducing the spacing of the transverse stiffeners, or by providing multiple longitudinal stiffeners. A combination of closely spaced transverse and multiple longitudinal stiffeners will result in a slender plate girder having a high strength-weight ratio. However, because of the additional fabrication cost involved, such solutions may not always be cost-effective. Examples of plate girders with multiple longitudinal stiffeners are presented in Sec. 9.3.4.

From an analytical standpoint, the strength determination of a web with multiple longitudinal stiffeners is a mathematically complex problem. Theoretical treatment of this problem has been provided by Timoshenko [1961] and Bleich [1952], which deals with longitudinally stiffened plates with up to three stiffeners placed symmetrically about the centerline of a plate under uniform edge compression. Kloppel and Scheer [1956, 1957] have given solutions for simply supported rectangular plates under combined bending and compression, for the cases of one and two longitudinal stiffeners. But the web plate of a girder is subjected to flexural stresses that vary linearly from compression to tension. Buckling of a plate girder web under flexure, when the web is reinforced by a single longitudinal stiffener, has been discussed by Rockey and Legget [1962] (discussed earlier). The strength of plate girders with multiple longitudinal stiffeners has been discussed by Rockey and Cook [1965a,b]; Owen, Skaloud, and Rockey [1970]; and Ardali [1980]. A handbook by Kloppel and Scheer [1960] presents extensive charts and tables for designing plate girders with multiple longitudinal stiffeners, which forms the basis for the German design practice.

Rockey and Cook [1965a,b] have provided design methods for plate girders having webs with multiple longitudinal stiffeners (up to six stiffeners) based on the following assumptions:

1. The stresses in the extreme fibers of the web are equal and opposite.
2. The longitudinal stiffeners are placed symmetrically about the midplane of the web.
3. All longitudinal stiffeners have equal flexural stiffness.
4. Torsional rigidity of the longitudinal stiffeners is negligible.
5. Transverse stiffeners provide a simple support to the web plate of the panel in which the longitudinal stiffeners are provided.

6. When the stiffeners are at their optimum position, the buckling resistances of the subpanels are equal. Therefore, for finding approximate optimum position of the stiffeners, it is assumed that the buckling stresses in the subpanels are equal.

The solution provided by Rockey and Cook [1965a,b] involves tables, charts, and equations for the optimum locations of up to six longitudinal stiffeners placed in the compression zone of the web, for the two cases of boundary conditions (at the flange-web junctures):

1. Flanges providing clamped (fixed) support
2. Flanges providing simple support

The main effect of providing a web with multiple longitudinal stiffeners is the increased value of the buckling coefficient k, which increases the buckling strength of the subpanels. Rockey and Cook [1965a,b] have shown that the value of k can vary from over 300 for a web with two longitudinal stiffeners to over 1200 for a web with five longitudinal stiffeners, for the case of simply supported boundary conditions at the flanges. For the case of clamped boundary conditions at the flanges, the values of k are even higher (as expected). The values of k for a web with up to six longitudinal stiffeners, and their optimum locations, are shown in Table 9.9. It is instructive to note that both the large values of the buckling coefficients K_s[39] and the associated limiting

TABLE 9.9
Optimum placing of multiple longitudinal stiffeners [Rockey and Cook, 1965b]

No. of stiffeners	Stiffener locations from the compression flange						Buckling coefficient	Limiting d/t_w ratios for $F_{y, ksi}$		
	η_1	η_2	η_3	η_4	η_5	η_6	K_s	36	50	90
	Flanges provide simple support									
0							23.9	134	113	85
1	.20						129	311	264	197
2	.123	.275					313	484	412	306
3	.093	.198	.323				532	631	535	399
4	.073	.152	.242	.349			842	793	673	502
5	.060	.124	.194	.273	.367		1220	956	811	604
6*	.051	.104	.162	.225	.296	.381	1670	1117	948	707
	Flanges provide clamped support									
0							42.7	179	152	113
1	.22						161	347	295	219
2	.136	.284					356	517	438	326
3	.101	.204	.327				597	668	567	422
4	.080	.158	.246	.352			926	832	707	527
5	.066	.129	.198	.278	.369		1322	995	845	629
6*	.056	.109	.166	.228	.298	.382	1800	1160	983	733

η_i = fraction of the web depth from the compression flange.
d = height of web, t_w = thickness of web.
K_s = exact value of the buckling coefficient for the given configuration of longitudinal web stiffening.
*Values of the limiting d/t_w ratios shown for the case of six longitudinal stiffeners are approximate, as given in O'Connor [1971].

---

[39]Rockey and Cook [1965b] have used the symbol K_s to denote the buckling coefficient k for the exact configuration of the stiffening.

d/t_w ratios for the web increase with the increase in the number of the longitudinal stiffeners.

Table 9.10 shows the requirements for the stiffness of the longitudinal stiffeners in terms of the flexural rigidity of the panel. These relationships approximate the theoretical relationships between the size and stiffness of the longitudinal stiffener, the size and stiffness of the web plate, and the aspect ratio and are valid for the aspect ratio α in the range of 0.5 and 1.6. For the values of the aspect ratios outside this range, curves shown in Figs. 9.77 and 9.78 have been recommended. It may be noted that for values of the aspect ratios less than 1.5, the buckling resistance and the stiffness of the longitudinal stiffeners are little affected by an increase in longitudinal restraint from that of a simple support to a clamped support. This is evident from the respective values of the buckling coefficient K_s in Table 9.9 and γ in Table 9.10.

In an effort to provide some guidance in designing plate girders with multiple longitudinal stiffeners, Ardali [1980], using the tension-field mechanism, carried out an extensive parametric study in which he analyzed some 15,000 girders. The girders were subjected to various combinations of shear and bending, but the study was restricted to failure in the shear mode. The study involved three design parameters: the web slenderness ratio (h/t_w), the web aspect ratio ($\alpha = a/h$), and the flange strength parameter (M_p*).[40] The range of variation of each parameter extended well beyond the values normally encountered in practice. The effects of introducing up to eight longitudinal stiffeners were studied in each case.

TABLE 9.10
Design of multiple longitudinal stiffeners [Rockey and Cook, 1965b]

No. of stiffeners	Value of $\gamma = EI_q/dD$
	Longitudinal edges simply supported
2	$(30.69 + 202.7\beta)\alpha^2 - (4.87 + 20.69\beta)\alpha^3$
3	$(35.54 + 422.9\beta)\alpha^2 - (4.278 + 73.72\beta)\alpha^3$
4	$(46.52 + 687.0\beta)\alpha^2 - (5.961 + 98.81\beta)\alpha^3$
5	$(57.58 + 1036\beta)\alpha^2 - (7.420 + 123.4\beta)\alpha^3$
	Longitudinal edges clamped
2	$(35.37 + 195.8\beta)\alpha^2 - (11.29 + 15.94\beta)\alpha^3$
3	$(37.18 + 423.5\beta)\alpha^2 - (7.852 + 87.98\beta)\alpha^3$
4	$(46.50 + 708.5\beta)\alpha^2 - (8.888 + 142.9\beta)\alpha^3$
5	$(58.02 + 1036\beta)\alpha^2 - (11.42 + 179.1\beta)\alpha^3$

I_q = moment of inertia of the qth longitudinal stiffener.
d = depth of web.
D = rigidity of plate $Et^3/12(1 - v^2)$.
α = aspect ratio
   = transverse stiffener spacing/web depth.
β = ratio of longitudinal stiffener to cross-sectional area of the panel.

---

[40]Ardali defined the flange strength parameter $M_p* = M_{pf}/d^2t\sigma_{yw}$, where M_{pf} = plastic moment of the flange plate, d = clear depth of web plate between flanges, t = web thickness, and σ_{yw} = yield stress of the web material.

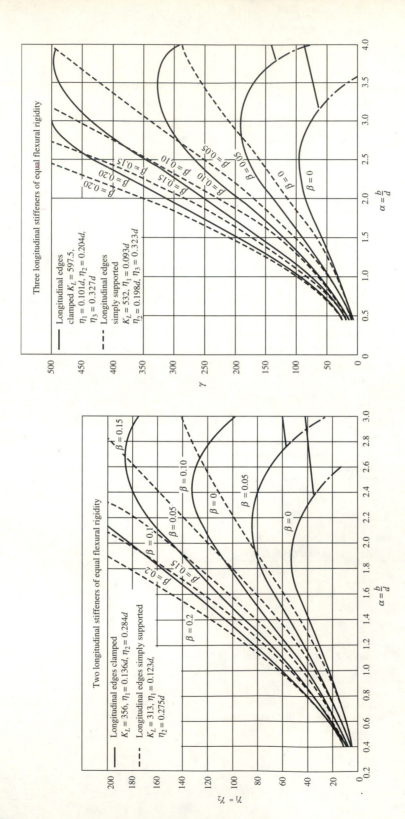

FIGURE 9.77

Curves showing γ–aspect ratio relationships [Rockey and Cook, 1965a,b].

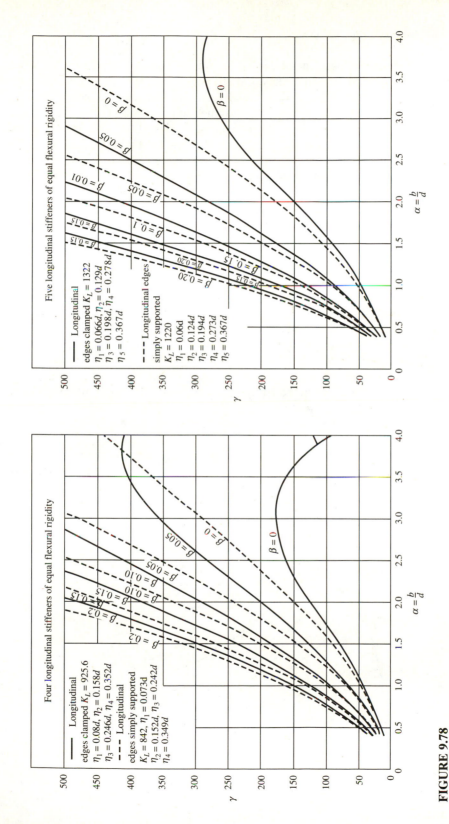

FIGURE 9.78

More curves showing γ–aspect ratio relationships [Rockey and Cook, 1965a,b].

1053

Effects of shear, and combined bending and shear, were considered in the Ardali study [1980]. In the case of pure shear, the stiffeners were spaced equally over the depth of the web, dividing the web into equal subpanels. Because the shear buckling capacity of each subpanel in such a case is assumed to be the same, this arrangement of stiffeners is considered as optimal. In the case of combined bending and shear, the stiffener spacing was adjusted so that the panels subjected to the highest compressive stress were smaller than the others.

Figure 9.79 shows, for the high–shear loading case, Ardali's [Ardali, 1980] plots of the interrelationship between the slenderness ratio of web and the increase in the ulti-mate load capacity. Each curve represents a different number of longitudinal stiffeners. Although plotted for webs having aspect ratio of 1.5 and specific flange strength (M_p^*), these curves are representative of all other curves obtained in the study. Such curves can be used by designers to choose the optimum number of stiffeners for a given web slenderness ratio. An examination of these curves leads to the following trend [Evans, 1973]:

1. All curves lie within an envelope that has a steep slope at low values of the web slenderness ratios but levels off as the slenderness ratio increases.
2. Typically, a curve corresponding to a given number of stiffeners branches down at a certain web slenderness ratio. Until this value of the slenderness ratio is reached, no advantage is gained by using more stiffeners. For more slender webs, additional longitudinal stiffeners must be added to increase the ultimate strength of the plate girder.

9.7.2.5 End panels

The portion of the girder between the bearing stiffeners at the support and the first intermediate transverse stiffener is called the end panel. In the context of tension-field

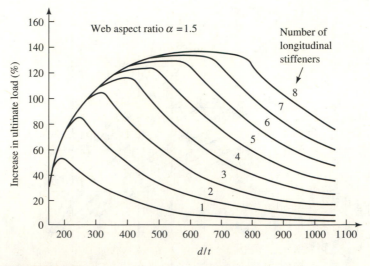

FIGURE 9.79
Increase in the strength of shear webs with number of longitudinal stiffeners [Ardali, 1980].

action, this panel is referred to as the anchor panel because it is thought to anchor the horizontal component of the tension field in the adjacent interior panel. Obviously, being the end panel, it has an adjacent panel on only one side, and there is no neighboring plate on the other side to serve as anchor for the tension field in the end panel itself. Thus, the end panel is assumed to have weak tension field and is considered ineffective as far as tension field is concerned. Consequently, shear in this panel must conform to the design criteria of a non-tension-field girder; i.e., it must be designed as a beam-shear panel, unless the end stiffeners are designed to resist the bending effect of the tributary tension field. From a practical standpoint, the end (or the anchor) panel of the girder designed on the basis of the tension field action should have a small enough aspect ratio (a/h or d_o/D) to eliminate the tension field in this panel. Should a tension field action develop in this panel, its horizontal component will induce bending of the end stiffener about its minor axis, causing it to deform permanently [Basler and Thurlimann, 1961]. As evidenced by tests, such an action essentially causes premature failure of the end post, leading to the premature failure of the plate girder itself [Basler et al., 1960].

Design of the end panel is an integral component of the design of a plate girder. Two approaches have been suggested by Basler and Thurlimann [1961] for eliminating the possibilities of the premature failure of the end panel in unframed plate girders, such as those supported on piers and abutments. The simplest and the most economical solution consists of avoiding the development of the tension-field action in the end panel by having a stiffener spacing small enough so that the end panel can be designed as a non-tension-field girder. This is the approach used in both the AASHTO and AISC specifications. This approach must be used for girders that are framed into other load-carrying structures such as trusses. The distance a between the end and the first intermediate stiffener has been suggested to be [Basler and Thurlimann, 1961, Eqs. 17a and 17b]

$$a < \frac{11,000}{\sqrt{\tau}}t \tag{9.286a}$$

where
$$\tau \le 4E\left(\frac{t}{a}\right)^2 \tag{9.286b}$$

In practice, this approach is followed by imposing an upper limit on the permitted shear stress in the end panel and also limiting the distance between the end stiffener and the first intermediate transverse stiffener. For service load design, the maximum spacing is limited to a maximum of $1.5D$ (AASHTO 10.34.4.3) [AASHTO, 1992], and the maximum permitted shear stress is [AASHTO, 1992, Eq. 10.28]

$$F_v = \frac{CF_y}{3} \le \frac{F_y}{3} \tag{9.287}$$

For the load factor design, it is required that the first stiffener space at the simple support of a plate girder be such that the shear force in the end panel does not exceed the plastic or buckling shear force given by the following equation [AASHTO, 1992, Eq. 10.112]:

$$V = CV_P \tag{9.288}$$

The AISC specifications [AISC, 1989] have a similar provision (Sec. G4) for design of plate girders.

Alternatively, the end post must be designed to resist the membrane tension in the web. As suggested by Basler and Thurlimann [1961], this can be done by bending down the top flange around the end of the girder or by welding an extra plate at the end. This extra plate, together with the end stiffener and certain portion of the web, forms a strong end post to resist the horizontal pull due to the tension field in the end panel (Fig. 9.80). The following expression for designing the end plate is due to Basler [1961a, Eq. 17c]:

$$A_e = \frac{hA_w(\tau - \tau_{cr})}{8e\sigma_{all}} \tag{9.289}$$

$$\tau_{cr} \le 4E\left(\frac{t}{a}\right)^2 \tag{9.290}$$

where A_e = area of cross section of the end plate
A_w = area of cross section of web
    = $ht(= Dt_w)$
h = depth of web
t = web thickness ($= t_w$)
e = distance between the end stiffener and the end plate
a = distance between the end and the first intermediate stiffener
τ = shear stress
τ_{cr} = critical shear stress
σ_{all} = allowable bending stress
E = modulus of elasticity of steel

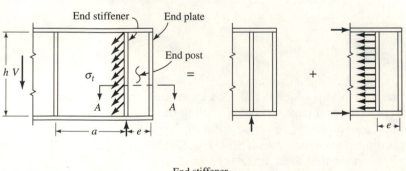

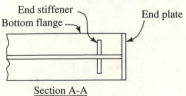

Section A-A

FIGURE 9.80
End post as an anchorage for tension field.

Alternatively, based on the ultimate load considerations, the required area A_e of the end plate can be computed from Eq. 9.291 [SSRC, 1988]:

$$A_e = \frac{hA_w(\tau - \tau_{cr})}{8e\sigma_y} \tag{9.291}$$

where σ_y is the yield stress of steel.

9.7.3 Transverse Stiffeners

The phenomenon of tension-field action has led to the development of two recognized procedures for design of plate girders: without considering the tension-field action and with the tension-field action. Development of tension-field action in a web is contingent on providing transverse stiffeners of adequate stiffness. Thus, transverse stiffeners are always required for a plate girder designed as a tension-field girder, but they may or may not be provided for a non-tension-field girder. Of course, if transverse stiffeners are not provided, the Pratt truss analogy becomes invalid, because the tension field cannot be developed.

With the exception of the end stiffeners, transverse stiffeners are intermediate stiffeners whose function is twofold: to preserve the shape of the girder's cross section (i.e., keep the web straight by preventing it from buckling), and to ensure its postbuckling strength. The first function requires a certain minimum stiffness, and the second requires a minimum strength (i.e., a certain minimum cross-sectional area) [Basler, 1961a].

An experimental investigation of the required stiffness of stiffeners was made by Massonet at the University of Liege, Belgium [Massonet, 1960; Massonet, Mazy, and Tanghe, 1960]. A discussion on analysis of transverse stiffeners has been provided by Cooper [1967]. The AASHTO requirements for the stiffness for transverse stiffeners are discussed in Sec. 9.5.6.

9.8
OPTIMUM DESIGN OF PLATE GIRDERS

9.8.1 Introduction

Design of a plate girder involves proportioning five components:

1. Flanges
2. Web
3. Longitudinal stiffener (if provided)
4. Transverse stiffeners (if provided)
5. Bearing stiffeners

In recognition of the vulnerability of webs of plate girders to buckling, two general design criteria are recognized for proportioning them: the *web buckling approach* and the *load-carrying capacity approach* [Cooper, 1974; SSRC, 1988]. In the web buckling approach, the proportions of a plate girder are governed by considerations of stability of the web; i.e., the web buckling stress forms the criterion for limit of usefulness. To improve the stability of web, various arrangements of stiffeners, as discussed in preceding paragraphs, are used to stiffen the web, enabling it to sustain higher buckling stress. This is the approach adopted by AASHTO [1992] and AREA [1980] specifications for webs of plate girders [Cooper, 1974; SSRC, 1988]. The main objection to this practice seems to be the inconsistent values for safety factors used in order to make the design agree better with the real behavior of the web plates [SSRC, 1988].

In cases where the plate girder design is based on the buckling strength, the existence of the postbuckling strength is tacitly recognized by the use of lower factors of safety against web buckling. This is known as the load-carrying capacity approach, introduced in 1961 for buildings [Basler, 1961c]. It forms the basis of AISC specifications [AISC, 1989] for design of plate girders. The validity of the postbuckling strength of plate girders is based on extensive analytical and experimental research [Basler, 1961a,b; Basler and Thurlimann, 1960a,b; Basler et al., 1960; Yen and Basler, 1962]. This approach has not been applied to bridge girders and other situations where repeated loads are encountered [Cooper, 1974].

A general discussion on the topic of optimum design of girders is presented in Chapter 7. The definition of "optimum design" is rather broad. Ignoring the life-cycle costs, some may define *optimum* design as one that reflects the minimum first cost. Others may define it as one that gives a least-weight design. Material and labor costs vary considerably worldwide. In countries such as the United States, the cost of labor and fabrication is very high and forms a paramount consideration in estimating the cost of the finished girder. The situation is different in countries of the Far East, where the labor is cheap and material relatively expensive. Because of the complexities and uncertainties involved in estimating the cost of fabrication of a plate girder, the mathematical model selected here for optimum design is a bisymmetric plate girder having the least weight. To some extent, this model is justified because the longitudinal welds between the flange plates and the web are common to all plate girders. The cost of stiffening details (transverse and longitudinal stiffeners), an important component of cost analysis that may offset any savings in a least-weight design, has been ignored in this model. The goal then is to select the optimum sizes of flanges and the web.

9.8.2 Preliminary Design of a Plate Girder

A simple formula giving a relationship between the area of the flange and the web of a bisymmetric plate girder may be derived by considering the effectiveness of the web in carrying moment in an elastic system, as shown in Fig. 9.81. Assuming that the resistance moment is equal to the couple formed by the C and T forces acting at the centroids of compression and tension flanges, respectively, one may write

$$\text{Arm of the couple } = \frac{1}{2}(h + d) \tag{9.292}$$

$$M = C\left(\frac{h + d}{2}\right) = T\left(\frac{h + d}{2}\right) \tag{9.293}$$

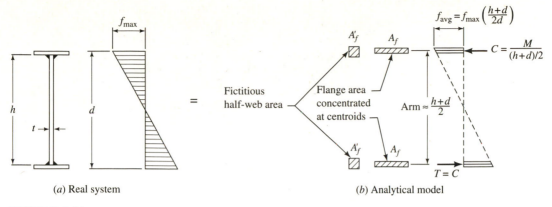

(a) Real system   (b) Analytical model

FIGURE 9.81
Model for the optimum design of a plate girder [Salmon, 1990].

so that

$$C = T = \frac{2M}{(h + d)} \qquad (9.294)$$

Let A_f = area of flange
A'_f = effective area of half web

The effective area of half web, A'_f, is defined as the *fictitious* area of half web located at the centroid of the flange, which gives the same moment of resistance as the actual web area. The total effective area in compression is $A_f + A'_f$. The average flexural stress, f_{avg}, on the total effective area is

$$f_{avg} = \frac{Force}{Area} = \frac{C(or\ T)}{(A_f + A'_f)} = \frac{2M}{(h + d)(A_f + A'_f)} \qquad (9.295)$$

from which

$$A_f + A'_f = \left(\frac{2M}{h + d}\right) f_{avg} \qquad (9.296)$$

The resisting moment, M'_w, of the fictitious web area A'_f is

$$M'_w = (force\ in\ the\ fictitious\ web\ area)(lever\ arm)$$

$$= [(f_{avg})(A'_f)]\left(\frac{h + d}{2}\right) \qquad (9.297)$$

From the stress distribution diagram (Fig. 9.82),

$$\frac{f_{avg}}{f_{max}} = \frac{(h + d)/4}{d/2} = \frac{h + d}{2d} \qquad (9.298)$$

from which

$$f_{avg} = \left(\frac{h + d}{2d}\right) f_{max} \qquad (9.299)$$

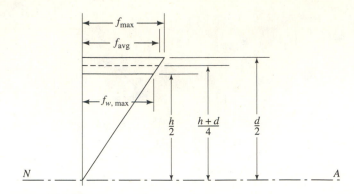

FIGURE 9.82
Stress distribution diagram.

Substitution for f_{avg} from Eq. 9.299 in Eq. 9.297 yields

$$
\begin{aligned}
M'_w &= \left[\left(\frac{h+d}{2d}\right)f_{max}A'_f\right]\left(\frac{h+d}{2}\right) \\
&= f_{max}A'_f\left[\frac{(h+d)^2}{4d}\right]
\end{aligned}
\tag{9.300}
$$

The bending stress at top of web is

$$
f_{w,max} = f_{max}\left(\frac{h}{d}\right)
$$

The resisting moment of the real web area is given by

$$
\begin{aligned}
M_w &= (f_{w,max})(\text{section modulus of web}) \\
&= \left[f_{max}\left(\frac{h}{d}\right)\right]\left(\frac{t_w h^2}{6}\right)
\end{aligned}
\tag{9.301}
$$

where $f_{w,max}$ is the maximum stress in the web. Equating the resisting moments of the fictitious and the real webs (Eqs. 9.300 and 9.301, respectively) yields

$$
M'_w = M_w
$$

$$
f_{max}A'_f\left[\frac{(h+d)^2}{4d}\right] = f_{max}\left(\frac{h}{d}\right)\left(\frac{t_w h^2}{6}\right)
$$

from which

$$
A'_f = \frac{t_w h}{6}\left(\frac{2h}{h+d}\right)^2
\tag{9.302}
$$

Assuming conservatively that $(h+d) \approx 2h$, and writing $A_w = t_w h$, Eq. 9.302 becomes

$$
A'_f = \frac{A_w}{6}
\tag{9.303}
$$

Substitution for A_f from Eq. 9.303 and f_{avg} in terms of f_{max} from Eq. 9.299 into Eq. 9.296 yields

$$A_f + A'_f = \left[\frac{2M}{h+d} \right] \left[\left(\frac{h+d}{2d} \right) f_{max} \right]$$

$$= \frac{Md}{f_{max}} \left(\frac{2}{h+d} \right)^2 \tag{9.304}$$

Substitution for A'_f from Eq. 9.302 in Eq. 9.304 yields

$$A_f = \frac{Md}{f_{max}} \left(\frac{2h}{h+d} \right)^2 - \frac{A_w}{6} \left(\frac{2h}{h+d} \right)^2$$

$$= \frac{M}{f_{max}} \left(\frac{d}{h^2} \right) \left(\frac{2h}{h+d} \right)^2 - \frac{A_w}{6} \left(\frac{2h}{h+d} \right)^2 \tag{9.305}$$

$$= \left(\frac{2h}{h+d} \right)^2 \left[\frac{M}{f_{max}h} \left(\frac{d}{h} \right) - \frac{A_w}{6} \right]$$

Again, assuming conservatively $d \approx h$, and expressing $f_{max} = F_b$, the allowable flexural stress, Eq. 9.305 can be expressed as

$$A_f = \frac{M}{F_b h} - \frac{A_w}{6} \tag{9.306}$$

Equation 9.306 can be used to make preliminary estimates for the flange and the web areas of homogeneous bisymmetric plate girders. However, it cannot be used for hybrid girders because the flange yield stress is different from (higher than) the web yield stress, and the web is much less effective than the flange in resisting moment. For example, for a hybrid girder with A514 steel flanges ($F_y = 100$ ksi, $F_u = 110$ to 130 ksi, available only for plates) and A36 steel web, the web may be taken as being only half as effective as in a homogeneous girder [Gaylord, Gaylord, and Stallmeyer, 1992, p. 500]. In such cases, Eq. 9.306 can be expressed as

$$A_f = \frac{M}{F_b h} - \frac{A_w}{12} \tag{9.307}$$

9.8.3 Optimum Girder Depth

The optimum depth h for a plate girder having total cross-sectional area A_g can be determined from the familiar minimization principle:

$$\frac{\partial A_g}{\partial h} = 0 \tag{9.308}$$

where

$$A_g = 2A_f + A_w \tag{9.309}$$

In general the moment resistance of the girder can be expressed as

$$M = f_b S_x \tag{9.310}$$

where S_x is the section modulus of the girder. Its value is obtained from Eq. 9.306 by noting that $M/F_b = S_x$ and $A_w = t_w h$. Thus,

$$S_x = A_f h + \frac{t_w h^2}{6} \tag{9.311}$$

where it is assumed that the flange area centroids are located a distance h apart (i.e., flange areas are concentrated in lines of zero thickness, an approximation). From Eq. 9.311 one obtains

$$A_f = \frac{S_x}{h} - \frac{A_w}{6} \tag{9.312}$$

The gross area of the girder can now be expressed by substituting Eq. 9.312 into Eq. 9.309:

$$
\begin{aligned}
A_g &= 2\left(\frac{S_x}{h} - \frac{A_w}{6}\right) + A_w \\
&= \frac{2S_x}{h} + \frac{2}{3} A_w \\
&= \frac{2S_x}{h} + \frac{2}{3} t_w h
\end{aligned}
\tag{9.313}
$$

By introducing a web slenderness ratio parameter, $\beta_w = h/t_w$, Eq. 9.313 can be expressed as

$$
\begin{aligned}
A_g &= \frac{2S_x}{h} + \frac{2}{3} \frac{h^2}{\left(\dfrac{h}{t_w}\right)} \\
&= \frac{2S_x}{h} + \frac{2}{3} \frac{h^2}{\beta_w}
\end{aligned}
\tag{9.314}
$$

Applying Eq. 9.308 to Eq. 9.314, one obtains

$$\frac{\partial A_g}{\partial h} = -\frac{2S_x}{h^2} + \frac{4}{3} \frac{h}{\beta_w} = 0$$

which yields

$$h^3 = 1.5 \beta_w S_x \tag{9.315}$$

Substituting $S_x = M/f$, Eq. 9.315 can be expressed as

$$h = \sqrt[3]{1.5 \beta_w \frac{M}{f}} \tag{9.316}$$

The section modulus of the web alone, S_w, can be expressed as

$$S_w = \frac{t_w h^2}{6} = \frac{h^3}{6\left(\dfrac{h}{t_w}\right)} = \frac{h^3}{6\beta_w} \tag{9.317}$$

Alternatively, S_w can also be expressed as

$$S_w = \frac{t_w h^2}{6} = \frac{A_w h}{6} \tag{9.318}$$

Substituting $h^3 = 1.5\beta_w S_x$ from Eq. 9.316 in Eq. 9.317, one obtains

$$S_w = \frac{1.5\beta_w S_x}{6\beta_w} = \frac{S_x}{4} \tag{9.319}$$

Equation 9.319 simply states that at the optimum, the moment resistance of the web is one-fourth of the total moment resistance of the girder. Therefore, the moment resistance of the flange must be three-fourths of the total moment resistance of the girder. Noting that the moment is proportional to the section modulus, we have

$$S_f = \tfrac{3}{4} S_x \tag{9.320}$$

Combining Eq. 9.318 and Eq. 9.319, we have

$$\frac{A_w h}{6} = \frac{S_x}{4}$$

or

$$A_w = \frac{1.5 S_x}{h} = \frac{1.5}{h}\left(\frac{M}{f}\right) \tag{9.321}$$

Because $S_f = A_f h = \tfrac{3}{4} S_x$, we have

$$A_f = \frac{3}{4}\frac{S_x}{h} = \frac{3}{4}\frac{M}{fh} \tag{9.322}$$

Substitution of Eq. 9.321 and 9.322 in Eq. 9.309, and writing $A_g = A_0 = $ optimum cross-sectional area of plate girder, yields

$$
\begin{aligned}
A_0 &= 2A_f + A_w \\
&= 2 \times \left(\frac{3}{4}\frac{M}{fh}\right) + \frac{1.5M}{fh} \\
&= \frac{3M}{fh}
\end{aligned} \tag{9.323}
$$

Equation 9.323 can also be expressed in terms of the web slenderness ratio β_w by substituting for h from Eq. 9.316:

$$A_0 = \frac{3M}{f\left(\sqrt[3]{1.5\beta_w \frac{M}{f}}\right)}$$

$$= \sqrt[3]{\frac{18M^2}{f^2\beta_w}}$$

(9.324)

Equation 9.324 may be used to examine variations in cost with allowable stress f. Cost differences are insensitive to moderate departures from the optimum girder depths. O'Connor [1971] has shown that for a variation of the web depth between 0.79 and 1.24 of the optimum depth, the total girder area varies within 5 percent of the optimum.

The discussion in the preceding paragraphs is focused on the optimum design of a bisymmetric, prismatic plate girder having an unstiffened web. Based on the model shown in Fig. 9.81, Schilling [1974] has developed a general procedure for optimum elastic design of girders with or without web stiffeners. For a stiffened girder, the section modulus and the moment of inertia are clearly functions of three geometric parameters: the total cross-sectional area A; the ratio of the web A_w to the total area A (i.e., $A_w A$); and the web slenderness ratio h/t_w. Schilling [1974] has shown that the section modulus and the moment of inertia of a plate girder can be expressed as

$$S = \left(\frac{3 - 2a}{6}\right)\sqrt{abA^3}$$

(9.325)

$$I = \left(\frac{3 - 2a}{12}\right)abA^2$$

(9.326)

where

$$a = \frac{A_w}{A} \quad \text{and} \quad b = \frac{h}{t_w} = \beta_w$$

The optimum values of the section modulus and the moment of inertia can be obtained from the minimization principle, i.e., partially differentiating Eqs. 9.325 and 9.326 with respect to a (the subscript "opt" indicates *optimum*):

$$\frac{\partial S}{\partial a} = \frac{1}{6}(1.5a^{-1/2} - 3a^{1/2})\sqrt{A^3} = 0$$

from which

$$a_{\text{opt}} = 0.5$$

(9.327)

$$\frac{\partial I}{\partial a} = \frac{1}{12}(3 - 4a)bA^2 = 0$$

from which

$$a_{\text{opt}} = 0.75$$

(9.328)

Substitution of Eqs. 9.327 and 9.328 in Eqs. 9.325 and 9.326, respectively, yields

$$S_{\text{opt}} = \frac{1}{3}\sqrt{\frac{bA^3}{2}} = \frac{2h_{\text{opt}}^3}{3b}$$

(9.329)

$$I_{\text{opt}} = \frac{3bA^2}{32} = \frac{h_{\text{opt}}^4}{6b} \tag{9.330}$$

Equations 9.329 and 9.330 show that for a constant value of slenderness parameter b (or β_w), the optimum section modulus varies as $A^{1.5}$, whereas the optimum value of the moment of inertia varies as A^2. Combining Eqs. 9.327 and 9.329, and Eqs. 9.328 and 9.330, we obtain the following dimensionless parameters:

$$\frac{S}{S_{\text{opt}}} = \left(\frac{3 - 2a}{\sqrt{2}}\right)\sqrt{a} \tag{9.331}$$

$$\frac{I}{I_{\text{opt}}} = \left(\frac{8(3 - 2a)}{9}\right)a \tag{9.332}$$

Plots of Eqs. 9.331 and 9.332 for various values of $a(= A_w/A)$ are shown in Fig. 9.83. For both plots, the total cross-sectional areas of the girder A and the web slenderness parameter b (or β_w) are kept constant. The peaks of both parabolic curves correspond to Eqs. 9.327 and 9.328. It can be seen that there is a range of values of A_w/A for which both S and I do not vary much. For values of a between 0.4 and 0.6, the value of the section modulus is between 98 and 99 percent of its optimum value. Similarly, for values of a between 0.65 and 0.85, the value of the moment of inertia is within 98 and 99 percent of its optimum value. Also, equating Eqs. 9.331 and 9.332 shows that for $a = 0.633$, both S and I are equal to 97.5 percent of their optimum values.

Of course, it should be realized that in practical cases, often a girder would have transverse web stiffeners that have not been considered in the foregoing discussion. This means that Eqs. 9.329 and 9.330 cannot be used directly for proportioning plate girders with stiffeners. In such cases, it has been suggested that Eq. 9.325 be corrected to

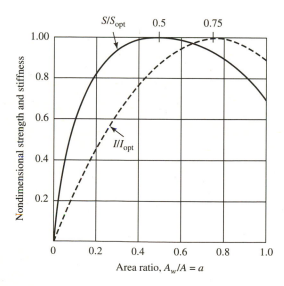

FIGURE 9.83
Variation of S/S_{opt} and I/I_{opt} with A/A_w, for constant values of cross-sectional area A, and the web slenderness ratio h/t_w [Schilling, 1974].

eliminate the effect of zero thickness of the flange, and that an additional cross-sectional area, ΔA, be included in the analysis to account for the area of transverse stiffeners. For further discussion on this topic, see Schilling [1974].

Breslar, Lin, and Scalzi [1968, p. 504] suggest a simple expression to select a preliminary optimum depth h_0 for a plate girder with constant h/t_w in terms of the known moment M and the allowable stress F:

$$h_0 = \left[\frac{3C_1KM}{C_4^2 F(3C_2 - C_1C_3)} \right]^{1/3} \tag{9.333}$$

where K = 120 to 180 for welded girders
$\quad\quad C_1 = 0.95$
$\quad\quad C_2 = 1.3$
$\quad\quad C_3 = 1.0$
$\quad\quad C_4 = 0.95$

Note that the optimum depth h_0 is not very sensitive to variation in the values of K. When K varies from a low of 120 to a high of 180, the maximum variation is less than 15 percent. Use of Eq. 9.333 is illustrated in Example 9.1.

Discussions on optimum plate girder design have been provided by Shedd [1934], Haaijer [1961], Krishnan and Shetty [1961], Razani and Goble [1966], Blodgett [1966], Bresler, Lin, and Scalzi [1968], Kuzmanovic and Willems [1983], and Salmon and Johnson [1990]. Schilling [1974], Azad [1980], Fleischer [1985], and Anderson and Chong [1986] have discussed the optimum design for both homogeneous and hybrid girders. Fleischer [1985] has provided mathematical and nomographic optimum design methods for bisymmetric plate girders for any moment-shear combination based on the web-buckling theory (no tension-field action). A discussion on the optimum design of composite plate girders and a girder with an upper flange of infinite area has been provided by O'Connor [1971].

While optimization of a plate girder (and for that matter, any structure) remains a cherished goal of designers, it is to be noted that AASHTO specifications [AASHTO, 1992, 1994] impose minimum thickness and slenderness requirements for the web which must be satisfied. These requirements are discussed in Sec. 9.5.3 (Eqs. 9.104, 9.108, 9.140, and 9.141). Furthermore, it is worth remembering that a least-weight design of a girder does not automatically (or necessarily) translate into a least-cost design. Fabrication costs and size limitations from the transportability standpoint are important considerations for cost analysis of a plate girder. These issues are discussed in the next section.

9.9
SOME PRACTICAL CONSIDERATIONS

9.9.1 General Considerations

Special attention should be paid to plate girders during erection because they are particularly vulnerable to severe damage or collapse during this phase, as a result of instability of the thin plate elements from which they are built. Structures are particularly vulnerable to failure during erection because the stiffening elements, such as the deck slab and lateral bracings, may not be in place at the time. Furthermore, the structure's strength may be compromised when certain connections are partially bolted or not fully welded to permit precise alignment of members. It was during erection that the Brazos River Bridge, Brazos, Texas, a 973-ft continuous plate girder bridge (Fig. 9.84), collapsed. The failure reportedly was initiated by overstress of the connections between the web and the flange during erection [Leet, 1988]. Failures of a few steel box girder bridges due to instability of flange and web plates are reported in the literature [Smith, 1977].

FIGURE 9.84
Collapse of the Brazos River Bridge, Texas.

9.9.2 Economic Considerations

Economic considerations for steel beam bridges discussed in Chapter 8 (e.g., wider girder spacings save fabrication costs) are also valid for plate girder bridges and will not be repeated here. However, a plate girder, unlike a rolled beam, happens to be a product of a designer's discretionary proportioning of flanges and web and should follow sound design practices to achieve economy, principles of optimization notwithstanding.

A final design is usually selected from several alternative designs involving variables such as flange splices versus common width and thickness of flanges, thicker un-stiffened web versus a thinner stiffened web, and ability to erect. A good design should consider the cost of the finished girder rather than the cost of the material alone. The input of a fabricator and contractor during the design phase should be encouraged with a view to minimizing fabrication costs. Fabrication costs for detail material are several times more expensive per pound than main material.

The greatest material savings is achieved in plate girders by properly designing top flanges. However, it should be noted that, in contrast to past practice, a least-weight design does not necessarily translate into a least-cost design. A major part of the total cost of a bridge—usually more than half—pertains to construction. Fabrication costs, handling and transportation, erection, and labor practices play a major role in the cost of a finished structure. Duplication and simplicity in detailing are essential ingredients of the design process for an economical structure. In addition, simpler details afford easy understanding of structural behavior and analysis. Fabricators should be given options, to achieve economy, for designing connections of the required strength. For example, a fabricator can be permitted to use either high-strength bolting or welding for attaching diaphragms, cross frames, and bracings.

Several guidelines are pertinent to economical proportioning of plate girders and splicing of plate components [Knight, 1984; Schilling, 1985; Foil, 1992; Guzek and Grzybowsky, 1992; Stupp, 1992; Mistry, 1994]. It is recommended that minimum flange thicknesses be in the $\frac{3}{4}$-in. to 1-in. range. Thinner flanges increase cost due to problems with heat distortion during welding. The most economical flange size often may be of single size. However, in some cases, when it may be economical to vary flange sizes to approximate variation in bending moment, it is more economical to achieve desired change in the flange areas by changing the plate thickness rather than

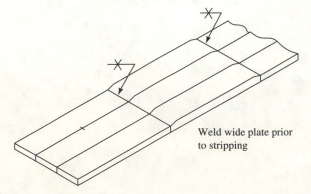

Weld wide plate prior to stripping

FIGURE 9.85
Multiple flange splicing scheme [Schilling, 1985].

flange width (i.e., a constant width is more desirable). Figure 9.85 illustrates a multiple splicing scheme in which plates of varying thicknesses are welded together as slabs received from the mill. This permits a fabricator to cut several duplicate flanges from wide plates of different thicknesses before the cuts are made. Cost-saving advantages offered by this scheme include handling of fewer members during fabrication, fewer run-off tabs and starts and stops for the welds, and straighter flanges as a result of cutting after the splices are welded [Schilling, 1985].

Bridge designers usually attempt to design a plate girder with a thin web and stiffen it transversely and longitudinally, in an attempt to achieve a least-weight solution. However, it should be recognized that providing stiffeners is one of the most labor-intensive (and therefore costly) operations in plate girder fabrication. In many cases, an unstiffened, thicker (and therefore heavier) web may be more economical, resulting from savings in fabrication costs of applying stiffeners.

Transverse stiffeners should be provided on only one side of the web, with the exceptions of the diaphragm locations and at the ends (bearing stiffeners), where they are required on both sides. Transverse stiffeners should not bear on both the top and bottom flanges unless this is a design requirement, such as for the end (bearing) stiffeners or at locations of concentrated loads. Fitting transverse stiffeners is a time- and labor-intensive operation because each stiffener has to be individually cut and ground to fit each location. As mentioned, intermediate transverse stiffeners provided on only one side of the web must be in bearing against the compression flange, but their attachment to it is not a design requirement and, therefore, should not be specified on fabrication drawings to save costs. However, due consideration should be given to the need for this attachment if the location of the stiffener or its use as a connector plate for a diaphragm or cross frame will produce out-of-plane movements in a welded web-to-flange connection (AASHTO, 1992, 10.34.4.6).

Plate girders for longer spans may sometimes necessitate deeper webs with both transverse and longitudinal stiffeners. In such cases, transverse stiffeners should be placed on the opposite side of the web from the longitudinal stiffeners. This eliminates transverse stiffeners intersecting with the longitudinal stiffeners, resulting in savings in shop labor costs. Studies of plate girders at Bethlehem Steel Corporation have shown that for reasons of economy, longitudinal stiffeners should not be considered for span lengths less than 300 ft [Knight, 1984].

A good knowledge of types of and procedures for welding are obviously helpful in specifying economic details. Because of lack of required knowledge, full-penetration groove welds are sometimes specified where fillet welds would be adequate, without recognizing that full-penetration welds require joint preparation, multiple-weld passes, and nondestructive testing, all of which greatly increase costs, often 150 to 200 percent more [Schilling, 1985]. For example, instead of specifying full-penetration welds on bearing stiffeners, they can be finished to bear, or finished to bear with fillet welds. Not only is this a cost-saving alternative; it will also prevent distortion of the bottom flange caused by the full-penetration weld, which must be straightened. Consequently, full-penetration welds should be avoided whenever possible.

A knowledge of availability of plates of various sizes and transportation limitations of the finished plate girder is important to determine splice locations and accomplish a good, constructible, and cost-effective design. AISC [1989] classifies plates as follows:

1. *Sheared* plates are those produced by rolling between horizontal rolls and trimmed, i.e., sheared or gas cut, on all edges.
2. *Universal* (UM) plates are produced by rolling between horizontal and vertical rolls and trimmed (sheared or gas cut) at ends only.
3. *Stripped* plates are furnished to required widths by shearing or gas cutting from wider sheared plates.

Sizes of plates produced by steel mills located in various parts of the country vary widely, and catalogs of individual mills should be consulted for their availability. The extreme width of UM plates currently rolled is 60 in., and for sheared plates 200 in. Typically, there is 48 in. minimum order width. Plates are typically produced in the following thicknesses:

Over 8 in. to 48 in. in width: 0.230 in. and over in thickness
Over 48 in. in width: 0.180 in. and over in thickness

The preferred increments in thicknesses of plates are

$\frac{1}{32}$ in. increments up to $\frac{1}{2}$ in.

$\frac{1}{16}$ in. increments over $\frac{1}{2}$ to 1 in.

$\frac{1}{8}$ in. increments over 1 in. to 3 in.

$\frac{1}{4}$ in. increments over 3 in.

Fabricators should be given some flexibility in flange splice locations so that they can use plate lengths that are available from mills in the area of the shop. Also, capacities of various shops vary in terms of maximum plate lengths that can be handled: some shops can efficiently handle plate lengths of over 100 ft whereas others are limited to 80 ft or less.

Girder lengths and depths should be limited to 120 and 15 ft, respectively, for convenient transportability. Larger sizes result in shipping from the fabrication shop to the job site being too expensive and difficult.

Cross frames and diaphragms are integral components of both rolled beam and plate girder bridges; if judiciously detailed, they can result in reduced fabrication costs. A discussion on this topic has been provided by Gatti [1994].

"Fracture-critical" requirements increase costs. It is cost-effective to take steps to minimize the number of members that must be classified as fracture-critical materials (FCM). Therefore, only material that must be fracture-critical should be labeled as such. Components such as diaphragms do not need to be fracture critical and would increase cost unnecessarily if labeled FCM.

9.10
AASHTO CRITERIA FOR DESIGN OF PLATE GIRDERS

9.10.1 General Considerations

The AASHTO [1992] specifications permit two different methods for designing plate girders: the service load design method and the load factor design method. In the near future, these methods are going to be replaced by the load and resistance design method [AASHTO, 1994]. A summary of the LRFD criteria for design of plate girders has been provided by Cooper, Galambos, and Ravindra [1978].

Various design parameters such as the width-to-thickness ratio (b/t), web slenderness ratio (D/t_w), web aspect ratio (d_o/D), and stiffeners (transverse and longitudinal), all of which affect the strength of a plate girder, are discussed in several preceding paragraphs. Various AASHTO equations defining the flexural and shear strengths of plate girders have been derived. A plate girder comprises three main components—two flanges and a web—whose proportioning constitutes a major portion of design. In the following paragraphs we discuss the design of these and other components by the service load and the load factor design methods, with pertinent references to the AASHTO specifications [AASHTO, 1992].

9.10.2 Service Load Design Method

The design of steel plate girders is governed by AASHTO 10.34. The following are the main requirements.

9.10.2.1 General design philosophy

The girders should be proportioned by the moment of inertia method (AASHTO 10.34.1.1). This simply means that the bending stress computed from the familiar flexural formula $f_b = Mc/I$ should not exceed the allowable bending stress value.

Due consideration for holes present in plate girder components should be given in computing the moment of inertia, I. Although a plate girder is usually a welded assembly of two flanges and a web (and stiffeners when present), holes may be present for high-strength bolts for field splicing. Specifications permit neglecting the presence of any holes not exceeding $1\frac{1}{4}$ in. in diameter, provided that the area removed from each flange does not exceed 15 percent of the flange area. Any area in excess of 15 percent is required to be deducted from the gross area when computing the moment of inertia.

9.10.2.2 Flanges

Design requirements for flanges of plate girders are covered in AASHTO 10.34.2. A flange may comprise a series of plates joined end to end by full-penetration welds (e.g., in a welded plate girder) or angles, or a combination of the two (e.g., a bolted plate girder). Three schemes can be used to accomplish changes in the flange areas: varying the thickness of flange plates, varying the width of flange plates, or adding cover plates. Preferences of one scheme over the other vary with designers. For example, the California Department of Transportation deleted the provision of "adding cover plates" in its August 1994 revision of its version of AASHTO specifications. Alternatively, flanges can be fabricated from higher-strength steel, resulting in a hybrid girder (Fig. 9.6).

The width-to-thickness ratio (b/t) requirements for compression flange are based on local buckling considerations, as discussed in Sec. 9.5.2, and are similar for both welded and bolted girders.

For welded girders, the ratio of compression flange plate width, b, to its thickness, t, is governed by AASHTO Eq. 10.19 (AASHTO 10.34.2.1.3):

$$\frac{b}{t} \leq \frac{3250}{\sqrt{f_{b,\text{psi}}}} \leq 24 \qquad \text{(9.83 repeated)}$$

where f_b is the calculated bending stress ($\leq 0.55F_y$).

For bolted girders (AASHTO 10.34.2.2.1), the width-to-thickness requirements are expressed in terms of the width b' and the thickness t of the outstanding leg of the angle. Because in this case $b' \approx b/2$ for the welded plate girder, the permitted b'/t ratio is just half of that permitted for welded girders. Maximum permitted values of b/t and b'/t ratios for steels of various yield strengths are given in Table 9.11.

The AASHTO specifications [AASHTO, 1992] do not provide any guidelines regarding the minimum thickness of the flange plates. The thinness of the flange plates is a matter of concern during fabrication, handling, and erection. Consequently, certain specifications mandate minimum thickness of the flange plates. For example, the Pennsylvania Department of Transportation [PennDOT, 1994] specifies that "for girders, the minimum flange plate thickness shall be $\frac{3}{4}$ in. unless the fabricator can demonstrate the ability to satisfactorily fabricate and erect plate girders with thinner flange plates." Such requirements should be kept in mind when selecting the thickness of the flange plates.

9.10.2.3 Web

Design of web is governed by three main requirements: stiffness, stability, and strength.

For providing adequate stiffness, the depth is limited by AASHTO 10.5.1, which stipulates that for beams or girders, the ratio of depth to length of span should not be less than 1/25. For composite plate girders, the ratio of the overall depth of girder (concrete slab plus steel girder) to length of span preferably should not be less than 1/25. However, the depth-span ratio for the steel girder alone should not be less than 1/30 (AASHTO 10.5.2).

TABLE 9.11
Maximum permitted values of b/t or b'/t ratios for compression flange (service load design)

Yield strength, $F_{y,\text{ksi}}$	Welded girder, b/t (AASHTO 10.34.2.1.3)	Bolted girder, b'/t (AASHTO 10.34.2.2.1)
36	23	11
50	20	10
70	17	8.5
90	15	7.5
100	14	7

b = width of flange plate.
b' = width of the outstanding leg of the flange angle.
t = thickness of plate or the outstanding leg of the angle.

In spite of its untraceable basis or evolution, the depth-to-span ratio ($\not< 1/25$) requirement has remained a part of the AASHTO specifications since its very inception [ASCE, 1958; Wright and Walker, 1971]. The depth-span requirements are discussed in Chapter 5 (Sec. 5.2.4).

To provide adequate stability (i.e., to prevent web buckling), the depth of the girder is governed by the permitted slenderness ratio (d/t_w) given by Eq. 9.104 (AASHTO Eq. 10.23) and Eq. 9.108 (AASHTO Eq. 10.24) for longitudinally unstiffened and stiffened girders, respectively (see Tables 9.7 and 9.8). For the longitudinally stiffened girders, the minimum value of the web thickness is half that required for girders without the longitudinal stiffeners.

It should be noted that the required web thickness is a function of the calculated bending stress. Graphical solutions of AASHTO Eqs. 10.23 and 10.24 are given in AASHTO [1992, Fig. 10.34.3.1A].

To provide adequate shear strength, the web must satisfy Eq. 9.155 (AASHTO Eq. 10.25) if it is unstiffened transversely. If transverse stiffeners are provided, the web must satisfy Eq. 9.210 (AASHTO Eq. 10.26). These equations are discussed in Secs. 9.5.4 and 9.5.7, respectively.

9.10.2.4 Transverse intermediate stiffeners

Requirements. Transverse intermediate stiffeners are not required if the average calculated unit shearing stress in the gross section of the web at the point considered, f_v, is less than that given by Eq. 9.155 (AASHTO Eq. 10.25) and $D/t_w < 150$ when the web is longitudinally unstiffened. Transverse intermediate stiffeners are required if either of these two requirements is not met.

Transverse stiffeners are required when the web is longitudinally unstiffened and $D/t_w > 150$. In this case the purpose of providing transverse stiffeners is to develop sufficient stiffness to ensure efficient handling, fabrication, and erection of girders. The spacing of these stiffeners (i.e., the aspect ratio) must conform to Eq. 9.221.

Transverse stiffeners are also required when the calculated shear stress exceeds that given by Eq. 9.155 (AASHTO Eq. 10.25). In this case the spacing of transverse stiffeners should conform to AASHTO 10.34.4.2.

Spacing of transverse stiffeners. The maximum spacing of transverse intermediate stiffeners is limited to $3D$ subject to the handling requirements given by Eq. 9.221. That is, the smaller spacing governs.

The portion of the girder between the end (or the bearing) stiffener and the first intermediate stiffener forms the end panel of the girder. The spacing of the first transverse stiffener should satisfy dual criteria: the spacing should not exceed $1.5D$ (as discussed in Sec. 9.7.2.5), and the shear stress in the end panel should not exceed that given by Eq. 9.287 (AASHTO Eq. 10.28).

If a girder panel is subjected to simultaneous shear and bending moment with the value of shear stress higher than $0.6F_v$, the bending stress F_s is to be limited to that given by Eq. 9.270b (AASHTO Eq. 10.29). When using this equation, the live load should be the load to produce maximum moment at the section under consideration.

Types of intermediate transverse stiffeners. Intermediate transverse stiffeners preferably should be made of plates for welded plate girders and of angles for riveted plate girders. They may be used in pairs (one stiffener fastened on each side of the web plate) with a tight fit at the compression flange. Alternatively, they may be made of single stiffeners fastened to only one side of the web plate, in which case they *must* be in bearing against the compression flange (to prevent its twisting) but need not be attached to the compression flange to be effective. When only single stiffeners are used, it is usual to place them on the inside face of the web for aesthetic reasons. In some cases a stiffener may be used as a connector plate for a diaphragm, a cross frame, or lateral supports, which could result in out-of-plane movement in the welded web-to-flange connection. In such cases, attachment of the stiffener to the compression flange may be necessary, and the connection should be adequately designed to transmit the lateral force developed at the connection.

Transverse intermediate stiffeners need not be in bearing with the tension flange, but they should be terminated within a distance of four to six times the web thickness from the near edge of the web-to-flange fillet weld (AASHTO 10.34.4.9). However, this unsupported distance of the web between the tension flange and the end of the transverse stiffener should not be exceeded to avoid local buckling of the web [Basler and Thurlimann, 1959; Basler et al., 1960]. Furthermore, welding of transverse stiffeners to tension flange may be objectionable from the standpoint of fatigue [Cooper, 1974].

When a concentrated load is applied on the flange of a plate girder, transverse stiffeners in pairs are required to prevent crippling in the web immediately adjacent to concentrated reaction or loads. These stiffeners, of necessity, are designed as bearing stiffeners (AASHTO 10.34.4.9).

Design of transverse intermediate stiffeners. Design requirements for transverse stiffeners, specified in AASHTO 10.34.4.7, are based on elastic buckling theory and are discussed in AASHTO 9.5.6 (Eqs. 9.198 through 9.204; AASHTO, 1992, Eqs. 10.30 and 10.31a). Requirements specified in AASHTO–LRFD [1994] (Eqs. 6.10.8.1.3-3 and 4) are identical. Transverse stiffeners should have sufficient cross-sectional area to resist the vertical component of the tension field in the panel. When single stiffeners are used, the moment of inertia should be taken about the face of the web. But when stiffeners are used in pairs, the moment of inertia should be taken about the centerline of the web (AASHTO 10.34.4.8).

To avoid local buckling, transverse stiffeners must meet certain width and thickness requirements. The width, b_t, of a plate or the outstanding leg of an angle-intermediate stiffener and the thickness, t_p, should conform to the following two requirements (AASHTO 10.34.4.10):

$$b_t \geq \left(2 \text{ in.} + \frac{d}{30}\right) \tag{9.334}$$

$$16.0t_p \geq b_t \geq 0.25b_f \tag{9.335}$$

where d = full depth of the girder
  b_f = width of compression flange

Identical requirements (Eqs. 6.10.8.1.2-1 and 2) are specified in AASHTO–LRFD [1994].

9.10.2.5 Bearing stiffeners

Design of bearing stiffeners is specified in AASHTO 10.34.6. Bearing stiffeners are required at locations where concentrated loads are transmitted to the web through flanges. Such locations are end bearings of welded plate girders and the intermediate bearings of continuous welded plate girders where the bottom flanges receive the reactions, or the points of concentrated loads applied to the top girder flanges.

The function of bearing stiffeners is to distribute reaction or concentrated loads into the web to create web shear (Fig. 9.86a). Additionally, they preclude the possibility of local crippling in the web adjacent to concentrated loads or reactions (Fig. 9.86b) and prevent general vertical buckling of the web (Fig. 9.86c).

To effectively perform these functions, bearing stiffeners should be sufficiently stiff against buckling. If the bearing stiffeners are provided on one side of the web only, they will be loaded eccentrically, and thus be subjected to both axial load and moment, and have reduced effectiveness. Therefore, it is preferable to have bearing stiffeners consisting of plates provided in pairs (i.e., placed on both sides of the web, AASHTO 10.34.6.1), and their connection with the web should be designed to transmit the entire reaction to the bearings. They must bear firmly on the flanges (i.e., fit tightly against the loaded flanges) through which they receive the reaction (or the concentrated load) and extend as far possible to the outer edges of the flanges. The ends of the bearing stiffeners are required to be milled (or ground) to fit against the flange through which they receive their reaction.

Alternatively, they should be attached to the flange by full-penetration welds. Such a tight fitting develops an end restraint that allows for the use of reduced effective length of the stiffener column ($0.75D$, instead of the full depth D of web), a concept introduced in the new AASHTO–LRFD 6.10.8.2.4a [AASHTO–LRFD, 1994]. The

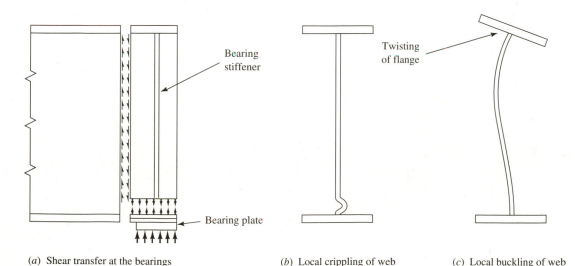

(a) Shear transfer at the bearings   (b) Local crippling of web   (c) Local buckling of web

FIGURE 9.86

Support conditions and possible distortion of web at the end of a girder [Johnston, Lin, and Galambos, 1986].

reduced effective length of the stiffener is not permitted in the 1992 AASHTO specifications, although such a provision exists in the AISC specifications [AISC, 1989] (Sec. K1.8).

The thickness requirement for the bearing stiffeners (plate or angles) is given by

$$t_{\text{bg st}} \nless \frac{b'}{12} \sqrt{\frac{F_{y,\text{psi}}}{33,000}} \qquad (9.336)$$

which is the same as AASHTO Eqs. 10.34 and 10.35.

To provide space for uninterrupted fillet welds at the web-flange juncture, the inside corner on one edge of the stiffeners must, of necessity, be clipped to ensure tight fit against the flange. This results in reduced contact width $b_1 (< b_t)$ of the stiffener and reduced contact area ($b_1 t_p$ in Fig. 9.87(b)) between the bottom flange and the bearing stiffeners, which is smaller than the gross cross-sectional area ($b_t t_p$) of the bearing stiffeners. This contact area of the stiffeners should be adequate to transmit the reaction (or the concentrated load) without exceeding the permitted bearing on either the flange material or the stiffener material, $0.80F_y$ according to AASHTO 10.32.1 (Table 10.32.1A). The *effective area in bearing* is considered to be only the portions of the stiffeners outside the flange-to-web fillet welds.

In case of bolted (or riveted) plate girders, bearing stiffeners are required to consist of angles, with outstanding legs extended as close to the edges of flange angles as possible. Bearing stiffener angles are proportioned for bearing on the outstanding legs of flange angles, considering the actual contact area of the legs. The portions of legs fitted to the fillet of the flange angles should be neglected (Fig. 9.87(c)). Crimping of the angle bearing stiffeners is not permitted. To preserve straightness, the space between their contact legs and web should be filled with *fillers*. The connection between the angle stiffeners and the web should be designed to transmit the entire reaction to the bearings.

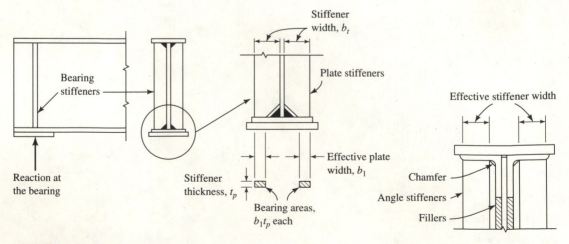

FIGURE 9.87
Bearing stiffeners for plate girders.

Bearing stiffeners are designed as concentrically loaded columns. A portion of the web extending longitudinally on both sides of the bearing stiffeners is considered participatory in carrying the reaction load. Depending on the magnitude of the end reaction to be transmitted, the design may require two (one on each side of the web) or four or more (symmetrically placed about the web) stiffeners. The cross-sectional area of this *fictitious column* is defined as follows (AASHTO 10.34.6.1):

1. When two stiffeners (one on each side of the web) are provided, the column section, resembling a + (plus) sign, consists of the two stiffeners and a centrally located strip of the web equal to $18t_w$ (Fig. 9.88(a)).
2. If there are four or more stiffeners, the column section consists of areas of all stiffeners and a centrally located strip of web plate whose width is equal to that enclosed by the stiffeners plus a width equal to $18t_w$ (Fig. 9.88(b)).

The actual compressive stress in the fictitious column should not exceed the allowable stress, which depends on its slenderness ratio, KL/r. This fictitious column may be an intermediate column ($KL/r \leq C_c$) or a long column ($KL/r \geq C_c$). For both cases, the allowable stresses are specified in AASHTO Table 10.32.1A (Appendix A, Table A.26) as follows:

When $KL/r \leq C_c$ (intermediate column):

$$F_a = \frac{F_y}{\text{FS}} \left[1 - \frac{(kL/r)^2 F_y}{4\pi^2 E} \right]$$

$$= 16,980 - 0.53(KL/r)^2 \text{ for A36 steel} \tag{9.337}$$

When $KL/r \geq C_c$ (long column):

$$F_a = \frac{\pi^2 E}{\text{FS}(KL/r)^2}$$

$$= \frac{135,008,740}{(KL/r)^2} \text{ (psi) with FS} = 2.12 \tag{9.338}$$

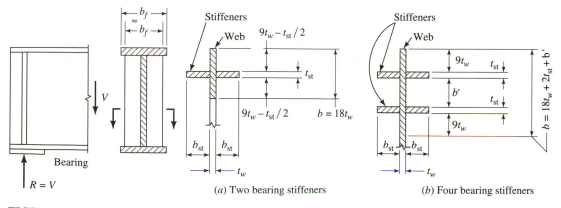

FIGURE 9.88
Column section for bearing stiffeners.

where

$$C_c = \sqrt{\frac{2\pi^2 E}{F_y}} \tag{9.339}$$

In AASHTO Table 10.32.1A [1992], the value of the numerator in Eq. 9.338 is given as 135,000,740 instead of 135,008,740.

9.10.2.6 Longitudinal stiffeners

Strength of longitudinally stiffened girders is discussed in Sec. 9.7.2.2. AASHTO 10.34.5 covers provision for a single longitudinal stiffener placed at $0.20D$ from the inside face of the compression flange. The principal design requirements are the moment of inertia and the width-to-thickness ratio. The first (Eq. 9.276, AASHTO Eq. 10.32) is provided to ensure sufficient stiffness to force a straight longitudinal node in the web. The second (Eq. 9.278a, AASHTO Eq. 10.33) is provided to prevent local buckling of the longitudinal stiffener.

Longitudinal stiffeners are usually placed on one side of the web. They need not be continuous, and they may be cut at their intersection with the transverse stiffeners when both are provided on the same side of the web. However, economics dictates that they be provided on the opposite sides of the web. The spacing requirements for transverse stiffeners in a longitudinally stiffened girder should conform to AASHTO 10.34.5.5 [AASHTO, 1992]. It is important to note that the maximum spacing of *all* transverse stiffeners (including the first intermediate stiffener) is limited to 1.5 times the maximum *subpanel depth*.

9.10.2.7 Deflection, camber, and fatigue

Deflection, camber, and fatigue pertaining to steel girders and the corresponding AASHTO requirements are discussed in Chapter 5 and illustrated in Chapter 8. Allowable deflection for steel girders and requirements governing camber are covered in AASHTO 10.6 and Secs. 10.14 and 10.15.3, respectively. Allowable fatigue stresses affect design of different parts of a plate girder differently: cover plates (AASHTO 10.13), connection design (AASHTO 10.3), and shear studs for composite action (AASHTO 10.38.5). These design considerations are illustrated in Example 8.3 (Chapter 8). The same requirements are also applicable to plate girders.

9.10.3 Load Factor Design

9.10.3.1 General design philosophy

The load factor design, also referred to as the strength design method, is based on the work of Vincent [1969] and is specified in AASHTO [1992, Part D]. This design method is discussed in detail in Chapter 8 (Sec. 8.6.2) and will not be repeated here. The three load levels (the maximum load, the service load, and the overload) to be used in design are defined as follows (see Table 8.8, Chapter 8):

$$\text{Maximum design load} = 1.30\left[D + \frac{5}{3}(L + I)\right]$$

$$\text{Service load} = D + (L + I) \tag{9.340}$$

$$\text{Overload} = D + \frac{5}{3}(L + I)$$

The moments, shears, and other forces due to service loads are computed by assuming the elastic behavior of the structure, as in the case of the service load design. Structural members are then proportioned for *factored* loads, which are simply multiples of the service loads.

9.10.3.2 Proportioning the cross section

The cross section of plate girder is proportioned for the maximum design load. The flexural strength of a member, which depends on whether the section is compact or noncompact, is given by the following expressions:

$$\text{Compact sections: } M_u = F_y Z \tag{9.341}$$

$$\text{Noncompact sections: } M_u = F_y S \tag{9.342}$$

where Z = plastic section modulus
S = elastic section modulus
F_y = minimum specified yield strength of steel

Equations 9.341 and 9.342 are AASHTO Eqs. 10.91 and 10.97, respectively.

In the case of a plate girder, the section is not likely to meet the compactness requirements as specified in AASHTO 10.48.2.1 (see discussion in Chapter 8 and Table 8.9). Consequently, the cross section of a plate girder is proportioned based on the following relationship, applicable for braced noncompact sections:

$$F_y S \geq 1.30\left[D + \frac{5}{3}(L + I)\right] \tag{9.343}$$

In Eqs. 9.342 and 9.343, the presence of the section modulus (S) indicates that the flexural stress distribution is linear. Therefore, the section criteria for flanges are the same as for the service load design. Equation 9.341 (AASHTO Eq. 10.98) is applicable only if the criteria as specified in AASHTO 10.48.2.1 are satisfied:

1. For the projecting compression flange element (i.e., half-width of the compression flange):

$$\frac{b'}{t} \leq \frac{2200}{\sqrt{F_y}} \tag{9.344}$$

2. For web, Eq. 9.139 (AASHTO Eq. 10.99) applies:

$$\frac{D_c}{t_w} \leq \frac{15{,}400}{\sqrt{F_y}} \tag{9.139}$$

where D_c = depth of web in compression
$\quad\quad\quad$ = $D/2$ for symmetrical girders

3. The compression flange is laterally braced at intervals L_b:

$$L_b \leq \frac{(20 \times 10^6)A_f}{F_y d} \tag{9.345}$$

If Eqs. 9.139 and 9.345 are not satisfied, Eq. 9.342 cannot be used for computing the flexural strength of the girder. Instead, the strength is to be computed from AASHTO Eq. 10.102a:

$$M_u = M_r R_b \tag{9.346}$$

where M_r and R_b are defined by AASHTO Eqs. 102b and 102c.[41]

9.10.3.3 Web

The web should be proportioned to resist shear caused by the maximum loads. Shear strength of a girder is computed as follows:

1. The shear strength of an unstiffened girder is limited by its plastic or buckling shear capacity (AASHTO Eq.10.112):

$$V_u = CV_P \tag{9.288 repeated}$$

2. The shear strength of a transversely stiffened girder, with aspect ratio not exceeding 3 (maximum permitted), is computed as the sum of its plastic or buckling shear capacity and the postbuckling shear resistance due to tension-field action, as given by Eq. 9.207 (AASHTO Eq. 10.113). In these equations, the values of the web buckling coefficient, C, depend on the D/t_w ratio and are given by Eqs. 9.215 through 9.217 (AASHTO Eqs. 10.115 and 10.116). It was pointed out earlier (Sec. 9.7.2.3) that increase in shear capacity due to presence of a longitudinal stiffener is small and neglected in computing shear strength of the girder.
3. Webs of girders with transverse stiffeners but without the longitudinal stiffener must conform to D/t_w requirements given by Eq. 9.140 (AASHTO Eq. 10.103). However, when a longitudinal stiffener is also provided at $D/5$ from the inside face of the compression flange, the governing D/t_w requirements are given by Eq. 9.141 (AASHTO Eq. 10.108). In this latter case, a web only half as thick as required for the longitudinally unstiffened web is required (discussed in Sec. 9.5.3.2; see Table 9.8).

9.10.3.4 Transverse stiffeners

The width-to-thickness (b'/t) requirements for the transverse stiffeners are given by Eq. 9.278b (AASHTO Eq. 10.104). Its cross-sectional area and the stiffness requirements are given, respectively, by Eq. 9.199 (AASHTO Eq. 10.105) and Eq. 9.203 (AASHTO Eq. 10.106). Other requirements for the transverse stiffeners are the same as in the case of the service load design.

---

[41] These equations are lengthy and are not excerpted here to preserve space.

9.10.3.5 Longitudinal stiffeners

As in the case of the service load design, the longitudinal stiffener is to be placed at $D/5$ from the *inside face* of the compression flange. The b'/t limits are the same as for the transverse stiffeners (Eq. 9.278b). The stiffness requirements are given by Eq. 9.276 (AASHTO Eq. 10.109), Eq. 9.283 (AASHTO Eq. 10.110), and Eq. 9.285b (AASHTO Eq. 10.111).

9.10.3.6 Bearing stiffeners

The design requirements for the bearing stiffeners are the same as in the case of the service load design.

9.10.3.7 Deflection, camber, and fatigue

Design requirements for deflection, camber, and fatigue are related to the service load behavior and are applied for the serviceability check in the load factor design. Therefore, these are the same as in the case of the service load design.

9.10.4 Composite Plate Girders

Composite construction of steel beam bridges by the two design methods presented in the preceding paragraphs is discussed in detail in Chapter 8. In general, composite construction adds to the stiffness of the girder significantly, resulting in improved performance. Consequently, it is economical and should be used whenever feasible. The design principles for plate girders are the same as for composite design with rolled W-shapes (discussed in Chapter 8). AASHTO design criteria for composite steel design are covered in AASHTO Secs. 10.38 and 10.50 for the service load design and load factor design methods, respectively.

9.11
CONNECTIONS

9.11.1 General Considerations

The purpose of this section is not to present a complete discussion on design of bolted connections, because it is assumed that readers are familiar with the design principles of both welded and bolted connections. The basic concepts used in connection design for bridges are the same as those used in other steel structures. However, because of the fluctuation in stress levels and stress reversals caused by the moving loads encountered in bridge structures, fatigue and slippage between the connected parts are matters of serious concern. Accordingly, special considerations that must be made for design of connections for bridges are discussed in this section. A general discussion on design of connections for steel structures can be found in many texts on steel design [Salmon and Johnson, 1990; Gaylord, Gaylord, and Stallmeyer, 1992; and many references given in these texts].

Connections, welded or bolted, must be designed to adequately transmit loads from one connected part to another. Because of great concern for fatigue- and distortion-induced damage as a result of secondary stresses [Fisher, 1977; NCHRP, 1990], methodology of providing connections plays a significant role in design of all steel bridges, including plate girders. Fatigue is discussed in Chapter 5. AASHTO's requirements for fatigue design are based on the work of Fisher [1977] conducted at Lehigh University. A comprehensive reading of Fisher [1977] and NCHRP [1990] is highly recommended to develop an understanding of connection design as related to fatigue. Typical fatigue-prone details and their locations in steel structural members of bridges are described and illustrated in Table A.12 (Appendix A) (AASHTO Table 10.3.1B and Fig. 10.3.1C). In general, they are as follows [Fisher, 1977].

Main load-carrying members:

1. Cover plate end transverse welds
2. Web and flange splices
3. Termination of cover plate longitudinal welds
4. Stringer-to-floor beam and floor beam-to-girder connections
5. Coping of flanges
6. Web cope holes
7. Pin and hanger connections

Secondary members:

1. Lateral connections to floor beams and girders
2. Intersecting welds of lateral connection plates
3. Transverse connection plates subjected to out-of-plane distortion
4. Rolled beam diaphragm connections
5. Backing bar splices
6. Repair holes with partial or complete plug welds
7. Tack welds

9.11.2 AASHTO Criteria for Connections—Service Load Design

Design of connections is covered in AASHTO 10.23 (welding) and 10.24 (fasteners, i.e., high-strength bolts). Steel base metal to be welded, weld metal, and welding design details are required to conform to the requirements of the ANSI/AASHTO/AWS D1.5 Bridge Welding Code and subsequent AASHTO Interim Specifications. Joints can be welded, bolted using high-strength bolts, or a combination of both.

The *maximum* weld size, as permitted by AASHTO, along the edges of the material less than $\frac{1}{4}$ in. thick, can be as thick as the material to be connected. Along the edges of the thicker material, the maximum weld size permitted is $\frac{1}{16}$ in. *smaller* than the thickness of the material to be connected.

The permitted *minimum* weld size depends on the thickness of the thicker part to be joined. If the thickness of the thicker part joined $\leq \frac{3}{4}$ in., the minimum weld size is limited to $\frac{1}{4}$ in. For thicker parts to be joined, the minimum weld size is to be limited to $\frac{5}{16}$ in. However, the weld size need not be larger than the thickness of the thinner part

TABLE 9.12
Recommended bolt sizes for connection angles

Width of the leg (in.)	Bolt diameter (in.)
2	$\frac{5}{8}$
$2\frac{1}{2}$	$\frac{3}{4}$
3	$\frac{7}{8}$
$3\frac{1}{2}$	1

joined. In all cases, smaller welds are permitted based on the applied stress and the use of the appropriate preheat.

Certain restrictions apply to sizes of high-strength bolts. In general, use of $\frac{3}{4}$-in. or $\frac{7}{8}$-in. diameter bolts is recommended. Use of $\frac{5}{8}$-in. diameter bolts is *not* permitted for connecting members carrying calculated stress, except in $2\frac{1}{2}$-in.-wide legs of angles and in flanges of sections requiring $\frac{5}{8}$-in. bolts.

Angles are one of the most common types of connection hardware used in joining two steel members by bolts. The diameter of the bolts in angles carrying calculated stress is not to exceed one-fourth the width of the leg in which they are placed. Examples of such connections are stringer–to–floor beam connections, floor beam–to–girder connections, and floor beam–to–truss connections (at the panel points). In all these connections, clip angles are used to connect the two members. For angles whose sizes are not determined by calculated stress, the recommended sizes of the bolts are shown in Table 9.12 (AASHTO 10.24.4.3):

The requirements for spacing of fasteners and the edge and end distances are the same for bearing-type and slip-critical joints (described later). They are covered, respectively, by AASHTO 10.24.5 and 10.24.7 [AASHTO, 1992] and are shown in Table A.27 (Appendix A).

Hole types for high-strength bolted connections are standard holes, oversize holes, short slotted holes, and long slotted holes. Their sizes are defined in AASHTO Table 10.24.2. Standard holes are made $\frac{1}{16}$ in. larger than the diameter of the bolt for easy placement of the bolts.

9.11.3 Types of Bolted Connections

Connections are typically characterized as connections between the main members (such as stringers–to–floor beam or floor beam–to–main girders or trusses) or as connections to the secondary members (such as diaphragms, bracings, and gusset plates). In terms of performance under loads, the connections are categorized as either *bearing-type* connections or *slip-critical* connections (known in the past as *friction-type* connections).[42] In bearing-type connections, the force is transferred by shear and bearing on the bolt. In slip-critical connections, the force is transferred by the friction produced

---

[42]The term *slip-critical,* chosen to replace the term *friction-type,* first appeared in AISC [1986] and AISC [1989].

between the faying surfaces. For this reason, the condition of the faying surfaces plays a defining role in the shear-resisting mechanism of slip-critical connections.

Both the bearing-type and the slip-critical connections are proportioned on the basis of the calculated shear on the gross area of the bolt. In both connections, the shear is transmitted across shear planes between steel components, and the strength of the connections is the same. However, in slip-critical connections, a serviceability requirement to preclude slip at the service load is specified in addition to the strength requirement, and resistance to slip[43] at service load is a defining design consideration. An excellent study of connection slip as a serviceability limit has been provided by Galambos, Reinhold, and Ellingwood [1982].

In general, the slip-critical joints are those that are subject to stress reversal, heavy impact loads, or severe vibration or where stress and strain due to joint slippage would impair the serviceability of the structure. Thus, the limit state of slip in the joint is a serviceability requirement, and joints, of necessity, are *required* to be designed for resistance to slippage (AASHTO 10.32.3.1.6). Included in this category are the following (AASHTO 10.24.1.4):

1. Joints subject to fatigue loading
2. Joints installed in oversize holes
3. Joints subject to significant stress reversal
4. Joints in which welds and bolts share in transmitting load at a common faying surface
5. Joints in which any slip would be critical to their performance or to the performance of the structure
6. Joints involving connections subject to computed tension or combined shear and tension

The use of bolted bearing-type connections is limited to members in compression and secondary members (AASHTO 10.24.1.6 and 10.32.3.1.8). In general, bearing-type connections are used where the service conditions preclude cyclic loading approaching complete stress reversal and member deformation due to slip of the connection into bearing is acceptable.

9.11.4 Design for Bolt Sizes

9.11.4.1 Service load design

Design of bolted joints according to the service load design method is covered in AASHTO 10.32.3. In determining the sizes of bolts, the cross-sectional area based on the *nominal* diameter (called the nominal, unthreaded, or the gross area, Table A.27, Appendix A) is to be used, except as otherwise noted. It is therefore necessary to ensure that the threads are excluded from shear planes of the contact surfaces. In determining whether the bolt threads are excluded from these shear planes, threaded length of the bolt is calculated as two pitches greater than the specified length as an allowance for

---

[43]"Slip" is defined as occurring when "the friction bond is definitely broken and the two surfaces slip with respect to one another by a relatively large amount" [Vesarhelyi and Chiang, 1967].

the thread runout. If the threads are present in the shear planes, the area at the root of the threads should be used in place of the nominal area. Because the area at the root of the threads is somewhat smaller than the tensile stress area, the root area is taken as 0.7 of the gross area [Salmon and Johnson, 1990, p. 121].

For designing connections, AASHTO [1992] specifications follow the "shear stress" approach, i.e., the allowable shear stress, F_v, on the threaded areas of high-strength bolts is specified. If the material thickness or joint details preclude threads in the shear planes, the tabulated shear stress can be increased by 40 percent ($1.00/0.7 \approx 1.4$), as noted in Table 10.32.3B, footnote d [AASHTO, 1994]. Allowable stresses on high-strength bolts (AASHTO Table 10.32.3B) are given in Table A.28 (Appendix A). It will be observed from this table that the allowable stress in bearing, F_P, on connected material with two or more bolts in line of force in standard or short slotted holes is greater than the ultimate strength of the connected material. This is so because this stress value does not represent a true stress on the surface in bearing but a fictitious stress on the projected area of the surface. It has been determined from tests that strength of the net section of a tension member remains unaffected if the bearing stress is not larger than 2.25 times the net-section stress [Gaylord, Gaylord, and Stallmeyer, 1992].

In bearing-type connections, pull-out shear in a plate between the end of the plate and the end row of the fasteners should also be checked, in addition to the check for the bearing strength.

In slip-critical joints, as in all high-strength bolted joints, loads are resisted by friction. The pretension force in the bolt equals the clamping force between the connected components. The resistance to shear is provided by the frictional force μT, where μ is the *slip coefficient* (known in the past as the *coefficient of friction*) and T is the pretension force in the bolt. The value of the slip coefficient (< 1.0 always) depends on the surface conditions of the faying surfaces and typically varies from 0.2 to 0.6 [Kulak, Fisher, and Struik, 1987]. These conditions refer to such items as mill scale, oil paint, and special surface treatments (e.g., special coatings, galvanizing). For design of slip-critical joints, AASHTO (Table 10.32.3C) specifies values of *allowable loads*[44] (Table A.29, Appendix A) instead of specifying the slip coefficients.

A slip-critical joint must be designed to satisfy the following two requirements:

1. Strength requirements, by satisfying the allowable stresses as specified in Table A.28 (Appendix A) (AASHTO Table 10.32.3.B)
2. Serviceability requirements, by limiting the force on the connection to the allowable slip resistance, P_s, given by (AASHTO 10.32.3.2.1)

$$P_s = F_s A_b N_b N_s \tag{9.347}$$

where F_s = nominal slip resistance per unit of bolt area from AASHTO Table 10.32.3C
　　　　(Table A.29, Appendix A)
　　A_b = area corresponding to the nominal body area of the bolt, in.^{2}
　　N_b = number of bolts in the joint
　　N_s = number of slip planes

---

[44]This is actually allowable stress rather than load (or force) and is defined as the slip load per unit of bolt area.

Equating the design force on the joint to the allowable slip resistance, the required number of bolts, N_b, can be computed by Eq. 9.349:

$$N_b = \frac{\text{Design shear}}{F_s A_b N_s} \qquad (9.348)$$

Of course, any fractional value of N_b should be rounded off to the next whole number.

The maximum acceptable service load shear stress, F_v, for bolts in slip-critical joints in steel buildings has been recommended by the Research Council on Structural Connections [RCSC, 1985]. The corresponding AASHTO values appear to be 90 percent of these values, rounded off to the nearest one-half ksi. The allowable stress values are smaller for joints with slotted or oversize holes because repeated loading results in reduced fatigue strength in such joints.

For designing a slip-critical joint, the appropriate or governing value of the allowable shear stress from Tables 10.32.3B and 10.32.3C [AASHTO, 1992] (Tables A.28 and A.29, Appendix A, respectively) should be carefully selected. It should be noted that the allowable stress values in Table 10.32.3B are different for high-strength bolts having threads excluded or included in the shear planes, but no such difference exists in Table 10.32.3C. For example, A325 bolts for slip-critical joints for Class B conditions are permitted to be stressed to 25 ksi (Table 10.32.3C). The allowable stress on bolts for the same joint is 19 ksi when the threads are included in the plane and $26.5 (= 19 \times 1.4 \approx 26.5)$ ksi (per footnote d in Table 10.32.3B) when the threads are excluded from the shear plane. Therefore, if the threads are included in the plane, the bolts must be proportioned for 19 ksi, but if the threads are not included in the plane, they should be proportioned for 25 ksi, not for 26.5 ksi. That is, the *smaller* of the two values from Tables 10.32.3B and 10.32.3C governs.

The slip resistance between the two connected parts depends on the condition of the faying surfaces, which, for highway bridges, must meet the requirements specified in AASHTO, Div. II—Construction, Art. 11.5.6.3. These surface conditions are classified as Class A, B, or C. Paint is permitted on the faying surfaces of joints unconditionally except in slip-critical connections. Coatings referred to as Class A and Class B include those coatings which provide a mean slip coefficient not less than 0.33 or 0.50, respectively, as determined by tests [Yura and Frank, 1985].

9.11.4.2 Load factor design

The fundamental principles of designing high-strength bolted joints remain the same regardless of the design method. The difference lies merely in the loads to be resisted and the maximum permitted values of the allowable shears.

Design of high-strength bolted joints by load factor design method is covered in AASHTO 10.56.1.3 [AASHTO, 1992]. The bolts in a joint are proportioned from Eq. 9.349:

$$N_b = \frac{\phi R}{(\phi F) A_b} \qquad (9.349)$$

where ϕR = design bearing strength, kips
ϕF = design strength (ksi) per unit of bolt area given in AASHTO Table 10.56A (Table A.30, Appendix A) for appropriate kind of load
A_b = area of bolt corresponding to the nominal diameter of bolt

The slip-critical joints are designed to prevent slip at the overload in accordance with AASHTO 10.57.3 [AASHTO, 1992]. Overload is the force caused by $[D + 5(L + I)/3]$, for H or HS trucks only. The number of bolts, N_b, required to resist this force is given by

$$N_b = \frac{\phi R_s}{(\phi F_s) A_b N_s} \qquad (9.350)$$

where ϕF_s = design slip resistance caused by the overload
  ϕF_s = design slip resistance (ksi) per unit of bolt area given in Table 10.57A
      (Table A.31, Appendix A)

It is reiterated that, as in the case of the service load design, the joints must be designed, at a minimum, for the minimum strength requirements in bearing as specified in AASHTO 10.18 and 10.19 [AASHTO, 1992].

9.12
DESIGN EXAMPLE

Example 9.4 illustrates application of the design principles discussed in this chapter. The example presents a complete design, by the service load method, of a two-span (125 and 125 ft), two-lane, continuous plate girder highway bridge for which the scheme shown in Fig. 9.13(a), instead of the simpler schemes shown in Figs. 9.11 and 9.12, has been selected. This scheme, which results in a redundant load path structure, has been purposely selected to illustrate the different load path involved and the difficulties involved in calculating design forces. In addition, it involves design of high-strength bolted and welded connections.

The deck slab is to be supported by several steel stringers running parallel to the traffic. The stringers are supported by the transverse floor beams placed perpendicular to the stringers. It is assumed that the geometry of the approach road requires the stringers and the floor beams to be at the same level. To fulfill this requirement, the stringers are *framed into* the floor beams, so that the top flanges of the stringers and the floor beams are at the same level. The scheme of Fig. 9.13(b), in which the stringers are supported on the top flanges of the floor beams, is considered nonfeasible for the purpose of this example. The floor beams, in turn, are supported by two plate girders, referred to as the main girders, placed parallel to the traffic, one on each side of the bridge, with their top flanges at the same level as those of the floor beams and stringers. These main girders are supported on the abutments and piers, which receive the loads from the superstructure and transmit it to the foundation below.

Design of the complete superstructure for the bridge in this example involves four different types of flexural members: reinforced concrete deck slab, longitudinal stringers, transverse floor beams, and longitudinal plate girders. Design procedure for transverse floor beams and plate girders is introduced for the first time in this example. Although design of the deck slab and the stringers is discussed and illustrated in Chapter 8, their design is included in this example also, to illustrate the logical sequence in the design procedure and to preserve completeness of design calculations.

In this example, it is assumed that the slab will be poured on the temporary false-work, which will be removed after the deck has hardened. For this reason, the dead weight of the falsework has not been included in the dead load for designing the stringers. However, if it is proposed to use *permanent stay-in-place* (*SIP*) forms (also referred to as formed steel deck, metal deck forms, Fig. 8.10, Chapter 8), or prestressed concrete deck panels (Fig. 7.70, Chapter 7) to support the slab during construction, their deadweight should be considered in design. Some specifications require that a dead load of 15 lb/ft^2 be included in design as an allowance for this purpose. The SIP forms are discussed in Chapter 7 (Sec. 7.7).

It is anticipated that due to the wear and tear of the deck surface over time, a new wearing surface will be required at some time in the future. Addition of this wearing surface on top of the existing deck will increase the dead load of the superstructure. Therefore, in compliance with AASHTO 3.3.3, a provision for the dead load (assumed 35 lb/ft^2) due to the future wearing surface has been made in this example. Also, an allowance of $\frac{1}{2}$ in. of additional concrete is included in the dead load calculations as an integral wearing surface, to allow for the abrasion of deck slab during its service life without impairing its strength (AASHTO 3.3.5).

Design aids are always helpful in selecting preliminary sizes of members, to be followed by substantive calculations. Design aids for slab-steel stringer superstructures are discussed in Chapter 8 (Sec. 8.8). For example, Fig. 8.31 can be used to select a trial section and reinforcing for deck slab. Similarly, Figs. 8.32 through 8.34 can be used for selecting trial sections of the steel stringers.

For determining moments and shears in the continuous plate girders of this example, the *method of influence coefficients* [AISC, 1966] has been used. This method is explained in detail in Chapter 8 (Example 8.6) and therefore is not repeated here. It is re-iterated that the load path in the superstructure of this example is different from the one in which loads from the deck slab are transferred directly to a system of parallel girders (Fig. 9.11). Calculations for determining maximum moments, shears, and reactions are tedious and time-consuming because of two reasons: (1) the loads are transferred to the girders at discrete points through transverse floor beams, which themselves receive loads from stringers; and (2) effects due to both the truck and the lane loading have to be investigated in order to determine the governing values of these parameters at critical locations in the span. Instead of plotting envelopes for moments and shears for the entire span, values of these parameters have been determined at critical locations only (as evidenced from maximum values of the "influence coefficients" or the "influence areas" in the tables of AISC [1966]). For a preliminary design presented in this example, this is considered sufficient. If desired, moment and shear envelopes can be plotted as explained in Chapter 8.

EXAMPLE 9.4. A preliminary design is required for the superstructure of a two-span, two-lane, continuous highway bridge to carry HS20-44 loading. Each span measures 125 ft between the centers of bearings. The bridge cross section should provide for a clear road-way having two 12-ft-wide traffic lanes in addition to 8-ft wide shoulders on each side, and standard parapets and railings. The bridge should be designed according to the AASHTO [1992] specifications for 2×10^6 cycles. A provision for 35 lb/ft^2 of dead load toward future wearing surface should be made in design. Use $f_c' = 4000$ psi and Gr. 40 reinforcement for the slab, and A36 steel for other structural members of the superstructure. For connections, use $\frac{7}{8}$-in.-diameter A-325 high-strength bolts where required, or welds. A typical cross section of the superstructure is shown in Fig. E9.4a.

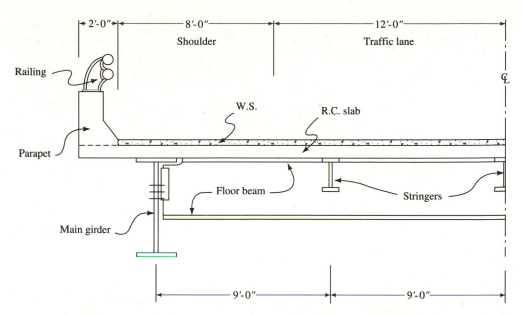

FIGURE E9.4a
Typical cross section.

Solution. All references made in this example pertain to the AASHTO 1992 specifications and are denoted by appropriate article numbers.

Design of deck slab. For the preliminary design, a stringer spacing of 9 ft 0 in. is selected and a flange width of 10 in. is assumed.
Effective span of deck slab, AASHTO 3.24.1.2(b):

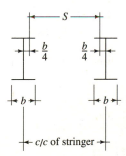

$$S = \text{distance between the top flanges} + \frac{b_f}{2}$$

$$= c/c \text{ of stringers} - \frac{b_f}{2}$$

$$= 9.0 - \tfrac{1}{2} \times \tfrac{10}{12}$$

$$= 8.58 \text{ ft}$$

Minimum slab thickness. The deck slab spans continuously over the stringers, with main reinforcement running perpendicular to traffic. For such a case, the AASHTO specifications do not provide any guidelines for the thickness of the slab. Because of the relatively short span and continuity of the deck slab, deflection is hardly a matter of concern. For a preliminary design, however, slab thickness is selected from AASHTO Table 8.9.2:

$$t_{s,\min} = \frac{S + 10}{30} \text{ ft} = \frac{8.58 + 10}{30} \times 12 = 7.43 \text{ in.}$$

Use $7\frac{1}{2}$-in.-thick slab (a practical minimum). In addition, include a $\frac{1}{2}$-in.-thick integral wearing surface, resulting in the total thickness of the slab as 8 in.

Dead load

Self-weight of slab $= (\frac{8}{12})(0.15)$	$= 0.100$ k/ft
Future wearing surface @ 35 lb/ft^2	$= 0.035$ k/ft
Total dead load	$= 0.135$ k/ft

$$M_D = \pm\frac{wS^2}{10} = \pm\frac{0.135 \times (8.58)^2}{10} = 0.99 \text{ k-ft}$$

Live load. For a deck slab having main reinforcement perpendicular to traffic, the live-load moment is (AASHTO 3.24.3.1)

$$M_L' = \left[\frac{S + 2}{32}\right]P = \frac{8.52 + 2}{32} \times 16 = 5.29 \text{ k-ft}$$

For a deck slab spanning three or more supports, a continuity factor of 0.8 applies. Therefore,

$$M_L = 0.8M_L' = (0.8)(5.29) = 4.23 \text{ k-ft}$$

Impact factor, $IF = 0.30$:

$$M_{L+I} = (4.23)(1 + 0.3) = 5.50 \text{ k-ft}$$

Total design moment, $M_{\text{Total}} = 0.99 + 5.50 = 6.49$ k-ft/ft.

Main reinforcement: transverse (top and bottom). Provide 2-in. cover (excluding integral wearing surface) for the top reinforcement and 1-in. cover for the bottom reinforcement (AASHTO 8.22.1). Assume that #6 Grade 40 bars are used.

$$d = 7.5 - 2 - 0.375 = 5.125 \text{ in. (for } -ve \text{ moments over supports)}$$

For Gr. 40 reinforcing bars, $F_s = 20$ k/in.^{2}.

$$f_c = 0.4f_c' = 0.4 \times 4 = 1.6 \text{ k/in.}^2$$

$$n = 8 \qquad \text{(Table A.14, Appendix A)}$$

From Table A.15 (Appendix A), the design coefficients are as follows ($k = 0.39$, $j = 0.87$):

$$M_R = \frac{f_c kjbd^2}{2}$$
$$= \frac{(1.6)(0.39)(0.87)(12)(5.125)^2}{2(12)}$$
$$= 7.13 \text{ k-ft} > 6.49 \text{ k-ft, OK}$$

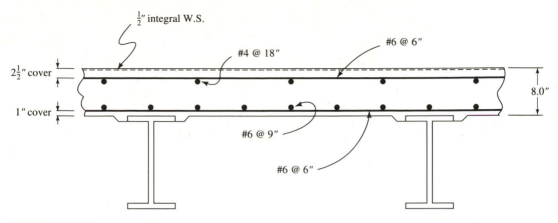

FIGURE E9.4b
Reinforcement details (transverse section).

$$A_s = \frac{M}{f_s\,jd} = \frac{(6.49)(12)}{(20)(0.87)(5.125)} = 0.87 \text{ in.}^2/\text{ft}$$

Provide #6 @ 6 in. o.c., $A_s = 0.88$ in.^{2}/ft (Table A.18, Appendix A).

Distribution steel. Longitudinal (at bottom), for main reinforcement perpendicular to traffic (AASHTO 3.10.24.2),

$$\text{Percentage of steel} = \frac{200}{\sqrt{S}} = \frac{200}{\sqrt{8.58}} = 68.3\% > 67\%$$

Therefore, 67 percent governs.

$$A_{s,\text{dist}} = 0.88 \times 0.67 = 0.59 \text{ in.}^2/\text{ft}$$

Provide #6 @ 9 in. o.c., $A_s = 0.59$ in.^{2}/ft, OK. The distribution reinforcement will be spaced to satisfy requirements of AASHTO 3.24.10.3.

Temperature steel: longitudinal, at top, AASHTO 8.20. Minimum steel area = $\frac{1}{8}$ in.^{2}/ft, maximum spacing = 18 in. Provide #4 @18 in. o.c., $A_s = 0.133$ in.^{2}/ft. > 0.125 in.^{2}, OK.

Shear and bond: Sec. 3.24.4. Slab designed to moment requirements is deemed to satisfy shear and bond requirements.

The reinforcement details are shown in Fig. E9.4b.

Design of stringers. A floor beam spacing of 25 ft 0 in. is selected, resulting in five even spacings for each 125-ft span of the main girders. Because of the relatively short span of stringers, noncomposite design is more likely to be economical. Accordingly, composite design is not considered for stringers in this example. A longitudinal section of a line of stringers is shown in Fig. E9.4c.

Interior stringers

Dead load. It is assumed that the pouring of the parapets and installation of the railings will commence after the slab has cured. Therefore, all the five stringers are assumed to participate in carrying dead load due to these elements (AASHTO 3.23.2.3.1.1). A typical section of parapet is assumed as shown in the adjoining figure. The dead load due to the two

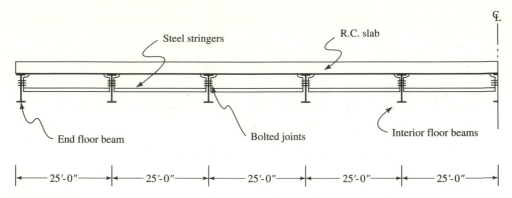

FIGURE E9.4c
Longitudinal section showing a line of stringers and the supporting transverse floor beams.

parapet sections, per stringer, is

$$w_{par} = (2)\left[(1.25)(2.25) + \left(\frac{0.167 + 1.25}{2}\right)(0.75)\right](0.15)\left(\frac{1}{5}\right)$$

$$= 0.201 \text{ k/ft}$$

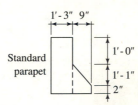

An allowance of 20 lb/ft is made for the dead load of the railings. The corresponding dead load per stringer is

$$w_{railing} @ 20 \text{ lb/ft} = \frac{(0.02)(2)}{5} = 0.008 \text{ k/ft}$$

A W27 × 84 is assumed for the preliminary design of the stringer. Therefore, dead load on the stringer is

Slab	= (8/12)(0.15)(9.0)	= 0.900 k/ft
Future wearing surface	= (0.035)(9.0)	= 0.315 k/ft
Parapet		= 0.201 k/ft
Railings		= 0.008 k/ft
Stringer (W27 × 84)		= 0.084 k/ft

$$\text{Total dead load, } w_D = 1.508 \text{ k/ft}$$

Therefore, moment due to the dead load is

$$M_D = \frac{wL^2}{8} = \frac{(1.508)(25)^2}{8} = 118 \text{ k-ft}$$

Live load. For concrete slab on steel I-beams carrying two or more lanes of traffic and $S < 14$ ft, the distribution factor is (Table A.7, Appendix A)

$$\text{DF} = \frac{S}{5.5} = \frac{9.0}{5.5} = 1.636$$

Maximum live-load moment (M_L) due to HS20-44 truck loading for a span of 25 ft (Table A.5, Appendix A) is 207.4 k-ft. Therefore, live-load moment per stringer is

$$M_L = (\tfrac{1}{2})(207.4)(1.636) = 170 \text{ k-ft}$$

$$\text{Impact factor, IF} = \frac{50}{L + 125} = \frac{50}{25 + 125} = 0.33 > 0.3$$

Hence, use IF $= 0.3$

$$M_{L+I} = (170)(1 + 0.30) = 221 \text{ k-ft}$$
$$M_{\text{Total}} = 118 + 221 \qquad = 339 \text{ k-ft}$$

The compression flanges of the stringers will be fully restrained by encasing them in concrete slab, which permits full allowable compressive stress to be used. For A36 steel,

$$F_b = 0.55F_y = (0.55)(36) = 20 \text{ ksi} \qquad \text{(Table A.26, Appendix A)}$$

Calculate the required section modulus for the stringer.

$$S_{\text{reqd}} = \frac{M}{F_b} = \frac{339}{20} = 203.4 \text{ in.}^3$$

For W27 × 84, $S_x = 213 \text{ in.}^3 > S_{\text{reqd}} = 203.4 \text{ in.}^3$, OK.

Exterior stringers. The arrangement of the floor system for this superstructure results in the exterior stringers becoming the main girders. Therefore, the main girders will be designed to carry the load of the exterior stringers.

Shear and joints (interior stringers only)—AASHTO 3.23.1

Dead load

$$\text{Total dead load, } w_d = 1.508 \text{ k/ft}$$

$$V_D = \tfrac{1}{2}w_D L = (\tfrac{1}{2})(1.508)(25) = 18.9 \text{ kips}$$

Live load. For the axles adjacent to the floor beam, three positions, as shown in Fig. E9.4d, are considered, and the maximum shear is computed by the lever rule method (AASHTO 3.23.1.2).

1. Position (a):

$$R_1 = 2\left(\tfrac{7}{9} + \tfrac{1}{9}\right)P = 1.78P$$

2. Position (b):

$$R_2 = \left(\tfrac{5}{9} + 1 + \tfrac{3}{9}\right)P = 1.89P$$

3. Position (c):

$$R_3 = \left[2\left(\tfrac{6}{9}\right) + \tfrac{2}{9}\right]P = 1.56P$$

Hence, $R = 1.89P$ governs, where $P = 16$ kips.

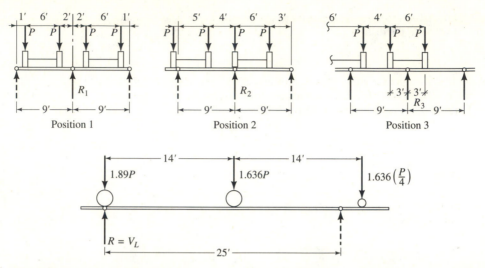

FIGURE E9.4d
Position of the axles close to the floor beams for maximum shear in the stringer.

Alternatively, the maximum value of DF can be computed from Eq. 4.4c (Chapter 4). Referring to Fig. 4.17c(ii),

$$DF = P\left(3 - \frac{10}{S}\right) = P\left(3 - \frac{10}{9}\right) = 1.89P$$

For axles away from the floor beams (i.e., the front and the middle axles), the distribution factor, DF = 1.636 (same as for the live-load moment) applies. Thus, the maximum live load shear in the stringer is

$$V_L = 1.89P + (1.636P)\left(\tfrac{11}{25}\right)$$
$$= 2.61P$$
$$= (2.61)(16) = 41.8 \text{ kips}$$

$IF = 0.30$

$V_{L+I} = (41.8)(1 + 0.30) = 54.3 \text{ kips}$

$V_{\text{Total}} = 54.3 + 188.9 = 73.2 \text{ kips}$

Calculate the number of high-strength bolts required to connect stringers to the floor beams. Slip-critical connection using $\frac{7}{8}$-in.-diameter A325 high-strength bolts will be used. Design of slip-critical joints is discussed in Sec. 9.11.4. The connection between the end floor beam and the stringer involves one shear plane only. Assuming conservatively that the threads will be included[45] in the shear plane, from Table A.28, Appendix A (AASHTO Table 10.32.3B), $F_v = 19$ ksi. The gross area, A_b, of a $\frac{7}{8}$-in.-diameter bolt is (Table A.27,

---

[45]Even if the threads are excluded from the shear plane, the same number of bolts will be required because the slip resistance governs.

Appendix A) 0.6013 in.^{2}. Therefore, based on the strength consideration,

$$N_b = \frac{\text{Total shear}}{F_v A_b} = \frac{73.2}{(19.0)(0.6013)} = 6.4, \qquad \text{say, 7 bolts.}$$

Based on the slip resistance consideration, the number of bolts will be computed from Eq. 9.348. Assuming Class A surface conditions for the faying surfaces, $F_s = 15.5$ ksi from Table A.27, Appendix A (AASHTO Table 10.32.3C). Therefore,

$$N_b = \frac{\text{Total shear}}{F_s A_B} = \frac{73.2}{15.5 \times 0.6013} = 7.8, \qquad \text{say, 8 bolts (governs)}$$

Hence, provide $8\frac{7}{8}$-in.-diameter A325 high-strength bolts.

Allowable shear will be checked for average shear on the gross web area, block shear in the web because the beam is coped, shear on plane through the bolt holes in the connection angles, and bearing on the connection angles. For the W27 $\times$ 84, $d = 26.71$ in., $t_w = 0.46$ in.

1. *Average shear on the web*

$$f_v = \frac{V}{dt_w}$$

$$= \frac{73.2}{(26.71)(0.46)}$$

$$= 5.95 \text{ ksi} < 0.33 F_y = (0.33)(36) = 12 \text{ ksi, OK}$$

2. *Block shear, R_{BS} (web tear-out) in the web.* The top flange of the stringer will be coped to place it at the same level as the top flange of the floor beam. From Table A.26 (Appendix A), the following arrangement of the bolts is established:

Spacing (distance between the centers of bolts) = 3 in.

Distance of the fastener from the coped end of
the web and from the end of the stringer   = 2 in.

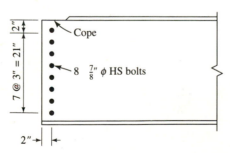

$$\text{Area in shear, } A_v = \left[23 - \left(\tfrac{7}{8} + \tfrac{1}{16}\right)(7.5)\right] \times 0.46 = 7.35 \text{ in.}^2$$

$$\text{Area in tension, } A_t = \left[2 - \left(\tfrac{7}{8} + \tfrac{1}{16}\right)\left(\tfrac{1}{2}\right)\right] = 0.70 \text{ in.}^2$$

$$\text{Allowable reaction, } R_{BS} = A_v F_v + A_t F_t$$

$$= (7.35)(12) + 0.70 \times 20$$

$$= 102.2 \text{ kips} > V = 73.2 \text{ kips, OK}$$

3. *Shear in the connection angles.*

Length of the connection angle $= 7 \times 3 + 2 \times 2 + 25$ in.

Minimum width of the leg of the
connection angle (Sec. 10.24.4.2) $= 4 \times$ diameter of bolt
$$= 4 \times \tfrac{7}{8} = 3.5 \text{ in.}$$

Use L4 $\times$ 3$\frac{1}{2}$ $\times$ $\frac{3}{8}$, with 4-in. leg outstanding. Check shear on plane through the bolt holes. The net shear area, A_n, is

$$
\begin{aligned}
A_n &= 2t\left[L - N_b\left(d + \tfrac{1}{16}\right)\right] \\
&= (2)\left(\tfrac{3}{8}\right)\left[25 - 8\left(\tfrac{7}{8} + \tfrac{1}{16}\right)\right] \\
&= 13.125 \text{ in.}^2
\end{aligned}
$$

$V_{\text{allow}} = A_n \times F_v = (13.125)(12) = 157.5$ kips $> V = 73.2$ kips, OK.

4. *Bearing on connection angles.* The total thickness of the two angles together $(= 2 \times \tfrac{3}{8} = \tfrac{3}{4}$ in.$)$ is greater than the thickness of the stringer web $(= 0.46$ in.$)$. Hence bearing on connection angles does not govern.

Alternatively, the connection angles may be welded to the stringers and field bolted to the floor beams.

Deflection. It will be conservatively assumed that the entire live load from the two lanes of HS20 trucks is carried by three stringers only. Deflection due to live load will be computed from Eq. 5.12 (Chapter 5):

$$\Delta = \frac{P_T}{90 I_s}(L^3 - 555L + 4780) \tag{5.12}$$

where P_T = (weight of the one front wheel) $\times$ (number of wheels per axle)
$\times$ (number of lanes) $\times$ (dist. factor) $\times$ (1 + impact factor)
$= (4)(2)(2)(1.636)(1.3)$
$= 34.03$ kips
$I_s = 2850$ in.^{4} for W27 $\times$ 84

Substituting for P_T and I_s in Eq. 5.12, we obtain

$$
\begin{aligned}
\Delta_L &= \frac{34.03}{(90)(2850)(3)}[(25)^3 - 555 \times 25 + 4780] \\
&= 0.3 \text{ in.} \\
\Delta_{L,\text{allow}} &= \frac{L}{800} \\
&= \frac{(25)(12)}{800} = 0.375 \text{ in.} > 0.3 \text{ in. OK}
\end{aligned}
$$

Hence, use W27 $\times$ 84 for stringers.

Design of floor beams. Figure E9.4e shows a typical transverse section of the bridge showing the floor beam in which the stringers are framed. The floor beams receive loads from the stringers, which are spaced at 9 ft o.c., so that three lines of stringers frame into each floor beam. Typically, each intermediate floor beam receives reaction loads from two stringers at each connection, whereas the end floor beams receive reaction loads from only one stringer at each connection. Dead load on the stringer was computed to be 1.508 k/ft.

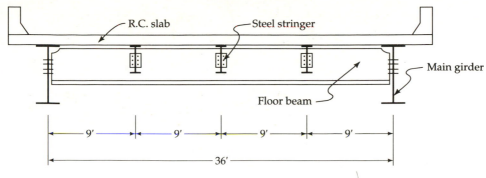

FIGURE E9.4e
Transverse section through stringers.

Intermediate floor beams

Dead load. At each stringer–floor beam connection, the reaction, R_D, due to dead load is

$$R_D = 2(\tfrac{1}{2} \times 1.508)(25) = 37.7 \text{ kips}$$

Because the beam is symmetrically loaded, the dead-load moment is

$$M_D' = Pa + \frac{PL}{4}, \qquad a = 9 \text{ ft}, L = 36 \text{ ft}$$

$$= 37.7 \times 9 + \frac{37.7 \times 36}{4} = 679 \text{ k-ft}$$

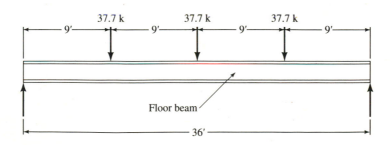

For estimating the self-weight of the floor beam, try W36 × 260.

$w_G = 260 \text{ lb/ft} = 0.26 \text{ k/ft}$
$M_G = (\tfrac{1}{8})(wL^2) = (\tfrac{1}{8})(0.26)(36)^2 = 42 \text{ k-ft}$

Total DL moment, $M_D = 679 + 42 = 721$ k-ft.

Live load. Consider the portion of truck load carried by each interior stringer. No transverse distribution of the wheel loads is permitted (AASHTO, 3.23.3.1). Two critical transverse positions of the HS20 trucks will be considered. *Case I:*

$$R_1 = \left(\tfrac{8}{9} + \tfrac{2}{9}\right) = 1.11P = R_3$$
$$R_3 = \left(\tfrac{7}{9} + \tfrac{1}{9}\right) = 1.78P$$

Case II:

$$R_1 = \left(\tfrac{8}{9} + \tfrac{4}{9}\right)P \quad\quad = 1.333P$$
$$R_2 = \left(\tfrac{5}{9} + 1 + \tfrac{3}{9}\right)P = 1.89P$$
$$R_3 = \left(\tfrac{6}{9}\right)P \quad\quad\quad = 0.667P$$

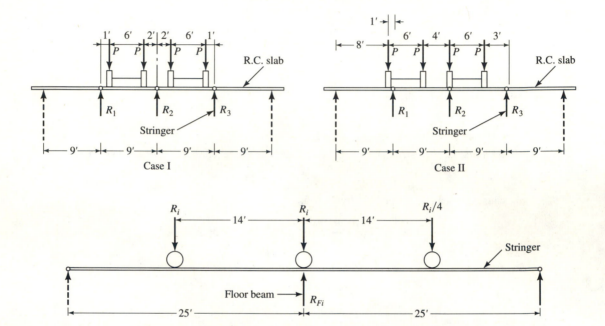

Case I

Case II

Stringer

Floor beam

In cases I and II, R_1, R_2, and R_3 are loads on the three stringers, which are equivalent to two trucks. To obtain the maximum live load on the floor beam, the longitudinal positions of the wheel loads will be as shown, the middle wheel being placed directly over the floor beam (see Fig. 4.22, Chapter 4). Calculate the reaction on the floor beam, R_{Fi}.

$$R_{\text{Fi}} = \left[\tfrac{11}{25} + 1 + \left(\tfrac{11}{25}\right)\left(\tfrac{1}{4}\right)\right] R_i = 1.55 R_i$$

Live-load moments at midspan. The equivalent loads on the floor beam as transferred from the three stringers through their reactions are as follows. *Case I:*

$$R_{F1} = 1.55 R_1 = 1.55 \times 1.11P = 1.72P$$
$$R_{F2} = 1.55 R_2 = 1.55 \times 1.78P = 2.76P$$
$$R_{F3} = 1.55 R_3 = 1.55 \times 1.11P = 1.72P$$

Because the floor beam is symmetrically loaded, the maximum moment is

$$M_{L1} = Pa + \frac{PL}{4}, \quad\quad a = 9 \text{ ft}, L = 36 \text{ ft}$$
$$= (1.72P)(9) + \frac{(2.76P)(36)}{4}$$
$$= 40.32P = (40.32)(16) = 645 \text{ k-ft}$$

Case II:

$$R_{F1} = 1.55R_1 = (1.55)(1.333P) = 2.07P$$
$$R_{F2} = 1.55R_2 = (1.55)(1.89P) = 2.93P$$
$$R_{F3} = 1.55R_3 = (1.55)(0.667P) = 1.03P$$

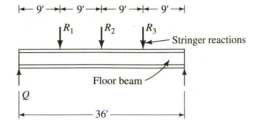

The reaction, R_L, at the left support is

$$R_L = \left[(2.07)\left(\tfrac{27}{36}\right) + (2.93)\left(\tfrac{18}{36}\right) + (1.03)\left(\tfrac{9}{36}\right)\right] P$$
$$= 3.28P$$

Therefore,

$$M_{L2} = (3.28P)(18) - (2.07P)(9) = 40.32P = 645 \text{ k-ft}$$

Hence, $M_L = 645$ k-ft.

For two lanes of traffic, no reduction in live load is permitted.

$$\text{Impact factor, } I = 0.30$$
$$M_{L+I} = (645)(1 + 0.30) = 839 \text{ k-ft}$$
$$M_{\text{Total}} = M_D + M_{L+I} = 721 + 839 = 1560 \text{ k-ft}$$

Compute the allowable stress, F_b, for W36 × 260. Assume that compression flanges of floor beams are laterally supported at connections with stringers only. The allowable stress in compression is given by the following formula (Table A.26, Appendix A)

$$F_b = \left(\frac{50 \times 10^6 C_b}{S_{xc}}\right)\left(\frac{I_{yc}}{l}\right)\sqrt{(0.772)\left(\frac{J}{I_{yc}}\right) + (9.87)\left(\frac{d}{l}\right)^2} \le 0.55F_y$$

where S_{xc} = section modulus with respect to compression flange, in.^{3}

    I_{yc} = moment of inertia of the compression flange about the vertical axis in the plane of the web, in.^{4}

     l = length of the unbraced segment, in.

    J = torsional constant

      = $\tfrac{1}{3}[(bt^3)_c + (bt^3)_t + Dt_w^3]$, in.^{4}

    D = height of web, in.

    d = depth of the girder, in.

The section properties of W36 × 260 are [AISC, 1989, p. 1-12] $b_f = 16.55$ in., $t_f = 1.44$ in., $d = 36.26$ in., $t_w = 0.84$ in., $S_{xc} = 953$ in.^{3}

$$I_{yc} = (1.44)\frac{(16.55)^3}{12} = 544 \text{ in.}^4$$
$$D = d - 2t_f = 36.26 - (2)(1.44) = 33.28 \text{ in.}$$

$$J = \tfrac{1}{3}[2(16.55)(1.44)^3 + (33.28)(0.84)^3] = 39.52 \text{ in.}^4$$
$$l = 9(12) = 108 \text{ in.}$$
$$C_b = 1.0$$

The values of the torsional constant, J, for all W shapes are listed in AISC [1989, pp. 1-117–1-124]. It may be noted that the AISC-listed values of J are higher than those computed from the AASHTO formula because the latter formula neglects the presence of fillets at the corners of the flange-web junctures. The AISC-listed value of J for W36 × 260 is 41.5 in.[4].

$$F_b = \left(\frac{(50)(10^6)(1.0)}{953}\right)\left(\frac{544}{108}\right)\sqrt{(0.772)\left(\frac{39.52}{544}\right) + (9.87)\left(\frac{36.26}{108}\right)}$$
$$= 285,690 \text{ psi} > 0.55F_y = (0.55)(36,000) = 20,000 \text{ psi}$$

Therefore, use $F_b = 20,000$ psi:

$$S_{\text{reqd}} = \frac{1560 \times 12}{20} = 936 \text{ in.}^3$$

Use W36 × 260, $S_x = 953$ in.$^3 > 936$ in.^{3}, OK.

End floor beams

Dead load. Dead load on the end floor beam is one-half of that on an intermediate floor beam. Therefore,

$$M_D' = \tfrac{1}{2}(M_D) \text{ for an intermediate floor beam}$$
$$= \tfrac{1}{2}(679) = 340 \text{ k-ft}$$

For estimating the self-weight of the floor beam, try W36 × 210:

$$w_G = 210 \text{ lb/ft}$$
$$M_G = (\tfrac{1}{8})(210)(36)^2 = 34 \text{ k-ft}$$
$$\text{Total dead-load moment, } M_D = 340 + 34 = 374 \text{ k-ft}$$

Live load. To obtain maximum values of the stringer reactions on the end floor beam, the wheels of the HS truck will be placed longitudinally such that the rear wheel is positioned directly over the end floor beam and the front wheel remains off the stringer (because $L = 25$ ft < 28 ft, the distance between the front and the rear axles).

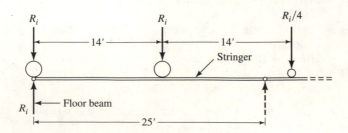

$$R_{\text{Fi}} = \left(1 + \tfrac{11}{25}\right)R_i = 1.44R_i$$

The value of R_{Fi} corresponding to the intermediate floor beam was found to be $1.55R_i$ in the previous calculations. The moment due to live load for the end floor beam can be determined from proportion of the live-load moment for the intermediate floor beam.

$$M_{L+I} = \left(\frac{1.44}{1.55}\right)(M_{L+I} \text{ for the intermediate floor beam})$$

$$= \left(\frac{1.44}{1.55}\right)(839)$$

$$= 779 \text{ k-ft}$$

Total moment, $M_{Total} = M_D + M_{L+I} = 374 + 779 = 1153$ k-ft.

Compute the allowable stress, F_b, for W36 $\times$ 210. Assume that compression flanges of the end floor beams are laterally supported at connections with stringers only. The section properties of W36 $\times$ 210 are [AISC, 1989, p. 1-12] $b_f = 12.18$ in., $t_f = 1.36$ in., $d = 36.69$ in., $t_w = 0.83$ in., $S_{xc} = 917$ in.[3].

$$I_{yc} = (1.36)\frac{(12.18)^3}{12} = 205 \text{ in.}^4$$

$$D = d - 2t_f = 36.69 - 2(1.36) = 33.97 \text{ in.}$$

$$J = \tfrac{1}{3}[2(12.18)(1.36)^3 + (33.97)(0.83)^3] = 33.97 \text{ in.}^4$$

$$l = 9(12) = 108 \text{ in.}$$

$$C_b = 1.0$$

$$F_b = \frac{(50)(10^6)(1.0)}{719}\left(\frac{205}{108}\right)\sqrt{(0.772)\left(\frac{26.90}{205}\right) + (9.87)\left(\frac{36.69}{108}\right)}$$

$$= 147{,}012 \text{ psi} > 0.55F_y = (0.55)(36{,}000) = 20{,}000 \text{ psi}$$

Therefore, use $F_b = 20{,}000$ psi:

$$S_{reqd} = \frac{(1153)(12)}{20} = 692 \text{ in.}^3$$

Use W36 $\times$ 210, $S_x = 719$ in.[3] > 692 in.[3], OK.

Shear and joints

Intermediate floor beam

Dead-load shear. Each intermediate floor beam carries load from three stringers. DL from one stringer $= 1.508 \times 25 = 37.7$ kips. Therefore, the DL shear in the intermediate floor beam is

$$V_D = \tfrac{1}{2}(37.7)(3) = 56.55 \text{ kips}$$

Shear due to the self-weight of the floor beam, W36$\times$260: $V_G = \tfrac{1}{2}(0.26)(36) = 4.68$ kips.

Live-load shear. Consider reactions from slab to stringers. Assume all trucks clear of shoulders as shown.

$$R_1 = P\left(\tfrac{6}{9} + \tfrac{6}{9} + \tfrac{2}{9}\right) = 1.56P$$

$$R_2 = P\left(\tfrac{3}{9} + \tfrac{7}{9} + \tfrac{5}{9}\right) = 1.67P$$

$$R_3 = P\left(\tfrac{4}{9}\right) = 0.44P$$

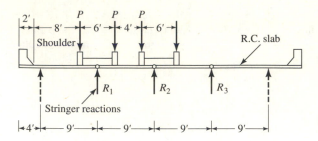

For stringer reactions on floor beams, $R_{Fi} = 1.55R_i$. For floor beam reactions to the main girder,

$$V_L = 1.55\left[(1.56)\left(\tfrac{27}{36}\right) + (1.67)\left(\tfrac{18}{36}\right) + (0.44)\left(\tfrac{9}{36}\right)\right] P$$

$$= 3.28P$$

$$= (3.28)(16) = 52.48 \text{ kips}$$

Impact factor, $I = 0.30$
$V_{L+I} = (52.48)(1 + 0.30) = 68.22$ kips
Total end shear, $V_{\text{Total}} = 56.55 + 4.68 + 68.22 = 129.45$ kips

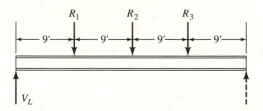

For connecting floor beams to the main girders, use $\tfrac{7}{8}$-in.-diameter A325 high-strength bolts, $A_b = 0.6013$ in.² (Table A.27, Appendix A). The joint will be designed as slip-critical. Based on the strength consideration, and assuming threads are included in the shear plane, the number of bolts required, N_b, is

$$N_b = \frac{V}{F_v A_b}$$

$$= \frac{129.45}{(19)(0.6013)} = 11.3, \text{ say 12 bolts}$$

Based on the slip resistance consideration, and assuming Class A surface condition of the faying surfaces, the number of bolts required, N_b, is

$$N_b = \frac{V}{F_s A_b N_s}$$

$$= \frac{129.45}{(15.5)(0.6013)(1)}$$

$$= 13.89, \text{ say 14 bolts (governs)}$$

Hence, provide fourteen $\tfrac{7}{8}$-in.-diameter A325 high-strength bolts. With spacing of 3 in. o.c., and 2 in. end distances, the minimum height of web required $= 13 \times 3 + 2 \times 2 = 43$ in., which is smaller than the depth of W36 × 260 ($d = 36.26$ in.). Hence, provide 14 bolts in two columns, seven in each column, and stagger them.

Shear will be checked as for the case of stringers explained earlier.

1. *Average shear on the gross area of web*

$$f_v = \frac{V}{dt_w} = \frac{129.45}{(36.26)(0.84)} = 4.25 \text{ ksi} < 12 \text{ ksi, OK}$$

2. *Block shear for web*

Net area in shear, $A_v = \left[21.5 - (6.5)\left(\frac{7}{8} + \frac{1}{16}\right)\right](0.84) = 13.18 \text{ in.}^2$

Net area in tension, $A_t = \left[5 - \left(\frac{7}{8} + \frac{1}{16}\right)\left(\frac{1}{2}\right)\right](0.84) = 3.81 \text{ in.}^2$

Allowable shear, $R_{BS} = A_v F_v + A_t F_t$

$$= (13.18)(12) + (3.81)(20)$$

$$= 234.36 \text{ kips} > V = 129.45 \text{ kips, OK}$$

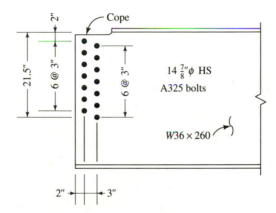

3. *Shear in the connection angles*

Length of the connection angle $\qquad = 6 \times 3 + 2 \times 2 + 22 \text{ in.}$

Minimum width of the leg of the
connection angle required (AASHTO 10.24.4.2) $= 4 \times$ diameter of bolt

$$= 4\left(\frac{7}{8}\right) = 3.5 \text{ in.}$$

Use L5 $\times$ 4 $\times \frac{1}{2}$, with 4-in. leg outstanding. Check shear on plane through the bolt holes. The net shear area, A_n, is

$$A_n = 2t\left[L - N_b\left(d + \frac{1}{16}\right)\right] = 2\left(\frac{1}{2}\right)\left[23.5 - 7\left(\frac{7}{8} + \frac{1}{16}\right)\right] = 16.94 \text{ in.}^2$$

$$V_{\text{allow}} = A_n \times F_v = (16.94)(12) = 203.3 \text{ kips} > V = 129.45 \text{ kips, OK}$$

4. *Bearing on the connection angles.* The total thickness of the two angles together ($= 2 \times \frac{1}{2} = 1$ in.) is greater than the thickness of the web ($= 0.84$ in.). Hence, bearing on the connection angles does not govern.

End floor beams

Dead-load shear

$$V_D = \tfrac{1}{2} \times V_D \text{ for intermediate floor beam}$$

$$= \left(\tfrac{1}{2}\right)(56.55) = 28.28 \text{ kips}$$

$$V_G = (\tfrac{1}{2})(0.210)(36)$$

$$= 3.78 \text{ kips (due to self-weight of the floor beam)}$$

Live-load shear. As for the LL moment, the LL shear is computed from proportion to LL shear for the intermediate floor beam. Thus,

$$V_{L+I} = \left(\frac{1.44}{1.55}\right) \times V_{L+I} \text{ for interior floor beam}$$

$$= \left(\frac{1.44}{1.55}\right) \times 68.22 = 63.38 \text{ kips}$$

Total end shear, $V = 28.28 + 3.78 + 63.38$

$$= 95.44 \text{ kips}$$

For connecting the end floor beams to the main girders, use $\frac{7}{8}$-in.-diameter A325 high-strength bolts, $A_b = 0.6013$ in.^{2}. The joint will be designed as slip-critical. Based on the strength consideration, and assuming threads included in the shear plane, the number of bolts required, N_b, is

$$N_b = \frac{V}{F_v A_b} = \frac{95.44}{9 \times 0.6013} = 8.35, \qquad \text{say, 9 bolts}$$

Based on the slip resistance consideration, and assuming Class A surface condition of the faying surfaces, the number of bolts required, N_b, is

$$N_b = \frac{V}{F_s A_b N_s}$$

$$= \frac{95.44}{(15.5)(0.6013)(1)}$$

$$= 10.24, \qquad \text{say, 11 bolts (governs)}$$

Hence, provide eleven $\frac{7}{8}$-in.-diameter A325 high-strength bolts. With spacing of 3 in. o.c., and 2 in. end distances, the minimum height of web required $= 10 \times 3 + 2 \times 2 = 34$ in., which is almost equal to the height of web of W36 $\times$ 210($D = 36.69 - 2 \times 1.36 \approx$ 34 in.). Hence, provide 11 bolts in one column, as shown.

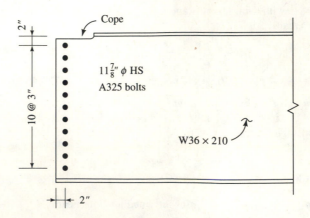

Shear will be checked as for the intermediate floor beams.

Average shear on the gross area of web

$$f_v = \frac{V}{dt_w}$$

$$= \frac{95.44}{(36.69)(0.83)} = 3.13 \text{ ksi} < 12 \text{ ksi, OK}$$

Block shear for web

$$\text{Net area in shear, } A_v = \left[32 - (10.5)\left(\tfrac{7}{8} + \tfrac{1}{16}\right)\right](0.83) = 18.39 \text{ in.}^2$$

$$\text{Net area in tension, } A_t = \left[2 - \left(\tfrac{7}{8} + \tfrac{1}{16}\right)\left(\tfrac{1}{2}\right)\right](0.83) = 1.27 \text{ in.}^2$$

$$\text{Allowable shear, } R_{BS} = A_v F_v + A_t F_t$$

$$= (18.39)(12) + (1.27)(20)$$

$$= 246.1 \text{ kips} > V = 95.44 \text{ kips, OK}$$

Shear in the connection angles

Length of the connection angle $= 10 \times 3 + 2 \times 2 + 34$ in.

Minimum width of the leg of the
connection angle (Sec. 10.24.4.2) $= 4 \times$ diameter of bolt

$$= 4 \times \tfrac{7}{8} = 3.5 \text{ in.}$$

Use $L4 \times 3\tfrac{1}{2} \times \tfrac{3}{8}$, with 4-in. leg outstanding. Check shear on plane through the bolt holes. The net shear area, A_n, is

$$A_n = 2t\left[L - N_b\left(d + \tfrac{1}{16}\right)\right]$$

$$= 2\left(\tfrac{1}{2}\right)\left[34 - 11\left(\tfrac{7}{8} + \tfrac{1}{16}\right)\right]$$

$$= 23.69 \text{ in.}^2$$

$$V_{\text{allow}} = A_n \times F_v = (23.69)(12) = 284.3 \text{ kips} > V = 95.44 \text{ kips, OK}$$

Bearing on the connection angles. The total thickness of the two angles together ($= 2 \times \tfrac{1}{2} = 1$ in.) is greater than the thickness of the web ($= 0.83$ in.). Hence, bearing on the connection angles does not govern.

Deflection

Intermediate floor beam. The floor beam is loaded by reactions from the three stringers spaced at 9 ft o.c., as shown. These loads are fixed in position. The live-load reactions transferred by the stringers to the floor beam are

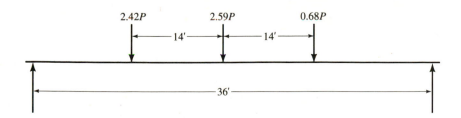

Load at 9 ft from left support $= 1.55 \times 1.56P = 2.42P$

Load at 18 ft from left support $= 1.55 \times 1.67P = 2.59P$

Load at 27 ft from left support $= 1.55 \times 0.44P = 0.68P$

where $P = 16$ kips.

Deflection at midspan of a simple beam due to a concentrated load at any point on the span is given by

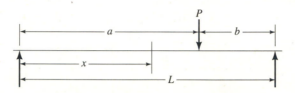

$$\Delta = \frac{Pbx}{6EIL}(L^2 - b^2 - x^2), \qquad x < a$$

Deflection due to each load is calculated separately. For W36 $\times$ 260, the moment of inertia, $I = 17,300$ in.[4]. Due to load on the left of midspan, load $= 2.42P$.

$$\Delta_1 = \left\{ \frac{(2.42 \times 16)(27 \times 12)(18 \times 12)}{6(29,000)(17,300)(36)(12)} \right\} [(36)^2 - (27)^2 - (18)^2](12)^2$$

$$= 0.12 \text{ in.}$$

Due to load at midspan, load $= 2.59P$.

$$\Delta_2 = \frac{PL^3}{48EI}$$

$$= \frac{(2.59 \times 16)(36 \times 12)^3}{(48)(29,000)(17,300)}$$

$$= 0.14 \text{ in.}$$

Due to load on the right of midspan, load $= 0.68P$. From proportion of deflection due to load on the left of span,

$$\Delta_3 = \frac{0.68}{2.42} \times 0.12 = 0.03 \text{ in.}$$

Total deflection,

$$\Delta = \Delta_1 + \Delta_2 + \Delta_3$$

$$= 0.12 + 0.14 + 0.03$$

$$= 0.29 \text{ in.}$$

$$\Delta_{\text{allow}} = \frac{L}{800} = \frac{(36)(12)}{800} = 0.54 \text{ in.} > 0.29 \text{ in., OK}$$

End floor beam.   The deflection in the end floor beam is computed from proportion of the live-load deflection in the intermediate floor beam. The ratio of the load on the end and the intermediate floor beam is 0.929($= 1.44/1.55$). The moment of inertia of W36 $\times$ 210 is 13,200 in.[4]. Therefore, the deflection at midspan is

$$\Delta = (0.29)(0.929)\left(\frac{13,200}{17,300}\right)$$

$$= 0.21 \text{ in.} < 0.54 \text{ in., OK}$$

Use W36×260 for the intermediate floor beams and W36×210 for the end floor beams.

Design of main girders. Moments, shears, and reactions in the main girders will be computed using the influence coefficients as given in AISC [1966]. The method of computing these values was illustrated in Chapter 8 (Example 8.6). Loads are transferred to the main girders through the floor beams, which are spaced at 25 ft o.c. (i.e., at 0.2L) as shown.

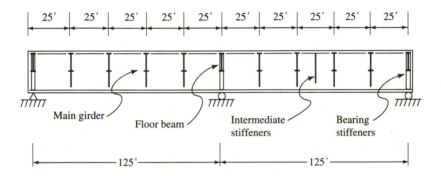

Positive moments.   Refer to Table A.2.0 of AISC [1966].

Dead load

1. *From the floor beams.* From calculations for the intermediate floor beams, reaction due to dead load transferred to the main girder is

$$V_D = 56.55 \text{ kips}$$

Note that for point loads, the maximum total area under the influence line occurs at 0.4L. Values of the IL ordinate at every 0.2L of span are listed in the Table E9.4a. Thus,

TABLE E9.4a
Influence coefficients for point loads

Load point	Ordinates for BM at					
	0.0L	0.2L	0.4L	0.6L	0.8L	1.0L
0.0L	0	0	0	0	0	0
0.2L	0	0.1504	0.1008	0.0512	0.0016	−0.0480
0.4L	0	0.1032	0.2064	0.1096	0.0128	−0.0840
0.6L	0	0.0608	0.1216	0.1824	0.0432	−0.0960
0.8L	0	0.0256	0.0512	0.0768	0.1024	−0.0720
1.0L	0	−0.0144	−0.0288	−0.0432	−0.0576	−0.0720
1.2L	0	−0.0144	−0.0288	−0.0432	0.0576	−0.0720
1.4L	0	−0.0192	−0.0384	−0.0576	−0.0768	−0.0960
1.6L	0	−0.0168	−0.0336	−0.0504	−0.0672	−0.0840
1.8L	0	−0.0096	−0.0192	−0.0288	−0.0384	−0.0480
2.0L	0	0	0	0	0	0

$$M_{D,0.4L} = 56.55(0.1008 + 0.2064 + 0.1216 + 0.0512 + 0 - 0.0288$$
$$- 0.0384 - 0.0336 - 0.0192)(125)$$
$$= 2545 \text{ k-ft}$$

2. *Self-weight of the main girder (assumed).* $w = 600$ lb/ft (including stiffeners, bracings, connections, etc.). Total area under the IL diagram at $0.4L = 0.0700$ as shown in Table E9.4b. Therefore, the moment due to the self-weight of the girder at $0.4L$ is

$$M_{G,0.4L} = 0.60 \times 0.0700 \times (125)^2$$
$$= 656 \text{ k-ft}$$

Live load

1. *Truck load.* Consider one truck per lane on the structure, placed laterally so as to produce maximum shear in floor beams (i.e., maximum reaction on girder) with the middle axles at $0.4L$, where the influence coefficient has maximum value.

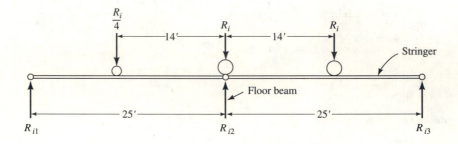

$$R_{i1} = \left(\tfrac{11}{25}\right)\frac{R_i}{4} = 0.14R_i$$
$$R_{i2} = \left[\left(\tfrac{11}{25}\right)\left(\tfrac{1}{4}\right) + 1 + \left(\tfrac{11}{25}\right)\right] R_i = 1.55R_i$$
$$R_{i3} = \left(\tfrac{11}{25}\right) = 0.56R_i$$

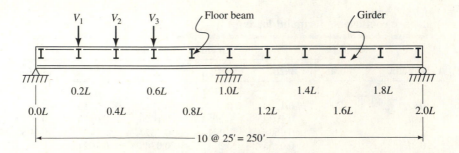

The live-load reaction from the floor beam was computed to be 52.48 kips. Therefore, the actual reaction loads transferred from the floor beams to the main girder are

$$V_1 = V_L\left(\frac{0.14}{1.55}\right) = (52.48)\left(\frac{0.14}{1.55}\right) = 11.39 \text{ kips}$$

TABLE E9.4b
Influence area for distributed loads

	Area under the influence-line diagram with unit load at					
	0	**0.2L**	**0.4L**	**0.6L**	**0.8L**	**1.0L**
+ve area	0	0.0675	0.0950	0.0825	0.0300	0
−ve area	0	0.0125	−0.0250	−0.0375	−0.0500	−0.1250
Total area	0	0.0550	0.0700	0.0450	−0.0200	−0.1250

$$V_2 = V_L = 52.48 \text{ kips}$$

$$V_3 = V_l\left(\frac{0.56}{1.55}\right) = (52.48)\left(\frac{0.56}{1.55}\right) = 18.96 \text{ kips}$$

Note that the smallest shear, V_1, is placed at 0.2L, the point where the value of the influence coefficient is the smallest. The maximum moment in the main girder at 0.4L, due to loads V_1, V_2, and V_3 placed as shown, is

$$M_L = \sum V_i \times \text{influence coefficient}$$
$$= [(11.39)(0.1008) + (52.48)(0.2064) + (18.96)(0.1216)](125)$$
$$= 1786 \text{ k-ft}$$

2. *Lane load.* The lane load will be placed on one span only with concentrated load at 0.4L. Transversely, the lane load will be placed as shown. Loads transferred to stringers are computed by the lever rule method.

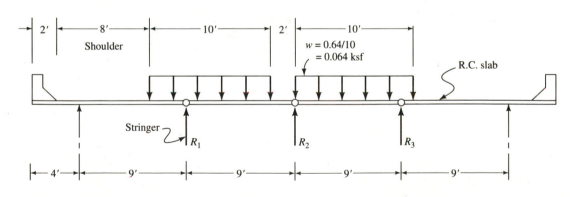

$$R_1 = 0.064\left[3\left(\frac{7.5}{9}\right) + 7\left(\frac{5.5}{9}\right)\right] = 0.434 \text{ k/ft}$$

$$R_2 = 0.064\left[7\left(\frac{3.5}{9}\right) + 9\left(\frac{4.5}{9}\right)\right] = 0.462 \text{ k/ft}$$

$$R_3 = 0.064\left[9\left(\frac{4.5}{9}\right) + 1\left(\frac{8.5}{9}\right)\right] = 0.348 \text{ k/ft}$$

The lane loads as transferred by the stringer reactions to the floor beam are obtained by multiplying the above values by the length of the stringer (= 25 ft). Thus,

$$R_{F1} = 0.434 \times 25 = 10.85 \text{ kips}$$
$$R_{F2} = 0.462 \times 25 = 11.55 \text{ kips}$$
$$R_{F3} = 0.348 \times 25 = 8.70 \text{ kips}$$

The stringer reactions, R_{F1}, R_{F2}, and R_{F3}, are placed at 9 ft o.c. on the floor beam as shown. The reaction, V, of the floor beam is the load transferred to the main girder.

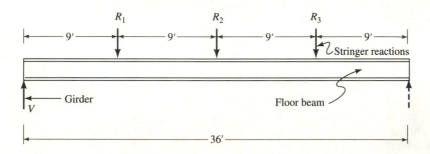

$$V = (10.85)\left(\tfrac{27}{36}\right) + (11.55)\left(\tfrac{18}{36}\right) + (8.70)\left(\tfrac{9}{36}\right) = 16.09 \text{ kips}$$

The reaction, V_c, in the floor beam due to the concentrated load of 18 kips (to be applied with the uniform lane load) is computed by proportion of the lane load. Thus,

$$V_c = (16.09)\left(\frac{18}{0.64 \times 25}\right) = 18.10 \text{ kips}$$

The maximum positive moment in the girder is obtained by placing floor beam reactions, each equal to V, as shown. Note that the reactions at $0.0L$ and $1.0L$ are each equal to $V/2$. The reaction due to the concentrated load, V_c, is positioned at $0.4L$, the point of the maximum value of the influence coefficient.

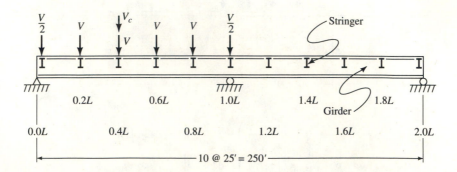

$$M_L^+ = (16.09)[(0.1008 + 0.2064 + 0.1216 + 0.0512)](125)$$
$$+ (18.10)(0.2064)(125)$$
$$= 1432 \text{ k-ft} < 1786 \text{ k-ft, the moment due to the truck loading}$$

Hence, the truck loading controls, and $M_L^+ = 1786$ k-ft.

$$\text{Impact factor, } I = \frac{50}{L + 125} = \frac{50}{125 + 125} = 0.2$$

$$M_{L+I}^+ = (1786)(1 + 0.20) = 2143 \text{ k-ft}$$

Total maximum $+ve$ moment $= 2545 + 656 + 2143 = 5344$ k-ft (at $0.4L$).

Negative moments. From Table E6.1 of influence coefficients, it is seen that the maximum $-ve$ moment occurs at $1.0L$, i.e., at the interior support.
Dead load

    1. *From the floor beams*

$$V_D = 56.55 \text{ kips as before.}$$
$$M_D = (56.55)[(0.0480 + 0.0840 + 0.0960 + 0.0720)](2)(125)$$
$$= 4241 \text{ k-ft}$$

    2. *Self-weight of the girder (assumed)*

$$w_G = 0.60 \text{ k/ft (including stiffeners, bracings, connections, etc.)}$$
From Table E6.2, influence area at $1.0L = -0.1250$
$$M_G^- = (0.660)(-0.125)(125)^2 = 1172 \text{ k-ft}$$

Live load

    1. *Truck load.* Consider only one truck on the structure. As the trailer is not long enough (30 ft maximum) to reach the maxima on both spans (at $0.6L$ and $1.4L$—100 ft apart), maximum $-ve$ moment at the interior support ($1.0L$) occurs when the middle wheels are at $0.6L$ (since associated with the largest $-ve$ influence coefficient), with front wheels closer to the interior support as shown. Note that the smallest reaction, V_1, is placed at $0.8L$, the point associated with the smaller influence coefficient. The following values of the floor beam reactions due to live load were computed earlier:

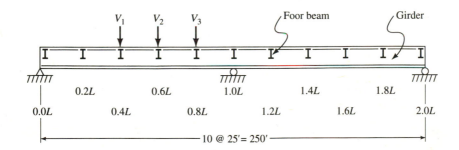

$$V_1 = 11.39 \text{ kips}$$
$$V_2 = 52.48 \text{ kips}$$
$$V_3 = 18.96 \text{ kips}$$

Therefore, the maximum $-ve$ moment is

$$M_L^- = [(18.96)(0.084) + (52.48)(0.096) + (11.39)(0.072)](125)$$
$$= 931 \text{ k-ft}$$

2. *Lane load.* Consider both spans as fully loaded as shown, with concentrated loads at 0.6L and 1.4L, both of which are the points associated with maximum values of the influence coefficients. The following values of V and V_c were computed earlier:

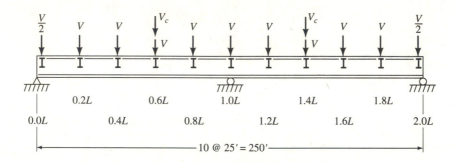

$$V = 16.09 \text{ kips}$$

$$V_c = 18.10 \text{ kips}$$

$$M_L^- = 16.09[(0.048 + 0.084 + 0.096 + 0.072) \times 2](125)$$
$$+ (18.10)(0.096 \times 2)(125)$$
$$= 1641 \text{ k-ft} > 931 \text{ k-ft, moment due to the truck loading}$$

Hence, the lane load controls, and $M_L^- = -1641$ k-ft.

For computing the impact factor to be used for maximum negative moment in a continuous span, the length L is taken as the average length of the two adjacent spans (AASHTO 3.8.2.2e). In the present case, $L_{avg} = \frac{1}{2} \times (125 + 125) = 125$ ft, the same as considered for the maximum positive moment. Hence, $I = 0.2$.

$$M_{L+I-} = (1641)(1 + 0.20) = 1969 \text{ k-ft}$$

Total maximum $-ve$ moment $= -(4241 + 1172 + 1969) = -7382$ k-ft (at $1.0L$).

Additional moment as exterior stringer

Dead load. The dead load will be computed by the lever rule method.

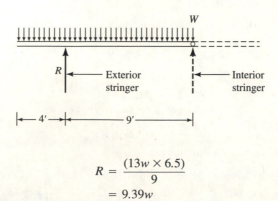

$$R = \frac{(13w \times 6.5)}{9}$$
$$= 9.39w$$

Slab $= \left(\frac{8}{12}\right)(0.15)(9.39) = 0.939$ k/ft
Wearing surface $= (0.035)(9.39)$ $= 0.329$ k/ft
Parapet $= 0.201$ k/ft
Railing $= 0.008$ k/ft

Total dead load $= 1.477$ k/ft

Influence area at $0.4L = 0.0700$

$$M^+_{D,0.4L} = (1.477)(0.0700)(125)^2 = 1615 \text{ k-ft}$$

Influence area at $1.0L = -0.1250$

$$M^-_{D,-1.0L} = (1.477)(-0.1250)(125)^2 = -2885 \text{ k-ft}$$

Live load. Because truck load and lane load are mutually exclusive, we must use truck load for maximum $+ve$ moment at $0.4L$ and lane load for maximum $-ve$ moment at $1.0L$, as before. The lever rule method will be used to compute loads.

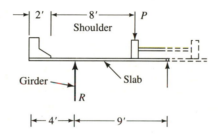

1. *Truck load*

$$R = \left(\frac{3}{9}\right)P = 0.33P$$

For a concrete deck slab supported by four or more steel stringers and $S > 6$ ft, the fraction of the wheel load (i.e., the distribution factor) must not be less than (AASHTO 3.23.2.3.1.5)

$$\frac{S}{4.0 + 0.25S} = \frac{9}{4.0 + 0.25 \times 9} = 1.44 > 0.33$$

Hence, $DF = 1.44$ governs, and

$$R = 1.44P = (1.44)(16) = 23.04 \text{ kips}$$

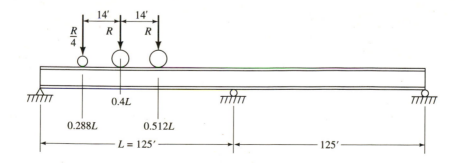

TABLE E9.4c
Influence coefficients for moment at 0.4L with load at various positions on span

IL coefficient	0.2L	0.3L	0.4L	0.5L	0.6L
Position of load	0.1008	0.1527	0.2064	0.1625	0.1216

With the middle axle positioned at $0.4L$ (= 50 ft from the left support), the front and the rear axles are positioned at $0.288L$ (= 36 ft) and $0.512L$ (= 64 ft), respectively, from the left support. The values of the influence coefficients at these locations are found by interpolation of values listed in Table E9.4c:

$$IL_{0.288L} = 0.1008 + \frac{0.088}{0.100}(0.1527 - 0.1008) = 0.1465$$

$$IL_{0.512L} = 0.1625 + \frac{0.012}{0.100}(0.1216 - 0.1625) = 0.1576$$

$$M^+_{L,0.4L} = (23.04)[\tfrac{1}{4}(0.1465) + 0.2064 + 0.1576](125) = 1153 \text{ k-ft}$$

$$M^+_{L+I,0.4L} = (1153)(1 + 0.2) = 1384 \text{ k-ft}$$

2. Lane load

$$R = 3(0.064)(1.5)/9 = 0.032 \text{ k/ft}$$

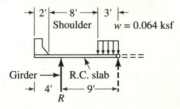

Due to the concentrated load of 18 kips, the equivalent uniform load is $18/10 = 1.8$ k/ft. Therefore,

$$R_c = [3(1.8)(1.5)]/9 = 0.90 \text{ kip}$$

$$\text{Influence area at } 1.0L = -0.1250 \text{ (Table E9.4b)}$$

$$M^-_{L,1.0L} = (0.032)(0.125)(125)^2 + 2(0.90)(0.2064)(125)$$
$$= 109 \text{ k-ft}$$

$$M^-_{L+I,1.0L} = 10(1 + 0.13) = 131 \text{ k-ft}$$

Thus, the maximum $+ve$ and $-ve$ moments in the main girder are

$$M^+_{max} = 1384 + 5344 = 6728 \text{ k-ft}$$

$$M^-_{max} = -(131 + 7382) = -7513 \text{ k-ft}$$

Shear and reactions.   Refer to AISC [1966, Table A.2.0] for the influence coefficients tabulated in Table E9.4d.

TABLE E9.4d
Influence coefficients for point loads

Load at	Reaction		Shear	
	R_A	R_B	V_{AB}	V_{BA}
0.0L	1.0	0	1.0	0
0.2L	0.7520	0.2960	0.7520	−0.2480
0.4L	0.5160	0.5680	0.5160	−0.4840
0.6L	0.3040	0.7920	0.3040	−0.6960
0.8L	0.1280	0.9440	0.1280	−0.8720
1.0L	0	1.0	0	−1.0
1.2L	−0.0720	0.9440	−0.0720	−0.0720
1.4L	−0.0960	0.7920	−0.0960	−0.0960
1.6L	−0.0840	0.5680	−0.0840	−0.0840
1.8L	−0.0480	0.2960	−0.0480	−0.0480
2.0L	0	0	0	0

Due to dead load (transmitted from floor beams)

$V_D = 56.55$ kips as computed earlier.

$R_{A,D} = (56.55)(0.7520 + 0.5160 + 0.3040 + 0.1280 − 0.0720 − 0.0960$
$\qquad − 0.0840 − 0.0480)$
$\qquad = (56.55)(1.4) = 79$ kips

$R_{B,D} = (56.55)(0.2960 + 0.5680 + 0.7920 + 0.9440)(2)$
$\qquad = (56.55)(5.2) = 294$ kips

$V_{AB,D} = R_{A,D} = 79$ kips

$V_{BA,D} = (56.55)(−0.2480 − 0.4840 − 0.6960 − 0.8720 − 0.0720$
$\qquad − 0.0960 − 0.0840 − 0.0480)$
$\qquad = (56.55)(−2.6) = −147$ kips

Due to self-weight of girder. The self-weight of the girder is assumed to be 600 lb/ft.

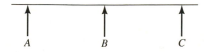

$w_G \quad = 0.6$ k/ft
$R_{A,G} \ = (0.6)(125)(0.375) \quad = 28$ kips
$R_{B,G} \ = (0.6)(125)(1.25) \quad\ \ = 94$ kips
$V_{AB,G} = (0.6)(125)(0.375) \quad = 28$ kips
$V_{BA,G} = (0.6)(125)(−0.625) = −47$ kips

Live load (from floor beams). Both truck and lane loadings would be investigated, and the maximum values given by either of the two loading conditions would be used for design.

1. *Due to truck loading.* For maximum reaction, $R_{A,L}$, at the end support A (at 0.0L) of the left span (AB), the HS truck is positioned such that the rear axle is placed directly over the end floor beam at A, as shown.

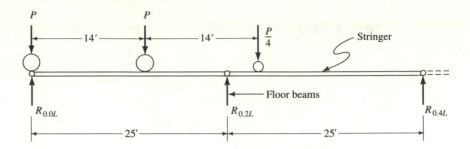

$$R_{0.0L} = P\left(1 + \tfrac{11}{25}\right) = 1.44P$$

$$R_{0.2L} = P\left[\left(\tfrac{14}{25}\right) + \left(\tfrac{22}{25}\right)\left(\tfrac{1}{4}\right)\right] = 0.78P$$

$$R_{0.4L} = \frac{P}{4}\left(\frac{3}{25}\right) = 0.03P$$

Recall *LL* shear in the end floor beams. The *LL* shear, including impact ($I = 0.3$), was computed to be 63.38 kips. Without impact, the *LL* shear would be

$$V_{L,0.0L} = \frac{63.38}{1.3} = 48.75 \text{ kips} = 1.44P \quad \text{(computed above)}$$

By proportion, *LL* shear at 0.2*L* and 0.4*L* is computed as follows:

$$V_{L,0.2L} = (48.75)\left(\frac{0.78}{1.44}\right) = 26.41 \text{ kips}$$

$$V_{L,0.4L} = (48.75)\left(\frac{0.03}{1.44}\right) = 1.02 \text{ kips}$$

With the above three loads positioned, respectively, at 0.0*L*, 0.2*L*, and 0.4*L* from the left support, the reaction due to the live load at the left support, $R_{A,L}$, is

$$R_{A,L} = \sum (\text{load}) \times (\text{IC for } R_A)$$
$$= (48.75)(1.0) + (26.41)(0.752) + (1.02)(0.5160)$$
$$= 69.14 \text{ kips}$$

Impact factor, $I = 0.20$

$$R_{A,L+I} = (69.14)(1 + 0.2) = 83 \text{ kips}$$

For maximum $-ve$ shear at B, the loads computed above are positioned so that

$$V_{1.0L} = 48.75 \text{ kips}$$
$$V_{0.8L} = 26.41 \text{ kips}$$
$$V_{0.6L} = 1.02 \text{ kips}$$

Therefore, the maximum $-ve$ shear at B is

$$V_{B,L} = \sum (\text{load}) \times (\text{IC for } V_{BA})$$
$$= (48.75)(-1.0) + (26.41)(-0.8720) + (1.02)(-0.6960)$$
$$= -72.49 \text{ kips}$$

Impact factor, $I = 0.20$

$$V_{B,L+I} = (-72.49)(1 + 0.2) = -87 \text{ kips}$$

For maximum reaction, $R_{B,L}$, at the interior support B (at $1.0L$) of the left span (AB), the HS truck is positioned such that the rear axle is placed directly over the interior floor beam at B, as shown.

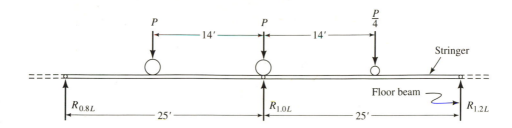

$$R_{0.8L} = P\left(\tfrac{14}{25}\right) = 0.56P$$

$$R_{1.0L} = P\left[\left(\tfrac{11}{25}\right) + 1 + \left(\tfrac{11}{25}\right)\left(\tfrac{1}{4}\right)\right] = 1.55P$$

$$R_{1.2L} = \frac{P}{4}\left(\frac{14}{25}\right) = 0.14P$$

Recall LL shear in the interior floor beams. V_L was computed to be 52.48 kips (without impact), so that $1.55P = 52.48$ kips. From Table E9.4d, the IL coefficients for R_B, with points loads at B at $0.8L$ and $1.2L$, are 1.0, 0.944, and 0.944 respectively. Therefore,

$$\begin{aligned}
R_{B,L} &= \text{load} \times \sum \text{IC} \\
&= (52.48)\left[\left(\frac{0.56}{1.55}\right)(0.9440) + (1)(1.0) + \left(\frac{0.14}{1.55}\right)(0.9440)\right] \\
&= 75.08 \text{ kips}
\end{aligned}$$

With $I = 0.2$, $R_{B,L} = 75.08 \times 1.2 = 90.1$ kips. Hence, the maximum shears, including impact, in the left span (AB) due to the HS truck loading are

$$V_{AB,L+I} = R_{A,L+I} = 83 \text{ kips}$$

$$V_{BA,L+I} = R_{B,L+I} = -87 \text{ kips}$$

2. *Due to lane loading.* Recall that the maximum shear in the floor beam due to the lane loading was computed to be

$$V = 16.09 \text{ kips due to uniform load of } 0.064 \text{ k/ft}^2$$

$$V_c = 18.10 \text{ kips due to a concentrated load of 18 kips (for moment)}$$

For shear computations, the concentrated load to be used in conjunction with the uniform lane load is 26 kips (instead of 18 kips used for moment computations). The shear corresponding to the concentrated load of 26 kips is found by proportion:

$$V_c = (18.10)\left(\tfrac{26}{18}\right) = 26.14 \text{ kips}$$

Note that reaction and shear at end supports are maximum when *only one span is loaded*. Therefore, reaction at the left support, A, of the left span, AB, is

$$R_{A,L} = (\text{load}) \sum (\text{IC for } V_{AB})$$
$$= 16.09(0.7520 + 0.5160 + 0.3040 + 0.1280) + (26.14)(1.0)$$
$$= 53.49 \text{ kips} < 69.14 \text{ kips due to the truck loading}$$

Hence, the truck loading governs.

Reaction at the central support is maximum when both spans are loaded.

$$R_{B,L} = \sum (\text{load})(\text{IC for } R_B)$$
$$= (16.09)(0.2960 + 0.5680 + 0.7920 + 0.9440) \times 2 + (26.14)(1.0)$$
$$= 109.81 \text{ kips} > 75.08 \text{ kips due to truck loading}$$

$$\text{Impact factor, } I = 0.20$$
$$R_{B,L+I} = (109.81)(1 + 0.20) = 132.0 \text{ kips}$$

Shear at the interior support is maximum when only one span is loaded (larger IC). Therefore,

$$V_{BA,L} = \sum (\text{load})(\text{IC for } R_B)$$
$$= 16.09(0.2960 + 0.5680 + 0.7920 + 0.9440) + (26.14)(1.0)$$
$$= 67.97 < 72.49 \text{ kips due to truck loading}$$

Hence, the truck loading governs.

Additional shear and reaction due to exterior stringer action

Due to dead load. Dead load due to the action as exterior stringer was computed earlier to be 1.477 k/ft. Reactions and shears due to that load are computed as follows. The influence areas for distributed load are given in Table E9.4e.

$$R \text{ or } V = (\text{load/ft})(\text{span length})(\text{influence area})$$
$$R'_{A,D} = (1.477)(125)(0.375) = 69 \text{ kips}$$
$$R'_{B,D} = (1.477)(125)(1.250) = 231 \text{ kips}$$
$$V'_{AB,D} = (1.477)(125)(0.375) = 69 \text{ kips}$$
$$V'_{BA,D} = (1.477)(125)(-0.625) = -115 \text{ kips}$$

Due to live load

1. *Truck loading.* Use truck loading for maximum reaction and shear at the left support (*A*). The rear axle is positioned directly over the end floor beam (at 0.0*L*), and the middle and front axles are positioned at 14 ft and 28 ft (0.112*L* and 0.224*L*, respectively) from

TABLE E9.4e
Influence area for distributed loads

	Reaction		Shear	
	R_A	R_B	V_{AB}	V_{BA}
+*ve* area	0.4375	1.2500	0.4375	0
−*ve* area	−0.0625	0	−0.0625	−0.6250
Total area	0.3750	1.2500	0.3750	−0.6250

TABLE E9.4f
Influence coefficients for 0.0L with load at various points on span

Position of load	0.0L	0.1L	0.2L	0.3L
IL coefficients	1.0	0.8753	0.7520	0.6318

the left end as shown. Influence coefficients at these intermediate points are computed by interpolation starting with the data in Table E9.4f:

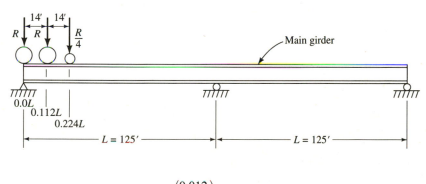

$$IL_{0.112L} = 0.8753 + \left(\frac{0.012}{0.010}\right)(0.7520 - 0.8753) = 0.8605$$

$$IL_{0.224L} = 0.7520 + \left(\frac{0.024}{0.100}\right)(0.6318 - 0.7520) = 0.7232$$

$$R = 23.04 \text{ kips}$$

$$R'_{A,L} = V'_{AB,L}$$

$$= (23.04)(1.0) + (23.04)(0.8605) + (\tfrac{1}{4})(23.04)(0.7232)$$

$$= 47 \text{ kips}$$

Impact factor, $I = 0.20$

$$R'_{A,L+I} = V'_{AB,L+I} = 47(1 + 0.2) = 56.0 \text{ kips}$$

For maximum shear at the interior support in the left span, $V'_{BA,L}$, the HS truck is positioned as close to the interior support as possible. Accordingly, the rear axle is positioned directly over that support and the middle and the front axles at 14 ft and 28 ft, respectively, to the left of the support as shown. These positions correspond to 0.776L (97 ft) and 0.888L (111 ft), respectively, from the left support. The influence coefficients at these locations are found by interpolation starting with the data in Table E9.4g:

$$IC_{0.776L} = -0.7892 - \left(\frac{0.076}{0.100}\right)(0.8720 - 0.7892) = -0.8521$$

$$IC_{0.888L} = -0.8720 - \left(\frac{0.088}{0.100}\right)(0.9427 - 0.8720) = -0.9342$$

TABLE E9.4g
Influence coefficients for 1.0L (V_{BA}) with load at various points on span

Position of load	0.7L	0.8L	0.9L	1.0L
IL coefficient	−0.7892	−0.8720	−0.9427	−1.0

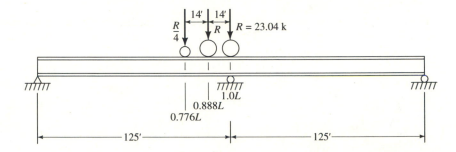

Therefore,

$$V'_{BA,L} = (\tfrac{1}{4})(23.04)(-0.8521) + (23.04)(-0.9342) + (56.04)(-1.0)$$
$$= -64.20 \text{ kips}$$

Impact factor $I = 0.20$

$$V'_{BA,L+I} = (-64.2)(1 + 0.2) = -77.0 \text{ kips}$$

2. *Lane loading.* For computing the maximum value of $R'_{B,L}$, apply lane loading to both spans. The equivalent loads of 0.032 k/ft due to the uniform load and 0.90 k/ft due to the concentrated load of 18 kips were computed earlier. Noting that for shear, the concentrated load is 26 kips, the corresponding value of the reaction is found by proportion:

$$R'_{B,L} = (0.032)(125)(1.250) + (0.90)(26/18)1.0 = 6.3 \text{ kips}$$

Impact factor, $I = 0.20$

$$R'_{B,L+I} = (6.3)(1 + 0.20) = 8.0 \text{ kips}$$

The maximum values of reactions and shears are given by the sum of effects due to (1) dead load of superstructure as transferred from stringers and floor beams, (2) self-weight of the girder, (3) live load plus impact as transferred from the floor beams, (4) dead load from the superstructure due to the main girder acting as the exterior stringer, and (5) live load plus impact due to the main girder acting as the exterior stringer. Values of these effects were computed earlier. The final values to be used for design are

$$R_{A,\max} = V_{AB,\max}$$
$$= 79 + 28 + 83 + 69 + 56 = 315 \text{ kips}$$
$$R_{B,\max} = 294 + 94 + 132 + 231 + 8 = 759 \text{ kips}$$
$$V_{BA,\max} = -147 - 47 - 87 - 115 - 77 = -473 \text{ kips}$$

Design of cross section of the main girder

$$M_{\text{pos}} = 6728 \text{ k-ft}$$
$$M_{\text{neg}} = 7513 \text{ k-ft} > M_{\text{pos}}$$

Because the difference between maximum positive and maximum negative moment is small (approximately 10 percent), prismatic girders are used for an economical design.

Determination of the section of the plate girder is a bit tricky. The allowable bending stress, F_b (Table A.26, Appendix A), is a complex function of several geometric properties of the section (S_{xc}, I_{yc}, J, d and l) and loading conditions (C_b) as demonstrated earlier for the design of floor beams. Also, the allowable bending stress must be reduced if the actual stress, f_v, exceeds $0.6F_v$, where F_v is the allowable shear stress. Consequently, certain assumptions will be made to determine F_b.

Girder depth, d.   Assume width of flange $b = 24$ in. Also assume that the compression bottom flange near the interior support is laterally supported at the locations of floor beams, so that the length of the unsupported segment of the girder is $l = 25$ ft $= 300$ in.

Assuming $F_b = 0.55F_y = (0.55)(36) = 20$ ksi, the required section modulus is

$$S_x = \frac{(7513)(12)}{20} = 4508 \text{ in.}^3$$

For a girder having a constant t_w/D, the optimum girder depth, h_0, can be computed from Eq. 9.333:

$$h_0 = \sqrt[3]{\frac{3C_1KM}{C_4^2 F_b(3C_2 - C_1 C_3)}}$$

For a welded girder, the values of the constants are given as: $C_1 = 0.95$, $C_2 = 1.3$, $C_3 = 1.0$, and $C_4 = 0.95$. The value of K varies between 120 and 180; an average value of 150 is used.

$$h_0 = \sqrt[3]{\frac{3(0.95)(150)M}{(0.95)^2(F_b)(3 \times 1.3 - 0.95 \times 1.0)}}$$

$$= 5.44\left(\frac{M}{F_b}\right)^{1/3}$$

h_0 is computed for both maximum negative and positive moments, and the average of the two values of h_0 is used. Maximum $-ve$ moment $= 7513$ k-ft.

$$h_{0,\text{reqd}} = 5.44\left[\frac{(7513)(12)}{20}\right]^{1/3} = 90 \text{ in.}$$

Max $+ve$ moment $= 6728$ k-ft.

$$h_{0,\text{reqd}} = 5.44\left(\frac{6728 \times 12}{20}\right)^{1/3} = 86.6 \text{ in.}$$

$$\text{Average } h_0 = (\tfrac{1}{2})(90 + 86.6) = 88.3 \text{ in.}$$

$$\text{Use } h_0 = 90 \text{ in.} > L/25 = (125 \times 12)/25 = 60 \text{ in., OK}$$

Web thickness, t_w

$$F_{v,\text{max}} = 0.33F_y = (0.33)(36) = 12 \text{ ksi (Eq. 9.287)}$$

$$V_{\text{max}} = 473 \text{ kips}$$

$$f_v = \frac{V}{Dt_w}$$

from which

$$t_w = \frac{V}{DF_v}$$

$$= \frac{473}{90 \times 12} = 0.438 \text{ in.}$$

Try a web $\frac{1}{2} \times 90$ so that $D = 90$ in. and $t_w = 0.5$ in. This gives

$$\frac{D}{t_w} = \frac{90}{0.5} = 180 > 165, \text{ but} < 330 \text{ (Table 9.7).}$$

Hence, a longitudinal stiffener will be required. Because $D = 90$ in. > 7 ft, a longitudinal stiffener may likely result in an economical design. The permitted values of D/t_w ratios for girders with and without a longitudinal stiffener are given in Table 9.7.

Flange plates.   Try a 2-in.-thick flange plate, $t_f = 2$ in. With a 90-in.-deep web, distance from the neutral axis to the extreme compression fibers is

$$\tfrac{1}{2}d = 45 + 2 = 47 \text{ in.}$$

Therefore

$$I_{\text{reqd}} = (S_{\text{reqd}})\left(\frac{d}{2}\right)$$

$$= (4508)(47) = 211,876 \text{ in.}^4$$

The moment of the girder equals the sum of the moment of inertia due to the flange and the web: $I_G = I_f + I_w$. The moment of inertia contributed by the web, I_w, is

$$I_w = \frac{t_w D^3}{12}$$

$$= \frac{(0.5)(90)^3}{12} = 30,375 \text{ in.}^3$$

Therefore, $I_{f,\text{reqd}} = I_G - I_w = 211,876 - 30,375 = 181,501 \text{ in.}^4$
Calculate the required flange area, A_f.

$$A_{f,\text{reqd}} = \frac{I_{f,\text{reqd}}}{2(d/2 - t_f/2)^2}$$

$$= \frac{181,501}{2(47 - 1)^2} = 43 \text{ in.}^2$$

In the above calculation, the moment of inertia of the flange about its centroidal axis has been ignored because it is very small.
Assume flange width $b = 24$ in. and calculate the required flange thickness.

$$t_f = \tfrac{43}{24} = 1.8 \text{ in.}$$

Provide two 2×24 flanges, $A_f = 2 \times 24 = 48$ in.$^2 > 43$ in.^{2}, OK. Thus, we have a preliminary trial section: flanges, 2×24; web, $\frac{1}{2} \times 90$; total girder depth, $d = 2 \times 2 + 90 = 94$ in.

Calculate the allowable bending stress, F_b, given by the following formula (Table A.26, Appendix A):

$$F_b = \frac{(50 \times 10^6)C_b}{S_{xc}}\left(\frac{I_{yc}}{l}\right)\sqrt{0.722\frac{J}{I_{yc}} + 9.87\left(\frac{d}{l}\right)^2} \leq 0.55F_y$$

Calculate section properties required in the above formula.

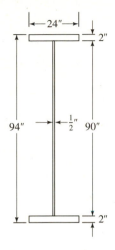

$$I_x = 2\left[\frac{(24)(2)^3}{12} + (24)(2)(46)^2 + \left(\frac{1}{3}\right)\left(\frac{1}{2}\right)(45)^3\right]$$

$$= 233{,}543 \text{ in.}^4$$

$$S_x = \frac{I_x}{d/2} = \frac{233{,}543}{47} = 4969 \text{ in.}^3$$

$$I_{yc} = 2(24)^3/12 = 2304 \text{ in.}^4$$

$$J = \frac{(bt^3)_c + (bt^3)_t + Dt_w^3}{3}$$

$$= \frac{2(24)(2)^3 + (90)(0.5)^3}{3} = 131.8 \text{ in.}^4$$

where $d = 94$ in., $l = 25$ ft $= 300$ in., and $C_b = 1$ (conservative assumption). Substituting these values in the above formula,

$$F_b = \left(\frac{(50 \times 10^6)(1.0)}{4969}\right)\left(\frac{2304}{300}\right)\sqrt{(0.722)\left(\frac{131.8}{2304}\right) + (9.87)\left(\frac{94}{300}\right)^2}$$

$$= 77{,}677 \text{ psi}$$

which is much greater than $F_{b,\text{allow}} = 20{,}000 \text{ lb/in.}^2$. Hence, use $F_b = 20{,}000 \text{ lb/in.}^2$. The actual bending stress is

$$f_b = \frac{M_{\text{max}}}{S_x} = \frac{(7513)(12)}{4969} = 18.14 \text{ ksi}$$

The selected flange and the web sizes were based on the assumed value of $F_b = 20{,}000$ lb/in.², and therefore need not be revised for now. However, the value of $F_b = 20$ ksi may need to be reduced according to AASHTO 10.34.4.4 if the actual shear stress, f_v, exceeds $0.6F_v$ (checked later), and that may require a revised section.

Check the b/t ratio for the compression flange. For A36 steel and $F_b = 20{,}000$ lb/in.², $(b/t)_{\text{max}} = 23$ for welded girders (see Table 9.11). Actual $b/t = 24/2 = 12 < 23$, OK.

Check the self-weight of the girder.

$$w_G = (2A_f + A_w)^\gamma_{steel}/144 = (2 \times 2 \times 24 + \tfrac{1}{2} \times 90) \times \tfrac{490}{144}$$
$$= 480 \text{ lb/ft}$$

which is < 600 lb/ft (assumed), with ample allowance for bracings, stiffeners, jointing, etc.

Check for shear. For a web with a D/t_w ratio of 180, the maximum permitted shear stress is given by Eq. 9.155:

$$F_v = \frac{(7.33)(10^7)}{(D/t_w)^2} = \frac{(7.33)(10^7)}{(180)^2} = 2262 \text{ psi}$$

The actual shear stress, f_v, is

$$f_v = \frac{V}{Dt_w} = \frac{473}{(90)(0.5)} = 10.51 \text{ ksi}$$

which is much higher than $F_v = 2262$ psi. Hence, transverse stiffeners will be required (AASHTO 10.34.4.1).

Maximum permitted aspect ratios, d_o/D (d_o = spacing of intermediate stiffeners), are given by Eq. 9.221:

$$\frac{d_o}{D} \leq \left(\frac{260}{D/t_w}\right)^2 = \left(\frac{260}{180}\right)^2 = 2.09$$

which is $< d_o/D$ of 3. Hence, $(d_o/D)_{max} = 2$ can be used.

Try $d_o/D = 1$. The plate buckling coefficient, k, is (Eq. 9.147)

$$k = 5 + \frac{5}{(d_o/D)^2} = 5 + \frac{5}{1} = 10$$

Compute the applicable value of the web buckling coefficient, C. Determine if Eq. 9.215, Eq. 9.216, or 9.217 applies.

$$\frac{7500\sqrt{k}}{\sqrt{F_y}} = \frac{7500 \times \sqrt{10}}{\sqrt{36,000}} = 125 < (D/t_w = 180)$$

Hence, the value of C is given by Eq. 9.217:

$$C = \frac{(4.5)(10^7)k}{(D/t_w)^2 F_y} = \frac{(4.5)(10^7)(10)}{(180)^2(36,000)} = 0.39$$

The allowable shear stress, F_v, is given by Eq. 9.210:

$$F_v = \frac{F_y}{3}\left[C + \frac{0.87(1 - C)}{\sqrt{1 + (d_o/D)^2}}\right]$$

$$= \frac{36}{3}\left[0.39 + \frac{0.87(1 - 0.39)}{\sqrt{1 + 1}}\right]$$

$$= 9.86 \text{ ksi} < f_v = 10.51 \text{ ksi, NG}$$

Hence, reduce the aspect ratio, d_o/D; i.e., reduce the spacing, d_o, of transverse stiffeners. Try $d_o = 60$ in., so that $d_o/D = 0.667$.

$$k = 5 + \frac{5}{(0.667)^2} = 16.24$$

Therefore

$$\frac{7500\sqrt{k}}{\sqrt{F_y}} = \frac{7500 \times \sqrt{16.24}}{\sqrt{36,000}} = 159 < (d/t_w = 180)$$

$$C = \frac{4.5 \times 10^7 k}{(D/t_w)^2 F_y}$$

$$= \frac{4.5 \times 10^7 \times 16.24}{(180)^2 \times 36,000} = 0.626$$

so that

$$F_v = \frac{F_y}{3}\left[C + \frac{0.87(1 - C)}{\sqrt{1 + (d_o/D)^2}} \right]$$

$$= \frac{36}{3}\left[0.626 + \frac{0.87(1 - 0.626)}{\sqrt{1 + (0.667)2}} \right]$$

$$= 11.25 \text{ ksi} > f_v = 10.51 \text{ ksi, OK}$$

Check whether the allowable bending stress, F_b, needs to be reduced according to Eq. 9.270b (AASHTO 10.34.4.4, Eq. 10.29):

$$f_v = 10.51 \text{ ksi} > 0.6F_v = 0.6 \times 11.25 = 6.75 \text{ ksi}$$

Hence, F_b must be reduced to F_s, which is given by

$$F_s = \left[0.754 - 0.34\left(\frac{f_v}{F_v}\right) \right]F_y$$

$$= \left[0.754 - (0.34)\left(\frac{10.51}{11.25}\right) \right] \times 36,000$$

$$= 15,709 \text{ psi} < f_b = 18.14 \text{ ksi, NG}$$

Therefore, the section should be revised to increase the section modulus, which will reduce the actual bending stress, f_b. This will be advantageously accomplished by providing a thicker web, which will also reduce the shear stress (and reduce f_v/F_v).

Try a web $\frac{5}{8} \times 90$. The section properties are

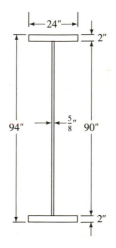

$$A = 2 \times 24 \times 2 + \tfrac{5}{8} \times 90$$

$$= 152.25 \text{ in.}^2$$

$$I_x = 2\left[(24)\left(\frac{2^3}{12}\right) + (24)(2)(46)^2 + \frac{5}{8} \times \frac{(46)^3}{3}\right]$$

$$= 241,137 \text{ in.}^4$$

$$S_x = \frac{241,137}{47} = 5130 \text{ in.}^3$$

$$\frac{D}{t_w} = \frac{90}{0.625} = 144$$

Calculate actual bending and shear stresses as before.

$$f_b = \frac{M_{\max}}{S_x} = \frac{7513 \times 12}{5130} = 17.57 \text{ ksi} < F_b = 20 \text{ ksi, OK}$$

$$f_v = \frac{V}{Dt_w} = \frac{473}{(90)(0.625)} = 8.41 \text{ ksi}$$

Try $D/d_o = 1.5$, so that $d_o/D = 0.667$ and $k = 16.24$ (computed earlier).

$$\frac{7500 \times \sqrt{k}}{\sqrt{F_y}} = \frac{(7500)(\sqrt{16.24})}{\sqrt{36,000}} = 159.3 > D/t_w = 144$$

$$\frac{6000 \times \sqrt{k}}{\sqrt{F_y}} = \frac{(6000)(\sqrt{16.24})}{\sqrt{36,000}} = 127.4 <= D/t_w = 144$$

Hence, the value of C is given by Eq. 9.216:

$$C = \frac{6000\sqrt{k}}{(D/t_w)F_y}$$

$$= \frac{6000(\sqrt{16.24})}{(144)(\sqrt{36,000})} = 0.885$$

The allowable shear stress is given by Eq. 9.210:

$$F_v = \frac{F_y}{3}\left[C + \frac{0.87(1 - C)}{\sqrt{1 + (d_o/D)^2}}\right]$$

$$= \frac{36}{3}\left[0.885 + \frac{0.87(1 - 0.885)}{\sqrt{1 + (0.667)^2}}\right]$$

$$= 11.62 \text{ ksi} > f_v = 8.41 \text{ ksi, OK}$$

Check whether the allowable bending stress, F_b, needs to be reduced according to Eq. 9.270b (AASHTO 10.34.4.4 Eq. 10.29):

$$f_v = 8.81 \text{ ksi} > 0.6F_v = (0.6)(11.62) = 6.97 \text{ ksi}$$

Hence, F_b must be reduced to F_s, which is given by

$$F_s = \left[0.754 - 0.34\left(\frac{f_v}{F_v}\right)\right]F_y$$

$$= \left[0.754 - (0.34)\left(\frac{8.41}{11.62}\right)\right](36)$$

$$= 18.29 \text{ ksi} > f_b = 17.57 \text{ ksi, OK}$$

Hence, the trial section is adequate for both bending and shear and will be adopted as the final section:

Flange: two plates—24 × 2
Web: $\frac{5}{8}$ × 90 with transverse stiffeners @ 60 in. o.c.

Check whether a longitudinal stiffener is required according to AASHTO 10.34.3.1. The value of f_b was computed to be 17.57 ksi. Refer to Table 9.6.

$$t_w = \frac{D\sqrt{f_b}}{23,000}$$

$$= \frac{(90)(\sqrt{17,570})}{23,000}$$

$$= 0.52 \text{ in.} < 0.625 \text{ in. provided, OK}$$

Hence, a longitudinal stiffener is *not* required.

Design of transverse stiffeners

Intermediate stiffeners. Intermediate transverse stiffeners will be provided at 60 in. o.c., required to control shear stresses.

Use a single stiffener on the inside of a girder with a tight fit against the compression flange. Intermediate stiffeners are designed to satisfy stiffness and strength requirements of AASHTO 10.34.4.7. Use Eq. 9.203 and 9.204:

$$I_{s,\text{reqd}} = d_o t_w^3 J \qquad\qquad \text{(Eq. 9.203)}$$

$$\text{where } J = 2.5(D/d_o)^2 - 2 \geq 0.5 \qquad\qquad \text{(Eq. 9.204)}$$

With an aspect ratio $d_o/D = \frac{2}{3}$,

$$J = (2.5)(1.5)^2 - 2 = 3.625 > 0.5, \text{ OK}$$

$$I_{s,\text{reqd}} = (60)(0.625)^3(3.625) = 53 \text{ in.}^4$$

Minimum width, b_t, should be the larger of the values given by Eqs. 9.334 and 9.335:

a. (2 in. + $d/30$) = (2 + 90/30) = 5 in.   (Eq. 9.335a)
b. $0.25b_f$ = 0.25 × 24 = 6 in.   (Eq. 9.335b)

Minimum thickness, t_p, should be the larger of the two values given by Eq. 9.335b:

1. width/16, i.e., $b_t/16$
2. $16t_p = 0.25b_f$ from which $(t_p)_\text{min} = b_f/64 = 24/64 = 0.375$ in.

Assuming $t_p = b_t/16$, the moment of inertia of the stiffener about the base is

$$I_s = \frac{t_p b_t^3}{3} = \frac{(b_t/16)b_t^3}{3} = \frac{b_t^4}{48} = 53 \text{ in.}^4$$

which yields $b_t = 7.1$ in.
Try $b_t = 7.5$ in.

$$t_p = \frac{b_t}{16} = \frac{7.5}{16} = 0.47 \text{ in.}$$

Try $t_p = 0.5$ in.

$$I = \frac{(0.5)(7.5)^3}{3} = 70.3 \text{ in.}^4 > 53 \text{ in.}^4, \text{OK}$$

The area of stiffener $A = 7.5 \times 0.5 = 3.75$ in.^{2}. The minimum required area of stiffener is given by Eq. 9.200:

$$A = [0.15 B D t_w (1 - C)(f_v/F_v) - 18 t_w^2]Y$$

where $B = 2.4$ for single plate stiffener
$D = 90$ in.
$t_w = 0.625$ in.
$C = 0.885$ (computed earlier)
$f_v/F_v = 8.41/11.62 = 0.724$
$Y = 1$ (same steel for web and stiffener)

Substitution of the above values in Eq. 9.200 yields

$$A = [(0.15)(2.4)(90)(0.625)(1 - 0.885)(0.724) - 18(0.625)^2](1.0)$$
$$= -5.35$$

Because the computed value of A is negative, only the width and the thickness requirements of the stiffener need to be satisfied. Hence, provide $7\frac{1}{2} \times \frac{1}{2}$ bars for the intermediate transverse stiffeners at 60 in. o.c. ($d_o = 60$ in.), on one side of the web only.

First intermediate stiffeners. Tension-field action is not permitted in the end panels, and the shear stress in the end panel is limited to the value given by Eq. 9.228a:

$$F_v = C F_y/3$$

End shear $= 315$ kips.

$$f_v = \frac{V}{D t_w} = \frac{315}{(90)(0.625)} = 5.6 \text{ ksi}$$

Assume that the first stiffener is located at $D/2 = 45$ in., so that

$$\frac{d_o}{D} = \frac{45}{90} = 0.5$$

$$k = 5 + \frac{5}{(d_o/D)^2} = 5 + \frac{5}{(0.5)^2} = 25$$

$$\frac{6000 \sqrt{k}}{\sqrt{F_y}} = \frac{6000 \times \sqrt{25}}{\sqrt{36,000}} = 158.1 > \frac{D}{t_w} = 144$$

Hence, $C = 1.0$, and

$$F_v = C F_y/3 = 1.0 \times 36/3 = 12 \text{ ksi} \gg f_v = 5.6 \text{ ksi}$$

Hence, the spacing can be reduced. Try $d_o = 60$ in., the same spacing as for the intermediate stiffeners. For this spacing, C was computed to be 0.886. Therefore,

$$F_v = C F_y/3 = 0.886 \times 36/3 = 10.63 \text{ ksi} > f_v = 5.6 \text{ ksi, OK}$$

Hence, provide the first transverse stiffener at 60 in. from the end bearing stiffener. This results in a uniform spacing of 60 in. for all transverse stiffeners. Note that the maximum spacing permitted for the first transverse stiffener is $1.5D$ or 135 in. ($= 11$ ft 3 in.).

Bearing stiffeners. Bearing stiffeners will be provided at the end, at the interior supports, and at all floor beam locations in accordance with AASHTO 10.34.6. At the supports, all bearing stiffeners will have tight fit against both flanges and be ground to fit against the flanges from which they receive reactions.

1. *End bearing stiffeners (also at floor beam locations).* The maximum value of the end reaction is $R_A = 315$ kips. Provide maximum stiffener width so that

$$b' = \frac{b_f - t_w}{2} = \frac{24 - 0.625}{2} = 11.69 \text{ in.}$$

Use stiffener width $b' = 11$ in.

Minimum thickness of the bearing stiffener is given by Eq. 9.336:

$$t = \frac{b'}{12}\sqrt{\frac{F_y}{33,000}} = \frac{11}{12}\sqrt{\frac{36,000}{33,000}} = 0.96 \text{ in.}$$

Use $t = 1$ in.

Check the strength of the bearing stiffener as a *column*. The participatory length of the web $= 18t_w = 18 \times 0.625 = 11.25$ in. The cross section of the fictitious column is as shown. Calculate section properties and the allowable compressive stress (Table A.26, Appendix A).

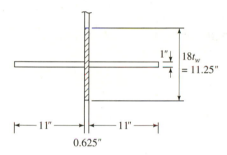

$$I = \frac{(1.0)(11 + 0.625 + 11)^3}{12} = 965 \text{ in.}^4$$

$$A = (11.25)(0.625) + 2(11)(1.0) = 29 \text{ in.}^2$$

$$r = \sqrt{\frac{I}{A}} = \sqrt{\frac{965}{29}} = 5.77 \text{ in.}$$

$$\frac{KL}{r} = \frac{(1.0)(90)}{5.77} = 15.6 < 126.1 \text{ for A36 steel}$$

$$F_a = 16,980 - 0.53(KL/r)^2$$
$$= 16,980 - (0.53)(15.6)^2$$
$$= 16,851 \text{ psi}$$

Compare with the actual compressive stress in the fictitious column.

$$f_a = \frac{R}{A} = \frac{315}{29} = 10.86 \text{ ksi} < F_a = 16.86 \text{ ksi, OK}$$

Check the bearing stress on the bottom flange caused by bearing stiffeners. Allowing 1 in. for cope for weld at the flange-web juncture leaves the net width of one bearing stiffener $= 11 - 1 = 10$ in. The area in bearing due to two stiffeners is

$$A_b = (2 \text{ stiffeners})(10)(1.0) = 20 \text{ in.}^2$$

The actual bearing stress is

$$f_p = \frac{R}{A_b} = \frac{315}{20} = 15.75 \text{ ksi}$$

The allowable bearing stress is (Table A.26, Appendix A)

$$F_p = 0.80F_y = 29.0 \text{ ksi} > f_p = 15.75 \text{ ksi, OK}$$

2. *Bearing stiffener at the interior support.* Maximum reaction is 759 kips. For only one pair of bearing stiffeners, as provided at the end supports, the following values were computed:

$$F_a = 16.85 \text{ ksi}, \qquad A = 29 \text{ in.}^2$$

Therefore, the axial load-carrying capacity is

$$P = F_a A = 16.85 \times 29 = 488.7 \text{ kips} < 759 \text{ kips}$$

Hence, two pairs of stiffeners will be required. Try two pairs of stiffeners 11×1 spaced at 9 in. between their outside faces. The cross section of the fictitious column is as shown. The total length of the web participating with the stiffeners is taken as $18t_w$ ($= 11.25$ in., 5.625 in. beyond each stiffener) plus the portion enclosed by the stiffeners. Check strength of the bearing stiffeners as a column.

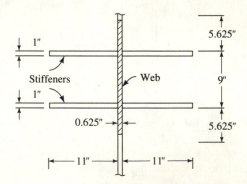

$$9t_w = (9)(0.625) = 5.625 \text{ in.}$$

$$I = (2)\left(\frac{1 \times (11 + 0.625 + 11)^3}{12}\right) = 1930 \text{ in.}^4$$

$$A = (20.25)(0.625) + 4(11)(1.0) = 56.7 \text{ in.}^2$$

$$r = \sqrt{\frac{I}{A}} = \sqrt{\frac{1930}{56.7}} = 5.83 \text{ in.}$$

$$\frac{L}{r} = \frac{90}{5.83} = 15.4$$

$$F_a = 16,980 - 0.53(15.4)^2 = 16,854 \text{ psi} = 16.85 \text{ ksi}$$

The actual stress is

$$f_a = \frac{R}{A} = \frac{759}{56.7} = 13.4 \text{ ksi} < F_a = 16.85 \text{ ksi, OK}$$

Check bearing on the stiffener ends. Allowing 1 in. for cope for welds at the flange-web junctures, the net width of each stiffener is $11 - 1 = 10$ in. The net area in bearing is $A_b = (4 \text{ stiffeners})(10)(1.0) = 40$ in.^{2}

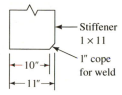

Stiffener
1×11

1" cope
for weld

$\leftarrow 10" \rightarrow$

$\leftarrow 11" \rightarrow$

The actual bearing stress is

$$f_p = \frac{R}{A_b} = \frac{759}{40} = 19 \text{ ksi} < F_p = 29 \text{ ksi, OK}$$

Design of welded connections

Welds for flange-web connection. Maximum shear at the interior support is 473 kips.

$$\text{Shear stress, } \tau = \frac{VQ}{Ib}$$

$$\text{Shear flow, } \tau b = \frac{VQ}{I}$$

$$Q = (2)(24)(46) = 2208 \text{ in.}^3$$

$$\tau b = \frac{(473)(2208)}{241,137} = 4.33 \text{ k/in. for two weld lines}$$

Strength of weld required $= 4.33/2 = 2.17$ kips/in.

For web to flange weld, the stress category is B (tensile stress, with reversal of stresses, continuous fillet welds parallel to direction of applied stress) as shown in AASHTO Illustrated Example 4 (Table A.12, Appendix A, and Figure 10.3.1C). For a redundant path structure, the allowable fatigue stress for 2×10^6 cycles is 16 ksi (Table A.10, Appendix A).

Throat thickness of weld required $= 2.17/18.0 = 0.12$ in.
Size of weld required $= 0.12/0.707 = 0.17$ in.

According to AASHTO 10.23.2.2, the minimum size of the fillet weld required for thickness of the thicker part to be joined $> \frac{3}{4}$ in. is $\frac{5}{16}$ in. Hence, the minimum weld size for 2-in.-thick flange $= \frac{5}{16}$ in. > 0.17 in. Provide $\frac{5}{16}$-in. fillet weld throughout.

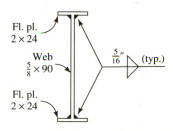

Fl. pl.
2×24

Web
$\frac{5}{8} \times 90$

$\frac{5}{16}"$ (typ.)

Fl. pl.
2×24

Weld for the end stiffeners

Number of weld lines $= 4$ ($= 2 \times 2$ stiffeners)

Stress in weld $= \dfrac{315}{(4)(90)} = 0.875$ k/in.

For a redundant load path structure, the allowable weld stress for transverse stiffener corresponds to stress category C (Table A.10, footnote b, Appendix A). For 2×10^6 cycles, the allowable fatigue stress is 13 ksi. Hence,

Weld size required $= \dfrac{0.875}{(13)(0.707)} = 0.1$ in.

Minimum weld size for 1-in. stiffener $= \frac{5}{16}$ in.

Hence, provide $\frac{5}{16}$-in. fillet welds.

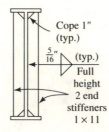

Cope 1″ (typ.)

$\frac{5}{16}$″ (typ.)

Full height
2 end stiffeners
1×11

Weld for bearing stiffeners at the interior support

Number of weld lines $= 8$ ($= 2 \times 4$ stiffeners)

Stress in weld $= \dfrac{759}{(8)(90)} = 1.05$ k/in.

Allowable weld stress $= 12.0$ ksi

Weld size required $= \dfrac{1.05}{(12)(0.707)} = 0.12$ in.

Minimum weld size for a 1-in. stiffener is $\frac{5}{16}$ in. Hence, provide $\frac{5}{16}$-in. fillet welds on both sides of all four stiffeners for their full height.

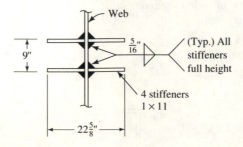

Web

9″

$\frac{5}{16}$″ (Typ.) All stiffeners full height

4 stiffeners
1×11

$22\frac{5}{8}$″

Lateral bracing and cross frames.   Lateral bracing is discouraged for plate girders in general. Bracing requirements can typically be handled by providing cross frames. The following calculations are provided only for illustrative purposes, when cross frames are not provided.

Top flanges.   Haunches are provided in the bottom of the concrete deck as shown, to provide lateral support to the top flanges of stringers and main girders for positive moment only.

Bottom flanges.   In the negative moment region, the bottom flanges of the main girders are under compression. Calculate stress in the bottom flange due to the lateral wind load according to AASHTO 10.20.2 (see discussion in Chapter 8, Sec. 8.4.2*b*).

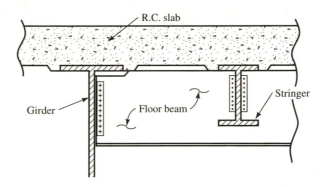

The lateral wind load at 50 lb/ft³ is applied to the exposed area of the bridge (in elevation) (AASHTO 10.21.2; see discussion in Chapter 3). The height from the bottom of girder to the top of parapet is

$H = 94 + 8 + 2 + 13 + 12 = 129$ in. $= 10.75$ ft
Wind load @ 50 lb/ft², $w = (50)(10.75) = 538$ lb/ft > 300 lb/ft, OK
Wind load to bottom flange $= (\frac{1}{2})(538) = 269$ lb/ft

Floor beams spaced at 25 o.c. will act as diaphragms. Therefore,

S_d = diaphragm spacing = 25 ft

$L = 125$ ft

$M_{cb} = 0.08WS_d^2$ lb-ft   (AASHTO Eq. 10.9)

$= (0.08)(269)(25)^2$

$= 13,450$ lb-ft

$$F_{cb} = \frac{72M_{cb}}{t_f b_f^2} \quad \text{(8.4, Chapter 8)}$$

$$= \frac{(72)(13,450)}{(2)(24)^2}$$

$$= 841 \text{ psi}$$

$R = [0.2272L - 11]S_d^{-2/3}$ (8.6, Chapter 8)

$= [(0.2272)(125) - 11](25)^{-2/3}$

$= 2.035$

The maximum stress induced in the bottom flange by the wind is

$$F = RF_{cb} \quad \text{(8.5, Chapter 8)}$$

$$= (2.035)(841) = 1711 \text{ psi} = 1.71 \text{ ksi}$$

Stress in the bottom flange due to loads from the superstructure was computed to be 17.57 ksi. Therefore, the total bending stress in the bottom flange is

$$f_b = 17.57 + 1.71$$

$$= 19.28 \text{ ksi} > F_s = 18.61 \text{ ksi}$$

Hence, lateral bracings may be provided as an option instead of cross frames. The value of R, when lateral bracings are provided, is

$$R = [0.059L - 0.64]S_d^{-1/2} \qquad (8.7, \text{Chapter 8})$$
$$= [(0.059)(125) - 0.64](25)^{-1/2}$$
$$= 1.35$$

The maximum stress induced in the bottom flange by the wind is

$$F = RF_{cb}$$
$$= (1.35)(841) = 1135 \text{ psi} = 1.14 \text{ ksi}$$

Therefore, the total bending stress in the bottom flange is

$$f_b = 17.57 + 1.14$$
$$= 18.71 \text{ ksi} \approx F_s = 18.61 \text{ ksi, OK}$$

The lateral wind load will be transmitted to bearings at the supports (i.e., at the abutments and the interior support), which, in turn, will transmit it to the substructure and finally to the foundation. The *horizontal reactions* due to the wind load at the supports can be computed from the influence area for reactions at supports at A and B (i.e., for R_A and R_B) due to uniform loads, which, respectively, are 0.375 (at the end support) and 1.25 (at the interior support). Accordingly, the horizontal reactions at these supports are

$$R_{AH} = (0.375)(0.269)(125) = 13.9 \text{ kips}$$
$$R_{BH} = (1.250)(0.269)(125) = 42 \text{ kips}$$

Provide bracing arrangement as shown. The force in the bottom chord will be 42 kips. The length of the diagonal member is

$$L = \sqrt{(18)^2 + (4.67)^2} = 18.6 \text{ ft}$$

Therefore, the force in the diagonal is

$$F = (42)\left(\frac{18.6}{18}\right) = 43.4 \text{ kips}$$

Try WT6 × 22.5 for the diagonal member. Its section properties are $A = 6.61$ in.^{2}, $r_x = 1.58$ in. $< r_y = 1.94$ in. Hence, KL/r_x governs.

$$\frac{KL}{r_y} = \frac{(1.0)(18.6)(12)}{1.58} = 141.3$$

$$F_a = 16,980 - 0.53(KL/r)^2$$
$$= 16,980 - 0.53(141.3)^2$$
$$= 6400 \text{ psi} = 6.4 \text{ ksi}$$

Therefore, the axial load capacity of WT6 × 22.5 is

$$P = (F_a)(A) = (6.4)(6.61) = 42.3 \text{ kips} < F = 43.4 \text{ kips, NG}$$

Try WT6 × 25 (next larger size). $A = 7.34$ in.^{2}, $r_x = 1.6$ in., $r_y = 1.96$ in. Since $r_x < r_y$, KL/r_x governs.

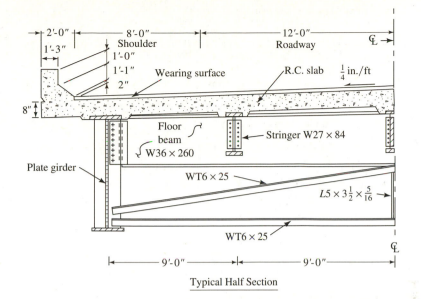

Typical Half Section

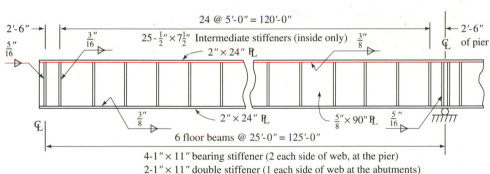

Main Girder Stiffeners

4-1″ × 11″ bearing stiffener (2 each side of web, at the pier)
2-1″ × 11″ double stiffener (1 each side of web at the abutments)

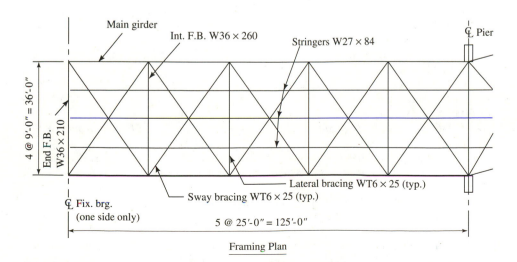

Framing Plan

FIGURE E9.4f
Typical details for the superstructure.

$$\frac{KL}{r_x} = \frac{(1)(18.6)(12)}{1.6} = 139.6$$

$$F_a = 16,980 - 0.53(139.5)^2$$

$$= 6666 \text{ psi} = 6.67 \text{ ksi}$$

Therefore, the axial load capacity of WT6 × 25 is

$$P = (F_a)(A) = (6.7)(7.34) = 48.9 \text{ kips} < F = 43.4 \text{ kips, OK}$$

Provide WT6 × 25 for both the bottom chord and the diagonals for the cross frame at the interior support. Use L5 × $3\frac{1}{2}$ × $\frac{5}{16}$ for the vertical post underneath the floor beam.

The horizontal force in the transverse diaphragms (i.e., at the floor beam locations) is given by Eq. 8.8 (Chapter 8) (AASHTO Eq. 10.10):

$$F_D = 1.14WS_d$$

$$= (1.14)(269)(25)$$

$$= 7667 \text{ lb} = 7.67 \text{ kips} \ll P = 48.9 \text{ kips}$$

For simplicity of connections and uniformity, provide the same arrangement of bracings at all floor beam locations, including those at the abutments. Note that the smallest member permitted for a lateral bracing is L3 × $2\frac{1}{2}$ (AASHTO 10.21.6).

Typical details for the bridge are shown in Fig. E9.4f.

REFERENCES

AASHTO. (1991). *Commentary on ANSI/AASHTO/AWS Bridge Welding Code,* AASHTO, Washington, DC.

——. (1992). *AASHTO Standard Specifications for Highway Bridges,* 15th ed., AASHTO, Washington, DC.

——. (1994). *Interim Specifications—Bridges—1994,* AASHTO, Washington, DC.

AASHTO–LFRD. (1994). *LRFD Bridge Design Specifications, Customary U.S. Units,* 1st ed., AASHTO, Washington, DC.

Adams, P. F. (1966). *Plastic Design in High-Strength Steel,* Ph.D. dissertation, Lehigh University, Bethlehem, PA.

AISC. (1963). *Design Manual for Orthotropic Steel Plate Deck Bridges,* ed., AISC, New York.

——. (1966). *Moments, Shears, and Reactions for Continuous Highway Bridges,* Pub. No. T106, AISC, Chicago.

——. (1986). *Manual of Steel Construction, Load and Resistance and Factor Design,* AISC, Chicago.

——. (1989). *Manual of Steel Construction, Allowable Stress Design,* 9th ed., AISC, Chicago.

——. (1994). *Manual of Steel Construction, Load and Resistance and Factor Design,* vol. I, 2nd ed., AISC, Chicago.

AISI. (1978). *Proposed Criteria for Load and Resistance Factor Design of Steel Building Structures,* Bull. No. 27, AISI, Washington, DC.

Akita, Y., and Fujii, T. (1966a). "Minimum Weight Design of Structures Based on Buckling Strength and Plastic Collapse—1st Rep., Plastic Collapsing Load of Plate Girders Accompanied by Web's Shear Buckling," *J. Soc. Naval Architects of Japan,* no. 119, June, pp. 200–226 (in Japanese).

———. (1966b). "Minimum Weight Design of Structures Based on Buckling Strength and Plastic Collapse—2nd Rep., Strength of Plate Girders in Postbuckling under Combined Bending and Shear," *J. Soc. Naval Architects of Japan,* no. 120, December, pp. 156–164 (in Japanese).

Anderson, K. E., and Chong, K. P. (1986). "Least Cost Computer-Aided Design of Steel Girders," *AISC Eng. J.,* 23(4), 4th Qtr., pp. 151–156.

Anonymous. (1955). "100 Years of Metal Working—Welding, Brazing and Joining," *Iron Age,* June.

ANSI/AASHTO/AWS. (1988). *ANSI/AASHTO/AWS Bridge Welding Code D.1.5-88.* AASHTO, Washington, D.C.

Ardali, S. (1980). *A Parametric Study of the Effect of Longitudinal Stiffeners on the Behaviour of Plate Girders,* MSc thesis, University College, Cardiff, England.

AREA. (1980). *Manual for Railway Engineering—Specifications for Railway Bridges,* AREA, Chicago.

ASCE. (1973). "Suggested Design Guides for Beams with Web Holes," Subcommittee on Beams with Web Openings of the Task Committee on Flexural Members, J. E. Bower, Chairman, *ASCE J. Struct. Div.,* 97(ST11), November, pp. 2702–2728. Disc. 99(ST6), June 1973, pp. 1312–1315.

———. (1974). "Deflection Limitations for Bridges," Progress Report of the Committee on Deflection Limitations of Bridges of the Structural Division, *ASCE Proc. J. Struct. Div.,* Paper 1633, May.

ASCE–AASHO. (1968). "Design of Hybrid Steel Beams," Report of Subcommittee on Hybrid Beams and Girders, Joint ASCE–AASHO Committee on Flexural Members, C. G. Schilling, Chairman, *ASCE J. Struct. Div.,* 94(ST6), June, pp. 1397–1426.

ASCE–AASHTO. (1978). "Theory and Design of Longitudinally Stiffened Plate Girders," Task Committee on Longitudinally Stiffened Plate Girders of the ASCE–AASHTO Committee on Flexural Members of the Committee on Metals of the Structural Division, Andrew Lally, Chairman, *ASCE J. Struct. Div.,* 104(ST4), April, pp. 697–716.

ASCE–WRC. (1971). "Plastic Design in Steel—A Guide and Commentary," *Manual and Reports on Engineering Practice—No. 41,* 2nd ed., ASCE, New York.

Azad, A. K. (1978). "Economic Design of Homogeneous I-Beams," *ASCE J. Struct. Div.,* 104(ST4), April, pp. 637–648.

———. (1980). "Continuous Steel I-Girders: Optimum Proportioning," *ASCE J. Struct. Div.,* 106(ST7), July, pp. 1543–1555.

Badtorf, S. B., and Stein, M. (1947). "Critical Combinations of Shear and Direct Stress for Simply Supported Rectangular Flat Plates," *NACA Tech. Note 1223.*

Barbre, R. (1936). "Beulspannungen in Rechteckplatten mit Langssteifen bei gleichmassiger Druckbeanspruchung," *Der Bauingenieur,* vol. 17, p. 268.

———. (1937). "Stabilitat gleichmassig gedruckter Rechteckplatten mit Langs-oder Quersteifen," *Ingenieur-Archiv,* vol. 8, p. 117.

Barker, M. G., and Hartnagel, B. A. (1994). "Large Scale Girder Testing for More Economical Steel Bridges," *AISC Modern Steel Constr.,* November, pp. 36–40.

Basler, K. (1961a). "Strength of Plate Girder in Shear," *Proc. ASCE, 87* (ST7), October, pp. 151–180 (Paper No. 2967); *Trans. ASCE,* vol. 128, pt. II, 1963, pp. 683–712.

Basler, K. (1961b). "Strength of Plate Girders under Combined Bending and Shear," *Proc. ASCE, 87* (ST7), October, pp. 181–197; *Trans. ASCE,* vol. 128, pt. II, 1963, pp. 720–735.

———. (1961c). "New Provisions for Plate Girder Design," *Proc. AISC Natnl. Eng. Conf.,* Chicago: AISC, pp. 65–74.

Basler, K., and Thurlimann, B. (1959). "Plate Girder Research," *AISC Natnl. Eng. Conf. Proc.*

———. (1960a). "Carrying Capacity of Plate Girders," *IABSE 6th Cong., Prel. Pub.,* vol. 16.

———. (1960b). "Buckling Tests on Plate Girders," *IABSE 6th Cong., Prel. Pub.,* vol. 17.

——. (1961). "Strength of Plate Girders in Bending," *Proc. ASCE, 87* (ST6), August, pp. 153–181 (Paper no. 2913); *Trans. ASCE,* vol. 128, pt. II, 1963, pp. 655–682.

Basler, K., Yen, B. T., Mueller, J. A., and Thurlimann, B. (1960). "Web Buckling Tests on Welded Plate Girders," *Welding Res. Council, Bull.,* no. 64, September.

Batford, S. B., and Stein, M. (1947). "Critical Combinations of Shear and Direct Stress for Simply Supported Rectangular Plates," *NACA Tech. Note 1223.*

Bazant, Z. P., and Cedolin, L. (1991). *Stability of Structures—Elastic, Inelastic, Fracture, and Damage Theories,* Oxford University Press, New York.

Beach, H. T. (1898). "A Theory for Spacing Stiffeners in Plate Girders," 39(20), May, p. 322; 39(23), p. 370; 40(1), p. 10; and 40(6), 1898, p. 90.

——. (1899). "Spacing Stiffeners in Plate Girders," *Engineering News,* 41(7), February, p. 106; discussions: *Engineering News,* 41(15), 1899, p. 234.

Beedle, L. S. (1974). "Introduction," in *Structural Steel Design,* Chapter 1, L. Tall, ed., Ronald Press, New York.

——, ed. (1991). *Stability of Metal Structures, A World View,* Structural Stability Research Council, National Science Foundation and U.S. Trade and Development Program, U.S. International Development Cooperation Agency, Washington, DC.

Beedle, L. S., and Tall, L. (1960). "Basic Column Strength," *ASCE J. Struct. Div.,* 86(ST7), Proc. Paper 2555, July, p. 139.

Bernoulli, J. (1789). "Essai theorique sur les vibrations de plaques elastiques rectangulaires et libres," *Nova Acta Acad. Petropolit,* vol. 5, St. Petersburg, Russia, pp. 197–219.

Bijlaard, P. P. (1940–1941). "Theory of Plastic Stability of Thin Plates," *IABSE Pub.,* vol. VI, p. 45.

——. (1947). "Some Contributions to the Theory of Elastic and Plastic Stability," *IABSE Pub.,* vol. VIII, p. 17.

Bishop, E. D. (1962). "Welded Plate Girder Bridge with 450 ft Main Span," *ASCE Civ. Eng.,* October, pp. 52–55.

Bleich, F. (1924). "Theorie und Berechnung der eisernen Brucken," Julius Springer, Berlin.

——. (1952). *Buckling Strength of Metal Structures,* Ch. 11, McGraw-Hill Companies, Inc., New York.

Blodgett, O. W. (1963). "Current Practices in Plate Girder Design," *Welding J.,* 42(5), pp. 411–420.

——. (1966). *Design of Welded Structures,* James F. Lincoln Arc Welding Foundation, Cleveland, OH.

Boobnov,[46] J. G. (1914). *Stoitel'nai Mekhanika Korablia, (Theory of Structure of Ships),* vol. 2, St. Petersburg, p. 515 (in Russian).

Bornscheuer, F. W. (1947). *Contribution to the Calculation of Flat Uniformly Loaded Rectangular Plates, Reinforced by a Longitudinal Stiffener* (in German), dissertation, Darmstadt.

Bower, J. E. (1966a). "Elastic Stresses around Holes in Wide-Flange Beams," *ASCE J. Struct. Div.,* 92(ST2), April, pp. 85–101.

——. (1966b). "Experimental Stresses in Wide-Flange Beams with Holes," *ASCE J. Struct. Div.,* 92(ST5), October, pp. 167–186.

——. (1968). "Ultimate Strength of Beams with Rectangular Holes," *ASCE J. Struct. Div.,* 94(ST6), June, pp. 1315–1337.

Breen, F. L. (1972). "Load Factor Design of W-Beams," in *Four Design Examples, Load Factor Design of Steel Highway Bridges,* AISI Pub. 123(PS010), AISI, New York, pp.1-1–1-14; 1-1E–1-16E.

---

[46]Frequently transliterated as Boobnoff or Bubnov.

Bresler, B., Lin, T. Y., and Scalzi, J. (1968). *Design of Steel Structures,* 2nd ed., John Wiley & Sons, New York, pp. 497–554.

Brockenbrough, R. L., and Johnston, B. G. (1974). *United States Steel Design Manual,* U.S. Steel Corp., Pittsburgh.

Bryan, G. H. (1891). "On the Stability of a Plane Plate under Thrusts in Its Own Plane with Application on the 'Buckling' of the Sides of a Ship," *Proc. London Math. Soc.,* vol. 22, p. 54.

BSI. (1982). *Steel, Concrete, and Composite Bridges,* British Standard BS5400: Part 3, *Code of Practice for Design of Steel Bridges,* British Standard Institution, London.

Budiansky, B., and Connor, R. W. (1948). "Buckling Stresses in Clamped Rectangular Flat Plates in Shear," *NACA Tech. Note 1559.*

Bulson, P. S. (1969). *Stability of Flat Plates,* American Elsevier, New York.

Burdette, E. G., and Goodpasture, D. W. (1971). *Full-Scale Bridge Testing and Evaluation of Bridge Design Criteria,* University of Tennessee, Knoxville.

Calladine, C. R. (1973). "A Plastic Theory of Collapse of Plate Girders under Combined Shearing Force and Bending Moment," *Struct. Engineer,* 51(4), April, pp. 147–154.

Carskaddan, P. S. (1958). "Shear Buckling of Unstiffened Hybrid Beams," *ASCE J. Struct. Div.,* 94(ST8), August, pp. 1965–1990.

Chan, P. B., and Redwood, R. G. (1974). "Stresses in Beams with Circular Eccentric Web Holes," *ASCE J. Struct. Div.,* 100(ST1), January, pp. 231–248.

Charlton, T. M. (1976). "Theoretical Work," in *The Works of Isambard Kingdom Brunel,* A. Pugsley, ed., Institute of Civil Engineers, University of Bristol, England, p. 191.

Chatterjee, S. (1981). "Design of Webs and Stiffeners in Plate Girders," in *The Design of Steel Bridges,* Granada Publishing, St. Albans, England.

Chern, C., and Ostapenko, A. (1969). "Ultimate Strength of Plate Girders under Shear," *Fritz Eng. Lab. Rep. No. 328.7,* Lehigh University, Bethlehem, PA, August.

———. (1970a). "Bending Strength of Unsymmetrical Plate Girders," *Fritz. Eng. Lab. Rep. No. 328.8,* Lehigh University, Bethlehem, PA, September.

———. (1970b). "Unsymmetric Plate Girders under Shear and Moment," *Fritz. Eng. Lab. Rep. No. 328.9,* Lehigh University, Bethlehem, PA, October.

———. (1971). "Ultimate Strength of Longitudinally Stiffened Plate Girders under Combined Loads," *IABSE Proc. Colloq. Design of Plate and Box Girders for Ultimate Strength,* London.

Chow, L., Conway, H. D., and Winter, G. (1952). "Stresses in Deep Beams," *Proc. ASCE, 78, Separate No. 127,* May.

Chwalla, E. (1936). "Beitrag zur stabilitatstheorie des Stegbleches vollwandiger Trager," *Der Stahlbau,* vol. 9, p. 161.

Clark, E. (1850). *The Britannia and Conway Tubular Bridges,* vols. 1 and 2, Day and Son, London.

Clark, J. W., and Sharp, M. L. (1971). "Limit Design of Aluminum Shear Web," *IABSE Proc. Colloq. Design of Plate and Box Girders for Ultimate Strength,* London.

Cooper, P. B. (1965). "Bending and Shear Strength of Longitudinally Stiffened Plate Girders," *Fritz Eng. Lab. Rep. No. 304.6,* Lehigh University, Bethlehem, PA, September.

———. (1967). "Strength of Longitudinally Stiffened Plate Girders," *ASCE J. Struct. Div.,* 93(ST2), Proc. Paper 5211, April, pp. 419–451.

———. (1974). "Plate Girders," in *Structural Steel Design,* 2nd ed., Chapter 8, L. Tall, ed., Ronald Press, New York.

Cooper, P. B., Galambos, T. V., and Ravindra, M. K. (1978). "LRFD Criteria for Plate Girders," *ASCE J. Struct. Div.,* 104(ST9), September, pp. 1389–1407.

Cooper, P. B., Lew, H. S., and Yen, B. T. (1964). "Welded Constructional Alloy Plate Girders," *Proc. ASCE J. Struct. Div.* 90(ST1), February, pt. 1, paper 3784, pp. 1–36.

Cooper, P. B., and Roychowdhury, J. (1990). "Shear Strength of Plate Girders with Web Openings," *ASCE J. Str. Eng.,* 116(7), July, pp. 2042–2048.

Cooper, P. B., and Snell, R. R. (1972). "Tests on Beams with Reinforced Web Openings," *ASCE J. Struct. Div.,* 98(ST3), March, pp. 611–632.

Cooper, P. B., Snell, R. R., and Knostman, H. D. (1977). "Failure Tests on Beams with Eccentric Web Holes," *ASCE J. Struct. Div.,* 103(ST9), September, pp. 1731–1738.

Cooper, S. C., and Chen, A. C. (1985). *Designing Steel Structures: Methods and Cases,* Prentice-Hall, Englewood Cliffs, NJ.

CRC. (1966). *Guide to Design Criteria for Metal Compression Members,* Column Research Council, 2nd ed., B. G. Johnston, ed., John Wiley & Sons, New York.

D'Apice, M. A., Fielding, D. J., and Cooper, P. B. (1966). "Static Tests on Longitudinally Stiffened Plate Girders," *Welding Research Council Bull. No. 117,* October; "Strength of Plate Girders with Longitudinal Stiffeners," *Bull. No. 16,* AISI, April 1969, Paper No. III (includes historical survey of bibliography on longitudinally stiffened plates).

Darwin, D. (1990). *Steel and Composite Beams with Web Openings,* AISC, Steel Design Guide Series 2, AISI, Chicago.

Davies, G., and Mandel, S. N. (1979). "The Collapse Behavior of Tapered Plate Girders Loaded within the Tip," *Proc. Inst. Civ. Engrs.,* London, vol. 67, part 2.

Desai, S. (1969a). "Tension Testing Procedure," *Fritz Eng. Lab. Rep. No. 273.44,* Lehigh University, Bethlehem, PA, February.

————. (1969b). "Mechanical Properties of A572 Grade 65 Steel," *Fritz Eng. Lab. Rep. No. 343.2,* Lehigh University, Bethlehem, PA, September.

Dhillon, B. S. (1991). "Optimum Design of Composite Hybrid Plate Girders," *ASCE J. Struct. Eng.,* 117(7), July, pp. 2088–2098.

Donahey, R. C. (1987). "Deflections of Composite Beams with Web Openings," *Building Structures, Proc. ASCE Structures Congress,* D. R. Shermon, ed., Orlando, FL, August, pp. 404–417.

Donahey, R. C., and Darwin, D. (1986). "Performance and Design of Composite Beams with Web Openings," *Struct. Eng. and Eng. Mat. SM Rep. No. 18,* University of Kansas for Research, Lawrence, KS.

Donnell, L. H. (1976). *Beams, Plates, and Shells,* McGraw-Hill Companies, Inc., New York.

Dornen, A. (1951). "Stahlbau-Tagung Stuttgard," in W. Dorn, ed. *Abhandungen aus dem Stahlbau.*

Dougherty, B. K. (1980), "Elastic Deformation of Beams with Web Openings," *ASCE J. Struct. Div.,* 106(ST1), January, pp. 301–312.

Dubas, C. (1948). "Contribution a L'etude du Voilement des Toles Raidies" ("A Contribution of the Study of Buckling of Stiffened Plates"), *IABSE Prelim. Pub., 3rd Congress,* Leige, p. 129.

Dubas, P. (1971). "Tests on Post-Critical Behavior of Stiffened Box Girders," *IABSE Proc. Colloq. Design of Plate and Box Girders for Ultimate Strength,* London.

Dwight, J. B., and Ratcliffe, A. T. (1967). "The Strength of Thin Plates in Compression," *Proc. Symp. at University College of Swansea on Thin-Walled Steel Structures,* September.

El Gaaly, M. A. (1983). "Web Design under Compressive Edge Loads," *AISC Eng. J.,* 20(4), 4th Qtr., pp. 153–171.

Elliott, A. L. (1960). "How to Use High-Strength Steel Effectively," *Eng. News-Rec.,* February 18, pp. 52–60.

————. (1962). "A Structural Future for Alloy Steels," National Research Council, *Hwy. Res. Board, Bull. 346,* January, pp. 27–40.

ENR. (1956). "Plate Girder Bridge Sets Record with 856-Foot Span," *Eng. News-Rec.,* 159(6), August 8, pp. 46–47.

Erickson, E. L., and VanEenam, N. (1957). "Application and Development of AASHO Specifications to Bridge Design," *Proc. ASCE,* 83 (ST4), July, p. 1320.

Errera, S. J. (1974). "Materials," in *Structural Steel Design,* L. Tall, ed., Ronald Press, New York.

Euler, L. (1766). "De Motu Vibratorio Tympanorum," *Novi Commentari Acad. Petropolit,* 10, pp. 243–260.

Evans, H. R. (1983). "Longitudinally and Transversely Reinforced Plate Girders," Ch. 1 in *Plated Structures, Stability and Strength,* R. Narayanan, ed., Applied Science Publishers, New York.

Evans, H. R., Rocky, K. C., and Porter, D. M. (1976). "Unifying Method for the Ultimate Load Design for Plate Girders Subject to Shear and Bending," *Report,* University College, Cardiff, Wales.

Evans, H. R., and Tang, K. H. (1981). "A Report on Five Tests Carried Out on a Large Scale Transversely Stiffened Plate Girder," *TRV3, Report No. DT/SC/8,* University College, Cardiff, England.

Fairbairn, W. (1849). *An Account of the Construction of the Britannia and Conway Tubular Bridges,* Longman, Brown, Green and Longmans, London.

———. (1854). *On the Application of Cast and Wrought Iron to Building Purposes,* Longmans, Green and Co., London.

Falby, W. E., and Lee, G. C. (1976). "Tension-Field Design of Tapered Webs," *AISC Eng. J.* 13(1), p. 11.

Fisher, J. W. (1977). *Bridge Fatigue Guide, Design and Details,* AISC, New York.

———. (1984). *Fatigue and Fracture in Steel Bridges—Case Studies,* John Wiley & Sons, New York.

Fisher, J. W., Galambos, T. V., Kulak, G. L., and Mayasandra, K. (1978). "Load and Resistance Design Criteria for Connectors," *ASCE J. Struct. Div.,* 104(ST9), September, pp. 1427–1441.

Fleischer, W. H. (1985). "Design and Optimization of Plate Girders and Weld-Fabricated Beams for Building Construction," *AISC Eng. J.,* 22(1), 1st Qtr., pp. 1–10.

Flint, A. R., and Edwards, L. S. (1970). "Limit State Design of Highway Bridges," *Struct. Engineer,* 48(3), March, pp. 93–198.

Foil, J. R. (1992). "What Engineers Can Do to Reduce Bridge Fabrication Costs," *AISC Modern Steel Constr.,* September, p. 28.

Frankland, J. M. (1940). "The Strength of Ship Plating under Edge Compression," *David Taylor Model Basin Report 469,* Washington, DC.

Frost, R. W., and Leffler, R. E. (1971). "Fatigue Tests of Beams with Rectangular Web Holes," *ASCE J. Struct. Div.,* 97 (ST2) February, pp. 509–527.

Frost, R. W., and Schilling, C. G. (1964). "Behavior of Hybrid Beams Subjected to Static Loads," *ASCE J. Struct. Div.,* 90(ST3), June, pt. 1, paper 3928, pp. 55–88.

Fujii, T. (1967). "Minimum Weight Design of Structures Based on Buckling Strength and Plastic Collapse—3rd Report: An Improved Theory on Post-Buckling Strength of Plate Girders in Shear," *J. Soc. Naval Architects of Japan, No. 122,* December, pp. 119–128 (in Japanese).

———. (1968a). "On an Improved Theory for Dr. Basler's Theory," *IABSE Proc. 8th Congress,* New York, September, pp. 477–487.

———. (1968b). "On Ultimate Strength of Plate Girders," *Japan Shipbuilding and Marine Engineering,* May.

———. (1971). "A Comparison between Theoretical Values and Experimental Results for the Ultimate Shear Strength of Plate Girders," *IABSE, Proc. Colloq. Design of Plate and Box Girders for Ultimate Strength,* London.

Galambos, T. V. (1972). "Load Factor Design of Steel Buildings," *AISC Eng. J.,* 9(3). July, pp. 108–113.

———. (1981). "Load and Resistance Factor Design," *AISC Eng. J.,* 18(3), pp. 74–82.

Galambos, T. V., and Ravindra, M. K. (1978). "Proposed Criteria for Load and Resistance Factor Design," *AISC Eng. J.,* 15(1), 1st Qtr., pp. 8–17.

Galambos, T. V., Reinhold, T. A., and Ellingwood, B. (1982). "Serviceability Limit States: Connection Slip," *ASCE J. Struct. Div.,* 108(ST2), December, pp. 2668–2680.

Gatti, W. (1994). "Economical Steel Bridge Details," *AISC Modern Steel Constr.,* September, pp. 24–29.

Gaylord, E. H., Jr. (1963b). "Discussion of 'Strength of Plate Girder in Shear,' " *Trans. ASCE,* vol. 128, pt. II, pp. 712–715.

Gaylord, E. H., Jr., and Gaylord, C. N., eds. (1990). *Structural Engineering Handbook,* 3rd ed., McGraw-Hill Companies, Inc., New York.

Gaylord, E. H., Jr., Gaylord, C. N., and Stallmeyer, J. E. (1957/1992). *Design of Steel Structures,* McGraw-Hill Companies, Inc., New York.

Gerard, G. (1957). "Handbook of Structural Stability," pt. IV, *NACA Tech. Note 3784,* Washington, DC.

———. (1960). "Strength and Efficiency Aspects of Plate Girders," *Proc. ASCE J. Eng. Mech. Div.,* 86(EM2), pt. 1, paper 2439, April, pp. 17–33.

———. (1962). *Introduction to Structural Stability Theory,* McGraw-Hill Companies, Inc., New York.

Gerard, G. and Becker, H. (1957). "Handbook of Structural Stability. Part I—Buckling of Flat Plates," *NACA Tech. Note 3871,* Washington, DC, July.

Gies, J. (1963). *Bridges and Men,* The Universal Library, Grosset and Dunlap, New York, p. 123.

Gonulsen, W. H. (1972). "Two-Span Continuous Composite Welded Girder Highway Bridge," in *Four Design Examples—Load Factor Design of Steel Highway Bridges,* Publication No. P123(PS010), AISI, New York.

Guzek, T. P., and Grzybowski, J. R. (1992). "Reducing Bridge Fabrication Costs," *AISC Modern Steel Constr.,* September, pp. 24–27.

Haaijer, G. (1959). "Plate Buckling in the Strain-Hardening Range," *Trans. ASCE,* vol. 124, Paper No. 2968, pp. 117–148. Also *ASCE J. Eng. Mech. Div.,* 83(EM2), Proc. Paper 1212, April 1957.

———. (1961). "Economy of High-Strength Steel Structural Members," *Proc. ASCE J. Struct. Div.,* 87(ST8), December, paper 3010, pp. 1–23.

Haaijer, G. and Thurlimann, B. (1959). "On Inelastic Buckling in Steel," *ASCE. J. Eng. Mech. Div.,* 84(EM2), Proc. Paper 1581, April; *Trans. ASCE,* vol. 125(I), 1960, p. 308.

Hadley, H. M. (1961a). "Exploratory Tests on Steel Delta Girder," *ASCE Civ. Eng.,* May, pp. 50–52.

———. (1961b). "Delta Girders for Short Steel Span," *Eng. News-Rec.,* May 25, pp. 27–28.

———. (1962). "Delta Girder Design Grows Up," *Eng. News-Rec.,* May 17, pp. 40–41.

———. (1964). "Bridge Delta Girder—Single-Webbed and Double-Webbed," *AISC Eng. J.,* 1(4), October, pp. 132–136.

Hall, L. R., and Stallmeyer, J. E. (1964). "Thin Web Girder Fatigue Behavior as Influenced by Boundary Rigidity," *University of Illinois, Dept. Civ. Eng., Struct. Research Series, 278,* January.

Hamilton, S. B. (1958). "Building Materials and Techniques," in *A History of Technology,* Singer, C., Holmyard, E. J., and Donaldson, J. M., eds., Clarendon Press, Oxford, England, vol. 5, p. 472.

Heins, C. P. (1980). "LRFD Criteria for Composite Steel I-Beam Bridges," *ASCE J. Struct. Div.,* 106(ST11), November, pp. 2297–2312.

Heins, C. P., and Firmage, D. A. (1979). *Design of Modern Steel Highway Bridges,* John Wiley & Sons, New York.

Heins, C. P., and Kuo, T. C. (1973). "Live-Load Distribution on Composite Highway Bridges at Ultimate Load," *Civ. Eng. Report No. 53,* University of Maryland, College Park, MD, April.

———. (1975). "Ultimate Live-Load Distribution Factor for Bridges," *ASCE J. Struct. Div.,* 101(ST7), July, pp. 1481–1496.

Heins, C. P., and Kurzweil, A. D. (1976). "Load Factor Design of Continuous Span Bridges," *ASCE J. Struct. Div.,* 102(ST6), June, pp. 1213–1228.

Herzog, M. A. M. (1974a). "Die Traglast unversteifter und versteifter dunnwandiger Blechtrager unter reinem Schub und Schub mit Biegung nach Versuchen," *Bauingenieur,* October.

———. (1974b). "Ultimate Strength of Plate Girders from Tests," *ASCE J. Struct. Div.,* 100(ST5), pp. 849–864.

Hoff, N. J. (1956). *The Analysis of Structures,* John Wiley & Sons, New York.

Hoglund, T. (1971a). "Behavior and Load Carrying Capacity of Thin-Plate I-Girders," *Royal Inst. of Tech. Bull. No. 93,* Stockholm, Sweden (in Swedish).

———. (1971b). "Simply Supported Thin-Plate I-Girders without Web Stiffeners Subjected to Distributed Transverse Load," *IABSE Proc. Colloq. Design of Plate and Box Girders for Ultimate Strength,* London.

———. (1971c). "Strength of Thin-Plate Girders with Circular or Rectangular Web Holes without Web Stiffeners," *IABSE Proc. Colloq. Design of Plate and Box Girders for Ultimate Strength,* London.

———. (1973). "Design of Thin-Plate I-Girders in Shear and Bending," *Royal Inst. of Tech. Bull. No. 94,* Stockholm, Sweden (in Swedish).

Hollister, L. C., and Sunbury, R. D. (1960). "High-Strength Steels Show Economy for Bridges," *ASCE Civ. Eng.,* June, pp. 60–63.

Hopkins, H. J. (1970). *A Span of Bridges,* Praeger Publishers, New York.

Ilyushin, A. A. (1947). "The Elasto-Plastic Stability of Plates," translation in *NACA Tech. Memo. 1188.*

Imbsen and Associates. (1991). *Distribution of Loads in Bridges,* NCHRP Project 12-26, Transportation Research Board, National Research Council, Washington, DC.

Jewett, R. A. (1967). "Structural Antecedents of the I-Beam, 1800–1850," *Technology and Culture,* 8, pp. 350–355.

Johnston, B. G., Lin, F. J., and Galambos, T. V. (1986). *Basic Steel Design,* Prentice Hall, Englewood Cliffs, NJ.

Jombock, J. R., and Clark, J. W. (1962). "Postbuckling Behavior of Flat Plates," *Trans. ASCE,* 127(II), p. 227.

Karol, J. (1963). "Calcasieu River Bridge," *Welding J.,* 42(11), November, pp. 867–870, 877–880.

Kerenshy, O. A., Flint, A. R., and Brown, W. C. (1956). "The Basis for Design of Beams and Plate Girders in the Revised British Standard 153," *Proc. Inst. Civ. Eng.* (London), pt. III, 5, August, pp. 396–444.

Kleeman, P. W. (1956). *The Buckling Strength of Simply Supported, Infinitely Long Plates with Transverse Stiffeners,* Her Majesty's Stationery Office, Aeronautical Research Council, Reports and Memoranda 2971, London.

Klitchieff, J. M. (1949). "On the Stability of Plates Reinforced by Ribs," *Trans. ASME J. Appl. Mech.,* vol. 71, March, pp. 74–76.

Kloppel, K. K., and Moller, K. H. (1968). *Beulwerte Ausgesteifter Rechteckplatten,* vol. 2, Verlag von Wilhelm Ernst und Sohn, Berlin.

Kloppel, K. K., and Scheer, J. (1956). *Stahlbau,* 25, p. 117 and 225.

———. (1957). *Stahlbau,* 26, p. 246 and 364.

———. (1960). *Beulwerte Ausgesteifter Rechteckplatten,* vol. 1, Verlag von Wilhelm Ernst und Sohn, Berlin.

Knight, R. P. (1984). "Economical Steel Plate Girder Bridges," *AISC Eng. J.,* 2nd Qtr., pp. 89–93; presented at the National Bridge Conference, Pittsburgh, PA, June 1, 1983.

Kollbrunner, C. F., and Meister, M. (1958). *Ausbeulen (Buckling of Plates),* Springer Verlag, Berlin.

Komatsu, S. (1971). "Ultimate Strength of Stiffened Plate Girders Subjected to Shear," *IABSE, Proc. Colloq. Design of Plate and Box Girders for Ultimate Strength,* London, pp. 49–65.

Komatsu, S., Moriwaki, Y., Fujino, M., and Takimoto, T. (1984). "Ultimate Strength of Girders in Combined Load," *ASCE J. Struct. Eng.,* 110(4), April, pp. 754–768.

Krishnan, S., and Shetty, K. V. (1961). "Method of Minimum Weight Design for Thin-Walled Beam," *Struct. Eng.,* 39(5), May, pp. 174–180.

Kroll, W. D. (1943). "Tables of Stiffness and Carry-Over Factor for Flat Rectangular Plates under Compression," *NACA Wartime Rept. L-398.*

Kromm, A., and Marguerre, K. (1937). "Verhalten eines von Schub und Druckkraften beanspruchten Plattenstreifens oberhalb Beulgrenze," *Luftfahrt-Forschung,* vol. 17, p. 62.

Kuhn, P., and Peterson, J. P. (1947). "Strength Analysis of Stiffened Beam Webs," *NACA Tech. Note 1364.*

Kuhn, P., Peterson, J. P., and Levin, R. L. (1952). "A Summary of Diagonal Tension," pt. 1, vol. 1, *NACA Tech. Note 2661.*

Kulak, G. L., Fisher, J. W., and Struik, J. H. (1987). *Guide to Design Criteria for Bolted and Riveted Joints,* 2nd ed., John Wiley & Sons, New York.

Kussman, R. L., and Cooper, P. B. (1976). "Design Example for Beams with Web Openings," *AISC Eng. J.,* 13(2), 2nd Qtr., pp. 48–56.

Kuzmanowic, B. O., and Williams, N. (1983). *Steel Design for Structural Engineers,* 2nd ed., Prentice Hall, Englewood Cliffs, NJ, pp. 450–451, 619–621.

Lahde, R., and Wagner, H. (1936). "Test for the Determination of Stress Concentration in Tension Fields," *NACA Tech. Memo. 809.*

Lambert, T., ed. (1974). *Structural Steel Design,* Ronald Press, New York.

Larson, M. A., and Shah, K. N. (1976). "Plastic Design of Web Openings in Steel Beams," *ASCE J. Struct. Div.,* 102(ST5), May, pp. 1031–1041.

Laviolette, M. (1968). "Bridge No. 34 on the Wallonia Motorway (Belgium)," *Acier-Stahl-Steel,* 33(6), June, pp. 288–293.

Lay, M. G. (1965). "Flange Local Buckling in Wide-Flange Shapes," *ASCE J. Struct. Div.,* 91(ST6), Proc. Paper 4554, December, pp. 95–116.

Lay, M. G., and Galambos, T. V. (1964). "The Inelastic Behavior of Steel Beams under Moment Gradient," *Fritz Eng. Lab. Rep. No. 297.12,* Lehigh University, Bethlehem, PA, July.

———. (1965). "Inelastic Steel Beams under Uniform Moment," *ASCE J. Struct. Div.,* 91(ST6), Proc. Paper 4566, December.

———. (1967). "Inelastic Steel Beams under Moment Gradient," *Proc. ASCE J. Struct. Div.,* 93(ST1), February, pp. 381–399.

Leet, K. M. (1988). *Fundamentals of Structural Analysis,* Macmillan, New York.

Leonhardt, F., and Pelikan, W. (1951). "Grundsatzliches zum Entwurf und zur baulichen Durchbildung—Die Neue Koln–Mulheimer Brucke," *Herausgegeben von der Stadt Koln,* p. 16.

Levy, S. K., Fienup, K. L., and Wooley, R. M. (1945). "Analysis of Square Shear Web above Buckling Load," *NACA Tech. Note 962.*

———. (1946). "Analysis of Deep Rectangular Shear Web above Buckling Load," *NACA Tech. Note 1009.*

Lew, H. S., and Toprac, A. A. (1967). "Fatigue Strength of Hybrid Plate Girders under Constant Moment," *Proc. Hwy. Res. Board,* 40th Annual Meeting.

Lim, L. C., Lu, L. W., and Beedle, L. S. (1969). "Mechanical Properties of ASTM A36 and A441 Steel," *Fritz Eng. Lab. Rep. No. 343.14,* Lehigh University, Bethlehem, PA, August.

Lincoln Electric Co. (1957). *Procedure Handbook of Arc Welding Design and Practice,* 11th ed., part 1 (reprinted 1967). James F. Lincoln Arc Welding Foundation, Cleveland, Ohio.

Lokshin, A. S. (1935). "On the Calculation of Plates with Ribs," *J. Applied Math. and Mechanics,* vol. 2, Moscow, p. 225 (in Russian).

Longbottom, E., and Heyman, J. (1956). "Experimental Verification of the Strengths of Plate Girders Designed in Accordance with the Revised British Standard 153: Tests on Full-Size and Model Plate Girders," *Proc. Inst. Civ. Eng.,* London, vol. 5, part III, p. 462.

Lundquist, E. E. (no year). "Comparison of Three Methods for Calculating the Compressive Strength of Flat and Slightly Curved Sheets and Stiffener Combination," *NACA Tech. Note 455.*

Lundquist, E. E., and Stowell, E. Z. (1942). "Critical Compressive Stress for Flat Rectangular Plates Supported along All Edges and Elastically Restrained against Rotation along the Unloaded Edges," *NACA Tech. Note 733;* "Critical Compressive Stress for Outstanding Flanges," *NACA Tech. Note 734.*

Lyse, I., and Godfrey, H. J. (1935). "Investigation of Web Buckling in Steel Beams," *Trans., ASCE,* 100, pp. 675–706.

Mandel, J. A., Brennen, P. J., Wasil, B. A., and Antoni, C. M. (1971). "Stress Distribution in Castellated Beams," *ASCE J. Struct. Div.,* 97(ST7), July, pp. 1947–1967.

Massonet, C. E. L. (1940–1941). "La stabilite de l'ame de poutres munies de raidisseurs horizontaux et sollicitees par flexion pure," *IABSE Pub. 6.,* p. 233.

———. (1960). "Stability Considerations in the Design of Steel Plate Girders," *ASCE J. Struct. Div.,* 86(ST1), Proc. Paper 2350, January, pp. 71–97; *Trans. ASCE,* vol. 127, pt. II, 1962, pp. 420–447.

Massonnet, C. E. L., Mas, E., and Maus, H. (1962). "Essais de voilment sur deux poutres a membrures et raidisseurs tubulaires," *IABSE Pub.,* vol. XXII.

Massonnet, C. E. L., Mazy, G., and Tanghe, A. (1960). "Theorie generale du voilement des plaques rectangulaires orthotropes, encastrees ou appuyees sur leur contour, munies de raidisseurs paralleles aux bords a grandes rigidites flexionnelle et torsionelle," *IABSE Pub. 20,* pp. 223–262.

McCormac, J. (1992). *Structural Steel Design, ASD Method,* 4th ed., HarperCollins Publishers, New York.

McMormic, M. M. (1972a). *Open Web Beams—Behavior, Analysis, and Design,* BHP Report, MRL 17/18, Melbourne Research Laboratories, The Broken Hill Proprietary Co. Ltd., Clayton, Victoria, Australia.

———. (1972b). "Discussion of 'Suggested Design Guides for Beams with Web Holes,' " *ASCE J. Struct Div.,* 98(ST12), December, pp. 2814–2816.

Merritt, F. S., ed. (1992). *Structural Steel Designer's Handbook,* McGraw-Hill Companies, Inc., New York.

Meszaros, I., and Djubek, J. (1966). "Vplyv Tuhosti Vystuh na Deformativ nost Stien," *Stavebnicky Caposis,* SAV XIV3, Bratislava.

Milosavljevitch, M. (1947). "Sur la stabilite des plaques rectangulaires reinforcees par des raidisseurs et sollicitees a al flexion et au cissaillement," *IABSE Pub., 8,* p. 141.

Mistry, V. (1994). "Economical Steel Bridge Construction," *AISC Modern Steel Constr.,* March, pp. 42–47.

Modjeski and Masters. (1991). *LRFD Bridge Design Code,* NCHRP Project 12-33, Transportation Research Board, National Research Council, Washington, DC.

Moisseiff, L. S., and Lienhard, F. (1941). "Theory of Elastic Stability Applied to Structural Design," *Trans. Am. Soc. Civil Engrs.,* 106, p. 1052.

Moon, T. J., and Maun, V. P. (1972). "Design of a Three-Span Noncomposite Plate Girder Using the Tentative Criteria for Load Factor Design of Steel Highway Bridges," in *Four Design Examples—Load Factor Design of Steel Highway Bridges,* Publication No. P123(PS010), AISI, New York, pp. 2-1–2-24.

Moore, H. F. (1913). "The Strength of I-Beams in Flexure," University of Illinois, Bull. 68, University of Illinois, Urbana, pp. 20–21.

Moore, H. F., and Wilson, W. M. (1916). *Strength of Webs of I-Beams and Girders,* University of Illinois, Bull. 86, University of Illinois, Urbana.

Moriwaki, Y., and Fujino, M. (1976). "Buckling Strength, Load-Carrying Capacity of Plate Girders with Initial Imperfections," *Proc. Symp. Fabrication and Erection of Structures,* 21st National Symposium on Bridge and Structural Engineering, Japan Society for the Promotion of Science, Tokyo, Japan, March, pp. 209–234.

Morris, J. L. (1954). *Welding Processes and Procedures,* Prentice Hall, Englewood Cliffs, NJ, p. 3.

Mueller, J. A., and Yen, B. T. (1968). "Girder Web Boundary Stresses and Fatigue," *WRC Bull.* 127, January.

Narayanan, R. (1980). *Ultimate Capacity of Plate Girders Containing Cutouts,* University College, Cardiff, Report.

Narayanan, R. (1983). "Ultimate Shear Capacity of Plate Girders with Openings in Their Webs," Chapter 2 in *Plated Structures—Stability and Strength,* R. Narayanan, ed., Applied Science Publishers, London and New York, pp. 39–76.

Narayanan, R., and Der-Avanessian, N. G. V. (1981a). *A Theoretical Model for the Prediction of Ultimate Capacity of Webs with Circular Cutouts,* University College, Cardiff, Report.

———. (1981b). *Theoretical Models for the Assessment of Ultimate Capacity of Plate Girders Containing Central Rectangular Cutouts and Eccentric Circular Cutouts,* University College, Cardiff, Report.

———. (1982a). *Elastic Buckling of Perforated Plates under Shear,* University College, Cardiff, Report.

———. (1982b). *Ultimate Capacity of Plate Girders Containing Holes in Webs,* University College, Cardiff, Report.

———. (1985). "Design of Slender Webs Having Rectangular Holes," *ASCE J. Struct. Eng.,* 111(4), April, pp. 777–787.

Narayanan, R., and Rockey, K. C. (1981). "Ultimate Capacity of Plate Girders with Webs Containing Circular Cutouts," *Proc. Inst. Civ. Engrs.,* part 2, 72, pp. 845–862, London.

Navier, L. M. H. (1823). *Bull. Soc. Philosophique-mathematique,* Paris, p. 92.

NCHRP. (1990). *Distortion-Induced Fatigue Cracking in Steel Bridges,* NCHRP Report 336, Transportation Research Board, Washington, DC.

Nylander, H. (1956). "Torsion, Bending and Lateral Buckling of I-Beams," Royal Stockholm Inst. Technology, *Trans. 102.*

O'Connor, C. (1964). "The Buckling of a Monosymmetric Beam Loaded in the Plane of Symmetry," *Australian J. Appl. Sci.,* 15(4), December, pp. 191–203.

———. (1971). *Design of Bridge Superstructures,* John Wiley & Sons, New York.

O'Connor, C., Goldsmith, P. R., and Ryall, J. T. (1965), "The Reinforcement of Slender Steel Beams to Improve Beam Buckling Strength," Inst. Civ. Engrs. (Australia), *Civ. Eng. Trans.,* CE7(1), April, pp. 29–38.

Osgood, W. R. (1939). "A Theory of Flexure for Beams with Nonparallel Extreme Fibers," *Trans. ASME J. Appl. Mech.,* vol. 61, pp. A122–A126.

Ostapenko, A. (1974). "Local Buckling," in *Structural Steel Design,* Ch. 17, 2nd ed., L. Tall, ed., The Ronald Press, New York.

Ostapenko, A., and Chern, C. (1970). "Strength of Longitudinally Stiffened Plate Girders," *Fritz Eng. Lab. Rep. No. 328.10,* Lehigh University, Bethlehem, PA, December.

Owen, D. R. J., Rockey, K. C., and Skaloud, M. (1970). "Ultimate Load Behavior of Longitudinally Reinforced Web Plates Subjected to Pure Bending," *IABSE Pub.,* Zurich, Switzerland, vol. 20/I, pp. 113–148.

Peery, D. J., and Azar, J. J. (1982). *Aircraft Structures,* McGraw-Hill Companies, Inc., 1982.

PennDOT. (1994). *Design Manual Part 4, Structures—Procedures—Designs—Plans— Presentation,* PDT Pub. No. 15, Commonwealth of Pennsylvania, Department of Transportation.

Petterson, P. J., Corrodo, J. A., Huang, J. S., and Yen, B. T. (1970). "Fatigue and Static Tests of Two Welded Plate Girders," *WRC Bull.* 155, October.

Pole, W., ed. (1877). *The Life of Sir William Fairbairn, Bart,* David and Charles, Newton Abbot, London, reprinted 1970.

Porter, D. M., Rockey, K. C., and Evans, H. R. (1975). "The Collapse Behavior of Plate Girders Loaded in Shear," *Struct. Eng.,* 53(8), August, pp. 313–325.

Praeger, E. H., and Kavanagh, T. C. (1959). "Longest Plate-Girder Span in U. S. Completed," *ASCE Civ. Eng.,* December, pp. 42–43.

Ravindra, M. K., and Galambos, T. V. (1978). "Load and Resistance Factor Design for Steel," *ASCE J. Struct. Div.,* 104(ST9), September, pp. 1337–1353.

Razani, R., and Goble, G. G. (1966). "Optimum Design of Constant-Depth Plate Girders," *Proc. ASCE J. Struct. Div.,* 92(ST2), April, paper 4787, pp. 253–281.

RCSC. (1985a). *Commentary on Specifications for Structural Joints Using ASTM A325 or A490 Bolts,* AISC, Chicago.

RCSC. (1985b). *Allowable Stress Design Specification for Structural Joints Using ASTM A325 or A490 Bolts,* AISC, Chicago.

RCSC. (1986). *Load and Resistance Design Specification for Structural Joints Using ASTM A325 or A490 Bolts,* AISC, Chicago.

Redwood, R. G. (1972). "Tables for Plastic Design of Beams with Rectangular Holes," *AISC Eng. J.,* 9(1), January, pp. 2–19.

———. (1983). "Design of I-Beams with Web Perforations," in *Beams and Beam-Columns— Stability and Strength,* Ch. 3, R. Narayanan, ed., Applied Science Publishers, London.

Redwood, R. G., Baranda, H., and Daly, M. (1978). "Tests of Thin-Webbed Beams with Unreinforced Holes," *ASCE J. Struct. Div.,* 104(ST3), March, pp. 577–595.

Redwood, R. G., and Chan, P. W. (1974). "Design Aides for Beams with Circular Eccentric Web Holes," *ASCE J. Struct. Div.,* 100(ST2), February, pp. 297–303.

Redwood, R. G., and Shrivastava, S. C. (1980). "Design Recommendations for Steel Beams with Holes," *Canadian J. Civ. Eng.,* 7(4), pp.642–650.

Redwood, R. G., and Uenoya, M. (1979). "Critical Loads for Webs with Holes," *ASCE J. Struct. Div.,* 105(ST10), October, pp. 2053–2067.

Reissner, H. (1909). "Uber die Knicksicherheit ebener Bleche," *Zentralblatt der Bauverwaltung,* p. 93.

Roberts, T. M., and Chong, C. K. (1981). "Collapse of Plate Girders under Edge Loading," *ASCE J. Struct. Div.,* 107(ST8), August, pp. 1503–1509.

Robinson, R. (1984). "Steel Girder Bridge Sets Record Length," *ASCE Civ. Eng.,* May, pp. 38–40.

Rockey, K. C. (1957). "Shear Buckling of Web Reinforced by Vertical Stiffeners and a Central Horizontal Stiffener," *IABSE Pub. 17,* pp. 161–171.

——. (1958). "Web Buckling and Design of Web Plates," *Struct. Eng.,* 36(2), February, pp. 45–60.

——. (1971a). "An Ultimate Load Method of Design for Plate Girders," *Proc. Conf. Dev. Bridge Des. Construct.,* Crosby Lockwood, London.

——. (1971b). "An Ultimate Load Method of Design for Plate Girders," *Proc. Conf. Dev. Bridge Des. Construct.,* Crosby Lockwood, London.

——. (1971c). Free discussion, in *IABSE Proc. Colloq. Design of Plate and Box Girders for Ultimate Strength,* London, p. 323.

Rockey, K. C., Anderson, R. G., and Cheung, Y. K. (1967). "The Behavior of Square Shear Webs Having a Circular Hole," *Proc. Swansea Symp. on Thin-Walled Str.,* Crosby, Lockwood and Sons, London, pp. 148–169.

Rockey, K. C., and Cook, I. T. (1965a). "Optimum Reinforcement by Two Longitudinal Stiffeners of a Plate Subjected to Pure Bending," *Intern. J. Solids Structures,* 1(1), February, pp. 79–92.

——. (1965b). "The Buckling under Pure Bending of a Plate Girder Reinforced by Multiple Longitudinal Stiffeners," *Intern. J. Solids Structures,* 1(2), April, pp. 147–156.

Rockey, K. C., Evans, H. R., and Porter, D. M. (1973). "Ultimate Load Capacity of Stiffened Webs Subjected to Shear and Bending," *Proc. Conf. Steel Box Girders,* Institute of Civil Engineers, London.

——. (1974). "The Ultimate Strength Behavior of Longitudinally Stiffened Reinforced Plate Girders," *Proc. Symp. Structural Analysis, Nonlinear Behavior, and Technique,* Transport and Road Research Laboratory, Crowthorne, England, December, pp. 163–174.

——. (1978). "A Design Method for Predicting the Collapse Behavior of Plate Girders," *Proc. Inst. Civ. Engrs.,* part 2, pp. 85–112.

Rockey, K. C., and Leggett, D. M. A. (1962). "The Buckling of a Plate Girder Web under Pure Bending When Reinforced by a Single Longitudinal Stiffener," *Proc. Inst. Civ. Engrs.,* London, vol. 21, January, p. 161.

Rockey, K. C., and Skaloud, M. (1968). "Influence of Flange Stiffeners upon the Load-Carrying Capacity of Webs in Shear," *IABSE Final Report, Proc. of the 8th Congress,* New York, September, pp. 429–439.

——. (1972). "The Ultimate Load Behavior of Plate Girders Loaded in Shear," *Struct. Eng.,* 50(11), January, pp. 29–48.

Rode, H. H. (1916). *Beitrage zur Theorie der Knickerscheinungen,* Wilhelm Englemann Verlag, Leipzig (dissertation); *Der Eisenbau,* vol. 7, 1916, pp. 121, 157, 210, 239, 296.

Roderick, J. W., Hawkins, N. M., and Lim, L. C. (1967). "The Behavior of Composite Steel and Lightweight Concrete Beams," *ASCE Civ. Eng. Trans.,* 9(2), October, pp. 265–275.

Rolt, L. T. C. (1957). *Isambard Kingdom Brunel,* Longmans, Green, and Company, London, p. 180.

Ros, M., and Eichinger, A. (1932). "Final Report," *IABSE First Congress,* Paris, p. 144.

Rosenberg, N., and Vincenti, W. G. (1978). *The Britannia Bridge: The Generation and Diffusion of Technical Knowledge,* MIT Press, Cambridge, MA.

Salmon, C. G., and Johnson, C. G. (1990). *Steel Structures: Design and Behavior,* 3rd ed., HarperCollins Publishers, New York.

Sattler, K. (1961). "Composite Construction in Theory and Practice," *Struct. Eng.,* 39(4), April, pp. 124–144.

Schafer, G. (1957). "The New Highway Bridge over the Sava between Belgrade and Zemun (Yugoslavia)," *Acier-Stahl-Steel,* 22(5), May, pp. 213–218.

Schedd, T. C. (1934). *Structural Design in Steel,* John Wiley & Sons, Inc., New York.

Schilling, C. G. (1967). "Web Crippling Tests on Hybrid Girders," *ASCE J. Struct. Div.,* 93(ST1), February, pp. 59–70.

——. (1974). "Optimum Proportions for I-Shaped Beams," *ASCE J. Struct. Div.,* 100(ST12), December, pp. 2385–2401.

——. (1985). "Steel Bridges: The Best of Current Practice," *AISC Pub. No. G-446-2/1/85.*

Schmidt, L. C. (1965). "Restraints against Lateral Buckling," *Proc. ASCE J. Eng. Mech. Div.,* 91, EM6, December, pt. 1, paper 4561, pp 1–10.

Schueller, W., and Ostapenko, A. (1970). "Tests on a Transversely Stiffened and on a Longitudinally Stiffened Unsymmetrical Plate Girder," *Welding Research Council Bull. 156,* New York, November.

Schuette, E. H., and McCulloch, J. C. (1947). "Charts for the Minimum-Weight Design of Multiweb Wings in Bending," *NACA Tech. Note 1323.*

Schussler, K., and Pelikan, W. (1951). "Die Neue Rheinbrucke Koln–Mulheim," *Der Stahlbau,* vol. 20, p. 141.

Sealey, A. (1976). *Bridges and Aqueducts,* Hugh Evelyn, London.

Seely, F. B., and Smith, J. O. (1952). *Advanced Mechanics of Materials,* John Wiley & Sons, Inc., New York.

Selberg, A. (1973). "On the Shear Capacity of Girder Webs," *University of Trondheim Report.*

Shanmugam, N. E., and Narayanan, R. (1982). "Elastic Buckling of Perforated Plates for Various Loading and Edge Conditions," *Intl. Conf. on Finite Element Methods,* Shanghai, Paper No. 103.

Sharp, M. L., and Clark, J. W. (1971). "Thin Aluminum Shear Webs," *ASCE J. Struct. Div.,* 97(ST4), pp. 1021–1038.

Shedd, T. C. (1934). *Structural Design in Steel,* Ch. 3, John Wiley & Sons, Inc., New York.

Singer, F. L. (1962). *Strength of Materials,* Harper and Row, New York.

Skaloud, M. (1962). "Design of Web Plates of Steel Girders with Regard to Postbuckling Behavior," *Struct. Eng.,* 40(9), September, pp. 279–284; 40(12), December, pp. 406–416.

——. (1971). "Ultimate Load and Failure Mechanism of Thin Webs in Shear," *IABSE Proc. Colloq. Design of Plate and Box Girders for Ultimate Strength,* London.

——. (1983). "Optimum Rigidity of Stiffeners of Webs and Flanges," in *Plated Structures, Stability and Strength,* Ch. 4, R. Narayanan, ed., Applied Science Publishers, New York.

Smiles, S. (1868). *The Life of George Stephenson and His Son Robert Stephenson,* rev. ed., Harper and Brothers, New York.

Smith, D. M. (1977). "Why Do Bridges Fail," *ASCE Civ. Eng.,* November, pp. 58–62.

SSRC. (1976). *Guide to Stability Design Criteria for Metal Structures,* 3rd ed., B. G. Johnston, ed., Structural Stability Research Council, John Wiley & Sons, New York.

——. (1988). *Guide to Stability Design Criteria for Metal Structures,* 4th ed., T. V. Galambos, ed., Structural Stability Research Council, John Wiley & Sons, New York.

Stein, M., and Fralich, R. W. (1949). "Critical Shear Stresses of Infinitely Long, Simply Supported Plate with Transverse Stiffeners," *NACA Tech. Note 1851,* April; *J. Aeronaut. Sci.,* vol. 17.

Stein, M., and Neff, J. (1947). "Buckling Stresses of Simply Supported Flat Plates in Shear," *NACA Tech. Note 1222.*

Stein, O. (1934). "Die Stabilitat Blechtragerstehbleche im zweiachsigen Spannungs zustand," *Der Stahlbau,* vol. 7, p. 57.

Steinhardt, O., and Schroter, W. (1971). "Postcritical Behavior of Aluminum Plate Girders with Transverse Stiffeners," *IABSE Proc. Colloq. Design of Plate and Box Girders for Ultimate Strength,* London.

Steinman, B. D., and Watson, S. R. (1957). *Bridges and Their Builders,* Dover Publications, New York.

Stowell, E. Z., Heimerl, G. J., Libove, C., and Lundquist, E. E. (1952). "Buckling Stresses for Flat Plates and Sections," *Trans. ASCE 117,* pp. 545–578.

Stowell, E. Z., and Schwartz, E. B. (1943). "Critical Stresses for an Infinitely Long Plate with Elastically Restrained Edges under Combined Shear and Direct Stress," *NACA Wartime Report L-340,* November.

Stupp, R. P. (1992). "What Engineers Can Do to Reduce Bridge Fabrication Costs," *AISC Modern Steel Constr.,* September, p. 28.

Subcommittee 3 on Prestressed Steel of Joint ASCE–AASHO Committee on Steel Flexural Members. (1968). "Development and Use of Prestressed Steel Flexural Members," *Proc. ASCE J. Struct. Div.,* September, pp. 2033–2059.

Sutherland, R. J. M. (1963). "The Introduction of Structural Wrought Iron," *Trans. Newcomen Soc.,* vol. 36, p. 80.

Szilard, R. (1974). *Theory and Analysis of Plates: Classical and Numerical Solutions,* Prentice Hall, Englewood Cliffs, NJ.

Takeuchi, T. (1964). *Investigation of the Load-Carrying Capacity of Plate Girders,* M.S. thesis, University of Kyoto (in Japanese).

Thurlimann, B. (1963). "Static Strength of Plate Girders," *Extract des Memoires de la Societe Royale dis' Sciences de Liege,* vol. VIII, p. 137.

Timoshenko, S. (1913). "Sur la stabilite des systems elastiques," *Annales des ponts et chaussees,* parts III, IV, V.

———. (1915). "Stability of Rectangular Plates with Stiffeners," *Mem. Inst. Engs., Ways of Commun.,* vol. 89, p. 23 (in Russian).

———. (1921). "Uber die Stabilitat versteifter Platten," *Der Eisenbau,* vol. 12, p. 147.

———. (1935). "Stability of the Webs of Plate Girders," *Engineering,* vol. 238, p. 207.

———. (1945). "Theory of Bending, Torsion and Buckling of Thin-Walled Members of Open Cross-Section," *J. Franklin Inst.,* 239(3), pp. 201–219; (4), pp. 249–268; (5), pp. 343–361.

———. (1953). *History of Strength of Materials,* McGraw-Hill Companies, Inc., New York.

Timoshenko, S. P., and Gere, J. M. (1961). *Theory of Elastic Stability,* McGraw-Hill Companies, Inc., New York.

Todhunter, I., and Pearson, K. (1960). *A History of the Theory of Elasticity,* vols. 1 and 2, Dover Publications, Inc., New York.

Toprac, A. A. (1963). "Fatigue Strength of Full-Size Hybrid Girders," *Proc. AISC Ntnl. Eng. Conf.,* Tulsa, OK.

———. (1965). "Strength of Three New Types of Composite Beams," *AISC Eng. J.,* 2(1), January, pp. 21–30.

Toprac, A. A., and Natrajan, M. (1971). "Fatigue Strength of Hybrid Plate Girders," *ASCE J. Struct. Div.,* 97(ST4), April, pp. 1203–1225.

Troitsky, M. S. (1967). *Orthotropic Bridges, Theory and Practice,* James F. Lincoln Arc Welding Society, Cleveland, OH.

———. (1976). *Stiffened Plates—Bending, Stability, and Vibrations,* Elsevier Scientific Publishing, New York.

———. (1989). *Prestressed Steel Structures,* James F. Lincoln Arc Welding Foundation, Cleveland, OH.

———. (1990). *Prestressed Steel Bridges—Theory and Design,* Van Nostrand Reinhold Co., New York.

Troitsky, M. S., and Rabbani, N. F. (1987). "Tendon Configurations of Prestressed Steel Girder Bridges," *Proc. Centennial Conf., Canadian Soc. Civil Eng.,* May 19–22, Montreal, Quebec, Canada, pp. 172–182.

Troitsky, M. S., Zielinski, Z. A., and Rabbani, N. F. (1989). "Prestressed-Steel Continuous-Span Girders," *ASCE J. Str. Engr.* 115(6), June.

Turneaure, F. E. (1898). "Tests of the Stress in Plate Girder Stiffeners," *Engineering News,* 40(12), September, p. 186.

Turner, C. A. P., and Shinner, F. G. (1898). "Spacing Stiffeners in Plate Girders," *Engineering News,* 40(25), December, p. 399.

Tyrell, H. G. (1911). *History of Bridge Engineering,* published by author, Chicago, IL.

Udea, Y. (1962). *Elastic, Elastic-Plastic, and Plastic Buckling of Plates with Residual Stresses,* Ph. D. dissertation, Lehigh University, Bethlehem, PA.

USS. (1986a). *Highway Structures Design Handbook,* vol. I, U.S. Steel Corp., Pittsburgh.

USS. (1986b). *Highway Structures Design Handbook,* vol. II, U.S. Steel Corp., Pittsburgh.

U.S. Steel Corp. (1983). "Determining the Need for Lateral Wind Bracing in Plate Girder Bridges," *Supplement to Chapter 5, Highway Structures Design Handbook, Vol. II,* U.S. Steel Corp., Pittsburgh, September.

Vasarhelyi, D. D., and Chiang, K. C. (1967). "Coefficient of Friction in Joints of Various Steels," *ASCE J. Struct. Div.,* 93(ST4), August, pp. 227–243.

Vincent, G. S. (1969). "Tentative Criteria for Load and Resistance Design of Steel Bridges," *AISI, Bull. No. 15,* AISI, March.

von Karman, T., Sechler, E. E., and Donnell, L. H. (1932). "The Strength of Thin Plates in Compression," *Trans. ASME,* vol. 54.

Wagner, H. (1929). "Ebene Blechwandtrager mit sehr dunnem Stegblech," *Zeitschrift fur Flugtechnik und Motorluftschiffahrt,* vol. 20, pp. 220, 227, 256, 279, 306.

——. (1931). "Flat Sheet Metal Girder with Very Thin Metal Web," *NACA Tech. Memo, Nos. 604, 605, 606.*

Wang, T. K. (1947). "Buckling of Transverse Stiffened Plates under Shear," *J. Applied Mechanics,* vol. 14, p. A-269.

Wang, T. M., Snell, R. R., and Cooper, P. B. (1975). "Strength of Beams with Eccentric Holes," *ASCE J. Struct. Div.,* 101(ST9), September, pp. 1783–1800.

Wastlund, G., and Bergman, S. G. A. (1947). "Buckling of Webs in Deep Steel I-Girders," *IABSE Pub.,* vol. 8, p. 291.

Weitz, F. R. (1966). "Entwicklungstendenzen des Stahlbruckenbaus am Beispiel der Rheinbrucke Wiesbaden–Schierstein," *Stahlbau,* 35(10), October, pp. 289–301; 35(12), December, pp. 357–365.

Wilson, J. M. (1886). "On Specifications for Strength of Iron Bridges," *Trans. ASCE,* vol. 15, pt. I, paper no. 335, pp. 401–403, 489–490.

——. (1898). "Spacing Stiffeners in Plate Girders," *Engineering News,* 40(6), August, p. 89; discussions: *Engineering News,* 40(10), September 1898, p. 154.

Winterton, K. (1962). "A Brief History of Welding Technology," *Welding and Metal Fabrication,* November, December.

Wolchuck, R. (1981). "Design Rules for Steel Girder Bridges," *IABSE Proc., P-41/81,* Zurich, Switzerland, May.

Wolchuck, R., and Mayrbaurl, R. M. (1980). *Consulting Engineers Proposed Design Specifications of Steel Box Girder Bridges,* Rep. No. FHWA-TS-80-205, U.S. Department of Transportation, FHWA, Office of Research and Development, Washington, DC, January.

Wright, R. N., and Walker, W. H. (1971). "Criteria for Deflection of Steel Bridges," *AISI Bull.,* 19, AISI, New York.

Yen, B. T., and Basler, K. (1962). "Static Carrying Capacity of Plate Girders," *Hwy. Res. Board Proc.,* vol. 41.

Yen, B. T., and Cooper, P. B. (1963). "Fatigue Tests of Welded Plate Girders," *Welding J.,* 42(6), 261s-3s, June.

Yen, B. T., and Mueller, J. A. (1966). "Fatigue Tests of Large-Size Welded Plate Girders," *WRC. Bull.,* 118, November.

Yonezawa, H., Miakami, I., Dogaki, M., and Uno, H. (1978). "Shear Strength of Plate Girders with Diagonally Stiffened Webs," *Trans. Japan Soc. Civ. Engrs.,* vol. 10.

Yura, J. A., and Frank, K. H. (1985). "Testing Method to Determine the Slip Coefficient for Coatings Used in Bolted Joints," *AISC Eng. J.,* 22(3), 3rd Qtr., pp. 151–155; *AISC–LRFD-1986,* p. 6-278.

Yura, J. A., Galambos, T. V., and Ravindra, M. K. (1978). "The Bending Resistance of Steel Beams," *ASCE J. Struct. Div.,* 104(ST9), September, pp. 1355–1370.

Zahn, C. J. (1987). "Plate Girder Design Using LRFD," *AISC Eng. J.,* 24(1), 1st Qtr., pp. 11–20.

Zuraski, P. D. (1991). "Continuous-Beam Analysis for Highway Bridges," *J. Struct Eng.,* vol. 117, January.

CHAPTER 10

Inspection, Evaluation, Rehabilitation, and Maintenance of Bridges

10.1
INTRODUCTION

On December 15, 1967, the Point Pleasant Bridge, which carried U.S. Highway 35 over the Ohio River, located between Point Pleasant, West Virginia, and Kanauga, Ohio, collapsed without any warning, killing 46 of the 64 passengers and drivers present on the bridge at the time [NTSB, 1968]. This sudden failure was caused by a stress–corrosion fracture at the pinhole of a single eyebar member [Ballard and Yakowitz, 1969; Scheffey and Cayes, 1974; Nishanian and Frank, 1972; Fisher, 1984]. Also known as the Silver Bridge because of the shiny aluminum paint used to prevent rusting of its steel members, it was a three-span (380, 700, and 380 ft) eyebar chain suspension bridge built in 1928. This historic catastrophe marked a turning point in the maintenance practices of the nation's bridges, for from it evolved our present bridge safety inspection and maintenance program. So powerful was the impact of this failure that, for fear of a similar catastrophe, a nearly identical and contemporary bridge, also spanning the Ohio River, at St. Mary's, West Virginia, was dismantled in 1969 [Fisher, 1984]. Several well-known highway bridge failures that occurred between 1876 and 1967—the Ashtabula Bridge in Ohio, the Firth of Tay Bridge in Scotland, the Quebec Bridge in Canada, and the Tacoma Narrows and the Silver bridges in the United States—were discussed in Chapter 1.

There are several causes of bridge failures: floods, scour, wind, earthquakes, corrosion, fatigue, failure of a fracture-critical member, overloading, poor design (buckling of compression members, lack of redundancy, etc.), collision with substructure, and fire. Floods marked the first bridge failure in American history. One of several bridges built by Hernando de Soto's Genoese engineer, Maese Francisco, during the Spanish exploration of the 1530s and 1540s was swept away by river currents during a flood [Gies, 1963]. A general discussion on bridge failures has been given by Smith [1977].

Although in old steel bridges, fatigue failures usually occur due to cyclic loading (see Chapter 5), an *early*-life fatigue failure can also occur under some conditions. For example, the Kings Bridge in Melbourne, Australia, failed only 15 months after it was put in service. Investigations identified a fatigue failure caused by use of unsuitable material, large pre-erection cracks, and poor fabrication and inspection practices [White, Minor, and Derucher, 1992].

In spite of the significant advances in structural and materials engineering, several bridges have failed due to various causes during the last few years, albeit mostly due to floods and scour. For example, the April 1985 collapse of the U.S. Route 43 bridge over Chacksawbougue Creek near Mobile, Alabama, was a classic example of failure due to underwater scour problems [White, Minor, and Derucher, 1992]. Local scour was also the cause of the collapse of the 35-year-old, 540-ft-long New York Thruway Bridge over Schoharie Creek on April 5, 1987, which killed 10 people [NTSB, 1988]. And, for similar reasons, the 55-year-old U.S. Route 51 bridge over the Hatchie River near Covington, Tennessee, collapsed on April 1, 1989, killing eight people [White, Minor, and Derucher, 1992]. The June 28, 1983 collapse of a suspended span of the Mianus River Bridge on Interstate 95 in Connecticut [NTSB, 1984] was a classic example of failure of a fracture-critical bridge, somewhat similar to that of the Point Pleasant Bridge collapse [Fisher, 1984]. Investigations of these tragedies revealed that they could have been prevented through timely inspection and corrective action on the deficiencies discovered. The importance of regular periodic safety inspections and reporting procedures, followed by corrective action, can hardly be overemphasized.

10.2
BRIDGE INSPECTION

The Point Pleasant Bridge disaster prompted President Lyndon Johnson to order a special task force to investigate the collapse of the bridge, to propose action for speedy reconstruction of the bridge, and to suggest procedures and preventative action to avoid future bridge failures. A committee, formed at the direction of this task force and under the leadership of the administrator of the Federal Highway Administration (FHWA), directed all 50 states to review and inventory all existing highway bridges by January 1970. All bridges longer than 20 ft were required to be described and registered in a national database, and thus the National Bridge Inventory (NBI) was established. Priority was to be given to the pre-1935 bridges (because of their age), to be followed by other structures. The general policy required inspection of all structures on a five-year cycle, and that of important structures every two years. Concerns brought by the revelations of deteriorated conditions of several bridges nationally resulted in the 1978 Surface Transportation Act, requiring all owners of highway bridges to conduct biennial inspections unless an exception was allowed [White, Minor, and Derucher, 1992]. The 1988 revision of the National Bridge Inspection Standard (NBIS) gave states the authority to vary the frequency of inspections. However, this policy required prior FHWA approval if the inspection frequency was to *exceed* two years [FHWA, 1988a].

Although safety inspection requirements and procedures [AASHTO, 1964] existed even prior to the Point Pleasant Bridge collapse, the federal mandate heralded a bridge safety inspection and recording program of unprecedented scale involving, as a starting point, in-depth inspections of all bridges, supervised by professional engineers. This resulted in significant funding for developing and organizing new procedures and guidelines for inspection and maintenance of the nation's bridges at a heightened pace

[Ahlskog, 1982; Guide, 1993; NSPE, 1988]. Several inspection and training manuals [AASHTO, 1970; AASHTO, 1994; FHWA, 1970, 1977, 1984a,b, 1986a,b; NCH SYN, 1985; USFS, 1979; PEN, 1987] and procedures covering various aspects of bridge inspection, such as inspection of superstructure (trusses, decks, joints, bearings, drainage systems, corrosion, etc.), substructure, and underwater portions of abutments and piers [FHWA, 1988a,b, 1989a; NCH SYN, 1981; TRB, 1988], were published to educate and train the inspection and engineering personnel. These inspection procedures were drawn mostly from reference [AASHO, 1964]. According to a survey conducted between 1978 and 1981 in 20 states and Ontario, Canada, fatigue cracks had developed at approximately 120 steel bridge sites [Fisher and Yuceoglu, 1981]. Procedures were developed for mitigating such problems [FHWA, 1986a; Fisher, 1981; NCHRP, 1987a,c, 1990b]. Considering the vital importance of the nation's infrastructure, guidelines were prescribed for recording the conditions of bridges at the national level [FHWA Guide, 1979, 1988].

Several studies about the nation's bridges have been published in the last few years [Dunker and Rabbat, 1990a,b; FHWA, 1989b; RBM, 1987]. A recent study [BRM, 1990] pointed out that, of more than 585,000 bridges, about 221,000, or 38 percent, are *substandard.* A jurisdictional breakdown of these figures indicates that, out of about 275,000 interstate and state highway bridges, about 75,000, or 27 percent, are substandard. Also, out of 310,000 city, county, and township highway bridges, a shocking 146,000, or 47 percent, are substandard. For preserving the safety and serviceability of such a vast number of bridges, there is an obvious need for a systematic inspection and reporting system for these bridges and a program for their maintenance and repairs [RBM, 1987].

TABLE 10.1

Twelve of the most common bridge types built 1950–1987 and percentages classified structurally deficient [Dunker and Rabbat, 1990a]

Bridge type	Number built 1950–1987	Percent of total built 1950–1987	Average year built	Percent structurally deficient 1950–1987	Percent structurally deficient 1980–1987
Steel stringer (SST)	69,885	24	1964	23	7
Continuous steel stringer (CSST)	32,227	11	1967	11	1
Timber stringer (TST)	31,083	10	1963	52	30
Prestressed concrete stringer (PCST)	27,923	9	1971	4	0
Reinforced concrete slab (RCSL)	24,162	8	1966	11	2
Continuous reinforced concrete slab (CRCSL)	18,573	6	1967	4	0
Prestressed concrete multiple box (PCMB)	16,377	5	1973	5	1
Reinforced concrete stringer (RCST)	12,500	4	1966	10	2
Reinforced concrete T (RCT)	11,361	4	1964	6	1
Continuous reinforced concrete T	5827	2	1963	3	1
Prestressed concrete slab (PCSL)	5706	2	1973	3	0
Prestressed concrete T (PCT)	5017	2	1972	5	0
Total of 12 types	260,641	88	—	—	—
Total of all types	296,668	—	—	—	—

The term *substandard* is rather broad. A substandard bridge is defined by its functional obsolescence, structural deficiencies, or both. According to FHWA [FHWA, 1989b], a bridge is deemed functionally obsolete if it has inadequate sight distance, substandard clearances, restricted lane widths, sharp curvatures, or poor highway geometrics. A bridge is judged to be structurally deficient if it has been restricted to light vehicles (i.e., it is incapable of permitting design loads), is closed, or requires immediate rehabilitation to permit traffic. Table 10.1 shows 12 of the most commonly built bridge types during the 1950–1987 period and the percentage classified as structurally deficient.

10.3
BRIDGE EVALUATION

10.3.1 Bridge Rating

Structural deficiency of a bridge may have resulted from several factors such as

- Designs for lighter loads (e.g., H15, HS15, H20, etc.) compared to loads in use at present (e.g., HS20 or HS25, etc.);
- Designs according to codes, specifications, or stress levels that are no longer applicable;
- Reduction of the live-load capacity as a result of aging, deterioration, or damage to structural members. An increase in dead load, such as that due to a thicker new deck or a new layer of wearing course on an old deck without removing the old layer of wearing course, would increase the dead-load moment, with consequent decrease in the live-load moment capacity of the bridge.

Any of these factors could cause overstress in some or all components of a deficient bridge. Since a structure is only as strong as its weakest link, overstressing of any bridge component would render a bridge structurally deficient and would compromise its safety. Consequently, such a bridge will either have to be closed or, at best, be permitted to carry light traffic (loads) only. Structural capacity analysis to determine the reduced loading that a structurally deficient bridge can safely carry is known as *rating*. Although the substructure components, such as abutments and piers, are also components of a bridge that must support total load transmitted from the superstructure, they generally have larger load-carrying capacities than the superstructure. Consequently, it is the load-carrying capacity of the superstructure that generally governs the rating of a bridge. Expressed as a number, the rating factor, *RF,* is simply the ratio of the actual live-load capacity to the required live-load capacity [White, Minor, and Derucher, 1992]:

$$RF = \frac{\text{Available capacity for live-load plus impact}}{\text{Capacity required for live-load plus impact}} \tag{10.1}$$

Note that for timber bridges the impact factor, *I*, is taken as zero (AASHTO 3.8.1.2).

A superstructure consists of several components, such as deck, stringers, floor beams (if any), bearings, and truss members (if any). For rating analysis of a superstructure, the load-carrying capacity and the rating factor of each bridge component or subcomponent (e.g., a truss member for a truss bridge) must be calculated; the smallest of the rating factors determines the rating factor of the bridge. The *required* load-carrying capacity chosen for comparison generally refers to the prescribed loading, such as the AASHTO H20 or the HS20 loading.

The required or actual load-carrying capacity may have to be expressed differently for different bridge components. For example, for a slab, the capacity will be expressed in terms of moment; for a beam, in terms of moment, shear, and deflection; for a truss member, in terms of stresses (or axial loads). The following step-by-step procedure may be followed for the rating analysis of a bridge [NCHRP, 1987b]:

1. Analyze the bridge completely for the service loads (H20, HS20, etc.); i.e., determine moments, shears, stresses, etc., in various bridge components.
2. Calculate the member forces (or stresses, as required) resulting from dead loads only.
3. Calculate load-carrying capacity of members based on their actual section properties and allowable (or code-prescribed) stresses.
4. Calculate the member capacity available to carry live-load. This quantity is simply the difference between the quantities calculated in steps 2 and 3:

$$\text{live-load capacity} = \text{Total member capacity (step 3)} - \text{Forces}$$
$$\text{due to dead loads (step 2)}$$

5. The rating factor is simply the ratio of quantities calculated in steps 4 and 1, and may be variously expressed as:
   a. For bending members, such as slabs, beams, and girders:

$$RF = \frac{\text{Available moment capacity to carry live-load}}{\text{Design moment due to live-load plus impact}} \tag{10.2}$$

   b. For axially loaded members such as truss members:

$$RF = \frac{\text{Stress available to carry live-load}}{\text{Design stress due to live-load plus impact}} \tag{10.3}$$

10.3.2 Types of Bridge Rating

In addition to regular service loads, bridges may occasionally be subjected to overloads. Accordingly, the AASHTO specifications recommend two levels of capacity ratings for bridges: inventory rating and operating rating [White, Minor, and Derucher, 1992]. The inventory rating relates to the loads under which a bridge can perform safely indefinitely. The operating rating relates to the absolute maximum loads that may be permitted on the bridge, which cannot be exceeded under any circumstance. Because of the differences in stress levels used for calculating the two rating factors, the factor values are different. For example, for the inventory rating, the stress levels used are $0.55F_y$, or the allowable stress, whereas for the operating rating, the stress levels used are $0.75F_y$, or $\frac{75}{55}$ times the allowable stress.

While it is simpler to use the stress concept for the inventory analysis of steel or timber bridges, such is not the case for reinforced or prestressed concrete bridges. For these bridges, it is simpler to use the load factor design method [AASHTO, 1976, 1989]. The general expressions for rating factors may be obtained from the formulas for moments due to factored loads (presented in earlier chapters) as follows:

10.3.2.1 Inventory level

$$M_u = 1.3[\beta_D D + \beta_L(L + I)] \tag{10.4}$$

where M_u is the required capacity of a bending member. Substitution of $\beta_D = 1.0$ and $\beta_L = \frac{5}{3}$ reduces Eq. 10.4 to

$$\begin{aligned}
M_u &= 1.3\left[M_D + \left(\tfrac{5}{3}\right)M_{L+I}\right] \\
&= 1.3M_D + 1.3\left(\tfrac{5}{3}\right)M_{L+I} \\
&= \text{(factored moment due to dead load} \\
&\quad + \text{factored moment due to live load)}
\end{aligned} \tag{10.5}$$

$$\text{For design:} \quad \phi M_n \geq M_u \tag{10.6}$$

Substitution of Eq. 10.6 in Eq. 10.5 yields

$$\text{Available live-load moment capacity} = \phi M_n - 1.3M_D \tag{10.7}$$

$$\text{Required live-load moment capacity} = 1.3\left(\tfrac{5}{3}\right)M_{L+I} \tag{10.8}$$

Hence, the rating factor, RF, is expressed as the ratio of the *available* live-load capacity to the *required* live-load capacity:

$$RF_{\text{in}} = \frac{\phi M_n - 1.3M_D}{1.3\,(5/3)\,M_{L+I}} \tag{10.9}$$

10.3.2.2 Operating level

For operating level, the value of β_L is taken as unity, so that Eq. 10.5 becomes

$$RF_{\text{op}} = \frac{\phi M_n - 1.3M_D}{1.3M_{L+I}} \tag{10.10}$$

where
R_{in} = inventory rating factor
R_{op} = operating rating factor
M_D = moment due to dead load
M_{L+I} = moment due to live load plus impact
M_u = ultimate moment capacity = ϕM_n
ϕ = capacity reduction (or resistance) factor
M_n = nominal moment capacity

The quantity M_{L+I} in Eq. 10.5 through Eq. 10.10 needs some explanation. FHWA requires that ratings be reported in terms of tons for truck loads with standard configuration, namely, H20, HS20, Type 3 (regular two-axle truck), Type 3S-2 (a trailer truck, 18-wheeler) and Type 3-3 (tandem truck). In recognition of the trend toward heavier loads, some states require rating in terms of the HS25 truck. Various kinds of legal and design loads for highway bridges were described in Chapter 3 and are discussed in AASHTO [1970]. It should be borne in mind that although some of the legal truck loads may be heavier than the HS20 truck, because of the vehicle configuration, the

TABLE 10.2

Maximum live load moments due to one line of wheels, one lane, simple spans

Span	Type of loading				
	HS20	H15	3	3S2	3-3
10	40.0	30.0	27.2	24.8	22.4
15	60.0	45.0	47.6	43.4	39.2
20	80.0	60.0	68.0	62.0	56.0
25	103.7	75.0	89.3	85.1	73.5
30	141.1	92.5	111.6	110.7	91.0
40	224.9	129.7	173.0	162.0	143.2
50	314.0	167.1	235.5	219.6	197.0
60	403.3	209.2	298.0	306.0	282.0
70	492.8	265.1	360.5	392.4	370.0
80	582.5	327.0	423.0	481.0	470.0
90	672.2	394.9	485.5	571.0	570.0
100	771.0	468.8	548.0	661.0	670.0
120	941.7	634.5	673.0	841.6	870.0
140	1121.4*	824.2	798.0	1021.0	1070.0
160	1384.0*	1038.0	923.0	1201.0	1270.0
180	1701.2*	1275.8	1048.0	1381.0	1470.0
200	2050.0*	1537.0	1173.0	1561.0	1670.0

*Lane load controls.

For existing steel and concrete bridges, AASHTO [1989] suggests the following equation:

$$\phi R_n = \mu_D D + \mu_L(RF)L(1 + I) \tag{10.11}$$

which can be expressed as

$$RF = \frac{\phi R_n - \mu_D D}{\mu_L L(1 + I)} \tag{10.12}$$

moments due to the HS20 truck are the largest, and should govern. A comparison of moments due to various loadings for a few selected spans is presented in Table 10.2, and the corresponding loadings are shown in Fig. 10.1.

For existing steel and concrete bridges, AASHTO [1989] suggests the following equation:

$$\phi R_n = \mu_D D + \mu_L(RF)L(1 + I) \tag{10.11}$$

which can be expressed as

$$RF = \frac{\phi R_n - \mu_D D}{\mu_L L(1 + I)} \tag{10.12}$$

where RF = rating factor

ϕ = resistance factor, a function of the condition of the superstructure that varies from 0.95 for a good condition to 0.55 for a heavily deteriorated bridge

R_n = nominal strength or resistance

μ_D = dead-load factor

μ_L = live-load factor

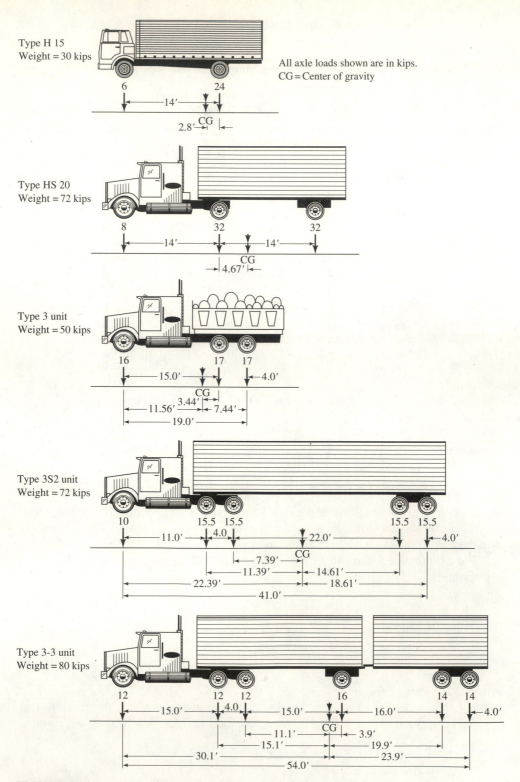

FIGURE 10.1
A comparison of some AASHTO standard and legal load types.

> I = impact factor, *based on the condition of the wearing surface* rather than the span length
>
> L = nominal live-load effect
>
> D = nominal dead-load effect

Values of various parameters to be used in Eq. 10.12 are rather involved and should be carefully selected. A discussion on the use of this equation can be found in references such as [AASHTO, 1989; White, Minor, and Derucher, 1992].

A bridge may often have to carry heavy vehicles with *nonstandard load configurations,* otherwise called *permit loads,* and a bridge needs to be analyzed for this loading as well. Permit loads refer to vehicles having nonstandard lengths and widths or gross weight *exceeding* 80,000 lb. Permits may be required for single-trip (infrequent) or for multiple-trip (frequent) loads. Requests for single-trip permits for vehicles with gross weights over 800,000 lb and for multiple-trip permits for vehicles with gross weights of 160,000 lb have been reported in New Mexico [White, Minor, and Derucher, 1992].

The AASHTO criteria [AASHTO, 1970; AASHTO, 1994] recommend issuance of permits for loads exceeding the inventory capacity, but not exceeding the operating capacity. Since it is critical that under no circumstances should the stress level in any bridge component exceed the operating rating stress level, the permitting authority should ensure that the permitted heavy loads are well distributed over the vehicle so as not to create unacceptable stress levels in the bridge. The single-trip permit should therefore be issued only if the pertinent load does not cause stress levels beyond the operating rating stress levels. In this case, however, caution should be exercised to strictly limit the number of such permits so as to preclude the possibility of fatigue failure [NCHRP, 1987a, 1988, 1989b]. On the other hand, multiple-trip permits can be issued if the stress levels caused by the pertinent load do not exceed the inventory rating stress levels. Since the operating rating for a bridge would already be known in terms of an HS truck, the rating for the permit load can be calculated without reanalyzing the entire bridge for the permit load. The required rating factor for the permit load, RF_{per}, can be derived for slabs and beams as follows [White, Minor, and Derucher, 1992].

The operating rating factor, RF_{op}, can be expressed as

$$RF_{op} = \frac{M_u - 1.3M_D}{1.3M_{L+I}} \qquad (10.13)$$

Similarly, the rating factor for the permit load, RF_{per}, can be expressed as

$$RF_{per} = \frac{M_u - 1.3M_D}{1.3M_{per}} \qquad (10.14)$$

Dividing Eq. 10.14 by Eq. 10.13 yields

$$\frac{RF_{per}}{RF_{op}} = \frac{M_{L+I}}{M_{per}} \qquad (10.15)$$

Expressing $M_{L+I} = M_{HS}$ = moment due to HS20 truck loading, Eq. 10.15 can be expressed as

$$RF_{per} = \left[\frac{M_{HS}}{M_{per}}\right] \times RF_{op} \qquad (10.16)$$

Since the rating factor for the operating rating, R_{op}, is always less than 1.0, an RF_{per} greater than 1.0 would indicate that the permit vehicle would cause stresses higher than the operating capacity of the bridge.

A comprehensive discussion on bridge rating, with several examples, is presented by White, Minor, and Derucher [1992]. Computer programs for rating analysis of highway bridges can be found in several references, of which [WHD, 1973; White and Minor, 1989; Woodward and Minor, 1990] are representative.

10.3.3 Bridge Posting

What is done after the rating analysis of a deficient bridge has been performed? Generally speaking, a sign indicating the safe load limit is posted near the approach of the bridge. The practice of posting safe loads varies widely, for the value of the load limit itself would have two values—one based on the inventory rating and the other based on the operating rating. Essentially, posting load limits for a bridge is a jurisdictional policy decision to be made by the bridge owners. Bridge posting may be made if

1. The legal load exceeds the inventory rating
2. The legal load exceeds the operating rating
3. Or the value of load lies in between the inventory and the operating ratings

One should remember, however, that a bridge may be posted for load limits for reasons other than structural deficiency. For example, a bridge may be posted for a lower level of loads to restrict or limit certain types of traffic. A discussion on bridge weight limit posting practices can be found in several references [NCH SYN, 1984, 1988b].

10.4
BRIDGE REHABILITATION

10.4.1 General Considerations

The Point Pleasant Bridge catastrophe of 1967 was a defining event for the nation's bridge engineers. It drew attention to the critical fact that bridges form a vital link in our infrastructure and need regular inspection and maintenance to be kept safe and serviceable for any length of time.

Many of the structurally deficient bridges are good candidates for *rehabilitation*. Experience has shown that old bridges, when properly rehabilitated, often serve as well as new bridges. A classic example of a rehabilitated bridge that has served over 150 years is Telford's suspension bridge over the Menai Straits in England, the world's first bridge over ocean waters. Opened to traffic on January 30, 1826, and retrofitted in 1839, the Menai Straits Bridge served well until 1939 when it was rehabilitated. It is still in satisfactory service [Gies, 1963]. Often, bridges are built with future expansion in mind.

New York's Verrazano Narrows Bridge was initially built in 1964 with six lanes on a single deck; the second deck was added in 1980 to accommodate the increased traffic.

The two terms generally used in the context of strengthening bridges are *rehabilitation* and *retrofitting*. They involve engineering solutions that are completely different from routine maintenance or repair work.

A distinction is made between *rehabilitation* and *repairs,* depending on the scope of the work involved. The term "repairs" often refers to corrective action or steps taken for common maintenance for an otherwise functional bridge. On the other hand, the term "rehabilitation" implies implementing a planned upgrade of a bridge to a desired level of service. It generally involves significant improvements in structurally deficient or functionally obsolete bridges to enhance their load or traffic-carrying capacities, or to prolong their service life. Common bridge repairs would include items such as patching a portion of the deck, repairing or replacing a damaged component of the superstructure, repairing and cleaning frozen bearings, etc. Rehabilitation, on the other hand, refers to, in layman's terms, giving new life to an otherwise structurally deficient or functionally obsolete bridge.

The term "retrofitting" also involves strengthening a bridge, and therefore may be considered simply as rehabilitation. The difference between rehabilitation and retrofitting is often blurred, and academic at best. The goal in both cases is to upgrade a bridge to a desired level of service. In the current engineering practice, however, the term "retrofitting" is generally used in the context of "strengthening" older bridges for seismic safety or upgrade, a task referred to as seismic retrofit. It involves uniquely engineered solutions to modify dynamic characteristics of bridge components and member connections. The goal of a seismic retrofit is to provide additional capacity requirements and, through modifications, to force the bridge to the desired behavior during a seismic event.

There is no such thing as an everlasting bridge; all bridges age. With aging of the nation's highway bridges, their rehabilitation has become a problem of significant dimension, which has been compounded by an ever-increasing demand for wider and heavier load-carrying vehicles. This development simply translates into a demand for increasing the load-carrying capacity of bridges by rehabilitating them. Rehabilitation of a bridge could often be a more cost-effective alternative than its replacement, an idea that has gained significant importance because of dwindling revenues and budgetary constraints. As a result, rehabilitation work has gained significant momentum, and increasing percentages of infrastructure budgets are being spent on this type of work.

Not all bridges can be rehabilitated economically, however. In some cases, a bridge may be evaluated as so deficient that its rehabilitation is precluded as a cost-effective alternative, justifying replacement of the entire bridge. A famous case in point is that of the first successful railway bridge in the world, the double-deck Niagara Bridge (a main span of 821 ft with the upper deck carrying the railroad and the lower deck for the foot and the carriageway) built in 1855 by John Roebling (discussed in Chapter 1). Over time, the trains had become too heavy (two and a half times the original design load) for this bridge to support without frequent and expensive repairs. As a result, it was simply removed from service and was replaced at an adjacent site in 1896 by a 500-foot double-deck arch span. This bridge was retrofitted in 1920 and is still in satisfactory service [Steinman and Watson, 1957]. Another well-known case is that of the 1969 dismantling of the eyebar suspension bridge over the Ohio River at St Mary's, West Virginia, and its replacement by a new bridge shortly after the 1967 collapse of the identical Point Pleasant Bridge [Fisher, 1984].

The problem of retrofitting the San Francisco–Oakland Bay Bridge in California (Fig. 1.56, Chapter 1; also referred to as the Bay Bridge for short), completed in 1936, is a case study in progress worth serious consideration. A portion of this bridge was seriously damaged during the M 7.1 Loma Prieta earthquake on October 17, 1989 (discussed later). A postearthquake investigation revealed that this bridge was seriously lacking in adequate seismic resistance. The cost to retrofit the bridge, based on initial investigations, was estimated at $650 million. Further investigations led to the revised (1996) estimated cost of retrofitting as $1.2 billion, approaching the cost of *replacing* the bridge. As a result, replacement, rather than retrofitting, of the entire eastern portion of the bridge—from Yerba Buena Island to the Oakland shoreline (also referred to as the East Bay Crossing)—is being contemplated.

Aside from the functional and structural deficiencies that are common to all types of bridges, some are unique to suspension bridges. These include deterioration of the protective systems of the main cables and suspenders, deterioration of the cable both inside and outside the anchorage and tower saddle, deterioration of cable bands, corrosion of suspenders, broken wires, cracked sockets, loose and missing bolts, and problems caused by vibrations.

Some old truss bridges are found to be structurally deficient in many respects: light trusses, frozen bearings, steel stringers, and girders corroded so severely that major repairs to or replacement of all components are required to keep the bridge safe and operational. Such bridges may be ideal candidates for replacement. During an in-depth inspection in 1972 of an old steel truss bridge in Berwick, Pennsylvania, the author observed severely corroded floor beams and stringers with perforations (as a result of corrosion) in webs of several stringers. Corrosion was so severe that thick scales of rust, formed on webs and flanges, could be scraped with fingernails (Figs. 10.2 and 10.3). The expansion bearings were also frozen as a result of severe corrosion and debris build-up. The rating analysis of the truss indicated obvious (because of age) structural deficiency. The entire bridge was replaced about five years later. Effects of corrosion on steel beams in highway bridge superstructures and its potential as a strength reducer were discussed in Chapter 8.

Decision making regarding rehabilitation versus replacement is at best difficult, for it depends on various factors that vary widely, both regionally and from state to state. Weissman et al. [1990] have discussed a procedure, based on the Texas bridge system and NBI data, that can be used to assist managers in selecting and prioritizing bridge rehabilitation and replacement projects. According to one model that assumes the useful service life of a bridge is 60 years, after which the structure needs to be replaced, and that the average bridge will need a rehabilitation activity at midlife or 30 years, the estimated cost of these activities is predicted as $215 per square meter for rehabilitation and $377 per square meter for replacement in 1988 dollar values [Weissman et al., 1990].

FIGURE 10.2
Severe corrosion of steel stringers supporting an open steel deck of a steel through-truss bridge.

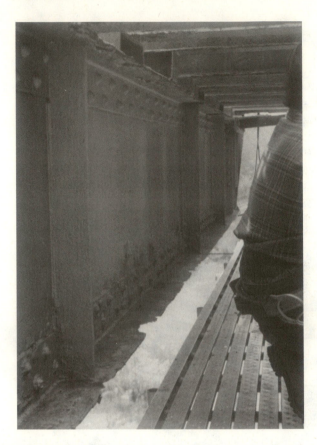

FIGURE 10.3
Severe corrosion of the bottom flange of a floor beam (a plate girder) of a steel through-truss bridge.

10.4.2 Rehabilitation of Superstructures

In recognition of the magnitude and the importance of rehabilitation work, considerable information has been published on the subject during the past few years [Mancarti, 1982; Warner, 1981; Park, 1984; FHWA, 1984a; ASTM STP, 1990; BERR, 1990; Golabi and Thompson, 1990; BR, 1992; Guide, 1993; NCHRP, 1980a,c; Xanthakos, 1996]. The nature and the scope of work involved in rehabilitation vary widely, depending on the nature and scope of the structural deficiency, or the nature of the functional obsolescence of a bridge. Structural strengthening techniques are generally divided into four categories [Klaiber et al., 1987; Wipf, Klaiber, and Hall, 1981]:

1. Addition or modification of a member or support
2. Reduction of dead load
3. Application of external post-tensioning
4. Increased bridge stiffness in either the transverse or the longitudinal direction

  Building a damage-resistant concrete deck remains an elusive goal. The most common form of rehabilitation work involves extensive repairs to or replacement of the concrete deck (partially or wholly), which may have deteriorated significantly, affecting its load-carrying capacity. This type of rehabilitation work is quite common in the snow regions, where deicing chemicals penetrate the concrete deck and cause damaging deterioration of steel reinforcing bars [Deithelm, Tracey, and Ingberg, 1972; Minor and White, 1988; NCHRP, 1983]. The rust layer formed on the reinforcing bars causes them to expand laterally, creating tension in concrete and consequent cracking and spalling. This leads to accelerated corrosion, resulting in the rapid deterioration and shortened service life of the deck. Often, such decks go through periodic protective overlays of asphalt or modified latex concrete, sometimes without removal of the existing wearing surface course. This practice results in increasing the dead load of the deck beyond that considered in the original design and lowers the live-load-carrying capacity of the bridge. In such situations, the entire deck may warrant replacement by a lighter one.

In some cases, even sound existing decks may be replaced by lighter decks in order to reduce dead load and thereby increase the live-load capacity of the superstructure. Such decks may be made of lightweight concrete, high-strength concrete, or steel grid flooring (open or filled with lightweight concrete, discussed in Chapter 8), or they may be steel [Chang, 1961] or aluminum orthotropic decks [Rogerson et al., 1967; Stahl, 1990]. Structural aluminum possesses the advantages of greater strength compared with structural steel, with only one-third the weight; consequently, it lends itself as a viable alternative for building lighter structures. In 1933, marking the very first use of aluminum in bridge work, the entire suspended flooring (including roadway, sidewalks, stringers, and floor beams) of the two 360-foot lenticular trusses of Pittsburgh's 50-year-old Smithfield Street Bridge over the Monongahela River was replaced with aluminum counterparts. The result was a superstructure that was about 800 tons lighter, with increased live-load capacity and enhanced service life [Steinman and Watson, 1957]. Open steel grid flooring (discussed in Chapter 8), in addition to being lighter, also offers the advantage of being free from drainage requirements, as snow and rain water can escape through the grid openings; a disadvantage is that it is slippery when wet. Recently, many varieties of cement-based composites (discussed in Chapters 2 and 8) have been used for deck replacement.

The second type of rehabilitation work involves the strengthening or replacement of existing damaged or deteriorated beams supporting a deck. For this, many innovative schemes have been developed and used throughout the world. The choice of a proper rehabilitation technique depends on several factors, including the type of deck, the type of beams or girders (steel, reinforced, or prestressed concrete), and the nature and scope of work involved. Generally, the work involved is cumbersome, and may be disruptive to traffic since this type of work may involve partial or complete closure of a bridge.

Strength of corroded [NCHRP, 1990a] or otherwise damaged steel beams can be evaluated, and they can be strengthened or replaced as necessary. Several methods for strengthening steel beams, such as stiffening by welding steel plates, prestressing, developing composite action, etc., have been developed [Klaiber et al., 1987; Wipf, Klaiber, and Hall, 1981] and have been successfully used in many projects. According to Klaiber et al. [1987], over 375 articles have been published on various techniques for strengthening and repairing various types of bridges.

Flanges and webs of steel beams can be strengthened by welding cover plates. This technique increases both cross-sectional area and stiffness of beams, and thus increases load-carrying capacity [Wipf, Klaiber, and Hall, 1981; Dunker, Klaiber, and

Sanders, 1987]. Stringers in the adjacent spans can be spliced to develop continuity under live load, resulting in reduced moments and deflections. Alternatively, steel beams can be post-tensioned using prestressing cables, a method for increasing the beams' load-carrying capacity, the successful use of which has been amply reported in the literature [ASCE–AASHO, 1968; Sterian, 1969; Ferjencik, 1971/1972; Kar, 1974; Wiley, Klaiber, and Dunker, 1981; Grace, 1981; Seim, 1983; Mancarti, 1984; Dunker, 1985; Dunker, Klaiber, and Sanders, 1985; Preston, 1985; Daoud, 1987; Troitsky, Zielinski, and Pimpriker, 1987; Troitsky and Rabbani, 1987; Ayyub, Sohn, and Saadatmanesh, 1988; Wiley, 1988; Troitsky, Zielinski, and Rabbani, 1989; Troitsky, 1989]. These methods can also be used to increase the load-carrying capacity of concrete deck–steel beam composite bridges. Several examples of applying the technique of post-tensioning single- and multiple-span steel, concrete, and composite bridges are reported in the literature [Ferjencik, 1971/1972; Troitsky, 1989; Wipf, Klaiber, and Hall, 1981]. Klaiber et al. [1987] have presented 33 examples of how post-tensioning techniques can be applied to single- and multiple-span bridges of steel, concrete, and composite construction. Sterian [1969] and Ferjencik [1971/1972] have discussed examples of post-tensioning techniques used for steel bridges in Europe. This technique can also be used for building new bridges, as evidenced by the 10-span, continuous, cable-stressed, composite, concrete and steel Bonners Ferry Bridge, Idaho, built in 1982 [Wiley, Klaiber, and Dunker, 1981].

A majority of bridges built in the last 50 years have combination decks (noncomposite reinforced concrete slab supported by steel stringers) that have proven deficient by today's standards. The live-load capacity of such bridges can be increased by converting them to composite bridges. This is accomplished by welding studs to the existing steel beams during replacement of the deteriorated deck, often with lightweight concrete. Noncomposite slabs can be converted into composite slabs even if they are judged to be sound and do not need to be replaced. In such cases, studs can be welded to the supporting beams with the slab still in place. Holes are drilled through the deck to the top of the beam flanges, to which studs are welded. Epoxy is injected between the deck and the beam to create bond, and the holes in the slab are grouted. Several examples of such projects, completed at less than 50 percent of the cost of demolishing and rebuilding a new bridge, are reported in the literature [Klaiber, Dunker, and Sanders, 1981; Klaiber et al., 1983; Dunker et al., 1985; Dunker, Klaiber, and Sanders, 1987; AISC, 1993a,b].

Reinforced concrete girders most commonly deteriorate as a result of corrosion of steel reinforcing bars, causing the superstructure to be structurally deficient. Several methods of repairing and rehabilitating cracked or deteriorated concrete, such as injecting epoxy in the cracks and external reinforcing, have been used, and new methods continue to be researched and developed. One good alternative is to replace girders containing highly corroded reinforcing bars (that may be seemingly irreparable) by fewer high-strength prestressed concrete girders, often using lightweight concrete decks. Recent developments in high-strength composite fibers have shown significant promise for use in rehabilitation of concrete structures. Because of their light weight and high modulus of elasticity, they are considered appropriate for strengthening and retrofitting bridge components. Polyaramid, glass, carbon, and similar materials (discussed in Chapter 2) have been used.

One of the methods of strengthening existing reinforced concrete beams is to bond steel plates to their tension faces. This is an economical and effective method successfully used for both bridges and buildings in many countries worldwide—England, France, Belgium, Poland, Switzerland, and South Africa [Barrett, 1985; Brown, 1973; Davies and Powell, 1984; Fleming and King, 1967; Hugenschimdt, 1976; Iion and Otokawa, 1981; Irwin, 1975; Jones et al., 1980; Jones and Swamy, 1984; Jones, Swamy, and Salman, 1985; Jones, Swamy, and Bloxham, 1986; Lerchental, 1967; MacDonald, 1978; Mander, 1974; Parkinson, 1978; Raithby, 1980; Ryback, 1981; Sommerard, 1971; Swamy and Jones, 1980; Swamy, Jones, and Ang, 1982; Swamy, Jones, and Bloxham, 1987; Van Germert, 1982]. Its main advantage is that the required operations are simple and can be carried out in a relatively short time without interrupting the use of the structure. Conceptually, the method used is similar to the coverplating of steel beams to increase their strength and stiffness, as mentioned earlier. The technique consists of epoxy-bonding steel plates, which serve as external reinforcements, to reinforced beams, not only in the tension zone but also in compression and shear. Studies by Fleming and King [1967] show that the addition of glued plates to existing reinforced concrete beams substantially increases their flexural stiffness and reduces cracking and structural deformations at all load levels. Furthermore, these plates increase the flexural strength of beams by 10 to 15 percent. With the advent of composite materials, research is under way to explore the possibilities of using fiber-reinforced plastic plates and laminates that can be epoxy-bonded to reinforced concrete beams [An, Saadatmanesh, and Ehsani, 1991; Brown, 1992; Neuerm and Kaiser, 1991; Saadatmanesh and Ehsani, 1991; Crasto, Kim, and Mistretta, 1996; Shahawy and Beitelman, 1996].

Generally, prestressed concrete bridges have been found to be rather trouble free, although corrosion of prestressing steel (discussed in Chapter 7) has become a matter of concern. Studies [Dunker and Rabbat, 1992; Gustaferro, Hillier, and Janney, 1983; Novokshchenov, 1993; Pfeifer, Landgren, and Zoob, 1987; NCHRP, 1980b, 1989a; NCH SYN, 1988a; Schupack and Suarez, 1991] indicate that most of them, although nearing their 50-year service life, are still in excellent condition. They have needed little repair work and, with regular maintenance, are expected to last for many more years. This view is based on several tests on prestressed girders removed from several replacement bridges that have shown them to be in reasonably good condition [Riessauw and Taerwe, 1980; PCI, 1984; Olsen and French, 1990; Shenoy and Frantz, 1991; Labia, Saiidi, and Douglas, 1993; Tabatabai and Dickson, 1993]. Methods of damage evaluation and repair for prestressed concrete members are discussed in several references [Koretzky, 1978; NCHRP, 1980b; NCH SYN, 1983]. Enhanced experience in mitigating corrosion of prestressing steels [Podolny, 1993] and advances in applications of FRP materials (fiber-reinforced plastics, discussed in Chapter 2) to prestressed concrete bridges [Minosaku, 1992; Tsuji, Kanda, and Tamura, 1993] should result in marked improvement in the service life performance of these bridges.

Under certain conditions, prestressed concrete girders may have been damaged so significantly as to warrant replacement. A case in point is the rehabilitation of the Walnut Lane Memorial Bridge, Philadelphia, Pennsylvania. Built in 1950, the post-tensioned girders of this three-span bridge had developed longitudinal cracks in the bottom flanges. As a result, they were replaced in 1990 by the new AASHTO Type VI prestressed girders [Zollman et al., 1992].

Often, the improvement of poor geometry in an existing bridge may justify its rehabilitation. A good many bridges throughout the country were designed during the early part of this century for H15 or HS15 truck loading. As a result of proper care and maintenance, many of these bridges have been functioning well. Some are magnificent structures that have become historic landmarks worthy of preservation [NCH SYN, 1983]. Unfortunately, however, many of these bridges have become functionally obsolete because they do not conform to today's geometric standards. Such bridges have to be either rehabilitated or posted for lighter loads and restricted traffic, reducing their usefulness.

Typically, poor bridge geometry is characterized by inadequacies such as substandard vertical or horizontal clearances, narrow width, or a combination of these factors, as compared with the current standards. Methods and schemes used in rehabilitating such bridges will depend on the nature and scope of rehabilitation work involved, and several schemes may be considered. An existing bridge can be widened either only on one side or on both sides of the centerline of the bridge. The desirable option will depend on factors such as the right-of-way, alignment of the approach roads, and sight distance. Existing vertical clearance, a problem typical of old through-truss bridges, can be increased by properly modifying the depth of portals and sway bracings or by lowering the floor system. The low overhead clearances on these bridges result in a lot of accidents due to overly high vehicles. Often these bridges have to be closed for necessary repairs, resulting in long detours, which exacerbates the traffic problem.

Where grade separation structures are involved, the vertical clearance can be increased by raising the overpass or lowering the roadway underneath. The width of the road underneath can often be increased by modifying the substructural components (relocation of bents) supporting the overhead structure. An innovative scheme was used for widening, in 1992, of the four-lane, 80-ft-wide I-5 highway under the Capital Boulevard Bridge in Olympia, Washington, to an eight-lane 146-ft-wide highway. The existing three-span (84, 110, and 84 ft) was a continuous steel bridge, supported on two 75-ft-high reinforced concrete columns. It was modified to a columnless structure supported by two elliptical two-hinged steel arches spaced 54 ft apart and spanning 184 ft (Fig. 10.4). With a rise of 49 ft, the depth of the two-cell 7-ft-wide nonprismatic cross section of the arches varies from 6 ft at the springings to 4 ft at the crown. The modified structure resulted not only in a wider highway, but also in an aesthetically superior structure [Van Lund et al., 1981]. The $34 million rehabilitation of the Belle Vernon Bridge, which carries Interstate 70 over the Monongahela River in Belle Vernon, Pennsylvania, completed in December 1992, is another example of innovative rehabilitation. Widening was achieved by a unique conversion of the existing deck trusses to trapezoidal space frames (Fig. 10.5), thus maximizing the effective use of the existing trusses while minimizing substructure widening and additional steel requirements. As an added advantage, it also eliminated hydraulic involvement with an adjacent stream and the related right-of-way costs [AISC, 1993b].

Innovative schemes and analytical methods can often be used to investigate and rehabilitate old bridges, with due considerations for the future. For example, future growth patterns and traffic safety considerations may require four traffic lanes in place of the existing two or three. In such a case, an existing two-lane bridge, with required modification, can be utilized as one-half of a new four-lane structure. Many truss bridges

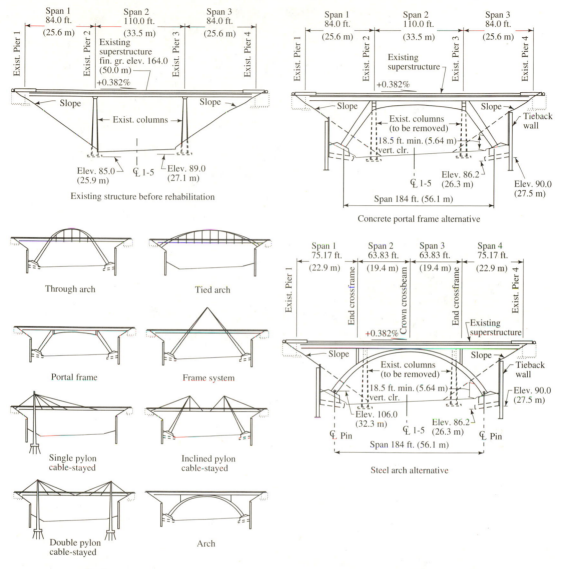

FIGURE 10.4
Rehabilitation of the Capital Boulevard Undercrossing, Olympia, Washington [Van Lund et al., 1981].

have been performing well for many years carrying full highway traffic (including some overloads) without any serviceability problems, indicating that they are perhaps not as deficient as predicted by the commonly used two-dimensional analysis. A three-dimensional truss analysis using the load factor method may give better insight into the member stresses as compared with the results of a two-dimensional analysis using the service load method. A bridge deck can be analyzed by the finite element method

(a)

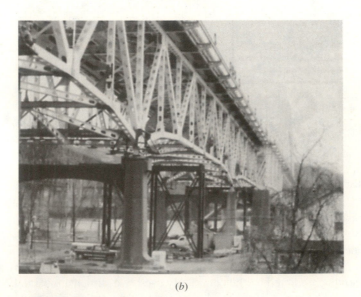

(b)

FIGURE 10.5
Rehabilitation of the Belle Vernon Bridge, Belle Vernon,
Pennsylvania (a) after construction, (b) prior to reconstruction
[AISC, 1993b].

to better predict its behavior under loads. An example where such methodologies have been used is the Apalachicola River Bridge between Bristol and Blountstown, Florida. A three-dimensional analysis of the truss using GTStrudl (a computer program) improved the truss rating from HS15 to HS22. A global three-dimensional finite element analysis of the existing noncomposite deck using a ribbed plate model (BRUFEM—Bridge Rating Using Finite Element Analysis) improved the deck rating from HS15 to HS21 [Sessions, Blanchard, and Locke, 1991].

10.4.3 Seismic Retrofit

10.4.3.1 Seismic damage to bridges

According to Webster's dictionary, "retrofit" means "to furnish (an automobile, airplane, etc.) with parts or equipment made available *after* the time of original manufacture." Structural *retrofitting* simply implies *reinforcing* or *strengthening* of an existing structure to resist loads and resulting deformations larger than those allowed by the original design values.

The idea of bridge retrofitting has been around for a long time. Many bridges had been retrofitted in the nineteenth century to improve stability under wind loads. A well-known example is the retrofitting of Telford's Menai Straits Bridge in 1839 [Gies, 1963; Steinman and Watson, 1957]. Several well-known suspension bridges had to be variously retrofitted to control dangerous oscillations due to wind loads during the early part of the twentieth century. Some of the important works include the 1945 retrofit of the Bronx–Whitestone Bridge, New York, at a cost of $1.3 million to change stiffening plate girders to trusses; the 1953 retrofit of the Golden Gate Bridge, San Francisco, at a cost of $3 million to provide an additional bracing system; and the insertion of diagonal stays in the Deer Island Bridge, Maine [O'Connor, 1971]. It is interesting to note that, with proper maintenance and structural preservation, the service lives of suspension bridges can approach 200 years.

The catastrophic damage to bridges during the February 8, 1971, M 6.6 San Fernando, California, earthquake [Fung et al., 1971; Jennings, 1971] marked a turning point in bridge design practices in the United States, for it spotlighted the little-known but extreme vulnerability of bridges to earthquake damage. From it evolved the present-day program of seismic retrofit of bridges in California and elsewhere in the country. Damage to transportation structures in the October 1, 1987, M 5.9 Whittier Narrows earthquake, which involved the near collapse of the I-605/I-5 Overcrossing in the Los Angeles area [Gates, Mellon, and Klien, 1988; Priestley, 1988], exacerbated the problem of seismically weak bridges.

The October 17, 1989, M 7.1 Loma Prieta earthquake, the largest to occur in the San Francisco Bay area since the great earthquake of 1906, caused 62 deaths, 3757 injuries, and property damage estimated at $5.6 billion [EERI, 1990]. Over 1300 buildings were destroyed and another 20,000 damaged. The damage to bridges was estimated at $1.8 billion [EERI, 1990; EQE, 1989; NIST, 1990; USGAO, 1990]. Thirteen bridges in the area had to be closed after the earthquake as a result of damage that varied from damaged bearings to complete collapse. Two of the most dramatic bridge failures during this earthquake were those of the Cypress Viaduct (Fig. 10.6) (built in 1957), in which

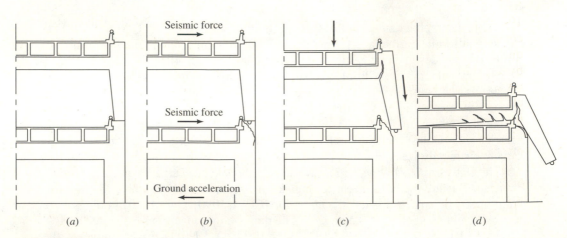

FIGURE 10.6
Collapse of the Cypress Viaduct during the 1989 Loma Prieta earthquake: photograph of the collapse
(above), the failure mode (below) [EERI, 1990].

41 people died, and the link span of the San Francisco–Oakland Bay Bridge (Fig. 10.7), both located about 60 miles from the earthquake's epicenter. Somewhat less spectacular was the collapse of several spans of the Struve Slough Bridge (Fig. 10.8), built in 1964. A complete discussion of the failure modes of these and other bridges is reported in the literature [EERI, 1990; NIST, 1990; Miranda and Bertero, 1991;]. While many portions and components of these multispan structures were variously damaged, a common characteristic failure was the collapse of decks as they pulled away from their supports. Huge losses caused by this earthquake provided the necessary impetus for a bridge retrofit program in California.

It is instructive to note that the damaged and collapsed bridges were built according to the available knowledge, seismic codes, and standards then used in engineering practice, but that have since changed substantially. As a result, many of the old bridges are now being discovered as seriously deficient in seismic resistance [Priestley and Seible, 1991,1994] and are therefore in need of costly retrofitting or replacement. For example, the San Francisco–Oakland Bay Bridge was designed in 1933 for 10% g earthquake accelerations, comparable to the levels specified in the 1930 Uniform Building Code for buildings. The knowledge of damaging earthquake motions was very limited at the time—the first few measurements of strong motions were not made until the 1933 Long Beach earthquake. There was some seismic strengthening of this bridge with the installation of cable restrainers in the 1970s. New design standards require the west side of the bridge to be strong enough to withstand an M 8.3 earthquake on the San Andreas Fault, and the eastern span is required to be strong enough to endure an M 7.5 earthquake on the Hayward Fault (Fig. 10.10), a significant departure from the seismic requirements of the 1930 Uniform Building Code then in use.

A brief history of seismic code development in the United States was presented in Chapter 3 and is reported in the literature [EERI, 1990; Miranda, 1993]. Historically, bridge builders in some European countries and New Zealand have considered seismic forces, but because of relatively low seismicity in those regions, vigorous research efforts toward earthquake-resistant bridges have not been made [ATC, 1982; Chapman, 1979; Ravara, 1979]. In Japan, a country of high seismicity, seismic forces have been considered in design since 1926, following the experience of the 1923 Kanto earthquake [Ohashi et al., 1979b]. In an effort to mitigate damages similar to those caused by the 1964 Niigata earthquake (Fig. 10.9), specifications for the design of earthquake-resistant highway bridges [JRA, 1971] were issued in Japan in 1971. However, because of the high seismicity in regions such as California, which has well over 22,000 bridges, it is in the United States where significant seismic code development has taken place. Studies have indicated that, although California bridges are more vulnerable to seismic problems because of the San Andreas Fault (Fig. 10.10) [Cluff, 1989], some regions in the eastern and central United States share similar problems [Atkinson, 1987; Saadeghvaziri, 1990].

10.4.3.2 California highway bridge retrofit program

In 1981, the Applied Technology Council developed the first guidelines [ATC, 1981] for retrofit of existing bridges. In 1983, it developed seismic design requirements for new bridges [ATC, 1983], which were national in scope and, therefore, were adopted by AASHTO as Guide Specifications [AASHTO, 1983]. These later became a

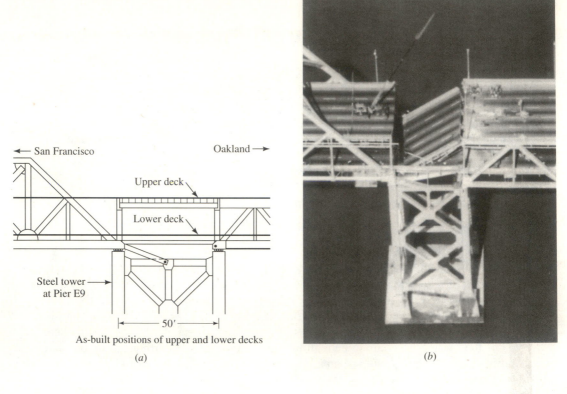

San Francisco ←

Oakland →

Upper deck

Lower deck

Steel tower
at Pier E9 →

├─── 50' ───┤

As-built positions of upper and lower decks

(a)

(b)

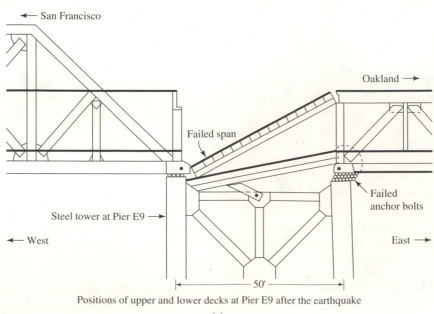

San Francisco ←

Oakland →

Failed span

Steel tower at Pier E9 →

← West

East →

Failed
anchor bolts

├─── 50' ───┤

Positions of upper and lower decks at Pier E9 after the earthquake

(c)

FIGURE 10.7
Collapse of the San Francisco–Oakland Bay Bridge Viaduct [EERI, 1990].

FIGURE 10.8
Collapse of the Struve Slough Bridge. Note the columns punching through the collapsed reinforced concrete spans.

part of the AASHTO standard [AASHTO, 1991]. Both past and continuing research directed toward developing better design codes and standards for new earthquake-resistant bridges has been amply discussed in the literature [Imbsen, 1981; ATC, 1986; Buckle, Mayes, and Button, 1987; Priestley and Park, 1987a; AASHTO, 1991; Mahin and Boroschek, 1991; Imbsen & Associates, Inc., 1992; Seyed, 1992], and summarized by Mayes et al. [1992]. Although retrofit needs were recognized soon after the 1971 San Fernando earthquake, it was the 1989 Loma Prieta earthquake that galvanized the seismic retrofitting effort. That earthquake sparked a keen interest in the engineering community that drove it to retrofitting research and practice with missionary zeal. Following the Loma Prieta earthquake, the California Department of Transportation (CALTRANS) embarked on a retrofitting and research program of unprecedented scale, recognized as one of the world's most extensive and technologically advanced retrofit programs for highway bridges. Some important aspects of this program are presented in the following paragraphs.

California's seismic retrofit program evolved from observations that the 1971 San Fernando earthquake [Fung et al., 1971; Jennings, 1971] collapsed portions of the nearly complete I-205/I-5 and I-5/SR-14 interchanges in Los Angeles County, and

FIGURE 10.9
Collapse of the Showa Bridge during the 1964 Niigata earthquake, Japan. Two piers in the middle of the river failed, causing three spans to drop. Two other spans slipped off piers that remained upright [EERI, 1990].

severely damaged several other bridges in the area. Typically, these bridges were continuous multispan elevated structures consisting of reinforced and prestressed concrete multicell box girders. The resultant damage was caused by the differential movement at the expansion joints as adjacent parts of the structures moved longitudinally in opposite directions, thus pulling a span off its supporting shelf or transferring damaging loads into the columns. This movement was sufficient for some bridges to displace the roadway decks off their supports (at the abutments or bents), causing them to collapse (because of the loss of the underlying support) to the ground, and also causing columns to fail. This observation led CALTRANS to conclude that restraining motions at the expansion joints would keep the decks from falling and would reduce forces in the supporting elements sufficiently to prevent collapse. This conclusion formed the basis of the hinge and bearing restrainer retrofit program developed and started by CALTRANS in 1972 [Degenkolb, 1978, 1979; ATC, 1979a; FHWA, 1979, 1983, 1987; EERI, 1990; Selna, Malvar, and Zelinski, 1989]. The technique, intended to limit the opening that could occur at expansion joints, consisted of installing cable restrainers or similar devices in existing bridges throughout the state.

The restrainer units are essentially *mechanical energy dissipators* that have also been used in bridges in Japan [Uyemae, Ikewaki, and Aoyama, 1977; Yamadera and Uyemae, 1979] and New Zealand [Blakeley, 1979]. The California restrainer units were designed to resist (elastically) an arbitrary force equal to 25 percent of the lighter deck section connected. In Japanese bridges, similar restrainers are provided at supports, but they are designed to resist a horizontal force of varying magnitudes—in some cases

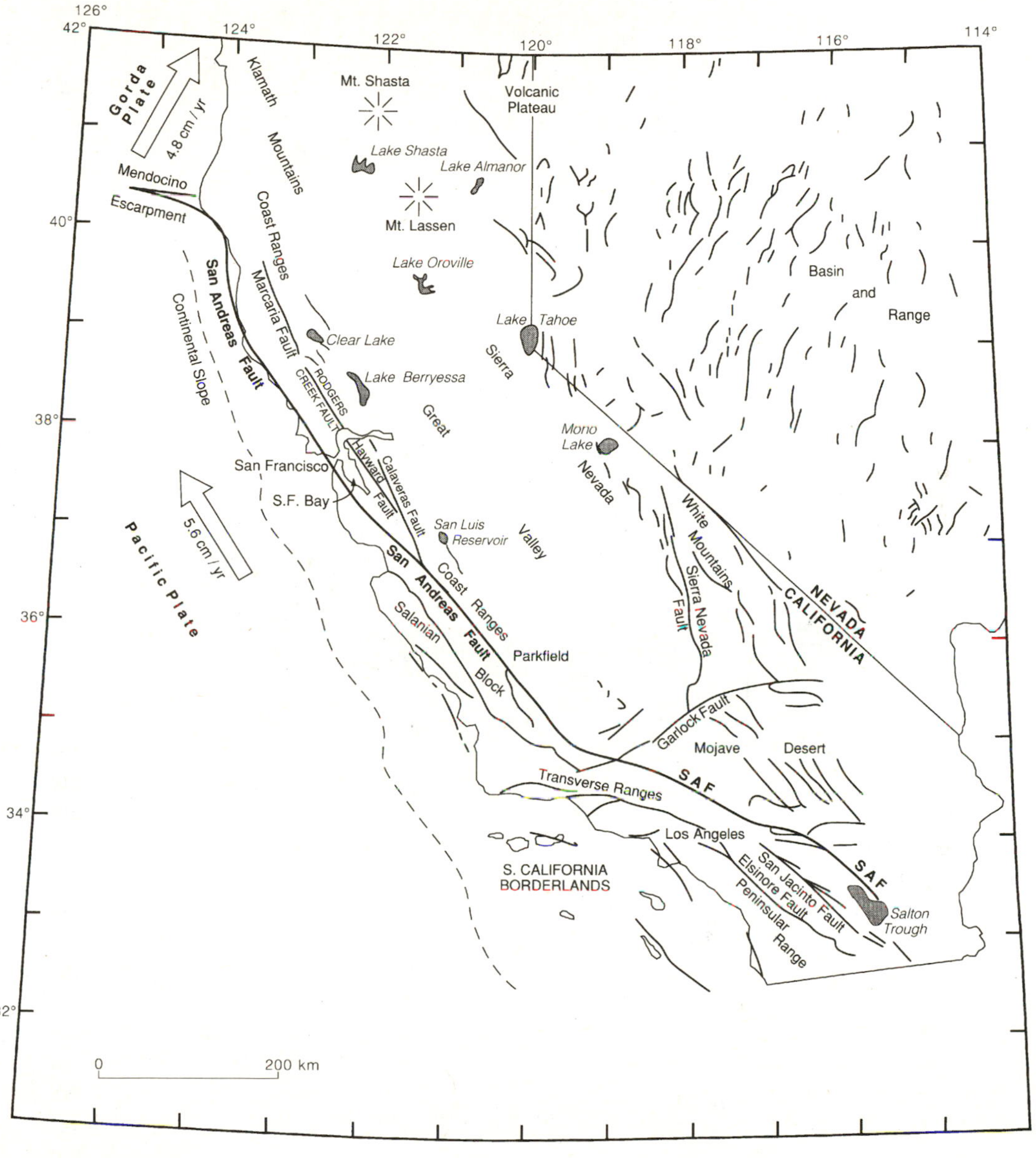

FIGURE 10.10
Map of California showing the San Andreas Fault [EERI, 1990].

as much as 100 percent of the dead-load reaction at support [Yamadera and Uyemae, 1979].

A typical retrofitting detail used for multicell concrete box girder bridges is shown in Fig. 10.11. It consists of seven $\frac{3}{4}$-in.-diameter preformed 6×19 galvanized cables (Federal Spec. RR W-410C), passing through a joint and attached to each side with special anchorages. The cables are tied to approximately 12-in.-square anchor plates

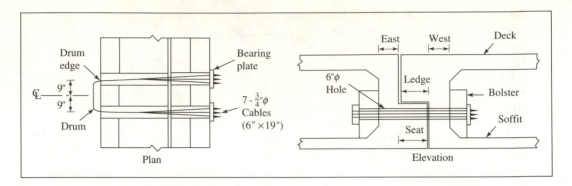

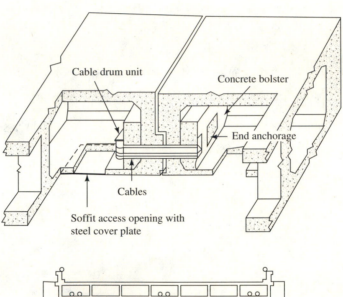

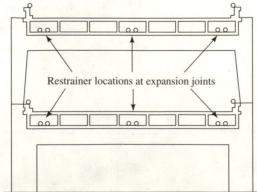

FIGURE 10.11
A cable restrainer device: (above) detail developed by CALTRANS after the 1971 San Fernando earthquake, (middle) a typical expansion joint retrofit, and (below) section of a typical bent showing cable restrainer locations [EERI, 1990].

that are $\frac{1}{2}$ in. thick, bearing on the end diaphragm of the box cells. Concrete bolsters were added to strengthen the diaphragms. Based on the working load of 50 percent of the ultimate, with an additional 33 percent overstress permitted for seismic conditions, each cable has a capacity of 30.6 kips (or 428 kips for the seven-cable unit). Customized restrainer details [Degenkolb, 1979] were developed to suit various types of bridges. Where cable restrainers are found to be undesirable or impractical, two $1\frac{1}{2}$-in. diameter high-strength steel bars ($F_y = 120$ ksi) per restrainer unit (Fig. 10.12) are used. Alternatively, cables could also be used for this scheme. Figure 10.13 shows the details of the restrainer units used for short-span T-beam bridges where the restraining force requirements are considerably lower. Figure 10.14 shows restrainer details for superstructures with steel girders: scheme (a) is used when the girders in the adjacent spans are aligned, and (b) is used when they are not aligned (offset). In the latter case, transverse beams are attached to the bottom girder flanges, which are used for anchoring the restrainer cables. Figure 10.15 shows a method of attaching the ends of steel girders directly to the supporting concrete bents.

For multicell box girders, at least two restrainer units are provided at each bent or hinge—one as close as possible to each edge of the superstructure. A minimum of one seven-cable restrainer unit placed in each exterior cell of the box girder at each hinge is generally considered sufficient to provide maximum resistance to transverse

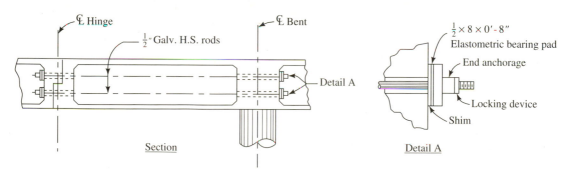

FIGURE 10.12
High-strength rod restrainer [Degenkolb, 1979].

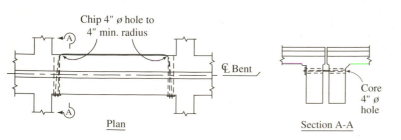

FIGURE 10.13
Restrainer unit detail used for short-span T-beam bridges [Degenkolb, 1979].

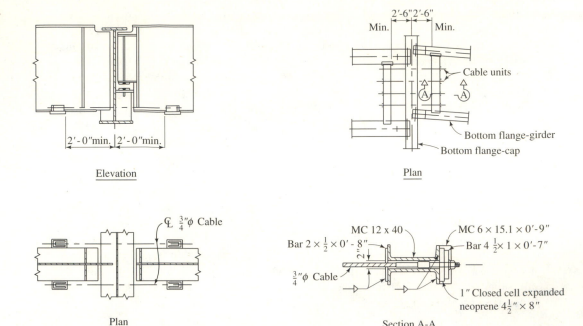

FIGURE 10.14
Restrainer details for superstructures with steel girders: (a) when the girders in the adjacent spans are aligned; (b) when the girders in the adjacent spans are not aligned [Degenkolb, 1979].

bending of the entire superstructure [Degenkolb, 1979]. In some cases, such as for the box girders of the Cypress Viaduct, an additional restrainer unit is placed in the middle cell. Necessary adjustments are made to permit normal movements of joints, such as those due to temperature changes, creep, or shrinkage, and to start acting as soon as maximum normal open joint width is exceeded. A ductility factor (explained later) of 1 is assumed for cable and bar restrainers.

In the 25 years since the 1971 earthquake, cable restrainers have been installed at expansion joints in over 1200 bridges [Degenkolb, 1979; Zelinski, 1985, 1990], but their strength and effectiveness had not been tested through research because of lack of funding. Tests [Selna and Malvar, 1987; Selna, Malvar, and Zelinski, 1989] that began in 1984 on three types of restrainers concluded that their ductility had been overestimated. Although all restrainers reached their design load during tests, two failed in anchorages rather than in the desired, more ductile mode of cable or bar elongation [EERI, 1990]. The general inadequacy of the installed restrainer devices was evident from their performance during the 1987 Whittier Narrows and the 1989 Loma Prieta earthquakes. A case in point is the performance of the I-605/I-5 Overcrossing during the Whittier Narrows earthquake. Although it did not lose any spans, the overcrossing had otherwise been badly damaged. It was concluded [EERI, 1990; Roberts, 1990] that, in spite of the presence of cable restrainer devices, a slightly greater shaking would have degraded the columns enough for complete failure to occur. In the case of the Cypress

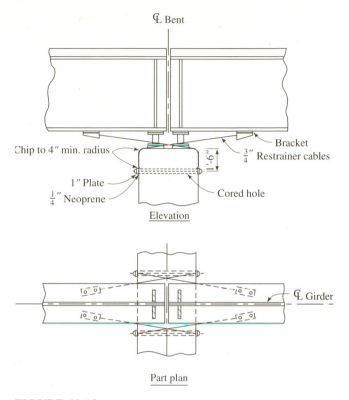

FIGURE 10.15
A method of attaching ends of steel girders directly to the supporting bents [Degenkolb, 1979].

Viaduct, a reinforced concrete structure with some prestressing and two levels of elevated roadway consisting of box girders supported by a series of 83 two-story bents, longitudinal cable restrainers were installed in 1977 at all transverse joints in the box girder bridge superstructure, to provide continuity. However, of these, 48 bents collapsed during the Loma Prieta earthquake. As one of the earliest uses of prestressed concrete in the United States, it had been designed according to state-of-the-art engineering practice at the time. But because of the insufficient knowledge of earthquake engineering at the time, it was designed as a nonductile structure. As ductility could not develop in the overstressed members of the structure under seismic loads, brittle failure of columns and joints resulted. Typical failure mode of one of the viaduct bents is shown in Fig. 10.6. In the case of the Struve Slough Bridge, 7 spans of the northbound structure and 10 spans of the southbound structure collapsed. Some of these spans were punched through, as shown in Fig. 10.8, by the supporting columns, which sheared at the transverse cap beams as the deck slabs fell to the ground. The cable restrainers, installed in 1984 at each expansion joint of this bridge, performed well, however, and held the structure together in spite of large displacements experienced by the collapsed structures. The primary cause of collapse was attributed to nonductile column and joint designs. This uncertain performance of the restrainers, originally thought to be failure-proof, led to the conclusion that joint restrainers were not by themselves sufficient to prevent collapse of some bridges supported on nonductile columns, not even for a modest-magnitude earthquake with a relatively short duration of moderate ground shaking [Zelinski, 1985; EERI, 1990; Roberts, 1990].

It is instructive to note that failure modes similar to those observed during the San Fernando earthquake were also observed in bridge failures during the Alaska and Niigata (Japan) earthquakes of 1964; the January 17, 1994, Northridge, California, M 6.7 earthquake [EERI, 1994]; and the January 17, 1995 Hygo–Ken Nanbu, Japan, M 6.8 earthquake [EERI, 1995]. Also during these earthquakes, bridge decks were displaced completely off their seats, causing decks to fall. But design deficiencies observed in these mishaps were not corrected in the pre-1971 bridges. Nevertheless, the observed performance of bridges during the San Fernando earthquake led to (1) revision of seismic design practices for new bridges in California that became and continue to be adapted for national standards, and (2) initiation of a retrofit program to correct the deficiencies of existing bridges. The revised specifications essentially incorporated more strength, ductility, and continuity into design details and, as a result, the post-1971-bridges are considered to have better seismic resistance than do their earlier counterparts. Also, as a result of the lessons learned from the 1971 San Fernando earthquake, CALTRANS introduced an improved seismic retrofit program for existing bridges.

10.4.3.3 Current seismic retrofit practices

Much has been learned through research and experience since the 1971 San Fernando earthquake, and the necessary changes involving the ductile detailing of bridges are being incorporated into new designs [ATC, 1983; EERI, 1990; Priestley and Seible, 1991; Seyed, 1991a; CALTRANS, 1992, 1995; Gamble, Hawkins, and Kaspur, 1996; Imbsen & Associates, Inc., 1992], so that these bridges would, through ductile behavior, sustain some damage, but not collapse, during an earthquake.

Lack of adequate confinement of concrete in bridge columns designed before the 1971 San Fernando earthquake has been a matter of serious concern with respect to their seismic resistance and ductility. Typically, these columns use #4 perimeter hoops at 12-in. centers placed uniformly up the column regardless of column dimensions. Out of concern for the nonductile behavior of these columns, several schemes for their retrofit were developed that included wrapping with prestressed steel hoops or with wire that is covered with a protective coat of shotcrete, and jacketing with a welded steel shell infilled with grout [Priestley and Park, 1987b; Chai, 1991; Chai, Priestley, and Seible, 1991a,b, 1994; Priestley, Seible, and Chai, 1992; Priestly, Seible, and Verma 1994; Priestley, et al., 1991a,b, 1994]. This is the current approach used extensively in California to retrofit deficient bridge columns. An extensive treatment of seismic design and retrofit of bridges has been presented by Priestley, Seible, and Calvi [1996].

The term *jacketing* refers to external encasement of concrete columns by prefabricated steel shells welded in situ. In the case of circular columns, the jacket is fabricated slightly oversized, and the gap between the steel shell and the column is filled with cement-based grout to ensure composite action between the jacket and the column. Depending on the dimensions of the jacket, the bonded steel jacket increases the lateral stiffness of the column and also the bond strength between the jacket and the grout infill. The increase in the lateral stiffness typically translates into an increase in the seismic design force for the structure. The presence of the steel jacket also reduces the effective plastic hinge length of the column, resulting in a large increase in the curvature demand at the critical section of the column. In the case of flexurally deficient *rectangular* concrete columns, strength can be enhanced by jacketing them with *elliptical* steel shells. Because the gap between the elliptical steel shell and the rectangular column would be larger than the gap in circular columns, it would typically be filled with normal-weight concrete [Chai, Priestley, and Seible, 1994].

Typical details of column retrofitting [Degenkolb, 1978, 1979] are shown in Fig. 10.16. Although test studies have demonstrated that, in the case of flexural retrofit, the steel jacket need not be extended to the full height of the column [Chai, Priestley, and Seible, 1991a,b], field applications tend to provide full extension of the steel jacket to ensure a uniform appearance to the column after retrofit. To prevent the jacket from bearing on the superstructure, the steel jacket is terminated about 2 in. short from the soffit of the superstructure. Similarly, a vertical gap is provided between the jacket and the top of the footing, although this is not apparent in Fig. 10.16.

Recently, as an alternative to steel jackets, a *fiberglass* jacket (referred to as a *high-strength fiber composite system* or *composite column casing*) has been developed for retrofitting concrete columns as a result of research at the University of California at San Diego. The technique involves wrapping continuous composite material (*E-glass* fabric or *prepreg* carbon fibers) around the existing reinforced concrete columns. After proper curing, these composite materials become sufficiently strong (similar to steel jackets) to prevent plastic shearing of column concrete. A discussion on this technique has been presented by Priestley, Seible, and Fyfe [1992, 1993].

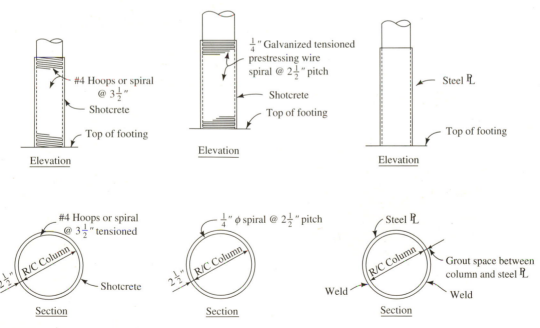

FIGURE 10.16
Various schemes for column retrofitting [Degenkolb, 1979].

In California, two types of fiber composites have been approved for column wrappings: *E-glass fiber* ($F_{ult} = 350$ ksi) and *carbon fiber* ($F_{ult} = 43,000$ ksi). Each can be provided in different thicknesses in three zones over the height of the column: (1) the upper portion of the column equal to 1.5 times the column diameter, or 1.5 times the larger lateral dimension of a rectangular column; (2) a transition zone equal to the column diameter, or equal to the larger lateral dimension of a rectangular column; and (3) the remainder as the lower portion of the column. The thickness of the fiberwrap is twice as much in the upper portion of the column as it is in the lower portion of the column, the change occurring gradually in the transition zone. The permitted fiberwrap thickness depends on the size of the column, as shown in Table 10.3. It will be noted that the minimum thickness is 0.05 in. for the carbon fiber composite and 0.10 in. for the E-glass composite. A few details of the fiberwrap column casings are shown in Fig. 10.17.

As steel jackets are the preferred standard for column retrofits in California, the composite column casings are to be used only as alternatives. The technique is considered desirable where partial-height columns or columns having limited construction access are involved [CALTRANS, 1995]. Although the fiber composite retrofit scheme has been used in many bridge retrofit projects in California [Fife and Arnold, 1996], CALTRANS [1996] imposes the following limitations for the use of composite fiber-wrap retrofit schemes:

1. Its use is limited typically to cases of ductility demands of 4 or less for circular columns and 3 or less for rectangular columns.
2. Its use is limited to circular columns of 48 in. diameter or less. For rectangular columns, the longer lateral dimension is limited to 36 in., and the sides aspect ratio should not be greater than 1.5.
3. A steel jacket is the only approved retrofit to confine (fully fix) a lap splice; however, composites may be used if a pin is assumed in the analysis at a splice.
4. Composites are not to be used for single-column bent structures.
5. Composites are not to be used if the axial dead load is greater than $0.15 f_c' A_g$.

TABLE 10.3
Thickness of the composite fiberwraps [CALTRANS, 1996]

| Column width/ diameter (in.) | Round columns | | | |
| | E-glass (in.) | | Carbon fiber (in.) | |
	t_1 minimum	t_2 minimum	t_1 minimum	t_2 minimum
12	0.20	0.10	0.05	0.05
24	0.40	0.20	0.08	0.05
36	0.60	0.30	0.12	0.06
48 maximum	0.80	0.40	0.16	0.08
	Rectangular columns			
12	0.30	0.15	0.06	0.05
24	0.60	0.30	0.12	0.06
36 maximum	0.88	0.44	0.18	0.09

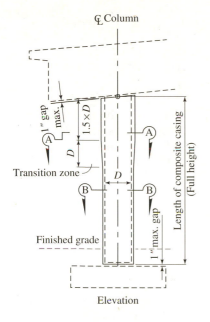

Elevation

Note:
   Existing rectangular concrete
   column surfaces shall be straight or
   slightly convex outward at all areas
   to be covered by jackets. Otherwise,
   the surface shall be filled with epoxy.

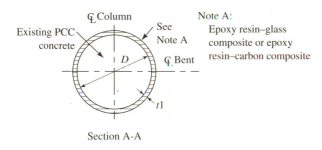

Note A:
   Epoxy resin–glass
   composite or epoxy
   resin–carbon composite

Section A-A

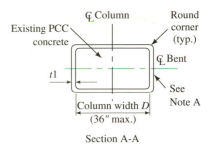

Section A-A

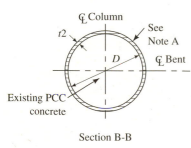

Section B-B

Circular column

(Not to scale)

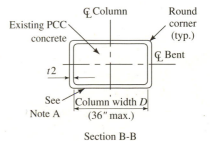

Section B-B

Rectangular column

FIGURE 10.17
Composite fiberwrap retrofit scheme for columns [CALTRANS, 1996].

SYSTEM 1
Fiber volume = 35% min.

E-glass		
Round column		
Column dia	$t1$ (min.)	$t2$ (min.)
12″	0.20″	0.20″
24″	0.35″	0.20″
36″	0.50″	0.25″
48″	0.65″	0.35″
60″	0.85″	0.40″
72″	1.00″	0.50″

E-glass		
Rectangular column		
Column width	$t1$ (min.)	$t2$ (min.)
12″	0.25″	0.20″
24″	0.50″	0.25″
36″ max.	0.75″	0.40″

SYSTEM 2
Fiber volume = 50% min.

Carbon		
Round column		
Column dia	$t1$ (min.)	$t2$ (min.)
12″	0.05″	0.05″
24″	0.07″	0.05″
36″	0.10″	0.05″
48″	0.13″	0.07″
60″	0.17″	0.08″
72″	0.20″	0.10″

Carbon		
Rectangular column		
Column width	$t1$ (min.)	$t2$ (min.)
12″	0.05″	0.05″
24″	0.10″	0.05″
36″ max.	0.15″	0.08″

General notes:

1. For column heights less than $5 \times D$, use constant thickness full height of $t1$.
2. For hexagonal or octagonal columns, use composite thickness specified in Rectangular Column table.
3. Remove any sharp corners to $1\frac{1}{2}$ in. radius minimum.
4. All materials shall be protected from moisture.
5. Drainage opening reinforcement shall be of the same material used for the column casing.
6. The casing thickness shall taper evenly the full length of the transition zone.
7. The composite casing shall adhere firmly to all surfaces of the existing column.

E-glass notes:

1. Each composite section shall be wrapped using continuous E-glass fabric not less than 2 ft in height. All wraps of continuous E-glass weave shall be terminated a minimum of 12 in. past the starting point of the initial wrap. Subsequent wraps shall be started (butted) at the ending point of the last wrap.
2. All cut edges shall be sealed with epoxy.

Carbon notes:

1. Pre-preg carbon jacket shall be completely cured by elevated temperature.
2. Pre-preg carbon fiber spools shall contain continuous strands not less than 100 ft in length.

FIGURE 10.17
(*continued*)

6. Composites are not permitted if the column longitudinal reinforcement ratio is greater than 2.5 percent.
7. Composites are not permitted for bridges that require flame-sprayed plastic.
8. Composites are permitted for prismatic columns only.
9. If any column of the bridge requires a steel casing retrofit, the entire bridge is to be detailed using steel column casings.

Most California bridges are multispan, continuous, reinforced and prestressed concrete multicell box girder structures. With recognition of the limited resources available to complete a task of such large magnitude, various bridges had to be prioritized for retrofit work. In this context, two support types for bridges were recognized early on: those supported by the single-column bents, and those with the multiple-column bents. Because of the obvious lack of redundancy in bridges with single-column bents, they were considered riskier than those with multiple-column bents and were therefore targeted for priority retrofitting [Gates and Maroney, 1990]. However, factors other than ductility deficiency dictate retrofitting a bridge. These factors include earthquake fault locations (bridges adjacent to or crossing major earthquake faults), foundation soil characteristics (deep soft soils or sands with liquefaction potential), importance to the transportation network (a key interchange or a bridge with few alternative routes), and cost considerations [ATC, 1983; EERI, 1990; Gates and Maroney, 1990].

The satisfactory response of a bridge supported on columns and/or bents depends heavily on their capacity to displace inelastically through several cycles of response without significant degradation of strength or stiffness, a quality termed *ductility*. Thus, the key to seismic safety of a structure is its ductility. The *ductility factor* is defined as the ratio of the maximum expected deformation during the design-level earthquake to deformation at yield. The term "deformation" is used in a generic sense to include displacements, strains, and rotations at joints. For example, in terms of displacement, the ductility factor is defined as

$$\mu_\Delta = \frac{\Delta_m}{\Delta_y} \tag{10.17}$$

where μ_Δ = displacement ductility factor

Δ_m = maximum displacement expected during the design-level earthquake

Δ_y = displacement at yield

In reinforced concrete structures, ductility is achieved by confining concrete through appropriate placement of steel reinforcing bars and ties. In steel sections, ductility is obtained by using compact sections capable of attaining plastic moment capacity before premature buckling. Properly designed, a ductile structure can retain its load-carrying ability even after overstressing has occurred as a result of repeated cyclic seismic deformations. Since seismic damage to highway bridges is caused primarily by lateral deformations, determination (and containment) of lateral inelastic displacements is very important for the design and retrofit of bridges in seismic regions. Ductile structural behavior is characterized by a large *displacement ductility ratio* (μ_Δ). A parameter often referred to in the context of design of ductile structures is the *demand-to-capacity ratio (D/C ratio)*. While the *demand* (or the *strength demand*) refers to the resistance a structure must develop when subjected to design overload (in this case, the force developed in a structural member as a result of seismic shaking), *capacity* refers to the structural strength available to resist the seismic force. A comprehensive discussion on ductility and related issues has been presented by Priestley, Seible, and Calvi [1996].

The current bridge retrofit practices followed in California, evolved over a period of about 20 years, are specified in a manual of the California Department of Transportation [CALTRANS, 1995], and are discussed in several other references [ATC, 1979a, 1983;

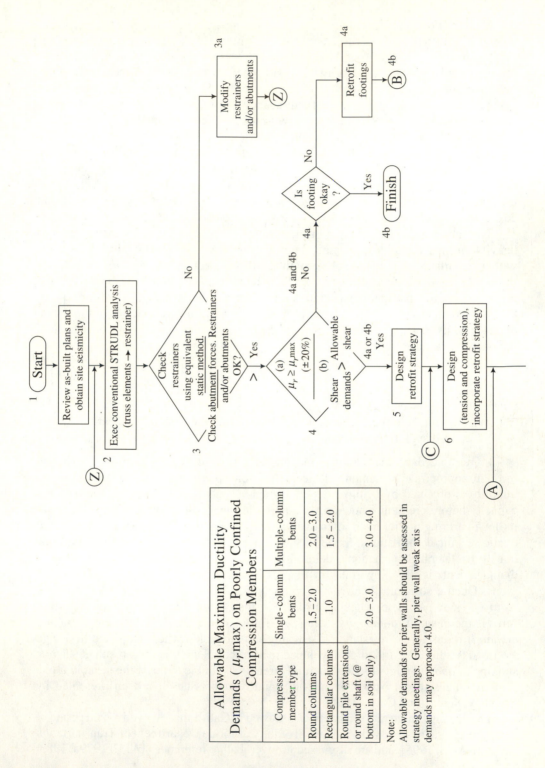

Allowable Maximum Ductility Demands (μ_r-max) on Poorly Confined Compression Members

Compression member type	Single-column bents	Multiple-column bents
Round columns	1.5 – 2.0	2.0 – 3.0
Rectangular columns	1.0	1.5 – 2.0
Round pile extensions or round shaft (@ bottom in soil only)	2.0 – 3.0	3.0 – 4.0

Note:
Allowable demands for pier walls should be assessed in strategy meetings. Generally, pier wall weak axis demands may approach 4.0.

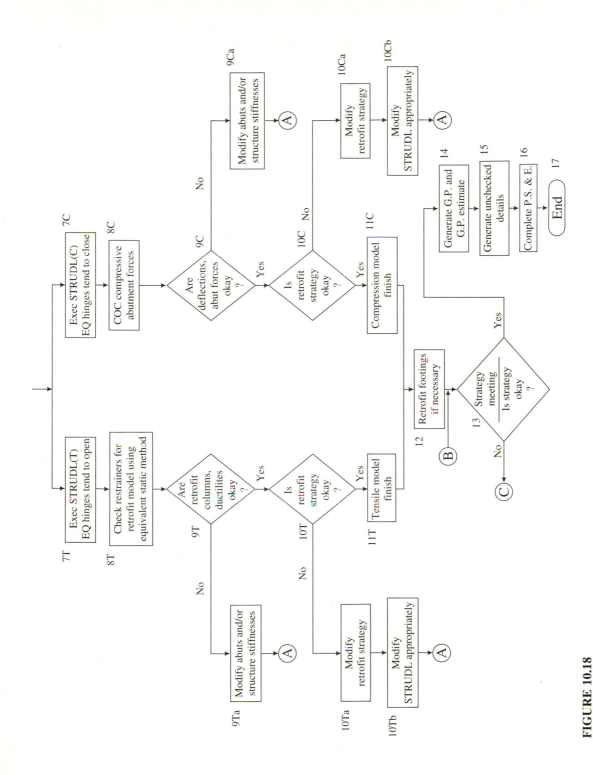

FIGURE 10.18
Flowchart showing the California methodology for seismic retrofitting [CALTRANS, 1995].

Federal Highway Administration, 1979, 1983; Ohashi et al., 1979a,b; Zelinski, 1995a,b, 1996]. A detailed description of the retrofit methodology is beyond the scope of this book. An exhaustive treatment of this topic has been provided by Priestley, Seible, and Calvi [1996]. A step-by-step procedure suggested by the California methodology [CALTRANS, 1995] is presented in the flowchart of Fig. 10.18. The procedure, in general, involves four major tasks:

1. Structural diagnostics (steps 1–4)
2. Retrofit strategy development (step 5)
3. Elastic analysis bounding nonlinear behavior (steps 6–11)
4. Retrofit design (steps 12–16)

In addition, the designer should consider all other possible variations in the failure modes. The basic task is to evaluate and retrofit the structure against all potential collapse modes. Typically, a retrofit candidate structure is first analyzed assuming linear behavior, i.e., assuming that strain levels in all structural components remain in the linear elastic range. Next, a dynamic analysis of the structure is performed, for both tension and compression states, to evaluate the state of structure under maximum credible earthquake loading. Based on this analysis, the demand is compared to capacity. For the purpose of dynamic analysis, several in-house computer programs [CYGNA, 1991; Seyed, 1992a,b,c] based on *STRUDL modeling* are used. The basic design approach followed is to accept some seismic damage in a bridge provided it does not lead to the collapse of the structure. All components of the structure, viz., the superstructure, bearings, abutments, piers, column bents, and footings, are systematically analyzed, and each is identified for potential retrofitting. Based on the *D/C* ratio, necessary retrofit schemes are suggested for implementation. Because of their unsatisfactory past performance, the existing hinge seats and restrainers, installed in box girder bridges of the 1950s and 1960s following the 1971 San Fernando earthquake, are also analyzed as part of the overall retrofit analysis. Permitted restrainer elongation should be small enough to prevent seat drop-off, and the restrainer forces should be small enough to preclude diaphragm failure. The diaphragms can fail if the seismic tensile forces generated in restrainers are larger than the superstructure's capacity to hold restrainers. A detailed description of this methodology can be found in the *Interim Memo to Designers* [CALTRANS, 1992, 1995].

The California retrofitting methodology was soon put to the test. Many California bridges in the regions of strong shaking had been retrofitted since the 1989 Loma Prieta earthquake. Several of these bridges were subjected to severe ground motion during the 1994 Northridge earthquake. *All* structures in the region of strong shaking that were retrofitted performed adequately, thus demonstrating the validity of the California retrofit procedures. There were 24 retrofitted bridges in the region of very strong shaking and a total of 60 in the region having peak accelerations of 0.25 *g* or greater. Performance of these bridges during this earthquake showed that they withstood the seismic forces well. The retrofitted structures resisted the earthquake motions much better than did the unretrofitted structures. At most, the retrofitted bridges suffered minor damage, and all have remained in service. Only seven bridges collapsed, and none of them had been retrofitted. Initially, these collapses were attributed to the unseating of the failed bridge sections from the narrow seat widths at the abutments and at the expansion joints. However, the post-earthquake studies [Priestley, Seible, and Wang, 1994] showed that the likely failure sequence started with either column shear or flexure shear, with unseating as a direct consequence of the shortening or collapse of the adjacent bents. A critical review of the performance of bridges during the Northridge earthquake has been presented by Priestley, Seible, and Uang [1994] and by Housner and Thiel [1995].

It should be noted that AASHTO presently has no standards for the seismic retrofit of existing bridges. Although the California methodology [CALTRANS, 1992, 1995] is being used as a state-of-the-art practice, and several reports and books [Robinson, Longinow, and Albert, 1979; Robinson, Longinow, and Chu, 1979; Kawashima, 1990; Imbsen & Associates, Inc., 1992; Caspe, 1993; Zelinski, 1995a,b, 1996; Priestley, Seible, and Calvi, 1996; Xanthakos, 1996] have been published on this subject, no code or national standard has been adopted for the seismic retrofit of existing bridges [EERI, 1990; Miranda, 1993]. Research continues to be done to develop ways of retrofitting long-span bridges such as the Golden Gate Bridge [EERC, 1993], San Francisco–Oakland Bay Bridge, and others. New techniques such as base isolation [Buckle and Mayes, 1990; Constantinou et al., 1992; Kartoum, Constantinou, and Reinhorn, 1992] are evolving that are expected to improve performance of bridges during earthquakes. The past shows that research efforts on earthquake engineering not only have been noncommensurate with the problem's magnitude, but the answers given have lagged behind their need by some 20 years. It is believed that knowledge of bridge behavior during very strong and long-duration shaking resulting from a major earthquake is still evolving [EERI, 1990].

10.5
MAINTENANCE OF BRIDGES

A bridge is like a piece of equipment in that it shows signs of wear and tear over time. Its endurance depends on several factors, chiefly, the original strength of its design and materials, the amount of strain from the traffic and weather, and maintenance. In addition to the wear and tear caused by traffic, bridges are always exposed to environmental hazards such as rain, snow, floods, fire, earthquakes, and debris accumulation. Signs of deterioration and decay become evident as they grow older. For example, the Brooklyn Bridge needed a general overhaul in the 1940s after over a half century of heavy duty. When the second deck was given to New York's George Washington Bridge, 22 of its 584 suspenders were found to have deteriorated.

All bridges, small or big, must be repaired now and then. Periodic and timely maintenance is vital to their satisfactory performance and service life. The "prevention is better than cure" philosophy is applicable to bridges as well. Proper maintenance of a bridge will cut down life cycle costs, increase its service life, and in all likelihood prove to be more cost-effective than building a new bridge [NCH SYN, 1989].

Numerous surveys [RBM, 1987; Federal Highway Administration Guide, 1988; Federal Highway Administration, 1989b; BRM, 1990; Dunker and Rabbat, 1990a,b] have shown that existing bridges are deteriorating faster than they can be repaired, rehabilitated, or replaced. Because of budgetary constraints, a lot of bridges are subject to deferred maintenance [NCH SYN, 1979]. Due to concerns over the serious-ness of bridge maintenance problems, considerable information on maintenance and re-habilitation has been published in recent years by the Federal Highway Administration (FHWA). A new field—"Bridge Management Systems"—has been created in an effort to handle these tasks, and considerable research efforts are being directed nationwide toward developing its effectiveness. A discussion on the many facets of bridge manage-ment programs can be found in the literature [Golabi, Kulkarni, and Way, 1982; Kansas DOT, 1984; Hoffman, 1986; Chen and Johnson, 1987; NCH SYN, 1987a; Penn DOT, 1987; FHWA, 1989c; Jiang and Sinha, 1989; O'Connor and Hyman, 1989; Golabi and Thompson, 1990; AASHTO, 1993].

The nature of the work involved in bridge maintenance varies with the bridge type, location, material, and the policies of bridge owner agencies (cities, counties, state high-way departments, etc.). Because of the diverse nature of the work involved, there exists no national or uniform maintenance policy, although general guidelines published by the FHWA and others [NMSHD, 1971; TRB, 1979; TRR, 1988] can be used by all. In recognition of the importance of bridge maintenance work, the FHWA has developed courses to train bridge inspectors in effective bridge maintenance.

A major cause of deterioration of steel bridge members is corrosion, a cause of nu-merous bridge failures. The 37-year-old West Side Highway Bridge in New York City collapsed under traffic in December 1973 as a result of severe corrosion and neglected painting [Freyermuth, 1992]. Corrosion can be prevented by timely inspection, and cleaning and repainting of the corroded surfaces. A proper surface protection practice will contribute greatly to the enhanced life of the structure [ENR, 1989; NCH SYN, 1987b]. In view of the increasing decay of the nation's infrastructure, combined with the reduction of resources for new construction, the preservation of new and existing steel bridges through surface protection has become extremely important. While paint-ing practices are as old as iron and steel, new methods such as thermal spraying with zinc or aluminum coatings are reported to have shown promise of protection for more than 20 years after first maintenance [Sulit, 1993]. A discussion on thermal spray metal-lic coating systems can be found in the steel structures painting manuals of the Steel Structures Painting Council [SSPC, 1982/1991].

Environmental and health concerns about removal and disposal of lead-based paints have resulted in increased costs related to the painting of bridges. New paint systems are now available, with either greatly reduced quantities of volatile organic compounds or none at all.

10.6
SUMMARY

Several published studies have indicated that about 38 percent of the nation's bridges suffer from some kind of deficiency. Consequently, assessment of these deficiencies through a comprehensive inspection program has become very important. Deficiency can be functional or structural, leading to a level of service at or below a specified min-imum. Examples of deficiencies are many. They include inadequate lane and shoulder widths, inadequate horizontal and vertical clearances, inadequate numbers of lanes causing traffic jams, absence of sidewalks, poor riding qualities of decks, deteriorated concrete decks, inadequate live load capacity according to present standards, and inadequate resistance to lateral loads (wind or seismic). While some of these conditions only cause inconvenience and human discomfort, others may seriously compromise public safety.

Bridge rating involves structural capacity analysis of bridges to determine their overall response to various live loading conditions. Inventory rating refers to the capacity rating that indicates the load level considered safe for a bridge for an indefinite amount of time. Operating rating is the capacity rating that indicates the absolute maximum load level that is safe but must not be exceeded during the service life of a bridge. Bridge rating is required to be performed on all bridges that do not measure up to the current AASHTO standard. Bridges with ratings below the inventory level would be restricted to reduced load levels, and posted as such. Such bridges would need to be rehabilitated (or retrofitted) to provide an improved level of service.

As bridges grow older, their rehabilitation and retrofitting becomes increasingly important. Deterioration of concrete, corrosion of steel, heavier live loads, increased traffic density, poor resistance to fatigue, wind and seismic loads, damage due to fire and collision, and normal wear due to aging are some of the reasons for rehabilitating or retrofitting a bridge. Experience with earthquakes has indicated serious inadequacies in many bridges worldwide in terms of their safety and integrity during earthquakes [Priestley and Seible, 1994]. Most of these bridges were designed when the state of knowledge required for earthquake-resistant design was still evolving. As a result, many bridges are now being retrofitted (or replaced) to endure seismic forces according to the new standards.

With the growing inventory of the nation's bridges, inspection, evaluation, rehabilitation, and maintenance of bridges have evolved into disciplines of special significance. Related to the life-cycle costs of a bridge, these functions now form the core of the bridge management systems across the country. With the continuing monetary and energy crisis, and as bridges continue to outperform their design lives, rehabilitation and maintenance of bridges have assumed new dimensions as viable money-saving alternatives. With new technologies and experience, the art of bridge repair and rehabilitation is continuing to be enhanced with worldwide applications. The topic of bridge strengthening and rehabilitation has been comprehensively discussed by several authors [Park, 1984; Warner, 1981; Xanthakos, 1996].

REFERENCES

AASHO. (1964). *Informational Guide for Maintenance Inspections,* AASHO, Washington, DC.
———. (1970). *Manual for Maintenance Inspection of Bridges,* AASHO, Washington, DC.
AASHTO. (1976). *Interim Specifications for Bridges, 1976,* AASHTO, Washington, DC.
———. (1983). *Guide Specifications for Seismic Design of Highway Bridges,* AASHTO, Washington, DC.
———. (1989). *Guide Specifications for Strength Evaluation of Existing Steel and Concrete Bridges, 1989,* AASHTO, Washington, DC.

——. (1991). *Specification for Seismic Design of Highway Bridges,* AASHTO, Washington, DC.

——. (1993). *Guidelines for Bridge Management Systems,* AASHTO, Washington, DC.

——. (1994). *Manual for Condition Evaluation of Bridges,* AASHTO, Washington, DC.

Ahlskog, J. J. (1982). "The Bridge Inspection Program—A Vital Bridge Planning Program Aid," IABSE *Proc. Symp. on Maintenance, Repair, and Rehabilitation of Bridges,* vol. 38, pp. 231–241.

AISC. (1993a). "Renovation: Small Bridge Projects Offer Big Savings," *AISC Modern Steel Construction,* February, pp. 32–33.

——. (1993b). "Reconstructed Prize Bridge Award: Belle Vernon Bridge," *AISC Modern Steel Construction,* November, pp. 70–72.

An, W., Saadatmanesh, H., and Ehsani, M. R. (1991). "RC Beams Strengthened with FRP Plates. II: Analysis and Parametric Study," *ASCE J. Struct. Eng.,* 117(11), pp. 3434–3455.

ASCE–AASHO. (1968). "Development and Use of Prestressed Steel Flexural Members," *Proc. ASCE., Subcommittee 3 on Prestressed Steel of Joint ASCE–AASHO Committee on Steel Flexural Members,* September, pp. 2033–2059.

ASTM STP. (1990). "Extending the Life of Bridges," in G. W. Maupin, B. C. Brown, and A. G. Lichtenstein, eds., *ASTM STP 1100,* Philadelphia, PA.

ATC. (1979a). *Retrofitting Existing Bridges,* Applied Technology Council, Report No. ATC–6–1, Working Group 4, *Proc. Conf. Earthquake Resistance of Highway Bridges,* San Diego, CA, January 29–31.

——. (1979b). *Earthquake Resistance of Highway Bridges, Proc. of a Workshop,* Applied Technology Council, November.

——. (1981). *Seismic Design Guidelines for Highway Bridges,* Applied Technology Council, Palo Alto, CA.

——. (1982). *Comparison of United States and New Zealand Seismic Design Practices for Highway Bridges,* Applied Technology Council, August.

——. (1983). *Seismic Retrofitting Guidelines for Highway Bridges,* Applied Technology Council, Report No. FHWA–RD–83–007 and ATC–6–2, U.S. Department of Transportations, Federal Highway Administration, Washington, DC, December.

——. (1986). *Seismic Resistance of Highway Bridges,* Proceedings of Second Joint U.S.–New Zealand Workshop, Applied Technology Council.

Atkinson, Gail M. (1987). "Implications of Eastern Ground Motion Characteristics for Seismic Hazard Assessment in Eastern North America." In *Proc. Symp. Seismic Hazards, Ground Motions, Soil-Liquefaction and Engineering Practice in Eastern North America,* Technical Report NCEER–87–0025, National Center for Earthquake Engineering Research, State University of New York at Buffalo, pp. 375–386.

Ayyub, B. M., Sohn, Y. G., and Saadatmanesh, H. (1988). *Static Strength of Prestressed Composite Steel Girders,* Final Report to National Science Foundation, Department of Civil Engineering, University of Maryland, College Park, May.

Ballard, D. B., and Yakowitz, H. (1969). *Mechanisms Leading to the Failure of the Point Pleasant, West Virginia Bridge—Part 3,* National Bureau of Standards Report No. 9981 to U.S. Bureau of Public Roads, September.

Barrett, N. (1985). "Plates Steel Leeds Floor," *New Civil Engineer,* June 20, p. 18.

BERR. (1990). *Bridge Evaluation, Repair and Rehabilitation, Series E: Applied Sciences,* vol. 187, Nowak, A. S., ed., Kluwer Academic Publishers, Dordrecht.

Blakeley, R. W. G. (1979). "Analysis and Design of Bridges Incorporating Mechanical Energy Dissipating Devices for Earthquake Resistance," *Proc. Workshop on Earthquake Resistance of Highway Bridges, Applied Technology Council,* San Diego, CA, January 29–31, pp. 313–342.

BR. (1992). "Bridge Rehabilitation," *Proc., 3rd Intl. Workshop on Bridge Rehabilitation,* organized by Technical University, Darmstadt and the University of Michigan, June 14–17.

BRM. (1990). "1990 Exclusive Bridge Inventory Update," *Better Roads Magazine,* November, p. 26.

Brown, K. (1973). "Japanese Style Strengthening for M5 Bridges," *Construction News,* October, p. 21.

Brown, S. (1992). "Fiber/Epoxy Composites Strengthen Bridge Columns," *Materials: Performance and Prevention of Deficiencies and Failures,* White, T. D., ed., pp. 691–695.

Buckle, I. G., and Mayes, R. L. (1990). "Seismic Isolation History, Application, and Performance—A World View," *Earthquake Spectra,* 6(2), pp. 455–474.

Buckle, I. G., Mayes, R. L., and Button, M. R. (1987). *Seismic Design and Retrofit Manual for Highway Bridges,* Report No. FHWA–IP–87–6, U.S. Department of Transportation, Federal Highway Administration, May.

CALTRANS. (1992). *Interim Memo to Designers 20-4,* State of California, Department of Transportation, Division of Structures, Sacramento, April.

———. (1995). *Interim Memo to Designers 20-4,* State of California, Department of Transportation, Division of Structures, Sacramento, March.

———. (1996). *Memo to Designers 20-4, Draft, Attachment B,* State of California, Department of Transportation, Division of Structures, Sacramento, March.

Caspe, M. S. (1993). "Passive Energy Dissipating Systems," Paper presented at the 1993 AASHTO Bridge Subcommittee Annual Meeting, Denver, CO, May.

Chai, Y. H. (1991). "Steel Jacketing of Circular Reinforced Concrete Bridge Columns for Enhanced Flexural Performance," Ph.D. thesis, University of California, San Diego.

Chai, Y. H., Priestley, M. J. N., and Seible, F. (1991a). "Seismic Retrofit of Circular Bridge Columns for Enhanced Flexural Performance," *ACI Structural Journal,* 88(5), September–October, pp. 572–584.

———. (1991b). *Flexural Retrofit of Circular Reinforced Concrete Bridge Columns by Steel Jacketing—Experimental Studies,* Res. Rept. no. SSRP 91-06, Department of Applied Mechanical and Engineering Science, University of California, San Diego, CA.

———. (1994). "Analytical Model for Steel-Jacketed RC Circular Bridge Columns," *ASCE, J. Struct. Eng.,* 120(8), August, pp. 2358–2376.

Chang, J. C. L. (1961). "Orthotropic-Plate Construction for Short-Span Bridges," *ASCE Civ. Eng.,* December, pp. 53–56.

Chapman, H. E. (1979). "An Overview of the State of Practices in Earthquake Design Of Bridges in New Zealand," *Proc. Workshop on Earthquake Resistance of Highway Bridges,* Applied Technology Council, January 29–31.

Chen, C., and Johnson, D. (1987). *Bridge Management Under a Level of Service Concept Providing Optimum Improvement Action, Time and Budget Prediction,* Report No. FHWA–NC–88–004, North Carolina State University, Center for Transp. Eng. Studies, Raleigh, September.

Cluff, L. S. (1989). *California at Risk: Reducing Earthquake Hazards, 1987–1992, Report SSC 89-02,* State of California, Seismic Safety Commission, September 1.

Constantinou, M. C., Kartoum, A., Reinhorn, A. M., and Bradford, P. (1992). "Sliding Isolation System for Bridges: Experimental Study," *Earthquake Spectra,* 8(3), August, pp. 321–344.

Crasto, A. S., Kim, R. Y., and Mistretta, J. P. (1996). "Rehabilitation of Concrete Bridge Beams with Externally Bonded Composite Plates," Presented at the 41st Intl. SAMPE Symp. & Exh., Anaheim, CA, March 24–28, Book 2 of 2, pp. 1269–1279.

CYGNA. (1991). "Seismic Modelling Parametric Studies," Submitted to State of California, Department of Transportation, Division of Structures, July.

Daoud, F. K. (1987). "Experimental Strengthening of a Three-Span Composite Model Bridge by Post-Tensioning," M.S. thesis, Iowa State University, Ames.

Davies, B. L., and Powell, J. (1984). "Strengthening of Brinsworth Road Bridge, Rotherham," *IABSE 12th Congress,* Vancouver, BC, Canada, September, pp. 401–407.

Degenkolb, O. H. (1978). "Retrofitting Techniques for Highway Bridges," *Bridge Notes,* California Department of Transportation, 20(1), August.

Degenkolb, O. H. (1979). "Retrofitting of Existing Highway Bridges Subject to Seismic Loading—Practical Considerations," Report No. ATC-6-1, *Proceedings, Conference on Earthquake Resistance of Highway Bridges, Applied Technology Council,* San Diego, CA, Jan. 29–31, pp. 344–359.

Deithelm, P. J., Tracey, R. G., and Ingberg, R. C. (1972). *Bridge Deck Deterioration and Restoration,* Minnesota Department of Highways, St. Paul.

Dunker, K. F. (1985). "Strengthening of Simple-Span Composite Bridges by Post-Tensioning," Ph.D. dissertation, Iowa State University, Ames.

Dunker, K. F., Klaiber, F. W., Beck, B. L., and Sanders, W. W. (1985). *Strengthening of Existing Single-Span Steel Beam and Concrete Deck Bridges,* Part II, ERI Project 1536, ISU-ERI-Ames-85231, Final Report, Engineering Research Institute, Iowa State University, Ames.

Dunker, K. F., Klaiber, F. W., and Daoud, F. K. (1987). *Strengthening of Existing Continuous Composite Bridges,* ERI Project 1846, ISU-ERI-Ames-88007, Final Report, Engineering Research Institute, Iowa State University, Ames.

Dunker, K. F., Klaiber, F. W., and Sanders, W. W. Jr. (1985). *Design Manual for Strengthening Single-Span Composite Bridges by Post-Tensioning,* Part III, ERI Project 1536, ISU-ERI-Ames-85229, Final Report, Engineering Research Institute, Iowa State University, Ames.

——. (1987). "Strengthening of Steel Stringer Bridges by Selective Stiffening," *Trans. Res. Rec. 1118,* Transportation Research Board, Washington, DC, pp. 43–48.

Dunker, K. F., and Rabbat, B. G. (1990a). "Highway Bridge Type and Performance Patterns," *ASCE J. Performance of Constructed Facilities,* 4(3), August, pp. 161–173.

——. (1990b). "Performance of Highway Bridges," *Concrete Intl.* 12(8), August, pp. 40–43.

——. (1992). "Performance of Prestressed Concrete Highway Bridges in the United States—The First 40 Years," *PCI J.,* 37(3), May–June, pp. 48–64.

EERC. (1993). "Critical Components of Golden Gate Bridge Tested," *NEWS,* 14(2), Earthquake Engineering Research Center, University of California, Berkeley, July.

EERI. (1990). *Competing Against Time,* Governor's Board of Inquiry on the 1989 Loma Prieta Earthquake, Report to Governor George Deukmejian, May 31, 1990, second printing with minor corrections, August.

——. (1994). *Northridge Earthquake January 17, 1994, Preliminary Reconnaissance Report,* Pub. No. 94-01, Earthquake Engineering Research Institute, Oakland, CA, March.

——. (1995). *The Hygo-Ken Nanbu Earthquake January 17, 1995, Preliminary Reconnaissance Report,* Pub. No. 95-04, Earthquake Engineering Research Institute, Oakland, CA, February.

ENR. (1989). "Regulators Putting Lid on Paint," *Eng. News Record,* 223(14), October 5, pp. 30–33.

EQE. (1989). *The October 17, 1989, Loma Prieta Earthquake,* EQE Engineering, Inc., San Francisco, CA.

Ferjencik, P. (1971/1972). "Czechoslovak Contribution in the Field of Prestressed Steel Structures," *I.C.E. Monthly,* Vol. II, no. 11.

FHWA. (1970). *Bridge Inspector's Training Manual 70,* U.S. Department of Transportation, Federal Highway Administration, Washington, DC.

——. (1977). *Bridge Inspectors Manual for Movable Bridges,* U.S. Department of Transportation, Federal Highway Administration, Washington, DC.

———. (1979). *Seismic Retrofit for Highway Bridges,* U.S. Department of Transportation, Federal Highway Administration, Report No. Federal Highway Administration-TS-79-217, Washington, DC.

———. (1983). *Seismic Retrofitting Guidelines for Highway Bridges,* Report No. FHWA/RD-83/007, U.S. Department of Transportation, Federal Highway Administration, Washington, DC, December.

———. (1984a). *Rehabilitation of Existing Bridges Workshop,* U.S. Department of Transportation, Federal Highway Administration, Washington, DC.

———. (1984b). *Bridge Maintenance Manual,* U.S. Department of Transportation, Federal Highway Administration, Washington, DC.

———. (1986a). *Inspection of Fracture Critical Bridge Member, Supplement to the Bridge Inspector's Training Manual,* GPO Stock no. 050-001-00302-3, U.S. Department of Transportation, Federal Highway Administration, Washington, DC.

———. (1986b). *Culvert Inspection Manual,* Report No. FHWA-IP-86-2, U.S. Department of Transportation, Federal Highway Administration, Washington, DC, July.

———. (1987). *Seismic Design and Retrofit Manual for Highway Bridges,* Report No. FHWA-1P-87-6, Federal Highway Administration, Washington, DC.

———. (1988a). *Technical Advisory—Revisions to the National Bridge Inspection Standards,* U.S. Department of Transportation, Federal Highway Administration, Washington, DC.

———. (1988b). *Interim Procedures for Evaluating Scour at Bridges,* Bridge Division, Office of Engineering, U.S. Department of Transportation, Federal Highway Administration, Washington, DC, September.

———. (1989a). *Underwater Inspection of Bridges,* Report No. FHWA-DP-80-1, Federal Highway Administration, Washington, DC, November.

———. (1989b). *The Status of Nation's Highways and Bridges: Conditions and Performance and Highway Bridge Replacement and Rehabilitation Program,* Report to the U.S. Congress, U.S. Department of Transportation, Federal Highway Administration, Washington, DC.

———. (1989c). *Bridge Management Systems,* Report No. FHWA-Dp-71-01R, Federal Highway Administration, Washington, DC.

FHWA Guide. (1979). *Recording and Coding Guide for the Structure Inventory and Appraisal of the Nation's Bridges,* Bridge Management Branch, Bridge Division, Federal Highway Administration, Washington, DC.

———. (1988). *Recording and Coding Guide for the Structure Inventory and Appraisal of the Nation's Bridges,* Bridge Management Branch, Bridge Division, Federal Highway Administration, Washington, DC.

Fife, E. R., and Arnold, S. (1996). "The Concept of the Composite System and Column Retrofit at I-5 and Hwy. 2 Using TYFOS Fiberwrap System," *41st Intl. SAMPE Symp. and Exh.,* Anaheim, CA, March 24–28, Book 2 of 2, pp. 1304–1310.

Fisher, J. W. (1981). *Inspecting Steel Bridges for Fatigue Damage,* Fritz Engineering Laboratory Report No. 386-15(81), Lehigh University, Bethlehem, PA, March.

———. (1984). *Fatigue and Fracture in Steel Bridges—Case Studies,* John Wiley & Sons, New York.

Fisher, J. W., and Yuceoglu, V. (1981). *A Survey of Localized Cracking in Steel Bridges,* Interim Report, DOT-FH-11-9506, Federal Highway Administration, December.

Fleming, C. J., and King, G. E. M. (1967). "The Development of Structural Adhesives for Three Original Uses in South Africa," RILEM International Symposium, *Synthetic Resins in Building Construction,* Paris, France, pp. 75–92.

Freyermuth, C. L. (1992). "Building Better Bridges: Concrete vs. Steel," *ASCE Civ. Eng.,* July, pp. 68–69.

Fung, G. C., LeBeau, R. J., Klein, E. D., Belvedere, J., and Goldschimdt, A. F. (1971). *The San Fernando Earthquake, Field Investigation of Bridge Damage,* California Department of Transportation, February.

Gamble, W. L., Hawkins, N. M., and Kaspur, I. I. (1996). "Seismic Retrofitting of Bridge Pier Columns," *41st Intl. SAMPE Symp. and Exh.,* Anaheim, CA, March 24–28, 1996, Book 2 of 2, pp. 1004–1015.

Gates, J., and Maroney, B. (1990). "Prioritizing Bridges for Seismic Retrofit," *Proceedings of the U.S.–Japan Workshop on Retrofitting Bridges,* December 17–18, Tsukuba, Japan.

Gates, J. H., Mellon, S., and Klien, G. (1988). "The Whittier Narrows, California Earthquake of October 1, 1987—Damage to State Highway Bridges," *EERI, Earthquake Spectra,* 4(2).

Gies, J. (1963). *Bridges and Men,* Grosset & Dunlap, New York.

Golabi, K., Kulkarni, R., and Way, G. (1982). "A Statewide Management System," *Interfaces,* 12(6), December, pp. 5–21.

Golabi, K., and Thompson, P. D. (1990). "A Network Optimization System for Maintenance and Improvement of California's Bridges," in *Bridge Evaluation, Repair and Rehabilitation,* Kluwer Academic Publishers, Dordrecht, pp. 41–55.

Grace, N. F. F. (1981). "Effect of Prestressing the Deck in Continuous Bridge of Composite Construction," M.A. thesis, University of Windsor, Windsor, Ontario.

Guide. (1993). *Bridge Inspection and Rehabilitation: A Practical Guide,* Silano, L. G., ed., John Wiley & Sons, New York.

Gustaferro, A., Hillier, M. A., and Janney, J. R. (1983). "Performance of Prestressed Concrete on the Illinois Tollway after 25 Years of Service," *PCI J.,* 28(1), January–February, pp. 50–67.

Hoffman, G. L. (1986). "Bridge Management: Computer Aided Priorities," *ASCE Civ. Eng.,* May, pp. 62–64.

Housner, G., and Thiel, C. C., Jr. (1995). "The Continuing Challenge: Report on the Performance of State Bridges in the Northridge Earthquake," *Earthquake Spectra,* 11(4), November, pp. 607–636.

Hugenschmidt, H. (1976). "Epoxy Adhesive for Concrete and Steel," in *Proc., First International Congress on Polymers in Concrete,* London, England, May 1975, The Construction Press, Ltd., Hornby, England, pp. 195–209.

Iion, T., and Otokawa, K. (1981). "Application of Epoxy Resins in Strengthening of Concrete Structures," *Proc. Third Intl. Congress on Polymers in Concrete,* Koriyama, Japan, May, vol. II, pp. 997–1011.

Imbsen, R. A. (1981). *Seismic Design of Highway Bridges Workshop Manual,* Design and Retrofitting Concepts, Report No. FHWA-IR-81-2, U.S. Department of Transportation, Federal Highway Administration, Washington, DC, January.

Imbsen & Associates, Inc. (1992). *Seismic Design of Highway Bridges—Training Course Participant Workbook,* Prepared for U.S. Department of Transportation, Federal Highway Administration, Washington, DC, March.

Irwin, C. A. K. (1975). *The Strengthening of Concrete Beams by Bonded Steel Plates,* TRRL Supp. Report 160, UC, Transport and Road Research Laboratory, Department of Environment, Crowthorne, England, p. 8.

Jennings, P. C. (1971). *Engineering Features of the San Fernando Earthquake of February 9, 1971,* Report No. EERL 71-02, California Institute of Technology, Pasadena, CA, June.

Jiang, Y., and Sinha, K. C. (1989). "Dynamic Optimization Model for Bridge Management Systems," *Transportation Research Record 1211,* Transportation Research Board, Washington, DC, pp. 92–100.

Jones, R., and Swamy, R. N. (1984). "In Situ Strengthening Concrete Structural Members Using Epoxy-Bonded Steel Plates," *Proc. 4th Intl. Congress Polymers in Concrete,* Darmstadt, September, pp. 251–255.

Jones, R., Swamy, R. N., and Bloxham, J. (1986). "Crack Control of Reinforced Concrete Beams Through Epoxy-Bonded Steel Plates," *Proc. Intl. Conf. Adhesion between Polymers and Concrete,* Aixen Provence, September, pp. 542–555.

Jones, R., Swamy, R. N., Bloxham, J., and Bouderbalah, A. (1980). "Composite Behavior of Concrete Beams with Epoxy-Bonded External Reinforcement," *Int. J. Cement Composites,* 2(2), May, pp. 91–107.

Jones, R., Swamy, R. N., and Salman, F. A. R. (1985). "Structural Implications of Repairing by Epoxy-Bonded Steel Plates," *Proc. 2nd Intl. Conf. Structural Faults and Repair,* London, England, April–May, Engineering Technics Press, pp. 75–80.

JRA. (1971). *Specifications for Earthquake Resistant Design of Highway Bridges,* Japan Road Association.

Kansas DOT. (1984). *Development of Highway Improvement Priority System for Kansas,* Division of Planning and Development, Office of Analysis and Evaluation, Kansas DOT, December.

Kar, Anil. (1974). "Prestressing Applications in Distressed Structures," *PCI J.,* March–April.

Kartoum, A., Constantinou, M. C., and Reinhorn, M. A. (1992). "Sliding Isolation System for Bridges: Analytical Study," *Earthquake Spectra,* 8(3), August, pp. 345–372.

Kawashima, K. (1990). "Present Earthquake Engineering Efforts to Mitigate Earthquake Hazards of Road Transportation Facilities in Japan," *ASCE San Francisco 1990 Annual Civil Engineering Convention,* November.

Klaiber, F. W., Dedic, D. J., Dunker, K. F., and Sanders, W. W. (1983). *Strengthening of Existing Single-Span Steel Beam and Concrete Deck Bridges,* Part I, ERI Project 1536, ISU-ERI-Ames-83185, Final Report, Engineering Research Institute, Iowa State University, Ames.

Klaiber, F. W., Dunker, K. F., and Sanders, W. W., Jr. (1981). *Feasibility Study of Strengthening Existing Single-Span Steel Beam Concrete Deck Bridges,* ERI Project 1460, ISU-ERI-Ames-81251, Final Report, Engineering Research Institute, Iowa State University, Ames.

Klaiber, F. W., Dunker, K. F., Wipf, T. J., and Sanders, W. W. (1987). *Methods of Strengthening Existing Highway Bridges,* National Cooperative Highway Research Program Report No. 293, Transportation Research Board, Washington, DC.

Koretzky, H. P. (1978). "What Has Been Learned from the First Prestressed Concrete Bridges—Repair of Such Bridges," *Transportation Research Record 664,* Transportation Research Board, St. Louis, MO.

Labia, Y., Saiidi, M., and Douglas, B. (1993). *Retrofitting and Structural Evaluation of Prestressed Concrete Bridges,* Progress Report, Department of Civil Engineering, University of Nevada, Reno, March.

Lerchental, H. (1967). "Bonded Sheet Metal Reinforcement for Concrete Slabs," *RILEM Intl. Symp., Resins in Building Construction,* Paris, France, pp. 165–173.

MacDonald, M. D. (1978). *The Flexural Behavior of Concrete Beams with Bonded External Reinforcement,* TRRL Supp. Report 415, Transport and Road Research Laboratory, Department of Environment, Crowthorne, England.

Mahin, S., and Boroschek, R. (1991). *Influence of Geometric Nonlinearities on the Seismic Response and Design of Bridge Structures,* Report to State of California, Department of Transportation, Division of Structures, October.

Mancarti, G. D. (1982). "Resurfacing, Restoring and Rehabilitating Bridges in California," in *Proc. Intl. Conf. Short- and Medium-Span Bridges,* Toronto, Ontario, August 8–12.

———. (1984). "Strengthening California's Steel Bridges by Prestressing," *Transportation Research Record 950,* Transportation Research Board, Washington, DC, pp. 183-187.

Mander, R. F. (1974). *Bonded External Reinforcement, A Method of Strengthening Structures,* Department of the Environment Report on Quinton Interchange for the M5 Motorway, London, England.

Mayes, R. L., Buckle, I. G., Kelly, T. E., and Jones, L. R. (1992). "AASHTO Seismic Isolation Design Requirements for Highway Bridges," *ASCE J. Struct. Eng.,* 118(1), January, pp. 284–304.

Minor, J., and White, K. R. (1988). *Condition Surveys of Concrete Bridge Components—User's Manual,* National Cooperative Highway Research Program Report No. 312, Transportation Research Board, Washington, DC.

Minosaku, K. (1992). "Using FRP Materials in Prestressed Concrete Structures," *Concrete Intl.,* 14(8), August, pp. 41–44.

Miranda, E. (1993). "Evaluation of Seismic Design Criteria for Highway Bridges," *Earthquake Spectra,* 9(2), May, pp. 233–250.

Miranda, E., and Bertero, V. V. (1991). "Evaluation of the Failure of the Cypress Viaduct in the Loma Prieta Earthquake," *Bull. Seismological Society of America,* 118(5), October, pp. 2070–2086.

NCHRP (1980a). *Bridges on Secondary Highways and Local Roads: Rehabilitation and Replacement,* National Cooperative Highway Research Program Report No. 222, Transportation Research Board, Washington, DC.

———. (1980b). *Damage Evaluation and Repair Methods for Prestressed Concrete Members,* National Cooperative Highway Research Program Report No. 226, Transportation Research Board, Washington, DC.

———. (1980c). *Rehabilitation and Replacement of Bridges on Secondary Highways and Local Roads,* National Cooperative Highway Research Program Report No. 243, Transportation Research Board, Washington, DC.

———. (1983). *Long-Term Rehabilitation of Salt-Contaminated Decks,* National Cooperative Highway Research Program Report No. 257, Transportation Research Board, Washington, DC.

———. (1987a). *Fatigue Evaluation Procedures for Steel Bridges,* National Cooperative Highway Research Program Report No. 299, Transportation Research Board, Washington, DC.

———. (1987b). *Load Evaluation of Existing Bridges,* National Cooperative Highway Research Program Report No. 301, Transportation Research Board, Washington, DC.

———. (1987c). *Fatigue and Fracture Evaluation for Rating Riveted Bridges,* National Cooperative Highway Research Program Report No. 302, Transportation Research Board, Washington, DC.

———. (1988). *Condition Surveys of Concrete Bridge Components—User's Manual,* National Cooperative Highway Research Program Report No. 312, Washington, DC.

———. (1989a). *Corrosion Protection of Prestressed Systems in Concrete Bridges,* National Cooperative Highway Research Program, Report No. 313, Transportation Research Board, Washington, DC.

———. (1989b). *Guidelines for Redundancy Design and Rating of Two-Girder Steel Bridges,* National Cooperative Highway Research Program Report No. 319, Transportation Research Board, Washington, DC, October.

———. (1990a). *Guidelines for Evaluating Corrosion Effects in Existing Steel Bridges,* National Cooperative Highway Research Program Report No. 333, Transportation Research Board, Washington, DC.

———. (1990b). *Distortion-Induced Fatigue Cracking in Steel Bridges,* National Cooperative Highway Research Program Report No. 336, Transportation Research Board, Washington, DC.

NCH SYN. (1979). *Consequences of Deferred Maintenance,* National Cooperative Highway Research Program Synthesis of Highway Practice, Report No. 58, Transportation Research Board, Washington, DC.

———. (1981). *Underwater Inspection and Repair of Bridge Substructures,* National Cooperative Highway Research Program Synthesis of Highway Practice Report No. 88, Transportation Research Board, Washington, DC.

———. (1983). *Historic Bridges—Criteria for Decision Making,* National Cooperative Highway Research Program Synthesis of Highway Practice Report No. 101, Transportation Research Board, Washington, DC.

———. (1984). *Bridge Weight-Limit Posting,* National Cooperative Highway Research Program Synthesis of Highway Practice Report No. 108, Transportation Research Board, Washington, DC.

———. (1985). *Detecting Defects in Highway Structures,* National Cooperative Highway Research Program Synthesis of Highway Practice Report No. 118, Transportation Research Board, Washington, DC.

———. (1987a). *Bridge Management Systems,* National Cooperative Highway Research Program Synthesis of Highway Practice, Report No. 300, Transportation Research Board, Washington, DC, December.

———. (1987b). *Protective Coatings for Bridge Steel,* National Cooperative Highway Research Program Synthesis of Highway Practice Report No. 136, Transportation Research Board, Washington, DC.

———. (1988a). *Durability of Prestressed Concrete Highway Structures,* National Cooperative Highway Research Program Synthesis of Highway Practice Report No. 140, Transportation Research Board, Washington, DC.

———. (1988b). *Uniformity Efforts in Oversize/Overweight Permits,* National Cooperative Highway Research Program Synthesis of Highway Practice Report No. 143, Transportation Research Board, Washington, DC.

———. (1989). *Evolution and Benefits of Preventative Maintenance Strategies,* National Cooperative Highway Research Program Synthesis of Highway Practice Report No. 153, Transportation Research Board, Washington, DC.

Neuerm, Y. and Kaiser, H. (1991). "Strengthening of Structures with CFRP Laminates," in S. L. Iyer and R. Sen, eds., *Advanced Composites Materials in Civil Engineering Structures,* pp. 224–232.

Nishanian, J., and Frank, K. H. (1972). *Fatigue Characteristics of Steel Used in the Eyebars of the Point Pleasant Bridge, Final Rep.,* Federal Highway Administration, Report No. FHWA-RD-7, No. FHWA-RD-73-18, U.S. Department of Transportation, Washington, DC, June.

NIST. (1990). *Performance of Structures During the Loma Prieta Earthquake of October 17, 1989,* Lew, H.S., ed., NIST Special Publication 778 (ICCSSC TR11), U.S. Department of Commerce, National Institute of Standards and Technology, January.

NMSHD. (1971). *Guidelines for Maintenance Operation,* New Mexico State Highway Department, Maintenance Division, Santa Fe.

Novokshchenov, V. (1993). "Prestressed Concrete Bridges in Adverse Environments," *Concrete Intl.,* 13(5), May, pp. 44–48.

NSPE. (1988). "Safety Board Critical of Bridge-Inspection Agenda," *Engineering Times,* National Society of Professional Engineers, Alexandria, VA, January, p. 5.

NTSB. (1968). *Collapse of US 35 Highway Bridge at Point Pleasant, West Virginia, December 15, 1967,* National Transportation Safety Board, U.S. Department of Transportation, Washington, DC, October.

———. (1984). *Highway Accident Report—Collapse of a Suspended Span of Interstate Route 95 Highway Bridge over the Mianus River, Greenwich, Connecticut, June 28, 1983,* National Transportation Safety Board, U.S. Government, Washington DC, July.

———. (1988). *Highway Accident Report—Collapse of New York Thruway (I-90) Bridge over the Schoharie Creek, near Amsterdam, New York, April 5, 1987,* National Transportation Safety Board, Report No. NTSB/HAR-88-02, U.S. Government, Washington, DC, April.

O'Connor, C. (1971). *Design of Bridge Superstructures,* John Wiley & Sons, New York.

O'Connor, D., and Hyman, W. A. (1989). *Bridge Management Systems,* Report No. FHWA-DP-71-01, Federal Highway Administration, Washington, DC.

Ohashi, M., Fujii, T., Kuribayashi, E., and Tazaki, T. (1979a). "Inspection and Retrofitting of Earthquake Resistance Vulnerability of Highway Bridges—Japanese Approach," Report No. ATC-6-1, *Proc. Conf. Earthquake Resistance of Highway Bridges,* Applied Technology Council, San Diego, CA, January 29–31, pp. 391–407.

Ohashi, M., Kurubayashi, E., Iwasaki, T., and Kawashima, K. (1979b). "An Overview of the State of Practices in Earthquake Resistant Design of Highway Bridges," *Proc. Workshop Earthquake Resistance of Highway Bridges,* Applied Technology Council, San Diego, CA, January 29–31.

Olson, S. A., and French, C. W. (1990). "Prestressed Concrete Girders after 20 Years in Service," *Bridge Evaluation, Repair, and Rehabilitation,* Nowak, A. S., ed., University of Michigan, Ann Arbor, pp. 391–403.

Park. (1984). *Bridge Rehabilitation and Replacement (Bridge Repair Practice),* S. H. Park, Trenton, NJ.

Parkinson, J. (1978). "Glue Solves a Sticky Problem for Gestetner," *New Civil Engineer,* September 14, pp. 26–27.

PCI. (1984). "25-Year-Old Prestressed Concrete Girder Tested," *PCI J.,* January–February, pp. 177–179.

PEN. (1987). "FHWA Proposes NICET Certification for Bridge Inspectors," *Professional Engineering News,* National Society of Professional Engineers, Alexandria, VA, fall, p. 2.

Penn DOT. (1987). *The Pennsylvania Bridge Management System, Final Report,* Bridge Management Work Group, Pennsylvania Department of Transportation, Bureau of Bridge and Roadway Technology, February.

Pfeifer, D. W., Landgren, J. R., and Zoob, A. (1987). *Protective Systems for New Prestressed and Substructure Concrete,* Report No. FHWA/RD-86/193, U.S. Department of Transportation, Federal Highway Administration, Washington, DC, April, 113 pp.

Podolny, W. (1993). "Corrosion of Prestressing Steels and Its Mitigation," *PCI J.,* 37(5), September–October, pp. 34–55.

Preston, R. L. (1985). *Strengthening Methods for Bridge Superstructures,* National Roads Board, Wellington, New Zealand.

Priestley, M. J. N. (1988). "Damage to the I-5, I-605 Separator," *Earthquake Spectra,* 4(2), Earthquake Engineering Research Institute, May.

———. (1991). "Retrofit of the San Francisco Double Deckers: Design of Joints for Shear Force," in *Seismic Assessment and Retrofit of Bridges,* Report SSRP 91/03, University of California, San Diego, Structural Systems Research Project.

Priestley, M. J. N., and Park, R. (1987a). "Strength and Ductility of Concrete Bridge Columns under Seismic Loading," *ACI Struct. J.,* 84(1), January–February, pp. 61–76.

———. (1987b). "Strength and Ductility of Concrete Bridge Columns under Seismic Loading," *ACI Struct. J.,* 84(1), pp. 61–76.

Priestley, M. J. N., and Seible, F. (1991). *Seismic Assessment and Retrofit of Bridges,* Report No. SSRP-91/03, University of California at San Diego, La Jolla, July.

———. (1994). "Seismic Assessment of Existing Bridges," *Proc. 2nd Intl. Workshop Seismic Design of Bridges,* vol. 2, Queenstown, New Zealand, August, pp. 46–70.

Priestley, M. J. N., Seible, F., and Calvi, G. M. (1996). *Seismic Design and Retrofit of Bridges,* John Wiley & Sons, New York.

Priestley, M. J. N., Seible, F., and Chai, Y. H. (1992). *Design Guidelines for Assessment Retrofit and Repair of Bridges for Seismic Performance,* Research Report No. SSRP 92-01, Department of Applied Mechanical and Engineering Science, University of California, San Diego.

Priestley, M. J. N., Seible, F., and Fyfe, E. (1992). "Column Seismic Retrofit Using Fiberglass/Epoxy Jackets," *Proc. 3rd NSF Workshop Bridge Engineering Research in Progress,* La Jolla, CA, November, pp. 247–251.

———. (1993) "Column Retrofit Using Fiberglass/Epoxy Jackets," *Proc. 1993 FIP Symp.,* Kyoto, Japan, October, pp. 147–160.

Priestley, M. J. N., Seible, F., and Verma, R. (1994). "Steel Jacket Retrofitting of Reinforced-Concrete Bridge Columns for Enhanced Shear Strength, Part I: Theoretical Considerations and Test Design," *ACI Struct. J.,* 91(4), July/August, pp. 394–405.

Priestley, M. J. N., Seible, F., Xiao, Y., and Verma, R. (1994). "Steel Jacket Retrofitting of Reinforced-Concrete Bridge Columns for Enhanced Shear Strength, Part II: Test Results and Comparison with Theory," *ACI Struct. J.,* 91(5), September/October, pp. 537–551.

Priestley, M. J. N., Seible, F., Chai, Y. H., and Sun, Z. L. (1991a). "Flexural Retrofit of Bridge Columns by Steel Jacketing," in *Proc. First Annual Seismic Res. Workshop,* Department of Transportation, Division of Structures, Sacramento, CA, December 3–4.

Priestley, M. J. N., Seible, F., and Uang, C. M. (1994). *The Northridge Earthquake of January 17, 1994—Damage Analysis of Selected Bridges,* Structural Systems Report No. SSRP-94/06, University of California at San Diego, February.

Priestley, M. J. N., Seible, F., Xiao, Y., and Verma, R. (1991b). "Shear Retrofit of Bridge Columns by Steel Jacketing," in *Proc. First Annual Seismic Res. Workshop,* Department of Transportation, Division of Structures, Sacramento, CA, December 3–4.

Raithby, K. D. (1980). *External Strengthening of Concrete Bridges with Bonded Plates,* TRRL Supp. Report 612, Transport and Road Research Laboratory, Department of Environment, Crowthorne, England.

Ravara, A. (1979). "A European View of the Earthquake Resistant Design of Bridges," in *Proc. Workshop Earthquake Resistance of Highway Bridges,* Applied Technology Council, January 29–31.

RBM. (1987). "FHWA Considers Bridge Ailments, Remedies," *Roads and Bridges Magazine,* Des Plaines, IL, November, pp. 45–46.

Riessauw, F. G., and Taerwe, L. (1980). "Tests on Two 30-Year-Old Prestressed Concrete Beams," *PCI J.,* November–December, pp. 70–73.

Roberts, J. E. (1990). "Presentation by CALTRANS to Governor's Board of Inquiry," Testimony Presented to the Board of Inquiry, March 15, 1990.

Robinson, R. R., Longinow, A., and Albert, D. S. (1979). *Seismic Retrofit Measures for Highway Bridges, vol. 2, Earthquake and Structural Analysis,* Report No. FHWA-TS-79-217, U.S. Department of Transportation, Federal Highway Administration, Washington, DC, April.

Robinson, R. R., Longinow, A., and Chu, K. H. (1979). *Seismic Retrofit Measures for Highway Bridges, vol. 1, Earthquake and Structural Analysis,* Rep. no. FHWA-TS-79-216, U.S. Department of Transportation, Federal Highway Administration, Washington, DC., April.

Robinson, R. R., Privitzer, E., Longinow, A., and Chu, K. H. (1975). *Structural Analysis and Retrofitting of Existing Highway Bridges Subjected to Strong Motion Seismic Loading,* Report No. FHWA-RD-75-94, U.S. Department of Transportation, Federal Highway Administration, Washington, DC, May.

Rogerson, W. M., Sharp, M. L., Stemler, J. R., and Sommer, R. J. (1967). "Aluminum Orthotropic Bridge Deck," *ASCE Civ. Eng.,* November, pp. 65–70.

Ryback, M. (1981). "Reinforcement of Bridges by Gluing of Reinforcing Steel," *RILEM Materials and Structures,* 16(91), January, pp. 13–17.

Saadatmanesh, H., and Ehsani, M. R. (1991). "RC Beams Strengthened with GFRP Plates. I: Experimental Study," *ASCE J. Struct. Eng.,* 117(11), pp. 3417–3433.

Saadeghvaziri, M. A. (1990). "Seismic Damage Assessment for Eastern United States," *Fall Seminar 1990 Buildings and Bridges: Seismic Analysis and Design of Structural Systems in the Eastern United States,* presented by the Structural Group, ASCE North Jersey Branch, New Jersey Section.

Scheffey, C. F., and Cayes, L. R. (1974). *Model Tests of Modes of Failure of Joint C13N of Eyebar Chain—Point Pleasant Bridge Investigation,* Federal Highway Administration Report No. FHWA-RD-74-19, U.S. Department of Transportation, Washington, DC, January.

Schupack, M., and Suarez, M. G. (1991). Discussion of "Prestressed Concrete Bridges in Adverse Environments" by V. Novokshchenov, *Concrete International,* 13(12), December, pp. 11–14.

Seim, C. (1983). "Steel Beats Concrete for Idaho Bridge," *ASCE, Civ. Eng.,* 53(8), August, pp. 28–32.

Selna, L., and Malvar, J. (1987). *Full Scale Experimental Testing of Retrofit Devices Used for Reinforced Concrete Bridges,* Report No. UCLA/EQSE-87/01, University of California, Los Angeles, June.

Selna, L. G., Malvar, L. J., and Zelinski, R. J. (1989a). "Box Girder Bar and Bracket Seismic Retrofit Devices," *ACI Structural Journal, American Concrete Institute,* 86(5), September–October.

———. (1989b). "Bridge Retrofit Testing: Hinge Cable Restrainers," *ASCE, J. Struct. Eng.,* 115(4), April.

Sessions, L., Blanchard, B., and Locke, J. (1991). "Renovation: Over the Hill Bridges," *AISC Modern Steel Construction,* February, pp. 28–31.

Seyed, M. (1991a). *Seismic Design Criteria for Cypress St. Viaduct,* Special Analysis Section, State of California, Department of Transportation, Division of Structures, October 31.

———. (1991b). *Foundation Stiffness Issues for Cypress St. Viaduct,* Special Analysis Section, State of California, Department of Transportation, Division of Structures, December 16.

———. (1992a). *User's Manual for COLx, Column Ductility Program,* Special Analysis Section, State of California, Department of Transportation, Division of Structures, January 24.

———. (1992b). *User's Manual for BEAMx, Beam Ductility Program,* Special Analysis Section, State of California, Department of Transportation, Division of Structures, January 27.

———. (1992c). *Seismic Behavior of Single Column Bents in Transverse Direction,* Special Analysis Section, State of California, Department of Transportation, Division of Structures, January 30.

———. (1992d). *User's Manual for FRAMEx, Frame Ductility Program,* Special Analysis Section, State of California, Department of Transportation, Division of Structures, February 2.

Shahawy, M. A., and Bietelman, T. (1996). "Structural Repair and Strengthening of Damages to Prestressed Concrete Bridges Utilizing Externally Bonded Carbon Materials," *41st Intl. SAMPE Symp. and Exh.,* Anaheim, CA, March 24–28, Book 2 of 2, pp. 1311–1318.

Shenoy, C. V., and Frantz, G. C. (1991). "Structural Tests of 27-Year-Old Prestressed Concrete Bridge Beams," *PCI J.,* 36(5), September–October, pp. 80–90.

Smith, D. W. (1977). "Why Do Bridges Fail?," *ASCE, Civ. Eng.,* November, pp. 58–62.

Sommerard, T. (1971). "Swanley's Steel Plate Patch Up," *New Civil Engineer,* No. 247, June 16, pp. 18–19.

Soto, M. H. (1978). "Some Considerations in Widening and Rehabilitation of Bridges," *Transportation Research Record 664,* Transportation Research Board, St. Louis, MO.

SSPC. (1982/1991). *Steel Structures Painting Manual,* Steel Structures Painting Council, Pittsburgh, PA, vol. I, *Good Painting Practice,* 2nd ed., 1982, vol. II, *Systems and Specifications,* 6th ed., 1991.

Stahl, F. L. (1990). "Orthotropic Steel Plates for Bridge Deck Replacement," in G. W. Maupin, B. C. Brown, and A. G. Lichtenstein, eds., *Extending the Life of Bridges, STP 1100,* ASTM, Philadelphia, PA, pp. 109–120.

Steinman, D. B., and Watson, S. R. (1957). *Bridges and Their Builders,* Putnam, New York.

Sterian, D. (1969). "Introducing Artificial Initial Forces into Steel Bridge Decks," *Acier-Stahl-Steel,* No. 1, pp. 31–37.

Sulit, R. A. (1993). "Thermal Spraying for Steel Bridges," *AISC Modern Steel Construction,* February, pp. 34–35.

Swamy, R. N., and Jones, R. (1980). "Behavior of Plated Reinforced Concrete Beams Subjected to Cyclic Loading During Glue Hardening," *Int. J. of Cement Composites,* 2(4), November, pp. 233–234.

Swamy, R. N., Jones, R., and Ang, T. H. (1982). "Under- and Over-Reinforced Concrete Beams with Glued Steel Plates," *Intl. J. Cement Composites and Lightweight Conc.,* 4(1), February, pp. 19–32.

Swamy, R. N., Jones, R., and Bloxham, J. W. (1987). "Structural Behavior of Reinforced Concrete Beams Strengthened by Epoxy-Bonding Steel Plates," *Structural Engineer,* 65A(2), February, London, England, pp. 59–68.

Tabatabai, H., and Dickson, T. J. (1993). "Structural Evaluation of a 34-Year-Old Precast Post-Tensioned Concrete Girder," *PCI J.,* 38(5), September–October, pp. 50–63.

TRB. (1979). *Snow Removal and Ice Control Research,* Special Report 185, Transportation Research Board, Washington, DC.

TRB. (1988). *Underwater Bridge Inspection Programs,* Circular 330, Transportation Research Board, Washington, DC.

Troitsky, M. S. (1989). *Prestressed Steel Structures,* Lincoln Arc Welding Foundation, Cleveland, OH.

Troitsky, M. S., and Rabbani, N. F. (1987). "Tendon Configurations of Prestressed Steel Girders," *Proc. Centennial Conf. Canadian Soc. Civil Engrs.,* May 19–22, Montreal, Quebec, pp. 171–182.

Troitsky, M. S., Zielinski, Z. A., and Pimpriker, M. S. (1987). "Experimental Evaluation of Prestressed Steel and Plate Girder Bridges," *ASCE Proc. Experimental Assessment of Performances of Bridges,* Boston, MA, October 27, pp. 1–6.

Troitsky, M. S., Zielinski, Z. A., and Rabbani, N. F. (1989). "Prestressed-Steel Continuous-Span Girders," *ASCE J. Struct. Eng.,* 115(6), June, pp. 1357–1370.

TRR. (1988). *Structures Maintenance,* Transportation Research Record Rep. no. 1184, Transportation Research Board, Washington, DC.

Tsuji, Y., Kanda, M., and Tamura, T. (1993). "Applications of FRP Materials to Prestressed Concrete Bridges and Other Structures in Japan," *PCI J.,* 38(4), July–August, pp. 50–58.

USFS. (1979). *Wood Bridges—Decay Inspection and Control,* Agricultural Handbook No. 557, Forest Service, U.S. Department of Agriculture, Madison, WI.

USGAO. (1990). *Loma Prieta Earthquake: Collapse of the Bay Bridge and the Cypress Viaduct,* Report GAO/RCED-90-177, United States General Accounting Office.

Uyemae, Y., Ikewaki, K., and Aoyama, K. (1977). "New Proposals on Fall-Proof Devices for Prestressed Concrete Girder," *J. Japan Prestressed Concrete Engineering Association,* 19(6), December.

Van Germert, D. A. (1982). "Repairing of Concrete Structures by Externally Bonded Steel Plates," in *Proc. ICP/RILEM/IBK International Symposium on Plastics in Material and Structural Engineering,* Elsevier Scientific Publishing Co., Prague, June, pp. 519–526.

Van Lund, J. A., Chen, R. L., Mhatre, Y. A., and Vashisth, U. C. (1981). "Steel Arches Used in Bridge Reconstruction over I-5," *Transportation Research Record 1223,* Transportation Research Board, Washington, DC, pp. 47–53.

Warner, R. F. (1981). "Strengthening, Stiffening, and Repair of Concrete Structures," *IABSE Surveys,* vol. 17, May, pp. 25–41.

Weissman, J., Harrison, R., Burns, N. H., and Hudson, W. R. (1990). "A Bridge Management System Model for the Selection of Rehabilitation and Replacement Projects," in Kenneth S. Opiela, ed., *Microcomputer Applications in Transportation III,* ASCE, New York, pp. 784–793.

WHD. (1973). *System Orientation Manual for Load Rating of Bridge Structures,* Wyoming Highway Department, Bridge Division.

White, K. R., and Minor, J. (1989). *User's Manual, Microcomputer Program for Bridge Analysis and Rating,* Federal Highway Administration, Washington, DC.

White, K. R., Minor, J., and Derucher, K. N. (1992). *Bridge Maintenance, Inspection and Evaluation,* 2nd ed., Marcel Dekker, New York.

Wiley, W. E. (1988). "Post-Tensioning of Composite T-Beam Subjected to Negative Moment," M.S. thesis, Iowa State University, Ames.

Wiley, W. E., Klaiber, F. W., and Dunker, K. F. (1981). "Behavior of Composite Steel Bridge Beams Subjected to Various Posttensioning Schemes," *Transportation Research Record 1223,* Transportation Research Board, Washington DC, pp. 63–72.

Wipf, T. J., Klaiber, F. K., and Hall, M. J. (1981). "Strengthening of Steel Stringer Bridges by Transverse and Longitudinal Stiffening," *Transportation Research Record 1223,* Transportation Research Board, Washington DC, pp. 54–62.

Woodward, C. B., and Minor, J. (1990). *User's Manual, TIMBRE,* Louisiana Transportation Research Center, Louisiana State University.

Xanthakos, P. P. (1996). *Bridge Strengthening and Rehabilitation,* Prentice Hall, Upper Saddle River, NJ.

Yamadera, N., and Uyemae, Y. (1979). "Special Considerations and Requirements for the Seismic Design of Bridges in Japan," *Proc. Workshop Earthquake Resistance of Highway Bridges,* Applied Technology Council, San Diego, CA, January 29–31, pp. 286–312.

Zelinski, R. J. (1985). *California Department of Transportation Bridge Earthquake Retrofitting Program,* U.S./New Zealand Workshop, May.

——. (1990). "California Highway Bridge Retrofit Strategy and Details," in *2nd Workshop on Bridge Engineering Research in Progress,* National Science Foundation and Civil Engineering Department, University of Nevada, Reno, October 29–30.

——. (1995a). "Northridge Earthquake Influence on Bridge Design Code," *ACI Conf.,* Montreal, November 9.

——. (1995b). "CALTRANS Seismic Design Commentary on New Bridges," *FIGG Engineering Group Symp.,* Tallahassee, FL, September 29.

——. (1996b). "Bridge Retrofit Concepts," *41st Intl. SAMPE Symp. and Exh.,* Anaheim, CA, March 24–28, 1996, Book 2 of 2, pp. 990–1003.

Zollman, C. C., Depman, F., Nagle, J., and Hollander, E. F. (1992). "Building and Rebuilding of Philadelphia's Walnut Lane Memorial Bridge—Part 1: A History of Design, Construction, and Service Life," *PCI J.,* 37(3), May–June, pp. 66–82.

CHAPTER 11

Aesthetics of Bridges

11.1
INTRODUCTION

The word *aesthetic*[1] can be etymologized to the Greek word "$\alpha\iota\sigma\theta\eta\tau\iota\kappa\acute{o}$s," which means perceptive, or fitted to be perceptive. In 1750, A. G. Baumgarten published a work entitled *Aesthetica,* dealing with beauty, and the term *aesthetics* has since been used to mean the study of such matters as art and the beautiful [Ducasse, 1966]. Accordingly, Webster's College Dictionary defines "aesthetics" as the study or theory of beauty, or the branch of philosophy dealing with art, its creative sources, its forms, and its effects.

Since the dawn of civilization, philosophers, artists, art critics, social scientists, architects, and many others have engaged in an endless endeavor to define and discuss beauty, art, and aesthetics, and the interrelationships thereof [Parker, 1929; Gideon, 1952; Anderson, 1958; Torroja, 1958; Schlaepfer, 1959; Arnheim, 1965; Dunican, 1966; Heyer, 1966; Scott, 1969; Medwadowski, 1971; Collingwood, 1979; Tassios, 1980]. Literature on bridge aesthetics, because of the intrinsically subjective nature and philosophical domain of aesthetics, is replete with treatises, books, and journals. In view of the changing perspectives, social demands, and advancements in materials and building technology, the literature on aesthetics will continue to grow [Boller, 1881; Young, 1911; Brangwyn and Sparrows, 1920; Hayden and Barron, 1931; Faber, 1941,1945; Inglis, 1945; Mumford, 1955; Torroja, 1958; Evans and Houghton-Evans, 1964; Billington, 1969, 1973a,b, 1974, 1981; Le Corbusier, 1970; Whitney, 1983].

---

[1]The British spelling for this word is "esthetics." The British variants of words derived from *aesthetics* have the letter "a" missing and begin with "e." Various variants, for example, are *aesthete* and *esthete* (Brit.), *aesthetical* and *esthetical* (Brit.), *aestheticism* and *estheticism* (Brit.). In this book, the word *aesthetics* and its derivatives are used throughout.

Many authors have focused on fundamental philosophical and psychological aspects of aesthetics of bridges and other structures [Hool and Thissen, 1916; Wadell, 1916; Wendell, 1953; Leonhardt, 1968, 1980, 1984, 1991; Wengenroth, 1971; Keisling and Whetstone, 1972; Elliot, 1973; Zuk, 1976, Slatter, 1980; Tahara and Naka-mura, 1980; Tassios, 1980; O'Connor, 1991; Revelo, 1991]. Others dwell on the aesthetical analysis and visual aspects of existing bridges [Murray, 1981, 1991; Glomb, 1991; Gottemoeller, 1991; Liebenberg, 1991]. Architectural principles of bridge design have been presented in many books and papers [Watson, 1938; Elliot, 1968; Leonhardt, 1968, 1984, 1991; Bakht and Jaeger, 1983; Zuk, 1983; De Miranda, 1991; Menn, 1991]. Billington has provided a discussion on history and aesthetics in suspension [1977a] and concrete arch bridges [1977b]. A discussion on history and aesthetics of cable-stayed bridges has been provided by Billington and Nazmi [1991]. Discussions on the aesthetics of selected bridges have been presented by several authors. Muller [1991] has presented a perspective on the aesthetics of concrete segmental bridges. White and von Bernwitz [1928] have discussed the aesthetics of Pittsburgh's bridges. Kavanagh [1975] has presented aesthetic considerations for steel bridges. Warton and Hurd [1990] have focused on the aesthetics of concrete bridges. Billington [1990] and Tajima and Sugiyama [1991] have discussed the significance of the forms of towers, regarding the aesthetics of suspension bridges in Japan. Leonhardt [1984] has presented an excellent treatise on the aesthetics of bridges worldwide. His book *Bridges—Aesthetics and Design* [Leonhardt, 1984], originally written in German and translated to English, remains the most detailed study and one of the best guides on the aesthetics of bridges. At the end of his book, Leonhardt provides an alphabetical listing of all bridges discussed in the book, with the names of engineers and architects responsible for those bridges.

While many authors have repeatedly discussed beauty and the aesthetics of long-span bridges such as arch, cable-stayed, and suspension bridges, others have presented aesthetic considerations for short- and medium-span bridges. Because of their large numbers, short- and medium-span bridges form a very important and integral part of both urban and suburban surroundings. Thus, their appearance is very important to the surrounding communities [Billington, 1981]. Specific problems related to the aesthetics of short- and medium-span bridges have been addressed by several authors [Shureman, 1938; Hayden and Barron, 1950; Dorton, 1991; Wasserman, 1991; Harbeson, 1991; Murray, 1991; von Olnhausen, 1991; Elliot, 1991]. Concern for aesthetics and for the acceptable appearance of bridges is often expressed as a part of the design policies of bridge owners, such as California's *Bridge Design Practice Manual* [CALTRANS, 1970, 1993].

Prompted by worldwide concern for bridge aesthetics, the Transportation Research Board published *Bridge Aesthetics around the World* [TRB, 1991], an illustrated compendium of papers on bridge aesthetics. It contains 23 papers from well-known engineers, authors, and designers of distinctive bridges from 16 countries. It also contains an annotated bibliography [Burke and Teach, 1991] of 254 references. This beautifully illustrated book not only reflects the concern and thinking of bridge engineers worldwide, but it also provides valuable advice, recommendations, guidelines, and examples for the aesthetic design of bridges. This book, as well as Leonhardt's *Bridges—Aesthetics and Design* [1984] are highly recommended for developing an awareness of fundamentals and practices of bridge aesthetics around the world. Liebenberg [1991] has discussed the process of aesthetic evaluation of bridges. Ito [1991] has provided an interesting insight into the beauty of spiral bridges. The aesthetics of Japanese pedestrian bridges has been discussed by Nakamura and Kubota [1991]. Ghaswala [1991] has provided a discussion on the *Golden Section* and bridge aesthetics in India. Aesthetics, history, and the nature of Spanish bridges have been discussed by Ordonez [1991]. A Canadian perspective on aesthetic considerations for bridge overpasses has been presented by Dorton [1991]. von Olnhausen [1991] has discussed the Swedish perspective of bridge aesthetics. Elliot [1983] has presented a discussion of the aesthetic development of California bridges. All combined, this effort appears to be a repetition in establishing the interdependence of bridge aesthetics, economics, and structural performance. While some of the writings have helped engineers experience the fascinating field of bridge aesthetics through illustrations and photographic presentations, others are so vague and abstract that they can be characterized as "tiresome empirical twaddle" [Nobbs, 1911]. Bridges of Eiffel [Billington, 1983], Maillart [Bill, 1969; Billington, 1974, 1979], Eads [Girbert and Billington, 1970], Roebling [McCullough, 1972], and Menn [Billington, 1978] have been extolled because of the grandiose display of their bridges' equipoise, which has never been surpassed. Some of these bridges (Figs. 11.1–11.5) are known worldwide for their aesthetic appeal. Figures 11.6 and 11.7 are other examples of bridges having aesthetic merits.

11.2
PHILOSOPHICAL ASPECTS OF BEAUTY, AESTHETICS, AND ART

Beauty has undeniable universal appeal and remains a cherished goal toward creative achievement, as observed by Hayden and Barron [1950]:

> If you get beauty, and naught else, you get about the best thing the God Invents.

Beauty has been defined as the capacity of an object aesthetically contemplated to yield feelings that are pleasant. Yet beauty cannot be proved by appeal or consensus, or by the "test of time," or by the type of person who experiences it in a given way. Beauty also cannot be proved by appeal to technical principles or canons. However, it may be that there are certain narrower and more technical requirements in the various fields of art, without the fulfillment of which no work can be beautiful [Ducasse, 1966]. Beauty, according to Ducasse [1966], can be expressed as the "science of mathematical aesthetics, which gives a physical interpretation of functionalistic behavior through aesthetic expression." Ducasse [1966] defines beauty as "a character that anything has in so far as it gives pleasure to someone in aesthetic contemplation," and "art—the critically controlled objective expression by the artist of a feeling in him." Le Corbusier [1970] gives the scientific definition of beauty: "Where economic law reigns supreme and mathematical exactness is joined to daring and imagination, that is beauty."

In the past, the aesthetic was considered to be "a property of an object, like function or pleasure, a property that manifested itself in the harmonious proportions of the dimensions" [Menn, 1991]. It was the German philosopher Immanuel Kant (1724–1804)

FIGURE 11.1
John Roebling's Brooklyn Bridge, New York City—the East Coast symbol: (*top*) a view facing towers, and (*bottom*) overall view [Billington and Nazmi, 1991].

FIGURE 11.2
Maillart's Salginatobel Bridge near Scgiers, Switzerland, a reinforced concrete arch spanning 90 m (295.3 ft) built in 1930, most famous for its aesthetic expressiveness. Maillart won the contract for the bridge by submitting the lowest bid out of 18 designs [Billington, 1991].

FIGURE 11.3
A reinforced concrete arch bridge built by Robert Maillart in 1933. Its very thin arch, spanning 37.4 m (122.7 ft), is stiffened by the horizontally curved roadway, and the two parts are integrated by vertical trapezoidal cross walls [Billington, 1991].

FIGURE 11.4
The Reichenau Bridge, spanning 100 m (328.1 ft) and built in 1964 by Christian Menn. Note the expressiveness of the funicular line, the delicacy of the members, and the transparency (openness through substructure) [Billington, 1991].

FIGURE 11.5
The Gantor Bridge on the Simpson Road above Brig, Switzerland, designed by Christian Menn in 1980. Note the expressiveness of the new form in which the prestressed cables are embedded in the triangular wall above the roadway. Main span 174 m (570.9 ft), and maximum column height 150 m (492.1 ft) [Billington, 1991].

FIGURE 11.6
The Bacunayagua River Bridge, Cuba, designed by Luis P. Saenz. Note the transparency, the slenderness of the members, and the aesthetic expressiveness through the funicular line [Martin, 1974].

FIGURE 11.7
Adams Avenue Overcrossing, San Diego, California. The
expressiveness of the arch is produced by curving the inclined
supports of this rigid-frame bridge. For safety considerations, the
supports are placed high up on the side slopes where they are not
a menace to traffic [Elliot, 1991].

who, along with ethics and the theory of cognition, ranked aesthetics as an actual philosophical discipline. He "visualized a close connection between aesthetics and optimum
functionalism of organic nature" [Menn, 1991].

The word *aesthetic* today has become obscured. Sometimes it is used in its et-
ymological sense of "perceptible" or having to do with perception. It is also used to
designate several more or less distinct sorts of inquiries, such as philosophy or art, and
beauty; empirical investigations of the things judged beautiful by certain persons (e.g.,
statistical investigations for preferences of color, proportions in rectangles); and also
art criticism. The term *aesthetic* is also loosely used as more or less synonymous with
"beautiful" [Ducasse, 1966]. Some are quick to confuse aesthetics with something superficial or artificial, like cosmetics.

Since bridges are created objects, they may be looked upon as works of art—good
and bad. However, the aestheticians have never been unanimous on the definition of
"art," for the judgmental values of artist-aestheticians (artists with a leaning toward
philosophy) and philosopher-aestheticians (philosophers with a taste for art) have often
been contradictory [Collingwood, 1979]. Ducasse [1966] points out: "Art is not a quality of things but an activity of man. Art is not an activity aiming at creation of beauty.
The artist does not aim at beauty but at objective self expression. The deliberate creation of beauty is not art." For Tolstoy, "the essence of art is transmission of emotion" (as
quoted in [Ducasse, 1966]). Beauty can be expressed through architecture, but as Scott
[1969] points out, "What we feel as beauty in architecture is not a matter for logical
demonstration." Among such alleged canons of beauty may be mentioned the rules of
so called "harmony" in music; various precepts concerning literary composition, unity,
truth to nature; such requirements as consistency, relevance, unambiguity; and so on
[Ducasse, 1966].

11.3
SOCIAL IMPACT OF BRIDGES

Bridge building evolved as an esteemed and revered profession, as observed by Michelangelo in the sixteenth century: "A bridge ought to be built as though it were intended to be a cathedral, with the same care and the same materials" (as quoted in [Liebenberg, 1991]). Long-span bridges, such as suspension, cable-stayed, and arch, stand as monumental structures and have been dubbed "index of civilization" and "the epitome of the progress of humanity throughout the ages" [Steinman and Watson, 1957]. The world has long extolled their builders—Telford, Eiffel, Eads, Roebling, Maillart, Menn, Steinman, and Leonhardt, to name a few. "The art of building, and bridge construction in particular, is one of the most expressive synthesis of the capacity of a people, one of the more meaningful elements that distinguish a nation's genius and level of civilization" [De Miranda, 1991]. Civilization and architecture reflect each other, for as Lethaby points out, "architecture, properly understood, is civilization itself," and, as defined by Matthew Arnold (1822–1888), civilization is but humanization of man in society [Mumford, 1955]. Bridges in urban areas—the omnipresent inner-city interchanges, underpasses, overpasses, and pedestrian bridges [Nakamura and Kubota, 1991]—symbolize social impact landmarks, a sentiment echoed throughout the world [TRB, 1991]. They represent legacies to the future generations, as observed by Ruskin (1819–1900) (as quoted in [Steinman and Watson, 1957, pp. 392–393]):

> Therefore when we build, let us think that we build forever. Let it not be for present delight, nor for present use alone; let it be such work as our descendants will thank us for, and let us think, as we lay stone on stone, that a time is to come when those stones will be held sacred because our hands have touched them, and that men will say as they look upon the labor and wrought substance on them, "See, this our fathers did for us."

Ruskin's sentiments are echoed by architect Russell Sturgis (1836–1909): "Instead of concentrating their attention upon the question whether their works would stand, they should direct some of it to the question whether they are fit to stand," for, as Murray [1981] points out, "Works produced by the great majority, the poor artist, are destroyed or cast aside, and we are therefore spared the pain of having to live with them. Not so with bad structures designed by engineers."

Bridges form some of the most important civil engineering creations [Bill, 1969]. Construction of bridges over formidable spans such as Verrazano Narrows, Golden Gate, or, for that matter, the New River Gorge, came as challenges to the technical skill and ingenuity of engineers. Their completion symbolized the glorious triumph of their builders over the forces of nature. As a result, there is a lot of pride and glory associated with the design and construction of these monumental structures. Engineers, designers, fabricators, the owner agencies, and the workers take pride in associating themselves with these bridges. One of the greatest art critics of his time, Montgomery Schuyler, wrote in 1883 [Schuyler, 1883] (perhaps impressed by the Brooklyn Bridge, also completed in 1883), "It so happens that the work which is likely to be foremost a durable monument, and convey some knowledge of us to the most remote posterity, is a work of bare utility, not a shrine, not a fortress, not a palace, but a bridge."

In the opinion of Thomas Hastings, the greatest injustice to the public taste or feeling is the building of an ugly bridge, for the most prominent and useful structure should be the most beautiful; yet the reverse has been the custom, particularly in America [Tyrell, 1912, p. 16]. Hastings also observed, "while houses have been adorned and made architecturally attractive, the beautifying of bridges has not advanced in proportion to other arts" [Tyrell, 1912, p. 10].

Bridges are built essentially as utilitarian structures to serve a transportation system for a certain life span, beyond which, because of changes in traffic patterns and transportation systems, bridges cease to serve their function, and are, hypothetically, to be abandoned. For economic reasons, however, this philosophy of continual replacement is being replaced by one of conservation and adaptation to future needs through rehabilitation. This calls for building bridges that would have some aesthetic merits and ideological balance not only for the present but also for the future, for, once built,

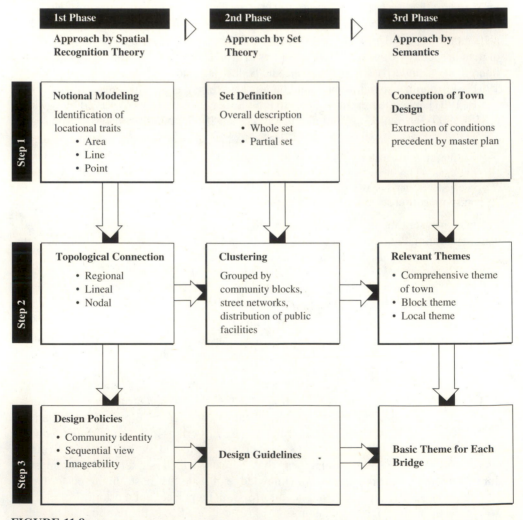

FIGURE 11.8

Framework of contextual approach for aesthetic design of bridges [Nakamura and Kubota, 1991].

they would stand as legacies for several generations. As social scientist Lewis Mumford (1895–1990) pointed out, "Ideological obsolescence is worse than functional obsolescence (for which it was created), and even worse than technical obsolescence (which may be remedied by reconversion, reinforcement, or redoing the structure with new forms and materials)" (as quoted in [Ordonez, 1991]). This calls for building bridges, albeit presciently, with a touch of yet unknown futuristic aesthetics, which may be markedly different from that of the past or the present and cannot be postulated. One way to accomplish this goal would be to design within the guidelines of contemporary aesthetics. Methods of aesthetic design of bridges have been discussed by Ohata [1984] and by Ohata, Takahashi, and Yamane [1987]. An interesting framework of the thinking process for developing aesthetic bridges has been described by Nakamura and Kubota [1991] (Fig. 11.8).

11.4
AESTHETIC POLICIES AND ENGINEERS' TRAINING

Beauty and its study, aesthetics, are highly controversial subjects to which each critical observer brings an abundance of preconceptions, based on personal likes and dislikes, and conflicting aesthetic perceptions that burden objectivity in judgment. Beauty is an emotional concept that is relative to the individual observer, from which stems the old axiom "beauty lies in the eyes of the beholder." What is pleasant and acceptable to one might be offensive and unacceptable to another. "Likewise, aesthetics is not an exact science for which rules can be laid down to ensure universal satisfaction" [Wasserman, 1991], or, in the words of the German philosopher Hegel (1770–1831), "It is impossible to discover a rule that can be used to judge what is beautiful and what is not."

Over the years, many factors have contributed to a decline in the creation of aesthetic bridges. The concept of strict functionalism, which treated bridges as pure structures, first appeared in eighteenth-century Italy when Lodoli proposed that "only that shall follow in a building that has a definite function and derives from the strictest necessity" (as quoted in [Schlaepfer, 1959, pp. 69–70]). This doctrine proved impractical to follow and few practiced it. To functionalism, the French architect Villet Le Duc added the thesis that taste and artistic sensitivity must have a role in design, but that their influence must be exerted through a rational process rather than through the subconscious (as quoted in [Medwadowski, 1971]).

Other factors also contributed to a decline in the aesthetics of bridges. Until the nineteenth century, the responsibilities for engineering, architecture, and construction of a bridge were centered in one man. That began to change with the advent of new materials such as steel and concrete. Designing with these new materials demanded a thorough study of their properties and behavior, leading to a science of engineering separate from architecture. This was followed by the separation between the engineer and the contractor. This separation of responsibilities led to the worldwide decline in the aesthetic merits of bridges [Potyondy, 1969]. The reasons for lack of beauty in old American bridges are discussed by Tyrell [1912].

Practically speaking, the shape of a bridge is a logical result of many contradictory factors such as economic, functional, social, and environmental, the economic factor often being the paramount design criterion. Conventionally, public agencies approach design on a least-cost basis, separate from construction. For expediency, their bridges are generally a rehash of previous designs that can be easily duplicated, incorporating a maximum number of standard details, regardless of the aesthetic implications for the problem at hand. The result is usually an unattractive bridge that is utilitarian but lacking in aesthetic merits and not in harmony with its surroundings.

In a design office, engineering projects are quite often overwhelmed with considerations of geometrics, analysis, design alternatives, schedules, and costs, which together temper with the art of structural engineering in the design and building of an aesthetically pleasant bridge. This calls for maintaining a balance between engineering skills and aestheticism. In a structure, art and engineering should be conjunctional to produce something that is not necessarily sensational but certainly visually impressive and technically refined and sound. It should symbolize unity of utility, harmony, and beauty. A bridge should symbolize not only functional fitness, but also the engineer's aesthetic expression.

Bridges form a part of public works for which decision making requires agreed-upon criteria, and Goethe's dictum "the artist must create what the public *ought* to like, not what it *does* like" [Gideon, 1952] is no longer practical. In modern times, aesthetic qualities are subject to acceptance by viewers and evaluators, and their standards are not necessarily the same and will continue to change. The trend is to treat the public as a paying client to whom the concept of a bridge under design is to be sold. Diversity in viewers' reactions to appearance leads to the belief that there is insufficient common ground on which to base criteria for aesthetics [Gottemoeller, 1991]. Decision making is further complicated by the fact that aesthetic attributes can be only qualitative and not quantitative, for "the aesthetics is, to a certain degree, an intrinsic property of the object itself" [Menn, 1991]. While it is indeed difficult, if not impossible, to make hard and fast rules in aesthetics, based on some objectivity, "good" and "bad" taste can be defined [Broachman, 1955] and principles of aesthetics formulated. From these principles, consensus guidelines can be formed to bring about transformation of an abstract sense of beauty to elegant engineering creativity, instead of applying some quaint notions of embellishments.

The main impediment to creating aesthetic bridges appears to be the engineers' lack of training in art and architecture; their work is driven by the inertia of their training in the mathematics of functionality. Engineers need not be omniscient in art and architecture; however, aesthetic sensitivity and awareness are mental attributes that cannot be gained blindly, impulsively, or inspirationally [Tang, 1991]. Nor are they likely to grow through an osmotic process. Thinking aesthetically should be a part of structural engineering [Law, 1976]. As Billington [1969] points out, for most people it can be accomplished through proper learning: "Education in structures should begin by returning to a study of the great masterworks of the recent past," and engineers should learn to contemplate them [Revelo, 1991]. This initial experience can be extremely helpful in learning appreciation for visual arts and developing aesthetic sensitivity, which may be enhanced in one's working life through practice [Murray, 1991]. Hopefully, this will lead to a general creativity in designing beautiful bridges, rather than sporadic works of artistic brilliance created by only a few. But without any guidelines, generations of engineers could simply continue to build ugly bridges [Ghaswala, 1991].

While some experts on aesthetics feel that economic considerations should not be subordinate to those of aesthetics when the two are at odds [Menn, 1991], the realities of budgetary constraints may render achieving such a goal difficult, if not impossible. Unfortunately, most believe in the perpetuating myth that aesthetics involves additional costs. However, aesthetic elegance does not have to be expensive. The world-famous Maillart's bridges are perfect examples of twentieth-century structural art that combine minimum material, minimum cost, and maximum aesthetic expression. That reasonable additional expenditures should be advocated to achieve acceptable aesthetic qualities is a sentiment echoed by engineers worldwide [CE, 1970, 1975, 1976; IH, 1984; TRB, 1991].

11.5
AESTHETICS AND ORNAMENTATION

The difference between ornamentation and aesthetics is often blurred. Creating an aesthetic bridge is not synonymous with creating an ornate bridge. Ornamentation or embellishment refers to decorative additions purely for the sake of appearance or beauty and should be used only as a last resort to secure an aesthetic structure. The contemporary trend in civil engineering to design structures that are free of superfluous embellishment should be also reflected in bridges.

Bridges are considered as pure structures in that they are free of all intricate considerations that must be made for buildings, such as electric and heating installations, partitions, doors, windows, and bathrooms. Thus, they are, in a sense, physical and visual presentations of an engineer's mathematics. To satisfy aesthetic principles, the design should not mask the type of structure being used. For example, joints and hinges, whether in arches or in beams, should not be concealed; a hinged arch should not resemble a fixed arch; and vertical members designed to resist tension (for example, in a truss or hangers of a bowstring girder) should not be dimensioned like compression members [Potyondy, 1969].

Bridges should never be imbued ornamentally. Figures 11.9 and 11.10 show examples of ornamentation of bridges. The purpose of ornamentation, if used, should be to emphasize the structural parts and impress the observer, without masking the true nature of form and material, and Ruskin's rule "to decorate construction without constructing decoration" should be applied [Tyrell, 1912]. The absence of superfluous and irritating details is in itself considered a measure of aesthetics.

Ornamentation should not be used to compensate for the aesthetic shortcomings. However, where the public can draw near and observe a structure at close range, an architectural treatment or judicious ornamentation are of primary importance [Ito, 1991; Muller, 1991]. As Menn [1991] points out, "One cannot deny that decoration by an engineer endowed with artistic talent may have an appealing effect. Even dalliance and static nonsense like a pinch of salt can revive the aesthetic appeal of a secondary element." He advises, however, that such variations and details be left to true artists, not to ordinary engineers and architects. This thinking may be viewed by some as deviating from the rules of aesthetic design; but "aesthetic rules are not absolute; they only serve as a framework upon which the engineer must superimpose his originality and artistic sensibilities" [Menn, 1991].

FIGURE 11.9
Old Lu Gou Bridge, Beijing, China, showing embellishment through carved stone lions in different sizes and positions [Tang, 1991].

FIGURE 11.10
The Wahan Yangtze Bridge, China, showing embellishment through cast-iron railing panels [Tang, 1991].

11.6
PRINCIPLES OF AESTHETIC DESIGN

Principles of aesthetics in some form or other have been in the works since ancient times. The first-century B.C. Roman soldier-architect Vitruvius, in addition to building materials and methods, also considered the aims of architecture, which, paraphrased in the time-honored English Renaissance formulation, came to be known as *commodity, firmness,* and *delight.* It is the third aim that we call aesthetics [Medwadowski, 1971]. Le Corbusier observed,

> The engineer, inspired by the law of economy and governed by mathematical calculation puts us in accord with universal law, and our engineers produce architecture, for they employ a mathematical calculation which derives from natural law and their works give us a feeling of harmony. The engineer, therefore, has his own aesthetics, for he must, in making his calculations, qualify some of the terms of his equations, and it is here that taste intervenes.

Along the same lines, Professor Nervi concludes [Nervi, 1956],

> The true essence of good design consists in the full satisfaction of functional, statical, constructional and economic means, and the creation of a well balanced arrangement; a project which satisfies these conditions may be aesthetically significant or expressively beautiful but will never be aggressively annoying.

These remarks simply recognize bridge design as a solution-oriented problem with optimization as the desired objective, an optimum solution being the one that is most economical among all those that are aesthetically and technically acceptable. And in the words of Ricardo Morandi (as quoted in [Dunican, 1996]), "It is in fact only necessary to be moderately familiar with the design of structures to realize that it is always possible, within certain limits, to solve a problem—functionally, structurally, and economically—in several valid ways." The art of successful bridge design has been aptly summarized by Elizabeth Mock [1949, p. 7]:

> Since the reality of a bridge lies in its structure, the art of bridge building lies in the recognition and development of the beauty latent in those forms that most effectively exploit the strength and special properties of a given material. Beauty is not automatic; technical perfection alone is not enough. A great engineer is not a slave of his formulas. He is an artist who uses calculations as tools to create working shapes as inevitable and harmonious in their appearance as the natural laws behind them.

Menn [1991] summarizes it quite succinctly: "In principle, bridge aesthetics involves two aspects that are largely independent of each other: integration of the bridge into its surroundings and design of the bridge as a structure itself."

Aesthetic bridges can be built through fusion of engineering and art. Consequently, engineers need to possess aesthetic sensibility and work in an environment that fosters sensitivity to art and architecture. But "unless the engineer...knows something of the underlying principles of architecture, we cannot obtain the degree of attention to aesthetics...which the time, or rather an enlightened public, now demands" [Watson, 1938]. "Harmony, unity, variety and balance are the basic elements of creative composition common to all fine arts as well as bridge architecture. These elements are physically produced in a bridge by proper shaping and treating the structure's component parts to give form, line, space, light and shadow, texture and color. These are the technical means for creating all visual artistic expression" [CALTRANS, 1970].

The doctrine of the engineer's aesthetic has been aptly summarized by Medwadowski [1971]: "If the laws of nature are applied to the materials involved in construction, the resulting structure will be inevitably beautiful." From this follows the well-known philosophy echoed in Sullivan's famous maxim: "Form follows function." This is not to say that such a creation will also be efficient. As pointed out by Schlaepher [1959], structural efficiency is not synonymous with beauty. Le Corbusier [1970] recognizes this notion by noting the intervention of taste in the engineer's design process. The current trend to build prestressed and cable-stayed bridges as the preferred types is an example of this truth. Budgetary constraints often dictate the bridge type selection process.

Discussion on general but time-honored principles of aesthetic design continues to be repeated by many authors [Harbeson, 1991; Leonhardt, 1984, 1991; Menn, 1991; Murray, 1991; Wasserman, 1991]. Tyrell [1912, p. 42] prescribes the following requirements for an aesthetic bridge design:

1. Selection of the most artistic form consistent with economy
2. Expressiveness
3. Symmetry
4. Simplicity
5. Harmony and contrast
6. Conformity with environment
7. Proper combination of materials
8. Judicious use of applied ornament to make the overall appearance pleasant

A good bridge design should satisfy a duality: functionalism and aesthetics. Right from the beginning of their education, engineers are indoctrinated with ideas of optimal design. They are trained to focus on functional fitness, i.e., designing for loads and resistance, with due regard to safety, serviceability, and economics, but with little, if any, regard for aesthetics [Menn, 1991]. It is believed that most of the doctrinaire engineers, because of their almost total lack of training in aesthetics, tend to adhere to this dogma cardinally.

Since the dawn of the twentieth century, the importance of aesthetics in civil engineering has been vanishing. The old book *Theory and Practice of Modern Structures* [Johnson, Bryan, and Turneaure, 1916] is an example of engineers' declining interest in aesthetics. Its first (1893) edition included a well-illustrated chapter, "The Aesthetic Design of Bridges." Authored by David A. Moliter, this chapter appeared in each of the first eight editions of this book. But it was omitted in the ninth (1916) edition, with this remark included in the preface to Part III of the book: "Owing to the increased development and specialization of many lines of structural engineering, it has been thought best to omit certain topics treated in the earlier works." Today, aesthetics has become an alien subject to engineers.

Furthermore, guidelines for dealing with various aspects of bridge design, as discussed earlier, should be developed through aesthetics-sensitive engineering education and practice, as no set of rules or formulas can be found for the purpose [Billington,

1969]. Formulas are tools, not answers, for "a formula may be a good servant, but it is a bad master at any time," as pointed out by the British architect Charles Holden (1875–1960) [TRB, 1991]. Designing an aesthetic bridge is not only a social demand, it is our social obligation. Recognition that bridges are symbols of structural art and that beauty of constructional work is known through sight is essential. As Eduardo Torroja [1958, Ch. 17, p. 287] points out,

> The best possible rule for the creation of a truly beautiful structure is that the designer shall have a serene and acute artistic sensibility and fecund creative imagination, served by the requisite technical skill to understand the purpose and mechanism of its strength and behavior.

We should also have an open mind and be receptive to better ideas, forms, and styles, and not be captives of trends. The standards of aesthetics have changed over the years; with advances and innovations in building technology and materials (composites, for example), these standards are likely to change in the future.

In the United States, bridge construction work is usually awarded thorough a competitive bidding process. In addition to the engineer's pursuit of designing an aesthetic bridge, it should be possible to include, in our advertisements for competitive bidding or in contract regulations, recommendations of an aesthetic nature in order to direct designers and builders toward general design principles that take into account the architectural appearance of the bridges. This effort should be conducive to bringing out the best in both designers and builders, leading to a common goal of achieving a structure with a balance in structural function and aesthetics.

11.7
GUIDELINES FOR AESTHETIC DESIGN

While the nonquantifiable nature of aesthetics as an intrinsic property of objects cannot be disputed, aesthetic qualities invariably evoke measurable emotions that, when viewed objectively, are much the same in all people. As a corollary to Kant's theory, Menn [1991] views bridge design as a creativity that combines functionalism (safety, serviceability, and economy—in that order) and aesthetics. It was first proposed by the Pythagorean school that rules of form are based on mathematics [Tang, 1991]. In the past 200 years, bridge engineering has been transformed from a handcraft tradition to a discipline of complex techniques based on science and engineering, but the artistic aspects of this discipline have lagged. True, mathematics and structural analysis form the theoretical foundation of all utilitarian structures. But the formulas, numerical calculations, and ready-made patterns cannot accomplish aesthetic shaping of bridges. Nor can this goal be achieved blindly, impulsively, or inspirationally.

In addition to engineering training, two fundamental requirements must be met in order to create aesthetically pleasing structures. The first requirement is to have some objective laws of aesthetics—general principles and rules that, when followed, will, in most cases, improve the design of an engineering structure. "The rules and guidelines provide us with a better point of departure and help us with the critical appraisal of our designs, thus making us aware of aesthetic design errors" [Leonhardt, 1984]. Second, one must not assume that a simple application of these rules in itself will lead to the creation of beautiful bridges. The designer must still possess imagination, intuition, and a sense of both form and beauty, qualities that must be practiced and perfected. As Leonhardt [1991] points out, "The artistically gifted may be able to produce masterpieces of beauty intuitively without reference to any rules and without rational procedures. However, the many functional requirements imposed on today's structures demand that our work must include a significant degree of conscious, rational and methodical reasoning."

To achieve aesthetic qualities in a bridge, Murray proposes 10 basic elements that should be satisfied: expression of function, form, rhythm, scale, harmony, proportions, visual stability, light and shade, texture, and color [Murray, 1991].

A bridge consists of two major parts: superstructure and substructure. The deck, beams and girders, parapets, railings, trusses, arches, suspension cables, towers, etc. are components of the superstructure. The abutments, piers, columns, bents, etc. are components of the substructure. In most cases, it is the superstructure that is the target of viewers' eyes; consequently, it gets the most attention for aesthetic design and detailing. In elevated structures, however, the appearance of elements of substructure has a significant influence on the overall appearance of the entire structure; consequently, they too should be given the required attention.

The terms *function, form, order, harmony,* etc. have been defined differently in the context of their usage, e.g., in fine art, music, and poetry. Their meanings in relation to civil engineering works are defined by architects and critics of architecture. Discussions of these terms specifically in the context of aesthetic qualities of bridges have been presented in several papers [Harbeson, 1991; Leonhardt, 1991; Menn, 1991; Murray, 1991].

11.7.1 Form and Function

Form is the quintessence of aesthetics, and it refers to the type of load-bearing systems, such as beams, arches, and suspensions. Principles of aesthetics require that the form used in a structure correspond to the construction material used. The use of material, shape, and form should be such that the concept "form follows function" is realized through construction. In one bridge it is the power and strength of the arch that impresses; in another it is the grace of the cables creating the wonder that such slight material can carry so great a load. The use of masonry or reinforced concrete in arches and vertical load-bearing elements expresses their compressive strength. On the other hand, the use of steel cables in suspension and cable-stayed bridges expresses their ability to carry large tensile loads. Likewise, a prestressed concrete beam displays its ability to carry bending loads over relatively large spans.

A bridge is a utilitarian structure. Its functions include transmitting various loads to the foundation as well as providing adequate protection against deformation, oscillation, and weather. A good form should reflect an optimal solution to this design problem. The oft-quoted Sullivan's maxim "form follows function" implies, in the context of bridges, that if a bridge and its components—deck, abutments, piers, etc.—are shaped and proportioned to carry their loads by minimum and obvious means, they will be inherently beautiful. However, critics point out that, in view of modern advanced and stronger materials, this view is questionable. This is aptly pointed out by Faber [1941]: "The second fallacy is occasionally heard from young engineers and may, perhaps, be expressed in the statement that if a structure is honestly designed to satisfy all its scientific or engineering requirements, the result will be necessarily beautiful. This is probably the perfect example of wishful thinking."

11.7.2 Proportion

Conceptually, the term *proportion* is a relational property between two aspects of an object and is expressed as *ratio* for comparison purposes in engineering. Architecturally, "it is a function of the visual relationships of the components of a structure, each to the other, and of the structure to its setting" [Harbeson, 1991].

Proportion is the fundamental bearer of the aesthetic merits of a bridge. It is an aspect of architecture that has been used for centuries and stems from the perception that well-proportioned objects possess visual appeal. The ancients called it the "Golden Section" (or "golden ratio"). It is defined as a line segment of two parts—a longer part a and a shorter part b (i.e., $b < a$)—such that the ratio $(a + b)/a = a/b = \phi$. Mathematically, it is the positive root of the quadratic equation $x^2 = x + 1$ and is equal to 1.618. The equality of the ratios 0.618:1, 1:1.618 ($= 0.618$), 1.618:2.618 ($= 0.618$), etc., a relationship that can be advanced to infinity, is noteworthy. This historically important concept formed a tenet in aesthetics, art, and architecture, for it has often been thought that a form, including the human form, is most pleasing when its parts divide it in *golden sections* [Ghaswala, 1991; Tang, 1991]. A related concept is the *golden rectangle,* whose adjacent sides are in golden ratio and which the ancient Greeks felt had the most pleasing proportions of all rectangles. Consequently, the shape appears in many works and was especially prevalent in Renaissance art and architecture.

The Pythagorean school professed principles of mathematics for art and architecture. Greek and Roman architects used the concept of the golden section to control the dimensions of buildings [Borissavlietch, 1958; Ghyka, 1946]. No new systematic study of the application of the golden section to bridges has been reported in the literature [Ghaswala, 1991; Tang, 1991]. Some coincidental relationships of the golden section to modern bridges is briefly discussed by Ghaswala [1991]. For example, he suggests that the ratio of the main span to the side spans of some cable-stayed bridges satisfies $\phi^2 = 2.618$ and that the span-to-cable sag ratio of suspension bridges satisfies $\phi^3 = 4.236$, albeit approximately. Referring to the golden ratio as the *golden mean,* Leonhardt [1984, p. 19] suggests that "this does not fit into the series of whole number relationships and does not play the important role in architecture which is often ascribed to it."

The mathematician Leonardo Fibonacci (1175–1240) introduced a set of whole numbers [1, 2, 3 ($= 1 + 2$), 5 ($= 2 + 3$), 8 ($= 3 + 5$), 13 ($= 5 + 8$), 21 ($= 8 + 13$), 34 ($= 13 + 21$), 55 ($= 21 + 34$), 89 ($= 34 + 55$), etc.] called the Fibonacci series, which has been used to analyze the proportion of the human body. It is also used to construct a logarithmic spiral, which occurs in nature in snail and ammonite shells and which is considered particularly beautiful for ornaments [Leonhardt, 1984, p. 19]. Note that $21:34 = 34:55 = 55:89 = 0.618$, the value of the golden ratio.[2]

In a physical sense, *proportion* means the relationship between the dimensions of two parts, or those of a part and the whole. In engineering, it depends on factors such as strength, stiffness, and economic considerations. In design, one has to deal with such ratios as girder depth to span, end span to center span of a continuous bridge, cantilever span to anchor span of a cantilever bridge, and sag to span of a suspension bridge. The ancient Chinese architects used the series $(3, 6, 9, 27, 81, \dots)$ for dimensioning structural parts. The appropriateness of these numbers, the golden ratio, or any other series of exact numbers for building with modern materials such as steel, reinforced and pre-stressed concrete, and the emerging composites is highly questionable [Revelo, 1991; Tang, 1991], particularly considering the fact that safety concerns have significantly influenced design codes. For example, modern bridges must routinely be designed for adequate resistance to collision and to seismic loads, a practice that has led to increased pier diameters.

Considerations for proportion vary with bridge type, since they deal with the inter-relationship of sizes of various bridge members or components. Engineers unanimously opine that the most important criterion for the grace of a bridge is the slenderness of the beam, referred to as *depth-span* ratio in most specifications. In the early 1900s, improvements in analysis, the demands of economy, and aesthetic considerations combined to accelerate the trend toward increased slenderness of proportions. However, slenderness taken to extremes led to unhappy and disastrous results. Increased emphasis on artistic appearance placed a premium on grace and slenderness, a trend culminating in 1940 in the design of the Tacoma Narrows Bridge, with a slenderness ratio of span/350. The result was an extremely flexible structure and by far the most flexible of all modern suspension bridges. Its stiffening girders were only 8 ft deep in a span of 2800 ft. The resulting extreme vertical flexibility was compounded by the high flexible towers and long side spans, which *added* to the flexibility of the design. This factor, combined with the aerodynamic instability of the bridge's deck, led to its catastrophic failure only four months after completion.

Tassios [1980] prefers "expressive proportions which emphasize the desired character for a structure" (as quoted in [Leonhardt, 1991]). In bridges, it is related to the depth-span ratios of beams, height-to-width (or diameter) ratios of columns (slenderness ratio), aspect ratios of rectangular spaces between columns of a continuous bridge, span-rise ratio of an arch, cable sag-span ratio in a suspension bridge, ratio of end span to intermediate span, etc. For all these visual characteristics, certain ratios, referred to as harmonious ratios (or proportions), lend themselves to more visually pleasant structures than others.

Concepts of good proportion change with time and are greatly influenced by the nature of bridge materials (steel, reinforced concrete, prestressed concrete, composites, timber, etc.), the type of forces to be carried by members (tension, compression,

---

[2]Leonardo's friend Luca Pacioli called it "the Divine Proportion" and Johannes Kepler (1571–1630) referred to it as "one of the two jewels of Geometry."

bending), and the methods of construction. Proportions exercise significant visual impact. For example, a deck that appears to be too thin would likely convey the perception of an unsafe bridge.

11.7.3 Scale

Scale is a function of relative size as perceived in the components of a structure and its overall unity. The essential objective of scale in the design of bridges is rightness of appearance. If, through the design of a structure or some of its members, the resulting visual impression is of a structure either larger or smaller than it actually is, then it will be "out of scale and its visual impact one of false impression" [Harbeson, 1991].

A bridge should always dominate as well as conform. A bridge among rugged hills or rocky cliffs should have a simple and bold outline so that it will not be dwarfed by its surroundings [Hool and Thissen, 1916, p. 492]. On the other hand, a large bridge in a residential area is likely to look out of place. Several examples have been discussed by Leonhardt [1991] and De Miranda [1991].

11.7.4 Order

Leonhardt [1991] refers to *order* as the characteristic of arrangement of certain things in a structure. These include lines and edges and their directions in a bridge, sizes of beams in adjacent spans, aspect ratios of rectangles between piers of adjacent span, and symmetry. For example, the directions of various truss members should be limited to only a few. The difference between the visible depths of beams in the adjacent span should not be excessive. Likewise, the span ratios of various arches in a bridge should be comparable. When repetitiveness is required, e.g., in multispan bridges, equal elements should be provided to create satisfactory visual appeal, although too much repetition leads to monotony. The principle of order is very important for creating a structure of aesthetic merit.

Continuity in a superstructure can often be used as an effective means to create an elegant bridge. With uninterrupted lines and the absence of joints, allowing smooth transition of girder depths at adjacent supports, continuity can lead to an optimal design. Because of the higher negative moments, a larger-depth girder is required at the intermediate support than at the ends. This statical requirement is easily met by providing haunched girders, with haunched ends at the intermediate supports. By comparison, simple-span bridges lack fluidity of line and appear clumsy [Menn, 1991; Wasserman, 1991] and should be avoided for aesthetic reasons. While a two-span layout is considered objectionable because of the "split composition effect" it produces (as quoted in [Dorton, 1991] based on [Ritner, 1986]), an odd number of spans is preferred over an even number of spans as an accepted architectural practice [Leonhardt, 1991; Liebenberg, 1991; Glomb, 1991]. They provide more appealing visual appearance, according to a public survey [O'Connor, 1991].

Guidelines for the haunch forms are discussed by Leonhardt [1991]. For horizontal, straight, or slightly inclined roadway alignments, straight haunches (Fig. 11.11)

FIGURE 11.11
A three-span beam bridge with straight haunches [Leonhardt, 1991].

FIGURE 11.12
A three-span beam bridge with vertical curve and curved haunches [Leonhardt, 1991].

are considered to look good. Haunches should be limited to 0.2 of the span length, and slope limited to 1:8. For curved vertical alignment of the deck, parabolic curved haunches, with curvature decreasing toward the midspan, are preferred (Fig. 11.12). A slight positive camber in roadway is preferred even when curved vertical alignment is not a requirement, simply to prevent a sagging appearance. However, some prefer a constant curvature between piers and midspan instead of abbreviated haunches with tangents.

Good order also requires proper arrangement of enclosed spaces. Leonhardt [1991] suggests that stout rectangles of 0.8:1 should not be placed next to slim rectangles of 1:3. The same logic applies to various arches of a multi-arch bridge. Likewise, different kinds of supports (V-type, hammerhead, tapered shafts, multiple columns, braced column, etc.) used in the same bridge indicate poor order, resulting in an ugly structure (Fig. 11.13).

11.7.5 Rhythm

Rhythm is defined as a patterned repetition of a motif or formal element. An example of rhythm is the pattern of regular or irregular pulses caused in music by the occurrence of strong and weak melodic and harmonic beats. In a bridge, rhythm is essential for organization of details and can be achieved by ordered repetition in the spacing of superstructure and substructure elements or components. These include proper spacing of supports (bents and piers), giving equal span lengths in a multispan bridge using the same girder system throughout the bridge, and the proper spacing of expansion and construction joints in spans (if provided), walls, parapets, and safety curbs. However, too many repetitions create monotony, which should be interrupted by other design elements [Leonhardt, 1991; Liebenberg, 1991; Harbeson, 1991]. Note that because of the costly maintenance and repair problems caused by leakage through joints, the present trend is to avoid joints altogether.

FIGURE 11.13
(*top*) Lack of harmony and order is displayed through use of different kinds of supports in the same bridge. (*bottom*) A bridge with an annoying mixture of supports [Murray, 1991].

11.7.6 Harmony

The importance of *harmony* has been known since the dawn of civilization, as evidenced by the following time-honored poem (the *Kuan-tzu*, Chapter 55, Book IX, 4th Century B.C., translated by Gustav Haloun, 1951 [Dunican, 1966]):

> Reality is the embodiment of structure;
> Structures are the embodiment of properties;
> Properties are the embodiment of harmony;
> Harmony is the embodiment of congruity.

In aesthetic bridge design context, the term *harmony* is used to describe several desirable elements—consistent and orderly arrangements of parts, agreement and accord, compatibility, etc. A bridge of aesthetic merit should befit its surroundings. This element of aesthetic design is variously referred to as "integrating a structure into its environment, landscape or cityscape" [Leonhardt, 1991], "visual harmony of bridge and its surrounding" [Murray, 1991], and "matching or compatibility with surroundings so that it does not appear to be an eyesore" [Elliot, 1991]. Various components and their proportions should not be too dissimilar. Bridges within a short distance of each

FIGURE 11.14
Lack of harmony and order displayed by the poor depth transitions and awkward configurations of girders in the adjacent spans [Wasserman, 1991].

other should have features that are in harmony with each other. Harmony is also related to the proportion of the whole structure in relation to its surroundings (dwarfness or dominance), of the whole structure to its parts, and between various parts themselves. For example, large variations in the depths of girders in adjacent spans will give the appearance of disharmony and lack of visual appeal (Fig. 11.14).

11.7.7 Light and Shade

Visual slenderness of the superstructure is one of the most important features affecting the overall appearance of a bridge. Visual (or apparent) slenderness is defined as the ratio of the visible continuous girder to the visually distinguishable height or width of the superstructure. It is different from the actual slenderness, the ratio of span length to girder depth [Menn, 1991]. The angle of the sun and the shades created on the viewer side of the superstructure affect the apparent or visual slenderness of the bridge. When a superstructure is in partial shadow, the lighted depth (shallower than actual) of the superstructure appears more slender than it really is. In totally shadowed superstructures slenderness is enhanced tremendously.

Desirable effects of light and shade in a bridge superstructure can be produced by suitable sizing, shaping, and the location of its various elements. Figures 11.15 and 11.16 show various effects that can be produced to enhance the visual slenderness of

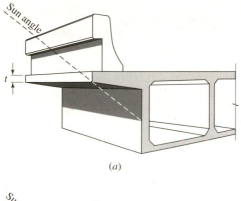

(a)

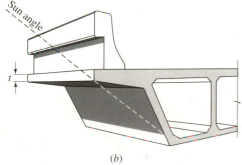

(b)

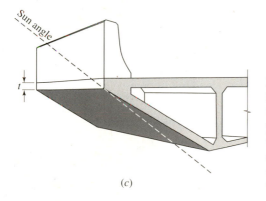

(c)

FIGURE 11.15
Effects of light and shade. Shadows cast
by the overhang on the exterior girder
place the girder in the shadow, similar
to the shade always present on the soffit:
concrete box girder with (a) vertical sides,
(b) sloping sides, and (c) sloping sides
without overhang [CALTRANS, 1993].

a bridge. A longitudinal shadow on the entire superstructure can be cast with a horizontal projection of some sort, e.g., by providing an overhang of the deck slab. Short
overhangs, however, are not very helpful in this respect. Menn [1991] recommends
that the ratio of overhang projection to girder depth must be at least 1:1 to produce
the desirable effect of reduced visual slenderness. Safety considerations require about
3-ft-high curbed parapets on both sides of the deck. If improperly placed, they considerably reduce the visual slenderness (Fig. 11.17). As a general rule, the slenderness
of short simple-span bridges is less than that of continuous bridges, a reason to avoid
simple spans whenever possible. In a continuous bridge, the visual slenderness can be
significantly improved by slightly tapering the girder depth toward the abutments.

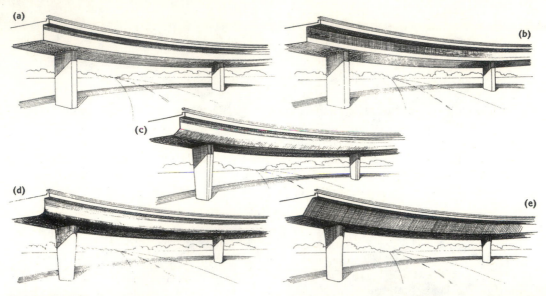

FIGURE 11.16

Effects of light and shade. (*a*) Vertical face of a structure with a short overhang (and hence a shorter shadow on the exterior face of the structure) giving the impression of a deeper structure. (*b*) Deeper shadow of a wider overhang reduces the visual depth and gives the impression of a slender structure. (*c*) Chamfering and (*d*) rounded edges enhance the slenderness by deemphasizing the depth. (*e*) Sloping girders recede into the shadow, enhancing the slenderness of the structure. The brightly lit face of the barrier rail contrasts with shadow and stands out as a continuous, slender band of light, accentuating the flow of the structure. The structure appears subdued, inviting the flow of traffic beneath [CALTRANS, 1970].

Parapets built in the plane of exterior girders increase the apparent depth of the girder and reduce the visual slenderness, a detail that should be avoided.

11.7.8 Surface Treatment

Surface treatment involves two aspects: color and texture.

11.7.8.1 Color

The effect of color on a viewer is very important, but the definition of good color and viewers' responses to various colors have always been controversial. A study by

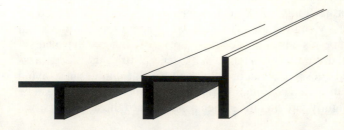

FIGURE 11.17

A parapet placed in the plane of the edge beam increases the visual depth and hence the visual slenderness of the structure, resulting in a blunt appearance [Leonhardt, 1991].

Zuk [1974] showed that most viewers preferred white, yellow, light blue, and green over brown, black, and aluminum colors. It also showed that while red and dark blue were liked by aesthetically trained people, others did not find them as appealing. Ideally, the color should harmonize with its surroundings; green with a touch of yellow would blend well. However, aesthetic treatment of surfaces with color, particularly in natural surroundings, is faced with a dichotomy, as some feel that man-made objects should look man-made. Such a controversy can be avoided by the careful selection of and use of color in paints for the protection of steel structures from corrosion, and in concrete aggregates, cement, and admixtures for concrete surfaces. A brief discussion on the aesthetic aspects of color has been presented by Harbeson [1991]. Coloring of concrete has been found to be expensive [Elliot, 1991] and has a perpetual maintenance problem associated with peeling [Murray, 1991].

11.7.8.2 Texture

Texture refers to the architectural treatment of a surface to improve or enhance its importance and create a visual interest. Such a treatment is important for surfaces of retaining walls, concrete barriers, abutment walls, pier walls, and columns. A discussion on texturing surfaces of bridge components along with several examples are reported in the literature [Shureman, 1938; Brown, 1975; Leonhardt, 1984; Elliot, 1991; Harbeson, 1991; Muller, 1991; Murray, 1991; von Olnhausen, 1991; O'Connor, 1991]. These surfaces are readily visible to viewers from a short distance, particularly in pedestrian bridges [Nakamura and Kubota, 1991], and can be made more attractive by judiciously texturing them, thus enhancing the overall visual appeal of a bridge [Muller, 1991]. Textured surfaces also appeal to the sense of touch.

Concrete surfaces are adaptable to easy texturing. The function of texture is to break the monotony of plainness of large surfaces such as faces of parapets, retaining walls, and piers. Texturing accomplishes this by creating shadows that will give certain areas a darker color. The shadow producing irregularity should be large, usually in the 1- to 4-in. range, to be effective, and large enough to be visible from a distance of 100 to 500 ft or more [Elliot, 1991]. Because texturing curved surfaces, such as round columns, column flares, and rounded ends of pier walls, is both difficult and expensive, texture patterns should be limited to flat surfaces.

Textured surfaces can be created in a variety of ways, and their appearance may vary. These include coarse aggregate surfaces [Freyermuth, 1966; Leonhardt, 1984]; simple horizontal, vertical, or inclined ribbing on the exposed surface (Figs. 11.18 and 11.19); and sculptured surfaces (Fig. 11.20), which may be quite appropriate for inner-city pedestrian bridges [Brady, 1942; Concrete, 1973, 1974; March, 1973; North, 1973; Strong, 1973; Brown, 1975; ACI, 1976; Scuri, 1992].

A coarse aggregate surface can be created by using precast exposed aggregate panels [Freyermuth, 1966; PCI, 1987a,b]. A PCI report [PCI, 1987a] describes use of architectural precast fascia panels for the three-span Research Boulevard Bridge, Kettering, Ohio (Fig. 11.21), which won a 1987 Prestressed Concrete Institute award for aesthetics [PCI, 1987b]. Colored exposed aggregate, selected to blend with the surrounding buildings, was used for these panels. Figure 11.21 also shows the details of attaching these panels to the precast prestressed fascia box girders of the bridge. Another PCI report [PCI, 1989] describes the use of adhered multicolored stone dimensioned veneer

FIGURE 11.18
Textured surfaces to enhance aesthetics: (*top*) precast exposed aggregate panels on faces of parapets, retaining walls, and abutments [Freyermuth, 1966]; (*center*) vertical ribbing; (*bottom*) inclined ribbing [von Olnhausen, 1991].

FIGURE 11.18 (continued)
Texture surfaces to enhance aesthetics: Texture shown by horizontal ribbing on piers [Harbeson, 1991].

for three multispan arch pedestrian bridges in Canada (Fig. 11.22) that won a 1988 PCI award for its excellent aesthetics [PCI, 1988].

Ribbed surfaces can be produced by using manufactured form lines or by the application of vertical ribbing (such as 4×4 timbers cut diagonally) to forms. Sculptured patterns can be produced by use of profiled formwork built up in plywood. Advances in computer-aided design, mold making, and precast concrete technology have added new dimensions to creating structural patterns. Several innovative methods and applications are discussed by Scuri [1992].

A coarse surface can be created by exposing a large aggregate on the face of the concrete. A practice used by the California Department of Transportation is to cast deep vertical corrugations in concrete and then break their edges off with hammers (Fig. 11.23) [CALTRANS, 1993; Elliot, 1991]. California's guidelines for spacing and depth of these corrugations are specified in its *Bridge Design Practice Manual* [CALTRANS, 1993].

FIGURE 11.19
Texture on faces of (*top*) columns and (*bottom*) piers
[Harbeson, 1991].

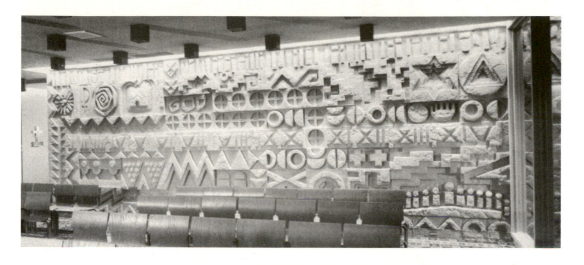

FIGURE 11.20
Aesthetic patterns created by using sculptured forms: (*top*)
[PCI, 1987a], (*bottom*) [North, 1973].

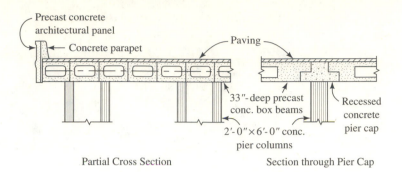

Precast concrete
architectural panel

Concrete parapet

Paving

33″-deep precast
conc. box beams

Recessed
concrete
pier cap

2′-0″×6′-0″ conc.
pier columns

Partial Cross Section

Section through Pier Cap

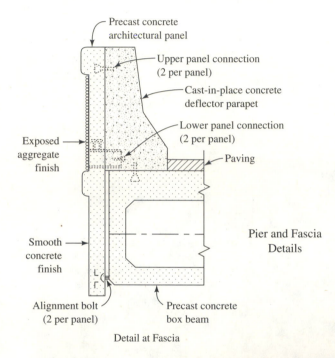

Precast concrete
architectural panel

Upper panel connection
(2 per panel)

Cast-in-place concrete
deflector parapet

Lower panel connection
(2 per panel)

Exposed
aggregate
finish

Paving

Smooth
concrete
finish

Pier and Fascia
Details

Alignment bolt
(2 per panel)

Precast concrete
box beam

Detail at Fascia

FIGURE 11.21
Details of the precast
fascia panels for the
Research Boulevard Bridge,
Kettering, Ohio [PCI,
1987a].

FIGURE 11.22
Adhered multicolored dimensioned stone veneer for multispan pedestrian
arch bridges, Winnipeg, Manitoba, Canada [PCI, 1989].

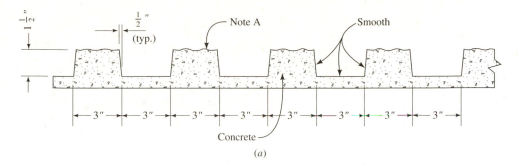

(a)

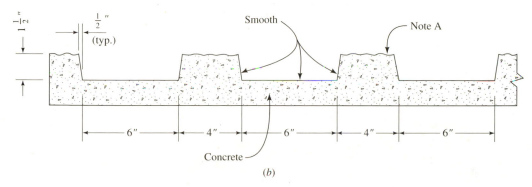

(b)

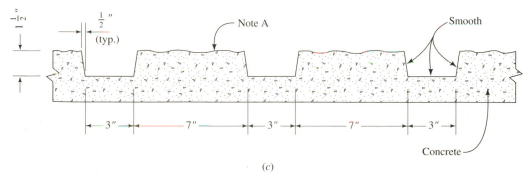

(c)

Note: A — Fractured surface max. relief $\frac{3}{16}$"

FIGURE 11.23
A practice used by California Department of Transportation for creating vertical ribbing on faces of walls [CALTRANS, 1993].

Narer and Freedman [1992] have suggested the use of *removable* precast brick veneer facing panels (Fig. 11.24), which afford easy initial installation (placement and anchorage) and subsequent maintenance and repairs. Typically, the panels are formed by placing the cored bricks face down in a prepared formwork, vibrating high-strength mortar between and into the cores of the bricks, and immediately pouring the precast concrete over the brick facing without the aid of special bonding agents. This method is similar to the one described by Walton [1986].

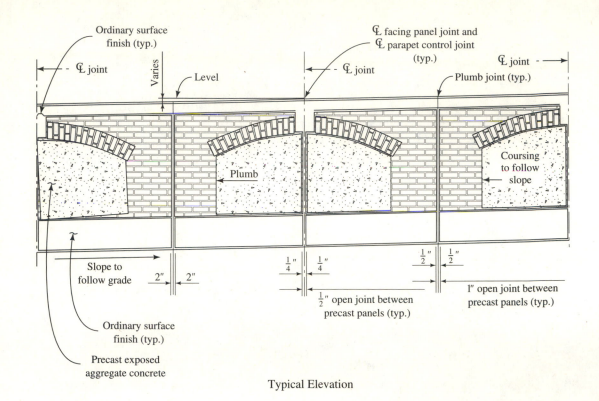

Typical Elevation

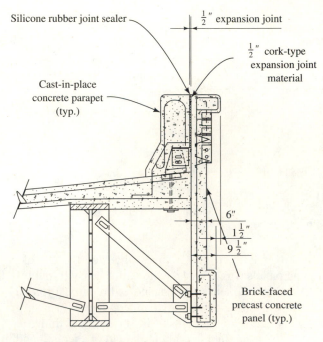

Precast Panel Mounting Detail

FIGURE 11.24
Precast brick veneer facing panels used on parapet faces for aesthetic enhancement [Narer and Freedman, 1992].

While textured surfaces of abutments, retaining walls, etc. enhance the elegance of a bridge, such a treatment may be considered unnecessary for surfaces of exterior beams, girders, or slender columns, for which smooth surfaces with good finish but that are not glossy, work well [Leonhardt, 1991]. In the past two decades, the use of weathering steel for bridges has increased as a means of economizing through elimination of painting. With time, rusting changes its color to brown, unfortunately one of the least preferred colors [Zuk, 1973, 1974]. Necessary care must be taken during construction to prevent rust from staining abutments and piers in the future, rendering them unsightly.

11.8
SUBSTRUCTURE

While the superstructure is the dominant part of a bridge, the appearance of the substructure components—abutment, wingwalls, bents, and piers—markedly influences the overall appearance of the bridge. Therefore, careful consideration should be given to their design and appearance.

11.8.1 Abutments

Guidelines for aesthetic treatment of abutments and wing walls are discussed briefly by Elliot [1991], Harbeson [1991], and Murray [1991]. Abutments that are large and located just off the shoulders of the road, to minimize span lengths, are considered dangerous and a "lethal obstruction" [Elliot, 1991] to traffic. Accordingly, the present trend is to make small abutments, also referred to as spill-through abutments. Typically, these abutments are located on the sloped fill, away from the shoulders, often in the form of a small bearing slab supported on piles high up on the tip of the approach fill (Fig. 11.25) [Elliot, 1991; Wasserman, 1991]. However, heavy sloping abutments (Fig. 11.26) are considered objectionable, as they portray lack of visual stability [Murray, 1991].

11.8.2 Piers

Piers are intermediate supports in a multispan bridge. Their number and shape play an important role in creating a visual aspect referred to as "transparency" [Menn, 1991]. Their locations, size, shapes, numbers, and arrangement should not be such as to reduce or block visibility through the open spaces between them.

Various cross sections and profiles of columns and piers, depending on the structural needs and designer's preferences, are in use. These include single columns of various cross sections (vertical or inclined), narrow rectangular (straight or tapered) columns, multiple columns, hammerhead piers, singly and multiply braced pier columns, multiple column bents, and so on (Fig. 11.27). In elevation, these columns can be vertical or inclined, and in each case they may be flared (Figs. 11.28 and 11.29). Inclined columns, usually having V, X, or Y shapes, seem to enhance the overall visual

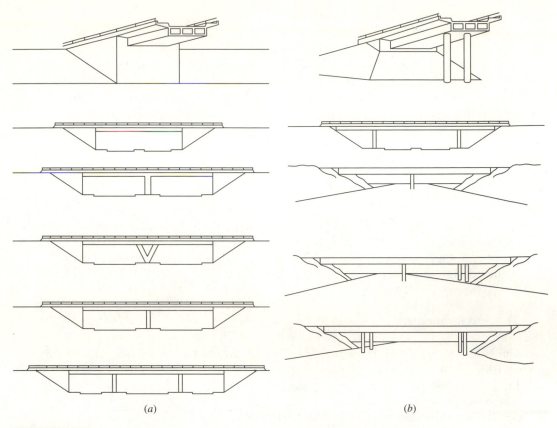

(a)   (b)

FIGURE 11.25
(a) Heavy and (b) spill-through abutments [CALTRANS, 1970].

FIGURE 11.26
Visual instability displayed through sloping abutments
[Murray, 1991].

FIGURE 11.27
Various kinds of supports: (*a*) tapered shaft, (*b*) multiple columns, (*c*) hammerhead piers, (*d*) multiple column bents, (*e*) singly braced pier columns, (*f*) multiply braced pier columns, (*g*) single hammerhead pier, and (*h*) application of flair [Wasserman, 1991].

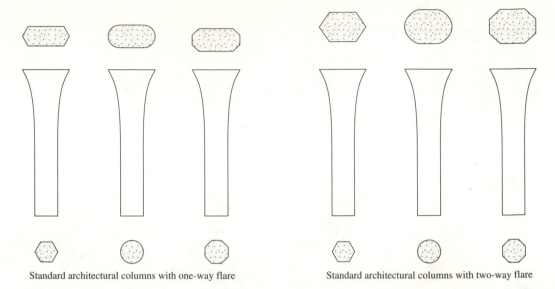

Standard architectural columns with one-way flare   Standard architectural columns with two-way flare

FIGURE 11.28
Various profiles of piers and columns [CALTRANS, 1993].

appeal of bridges [Elliot, 1991]. For safety considerations, the present trend is to place columns on the side slopes, far away from the traffic.

Guidelines for the aesthetics of piers have been discussed in several references [Elliot, 1991; Harbeson, 1991; Leonhardt, 1984, 1991; Menn, 1991], and are summarized as follows:

1. Columns with round cross section offer the most slender design and are easy to build. However, in long bridges, they seem to create an illusion of punching effect and instability. This has led to the preference for rectangular columns.
2. The ratio of bridge width to column width of 3:1 or 3.5:1 results in harmonious proportion [Menn, 1991]. The column width should also not exceed about one-eighth of the span [Leonhardt, 1984, 1991].
3. For long bridges, framed or hammerhead columns should not be used.
4. Single columns are considered unsuitable for low, broad bridges with decks wider than 12 m (39 ft). For such bridges a pair of slender circular columns should be used to enhance aesthetics.
5. For high bridges, single columns should be used, irrespective of bridge width, to improve bridge transparency.
6. When multicolumn bents are used, careful consideration should be given to the distance between the columns in the bent to preserve transparency. Fewer columns, preferably two, should be used, with the longitudinal distance between them being at least three times their lateral spacing (Fig. 11.30). Lack of attention to the proper location of more columns in a bent presents an "entangled impression—a forest of columns, especially if the bridge is on a curve" [Leonhardt, 1991].

FIGURE 11.29
Various profiles of piers [Elliot, 1991].

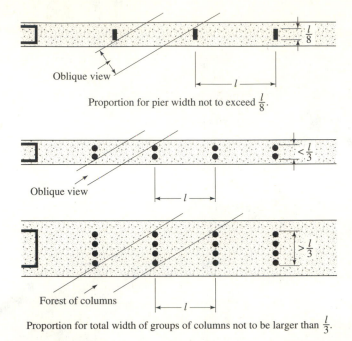

Oblique view

Proportion for pier width not to exceed $\frac{l}{8}$.

Oblique view

Forest of columns

Proportion for total width of groups of columns not to be larger than $\frac{l}{3}$.

FIGURE 11.30
Proportion and arrangement of supports to preserve transparency and scale [Leonhardt, 1991].

11.9
SUMMARY

For a visually expressive bridge, aesthetics should be a component of the overall design process. Design details should reflect the fact that art and science can meet in harmony. These details embody considerations of form, proportion, harmony, rhythm, continuity, order, color, texture, environmental compatibility, strength, stiffness, durability, and attractiveness. These characteristics should be conjunctional, to attain beauty as defined by the Italian Renaissance architect Leone Alberti (1404–1472) [Harbeson, 1991]: "I shall define beauty to be a harmony of all the parts, in whatever subject it appears, fitted together with such proportion and connection, that nothing could be added, diminished, or altered, but for worse."

Engineers should not only think aesthetically [Law, 1976] but should also make a conscious effort to learn art and architecture [Billington, 1990, 1991; Elliot, 1991] as an ongoing process. Within the restrictions of materials science and the costs inherent in designing a utilitarian work such as a bridge, the designer should judiciously apply his mathematical and engineering skill with artistic sensitivity to create structures that will integrate harmoniously with the surroundings. As pointed out by De Miranda [1991], every bridge designer should take to heart the maxim of the great French builder Sejourne: "The creation of ugliness is not permissible." Toward that goal, the Board of

Directors of the American Society of Civil Engineers (ASCE) passed a fitting resolution in 1969 [CE, 1970]:

> Recognizing that functional civil engineering designs often produce forms that are totally pleasing to the human eye;
>
> that structures conversely can be functional but not at all pleasant to behold;
>
> that excellence of appearance need not be costly;
>
> that natural beauty can be destroyed in the creation of man-made facilities;
>
> but that through care in design natural beauty can be preserved or enhanced in the construction of things;
>
> the American Society of Civil Engineers, through action of its Board of Directors, urges an even greater concern for esthetics among all of its members involved in the design decisions affecting the physical environment;
>
> urges all its members to advocate reasonable additional expenditures if needed to achieve esthetic quality in their work;
>
> and assures the public that concern for esthetics continues to be the policy of this society, as stated for the guidance of all its Councils, Divisions, Sections and individual members.

Bridges generally are more monumental in character than other structures. They should be built so as to make bold aesthetic statements. As a legacy, a beautiful bridge is destined to stand as a proud symbol of civil engineering accomplishment and a source of inspiration for generations to come. Steinman and Watson [1957] have aptly expressed this sentiment: "A bridge is more than the sum of stresses and strains: it is an expression of man's creative urge—a challenge and an opportunity to create the beautiful. A bridge is the fulfillment of human dreams and hopes and aspirations.... A bridge is a monument to mankind's indomitable will to achieve. Bridges symbolize the ideals and aspirations of humanity." The importance of this accomplishment is described by a tribute to bridge builders by Gurnie Hobbs [1960]:

> A Bridge is a great and a marvelous thing,
> A wonder, an inspiration to behold.
> It soars—it reaches—like the bridges of the mind,
> Of human communication, the fairest bridge of them all.
> His influence, his knowledge of his companions
> On this sphere, and thus, hopefully, of himself.
> Lord, could any man ask a higher goal,
> Than to be a builder of bridges?

REFERENCES

ACI. (1976). "Precast Murals for Structure and Design," *ACI J.,* February, pp. 73–75.

Anderson, S. O. (1958). "An Enquiry Concerning the Basis of Design Decision in Architecture," M.A. thesis, School of Architecture, University of California, Berkeley.

Arnheim, R. (1965). *Art and Visual Perception,* University of California Press, Berkeley.

Bakht, B., and Jaeger, L. G. (1983). "Bridge Aesthetics," *Canadian J. Civ. Eng.,* 10(3), pp. 408–414.

Bill, M. (1969). *Robert Maillart, Bridges and Construction,* 3rd ed., Frederick A. Praeger, New York.

Billington, D. P. (1969). "Engineering Education and the Origins of Modern Structures," *ASCE Civ. Eng.,* January, pp. 52–57.

———. (1973a). "Public Works—Higher Aesthetic Standards Needed," *ASCE Civ. Eng.,* October, pp. 36–40.

———. (1973b). "Art in Engineering—The Need for a New Criticism," *ASCE J. Struct. Div.,* 99(ST10), October, pp. 499–511.

———. (1974). "An Example of Structural Art: The Salginatobel Bridge of Robert Maillart," *J. Soc. Architectural Historians,* 33(1), pp. 61–72.

———. (1977a). "History and Esthetics in Suspension Bridges," *ASCE J. Struct. Div.,* 103(ST8), August, pp. 1655–1672.

———. (1977b). "History and Esthetics in Concrete Arch Bridges," *ASCE J. Struct. Div.,* 103(ST8), August, pp. 2129–2143.

———. (1978). *Bridges of Christian Menn,* Princeton University Art Museum, Princeton, NJ.

———. (1979). *Robert Maillart's Bridges: The Art of Engineering,* Princeton University Press, Princeton, NJ.

———. (1981). "Bridge Design and Regional Esthetics," *ASCE J. Struct. Div.,* 107(ST3), pp. 473–486.

———. (1983). *The Tower and the Bridge,* Basic Books, New York.

———. (1990). "Bridges as Art," *ASCE Civ. Eng.,* March, pp. 50–53.

———. (1991). "Bridges and New Art of Bridge Engineering," in *Bridge Aesthetics around the World,* Committee on General Structures, Subcommittee on Bridge Aesthetics, Transportation Research Board, Washington DC, pp. 67–79.

Billington, D. P., and Nazmi, A. (1991). "History and Aesthetics of Cable-Stayed Bridges," *ASCE J. Struct. Eng.,* 117(10), October.

Boller, A. P. (1881). *The Architecture of Bridges: Practical Treatise on the Construction of Iron Highway Bridges,* John Wiley & Sons, New York, pp. 82–87.

Borissavlietch, M. (1958). *The Golden Number,* Alec Tivanti, London.

Brady, F. L. et al. (1942). "The Surface Finishing of Concrete Structures" (correspondence), *J. Inst. Civ. Engrs.,* v. 18, pp. 522–534.

Brangwyn, F., and Sparrows, W. S. (1920). *A Book of Bridges,* John Lane Co., New York.

Broachman, O. (1955). *Good and Bad Taste.* Translated from the Norwegian by M. A. Michael, Macmillan, New York.

Brown, H. E. (1975). "Concrete Finishes for Highway Structures," Virginia Highway and Transportation Research Council, Charlottesville.

Burke, M. (1989). "Bridge Design and the 'Bridge Aesthetics Bibliography,'" *ASCE J. Struct. Eng.,* 115(4), pp. 883–899.

Burke, M. P. and Teach, A. (1991). "Annotated Bibliography on Bridge Aesthetics," *Bridge Aesthetics around the World,* Committee on General Structures, Subcommittee on Bridge Aesthetics, Transportation Research Board, Washington, DC, pp. 242–263.

CALTRANS. (1970). "Aesthetics in Bridge Design," in *Bridge Design Practice,* California Department of Transportation, Sacramento, CA, Section 16.

———. (1993). "Bridge Design Aesthetics," in *Bridge Design Practice,* California Department of Transportation, Sacramento, CA, February, Section 7.

CE. (1970). "Handsome Civil Engineering Structures," *ASCE Civ. Eng.,* May, pp. 56–59.

———. (1975). "Esthetics: a Premium on Four-Level Interchange," *ASCE Civ. Eng.,* September, p. 51.

———. (1976). "Bridge Bid Is Lowest on Aesthetic Choice," *ASCE Civ. Eng.,* May 27, p. 11.

Collingwood, R. G. (1979). *The Principles of Art,* Oxford University Press, New York.

Concrete. (1973). "Sculptured Retaining Wall," *Concrete,* 7(3), March, p. 43.

———. (1974). "No Hesitation in This Year's Innovation Award," *Concrete,* 8(9), September, pp. 32–33.

De Miranda, F. (1991). "The Three Mentalities of Successful Bridge Design," in *Bridge Aesthetics around the World,* Committee on General Structures, Subcommittee on Bridge Aesthetics, Transportation Research Board, Washington, DC, pp. 89–94.

Dorton, R. A. (1991). "Aesthetic Considerations for Bridge Overpass Design," in *Bridge Aesthetics around the World,* Committee on General Structures, Subcommittee on Bridge Aesthetics, Transportation Research Board, Washington, DC, pp. 10–17.

Ducasse, J. C. (1966). *The Philosophy of Art,* Dover, New York.

Dunican, P. (1966). "The Art of Structural Engineering," *Structural Engineer,* 44(3), March, pp. 97–108.

Elliot, A. L. (1968). "Aesthetics of Highway Bridges," *ASCE Civ. Eng.,* pp. 64–66.

———. (1973). *Aesthetics in Structures,* Special Report 138, Highway Research Board, pp. 101–105.

———. (1983). "Aesthetic Development of California's Bridges," *ASCE J. Struct. Eng.,* 109(9), September, pp. 2159–2174.

———. (1991). "Creating a Beautiful Bridge," *Bridge Aesthetics around the World,* Committee on General Structures, Subcommittee on Bridge Aesthetics, Transportation Research Board, Washington, DC, pp. 215–229.

Evans, R. H., and Houghton-Evans, W. (1964). "Form and Structure in Engineering," *Proc. Inst. Civil Engrs.,* London, vol. 27, pp. 263–290.

Faber, O. (1941). "Aesthetics in Engineering Structures," *J. Inst. Civ. Engrs.,* London, vol. 16, pp. 139–168.

———. (1945). First Lecture in *The Aesthetic Aspect of Civil Engineering Design,* Institute of Civil Engineers, London, pp. 1–23.

Freyermuth, C. L. (1966). "Developments in Concrete Bridge Construction," PCA, presented at the Southeastern Association of State Highway Officials Bridge Committee Meeting, Nashville, TN, September 19.

Ghaswala, S. K. (1991). "Bridge Aesthetics in India," in *Bridge Aesthetics around the World,* Committee on General Structures, Subcommittee on Bridge Aesthetics, Transportation Research Board, Washington, DC, pp. 189–196.

Ghyka, M. (1946). *The Geometry of Art and Life,* Sheed & Ward, New York.

Gideon, S. (1952). *Space, Time, and Architecture,* Harvard University Press, Cambridge, MA.

Girbert, R. W., and Billington, D. P. (1970). "The Eads Bridge and Nineteenth Century River Politics," in *Civil Engineering: History, Heritage, and the Humanities,* Princeton University Press, Princeton, NJ.

Glomb, J. (1991). "Aesthetics Aspects of Contemporary Bridge Design," in *Bridge Aesthetics around the World,* Committee on General Structures, Subcommittee on Bridge Aesthetics, Transportation Research Board, Washington, DC, pp. 95–104.

Gottemoeller, F. (1991). "Aesthetics and Engineers: Providing for Aesthetic Quality in Bridge Design," in *Bridge Aesthetics around the World,* Committee on General Structures, Subcommittee on Bridge Aesthetics, Transportation Research Board, Washington, DC, pp. 80–88.

Harbeson, P. C. (1991). "Architecture in Bridge Design," in *Bridge Aesthetics around the World,* Committee on General Structures, Subcommittee on Bridge Aesthetics, Transportation Research Board, Washington, DC, pp. 105–121.

Hayden, A. G., and Barron, M. (1931). *The Rigid Frame Bridge,* John Wiley & Sons, New York.

———. (1950). *The Rigid Frame Bridge,* John Wiley & Sons, New York.

Heyer, P. (1966). *Architects on Architecture,* Walker & Co., New York.

Hobbs, G. C. (1960). "Bridges," in *Reflections in Lafayette Park and Other Poems,* Valhalla Press, Napa Valley, CA., 1960.

Hool, G. A., and Thissen, F. C. (1916). *Reinforced Concrete Construction,* McGraw-Hill Companies, Inc., New York.

IH. (1984). "Toward Better Bridges" (editorial), *Indian Highways,* 12(6), June.

Inglis, Sir Charles. (1945). Third Lecture in *The Aesthetic Aspect of Civil Engineering Design,* Institute of Civil Engineers, London, pp. 236–245.

Ito, M. (1991). "Spiral Bridges," in *Bridge Aesthetics around the World,* Committee on General Structures, Subcommittee on Bridge Aesthetics, Transportation Research Board, Washington, DC, pp. 133–136.

Johnson, J. B., Bryan, C. W., and Turneaure, F. E. (1916). *The Theory and Practice of Modern Framed Structures,* 9th ed., John Wiley & Sons, New York.

Kavanaugh, T. C. (1975). "Some Esthetics Considerations in Steel Design," *ASCE J. Struct. Div.,* 101 (ST11), pp. 2257–2275.

Keisling, E. W., and Whetstone, G. A. (1972). "Civil Engineering for Recreation," *ASCE Civ. Eng.,* April.

Law, F. M. (1976). "Thinking Aesthetically Is a Part of Structural Engineering," *ASCE, Methods of Structural Analysis,* v. 1, pp. 1–18.

Le Corbusier (1970). *Towards a New Architecture,* 4th ed., Frederick A. Praeger Inc., New York.

Leonhardt, F. (1968). "Aesthetics of Bridge Design," *J. Prestressed Conc. Inst.,* 13(1), February, pp. 14–31.

——. (1980). "Aesthetics in Structural Engineering," *Proc. 11th Congress of the IABSE,* Vienna, Austria, pp. 3–8.

——. (1984). *Bridges—Aesthetics and Design,* MIT Press, Cambridge, MA. (This edition is combined with the original German version of this book "*Brucken—Aesthetic und Gestaltung,*" Deutsche Verlags–Anstalt GmbH DVA, Stuttgart, Germany.)

——. (1991). "Developing Guidelines for Aesthetic Design," in *Bridge Aesthetics around the World,* Committee on General Structures, Subcommittee on Bridge Aesthetics, Transportation Research Board, Washington, DC, pp. 32–57.

Liebenberg, A. C. (1991). "Aesthetic Evaluation of Bridges," in *Bridge Aesthetics around the World,* Committee on General Structures, Subcommittee on Bridge Aesthetics, Transportation Research Board, Washington, DC, pp. 1–9.

Marsh, P. (1973). "Concrete Too Is Beautiful," *Concrete,* 1(7), July, pp. 22–25.

Martin, I. (1974). "Good Esthetics a 'Happy Accident,'" *ASCE Civ. Eng.,* December, pp. 71–73.

McCullough, D. (1972). *The Great Bridge,* Simon & Schuster, New York.

Medwadowski, S. J. (1971). "Conceptual Design of Shells," in *Concrete Thin Shells,* ACI Pub. SP-28, Paper 28–2, ACI, pp. 15–39.

Menn, C. (1991). "Aesthetics in Bridge Design," in *Bridge Aesthetics around the World,* Committee on General Structures, Subcommittee on Bridge Aesthetics, Transportation Research Board, Washington, DC, pp. 177–188.

Mock, E. B. (1949). *The Architecture of Bridges,* The Museum of Modern Art, New York.

Muller, J. M. (1991). "Aesthetics in Concrete Segmental Bridges," in *Bridge Aesthetics around the World,* Committee on General Structures, Subcommittee on Bridge Aesthetics, Transportation Research Board, Washington, DC, pp. 18–31.

Mumford, L. (1955). *Sticks and Stones,* 2nd ed., Dover, New York.

Murray, J. (1981). "Visual Aspects of Motorway Bridges," *Proc. Inst. Civ. Engrs.,* London, vol. 70, pp. 755–788.

——. (1991). "Visual Aspects of Bridge Design," in *Bridge Aesthetics around the World,* Committee on General Structures, Subcommittee on Bridge Aesthetics, Transportation Research Board, Washington, DC, pp. 155–166.

Nakamura, Y., and Kubota, Y. (1991). "Pedestrian Bridges in the City," in *Bridge Aesthetics around the World,* Committee on General Structures, Subcommittee on Bridge Aesthetics, Transportation Research Board, Washington, DC, pp. 137–146.

Narer, J. W., and Freedman, E. S. (1992). "Aesthetic Enhancement of Highway Bridges in Maryland Utilizing Precast Brick Veneer Facing Panels," *PCI J.,* 37(2), March/April, pp. 24–29.

Nervi, P. L. (1956). *Structures,* F. W. Dodge Corp., New York.

Nobbs, et al. (1911). "Aesthetics in Bridge Design," *Trans. Canadian Soc. Civ. Engrs.,* Montreal, Canada, vol. 25, pp. 277–288.

North, B. H. (1973). "Appearance Matters," *Concrete,* 7(5), May, pp. 18–23.

O'Connor, C. (1991). "Empirical Assessment of Bridge Aesthetics: An Australian View," in *Bridge Aesthetics around the World,* Committee on General Structures, Subcommittee on Bridge Aesthetics, Transportation Research Board, Washington, DC, pp. 230–240.

Ohata, T. (1984). "Studies on Aesthetic Design of Double-Deck Bridges with Different Types Constructed Contiguously and Its Application," *Proc. Japan Soc. Civ. Engrs.,* 344(I-1), April, pp. 205–213 (in Japanese).

Ohata, T., Takahashi, N., and Yamane, T. (1987). "Aesthetic Design Method for Bridges," *ASCE J. Str. Eng.,* 113(8), August, pp. 1678–1687.

Ordonez, J. A. F. (1991). "Spanish Bridges: Aesthetics, History, and Nature," in *Bridge Aesthetics around the World,* Committee on General Structures, Subcommittee on Bridge Aesthetics, Transportation Research Board, Washington, DC, pp. 205–214.

Parker, D. H. (1929). *The Principles of Aesthetics,* Silver Publishers, Boston.

PCI. (1987a). "Research Boulevard Bridge," *PCI J.,* 32(6), November–December, pp. 132–136.

———. (1987b), "1987 PCI Professional Design Awards Program, Research Boulevard Bridge, Kettering, Ohio," *PCI J.,* 32(5), September–October, p. 38.

———. (1988). "1988 PCI Professional Awards Program—Kil-Cona Park Pedestrian Bridges, Winnipeg, Manitoba, Canada," *PCI J.,* 33(5), September–October, p. 47.

———. (1989). "Kil-Cona Park Pedestrian Bridges," *PCI J.,* 34(2), January–February, pp. 136–147.

Potyondy, J. G. (1969). "Aesthetic Problems in Contemporary Concrete Bridge Design," in *Concrete Bridge Design,* ACI Pub. SP-23, pp. 7–18.

Revelo, C. K. (1991). "Form, Modeling, and Composition in Bridge Aesthetics," in *Bridge Aesthetics around the World,* Committee on General Structures, Subcommittee on Bridge Aesthetics, Transportation Research Board, Washington, DC, pp. 147–154.

Ritner, J. C. (1986). "Bridges Produced by an Architectural Engineering Team," in *Trans. Res. Rec. 1044,* Transportation Research Board, Washington, DC, pp. 26–34.

Schlaepfer, F. J. (1959). "The Interrelation of Structure and Beauty in Architecture," M.A. thesis, School of Architecture, University of California, Berkeley.

Schodeck, D. L. (1987). *Landmarks in American Civil Engineering,* MIT Press, Cambridge, MA.

Schuyler, M. (1883). "The Bridge as a Monument," *Harper's Weekly,* 27, May 24.

Scott, G. (1969). *The Architecture of Humanism,* 2nd ed., Charles Schriber's Sons, New York, p. 184.

Scuri, V. (1992). "Applications of Sculptural Art Forms in Precast Concrete Structures," *J. Prestressed Conc. Inst.,* 37(1), January/February, pp. 37–49.

Shureman, L. R. (1938). "Beauty in Short-Span Highway Bridges," *ASCE Civ. Eng.,* May, pp. 318–319.

Slatter, R. E. (1980). "Bridge Aesthetics," in *The Final Report of the 11th Congress,* Vienna, Austria, IABSE, Zurich, Switzerland, pp. 115–120.

Steinman, D. B., and Watson, S. R. (1957). *Bridges and Their Builders,* Putnam, New York.

Strong, P. (1973). "Art in Architecture," *Concrete,* 7(1), January, pp. 22–23.

Tahara, Y., and Nakamura, Y. (1980). "On the Manual for Aesthetic Design of Bridges," in *The Final Report of the 11th Congress,* Vienna, Austria, IABSE, Zurich, Switzerland, pp. 101–108.

Tajima, J., and Sugiyama, K. (1991). "Historical Transition of Suspension Bridge Forms in Japan," in *Bridge Aesthetics around the World,* Committee on General Structures, Subcommittee on Bridge Aesthetics, Transportation Research Board, Washington, DC, pp. 122–132.

Tang, H. C. (1991). "Philosophical Basis for Chinese Bridge Aesthetics," in *Bridge Aesthetics around the World,* Committee on General Structures, Subcommittee on Bridge Aesthetics, Transportation Research Board, Washington, DC, pp. 167–176.

Tassios, T. P. (1980). "Relativity and Optimization of Aesthetic Rules for Structures," in *The Final Report of the 11th Congress,* Vienna, Austria, IABSE, Zurich, Switzerland, pp. 59–67.

TRB. (1991). *Bridge Aesthetics around the World,* Committee on General Structures, Subcommittee on Bridge Aesthetics, Transportation Research Board, National Research Council, Washington, DC.

Torroja, E. (1958). "The Beauty of Structures," in *Philosophy of Structures,* University of California Press, Berkeley, pp. 268–289.

———. (1958). *Philosophy of Structures,* University of California Press, Berkeley.

Tyrell, H. G. (1912). *Artistic Bridge Design,* Myron C. Clark Publishing Co., New York, p. 16.

von Olnhausen, W. (1991). "Bridges in Sweden: Should We Do More about Bridge Aesthetics?" in *Bridge Aesthetics around the World,* Committee on General Structures, Subcommittee on Bridge Aesthetics, Transportation Research Board, Washington, DC, pp. 197–204.

Wadell, J. A. L. (1916). "Aesthetics in Bridge Design," in *Bridge Engineering,* vol. 2, John Wiley & Sons, New York.

Walton, A. E. (1986). "Production of Brick Veneer Precast Concrete Panels," *PCI J.,* 31(3), May–June, pp. 48–63.

Warton, S. C., and Hurd, M. K. (1990). *Esthetics in Concrete Bridge Design,* ACI, Detroit, MI.

Wasserman, E. P. (1991). "Aesthetics for Short- and Medium-Span Bridges," in *Bridge Aesthetics around the World,* Committee on General Structures, Subcommittee on Bridge Aesthetics, Transportation Research Board, Washington, DC, pp. 58–66.

Watson, W. J. (1938). "Architectural Principles of Bridge Design," *ASCE Civ. Eng.,* March, pp. 181–184.

Wendell, E. W. (1953). "Bridge Design Is Guided by Esthetics as Well as Functional Considerations," *ASCE Civ. Eng.,* November, pp. 47–50.

Wengenroth, R. H. (1971). "Bridge Engineer Looks at Esthetics of Structures," *ASCE J. Struct. Div.,* 97(ST4), April, pp. 1227–1237.

White, J., and von Bernwitz, M. W. (1928). *The Bridges of Pittsburgh* (foreword), Cramer Printing and Publishing Co., Pittsburgh.

Whitney, C. S. (1983). *Bridges: Their Art, Science, and Evolution,* Greenwich House, New York.

Young, C. R. (1911). "Aesthetics in Bridge Design," *Trans. Canadian Soc. Civ. Engrs.,* Montreal, vol. 25, pp. 254–276.

Zuk, W. (1973). "Methodology for Evaluating the Aesthetic Appeal of Bridge Designs," *Highway Research Record 428,* Transportation Research Board, Washington, DC, pp. 1–4.

———. (1974). "Public Response to Bridge Colors," *Transportation Research Record 507,* Transportation Research Board, Washington, DC.

———. (1976). "How Almost Anyone Can Design a Good-Looking Bridge in One Easy Lesson," *ASCE Methods of Structural Analysis,* vol. 1, pp. 19–32.

———. (1983). "The Architecture of Bridges," *Progressive Architecture,* Reinhold, New York, March, pp. 96–99.

APPENDIX A

TABLE A.1
Weights of materials used in bridge construction

	Material	lb/cu. ft
1.	Steel or cast steel	490
2.	Cast iron	450
3.	Aluminum alloys	175
4.	Timber (treated or untreated)	50
5.	Concrete, plain or reinforced	150
6.	Compacted sand, earth, gravel, or ballast	120
7.	Loose sand, earth, and gravel	100
8.	Macadam or gravel, rolled	140
9.	Cinder filling	60
10.	Pavement, other than wood block	150
11.	Railway rails, guard rails, and fastenings (per linear ft of track)	200
12.	Stone masonry	170
13.	Asphalt plank, 1 in. thick	9 lb/ft^2

TABLE A.2

Approximate C_D values for various bodies[Roberson and Crowe, 1990]*

Type of body	Length ratio	Re	C_D
Rectangular plate	$l/b = 1$	$>10^4$	1.18
	$l/b = 5$	$>10^4$	1.20
	$l/b = 10$	$>10^4$	1.30
	$l/b = 20$	$>10^4$	1.50
	$l/b = \infty$	$>10^4$	1.98
Circular cylinder— axis parallel to flow	$l/d = 0$ (disk)	$>10^4$	1.17
	$l/d = 0.5$	$>10^4$	1.15
	$l/d = 1$	$>10^4$	0.90
	$l/d = 2$	$>10^4$	0.85
	$l/d = 4$	$>10^4$	0.87
	$l/d = 8$	$>10^4$	0.99
Square rod	∞	$>10^4$	2.00
Square rod	∞	$>10^4$	1.50
Triangular cylinder	∞	$>10^4$	1.39
Semicircular shell	∞	$>10^4$	1.20
Semicircular shell	∞	$>10^4$	2.30
Hemispherical shell		$>10^4$	0.39
Hemispherical shell		$>10^4$	1.40
Cube		$>10^4$	1.10
Cube		$>10^4$	0.81
Cone—60° vertex		$>10^4$	0.49
Parachute		$\approx 3 \times 10^7$	1.20

*Reprinted with permission from Houghton Mifflin Co.

TABLE A.3

Maximum moments, shears, and reactions—H15-44 loading, simple spans, one lane

Span in feet; moments in thousands of foot-pounds; shears and reactions in thousands of pounds. Values are subject to specification reduction for loading of multiple lanes. Impact not included.

Span	Moment	End shear and end reaction[a]	Span	Moment	End shear and end reaction[a]
1	6.0[b]	24.0[b]	42	274.4[b]	29.6
2	12.0[b]	24.0[b]	44	289.3[b]	30.1
3	18.0[b]	24.0[b]	46	304.3[b]	30.5
4	24.0[b]	24.0[b]	48	319.2[b]	31.0
5	30.0[b]	24.0[b]	50	334.2[b]	31.5
6	36.0[b]	24.0[b]	52	349.1[b]	32.0
7	42.0[b]	24.0[b]	54	364.1[b]	32.5
8	48.0[b]	24.0[b]	56	379.1[b]	32.9
9	54.0[b]	24.0[b]	58	397.6	33.4
10	60.0[b]	24.0[b]	60	418.5	33.9
11	66.0[b]	24.0[b]	62	439.9	34.4
12	72.0[b]	24.0[b]	64	461.8	34.9
13	78.0[b]	24.0[b]	66	484.1	35.3
14	84.0[b]	24.0[b]	68	506.9	35.8
15	90.0[b]	24.0[b]	70	530.3	36.3
16	96.0[b]	24.8[b]	75	590.6	37.5
17	102.0[b]	25.1[b]	80	654.8	38.7
18	108.0[b]	25.3[b]	85	720.4	39.9
19	114.0[b]	25.6[b]	90	789.8	41.1
20	120.0[b]	25.8[b]	95	862.1	42.3
21	126.0[b]	26.0[b]	100	937.5	43.5
22	132.0[b]	26.2[b]	110	1097.3	45.9
23	138.0[b]	26.3[b]	120	1269.0	48.3
24	144.0[b]	26.5[b]	130	1452.8	50.7
25	150.0[b]	26.6[b]	140	1648.5	53.1
26	156.0[b]	26.8[b]	150	1856.3	55.5
27	162.7[b]	26.9[b]	160	2076.0	57.9
28	170.1[b]	27.0[b]	170	2307.8	60.3
29	177.5[b]	27.1[b]	180	2551.5	62.7
30	177.5[b]	27.2[b]	190	2807.3	65.1
31	192.4[b]	27.3[b]	200	3075.0	67.5
32	199.8[b]	27.4[b]	220	3646.5	72.3
33	207.3[b]	27.5	240	4266.0	77.1
34	214.7[b]	27.7	260	4933.5	81.9
35	222.2[b]	27.9	280	5649.0	86.7
36	229.6[b]	28.1	300	6412.5	91.5
37	237.1[b]	28.4			
38	244.5[b]	28.6			
39	252.0[b]	28.9			
40	259.5[b]	29.1			

[a] Concentrated load is considered placed at the support. Loads used are those stipulated for shear.
[b] Maximum value determined by standard truck loading. Otherwise the standard lane loading governs.

TABLE A.4

Maximum moments, shears, and reactions—HS15-44 loading, simple spans, one lane

Span in feet; moments in thousands of foot-pounds; shears and reactions in thousands of pounds. Values are subject to specification reduction for loading of multiple lanes. Impact not included.

Span	Moment	End shear and end reaction[a]	Span	Moment	End shear and end reaction[a]
1	6.0[b]	24.0[b]	42	364.0[b]	42.0[b]
2	12.0[b]	24.0[b]	44	390.7[b]	42.5[b]
3	18.0[b]	24.0[b]	46	417.4[b]	43.0[b]
4	24.0[b]	24.0[b]	48	444.1[b]	43.5[b]
5	30.0[b]	24.0[b]	50	470.9[b]	43.9[b]
6	36.0[b]	24.0[b]	52	497.7[b]	44.3[b]
7	42.0[b]	24.0[b]	54	524.5[b]	44.7[b]
8	48.0[b]	24.0[b]	56	551.3[b]	45.0[b]
9	54.0[b]	24.0[b]	58	578.1[b]	45.3[b]
10	60.0[b]	24.0[b]	60	604.9[b]	45.6[b]
11	66.0[b]	24.0[b]	62	631.8[b]	45.9[b]
12	72.0[b]	24.0[b]	64	658.6[b]	46.1[b]
13	78.0[b]	24.0[b]	66	685.5[b]	46.4[b]
14	84.0[b]	24.0[b]	68	712.3[b]	46.6[b]
15	90.0[b]	25.6[b]	70	739.2[b]	46.8[b]
16	96.0[b]	27.0[b]	75	806.3[b]	47.3[b]
17	102.0[b]	28.2[b]	80	873.7[b]	47.7[b]
18	108.0[b]	29.3[b]	85	941.0[b]	48.1[b]
19	114.0[b]	30.3[b]	90	1008.3[b]	48.4[b]
20	120.0[b]	31.2[b]	95	1074.9[b]	48.7[b]
21	126.0[b]	32.0[b]	100	1143.0[b]	49.0[b]
22	132.0[b]	32.7[b]	110	1277.7[b]	49.4[b]
23	138.0[b]	33.4[b]	120	1412.5[b]	49.8[b]
24	144.5[b]	34.0[b]	130	1547.3[b]	50.7
25	155.5[b]	34.6[b]	140	1682.1[b]	53.1
26	166.6[b]	35.1[b]	150	1856.3	55.5
27	177.8[b]	35.6[b]	160	2076.0	57.9
28	189.0[b]	36.0[b]	170	2307.8	60.3
29	200.3[b]	36.6[b]	180	2551.5	62.7
30	211.6[b]	37.2[b]	190	2807.3	65.1
31	223.0[b]	37.7[b]	200	3075.0	67.5
32	234.4[b]	38.3[b]	220	3646.5	72.3
33	245.8[b]	38.7[b]	240	4266.0	77.1
34	257.7[b]	39.2[b]	260	4933.5	81.9
35	270.9[b]	39.6[b]	280	5649.0	86.7
36	284.2[b]	40.0[b]	300	6412.5	91.5
37	297.5[b]	40.4[b]			
38	310.7[b]	40.7[b]			
39	324.0[b]	41.1[b]			
40	337.4[b]	41.4[b]			

[a] Concentrated load is considered placed at the support. Loads used are those stipulated for shear.

[b] Maximum value determined by standard truck loading. Otherwise the standard lane loading governs.

TABLE A.5

Maximum moments, shears, and reactions—H20-44 loading, simple spans, one lane

Span in feet; moments in thousands of foot-pounds; shears and reactions in thousands of pounds. Values are subject to specification reduction for loading of multiple lanes. Impact not included.

Span	Moment	End shear and end reaction[a]	Span	Moment	End shear and end reaction[a]
1	8.0[b]	32.0[b]	42	365.9[b]	39.4
2	16.0[b]	32.0[b]	44	385.8[b]	40.1
3	24.0[b]	32.0[b]	46	405.7[b]	40.7
4	32.0[b]	32.0[b]	48	425.6[b]	41.4
5	40.0[b]	32.0[b]	50	445.6[b]	42.0
6	48.0[b]	32.0[b]	52	465.5[b]	42.6
7	56.0[b]	32.0[b]	54	485.5[b]	43.3
8	64.0[b]	32.0[b]	56	505.4[b]	43.9
9	72.0[b]	32.0[b]	58	530.1	44.6
10	80.0[b]	32.0[b]	60	558.0	45.2
11	88.0[b]	32.0[b]	62	586.5	45.8
12	96.0[b]	32.0[b]	64	615.7	46.5
13	104.0[b]	32.0[b]	66	645.5	47.1
14	112.0[b]	32.0[b]	68	675.9	47.8
15	120.0[b]	32.5[b]	70	707.0	48.4
16	128.0[b]	33.0[b]	75	787.5	50.0
17	136.0[b]	33.4[b]	80	872.0	51.6
18	144.0[b]	33.8[b]	85	960.5	53.2
19	152.0[b]	34.1[b]	90	1053.0	54.8
20	160.0[b]	34.4[b]	95	1149.5	56.4
21	168.0[b]	34.7[b]	100	1250.0	58.0
22	176.0[b]	34.9[b]	110	1463.0	61.2
23	184.0[b]	35.1[b]	120	1692.0	64.4
24	192.0[b]	35.3[b]	130	1937.0	67.6
25	200.0[b]	35.5[b]	140	2198.0	70.8
26	208.0[b]	35.7[b]	150	2475.0	74.0
27	216.9[b]	35.9[b]	160	2768.0	77.2
28	226.8[b]	36.0[b]	170	3077.0	80.4
29	236.7[b]	36.1[b]	180	3402.0	83.6
30	246.6[b]	36.3[b]	190	3743.0	86.8
31	256.5[b]	36.4[b]	200	4100.0	90.0
32	266.5[b]	36.5[b]	220	4862.0	96.4
33	276.4[b]	36.6[b]	240	5688.0	102.8
34	286.3[b]	36.9	260	6578.0	109.2
35	296.2[b]	37.2	280	7532.0	115.6
36	306.2[b]	37.5	300	8550.0	122.0
37	316.1[b]	37.8			
38	326.1[b]	38.2			
39	336.0[b]	38.5			
40	346.0[b]	38.8			

[a] Concentrated load is considered placed at the support. Loads used are those stipulated for shear.
[b] Maximum value determined by standard truck loading. Otherwise the standard lane loading governs.

TABLE A.6

Maximum moments, shears, and reactions—HS20-44 loading, simple spans, one lane

Span in feet; moments in thousands of foot-pounds; shears and reactions in thousands of pounds. Values are subject to specification reduction for loading of multiple lanes. Impact not included.

Span	Moment	End shear and end reaction[a]	Span	Moment	End shear and end reaction[a]
1	8.0[b]	32.0[b]	42	485.3[b]	56.0[b]
2	16.0[b]	32.0[b]	44	520.9[b]	56.7[b]
3	24.0[b]	32.0[b]	46	556.5[b]	57.3[b]
4	32.0[b]	32.0[b]	48	592.1[b]	58.0[b]
5	40.0[b]	32.0[b]	50	627.9[b]	58.5[b]
6	48.0[b]	32.0[b]	52	663.6[b]	59.1[b]
7	56.0[b]	32.0[b]	54	699.3[b]	59.6[b]
8	64.0[b]	32.0[b]	56	735.1[b]	60.0[b]
9	72.0[b]	32.0[b]	58	770.8[b]	60.4[b]
10	80.0[b]	32.0[b]	60	806.5[b]	60.8[b]
11	88.0[b]	32.0[b]	62	842.4[b]	61.2[b]
12	96.0[b]	32.0[b]	64	878.1[b]	61.5[b]
13	104.0[b]	32.0[b]	66	914.0[b]	61.9[b]
14	112.0[b]	32.0[b]	68	949.7[b]	62.1[b]
15	120.0[b]	34.1[b]	70	985.6[b]	62.4[b]
16	128.0[b]	36.0[b]	75	1075.1[b]	63.1[b]
17	136.0[b]	37.7[b]	80	1164.9[b]	63.6[b]
18	144.0[b]	39.1[b]	85	1254.7[b]	64.1[b]
19	152.0[b]	40.4[b]	90	1344.4[b]	64.5[b]
20	160.0[b]	41.6[b]	95	1434.1[b]	64.9[b]
21	168.0[b]	42.7[b]	100	1524.0[b]	65.3[b]
22	176.0[b]	43.6[b]	110	1703.6[b]	65.9[b]
23	184.0[b]	44.5[b]	120	1883.3[b]	66.4[b]
24	192.7[b]	45.3[b]	130	2063.1[b]	67.6
25	207.4[b]	46.1[b]	140	2242.8[b]	70.8
26	222.2[b]	46.8[b]	150	2475.1	74.0
27	237.0[b]	47.4[b]	160	2768.0	77.2
28	252.0[b]	48.0[b]	170	3077.1	80.4
29	267.0[b]	48.8[b]	180	3402.1	83.6
30	282.1[b]	49.6[b]	190	3743.1	86.8
31	297.3[b]	50.3[b]	200	4100.0	90.0
32	312.5[b]	51.0[b]	220	4862.0	96.4
33	327.8[b]	51.6[b]	240	5688.0	102.8
34	343.5[b]	52.2[b]	260	6578.0	109.2
35	361.2[b]	52.8[b]	280	7532.0	115.2
36	378.9[b]	53.3[b]	300	8550.0	122.0
37	396.6[b]	53.8[b]			
38	414.3[b]	54.3[b]			
39	432.1[b]	54.8[b]			
40	449.8[b]	55.2[b]			

[a] Concentrated load is considered placed at the support. Loads used are those stipulated for shear.

[b] Maximum value determined by standard truck loading. Otherwise the standard lane loading governs.

Distribution of wheel loads in longitudinal beams (AASHTO Table 3.23.1)

Kind of floor	Bridge designed for one traffic lane	Bridge designed for two or more traffic lanes
Timber[a]:		
Plank[b]	$S/4.0$	$S/3.75$
Nail-laminated[c]		
4"-thick or multiple-layer[d]		
floors over 5" thick	$S/4.5$	$S/4.0$
Nail-laminated[c]		
6" or more thick	$S/5.0$	$S/4.25$
	If S exceeds 5', use footnote f.	If S exceeds 6.5', use footnote f.
Glued-laminated[e] panels		
on glued-laminated stringers		
4" thick	$S/4.5$	$S/4.0$
6" or more thick	$S/6.0$	$S/5.0$
	If S exceeds 6', use footnote f.	If S exceeds 7.5', use footnote f.
On steel stringers:		
4" thick	$S/4.5$	$S/4.0$
6" or more thick	$S/5.25$	$S/4.5$
	If S exceeds 5.5', use footnote f.	If S exceeds 7', use footnote f.
Concrete:		
On steel I-beam stringers[g] and		
prestressed concrete girders	$S/7.0$	$S/5.5$
	If S exceeds 10', use footnote f.	If S exceeds 14', use footnote f.
On concrete T-beam	$S/6.5$	$S/6.0$
	If S exceeds 6', use footnote f.	If S exceeds 10', use footnote f.
On timber stringers	$S/6.0$	$S/5.0$
	If S exceeds 6', use footnote f.	If S exceeds 10', use footnote f.
Concrete box girders[h]	$S/8.0$	$S/7.0$
	If S exceeds 12', use footnote f.	If S exceeds 16', use footnote f.
On steel box girders	See Article 39.2	
On prestressed concrete		
spread box beams	See Article 3.28	
Steel grid:		
(Less than 4" thick)	$S/4.5$	$S/4.0$
(4" or more)	$S/6.0$	$S/5.0$
	If S exceeds 6', use footnote f.	If S exceeds 10.5', use footnote f.
Steel bridge corrugated plank[i]		
(2" min. depth)	$S/5.5$	$S/4.5$

S = average stringer spacing in feet.

[a] Timber dimensions shown are for nominal thickness.

[b] Plank floors consist of pieces of lumber laid edge to edge with the wide faces bearing on the supports (see Article 20.17, Divison II).

[c] Nail-laminated floors consist of pieces of lumber laid face to face with the narrow edges bearing on the supports, each piece being nailed to the preceding piece (see Article 20.18, Division II).

[d] Multiple-layer floors consist of two or more layers of planks, each layer being laid at an angle to the other (see Article 20.17, Division II).

[e] Glued-laminated panel floors consist of vertically glued-laminated members with narrow edges of the laminations bearing on the supports (see Article 20.1.1, Division II).

[f] In this case the load on each stringer shall be the reaction of the wheel loads, assuming the flooring between the stringers acts as a simple beam.

[g] "Design of I-Beam Bridges" by N. M. Newmark, *Proc. ASCE,* March 1948.

[h] The sidewalk live load (see Article 3.15) shall be omitted for interior and exterior box girders designed in accordance with the wheel load distribution indicated herein.

[i] Distribution factors for steel bridge corrugated plank set forth in Table A.7 are based substantially on the following reference: *Journal of Washington Academy of Sciences,* Vol. 67, No. 2, 1977, "Wheel Load Distribution of Steel Bridge Plank," by Conrad P. Heins, professor of civil engineering, University of Maryland. These distribution factors were developed based on studies using 6" × 2" steel corrugated plank. The factors should yield safe results for other corrugation configurations provided primary bending stiffness is the same as or greater than the 6" × 2" corrugated plank used in the studies.

TABLE A.8

Distribution of wheel loads in longitudinal beams for calculation of bending moments in interior longitudinal stringers (AASHTO Table 3.23.1[*])

Kind of floor	Bridge designed for one traffic lane	Bridge designed for two or more traffic lanes	Range of applicability[j]
Timber:[a]			
Plank[b]	$S/4.0$	$S/3.75$	N/A
Nail-laminated[c] 4″-thick or multiple-layer[d] floors over 5″ thick	$S/4.5$	$S/4.0$	N/A
Nail-laminated[c] 6″ or more thick	$S/5.0$	$S/4.25$	N/A
	If S exceeds 5′, use footnote f.	If S exceeds 6.5′, use footnote f.	
Glued-laminated[e] panels on glued-laminated stringers			
4″ thick	$S/4.5$	$S/4.0$	N/A
6″ or more thick	$S/6.0$	$S/5.0$	N/A
	If S exceeds 6′, use footnote f.	If S exceeds 7.5′, use footnote f.	
On steel stringers			
4″ thick	$S/4.5$	$S/4.0$	N/A
6″ or more thick	$S/5.25$	$S/4.5$	N/A
	If S exceeds 5.5′, use footnote f.	If S exceeds 7′, use footnote f.	
Concrete:			
On timber stringers	$S/6.0$	$S/5.0$	N/A
	If S exceeds 6′, use footnote f.	If S exceeds 5′, use footnote f.	
On steel I-beam stringers and prestressed concrete girders; concrete T-beams[g]	$0.1 + \left(\dfrac{S}{4'}\right)^{0.4}\left(\dfrac{S}{L}\right)^{0.3}\left(\dfrac{K_g}{Lt_s^3}\right)^{0.1}$ or $\quad 0.1 + \left(\dfrac{S}{4'}\right)^{0.4}\left(\dfrac{S}{L}\right)^{0.3}$	$0.15 + \left(\dfrac{S}{3'}\right)^{0.6}\left(\dfrac{S}{L}\right)^{0.2}\left(\dfrac{K_g}{Lt_s^3}\right)^{0.1}$ or $\quad 0.15 + \left(\dfrac{S}{3'}\right)^{0.6}\left(\dfrac{S}{L}\right)^{0.2}$	$3'6'' \leq S \leq 16'0''$ $20' \leq L \leq 240'$ $4.5'' \leq t_s \leq 12.0''$ $10,000 \leq K_g$ $\leq 7,000,000$ in.^{4} $N_b \leq 4$
	If S exceeds 16′, use footnote f.	If S exceeds 16′, use footnote f. If $N_b < 4$, use footnote f.	
Prestressed and reinforced concrete box girders[g,h]	$\left(3 + \dfrac{S}{2.2'}\right)\left(\dfrac{1'}{L}\right)0.35\left(\dfrac{1}{N_c}\right)0.45$	$\dfrac{2.5}{N_c} - \dfrac{1}{N_L} + \dfrac{L}{800'} + \left(\dfrac{S}{9'}\right)\left(\dfrac{90'}{L}\right)0.25$	$7' \leq S \leq 13'$ $60' \leq L \leq 240'$ $3 \leq N_c$
	If S exceeds 13′, use footnote f. If $S \leq 7'$, use 7′ to be conservative. If $L \leq 60'$ use L, but distribution factor will be more conservative.		
On steel box girders	(See Article 10.29.2.)		N/A
On prestressed concrete spread box beams[g]	$2\left(\dfrac{S}{5'}\right)^{0.35}\left[\left(\dfrac{S}{L}\right)\left(\dfrac{d}{L}\right)\right]^{0.25}$	$\left(\dfrac{S}{2'}\right)^{0.6}\left[\left(\dfrac{S}{L}\right)\left(\dfrac{d}{L}\right)\right]0.125$	$6' \leq S \leq 11'6''$ $20' \leq L \leq 140'$ $1'6'' \leq d \leq 5'6''$ $N_b \geq 3$
	If S exceeds 11′6″, use footnote f.		

(continued)

TABLE A.8
(continued)

Kind of floor	Bridge designed for one traffic lane	Bridge designed for two or more traffic lanes	Range of Applicability[j]
Precast box beams used in multibeam decks[g]	$k\left(\dfrac{b}{L}\right)^{0.5}\left(\dfrac{I}{J}\right)^{0.25}$ or $\quad k\left(\dfrac{b}{L}\right)^{0.5}$	$\left(\dfrac{2b}{3'}\right)^{0.6}\left[\left(\dfrac{b}{L}\right)\left(\dfrac{1}{N_b}\right)\right]^{0.2}\left(\dfrac{I}{J}\right)^{0.06}$ or $\quad\left(\dfrac{2b}{3'}\right)^{0.6}\left[\left(\dfrac{b}{L}\right)\left(\dfrac{1}{N_b}\right)\right]^{0.2}$	$3' \le b \le 5'$ $20' \le L \le 120'$ $5 \le N_b \le 20$ $25{,}000 \le J$ $\le 610{,}000$ in.^{4} $40{,}000 \le I$ $\le 610{,}000$ in.^{4}
Precast beam other than box beams used in multi-beam decks	(See Article 3.23.2.7.)		N/A
Steel grid:			
(Less than 4″ thick)	$S/4.5$	$S/4.0$	
(4″ or more)	$S/6.0$	$S/5.0$	
	If S exceeds 6′, use footnote f.	If S exceeds 10.5′, use footnote f.	
Steel bridge corrugated plank[i] (2″ min. depth)	$S/5.5$	$S/4.5$	

[*] See *Guide Specifications for Distribution of Loads for Highway Bridges, 1994,* AASHTO, Washington, DC.

S = average stringer spacing in feet.

[a] Timber dimensions shown are for nominal thickness.

[b] Plank floors consist of pieces of lumber laid edge to edge with the wide faces bearing on the supports (see Article 16.3.11, Divison II).

[c] Nail-laminated floors consist of pieces of lumber laid edge to edge with the narrow edges bearing on the supports, each piece being nailed to the preceding piece (see Article 16.3.12, Division II).

[d] Multiple-layer floors consist of two or more layers of planks, each layer being laid at an angle to the other (see Article 16.3.11, Division II).

[e] Glued-laminated panel floors consist of vertically glued-laminated members with narrow edges of the laminations bearing on the supports (see Article 16.3.13, Division II).

[f] In this case the load on each stringer shall be the reaction of the wheel loads, assuming the flooring between the stringers acts as a simple beam.

[g] From Imbsen & Associates, Inc. (NCHRP Project 12-26).

[h] The sidewalk live load (see Article 3.14) shall be omitted for interior and exterior box girders designed in accordance with the wheel load distribution indicated herein.

[i] Distribution factors for steel bridge corrugated plank set forth in Table A.8 are based substantially on the following reference: *Journal of Washington Academy of Sciences,* Vol. 67, No. 2, 1977, "Wheel Load Distribution of Steel Bridge Plank," by Conrad P. Heins, Professor of Civil Engineering, University of Maryland. These distribution factors were developed based on studies using 6″ × 2″ steel corrugated plank. The factors should yield safe results for other corrugation configurations provided primary bending stiffness is the same as or greater than the 6″ × 2″ corrugated plank used in the studies.

[j] The range of applicability was established in NCHRP Project 12-26 from a database of bridges gathered from several states. These ranges were used to establish the formulas and do not necessarily represent the limits that can be used for design.

TABLE A.9
Distribution of wheel loads in transverse beams (AASHTO Table 3.23.3.1)

Kind of floor	Fraction of wheel load to each floor beam
Plank[a,b]	$\dfrac{S}{4}$
Nail-laminated[c] or glued-laminated[e] 4 in. in thickness, or multiple-layer[d] floors more than 5 in. thick	$\dfrac{S}{4.5}$
Nail-laminated[c] or glued-laminated[e] 6 in. or more in thickness	$\dfrac{S^{f}}{5}$
Concrete	$\dfrac{S^{f}}{6}$
Steel grid (less than 4 in. thick)	$\dfrac{S}{4.5}$
Steel grid (4 in. or more thick)	$\dfrac{S^{f}}{6}$
Steel bridge corrugated plank (2 in. minimum depth)	$\dfrac{S}{5.5}$

S = spacing of floor beams in feet.
For footnotes a through e, see AASHTO [1992] Table 3.23.1.
[f] If S exceeds denominator, the load on the beam shall be the reaction of the wheel loads, assuming the flooring between beams acts as a simple span.

TABLE A.10
Allowable fatigue stress range (AASHTO Table 10.3.1A)
Redundant load path structures[*]

	Allowable stress range, F_{sr} (ksi)[a]			
Stress category	For 100,000 cycles	For 500,000 cycles	For 2,000,000 cycles	Over 2,000,000 cycles
A	63 (49)[c]	37 (29)[c]	24 (18)[c]	24 (16)[c]
B	49	29	18	16
B'	39	23	14.5	12
C	35.5	21	13	10 12[b] 12[b]
D	28	16	10	7
E	22	13	8	4.5
E'	16	9.2	5.8	2.6
F	15	12	9	8

[*] Structure types with multiload paths where a single fracture in a member cannot lead to collapse. For example, a simply supported single-span multibeam bridge or a multi-element eye-bar truss member has redundant load paths.
[a] The range of stress is defined as the algebraic difference between the maximum stress and the minimum stress. Tension stress is considered to have the opposite algebraic sign from compression stress.
[b] For transverse stiffener welds on girder webs or flanges.
[c] For unpainted weathering steel, A709, all grades, when used in conformance with the FHWA *Technical Advisory on Uncoated Weathering Steel in Structures,* October 3, 1989.

TABLE A.11
Allowable fatigue stress range (AASHTO Table 10.3.1A)
Nonredundant load path structures*

Stress category	Allowable stress range, F_{sr} (ksi)[a]			
	For 100,000 cycles	For 500,000 cycles	For 2,000,000 cycles	Over 2,000,000 cycles
A	50 (39)[d]	29 (23)[d]	24 (16)[d]	24 (16)[d]
B	39	23	16	16
B'	31	18	11	11
C	28	16	10 (12)[b]	9 (11)[b]
D	22	13	8	5
E[c]	17	10	6	2.3
E'	12	7	4	1.3
F	12	9	7	6

* Structure types with multiload paths where a single fracture in a member cannot lead to collapse. For example, a simply supported single-span multibeam bridge or a multi-element eye-bar truss member has redundant load paths.
For footnotes a through d, see Table A.10 (AASHTO Table 10.3.1A).
[a] The range of stress is defined as the algebraic difference between the maximum stress and the minimum stress. Tension stress is considered to have the opposite algebraic sign from compression stress.
[b] For transverse stiffener welds on girder webs or flanges.
[c] Partial length welded cover plates shall not be used on flanges more than 0.8 in. thick for nonredundant load path structures.
[d] For unpainted weathering steel, A709, all grades, when used in conformance with the FHWA *Technical Advisory on Uncoated Weathering Steel in Structures,* October 3, 1989.

TABLE A.12
Fatigue categories (AASHTO Table 10.3.1B)

General condition	Situation	Kind of stress	Stress category (See Table 10.3.1A)	Illustrative example (See Fig. 10.3.1C)
Plain member	Base metal with rolled or cleaned surface. Flame-cut edges with ANSI smoothness of 1000 or less.	T or Rev[a]	A	1, 2
Built-up members	Base metal and weld metal in members of built-up plates or shapes (without attachments) connected by continuous full penetration groove welds (with backing bars removed) or by continuous fillet welds parallel to the direction of the applied stress.	T or Rev	B	3, 4, 5, 7
	Base metal and weld metal in members of built-up plates or shapes (without attachments) connected by continuous full penetration groove welds (with backing bars not removed) or by continuous partial penetration groove welds parallel to the direction of the applied stress.	T or Rev	B'	3, 4, 5, 7
	Calculated flexural stress at the toe of transverse stiffener welds on girder webs or flanges.	T or Rev	C	6
	Base metal at ends of partial-length welded coverplates with high-strength bolted slip-critical end connections.[f]	T or Rev	B	22

(continued)

General condition	Situation	Kind of stress	Stress category (See Table 10.3.1A)	Illustrative example (See Fig. 10.3.1C)
	Base metal at ends of partial-length welded cover plates narrower than the flange having square or tapered ends, with or without welds across the ends, or wider than flange with welds across the ends: (a) Flange thickness ≤ 0.8 in. (b) Flange thickness > 0.8 in.	 T or Rev T or Rev	 E E′	 7 7
	Base metal at ends of partial-length welded cover plates wider than the flange without welds across the ends.	T or Rev	E′	7
Groove-welded connections	Base metal and weld metal in or adjacent to full penetration groove weld splices of rolled or welded sections having similar profiles when welds are ground flush with grinding in the direction of applied stress, and weld soundness established by nondestructive inspection.	T or Rev	B	8, 10
	Base metal and weld metal in or adjacent to full penetration groove weld splices at transitions in width or thickness, with welds ground to provide slopes no steeper than 1 to $2\frac{1}{2}$, with grinding in the direction of applied stress, and weld soundness established by nondestructive inspection: (a) AASHTO M270 Grades 100/100W (ASTM A709) base metal (b) Other base metals	 T or Rev T or Rev	 B′ B	 11, 12 11, 12
	Base metal and weld metal in or adjacent to full penetration groove weld splices, with or without transitions having slopes no greater than 1 to $2\frac{1}{2}$, when the reinforcement is not removed and weld soundness is established by nondestructive inspection.	T or Rev	C	8, 10, 11, 12
Groove-welded attachments— longitudinally loaded[b]	Base metal adjacent to details attached by full or partial penetration groove welds when the detail length, L, in the direction of stress is less than 2 in.	T or Rev	C	6, 15
	Base metal adjacent to details attached by full or partial penetration groove welds when the detail length, L, in the direction of stress is between 2 in. and 12 times the plate thickness but less than 4 in.	T or Rev	D	15
	Base metal adjacent to details attached by full or partial penetration groove welds when the detail length, L, in the direction of stress is greater than 12 times the plate thickness or greater than 4 in.: (a) Detail thickness < 1.0 in. (b) Detail thickness ≥ 1.0 in.	 T or Rev T or Rev	 E E′	 15 15
	Base metal adjacent to details attached by full or partial penetration groove welds with a transition radius, R, regardless of the detail length:			

(continued)

General condition	Situation	Kind of stress	Stress category (See Table 10.3.1A)	Illustrative example (See Fig. 10.3.1C)
	With the end welds ground smooth	T or Rev		16
	(a) Transition radius ≥ 24 in.		B	
	(b) 24 in. > transition radius ≥ 6 in.		C	
	(c) 6 in. > transition radius ≥ 2 in.		D	
	(d) 2 in. > transition radius ≥ 0 in.		E	
	For all transition radii without end welds ground smooth.	T or Rev	E	16
Groove-welded attachments— transversely loaded[b,c]	Detail base metal attached by full penetration groove welds with a transition radius, R, regardless of the detail length and with weld soundness transverse to the direction of stress established by nondestructive inspection:			
	With equal plate thickness and reinforcement removed	T or Rev		16
	(a) Transition radius ≥ 24 in.		B	
	(b) 24 in. > transition radius ≥ 6 in.		C	
	(c) 6 in. > transition radius ≥ 2 in.		D	
	(d) 2 in. > transition radius ≥ 0 in.		E	
	With equal plate thickness and reinforcement not removed	T or Rev		16
	(a) Transition radius ≥ 6 in.		C	
	(b) 6 in. > transition radius ≥ 2 in.		D	
	(c) 2 in. > transition radius ≥ 0 in.		E	
	With equal plate thickness and reinforcement removed	T or Rev		16
	(a) Transition radius ≥ 2 in.		D	
	(b) 2 in. > transition radius ≥ 0 in.		E	
	For all transition radii with unequal plate thickness and reinforcement not removed.	T or Rev	E	16
Fillet-welded connections	Base metal at details connected with transversely loaded welds, with the welds perpendicular to the direction of stress:			
	(a) Detail thickness ≤ 0.5 in.	T or Rev	C	14
	(b) Detail thickness > 0.5 in.	T or Rev	See note[d]	
	Base metal at intermittent fillet welds.	T or Rev	E	—
	Shear stress on throat of fillet welds.	Shear	F	9
Fillet-welded attachments— longitudinally loaded[b,c,e]	Base metal adjacent to details attached by fillet welds with length, L, in the direction of stress is less than 2 in. and stud-type shear connectors.	T or Rev	C	15, 17, 18, 20
	Base metal adjacent to details attached by fillet welds with length, L, in the direction of stress between 2 in. and 12 times the plate thickness but less than 4 in.	T or Rev	D	15, 17
	Base metal adjacent to details attached by fillet welds with length, L, in the direction of stress			

(*continued*)

General condition	Situation	Kind of stress	Stress category (See Table 10.3.1A)	Illustrative example (See Fig. 10.3.1C)
	greater than 12 times the plate thickness or greater than 4 in.			
	(a) Detail thickness < 1.0 in.	T or Rev	E	7, 9, 15, 17
	(b) Detail thickness ≥ 1.0 in.	T or Rev	E′	7, 9, 15
	Base metal adjacent to details attached by fillet welds with a transition radius, R, regardless of the detail length:			
	With the end welds ground smooth	T or Rev		16
	(a) Transition radius ≥ 2 in.		D	
	(b) 2 in. > transition radius ≥ 0 in.		E	
	For all transition radii without the end welds ground smooth.	T or Rev	E	16
Fillet-welded attachments— transversely loaded with the weld in the direction of principal stress[b,e]	Detail base metal attached by fillet welds with a transition radius, R, regardless of the detail length (shear stress on the throat of fillet welds governed by Category F):			
	With the end welds ground smooth	T or Rev		16
	(a) Transition radius ≥ 2 in.		D	
	(b) 2 in. > transition radius ≥ 0 in.		E	
	For all transition radii without the end welds ground smooth.	T or Rev	E	16
Mechanically fastened connections	Base metal at gross section of high-strength bolted slip-resistant connections, except axially loaded joints which induce out-of-plane bending in connecting materials.	T or Rev	B	21
	Base metal at net section of high-strength bolted bearing-type connections.	T or Rev	B	21
	Base metal at net section of riveted connections.	T or Rev	D	21
	Base metal at the net section of eye-bar head, or pin plate.	T	E	23, 24
Eye-bar or pin plates	Base metal in the shank of eye-bars, or through the gross section of pin plates with:			
	(a) Rolled or smoothly ground surfaces	T	A	23, 24
	(b) Flame-cut edges	T	B	23, 24

[a] "T" signifies range in tensile stress only; "Rev" signifies a range of stress involving both tension and compression during a stress cycle.

[b] "Longitudinally loaded" signifies direction of applied stress is parallel to the longitudinal axis of the weld. "Transversely loaded" signifies direction of applied stress is perpendicular to the longitudinal axis of the weld.

[c] Transversely loaded partial penetration groove welds are prohibited.

[d] Allowable fatigue stress range on throat of fillet welds transversely loaded is a function of the effective throat and plate thickness. (See Frank, K. H., and Fisher, J. W., "Fatigue strength of Fillet Welded Cruciform Joints," *Journal of the Structural Division,* ASCE, Vol. 105, No. ST9, September 1979.)

$$S_r = S_r^c \left(\frac{0.06 + 0.79H/t_p}{1.1(t_p)^{1/6}} \right)$$

where S_r^c is equal to the allowable stress range for Category C given in Table 10.3.1A. This assumes no penetration at the weld root.

[e] Gusset plates attached to girder flange surfaces with only transverse fillet welds are prohibited.

[f] See Watter, F., Albrecht, P., and Sahli, A. H., "End-Bolted Cover Plates," *Journal of Structural Engineering,* ASCE, Vol. 111, No. 6, June 1985, pp. 1235–1249.

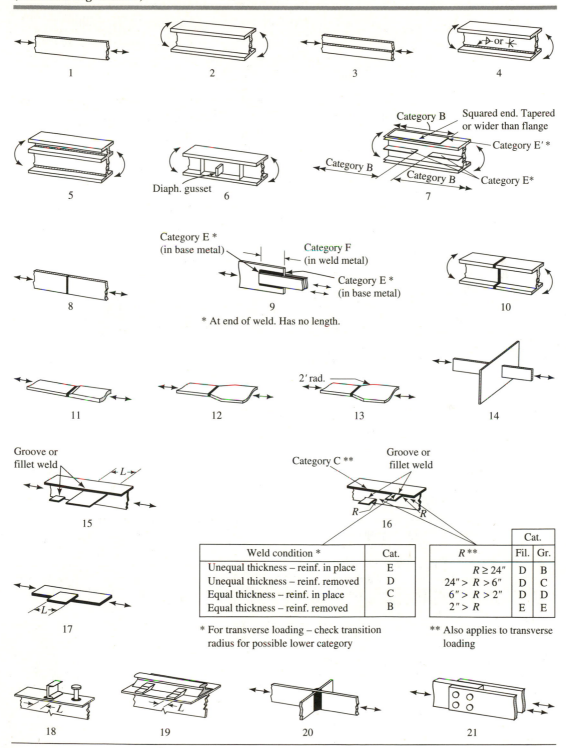

Category B — Squared end. Tapered or wider than flange

Category E′ *

Category B

Category B

Category E*

Diaph. gusset 6

Category E *
(in base metal)

Category F
(in weld metal)

Category E *
(in base metal)

* At end of weld. Has no length.

Groove or fillet weld

← L →

Category C **

Groove or fillet weld

R

R

2′ rad.

Cat.		
Weld condition *	Cat.	
Unequal thickness – reinf. in place	E	
Unequal thickness – reinf. removed	D	
Equal thickness – reinf. in place	C	
Equal thickness – reinf. removed	B	

R **	Fil.	Gr.
$R \geq 24''$	D	B
$24'' > R > 6''$	D	C
$6'' > R > 2''$	D	D
$2'' > R$	E	E

* For transverse loading – check transition radius for possible lower category

** Also applies to transverse loading

1   2   3   4   5   7   8   9   10   11   12   13   14   15   16   17   18   19   20   21

TABLE A.13.1
Stress cycles (AASHTO Table 10.3.2A)

Main (longitudinal) load-carrying members				
Type of road	Case	ADTT[a]	Truck loading	Lane loading[b]
Freeways, expressways, major highways, and streets	I	2500 or more	2,000,000[c]	500,000
Freeways, expressways, major highways, and streets	II	less than 2500	500,000	100,000
Other highways and streets not included in Case I or II	III		100,000	100,000

TABLE A.13.2
Stress cycles (AASHTO Table 10.3.2A)

Transverse members and details subjected to wheel loads			
Type of road	Case	ADTT[a]	Truck loading
Freeways, expressways, major highways, and streets	I	2500 or more	2,000,000
Freeways, expressways, major highways, and streets	II	less than 2500	2,000,000
Other highways and streets not included in Case I or II	III		500,000

* Structure types with multiload paths where a single fracture in a member cannot lead to collapse. For example, a simply supported single-span multibeam bridge or a multi-element eye-bar truss member has redundant load paths.

[a] The range of stress is defined as the algebraic difference between the maximum stress and the minimum stress. Tension stress is considered to have the opposite algebraic sign from compression stress.

[b] For transverse stiffener welds on girder webs or flanges.

[c] Partial-length welded cover plates shall not be used on flanges more than 0.8 in. thick for nonredundant load path structures.

TABLE A.14
Values of modular ratio, n (AASHTO 10.38.1.3)

f_c' (psi)	n	f_c' (psi)	n
2000–2300	11	3600–4500	8
2400–2800	10	4600–5900	7
2900–3500	9	Over 6000	6

TABLE A.15

Review of rectangular beams by the service load method

$k = [pn + (pn)^2]^{0.5} - pn; \quad j = 1 - \frac{1}{3}k$

	$n = 7$		$n = 8$		$n = 9$		$n = 10$	
p	k	j	k	j	k	j	k	j
0.0010	0.112	0.963	0.119	0.960	0.125	0.958	0.132	0.956
0.0020	0.154	0.949	0.164	0.945	0.173	0.942	0.181	0.940
0.0030	0.185	0.938	0.196	0.935	0.207	0.931	0.217	0.928
0.0040	0.210	0.930	0.223	0.926	0.235	0.922	0.246	0.918
0.0050	0.232	0.923	0.246	0.918	0.258	0.914	0.270	0.910
0.0054	0.240	0.920	0.254	0.915	0.267	0.911	0.279	0.907
0.0058	0.247	0.918	0.262	0.913	0.275	0.908	0.287	0.904
0.0062	0.254	0.915	0.269	0.910	0.283	0.906	0.296	0.901
0.0066	0.261	0.913	0.276	0.908	0.290	0.903	0.303	0.899
0.0070	0.268	0.911	0.283	0.906	0.298	0.901	0.311	0.896
0.0072	0.271	0.910	0.287	0.904	0.301	0.900	0.314	0.895
0.0074	0.274	0.909	0.290	0.903	0.304	0.899	0.318	0.894
0.0076	0.277	0.908	0.293	0.902	0.308	0.897	0.321	0.893
0.0078	0.280	0.907	0.296	0.901	0.311	0.896	0.325	0.892
0.0080	0.283	0.906	0.299	0.900	0.314	0.895	0.328	0.891
0.0082	0.286	0.905	0.303	0.899	0.317	0.894	0.331	0.890
0.0084	0.289	0.904	0.306	0.898	0.321	0.893	0.334	0.889
0.0086	0.292	0.903	0.308	0.897	0.324	0.892	0.338	0.887
0.0088	0.295	0.902	0.311	0.896	0.327	0.891	0.341	0.886
0.0090	0.298	0.901	0.314	0.895	0.330	0.890	0.344	0.885
0.0092	0.300	0.900	0.317	0.894	0.332	0.889	0.347	0.884
0.0094	0.303	0.899	0.320	0.893	0.335	0.888	0.350	0.883
0.0096	0.306	0.898	0.323	0.892	0.338	0.887	0.353	0.882
0.0098	0.308	0.897	0.325	0.892	0.341	0.886	0.355	0.882
0.0100	0.311	0.896	0.328	0.891	0.344	0.885	0.358	0.881
0.0104	0.316	0.895	0.333	0.889	0.349	0.884	0.364	0.879
0.0108	0.321	0.893	0.338	0.887	0.354	0.882	0.369	0.877
0.0112	0.325	0.892	0.343	0.886	0.359	0.880	0.374	0.875
0.0116	0.330	0.890	0.348	0.884	0.364	0.879	0.379	0.874
0.0120	0.334	0.889	0.353	0.882	0.369	0.877	0.384	0.872
0.0124	0.339	0.887	0.357	0.881	0.374	0.875	0.389	0.870
0.0128	0.343	0.886	0.362	0.879	0.378	0.874	0.394	0.869
0.0132	0.347	0.884	0.366	0.878	0.383	0.872	0.398	0.867
0.0136	0.351	0.883	0.370	0.877	0.387	0.871	0.403	0.866
0.0140	0.355	0.882	0.374	0.875	0.392	0.869	0.407	0.864
0.0144	0.359	0.880	0.378	0.874	0.396	0.868	0.412	0.863
0.0148	0.363	0.879	0.382	0.873	0.400	0.867	0.416	0.861
0.0152	0.367	0.878	0.386	0.871	0.404	0.865	0.420	0.860
0.0156	0.371	0.876	0.390	0.870	0.408	0.864	0.424	0.859
0.0160	0.374	0.875	0.394	0.869	0.412	0.863	0.428	0.857
0.0170	0.383	0.872	0.403	0.866	0.421	0.860	0.437	0.854
0.0180	0.392	0.869	0.412	0.863	0.430	0.857	0.446	0.851
0.0190	0.400	0.867	0.420	0.860	0.438	0.854	0.455	0.848
0.0200	0.407	0.864	0.428	0.857	0.446	0.851	0.463	0.846

TABLE A.16
Design coefficients for rectangular beams

n and f_c'	f_s (psi)	f_c (psi)	k	j	ρ_s	R (psi)
10 (2500)	20,000	1000	0.333	0.889	0.0083	148
		1125	0.360	0.880	0.0101	178
	24,000	1000	0.294	0.902	0.0061	133
		1125	0.319	0.894	0.0075	160
9 (3000)	20,000	1200	0.351	0.883	0.0105	186
		1350	0.377	0.874	0.0128	223
	24,000	1200	0.310	0.897	0.0078	167
		1350	0.336	0.888	0.0095	201
8 (4000)	20,000	1600	0.390	0.870	0.0156	272
		1800	0.419	0.860	0.0188	324
	24,000	1600	0.348	0.884	0.0116	246
		1800	0.375	0.875	0.0141	295
7 (5000)	20,000	2000	0.412	0.863	0.0206	355
		2250	0.441	0.853	0.0248	423
	24,000	2000	0.368	0.877	0.0154	323
		2250	0.396	0.868	0.0186	387

$$k = \frac{n}{(n+r)}; \qquad j = 1 - \frac{k}{3}; \qquad \rho_s = \frac{n}{2r(n+r)}; \qquad R = \tfrac{1}{2} f_c k j$$

where $\quad r = \dfrac{f_s}{f_c}; \qquad M = Rbd^2$

TABLE A.17
Values of flexural resistance factor

$$\frac{M_u}{\phi bd^2} = \rho f_y \left[1 - 0.60 \left(\frac{\rho f_y}{f_c'} \right) \right]$$

ρ	$f_y = 40,000$				$f_y = 60,000$			
	3000	4000	5000	6000	3000	4000	5000	6000
0.0000	0	0	0	0	0	0	0	0
0.0005	20	20	20	20	30	30	30	30
0.0010	40	40	40	40	59	59	60	60
0.0015	59	59	60	60	88	89	89	89
0.0020	79	79	79	79	117	118	118	119
0.0025	98	99	99	99	146	147	147	148
0.0030	117	118	118	119	174	175	176	177
0.0035	136	137	138	138	201	203	205	206
0.0040	155	156	157	157	228	231	233	234
0.0045	174	175	176	177	255	259	261	263
0.0050	192	194	195	196	282	287	289	291
0.0055	210	213	214	215	308	314	317	319
0.0060	228	231	233	234	334	341	344	347

(continued)

TABLE A.17
(*continued*)

ρ	$f_y = 40,000$				$f_y = 60,000$			
	3000	**4000**	**5000**	**6000**	**3000**	**4000**	**5000**	**6000**
0.0065	246	250	252	253	360	367	372	375
0.0070	264	268	271	272	385	394	399	402
0.0075	282	287	289	291	410	420	425	430
0.0080	300	305	308	310	434	445	452	457
0.0085	317	323	326	328	458	471	478	484
0.0090	334	341	344	347	482	496	505	511
0.0095	351	358	363	366	505	521	531	538
0.0100	368	376	381	384	528	546	556	564
0.0105	385	394	399	402	551	570	582	590
0.0110	401	411	417	421	573	595	607	616
0.0115	418	428	435	439	595	619	632	642
0.0120	434	445	452	457	616	642	657	668
0.0125	450	463	470	475	638	666	682	694
0.0130	466	479	488	493	658	689	706	719
0.0135	482	496	505	511	679	712	730	744
0.0140	497	513	522	529	699	734	754	769
0.0145	513	530	540	546	719	756	778	794
0.0150	528	546	557	564	738	779	802	819
0.0155	543	562	574	582	757	800	825	844
0.0160	558	579	591	599	776	822	848	868
0.0165	573	595	608	616	794	843	871	892
0.0170	588	611	625	634	812	864	894	916
0.0175	602	627	641	651	830	885	916	940
0.0180	616	642	658	668	847	905	938	963
0.0185	630	658	674	685	864	925	960	987
0.0190	644	673	691	702	880	945	982	1010
0.0195	658	689	707	719	896	965	1004	1033
0.0200	672	704	723	736	912	984	1025	1056
0.0050	192	194	195	196	282	287	289	291
0.0060	228	231	233	234	334	341	344	347
0.0070	264	268	271	272	385	394	399	402
0.0080	300	305	308	310	434	445	452	457
0.0090	334	341	344	347	482	496	505	511
0.0100	368	376	381	384	528	546	556	564
0.0110	401	411	417	421	573	595	607	616
0.0120	434	445	452	457	616	642	657	668
0.0130	466	479	488	493	658	689	706	719
0.0140	497	513	522	529	699	734	754	769
0.0150	528	546	557	564	738	779	802	819
0.0160	558	579	591	599	776	822	848	868
0.0170	588	611	625	634	812	864	894	916
0.0180	616	642	658	668	847	905	938	963
0.0190	644	673	691	702	880	945	982	1010
0.0200	672	704	723	736	912	984	1025	1056
0.0210	699	734	755	769	942	1022	1067	1101
0.0220	725	764	787	803		1059	1108	1146
0.0230	751	793	818	835		1094	1149	1190
0.0240	776	822	849	868		1129	1188	1233
0.0250	800	850	880	900		1163	1227	1275

(*continued*)

TABLE A.17
(*continued*)

ρ	$f_y = 40,000$				$f_y = 60,000$			
	3000	**4000**	**5000**	**6000**	**3000**	**4000**	**5000**	**6000**
0.0260	824	878	910	932		1195	1264	1317
0.0270	847	905	940	963		1226	1301	1358
0.0280	869	932	969	995		1257	1337	1398
0.0290	891	958	999	1025			1372	1437
0.0300	912	984	1027	1056			1406	1476
0.0310	932	1009	1055	1086			1440	1514
0.0320	952	1034	1083	1116			1472	1551
0.0330	972	1059	1111	1146			1504	1588
0.0340	990	1083	1138	1175				1624
0.0350	1008	1106	1165	1204				1659
0.0360	1025	1129	1191	1233				1693
0.0370	1042	1151	1217	1261				1727
0.0380		1173	1243	1289				
0.0390		1195	1268	1317				
0.0400		1216	1293	1344				

TABLE A.18
Limiting steel ratios for flexural design

f_y	f_c'	β_1	$\rho_b{}^*$	$\rho_{max} = 0.75\rho_b$	$\rho_{min} = 200/f_y$
40,000	3000	0.85	0.0371	0.0278	0.0050
40,000	4000	0.85	0.0495	0.0371	0.0050
40,000	5000	0.80	0.0582	0.0437	0.0050
40,000	6000	0.75	0.0655	0.0491	0.0050
40,000	7000	0.70	0.0713	0.0535	0.0050
40,000	8000	0.65	0.0757	0.0568	0.0050
50,000	3000	0.85	0.0275	0.0206	0.0040
50,000	4000	0.85	0.0367	0.0275	0.0040
50,000	5000	0.80	0.0432	0.0324	0.0040
50,000	6000	0.75	0.0486	0.0364	0.0040
50,000	7000	0.70	0.0529	0.0397	0.0040
50,000	8000	0.65	0.0561	0.0421	0.0040
60,000	3000	0.85	0.0214	0.0160	0.0033
60,000	4000	0.85	0.0285	0.0214	0.0033
60,000	5000	0.80	0.0335	0.0252	0.0033
60,000	6000	0.75	0.0377	0.0283	0.0033
60,000	7000	0.70	0.0411	0.0308	0.0033
60,000	8000	0.65	0.0436	0.0327	0.0033
80,000	3000	0.85	0.0141	0.0106	0.0025
80,000	4000	0.85	0.0188	0.0141	0.0025
80,000	5000	0.80	0.0221	0.0166	0.0025
80,000	6000	0.75	0.0249	0.0187	0.0025
80,000	7000	0.70	0.0271	0.0203	0.0025
80,000	8000	0.65	0.0288	0.0216	0.0025

$$^*\rho_b = \frac{0.85\beta_1 f_c'}{f_y}\left(\frac{87,000}{87,000 + f_y}\right)$$

TABLE A.19
Spacing of bars for slab reinforcement (in.² per ft)

Spacing	Bar no.								
(in.)	3	4	5	6	7	8	9	10	11
3	0.44	0.78	1.23	1.77	2.40	3.14	4.00	5.06	6.25
3.5	0.38	0.67	1.05	1.51	2.06	2.69	3.43	4.34	5.36
4	0.33	0.59	0.92	1.32	1.80	2.36	3.00	3.80	4.68
4.5	0.29	0.52	0.82	1.18	1.60	2.09	2.67	3.37	4.17
5	0.26	0.47	0.74	1.06	1.44	1.88	2.40	3.04	3.75
5.5	0.24	0.43	0.67	0.96	1.31	1.71	2.18	2.76	3.41
6	0.22	0.39	0.61	0.88	1.20	1.57	2.00	2.53	3.12
6.5	0.20	0.36	0.57	0.82	1.11	1.45	1.85	2.34	2.89
7	0.19	0.34	0.53	0.76	1.03	1.35	1.71	2.17	2.68
7.5	0.18	0.31	0.49	0.71	0.96	1.26	1.60	2.02	2.50
8	0.17	0.29	0.46	0.66	0.90	1.18	1.50	1.89	2.34
9	0.15	0.26	0.41	0.59	0.80	1.05	1.33	1.69	2.08
10	0.13	0.24	0.37	0.53	0.72	0.94	1.20	1.52	1.87
11	0.12	0.22	0.34	0.48	0.65	0.86	1.09	1.39	1.70
12	0.11	0.20	0.31	0.44	0.60	0.78	1.00	1.27	1.56
13	0.10	0.18	0.29	0.41	0.55	0.73	0.92	1.17	1.44
14	0.09	0.17	0.27	0.38	0.51	0.68	0.86	1.09	1.34
15	0.09	0.16	0.25	0.35	0.48	0.63	0.80	1.02	1.25
16	0.08	0.15	0.23	0.33	0.45	0.59	0.75	0.95	1.17
17	0.08	0.14	0.22	0.31	0.42	0.56	0.71	0.90	1.10
18	0.07	0.13	0.21	0.29	0.40	0.53	0.67	0.85	1.04

TABLE A.20
Areas of groups of standard bars (in.²)

No. of	Bar no.									
bars	4	5	6	7	8	9	10	11	14	18
1	0.20	0.31	0.44	0.60	0.79	1.00	1.27	1.56	2.25	4.00
2	0.39	0.61	0.88	1.20	1.57	2.00	2.53	3.12	4.50	8.00
3	0.58	0.91	1.32	1.80	2.35	3.00	3.79	4.68	6.75	12.00
4	0.78	1.23	1.77	2.41	3.14	4.00	5.06	6.25	9.00	16.00
5	0.98	1.53	2.21	3.01	3.93	5.00	6.33	7.81	11.25	20.00
6	1.18	1.84	2.65	3.61	4.71	6.00	7.59	9.37	13.50	24.00
7	1.37	2.15	3.09	4.21	5.50	7.00	8.86	10.94	15.75	28.00
8	1.57	2.45	3.53	4.81	6.28	8.00	10.12	12.50	18.00	32.00
9	1.77	2.76	3.98	5.41	7.07	9.00	11.39	14.06	20.25	36.00
10	1.96	3.07	4.42	6.01	7.85	10.00	12.66	15.62	22.50	40.00
11	2.16	3.37	4.86	6.61	8.64	11.00	13.92	17.19	24.75	44.00
12	2.36	3.68	5.30	7.22	9.43	12.00	15.19	18.75	27.00	48.00

TABLE A.21
Minimum required beam widths (in.)[a]

Number of bars in one layer	Bar no.							
	3 and 4	5	6	7	8	9	10	11
2	6.0	6.0	6.5	6.5	7.0	7.5	8.0	8.0
3	7.5	8.0	8.0	8.5	9.0	9.5	10.5	11.0
4	9.0	9.5	10.0	10.5	11.0	12.0	13.0	14.0
5	10.5	11.0	11.5	12.5	13.0	14.0	15.5	16.5
6	12.0	12.5	13.5	14.0	15.0	16.5	18.0	19.5
7	13.5	14.5	15.0	16.0	17.0	18.5	20.5	22.5
8	15.0	16.0	17.0	18.0	19.0	21.0	23.0	25.0
9	16.5	17.5	18.5	20.0	21.0	23.0	25.5	28.0
10	18.0	19.0	20.5	21.5	23.0	25.5	28.0	31.0

[a] Tabulated values based on No. 3 stirrups, minimum clear distance of 1 in., and $1\frac{1}{2}$-in. cover.

TABLE A.22
Maximum number of bars in a single layer in a beam

$\frac{3}{4}$-in. maximum size aggregate, No. 4 stirrups[a]

Bar no.	Beam width b_w (in.)											
	8	10	12	14	16	18	20	22	24	26	28	30
5	2	4	5	6	7	8	10	11	12	13	15	16
6	2	3	4	6	7	8	9	10	11	12	14	15
7	2	3	4	5	6	7	8	9	10	11	12	13
8	2	3	4	5	6	7	8	9	10	11	12	13
9	1	2	3	4	5	6	7	8	9	9	10	11
10	1	2	3	4	5	6	6	7	8	9	10	10
11	1	2	3	3	4	5	5	6	7	8	8	9
14	1	2	2	3	3	4	5	5	6	6	7	8
18[b]	1	1	2	2	3	3	4	4	4	5	5	6

1-in. maximum size aggregate, No. 4 stirrups[a]

Bar no.	Beam width b_w (in.)											
	8	10	12	14	16	18	20	22	24	26	28	30
5	2	3	4	5	6	7	8	9	10	11	12	13
6	2	3	4	5	6	7	8	9	9	10	11	12
7	1	2	3	4	5	6	7	8	9	10	10	11
8	1	2	3	4	5	6	7	7	8	9	10	11
9	1	2	3	4	5	6	7	7	8	9	9	10
10	1	2	3	4	5	6	6	7	7	8	9	10

[a] Minimum concrete cover assumed to be 1.5 in. to the No. 4 stirrup.
[b] Tension reinforcement must be well distributed in flexural zone in accordance with AASHTO 8.16.8.4, Eq. 8.61.

Source: Adapted from *ACI Detailing Manual,* ACI Special Pub. SP-66(88), ACI, Farmington Hills, MI, 1988. Used by permission of American Concrete Institute.

TABLE A.23
Gross moments of inertia for T-beams

| | | | | | Values of C for $I_g = C(bh^3/12)$ | | | | | | |
| | | | | | b'/b | | | | | | | |
t/h	0.10	0.12	0.14	0.16	0.18	0.20	0.22	0.24	0.26	0.28	0.30	t/h
0.05	0.18414	0.20728	0.22917	0.25018	0.27052	0.29035	0.30979	0.32892	0.34779	0.36646	0.38495	0.05
0.06	0.19314	0.21739	0.24013	0.26178	0.28260	0.30278	0.32246	0.34174	0.36069	0.37936	0.39781	0.06
0.07	0.20059	0.22592	0.24953	0.27186	0.29321	0.31379	0.33377	0.35325	0.37233	0.39107	0.40953	0.07
0.08	0.20675	0.23311	0.25757	0.28060	0.30250	0.32352	0.34383	0.36357	0.38282	0.40167	0.42019	0.08
0.09	0.21183	0.23917	0.26445	0.28816	0.31063	0.33210	0.35278	0.37279	0.39225	0.41125	0.42986	0.09
0.10	0.21601	0.24425	0.27032	0.29469	0.31772	0.33966	0.36071	0.38102	0.40072	0.41989	0.43862	0.10
0.11	0.21942	0.24849	0.27530	0.30031	0.32388	0.34628	0.36772	0.38835	0.40830	0.42766	0.44654	0.11
0.12	0.22218	0.25202	0.27950	0.30512	0.32922	0.35208	0.37390	0.39485	0.41506	0.43464	0.45367	0.12
0.13	0.22441	0.25492	0.28304	0.30922	0.33383	0.35712	0.37932	0.40059	0.42107	0.44087	0.46008	0.13
0.14	0.22617	0.25729	0.28599	0.31270	0.33778	0.36149	0.38406	0.40565	0.42640	0.44643	0.46582	0.14
0.15	0.22755	0.25921	0.28842	0.31562	0.34115	0.36526	0.38819	0.41009	0.43111	0.45136	0.47095	0.15
0.16	0.22861	0.26074	0.29042	0.31806	0.34400	0.36849	0.39175	0.41396	0.43524	0.45572	0.47550	0.16
0.17	0.22940	0.26194	0.29203	0.32007	0.34639	0.37123	0.39482	0.41731	0.43885	0.45956	0.47953	0.17
0.18	0.22998	0.26286	0.29331	0.32171	0.34837	0.37355	0.39743	0.42020	0.44199	0.46291	0.48307	0.18
0.19	0.23037	0.26354	0.29431	0.32303	0.35000	0.37548	0.39964	0.42267	0.44469	0.46583	0.48618	0.19
0.20	0.23063	0.26403	0.29506	0.32407	0.35132	0.37707	0.40149	0.42476	0.44700	0.46834	0.48887	0.20
0.21	0.23078	0.26437	0.29562	0.32487	0.35237	0.37836	0.40302	0.42651	0.44896	0.47049	0.49120	0.21
0.22	0.23085	0.26458	0.29602	0.32546	0.35318	0.37939	0.40426	0.42796	0.45061	0.47232	0.49319	0.22
0.23	0.23088	0.26471	0.29628	0.32589	0.35379	0.38019	0.40526	0.42914	0.45197	0.47385	0.49488	0.23
0.24	0.23089	0.26476	0.29644	0.32618	0.35424	0.38080	0.40604	0.43009	0.45308	0.47511	0.49629	0.24
0.25	0.23089	0.26478	0.29652	0.32637	0.35455	0.38125	0.40663	0.43083	0.45396	0.47614	0.49745	0.25
0.26	0.23091	0.26478	0.29655	0.32647	0.35475	0.38156	0.40707	0.43139	0.45466	0.47696	0.49840	0.26
0.27	0.23098	0.26479	0.29656	0.32652	0.35486	0.38177	0.40737	0.43181	0.45519	0.47760	0.49915	0.27
0.28	0.23109	0.26482	0.29656	0.32653	0.35492	0.38188	0.40757	0.43210	0.45557	0.47809	0.49973	0.28
0.29	0.23129	0.26490	0.29658	0.32653	0.35494	0.38194	0.40769	0.43229	0.45584	0.47844	0.50017	0.29
0.30	0.23157	0.26504	0.29663	0.32654	0.35494	0.38196	0.40775	0.43240	0.45601	0.47869	0.50049	0.30
0.31	0.23196	0.26525	0.29673	0.32658	0.35494	0.38197	0.40777	0.43245	0.45611	0.47884	0.50070	0.31
0.32	0.23246	0.26556	0.29690	0.32666	0.35497	0.38197	0.40777	0.43247	0.45616	0.47893	0.50084	0.32
0.33	0.23309	0.26598	0.29716	0.32680	0.35504	0.38199	0.40777	0.43247	0.45618	0.47897	0.50091	0.33
0.34	0.23387	0.26651	0.29752	0.32703	0.35517	0.38206	0.40780	0.43248	0.45618	0.47898	0.50094	0.34
0.35	0.23480	0.26719	0.29799	0.32734	0.35537	0.38218	0.40786	0.43250	0.45619	0.47898	0.50095	0.35
0.36	0.23589	0.26800	0.29859	0.32777	0.35566	0.38236	0.40797	0.43256	0.45621	0.47899	0.50095	0.36
0.37	0.23716	0.26898	0.29933	0.32832	0.35605	0.38264	0.40815	0.43268	0.45628	0.47902	0.50096	0.37
0.38	0.23861	0.27013	0.30022	0.32900	0.35657	0.38301	0.40842	0.43286	0.45639	0.47909	0.50100	0.38
0.39	0.24027	0.27145	0.30127	0.32983	0.35721	0.38350	0.40879	0.43312	0.45658	0.47921	0.50108	0.39
0.40	0.24212	0.27297	0.30250	0.33082	0.35800	0.38412	0.40926	0.43349	0.45685	0.47941	0.50121	0.40

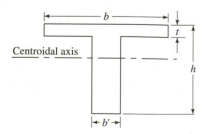

TABLE A.24
Concrete stresses as functions of f_c' and $\sqrt{f_c'}$

f_c'	$0.45f_c'$	$0.6f_c'$	$\sqrt{f_c'}$	$0.6\sqrt{f_c'}$	$2\sqrt{f_c'}$	$3\sqrt{f_c'}$	$3.5\sqrt{f_c'}$	$4\sqrt{f_c'}$	$5\sqrt{f_c'}$	$6\sqrt{f_c'}$	$7.5\sqrt{f_c'}$	$12\sqrt{f_c'}$
3000	1350	1800	55	33	110	164	192	219	274	329	411	657
3500	1575	2100	59	35	118	177	207	237	296	355	444	710
4000	1800	2400	63	38	126	190	221	253	316	379	474	759
4500	2025	2700	67	40	134	201	235	268	335	402	503	805
5000	2250	3000	71	42	141	212	247	283	354	424	530	849
5500	2475	3300	74	44	148	222	260	297	371	445	556	890
6000	2700	3600	77	46	155	232	271	310	387	465	581	930
6500	2925	3900	81	48	161	242	282	322	403	484	605	967
7000	3150	4200	84	50	167	251	293	335	418	502	627	1004
7500	3375	4500	87	52	173	260	303	346	433	520	650	1039
8000	3600	4800	89	54	179	268	313	358	447	537	671	1073

Adapted from *Post-Tensioned Box Girder Bridge Manual,* Post-Tensioning Institute, 1978, Phoenix, AZ. Reprinted with permission.

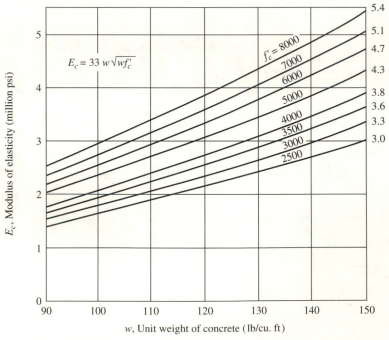

Concrete modulus of elasticity as affected by unit weight and strength

$E_c = 33\, w\sqrt{wf_c''}$

TABLE A.25

Properties and design strengths of prestressing strand and wire

Seven-wire, strand $f_{pu} = 270$ ksi				
Normal diameter (in.)	3/8	7/16	1/2	0.600
Area (sq in.)	0.085	0.115	0.153	0.217
Weight (plf)	0.29	0.39	0.52	0.74
$0.7 f_{pu} A_{ps}$ (kips)	16.1	21.7	28.9	41.0
$0.8 f_{pu} A_{ps}$ (kips)	18.4	24.8	33.0	46.9
$f_{pu} A_{ps}$ (kips)	23.0	31.0	41.3	58.6

Seven-wire, strand $f_{pu} = 250$ ksi						
Normal diameter (in.)	1/4	5/16	3/8	7/16	1/2	0.600
Area (sq in.)	0.036	0.058	0.080	0.108	0.144	0.215
Weight (plf)	0.12	0.20	0.27	0.37	0.49	0.74
$0.7 f_{pu} A_{ps}$ (kips)	6.3	10.2	14.0	18.9	25.2	37.6
$0.8 f_{pu} A_{ps}$ (kips)	7.2	11.6	16.0	21.6	28.8	43.0
$f_{pu} A_{ps}$ (kips)	9.0	14.5	20.0	27.0	36.0	54.0

Prestressing wire				
Diameter (in.)	0.192	0.196	0.25	0.276
Area (sq in.)	0.0289	0.0302	0.0491	0.0598
Weight (plf)	0.098	0.10	0.17	0.2
Ult. strength f_{pu} (ksi)	250	250	240	235
$0.7 f_{pu} A_{ps}$ (kips)	5.05	5.28	8.25	9.84
$0.8 f_{pu} A_{ps}$ (kips)	5.78	6.04	9.42	11.24
$f_{pu} A_{ps}$ (kips)	7.22	7.55	11.78	14.05

Adapted from *Post-Tensioned Box Girder Bridge Manual,* Post-Tensioned Institute, 1978, Phoenix, AZ. Reprinted with permission.

TABLE A.26
Allowable stresses (psi) in structural steel (AASHTO Table 10.32.1A)

Type	Structural carbon steel	High-strength low-alloy steel (Grade 50)	High-strength low-alloy steel (Grade 50W)	Quenched and tempered low-alloy steel	High yield strength quenched and tempered alloy steel[f]
AASHTO designation[e,h]	M270 Grade 36	M270 Grade 50	M270 Grade 50W	M270 Grade 70W	M270 Grade 100/100W
Equivalent ASTM designation[h]	A709 Grade 36	A709 Grade 50	A709 Grade 50W	A709 Grade 70W	A709 Grade 100/100W
Thickness of plates	Up to 4 in. incl.	Up to 4 in. incl.	Up to 4 in. incl.	Up to 4 in. incl.	Up to 2½ in. incl. / Over 2½ in. to 4 in. incl.
Shapes	All groups	All groups	All groups	Not applicable	Not applicable
Axial tension in members with no holes for high-strength bolts or rivets. ($0.55F_y$)	20,000	27,000	27,000	38,000	Not applicable
Use net section when member has any open holes larger than $1\frac{1}{4}$-in. diameter, such as perforations. ($0.46F_u$)	Not applicable	Not applicable	Not applicable	Not applicable	51,000 / 46,000
Axial tension in member with holes for high-strength bolts or rivets and tension in extreme fiber of rolled shapes, girders, and built-up sections subject to bending. Satisfy both gross and net section criteria. — Gross[i] section $0.55F_y$	20,000	27,000	27,000	38,000	Not applicable
Net section $0.50F_u$	29,000	32,500	35,000	45,000	Not applicable
Net section $0.46F_u$					51,000 / 46,000

1280

Axial compression, gross section: stiffeners of plate girders. Compression in splice material, gross section. — 20,000 | 27,000 | 27,000 | 38,000 | 55,000 | 49,000

Compression in extreme fibers of rolled shapes, girders, and built-up sections, subject to bending, gross section, when compression flange is:

(A) Supported laterally its full length by embedment in concrete $0.55F_y$ — 20,000 | 27,000 | 27,000 | 38,000 | 55,000 | 49,000

(B) Partially supported or is unsupported [a,b]

$$F_b = \frac{50 \times 10^6 C_b}{S_{xc}}\left(\frac{I_{yc}}{l}\right)\sqrt{0.772\frac{J}{I_{yc}} + 9.87\left(\frac{d}{l}\right)^2}$$

$$\leq 0.55F_y$$

$C_b = 1.75 + 1.05(M_1/M_2) + 0.3(M_1/M_2)^2 \leq$ 2.3 where M_1 is the smaller and M_2 the larger end moment in the unbraced segment of the beam; M_1/M_2 is positive when the moments cause reverse curvature and negative when bent in single curvature.

$C_b = 1.0$ for unbraced cantilevers and for members where the moment within a significant portion of the unbraced segment is greater than or equal to the larger of the segment end moments.

(continued)

1281

TABLE A.26
(*continued*)

		126.1	107	107	90.4	75.5	79.8
Compression in concentrically loaded columns[c]							
with $C_c = (2\pi^2 E/F_y)^{1/2}$ =							
when $KL/r \le C_c$		126.1	107	107	90.4	75.5	79.8
$F_a = \dfrac{F_y}{F.S.}\left[1 - \dfrac{(KL/r)^2 F_y}{4\pi^2 E}\right] =$		$16{,}980 - 0.53(L/r)^2$	$23{,}580 - 1.03(L/r)^2$	$23{,}580 - 1.03(L/r)^2$	$33{,}020 - 2.02(L/r)^2$	$47{,}170 - 4.12(L/r)^2$	$42{,}450 - 3.33(L/r)^2$
when $KL/r > C_c$							
$F_a = \pi^2 E/F.S.(KL/r)^2 =$ with F.S. = 2.12			$135{,}000{,}740/(KL/r)^2$				
Shear in girder webs, gross section	$F_v = 0.33F_y$	12,000	17,000	17,000	23,000	33,000	30,000
Bearing on milled stiffeners and other steel parts in contact (rivets and bolts excluded)	$0.80F_y$	29,000	40,000	40,000	56,000	80,000	72,000
Stress in extreme fiber of pins[d]	$0.80F_y$	29,000	40,000	40,000	56,000	80,000	72,000
Shear in pins	$F_v = 0.40F_y$	14,000	20,000	20,000	28,000	40,000	36,000
Bearing on pins not subject to rotation[g]	$0.80F_y$	29,000	40,000	40,000	56,000	80,000	72,000
Bearing on pins subject to rotation (such as used in rockers and hinges)	$0.40F_y$	14,000	20,000	20,000	28,000	40,000	36,000
Bearing on connected material at low carbon steel bolts (ASTM A307), turned bolts, ribbed bolts, and rivets (ASTM A502 Grades 1 and 2—governed by Table 10.32A)							

[a] Continuous or cantilever beams or girders may be proportioned for negative moment at interior supports for an allowable unit stress 20 percent higher than permitted by this formula but in no case exceeding allowable unit stress for compression flange supported its full length. If cover plates are used, the allowable static stress at the point of theoretical cutoff shall be as determined by the formula.

[b] l = length, in inches, of unsupported flange between lateral connections, knee braces, or other points of support.

I_{yc} = moment of inertia of compression flange about the vertical axis in the plane of the web in.[4]

d = depth of girder, in.

$J = \dfrac{[(bt^3)_c+(bt^3)_t+Dt_w^3]}{3}$ where b and t represent the flange width and thickness of the compression and tension flange, respectively (in.[4]).

S_{xc} = section modulus with respect to compression flange (in.[3]).

1282

[c] E = modulus of elasticity of steel
r = governing radius of gyration
L = actual unbraced length
K = effective length factor (see Appendix C)
$F.S.$ = factor of safety = 2.12

For graphic representation of these formulas, see Appendix C.

The formulas do not apply to members with variable moment of inertia. Procedures for designing members with variable moment of inertia can be found in the following references: *Engineering Journal*, AISC, January 1969, Vol. 6, No. 1, and October 1972, Vol. 9, No. 4; and *Steel Structures*, by William McGuire, 1968, Prentice Hall, Englewood Cliffs, New Jersey. For members with eccentric loading, see Article 10.36.

[d] See also Article 10.32.4.

[e] Except for the mandatory notch toughness and weldability requirements, the ASTM designations are similar to the AASHTO designations. Steels meeting the AASHTO requirements are prequalified for use in welded bridges.

[f] Quenched and tempered alloy steel structural shapes and seamless mechanical tubing meeting all mechanical and chemical requirements of A709 Grades 100/100W (except that the specified maximum tensile strength may be 140,000 psi for structural shapes and 145,000 psi for seamless mechanical tubing) shall be considered A709 Grades 100/100W steel.

[g] This shall apply to pins used primarily in axially loaded members, such as truss members and cable adjusting links. It shall not apply to pins used in members having rotation caused by expansion or deflection.

[h] M 270 Gr. 36 and A709 Gr. 36 are equivalent to M 183 and A36.
M 270 Gr. 50 and A709 Gr. 50 are equivalent to M 223 Gr. 50 and A572 Gr. 50.
M 270 Gr. 50W and A709 Gr. 50W are equivalent to M 222 and A588.
M 270 Gr. 50W and A709 Gr. 50W are equivalent to M 000 and A852.
M 270 Gr. 100/100W and A709 Gr. 100/100W are equivalent to M 244 and A514.

[i] When the area of holes deducted for high-strength bolts or rivets is more than 15 percent of the gross area, that area in excess of 15 percent shall be deducted from the gross area in determining stress on the gross section. In determining gross section, any open holes larger than $1\frac{1}{4}$-in. diameter, such as perforations, shall be deducted.

TABLE A.27

Nominal (or gross) areas of bolts, spacing, and edge distances

Description				
Diameter of bolt (in.)	$\frac{5}{8}$	$\frac{3}{4}$	$\frac{7}{8}$	1
Area of bolt (in.^{2})	0.3068	0.4418	0.6013	0.7854
Minimum c/c spacing (in.) (AASHTO 10.24.5.2)	$2\frac{1}{4}$	$2\frac{1}{2}$	3.0	$3\frac{1}{2}$
Minimum edge distance (in.) (AASHTO 10.24.7)				
From the center of a standard hole to a sheared or a flame-cut edge	$1\frac{1}{8}$	$1\frac{1}{4}$	$1\frac{1}{2}$	$1\frac{3}{4}$
From the center of a standard hole to a rolled or planed edge, except in flanges of beams and channels	1	$1\frac{1}{8}$	$1\frac{1}{4}$	$1\frac{1}{2}$
From the center of a standard hole to the edges of flanges of beams and channels	$\frac{7}{8}$	1	$1\frac{1}{8}$	$1\frac{1}{4}$

TABLE A.28

Allowable stress[a] on high-strength bolts or connected material (ksi), (AASHTO Interim, 1994, Table 10.32.3B)

Load condition	AASHTO M164 (ASTM A325)[h]	AASHTO M253 (ASTM A490)[h]
Applied static tension[b,c] shear, F_v, on bolt with threads in shear plane[d]	39.5 19	48.5 25
Bearing, F_p, on connected material with single bolt in line of force in a standard or short slotted hole	$0.9F_u$[e,f,g]	$0.9F_u$[e,f,g]
Bearing, F_p, on connected material with two or more bolts in line of force in standard or short slotted holes	$1.1F_u$[e,f,g]	$1.1F_u$[e,f]
Bearing, F_p, on connected material in long slotted holes	$0.9F_u$[e,f,g]	$0.9F_u$[e,f]

[a] Ultimate failure load divided by factor of safety.

[b] Bolts must be tensioned to requirements of Table 11.5A, Div. II.

[c] See Article 10.32.3.4 for bolts subject to tensile fatigue.

[d] If material thickness or joint details preclude threads in the shear plane, multiply tabulated values by 1.4.

[e] F_u = specified minimum tensile strength of connected part.

[f] Connections using high-strength bolts in slotted holes with load applied in a direction other than approximately normal (between 80 and 100 degrees) to the axis of the hole and connections with bolts in oversize holes shall be designed for resistance against slip in accordance with Article 10.32.3.2.1.

[g] Tabulated values apply when the distance L parallel to the line of force from the center of the bolt to the edge of the connected part is not less than $1\frac{1}{2}d$ and the distance from the center of a bolt to the center of an adjacent bolt is not less than $3d$.

[h] AASHTO M164 (ASTM A325) and AASHTO M253 (ASTM A490) high-strength bolts are available in three types, designated as Types 1, 2, or 3. Type 3 shall be required on the plans when using unpainted AASHTO M270 Grade 50W (ASTM A 709 Grade 50W).

TABLE A.29
Allowable load for slip-critical connections
(slip load per unit of bolt area (ksi)) (AASHTO Table 10.32.3C)

	Hole type and direction of load application							
	Any direction				Transverse		Parallel	
	Standard		Oversize and short slots		Long slots		Long slots	
Contact surface of bolted parts	AASHTO M164 (ASTM A325)	AASHTO M253 (ASTM A490)	AASHTO M164 (ASTM A325)	AASHTO M253 (ASTM A490)	AASHTO M164 (ASTM A325)	AASHTO M253 (ASTM A490)	AASHTO M164 (ASTM A325)	AASHTO M253 (ASTM A490)
Class A (slip coefficient 0.33) Clean mill scale and blast-cleaned surfaces with Class A coatings[a]	15.5	19	13.5	16	11	13.5	9	11.5
Class B (slip coefficient 0.50) Blast-cleaned surfaces and blast-cleaned surfaces with Class B coatings[a]	25	30.5	21.5	26	18	21.5	15.5	18
Class C (slip coefficient 0.40) Hot dip galvanized and rough-ended surfaces	20	24.5	17	20.5	14.5	17	12.5	14.5

[a] Coatings classified as Class A or Class B include those coatings that provide a mean slip coefficient not less than 0.33 or 0.50, respectively, as determined by "Testing Method to Determine the Slip Coefficient for Coatings Used in Bolted Joints." See Article 10.32.3.2.3.

TABLE A.30
Design strength of connectors (AASHTO Table 10.56A)

Type of fastener	Strength (ϕF)
Groove weld[a]	$1.00F_y$
Fillet weld[b]	$0.45F_u$
Low-carbon steel bolts	
ASTM A307	
Tension	30 ksi
Shear on bolt with	
threads in shear plane	22 ksi
Power-driven rivets	
ASTM A502	
Shear—Grade 1	25 ksi
Shear—Grade 2	30 ksi
High-strength bolts	
AASHTO M164	
(ASTM A325)	
Applied static tension[c]	67 ksi
Shear on bolt with	
threads in shear plane[d,e]	36 ksi
AASHTO M253	
(ASTM A490)	
Applied static tension[c]	84 ksi
Shear on bolt with	
threads in shear plane[d,e]	45 ksi

[a] F_y = yield point of connected material.
[b] F_u = minimum strength of the welding rod metal but not greater than the tensile strength of the connected parts.
[c] For M164 (A325) bolts, the tensile strength decreases for diameters greater than 1 in. The design value listed is for bolts up to 1 in. diameter. For diameters greater than 1 in., the design value shall be multiplied by 0.875.
[d] Tabulated values shall be reduced by 20 percent in bearing-type connections whose length between extreme fasteners in each of the spliced parts measured parallel to the line of axial force exceeds 50 in.
[e] If material thickness or joint details preclude threads in the shear plane, multiply values by 1.25.

TABLE A.31
Design slip resistance for slip-critical joints
Value of $\phi T_b \mu$ slip resistance per unit area of bolt (ksi), (AASHTO Table 10.57A)

	Hole type and direction of load application							
	Any direction				Transverse		Parallel	
	Standard		Oversize and short slots		Long slots		Long slots	
Contact surface of bolted parts	AASHTO M164 (ASTM A325)	AASHTO M253 (ASTM A490)	AASHTO M164 (ASTM A325)	AASHTO M253 (ASTM A490)	AASHTO M164 (ASTM A325)	AASHTO M253 (ASTM A490)	AASHTO M164 (ASTM A325)	AASHTO M253 (ASTM A490)
Class A (slip coefficient 0.33) Clean mill scale and blast-cleaned surfaces with Class A coatings[a]	21	27	18	23	15	19	13	16
Class B (slip coefficient 0.50) Blast-cleaned surfaces and blast-cleaned surfaces with Class B coatings[a]	32.5	41	28	35	23	28.5	19	24.5
Class C (slip coefficient 0.40) Hot dip galvanized and rough-ended surfaces	26	33	22	28	18	23	16	20

[a] Coatings classified as Class A or Class B include those coatings that provide a mean slip coefficient not less than 0.33 or 0.50, respectively, as determined by "Testing Method to Determine the Slip Coefficient for Coatings Used in Bolted Joints." See Article 10.32.2.3.

APPENDIX B

Moment Coefficients for Continuous Post-Tensioned Structures*

Tables are presented to simplify the computation of moments over the supports in continuous structures under post-tensioning loads. Coefficients are provided for two-span structures and for symmetric structures of three or more spans. Tendon profiles are parabolic segments. A procedure accounting for friction losses is included.

The bending moments in a beam continuous over several supports produced by post-tensioned prestressing tendons are usually computed by the equivalent load method as presented by Moorman.[1] All the forces between the tendon and the concrete are applied to the concrete beam, in effect as an exterior load, assuming the tendons to be omitted. The elastic analysis of continuous beams under these loads presents no theoretical difficulties; however, it is tedious if performed manually by moment distribution, slope deflection, or similar methods. Generally, these methods involve two steps: the computation of fixed end moments and the elastic distribution of these moments. The second step is explained in any text on structural analysis.[2] The computation of fixed end moments is simplified by various charts and tables. Formulas and graphs for a variety of conditions are presented by Parme and Paris[3] and tables for beams of constant cross section are presented by Bailey and Ferguson.[4]

This paper presents tables which simplify the bending moment computations for multispan beams with typical draped parabolic profile tendons. The restrictions are that the beams must be prismatic between supports; moreover, for three or more spans, the geometry of the structure must be symmetric. Except for the two-span case, coefficients are given only for tendon geometry that is symmetric about the centerline of the structure. Within these restrictions, the coefficients are given for a range of geometry parameters which covers the designs usually encountered. The determination of moments in beams with long tendons, where friction losses must be taken into account,

*From the paper "Moment Coefficients for Continuous Post-Tensioned Structures," in *J. Prestressed Concrete Institute,* 17(1), January–February, 1972, by P. Turula and C. L. Freyermuth, pp. 35–57.

is also considered, both for symmetric tensioning from both ends and for tensioning from only one end. The method presented here is not very cumbersome and should be suitable for general engineering use.

Problems beyond the scope of this paper, such as general variation of cross section of non-symmetric structures with more than two spans, can be analyzed by slope deflection methods with the fixed end moments computed using the curves developed by Parme and Paris.[3] Fixed end moments for cubic parabola tendon profiles can be computed using formulas presented by Fiesenheiser[5] and those for sine curve tendon profiles can be computed using graphs presented by Parme and Paris. The moments due to post-tensioning can also be obtained by using a general digital computer program for frame analysis, such as STRUDL,[6] if it allows members of the desired shape with the equivalent loads as the applied loading. None of these methods considers the continuity between the beam and its supporting columns, except for STRUDL, where this effect may be taken into account.

The load-balancing approach presented by Lin[7] is particularly applicable when the tendon profile in each span is one parabola, i.e., does not have a reversed curve over the supports. In this method, the equivalent load is considered to counteract a portion of the dead load, or the total dead load and a portion of the live load. For beams with reversed tendons, the methods can still be used in one of two ways:

1. As an exact method, add the equivalent load to the dead load and analyze the beam under the resulting "balanced" dead load. This method is rather tedious unless a suitable computer program is available.
2. As an approximate method, replace the actual tendon profile geometry throughout the span by a single parabola. In many cases, this will not be accurate enough for a final engineering analysis.

EQUIVALENT LOADS

The equivalent vertical distributed tendon load imposed on any point of the beam is computed as the product of the curvature of the tendon profile and the horizontal component of the tendon force at that point. It is usually accurate enough to consider the horizontal tendon force at each point equal to the total tendon force, particularly if the drape of the tendon profile is less than 4 percent of the span length.

The tendon profile in an interior span is in the shape of three parabolic segments, shown in Fig. 1(a) as ef, fgh, and hi. Segments ef and hi are the reversed parabolas. Points e, g, and i are the horizontal points of the parabolas, and points f and h are points of common tangency. The profile is assumed to be symmetric about the centerline of the span with its high point over the supports and low point at the span centerline.

The corresponding idealized structure, with the equivalent loads applied, is shown in Fig. 1(b). The magnitude of the upward distributed loads from the main portion of the tendon is

$$w = \frac{8Pc}{(1 - 2a)L_1^2} \tag{1}$$

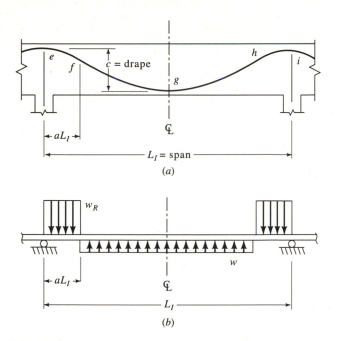

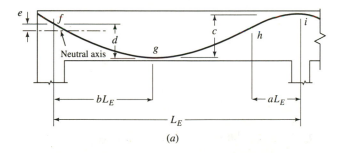

FIGURE 1
Typical interior span: (*a*) tendon profile geometry,
(*b*) equivalent load.

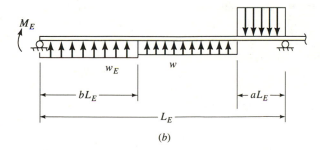

FIGURE 2
Typical exterior span: (*a*) tendon profile geometry,
(*b*) equivalent load.

where P is the horizontal tendon force component. The downward load at the reverse parabola segment is

$$w_R = \frac{1 - 2a}{2a} w \tag{2}$$

However, it need not be considered separately when using the tables presented in this paper.

A typical exterior span, as shown in Fig. 2(a), has a tendon profile which consists of three parabolic segments: fg, gh, and hi. Segments fg and gh have a common horizontal low point at g; segments gh and hi have a common tangent at h; and the reversed parabola segment, hi, has a horizontal high point at i directly over the support.

The equivalent tendon load acting on the exterior span is considered in three parts (Fig. 2(b)). First, the end moment

$$M_E = Pe \tag{3}$$

second, the upward load due to the tendons in the external parabola segment where the upward prestress load is given by

$$W_E = \frac{2Pd}{b^2 L_E^2} \tag{4}$$

and, third, the load due to the remaining part of the tendons for which the upward segment of the prestress load is given by

$$w = \frac{2Pc}{(1 - b)(1 - b - a)L_E^2} \tag{5}$$

MOMENT INFLUENCE COEFFICIENTS

Tables I through VI are to be used in computation of beam moments at the support points. These tables are intended for beams of constant cross section over all spans but may be used if the section changes from span to span, as explained later. Table I covers the two-span beam for which the two spans may or may not be the same. Tables II to VI cover three-, four- and five-span beams for which geometry of the structure must be symmetric. A beam of more than five spans can be analyzed by taking the additional interior spans as equivalent to the center span of the five-span beam. For the three-span case, coefficients are given only for the first interior support moment, and for the four- and five-span cases they are given for the first two interior supports. The moment over any other support is the same as the corresponding symmetric support moment if the loading is symmetric. If the loading is not symmetric, e.g., due to friction losses in a long beam tensioned from one end only, the moment is obtained by reversing the sign of the corresponding anti-symmetric component load coefficient, as explained in the full *J. PCI* article.

Within each of the tables, the loadings considered consist of either uniformly distributed load segments or applied end moments. In the final case, the moment, M, is obtained by multiplying the coefficient by both the intensity of the load, w, and the

TABLE I

Influence segment coefficients for two spans—1st interior support

Loading description*	Reverse curve*	\multicolumn{8}{c}{Ratio of left span length to right span length}							
		0.650	0.700	0.750	0.800	0.850	0.900	0.950	1.000
Load on one span only									
First 30 of first span	00	0.003576	0.004335	0.005180	0.006111	0.007132	0.008244	0.009447	0.010743
Last 70 of first span	05	0.014459	0.017528	0.020943	0.024711	0.028839	0.033333	0.038197	0.043438
Last 70 of first span	10	0.011971	0.014511	0.017339	0.020458	0.023876	0.027596	0.031623	0.035962
Last 70 of first span	15	0.009751	0.011821	0.014124	0.016666	0.019450	0.022480	0.025761	0.029295
First 40 of first span	00	0.006124	0.007424	0.008871	0.010467	0.012216	0.014119	0.016180	0.018399
Last 60 of first span	05	0.012306	0.014918	0.017824	0.021031	0.024545	0.028369	0.032510	0.036970
Last 60 of first span	10	0.010173	0.012332	0.014735	0.017386	0.020290	0.023452	0.026875	0.030562
Last 60 of first span	15	0.008271	0.010027	0.011980	0.014135	0.016497	0.019067	0.021850	0.024848
First 50 of first span	00	0.009102	0.011034	0.013183	0.015555	0.018154	0.020982	0.024044	0.027343
Last 50 of first span	05	0.009724	0.011789	0.014085	0.016619	0.019396	0.022418	0.025690	0.029214
Last 50 of first span	10	0.007947	0.009634	0.011511	0.013582	0.015851	0.018320	0.020994	0.023874
Last 50 of first span	15	0.006362	0.007712	0.009215	0.010873	0.012689	0.014667	0.016807	0.019113
Last 30 of last span	00	0.013022	0.012639	0.012278	0.011937	0.011614	0.011309	0.011019	0.010743
First 70 of last span	05	0.052652	0.051103	0.049643	0.048264	0.046960	0.045724	0.044552	0.043438
First 70 of last span	10	0.043590	0.042308	0.041099	0.039958	0.038878	0.037855	0.036884	0.035962
First 70 of last span	15	0.035510	0.034465	0.033481	0.032551	0.031671	0.030837	0.030047	0.029295
Last 40 of last span	00	0.022303	0.021647	0.021028	0.020444	0.019891	0.019368	0.018871	0.018400
First 60 of last span	05	0.044812	0.043494	0.042251	0.041078	0.039967	0.038916	0.037918	0.036970
First 60 of last span	10	0.037045	0.035955	0.034928	0.033958	0.033040	0.032171	0.031346	0.030562
First 60 of last span	15	0.030119	0.029233	0.028398	0.027609	0.026863	0.026156	0.025485	0.024848
Last 50 of last span	00	0.033143	0.032169	0.031250	0.030381	0.029560	0.028782	0.028044	0.027343
First 50 of last span	05	0.035411	0.034370	0.033388	0.032460	0.031583	0.030752	0.029963	0.029214
First 50 of last span	10	0.028939	0.028088	0.027285	0.026527	0.025810	0.025131	0.024487	0.023875
First 50 of last span	15	0.023167	0.022486	0.021843	0.021237	0.020663	0.020119	0.019603	0.019113
Unit moment on left end		−0.196969	−0.205882	−0.214285	−0.222222	−0.229729	−0.236842	−0.243589	−0.250000
Unit moment on right end		−0.303030	−0.294117	−0.285714	−0.277777	−0.270270	−0.263157	−0.256410	−0.250000
Applied loads									
Unit dead load on 1st span		−0.020804	−0.025220	−0.030133	−0.035555	−0.041494	−0.047960	−0.054959	−0.062500
Unit dead load on 2nd span		−0.075757	−0.073529	−0.071428	−0.069444	−0.067567	−0.065789	−0.064102	−0.062500
Unit dead load on both spans		−0.096562	−0.098749	−0.101562	−0.104999	−0.109062	−0.113749	−0.119062	−0.125000

*Numbers refer to percent of span. For example, in the third line of coefficients, the 70 and 10 indicate 70% and 10% of the first span.

$$M = \left[\sum w \cdot \text{coef.}\right] \cdot L_R^2 + \sum M_E \cdot \text{coef.}$$

square of the interior span length, L_1; that is, the coefficients are moments for a unit load intensity applied to a structure with unit interior span length. In the second case, the moment, M, is obtained by multiplying the coefficient by the applied end moment, M_E.

The algebraic signs of all moments follow the beam convention: positive for a moment giving compression in the top fiber. The moments obtained from the tabulated influence coefficients will follow this sign convention provided the sign of the distributed load is positive if it is applied in its usual direction. That is, a distributed dead load acting upward over the major portion of the tendons is also positive. The distributed load due to the prestressing tendon is always expressed as that of the major (upward curvature) portion. The effect of the reverse curvature portion is already included in the tabulated moment coefficients.

TABLE II

Influence segment coefficients for three spans—1st interior support

Loading description*	Reverse curve*	Ratio of exterior span length to interior span length							
		0.650	0.700	0.750	0.800	0.850	0.900	0.950	1.000
Symmetric prestress									
End 30 of end spans (sym.)	00	0.002744	0.003350	0.004028	0.004783	0.005615	0.006526	0.007519	0.008594
Inner 70 of end spans	05	0.011096	0.013544	0.016289	0.019339	0.022703	0.026388	0.030402	0.034750
Inner 70 of end spans	10	0.009187	0.011213	0.013485	0.016011	0.018796	0.021847	0.025170	0.028769
Inner 70 of end spans	15	0.007484	0.009134	0.010985	0.013043	0.015311	0.017797	0.020504	0.023436
End 40 of end spans	00	0.004700	0.005737	0.006899	0.008191	0.009616	0.011177	0.012878	0.014719
Inner 60 of end spans	05	0.009444	0.011527	0.013863	0.016459	0.019322	0.022459	0.025875	0.029576
Inner 60 of end spans	10	0.007807	0.009529	0.011460	0.013606	0.015973	0.018566	0.021390	0.024449
Inner 60 of end spans	15	0.006347	0.007748	0.009318	0.011062	0.012987	0.015095	0.017391	0.019878
End 50 of end spans	00	0.006985	0.008526	0.010253	0.012173	0.014291	0.016611	0.019137	0.021875
Inner 50 of end spans	05	0.007463	0.009109	0.010955	0.013006	0.015269	0.017747	0.020447	0.023371
Inner 50 of end spans	10	0.006099	0.007444	0.008953	0.010629	0.012478	0.014504	0.016710	0.019099
Inner 50 of end spans	15	0.004882	0.005959	0.007167	0.008509	0.009989	0.011611	0.013377	0.015290
Center span	05	0.049709	0.048579	0.047499	0.046467	0.045478	0.044531	0.043622	0.042749
Center span	10	0.041860	0.040909	0.039999	0.039130	0.038297	0.037499	0.036734	0.035999
Center span	15	0.034593	0.033806	0.033055	0.032337	0.031649	0.030989	0.030357	0.029750
Unit moments on the ends		−0.151162	−0.159090	−0.166666	−0.173913	−0.180851	−0.187499	−0.193877	−0.200000
Anti-symmetric prestress									
End 30 of end spans (anti-sym.)	00	0.005131	0.006141	0.007252	0.008462	0.009774	0.011188	0.012705	0.014324
Inner 70 of end spans	05	0.020746	0.024832	0.029320	0.034215	0.039520	0.045237	0.051369	0.057917
Inner 70 of end spans	10	0.017175	0.020558	0.024274	0.028327	0.032719	0.037452	0.042528	0.047949
Inner 70 of end spans	15	0.013990	0.016745	0.019772	0.023073	0.026650	0.030506	0.034641	0.039056
End 40 of end spans	00	0.008787	0.010518	0.012419	0.014493	0.016740	0.019162	0.021759	0.024533
Inner 60 of end spans	05	0.017657	0.021134	0.024954	0.029121	0.033636	0.038501	0.043720	0.049293
Inner 60 of end spans	10	0.014596	0.017471	0.020629	0.024073	0.027806	0.031828	0.036142	0.040749
Inner 60 of end spans	15	0.011867	0.014204	0.016772	0.019572	0.022607	0.025877	0.029385	0.033131
End 50 of end spans	00	0.013059	0.015631	0.018457	0.021538	0.024877	0.028476	0.032336	0.036458
Inner 50 of end spans	05	0.013953	0.016701	0.019719	0.023012	0.026580	0.030425	0.034548	0.038953
Inner 50 of end spans	10	0.011402	0.013648	0.016115	0.018806	0.021721	0.024864	0.028234	0.031833
Inner 50 of end spans	15	0.009130	0.010928	0.012903	0.015058	0.017392	0.019908	0.022607	0.025488
Unit moments on the ends		−0.282608	−0.291666	−0.300000	−0.307692	−0.314814	−0.321428	−0.327586	−0.333333
Applied loads									
Unit dead load on 1st span		−0.022908	−0.027608	−0.032812	−0.038528	−0.044764	−0.051528	−0.058827	−0.066666
Unit dead load on 2nd span		−0.058139	−0.056818	−0.055555	−0.054347	−0.053191	−0.052083	−0.051020	−0.050000
Unit dead load on 3rd span		0.006941	0.008120	0.009375	0.010702	0.012098	0.013560	0.015084	0.016666
Unit dead load on all spans		−0.074106	−0.076306	−0.078993	−0.082173	−0.085857	−0.090052	−0.094764	−0.100000
Unit dead load on spans 1 and 2		−0.081048	−0.084427	−0.088368	−0.092876	−0.097956	−0.103612	−0.109848	−0.116666
Unit dead load on spans 1 and 3		−0.015966	−0.019488	−0.023437	−0.027826	−0.032666	−0.037968	−0.043743	−0.050000

*Numbers refer to percent of span.

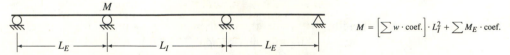

$$M = \left[\sum w \cdot \text{coef.}\right] \cdot L_I^2 + \sum M_E \cdot \text{coef.}$$

Four types of distributed loads are considered in the tables:

1. Loads applied to the end portion of the exterior spans over segment fg denoted by bL_E in Fig. 2(a). Coefficients are given for a b of 30 percent, 40 percent, and 50 percent.

2. Loads applied to the remaining (interior) portion of the exterior spans. The reverse curvature portion is segment hi in Fig. 2(a), denoted by aL_E in Fig. 2(a). Coefficients are tabulated for an a of 5 percent, 10 percent, and 15 percent.

TABLE III
Influence segment coefficients for four spans—1st interior support

Loading description*	Reverse curve*	Ratio of exterior span length to interior span length							
		0.650	0.700	0.750	0.800	0.850	0.900	0.950	1.000
Symmetric prestress									
End 30 of end spans (sym.)	00	0.004215	0.005082	0.006043	0.007097	0.008247	0.009493	0.010836	0.012278
Inner 70 of end spans	05	0.017041	0.020550	0.024433	0.028697	0.033345	0.038383	0.043815	0.049643
Inner 70 of end spans	10	0.014108	0.017013	0.020228	0.023758	0.027606	0.031777	0.036274	0.041099
Inner 70 of end spans	15	0.011493	0.013859	0.016478	0.019354	0.022489	0.025886	0.029550	0.033480
End 40 of end spans	00	0.007218	0.008705	0.010349	0.012155	0.014124	0.016258	0.018559	0.021028
Inner 60 of end spans	05	0.014504	0.017490	0.020795	0.024424	0.028380	0.032668	0.037290	0.042251
Inner 60 of end spans	10	0.011990	0.014459	0.017191	0.020190	0.023461	0.027006	0.030827	0.034928
Inner 60 of end spans	15	0.009748	0.011755	0.013977	0.016415	0.019075	0.021956	0.025063	0.028398
End 50 of end spans	00	0.010727	0.012936	0.015380	0.018064	0.020990	0.024161	0.027580	0.031250
Inner 50 of end spans	05	0.011461	0.013821	0.016433	0.019300	0.022426	0.025815	0.029468	0.033388
Inner 50 of end spans	10	0.009366	0.011295	0.013429	0.015772	0.018327	0.021096	0.024082	0.027285
Inner 50 of end spans	15	0.007498	0.009042	0.010751	0.012627	0.014672	0.016889	0.019279	0.021843
Two middle spans	05	0.038169	0.036853	0.035624	0.034475	0.033398	0.032386	0.031433	0.030535
Two middle spans	10	0.032142	0.031034	0.029999	0.029032	0.028124	0.027272	0.026470	0.025714
Two middle spans	15	0.026562	0.025646	0.024791	0.023992	0.023242	0.022537	0.021875	0.021250
Unit moments on the ends		−0.232142	−0.241379	−0.250000	−0.258064	−0.265625	−0.272727	−0.279411	−0.285714
Anti-symmetric prestress									
End 30 of end spans (anti-sym.)	00	0.003576	0.004335	0.005180	0.006111	0.007132	0.008244	0.009447	0.010743
Inner 70 of end spans	05	0.014459	0.017528	0.020943	0.024711	0.028839	0.033333	0.038197	0.043438
Inner 70 of end spans	10	0.011971	0.014511	0.017339	0.020458	0.023876	0.027596	0.031623	0.035962
Inner 70 of end spans	15	0.009746	0.011815	0.014117	0.016657	0.019439	0.022468	0.025747	0.029279
End 40 of end spans	00	0.006124	0.007424	0.008871	0.010467	0.012216	0.014119	0.016180	0.018399
Inner 60 of end spans	05	0.012306	0.014918	0.017824	0.021031	0.024545	0.028369	0.032510	0.036970
Inner 60 of end spans	10	0.010173	0.012332	0.014735	0.017386	0.020291	0.023452	0.026875	0.030562
Inner 60 of end spans	15	0.008271	0.010027	0.011980	0.014135	0.016497	0.019067	0.021850	0.024848
End 50 of end spans	00	0.009102	0.011034	0.013183	0.015555	0.018154	0.020982	0.024044	0.027343
Inner 50 of end spans	05	0.009724	0.011789	0.014085	0.016619	0.019396	0.022418	0.025690	0.029214
Inner 50 of end spans	10	0.007947	0.009634	0.011511	0.013582	0.015851	0.018320	0.020994	0.023874
Inner 50 of end spans	15	0.006367	0.007719	0.009223	0.010882	0.012700	0.014679	0.016821	0.019129
Two middle spans	05	0.064772	0.062867	0.061071	0.059374	0.057770	0.056249	0.054807	0.053437
Two middle spans	10	0.054545	0.052941	0.051428	0.049999	0.048648	0.047368	0.046153	0.044999
Two middle spans	15	0.045106	0.043779	0.042528	0.041347	0.040229	0.039171	0.038166	0.037212
Unit moments on the ends		−0.196969	−0.205882	−0.214285	−0.222222	−0.229729	−0.236842	−0.243589	−0.249999
Applied loads									
Unit dead load on 1st span		−0.022662	−0.027394	−0.032645	−0.038422	−0.044736	−0.051593	−0.059001	−0.066964
Unit dead load on 2nd span		−0.060200	−0.058316	−0.056547	−0.054883	−0.053315	−0.051834	−0.050433	−0.049107
Unit dead load on 3rd span		0.015557	0.015212	0.014880	0.014560	0.014252	0.013955	0.013668	0.013392
Unit dead load on 4th span		−0.001857	−0.002174	−0.002511	−0.002867	−0.003241	−0.003633	−0.004041	−0.004464
Unit dead load on all spans		−0.069162	−0.072672	−0.076822	−0.081612	−0.087040	−0.093106	−0.099806	−0.107142
Unit dead load on spans 1, 2, and 4		−0.084720	−0.087885	−0.091703	−0.096173	−0.101293	−0.107061	−0.113475	−0.120535
Unit dead load on spans 2 and 3		−0.044642	−0.043103	−0.041666	−0.040322	−0.039062	−0.037878	−0.036764	−0.035714
Unit dead load on spans 1 and 3		−0.007105	−0.012181	−0.017764	−0.023861	−0.030484	−0.037638	−0.045332	−0.053571
Unit dead load on spans 2 and 4		−0.062057	−0.060490	−0.059058	−0.057750	−0.056556	−0.055467	−0.054474	−0.053571

*Numbers refer to percent of span.

3. Loads applied to the interior spans. Here the reverse curvature segments of ef and hi are denoted by aL, in Fig. 1(a), with coefficients given for the above percentages for a. Note that the tendon profile is assumed to be symmetric within each interior span.

4. Uniform loads applied to specific spans for use in computing moments due to dead load as well as live load.

In this discussion L and I refer to span length and moment of inertia, respectively; subscripts E, I, L, R, and C denote exterior, interior, left, right, and center, respectively.

TABLE IV

Influence segment coefficients for four spans—2nd interior support

Loading description*	Reverse curve*	Ratio of exterior span length to interior span length							
		0.650	0.700	0.750	0.800	0.850	0.900	0.950	1.000
Symmetric prestress									
End 30 of end spans (sym.)	00	−0.002107	−0.002541	−0.003021	−0.003548	−0.004123	−0.004746	−0.005418	−0.006139
Inner 70 of end spans	05	−0.008520	−0.010275	−0.012216	−0.014348	−0.016672	−0.019191	−0.021907	−0.024821
Inner 70 of end spans	10	−0.007054	−0.008506	−0.010114	−0.011879	−0.013803	−0.015888	−0.018137	−0.020549
Inner 70 of end spans	15	−0.005746	−0.006929	−0.008239	−0.009677	−0.011244	−0.012943	−0.014775	−0.016740
End 40 of end spans	00	−0.003609	−0.004352	−0.005175	−0.006077	−0.007062	−0.008129	−0.009279	−0.010514
Inner 60 of end spans	05	−0.007252	−0.008745	−0.010397	−0.012212	−0.014190	−0.016334	−0.018645	−0.021125
Inner 60 of end spans	10	−0.005995	−0.007229	−0.008595	−0.010095	−0.011730	−0.013503	−0.015413	−0.017464
Inner 60 of end spans	15	−0.004874	−0.005877	−0.006988	−0.008207	−0.009537	−0.010978	−0.012531	−0.014199
End 50 of end spans	00	−0.005363	−0.006468	−0.007690	−0.009032	−0.010495	−0.012080	−0.013790	−0.015625
Inner 50 of end spans	05	−0.005730	−0.006910	−0.008216	−0.009650	−0.011213	−0.012907	−0.014734	−0.016694
Inner 50 of end spans	10	−0.004683	−0.005647	−0.006714	−0.007886	−0.009163	−0.010548	−0.012041	−0.013642
Inner 50 of end spans	15	−0.003749	−0.004521	−0.005375	−0.006313	−0.007336	−0.008444	−0.009639	−0.010921
Two middle spans	05	0.087789	0.088448	0.089062	0.089636	0.090175	0.090681	0.091157	0.091606
Two middle spans	10	0.073928	0.074482	0.074999	0.075483	0.075937	0.076363	0.076764	0.077142
Two middle spans	15	0.061094	0.061552	0.061979	0.062379	0.062754	0.063106	0.063437	0.063750
Unit moments on the ends		0.116071	0.120689	0.125000	0.129032	0.132812	0.136363	0.139705	0.142857
Anti-symmetric prestress									
		0.000000	0.000000	0.000000	0.000000	0.000000	0.000000	0.000000	0.000000
Applied loads									
Unit dead load on 1st span		0.006130	0.007392	0.008789	0.010322	0.011994	0.013806	0.015760	0.017857
Unit dead load on 2nd span		−0.051339	−0.051724	−0.052083	−0.052419	−0.052734	−0.053030	−0.53308	−0.053571
Unit dead load on 3rd span		−0.051339	−0.051724	−0.052083	−0.052419	−0.052734	−0.053030	−0.53308	−0.053571
Unit dead load on 4th span		0.006130	0.007392	0.008789	0.010322	0.011994	0.013806	0.015760	0.017857
Unit dead load on all spans		−0.090418	−0.088663	−0.086588	−0.084193	−0.081479	−0.078446	−0.075096	−0.071428
Unit dead load on spans 1, 2, and 4		−0.039079	−0.036939	−0.034505	−0.031774	−0.028745	−0.025416	−0.021787	−0.017857
Unit dead load on spans 2 and 3		−0.102678	−0.103448	−0.104166	−0.104838	−0.105468	−0.106060	−0.106617	−0.107142
Unit dead load on spans 1 and 3		−0.045209	−0.044331	−0.043294	−0.042096	−0.040739	−0.039223	−0.037548	−0.035714
Unit dead load on spans 2 and 4		−0.045209	−0.044331	−0.043294	−0.042096	−0.040739	−0.039223	−0.037548	−0.035714

*Numbers refer to percent of span.

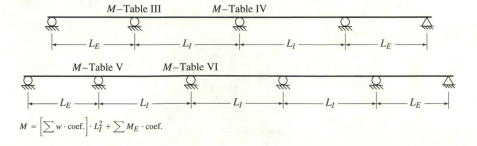

$$M = \left[\sum w \cdot \text{coef.}\right] \cdot L_I^2 + \sum M_E \cdot \text{coef.}$$

   Coefficients for reverse curvature segment lengths, other than those tabulated, can be obtained by linear interpolation. For reverse curvatures of less than 5 percent, the coefficient for the 0 percent case can be extrapolated by taking the corresponding 15 percent coefficient plus three times the difference between the 5 percent coefficient and the 10 percent coefficient. Similarly, the 20 percent case can be obtained by adding to the 5 percent case three times the difference between the 15 percent and the 10 percent cases. These extrapolations give results accurate to about 0.1 percent. The error due to linear interpolation is at most 0.3 percent.

TABLE V

Influence segment coefficients for five spans—1st interior support

Loading description*	Reverse curve*	Ratio of exterior span length to interior span length							
		0.650	0.700	0.750	0.800	0.850	0.900	0.950	1.000
Symmetric prestress									
End 30 of end spans (sym.)	00	0.003807	0.004606	0.005493	0.006471	0.007540	0.008702	0.009958	0.011309
Inner 70 of end spans	05	0.015392	0.018624	0.022212	0.026165	0.030487	0.035184	0.040262	0.045724
Inner 70 of end spans	10	0.012743	0.015418	0.018389	0.021662	0.025240	0.029129	0.033333	0.037855
Inner 70 of end spans	15	0.010381	0.012560	0.014980	0.017646	0.020561	0.023729	0.027154	0.030837
End 40 of end spans	00	0.006520	0.007888	0.009409	0.011083	0.012914	0.014903	0.017054	0.019368
Inner 60 of end spans	05	0.013100	0.015850	0.018905	0.022269	0.025947	0.029945	0.034267	0.038916
Inner 60 of end spans	10	0.010829	0.013103	0.015628	0.018409	0.021450	0.024755	0.028328	0.032171
Inner 60 of end spans	15	0.008805	0.010653	0.012706	0.014967	0.017439	0.020127	0.023031	0.026156
End 50 of end spans	00	0.009689	0.011723	0.013982	0.016470	0.019191	0.022148	0.025344	0.028782
Inner 50 of end spans	05	0.010352	0.012525	0.014939	0.017597	0.020504	0.023663	0.027078	0.030752
Inner 50 of end spans	10	0.008460	0.010236	0.012208	0.014381	0.016756	0.019338	0.022129	0.025131
Inner 50 of end spans	15	0.006772	0.008194	0.009773	0.011513	0.013414	0.015481	0.017716	0.020119
2nd and 4th spans	05	0.055161	0.053437	0.051818	0.050294	0.048857	0.047499	0.046216	0.044999
2nd and 4th spans	10	0.046451	0.044999	0.043636	0.042352	0.041142	0.039999	0.038918	0.037894
2nd and 4th spans	15	0.038387	0.037187	0.036060	0.035000	0.034000	0.033055	0.032162	0.031315
Center span	05	−0.013790	−0.013359	−0.012954	−0.012573	−0.012214	−0.011874	−0.011554	−0.011249
Center span	10	−0.011612	−0.011249	−0.010909	−0.010588	−0.010285	−0.009999	−0.009729	−0.009473
Center span	15	−0.009596	−0.009296	−0.009015	−0.008750	−0.008500	−0.008263	−0.008040	−0.007828
Unit moments on the ends		−0.209677	−0.218750	−0.227272	−0.235294	−0.242857	−0.249999	−0.256756	−0.263157
Anti-symmetric prestress									
End 30 of end spans (anti-sym.)	00	0.003978	0.004806	0.005725	0.006735	0.007839	0.009037	0.010330	0.011720
Inner 70 of end spans	05	0.016084	0.019433	0.023147	0.027233	0.031694	0.036538	0.041767	0.047387
Inner 70 of end spans	10	0.013316	0.016089	0.019164	0.022546	0.026240	0.030249	0.034579	0.039231
Inner 70 of end spans	15	0.010847	0.013106	0.015611	0.018366	0.021375	0.024642	0.028168	0.031958
End 40 of end spans	00	0.006813	0.008231	0.009805	0.011535	0.013425	0.015477	0.017692	0.020072
Inner 60 of end spans	05	0.013689	0.016540	0.019701	0.023178	0.026975	0.031097	0.035548	0.040331
Inner 60 of end spans	10	0.011316	0.013673	0.016286	0.019160	0.022300	0.025707	0.029387	0.033340
Inner 60 of end spans	15	0.009200	0.011116	0.013241	0.015578	0.018130	0.020901	0.023892	0.027107
End 50 of end spans	00	0.010124	0.012233	0.014571	0.017142	0.019951	0.023000	0.026292	0.029829
Inner 50 of end spans	05	0.010817	0.013070	0.015568	0.018315	0.021316	0.024574	0.028091	0.031870
Inner 50 of end spans	10	0.008840	0.010681	0.012722	0.014968	0.017420	0.020082	0.022956	0.026045
Inner 50 of end spans	15	0.007077	0.008551	0.010185	0.011983	0.013946	0.016077	0.018378	0.020851
2nd and 4th spans	05	0.048033	0.046467	0.044999	0.043622	0.042326	0.041105	0.039953	0.038863
2nd and 4th spans	10	0.040449	0.039130	0.037894	0.036734	0.035643	0.034615	0.033644	0.032727
2nd and 4th spans	15	0.033425	0.032335	0.031314	0.030355	0.029454	0.028604	0.027802	0.027044
Unit moments on the ends		−0.219101	−0.228260	−0.236842	−0.244897	−0.252475	−0.259615	−0.266355	−0.272727
Applied loads									
Unit dead load on 1st span		−0.022644	−0.027379	−0.032633	−0.038415	−0.044734	−0.051598	−0.059013	−0.066985
Unit dead load on 2nd span		−0.060347	−0.058423	−0.056618	−0.054921	−0.053323	−0.051816	−0.050391	−0.049043
Unit dead load on 3rd span		0.016129	0.015625	0.015151	0.014705	0.014285	0.013888	0.013513	0.013157
Unit dead load on 4th span		−0.004168	−0.004076	−0.003987	−0.003901	−0.003818	−0.003739	−0.003662	−0.003588
Unit dead load on 5th span		0.000497	0.000582	0.000672	0.000768	0.000868	0.000973	0.001082	0.001196
Unit dead load on all spans		−0.070534	−0.073671	−0.077414	−0.081764	−0.086723	−0.092291	−0.098471	−0.105263
Unit dead load on spans 1, 2, and 4		−0.087160	−0.089879	−0.093239	−0.097238	−0.101877	−0.107154	−0.113067	−0.119617
Unit dead load on spans 2, 3, and 5		−0.043721	−0.042216	−0.040794	−0.039447	−0.038169	−0.036953	−0.035795	−0.034688
Unit dead load on spans 1, 3, and 5		−0.006018	−0.011171	−0.016808	−0.022941	−0.029580	−0.036736	−0.044417	−0.052631
Unit dead load on spans 2 and 4		−0.064516	−0.062500	−0.060606	−0.058823	−0.057142	−0.055555	−0.054054	−0.052631

*Numbers refer to percent of span.

TABLE VI

Influence segment coefficients for five spans—2nd interior support

Loading description*	Reverse curve*	Ratio of exterior span length to interior span length							
		0.650	0.700	0.750	0.800	0.850	0.900	0.950	1.000
Symmetric prestress									
End 30 of end spans (sym.)	00	−0.000761	−0.000921	−0.001098	−0.001294	−0.001508	−0.001740	−0.001991	−0.002261
Inner 70 of end spans	05	−0.003078	−0.003724	−0.004442	−0.005233	−0.006097	−0.007036	−0.008052	−0.009144
Inner 70 of end spans	10	−0.002548	−0.003083	−0.003677	−0.004332	−0.005048	−0.005825	−0.006666	−0.007571
Inner 70 of end spans	15	−0.002076	−0.002512	−0.002996	−0.003529	−0.004112	−0.004745	−0.005430	−0.006167
End 40 of end spans	00	−0.001304	−0.001577	−0.001881	−0.002216	−0.002582	−0.002980	−0.003410	−0.003873
Inner 60 of end spans	05	−0.002620	−0.003170	−0.003781	−0.004453	−0.005189	−0.005989	−0.006853	−0.007783
Inner 60 of end spans	10	−0.002165	−0.002620	−0.003125	−0.003681	−0.004290	−0.004951	−0.005665	−0.006434
Inner 60 of end spans	15	−0.001761	−0.002130	−0.002541	−0.002993	−0.003487	−0.004025	−0.004606	−0.005231
End 50 of end spans	00	−0.001937	−0.002344	−0.002796	−0.003294	−0.003838	−0.004429	−0.005068	−0.005756
Inner 50 of end spans	05	−0.002070	−0.002505	−0.002987	−0.003519	−0.004100	−0.004732	−0.005415	−0.006150
Inner 50 of end spans	10	−0.001692	−0.002047	−0.002441	−0.002876	−0.003351	−0.003867	−0.004425	−0.005026
Inner 50 of end spans	15	−0.001354	−0.001638	−0.001954	−0.002302	−0.002682	−0.003096	−0.003543	−0.004023
2nd and 4th spans	05	0.031717	0.032062	0.032386	0.032691	0.032978	0.033249	0.033506	0.033749
2nd and 4th spans	10	0.026709	0.026999	0.027272	0.027529	0.027771	0.027999	0.028216	0.028421
2nd and 4th spans	15	0.022072	0.022312	0.022537	0.022750	0.022950	0.023138	0.023317	0.023486
Center span	05	0.045507	0.045421	0.045340	0.045264	0.045192	0.045124	0.045060	0.044999
Center span	10	0.038322	0.038249	0.038181	0.038117	0.038057	0.037999	0.037945	0.037894
Center span	15	0.031669	0.031609	0.031553	0.031500	0.031450	0.031402	0.031358	0.031315
Unit moments on the ends		0.041935	0.043750	0.045454	0.047058	0.048571	0.049999	0.051351	0.052631
Anti-symmetric prestress									
End 30 of end spans (anti-sym.)	00	−0.001326	−0.001602	−0.001908	−0.002245	−0.002613	−0.003012	−0.003443	−0.003906
Inner 70 of end spans	05	−0.005361	−0.006477	−0.007715	−0.009077	−0.010564	−0.012179	−0.013922	−0.015795
Inner 70 of end spans	10	−0.004438	−0.005363	−0.006388	−0.007515	−0.008746	−0.010083	−0.011526	−0.013077
Inner 70 of end spans	15	−0.003615	−0.004368	−0.005203	−0.006121	−0.007124	−0.008213	−0.009388	−0.010651
End 40 of end spans	00	−0.002271	−0.002743	−0.003268	−0.003845	−0.004475	−0.005159	−0.005897	−0.006690
Inner 60 of end spans	05	−0.004563	−0.005513	−0.006567	−0.007726	−0.008991	−0.010365	−0.011849	−0.013443
Inner 60 of end spans	10	−0.003772	−0.004557	−0.005428	−0.006386	−0.007433	−0.008569	−0.009795	−0.011113
Inner 60 of end spans	15	−0.003066	−0.003705	−0.004413	−0.005192	−0.006043	−0.006967	−0.007964	−0.009035
End 50 of end spans	00	−0.003374	−0.004077	−0.004857	−0.005714	−0.006650	−0.007666	−0.008764	−0.009943
Inner 50 of end spans	05	−0.003605	−0.004356	−0.005189	−0.006105	−0.007105	−0.008191	−0.009363	−0.010623
Inner 50 of end spans	10	−0.002946	−0.003560	−0.004240	−0.004989	−0.005806	−0.006694	−0.007652	−0.008681
Inner 50 of end spans	15	−0.002359	−0.002850	−0.003395	−0.003995	−0.004649	−0.005360	−0.006127	−0.006951
2nd and 4th spans	05	0.055238	0.055760	0.056249	0.056709	0.057140	0.057547	0.057932	0.058295
2nd and 4th spans	10	0.046516	0.046956	0.047368	0.047755	0.048118	0.048461	0.048784	0.049090
2nd and 4th spans	15	0.038446	0.038810	0.039150	0.039470	0.039770	0.040053	0.040321	0.040574
Unit moments on the ends		0.073033	0.076086	0.078947	0.081632	0.084158	0.086538	0.088785	0.090909
Applied loads									
Unit dead load on 1st span		0.006071	0.007340	0.008747	0.010295	0.011987	0.013824	0.015809	0.017942
Unit dead load on 2nd span		−0.050851	−0.051358	−0.051834	−0.052280	−0.052701	−0.053098	−0.053473	−0.053827
Unit dead load on 3rd span		−0.053225	−0.053125	−0.053030	−0.052941	−0.052857	−0.052777	−0.052702	−0.052631
Unit dead load on 4th span		0.013754	0.013858	0.013955	0.014045	0.014130	0.014209	0.014283	0.014354
Unit dead load on 5th span		−0.001642	−0.001980	−0.002354	−0.002765	−0.003213	−0.003699	−0.004222	−0.004784
Unit dead load on all spans		−0.085893	−0.085265	−0.084517	−0.083647	−0.082655	−0.081541	−0.080305	−0.078947
Unit dead load on spans 1, 2, and 4		−0.031024	−0.030159	−0.029131	−0.027939	−0.026584	−0.025064	−0.023380	−0.021531
Unit dead load on spans 2, 3, and 5		−0.105719	−0.106464	−0.107219	−0.107987	−0.108772	−0.109575	−0.110398	−0.111244
Unit dead load on spans 1, 3, and 5		−0.048796	−0.047765	−0.046638	−0.045411	−0.044083	−0.042652	−0.041116	−0.039473
Unit dead load on spans 2 and 4		−0.037096	−0.037500	−0.037878	−0.038235	−0.038571	−0.038888	−0.039189	−0.039473

*Numbers refer to percent of span.

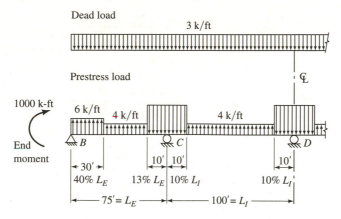

FIGURE 3
Four-span structure for Example 1.

Each table for the moment coefficients over a support is developed from the influence line for the moment in the beam over that support. The coefficients are obtained by computing the area under the influence line over the segment that is loaded by a constant distributed load. If the coefficient represents the effect of several load segments, then it is the sum of the area under each of the segments multiplied by the ratio of the equivalent loads.

EXAMPLE 1. Consider the four-span structure shown in Fig. 3. The moment at support C is to be computed for each of the following loads:

a = distributed prestress load as shown
b = a 1000 k-ft end moment acting on both ends
c = a 3 k/ft uniform dead load

The end to interior span ratio is 0.75. From Table III, the coefficient for the end 40 percent of the end span is 0.0103. The coefficient for the inner 60 percent with 13.3 percent reverse curve is interpolated as 0.0150. The coefficient for the middle spans is 0.0300. So the moment at support C due to the distributed prestress load a is

$$M - (0.0103 \times 6 + 0.0150 \times 4 + 0.0300 \times 4)100^2 = 2424 \text{ k-ft}$$

The coefficient for end moments is -0.25, so the desired moment due to loading b is $M = -250$ k-ft. The coefficient for unit dead load on all spans is -0.0768, so the moment due to the 3 k/ft dead load is $M = -2304$ k-ft.

NON-SYMMETRIC LOADINGS

As pointed out previously, symmetry is not a consideration in the two-span case, so only structures of three or more spans are considered in this section. As long as a structure is symmetric, any loading can be separated into two loadings, one of which is symmetric and the other anti-symmetric. This division is usually obvious. However, if not, it can be obtained by reversing the original loading, taking half of the sum of the original and reversed loadings as the symmetric part. The moments are then computed for both parts using the appropriate coefficients. The moments for the left half of the structure are equal to the sum of the computed moments; those for the right are equal to the difference.

EXAMPLE 2. The moments at the supports of a beam of constant cross section with four equal spans are to be computed. A typical non-symmetric equivalent prestress loading as produced when tensioning long beams from one end is considered. End moments, as considered in this example, would appear only if the tendons are anchored away from the neutral axis of the cross section, or if the beam is cantilevered. The loading diagram is shown in Fig. 4(a). Loading diagrams in (b), (c), and (d) show the reversed, the symmetric, and the anti-symmetric portion, respectively. Note that only the left half of the beam need be considered for these three loadings. Load diagram (b) was derived by folding the right part of the structure about its centerline. Load diagram (c) is half the sum of (a) and (b). Load diagram (d) can be computed either as the difference between (a) and (c) or as half the difference between (a) and (b). The moment at support B caused by the symmetric part of the loading is computed by using the coefficients in the symmetric prestress portion of Table III.

$$M_{BS} = (2.6 \times 0.02103 + 2.0 \times 0.03493 + 2.0 \times 0.0257)(50)^2 + 600 \times (-0.2857)$$
$$= 268.5 \text{ k-ft}$$

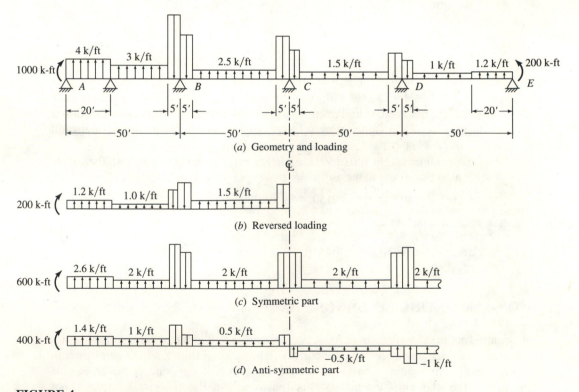

(a) Geometry and loading

(b) Reversed loading

(c) Symmetric part

(d) Anti-symmetric part

FIGURE 4
Four-span structure with non-symmetric loading for Example 2.

The moment at support B due to the anti-symmetric prestress is

$$M_{BA} = (1.4 \times 0.01840 + 1.0 \times 0.03056 + 0.5 \times 0.04500)(50)^2 + 400 \times (-0.2500)$$
$$= 97 \text{ k-ft}$$

The moment at support C due to the symmetric load (Table IV) is

$$M_{CS} = (-2.6 \times 0.01051 - 2.0 \times 0.01746 + 2.0 \times 0.07714)(50)^2 + 600 \times 0.1429$$
$$= 316 \text{ k-ft}$$

The moment at support C due to anti-symmetric prestress is zero

$$M_{CA} = 0$$

Finally, the moments at the three supports are

Left:
$$M_A = M_{BS} + M_{BA} = 365.5 \text{ k-ft}$$
$$M_C = M_{CS} + M_{CA} = 316 \text{ k-ft}$$
Right:
$$M_D = M_{BS} - M_{BA} = 171.5 \text{ k-ft}$$
$$M_C = M_{CS} - M_{CA} = 316 \text{ k-ft}$$

SPAN WITH DIFFERENT MOMENTS OF INERTIA

Two cases of spans with different moments of inertia may be analyzed using the tables. First, the cross section of the end spans may be different (e.g., the cross section of the spans in a two-span beam). Second, the center span cross section of a five-span beam may be different from the other two interior spans.

If the cross sections of the end spans differ, replace the end span ratio computation L_E/L_I by $L_E I_I/L_I I_E$ for selecting coefficients in the tables. Then multiply each distributed load applied to the end spans by $(I_E/I_I)^2$. For the two-span case, the ratio is $L_L I_R/L_R I_L$ and the multiplying factor is $(I_L/I_R)^2$ applied to a distributed load on the left span.

The center span section of a five-span beam may be different only to the extent that its stiffness remains the same as for the other interior spans. That is $I_C/L_C = I_I/L_I$ where C refers to the center span and I refers to the other interior spans. Any distributed loading applied to the center span must then be multiplied by $(I_C/I_I)^2$.

EXAMPLE 3. The moment at point C of the symmetric beam shown in Fig. 5 is to be computed. The end span ratio to be used is

$$100 \times I_I/100 \times 1.25 I_I = 0.8$$

The distributed load factor $(I_E/I_I)^2$ is 1.5625. The center span stiffness requirement is satisfied since $I_C/L_C = I_I/L_I$. Its distributed load factor is 4.0. Hence the required moment is obtained by using Table VI.

$$M_C = 0.04706 \times 1000 + (-0.00222 \times 5 \times 1.56 - 0.00368 \times 4 \times 1.56 + 0.02753 \times 5$$
$$+ 0.03812 \times 2 \times 4.0)(100)^2 = 4070 \text{ k-ft}$$

Similarly, from Table V, the moment at point B is

$$M_B = 3048 \text{ k-ft}$$

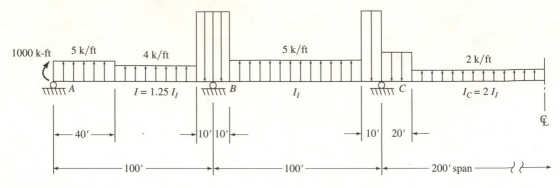

FIGURE 5
Five-span structure with varying moments of inertia for Example 3.

BENDING MOMENTS BETWEEN THE SUPPORTS

Bending moments between the supports can be computed by two methods. The first method is simply to compute the moment at any point by statics using the applied equivalent loads and the computed moments at the supports. The second method, which requires considerably less computation, is to compute a primary moment which is the moment produced by restoring beam continuity over the supports.

M'_x, the primary moment at any point x, is the horizontal component of the prestress force at that point times the eccentricity of the tendon profile from the neutral axis

$$M'_x = P_x e_x \tag{6}$$

The secondary moment is linear between the supports and, for a typical span AB,

$$M''_x = M''_A \left(1 - \frac{x'}{L}\right) + M''_B \frac{x'}{L} \tag{7}$$

where x' is the distance from support point A to the point x, L is the length of span AB, M'' is the secondary moment at the point indicated by the subscript. The secondary moment at a support, as required in Eq. (7), is computed by subtracting the primary moment influence coefficients. So the total moment at any point x is obtained from Eqs. (6) and (7) as

$$M_x = P_x e_x + (M_A - P_A e_A) \times \left(1 - \frac{x'}{L}\right) + (M_B - P_B e_B)\frac{x'}{L} \tag{8}$$

EXAMPLE 4. The moment in the first span of Example 3 is to be computed. The tendon profile is shown in Fig. 6(a), and the horizontal component of the tendon force is 1000 k. The primary moments as computed by Eq. (6) are shown in Fig. 6(b). The secondary moments at the ends are

$$M''_A = M_A - M'_A = 1000 \text{ k-ft} - 1000 \text{ k-ft} = 0 \text{ (free rotation)}$$
$$M''_B = M_B - M'_B = 3048 \text{ k-ft} - 3000 \text{ k-ft} = 48 \text{ k-ft}$$

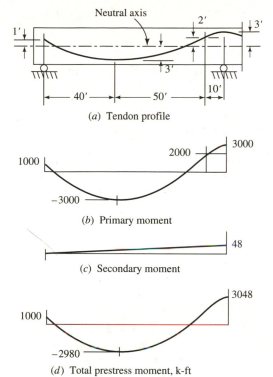

(a) Tendon profile

(b) Primary moment

(c) Secondary moment

(d) Total prestress moment, k-ft

FIGURE 6
Bending moments between supports for
Example 4.

and the secondary moment for the span as computed by Eq. (7) is shown in Fig. 6(c). The moment at any point of this curve can be computed directly from Eq. (8).

FRICTION LOSSES

The equivalent load due to prestressing, as given by Eqs. (1) through (5), is proportional to P, the horizontal component of the force in the prestressing tendons. However, P is not constant along the beam since it is reduced by friction losses along the tendons. A further variation of force is caused by anchor set as the load is transferred from the jacking device. Anchor set causes a reversal of friction forces in the end sections.

For short prestressing tendons, the friction losses can usually be neglected provided the total angular change of the tendon profile is small. However, anchor set losses may be large. In this case both effects may be accommodated by using a reduced constant value of P for the length of the beam.

For long post-tensioned tendons, the friction losses cannot be neglected in the final analysis. An ACI Building Code[8] formula gives the following value for P at any section x in the beam:

$$P_x = P_o e^{-(KL + \mu\alpha)} \qquad (9)$$

If the value of $KL + \mu\alpha$ is below 0.3, in accordance with ACI Code, Eq. (9) may be replaced by

$$P_x = \frac{P_o}{1 + KL + \mu\alpha} \tag{10}$$

Eqs. (9) or (10) may also be used to compute friction losses through any segment of the beam,[7] in which case the reference section is that end of the segment at which the tendon force P_o has already been computed. For reasonable accuracy in this case, Eq. (10) should not be used if the value of $KL + \mu\alpha$ for the segment is greater than about 0.1.

The computed tendon force at various sections along the beam can now be plotted. If the slope of the tendon is large, the horizontal component can be computed by multiplying the tendon force by $(1 - \frac{1}{2}s^2)$, where s is the tendon slope. A linear approximation for the tendon force variation with distance along the beam is sufficiently accurate for most cases and can be obtained by a straight-line approximation of the plotted tendon force.

The loss of prestress force at the anchor section due to anchor set is

$$\Delta P_o = 2\sqrt{rAE\Delta L} \tag{11}$$

However, if the computed ΔP_o is greater than $2 \times (P_o - P_{min})$, where P_o is the jacking force and P_{min} is the lowest computed prestress force in the beam—either at the non-jacking end for post-tensioning from one end, or near the midpoint for post-tensioning from both ends—then

$$\Delta P_o = P_o - P_{min} + \frac{rAE\Delta L}{P_o - P_{min}} \tag{12}$$

This value will be greater than the ΔP_o computed by Eq. (11). The prestress force plot can be revised to include the anchor set loss by noting that the friction losses will be reversed in the regions affected. The prestress force at the anchor will be $P_o - \Delta P_o$ and will increase with distance from the anchor at a rate of r.

NOTATION

A = cross-sectional area of the prestressing tendons
E = elastic modulus of the prestressing tendons
I_E, I_I = moment of intertia of the cross section in the span indicated
K = friction loss factor related to length
L = length of the segment over which friction loss is computed
L_E, L_I = length of the span indicated
ΔL = tendon movement at the anchor due to anchor set
M_E = end moment due to eccentricity of the tendon over the exterior support
M_x, M_A = bending moment at the point indicated

M' and M'' = primary and secondary bending moments, respectively

P_o = jacking force

ΔP_o = loss of prestress force at the jacking end due to anchor set

P_{min} = lowest prestress force considering friction losses

P_x, P_A = horizontal component of the prestressing tendon force at the point indicated

a = ratio of the reverse curve length to the span length

b = ratio of the end segment length to the span length in an exterior span

c = drape of the tendon profile, high point to low point

d = drape of the tendon profile in the end segment of an exterior span

e = eccentricity of the tendon profile above the neutral axis at the exterior support

e_x, e_A, etc. = eccentricity of the tendon profile above the neutral axis at the point indicated

r = loss of prestress force per unit length of beam

s = slope of the tendon profile

w = equivalent upward distributed load over the major segment of the tendon profile

w_E = equivalent upward distributed load in the end segment of an exterior span

w_R = equivalent downward distributed load over the reverse curvature segment of the tendon profile

x' = distance from the end of a span to a point x

α = angular change of the tendon profile in the segment over which friction loss is computed

μ = friction loss factor related to angular change of the tendon profile

Subscripts

A and S designate anti-symmetric and symmetric, respectively.

x, A, B, C, etc. designate points along the beam.

L, R, E, I, and C designate left, right, exterior, interior, and center spans, respectively.

REFERENCES

1. Moorman, R. B., "Equivalent Load Method for Analyzing Prestressed Concrete Structures," *Journal of the American Concrete Institute,* Vol. 23, No. 5, Jan. 1952, pp. 405–416.
2. Norris, C. H., and Wilbur, J. B., *Elementary Structural Analysis,* McGraw-Hill, Inc. New York, 1960.
3. Parme, A. L., and Paris, G. H., "Analysis of Continuous Prestressed Concrete Structures," *Proceedings of the First U.S. Conference on Prestressed Concrete,* Cambridge, Mass., 1951, p. 195.
4. Bailey, D. M., and Ferguson, P. M., "Fixed-End Moment Equations for Continuous Prestressed Concrete Beams," *Journal of the Prestressed Concrete Institute,* Vol. 11, No. 1, Feb. 1966, pp. 76–94.

5. Fiesenheiser, E. I., "Rapid Design of Continuous Prestressed Members," *Journal of the American Concrete Institute,* Vol. 25, No. 8, April 1954, pp. 669–676.
6. "ICES STRUDL-II, Engineering User's Manual, Vol. 1, Frame Analysis," *Report R68-91,* Department of Civil Engineering, Massachusetts Institute of Technology, Cambridge, Mass., Nov. 1968.
7. Lin, T. Y., *Design of Prestressed Concrete Structures,* John Wiley & Sons, Inc., New York, 1963.
8. *Building Code Requirements for Reinforced Concrete* (ACI 318-63), American Concrete Institute, Detroit, Mich., 1963.

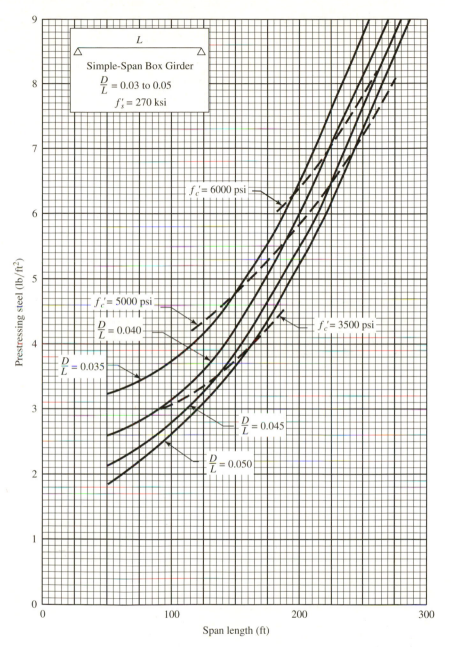

FIGURE B.1
CIP prestressed concrete box girder prestressing steel.

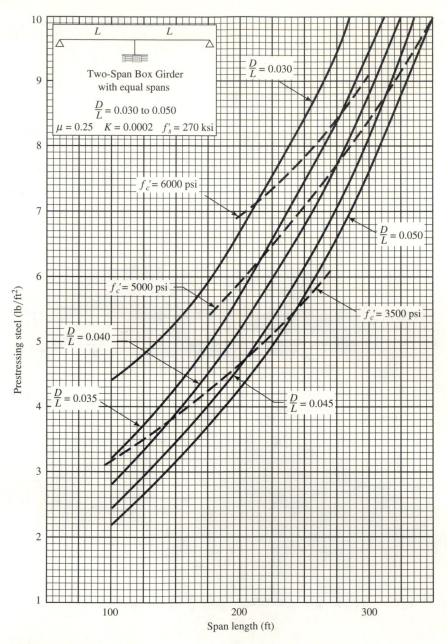

FIGURE B.2
CIP prestressed concrete box girder prestressing steel.

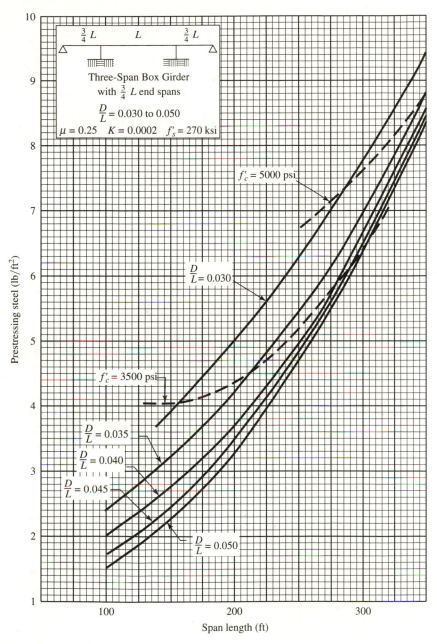

FIGURE B.3
CIP prestressed concrete box girder prestressing steel.

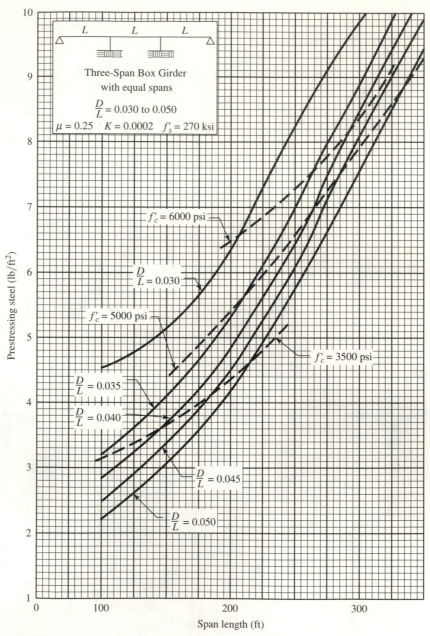

FIGURE B.4
CIP prestressed concrete box girder prestressing steel.

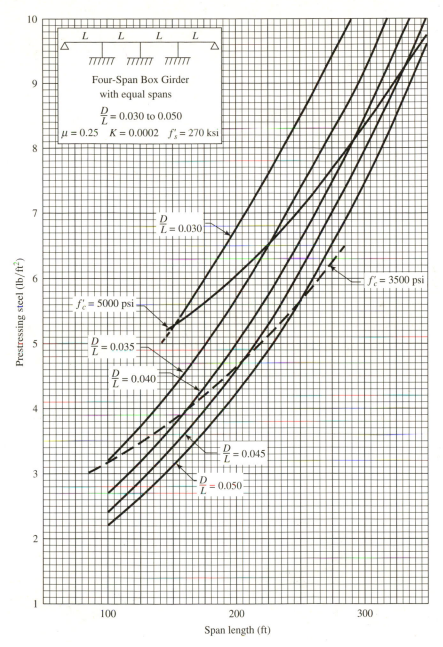

FIGURE B.5
CIP prestressed concrete box girder prestressing steel.

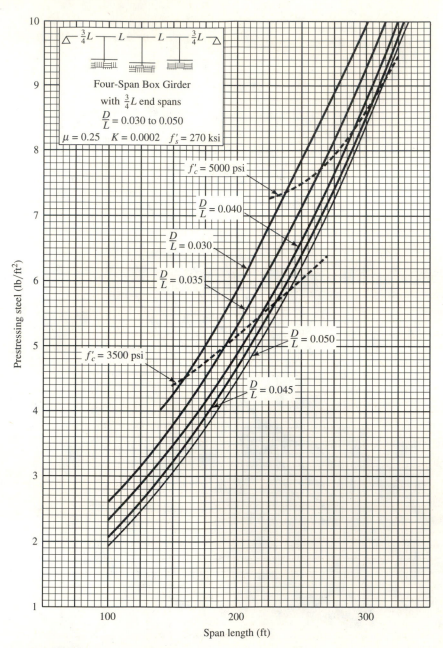

FIGURE B.6
CIP prestressed concrete box girder prestressing steel.

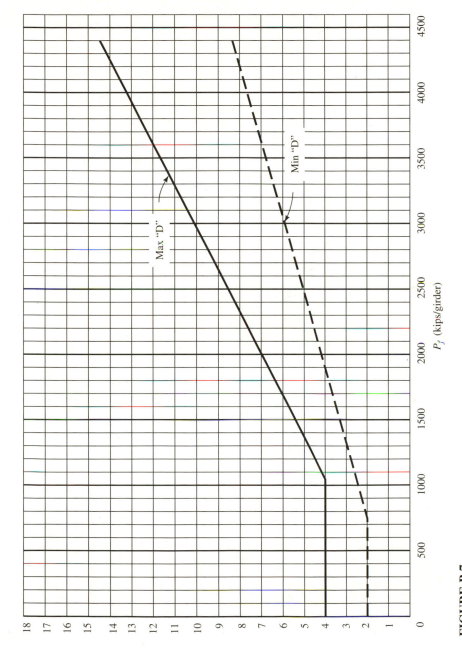

FIGURE B.7

D chart for simple spans.

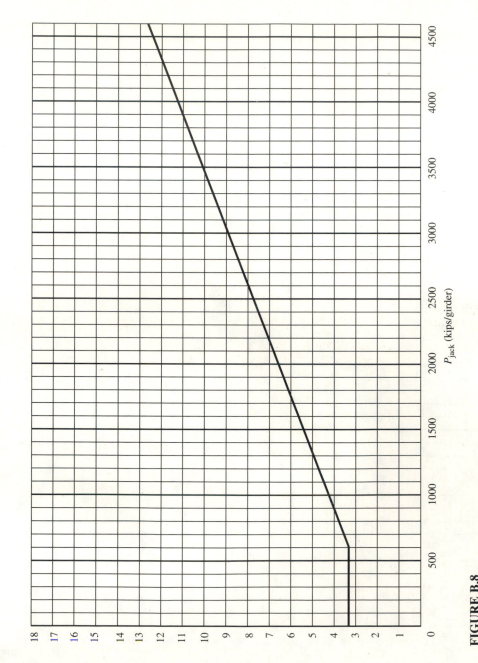

FIGURE B.8
D chart for continuous spans.

TABLE C.1
Cable-stayed bridges of the world

Name[a]	Location	Length of main or major span (ft)	(m)	Year completed[b]	Name[a]	Location	Length of main or major span (ft)	(m)	Year completed[b]
Tatara [1]	Ehime, Japan	2920	890	(1999)	Kap Shui Mun [1, 2, 12]	Hong Kong	1411	430	(1997)
Normandy	Le Havre, France	2808	856	1995	Helgeland	Sandnessjoen, Nordland, Norway	1394	425	1991
Qingzhou Minjiang [1]	Fuzhou, China	1985	605	1996					
Yang Pu	Shanghai, China	1975	602	1993	Quetzalapa Bridge	Quetzalapa, Mexico	1391	424	1993
Xupu [1]	Shanghai, China	1936	590	(1997)	Nan Pu	Shanghai, China	1388	423	1991
Meiko Chuo [1]	Aichi, Japan	1936	590	(1997)	Vasco da Gama [1]	Lisbon, Portugal	1378	420	(1998)
Skarnsundet Bridge	near Trondheim, Norway	1739	530	1991	Hitsuishijima [2]	Kanagawa, Japan	1378	420	1988
					Iwagurojima [2]	Kanagawa, Japan	1378	420	1988
Tsurumi Tsubasa [1]	Kanagawa, Japan	1673	510	1995	Yunyang over Hanjiang R.	Yunyang, Hubei Prov., China	1358	414	1994
Oresund [1]	Denmark/Sweden	1614	492	(2000)					
Ikuchi	Hiroshima, Ehime, Japan	1608	490	1991	Meiko Higashi [1]	Aichi, Japan	1345	410	(1997)
					Volga R. [1]	Ulyanovsk, Russia	1335	407	XXX
Higashi Kobe	Hyogo, Japan	1591	485	1994	Wadi Leban [1]	Riyadh, Saudi Arabia	1329	405	(1996)
Ting Kau [1, 14]	Hong Kong	1558	475	(1997)	Meiko–Nishi	Nagoya, Aichi, Japan	1329	405	1985
Seohae [1]	Korea	1542	470	(1998)	Bridge over Waal R.	Ewijck, Netherlands	1325	404	1976
Annacis (Alex Fraser)	Vancouver, B.C., Canada	1526	465	1986	Saint Nazaire	Saint Nazaire, France	1325	404	1975
					Rande	Vigo, Spain	1313	400	1977
Yokohama Bay	Kanagawa, Japan	1509	460	1989	Elorn R.	Brest/Quimper, France	1312	400	1994
Second Hooghly R.	Calcutta–Howrah, India	1499	457	1992	Wuhan Bridge over Yangtze R.	Wuhan, Hubei Prov., China	1312	400	1995
Second Severn Crossing	Severn R., England/Wales	1496	456	1995	Dame Point	Jacksonville, FL, USA	1300	396	1988
Dartford	Thames R., Dartford, England	1476	450	1991	Sidney Lanier Bridge [1]	Brunswick R., GA, USA	1250	381	XXX
Dao Kanong, Chao Phraya R.	Bangkok, Thailand	1476	450	1987	Houston Ship Channel	Baytown, TX, USA	1250	381	1995
					Hale Boggs Memorial	Luling, LA, USA	1222	372	1983
Chongqing Second Bridge over Yangtze R. [1]	Chongqing, Sichuan Prov., China	1457	444	1996	Dusseldorf–Flehe	Rhine R., Germany	1207	368	1979
					Tjorn Bridge, Askerofjord	near Gothenburg, Sweden	1201	366	1982
Barrios De Luna	Cordillera, Spain	1444	440	1983	Owensboro [1]	Ohio R., Owensboro, KY, USA	1200	366	XXX
Tongling over Yangtze R. [1]	Tongling, Anhui Prov., China	1417	432	1995					
					Sunshine Skyway	Tampa, FL, USA	1200	366	1987

[a] Notes for this column are listed at end of table, p. 1321.
[b] Parentheses indicate projected completion date.
*Collapse date.
XXX Completion date unknown.

(*continued*)

TABLE C.1
(*continued*)

Name[a]	Location	(ft)	(m)	Year completed[b]	Name[a]	Location	(ft)	(m)	Year completed[b]
Tampico	Panuco R., Mexico	1181	360	1988	Waal	Tiel, Netherlands	876	267	1975
Yamatogawa	Osaka, Japan	1165	355	1982	Ikarajima [1]	Japan	853	260	(1996)
Novi Sad	Yugoslavia	1152	351	1981	Yonghe	Tianjin, China	853	260	1987
Cape Girardeau [1]	Rt. 74 over Mississippi R., MO, USA	1150	350.5	XXX	Theodor Heuss	Dusseldorf, Germany	853	260	1957
					Burton	New Brun., Canada	850	259	1970
Batam–Tonton [1]	Indonesia	1148	350	1995	Oberkassel	Dusseldorf, Germany	846	258	1976
Ajigawa (Tempozan)	Osaka, Japan	1148	350	1991	Waal R. [1]	Zaltbommel, Netherlands	840	256	(1994)
Duisburg–Neuenkamp	Rhine R., Germany	1148	350	1970	Arade Bridge	Portimao, Portugal	840	256	1992
Glebe Island Bridge [1]	Sydney, Australia	1132	345	1994	Rees	Rees–Kalkar, Germany	837	255	1967
Jindo Bridge	Uldolmok Straits, Korea	1129	344	1985	Duisburg–Rheinhausen	Rhine R., Germany	837	255	1965
ALRT Fraser R. Bridge	Vancouver, B.C., Canada	1115	340	1988	Save River Railroad	Belgrade, Yugoslavia	833	254	1977
Mesopotamia	Parana, Argentina	1115	340	1972	Tokachi	Japan	823	251	1995
West Gate	Melbourne, Australia	1102	336	1978	Weirton–Steubenville	WV, USA	820	250	1990
Talmadge Memorial Bridge	Savannah, GA, USA	1100	335	1990	Tokachi Chuo	Obihiro, Hokkaido, Japan	820	250	1989
Hao Ping Hsi	Taiwan	1083	330	XXX	Yobuko	Saga, Japan	820	250	1988
Posadas Encarnacion	Argentina	1083	330	1986	Suehiro	Tokushima, Japan	820	250	1975
Puente Brazo Largo [2]	Rio Parana, Argentina	1083	330	1976	Chaco/Corrientes	Parana R., Argentina	804	245	1973
Zarate [2]	Rio Parana, Argentina	1083	330	1975	Papineau–Leblanc	Montreal, Canada	790	241	1969
Karnali R. Bridge	Chisapani, Nepal	1066	325	1993	Karkistensalml [1]	Finland	787	240	XXX
Kohlbrand	Hamburg, Germany	1066	325	1974	Aomori	Aomon, Japan	787	240	1992
Intl. Guadiana Bridge	Portugal/Spain	1063	324	1991	Jianwei	Sichuan Prov., China	787	240	1990
Pont de Brotonne, Seine R.	Rouen, France	1050	320	1977	Kessock	Inverness, Scotland	787	240	1982
Kniebrucke	Rhine R., Dusseldorf, Germany	1050	320	1969	Yasaka Bridge	Ohtake, Yamaguchi, Japan	787	240	1987
Mezcala	Mexico City/Acapulco Highway	1024	312	1993	Kamone	Osaka, Japan	787	240	1975
Daugava R.	Riga, Latvia	1024	312	1981	Sun Bridge	Japan	784	239	1993
Emscher	Rhine R., Germany	1017	310	1990	Kemi [1]	Wakayama, Japan	784	239	XXX
Dartford–Thurrock Bridge	Thames R., Great Britain	1001	305	1991	Sugawara–Shirokita	Osaka, Japan	780	238	1989
Erskine, R. Clyde	Glasgow, Scotland	1000	305	1971	Cochrane	Mobile, AL, USA	780	238	1991
Ombla Bay	Dubrovnik, Yugoslavia	998	304	XXX	Lake Maracaibo	Venezuela	771	235	1962
Bratislava	Danube R., Czech Republic	994	303	1972	Neuwied	Rhine R., Germany	770	235	1978
Severin	Cologne, Germany	990	302	1959	Wye R. Bridge	England	770	235	1966
Moscovsky, Dnieper R.	Kiev, Ukraine	984	300	1976	Albert Canal Bridge	Lanaye, Belgium	761	232	1985
Pasco–Kennewick	WA, USA	981	299	1978	Clark Bridge Replacement	Alton, IL, USA	756	230	1994
Neuwied	Rhine R., Germany	958	292	1977	Shimen	Chongqing, Sichuan Prov., China	755	230	1988
Faro Bridge	Denmark	951	290	1985	Chesapeake and Delaware Canal Bridge	DE, USA	750	229	1995
Donaubrucke	Deggenau, Germany	951	290	1975	Donaubrucke	Hainburg, Austria	748	228	1972
Dongying Bridge over Yellow R., Kenli	Shandong, China	945	288	1987	Penang	Malaysia	738	225	1985
Kurt–Schumacher	Mannheim–Ludwigshafen, Germany	941	287	1972	Fengtai	Anhui, China	735	224	1990
					Bengbu over Huaihe R.	Bengbu, Anhui Prov., China	735	224	1989
Wadi Kuf	Sipac, Libya	925	282	1971	Luangawa	Zambia	730	223	1968
Oved Dib [1]	Algeria	919	280	1994	Jinan Bridge over Yellow R.	Jinan, Shandong Prov., China	722	220	1982
Coatzacoalcos R.	Mexico	919	280	1984	Katsushika	Katsushika, Tokyo, Japan	722	220	1987
Dolsan	Yeosu, Korea	919	280	1984	Rokko	Hyogo, Japan	722	220	1976
Leverkusen	Germany	919	280	1964	Hawkshaw	New Brun., Canada	713	217	1967
Friedrich–Ebert (Bonn–Nord)	Bonn, Germany	919	280	1967	Longs Creek	New Brun., Canada	713	217	1966
Rheinbrucke	Speyer, Germany	902	275	1974	Toyosato	Osaka, Japan	709	216	1970
East Huntington	East Huntington, WV, USA	900	274	1985	Evripos Bridge	Greece	707	215	1988
					Onomichi	Hiroshima, Japan	705	215	1968
Bayview Bridge	Quincy, IL, USA	900	274	1987	Donaubrucke	Linz, Austria	705	215	1972
South Bridge, Dnieper R.	Kiev, Ukraine	889	271	1993	Quetzalapa Bridge	Mexico	699	213	1993
					Chuo	Japan	692	211	1993
Willems	Rotterdam, Netherlands	886	270	1981	Godsheide	Hasselt, Belgium	690	210	1978
Ewijck, Waal R.	near Ewijck, Netherlands	886	270	1976	Ohshiba [1]	Japan	689	210	(1998)

TABLE C.1
(*continued*)

Name[a]	Location	Length of main or major span (ft)	(m)	Year completed[b]	Name[a]	Location	Length of main or major span (ft)	(m)	Year completed[b]
Xiangjiang North Bridge	Changshu, Hunan Prov., China	689	210	1990	Salhus Bridge [13]	near Bergen, Norway	551	168	1994
Chalkis	Greece	689	210	1989	Tajiri Sky	Japan	551	168	1994
Erasmus	Rotterdam, Netherlands	682	208	1996	La Barqueta	Spain	551	168	1991
Polcevera Viaduct	Genoa, Italy	682	208	1969	Wandre, Meuse R.	Belgium	551	168	1989
Arno	Florence, Italy	676	206	1977	Ben–Ahin, Meuse R.	Belgium	551	168	1989
Batman	Tasmania, Australia	675	206	1968	Osaka Port	Japan	548	167	1993
Burlington Bridge	Burlington, IA, USA	660	201	1993	El Canon	Mexico	545	166	1993
Ayunose [1]	Japan	656	200	(1999)	Tahtiniemi	Heinola, Finland	541	165	1993
Alamillo	Guadalquivir R., Seville, Spain	656	200	1992	Daikoku	Kanagawa, Japan	541	165	1974
Shin Inagawa [1]	Osaka, Japan	656	200	XXX	Val Benoit	Meuse R., Liege, Belgium	531	162	XXX
Torikai–Niwaji (Yodogawa)	Settsu, Osaka, Japan	656	200	1987	Shin Mandai	Japan	531	162	1993
Chung Yang	Taiwan	656	200	1984	Paris–Massena	Paris, France	529	161	1969
Maogang	Shanghai, China	656	200	1982	Steyregger	Danube R., Austria	529	161	1979
Chichibu Park Bridge	Arakawa R., Saitama Pref., Japan	640	195	XXX	Risscoff [1]	Spain	525	160	XXX
Neches R. Bridge	TX, USA	640	195	1991	Alcaravaneras [1]	Spain	525	160	XXX
Ijssel Bridge	Kampen, Netherlands	635	194	1983	Umezawa	Japan	525	160	XXX
James River Bridge	near Richmond, VA, USA	630	192	1989	Nanhai over Jiujiang R.	Nanhai, Guangdong Prov., China	525	160	1988
Sakitama	Sakitama, Japan	623	190	1991	Ishikarikako	Hokkaido, Japan	525	160	1972
Ashigara	Kanagawa, Japan	607	185	1991	Arakawa	Tokyo, Japan	525	160	1970
Bybrua	Norway	607	185	1978	Okutama	Japan	522	159	1994
Aratsu Bridge	Fukuoka, Japan	604	184	1988	Krasnojarsk	Eastern Siberia	515	157	1991
Wandre	Belgium	600	183	1989	Cassagne	Cassagne, France	512	156	1899
Stromsund	Sweden	600	183	1955	Saame Bridge	Finland/Norway border	509	155	XXX
Adhmiyah	Baghdad, Iraq	599	183	1983	Utsjoki over Teno R.	Finland	509	155	1993
Carpineto	Prov. Poetenza, Italy	594	181	1977	Kannon [5]	Japan	509	155	1991
Tskuhara	Japan	591	180	(1997)	George Street	Newport, Gwent, Wales	500	152	1964
Kanisawa	Japan	591	180	XXX	Fureai	Japan	499	152	1993
Sanshui over Xijiang R. [1]	Guangdong Prov., China	591	180	XXX	Bourgone Bridge	Chalon-Sur-Saone, France	499	152	1992
Galecopper	Utrecht, Netherlands	590	180	1972	Chichibu	Saitama, Japan	499	152	1985
Suigo	Chiba, Japan	587	179	1977	Toyomi [1]	Japan	492	150	(1997)
Tulln	Danube R., Tulln, Austria	581	177	XXX	Third Qiantang R. Crossing	Hangzhou, Zhejiang Prov., China	492	150	XXX
Yohkura (Intl. Airport) [10]	Hiroshima, Japan	581	177	1992	Colindres	Spain	492	150	XXX
					Shiba Channel	Japan	492	150	1993
Lanaye	Belgium	581	177	1987	Yelcho R. Bridge	Chile	492	150	1989
Barranca el Zapote	Mexico	577	176	1993	Olympic Bridge	Korea	492	150	1989
Changxindao	Fuxian, Liaoning Prov., China	577	176	1981	Salvador (Bahia)	Brazil	492	150	1980
Mosul	Iraq	577	176	1981	Yanango	Peru	489	149	XXX
Maxau	Maxau, Germany	575	175	1966	Isere Viaduct	Valence–Grenoble, France	486	148	1991
Haiyin	Guangzhou, Guangdong Prov., China	574	175	1988	Mainbrucke [2]	Hoechst, Germany	486	148	1972
Karlsruhe	Germany	574	175	1965	Ebro R.	Navarra, Spain	480	146	1981
Iwazu	Japan	571	174	1993	Major	Spain	480	146	1980
Ganter	Switzerland	571	174	1980	Matsukawa [1]	Fukushima, Japan	476	145	1993
Nordhordland	between Kristiansand and Trondheim, Norway	564	172	1994	Danube Bridge	Metten, Germany	476	145	1982
					Ansa de Magliana	Rome, Italy	476	145	1967
Norderelbe	Hamburg, Germany	564	172	1963	Hattabara [1]	Hiroshima, Japan	472	144	1992
Utagenka	Japan	558	170	1993	Gassho	Toyama, Japan	472	144	1979
Minami Tahara	Japan	558	170	1993	Eisai	Kanagawa, Japan	472	144	1977
Paldang Grand Bridge [1]	Seoul, Korea	558	170	1995	Dnieper R.	Kiev, Ukraine	472	144	1964
					Nanguh	Japan	463	141	1995
Third Qiantang R. Bridge [1]	Hangzhou, Zhejiang Prov., China	551	168	XXX	Chandoline Bridge	Sion, Switzerland	459	140	XXX
					Karabitsu [1]	Japan	459	140	(1997)
					Toko	Hokkaido, Japan	459	140	1992
					Twin Harp Bridge	Japan	459	140	1991
					Bannaguro	Hokkaido, Japan	459	140	1990

[a] Notes for this column are listed at end of table, p. 1321.
[b] Parentheses indicate projected completion date.
*Collapse date.
XXX Completion date unknown.

(*continued*)

TABLE C.1
(continued)

Name[a]	Location	Length of main or major span (ft)	(m)	Year completed[b]	Name[a]	Location	Length of main or major span (ft)	(m)	Year completed[b]
Barranquilla	Barranquilla, Colombia	459	140	1974	Ogawa	Gunma Pref., Japan	375	114	1995
Neckarcenter Bridge [5]	Mannheim, Germany	458	140	1975	Tanaro R.	Alba, Italy	375	114	1983
Ludwigshafen	Ludwigshafen, Germany	458	140	1968	Fusetaura	Mie, Japan	374	114	1989
Maya	Koebe, Japan	457	139	1966	Notojima [1]	Japan	372	113.5	(1997)
John O'Connel Memorial	Sitka, AK, USA	450	137	1972	Macau/Taipa	Macau	367	112	1994
Chikumagawa [1, 6]	Japan	443	135	(1998)	Denden [17]	Japan	367	112	1989
Bidouze Valley	Orthez–Briscous, France	440	134	1991	Lezardrieux	Lezardrieux, France	367	112	1925
Toda Park	Japan	440	134	1990	Usui	Gunma, Japan	365	111	1992
Kwang Fu	Taiwan	440	134	1978	Rhône R.	St. Maurice, Switzerland	365	111	1986
Linjiangmen over Songhuajiang R. [1]	Jilin City, China	435	132.5	XXX	Las Americas	La Paz, Bolivia	361	110	1993
Pertuiset	France	433	132	1988	Shin Tamba	Kyoto, Japan	361	110	1987
Alcoy	Spain	433	132	1986	Alcoy Bridge	Spain	361	110	1985
Santa Rosa	Santa Cruz, Bolivia	427	130	1994	Shunda [1]	Fukushima, Japan	356	109	XXX
Alzette R.	Howald/Hesperange, Luxembourg	427	130	1994	Harmsenburg	Rotterdam, Netherlands	356	109	1968
Sanuki Fuchuko [1]	Kanagawa, Japan	427	130	1992	Tiber Bridge	Rome, Italy	355	108	1981
Sama de Langreo	Spain	427	130	1988	Natorigawa [1, 6]	Japan	354	108	(1996)
Nalon R.	Spain	427	130	XXX	Harata	Japan	354	108	1993
Fujiang	Santai, Sichuan Prov., China	420	128	1980	Sambre	Belgium	354	108	1988
Katsuse	Kanagawa, Japan	420	128	1960	Kamitsu [1]	Japan	351	107	(1996)
Hinoura	Aioi, Hyogo, Japan	418	127	1980	Kamitsu	Hyogo, Japan	351	107	1990
Martyrs Bridge	Grenoble, France	413	126	1991	Sapporo Munchen [1]	Sapporo, Hokkaido, Japan	351	107	1991
Kemijoki R. Bridge	Rovaniemi, Finland	413	126	1989	Flo er	Germany	350	107	1986
Jundushan Aqueduct [9]	Yanging County, Beijing, China	413	126	1988	Socorridos Bridge	Madeira Island, Portugal	348	106	1993
Rhine R. Bridge, Rt. N4	Schaffhausen, Switzerland	411	125.26	1995	Bridge over Sambre R. [15]	Belgium	348	106	1988
Colindres [14]	Spain	410	125	1993	Colindres	Spain	344	105	1993
Evripos	Athens, Greece	410	125	1991	La Arena [16]	Spain	344	105	1993
Franklinstrasse	Dusseldorf, Germany	410	125	1974	Yashiro-minami [6]	Japan	344	105	1991
Xigiao	Namhai, Guangdong Prov., China	409	125	1987	Yongjiang	Ningbo, Zhejiang Prov., China	344	105	1988
Lerez [1]	Spain	407	124	1994	Saint Maurice	Switzerland	344	105	1986
Heisei [1]	Gunma, Japan	407	124	1991	Bridge of the Isles	Montreal, Canada	344	105	1967
Shiraya	Nara, Japan	407	124	1991	Dagu R.	Shandong Prov., China	341	104	1977
Hikihara	Hyogo, Japan	407	124	1991	Shin–Ohashi	Tokyo, Japan	341	104	1976
Yasaka	Yamaguchi, Japan	407	124	1987	Okuwaka	Japan	341	104	1968
Karauko	Japan	404	123	1994	Saint-Florent-Le-Vieil	France	341	104	1965
Elbe R.	Podebrady, Czech Republic	404	123	1990	Suwa-kyo	Japan	338	103	1993
Heer Agimont	Meuse R., Belgium	404	123	1975	Kamitsuma	Gunma, Japan	338	103	1990
Odawara Blueway	Japan	400	122	1988	Kashima [5]	Japan	338	103	1988
Haengju, Han R.	Seoul, Korea	394	120	1995	Vrsovice	Prague, Czech Republic	332	101	1992
Martyrs	Grenoble, France	394	120	1991	Nitchu	Fukushima, Japan	331	101	1989
Tongzilin	Sichuan Prov., China	394	120	1990	Kasai Nagisa	Japan	328	100	1992
Fujito	Aioi, Hyogo, Japan	394	120	1980	Suho	Japan	328	100	1991
Ankang, Power Station	Shanxi Prov., China	394	120	1979	Dongfeng	Yunnan Prov., China	328	100	1985
Lake Jordan	Tabor, Czech Republic	390	119	1990	Takanashi	Shimane, Japan	328	100	1984
Strallato, Danube Canal	Vienna, Austria	390	119	1975	Zurhoff	Netherlands	328	100	1976
Neris River [1]	Vilnius, Lithuania	389	118.5	1984	Safti	Singapore	327	100	1995
Nishihaga	Fukushima, Japan	381	116	1989	Hachinohe	Japan	324	99	1996
Western Distributor Rd.	Leven R., Edinburgh, Scotland	377	115	1995	Tokimeki	Japan	324	99	1993
Veterans Admin. Skybridge [5]	Portland, OR, USA	377	115	1993	Julicherstrasse	Dusseldorf, Germany	324	99	1963
Seyssel	Lyon, France	377	115	1987	Taira	Japan	323	98.5	1995
Fuji Country Club [5]	Japan	377	115	1981	Sele R. [8]	Italy	322	98	1980
Foss Waterway	Tacoma, WA, USA	375	114	1996	Miyamoto	Japan	318	97	1994
					Rhine R.	Diepoldsau–Widnau, Switzerland	318	97	1985
					Matsugayama	Kanagawa, Japan	318	97	1978
					Laibin over Hongshui R. [6]	Guangxi Prov., China	315	96	1981
					Shin-watashi	Japan	308	94	1994
					Cycling Road [18]	Japan	308	94	1993
					Fukiagehama	Japan	308	94	1993

TABLE C.1
(continued)

Name[a]	Location	(ft)	(m)	Year completed[b]	Name[a]	Location	(ft)	(m)	Year completed[b]
Fushinogawa [9]	Japan	307	93.5	1983	Wilmersdorf Stadium [5]	Berlin, Germany	256	78	1974
Rhône R.	St. Maurice, Switzerland	305	93	1987	Saale R.	Nienburg, Germany	256	78	1824*
RW16 Overpass [5]	Rotterdam, Netherlands	299	91	1993	Henfeng North Rd.	Shanghai, China	253	77	1987
Gosyogawara [9]	Japan	299	91	1985	Sango [5]	Japan	253	77	1970
Yashiro-kita [6]	Japan	295	90	1996	Neckar R. [6]	Unterturkheim, Germany	253	77	1967
Garigliano R.	Italy	295	90	XXX	Haneda Sky Arch	Japan	249	76	1993
Huaiyin	Jiangsu Prov., China	295	90	1991	Yunyang	Sichuan Prov., China	249	76	1975
Kamome Bridge	Shinagawa, Tokyo, Japan	295	90	1986	Heisei	Nakano City, Japan	246	75	1994
Sanyuan	Shanxi Prov., China	291	89	1986	Susobana	Japan	246	75	1993
Heinrich Ehrhard	Germany	291	89	1981	Volta–Steg [5]	Neckar R., Stuttgart, Germany	246	75	1957
Jamatu Shirogane	Japan	291	89	1980	Akkar	India	246	75	XXX
Air Side Bridge	Tokyo Intl. Airport, Japan	290	88.5	1991	Sumoto	Japan	243	74	1993
Kawasaki–Bashi [5]	Old-Yodo R., Osaka, Japan	287	88	1978	Shin Moji	Fukuoka, Japan	243	74	1987
Access Road Bridge	Tokyo Intl. Airport, Japan	287	87.5	1992	Fureai [5]	Japan	243	74	1987
Footbridge, M-30 Motorway [5]	Madrid, Spain	282	86		Fishing Pier Bridge	Amagasaki, Hyogo, Japan	243	74	1982
Sieglanger [5]	Innsbruck, Austria	282	86	1977	Pont de la Bourse [5]	Le Havre, France	241	73	1969
M-25 Footbridge [5]	Spain	281	86	1967	Liuzhuang over Haihe R.	Tianjin City, China	236	72	1991
Tsukuhara	Kobe, Hyogo, Japan	281	86	1986	Marbella	Spain	236	72	1989
Hirosegawa [9]	Japan	279	85	1994	Zhangzhen	Zhejiang Prov., China	236	72	1983
Koshiki Daimyojin	Kagoshima Pref., Japan	279	85	1993	Mabito	Japan	234	71	1995
Neckar R. [5]	Ludwigsburg, Germany	279	85	1980	Ganga Canal [5]	Roorkee, India	234	71	1981
Omotogawa [6]	Iawate, Japan	279	85	1979	Jiali jiang	Sichuan Prov., China	233	71	1981
Kokubugawa [9]	Japan	277	84.5	1983	Flaming Geyser #3024	Green R., King County, WA, USA	230	70	1993
Vrbas R.	Banja Luka, Yugoslavia	276	84	XXX	Ville-sur-Haine [5]	Belgium	230	70	1988
Ishikawa Cycle [18]	Japan	276	84	1993	Pforzheim Bridge	Germany	230	70	1987
Hayes Footbridge [5]	Hayes, Middlesex, UK	276	84	1993	Zengda	Jinchuan, Sichuan Prov., China	230	70	1981
Hiroshima Airport Bridge [10]	Hiroshima, Japan	273	83	1995	Bosna R. (upstream) [5]	Zenica, Yugoslavia	226	69	1985
Captain William Moore	near Skagway, AK, USA	271	83	1974	Schillerstrasse [5]	Stuttgart, Germany	226	69	1961
Yamato	Osaka, Japan	271	83	1974	Pas du Lac [5]	France	223	68	1992
Barwon R. [5, 8]	Geelong, Australia	270	82	1969	Nakayoshi Bridge	Yachiyo, Chiba, Japan	223	68	1984
Saudi Arabia	Saudi Arabia	268	82	XXX	Lodemann Bridge [5]	Hanover, Germany	223	68	1965
Neto R. [9]	Italy	268	82	1973	Bidouze R.	France	220	67	1991
Shirakobato	Japan	266	81	1994	Futago [5]	Japan	220	67	1986
Le pont de Donzere	France	266	81	1951	Eimeikan (Horikoshi)	Tokyo, Japan	220	67	1984
Rw 16 Rotterdam	Netherlands	262	80	1994	Orizuru [5]	Japan	220	67	1980
Alende	Spain	262	80	1993	Isamu [5]	Japan	220	67	1975
Takino	Hokkaido, Japan	262	80	1992	Canal du Centre [5]	Obourg, Belgium	220	67	1966
Ayumi	Japan	262	80	1983	Prince's Island [5]	Calgary, Alb., Canada	220	67	XXX
Eric Harvie Bridge [5]	Calgary, Alb., Canada	262	80	1983	Bickensteg Bridge	Villingen, Germany	218	67	1972
Jinno	Hokkaido, Japan	262	80	1963	6 October Bridge	Cairo, Egypt	218	66.5	1995
Shinhama Bridge	Saga Pref., Japan	259	79	1994	Reuss R. [5, 9]	Bremgarten, Switzerland	217	66	1975
Melan [5]	Isere R., Melan, France	259	79	1980	Fontelle	Trith Saint Leger, France	217	66	XXX
Tweed R. [5]	Dryburgh–Abbey, England	259	79	1818*	Menomonee Falls [5]	Menomonee Falls, WI, USA	217	66	1971
Ryogun	Japan	256	78	1994	Reuss Bridge	Bremgarten, Switzerland	217	66	1970
Miyamoto	Japan	256	78	1994					
Pont Sur L'Allen	France	256	78	1994	Nackawic R.	New Brun., Canada	216	66	1967
Matsudagawa [9]	Japan	256	78	1987	Nakoyoi	Shizuoka, Japan	213	65	1989
Bosna R. (downstream) [5]	Zenica, Yugoslavia	256	78	1985	New Supply Channel Bridge	Hardwar, India	213	65	XXX

[a] Notes for this column are listed at end of table, p. 1321.
[b] Parentheses indicate projected completion date.
*Collapse date.
XXX Completion date unknown.

(continued)

TABLE C.1
(*continued*)

Name[a]	Location	(ft)	(m)	Year completed[b]	Name[a]	Location	(ft)	(m)	Year completed[b]
Nishi-sanjo Viaduct [6]	Japan	212	64.5	1996	Shintenjin	Japan	174	53	1995
Loir R.	La Fleche, France	210	64	XXX	The Rojo Gomez Bridge	Patitlan–La Paz, Mexico	174	53	1991
Patema Bridge	Provincia de Valencia, Spain	210	64	1991	Tilff Bridge	Belgium	174	53	1975
Yasuragi [5]	Fukko, Toyama, Japan	210	64	1981	Kodomo-no-kuni [5]	Japan	174	53	1971
Illhof [5]	Ill R., Strasbourg, France	208	64	1980	Nishikigaoka No. 3 Bridge	Hokkaido, Japan	172	52.5	1982
Aberfeldy [5,11]	Aberfeldy golf course, UK	207	63	1992	Benton City [7]	Yakima R., WA, USA	170	52	1957
					Uragami [5]	Japan	167	51	1990
Bandai [18]	Japan	205	62.5	1991	Yana	Shimane, Japan	167	51	1990
Kortrijk	Belgium	203	62	XXX	Luino over Tresa R.	Luino City, Varesa, Italy	166	50.5	1994
Winterthur [19]	Winterthur, Switzerland	200	61	XXX					
Hakusan	Japan	200	61	1996	Ohshiroike	Japan	166	50.5	1993
White Mountain Bridge	Nigata Pref., Japan	200	61	1994	The Crisostomo Bonilla	Patitlan-La Paz, Mexico	164	50	1991
L'Humanite	Belgium	200	61	1994	Republica Federal Bridge	Patitlan-La Paz, Mexico	164	50	1991
Ichibasaka	Japan	200	61	1993	Pulandian Bridge	Dalian, Liaoning Prov., China	164	50	1990
North Romaine R. [6]	Quebec, Canada	200	61	1960					
Oyama Gate	Japan	198	60	1993	Funade [5]	Japan	164	50	1989
Rhône R.	Riddes and Leytron, Switzerland	198	60	1992	Fureai [5]	Japan	164	50	1987
					Universiade Mwm. [5]	Japan	164	50	1984
Majitang	Taojiang, Hunan Prov., China	198	60	1985	Diekirch Bridge	Luxembourg	164	50	1974
					Birs Bridge [5]	Basel, Switzerland	164	50	1962
Santo Domingo Bridge	Santo Domingo, Dominican R.	198	60	1975	Botan [5]	Japan	163	49.5	1982
Tempul Aqueduct	Guadalete R., Spain	198	60	1925	Sohsui [9]	Japan	162	49	1994
Ponte Sul Tresa	Luino, Italy	197	60	1993	Maeda Forest Park	Japan	162	49	1994
Labofina	Belgium	195	59.5	1991	Yamanobe [5]	Takasaka, Saitama, Japan	162	49	1982
Lyne over M-25 Overpass [6]	Chertsey, England	195	59.5	1979					
Fureai	Japan	193	59	1993	Cotton Tree Drive [5]	Hong Kong	162	49	1979
Farges Allichamps	France	193	59	1992	Airport Hotel [5]	Hong Kong	157	48	1982
Buchenauer	Germany	193	58.8	1956	Hakucho [5]	Japan	156	47.5	1987
Jackfield Bridge,. Severn R.	Telford near Shropshire, UK	190	58	1995	Kita Kawauchi	Japan	154	47	1994
Uchiage	Japan	190	58	1995	Kaiseraugst [5] (Liebruti)	Basel, Switzerland	154	47	1978
Chikumagawa	Japan	190	58	1995					
Deai [5]	Japan	190	58	1993	Heisei	Japan	151	46	1989
Shotaisan Country Club [5]	Japan	189	57.5	1991	Aisen [5]	Japan	151	46	1984
					Reservoir Intake Tower [5]	Granada, Spain	147.6	45	1996
Yutani [5]	Japan	187	57	1989	Poplar Transit Station [5]	London, England	146	45	1992
Araki [9]	Japan	187	57	1986	Tanteba	Japan	146	45	1990
Yukitsuri [5]	Japan	187	57	1985	Fudokutsu	Nara, Japan	146	45	1989
Shimeno	Japan	187	57	1985	Fo Tan [5]	Hong Kong	146	45	1988
Ipponsugi [5]	Japan	187	57	1981	Yoshimi [5]	Japan	146	44.5	1998
Center Bridge [5]	Japan	182	56	1987	Sud III Expressway [5]	Rouen, France	146	44.4	
Myton Bridge [4]	Kingston upon Hull, England	182	56	1981	Nakao	Japan	144	44	1993
					Fukuoka Roman [5]	Japan	144	44	1990
					Kanazawa-chisake [5]	Japan	144	44	1986
Yamaguchi Reservoir [5]	Japan	182	56	1975	Ichinose	Hyogo, Japan	144	44	1985
Sun-marine	Japan	180	55	1996	Kotaki	Japan	144	44	1985
Canal San Juan	Patitlan–La Paz, Mexico	180	55	1991	Saiwai [5]	Japan	144	44	1981
					Bundesallee [5]	Berlin, Germany	144	44	1971
Okuno Echo [5]	Japan	180	55	1990	Tsuruoh [5]	Japan	142	43	1989
Grand Slum Country Club [5]	Japan	180	55	1985	Mitsuya Bridge [5]	Morioka, Iwate, Japan	142	43	1987
					Kawahara [5]	Morioka, Iwate,	142	43	1979
Merridian [4]	Merridian, CA, USA	180	55	1977	Mizumoto Park [5]	Japan	142	43	1973
Obourg [5]	Obourg, Belgium	180	55	1975	Ibor	Spain	138	42	1994
Asunaro [5]	Japan	179	54.5	1990	Pyrmont	Australia	138	42	1993
Central [5]	Japan	178	54	1982	Galgenberg Bridge	Waiblingen, Germany	138	42	1988
Shinbashi [5]	Japan	178	54	1978	Nakanohashi [5]	Japan	138	42	1981
Glacischaussee [5]	Hamburg, Germany	178	54	1963	Alende	Spain	137	41.7	1993
Xinwu	Shanghai, China	177	54	1975	Dahu Second Bridge	Liuyang, Hunan Prov., China	135	41	1989
Raxstrasse [5]	Vienna, Austria	177	54	1969					

TABLE C.1
(continued)

Name[a]	Location	Length of main or major span (ft)	(m)	Year completed[b]	Name[a]	Location	Length of main or major span (ft)	(m)	Year completed[b]
Yuhyake [5]	Japan	131	40	1990	Fureai Bridge [5]	Nara, Japan	115	35	1986
Momiji [5]	Japan	131	40	1989	Rother Valley Park [5]	North Sheffield, UK	115	35	1985
Salpasilta [1]	Joenssu, Finland	131	40	1994					
Akebono [5]	Japan	135	41	1983	King's Meadow [5]	Tees R., England	110	34	1817
Les Gures	France	131	40	1988	Fukaura [5]	Japan	108	33	1994
Namiki [5]	Japan	131	40	1978	Scripps Crossing [5]	La Jolla, California, USA	108	33	1993
Ichirihoki [5]	Japan	131	40	1978					
Kenzan Chuo [5]	Japan	131	40	1974	Beaune Overpass	France	108	33	1992
Shimada	Gifu, Japan	131	40	1963*	Duisburg [5]	Germany	106	32	1958
Makino [5]	Japan	128	39	1994	Leehsteg [1]	Reutta, Austria	105	32	1995
Chinaigawa [5]	Japan	128	39	1994	Loscher, C. J.	Switzerland	105	32	1784
Zosui	Nagano, Japan	128	39	1987	Preston Docks [4]	Preston, UK	102	31	1985
Apollon [5]	Japan	128	39	1985	Sileda	Spain	98	30	1993
Fureai [5]	Japan	125	38	1991	Gures Overpass	France	98	30	1988
Bungo	Fukuoka, Japan	125	38	1983	Pretoria [8]	Pretoria, S. Africa	93	28	1968
Ube Country Club [5]	Japan	125	38	1980	Bird Sanctuary Bridge [5,10]	Hikichi R., Yamoto City, Kanagawa Pref., Japan	90	27	1992
Juan Carlos	Dominican Republic	125	38	1977					
Expo Higashi Gate [5]	Japan	125	38	1969					
Bridge of "R" [5]	Japan	122	37	1993	Chongqing Bridge [5,11]	China	90	27	1986
Rosewood Golf Club [5]	Ono City near Kyoto, Japan	122	37	1993	Katsumoto Dam	Nagasaki, Japan	89	27	1981
Grand Tressan [5]	France	121	37	1989	Iwafune Country Club [5]	Japan	85	26	1992
Mount Street [5]	Perth, Australia	117	36	1969					
Kohen [5]	Japan	115	35	1994	Kaminozoki	Nagaoka, Niigata, Japan	64	20	1991
Overpass 73 over A6 Motorway	Beaune, France	115	35	1992	Tschachen R.	Switzerland	60	18	1973
					Ghent Opera House	Ghent, Belgium	57.4	17.5	1993

[1] Under construction [2] Railroad and highway [3] Twin bridges [4] Swing span [5] Pedestrian [6] Rail [7] Structural steel shape stay [8] Pipe bridge [9] Aqueduct [10] Timber girder [11] Fiber composite [12] Double deck [13] Connects to a 1246-m-long floating bridge [14] Three pylons, four-span continuous [15] Railway [16] Six pylons, seven-span continuous [17] Telecommunication pipe bridge [18] Bicycle bridge [19] CFRP stays

Database lists 600 cable-stayed bridges. Eight bridges were completed before 1950 and/or collapsed; they are only of historical significance or no longer exist. If these are excluded from consideration, the database reduces to 592 bridges either completed or under construction, distributed among 54 countries as follows:

Japan	228	Austria	8
China	46	Australia, Finland, Korea, and Yugoslavia, each	6
Germany	41	Argentina, Hong Kong, and Norway, each	5
France	29	Czech Republic, India, and Portugal, each	4
United States	27	Ukraine, Greece, and Taiwan, each	3
Spain	26	Bolivia, Denmark, Dominican Republic, Iraq,	
Belgium	18	Luxembourg, Saudi Arabia, and Sweden, each	2
United Kingdom	16	Algeria, Brazil, Chile, Colombia, Egypt,	
Switzerland	14	Indonesia, Latvia, Libya, Lithuania, Macau,	
Netherlands	12	Malaysia, Nepal, Peru, Russia, Siberia, Singapore,	
Canada, Italy, and Mexico, each	11	South Africa, Thailand, Venezuela, and Zambia, each	1

Note: Data compiled by Dr. Walter Podolny, Jr., senior structural engineer, Bridge Management Group, HNG-32, Federal Highway Administration, Washington, D. C., March 1997.

TABLE C.2
Suspension bridges of the world

Name[a]	Location	Length of main or major span (ft)	(m)	Year completed[b]	Name[a]	Location	Length of main or major span (ft)	(m)	Year completed[b]
Akashi Kaikyo [1]	Japan	6529	1990	(1998)	Skyway [3]	World's Fair, Chicago, IL, USA	1850	564	1933
Storebelt [1]	Zealand–Sprago, Denmark	5328	1624	(1997)	Hakata-Oshima	Japan	1837	560	1988
Humber River	Hull, England	4626	1410	1981	Throgs Neck	New York City, USA	1800	549	1961
Jiangyin Bridge	Yangtze R., Jiangsu Prov., China	4544	1385	XXX	Benjamin Franklin [2]	PA, USA	1750	533	1926
Tsing Ma Bridge [1]	Hong Kong	4518	1377	(1997)	Skjomen	Narvik, Norway	1722	525	1972
Hardanger Fjord	Norway	4347	1325	XXX	Kvalsund	Hammerfest, Norway	1722	525	1977
Verrazano Narrows	New York City, USA	4260	1298	1964	Dazi Bridge	Lasa, Xizang Region, China	1640	500	1984
Golden Gate	San Francisco, USA	4200	1280	1937	Kleve–Emmerich	Emmerich, Germany	1640	500	1965
Hoga Kusten [1]	400 km north of Stockholm, Sweden	3970	1210	(1997)	Bear Mountain	Peekskill, NY, USA	1632	497	1924
Mackinac Straits	MI, USA	3800	1158	1957	William Preston Lane, Jr. [5]	near Annapolis, MD, USA	1600	488	1952
Minami Bisan–Seto	Japan	3609	1100	1988	William Preston Lane, Jr. [5]	near Annapolis, MD, USA	1600	488	1973
Second Bosporus [1]	Istanbul, Turkey	3576	1090	1988	Williamsburg [2]	New York City, USA	1600	488	1903
First Bosporus	Istanbul, Turkey	3524	1074	1973	Newport	Newport, RI, USA	1600	488	1969
George Washington	New York City, USA	3500	1067	1931	Chesapeake Bay	Sandy Point, MD, USA	1600	488	1952
Third Kurushima Bridge	Japan	3379	1030	(1999)	Brooklyn [2]	New York City, USA	1595	486	1883
Second Kurushima Bridge	Japan	3346	1020	(1999)	Lions Gate	Vancouver, B. C., Canada	1550	472	1939
Tagus River [2]	Lisbon, Protugal	3323	1013	1966					
Forth Road	Queensferry, Scotland	3300	1006	1964	Hirato Ohashi	Hirato, Japan	1536	468	1977
Kita Bisan-Seto	Japan	3248	990	1988	Sotra	Bergen, Norway	1535	468	1971
Severn	Beachley, England	3240	988	1966	Hirato	Japan	1526	465	1977
Shimotsui Straits	Japan	3084	940	1988	Vincent Thomas	San Pedro–Terminal Islands, CA, USA	1500	457	1963
Xiling Bridge	Yangtze R., Xiling Gorge, China	2953	900	XXX	Mid-Hudson	Poughkeepsie, NY, USA	1495	457	1930
Tigergate (Humen)	Pearl R., Guangdong Prov., China	2913	888	XXX	Shantou Bay Bridge	Shantou, Guangdong Prov., China	1483	452	1995
Ohnaruto	Japan	2874	876	1985	Manhattan [2]	New York City, USA	1470	448	1909
Tacoma Narrows I [3]	Tacoma, WA, USA	2800	853	1940	MacDonald Bridge	Halifax, Nov. Scot., Canada	1447	441	1955
Tacoma Narrows II	Tacoma, WA, USA	2800	853	1950					
Askøy	near Bergen, Norway	2787	850	1992	A. Murray Mackay	Halifax, Nov. Scot., Canada	1400	426	1970
Innoshima	Japan	2526	770	1983					
Akinada [1]	Japan	2461	750	XXX	Triborough	New York City, USA	1380	421	1936
Hakucho [1]	Japan	2362	720	XXX	Alvsborg	Goteborg, Sweden	1370	418	1966
Kanmon Straits	Kyushu–Honshu, Japan	2336	712	1973	Hadong-Namhae	Pusan, South Korea	1325	404	1973
					Aquitaine	Bordeaux, France	1292	394	XXX
Angostura	Ciudad Bolivar, Venezuela	2336	712	1967	Baclan	Garrone R., Bordeaux, France	1292	394	1967
San Francisco–Oakland Bay [4]	San Francisco, USA	2310	704	1936	Ame–Darja R.	Buhara–Ural, Russia	1280	390	1964
Bronx–Whitestone	New York City, USA	2300	701	1939	Clifton [3]	Niagara Falls, NY, USA	1268	386	1869
Pierre Laporte	Quebec, Canada	2190	668	1970	Cologne–Rodenkirchen I [3]	Cologne, Germany	1240	378	1941
Delaware Memorial [5]	Wilmington, DE, USA	2150	655	1951					
Delaware Memorial [5]	Wilmington, DE, USA	2150	655	1968	Cologne–Rodenkirchen II [10]	Cologne, Germany	1240	378	1955
Seaway Skyway	Ogdensburg, NY, USA	2150	655	1960	St. Johns	Portland, OR, USA	1207	368	1931
Gjemnessund	Norway	2044	623	1992	Wakato	Kit-Kyushu City, Japan	1205	367	1962
Walt Whitman	Philadelphia, PA, USA	2000	610	1957	Mount Hope	Bristol, RI, USA	1200	366	1929
Tancarville	Tancarville, France	1995	608	1959	St. Lawrence R.	Ogdensburg, NY–Prescot, Ont., Canada	1150	351	1960
First Kurushima Bridge	Japan	1969	600	(1999)	Ponte Hercilio [2,6]	Florianapolis, Brazil	1114	340	1926
Lillebaelt	Lillebaelt Strait, Denmark	1969	600	1970	Bidwell Bar Bridge	Oroville, CA, USA	1108	338	1965
Kvisti [1]	Bergen, Nordland, Norway	1952	595		Middle Fork Feather R.	CA, USA	1105	337	1964
					Varodd, Topdalsfjord	Kristiansand, Norway	1105	337	1956
Tokyo Port Connect. Bridge [1]	Tokyo, Japan	1870	570	1993	Tamar Road	Plymouth, Great Britain	1100	335	1961
					Deer Isle	Deer Isle, ME, USA	1080	329	1939
Ambassador	Detroit, MI, USA–Canada	1850	564	1929	Rombaks	Narvik, Nordland, Norway	1066	325	1964

TABLE C.2
(*continued*)

Name[a]	Location	(ft)	(m)	Year completed[b]	Name[a]	Location	(ft)	(m)	Year completed[b]
		Length of main or major span					Length of main or major span		
Maysville	Maysville, KY, USA	1060	323	1931	Ohio R.	East Liverpool, OH, USA	705	215	1896
Ile d'Orleans	St. Lawrence R., Quebec, Canada	1059	323	1936	Clifton [3,6]	Bristol, England	702	214	1864
Ohio R.	Cincinnati, OH, USA	1057	322	1867	Ohio R. [6]	St. Mary's, OH, USA	700	213	1929
Otto Beit	Zambezi R., Rhodesia	1050	320	1939	Ohio R. [3,6]	Point Pleasant, OH, USA	700	213	1928
Dent	North Fork, Clearwater R., ID, USA	1050	320	1971	Sixth Street	Pittsburgh, PA, USA	700	213	1928
Niagara [3]	Lewiston, NY, USA	1040	317	1850	General U.S. Grant	Ohio R., Portsmouth, OH, USA	700	213	1927
Cologne–Mulheim I [3]	Cologne, Germany	1033	315	1929	Airline	St. Jo, TX, USA	700	213	1927
Cologne–Mulheim II	Cologne, Germany	1033	315	1951	Red R.	Nocona, TX, USA	700	213	1924
Miampimi	Mexico	1030	314	1900	Ohio R.	Steubenville, OH, USA	700	213	1904
Wheeling	WV, USA	1010	308	1848	Ohio R.	Steubenville, OH, USA	689	210	1928
Wheeling	WV, USA	1010	308	1856	Isere	Veurey, France	688	210	1934
Konohana [8,9]	Osaka, Japan	984	300	1990	Hungerford [3,6]	London, England	676	206	1845
Elizabeth [6]	Budapest, Hungary	951	290	1903	Mississippi R. [3]	Minneapolis, MN, USA	675	206	1877
Tjeldsund	Harstad, Norway	951	290	1967	Meixihe Bridge	Fengjie, Sichuan Prov., China	673	205	1990
Grand Mere	Quebec, Canada	948	289	1929	Lancz [6]	Budapest, Hungary	663	202	1845
Cauca R.	Colombia	940	287	1894	White R.	Des Arc, AR, USA	650	198	1928
Jinhu Bridge	Taining, Fujian Prov., China	932	284	1989	Roche Bernard [3]	Vilaine, France	650	198	1836
Peace R.	B.C., Canada	932	284	1950	Missouri R.	IL, USA	643	196	1956
Aramon	France	902	275	1901	Caille [3]	Annecy, France	635	194	1839
Cornwall–Masena	St. Lawrence R., NY–Ont., Canada	900	274	1958	Columbia R.	Beegee, WA, USA	632	193	1919
Fribourg [3]	Switzerland	896	273	1834	Rio Grande	Roma, TX, USA	630	192	1928
Brevik	Telemark, Norway	892	272	1962	St. John [3]	New Brun., Canada	628	191	1852
Royal George	Arkansas R., Canon City, CO, USA	880	268	1929	Bernardo Arango	Colombia	627	191	1929
Kjerrringstraumen	Nordland, Norway	853	260	1975	Osage R.	Tuscumbia, MO, USA	627	191	1905
Vranov Lake Bridge	Czech Republic	827	252	1993	Hennepin Avenue	Minneapolis, MN, USA	625	191	1990
Railway Bridge [3]	Niagara R., NY, USA	821	250	1854	...	Colombia	623	190	1926
Dome, Grand Canyon	Dome, AZ, USA	800	244	1929	Mississippi R. [3]	Minneapolis, MN, USA	620	189	1855
Point [3,6]	Pittsburgh, PA, USA	800	244	1877	Missouri R.	MO, USA	617	188	1954
Rochester	Rochester, PA, USA	800	244	1896	Chaoyang Bridge	Chongqing, Sichuan Prov., China	610	186	1969
Niagara R.	Lewiston, NY, USA	800	244	1899	Morgantown [3]	Morgantown, WV, USA	608	185	1855
Thousand Islands, Intl.	St. Lawrence R., USA–Canada	800	244	1938	Rhône R.	Serrieres, France	607	185	1934
Waldo Hancock	Penobscot R., Bucksport, ME, USA	800	244	1931	Rhône R. [3,6,8]	Cologne, Germany	605	184	1915
Anthony Wayne	Maumee R., Toledo, OH, USA	785	239	1931	St. Christophe	Lorient, France	604	184	1847
Parkersburg	Parkersburg, WV, USA	775	236	1916	Guy A. West	CA, USA	600	183	1968
Footbridge [3]	Niagara R., NY, USA	770	235	1847	Georgia–Florida	Donaldsonville, GA, USA	600	183	1927
Vernaison	France	764	233	1902	Bridgeport	Bridgeport, OK, USA	600	183	1921
Cannes Ecluse	France	760	232	1900	Panama Canal	Empire, Panama	600	183	1909
Ohio R.	East Liverpool, OH, USA	750	229	1905	Elverun	Norway	590	180	1932
Gotteron	Freiburg, Germany	746	227	1840	Voulte	Ardeche, France	590	180	1891
Iowa–Illinois Memorial I [3]	Moline, IL, USA	740	226	1934	Crooked R.	OR, USA	587	179	1963
Iowa–Illinois Memorial II	Moline, IL, USA	740	226	1959	Groslee Bridge	France	581	177	XXX
Davenport	IL, USA	740	226	1935	Menai [6]	Bangor, Wales	580	177	1826
Monongahela R.	South 10th Street, Pittsburgh, PA, USA	725	221	1933	98th Meridian	Byers, TX, USA	568	173	1914
Rondout	Kingston, NY, USA	705	215	1922	Vestfold	Norway	558	170	1932
					Invalides [3,6]	Seine R., Paris, France	558	170	1826
					Douro [3]	Oporto, Portugal	557	170	1842
					Fonda	Tribes Hill, NY, USA	556	169	1853
					Inn R.	Brail, Switzerland	550	168	1911
					Rio Higuamo	Santo Domingo, Dominican Republic	544	166	1934
					Cumberland R.	Nashville, TN, USA	540	165	1919
					Elche	Vinalopo R., Elche, Spain	540	164.5	1994
					Osage R.	Linn Creek, MO, USA	525	160	1911

[a] Notes for this column are listed at end of table, p. 1325.
[b] Parentheses indicate projected completion date.
... Unnamed birdge.
XXX Completion date unknown.

(*continued*)

TABLE C.2
(continued)

Name[a]	Location	Length of main or major span (ft)	(m)	Year completed[b]	Name[a]	Location	Length of main or major span (ft)	(m)	Year completed[b]
Bonhomme	Blavet R., France	525	160	1904	Mediacanoa	Colombia	380	116	1927
Villefranche	France	512	156	1906	Rio Cauca	Colombia	380	116	1923
Caperton	WV, USA	510	155	1903	Kellams	Hawkins, NY, USA	380	116	1890
Colorado R.	CO, USA	500	152	1929	Lamothe	Brioude, France	377	115	1884
Sowells Bluff	Durant, OK, USA	500	152	1928	Tetschen [6]	Elbe R., Bohemia	373	114	1855
North Sydney	Australia	500	152	1891	Lezardrieux	Trieux, France	367	112	1924
Windsor Locks	Connecticut R., CT, USA	500	152	1884	Dordogne [3]	Cubzac, France	360	110	1839
Allegheny R.	Oil City, PA, USA	500	152	1877	Schuylkill R. [3]	Philadelphia, PA, USA	358	109	1842
Garonne	Verdun, France	500	152	1846					
Lezardrieux [3]	Trieux, France	500	152	1840	Qileharen Bridge [11]	Eerqisi R., Qilegaren, China	350	108	1992
Whitewater R.	Valley Junction, USA	498	152	1889	Rio Grande	Hidalgo, TX, USA	350	107	1928
Framnes	Norway	492	150	1931	Equinunk [6]	Lordville, NY, USA	345	105	1870
Rio Quequen	Argentina	492	150	1929	Mass [6]	Seraing, Belgium	345	105	1843
Glommen R.	Norway	492	150	1923	Allegheny R.	Pittsburgh, PA, USA	344	105	1857
Franz Joseph [6]	Moldau R., Prague, Czech Republic	482	147	1868	Maine [3]	Angers, France	344	105	1838
					Dordogne	Argentat, France	344	105	1828
Loschwitz [6]	Germany	481	147	1893	Rio Cauca	Colombia	339	103	1920
Elk R. [3]	Charleston, WV, USA	478	146	1852	Saone [3]	Lyon, France	335	102	1828
Est R.	Reunion Island	475	145	1893	Victoria [6]	Chelsea, London, England	333	101	1857
Warren [3,6]	Warren, PA, USA	470	143	1871					
Waco	Waco, TX, USA	470	143	1870	Serrieres	Rhône R., France	332	101	1829
Bulkley R.	Hagwilet, B.C., Canada	460	140	1931	Brilliant	B.C., Canada	331	101	1913
Manawatu R.	New Zealand	460	140	1919	Seventh Street [3,6]	Pittsburgh, PA, USA	330	101	1884
Connecticut R.	Turners Falls, MA, USA	452	138	1870	Aare [6]	Switzerland	330	101	1854
San Rafael	Santo Domingo, Dominican Republic	451	137	1933	Podebrady [6]	Elbe R., Bohemia	330	101	1844
					...	Chile	328	100	1918
Terrall	Ringold, TX, USA	450	137	1917	Constantine [3]	Seine R., Paris, France	328	100	1837
Muskingum R. [6]	Dresden, OH, USA	450	137	1915	Conway [6]	North Wales	327	100	1826
Guyandot	WV, USA	450	137	1848	Mulheim [3,6]	Ruhr R., Germany	320	98	1844
Tweed [6]	Berwick, England	449	137	1819	Gulsvik	Norway	318	97	1904
Seventh Street [6,8]	Pittsburgh, PA, USA	442	135	1926	Humboldthafen [3,6,8]	Berlin, Germany	315	96	1927
Dnieper [6]	Kiev, Ukraine	440	134	1853	Footbridge [6]	Moldau R., Prague, Czech Republic	315	96	1869
Moldau R. [3,6]	Prague, Czech Republic	435	133	1842					
North Bridge	Dalian, Liaoning Prov., China	432	132	1987	Gjeithus	Norway	312	95	1909
Montrose [6]	Scotland	432	132	1829	Weser [3,6]	Hamelin, Germany	312	95	1839
Klamath R. II	CA, USA	430	131	1967	Karl [3,6]	Vienna, Austria	312	95	1828
Ninth Street [6,8]	Pittsburgh, PA, USA	430	131	1928	Loire	Montjean, France	302	92	1927
Ninth Street [6,8]	Pittsburgh, PA, USA	430	131	1927	Tower [6]	London, England	302	92	1895
Noresund	Norway	426	130	1930	Klamath R.	Happy Camp, CA, USA	300	91	1933
Mayo	FL, USA	423	129	1947	Lewis R.	Yale, WA, USA	300	91	1932
Anacaro	Colombia	417	127	1928	Sumida R. [6]	Tokyo, Japan	300	91	1928
...	Colombia	417	127	1927	Cowlitz [3]	Kelso, WA, USA	300	91	1905
Grand Audglauze	MO, USA	415	126	1920	Rio Claro	Chile	295	90	1916
Breslau [6]	Germany	415	126	1910	St. Pierre	Toulouse, France	295	90	1845
Donau R.	Germany	413	126	1910	Charente	Rochefort, France	295	90	1841
Rio Chiriqui	Panama	410	125	1917	Avignon	France	282	86	1888
Schuylkill Falls [3]	Philadelphia, PA, USA	408	124	1816	Neckar [3,6]	Mannheim, Germany	282	86	1845
Bryan–Fannin	Bonham, TX, USA	400	122	1927	River Tees [3,6]	England	281	86	1830
Ada–Kanawa	Oklahoma, USA	400	122	1922	...	Jamaica, West Indies	280	85	1920
Massena	New York City, USA	400	122	1910	Lambeth	London, England	280	85	1824
Ticonic	Waterville, ME, USA	400	122	1904	Tain–Tournon [6]	Rhône R., France	280	85	1863
Kennebec R.	Waterville, ME, USA	400	122	1903	Lehigh R.	Easton, PA, USA	279	85	1900
Grand Avenue [6]	St. Louis, MO, USA	400	122	1890	Canyon	Ecuador	275	84	1888
Alber [6,7]	London, England	400	122	1873	Franz [6]	Vienna, Austria	274	84	1848
Hammersmith [3,6]	London, England	400	122	1827	Elk R. [3]	Charleston, WV, USA	273	83	1884
Midi	Lyon, France	398	121	1849					
Beaucaire	Rhône R., France	394	120	1828	Frankfort [3,6]	Germany	262	80	1869
...	Colombia	390	119	1916	Garonne [6]	Langon, France	262	80	1831
Rhône	Valence, France	384	117	1828	Saone R.	Lyon, France	261	80	1888
...	Panama	380	116	1928					

TABLE C.2
(*continued*)

Name[a]	Location	(ft)	(m)	Year completed[b]	Name[a]	Location	(ft)	(m)	Year completed[b]
Kirkenes	Norway	260	79	1912	Marne [6]	Luzancy, France	180	55	1925
Dryburg Abbey [3,6,7]	Twee, England	260	79	1818	...	Guatemala	180	55	1913
					Egyptian [3,6]	St. Petersburg, Russia	180	55	1826
Auburn–Coloma	CA, USA	258	79	1862	Asre R.	Switzerland	179	55	1916
Railway Bridge [3,6]	Vienna, Austria	255	78	1860	Upper Salangen	Norway	177	54	1913
					Spree [6]	Berlin, Germany	175	53	1905
Hinche	Haiti	250	76	1934	Inverness	Scotland	173	53	1877
Railway and Highway	Costa Rica	250	76	1925	Aare [3]	Brugg, Switzerland	169	52	1875
					Borsig [6]	Berlin, Germany	167	51	1905
...	Panama	250	76	1924	Aqueduct, Allegheny R. [3]	Pittsburgh, PA, USA	162	49	1845
Darjeeling	India	250	76	1922					
Bry-sur-Marne [3]	France	250	76	1832	Sacramento R.	Castella, CA, USA	160	49	1933
...	Packwood, WA, USA	249	76	1934	Gotha [6]	Germany	160	49	1872
					Newburyport [6]	MA, USA	160	49	1827
Passau	Germany	246	75	1869	...	Colombia	156	48	1926
Newburyport	MA, USA	244	74	1909	Schuylkill Falls [3,6]	Philadelphia, PA, USA	153	47	1809
Newburyport [3,6]	MA, USA	244	74	1809					
Langenargen	Germany	236	72	1898	Railway and Highway	Costa Rica	150	46	1925
Lahn R.	Germany	233	71	1926					
St. Ilpize	France	232	71	1879	Alum Creek	Columbus, OH, USA	150	46	1922
Sophia [3,6]	Vienna, Austria	232	71	1825	Richmond	Richmond, IN, USA	150	46	1889
Louis Philippe [3]	Seine R., Paris, France	231	70	1833	Port Gibson [3,6]	MI, USA	150	46	1860
					Bercy [3,6]	Seine R., Paris, France	148	45	1832
...	Colombia	230	70	1923					
Invalides [3,6]	Seine R., Paris, France	230	70	1829	Muhlentor [6]	Lubeck, Germany	147	45	1899
					Tara R.	Yugoslavia	138	42	1932
Allentown [3,6]	Allentown, PA, USA	230	70	1815	Irwell [3,6]	Manchester, England	138	42	1825
					...	Peru	137	42	1921
Little Niangua R. [8]	MO, USA	225	69	1933	Strakonice [6]	Elbe R., Bohemia	137	42	1846
					Railway Bridge [3]	Saone R., France	137	42	1840
Ellbogen [6]	Eger, Bohemia	222	68	1836	Salzach R. [6]	Austria	135	41	1905
Ostrawitza [3,6]	Ostrau, Bohemia	216	66	1850	Lackawaxen	Minisink, NY, USA	135	41	1898
Karl Franz [6]	Granz, Austria	214	65	1845	Bourbon Island [6]	France	132	40	1823
Regnitz [3,6]	Bamberg, Germany	211	64	1829	Fosse	Geneva, Switzerland	132	40	1823
...	Ecuador	210	64	1924	...	Bolivia	131	40	1904
...	Venezuela	210	64	1921	Arcole [3,6]	Seine R., Paris, France	131	40	1827
Eger [3,6]	Saaz, Bohemia	210	64	1827					
...	Costa Rica	208	63	1909	Potomac R. [3,6]	Washington, DC, USA	130	40	1807
City Bridge [3]	Seine R., Paris, France	207	63	1842					
					Ogden Park	Chicago, IL, USA	125	38	1929
Augarten [6]	Vienna, Austria	202	62	1873	Fontanka	St. Petersburg, Russia	120	37	1824
Boquet Canyon	Los Angeles, CA, USA	200	61	1934	Aisne R. [6]	Vaux-sous-Laon, France	115	35	1927
Singapore [6]	Straits Settlements, Singapore	200	61	1870	Footbridge [6]	Nuremberg, Germany	112	34	1824
					Galashiel	England	112	34	1816
Weser [6]	Porta, Germany	200	61	1864	Rudolfs [3,6]	Vienna, Austria	110	34	1828
Aspern [3,6]	Vienna, Austria	200	61	1864	Northampton [6]	PA, USA,	100	30	1811
Aare [6]	Bern, Switzerland	200	61	1857	Strassnitz [3,6]	Germany	98	30	1824
Boevra	Norway	197	60	1918	Lahn [6]	Weilburg, Germany	98	30	1785
Neja	Norway	197	60	1918					
Wenatchee R.	Chiwaukum, WA, USA	190	58	1915	Mill Creek Park [6]	Youngstown, OH, USA	90	27	1894
Smithfield Street [3]	Pittsburgh, PA, USA	188	57	1847	Schikaneder [3,6]	Vienna, Austria	85	26	1830
Jalapa	Mexico	184	56	1908	Uniontown [6]	PA, USA,	72	22	1796
Hamm-Lip Canal [6]	Westphalia, Germany	181	55	1923	River Tees [3,6]	England	70	21	1741
					...	Colombia	66	20	1916
...	Venezuela	180	55	1927	Lions' Bridge	Berlin, Germany	57	17	1837

[1] Under construction [2] Railroad and highway [3] Not standing [4] Twin spans [5] Twin bridges [6] I-bar chain [7] Includes cable stays [8] Self-anchored [9] Mono-cable [10] Structure widened by addition of third cable (1994) [11] Highway and pedestrian, ferro-cement

Database lists 393 suspension bridges completed or under construction distributed amoung 45 countries as follows:

United States	144	Switzerland	8
France	47	Bohemia	6
Germany	28	Panama and Czech Republic, each	4
Norway	22	Costa Rica, Russia, and Venezuela, each	3
United Kingdom	21	Chile, Denmark, Dominican Republic, Ecuador, Hungary, Mexico,	
Japan	19	Portugal, Sweden, and Turkey, each	2
Colombia	12	Argentina, Australia, Belgium, Bolivia, Brazil, Guatemala,	
China	11	Haiti, Hong Kong, India, Jamaica, Yugoslavia, South Korea,	
Austria	10	New Zealand, Norway, Peru, Reunion Island, Rhodesia, Singapore,	
Canada	10	Spain, and Ukraine, each	1

Note: Data compiled by Dr. Walter Podolny, Jr., senior structural engineer, Bridge Management Group, HNG-32, Federal Highway Administration, Washington, D. C., March 1997.

TABLE C.3
Results of the spliced-girder bridge survey: summary of key design parameters[†]

Bridge name (source number)[*]	Location	Year completed (designed)	Span range (ft)	Girder type[**]	Span/ depth[a]	Girder spacing (ft)	Deck overhang (ft)
1. 36 Steel Bridge (31)	Calgary, Canada	1982	108–122	2 pier: 4 span: 1	20	14	0
2. 128 Steel Bridge (10, 34)	Snohomish, WA	1985	172		25	6	3
3. Airport Hwy. 2 Bridge (6, 19)	Alb., Canada	1982	148	2	20	17	4
4. Annacis Channel Bridge (24)	Vancouver, B.C., Canada	1984	197–233	1	24	10	6
5. Apalachicola River Bridge (11)	Franklin Cnty., FL	1986	164–200	1 (var.)	27	5	4
6. Overpass No. 2 (14, 27)	Vancouver, B.C., Canada	1986	138	3	22	24	5
7. Bow River Bridge (31)	Calgary, Canada	1985	112–150	2	20	16	0
8. Carmine–Smith Bridge (23)	McKenzie River, OR	1960	45–90	1	24	7	5
9. Choctawhachee Bridge (9)	Walton, FL	1988[b]	142–200	1	28	10	4
10. Cockshutt Road Bridge (32)	Brantford, Ont., Canada	1977	127–160	1	20	11	3
11. Congaree River Bridge (21)	Columbia, SC	1983[b]	94–160	1 (var.)	23	8	4
12. Floods Underpass (14)	Hope, B.C., Canada	1985	116	1	19	10	4
13. Credit River Bridge (3, 25)	Mississauga, Ont., Canada	1982	120–160	1	20	10	4
14. Dawhoo River Bridge (7)	Charleston Cnty., SC	1990	160–200	1 (var.)	25	6	3
15. Eglinton Ave. Bridge (3)	Mississauga, Ont., Canada	1990	148–174	1	21	9	4
16. Esker Overhead (14)	Skeena District, B.C., Canada	1990	164	1	20	10	4
17. FAI Route 72 Bridge (8, 18)	Piatt Cnty., IL	1973	106	1	23	6	3
18. Great Neck Road Bridge (21)	Virginia Beach, VA	1984[b]	128–215	1 (var.)	26	8	3
19. Harbor Blvd. Overcrossing (17)	Sacramento, CA	1968	139	3	22	13	3
20. Harbor Drive Bridge (22)	Oceanside, CA	1975	100	3	27	10	2
21. James McDonald Bridge (29)	Edmonton, Canada	1970	185–250	1 (var.)	19	15	4
22. Joseph Palmer Knapp Bridge (26)	Coinjock, NC	1986	78–150	1 (var.)	21	8	3
23. Kildonan Corridor (35)	Winnipeg, Canada	1989	205–269	1 (var.)	23	8	3
24. King George Flyover (14, 24)	Surrey, B.C., Canada	1989	118–141	2	26	19	5
25. Kingston Road Bridge (3, 12)	Scarborough, Ont., Canada	1977	130–166	1	21	9	4
26. Loy Lake Road Underpass (1, 36)	Grayson Cnty., TX	1985	150	1	23	7	3
27. McKenzie River Bridge (13, 16)	Armitage, OR	1984	220	Pier: 4 Span: 1	23	9	4
28. Missouri River Bridge #1 (20)	MO	1989	130–160	1	23	9	3
29. Missouri River Bridge #2 (20)	MO	1989	125	1	23	8	3
30. Napa River Bridge (5)	Vallejo, CA	1966	126–188	1 (var.)	24	N/A	N/A
31. Nine-Mile Bridge (28)	Spokane Cnty., WA	1975	86–136	1	25	8	3
32. Oak Avenue Bridge (13, 16)	Douglas Cnty., OR	1971	200–260	Pier: 4 Span: 1	26	8	3
33. Provencher Bridge (35)	Winnipeg, Manitoba, Canada	1990[b]	167–195	1	20	Var.	Var.
34. Pullen Creek Bridge (10, 34)	WA	1988	84–124	1	19	7	2
35. Rainbow Valley Bridge (29)	Edmonton, Canada	1980	140–170	3	24	9	3
36. Salt River Bridge (33)	Fort Knox, KY	1987	85–160	1	21	9	3
37. Sebastian Inlet Bridge (4)	Brevard Cnty., FL	1964	100–180	1 (var.)	23	9	1
38. Shelby Creek Bridge (33)	Pike Cnty., KY	1989	162–218	1	26	13	5
39. Shui Ribe Bridge (30)	Taipei, Taiwan	1982	170–263	5	18	9	1
40. Stewart Park Bridge (13, 16)	Douglas Cnty., OR	1967	185–260	Pier: 4 Span: 1	25	8	3
41. Talmadge Memorial Bridge (15)	Savannah, GA	1990	155–190	1 (var.)	24	9	3
42. Thacker Creek Overpass (14)	Chilliwack District, B.C., Canada	1985	60–98	1	18	10	3
43. Trosper Road Underpass (10, 34)	Thurston Cnty., WA	1991	116–126	3	25	16	3
44. Twelve Mile Creek Bridge (33)	Campbell Cnty., KY	1987[c]	145–182	1	24	13	4
45. Umpqua River Bridge (13, 16)	Sutherlin, OR	1970	65–220	Pier: 4 Span: 1	22	8	3

[†] *Source:* Abdel-Karim, A. M., and Tadros, M. K. (1992). "State of the Art of Precast/Prestressed Concrete Spliced-Girder Bridges," Precast/Prestressed Concrete Institute, Chicago, October.

[*] Paranthetical numbers refer to references in the original reference.

[**] See Fig. C3.1 for the girder type.

[a] The span-depth ratio is given for the longest span; an average value is given for spans with variable-depth pier segments.

[b] Proposed as an alternative or designed but not constructed.

[c] Bridge failed during construction and was redesigned in steel.

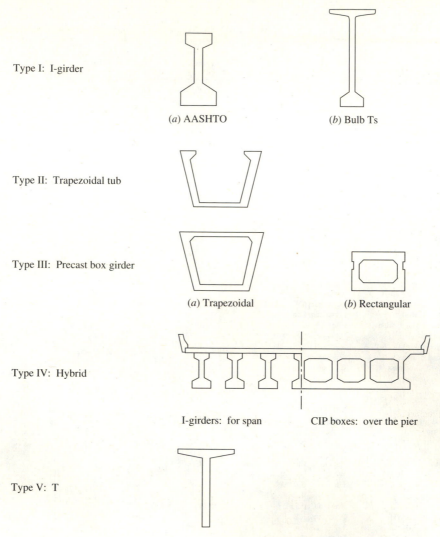

Type I: I-girder

(a) AASHTO

(b) Bulb Ts

Type II: Trapezoidal tub

Type III: Precast box girder

(a) Trapezoidal

(b) Rectangular

Type IV: Hybrid

I-girders: for span

CIP boxes: over the pier

Type V: T

FIGURE C3.1

Index*

Note: Italic page number indicates figure. "*n*" indicates footnote.

Permissions

Figure 1.1:   From Edwards, L. N.: *A Record of the History and Evolution of Early American Bridges,* C. H. Edwards (publisher), University Press, Orono, ME. Copyright ©1959 by University of Maine Press.

Figure 1.2:   From Gies, J.: *Bridges and Men,* Grosset and Dunlap, New York. Copyright ©1963 by Doubleday—Div. of Bantam, Doubleday Dell Publishing Group, Inc.

Figure 1.3:   From Smith, H. S.: *The World's Great Bridges,* Harper & Brothers, New York, 1953. Copyright ©1965 by HarperCollins Publishers.

Figure 1.4:   From Gies, J.: *Bridges and Men,* Grosset and Dunlap, New York. Copyright ©1963 by Doubleday—Div. of Bantam, Doubleday Dell Publishing Group, Inc.

Figure 1.5:   From Smith, H. S.: *The World's Great Bridges,* Harper & Brothers, New York, 1953. Copyright ©1965 by HarperCollins Publishers.

Figure 1.6:   From Steinman, D. B., and Watson, S. R.: *Bridges and Their Builders,* Dover, New York. Copyright ©1957 by Dover Publications, Inc.

Figure 1.7:   From Gies, J.: *Bridges and Men,* Grosset and Dunlap, New York. Copyright ©1963 by Doubleday—Div. of Bantam, Doubleday Dell Publishing Group, Inc.

Figure 1.8:   From Edwards, L. N.: *A Record of the History and Evolution of Early American Bridges,* C. H. Edwards (publisher), University Press, Orono, ME. Copyright ©1959 by University of Maine Press.

Figures 1.9, 1.10:   From Gies, J.: *Bridges and Men,* Grosset and Dunlap, New York. Copyright ©1963 by Doubleday—Div. of Bantam, Doubleday Dell Publishing Group, Inc.

Figures 1.11, 1.12:   From Steinman, D. B., and Watson, S. R.: *Bridges and Their Builders,* Dover, New York. Copyright ©1957 by Dover Publications, Inc.

Figure 1.14:   From Gies, J.: *Bridges and Men,* Grosset and Dunlap, New York. Copyright ©1963 by Doubleday—Div. of Bantam, Doubleday Dell Publishing Group, Inc.

Figures 1.15, 1.16:   From Hopkins, H. J.: *A Span of Bridges,* Praeger, New York. Copyright ©1970 by Praeger Publishers.

Figure 1.17:   From Edwards, L. N.: *A Record of the History and Evolution of Early American Bridges,* C. H. Edwards (publisher), University Press, Orono, ME. Copyright ©1959 by University of Maine Press.

Figure 1.18:   From Smith, H. S.: *The World's Great Bridges,* Harper & Brothers, New York, 1953. Copyright ©1965 by HarperCollins Publishers.

Figures 1.19, 1.23, 1.24:   From Hopkins, H. J.: *A Span of Bridges,* Praeger, New York. Copyright ©1970 by Praeger Publishers.

Figures 1.36 part (*b*), and 1.37:   From O'Connor, C.: *Design of Bridge Superstructures,* John Wiley & Sons, New York. Copyright ©1971 by John Wiley & Sons, Inc.

Figure 1.46:   From Smith, H. S.: *The World's Great Bridges,* Harper & Brothers, New York, 1953. Copyright ©1965 by HarperCollins Publishers.

Figures 1.62, 1.63:   From McCormac, J. C.: *Structural Steel Design,* 3rd ed., HarperCollins, New York. Copyright ©1981 by HarperCollins Publishers.

Figure 1.68:   From O'Connor, C.: *Design of Bridge Superstructures,* John Wiley & Sons, New York. Copyright ©1971 by John Wiley & Sons, Inc.

Figures 2.3, 2.4:   From Nawy, E. G.: *Prestressed Concrete: A Fundamental Approach,* Prentice Hall, Englewood Cliffs, NJ. Copyright ©1989 by Prentice Hall.